Praise for Danny G

"*JavaScript Bible* is the definitive resource in JavaScript programming. I am never more than three feet from my copy."

—*Steve Reich, CEO, PageCoders*

"This book is a must-have for any Web developer or programmer."

—*Thoma Lile, President, Kanis Technologies, Inc.*

"Outstanding book. I would recommend this book to anyone interested in learning to develop advanced Web sites. Mr. Goodman did an excellent job of organizing this book and writing it so that even a beginning programmer can understand it."

—*Jason Hensley, Director of Internet Services, NetVoice, Inc.*

"Goodman is always great at delivering clear and concise technical books!"

—*Dwayne King, Chief Technology Officer, White Horse*

"*JavaScript Bible* is well worth the money spent!"

—*Yen C.Y. Leong, IT Director, Moo Mooltimedia, a member of SmartTransact Group*

"A must-have book for any Internet developer."

—*Uri Fremder, Senior Consultant, TopTier Software*

"I love this book! I use it all the time, and it always delivers. It's the only JavaScript book I use!"

—*Jason Badger, Web Developer*

"Whether you are a professional or a beginner, this is a great book to get."

—*Brant Mutch, Web Application Developer, Wells Fargo Card Services, Inc.*

"I never thought I'd ever teach programming before reading your book [*JavaScript Bible*]. It's so simple to use—the Programming Fundamentals section brought it all back! Thank you for such a wonderful book, and for breaking through my programming block!"

—*Susan Sann Mahon, Certified Lotus Instructor, TechNet Training*

"I continue to get so much benefit from *JavaScript Bible*. What an amazing book! Danny Goodman is the greatest!"

—*Patrick Moss*

"Danny Goodman is very good at leading the reader into the subject. *JavaScript Bible* has everything we could possibly need."

—*Philip Gurdon*

"An excellent book that builds solidly from whatever level the reader is at. A book that is both witty and educational."

—*Dave Vane*

"I continue to use the book on a daily basis and would be lost without it."

—*Mike Warner, Founder, Oak Place Productions*

"*JavaScript Bible* is by *far* the best JavaScript resource I've ever seen (and I've seen quite a few)."

—*Robert J. Mirro, Independent Consultant, RJM Consulting*

JavaScript™
Examples Bible:
The Essential Companion to *JavaScript Bible*

JavaScript™ Examples Bible:
The Essential Companion to *JavaScript Bible*

Danny Goodman

Hungry Minds™

Best-Selling Books • Digital Downloads • e-Books • Answer Networks • e-Newsletters • Branded Web Sites • e-Learning

Indianapolis, IN ✦ Cleveland, OH ✦ New York, NY

JavaScript™ Examples Bible: The Essential Companion to *JavaScript™ Bible*

Published by:
Hungry Minds, Inc.
909 Third Avenue
New York, NY 10022
www.hungryminds.com

Library of Congress Control No.: 2001091964

ISBN: 0-7645-4855-7

Printed in the United States of America

10 9 8 7 6 5 4 3 2 1

1B/RY/QX/QR/IN

Distributed in the United States by Hungry Minds, Inc.

Distributed by CDG Books Canada Inc. for Canada; by Transworld Publishers Limited in the United Kingdom; by IDG Norge Books for Norway; by IDG Sweden Books for Sweden; by IDG Books Australia Publishing Corporation Pty. Ltd. for Australia and New Zealand; by TransQuest Publishers Pte Ltd. for Singapore, Malaysia, Thailand, Indonesia, and Hong Kong; by Gotop Information Inc. for Taiwan; by ICG Muse, Inc. for Japan; by Intersoft for South Africa; by Eyrolles for France; by International Thomson Publishing for Germany, Austria, and Switzerland; by Distribuidora Cuspide for Argentina; by LR International for Brazil; by Galileo Libros for Chile; by Ediciones ZETA S.C.R. Ltda. for Peru; by WS Computer Publishing Corporation, Inc., for the Philippines; by Contemporanea de Ediciones for Venezuela; by Express Computer Distributors for the Caribbean and West Indies; by Micronesia Media Distributor, Inc. for Micronesia; by Chips Computadoras S.A. de C.V. for Mexico; by Editorial Norma de Panama S.A. for Panama; by American Bookshops for Finland.

For general information on Hungry Minds' products and services please contact our Customer Care department; within the U.S. at 800-762-2974, outside the U.S. at 317-572-3993 or fax 317-572-4002.

For sales inquiries and resellers information, including discounts, premium and bulk quantity sales and foreign language translations please contact our Customer Care department at 800-434-3422, fax 317-572-4002 or write to Hungry Minds, Inc., Attn: Customer Care department, 10475 Crosspoint Boulevard, Indianapolis, IN 46256.

For information on licensing foreign or domestic rights, please contact our Sub-Rights Customer Care department at 212-884-5000.

For information on using Hungry Minds' products and services in the classroom or for ordering examination copies, please contact our Educational Sales department at 800-434-2086 or fax 317-572-4005.

For press review copies, author interviews, or other publicity information, please contact our Public Relations department at 317-572-3168 or fax 317-572-4168.

For authorization to photocopy items for corporate, personal, or educational use, please contact Copyright Clearance Center, 222 Rosewood Drive, Danvers, MA 01923, or fax 978-750-4470.

Hungry Minds™ is a trademark of Hungry Minds, Inc.

About the Author

Danny Goodman is the author of numerous critically acclaimed and bestselling books, including *The Complete HyperCard Handbook*, *Danny Goodman's AppleScript Handbook*, and *Dynamic HTML: The Definitive Reference*. He is a renowned authority and expert teacher of computer scripting languages and is widely known for his "JavaScript Apostle" articles in Netscape's *ViewSource* online developer newsletter. His writing style and pedagogy continue to earn praise from readers and teachers around the world. To help keep his finger on the pulse of real-world programming challenges, Goodman frequently lends his touch as consulting programmer and designer to leading-edge World Wide Web and intranet sites from his home base in the San Francisco area.

Credits

Acquisitions Editor
Sharon Cox

Project Editor
Neil Romanosky

Technical Editor
David Wall

Copy Editors
Jerelind Charles
Victoria Lee O'Malley

Editorial Manager
Colleen Totz

Project Coordinator
Regina Snyder

Graphics and Production Specialists
Gabriele McCann
Betty Schulte
Jeremey Unger
Erin Zeltner

Quality Control Technicians
Laura Albert
David Faust
Andy Hollandbeck

Permissions Editor
Laura Moss

Media Development Specialist
Greg Stephens

Media Development Coordinator
Marisa Pearman

Book Designer
Kurt Krames

Proofreading and Indexing
TECHBOOKS Production Services

Cover Illustrator
Kate Shaw

Preface

Acommon thread running throughout most of my computer-book–writing career is that I tend to write a book I wish I had had in order to learn a new technology in the first place. Because I must write that book without the benefit of existing models, I begin by doing my best to master the technology, and then I write the book to help other newcomers learn as much as I did, but more quickly and with less pain, anguish, and confusion. To accomplish that goal, I write as much content as I feel is necessary to cover the topic in the depth that my readers require.

When I started on what became the 4th and Gold editions of the *JavaScript Bible*, there were models to follow (my previous three editions) plus a substantial amount of brand new material, much of which had not yet been documented anywhere. I also assumed the responsibility of integrating the frequently conflicting and competing philosophies of the ways the JavaScript language is applied to a variety of browser brands and versions. Resolving these conflicts is a challenge that I face in my own programming work with clients, and I take great pleasure in sharing my solutions and approaches with other programmers floating in the same boat.

As my editor and I began counting the pages I had assembled for these new editions, we discovered that the number of pages far outstripped the printer's binding capabilities, even in a thicker volume made possible by using a hard cover (the Gold edition). Certainly not all of the words that I had written were so precious that some of them couldn't be cut. But we were hundreds of pages beyond capacity. To cut that much content would have forced exclusion of coverage of language or document object model vocabulary.

Fortunately, as had been done in previous editions, the plan for the new editions included Adobe Acrobat versions of the books on the accompanying CD-ROM. Although a significant compromise to ease of reading, it was possible to move some of the book's content to the CD-ROM and leave the most important parts on the printed page. For the softcover 4th edition, reference chapters covering less-used or advanced subjects were pulled from print; for the hardcover Gold edition, which was longer and targeted more for professional scripters, the advanced chapters were put back into the book (along with 15 additional chapters for that edition), and the JavaScript tutorial was exiled to the CD-ROM.

But even after making the difficult decisions about which chapters could go to the CD-ROMs, the page counts for both volumes were still excessive. Something else — something big — had to go. The remaining bundle that could free us from the page count devil was all of the Example sections from the reference vocabulary. By being nondiscriminatory about these extractions — that is, extracting all of them instead of only selected sections — we could convey to readers a consistent organizational model.

In the end, the extracted Example sections from Parts III and IV found their way into Appendix F on the CD-ROMs of both editions of the larger tome. I knew that as a reader of my own books (and one of a certain age at that) I would not enjoy having to flip back and forth between book and screen to refresh my memory about a term and see it in action. A more pleasing solution for many *JavaScript Bible* readers would be a separate volume containing a printed version of the Examples sections. The new volume would act as a companion to both the 4th and Gold editions of the *JavaScript Bible*.

Using Appendix F as a starting point, I divided the content into chapters along the same lines as the *JavaScript Bible* reference sections. This also gave me a chance to study the examples for each chapter with fresh eyes. The examples haven't changed, but I had the opportunity to direct the reader's attention to examples that I thought were particularly helpful in mastering a document-level or core language object. Thus, each chapter of this book begins with a scene-setting introduction and a list of highlights to which you should pay special attention. Also, since you will likely be scanning through the book from time to time, I added many illustrations of the pages produced from the code listings. These figures will help you visualize what important listing code does when the page is loaded into a browser.

Now you know the story behind the *JavaScript Examples Bible*. Some budget-conscious readers may not be thrilled to pay more for what appears to be a printout of content they already own in electronic format. If so, then please continue using the Acrobat version. But if, like me, you enjoy the portability and visual scanability of a printed work, then keeping this book near your *JavaScript Bible* volume will enhance your learning and research activities.

Organization and Features of This Book

Almost all chapters in this book correspond to similarly named chapters in Parts III and IV from the *JavaScript Bible* 4th and Gold editions. Although chapters in this book are consecutively numbered starting with Chapter 1, each chapter title includes a reference to the corresponding chapter number from the big books. For example, Chapter 1 of this book provides the Examples sections for terms related to generic HTML elements. That subject is covered in Chapter 15 of the big books. There is not always a one-to-one relationship between chapters. Several chapters of the big books have no Examples sections in them because sample code is embedded as part of the big book text. Therefore, don't be surprised to see gaps in pointers to *JavaScript Bible* reference chapters.

Listing numbers are derived from their original order in what had been planned as a contiguous volume. Such listing numbers are the ones referred to in the "On the CD-ROM" pointers throughout Parts III and IV of the big books. This should help you locate an example's listing when you reach one of those pointers in the *JavaScript Bible*. Notice, too, that the big books' running footers with property, method, and event handler names appear in this book, too. Therefore, if you should be looking at an example listing of this book and wish to consult the more detailed discussion of the subject in the large book, turn to the corresponding big book chapter and locate the corresponding terminology within the object's chapter.

Many examples throughout this book refer to The Evaluator. This Web page application is described at length in Chapter 13 of the big books. You can find the file for The Evaluator within the Listings\Chap13 folder on the CD-ROM for either the big book or this book.

CD-ROM

The accompanying CD-ROM contains the complete set of over 300 ready-to-run HTML documents from the *JavaScript Bible, Gold Edition*. These include listings for both the Examples sections in this book and all other listings from the Gold edition. You can run these examples with your JavaScript-enabled browser, but be sure to use the `index.html` page in the Listings folder as a gateway to running the listings. This page shows you the browsers that are compatible with each example listing.

The Quick Reference from Appendix A of the big books is in `.pdf` format on the CD-ROM for you to print out and assemble as a handy reference, if desired. Adobe Acrobat Reader is included on the CD-ROM so that you can read this `.pdf` file. Finally, the text of the book is in a `.pdf` file format on the CD-ROM for easy searching.

Formatting and Naming Conventions

The script listings and words in this book are presented in a `monospace font` to set them apart from the rest of the text. Because of restrictions in page width, lines of script listings may, from time to time, break unnaturally. In such cases, the remainder of the script appears in the following line, flush with the left margin of the listing, just as they would appear in a text editor with word wrapping turned on. If these line breaks cause you problems when you type a script listing into a document yourself, I encourage you to access the corresponding listing on the CD-ROM to see how it should look when you type it.

To make it easier to spot in the text when a particular browser and browser version is required, most browser references consist of a two-letter abbreviation and a version number. For example, IE5 means Internet Explorer 5 for any operating system;

NN6 means Netscape Navigator 6 for any operating system. If a feature is introduced with a particular version of browser and is supported in subsequent versions, a plus symbol (+) follows the number. For example, a feature marked IE4+ indicates that Internet Explorer 4 is required at a minimum, but the feature is also available in IE5, IE5.5, and so on. Occasionally, a feature or some highlighted behavior applies to only one operating system. For example, a feature marked IE4+/Windows means that it works only on Windows versions of Internet Explorer 4 or later. As points of reference, the first scriptable browsers were NN2, IE3/Windows, and IE3.01/Macintosh. Moreover, IE3 for Windows can be equipped with one of two versions of the JScript.dll file. A reference to the earlier version is cited as IE3/J1, while the later version is cited as IE3/J2. You will see this notation primarily in the compatibility charts throughout the reference chapters.

Acknowledgments

Because most of the content of this volume was created as part of the *JavaScript Bible*, the acknowledgments that you see in your copy of the 4th or Gold editions apply equally to this volume. But this *JavaScript Examples Bible* did not come into being without additional effort on the part of dedicated Hungry Minds, Inc., staff. In particular, I want to thank Sharon Cox for turning my idea into a title, and editor Neil Romanosky, who, even after marshaling over 4,000 pages of content for the 4th and Gold editions, took charge of this volume to maintain continuity across the entire series. Thanks, too, to my friends and family, who certainly must have grown weary of my tales of reaching schedule milestones on this project not once, not twice, but three times over many, many months.

Contents at a Glance

Contents

Generic HTML Element Objects (Chapter 15)

✦ ✦ ✦ ✦

In This Chapter

Understanding element containment relationships

Common properties and methods of all HTML element objects

Event handlers of all element objects

✦ ✦ ✦ ✦

Document object models for both IE4+ and NN6 expose all HTML elements as scriptable objects. A beneficial byproduct of this concept is that object model designers find it easier to implement their models according to genuinely object-oriented principles. (In truth, modern HTML and DOM industry standards encourage browser makers to think in object-oriented terms anyway.) The object-oriented principle most applicable to the way we work with objects is that all HTML elements inherit properties, methods, and event handlers from a generic (and unseen) HTML element object. Thus, specifications for any HTML element object start with those of the generic object, and then pile on element-specific features, such as the `src` property of an IMG element. This chapter deals almost exclusively with the properties, methods, and event handlers that all HTML elements have in common.

Examples Highlights

✦ Modern object models and the scripting world now pay much attention to the containment hierarchy of elements and text nodes in a document. The function shown in Listing 15-3 demonstrates how vital the `childNodes` property is to scripts that need to inspect (and then perhaps modify) page content.

✦ Element containment is also at the forefront in Listing 15-10, where W3C DOM syntax demonstrates how to use the `firstChild` and `lastChild` properties, plus the `insertBefore()`, `appendChild()`, and `replaceChild()` methods, to change portions of page content on the fly.

✦ In the IE/Windows world, data binding can be a powerful tool that requires only tiny amounts of your code in a page. You can get a good sense of the possibilities in the extended examples for the `dataFld` and related properties.

✦ Follow the steps for the `disabled` property to see how form controls can be disabled in IE4+ and NN6. IE5.5 lets you disable any element on the page, as you can witness in real time when you follow the example steps.

✦ Long-time IE scripters know the powers of the `innerHTML` and `innerText` properties. Listing 15-11 solidifies by example the precise differences between the two related properties. Only one of these properties, `innerHTML`, is implemented in NN6.

✦ Grasping the details of properties that govern element positions and dimensions is not easy, as noted in the *JavaScript Bible* text. But you can work through the examples of the client-, offset-, and scroll-related properties for IE4+ and the offset-related properties in NN6 to help you visualize what these properties control. If you are scripting cross-browser applications, be sure to work through the offset-related properties in both browsers to compare the results.

✦ Compare the IE5+ `attachEvent()` method and NN6 `addEventListener()` method for modern ways to assign event handlers to element objects. Although the method names are different, the two work identically.

✦ Observe how the `getAttribute()` method returns an object's property value when the property name is a string and the name is the same as an assigned element attribute name. The `getAttribute()` method is the prescribed way to retrieve property values according to the W3C DOM.

✦ You can see how the `getElementsByTagName()` method returns an array of nested elements with a particular tag. This is a great way, for example, to get a one-dimensional array of all cells within a table.

✦ Spend time comparing how the various insert- and replace-related methods operate from different points of view. In the IE world, most operate on the current element; in the W3C DOM world, the methods operate on child nodes of the current element.

✦ For IE5+/Windows, check out the way dynamic properties are managed through the `getExpression()`, `setExpression()`, and `recalc()` methods. Listing 15-32 demonstrates a neat graphical clock that employs these methods.

✦ IE5+/Windows provides a number of event handlers, such as `onBeforeCopy`, `onBeforePaste`, `onCopy`, `onCut`, and `onPaste` that let scripts manage the specific information preserved in the clipboard. These event handlers can also be used with the `onContextMenu` event handler to facilitate custom context menus.

✦ Another set of IE5+/Windows event handlers provides excellent control over user dragging and dropping of elements on a page. Listing 15-37 is particularly interesting in this regard.

✦ Listing 15-41 shows a cross-browser laboratory for understanding the three keyboard events and how to get key and character information from the event. You see event-handling that works with IE4+, NN4, and NN6 event models.

✦ Numerous mouse-related events belong to all HTML elements. Listings 15-42 and 15-43 demonstrate simplified image swapping and element dragging.

Generic Objects

Properties

accessKey

	NN2	NN3	NN4	NN6	IE3/J1	IE3/J2	IE4	IE5	IE5.5
Compatibility							✓	✓	✓

Example

When you load the script in Listing 15-1, adjust the height of the browser window so that you can see nothing below the second dividing rule. Enter any character into the Settings portion of the page and press Enter. (The Enter key may cause your computer to beep.) Then hold down the Alt (Windows) or Ctrl (Mac) key while pressing the same keyboard key. The element from below the second divider should come into view.

Listing 15-1: **Controlling the accessKey Property**

```
<HTML>
<HEAD>
<TITLE>accessKey Property</TITLE>
<SCRIPT LANGUAGE="JavaScript">
function assignKey(type, elem) {
    if (window.event.keyCode == 13) {
        switch (type) {
            case "button":
                document.forms["output"].access1.accessKey = elem.value
                break
            case "text":
                document.forms["output"].access2.accessKey = elem.value
                break
            case "table":
                document.all.myTable.accessKey = elem.value
        }
        return false
    }
}
</SCRIPT>
</HEAD>
<BODY>
<H1>accessKey Property Lab</H1>
<HR>
Settings:<BR>
```

Continued

Listing 15-1 *(continued)*

```
<FORM NAME="input">
Assign an accessKey value to the Button below and press Return:
<INPUT TYPE="text" SIZE=2 MAXLENGTH=1
onKeyPress="return assignKey('button', this)">
<BR>
Assign an accessKey value to the Text Box below and press Return:
<INPUT TYPE="text" SIZE=2 MAXLENGTH=1
onKeyPress="return assignKey('text', this)">
<BR>
Assign an accessKey value to the Table below (IE5.5 only) and press Return:
<INPUT TYPE="text" SIZE=2 MAXLENGTH=1
onKeyPress="return assignKey('table', this)">
</FORM>
<BR>
Then press Alt (Windows) or Control (Mac) + the key.
<BR>
<I>Size the browser window to view nothing lower than this line.</I>
<HR>

<FORM NAME="output" onSubmit="return false">
<INPUT TYPE="button" NAME="access1" VALUE="Standard Button">
<P></P>
<INPUT TYPE="text" NAME="access2">
<P></P>
</FORM>
<TABLE ID="myTable" CELLPADDING="10" BORDER=2>
<TR>
<TH>Quantity<TH>Description<TH>Price
</TR>
<TBODY BGCOLOR="red">
<TR>
    <TD WIDTH=100>4<TD>Primary Widget<TD>$14.96
</TR>
<TR>
    <TD>10<TD>Secondary Widget<TD>$114.96
</TR>
</TBODY>
</TABLE>

</BODY>
</HTML>
```

Note   In IE5, the keyboard combination may bring focus to the input field. This anomalous behavior does not affect the normal script setting of the accessKey property.

all

	NN2	NN3	NN4	NN6	IE3/J1	IE3/J2	IE4	IE5	IE5.5
Compatibility							✓	✓	✓

Example

Use The Evaluator (Chapter 13 in the *JavaScript Bible*) to experiment with the all collection. Enter the following statements one at a time into the lower text box, and review the results in the textarea for each.

```
document.all
myTable.all
myP.all
```

If you encounter a numbered element within a collection, you can explore that element to see which tag is associated with it. For example, if one of the results for the document.all collection says document.all.8=[object], enter the following statement into the topmost text box:

```
document.all[8].tagName
```

attributes

	NN2	NN3	NN4	NN6	IE3/J1	IE3/J2	IE4	IE5	IE5.5
Compatibility				✓				✓	✓

Example

Use The Evaluator (Chapter 13 in the *JavaScript Bible*) to examine the values of the attributes array for some of the elements in that document. Enter each of the following expressions into the lower text field, and see the array contents in the Results textarea for each:

```
document.body.attributes
document.getElementById("myP").attributes
document.getElementById("myTable").attributes
```

If you have both NN6 and IE5, compare the results you get for each of these expressions. To view the properties of a single attribute in IE5/Windows, enter the following statement into the bottom text field:

```
document.getElementById("myP").attributes["class"]
```

For NN6 and IE5/Mac, use the W3C DOM syntax:

```
document.getElementById("myP").attributes.getNamedItem("class")
```

behaviorUrns

	NN2	NN3	NN4	NN6	IE3/J1	IE3/J2	IE4	IE5	IE5.5
Compatibility								✓	✓

Example

The following function is embedded within a more complete example of IE/Windows HTML behaviors (Listing 15-19 in this chapter). It reports the length of the `behaviorUrns` array and shows — if the values are returned — the URL of the attached behavior.

```
function showBehaviors() {
    var num = document.all.myP.behaviorUrns.length
    var msg = "The myP element has " + num + " behavior(s). "
    if (num > 0) {
        msg += "Name(s): \r\n"
        for (var i = 0; i < num; i++) {
            msg += document.all.myP.behaviorUrns[i] + "\r\n"
        }
    }
    alert(msg)
}
```

canHaveChildren

	NN2	NN3	NN4	NN6	IE3/J1	IE3/J2	IE4	IE5	IE5.5
Compatibility								✓	✓

Example

Listing 15-2 uses color to demonstrate the difference between an element that can have children and one that cannot. The first button sets the `color` style property of every visible element on the page to red. Thus, elements (including the normally non-childbearing ones such as HR and INPUT) are affected by the color change. But if you reset the page and click the largest button, only those elements that can contain nested elements receive the color change.

Listing 15-2: **Reading the canHaveChildren Property**

```
<HTML>
<HEAD>
<TITLE>canHaveChildren Property</TITLE>
<SCRIPT LANGUAGE="JavaScript">
```

```
function colorAll() {
    for (var i = 0; i < document.all.length; i++) {
        document.all[i].style.color = "red"
    }
}

function colorChildBearing() {
    for (var i = 0; i < document.all.length; i++) {
        if (document.all[i].canHaveChildren) {
            document.all[i].style.color = "red"
        }
    }
}
</SCRIPT>
</HEAD>
<BODY>
<H1>canHaveChildren Property Lab</H1>
<HR>
<FORM NAME="input">
<INPUT TYPE="button" VALUE="Color All Elements" onClick="colorAll()">
<BR>
<INPUT TYPE="button" VALUE="Reset" onClick="history.go(0)">
<BR>
<INPUT TYPE="button" VALUE="Color Only Elements That Can Have Children"
onClick="colorChildBearing()">
</FORM>
<BR>
<HR>

<FORM NAME="output">
<INPUT TYPE="checkbox" CHECKED>Your basic checkbox
<P></P>
<INPUT TYPE="text" NAME="access2" VALUE="Some textbox text.">
<P></P>
</FORM>
<TABLE ID="myTable" CELLPADDING="10" BORDER=2>
<TR>
<TH>Quantity<TH>Description<TH>Price
</TR>
<TBODY>
<TR>
    <TD WIDTH=100>4<TD>Primary Widget<TD>$14.96
</TR>
<TR>
    <TD>10<TD>Secondary Widget<TD>$114.96
</TR>
</TBODY>
</TABLE>

</BODY>
</HTML>
```

canHaveHTML

	NN2	NN3	NN4	NN6	IE3/J1	IE3/J2	IE4	IE5	IE5.5
Compatibility									✓

Example

Use The Evaluator (Chapter 13 in the *JavaScript Bible*) to experiment with the canHaveHTML property. Enter the following statements into the top text field and observe the results:

```
document.all.input.canHaveHTML
document.all.myP.canHaveHTML
```

The first statement returns false because an INPUT element (the top text field in this case) cannot have nested HTML. But the myP element is a P element that gladly accepts HTML content.

childNodes

	NN2	NN3	NN4	NN6	IE3/J1	IE3/J2	IE4	IE5	IE5.5
Compatibility				✓			✓	✓	

Example

The walkChildNodes() function shown in Listing 15-3 accumulates and returns a hierarchical list of child nodes from the point of view of the document's HTML element (the default) or any element whose ID you pass as a string parameter. This function is embedded in The Evaluator so that you can inspect the child node hierarchy of that page or (when using evaluator.js for debugging as described in Chapter 45 of the *JavaScript Bible*) the node hierarchy within any page you have under construction. Try it out in The Evaluator by entering the following statements into the top text field:

```
walkChildNodes()
walkChildNodes(getElementById("myP"))
```

The results of this function show the nesting relationships among all child nodes within the scope of the initial object. It also shows the act of drilling down to further childNodes collections until all child nodes are exposed and catalogued. Text nodes are labeled accordingly. The first 15 characters of the actual text are placed in the results to help you identify the nodes when you compare the results against your HTML source code. The early NN6 phantom text nodes that contain carriage returns display <cr> in the results for each return character.

Listing 15-3: **Collecting Child Nodes**

```
function walkChildNodes(objRef, n) {
    var obj
    if (objRef) {
        if (typeof objRef == "string") {
            obj = document.getElementById(objRef)
        } else {
            obj = objRef
        }
    } else {
        obj = (document.body.parentElement) ?
            document.body.parentElement : document.body.parentNode
    }
    var output = ""
    var indent = ""
    var i, group, txt
    if (n) {
        for (i = 0; i < n; i++) {
            indent += "+---"
        }
    } else {
        n = 0
        output += "Child Nodes of <" + obj.tagName
        output += ">\n=====================\n"
    }
    group = obj.childNodes
    for (i = 0; i < group.length; i++) {
        output += indent
        switch (group[i].nodeType) {
            case 1:
                output += "<" + group[i].tagName
                output += (group[i].id) ? " ID=" + group[i].id : ""
                output += (group[i].name) ? " NAME=" + group[i].name : ""
                output += ">\n"
                break
            case 3:
                txt = group[i].nodeValue.substr(0,15)
                output += "[Text:\"" + txt.replace(/[\r\n]/g,"<cr>")
                if (group[i].nodeValue.length > 15) {
                    output += "..."
                }
                output += "\"]\n"
                break
            case 8:
                output += "[!COMMENT!]\n"
                break
            default:
                output += "[Node Type = " + group[i].nodeType + "]\n"
    }
```

Continued

Listing 15-3 *(continued)*

```
        if (group[i].childNodes.length > 0) {
            output += walkChildNodes(group[i], n+1)
        }
    }
    return output
}
```

children

	NN2	NN3	NN4	NN6	IE3/J1	IE3/J2	IE4	IE5	IE5.5
Compatibility							✓	✓	✓

Example

The walkChildren() function in Listing 15-4 accumulates and returns a hierarchical list of child elements from the point of view of the document's HTML element (the default) or any element whose ID you pass as a string parameter. This function is embedded in The Evaluator so that you can inspect the parent–child hierarchy of that page or (when using evaluator.js for debugging, as described in Chapter 45 of the *JavaScript Bible*) the element hierarchy within any page you have under construction. Try it out in The Evaluator in IE5+ by entering the following statements into the top text field:

```
walkChildren()
walkChildren("myP")
```

The results of this function show the nesting relationships among all parent and child elements within the scope of the initial object. It also shows the act of drilling down to further children collections until all child elements are exposed and catalogued. The element tags also display their ID and/or NAME attribute values if any are assigned to the elements in the HTML source code.

Listing 15-4: Collecting Child Elements

```
function walkChildren(objRef, n) {
    var obj
    if (objRef) {
        if (typeof objRef == "string") {
            obj = document.getElementById(objRef)
        } else {
            obj = objRef
```

```
        }
    } else {
        obj = document.body.parentElement
    }
    var output = ""
    var indent = ""
    var i, group
    if (n) {
        for (i = 0; i < n; i++) {
            indent += "+---"
        }
    } else {
        n = 0
        output += "Children of <" + obj.tagName
        output += ">\n=====================\n"
    }
    group = obj.children
    for (i = 0; i < group.length; i++) {
        output += indent + "<" + group[i].tagName
        output += (group[i].id) ? " ID=" + group[i].id : ""
        output += (group[i].name) ? " NAME=" + group[i].name : ""
        output += ">\n"
        if (group[i].children.length > 0) {
            output += walkChildren(group[i], n+1)
        }
    }
    return output
}
```

className

	NN2	NN3	NN4	NN6	IE3/J1	IE3/J2	IE4	IE5	IE5.5
Compatibility				✓			✓	✓	✓

Example

The style of an element toggles between "on" and "off" in Listing 15-5 by virtue of setting the element's `className` property alternatively to an existing style sheet class selector name and an empty string. When you set the `className` to an empty string, the default behavior of the H1 element governs the display of the first header. A click of the button forces the style sheet rule to override the default behavior in the first H1 element.

Listing 15-5: **Working with the className Property**

```
<HTML>
<HEAD>
<TITLE>className Property</TITLE>
<STYLE TYPE="text/css">
.special {font-size:16pt; color:red}
</STYLE>
<SCRIPT LANGUAGE="JavaScript">
function toggleSpecialStyle(elemID) {
    var elem = (document.all) ? document.all(elemID) :
document.getElementById(elemID)
    if (elem.className == "") {
        elem.className = "special"
    } else {
        elem.className = ""
    }
}
</SCRIPT>
</HEAD>
<BODY>
<H1>className Property Lab</H1>
<HR>
<FORM NAME="input">
<INPUT TYPE="button" VALUE="Toggle Class Name"
onClick="toggleSpecialStyle('head1')">
</FORM>
<BR>
<H1 ID="head1">ARTICLE I</H1>
<P>Congress shall make no law respecting an establishment of religion, or
prohibiting the free exercise thereof; or abridging the freedom of speech, or of
the press; or the right of the people peaceably to assemble, and to petition the
government for a redress of grievances.</P>

<H1>ARTICLE II</H1>
<P>A well regulated militia, being necessary to the security of a free state,
the right of the people to keep and bear arms, shall not be infringed.</P>
</BODY>
</HTML>
```

You can also create multiple versions of a style rule with different class selector identifiers and apply them at will to a given element.

clientHeight
clientWidth

	NN2	NN3	NN4	NN6	IE3/J1	IE3/J2	IE4	IE5	IE5.5
Compatibility							✓	✓	✓

Example

Listing 15-6 calls upon the clientHeight and clientWidth properties of a DIV element that contains a paragraph element. Only the width of the DIV element is specified in its style sheet rule, which means that the paragraph's text wraps inside that width and extends as deeply as necessary to show the entire paragraph. The clientHeight property describes that depth. The clientHeight property then calculates where a logo image should be positioned immediately after DIV, regardless of the length of the text. As a bonus, the clientWidth property helps the script center the image horizontally with respect to the paragraph's text.

Listing 15-6: **Using clientHeight and clientWidth Properties**

```
<HTML>
<HEAD>
<TITLE>clientHeight and clientWidth Properties</TITLE>
<SCRIPT LANGUAGE="JavaScript">
function showLogo() {
    var paragraphW = document.all.myDIV.clientWidth
    var paragraphH = document.all.myDIV.clientHeight
    // correct for Windows/Mac discrepancies
    var paragraphTop = (document.all.myDIV.clientTop) ?
        document.all.myDIV.clientTop : document.all.myDIV.offsetTop
    var logoW = document.all.logo.style.pixelWidth
    // center logo horizontally against paragraph
    document.all.logo.style.pixelLeft = (paragraphW-logoW)/2
    // position image immediately below end of paragraph
    document.all.logo.style.pixelTop = paragraphTop + paragraphH
    document.all.logo.style.visibility = "visible"
}
</SCRIPT>
</HEAD>
<BODY>
<BUTTON onClick="showLogo()">Position and Show Logo Art</BUTTON>
<DIV ID="logo" STYLE="position:absolute; width:120px; visibility:hidden"><IMG
SRC="logo.gif"></DIV>
<DIV ID="myDIV" STYLE="width:200px">
```

Continued

Listing 15-6 *(continued)*

```
<P>Lorem ipsum dolor sit amet, consectetaur adipisicing elit, sed do eiusmod
tempor incididunt ut labore et dolore magna aliqua. Ut enim adminim veniam, quis
nostrud exercitation ullamco laboris nisi ut aliquip ex ea commodo consequat.
Duis aute irure dolor in reprehenderit involuptate velit esse cillum dolore eu
fugiat nulla pariatur. Excepteur sint occaecat cupidatat non proident.</P>
</DIV>
</BODY>
</HTML>
```

To assist in the vertical positioning of the logo, the offsetTop property of the DIV object provides the position of the start of the DIV with respect to its outer container (the BODY). Unfortunately, IE/Mac uses the clientTop property to obtain the desired dimension. That measure (assigned to the paragraphTop variable), plus the clientHeight of the DIV, provides the top coordinate of the image.

If you use only IE5, you can eliminate the DIV wrapper around the P element and assign the STYLE attribute directly to the P element. The script can then read the clientHeight and clientWidth of the P object.

contentEditable

	NN2	NN3	NN4	NN6	IE3/J1	IE3/J2	IE4	IE5	IE5.5
Compatibility									✓

Example

Listing 15-7 is a simplified demonstration of how to turn some text inside a document into an editable element. When you click the button of a freshly loaded page, the toggleEdit() function captures the opposite of the current editable state via the isContentEditable property of the DIV that is subject to edit. You switch on editing for that element in the next statement by assigning the new value to the contentEditable property of the DIV. For added impact, turn the text of the DIV to red to provide additional user feedback about what is editable on the page. You can also switch the button label to one that indicates the action invoked by the next click on it.

Listing 15-7: **Using the contentEditable Property**

```
<HTML>
<HEAD>
<STYLE TYPE="text/css">
.normal {color: black}
.editing {color: red}
```

```
</STYLE>
<SCRIPT LANGUAGE="JavaScript">
function toggleEdit() {
    var newState = !editableText.isContentEditable
    editableText.contentEditable = newState
    editableText.className = (newState) ? "editing" : "normal"
    editBtn.innerText = (newState) ? "Disable Editing" : "Enable Editing"
}
</SCRIPT>
<BODY>
<H1>Editing Contents</H1>
<HR>
<P>Turn on editing to modify the following text:</P>
<DIV ID="editableText">Edit this text on the fly....</DIV>
<P><BUTTON ID="editBtn" onClick="toggleEdit()" onFocus="this.blur()">
Enable Editing
</BUTTON></P>
</BODY>
</HTML>
```

The BUTTON element has an `onFocus` event handler that immediately invokes the `blur()` method on the button. This prevents a press of the spacebar (during editing) from accidentally triggering the button.

currentStyle

	NN2	NN3	NN4	NN6	IE3/J1	IE3/J2	IE4	IE5	IE5.5
Compatibility								✓	✓

Example

Use The Evaluator (Chapter 13 in the *JavaScript Bible*) to compare the properties of the `currentStyle` and `style` objects of an element. For example, an unmodified copy of The Evaluator contains an EM element whose ID is `"myEM"`. Enter `document.all.myEM.style` into the bottom property listing text box and press Enter. Notice how most of the property values are empty. Now enter `document.all.myEM.currentStyle` into the property listing text box and press Enter. Every property has a value associated with it.

```
dataFld
dataFormatAs
dataSrc
```

	NN2	NN3	NN4	NN6	IE3/J1	IE3/J2	IE4	IE5	IE5.5
Compatibility							✓	✓	✓

Example

Listing 15-8 is a simple document that has two TDC objects associated with it. The external files are different formats of the U.S. Bill of Rights document. One file is a traditional, tab-delimited data file consisting of only two records. The first record is a tab-delimited sequence of field names (named "Article1", "Article2", and so on); the second record is a tab-delimited sequence of article content defined in HTML:

```
<H1>ARTICLE I</H1><P>Congress shall make...</P>
```

The second file is a raw text file consisting of the full Bill of Rights with no HTML formatting attached.

When you load Listing 15-8, only the first article of the Bill of Rights appears in a blue-bordered box. Buttons enable you to navigate to the previous and next articles in the series. Because the data source is a traditional, tab-delimited file, the nextField() and prevField() functions calculate the name of the next source field and assign the new value to the dataFld property. All of the data is already in the browser after the page loads, so cycling through the records is as fast as the browser can reflow the page to accommodate the new content.

Listing 15-8: **Changing dataFld and dataSrc Properties**

```
<HTML>
<HEAD>
<TITLE>Data Binding</TITLE>
<STYLE TYPE="text/css">
#display {width:500px; border:10px ridge blue; padding:20px}
.hiddenControl {display:none}
</STYLE>
<SCRIPT LANGUAGE="JavaScript">
function nextField() {
    var elem = document.all.display
    var fieldName = elem.dataFld
    var currFieldNum = parseInt(fieldName.substring(7, fieldName.length),10)
    currFieldNum = (currFieldNum == 10) ? 1 : ++currFieldNum
    elem.dataFld = "Article" + currFieldNum
}
```

```
function prevField() {
    var elem = document.all.display
    var fieldName = elem.dataFld
    var currFieldNum = parseInt(fieldName.substring(7, fieldName.length),10)
    currFieldNum = (currFieldNum == 1) ? 10 : --currFieldNum
    elem.dataFld = "Article" + currFieldNum
}

function toggleComplete() {
    if (document.all.buttonWrapper.className == "") {
        document.all.display.dataSrc = "#rights_raw"
        document.all.display.dataFld = "column1"
        document.all.display.dataFormatAs = "text"
        document.all.buttonWrapper.className = "hiddenControl"
    } else {
        document.all.display.dataSrc = "#rights_html"
        document.all.display.dataFld = "Article1"
        document.all.display.dataFormatAs = "HTML"
        document.all.buttonWrapper.className = ""
    }
}
</SCRIPT>
</HEAD>
<BODY>
<P><B>U.S. Bill of Rights</B></P>
<FORM>
<INPUT TYPE="button" VALUE="Toggle Complete/Individual"
onClick="toggleComplete()">
<SPAN ID="buttonWrapper" CLASS="">
<INPUT TYPE="button" VALUE="Prev" onClick="prevField()">
<INPUT TYPE="button" VALUE="Next" onClick="nextField()">
</SPAN>
</FORM>


<DIV ID="display" DATASRC="#rights_html" DATAFLD="Article1"
DATAFORMATAS="HTML"></DIV>

<OBJECT ID="rights_html" CLASSID="clsid:333C7BC4-460F-11D0-BC04-0080C7055A83">
    <PARAM NAME="DataURL" VALUE="Bill of Rights.txt">
    <PARAM NAME="UseHeader" VALUE="True">
    <PARAM NAME="FieldDelim" VALUE="&#09;">
</OBJECT>
<OBJECT ID="rights_raw" CLASSID="clsid:333C7BC4-460F-11D0-BC04-0080C7055A83">
    <PARAM NAME="DataURL" VALUE="Bill of Rights (no format).txt">
    <PARAM NAME="FieldDelim" VALUE="\">
    <PARAM NAME="RowDelim" VALUE="\">
</OBJECT>
</BODY>
</HTML>
```

Another button on the page enables you to switch between the initial piecemeal version of the document and the unformatted version in its entirety. To load the entire document as a single record, the `FieldDelim` and `RowDelim` parameters of the second OBJECT element eliminate their default values by replacing them with characters that don't appear in the document at all. And because the external file does not have a field name in the file, the default value (`column1` for the lone column in this document) is the data field. Thus, in the `toggleComplete()` function, the `dataSrc` property is changed to the desired OBJECT element ID, the `dataFld` property is set to the correct value for the data source, and the `dataFormatAs` property is changed to reflect the different intention of the source content (to be rendered as HTML or as plain text). When the display shows the entire document, you can hide the two radio buttons by assigning a `className` value to the SPAN element that surrounds the buttons. The `className` value is the identifier of the class selector in the document's style sheet. When the `toggleComplete()` function resets the `className` property to empty, the default properties (normal inline display style) take hold.

One further example demonstrates the kind of power available to the TDC under script control. Listing 15-9 displays table data from a tab-delimited file of Academy Award information. The data file has eight columns of data, and each column heading is treated as a field name: Year, Best Picture, Best Director, Best Director Film, Best Actress, Best Actress Film, Best Actor, and Best Actor Film. For the design of the page, only five fields from each record appear: Year, Film, Director, Actress, and Actor. Notice in the listing how the HTML for the table and its content is bound to the data source object and the fields within the data.

The "dynamic" part of this example is apparent in how you can sort and filter the data, once loaded into the browser, without further access to the original source data. The TDC object features `Sort` and `Filter` properties that enable you to act on the data currently loaded in the browser. The simplest kind of sorting indicates on which field (or fields, via a semicolon delimited list of field names) the entire data set should be sorted. Leading the name of the sort field is either a plus (to indicate ascending) or minus (descending) symbol. After setting the `data` object's `Sort` property, invoke its `Reset()` method to tell the object to apply the new property. The data in the bound table is immediately redrawn to reflect any changes.

Similarly, you can tell a data collection to display records that meet specific criteria. In Listing 15-9, two select lists and a pair of radio buttons provide the interface to the `Filter` property's settings (see Figure 1-1). For example, you can filter the output to display only those records in which the Best Picture was the same picture of the winning Best Actress's performance. Simple filter expressions are based on field names:

```
dataObj.Filter = "Best Picture" = "Best Actress Film"
```

Listing 15-9: **Sorting and Filtering Bound Data**

```
<HTML>
<HEAD>
<TITLE>Data Binding—Sorting</TITLE>
<SCRIPT LANGUAGE="JavaScript">
```

```
function sortByYear(type) {
    oscars.Sort = (type == "normal") ? "-Year" : "+Year"
    oscars.Reset()
}
function filterInCommon(form) {
    var filterExpr1 = form.filter1.options[form.filter1.selectedIndex].value
    var filterExpr2 = form.filter2.options[form.filter2.selectedIndex].value
    var operator = (form.operator[0].checked) ? "=" : "<>"
    var filterExpr = filterExpr1 + operator + filterExpr2
    oscars.Filter = filterExpr
    oscars.Reset()
}
</SCRIPT>

</HEAD>
<BODY>
<P><B>Academy Awards 1978-1997</B></P>
<FORM>
<P>Sort list by year <A HREF="javascript:sortByYear('normal')">from newest to
oldest</A> or <A HREF="javascript:sortByYear('reverse')">from oldest to
newest</A>.</P>
<P>Filter listings for records whose
<SELECT NAME="filter1" onChange="filterInCommon(this.form)">
    <OPTION VALUE="">
    <OPTION VALUE="Best Picture">Best Picture
    <OPTION VALUE="Best Director Film">Best Director's Film
    <OPTION VALUE="Best Actress Film">Best Actress's Film
    <OPTION VALUE="Best Actor Film">Best Actor's Film
</SELECT>
<INPUT TYPE="radio" NAME="operator" CHECKED
onClick="filterInCommon(this.form)">is
<INPUT TYPE="radio" NAME="operator" onClick="filterInCommon(this.form)">is not
<SELECT NAME="filter2" onChange="filterInCommon(this.form)">
    <OPTION VALUE="">
    <OPTION VALUE="Best Picture">Best Picture
    <OPTION VALUE="Best Director Film">Best Director's Film
    <OPTION VALUE="Best Actress Film">Best Actress's Film
    <OPTION VALUE="Best Actor Film">Best Actor's Film
</SELECT>
</P>
</FORM>
<TABLE DATASRC="#oscars" BORDER=1 ALIGN="center">
<THEAD STYLE="background-color:yellow; text-align:center">
<TR><TD>Year</TD>
    <TD>Film</TD>
    <TD>Director</TD>
    <TD>Actress</TD>
    <TD>Actor</TD>
</TR>
</THEAD>
<TR>
```

Continued

Listing 15-9 *(continued)*

```
    <TD><DIV ID="col1" DATAFLD="Year" ></DIV></TD>
    <TD><DIV ID="col2" DATAFLD="Best Picture"></DIV></TD>
    <TD><DIV ID="col3" DATAFLD="Best Director"></DIV></TD>
    <TD><DIV ID="col4" DATAFLD="Best Actress"></DIV></TD>
    <TD><DIV ID="col5" DATAFLD="Best Actor"></DIV></TD>
</TR>
</TABLE>

<OBJECT ID="oscars" CLASSID="clsid:333C7BC4-460F-11D0-BC04-0080C7055A83">
    <PARAM NAME="DataURL" VALUE="Academy Awards.txt">
    <PARAM NAME="UseHeader" VALUE="True">
    <PARAM NAME="FieldDelim" VALUE="&#09;">
</OBJECT>
</BODY>
</HTML>
```

For more detailed information on Data Source Objects and their properties, visit `http://msdn.microsoft.com` and search for "Data Binding."

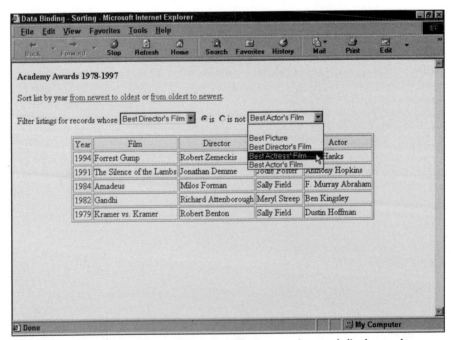

Figure 1-1: IE/Windows data binding puts filtering, sorting, and display under script control.

dir

	NN2	NN3	NN4	NN6	IE3/J1	IE3/J2	IE4	IE5	IE5.5
Compatibility				✓				✓	✓

Example

Changing this property value in a standard U.S. version of the browser only makes the right margin the starting point for each new line of text (in other words, the characters are not rendered in reverse order). You can experiment with this in The Evaluator by entering the following statements into the expression evaluation field:

```
document.getElementById("myP").dir = "rtl"
```

disabled

	NN2	NN3	NN4	NN6	IE3/J1	IE3/J2	IE4	IE5	IE5.5
Compatibility				(✓)			✓	✓	✓

Example

Use The Evaluator (Chapter 13 in the *JavaScript Bible*) to experiment with the disabled property on both form elements (IE4+ and NN6) and regular HTML elements (IE5.5). For IE4+ and NN6, see what happens when you disable the output textarea by entering the following statement into the top text box:

```
document.forms[0].output.disabled = true
```

The textarea is disabled for user entry, although you can still set the field's value property via script (which is how the true returned value got there).

If you have IE5.5+, disable the myP element by entering the following statement into the top text box:

```
document.all.myP.disabled = true
```

The sample paragraph's text turns gray.

document

	NN2	NN3	NN4	NN6	IE3/J1	IE3/J2	IE4	IE5	IE5.5
Compatibility							✓	✓	✓

Example

The following simplified function accepts a parameter that can be any object in a document hierarchy. The script finds out the reference of the object's containing document for further reference to other objects:

```
function getCompanionFormCount(obj) {
    var ownerDoc = obj.document
    return ownerDoc.forms.length
}
```

Because the `ownerDoc` variable contains a valid reference to a `document` object, the `return` statement uses that reference to return a typical property of the document object hierarchy.

firstChild
lastChild

	NN2	NN3	NN4	NN6	IE3/J1	IE3/J2	IE4	IE5	IE5.5
Compatibility				✓				✓	✓

Example

These two properties come in handy for Listing 15-10, whose job it is to either add or replace `LI` elements to an existing `OL` element. You can enter any text you want to appear at the beginning or end of the list. Using the `firstChild` and `lastChild` properties simplifies access to the ends of the list. For the functions that replace child nodes, the example uses the `replaceChild()` method. Alternatively for IE4+, you can modify the `innerText` property of the objects returned by the `firstChild` or `lastChild` property. This example is especially interesting to watch when you add items to the list: The browser automatically renumbers items to fit the current state of the list.

Listing 15-10: **Using firstChild and lastChild Properties**

```
<HTML>
<HEAD>
<TITLE>firstChild and lastChild Properties</TITLE>
<SCRIPT LANGUAGE="JavaScript">
// helper function for prepend() and append()
function makeNewLI(txt) {
    var newItem = document.createElement("LI")
    newItem.innerHTML = txt
    return newItem
}
function prepend(form) {
    var newItem = makeNewLI(form.input.value)
    var firstLI = document.getElementById("myList").firstChild
    document.getElementById("myList").insertBefore(newItem, firstLI)
```

```
    }
    function append(form) {
        var newItem = makeNewLI(form.input.value)
        var lastLI = document.getElementById("myList").lastChild
        document.getElementById("myList").appendChild(newItem)
    }
    function replaceFirst(form) {
        var newItem = makeNewLI(form.input.value)
        var firstLI = document.getElementById("myList").firstChild
        document.getElementById("myList").replaceChild(newItem, firstLI)
    }
    function replaceLast(form) {
        var newItem = makeNewLI(form.input.value)
        var lastLI = document.getElementById("myList").lastChild
        document.getElementById("myList").replaceChild(newItem, lastLI)
    }
</SCRIPT>

</HEAD>
<BODY>
<H1>firstChild and lastChild Property Lab</H1>
<HR>
<FORM>
<LABEL>Enter some text to add to or replace in the OL element:</LABEL><BR>
<INPUT TYPE="text" NAME="input" SIZE=50><BR>
<INPUT TYPE="button" VALUE="Insert at Top" onClick="prepend(this.form)">
<INPUT TYPE="button" VALUE="Append to Bottom" onClick="append(this.form)">
<BR>
<INPUT TYPE="button" VALUE="Replace First Item"
onClick="replaceFirst(this.form)">
<INPUT TYPE="button" VALUE="Replace Last Item" onClick="replaceLast(this.form)">
</FORM>
<P></P>
<OL ID="myList"><LI>Initial Item 1
<LI>Initial Item 2
<LI>Initial Item 3
<LI>Initial Item 4
<OL>
</BODY>
</HTML>
```

height
width

	NN2	NN3	NN4	NN6	IE3/J1	IE3/J2	IE4	IE5	IE5.5
Compatibility			✓	✓			✓	✓	✓

Example

The following example increases the width of a table by 10 percent.

```
var tableW = parseInt(document.all.myTable.width)
document.all.myTable.width = (tableW * 1.1) + "%"
```

Because the initial setting for the WIDTH attribute of the TABLE element is set as a percentage value, the script calculation extracts the number from the percentage width string value. In the second statement, the old number is increased by 10 percent and turned into a percentage string by appending the percentage symbol to the value. The resulting string value is assigned to the width property of the table.

hideFocus

	NN2	NN3	NN4	NN6	IE3/J1	IE3/J2	IE4	IE5	IE5.5
Compatibility									✓

Example

Use The Evaluator (Chapter 13 in the *JavaScript Bible*) to experiment with the hideFocus property in IE5.5. Enter the following statement into the top text field to assign a tabIndex value to the myP element so that, by default, the element receives focus and the dotted rectangle:

```
document.all.myP.tabIndex = 1
```

Press the Tab key several times until the paragraph receives focus. Now, disable the focus rectangle:

```
document.all.myP.hideFocus = true
```

If you now press the Tab key several times, the dotted rectangle does not appear around the paragraph. To prove that the element still receives focus, scroll the page down to the bottom so that the paragraph is not visible (you may have to resize the window). Click one of the focusable elements at the bottom of the page, and then press the Tab key slowly until the Address field toolbar has focus. Press the Tab key once. The page scrolls to bring the paragraph into view, but there is no focus rectangle around the element.

id

	NN2	NN3	NN4	NN6	IE3/J1	IE3/J2	IE4	IE5	IE5.5
Compatibility				✓			✓	✓	✓

Example

Rarely do you need to access this property in a script — unless you write an authoring tool that iterates through all elements of a page to extract the IDs assigned by the author. You can retrieve an object reference once you know the object's `id` property (via the `document.getElementById(elemID)` method). But if for some reason your script doesn't know the ID of, say, the second paragraph of a document, you can extract that ID as follows:

```
var elemID = document.all.tags("P")[1].id
```

innerHTML
innerText

	NN2	NN3	NN4	NN6	IE3/J1	IE3/J2	IE4	IE5	IE5.5
Compatibility				(✓)			✓	✓	✓

Example

The IE4+ page generated by Listing 15-11 contains an H1 element label and a paragraph of text. The purpose is to demonstrate how the `innerHTML` and `innerText` properties differ in their intent. Two text boxes contain the same combination of text and HTML tags that replaces the inner content of the paragraph's label.

If you apply the default content of the first text box to the `innerHTML` property of the `label1` object, the italic style is rendered as such for the first word. In addition, the text in parentheses is rendered with the help of the small style sheet rule assigned by virtue of the surrounding `<SPAN>` tags. But if you apply that same content to the `innerText` property of the `label` object, the tags are rendered as is.

Use this as a laboratory to experiment with some other content in both text boxes. See what happens when you insert a `<BR>` tag within some text of both text boxes.

Listing 15-11: **Using innerHTML and innerText Properties**

```
<HTML>
<HEAD>
<TITLE>innerHTML and innerText Properties</TITLE>
<STYLE TYPE="text/css">
H1 {font-size:18pt; font-weight:bold; font-family:"Comic Sans MS", Arial, sans-
serif}
.small {font-size:12pt; font-weight:400; color:gray}
</STYLE>
<SCRIPT LANGUAGE="JavaScript">

function setGroupLabelAsText(form) {
    var content = form.textInput.value
```

Continued

Listing 15-11 *(continued)*

```
    if (content) {
        document.all.label1.innerText = content
    }
}
function setGroupLabelAsHTML(form) {
    var content = form.HTMLInput.value
    if (content) {
        document.all.label1.innerHTML = content
    }
}
</SCRIPT>
</HEAD>

<BODY>
<FORM>
<P>
    <INPUT TYPE="text" NAME="HTMLInput"
    VALUE="<I>First</I> Article <SPAN CLASS='small'>(of ten)</SPAN>"
    SIZE=50>
    <INPUT TYPE="button" VALUE="Change Heading HTML"
    onClick="setGroupLabelAsHTML(this.form)">
</P>
<P>
    <INPUT TYPE="text" NAME="textInput"
    VALUE="<I>First</I> Article <SPAN CLASS='small'>(of ten)</SPAN>"
    SIZE=50>
    <INPUT TYPE="button" VALUE="Change Heading Text"
    onClick="setGroupLabelAsText(this.form)">
</P>
</FORM>
<H1 ID="label1">ARTICLE I</H1>
<P>
Congress shall make no law respecting an establishment of religion, or
prohibiting the free exercise thereof; or abridging the freedom of speech, or of
the press; or the right of the people peaceably to assemble, and to petition the
government for a redress of grievances.
</P>
</BODY>
</HTML>
```

isContentEditable

	NN2	NN3	NN4	NN6	IE3/J1	IE3/J2	IE4	IE5	IE5.5
Compatibility									✓

Example

Use The Evaluator (Chapter 13 in the *JavaScript Bible*) to experiment with both the `contentEditable` and `isContentEditable` properties on the `myP` and nested `myEM` elements (reload the page to start with a known version). Check the current setting for the `myEM` element by typing the following statement into the top text field:

```
myEM.isContentEditable
```

This value is `false` because no element upward in the element containment hierarchy is set to be editable yet. Next, turn on editing for the surrounding `myP` element:

```
myP.contentEditable = true
```

At this point, the entire `myP` element is editable because its child element is set, by default, to inherit the edit state of its parent. Prove it by entering the following statement into the top text box:

```
myEM.isContentEditable
```

While the `myEM` element is shown to be editable, no change has accrued to its `contentEditable` property:

```
myEM.contentEditable
```

This property value remains the default `inherit`. You can see an additional example of these two properties in use in Listing 15-7.

isDisabled

	NN2	NN3	NN4	NN6	IE3/J1	IE3/J2	IE4	IE5	IE5.5
Compatibility									✓

Example

Use The Evaluator (Chapter 13 in the *JavaScript Bible*) to experiment with both the `disabled` and `isDisabled` properties on the `myP` and nested `myEM` elements (reload the page to start with a known version). Check the current setting for the `myEM` element by typing the following statement into the top text field:

```
myEM.isDisabled
```

This value is `false` because no element upward in the element containment hierarchy is set for disabling yet. Next, disable the surrounding `myP` element:

```
myP.disabled = true
```

At this point, the entire `myP` element (including its children) is disabled. Prove it by entering the following statement into the top text box:

```
myEM.isDisabled
```

While the `myEM` element is shown as disabled, no change has accrued to its `disabled` property:

```
myEM.disabled
```

This property value remains the default `false`.

isMultiLine

	NN2	NN3	NN4	NN6	IE3/J1	IE3/J2	IE4	IE5	IE5.5
Compatibility									✓

Example

Use The Evaluator (Chapter 13 in the *JavaScript Bible*) to read the `isMultiLine` property for elements on that page. Try the following statements in the top text box:

```
document.body.isMultiLine
document.forms[0].input.isMultiLine
myP.isMultiLine
myEM.isMultiLine
```

All but the text field form control report that they are capable of occupying multiple lines.

isTextEdit

	NN2	NN3	NN4	NN6	IE3/J1	IE3/J2	IE4	IE5	IE5.5
Compatibility							✓	✓	✓

Example

Good coding practice dictates that your script check for this property before invoking the `createTextRange()` method on any object. A typical implementation is as follows:

```
if (document.all.myObject.isTextEdit) {
    var myRange = document.all.myObject.createTextRange()
    [more statements that act on myRange]
}
```

lang

	NN2	NN3	NN4	NN6	IE3/J1	IE3/J2	IE4	IE5	IE5.5
Compatibility				✓			✓	✓	✓

Example

Values for the `lang` property consist of strings containing valid ISO language codes. Such codes have, at the minimum, a primary language code (for example, `"fr"` for French) plus an optional region specifier (for example, `"fr-ch"` for Swiss French). The code to assign a Swiss German value to an element looks like the following:

```
document.all.specialSpan.lang = "de-ch"
```

language

	NN2	NN3	NN4	NN6	IE3/J1	IE3/J2	IE4	IE5	IE5.5
Compatibility							✓	✓	✓

Example

Although it is unlikely that you will modify this property, the following example shows you how to do it for a table cell object:

```
document.all.cellA3.language = "vbs"
```

lastChild

See `firstchild`.

length

	NN2	NN3	NN4	NN6	IE3/J1	IE3/J2	IE4	IE5	IE5.5
Compatibility	✓	✓	✓	✓	✓	✓	✓	✓	✓

Example

You can try the following sequence of statements in the top text box of The Evaluator (Chapter 13 in the *JavaScript Bible*) to see how the `length` property returns values (and sets them for some objects). Note that some statements work in only some browser versions.

```
(All browsers)   document.forms.length
(All browsers)   document.forms[0].elements.length
(NN3+, IE4+)     document.images.length
(NN4+)           document.layers.length
(IE4+)           document.all.length
(IE5+, NN6)      document.getElementById("myTable").childNodes.length
```

nextSibling
previousSibling

	NN2	NN3	NN4	NN6	IE3/J1	IE3/J2	IE4	IE5	IE5.5
Compatibility				✓				✓	✓

Example

The following function assigns the same class name to all child nodes of an element:

```
function setAllChildClasses(parentElem, className) {
    var childElem = parentElem.firstChild
    while (childElem.nextSibling) {
        childElem.className = className
        childElem = childElem.nextSibling
    }
}
```

This example is certainly not the only way to achieve the same results. Using a `for` loop to iterate through the `childNodes` collection of the parent element is an equally valid approach.

nodeName

	NN2	NN3	NN4	NN6	IE3/J1	IE3/J2	IE4	IE5	IE5.5
Compatibility				✓				✓	✓

Example

The following function demonstrates one (not very efficient) way to assign a new class name to every P element in an IE5+ document:

```
function setAllPClasses(className) {
    for (var i = 0; i < document.all.length; i++) {
        if (document.all[i].nodeName == "P") {
            document.all[i].className = className
        }
    }
}
```

A more efficient approach uses the `getElementsByTagName()` method to retrieve a collection of all P elements and then iterate through them directly.

nodeType

	NN2	NN3	NN4	NN6	IE3/J1	IE3/J2	IE4	IE5	IE5.5
Compatibility				✓				✓	✓

Example

You can experiment with viewing nodeType property values in The Evaluator. The P element whose ID is myP is a good place to start. The P element itself is a nodeType of 1:

```
document.getElementById("myP").nodeType
```

This element has three child nodes: a string of text (nodeName #text); an EM element (nodeName EM); and the rest of the text of the element content (nodeName #text). If you view the nodeType of either of the text portions, the value comes back as 3:

```
document.getElementById("myP").childNodes[0].nodeType
```

In NN6 and IE5/Mac, you can inspect the nodeType of the one attribute of this element (the ID attribute):

```
document.getElementById("myP").attributes[0].nodeType
```

With NN6 and IE5/Mac, you can see how the document object returns a nodeType of 9:

```
document.nodeType
```

When IE5 does not support a nodeType constant for a node, its value is sometimes reported as 1. However, more likely the value is undefined.

nodeValue

	NN2	NN3	NN4	NN6	IE3/J1	IE3/J2	IE4	IE5	IE5.5
Compatibility				✓				✓	✓

Example

The first example increases the width of a TEXTAREA object by 10 percent. The nodeValue is converted to an integer (for NN6's string values) before performing the math and reassignment:

```
function widenCols(textareaElem) {
    var colWidth = parseInt(textareaElem.attributes["cols"].nodeValue, 10)
    textareaElem.attributes["cols"].nodeValue = (colWidth * 1.1)
}
```

The second example replaces the text of an element, assuming that the element contains no further nested elements:

```
function replaceText(elem, newText) {
    if (elem.childNodes.length == 1 && elem.firstChild.nodeType == 3) {
        elem.firstChild.nodeValue = newText
    }
}
```

The function builds in one final verification that the element contains just one child node and that it is a text type. An alternative version of the assignment statement of the second example uses the `innerText` property in IE with identical results:

```
elem.innerText = newText
```

offsetHeight
offsetWidth

	NN2	NN3	NN4	NN6	IE3/J1	IE3/J2	IE4	IE5	IE5.5
Compatibility				✓			✓	✓	✓

Example

With IE4+, you can substitute the `offsetHeight` and `offsetWidth` properties for `clientHeight` and `clientWidth` in Listing 15-6. The reason is that the two elements in question have their widths hard-wired in style sheets. Thus, the `offsetWidth` property follows that lead rather than observing the default width of the parent (BODY) element.

With IE5+ and NN6, you can use The Evaluator to inspect the `offsetHeight` and `offsetWidth` property values of various objects on the page. Enter the following statements into the top text box:

```
document.getElementById("myP").offsetWidth
document.getElementById("myEM").offsetWidth
document.getElementById("myP").offsetHeight
document.getElementById("myTable").offsetWidth
```

offsetLeft
offsetTop

	NN2	NN3	NN4	NN6	IE3/J1	IE3/J2	IE4	IE5	IE5.5
Compatibility				✓			✓	✓	✓

Example

The following IE script statements utilize all four "offset" dimensional properties to size and position a DIV element so that it completely covers a SPAN element located within a P element. This can be for a fill-in-the-blank quiz that provides text entry fields elsewhere on the page. As the user gets an answer correct, the blocking DIV element is hidden to reveal the correct answer.

```
document.all.blocker.style.pixelLeft = document.all.span2.offsetLeft
document.all.blocker.style.pixelTop = document.all.span2.offsetTop
document.all.blockImg.height = document.all.span2.offsetHeight
document.all.blockImg.width = document.all.span2.offsetWidth
```

Because the offsetParent property for the SPAN element is the BODY element, the positioned DIV element can use the same positioning context (it's the default context, anyway) for setting the pixelLeft and pixelTop style properties. (Remember that positioning properties belong to an element's style object.) The offsetHeight and offsetWidth properties can read the dimensions of the SPAN element (the example has no borders, margins, or padding to worry about) and assign them to the dimensions of the image contained by the blocker DIV element.

This example is also a bit hazardous in some implementations. If the text of span2 wraps to a new line, the new offsetHeight value has enough pixels to accommodate both lines. But the blockImg and blocker DIV elements are block-level elements that render as a simple rectangle. In other words, the blocker element doesn't turn into two separate strips to cover the pieces of span2 that spread across two lines.

offsetParent

	NN2	NN3	NN4	NN6	IE3/J1	IE3/J2	IE4	IE5	IE5.5
Compatibility				✓			✓	✓	✓

Example

You can use the offsetParent property to help you locate the position of a nested element on the page. Listing 15-12 demonstrates how a script can "walk" up the hierarchy of offsetParent objects in IE for Windows to assemble the location of a nested element on a page. The goal of the exercise in Listing 15-12 is to position an image at the upper-left corner of the second table cell. The entire table is centered on the page.

The onLoad event handler invokes the setImagePosition() function. The function first sets a Boolean flag that determines whether the calculations should be based on the client or offset sets of properties. IE4/Windows and IE5/Mac rely on client properties, while IE5+/Windows works with the offset properties. The discrepancies even out, however, with the while loop. This loop traverses the offsetParent hierarchy starting with the offsetParent of the cell out to, but not including, the document.body object. The body object is not included because that is the positioning context for the image. In IE5, the while loop executes only once because just the TABLE element exists between the cell and the body; in IE4, the loop executes twice to account for the TR and TABLE elements up the hierarchy. Finally, the cumulative values of left and top measures are applied to the positioning properties of the DIV object's style and the image is made visible.

Listing 15-12: **Using the offsetParent Property**

```
<HTML>
<HEAD>
<TITLE>offsetParent Property</TITLE>
<SCRIPT LANGUAGE="JavaScript">
function setImagePosition(){
    var cElement = document.all.myCell
    // Set flag for whether calculations should use
    // client- or offset- property measures. Use
    // client- for IE5/Mac and IE4/Windows; otherwise
    // use offset- properties. An ugly, but necessary
    // workaround.
    var useClient = (cElement.offsetTop == 0) ?
        ((cElement.offsetParent.tagName == "TR") ? false : true) : false
    if (useClient) {
        var x = cElement.clientLeft
        var y = cElement.clientTop
    } else {
        var x = cElement.offsetLeft
        var y = cElement.offsetTop
    }
    var pElement = document.all.myCell.offsetParent
    while (pElement != document.body) {
        if (useClient) {
            x += pElement.clientLeft
            y += pElement.clientTop
        } else {
            x += pElement.offsetLeft
            y += pElement.offsetTop
        }
        pElement = pElement.offsetParent
    }
    document.all.myDIV.style.pixelLeft = x
    document.all.myDIV.style.pixelTop = y
    document.all.myDIV.style.visibility = "visible"
}
</SCRIPT>
</HEAD>
<BODY onload="setImagePosition()">
<SCRIPT LANGUAGE="JavaScript">
</SCRIPT>
<H1>The offsetParent Property</H1>
<HR>
<P>After the document loads, the script positions a small image in the upper
left corner of the second table cell.</P>
<TABLE BORDER=1 ALIGN="center">
```

```
<TR>
    <TD>This is the first cell</TD>
    <TD ID="myCell">This is the second cell.</TD>
</TR>
</TABLE>
<DIV ID="myDIV" STYLE="position:absolute; visibility:hidden; height:12;
width:12">
<IMG SRC="end.gif" HEIGHT=12 WIDTH=12></DIV>
</BODY>
</HTML>
```

outerHTML
outerText

	NN2	NN3	NN4	NN6	IE3/J1	IE3/J2	IE4	IE5	IE5.5
Compatibility							✓	✓	✓

Example

The page generated by Listing 15-13 (IE4+/Windows only) contains an H1 element label and a paragraph of text. The purpose is to demonstrate how the outerHTML and outerText properties differ in their intent. Two text boxes contain the same combination of text and HTML tags that replaces the element that creates the paragraph's label.

If you apply the default content of the first text box to the outerHTML property of the label object, the H1 element is replaced by a SPAN element whose CLASS attribute acquires a different style sheet rule defined earlier in the document. Notice that the ID of the new SPAN element is the same as the original H1 element. This allows the script attached to the second button to address the object. But this second script replaces the element with the raw text (including tags). The element is now gone, and any attempt to change the outerHTML or outerText properties of the label object causes an error because there is no longer a label object in the document.

Use this laboratory to experiment with some other content in both text boxes.

Listing 15-13: **Using outerHTML and outerText Properties**

```
<HTML>
<HEAD>
<TITLE>outerHTML and outerText Properties</TITLE>
<STYLE TYPE="text/css">
```

Continued

Listing 15-13 *(continued)*

```
H1 {font-size:18pt; font-weight:bold; font-family:"Comic Sans MS", Arial, sans-
serif}
.heading {font-size:20pt; font-weight:bold; font-family:"Arial Black", Arial,
sans-serif}
</STYLE>
<SCRIPT LANGUAGE="JavaScript">

function setGroupLabelAsText(form) {
    var content = form.textInput.value
    if (content) {
        document.all.label1.outerText = content
    }
}
function setGroupLabelAsHTML(form) {
    var content = form.HTMLInput.value
    if (content) {
        document.all.label1.outerHTML = content
    }
}
</SCRIPT>
</HEAD>

<BODY>
<FORM>
<P>
    <INPUT TYPE="text" NAME="HTMLInput"
    VALUE="<SPAN ID='label1' CLASS='heading'>Article the First</SPAN>" SIZE=55>
    <INPUT TYPE="button" VALUE="Change Heading HTML"
    onClick="setGroupLabelAsHTML(this.form)">
</P>
<P>
    <INPUT TYPE="text" NAME="textInput"
    VALUE="<SPAN ID='label1' CLASS='heading'>Article the First</SPAN>" SIZE=55>
    <INPUT TYPE="button" VALUE="Change Heading Text"
    onClick="setGroupLabelAsText(this.form)">
</P>
</FORM>
<H1 ID="label1">ARTICLE I</H1>
<P>
Congress shall make no law respecting an establishment of religion, or
prohibiting the free exercise thereof; or abridging the freedom of speech, or of
the press; or the right of the people peaceably to assemble, and to petition the
government for a redress of grievances.
</P>
</BODY>
</HTML>
```

ownerDocument

	NN2	NN3	NN4	NN6	IE3/J1	IE3/J2	IE4	IE5	IE5.5
Compatibility				✓					

Example

Use The Evaluator (Chapter 13 in the *JavaScript Bible*) to explore the `ownerDocument` property in NN6. Enter the following statement into the top text box:

```
document.body.childNodes[5].ownerDocument
```

The result is a reference to the `document` object. You can use that to inspect a property of the document, as shown in the following statement you should enter into the top text box:

```
document.body.childNodes[5].ownerDocument.URL
```

This returns the `document.URL` property for the document that owns the child node.

parentElement

	NN2	NN3	NN4	NN6	IE3/J1	IE3/J2	IE4	IE5	IE5.5
Compatibility							✓	✓	✓

Example

You can experiment with the `parentElement` property in The Evaluator. The document contains a P element named myP. Type each of the following statements from the left column into the upper expression evaluation text box and press Enter to see the results.

Expression	*Result*
`document.all.myP.tagName`	P
`document.all.myP.parentElement`	[object]
`document.all.myP.parentElement.tagName`	BODY
`document.all.myP.parentElement.parentElement`	[object]
`document.all.myP.parentElement.parentElement.tagName`	HTML
`document.all.myP.parentElement.parentElement.parentElement`	null

parentNode

	NN2	NN3	NN4	NN6	IE3/J1	IE3/J2	IE4	IE5	IE5.5
Compatibility				✓				✓	✓

Example

Use The Evaluator to examine the `parentNode` property values of both an element and a non-element node. Begin with the following two statements and watch the results of each:

```
document.getElementById("myP").parentNode.tagName
document.getElementById("myP").parentElement.tagName    (IE only)
```

Now examine the properties from the point of view of the first text fragment node of the `myP` paragraph element:

```
document.getElementById("myP").childNodes[0].nodeValue
document.getElementById("myP").childNodes[0].parentNode.tagName
document.getElementById("myP").childNodes[0].parentElement    (IE only)
```

Notice (in IE) that the text node does not have a `parentElement` property.

parentTextEdit

	NN2	NN3	NN4	NN6	IE3/J1	IE3/J2	IE4	IE5	IE5.5
Compatibility							✓	✓	✓

Example

The page resulting from Listing 15-14 contains a paragraph of Greek text and three radio buttons that select the size of a paragraph chunk: one character, one word, or one sentence. If you click anywhere within the large paragraph, the `onClick` event handler invokes the `selectChunk()` function. The function first examines which of the radio buttons is selected to determine how much of the paragraph to highlight (select) around the point at which the user clicks.

After the script employs the `parentTextEdit` property to test whether the clicked element has a valid parent capable of creating a text range, it calls upon the property again to help create the text range. From there, `TextRange` object methods shrink the range to a single insertion point, move that point to the spot nearest the cursor location at click time, expand the selection to encompass the desired chunk, and select that bit of text.

Notice one workaround for the `TextRange` object's `expand()` method anomaly: If you specify a sentence, IE doesn't treat the beginning of a P element as the starting end of a sentence automatically. A camouflaged (white text color) period is appended to the end of the previous element to force the `TextRange` object to expand only to the beginning of the first sentence of the targeted P element.

Listing 15-14: **Using the parentTextEdit Property**

```
<HTML>
<HEAD>
<TITLE>parentTextEdit Property</TITLE>
<STYLE TYPE="text/css">
P {cursor:hand}
</STYLE>
<SCRIPT LANGUAGE="JavaScript">
function selectChunk() {
    var chunk, range
    for (var i = 0; i < document.forms[0].chunk.length; i++) {
        if (document.forms[0].chunk[i].checked) {
            chunk = document.forms[0].chunk[i].value
            break
        }
    }
    var x = window.event.clientX
    var y = window.event.clientY
    if (window.event.srcElement.parentTextEdit) {
        range = window.event.srcElement.parentTextEdit.createTextRange()
        range.collapse()
        range.moveToPoint(x, y)
        range.expand(chunk)
        range.select()
    }
}
</SCRIPT>
</HEAD>

<BODY BGCOLOR="white">
<FORM>
<P>Choose how much of the paragraph is to be selected when you click anywhere in
it:<BR>
<INPUT TYPE="radio" NAME="chunk" VALUE="character" CHECKED>Character
<INPUT TYPE="radio" NAME="chunk" VALUE="word">Word
<INPUT TYPE="radio" NAME="chunk" VALUE="sentence">Sentence
<FONT COLOR="white">.</FONT></P>
</FORM>

<P onClick="selectChunk()">
Lorem ipsum dolor sit amet, consectetaur adipisicing elit, sed do eiusmod tempor
incididunt ut labore et dolore magna aliqua. Ut enim adminim veniam, quis
nostrud exercitation ullamco laboris nisi ut aliquip ex ea commodo consequat.
Duis aute irure dolor in reprehenderit involuptate velit esse cillum dolore eu
fugiat nulla pariatur. Excepteur sint occaecat cupidatat non proident, sunt in
culpa qui officia deserunt mollit anim id est laborum.
</P>
</BODY>
</HTML>
```

previousSibling

See nextSibling.

readyState

	NN2	NN3	NN4	NN6	IE3/J1	IE3/J2	IE4	IE5	IE5.5
Compatibility							✓	✓	✓

Example

To witness a readyState property other than complete for standard HTML, you can try examining the property in a script that immediately follows an <IMG> tag:

```
...
<IMG ID="myImg" SRC="someImage.gif">
<SCRIPT LANGUAGE="JavaScript">
alert(document.all.myImg.readyState)
</SCRIPT>
...
```

Putting this fragment into a document that is accessible across a slow network helps. If the image is not in the browser's cache, you might get the uninitialized or loading result. The former means that the IMG object exists, but it has not started receiving the image data from the server yet. If you reload the page, chances are that the image will load instantaneously from the cache and the readyState property will report complete.

recordNumber

	NN2	NN3	NN4	NN6	IE3/J1	IE3/J2	IE4	IE5	IE5.5
Compatibility							✓	✓	✓

Example

You can see the recordNumber property in action in Listing 15-15. The data source is a small, tab-delimited file consisting of 20 records of Academy Award data. Thus, the table that displays a subset of the fields is bound to the data source object. Also bound to the data source object are three SPAN objects embedded within a paragraph near the top of the page. As the user clicks a row of data, three fields from that clicked record are placed into the bound SPAN objects.

The script part of this page is a mere single statement. When the user triggers the onClick event handler of the repeated TR object, the function receives a reference to the TR object as a parameter. The data store object maintains an internal copy of the data in a recordset object. One of the properties of this recordset object is the `AbsolutePosition` property, which is the integer value of the current record that the data object points to (it can point to only one row at a time, and the default row is the first row). The statement sets the `AbsolutePosition` property of the `recordset` object to the `recordNumber` property for the row that the user clicks. Because the three SPAN elements are bound to the same data source, they are immediately updated to reflect the change to the data object's internal pointer to the current record. Notice, too, that the third SPAN object is bound to one of the data source fields not shown in the table. You can reach any field of a record because the Data Source Object holds the entire data source content.

Listing 15-15: **Using the Data Binding recordNumber Property**

```
<HTML>
<HEAD>
<TITLE>Data Binding (recordNumber)</TITLE>
<STYLE TYPE="text/css">
.filmTitle {font-style:italic}
</STYLE>
<SCRIPT LANGUAGE="JavaScript">
// set recordset pointer to the record clicked on in the table.
function setRecNum(row) {
    document.oscars.recordset.AbsolutePosition = row.recordNumber
}
</SCRIPT>

</HEAD>
<BODY>
<P><B>Academy Awards 1978-1997</B> (Click on a table row to extract data from
one record.)</P>
<P>The award for Best Actor of <SPAN DATASRC="#oscars" DATAFLD="Year"></SPAN>
 went to <SPAN DATASRC="#oscars" DATAFLD="Best Actor"></SPAN>
 for his outstanding achievement in the film
<SPAN CLASS="filmTitle" DATASRC="#oscars" DATAFLD="Best Actor Film"></SPAN>.</P>
<TABLE BORDER=1 DATASRC="#oscars" ALIGN="center">
<THEAD STYLE="background-color:yellow; text-align:center">
<TR><TD>Year</TD>
    <TD>Film</TD>
    <TD>Director</TD>
    <TD>Actress</TD>
    <TD>Actor</TD>
</TR>
</THEAD>
<TR ID=repeatableRow onClick="setRecNum(this)">
    <TD><DIV ID="col1" DATAFLD="Year"></DIV></TD>
    <TD><DIV CLASS="filmTitle" ID="col2" DATAFLD="Best Picture"></DIV></TD>
    <TD><DIV ID="col3" DATAFLD="Best Director"></DIV></TD>
    <TD><DIV ID="col4" DATAFLD="Best Actress"></DIV></TD>
    <TD><DIV ID="col5" DATAFLD="Best Actor"></DIV></TD>
```

Continued

Listing 15-15 *(continued)*

```
</TR>
</TABLE>

<OBJECT ID="oscars" CLASSID="clsid:333C7BC4-460F-11D0-BC04-0080C7055A83">
    <PARAM NAME="DataURL" VALUE="Academy Awards.txt">
    <PARAM NAME="UseHeader" VALUE="True">
    <PARAM NAME="FieldDelim" VALUE="&#09;">
</OBJECT>
</BODY>
</HTML>
```

runtimeStyle

	NN2	NN3	NN4	NN6	IE3/J1	IE3/J2	IE4	IE5	IE5.5
Compatibility								✓	✓

Example

Use The Evaluator (Chapter 13 in the *JavaScript Bible*) to compare the properties of the runtimeStyle and style objects of an element. For example, an unmodified copy of The Evaluator contains an EM element whose ID is "myEM". Enter both

document.all.myEM.style.color

and

document.all.myEM.runtimeStyle.color

into the top text field in turn. Initially, both values are empty. Now assign a color to the style property via the upper text box:

document.all.myEM.style.color = "red"

If you now type the two earlier statements into the upper box, you can see that the style object reflects the change, while the runtimeStyle object still holds onto its original (empty) value.

scopeName

	NN2	NN3	NN4	NN6	IE3/J1	IE3/J2	IE4	IE5	IE5.5
Compatibility								✓	✓

Example

If you have a sample document that contains XML and a namespace spec, you can use `document.write()` or `alert()` methods to view the value of the `scopeName` property. The syntax is

```
document.all.elementID.scopeName
```

scrollHeight
scrollWidth

	NN2	NN3	NN4	NN6	IE3/J1	IE3/J2	IE4	IE5	IE5.5
Compatibility							✓	✓	✓

Example

Use The Evaluator (Chapter 13 in the *JavaScript Bible*) to experiment with these two properties of the TEXTAREA object, which displays the output of evaluations and property listings. To begin, enter the following into the bottom one-line text field to list the properties of the `body` object:

```
document.body
```

This displays a long list of properties for the `body` object. Now enter the following property expression in the top one-line text field to see the `scrollHeight` property of the output TEXTAREA when it holds the dozens of lines of property listings:

```
document.all.output.scrollHeight
```

The result, some number probably in the hundreds, is now displayed in the output TEXTAREA. This means that you can scroll the content of the `output` element vertically to reveal that number of pixels. Click the Evaluate button once more. The result, 13 or 14, is a measure of the `scrollHeight` property of the TEXTAREA that had only the previous result in it. The scrollable height of that content was only 13 or 14 pixels, the height of the font in the TEXTAREA. The `scrollWidth` property of the output TEXTAREA is fixed by the width assigned to the element's `COLS` attribute (as calculated by the browser to determine how wide to make the textarea on the page).

scrollLeft
scrollTop

	NN2	NN3	NN4	NN6	IE3/J1	IE3/J2	IE4	IE5	IE5.5
Compatibility							✓	✓	✓

Example

Use The Evaluator (Chapter 13 in the *JavaScript Bible*) to experiment with these two properties of the TEXTAREA object, which displays the output of evaluations and property listings. To begin, enter the following into the bottom one-line text field to list the properties of the body object:

```
document.body
```

This displays a long list of properties for the body object. Use the TEXTAREA's scrollbar to page down a couple of times. Now enter the following property expression in the top one-line text field to see the scrollTop property of the output TEXTAREA after you scroll:

```
document.all.output.scrollTop
```

The result, some number, is now displayed in the output TEXTAREA. This means that the content of the output element was scrolled vertically. Click the Evaluate button once more. The result, 0, is a measure of the scrollTop property of the TEXTAREA that had only the previous result in it. There wasn't enough content in the TEXTAREA to scroll, so the content was not scrolled at all. The scrollTop property, therefore, is zero. The scrollLeft property of the output is always zero because the TEXTAREA element is set to wrap any text that overflows the width of the element. No horizontal scrollbar appears in this case, and the scrollLeft property never changes.

sourceIndex

	NN2	NN3	NN4	NN6	IE3/J1	IE3/J2	IE4	IE5	IE5.5
Compatibility							✓	✓	✓

Example

While the operation of this property is straightforward, the sequence of elements exposed by the document.all property may not be. To that end, you can use The Evaluator (Chapter 13 in the *JavaScript Bible*) to experiment in IE4+ with the values that the sourceIndex property returns to see how the index values of the document.all collection follow the source code.

To begin, reload The Evaluator. Enter the following statement in the top text box to set a preinitialized global variable:

```
a = 0
```

When you evaluate this expression, a zero should appear in the Results box. Next, enter the following statement into the top text box:

```
document.all[a].tagName + " [" + a++ + "]"
```

There are a lot of plus signs in this statement, so be sure you enter it correctly. As you successively evaluate this statement (by repeatedly clicking the Evaluate button), the global variable (a) is incremented, thus enabling you to "walk through" the elements in source code order. The `sourceIndex` value for each HTML tag appears in square brackets in the Results box. You generally begin with the following sequence:

```
HTML [0]
HEAD [1]
TITLE [2]
```

You can continue until there are no more elements, at which point an error message appears because the value of a exceeds the number of elements in the `document.all` array. Compare your findings against the HTML source code view of The Evaluator.

style

	NN2	NN3	NN4	NN6	IE3/J1	IE3/J2	IE4	IE5	IE5.5
Compatibility				✓			✓	✓	✓

Example

Most of the action with the `style` property has to do with the `style` object's properties, so you can use The Evaluator here to simply explore the lists of `style` object properties available on as many DHTML-compatible browsers as you have running. To begin, enter the following statement into the lower, one-line text box to inspect the `style` property for the `document.body` object:

```
document.body.style
```

Now inspect the `style` property of the table element that is part of the original version of The Evaluator. Enter the following statement into the lower text box:

```
document.getElementById("myTable").style
```

In both cases, the values assigned to the `style` object's properties are quite limited by default.

tabIndex

	NN2	NN3	NN4	NN6	IE3/J1	IE3/J2	IE4	IE5	IE5.5
Compatibility				✓			✓	✓	✓

Example

The HTML and scripting in Listing 15-16 demonstrate not only the way you can modify the tabbing behavior of a form on the fly, but also how to force form elements out of the tabbing sequence entirely in IE. In this page, the upper form (named `lab`) contains four elements. Scripts invoked by buttons in the lower form control the tabbing sequence. Notice that the `TABINDEX` attributes of all lower form elements are set to `-1`, which means that these control buttons are not part of the tabbing sequence in IE.

When you load the page, the default tabbing order for the `lab` form control elements (default setting of zero) takes charge. If you start pressing the Tab key, the precise results at first depend on the browser you use. In IE, the Address field is first selected; next the Tab sequence gives focus to the window (or frame, if this page were in a frameset); finally the tabbing reaches the `lab` form. Continue pressing the Tab key and watch how the browser assigns focus to each of the element types. In NN6, however, you must click anywhere on the content to get the Tab key to start working on form controls.

The sample script inverts the tabbing sequence with the help of a `for` loop that initializes two variables that work in opposite directions as the looping progresses. This gives the last element the lowest `tabIndex` value. The `skip2()` function simply sets the `tabIndex` property of the second text box to -1, removing it from the tabbing entirely (IE only). Notice, however, that you can click in the field and still enter text. (See the `disabled` property earlier in this chapter to see how to prevent field editing.) NN6 does not provide a `tabIndex` property setting that forces the browser to skip over a form control. You should disable the control instead.

Listing 15-16: **Controlling the tabIndex Property**

```
<HTML>
<HEAD>
<TITLE>tabIndex Property</TITLE>
<SCRIPT LANGUAGE="JavaScript">
function invert() {
    var form = document.lab
    for (var i = 0, j = form.elements.length; i < form.elements.length;
    i++, j--) {
        form.elements[i].tabIndex = j
    }
}

function skip2() {
    document.lab.text2.tabIndex = -1
}

function resetTab() {
    var form = document.lab
    for (var i = 0; i < form.elements.length; i++) {
        form.elements[i].tabIndex = 0
    }
}
</SCRIPT>
</HEAD>

<BODY>
<H1>tabIndex Property Lab</H1>
<HR>
<FORM NAME="lab">
Text box no. 1: <INPUT TYPE="text" NAME="text1"><BR>
Text box no. 2: <INPUT TYPE="text" NAME="text2"><BR>
<INPUT TYPE="button" VALUE="A Button"><BR>
```

```
<INPUT TYPE="checkbox">And a checkbox
</FORM>
<HR>
<FORM NAME="control">
<INPUT TYPE="button" VALUE="Invert Tabbing Order" TABINDEX=-1
onClick="invert()"><BR>
<INPUT TYPE="button" VALUE="Skip Text box no. 2 (IE Only)" TABINDEX=-1
onClick="skip2()"><BR>
<INPUT TYPE="button" VALUE="Reset to Normal Order" TABINDEX=-1
onClick="resetTab()">
</FORM>
</BODY>
</HTML>
```

The final function, resetTab(), sets the tabIndex property value to zero for all lab form elements. This restores the default order; but in IE5.5/Windows, you may experience buggy behavior that prevents you from tabbing to items after you reset them. Only the reloading of the page provides a complete restoration of default behavior.

tagName

	NN2	NN3	NN4	NN6	IE3/J1	IE3/J2	IE4	IE5	IE5.5
Compatibility				✓			✓	✓	✓

Example

You can see the tagName property in action for the example associated with the sourceIndex property discussed earlier. In that example, the tagName property is read from a sequence of objects in source code order.

tagUrn

	NN2	NN3	NN4	NN6	IE3/J1	IE3/J2	IE4	IE5	IE5.5
Compatibility								✓	✓

Example

If you have a sample document that contains XML and a Namespace spec, you can use document.write() or alert() methods to view the value of the tagUrn property. The syntax is

```
document.all.elementID.tagUrn
```

title

	NN2	NN3	NN4	NN6	IE3/J1	IE3/J2	IE4	IE5	IE5.5
Compatibility				✓			✓	✓	✓

Example

You can see how dynamic a tooltip is in Listing 15-17. A simple paragraph element has its TITLE attribute set to "First Time!", which is what the tooltip displays if you roll the pointer atop the paragraph and pause after the page loads. But an onMouseOver event handler for that element increments a global variable counter in the script, and the title property of the paragraph object is modified with each mouseover action. The count value is made part of a string assigned to the title property. Notice that there is not a live connection between the title property and the variable; instead, the new value explicitly sets the title property.

Listing 15-17: **Controlling the title Property**

```
<HTML>
<HEAD>
<TITLE>title Property</TITLE>
<SCRIPT LANGUAGE="JavaScript">
// global counting variable
var count = 0

function setToolTip(elem) {
    elem.title = "You have previously rolled atop this paragraph " +
        count + " time(s)."
}

function incrementCount(elem) {
    count++
    setToolTip(elem)
}
</SCRIPT>

</HEAD>
<BODY>
<H1>title Property Lab</H1>
<HR>
<P ID="myP" TITLE="First Time!" onMouseOver="incrementCount(this)">
Roll the mouse over this paragraph a few times.<BR>
Then pause atop it to view the tooltip.</P>
</BODY>
</HTML>
```

uniqueID

	NN2	NN3	NN4	NN6	IE3/J1	IE3/J2	IE4	IE5	IE5.5
Compatibility								✓	✓

Example

Listing 15-18 demonstrates the recommended syntax for obtaining and applying a browser-generated identifier for an object. After you enter some text into the text box and click the button, the addRow() function appends a row to the table. The left column displays the identifier generated via the table row object's uniqueID property. IE5+ generates identifiers in the format "ms__id$n$", where n is an integer starting with zero for the current browser session. Because the addRow() function assigns uniqueID values to the row and the cells in each row, the integer for each row is three greater than the previous one. There is no guarantee that future generations of the browser will follow this format, so do not rely on the format or sequence in your scripts.

Listing 15-18: **Using the uniqueID Property**

```
<HTML>
<HEAD>
<TITLE>Inserting an IE5+/Windows Table Row</TITLE>
<SCRIPT LANGUAGE="JavaScript">
function addRow(item1) {
    if (item1) {
        // assign long reference to shorter var name
        var theTable = document.all.myTable
        // append new row to the end of the table
        var newRow = theTable.insertRow(theTable.rows.length)
        // give the row its own ID
        newRow.id = newRow.uniqueID

        // declare cell variable
        var newCell

        // an inserted row has no cells, so insert the cells
        newCell = newRow.insertCell(0)
        // give this cell its own id
        newCell.id = newCell.uniqueID
        // display the row's id as the cell text
        newCell.innerText = newRow.id
        newCell.bgColor = "yellow"
        // reuse cell var for second cell insertion
        newCell = newRow.insertCell(1)
        newCell.id = newCell.uniqueID
```

Continued

elementObject.**uniqueID**

Listing 15-18 *(continued)*

```
        newCell.innerText = item1
    }
}
</SCRIPT>
</HEAD>

<BODY>
<TABLE ID="myTable" BORDER=1>
<TR>
<TH>Row ID</TH>
<TH>Data</TH>
</TR>

<TR ID="firstDataRow">
<TD>firstDataRow
<TD>Fred
</TR>
<TR ID="secondDataRow">
<TD>secondDataRow
<TD>Jane
</TR>
</TABLE>
<HR>
<FORM>
Enter text to be added to the table:<BR>
<INPUT TYPE="text" NAME="input" SIZE=25><BR>
<INPUT TYPE='button' VALUE='Insert Row' onClick='addRow(this.form.input.value)'>
</FORM>
</BODY>
</HTML>
```

Methods
addBehavior("*URL*")

	NN2	NN3	NN4	NN6	IE3/J1	IE3/J2	IE4	IE5	IE5.5
Compatibility								✓	✓

Example

Listing 15-19a is the JavaScript code for an external component named
makeHot.htc. Its purpose is to turn the color style property of an object to either a

default color ("red") or any other color that is passed to the component. For details on the syntax of the <PUBLIC> tags, see Chapter 48 of the *JavaScript Bible*. The code presented here helps you see how the page and scripts in Listing 15-19b work.

Listing 15-19a: **The makeHot.htc Behavior Component**

```
<PUBLIC:ATTACH EVENT="onmousedown" ONEVENT="makeHot()" />
<PUBLIC:ATTACH EVENT="onmouseup" ONEVENT="makeNormal()" />
<PUBLIC:PROPERTY NAME="hotColor" />
<PUBLIC:METHOD NAME="setHotColor" />
<SCRIPT LANGUAGE="JScript">
var oldColor
var hotColor = "red"

function setHotColor(color) {
    hotColor = color
}

function makeHot() {
    if (event.srcElement == element) {
        oldColor = style.color
        runtimeStyle.color = hotColor
    }
}

function makeNormal() {
    if (event.srcElement == element) {
        runtimeStyle.color = oldColor
    }
}
</SCRIPT>
```

The object to which the component is attached is a simple paragraph object, shown in Listing 15-19b. When the page loads, the behavior is not attached, so clicking the paragraph text has no effect.

When you turn on the behavior by invoking the turnOn() function, the addBehavior() method attaches the code of the makeHot.htc component to the myP object. At this point, the myP object has one more property, one more method, and two more event handlers that are written to be made public by the component's code. If you want the behavior to apply to more than one paragraph in the document, you have to invoke the addBehavior() method for each paragraph object.

After the behavior file is instructed to start loading, the setInitialColor() function is called to set the new color property of the paragraph to the user's choice from the SELECT list. But this can happen only if the component is fully loaded. Therefore, the function checks the readyState property of myP for completeness before invoking the component's function. If IE is still loading the component, the function is invoked again in 500 milliseconds.

As long as the behavior is loaded, you can change the color used to turn the paragraph "hot." The function first ensures that the component is loaded by checking that the object has the new color property. If it does, then (as a demonstration of how to expose and invoke a component method) the method of the component is invoked. You can also simply set the property value.

Listing 15-19b: **Using addBehavior() and removeBehavior()**

```
<HTML>
<HEAD>
<TITLE>addBehavior() and removeBehavior() Methods</TITLE>
<SCRIPT LANGUAGE="JavaScript">
var myPBehaviorID

function turnOn() {
    myPBehaviorID = document.all.myP.addBehavior("makeHot.htc")
    setInitialColor()
}

function setInitialColor() {
    if (document.all.myP.readyState == "complete") {
        var select = document.forms[0].colorChoice
        var color = select.options[select.selectedIndex].value
        document.all.myP.setHotColor(color)
    } else {
        setTimeout("setInitialColor()", 500)
    }
}

function turnOff() {
    document.all.myP.removeBehavior(myPBehaviorID)
}

function setColor(select, color) {
    if (document.all.myP.hotColor) {
        document.all.myP.setHotColor(color)
    } else {
        alert("This feature is not available. Turn on the Behavior first.")
        select.selectedIndex = 0
    }
}
function showBehaviorCount() {
    var num = document.all.myP.behaviorUrns.length
    var msg = "The myP element has " + num + " behavior(s). "
    if (num > 0) {
        msg += "Name(s): \r\n"
        for (var i = 0; i < num; i++) {
            msg += document.all.myP.behaviorUrns[i] + "\r\n"
        }
    }
    alert(msg)
}
```

```
</SCRIPT>
</HEAD>
<BODY>
<H1>addBehavior() and removeBehavior() Method Lab</H1>
<HR>
<P ID="myP">This is a sample paragraph. After turning on the behavior,
it will turn your selected color when you mouse down anywhere in this
paragraph.</P>
<FORM>
<INPUT TYPE="button" VALUE="Switch On Behavior" onClick="turnOn()">
Choose a 'hot' color:
<SELECT NAME="colorChoice" onChange="setColor(this, this.value)">
<OPTION VALUE="red">red
<OPTION VALUE="blue">blue
<OPTION VALUE="cyan">cyan
</SELECT><BR>
<INPUT TYPE="button" VALUE="Switch Off Behavior" onClick="turnOff()">
<P><INPUT TYPE="button" VALUE="Count the URNs"
onClick="showBehaviorCount()"></P>
</BODY>
</HTML>
```

To turn off the behavior, the removeBehavior() method is invoked. Notice that the removeBehavior() method is associated with the myP object, and the parameter is the ID of the behavior added earlier. If you associate multiple behaviors with an object, you can remove one without disturbing the others because each has its own unique ID.

addEventListener("*eventType*", *listenerFunc*, *useCapture*)
removeEventListener("*eventType*", *listenerFunc*, *useCapture*)

	NN2	NN3	NN4	NN6	IE3/J1	IE3/J2	IE4	IE5	IE5.5
Compatibility				✓					

Example

Listing 15-20 provides a compact workbench to explore and experiment with the basic W3C DOM event model. When the page loads, no event listeners are registered with the browser (except for the control buttons, of course). But you can add an event listener for a click event in bubble and/or capture mode to the BODY element or the P element that surrounds the SPAN holding the line of text. If you add an event listener and click the text, you see a readout of the element processing the event and information indicating whether the event phase is bubbling (3) or capture (1). With all event listeners engaged, notice the sequence of events being processed. Remove listeners one at a time to see the effect on event processing.

 Note   Listing 15-20 includes code for event capture that does not operate in NN6. Event capture facilities should work in a future version of the browser.

Listing 15-20: **W3C Event Lab**

```
<HTML>
<HEAD>
<TITLE>W3C Event Model Lab</TITLE>
<STYLE TYPE="text/css">
TD {text-align:center}
</STYLE>
<SCRIPT LANGUAGE="JavaScript">
// add event listeners
function addBubbleListener(elemID) {
    document.getElementById(elemID).addEventListener("click", reportEvent, false)
}
function addCaptureListener(elemID) {
    document.getElementById(elemID).addEventListener("click", reportEvent, true)
}
// remove event listeners
function removeBubbleListener(elemID)  {
    document.getElementById(elemID).removeEventListener("click", reportEvent, false)
}
function removeCaptureListener(elemID) {
    document.getElementById(elemID).removeEventListener("click", reportEvent, true)
}
// display details about any event heard
function reportEvent(evt) {
    if (evt.target.parentNode.id == "mySPAN") {
        var msg = "Event processed at " + evt.currentTarget.tagName +
            " element (event phase = " + evt.eventPhase + ").\n"
        document.controls.output.value += msg
    }
}
// clear the details textarea
function clearTextArea() {
    document.controls.output.value = ""
}
</SCRIPT>
</HEAD>
<BODY ID="myBODY">
<H1>W3C Event Model Lab</H1>
<HR>
<P ID="myP"><SPAN ID="mySPAN">This paragraph (a SPAN element nested inside a P
element) can be set to listen for "click" events.</SPAN></P>
<HR>
<TABLE CELLPADDING=5 BORDER=1>
```

```
<CAPTION STYLE="font-weight:bold">Control Panel</CAPTION>
<FORM NAME="controls">
<TR STYLE="background-color:#ffff99"><TD ROWSPAN=2>"Bubble"-type click listener:
    <TD><INPUT TYPE="button" VALUE="Add to BODY"
        onClick="addBubbleListener('myBODY')">
    <TD><INPUT TYPE="button" VALUE="Remove from BODY"
        onClick="removeBubbleListener('myBODY')">
</TR>
<TR STYLE="background-color:#ffff99">
    <TD><INPUT TYPE="button" VALUE="Add to P"
        onClick="addBubbleListener('myP')">
    <TD><INPUT TYPE="button" VALUE="Remove from P"
        onClick="removeBubbleListener('myP')">
</TR>
<TR STYLE="background-color:#ff9999"><TD ROWSPAN=2>"Capture"-type click
listener:
    <TD><INPUT TYPE="button" VALUE="Add to BODY"
        onClick="addCaptureListener('myBODY')">
    <TD><INPUT TYPE="button" VALUE="Remove from BODY"
        onClick="removeCaptureListener('myBODY')">
</TR>
<TR STYLE="background-color:#ff9999">
    <TD><INPUT TYPE="button" VALUE="Add to P"
        onClick="addCaptureListener('myP')">
    <TD><INPUT TYPE="button" VALUE="Remove from P"
        onClick="removeCaptureListener('myP')">
</TR>
<P>Examine click event characteristics: <INPUT TYPE="button" VALUE="Clear"
onClick="clearTextArea()"><BR>
<TEXTAREA NAME="output" COLS="80" ROWS="6" WRAP="virtual"></TEXTAREA>
</FORM>
</TABLE>
</BODY>
</HTML>
```

appendChild(*elementObject*)

	NN2	NN3	NN4	NN6	IE3/J1	IE3/J2	IE4	IE5	IE5.5
Compatibility				✓				✓	✓

Example

Scripts in Listing 15-21 demonstrate how the three major child-related methods work in IE5+ and NN6. The page includes a simple, two-item list. A form enables you to add items to the end of the list or replace the last item with a different entry.

The append() function creates a new LI element and then uses the appendChild() method to attach the text box text as the displayed text for the item. The nested expression, document.createTextNode(form.input.value), evaluates to a legitimate node that is appended to the new LI item. All of this occurs before the new LI item is added to the document. In the final statement of the function, appendChild() is invoked from the vantage point of the UL element — thus adding the LI element as a child node of the UL element.

Invoking the replaceChild() method in the replace() function utilizes some of the same code. The main difference is that the replaceChild() method requires a second parameter: a reference to the child element to be replaced. This demonstration replaces the final child node of the UL list, so the function takes advantage of the lastChild property of all elements to get a reference to that final nested child. That reference becomes the second parameter to replaceChild().

Listing 15-21: **Various Child Methods**

```
<HTML>
<HEAD>
<TITLE>appendChild(), removeChild(), and replaceChild() Methods</TITLE>
<SCRIPT LANGUAGE="JavaScript">
function append(form) {
    if (form.input.value) {
        var newItem = document.createElement("LI")
        newItem.appendChild(document.createTextNode(form.input.value))
        document.getElementById("myUL").appendChild(newItem)
    }
}

function replace(form) {
    if (form.input.value) {
        var newItem = document.createElement("LI")
        var lastChild = document.getElementById("myUL").lastChild
        newItem.appendChild(document.createTextNode(form.input.value))
        document.getElementById("myUL").replaceChild(newItem, lastChild)
    }
}

function restore() {
    var oneChild
    var mainObj = document.getElementById("myUL")
    while (mainObj.childNodes.length > 2) {
        oneChild = mainObj.lastChild
        mainObj.removeChild(oneChild)
    }
}
</SCRIPT>
</HEAD>
<BODY>
<H1>Child Methods</H1>
<HR>
Here is a list of items:
<UL ID="myUL"><LI>First Item
```

```
<LI>Second Item
</UL>
<FORM>
Enter some text to add/replace in the list:
<INPUT TYPE="text" NAME="input" SIZE=30><BR>
<INPUT TYPE="button" VALUE="Append to List" onClick="append(this.form)">
<INPUT TYPE="button" VALUE="Replace Final Item" onClick="replace(this.form)">
<INPUT TYPE="button" VALUE="Restore List" onClick="restore()">
</BODY>
</HTML>
```

The final part of the demonstration uses the `removeChild()` method to peel away all children of the UL element until just the two original items are left standing. Again, the `lastChild` property comes in handy as the `restore()` function keeps removing the last child until only two remain. Upon restoring the list, IE5/Mac fails to render the list bullets; but in the browser's object model, the UL element still exists.

applyElement(*elementObject*[, *type*])

	NN2	NN3	NN4	NN6	IE3/J1	IE3/J2	IE4	IE5	IE5.5
Compatibility								✓	✓

Example

To help you visualize the impact of the `applyElement()` method with its different parameter settings, Listing 15-22 enables you to apply a new element (an EM element) to a SPAN element inside a paragraph. At any time, you can view the HTML of the entire P element to see where the EM element is applied, as well as its impact on the element containment hierarchy for the paragraph.

After you load the page, inspect the HTML for the paragraph before doing anything else. Notice the SPAN element and its nested FONT element, both of which surround the one-word content. If you apply the EM element inside the SPAN element (click the middle button), the SPAN element's first (and only) child element becomes the EM element; the FONT element is now a child of the new EM element.

> ### Listing 15-22: **Using the applyElement() Method**

```
<HTML>
<HEAD>
<TITLE>applyElement() Method</TITLE>
<SCRIPT LANGUAGE="JavaScript">
function applyOutside() {
    var newItem = document.createElement("EM")
    newItem.id = newItem.uniqueID
    document.all.mySpan.applyElement(newItem)
```

Continued

Listing 15-22 *(continued)*

```
}

function applyInside() {
    var newItem = document.createElement("EM")
    newItem.id = newItem.uniqueID
    document.all.mySpan.applyElement(newItem, "inside")
}

function showHTML() {
    alert(document.all.myP.outerHTML)
}
</SCRIPT>
</HEAD>
<BODY>
<H1>applyElement() Method</H1>
<HR>
<P ID="myP">A simple paragraph with a <SPAN ID="mySpan">
<FONT SIZE=+1>special</FONT></SPAN> word in it.</P>
<FORM>
<INPUT TYPE="button" VALUE="Apply <EM> Outside" onClick="applyOutside()">
<INPUT TYPE="button" VALUE="Apply <EM> Inside" onClick="applyInside()">
<INPUT TYPE="button" VALUE="Show <P> HTML..." onClick="showHTML()"><BR>
<INPUT TYPE="button" VALUE="Restore Paragraph" onClick="location.reload()">
</FORM>
</BODY>
</HTML>
```

The visible results of applying the EM element inside and outside the SPAN element in this case are the same. But you can see from the HTML results that each element impacts the element hierarchy quite differently.

attachEvent("*eventName*", *functionRef*)
detachEvent("*eventName*", *functionRef*)

	NN2	NN3	NN4	NN6	IE3/J1	IE3/J2	IE4	IE5	IE5.5
Compatibility								✓	✓

Example

Use The Evaluator (Chapter 13 in the *JavaScript Bible)* to create an anonymous function that is called in response to an `onmousedown` event of the first paragraph on the page. Begin by assigning the anonymous function to global variable a (already initialized in The Evaluator) in the upper text box:

```
a = new Function("alert('Function created at " + (new Date()) + "')")
```

The quote marks and parentheses can get jumbled easily, so enter this expression carefully. When you enter the expression successfully, the Results box shows the function's text. Now assign this function to the `onmousedown` event of the `myP` element by entering the following statement into the upper text box:

```
document.all.myP.attachEvent("onmousedown", a)
```

The Results box displays `true` when successful. If you mouse down on the first paragraph, an alert box displays the date and time that the anonymous function was created (when the `new Date()` expression was evaluated).

Now, disconnect the event relationship from the object by entering the following statement into the upper text box:

```
document.all.myP.detachEvent("onmousedown", a)
```

blur()
focus()

	NN2	NN3	NN4	NN6	IE3/J1	IE3/J2	IE4	IE5	IE5.5
Compatibility	✓	✓	✓	✓	✓	✓	✓	✓	✓

Example

To show how both the `window.focus()` method and its opposite (`window.blur()`) operate, Listing 15-23 for NN3+ and IE4+ creates a two-window environment. From each window, you can bring the other window to the front. The main window uses the object returned by `window.open()` to assemble the reference to the new window. In the subwindow (whose content is created entirely on the fly by JavaScript), `self.opener` is summoned to refer to the original window, while `self.blur()` operates on the subwindow itself (except for the buggy behavior of NN6 noted earlier). Blurring one window and focusing on another window yields the same result of sending the window to the back of the pile.

Listing 15-23: **The window.focus() and window.blur() Methods**

```
<HTML>
<HEAD>
<TITLE>Window Focus() and Blur()</TITLE>
<SCRIPT LANGUAGE="JavaScript1.1">
// declare global variable name
var newWindow = null
function makeNewWindow() {
    // check if window already exists
    if (!newWindow || newWindow.closed) {
        // store new window object in global variable
```

Continued

Listing 15-23 *(continued)*

```
            newWindow = window.open("","","width=250,height=250")
            // pause briefly to let IE3 window finish opening
            setTimeout("fillWindow()",100)
    } else {
            // window already exists, so bring it forward
            newWindow.focus()
    }
}
// assemble new content and write to subwindow
function fillWindow() {
    var newContent = "<HTML><HEAD><TITLE>Another Subwindow</TITLE></HEAD>"
    newContent += "<BODY bgColor='salmon'>"
    newContent += "<H1>A Salmon-Colored Subwindow.</H1>"
    newContent += "<FORM><INPUT TYPE='button' VALUE='Bring Main to Front'
onClick='self.opener.focus()'>"
    // the following button doesn't work in NN6
    newContent += "<FORM><INPUT TYPE='button' VALUE='Put Me in Back'
onClick='self.blur()'>"
    newContent += "</FORM></BODY></HTML>"
    // write HTML to new window document
    newWindow.document.write(newContent)
    newWindow.document.close()
}
</SCRIPT>
</HEAD>
<BODY>
<H1>Window focus() and blur() Methods</H1>
<HR>
<FORM>
<INPUT TYPE="button" NAME="newOne" VALUE="Show New Window"
onClick="makeNewWindow()">
</FORM>
</BODY>
</HTML>
```

A key ingredient to the success of the makeNewWindow() function in Listing 15-23 is the first conditional expression. Because newWind is initialized as a null value when the page loads, that is its value the first time through the function. But after you open the subwindow the first time, newWind is assigned a value (the subwindow object) that remains intact even if the user closes the window. Thus, the value doesn't revert to null by itself. To catch the possibility that the user has closed the window, the conditional expression also sees if the window is closed. If it is, a new subwindow is generated, and that new window's reference value is reassigned to the newWind variable. On the other hand, if the window reference exists and the window is not closed, the focus() method brings that subwindow to the front. You can see the focus() method for a text object in action in *JavaScript Bible* Chapter 25's description of the select() method for text objects.

clearAttributes()

	NN2	NN3	NN4	NN6	IE3/J1	IE3/J2	IE4	IE5	IE5.5
Compatibility								✓	✓

Example

Use The Evaluator (Chapter 13 in the *JavaScript Bible*) to examine the attributes of an element before and after you apply clearAttributes(). To begin, display the HTML for the table element on the page by entering the following statement into the upper text field:

```
myTable.outerHTML
```

Notice the attributes associated with the <TABLE> tag. Look at the rendered table to see how attributes such as BORDER and WIDTH affect the display of the table. Now, enter the following statement in the top text box to remove all removable attributes from this element:

```
myTable.clearAttributes()
```

First, look at the table. The border is gone, and the table is rendered only as wide as is necessary to display the content with no cell padding. Lastly, view the results of the clearAttributes() method in the outerHTML of the table again:

```
myTable.outerHTML
```

The source code file has not changed, but the object model in the browser's memory reflects the changes you made.

click()

	NN2	NN3	NN4	NN6	IE3/J1	IE3/J2	IE4	IE5	IE5.5
Compatibility	✓	✓	✓	✓	✓	✓	✓	✓	✓

Example

Use The Evaluator (Chapter 13 in the *JavaScript Bible*) to experiment with the click() method. The page includes various types of buttons at the bottom. You can "click" the checkbox, for example, by entering the following statement in the topmost text field:

```
document.myForm2.myCheckbox.click()
```

If you use a recent browser version, you most likely can see the checkbox change states between checked and unchecked each time you execute the statement.

cloneNode(*deepBoolean*)

	NN2	NN3	NN4	NN6	IE3/J1	IE3/J2	IE4	IE5	IE5.5
Compatibility				✓				✓	✓

Example

Use The Evaluator (Chapter 13 in the *JavaScript Bible*) to clone, rename, and append an element found in The Evaluator's source code. Begin by cloning the paragraph element named myP along with all of its content. Enter the following statement into the topmost text field:

```
a = document.getElementById("myP").cloneNode(true)
```

The variable a now holds the clone of the original node, so you can change its ID attribute at this point by entering the following statement:

```
a.setAttribute("ID", "Dolly")
```

If you want to see the properties of the cloned node, enter a into the lower text field. The precise listing of properties you see depends on whether you use NN or IE; in either case, you should be able to locate the id property, whose value is now Dolly.

As a final step, append this newly named node to the end of the body element by entering the following statement into the topmost text field:

```
document.body.appendChild(a)
```

You can now scroll down to the bottom of the page and see a duplicate of the content. But because the two nodes have different ID attributes, they cannot confuse scripts that need to address one or the other.

componentFromPoint(*x,y*)

	NN2	NN3	NN4	NN6	IE3/J1	IE3/J2	IE4	IE5	IE5.5
Compatibility								✓	✓

Example

You can experiment with this method in the code supplied with Listing 15-24. As presented, the method is associated with a TEXTAREA object that is specifically sized to display both vertical and horizontal scrollbars. As you click various areas of the TEXTAREA and the rest of the page, the status bar displays information about the location of the event with the help of the componentFromPoint() method.

The script utilizes a combination of the event.srcElement property and the componentFromPoint() method to help you distinguish how you can use each one for different types of event processing. The `srcElement` property is used initially as a filter to decide whether the status bar will reveal further processing about the TEXTAREA element's event details.

The `onMouseDown` event handler in the BODY element triggers all event processing. IE events bubble up the hierarchy (and no events are cancelled in this page), so all `mouseDown` events eventually reach the BODY element. Then, the `whereInWorld()` function can compare each `mouseDown` event from any element against the textarea's geography.

Listing 15-24: **Using the componentFromPoint() Method**

```
<HTML>
<HEAD>
<TITLE>componentFromPoint() Method</TITLE>
<SCRIPT LANGUAGE="JavaScript">
function whereInWorld(elem) {
    var x = event.clientX
    var y = event.clientY
    var component = document.all.myTextarea.componentFromPoint(x,y)
    if (window.event.srcElement == document.all.myTextarea) {
        if (component == "") {
            status = "mouseDown event occurred inside the element"
        } else {
            status = "mouseDown occurred on the element\'s " + component
        }
    } else {
        status = "mouseDown occurred " + component + " of the element"
    }
}
</SCRIPT>
</HEAD>
<BODY onMouseDown="whereInWorld()">
<H1>componentFromPoint() Method</H1>
<HR>
<P>Tracking the mouseDown event relative to the textarea object. View results in
status bar.</P>
<FORM>
<TEXTAREA NAME="myTextarea" WRAP="off" COLS=12 ROWS=4>
This is Line 1
This is Line 2
This is Line 3
This is Line 4
This is Line 5
This is Line 6
</TEXTAREA>
</FORM>
</BODY>
</HTML>
```

contains(*elementObjectReference*)

	NN2	NN3	NN4	NN6	IE3/J1	IE3/J2	IE4	IE5	IE5.5
Compatibility							✓	✓	✓

Example

Using The Evaluator (Chapter 13 in the *JavaScript Bible*), see how the contains()
method responds to the object combinations in each of the following statements as
you enter them into the upper text box:

```
document.body.contains(document.all.myP)
document.all.myP.contains(document.all.item("myEM"))
document.all.myEM.contains(document.all.myEM)
document.all.myEM.contains(document.all.myP)
```

Feel free to test other object combinations within this page.

detachEvent()

See attachEvent().

dispatchEvent(*eventObject*)

	NN2	NN3	NN4	NN6	IE3/J1	IE3/J2	IE4	IE5	IE5.5
Compatibility				✓					

Example

Listing 15-25 demonstrates the dispatchEvent() method as defined in the W3C
DOM Level 2. The behavior is identical to that of Listing 15-26, which demonstrates
the IE5.5 equivalent: fireEvent(). This example does not perform all intended
actions in the first release of NN6 because the browser does not fully implement the
document.createEvent() method. The example is designed to operate more completely in a future version that supports event generation.

Listing 15-25: **Using the dispatchEvent() Method**

```
<HTML>
<HEAD>
<STYLE TYPE="text/css">
#mySPAN {font-style:italic}
</STYLE>
<SCRIPT LANGUAGE="JavaScript">
// assemble a couple event object properties
```

```
function getEventProps(evt) {
    var msg = ""
    var elem = evt.target
    msg += "event.target.nodeName: " + elem.nodeName + "\n"
    msg += "event.target.parentNode: " + elem.parentNode.id + "\n"
    msg += "event button: " + evt.button
    return msg
}

// onClick event handlers for body, myP, and mySPAN
function bodyClick(evt) {
    var msg = "Click event processed in BODY\n\n"
    msg += getEventProps(evt)
    alert(msg)
    checkCancelBubble(evt)
}
function pClick(evt) {
    var msg = "Click event processed in P\n\n"
    msg += getEventProps(evt)
    alert(msg)
    checkCancelBubble(evt)
}
function spanClick(evt) {
    var msg = "Click event processed in SPAN\n\n"
    msg += getEventProps(evt)
    alert(msg)
    checkCancelBubble(evt)
}

// cancel event bubbling if check box is checked
function checkCancelBubble(evt) {
    if (document.controls.bubbleOn.checked) {
        evt.stopPropagation()
    }
}

// assign onClick event handlers to three elements
function init() {
    document.body.onclick = bodyClick
    document.getElementById("myP").onclick = pClick
    document.getElementById("mySPAN").onclick = spanClick
}

// invoke fireEvent() on object whose ID is passed as parameter
function doDispatch(objID, evt) {
    // don't let button clicks bubble
    evt.stopPropagation()
    var newEvt = document.createEvent("MouseEvent")
    if (newEvt) {
        newEvt.button = 3
        document.getElementById(objID).dispatchEvent(newEvt)
    } else {
```

Continued

Listing 15-25 *(continued)*

```
        alert("This browser version does not support the feature.")
    }
}
</SCRIPT>
</HEAD>
<BODY ID="myBODY" onLoad="init()">
<H1>fireEvent() Method</H1>
<HR>
<P ID="myP">This is a paragraph <SPAN ID="mySPAN">(with a nested SPAN)</SPAN>
that receives click events.</SPAN></P>
<HR>
<P><B>Control Panel</B></P>
<FORM NAME="controls">
<P><INPUT TYPE="checkbox" NAME="bubbleOn"
onClick="event.stopPropagation()">Cancel event bubbling.</P>
<P><INPUT TYPE="button" VALUE="Fire Click Event on BODY"
onClick="doDispatch('myBODY', event)"></P>
<P><INPUT TYPE="button" VALUE="Fire Click Event on myP"
onClick="doDispatch('myP', event)"></P>
<P><INPUT TYPE="button" VALUE="Fire Click Event on mySPAN"
onClick="doDispatch('mySPAN', event)"></P>
</FORM>
</BODY>
</HTML>
```

---

fireEvent("*eventType*"[, *eventObjectRef*])

	NN2	NN3	NN4	NN6	IE3/J1	IE3/J2	IE4	IE5	IE5.5
Compatibility									✓

Example

The small laboratory of Listing 15-26 enables you to explore the possibilities of the IE5.5 fireEvent() method while reinforcing event bubbling concepts in IE. Three nested element objects are assigned separate onClick event handlers (via the init() function invoked after the page loads — although you can also set these event handlers via onClick attributes in the tags). Each handler displays an alert whose content reveals which object's event handler was triggered and the tag name and ID of the object that received the event. The default behavior of the page is to allow event bubbling, but a checkbox enables you to turn off bubbling.

After you load the page, click the italic segment (a nested SPAN element) to receive a series of three alert boxes. The first advises you that the SPAN element's onClick event handler is processing the event and that the SPAN element (whose ID is mySPAN) is, indeed, the source element of the event. Because event bubbling is enabled by default, the event bubbles upward to the SPAN element's next outermost container: the myP paragraph element. (However, mySPAN is still the source element.) Finally, the event reaches the BODY element. If you click in the H1 element at the top of the page, the event is not processed until it reaches the BODY element — although the H1 element is the source element because that's what you clicked. In all cases, when you explicitly click something to generate the onclick event, the event's button property shows zero to signify the primary mouse button in IE.

Now onto the real purpose of this example: the fireEvent() method. Three buttons enable you to direct a click event to each of the three elements that have event handlers defined for them. The events fired this way are artificial, generated via the createEventObject() method. For demonstration purposes, the button property of these scripted events is set to 3. This property value is assigned to the event object that eventually gets directed to an element. With event bubbling left on, the events sent via fireEvent() behave just like the physical clicks on the elements. Similarly, if you disable event bubbling, the first event handler to process the event cancels bubbling, and no further processing of that event occurs. Notice that event bubbling is cancelled within the event handlers that process the event. To prevent the clicks of the checkbox and action buttons from triggering the BODY element's onClick event handlers, event bubbling is turned off for the buttons right away.

Listing 15-26: **Using the fireEvent() Method**

```
<HTML>
<HEAD>
<STYLE TYPE="text/css">
#mySPAN {font-style:italic}
</STYLE>
<SCRIPT LANGUAGE="JavaScript">
// assemble a couple event object properties
function getEventProps() {
    var msg = ""
    var elem = event.srcElement
    msg += "event.srcElement.tagName: " + elem.tagName + "\n"
    msg += "event.srcElement.id: " + elem.id + "\n"
    msg += "event button: " + event.button
    return msg
}

// onClick event handlers for body, myP, and mySPAN
function bodyClick() {
    var msg = "Click event processed in BODY\n\n"
    msg += getEventProps()
    alert(msg)
    checkCancelBubble()
}
function pClick() {
    var msg = "Click event processed in P\n\n"
    msg += getEventProps()
    alert(msg)
```

Continued

Listing 15-26 *(continued)*

```
        checkCancelBubble()
}
function spanClick() {
    var msg = "Click event processed in SPAN\n\n"
    msg += getEventProps()
    alert(msg)
    checkCancelBubble()
}

// cancel event bubbling if check box is checked
function checkCancelBubble() {
    event.cancelBubble = document.controls.bubbleOn.checked
}

// assign onClick event handlers to three elements
function init() {
    document.body.onclick = bodyClick
    document.all.myP.onclick = pClick
    document.all.mySPAN.onclick = spanClick
}

// invoke fireEvent() on object whose ID is passed as parameter
function doFire(objID) {
    var newEvt = document.createEventObject()
    newEvt.button = 3
    document.all(objID).fireEvent("onclick", newEvt)
    // don't let button clicks bubble
    event.cancelBubble = true
}
</SCRIPT>
</HEAD>
<BODY ID="myBODY" onLoad="init()">
<H1>fireEvent() Method</H1>
<HR>
<P ID="myP">This is a paragraph <SPAN ID="mySPAN">(with a nested SPAN)</SPAN>
that receives click events.</SPAN></P>
<HR>
<P><B>Control Panel</B></P>
<FORM NAME="controls">
<P><INPUT TYPE="checkbox" NAME="bubbleOn"
onClick="event.cancelBubble=true">Cancel event bubbling.</P>
<P><INPUT TYPE="button" VALUE="Fire Click Event on BODY"
onClick="doFire('myBODY')"></P>
<P><INPUT TYPE="button" VALUE="Fire Click Event on myP"
onClick="doFire('myP')"></P>
<P><INPUT TYPE="button" VALUE="Fire Click Event on mySPAN"
onClick="doFire('mySPAN')"></P>
</FORM>
</BODY>
</HTML>
```

focus()

See blur().

getAdjacentText("*position*")

	NN2	NN3	NN4	NN6	IE3/J1	IE3/J2	IE4	IE5	IE5.5
Compatibility								✓	✓

Example

Use The Evaluator (Chapter 13 in the *JavaScript Bible*) to examine all four adjacent text possibilities for the myP and nested myEM elements in that document. Enter each of the following statements into the upper text box, and view the results:

```
document.all.myP.getAdjacentText("beforeBegin")
document.all.myP.getAdjacentText("afterBegin")
document.all.myP.getAdjacentText("beforeEnd")
document.all.myP.getAdjacentText("afterEnd")
```

The first and last statements return empty strings because the myP element has no text fragments surrounding it. The afterBegin version returns the text fragment of the myP element up to, but not including, the EM element nested inside. The beforeEnd string picks up after the end of the nested EM element and returns all text to the end of myP.

Now, see what happens with the nested myEM element:

```
document.all.myEM.getAdjacentText("beforeBegin")
document.all.myEM.getAdjacentText("afterBegin")
document.all.myEM.getAdjacentText("beforeEnd")
document.all.myEM.getAdjacentText("afterEnd")
```

Because this element has no nested elements, the afterBegin and beforeEnd strings are identical: the same value as the innerText property of the element.

getAttribute("*attributeName*" [, *caseSensitivity*])

	NN2	NN3	NN4	NN6	IE3/J1	IE3/J2	IE4	IE5	IE5.5
Compatibility				✓			✓	✓	✓

Example

Use The Evaluator (Chapter 13 in the *JavaScript Bible*) to experiment with the getAttribute() method for the elements in the page. For IE4, use the document.all notation. IE5 and NN6 understand the W3C standard `getElementById()` method of addressing an element. You can enter the following sample statements into the top text box to view attribute values.

IE4:

```
document.all.myTable.getAttribute("width")
document.all.myTable.getAttribute("border")
```

IE5/NN6:

```
document.getElementById("myTable").getAttribute("width")
document.getElementById("myTable").getAttribute("border")
```

getAttributeNode("*attributeName*")

	NN2	NN3	NN4	NN6	IE3/J1	IE3/J2	IE4	IE5	IE5.5
Compatibility				✓					

Example

Use The Evaluator (Chapter 13 in the *JavaScript Bible*) to explore the `getAttributeNode()` method in NN6. The Results TEXTAREA element provides several attributes to check out. Because the method returns an object, enter the following statements into the bottom text field so you can view the properties of the attribute node object returned by the method:

```
document.getElementById("output").getAttributeNode("COLS")
document.getElementById("output").getAttributeNode("ROWS")
document.getElementById("output").getAttributeNode("wrap")
document.getElementById("output").getAttributeNode("style")
```

All (except the last) statements display a list of properties for each attribute node object. The last statement, however, returns nothing because the STYLE attribute is not specified for the element.

getBoundingClientRect()

	NN2	NN3	NN4	NN6	IE3/J1	IE3/J2	IE4	IE5	IE5.5
Compatibility								✓	✓

Example

Listing 15-27 employs both the `getBoundingClientRect()` and `getClientRects()` methods in a demonstration of how they differ. A set of elements is grouped within a SPAN element named `main`. The group consists of two paragraphs and an unordered list.

Two controls enable you to set the position of an underlying highlight rectangle to any line of your choice. A checkbox enables you to set whether the highlight rectangle should be only as wide as the line or the full width of the bounding rectangle for the entire SPAN element.

All the code is located in the `hilite()` function. The SELECT and checkbox elements invoke this function. Early in the function, the `getClientRects()` method is invoked for the `main` element to capture a snapshot of all `TextRectangles` for the entire element. This array comes in handy when the script needs to get the coordinates of a rectangle for a single line, as chosen in the SELECT element.

Whenever the user chooses a number from the SELECT list and the value is less than the total number of `TextRectangle` objects in `clientRects`, the function begins calculating the size and location of the underlying yellow highlighter. When the Full Width checkbox is checked, the left and right coordinates are obtained from the `getBoundingClientRect()` method because the entire SPAN element's rectangle is the space you're interested in; otherwise, you pull the `left` and `right` properties from the chosen rectangle in the `clientRects` array.

Next comes the assignment of location and dimension values to the `hiliter` object's `style` property. The top and bottom are always pegged to whatever line is selected, so the `clientRects` array is polled for the chosen entry's `top` and `bottom` properties. The previously calculated `left` value is assigned to the `hiliter` object's `pixelLeft` property, while the width is calculated by subtracting the `left` from the `right` coordinates. Notice that the `top` and `left` coordinates also take into account any vertical or horizontal scrolling of the entire body of the document. If you resize the window to a smaller size, line wrapping throws off the original line count. However, an invocation of `hilite()` from the `onResize` event handler applies the currently chosen line number to whatever content falls in that line after resizing.

Listing 15-27: **Using getBoundingClientRect()**

```
<HTML>
<HEAD>
<TITLE>getClientRects() and getBoundClientRect() Methods</TITLE>
<SCRIPT LANGUAGE="JavaScript">
function hilite() {
    var hTop, hLeft, hRight, hBottom, hWidth
    var select = document.forms[0].choice
    var n = parseInt(select.options[select.selectedIndex].value) - 1
    var clientRects = document.all.main.getClientRects()
    var mainElem = document.all.main
    if (n >= 0 && n < clientRects.length) {
        if (document.forms[0].fullWidth.checked) {
            hLeft = mainElem.getBoundingClientRect().left
            hRight = mainElem.getBoundingClientRect().right
        } else {
            hLeft = clientRects[n].left
            hRight = clientRects[n].right
        }
        document.all.hiliter.style.pixelTop = clientRects[n].top +
```

Continued

Listing 15-27 *(continued)*

```
                document.body.scrollTop
        document.all.hiliter.style.pixelBottom = clientRects[n].bottom
        document.all.hiliter.style.pixelLeft = hLeft + document.body.scrollLeft
        document.all.hiliter.style.pixelWidth = hRight - hLeft
        document.all.hiliter.style.visibility = "visible"
    } else if (n > 0) {
        alert("The content does not have that many lines.")
        document.all.hiliter.style.visibility = "hidden"
    }
}
</SCRIPT>
</HEAD>
<BODY onResize="hilite()">
<H1>getClientRects() and getBoundClientRect() Methods</H1>
<HR>
<FORM>
Choose a line to highlight:
<SELECT NAME="choice" onChange="hilite()">
<OPTION VALUE=0>
<OPTION VALUE=1>1
<OPTION VALUE=2>2
<OPTION VALUE=3>3
<OPTION VALUE=4>4
<OPTION VALUE=5>5
<OPTION VALUE=6>6
<OPTION VALUE=7>7
<OPTION VALUE=8>8
<OPTION VALUE=9>9
<OPTION VALUE=10>10
<OPTION VALUE=11>11
<OPTION VALUE=12>12
<OPTION VALUE=13>13
<OPTION VALUE=14>14
<OPTION VALUE=15>15
</SELECT><BR>

<INPUT NAME="fullWidth" TYPE="checkbox" onClick="hilite()">
Full Width (bounding rectangle)
</FORM>
<SPAN ID="main">
<P>Lorem ipsum dolor sit amet, consectetaur adipisicing elit, sed do
eiusmod tempor incididunt ut labore et dolore magna aliqua.
Ut enim adminim veniam, quis nostrud exercitation ullamco:</P>
<UL>
<LI>laboris
<LI>nisi
<LI>aliquip ex ea commodo
</UL>
<P>Duis aute irure dolor in reprehenderit involuptate velit esse
cillum dolore eu fugiat nulla pariatur. Excepteur sint occaecat
cupidatat non proident, sunt in culpa qui officia deseruntmollit
```

```
anim id est laborum Et harumd und lookum like Greek to me, dereud
facilis est er expedit distinct.</P>
</SPAN>
<DIV ID="hiliter"
STYLE="position:absolute; background-color:yellow; z-index:-1;
visibility:hidden">
</DIV>
</BODY>
</HTML>
```

Because the z-index style property of the hiliter element is set to -1, the element always appears beneath the primary content on the page. If the user selects a line number beyond the current number of lines in the main element, the hiliter element is hidden.

getClientRects()

	NN2	NN3	NN4	NN6	IE3/J1	IE3/J2	IE4	IE5	IE5.5
Compatibility								✓	✓

Example

See Listing 15-27, which demonstrates the differences between getClientRects() and getBoundingClientRect() and shows how you can use the two together.

getElementsByTagName("*tagName*")

	NN2	NN3	NN4	NN6	IE3/J1	IE3/J2	IE4	IE5	IE5.5
Compatibility				✓				✓	✓

Example

Use The Evaluator (Chapter 13 in the *JavaScript Bible*) to experiment with the getElementsByTagName() method. Enter the following statements one at a time into the upper text box and study the results:

```
document.body.getElementsByTagName("DIV")
document.body.getElementsByTagName("DIV").length
document.getElementById("myTable").getElementsByTagName("TD").length
```

Because the getElementsByTagName() method returns an array of objects, you can use one of those returned values as a valid element reference:

```
document.getElementsByTagName("FORM")[0].getElementsByTagName("INPUT").length
```

getExpression("*attributeName*")

	NN2	NN3	NN4	NN6	IE3/J1	IE3/J2	IE4	IE5	IE5.5
Compatibility								✓	✓

Example

See Listing 15-32 for the setExpression() method. This listing demonstrates the kinds of values returned by getExpression().

hasChildNodes()

	NN2	NN3	NN4	NN6	IE3/J1	IE3/J2	IE4	IE5	IE5.5
Compatibility				✓				✓	✓

Example

Use The Evaluator (Chapter 13 in the *JavaScript Bible*) to experiment with the hasChildNodes() method. If you enter the following statement into the topmost text box:

```
document.getElementById("myP").hasChildNodes()
```

the returned value is true. You can find out how many nodes there are by getting the length of the childNodes array:

```
document.getElementById("myP").childNodes.length
```

This expression reveals a total of three nodes: the two text nodes and the EM element between them. Check out whether the first text node has any children:

```
document.getElementById("myP").childNodes[0].hasChildNodes()
```

The response is false because text fragments do not have any nested nodes. But check out the EM element, which is the second child node of the myP element:

```
document.getElementById("myP").childNodes[1].hasChildNodes()
```

The answer is true because the EM element has a text fragment node nested within it. Sure enough, the statement

```
document.getElementById("myP").childNodes[1].childNodes.length
```

yields a node count of 1. You can also go directly to the EM element in your references:

```
document.getElementById("myEM").hasChildNodes()
document.getElementById("myEM").childNodes.length
```

If you want to see the properties of the text fragment node inside the EM element, enter the following into the lower text box:

```
document.getElementById("myEM").childNodes[0]
```

You can see that the `data` and `nodeValue` properties for the text fragment return the text `"all"`.

insertAdjacentElement("*location*", *elementObject*)

	NN2	NN3	NN4	NN6	IE3/J1	IE3/J2	IE4	IE5	IE5.5
Compatibility								✓	✓

Example

Use The Evaluator (Chapter 13 in *JavaScript Bible*) to experiment with the `insertAdjacentElement()` method. The goal of the experiment is to insert a new H1 element above the `myP` element.

All actions require you to enter a sequence of statements in the topmost text box. Begin by storing a new element in the global variable `a`:

```
a = document.createElement("H1")
```

Give the new object some text:

```
a.innerText = "New Header"
```

Now, insert this element before the start of the `myP` object:

```
myP.insertAdjacentElement("beforeBegin", a)
```

Notice that you have not assigned an `id` property value to the new element. But because the element was inserted by reference, you can modify the inserted object by changing the object stored in the `a` variable:

```
a.style.color = "red"
```

The inserted element is also part of the document hierarchy, so you can access it through hierarchy references such as `myP.previousSibling`.

The parent element of the newly inserted element is the BODY. Thus, you can inspect the current state of the HTML for the rendered page by entering the following statement into the topmost text box:

```
document.body.innerHTML
```

If you scroll down past the first form, you can find the `<H1>` element that you added along with the `STYLE` attribute.

insertAdjacentHTML("*location*", "*HTMLtext*")
insertAdjacentText("*location*", "*text*")

	NN2	NN3	NN4	NN6	IE3/J1	IE3/J2	IE4	IE5	IE5.5
Compatibility							✓	✓	✓

Example

Use The Evaluator (Chapter 13 in the *JavaScript Bible*) to experiment with these two methods. The example here demonstrates the result of employing both methods in an attempt to add some HTML to the beginning of the myP element.

Begin by assigning a string of HTML code to the global variable a:

```
a = "<B ID='myB'>Important News!</B>"
```

Because this HTML is to go on the same line as the start of the myP paragraph, use the afterBegin parameter for the insert method:

```
myP.insertAdjacentHTML("afterBegin", a)
```

Notice that there is no space after the exclamation mark of the inserted HTML. But to prove that the inserted HTML is genuinely part of the document's object model, you can now insert the text of a space after the B element whose ID is myB:

```
myB.insertAdjacentText("afterEnd", " ")
```

Each time you evaluate the preceding statement (by repeatedly clicking the Evaluate button or pressing Enter with the cursor in the topmost field), an additional space is added.

You should also see what happens when the string to be inserted with insertAdjacentText() contains HTML tags. Reload The Evaluator and enter the following two statements into the topmost field, evaluating each one in turn:

```
a = "<B ID='myB'>Important News!</B>"
myP.insertAdjacentText("afterBegin", a)
```

The HTML is not interpreted but is displayed as plain text. There is no object named myB after executing this latest insert method.

insertBefore(*newChildNodeObject*[, *referenceChildNode*])

	NN2	NN3	NN4	NN6	IE3/J1	IE3/J2	IE4	IE5	IE5.5
Compatibility				✓				✓	✓

Example

Listing 15-28 demonstrates how the `insertBefore()` method can insert child elements (LI) inside a parent (OL) at different locations, depending on the second parameter. A text box enables you to enter your choice of text and/or HTML for insertion at various locations within the OL element. If you don't specify a position, the second parameter of `insertBefore()` is passed as `null`—meaning that the new child node is added to the end of the existing children. But choose a spot from the select list where you want to insert the new item. The value of each SELECT list option is an index of one of the first three child nodes of the OL element.

Listing 15-28: **Using the insertBefore() Method**

```
<HTML>
<HEAD>
<TITLE>insertBefore() Method</TITLE>
<SCRIPT LANGUAGE="JavaScript">
function doInsert(form) {
    if (form.newText) {
        var newChild = document.createElement("LI")
        newChild.innerHTML = form.newText.value
        var choice = form.itemIndex.options[form.itemIndex.selectedIndex].value
        var insertPoint = (isNaN(choice)) ?
            null : document.getElementById("myUL").childNodes[choice]
        document.getElementById("myUL").insertBefore(newChild, insertPoint)
    }
}
</SCRIPT>
</HEAD>
<BODY>
<H1>insertBefore() Method</H1>
<HR>
<FORM onSubmit="return false">
<P>Enter text or HTML for a new list item:
<INPUT TYPE="text" NAME="newText" SIZE=40 VALUE=""></P>
<P>Before which existing item?
<SELECT NAME="itemIndex">
    <OPTION VALUE=null>None specified
    <OPTION VALUE=0>1
    <OPTION VALUE=1>2
    <OPTION VALUE=2>3
</SELECT></P>
<INPUT TYPE="button" VALUE="Insert Item" onClick="doInsert(this.form)">
</FORM>

<OL ID="myUL">
    <LI>Originally the First Item
    <LI>Originally the Second Item
    <LI>Originally the Third Item
</OL>
</BODY>
</HTML>
```

---

item(*index* | *"index"* [, *subIndex*])

	NN2	NN3	NN4	NN6	IE3/J1	IE3/J2	IE4	IE5	IE5.5
Compatibility				✓			✓	✓	✓

Example

Use The Evaluator (Chapter 13 in the *JavaScript Bible*) to experiment with the item() method. Type the following statements into the topmost text box and view the results for each:

NN6 and IE5

```
document.getElementById("myP").childNodes.length
document.getElementById("myP").childNodes.item(0).data
document.getElementById("myP").childNodes.item(1).nodeName
```

NN6, IE4, and IE5

```
document.forms[1].elements.item(0).type
```

IE4 and IE5

```
document.all.item("myP").outerHTML
myP.outerHTML
```

In the last two examples, both statements return the same string. The first example is helpful when your script is working with a string version of an object's name. If your script already knows the object reference, then the second approach is more efficient and compact.

mergeAttributes(*"sourceObject"*)

	NN2	NN3	NN4	NN6	IE3/J1	IE3/J2	IE4	IE5	IE5.5
Compatibility								✓	✓

Example

Listing 15-29 demonstrates the usage of mergeAttributes() in the process of replicating the same form input field while assigning a unique ID to each new field. So you can see the results as you go, I display the HTML for each input field in the field.

The doMerge() function begins by generating two new elements: a P and an INPUT element. Because these newly created elements have no properties associated with them, a unique ID is assigned to the INPUT element via the uniqueID property. Attributes from the field in the source code (field1) are merged into the new INPUT element. Thus, all attributes except name and id are copied to the new element. The INPUT element is inserted into the P element, and the P element is appended to the document's form element. Finally, the `outerHTML` of the new element is displayed in its field. Notice that except for the NAME and ID attributes, all others are copied. This includes style sheet attributes and event handlers. To prove that the event handler works in the new elements, you can add a space to any one of them and press Tab to trigger the `onChange` event handler that changes the content to all uppercase characters.

Listing 15-29: **Using the mergeAttributes() Method**

```
<HTML>
<HEAD>
<TITLE>mergeAttributes() Method</TITLE>
<SCRIPT LANGUAGE="JavaScript">
function doMerge(form) {
    var newPElem = document.createElement("P")
    var newInputElem = document.createElement("INPUT")
    newInputElem.id = newInputElem.uniqueID
    newInputElem.mergeAttributes(form.field1)
    newPElem.appendChild(newInputElem)
    form.appendChild(newPElem)
    newInputElem.value = newInputElem.outerHTML
}
// called by onChange event handler of fields
function upperMe(field) {
    field.value = field.value.toUpperCase()
}
</SCRIPT>
</HEAD>
<BODY onLoad="document.expandable.field1.value =
document.expandable.field1.outerHTML">
<H1>mergeAttributes() Method</H1>
<HR>
<FORM NAME="expandable" onSubmit="return false">
<P><INPUT TYPE="button" VALUE="Append Field 'Clone'"
onClick="doMerge(this.form)"></P>
<P><INPUT TYPE="text" NAME="field1" ID="FIELD1" SIZE=120 VALUE="" STYLE="font-
size:9pt" onChange="upperMe(this)"></P>
</FORM>
</BODY>
</HTML>
```

normalize()

	NN2	NN3	NN4	NN6	IE3/J1	IE3/J2	IE4	IE5	IE5.5
Compatibility				✓					

Example

Use The Evaluator to experiment with the `normalize()` method in NN6. The following sequence adds a text node adjacent to one in the `myP` element. A subsequent invocation of the `normalize()` method removes the division between the adjacent text nodes.

Begin by confirming the number of child nodes of the `myP` element:

```
document.getElementById("myP").childNodes.length
```

Three nodes initially inhabit the element. Next, create a text node and append it as the last child of the `myP` element:

```
a = document.createTextNode("This means you!")
document.getElementById("myP").appendChild(a)
```

With the new text now rendered on the page, the number of child nodes increases to four:

```
document.getElementById("myP").childNodes.length
```

You can see that the last child node of `myP` is the text node you just created:

```
document.getElementById("myP").lastChild.nodeValue
```

But by invoking `normalize()` on `myP`, all adjacent text nodes are accumulated into single nodes:

```
document.getElementById("myP").normalize()
```

You can now see that the `myP` element is back to three child nodes, and the last child is a combination of the two previously distinct, but adjacent, text nodes:

```
document.getElementById("myP").childNodes.length
document.getElementById("myP").lastChild.nodeValue
```

releaseCapture()
setCapture(*containerBoolean*)

	NN2	NN3	NN4	NN6	IE3/J1	IE3/J2	IE4	IE5	IE5.5
Compatibility								✓	✓

Example

Listing 15-30 demonstrates the usage of `setCapture()` and `releaseCapture()` in a "quick-and-dirty" context menu for IE5+/Windows. The job of the context menu is to present a list of numbering styles for the ordered list of items on the page. Whenever the user brings up the context menu atop the OL element, the custom context menu appears. Event capture is turned on in the process to prevent mouse actions elsewhere on the page from interrupting the context menu choice. Even a click on the link set up as the title of the list is inhibited while the context menu is visible. A click anywhere outside of the context menu hides the menu. Clicking a choice in the menu changes the `listStyleType` property of the OL object and hides the menu. Whenever the context menu is hidden, event capture is turned off so that clicking on the page (such as the link) works as normal.

For this design, `onClick`, `onMouseOver`, and `onMouseOut` event handlers are assigned to the DIV element that contains the context menu. To trigger the display of the context menu, the OL element has an `onContextMenu` event handler. This handler invokes the `showContextMenu()` function. In this function, event capture is assigned to the context menu DIV object. The DIV is also positioned at the location of the click before it is set to be visible. To prevent the system's regular context menu from also appearing, the `event` object's `returnValue` property is set to `false`. The context menu is shown activated in Figure 1-2.

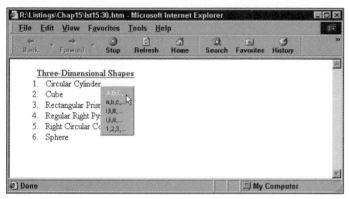

Figure 1-2: Displaying a customized context menu

Now that all mouse events on the page go through the `contextMenu` DIV object, let's examine what happens with different kinds of events triggered by user action. As the user rolls the mouse, a flood of `mouseover` and `mouseout` events fire. The event handlers assigned to the DIV manage these events. But notice that the two event handlers, `highlight()` and `unhighlight()`, perform action only when the `srcElement` property of the event is one of the menu items in the DIV. Because the page has no other `onMouseOver` or `onMouseOut` event handlers defined for elements up the containment hierarchy, you do not have to cancel event bubbling for these events.

When a user clicks the mouse button, different things happen depending on whether event capture is enabled. Without event capture, the `click` event bubbles up from wherever it occurred to the `onClick` event handler in the BODY element. (An alert dialog box displays to let you know when the event reaches the BODY.) But with event capture turned on (the context menu is showing), the `handleClick()` event handler takes over to apply the desired choice whenever the click is atop one of the context menu items. For all `click` events handled by this function, the context menu is hidden and the `click` event is canceled from bubbling up any higher (no alert dialog box appears). This takes place whether the user makes a choice in the context menu or clicks anywhere else on the page. In the latter case, all you need is for the context menu to go away like the real context menu does. For added insurance, the `onLoseCapture` event handler hides the context menu when a user performs any of the actions just listed that cancel capture.

Listing 15-30: **Using setCapture() and releaseCapture()**

```
<HTML>
<STYLE TYPE="text/css">
#contextMenu {position:absolute; background-color:#cfcfcf;
              border-style:solid; border-width:1px;
              border-color:#EFEFEF #505050 #505050 #EFEFEF;
              padding:3px 10px; font-size:8pt; font-family:Arial, Helvetica;
              line-height:150%; visibility:hidden}
.menuItem {color:black}
.menuItemOn {color:white}
OL {list-style-position:inside; font-weight:bold; cursor:nw-resize}
LI {font-weight:normal}
</STYLE>
<SCRIPT LANGUAGE="JavaScript">
function showContextMenu() {
    contextMenu.setCapture()
    contextMenu.style.pixelTop = event.clientY + document.body.scrollTop
    contextMenu.style.pixelLeft = event.clientX + document.body.scrollLeft
    contextMenu.style.visibility = "visible"
    event.returnValue = false
}

function revert() {
    document.releaseCapture()
    hideMenu()
}

function hideMenu() {
    contextMenu.style.visibility = "hidden"
}

function handleClick() {
    var elem = window.event.srcElement
    if (elem.id.indexOf("menuItem") == 0) {
        shapesList.style.listStyleType = elem.LISTTYPE
    }
    revert()
    event.cancelBubble = true
}

function highlight() {
    var elem = event.srcElement
    if (elem.className == "menuItem") {
        elem.className = "menuItemOn"
    }
}

function unhighlight() {
    var elem = event.srcElement
    if (elem.className == "menuItemOn") {
```

```
            elem.className = "menuItem"
     }
  }
</SCRIPT>
<BODY onClick="alert('You reached the document object.')" >
<OL ID="shapesList" onContextMenu="showContextMenu()">
<A HREF="javascript:alert('A sample link.')">Three-Dimensional Shapes</A>
<LI>Circular Cylinder</LI>
<LI>Cube</LI>
<LI>Rectangular Prism</LI>
<LI>Regular Right Pyramid</LI>
<LI>Right Circular Cone</LI>
<LI>Sphere</LI>
</OL>

<DIV ID="contextMenu" onLoseCapture="hideMenu()" onClick="handleClick()"
onMouseOver="highlight()" onMouseOut="unhighlight()">
<SPAN ID="menuItem1" CLASS="menuItem" LISTTYPE="upper-
alpha">A,B,C,...</SPAN><BR>
<SPAN ID="menuItem2" CLASS="menuItem" LISTTYPE="lower-
alpha">a,b,c,...</SPAN><BR>
<SPAN ID="menuItem3" CLASS="menuItem" LISTTYPE="upper-
roman">I,II,III,...</SPAN><BR>
<SPAN ID="menuItem4" CLASS="menuItem" LISTTYPE="lower-
roman">i,ii,iii,...</SPAN><BR>
<SPAN ID="menuItem5" CLASS="menuItem" LISTTYPE="decimal">1,2,3,...</SPAN><BR>
</DIV>
</BODY>
</HTML>
```

removeAttribute("*attributeName*" [, *caseSensitivity*])

	NN2	NN3	NN4	NN6	IE3/J1	IE3/J2	IE4	IE5	IE5.5
Compatibility				✓			✓	✓	✓

Example

Use The Evaluator (Chapter 13 in the *JavaScript Bible*) to experiment with the removeAttribute() method for the elements in the page. See the examples for the setAttribute() method later in this chapter, and enter the corresponding removeAttribute() statements in the top text box. Interlace statements using getAttribute() to verify the presence or absence of each attribute.

removeAttributeNode(*attributeNode*)
setAttributeNode(*attributeNode*)

	NN2	NN3	NN4	NN6	IE3/J1	IE3/J2	IE4	IE5	IE5.5
Compatibility				✓					

Example

Use The Evaluator (Chapter 13 in the *JavaScript Bible*) to experiment with the setAttributeNode() and removeAttributeNode() methods for the P element in the page. The task is to create and add a STYLE attribute to the P element. Begin by creating a new attribute and storing it temporarily in the global variable a:

```
a = document.createAttribute("style")
```

Assign a value to the attribute object:

```
a.nodeValue = "color:red"
```

Now insert the new attribute into the P element:

```
document.getElementById("myP").setAttributeNode(a)
```

The paragraph changes color in response to the newly added attribute.

Due to the NN6 bug that won't allow the method to return a reference to the newly inserted attribute node, you can artificially obtain such a reference:

```
b = document.getElementById("myP").getAttributeNode("style")
```

Finally, use the reference to the newly added attribute to remove it from the element:

```
document.getElementById("myP").removeAttribute(b)
```

Upon removing the attribute, the paragraph resumes its initial color. See the example for the setAttribute() method later in this chapter to discover how you can perform this same kind of operation with setAttribute().

removeBehavior(*ID*)

	NN2	NN3	NN4	NN6	IE3/J1	IE3/J2	IE4	IE5	IE5.5
Compatibility								✓	✓

Example

See Listings 15-19a and 15-19b earlier in this chapter for examples of how to use addBehavior() and removeBehavior().

removeChild(*nodeObject*)

	NN2	NN3	NN4	NN6	IE3/J1	IE3/J2	IE4	IE5	IE5.5
Compatibility				✓				✓	✓

Example

You can see an example of removeChild() as part of Listing 15-21 earlier in this chapter.

removeEventListener()

See addEventListener().

removeExpression("*propertyName*")

	NN2	NN3	NN4	NN6	IE3/J1	IE3/J2	IE4	IE5	IE5.5
Compatibility								✓	✓

Example

You can experiment with all three expression methods in The Evaluator (Chapter 13 in the *JavaScript Bible*). The following sequence adds an expression to a style sheet property of the myP element on the page and then removes it.

To begin, enter the number 24 in the bottom one-line text box in The Evaluator (but don't press Enter or click the List Properties button). This is the value used in the expression to govern the fontSize property of the myP object. Next, assign an expression to the myP object's style object by entering the following statement into the topmost text box:

```
myP.style.setExpression("fontSize","document.forms[0].inspector.value","JScript")
```

You can now enter different font sizes into the lower text box and have the values immediately applied to the fontSize property. (Keyboard events in the text box automatically trigger the recalculation.) The default unit is px, but you can also append other units (such as pt) to the value in the text field to see how different measurement units influence the same numeric value.

Before proceeding to the next step, enter a value other than 16 (the default fontSize value). Finally, enter the following statement in the topmost text box to disconnect the expression from the property:

```
myP.style.removeExpression("fontSize")
```

Notice that although you can no longer adjust the font size from the lower text box, the most recent value assigned to it still sticks to the element. To prove it, enter the following statement in the topmost text box to see the current value:

```
myP.style.fontSize
```

removeNode(*removeChildrenFlag*)

	NN2	NN3	NN4	NN6	IE3/J1	IE3/J2	IE4	IE5	IE5.5
Compatibility								✓	✓

Example

Examine Listing 15-21 for the `appendChild()` method to understand the difference between `removeChild()` and `removeNode()`. In the `restore()` function, you can replace this statement

```
mainObj.removeChild(oneChild)
```

in IE5+ with

```
oneChild.removeNode(true)
```

The difference is subtle, but it is important to understand. See Listing 15-31 later in this chapter for another example of the `removeNode()` method.

replaceAdjacentText("*location*", "*text*")

	NN2	NN3	NN4	NN6	IE3/J1	IE3/J2	IE4	IE5	IE5.5
Compatibility								✓	✓

Example

Use The Evaluator (Chapter 13 in the *JavaScript Bible*) to experiment with the `replaceAdjacentText()` method. Enter each of the following statements into the top text box and watch the results in the `myP` element (and its nested `myEM` element) below the solid rule:

```
document.all.myEM.replaceAdjacentText("afterBegin", "twenty")
```

Notice that the `myEM` element's new text picks up the behavior of the element. In the meantime, the replaced text (`all`) is returned by the method and displayed in the Results box.

```
document.all.myEM.replaceAdjacentText("beforeBegin", "We need ")
```

All characters of the text fragment, including spaces, are replaced. Therefore, you may need to supply a trailing space, as shown here, if the fragment you replace has a space.

```
document.all.myP.replaceAdjacentText("beforeEnd", " good people.")
```

This is another way to replace the text fragment following the myEM element, but it is also relative to the surrounding myP element. If you now attempt to replace text after the end of the myP block-level element,

```
document.all.myP.replaceAdjacentText("afterEnd", "Hooray!")
```

the text fragment is inserted after the end of the myP element's tag set. The fragment is just kind of floating in the document object model as an unlabeled text node.

replaceChild(*newNodeObject, oldNodeObject*)

	NN2	NN3	NN4	NN6	IE3/J1	IE3/J2	IE4	IE5	IE5.5
Compatibility				✓				✓	✓

Example

You can see an example of replaceChild() as part of Listing 15-21 earlier in this chapter.

replaceNode("*newNodeObject*")

	NN2	NN3	NN4	NN6	IE3/J1	IE3/J2	IE4	IE5	IE5.5
Compatibility								✓	✓

Example

Listing 15-31 demonstrates three node-related methods: removeNode(), replaceNode(), and swapNode(). These methods work in IE5+ only.

The page rendered from Listing 15-31 begins with a UL type list of four items. Four buttons control various aspects of the node structure of this list element. The first button invokes the replace() function, which changes the UL type to OL. To do this, the function must temporarily tuck away all child nodes of the original UL element so that they can be added back into the new OL element. At the same time, the old UL node is stored in a global variable (oldNode) for restoration in another function.

To replace the UL node with an OL, the replace() function creates a new, empty OL element and assigns the myOL ID to it. Next, the children (LI elements) are stored en masse as an array in the variable innards. The child nodes are then inserted into the empty OL element, using the insertBefore() method. Notice that as each child element from the innards array is inserted into the OL element, the child element is removed from the innards array. That's why the loop to insert the child nodes is a while loop that constantly inserts the first item of the innards array to the new element. Finally, the `replaceNode()` method puts the new node in the old node's place, while the old node (just the UL element) is stored in `oldNode`.

The `restore()` function operates in the inverse direction of the `replace()` function. The same juggling of nested child nodes is required.

The third button invokes the `swap()` function, whose script exchanges the first and last nodes. The `swapNode()` method, like the others in this discussion, operates from the point of view of the node. Therefore, the method is attached to one of the swapped nodes, while the other node is specified as a parameter. Because of the nature of the OL element, the number sequence remains fixed but the text of the LI node swaps.

To demonstrate the `removeNode()` method, the fourth function removes the last child node of the list. Each call to `removeNode()` passes the `true` parameter to guarantee that the text nodes nested inside each LI node are also removed. Experiment with this method by setting the parameter to `false` (the default). Notice how the parent–child relationship changes when you remove the LI node.

Listing 15-31: **Using Node-Related Methods**

```
<HTML>
<HEAD>
<TITLE>removeNode(), replaceNode(), and swapNode() Methods</TITLE>
<SCRIPT LANGUAGE="JavaScript">
// store original node between changes
var oldNode

// replace UL node with OL
function replace() {
    if (document.all.myUL) {
        var newNode = document.createElement("OL")
        newNode.id = "myOL"
        var innards = document.all.myUL.children
        while (innards.length > 0) {
            newNode.insertBefore(innards[0])
        }
        oldNode = document.all.myUL.replaceNode(newNode)
    }
}

// restore OL to UL
function restore() {
    if (document.all.myOL && oldNode) {
        var innards = document.all.myOL.children
        while (innards.length > 0) {
            oldNode.insertBefore(innards[0])
        }
        document.all.myOL.replaceNode(oldNode)

    }
}

// swap first and last nodes
function swap() {
```

```
        if (document.all.myUL) {
            document.all.myUL.firstChild.swapNode(document.all.myUL.lastChild)
        }
        if (document.all.myOL) {
            document.all.myOL.firstChild.swapNode(document.all.myOL.lastChild)
        }
    }

    // remove last node
    function remove() {
        if (document.all.myUL) {
            document.all.myUL.lastChild.removeNode(true)
        }
        if (document.all.myOL) {
            document.all.myOL.lastChild.removeNode(true)
        }
    }
</SCRIPT>
</HEAD>
<BODY>
<H1>Node Methods</H1>
<HR>
Here is a list of items:
<UL ID="myUL">
<LI>First Item
<LI>Second Item
<LI>Third Item
<LI>Fourth Item
</UL>
<FORM>
<INPUT TYPE="button" VALUE="Change to OL List" onClick="replace()">  
<INPUT TYPE="button" VALUE="Restore LI List" onClick="restore()">  
<INPUT TYPE="button" VALUE="Swap First/Last" onClick="swap()">  
<INPUT TYPE="button" VALUE="Remove Last" onClick="remove()">
</BODY>
</HTML>
```

You can accomplish the same functionality shown in Listing 15-31 in a cross-browser fashion using the W3C DOM. In place of the removeNode() and replaceNode() methods, use removeChild() and replaceChild() methods to shift the point of view (and object references) to the parent of the UL and OL objects: the document.body. Also, you need to change the document.all references to document.getElementById().

scrollIntoView(*topAlignFlag*)

	NN2	NN3	NN4	NN6	IE3/J1	IE3/J2	IE4	IE5	IE5.5
Compatibility							✓	✓	✓

Example

Use The Evaluator (Chapter 13 in the *JavaScript Bible*) to experiment with the `scrollIntoView()` method. Resize the browser window height so that you can see only the topmost text box and the Results textarea. Enter each of the following statements into the top text box and see where the `myP` element comes into view:

```
myP.scrollIntoView()
myP.scrollIntoView(false)
```

Expand the height of the browser window until you can see part of the table lower on the page. If you enter

```
myTable.scrollIntoView(false)
```

into the top text box, the page scrolls to bring the bottom of the table to the bottom of the window. But if you use the default parameter (`true` or empty),

```
myTable.scrollIntoView()
```

the page scrolls as far as it can in an effort to align the top of the element as closely as possible to the top of the window. The page cannot scroll beyond its normal scrolling maximum (although if the element is a positioned element, you can use dynamic positioning to place it wherever you want — including "off the page"). Also, if you shrink the window and try to scroll the top of the table to the top of the window, be aware that the TABLE element contains a CAPTION element so the caption is flush with the top of the window.

setActive()

	NN2	NN3	NN4	NN6	IE3/J1	IE3/J2	IE4	IE5	IE5.5
Compatibility									✓

Example

Use The Evaluator (Chapter 13 in the *JavaScript Bible*) to compare the `setActive()` and `focus()` methods. With the page scrolled to the top and the window sized so that you cannot see the sample check box near the bottom of the page, enter the following statement into the top text box:

```
document.forms[1].myCheckbox.setActive()
```

Scroll down to see that the checkbox has operational focus (press the spacebar to see). Now, scroll back to the top and enter the following:

```
document.forms[1].myCheckbox.focus()
```

This time, the checkbox gets focus and the page automatically scrolls the object into view.

setAttribute("*attributeName*", *value* [, *caseSensitivity*])

	NN2	NN3	NN4	NN6	IE3/J1	IE3/J2	IE4	IE5	IE5.5
Compatibility				✓			✓	✓	✓

Example

Use The Evaluator (Chapter 13 in the *JavaScript Bible*) to experiment with the `setAttribute()` method for the elements in the page. For IE4, use the `document.all` notation; IE5 and NN6 understand the W3C standard `getElementById()` method of addressing an element.

Setting attributes can have immediate impact on the layout of the page (just as setting an object's properties can). Enter these sample statements into the top text box to view attribute values:

IE4+:

```
document.all.myTable.setAttribute("width", "80%")
document.all.myTable.setAttribute("border", "5")
```

IE5+/NN6:

```
document.getElementById("myTable").setAttribute("width", "80%")
document.getElementById("myTable").setAttribute("border", "5")
```

setAttributeNode()

See `removeAttributeNode()`.

setCapture(*containerBoolean*)

See `releaseCapture()`.

setExpression("*propertyName*", "*expression*","*language*")

	NN2	NN3	NN4	NN6	IE3/J1	IE3/J2	IE4	IE5	IE5.5
Compatibility								✓	✓

Example

Listing 15-32 shows the `setExpression()`, `recalc()`, and `getExpression()` methods at work in a DHTML-based clock. Figure 1-3 shows the clock. As time clicks by, the bars for hours, minutes, and seconds adjust their widths to reflect the current time. At the same time, the `innerHTML` of SPAN elements to the right of each bar display the current numeric value for the bar.

The dynamically calculated values in this example are based on the creation of a new date object over and over again to get the current time from the client computer clock. It is from the date object (stored in the variable called `now`) that the hour, minute, and second values are retrieved. Some other calculations are involved so that a value for one of these time components is converted into a pixel value for the width of the bars. The bars are divided into 24 (for the hours) and 60 (for the minutes and seconds) parts, so the scale for the two types differs. For the 60-increment bars in this application, each increment is set to 5 pixels (stored in `shortWidth`); the 24-increment bars are 2.5 times the `shortWidth`.

As the document loads, the three SPAN elements for the colored bars are given no width, which means that they assume the default width of zero. But after the page loads, the `onLoad` event handler invokes the `init()` function, which sets the initial values for each bar's width and the text (`innerHTML`) of the three labeled spans. Once these initial values are set, the `init()` function invokes the `updateClock()` function.

In the `updateClock()` function, a new date object is created for the current instant. The `document.recalc()` method is called, instructing the browser to recalculate the expressions that were set in the `init()` function and assign the new values to the properties. To keep the clock "ticking," the `setTimeout()` method is set to invoke this same `updateClock()` function in one second.

To see what the `getExpression()` method does, you can click the button on the page. It simply displays the returned value for one of the attributes that you assign using `setExpression()`.

Listing 15-32: **Dynamic Properties**

```
<HTML>
<HEAD>
<TITLE>getExpression(), setExpression(), and recalc() Methods</TITLE>
<STYLE TYPE="text/css">
TH {text-align:right}
SPAN {vertical-align:bottom}
</STYLE>
<SCRIPT LANGUAGE="JavaScript">

var now = new Date()
var shortWidth = 5
var multiple = 2.5

function init() {
    with (document.all) {
        hoursBlock.style.setExpression("width",
            "now.getHours() * shortWidth * multiple","jscript")
        hoursLabel.setExpression("innerHTML",
            "now.getHours()","jscript")
        minutesBlock.style.setExpression("width",
            "now.getMinutes() * shortWidth","jscript")
```

```
            minutesLabel.setExpression("innerHTML",
                "now.getMinutes()","jscript")
            secondsBlock.style.setExpression("width",
                "now.getSeconds() * shortWidth","jscript")
            secondsLabel.setExpression("innerHTML",
                "now.getSeconds()","jscript")
        }

    updateClock()
}

function updateClock() {
    now = new Date()
    document.recalc()
    setTimeout("updateClock()",1000)
}

function showExpr() {
    alert("Expression for the \'Hours\' innerHTML property is:\r\n" +
document.all.hoursLabel.getExpression("innerHTML") + ".")
}
</SCRIPT>
</HEAD>
<BODY onLoad="init()">
<H1>getExpression(), setExpression(), recalc() Methods</H1>
<HR>
<P>This clock uses Dynamic Properties to calculate bar width and time
numbers:</P>
<TABLE BORDER=0>
<TR>
    <TH>Hours:</TH>
    <TD><SPAN ID="hoursBlock" STYLE="background-color:red"></SPAN>
 <SPAN ID="hoursLabel"></SPAN></TD>
</TR>
<TR>
    <TH>Minutes:</TH>
    <TD><SPAN ID="minutesBlock" STYLE="background-color:yellow"></SPAN>
 <SPAN ID="minutesLabel"></SPAN></TD>
</TR>
<TR>
    <TH>Seconds:</TH>
    <TD><SPAN ID="secondsBlock" STYLE="background-color:green"></SPAN>
 <SPAN ID="secondsLabel"></SPAN></TD>
</TR>
</TABLE>
<HR>
<FORM>
<INPUT TYPE="button" VALUE="Show 'Hours' number innerHTML Expression"
onClick="showExpr()"
</FORM>
</BODY>
</HTML>
```

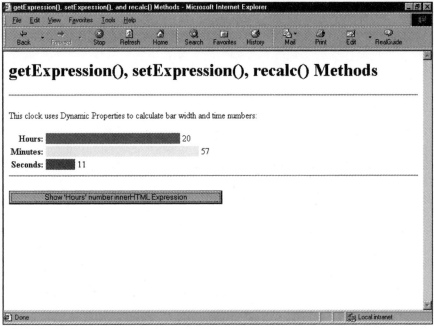

Figure 1-3: A clock controlled by dynamic properties

swapNode(*otherNodeObject*)

	NN2	NN3	NN4	NN6	IE3/J1	IE3/J2	IE4	IE5	IE5.5
Compatibility								✓	✓

Example

See Listing 15-31 (the `replaceNode()` method) for an example of the `swapNode()` method in action.

tags("*tagName*")

	NN2	NN3	NN4	NN6	IE3/J1	IE3/J2	IE4	IE5	IE5.5
Compatibility							✓	✓	✓

Example

Use The Evaluator (Chapter 13 in the *JavaScript Bible*) to experiment with the `tags()` method. Enter the following statements one at a time into the upper text box and study the results:

```
document.all.tags("DIV")
document.all.tags("DIV").length
myTable.all.tags("TD").length
```

Because the `tags()` method returns an array of objects, you can use one of those returned values as a valid element reference:

```
document.all.tags("FORM")[1].elements.tags("INPUT").length
```

urns("*behaviorURN*")

	NN2	NN3	NN4	NN6	IE3/J1	IE3/J2	IE4	IE5	IE5.5
Compatibility						-		✓	✓

Example

In case the `urns()` method is reconnected in the future, you can add a button and function to Listing 15-19b that reveals whether the `makeHot.htc` behavior is attached to the `myP` element. Such a function looks like this:

```
function behaviorAttached() {
    if (document.all.urns("makeHot")) {
        alert("There is at least one element set to \'makeHot\'.")
    }
}
```

Event handlers

onActivate
onBeforeDeactivate
onDeactivate

	NN2	NN3	NN4	NN6	IE3/J1	IE3/J2	IE4	IE5	IE5.5
Compatibility									✓

Example

You can modify Listing 15-34 later in this chapter by substituting `onActivate` for `onFocus` and `onDeactivate` for `onBlur`.

Use The Evaluator (Chapter 13 in the *JavaScript Bible*) to experiment with the `onBeforeDeactivate` event handler. To begin, set the `myP` element so it can accept focus:

```
myP.tabIndex = 1
```

If you repeatedly press the Tab key, the `myP` paragraph will eventually receive focus — indicated by the dotted rectangle around it. To see how you can prevent the element from losing focus, assign an anonymous function to the `onBeforeDeactivate` event handler, as shown in the following statement:

```
myP.onbeforedeactivate = new Function("event.returnValue=false")
```

Now you can press Tab all you like or click other focusable elements all you like, and the `myP` element will not lose focus until you reload the page (which clears away the event handler). Please do not do this on your pages unless you want to infuriate and alienate your site visitors.

onBeforeCopy

	NN2	NN3	NN4	NN6	IE3/J1	IE3/J2	IE4	IE5	IE5.5
Compatibility								✓	✓

Example

You can use the `onBeforeCopy` event handler to preprocess information prior to an actual copy action. In Listing 15-33, the function invoked by the second paragraph element's `onBeforeCopy` event handler selects the entire paragraph so that the user can select any character(s) in the paragraph to copy the entire paragraph into the clipboard. You can paste the results into the textarea to verify the operation. By assigning the paragraph selection to the `onBeforeCopy` event handler, the page notifies the user about what the copy operation will entail prior to making the menu choice. Had the operation been deferred to the `onCopy` event handler, the selection would have been made after the user chose Copy from the menu.

Listing 15-33: **The onBeforeCopy Event Handler**

```
<HTML>
<HEAD>
<TITLE>onBeforeCopy Event Handler</TITLE>
<SCRIPT LANGUAGE="JavaScript">
function selectWhole() {
    var obj = window.event.srcElement
    var range = document.body.createTextRange()
    range.moveToElementText(obj)
    range.select()
    event.returnValue = false
}
</SCRIPT>
```

```
</HEAD>
<BODY>
<H1>onBeforeCopy Event Handler</H1>
<HR>
<P>Select one or more characters in the following paragraph. Then
execute a Copy command via Edit or context menu.</P>
<P ID="myP" onBeforeCopy="selectWhole()">Lorem ipsum dolor sit amet,
consectetaur adipisicing elit, sed do eiusmod tempor incididunt ut
labore et dolore magna aliqua. Ut enim adminim veniam, quis nostrud
exercitation ullamco laboris nisi ut aliquip ex ea commodo consequat.</P>
<FORM>
<P>Paste results here:<BR>
<TEXTAREA NAME="output" COLS="60" ROWS="5"></TEXTAREA>
</P>
</FORM>
</BODY>
</HTML>
```

onBeforeCut

	NN2	NN3	NN4	NN6	IE3/J1	IE3/J2	IE4	IE5	IE5.5
Compatibility								✓	✓

Example

You can use the onBeforeCut event handler to preprocess information prior to an actual cut action. You can try this by editing a copy of Listing 15-33, changing the onBeforeCopy event handler to onBeforeCut. Notice that in its original form, the example does not activate the Cut item in either the context or Edit menu when you select some text in the second paragraph. But by assigning a function to the onBeforeCut event handler, the menu item is active, and the entire paragraph is selected from the function that is invoked.

onBeforeDeactivate

See onActivate.

onBeforeEditFocus

	NN2	NN3	NN4	NN6	IE3/J1	IE3/J2	IE4	IE5	IE5.5
Compatibility								✓	✓

Example

Use The Evaluator to explore the `onBeforeEditFocus` in IE5.5+. In the following sequence, you assign an anonymous function to the `onBeforeEditFocus` event handler of the `myP` element. The function turns the text color of the element to red when the event handler fires:

```
myP.onbeforeeditfocus = new Function("myP.style.color='red'")
```

Now turn on content editing for the `myP` element:

```
myP.contentEditable = true
```

If you now click inside the `myP` element on the page to edit its content, the text turns to red before you begin editing. In a page scripted for this kind of user interface, you would include some control that turns off editing and changes the color to normal.

If you wish to learn more about HTML content editing via the DHTML Editing ActiveX control, visit `http://msdn.microsoft.com/workshop/browser/mshtml/`.

onBeforePaste

	NN2	NN3	NN4	NN6	IE3/J1	IE3/J2	IE4	IE5	IE5.5
Compatibility								✓	✓

Example

See Listing 15-45 for the `onPaste` event handler (later in this chapter) to see how the `onBeforePaste` and `onPaste` event handlers work together.

onBlur

	NN2	NN3	NN4	NN6	IE3/J1	IE3/J2	IE4	IE5	IE5.5
Compatibility	✓	✓	✓	✓	✓	✓	✓	✓	✓

Example

More often than not, a page author uses the `onBlur` event handler to exert extreme control over the user, such as preventing a user from exiting out of a text box unless that user types something into the box. This is not a Web-friendly practice, and it is one that I discourage because there are intelligent ways to ensure a field has something typed into it before a form is submitted (see Chapter 43 of the *JavaScript Bible*). Listing 15-34 simply demonstrates the impact of the `TABINDEX` attribute in an IE5/Windows element with respect to the `onBlur` and `onFocus` events. Notice that as you press the Tab key, only the second paragraph issues the events even though all three paragraphs have event handlers assigned to them.

Listing 15-34: onBlur and onFocus Event Handlers

```
<HTML>
<HEAD>
<TITLE>onBlur and onBlur Event Handlers</TITLE>
<SCRIPT LANGUAGE="JavaScript">
function showBlur() {
    var id = event.srcElement.id
    alert("Element \"" + id + "\" has blurred.")
}
function showFocus() {
    var id = event.srcElement.id
    alert("Element \"" + id + "\" has received focus.")
}
</SCRIPT>
</HEAD>
<BODY>
<H1 ID="H1" TABINDEX=2>onBlur and onBlur Event Handlers</H1>
<HR>
<P ID="P1" onBlur="showBlur()" onFocus="showFocus()">Lorem ipsum
dolor sit amet, consectetaur adipisicing elit, sed do eiusmod tempor
incididunt ut labore et dolore magna aliqua. Ut enim adminim veniam,
quis nostrud exercitation ullamco laboris nisi ut aliquip ex ea
commodo consequat.</P>

<P ID="P2" TABINDEX=1 onBlur="showBlur()" onFocus="showFocus()">Bis
nostrud exercitation ullam mmodo consequet. Duis aute involuptate
velit esse cillum dolore eu fugiat nulla pariatur. At vver eos et
accusam dignissum qui blandit est praesent luptatum delenit
aigueexcepteur sint occae.</P>

<P ID="P3" onBlur="showBlur()" onFocus="showFocus()">Unte af phen
neigepheings atoot Prexs eis phat eit sakem eit vory gast te Plok
peish ba useing phen roxas. Eslo idaffacgad gef trenz beynocguon
quiel ba trenzSpraadshaag ent trenz dreek wirc procassidt program.</P>

</BODY>
</HTML>
```

onClick

	NN2	NN3	NN4	NN6	IE3/J1	IE3/J2	IE4	IE5	IE5.5
Compatibility	✓	✓	✓	✓	✓	✓	✓	✓	✓

Example

The onClick event handler is one of the simplest to grasp and use. Listing 15-35 demonstrates its interaction with the onDblClick event handler and shows you how to prevent a link's intrinsic action from activating when combined with click events. As you click and/or double-click the link, the status bar displays a message associated with each event. Notice that if you double-click, the click event fires first with the first message immediately replaced by the second. For demonstration purposes, I show both backward-compatible ways of cancelling the link's intrinsic action. In practice, decide on one style and stick with it.

Listing 15-35: **Using onClick and onDblClick Event Handlers**

```
<HTML>
<HEAD>
<TITLE>onClick and onDblClick Event Handlers</TITLE>
<SCRIPT LANGUAGE="JavaScript">
var msg = ""
function showClick() {
    msg = "The element has been clicked. "
    status = msg
}
function showDblClick() {
    msg = "The element has been double-clicked."
    status = msg
    return false

}
</SCRIPT>
</HEAD>
<BODY>
<H1>onClick and onDblClick Event Handlers</H1>
<HR>
<A HREF="#" onClick="showClick();return false"
onDblClick="return showDblClick()">
A sample link.</A>
</BODY>
</HTML>
```

onContextMenu

	NN2	NN3	NN4	NN6	IE3/J1	IE3/J2	IE4	IE5	IE5.5
Compatibility								✓	✓

Example

See Listing 15-30 earlier in this chapter for an example of using the `onContextMenu` event handler with a custom context menu.

onCopy
onCut

	NN2	NN3	NN4	NN6	IE3/J1	IE3/J2	IE4	IE5	IE5.5
Compatibility								✓	✓

Example

Listing 15-36 shows both the `onBeforeCut` and `onCut` event handlers in action (as well as `onBeforePaste` and `onPaste`). Notice how the `handleCut()` function not only stuffs the selected word into the `clipboardData` object, but it also erases the selected text from the table cell element from where it came. If you replace the `onBeforeCut` and `onCut` event handlers with `onBeforeCopy` and `onCopy` (and change `handleCut()` to not eliminate the inner text of the event source element), the operation works with copy and paste instead of cut and paste. I demonstrate this later in the chapter in Listing 15-45.

Listing 15-36: **Cutting and Pasting under Script Control**

```
<HTML>
<HEAD>
<TITLE>onBeforeCut and onCut Event Handlers</TITLE>
<STYLE TYPE="text/css">
TD {text-align:center}
TH {text-decoration:underline}
.blanks {text-decoration:underline}
</STYLE>
<SCRIPT LANGUAGE="JavaScript">
function selectWhole() {
    var obj = window.event.srcElement
    var range = document.body.createTextRange()
    range.moveToElementText(obj)
    range.select()
    event.returnValue = false
}
function handleCut() {
    var rng = document.selection.createRange()
    clipboardData.setData("Text",rng.text)
    var elem = event.srcElement
```

Continued

Listing 15-36 *(continued)*

```
    elem.innerText = ""
    event.returnValue = false
}

function handlePaste() {
    var elem = window.event.srcElement
    if (elem.className == "blanks") {
        elem.innerHTML = clipboardData.getData("Text")
    }
    event.returnValue = false
}
function handleBeforePaste() {
    var elem = window.event.srcElement
    if (elem.className == "blanks") {
        event.returnValue = false
    }
}
</SCRIPT>
</HEAD>
<BODY>
<H1>onBeforeCut and onCut Event Handlers</H1>
<HR>
<P>Your goal is to cut and paste one noun and one
adjective from the following table into the blanks
of the sentence. Select a word from the table and
use the Edit or context menu to cut it from the table.
Select one or more spaces of the blanks in the
sentence and choose Paste to replace the blank with
the clipboard contents.</P>

<TABLE CELLPADDING=5 onBeforeCut="selectWhole()" onCut="handleCut()" >
<TR><TH>Nouns</TH><TH>Adjectives</TH></TR>
<TR><TD>truck</TD><TD>round</TD></TR>
<TR><TD>doll</TD><TD>red</TD></TR>
<TR><TD>ball</TD><TD>pretty</TD></TR>
</TABLE>

<P ID="myP" onBeforePaste="handleBeforePaste()" onPaste="handlePaste()">
Pat said, "Oh my, the <SPAN ID="blank1" CLASS="blanks">
     </SPAN>
is so <SPAN ID="blank2" CLASS="blanks">
     </SPAN>!"</P>

<BUTTON onClick="location.reload()">Reset</BUTTON>
</BODY>
</HTML>
```

onDblClick

	NN2	NN3	NN4	NN6	IE3/J1	IE3/J2	IE4	IE5	IE5.5
Compatibility			✓	✓			✓	✓	✓

Example

See Listing 15-35 (for the onClick event handler) to see the onDblClick event in action.

onDrag

	NN2	NN3	NN4	NN6	IE3/J1	IE3/J2	IE4	IE5	IE5.5
Compatibility								✓	✓

Example

Listing 15-37 shows several drag-related event handlers in action. The page resembles the example in Listing 15-36, but the scripting behind the page is quite different. In this example, the user is encouraged to select individual words from the Nouns and Adjectives columns and drag them to the blanks of the sentence. To beef up the demonstration, Listing 15-37 shows you how to pass the equivalent of array data from a drag source to a drag target. At the same time, the user has a fixed amount of time (two seconds) to complete each drag operation.

The onDragStart and onDrag event handlers are placed in the <BODY> tag because those events bubble up from any element that the user tries to drag. The scripts invoked by these event handlers filter the events so that the desired action is triggered only by the "hot" elements inside the table. This approach to event handlers prevents you from having to duplicate event handlers (or IE <SCRIPT FOR=> tags) for each table cell.

The onDragStart event handler invokes setupDrag(). This function cancels the onDragStart event except when the target element (in other words, the one about to be dragged) is one of the TD elements inside the table. To make this application smarter about what kind of word is dragged to which blank, it passes not only the word's text, but also some extra information about the word. This lets another event handler verify that a noun has been dragged to the first blank, while an adjective has been dragged to the second blank. To help with this effort, class names are assigned to the TD elements to distinguish the words from the Nouns column from the words of the Adjectives column. The setupDrag() function generates an array consisting of the innerText of the event's source element plus the element's class name. But the event.dataTransfer object cannot store array data types, so the Array.join() method converts the array to a string with a colon separating the entries. This string, then, is stuffed into the event.dataTransfer object. The object is instructed to render the cursor display during the drag-and-drop operation so that when the cursor is atop a drop target, the cursor is the "copy" style. Figure 1-4 shows the cursor effect as the user drags a selected word from the columns to a blank field that is scripted as a drop target. Finally, the `setupDrag()` function is the first to execute in the drag operation, so a timer is set to the current clock time to time the drag operation.

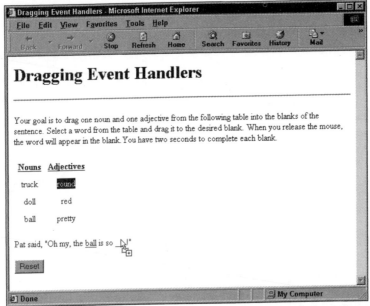

Figure 1-4: The cursor turns to a "copy" icon atop a designated drop target

The `onDrag` event handler (in the BODY) captures the `onDrag` events that are generated by whichever table cell element is the source element for the action. Each time the event fires (which is a lot during the action), the `timeIt()` function is invoked to compare the current time against the reference time (global `timer`) set when the drag starts. If the time exceeds two seconds (2,000 milliseconds), an alert dialog box notifies the user. To close the alert dialog box, the user must unclick the mouse button to end the drag operation.

To turn the blank SPAN elements into drop targets, their `onDragEnter`, `onDragOver`, and `onDrop` event handlers must set `event.returnValue` to `false`; also, the `event.dataTransfer.dropEffect` property should be set to the desired effect (`copy` in this case). These event handlers are placed in the P element that contains the two SPAN elements, again for simplicity. Notice, however, that the `cancelDefault()` functions do their work only if the target element is one of the SPAN elements whose ID begins with "blank."

As the user releases the mouse button, the `onDrop` event handler invokes the `handleDrop()` function. This function retrieves the string data from `event.dataTransfer` and restores it to an array data type (using the `String.split()` method). A little bit of testing makes sure that the word type ("noun" or "adjective") is associated with the desired blank. If so, the source element's text is set to the drop target's `innerText` property; otherwise, an error message is assembled to help the user know what went wrong.

Listing 15-37: **Using Drag-Related Event Handlers**

```
<HTML>
<HEAD>
<TITLE>Dragging Event Handlers</TITLE>
<STYLE TYPE="text/css">
TD {text-align:center}
TH {text-decoration:underline}
.blanks {text-decoration:underline}
</STYLE>
<SCRIPT LANGUAGE="JavaScript">
var timer
function setupDrag() {
    if (event.srcElement.tagName != "TD") {
        // don't allow dragging for any other elements
        event.returnValue = false
    } else {
        // setup array of data to be passed to drop target
        var passedData = [event.srcElement.innerText,
event.srcElement.className]
        // store it as a string
        event.dataTransfer.setData("Text", passedData.join(":"))
        event.dataTransfer.effectAllowed = "copy"
        timer = new Date()
    }
}
function timeIt() {
    if (event.srcElement.tagName == "TD" && timer) {
        if ((new Date()) - timer > 2000) {
            alert("Sorry, time is up. Try again.")
            timer = 0
        }
    }
}
function handleDrop() {
    var elem = event.srcElement
    var passedData = event.dataTransfer.getData("Text")
    var errMsg = ""
    if (passedData) {
        // reconvert passed string to an array
        passedData = passedData.split(":")
        if (elem.id == "blank1") {
            if (passedData[1] == "noun") {
                event.dataTransfer.dropEffect = "copy"
                event.srcElement.innerText = passedData[0]
            } else {
                errMsg = "You can't put an adjective into the noun placeholder."
            }
        } else if (elem.id == "blank2") {
            if (passedData[1] == "adjective") {
                event.dataTransfer.dropEffect = "copy"
```

Continued

Listing 15-37 *(continued)*

```
                event.srcElement.innerText = passedData[0]
            } else {
                errMsg = "You can't put a noun into the adjective placeholder."
            }
        }
        if (errMsg) {
            alert(errMsg)
        }
    }
}
function cancelDefault() {
    if (event.srcElement.id.indexOf("blank") == 0) {
        event.dataTransfer.dropEffect = "copy"
        event.returnValue = false
    }
}
</SCRIPT>
</HEAD>
<BODY onDragStart="setupDrag()" onDrag="timeIt()">
<H1>Dragging Event Handlers</H1>
<HR>
<P>Your goal is to drag one noun and one
adjective from the following table into the blanks
of the sentence. Select a word from the table and
drag it to the desired blank. When you release the
mouse, the word will appear in the blank. You have
two seconds to complete each blank.</P>

<TABLE CELLPADDING=5>
<TR><TH>Nouns</TH><TH>Adjectives</TH></TR>
<TR><TD class="noun">truck</TD><TD class="adjective">round</TD></TR>
<TR><TD class="noun">doll</TD><TD class="adjective">red</TD></TR>
<TR><TD class="noun">ball</TD><TD class="adjective">pretty</TD></TR>
</TABLE>

<P ID="myP" onDragEnter="cancelDefault()" onDragOver="cancelDefault()"
onDrop="handleDrop()">
Pat said, "Oh my, the <SPAN ID="blank1" CLASS="blanks">
     </SPAN>
is so <SPAN ID="blank2" CLASS="blanks">
     </SPAN>!"</P>

<BUTTON onClick="location.reload()">Reset</BUTTON>
</BODY>
</HTML>
```

One event handler not shown in Listing 15-37 is onDragEnd. You can use this event to display the elapsed time for each successful drag operation. Because the event fires on the drag source element, you can implement it in the `<BODY>` tag and filter events similar to the way the `onDragStart` or `onDrag` event handlers filter events for the TD element.

onDragEnter
onDragLeave

	NN2	NN3	NN4	NN6	IE3/J1	IE3/J2	IE4	IE5	IE5.5
Compatibility								✓	✓

Example

Listing 15-38 shows the `onDragEnter` and `onDragLeave` event handlers in use. The simple page displays (via the status bar) the time of entry to one element of the page. When the dragged cursor leaves the element, the `onDragLeave` event handler hides the status bar message. No drop target is defined for this page, so when you drag the item, the cursor remains as the "no drop" cursor.

> **Listing 15-38: Using onDragEnter and onDragLeave Event Handlers**

```
<HTML>
<HEAD>
<TITLE>onDragEnter and onDragLeave Event Handlers</TITLE>
<SCRIPT LANGUAGE="JavaScript">
function showEnter() {
    status = "Entered at: " + new Date()
    event.returnValue = false
}
function clearMsg() {
    status = ""
    event.returnValue = false
}
</SCRIPT>
</HEAD>
<BODY>
<H1 onDragEnter="showEnter()" onDragLeave="clearMsg()">
onDragEnter and onDragLeave Event Handlers
</H1>
<HR>
<P>Select any character(s) from this paragraph,
and slowly drag it around the page. When the dragging action enters the
large header above, the status bar displays when the onDragEnter
event handler fires. When you leave the header, the message is cleared
via the onDragLeave event handler.</P>
</BODY>
</HTML>
```

onDragOver

	NN2	NN3	NN4	NN6	IE3/J1	IE3/J2	IE4	IE5	IE5.5
Compatibility								✓	✓

Example

See Listing 15-37 of the onDrag event handler to see how the onDragOver event handler contributes to making an element a drop target.

onDragStart

	NN2	NN3	NN4	NN6	IE3/J1	IE3/J2	IE4	IE5	IE5.5
Compatibility							✓	✓	✓

Example

See Listing 15-37 of the onDrag event handler to see how to apply the onDragStart event handler in a typical drag-and-drop scenario.

onDrop

	NN2	NN3	NN4	NN6	IE3/J1	IE3/J2	IE4	IE5	IE5.5
Compatibility								✓	✓

Example

See Listing 15-37 of the onDrag event handler to see how to apply the onDrop event handler in a typical drag-and-drop scenario.

onFilterChange

	NN2	NN3	NN4	NN6	IE3/J1	IE3/J2	IE4	IE5	IE5.5
Compatibility							✓	✓	✓

Example

Listing 15-39 demonstrates how the onFilterChange event handler can trigger a second transition effect after another one completes. The onLoad event handler triggers the first effect. Although the `onFilterChange` event handler works with most of the same objects in IE4 as IE5, the filter object transition properties are not reflected in a convenient form. The syntax shown in Listing 15-39 uses the new ActiveX filter control found in IE5.5 (described in Chapter 30 of the *JavaScript Bible*).

Listing 15-39: **Using the onFilterChange Event Handler**

```
<HTML>
<HEAD>
<TITLE>onFilterChange Event Handler</TITLE>
<SCRIPT LANGUAGE=JavaScript>
function init() {
    image1.filters[0].apply()
    image2.filters[0].apply()
    start()
}

function start() {
    image1.style.visibility = "hidden"
    image1.filters[0].play()
}

function finish() {
    // verify that first transition is done (optional)
    if (image1.filters[0].status == 0) {
        image2.style.visibility = "visible"
        image2.filters[0].play()
    }
}
</SCRIPT>
</HEAD>
<BODY onLoad="init()">
<H1>onFilterChange Event Handler</H1>
<HR>
<P>The completion of the first transition ("circle-in")
triggers the second ("circle-out").
<BUTTON onClick="location.reload()">Play It Again</BUTTON></P>
<DIV ID="image1" STYLE="visibility:visible;
    position:absolute; top:150px; left:150px;
    filter:progID:DXImageTransform.Microsoft.Iris(irisstyle='CIRCLE',
    motion='in')"
    onFilterChange="finish()"><IMG SRC="desk1.gif" HEIGHT=90
    WIDTH=120></DIV>
<DIV ID="image2" STYLE="visibility:hidden;
    position:absolute; top:150px; left:150px;
    filter:progID:DXImageTransform.Microsoft.Iris(irisstyle='CIRCLE',
    motion='out')">
    <IMG SRC="desk3.gif" HEIGHT=90 WIDTH=120></DIV>
</BODY>
</HTML>
```

onFocus

	NN2	NN3	NN4	NN6	IE3/J1	IE3/J2	IE4	IE5	IE5.5
Compatibility	✓	✓	✓	✓	✓	✓	✓	✓	✓

Example

See Listing 15-34 earlier in this chapter for an example of the onFocus and onBlur event handlers.

onHelp

	NN2	NN3	NN4	NN6	IE3/J1	IE3/J2	IE4	IE5	IE5.5
Compatibility							✓	✓	✓

Example

Listing 15-40 is a rudimentary example of a context-sensitive help system that displays help messages tailored to the kind of text input required by different text fields. When the user gives focus to either of the text fields, a small legend appears to remind the user that help is available by a press of the F1 help key. IE5/Mac provides only generic help.

Listing 15-40: **Creating Context-Sensitive Help**

```
<HTML>
<HEAD>
<SCRIPT LANGUAGE="JavaScript">
function showNameHelp() {
    alert("Enter your first and last names.")
    event.cancelBubble = true
    return false
}
function showYOBHelp() {
    alert("Enter the four-digit year of your birth. For example: 1972")
    event.cancelBubble = true
    return false
}
function showGenericHelp() {
    alert("All fields are required.")
    event.cancelBubble = true
    return false
}
function showLegend() {
    document.all.legend.style.visibility = "visible"/
}
```

```
function hideLegend() {
    document.all.legend.style.visibility = "hidden"
}
function init() {
    var msg = ""
    if (navigator.userAgent.indexOf("Mac") != -1) {
        msg = "Press \'help\' key for help."
    } else if (navigator.userAgent.indexOf("Win") != -1) {
        msg = "Press F1 for help."
    }
    document.all.legend.style.visibility = "hidden"
    document.all.legend.innerHTML = msg
}
</SCRIPT>
</HEAD>

<BODY onLoad="init()" onHelp="return showGenericHelp()">
<H1>onHelp Event Handler</H1>
<HR>
<P ID="legend" STYLE="visibility:hidden; font-size:10px"> </P>
<FORM>
Name: <INPUT TYPE="text" NAME="name" SIZE=30
    onFocus="showLegend()" onBlur="hideLegend()"
    onHelp="return showNameHelp()">
<BR>
Year of Birth: <INPUT TYPE="text" NAME="YOB" SIZE=30
    onFocus="showLegend()" onBlur="hideLegend()"
    onHelp="return showYOBHelp()">
</FORM>
</BODY>
</HTML>
```

onKeyDown
onKeyPress
onKeyUp

	NN2	NN3	NN4	NN6	IE3/J1	IE3/J2	IE4	IE5	IE5.5
Compatibility			✓	✓			✓	✓	✓

Example

Listing 15-41 is a working laboratory that you can use to better understand the way keyboard event codes and modifier keys work in IE5+ and NN6. The actual code of the listing is less important than watching the page while you use it. For every key or key combination that you press, the page shows the keyCode value for the onKeyDown, onKeyPress, and onKeyUp events. If you hold down one or more modifier keys while performing the key press, the modifier key name is highlighted for each of the three events. Note that when run in NN6, the keyCode value is not the character code (which doesn't show up in this example for NN6). Also, you may need to click the NN6 page for the document object to recognize the keyboard events.

The best way to watch what goes on during keyboard events is to press and hold a key to see the key codes for the onKeyDown and onKeyPress events (see Figure 1-5). Then release the key to see the code for the onKeyUp event. Notice, for instance, that if you press the A key without any modifier key, the onKeyDown event key code is 65 (A) but the onKeyPress key code in IE (and the charCode property in NN6 if it were displayed here) is 97 (a). If you then repeat the exercise but hold the Shift key down, all three events generate the 65 (A) key code (and the Shift modifier labels are highlighted). Releasing the Shift key causes the onKeyUp event to show the key code for the Shift key.

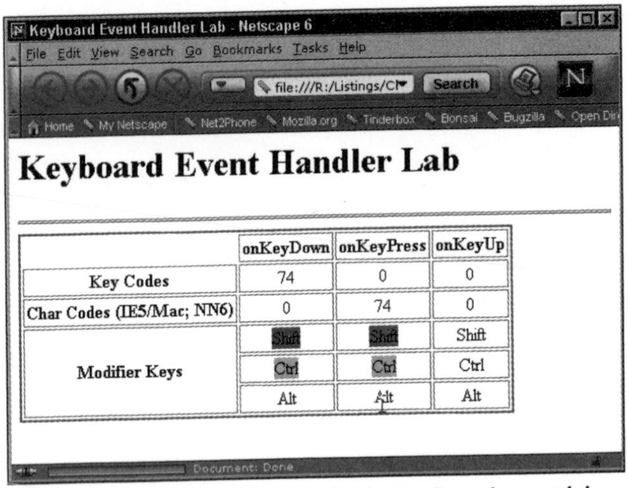

Figure 1-5: Pressing Ctrl+Alt+J in the keyboard event lab page

In another experiment, press any of the four arrow keys. No key code is passed for the onKeyPress event because those keys don't generate those events. They do, however, generate onKeyDown and onKeyUp events.

Listing 15-41: **Keyboard Event Handler Laboratory**

```
<HTML>
<HEAD>
<TITLE>Keyboard Event Handler Lab</TITLE>
<STYLE TYPE="text/css">
TD {text-align:center}
</STYLE>
<SCRIPT LANGUAGE="JavaScript">
function init() {
    document.onkeydown = showKeyDown
    document.onkeyup = showKeyUp
```

```
        document.onkeypress = showKeyPress
}

function showKeyDown(evt) {
    evt = (evt) ? evt : window.event
    document.getElementById("pressKeyCode").innerHTML = 0
    document.getElementById("upKeyCode").innerHTML = 0
    document.getElementById("pressCharCode").innerHTML = 0
    document.getElementById("upCharCode").innerHTML = 0
    restoreModifiers("")
    restoreModifiers("Down")
    restoreModifiers("Up")
    document.getElementById("downKeyCode").innerHTML = evt.keyCode
    if (evt.charCode) {
        document.getElementById("downCharCode").innerHTML = evt.charCode
    }
    showModifiers("Down", evt)
}
function showKeyUp(evt) {
    evt = (evt) ? evt : window.event
    document.getElementById("upKeyCode").innerHTML = evt.keyCode
    if (evt.charCode) {
        document.getElementById("upCharCode").innerHTML = evt.charCode
    }
    showModifiers("Up", evt)
    return false
}
function showKeyPress(evt) {
    evt = (evt) ? evt : window.event
    document.getElementById("pressKeyCode").innerHTML = evt.keyCode
    if (evt.charCode) {
        document.getElementById("pressCharCode").innerHTML = evt.charCode
    }
    showModifiers("", evt)
    return false
}
function showModifiers(ext, evt) {
    restoreModifiers(ext)
    if (evt.shiftKey) {
        document.getElementById("shift" + ext).style.backgroundColor = "#ff0000"
    }
    if (evt.ctrlKey) {
        document.getElementById("ctrl" + ext).style.backgroundColor = "#00ff00"
    }
    if (evt.altKey) {
        document.getElementById("alt" + ext).style.backgroundColor = "#0000ff"
    }
}
```

Continued

Listing 15-41 *(continued)*

```
function restoreModifiers(ext) {
    document.getElementById("shift" + ext).style.backgroundColor = "#ffffff"
    document.getElementById("ctrl" + ext).style.backgroundColor = "#ffffff"
    document.getElementById("alt" + ext).style.backgroundColor = "#ffffff"
}
</SCRIPT>
</HEAD>

<BODY onLoad="init()">
<H1>Keyboard Event Handler Lab</H1>
<HR>
<FORM>
<TABLE BORDER=2 CELLPADDING=2>
<TR><TH></TH><TH>onKeyDown</TH><TH>onKeyPress</TH><TH>onKeyUp</TH></TR>
<TR><TH>Key Codes</TH>
    <TD ID="downKeyCode">0</TD>
    <TD ID="pressKeyCode">0</TD>
    <TD ID="upKeyCode">0</TD>
</TR>
<TR><TH>Char Codes (IE5/Mac; NN6)</TH>
    <TD ID="downCharCode">0</TD>
    <TD ID="pressCharCode">0</TD>
    <TD ID="upCharCode">0</TD>
</TR>
<TR><TH ROWSPAN=3>Modifier Keys</TH>
    <TD><SPAN ID="shiftDown">Shift</SPAN></TD>
    <TD><SPAN ID="shift">Shift</SPAN></TD>
    <TD><SPAN ID="shiftUp">Shift</SPAN></TD>
</TR>
<TR>
    <TD><SPAN ID="ctrlDown">Ctrl</SPAN></TD>
    <TD><SPAN ID="ctrl">Ctrl</SPAN></TD>
    <TD><SPAN ID="ctrlUp">Ctrl</SPAN></TD>
</TR>
<TR>
    <TD><SPAN ID="altDown">Alt</SPAN></TD>
    <TD><SPAN ID="alt">Alt</SPAN></TD>
    <TD><SPAN ID="altUp">Alt</SPAN></TD>
</TR>
</TABLE>
</FORM>
</BODY>
</HTML>
```

Spend some time with this lab, and try all kinds of keys and key combinations until you understand the way the events and key codes work.

onLoseCapture

	NN2	NN3	NN4	NN6	IE3/J1	IE3/J2	IE4	IE5	IE5.5
Compatibility								✓	✓

Example

See Listing 15-30 earlier in this chapter for an example of how to use onLoseCapture with an event-capturing scenario for displaying a context menu. The onLoseCapture event handler hides the context menu when the user performs any action that causes the menu to lose mouse capture.

onMouseDown
onMouseUp

	NN2	NN3	NN4	NN6	IE3/J1	IE3/J2	IE4	IE5	IE5.5
Compatibility			✓	✓			✓	✓	✓

Example

To demonstrate a likely scenario of changing button images in response to rolling atop an image, pressing down on it, releasing the mouse button, and rolling away from the image, Listing 15-42 presents a pair of small navigation buttons (left- and right-arrow buttons). Because the image object is not part of the document object model for NN2 or IE3 (which reports itself as Navigator version 2), the page is designed to accept all browsers. Only those browsers that support precached images and image swapping (and thus pass the test for the presence of the document.images array) can execute those statements. For a browser with an image object, images are preloaded into the browser cache as the page loads so that response to the user is instantaneous the first time the user calls upon new versions of the images.

Listing 15-42: Using onMouseDown and onMouseUp Event Handlers

```
<HTML>
<HEAD>
<TITLE>onMouseDown and onMouseUp Event Handlers</TITLE>
<SCRIPT LANGUAGE="JavaScript">
if (document.images) {
    var RightNormImg = new Image(16,16)
    var RightUpImg = new Image(16,16)
```

Continued

Listing 15-42 *(continued)*

```
    var RightDownImg = new Image(16,16)
    var LeftNormImg = new Image(16,16)
    var LeftUpImg = new Image(16,16)
    var LeftDownImg = new Image(16,16)

    RightNormImg.src = "RightNorm.gif"
    RightUpImg.src = "RightUp.gif"
    RightDownImg.src = "RightDown.gif"
    LeftNormImg.src = "LeftNorm.gif"
    LeftUpImg.src = "LeftUp.gif"
    LeftDownImg.src = "LeftDown.gif"
}
function setImage(imgName, type) {
    if (document.images) {
        var imgFile = eval(imgName + type + "Img.src")
        document.images[imgName].src = imgFile
        return false
    }
}
</SCRIPT>
</HEAD>
<BODY>
<H1>onMouseDown and onMouseUp Event Handlers</H1>
<HR>
<P>Roll atop and click on the buttons to see how the link event handlers swap
images:</P>
<CENTER>
<A HREF="javascript:void(0)"
    onMouseOver="return setImage('Left','Up')"
    onMouseDown="return setImage('Left','Down')"
    onMouseUp="return setImage('Left','Up')"
    onMouseOut="return setImage('Left','Norm')"
>
<IMG NAME="Left" SRC="LeftNorm.gif" HEIGHT=16 WIDTH=16 BORDER=0></A>
  
<A HREF="javascript:void(0)"
    onMouseOver="return setImage('Right','Up')"
    onMouseDown="return setImage('Right','Down')"
    onMouseUp="return setImage('Right','Up')"
    onMouseOut="return setImage('Right','Norm')"
>
<IMG NAME="Right" SRC="RightNorm.gif" HEIGHT=16 WIDTH=16 BORDER=0></A>
</CENTER>
</BODY>
</HTML>
```

IE4+ and NN6+ simplify the implementation of this kind of three-state image button by allowing you to assign the event handlers directly to IMG element objects. Wrapping images inside links is a backward compatibility approach that allows older browsers to respond to clicks on images for navigation or other scripting tasks.

onMouseEnter
onMouseLeave

	NN2	NN3	NN4	NN6	IE3/J1	IE3/J2	IE4	IE5	IE5.5
Compatibility									✓

Example

You can modify Listing 15-43 with the IE5.5 syntax by substituting onMouseEnter for onMouseOver and onMouseLeave for onMouseOut. The effect is the same.

onMouseMove

	NN2	NN3	NN4	NN6	IE3/J1	IE3/J2	IE4	IE5	IE5.5
Compatibility			(✓)	✓			✓	✓	✓

Example

Listing 15-43 is a simplified example of dragging elements in IE4+. (See Chapter 31 of the *JavaScript Bible* for more dragging examples.) Three images are individually positioned on the page. Most of the scripting code concerns itself with the geography of click locations, the stacking order of the images, and the management of the onMouseMove event handler so that it is active only when an item is dragged.

Scripts assign the onMouseDown and onMouseUp event handlers to the document object, invoking the engage() and release() functions, respectively. When a user mouses down anywhere in the document, the engage() function starts by invoking setSelectedObj(). This function examines the target of the mouseDown event. If it is one of the map images, the selectedObj global variable is set to the image object and the element is brought to the front of the stacking order of images (any previously stacked image is returned to its normal position in the stack). MouseDown events on any other element simply make sure that the selectedObj variable is null. The presence of a value assigned to selectedObj serves as a kind of switch for other functions: When the variable contains a value, it means that the user is doing something associated with dragging an element.

Back at the engage() function—provided the user mouses down on one of the draggable images—the onMouseMove event handler is assigned to the document object, setting it to invoke the dragIt() function. For the sake of users, the offset of the mouse down event from the top-left corner of the image is preserved in the offsetX and offsetY variables (minus any scrolling that the body is subject to at that instant). These offset values are necessary to let the scripts set the location of the image during dragging (the location is set for the top-left corner of the image) while keeping the cursor in the same location within the image as when the user first presses the mouse.

As the user drags the image, the onMouseDown event handler fires repeatedly, allowing the dragIt() function to continually update the location of the element relative to the current cursor position (the event.clientX and event.clientY properties). The global offset variables are subtracted from the cursor position to preserve the relation of the image's top-left corner to the initial cursor position at mouse down.

Upon the user releasing the mouse button, the release() function turns off the onMouseMove event handler (setting it to null). This prevents the event from being processed at all during normal usage of the page. The selectedObj global variable is also set to null, turning off the "switch" that indicates dragging is in session.

Listing 15-43: **Dragging Elements with onMouseMove**

```
<HTML>
<HEAD><TITLE>onMouseMove Event Handler</TITLE>
<STYLE TYPE="text/css">
    #camap {position:absolute; left:20; top:120}
    #ormap {position:absolute; left:80; top:120}
    #wamap {position:absolute; left:140; top:120}
</STYLE>
<SCRIPT LANGUAGE="JavaScript">
// global variables used while dragging
var offsetX = 0
var offsetY = 0
var selectedObj
var frontObj

// set document-level event handlers
document.onmousedown = engage
document.onmouseup = release

// positioning an object at a specific pixel coordinate
function shiftTo(obj, x, y) {
    obj.style.pixelLeft = x
    obj.style.pixelTop = y
}

// setting the z-order of an object
function bringToFront(obj) {
    if (frontObj) {
        frontObj.style.zIndex = 0
    }
    frontObj = obj
    frontObj.style.zIndex = 1
}
```

```
// set global var to a reference to dragged element
function setSelectedObj() {
    var imgObj = window.event.srcElement
    if (imgObj.id.indexOf("map") == 2) {
        selectedObj = imgObj
        bringToFront(selectedObj)
        return
    }
    selectedObj = null
    return
}

// do the dragging (called repeatedly by onMouseMove)
function dragIt() {
    if (selectedObj) {
        shiftTo(selectedObj, (event.clientX - offsetX), (event.clientY -
offsetY))
        return false
    }
}

// set global vars and turn on mousemove trapping (called by onMouseDown)
function engage() {
    setSelectedObj()
    if (selectedObj) {
        document.onmousemove = dragIt
        offsetX = window.event.offsetX - document.body.scrollLeft
        offsetY = window.event.offsetY - document.body.scrollTop
    }
}

// restore everything as before (called by onMouseUp)
function release() {
    if (selectedObj) {
        document.onmousemove = null
        selectedObj = null
    }
}

</SCRIPT>
</HEAD>
<BODY>
<H1>onMouseMove Event Handler</H1>
<HR>
Click and drag the images:
<IMG ID="camap" SRC="camap.gif" WIDTH="47" HEIGHT="82" BORDER="0">
<IMG ID="ormap" SRC="ormap.gif" WIDTH="57" HEIGHT="45" BORDER="0">
<IMG ID="wamap" SRC="wamap.gif" WIDTH="38" HEIGHT="29" BORDER="0">
</SCRIPT>
</BODY>
</HTML>
```

onMouseOut
onMouseOver

	NN2	NN3	NN4	NN6	IE3/J1	IE3/J2	IE4	IE5	IE5.5
Compatibility	✓	✓	✓	✓	✓	✓	✓	✓	✓

Example

Listing 15-44 uses the U.S. Pledge of Allegiance with four links to demonstrate how to use the onMouseOver and onMouseOut event handlers. Notice that for each link, the handler runs a general-purpose function that sets the window's status message. The function returns a true value, which the event handler call evaluates to replicate the required return true statement needed for setting the status bar. In one status message, I supply a URL in parentheses to let you evaluate how helpful you think it is for users.

Listing 15-44: Using onMouseOver and onMouseOut Event Handlers

```
<HTML>
<HEAD>
<TITLE>onMouseOver and onMouseOut Event Handlers</TITLE>
<SCRIPT LANGUAGE="JavaScript">
function setStatus(msg) {
    status = msg
    return true
}
// destination of all link HREFs
function emulate() {
    alert("Not going there in this demo.")
}
</SCRIPT>
</HEAD>
<BODY>
<H1>onMouseOver and onMouseOut Event Handlers
</H1>
<HR>
<H1>Pledge of Allegiance</H1>
<HR>
```

```
I pledge <A HREF="javascript:emulate()" onMouseOver="return setStatus('View
dictionary definition')" onMouseOut="return setStatus('')">allegiance</A> to the
<A HREF="javascript:emulate()" onMouseOver="return setStatus('Learn about the
U.S. flag (http://lcweb.loc.gov)')" onMouseOut="return setStatus('')">flag</A>
of the <A HREF="javascript:emulate()" onMouseOver="return setStatus('View info
about the U.S. government')" onMouseOut="return setStatus('')">United States of
America</A>, and to the Republic for which it stands, one nation <A
HREF="javascript:emulate()" onMouseOver="return setStatus('Read about the
history of this phrase in the Pledge')" onMouseOut="return setStatus('')">under
God</A>, indivisible, with liberty and justice for all.
</BODY>
</HTML>
```

onPaste

	NN2	NN3	NN4	NN6	IE3/J1	IE3/J2	IE4	IE5	IE5.5
Compatibility								✓	✓

Example

Listing 15-45 demonstrates how to use the onBeforePaste and onPaste event handlers (in conjunction with onBeforeCopy and onCopy) to let scripts control the data transfer process during a copy-and-paste user operation. A table contains words to be copied (one column of nouns, one column of adjectives) and then pasted into blanks in a paragraph. The onBeforeCopy and onCopy event handlers are assigned to the TABLE element because the events from the TD elements bubble up to the TABLE container and there is less HTML code to contend with.

Inside the paragraph, two SPAN elements contain underscored blanks. To paste text into the blanks, the user must first select at least one character of the blanks. (See Listing 15-37, which gives a drag-and-drop version of this application.) The onBeforePaste event handler in the paragraph (which gets the event as it bubbles up from either SPAN) sets the event.returnValue property to false, thus allowing the Paste item to appear in the context and Edit menus (not a normal occurrence in HTML body content).

At paste time, the innerHTML property of the target SPAN is set to the text data stored in the clipboard. The event.returnValue property is set to false here, as well, to prevent normal system pasting from interfering with the controlled version.

Listing 15-45: **Using onBeforePaste and onPaste Event Handlers**

```
<HTML>
<HEAD>
<TITLE>onBeforePaste and onPaste Event Handlers</TITLE>
<STYLE TYPE="text/css">
TD {text-align:center}
TH {text-decoration:underline}
.blanks {text-decoration:underline}
</STYLE>
<SCRIPT LANGUAGE="JavaScript">
function selectWhole() {
    var obj = window.event.srcElement
    var range = document.body.createTextRange()
    range.moveToElementText(obj)
    range.select()
    event.returnValue = false
}
function handleCopy() {
    var rng = document.selection.createRange()
    clipboardData.setData("Text",rng.text)
    event.returnValue = false
}

function handlePaste() {
    var elem = window.event.srcElement
    if (elem.className == "blanks") {
        elem.innerHTML = clipboardData.getData("Text")
    }
    event.returnValue = false
}
function handleBeforePaste() {
    var elem = window.event.srcElement
    if (elem.className == "blanks") {
        event.returnValue = false
    }
}
</SCRIPT>
</HEAD>
<BODY>
<H1>onBeforePaste and onPaste Event Handlers</H1>
<HR>
<P>Your goal is to copy and paste one noun and one
adjective from the following table into the blanks
of the sentence. Select a word from the table and
copy it to the clipboard. Select one or more spaces
of the blanks in the sentence and choose Paste to
replace the blank with the clipboard contents.</P>

<TABLE CELLPADDING=5 onBeforeCopy="selectWhole()" onCopy="handleCopy()" >
<TR><TH>Nouns</TH><TH>Adjectives</TH></TR>
```

```
<TR><TD>truck</TD><TD>round</TD></TR>
<TR><TD>doll</TD><TD>red</TD></TR>
<TR><TD>ball</TD><TD>pretty</TD></TR>
</TABLE>

<P ID="myP" onBeforePaste="handleBeforePaste()" onPaste="handlePaste()">
Pat said, "Oh my, the <SPAN ID="blank1" CLASS="blanks">
     </SPAN>
is so <SPAN ID="blank2" CLASS="blanks">
     </SPAN>!"</P>

<BUTTON onClick="location.reload()">Reset</BUTTON>
</BODY>
</HTML>
```

onPropertyChange

	NN2	NN3	NN4	NN6	IE3/J1	IE3/J2	IE4	IE5	IE5.5
Compatibility								✓	✓

Example

The page generated by Listing 15-46 contains four radio buttons that alter the innerHTML and style.color properties of a paragraph. The paragraph's onPropertyChange event handler invokes the showChange() function, which extracts information about the event and displays the data in the status bar of the window. Notice how the property name includes style. when you modify the style sheet property.

Listing 15-46: **Using the onPropertyChange Property**

```
<HTML>
<HEAD>
<TITLE>onPropertyChange Event Handler</TITLE>
<SCRIPT LANGUAGE="JavaScript">
function normalText() {
    myP.innerText = "This is a sample paragraph."
}
function shortText() {
    myP.innerText = "Short stuff."
}
function normalColor() {
    myP.style.color = "black"
}
```

Continued

Listing 15-46 *(continued)*

```
function hotColor() {
    myP.style.color = "red"
}
function showChange() {
    var objID = event.srcElement.id
    var propName = event.propertyName
    var newValue = eval(objID + "." + propName)
    status = "The " + propName + " property of the " + objID
    status += " object has changed to \"" + newValue + "\"."
}
</SCRIPT>
</HEAD>
<BODY>
<H1>onPropertyChange Event Handler</H1>
<HR>
<P ID="myP" onPropertyChange = "showChange()">This is a sample paragraph.</P>
<FORM>
Text: <INPUT TYPE="radio" NAME="btn1" CHECKED onClick="normalText()">Normal
      <INPUT TYPE="radio" NAME="btn1" onClick="shortText()">Short
<BR>
Color: <INPUT TYPE="radio" NAME="btn2" CHECKED onClick="normalColor()">Black
       <INPUT TYPE="radio" NAME="btn2" onClick="hotColor()">Red
</FORM>
</BODY>
</HTML>
```

onReadyStateChange

	NN2	NN3	NN4	NN6	IE3/J1	IE3/J2	IE4	IE5	IE5.5
Compatibility							✓	✓	✓

Example

You can use the onReadyStateChange event handler to assist with a status display while a long external file, such as a Java applet, loads. For example, you might have a small image on a page that changes with the state change of an applet. The <APPLET> tag assigns a function to the onReadyStateChange event handler:

```
<APPLET ... onReadyStateChange="showState(this)">
```

Then the function changes the image for each state type:

```
function showState(obj) {
    var img = document.all.statusImage
    switch (obj.readyState) {
        case "uninitialized" :
            img.src = uninit.src
            break
        case "loading" :
            img.src = loading.src
            break
        case "complete" :
            img.src = ready.src
    }
}
```

The preceding function assumes that the state images are precached as the page loads.

onResize

	NN2	NN3	NN4	NN6	IE3/J1	IE3/J2	IE4	IE5	IE5.5
Compatibility			✓	✓			✓	✓	✓

Example

If you want to capture the user's resizing of the browser window (or frame), you can assign a function to the onResize event handler either via script

```
window.onresize = handleResize
```

or by an HTML attribute of the BODY element:

```
<BODY onResize="handleResize()">
```

onSelectStart

	NN2	NN3	NN4	NN6	IE3/J1	IE3/J2	IE4	IE5	IE5.5
Compatibility							✓	✓	✓

Example

Use the page from Listing 15-47 to see how the onSelectStart event handler works when a user selects across multiple elements on a page. As the user begins a selection anywhere on the page, the ID of the object receiving the event appears in the status bar. Notice that the event doesn't fire until you actually make a selection. When no other element is under the cursor, the BODY element fires the event.

Listing 15-47: **Using the onSelectStart Event Handler**

```
<HTML>
<HEAD>
<TITLE>onSelectStart Event Handler</TITLE>
<STYLE TYPE="text/css">
TD {text-align:center}
</STYLE>
<SCRIPT LANGUAGE="JavaScript">
function showObj() {
    var objID = event.srcElement.id
    status = "Selection started with object: " + objID
}
</SCRIPT>
</HEAD>
<BODY ID="myBody" onSelectStart="showObj()">
<H1 ID="myH1">onSelectStart Event Handler</H1>
<HR ID="myHR">
<P ID="myP">This is a sample paragraph.</P>
<TABLE BORDER="1">
<TR ID="row1">
    <TH ID="header1">Column A</TH>
    <TH ID="header2">Column B</TH>
    <TH ID="header3">Column C</TH>
</TR>
<TR ID="row2">
    <TD ID="cellA2">text</TD>
    <TD ID="cellB2">text</TD>
    <TD ID="cellC2">text</TD>
</TR>
<TR ID="row3">
    <TD ID="cellA3">text</TD>
    <TD ID="cellB3">text</TD>
    <TD ID="cellC3">text</TD>
</TR>
</TABLE>
</BODY>
</HTML>
```

◆   ◆   ◆

Window and Frame Objects (Chapter 16)

✦ ✦ ✦ ✦

In This Chapter

Scripting
communication
among multiple
frames

Creating and
managing new
windows

Controlling the size,
position, and
appearance of the
browser window

Dynamically
adjusting frame sizes
and frameset
compositions

✦ ✦ ✦ ✦

As physical containers of documents, window and frame objects play huge rolls in scripting. The `window` object has been scriptable in one form or another since the first scriptable browsers. Of course the object has gained numerous properties, methods, and event handlers over time, but you also often find many object-model-specific items that you probably wish were available across all browsers.

While scripts permit Web authors to manage multiple windows — and many of the examples in this chapter support that facility — try to think about your visitors, too. Very often multiple windows get in the way of site navigation and content, regardless of your good intentions. As some examples also demonstrate, you must include safety nets for your code to counteract the unpredictable actions of users who close or hide windows precisely when you don't want them to do so. Therefore, do not regard the multi-window examples here as user interface recommendations; rather consider them as recommended ways to handle a potentially tricky user-interface element.

Possible exceptions to my multi-window admonitions are the modal and modeless dialog box windows provided by various versions of IE for Windows. For other platforms, a modal dialog box can be simulated (search for details at `www.dannyg.com`). IE5.5 for Windows also adds a popup type window, which can be a helpful user interface element that exists between a tooltip and a modal dialog box.

Modern browsers, however, provide ample script control over framesets. As examples in this chapter demonstrate, your scripts can hide and show frames, or completely rearchitect a frameset without loading a new frameset.

Examples Highlights

+ Listing 16-4 for the `window.closed` property demonstrates an industrial-strength treatment of new window creation, which works with all scriptable browsers (taking into account shortcomings of earlier browsers).

+ NN4+ allows dynamic control over the presence of window chrome (statusbar, toolbar, et al.) with the help of signed scripts, as shown in Listing 16-6. Without signed scripts, or for IE, you must use `window.open()` to create a separate window with the characteristics of your choice.

+ The example listings for the `window.opener` property show you how scripts from a subwindow communicate with the window that opened it.

+ In the example listings for the `window.parent` property, you see how references to the various synonyms for a window object within a frameset evaluate. Thus, you can see what the references `window`, `top`, `parent`, and `self` mean within a frameset.

+ Compare Listings 16-20, 16-23, and 16-29 to understand not only the different looks of the three native dialog box windows (alert, confirm, and prompt), but also how values returned from two of them can influence script processing sequences.

+ A simple countdown timer in Listing 16-22 shows a practical application of the `window.clearTimeout()` method. Here the method stops the looping timer when the count reaches zero.

+ Watch the browser window dance in Listing 16-24. The `window.moveBy()` and `window.moveTo()` methods put window positioning through its paces.

+ Examples for `window.setInterval()` and `window.setTimeout()` apply these two similar methods to applications that are ideal for each one. You find other applications of `setTimeout()` in examples for the `window.closed` property and `window.open()` method.

+ Internet Explorer's modal and modeless dialog box windows get workouts in Listings 16-39 through 16-42.

+ The composition of a frameset, including the sizes of the frames, can be controlled dynamically in IE4+ and NN6, as shown in examples for the `FRAMESET.cols` and `FRAMESET.rows` properties.

Window Object

Properties

clipboardData

	NN2	NN3	NN4	NN6	IE3/J1	IE3/J2	IE4	IE5	IE5.5
Compatibility								✓	✓

Example

See Listings 15-30 and 15-39 (in Chapter 1 of this book) to see how the clipboardData object is used with a variety of edit-related event handlers.

closed

	NN2	NN3	NN4	NN6	IE3/J1	IE3/J2	IE4	IE5	IE5.5
Compatibility		✓	✓	✓			✓	✓	✓

Example

In Listing 16-4, I have created the ultimate cross-platform window opening and closing sample. It takes into account the lack of the opener property in Navigator 2, the missing closed property in Navigator 2 and Internet Explorer 3, and it even provides an ugly but necessary workaround for the inability of Internet Explorer 3 to gracefully see if a subwindow is still open.

The script begins by initializing a global variable, newWind, which is used to hold the object reference to the second window. This value needs to be global so that other functions can reference the window for tasks, such as closing. Another global variable, isIE3, is a Boolean flag that lets the window closing routines know whether the visitor is using Internet Explorer 3 (see details about the navigator. appVersion property in Chapter 28 of the *JavaScript Bible*).

For this example, the new window contains some HTML code written dynamically to it, rather than loading an existing HTML file into it. Therefore, the URL parameter of the window.open() method is left as an empty string. It is vital, however, to assign a name in the second parameter to accommodate the Internet Explorer 3 workaround for closing the window. After the new window is opened, an opener property is assigned to the object if one is not already assigned (this property is needed only for Navigator 2). Next comes a brief delay to allow Internet Explorer (especially versions 3 and 4) to catch up with opening the window so that content can be written to it. The delay (using the `setTimeout()` method described later in this chapter) invokes the `finishNewWindow()` function, which uses the global `newWind` variable to reference the window for writing. The `document.close()` method closes writing to the document — a different kind of close than a window close.

A separate function, `closeWindow()`, is responsible for closing the subwindow. To accommodate Internet Explorer 3, the script appears to create another window with the same characteristics as the one opened earlier in the script. This is the trick: If the earlier window exists (with exactly the same parameters and a name *other* than an empty string), Internet Explorer does not create a new window even with the `window.open()` method executing in plain sight. To the user, nothing unusual appears on the screen. Things look weird for Internet Explorer 3 users only if the user has closed the subwindow. The `window.open()` method momentarily creates that subwindow. This subwindow is necessary because a "living" `window` object must be available for the upcoming test of window existence. (Internet Explorer 3 displays a script error if you try to address a missing window, while NN2+ and IE4+ simply return friendly `null` values.)

As a final test, an `if` condition looks at two conditions: 1) if the `window` object has ever been initialized with a value other than `null` (in case you click the window closing button before ever having created the new window) and 2) if the window's `closed` property is `null` or `false`. If either condition is true, the `close()` method is sent to the second window.

Listing 16-4: **Checking Before Closing a Window**

```
<HTML>
<HEAD>
<TITLE>window.closed Property</TITLE>
<SCRIPT LANGUAGE="JavaScript">
// initialize global var for new window object
// so it can be accessed by all functions on the page
var newWind
// set flag to help out with special handling for window closing
var isIE3 = (navigator.appVersion.indexOf("MSIE 3") != -1) ? true : false
// make the new window and put some stuff in it
function newWindow() {
    newWind = window.open("","subwindow","HEIGHT=200,WIDTH=200")
    // take care of Navigator 2
    if (newWind.opener == null) {
        newWind.opener = window
    }
    setTimeout("finishNewWindow()", 100)
}
function finishNewWindow() {
    var output = ""
    output += "<HTML><BODY><H1>A Sub-window</H1>"
    output += "<FORM><INPUT TYPE='button' VALUE='Close Main Window'"
    output +="onClick='window.opener.close()'></FORM></BODY></HTML>"
```

```
      newWind.document.write(output)
      newWind.document.close()
}
// close subwindow, including ugly workaround for IE3
function closeWindow() {
    if (isIE3) {
        // if window is already open, nothing appears to happen
        // but if not, the subwindow flashes momentarily (yech!)
        newWind = window.open("","subwindow","HEIGHT=200,WIDTH=200")
    }
    if (newWind && !newWind.closed) {
        newWind.close()
    }
}
</SCRIPT>
</HEAD>
<BODY>
<FORM>
<INPUT TYPE="button" VALUE="Open Window" onClick="newWindow()"><BR>
<INPUT TYPE="button" VALUE="Close it if Still Open" onClick="closeWindow()">
</FORM>
</BODY>
</HTML>
```

To complete the example of the window opening and closing, notice that the sub-window is given a button whose onClick event handler closes the main window. In Navigator 2 and Internet Explorer 3, this occurs without complaint. But in NN3+ and IE4+, the user is presented with an alert asking to confirm the closure of the main browser window.

defaultStatus

	NN2	NN3	NN4	NN6	IE3/J1	IE3/J2	IE4	IE5	IE5.5
Compatibility	✓	✓	✓	✓	✓	✓	✓	✓	✓

Example

Unless you plan to change the default statusbar text while a user spends time at your Web page, the best time to set the property is when the document loads. In Listing 16-5, notice how I also read this property to reset the statusbar in an onMouseOut event handler. Setting the status property to empty also resets the statusbar to the defaultStatus setting.

Listing 16-5: Setting the Default Status Message

```
<HTML>
<HEAD>
<TITLE>window.defaultStatus property</TITLE>
<SCRIPT LANGUAGE="JavaScript">
window.defaultStatus = "Welcome to my Web site."
</SCRIPT>
</HEAD>
<BODY>
<A HREF="http://www.microsoft.com"
onMouseOver="window.status = 'Visit Microsoft\'s Home page.';return true"
onMouseOut="window.status = '';return true">Microsoft</A><P>
<A HREF="http://home.netscape.com"
onMouseOver="window.status = 'Visit Netscape\'s Home page.';return true"
onMouseOut="window.status = window.defaultStatus;return true">Netscape</A>
</BODY>
</HTML>
```

If you need to display single or double quotes in the statusbar (as in the second link in Listing 16-5), use escape characters (\' and \") as part of the strings being assigned to these properties.

dialogArguments

	NN2	NN3	NN4	NN6	IE3/J1	IE3/J2	IE4	IE5	IE5.5
Compatibility							✓	✓	✓

Example

See Listing 16-38 for the `window.showModalDialog()` method to see how arguments can be passed to a dialog box and retrieved via the `dialogArguments` property.

dialogHeight
dialogWidth

	NN2	NN3	NN4	NN6	IE3/J1	IE3/J2	IE4	IE5	IE5.5
Compatibility							✓	✓	✓

Example

Dialog boxes sometimes provide a button or icon that reveals more details or more complex settings for advanced users. You can create a function that handles the toggle between two sizes. The following function assumes that the document in the dialog box has a button whose label also toggles between "Show Details" and "Hide Details." The button's `onClick` event handler invokes the function as `toggleDetails(this)`.

```
function toggleDetails(btn) {
    if (dialogHeight == "200px") {
        dialogHeight = "350px"
        btn.value = "Hide Details"
    } else {
        dialogHeight = "200px"
        btn.value = "Show Details"
    }
}
```

In practice, you also have to toggle the `display` style sheet property of the extra material between `none` and `block` to make sure that the dialog box does not display scrollbars in the smaller dialog box version.

dialogLeft
dialogTop

	NN2	NN3	NN4	NN6	IE3/J1	IE3/J2	IE4	IE5	IE5.5
Compatibility							✓	✓	✓

Example

Although usually not a good idea because of the potentially jarring effect on a user, you can reposition a dialog box window that has been resized by script (or by the user if you let the dialog box be resizable). The following statements in a dialog box window document's script recenter the dialog box window.

```
dialogLeft = (screen.availWidth/2) - (parseInt(dialogWidth)/2) + "px"
dialogHeight = (screen.availHeight/2) - (parseInt(dialogHeight)/2) + "px"
```

Note that the `parseInt()` functions are used to read the numeric portion of the `dialogWidth` and `dialogHeight` properties so that the values can be used for arithmetic.

```
directories
locationbar
menubar
personalbar
scrollbars
statusbar
toolbar
```

	NN2	NN3	NN4	NN6	IE3/J1	IE3/J2	IE4	IE5	IE5.5
Compatibility			✓	✓					

Example

In Listing 16-6, you can experiment with the look of a browser window with any of the chrome elements turned on and off. To run this script, you must either sign the scripts or turn on codebase principals (see Chapter 46 of the *JavaScript Bible*). Java must also be enabled to use the signed script statements.

As the page loads, it stores the current state of each chrome element. One button for each chrome element triggers the toggleBar() function. This function inverts the visible property for the chrome object passed as a parameter to the function. Finally, the Restore button returns visibility to their original settings. Notice that the restore() function is also called by the onUnload event handler for the document. Also, if you load this example into NN6, non-fatal script errors occur when the scrollbars are turned on or off.

Listing 16-6: **Controlling Window Chrome**

```
<HTML>
<HEAD>
<TITLE>Bars Bars Bars</TITLE>
<SCRIPT LANGUAGE="JavaScript">
// store original outer dimensions as page loads
var originalLocationbar = window.locationbar.visible
var originalMenubar = window.menubar.visible
var originalPersonalbar = window.personalbar.visible
var originalScrollbars = window.scrollbars.visible
var originalStatusbar = window.statusbar.visible
var originalToolbar = window.toolbar.visible

// generic function to set inner dimensions
function toggleBar(bar) {
    netscape.security.PrivilegeManager.enablePrivilege("UniversalBrowserWrite")
    bar.visible = !bar.visible
    netscape.security.PrivilegeManager.revertPrivilege("UniversalBrowserWrite")
}
```

```
// restore settings
function restore() {
    netscape.security.PrivilegeManager.enablePrivilege("UniversalBrowserWrite")
    window.locationbar.visible = originalLocationbar
    window.menubar.visible = originalMenubar
    window.personalbar.visible = originalPersonalbar
    window.scrollbars.visible = originalScrollbars
    window.statusbar.visible = originalStatusbar
    window.toolbar.visible = originalToolbar
    netscape.security.PrivilegeManager.revertPrivilege("UniversalBrowserWrite")
}
</SCRIPT>
</HEAD>
<BODY onUnload="restore()">
<FORM>
<B>Toggle Window Bars</B><BR>
<INPUT TYPE="button" VALUE="Location Bar"
onClick="toggleBar(window.locationbar)"><BR>
<INPUT TYPE="button" VALUE="Menu Bar" onClick="toggleBar(window.menubar)"><BR>
<INPUT TYPE="button" VALUE="Personal Bar"
onClick="toggleBar(window.personalbar)"><BR>
<INPUT TYPE="button" VALUE="Scrollbars"
onClick="toggleBar(window.scrollbars)"><BR>
<INPUT TYPE="button" VALUE="Status Bar"
onClick="toggleBar(window.statusbar)"><BR>
<INPUT TYPE="button" VALUE="Tool Bar" onClick="toggleBar(window.toolbar)"><BR>
<HR>
<INPUT TYPE="button" VALUE="Restore Original Settings" onClick="restore()"><BR>
</FORM>
</BODY>
</HTML>
```

external

	NN2	NN3	NN4	NN6	IE3/J1	IE3/J2	IE4	IE5	IE5.5
Compatibility							✓	✓	✓

Example

The first example asks the user if it is okay to add a Web site to the Active Desktop. If Active Desktop is not enabled, the user is given the choice of enabling it at this point.

```
external.AddDesktopComponent("http://www.nytimes.com","website", 200, 100, 400, 400)
```

In the next example, the user is asked to approve the addition of a URL to the Favorites list. The user can follow the normal procedure for filing the item in a folder in the list.

```
external.AddFavorite("http://www.dannyg.com/update6.html",
"JSBible 4 Support Center")
```

The final example assumes that a user makes a choice from a SELECT list of items. The onChange event handler of the SELECT list invokes the following function to navigate to a fictitious page and locate listings for a chosen sports team on the page.

```
function locate(list) {
    var choice = list.options[list.selectedIndex].value
    external.NavigateAndFind("http://www.collegesports.net/scores.html", choice,
"scores")
}
```

frames

	NN2	NN3	NN4	NN6	IE3/J1	IE3/J2	IE4	IE5	IE5.5
Compatibility	✓	✓	✓	✓	✓	✓	✓	✓	✓

Example

Listings 16-7 and 16-8 demonstrate how JavaScript treats values of frame references from objects inside a frame. The same document is loaded into each frame. A script in that document extracts info about the current frame and the entire frameset. Figure 2-1 shows the results after loading the HTML document in Listing 16-7.

Listing 16-7: **Framesetting Document for Listing 1ð-8**

```
<HTML>
<HEAD>
<TITLE>window.frames property</TITLE>
</HEAD>
<FRAMESET COLS="50%,50%">
    <FRAME NAME="JustAKid1" SRC="lst16-08.htm">
    <FRAME NAME="JustAKid2" SRC="lst16-08.htm">
</FRAMESET>
</HTML>
```

A call to determine the number (length) of frames returns 0 from the point of view of the current frame referenced. That's because each frame here is a window that has no nested frames within it. But add the parent property to the reference, and the scope zooms out to take into account all frames generated by the parent window's document.

Listing 16-8: **Showing Various Window Properties**

```
<HTML>
<HEAD>
<TITLE>Window Revealer II</TITLE>
<SCRIPT LANGUAGE="JavaScript">
function gatherWindowData() {
    var msg = ""
    msg += "<B>From the point of view of this frame:</B><BR>"
    msg += "window.frames.length: " + window.frames.length + "<BR>"
    msg += "window.name: " + window.name + "<P>"
    msg += "<B>From the point of view of the framesetting document:</B><BR>"
    msg += "parent.frames.length: " + parent.frames.length + "<BR>"
    msg += "parent.frames[0].name: " + parent.frames[0].name
    return msg
}
</SCRIPT>
</HEAD>
<BODY>
<SCRIPT LANGUAGE="JavaScript">
document.write(gatherWindowData())
</SCRIPT>
</BODY>
</HTML>
```

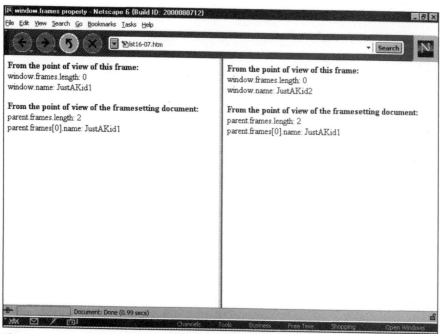

Figure 2-1: Property readouts from both frames loaded from Listing 16-7

The last statement in the example shows how to use the array syntax (brackets) to refer to a specific frame. All array indexes start with 0 for the first entry. Because the document asks for the name of the first frame (`parent.frames[0]`), the response is `JustAKid1` for both frames.

innerHeight
innerWidth
outerHeight
outerWidth

	NN2	NN3	NN4	NN6	IE3/J1	IE3/J2	IE4	IE5	IE5.5
Compatibility			✓	✓					

Example

In Listing 16-9, a number of buttons let you see the results of setting the `innerHeight`, `innerWidth`, `outerHeight`, and `outerWidth` properties.

Listing 16-9: **Setting Window Height and Width**

```
<HTML>
<HEAD>
<TITLE>Window Sizer</TITLE>
<SCRIPT LANGUAGE="JavaScript">
// store original outer dimensions as page loads
var originalWidth = window.outerWidth
var originalHeight = window.outerHeight
// generic function to set inner dimensions
function setInner(width, height) {
    window.innerWidth = width
    window.innerHeight = height
}
// generic function to set outer dimensions
function setOuter(width, height) {
    window.outerWidth = width
    window.outerHeight = height
}
// restore window to original dimensions
function restore() {
    window.outerWidth = originalWidth
    window.outerHeight = originalHeight
}
</SCRIPT>
</HEAD>
<BODY>
<FORM>
<B>Setting Inner Sizes</B><BR>
```

```
<INPUT TYPE="button" VALUE="600 Pixels Square" onClick="setInner(600,600)"><BR>
<INPUT TYPE="button" VALUE="300 Pixels Square" onClick="setInner(300,300)"><BR>
<INPUT TYPE="button" VALUE="Available Screen Space"
onClick="setInner(screen.availWidth, screen.availHeight)"><BR>
<HR>
<B>Setting Outer Sizes</B><BR>
<INPUT TYPE="button" VALUE="600 Pixels Square" onClick="setOuter(600,600)"><BR>
<INPUT TYPE="button" VALUE="300 Pixels Square" onClick="setOuter(300,300)"><BR>
<INPUT TYPE="button" VALUE="Available Screen Space"
onClick="setOuter(screen.availWidth, screen.availHeight)"><BR>
<HR>
<INPUT TYPE="button" VALUE="Cinch up for Win95" onClick="setInner(273,304)"><BR>
<INPUT TYPE="button" VALUE="Cinch up for Mac" onClick="setInner(273,304)"><BR>
<INPUT TYPE="button" VALUE="Restore Original" onClick="restore()"><BR>
</FORM>
</BODY>
</HTML>
```

As the document loads, it saves the current outer dimensions in global variables. One of the buttons restores the windows to these settings. Two parallel sets of buttons set the inner and outer dimensions to the same pixel values so that you can see the effects on the overall window and document area when a script changes the various properties.

Because Navigator 4 displays different-looking buttons in different platforms (as well as other elements), the two buttons contain script instructions to size the window to best display the window contents. Unfortunately, no measure of the active area of a document is available, so that the dimension values were determined by trial and error before being hard-wired into the script.

navigator

	NN2	NN3	NN4	NN6	IE3/J1	IE3/J2	IE4	IE5	IE5.5
Compatibility				✓			✓	✓	✓

Example

This book is littered with examples of using the navigator object, primarily for performing browser detection. Examples of specific navigator object properties can be found in Chapter 28 of the *JavaScript Bible* and Chapter 12 of this book.

offscreenBuffering

	NN2	NN3	NN4	NN6	IE3/J1	IE3/J2	IE4	IE5	IE5.5
Compatibility							✓	✓	✓

Example

If you want to turn off buffering for an entire page, include the following statement at the beginning of your script statements:

```
window.offscreenBuffering = false
```

onerror

	NN2	NN3	NN4	NN6	IE3/J1	IE3/J2	IE4	IE5	IE5.5
Compatibility		✓	✓	✓			✓	✓	✓

Example

In Listing 16-10, one button triggers a script that contains an error. I've added an error-handling function to process the error so that it opens a separate window and fills in a textarea form element (see Figure 2-2). If you load Listing 16-10 in NN6, some of the reporting categories report "undefined" because the browser unfortunately does not pass error properties to the `handleError()` function. A Submit button is also provided to mail the bug information to a support center e-mail address — an example of how to handle the occurrence of a bug in your scripts.

Listing 16-10: **Controlling Script Errors**

```
<HTML>
<TITLE>Error Dialog Control</TITLE>
<SCRIPT LANGUAGE="JavaScript1.1">
// function with invalid variable value
function goWrong() {
    var x = fred
}
// turn off error dialogs
function errOff() {
    window.onerror = doNothing
}
// turn on error dialogs with hard reload
function errOn() {
    window.onerror = handleError
}

// assign default error handler
window.onerror = handleError

// error handler when errors are turned off...prevents error dialog
function doNothing() {return true}

function handleError(msg, URL, lineNum) {
    var errWind = window.open("","errors","HEIGHT=270,WIDTH=400")
    var wintxt = "<HTML><BODY BGCOLOR=RED>"
```

```
      wintxt += "<B>An error has occurred on this page.    "
      wintxt += "Please report it to Tech Support.</B>"
      wintxt += "<FORM METHOD=POST ENCTYPE='text/plain' "
      wintxt += "ACTION=mailTo:support4@dannyg.com >"
      wintxt += "<TEXTAREA NAME='errMsg' COLS=45 ROWS=8 WRAP=VIRTUAL>"
      wintxt += "Error: " + msg + "\n"
      wintxt += "URL: " + URL + "\n"
      wintxt += "Line: " + lineNum + "\n"
      wintxt += "Client: " + navigator.userAgent + "\n"
      wintxt += "----------------------------------------\n"
      wintxt += "Please describe what you were doing when the error occurred:"
      wintxt += "</TEXTAREA><P>"
      wintxt += "<INPUT TYPE=SUBMIT VALUE='Send Error Report'>"
      wintxt += "<INPUT TYPE=button VALUE='Close' onClick='self.close()'>"
      wintxt += "</FORM></BODY></HTML>"
      errWind.document.write(wintxt)
      errWind.document.close()
      return true
}
</SCRIPT>
</HEAD>
<BODY>
<FORM NAME="myform">
<INPUT TYPE="button" VALUE="Cause an Error" onClick="goWrong()"><P>
<INPUT TYPE="button" VALUE="Turn Off Error Dialogs" onClick="errOff()">
<INPUT TYPE="button" VALUE="Turn On Error Dialogs" onClick="errOn()">
</FORM>
</BODY>
</HTML>
```

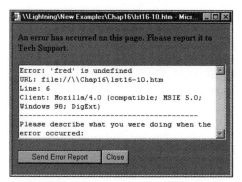

Figure 2-2: An example of a self-reporting error window

I provide a button that performs a hard reload, which, in turn, resets the window. onerror property to its default value. With error dialog boxes turned off, the error-handling function does not run.

opener

	NN2	NN3	NN4	NN6	IE3/J1	IE3/J2	IE4	IE5	IE5.5
Compatibility	✓	✓	✓	✓	✓	✓	✓	✓

Example

To demonstrate the importance of the opener property, take a look at how a new window can define itself from settings in the main window (Listing 16-11). The doNew() function generates a small subwindow and loads the file in Listing 16-12 into the window. Notice the initial conditional statements in doNew() to make sure that if the new window already exists, it comes to the front by invoking the new window's focus() method. You can see the results in Figure 2-3. Because the doNew() function in Listing 16-11 uses window methods and properties not available in IE3, this example does not work correctly in IE3.

Listing 16-11: **Contents of a Main Window Document That Generates a Second Window**

```
<HTML>
<HEAD>
<TITLE>Master of all Windows</TITLE>
<SCRIPT LANGUAGE="JavaScript1.1">
var myWind
function doNew() {
    if (!myWind || myWind.closed) {
        myWind = window.open("lst16-12.htm","subWindow",
            "HEIGHT=200,WIDTH=350,resizable")
    } else {
        // bring existing subwindow to the front
        myWind.focus()
    }
}
</SCRIPT>
</HEAD>
<BODY>
<FORM NAME="input">
Select a color for a new window:
<INPUT TYPE="radio" NAME="color" VALUE="red" CHECKED>Red
<INPUT TYPE="radio" NAME="color" VALUE="yellow">Yellow
<INPUT TYPE="radio" NAME="color" VALUE="blue">Blue
<INPUT TYPE="button" NAME="storage" VALUE="Make a Window" onClick="doNew()">
<HR>
This field will be filled from an entry in another window:
<INPUT TYPE="text" NAME="entry" SIZE=25>
</FORM>
</BODY>
</HTML>
```

The `window.open()` method doesn't provide parameters for setting the new window's background color, so I let the `getColor()` function in the new window do the job as the document loads. The function uses the `opener` property to find out which radio button on the main page is selected.

Listing 16-12: **References to the opener Property**

```
<HTML>
<HEAD>
<TITLE>New Window on the Block</TITLE>
<SCRIPT LANGUAGE="JavaScript">
function getColor() {
    // shorten the reference
    colorButtons = self.opener.document.forms[0].color
    // see which radio button is checked
    for (var i = 0; i < colorButtons.length; i++) {
        if (colorButtons[i].checked) {
            return colorButtons[i].value
        }
    }
    return "white"
}
</SCRIPT>
</HEAD>
<SCRIPT LANGUAGE="JavaScript">
document.write("<BODY BGCOLOR='" + getColor() + "'>")
</SCRIPT>
<H1>This is a new window.</H1>
<FORM>
<INPUT TYPE="button" VALUE="Who's in the Main window?"
onClick="alert(self.opener.document.title)"><P>
Type text here for the main window:
<INPUT TYPE="text" SIZE=25 onChange="self.opener.document.forms[0].entry.value =
this.value">
</FORM>
</BODY>
</HTML>
```

In the `getColor()` function, the multiple references to the radio button array can be very long. To simplify the references, the `getColor()` function starts out by assigning the radio button array to a variable I arbitrarily call `colorButtons`. That shorthand now stands in for lengthy references as I loop through the radio buttons to determine which button is checked and retrieve its value property.

A button in the second window simply fetches the title of the opener window's document. Even if another document loads in the main window in the meantime, the `opener` reference still points to the main window: Its `document` object, however, will change.

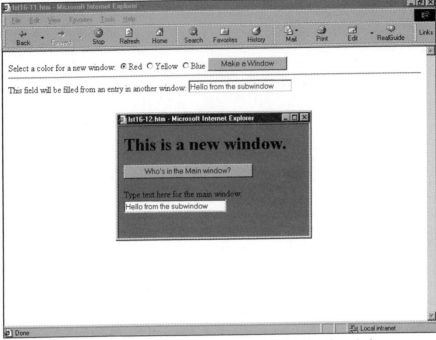

Figure 2-3: The main and subwindows, inextricably linked via the window.opener property

Finally, the second window contains a text input object. Enter any text there that you like and either tab or click out of the field. The onChange event handler updates the field in the opener's document (provided that document is still loaded).

pageXOffset
pageYOffset

	NN2	NN3	NN4	NN6	IE3/J1	IE3/J2	IE4	IE5	IE5.5
Compatibility			✓	✓					

Example

The script in Listing 16-13 is an unusual construction that creates a frameset and creates the content for each of the two frames all within a single HTML document (see "Frame Object" in Chapter 16 of the *JavaScript Bible* for more details). The purpose of this example is to provide you with a playground to become familiar with the page offset concept and how the values of these properties correspond to physical activity in a scrollable document.

In the left frame of the frameset are two fields that are ready to show the pixel values of the right frame's pageXOffset and pageYOffset properties. The content of the right frame is a 30-row table of fixed width (800 pixels). Mouse click events are captured by the document level (see Chapter 18 of the *JavaScript Bible*), allowing you to click any table or cell border or outside the table to trigger the showOffsets() function in the right frame. That function is a simple script that displays the page offset values in their respective fields in the left frame.

Listing 16-13: **Viewing the pageXOffset and pageYOffset Properties**

```
<HTML>
<HEAD>
<TITLE>Master of all Windows</TITLE>
<SCRIPT LANGUAGE="JavaScript">
function leftFrame() {
    var output = "<HTML><BODY><H3>Page Offset Values</H3><HR>\n"
    output += "<FORM>PageXOffset:<INPUT TYPE='text' NAME='xOffset' SIZE=4><BR>\n"
    output += "PageYOffset:<INPUT TYPE='text' NAME='yOffset' SIZE=4><BR>\n"
    output += "</FORM></BODY></HTML>"
    return output
}


function rightFrame() {
    var output = "<HTML><HEAD><SCRIPT LANGUAGE='JavaScript'>\n"
    output += "function showOffsets() {\n"
    output += "parent.readout.document.forms[0].xOffset.value =
self.pageXOffset\n"
    output += "parent.readout.document.forms[0].yOffset.value =
self.pageYOffset\n}\n"
    output += "document.captureEvents(Event.CLICK)\n"
    output += "document.onclick = showOffsets\n"
    output += "<\/SCRIPT></HEAD><BODY><H3>Content Page</H3>\n"
    output += "Scroll this frame and click on a table border to view " +
            "page offset values.<BR><HR>\n"
    output += "<TABLE BORDER=5 WIDTH=800>"
    var oneRow = "<TD>Cell 1</TD><TD>Cell 2</TD><TD>Cell 3</TD>" +
                "<TD>Cell 4</TD><TD>Cell 5</TD>"
    for (var i = 1; i <= 30; i++) {
        output += "<TR><TD><B>Row " + i + "</B></TD>" + oneRow + "</TR>"
    }
    output += "</TABLE></BODY></HTML>"
    return output
}
</SCRIPT>
</HEAD>
<FRAMESET COLS="30%,70%">
    <FRAME NAME="readout" SRC="javascript:parent.leftFrame()">
    <FRAME NAME="display" SRC="javascript:parent.rightFrame()">
</FRAMESET>
</HTML>
```

To gain an understanding of how the offset values work, scroll the window slightly in the horizontal direction and notice that the `pageXOffset` value increases; the same goes for the `pageYOffset` value as you scroll down. Remember that these values reflect the coordinate in the document that is currently under the top-left corner of the window (frame) holding the document. You can see an IE4+ version of this example in Listing 18-20 (in Chapter 4 of this book). A cross-browser version would require very little browser branching.

parent

	NN2	NN3	NN4	NN6	IE3/J1	IE3/J2	IE4	IE5	IE5.5
Compatibility	✓	✓	✓	✓	✓	✓	✓	✓	✓

Example

To demonstrate how various `window` object properties refer to window levels in a multiframe environment, use your browser to load the Listing 16-14 document. It, in turn, sets each of two equal-size frames to the same document: Listing 16-15. This document extracts the values of several window properties, plus the `document.title` properties of two different window references.

Listing 16-14: **Framesetting Document for Listing 16-15**

```
<HTML>
<HEAD>
<TITLE>The Parent Property Example</TITLE>
<SCRIPT LANGUAGE="JavaScript">
self.name = "Framesetter"
</SCRIPT>
</HEAD>
<FRAMESET COLS="50%,50%" onUnload="self.name = ''">
    <FRAME NAME="JustAKid1" SRC="lst16-15.htm">
    <FRAME NAME="JustAKid2" SRC="lst16-15.htm">
</FRAMESET>
</HTML>
```

Listing 16-15: **Revealing Various Window-Related Properties**

```
<HTML>
<HEAD>
<TITLE>Window Revealer II</TITLE>
<SCRIPT LANGUAGE="JavaScript">
function gatherWindowData() {
    var msg = ""
```

```
        msg = msg + "top name: " + top.name + "<BR>"
        msg = msg + "parent name: " + parent.name + "<BR>"
        msg = msg + "parent.document.title: " + parent.document.title + "<P>"
        msg = msg + "window name: " + window.name + "<BR>"
        msg = msg + "self name: " + self.name + "<BR>"
        msg = msg + "self.document.title: " + self.document.title
        return msg
}
</SCRIPT>
</HEAD>
<BODY>
<SCRIPT LANGUAGE="JavaScript">
document.write(gatherWindowData())
</SCRIPT>
</BODY>
</HTML>
```

In the two frames (Figure 2-4), the references to the `window` and `self` object names return the name assigned to the frame by the frameset definition (`JustAKid1` for the left frame, `JustAKid2` for the right frame). In other words, from each frame's point of view, the `window` object is its own frame. References to `self.document.title` refer only to the document loaded into that window frame. But references to the top and parent windows (which are one and the same in this example) show that those object properties are shared between both frames.

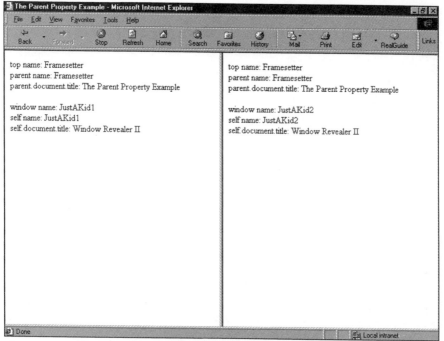

Figure 2-4: Parent and top properties being shared by both frames

A couple other fine points are worth highlighting. First, the name of the framesetting window is set as Listing 16-14 loads, rather than in response to an `onLoad` event handler in the `<FRAMESET>` tag. The reason for this is that the name must be set in time for the documents loading in the frames to get that value. If I had waited until the frameset's `onLoad` event handler, the name wouldn't be set until after the frame documents had loaded. Second, I restore the parent window's name to an empty string when the framesetting document unloads. This is to prevent future pages from getting confused about the window name.

returnValue

	NN2	NN3	NN4	NN6	IE3/J1	IE3/J2	IE4	IE5	IE5.5
Compatibility							✓	✓	✓

Example

See Listing 16-39 for the `showModalDialog()` method for an example of how to get data back from a dialog box in IE4+.

screenLeft
screenTop

	NN2	NN3	NN4	NN6	IE3/J1	IE3/J2	IE4	IE5	IE5.5
Compatibility								✓	✓

Example

Use The Evaluator (Chapter 13 in the *JavaScript Bible*) to experiment with the `screenLeft` and `screenTop` properties. Start with the browser window maximized (if you are using Windows). Enter the following property name into the top text box:

`window.screenLeft`

Click the Evaluate button to see the current setting. Unmaximize the window and drag it around the screen. Each time you finish dragging, click the Evaluate button again to see the current value. Do the same for `window.screenTop`.

screenX
screenY

	NN2	NN3	NN4	NN6	IE3/J1	IE3/J2	IE4	IE5	IE5.5
Compatibility				✓					

Example

Use The Evaluator (Chapter 13 in the *JavaScript Bible*) to experiment with the `screenX` and `screenY` properties in NN6. Start with the browser window maximized (if you are using Windows). Enter the following property name into the top text box:

```
window.screenY
```

Click the Evaluate button to see the current setting. Unmaximize the window and drag it around the screen. Each time you finish dragging, click the Evaluate button again to see the current value. Do the same for `window.screenY`.

scrollX
scrollY

	NN2	NN3	NN4	NN6	IE3/J1	IE3/J2	IE4	IE5	IE5.5
Compatibility				✓					

Example

Use The Evaluator (Chapter 13 in the *JavaScript Bible*) to experiment with the `scrollX` and `scrollY` properties in NN6. Enter the following property into the top text box:

```
window.scrollY
```

Now manually scroll the page down so that you can still see the Evaluate button. Click the button to see how far the window has scrolled along the y-axis.

self

	NN2	NN3	NN4	NN6	IE3/J1	IE3/J2	IE4	IE5	IE5.5
Compatibility	✓	✓	✓	✓	✓	✓	✓	✓	✓

Example

Listing 16-16 uses the same operations as Listing 16-5 but substitutes the `self` property for all `window` object references. The application of this reference is entirely optional, but it can be helpful for reading and debugging scripts if the HTML document is to appear in one frame of a multiframe window — especially if other JavaScript code in this document refers to documents in other frames. The `self` reference helps anyone reading the code know precisely which frame was being addressed.

Listing 16-16: **Using the self Property**

```
<HTML>
<HEAD>
<TITLE>self Property</TITLE>
<SCRIPT LANGUAGE="JavaScript">
self.defaultStatus = "Welcome to my Web site."
</SCRIPT>
</HEAD>
<BODY>
<A HREF="http:// www.microsoft.com"
onMouseOver="self.status = 'Visit Microsoft\'s Home page.';return true"
onMouseOut="self.status = '';return true">Microsoft</A><P>
<A HREF="http://home.netscape.com"
onMouseOver="self.status = 'Visit Netscape\'s Home page.';return true"
onMouseOut="self.status = self.defaultStatus;return true">Netscape</A>
</BODY>
</HTML>
```

status

	NN2	NN3	NN4	NN6	IE3/J1	IE3/J2	IE4	IE5	IE5.5
Compatibility	✓	✓	✓	✓	✓	✓	✓	✓	✓

Example

In Listing 16-17, the status property is set in a handler embedded in the onMouseOver attribute of two HTML link tags. Notice that the handler requires a return true statement (or any expression that evaluates to return true) as the last statement of the handler. This statement is required or the status message will not display, particularly in early browsers.

Listing 16-17: **Links with Custom Statusbar Messages**

```
<HTML>
<HEAD>
<TITLE>window.status Property</TITLE>
</HEAD>
<BODY>
<A HREF="http://www.dannyg.com" onMouseOver="window.status = 'Go to my Home
page. (www.dannyg.com)'; return true">Home</A><P>
<A HREF="http://home.netscape.com" onMouseOver="window.status = 'Visit Netscape
Home page. (home.netscape.com)'; return true">Netscape</A>
</BODY>
</HTML>
```

As a safeguard against platform-specific anomalies that affect the behavior of onMouseOver event handlers and the window.status property, you should also include an onMouseOut event handler for links and client-side image map area objects. Such onMouseOut event handlers should set the status property to an empty string. This setting ensures that the statusbar message returns to the defaultStatus setting when the pointer rolls away from these objects. If you want to write a generalizable function that handles all window status changes, you can do so, but word the onMouseOver attribute carefully so that the event handler evaluates to return true. Listing 16-18 shows such an alternative.

Listing 16-18: **Handling Status Message Changes**

```
<HTML>
<HEAD>
<TITLE>Generalizable window.status Property</TITLE>
<SCRIPT LANGUAGE="JavaScript">
function showStatus(msg) {
    window.status = msg
    return true
}
</SCRIPT>
</HEAD>
<BODY>
<A HREF="http:// www.dannyg.com " onMouseOver="return showStatus('Go to my Home
page (www.dannyg.com).')" onMouseOut="return showStatus('')">Home</A><P>
<A HREF="http://home.netscape.com" onMouseOver="return showStatus('Visit
Netscape Home page.')" onMouseOut="return showStatus('')">Netscape</A>
</BODY>
</HTML>
```

Notice how the event handlers return the results of the showStatus() method to the event handler, allowing the entire handler to evaluate to return true.

One final example of setting the statusbar (shown in Listing 16-19) also demonstrates how to create a simple scrolling banner in the statusbar.

Listing 16-19: **Creating a Scrolling Banner**

```
<HTML>
<HEAD>
<TITLE>Message Scroller</TITLE>
<SCRIPT LANGUAGE="JavaScript">
<!--
var msg = "Welcome to my world..."
var delay = 150
var timerId
var maxCount = 0
var currCount = 1
```

Continued

Listing 16-19 *(continued)*

```
function scrollMsg() {
    // set the number of times scrolling message is to run
    if (maxCount == 0) {
        maxCount = 3 * msg.length
    }
    window.status = msg
    // keep track of how many characters have scrolled
    currCount++
    // shift first character of msg to end of msg
    msg = msg.substring (1, msg.length) + msg.substring (0, 1)
    // test whether we've reached maximum character count
    if (currCount >= maxCount) {
        timerID = 0         // zero out the timer
        window.status = ""   // clear the status bar
        return              // break out of function
    } else {
        // recursive call to this function
        timerId = setTimeout("scrollMsg()", delay)
    }
}
// -->
</SCRIPT>
</HEAD>
<BODY onLoad="scrollMsg()">
</BODY>
</HTML>
```

Because the statusbar is being set by a standalone function (rather than by an onMouseOver event handler), you do not have to append a return true statement to set the status property. The scrollMsg() function uses more advanced JavaScript concepts, such as the window.setTimeout() method (covered later in this chapter) and string methods (covered in Chapter 34 of the *JavaScript Bible*). To speed the pace at which the words scroll across the statusbar, reduce the value of delay.

Many Web surfers (myself included) don't care for these scrollers that run forever in the statusbar. Rolling the mouse over links disturbs the banner display. Scrollers can also crash earlier browsers, because the setTimeout() method eats application memory in Navigator 2. Use scrolling bars sparingly or design them to run only a few times after the document loads.

Tip   Setting the status property with onMouseOver event handlers has had a checkered career along various implementations in Navigator. A script that sets the statusbar is always in competition against the browser itself, which uses the statusbar to report loading progress. When a "hot" area on a page is at the edge of a frame, many times the onMouseOut event fails to fire, thus preventing the statusbar from clearing itself. Be sure to torture test any such implementations before declaring your page ready for public access.

Methods

alert("*message*")

	NN2	NN3	NN4	NN6	IE3/J1	IE3/J2	IE4	IE5	IE5.5
Compatibility	✓	✓	✓	✓	✓	✓	✓	✓	✓

Example

The parameter for the example in Listing 16-20 is a concatenated string. It joins together two fixed strings and the value of the browser's `navigator.appName` property. Loading this document causes the alert dialog box to appear, as shown in several configurations in Figure 2-5. The JavaScript Alert: line cannot be deleted from the dialog box in earlier browsers, nor can the title bar be changed in later browsers.

Listing 16-20: Displaying an Alert Dialog Box

```
<HTML>
<HEAD>
<TITLE>window.alert() Method</TITLE>
</HEAD>
<BODY>
<SCRIPT LANGUAGE="JavaScript">
alert("You are running the " + navigator.appName + " browser.")
</SCRIPT>
</BODY>
</HTML>
```

Figure 2-5: Results of the alert() method in Listing 16-20 in Internet Explorer 5 (top) and Navigator 6 (bottom) for Windows 98

captureEvents(*eventTypeList*)

	NN2	NN3	NN4	NN6	IE3/J1	IE3/J2	IE4	IE5	IE5.5
Compatibility			✓						

Example

The page in Listing 16-21 is an exercise in capturing and releasing click events in the `window` object. Whenever the window is capturing click events, the `flash()` function runs. In that function, the event is examined so that only if the Control key is also being held down and the name of the button starts with "button" does the document background color flash red. For all click events (that is, those directed at objects on the page capable of their own `onClick` event handlers), the click is processed with the `routeEvent()` method to make sure the target buttons execute their own `onClick` event handlers.

Listing 16-21: **Capturing Click Events in the Window**

```
<HTML>
<HEAD>
<TITLE>Window Event Capture</TITLE>
<SCRIPT LANGUAGE="JavaScript1.2">
// function to run when window captures a click event
function flash(e) {
    if (e.modifiers = Event.CONTROL_MASK &&
    e.target.name.indexOf("button") == 0) {
        document.bgColor = "red"
        setTimeout("document.bgColor = 'white'", 500)
    }
    // let event continue to target
    routeEvent(e)
}
// default setting to capture click events
window.captureEvents(Event.CLICK)
// assign flash() function to click events captured by window
window.onclick = flash
</SCRIPT>
</HEAD>
<BODY BGCOLOR="white">
<FORM NAME="buttons">
<B>Turn window click event capture on or off (Default is "On")</B><P>
<INPUT NAME="captureOn" TYPE="button" VALUE="Capture On"
onClick="window.captureEvents(Event.CLICK)"> 
<INPUT NAME="captureOff" TYPE="button" VALUE="Capture Off"
onClick="window.releaseEvents(Event.CLICK)">
<HR>
<B>Ctrl+Click on a button to see if clicks are being captured by the window
(background color will flash red):</B><P>
<UL>
```

```
<LI><INPUT NAME="button1" TYPE="button" VALUE="Informix" onClick="alert('You
clicked on Informix.')">
<LI><INPUT NAME="button2" TYPE="button" VALUE="Oracle" onClick="alert('You
clicked on Oracle.')">
<LI><INPUT NAME="button3" TYPE="button" VALUE="Sybase" onClick="alert('You
clicked on Sybase.')">
</UL>
</FORM>
</BODY>
</HTML>
```

When you try this page, also turn off window event capture. Now only the buttons' onClick event handlers execute, and the page does not flash red.

clearInterval(*intervalIDnumber*)

	NN2	NN3	NN4	NN6	IE3/J1	IE3/J2	IE4	IE5	IE5.5
Compatibility			✓	✓			✓	✓	✓

Example

See Listings 16-36 and 16-37 for an example of how setInterval() and clearInterval() are used together on a page.

clearTimeout(*timeoutIDnumber*)

	NN2	NN3	NN4	NN6	IE3/J1	IE3/J2	IE4	IE5	IE5.5
Compatibility	✓	✓	✓	✓	✓	✓	✓	✓	✓

Example

The page in Listing 16-22 features one text field and two buttons (Figure 2-6). One button starts a countdown timer coded to last one minute (easily modifiable for other durations); the other button interrupts the timer at any time while it is running. When the minute is up, an alert dialog box lets you know.

Listing 16-22: **A Countdown Timer**

```
<HTML>
<HEAD>
<TITLE>Count Down Timer</TITLE>
<SCRIPT LANGUAGE="JavaScript">
<!--
var running = false
```

Continued

Listing 16-22 *(continued)*

```
var endTime = null
var timerID = null

function startTimer() {
    running = true
    now = new Date()
    now = now.getTime()
    // change last multiple for the number of minutes
    endTime = now + (1000 * 60 * 1)
    showCountDown()
}

function showCountDown() {
    var now = new Date()
    now = now.getTime()
    if (endTime - now <= 0) {
        stopTimer()
        alert("Time is up.  Put down your pencils.")
    } else {
        var delta = new Date(endTime - now)
        var theMin = delta.getMinutes()
        var theSec = delta.getSeconds()
        var theTime = theMin
        theTime += ((theSec < 10) ? ":0" : ":") + theSec
        document.forms[0].timerDisplay.value = theTime
        if (running) {
            timerID = setTimeout("showCountDown()",1000)
        }
    }
}

function stopTimer() {
    clearTimeout(timerID)
    running = false
    document.forms[0].timerDisplay.value = "0:00"
}
//-->
</SCRIPT>
</HEAD>

<BODY>
<FORM>
<INPUT TYPE="button" NAME="startTime" VALUE="Start 1 min. Timer"
onClick="startTimer()">
<INPUT TYPE="button" NAME="clearTime" VALUE="Clear Timer"
onClick="stopTimer()"><P>
<INPUT TYPE="text" NAME="timerDisplay" VALUE="">
</FORM>
</BODY>
</HTML>
```

Notice that the script establishes three variables with global scope in the window: `running`, `endTime`, and `timerID`. These values are needed inside multiple functions, so they are initialized outside of the functions.

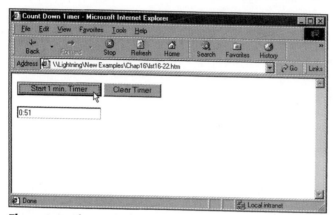

Figure 2-6: The countdown timer page as it displays the time remaining

In the `startTimer()` function, you switch the running flag on, meaning that the timer should be going. Using some date functions (see Chapter 36 of the *JavaScript Bible*), you extract the current time in milliseconds and add the number of milliseconds for the next minute (the extra multiplication by one is the place where you can change the amount to the desired number of minutes). With the end time stored in a global variable, the function now calls another function that compares the current and end times and displays the difference in the text field.

Early in the `showCountDown()` function, check to see if the timer has wound down. If so, you stop the timer and alert the user. Otherwise, the function continues to calculate the difference between the two times and formats the time in mm:ss format. As long as the `running` flag is set to `true`, the function sets the one-second timeout timer before repeating itself. To stop the timer before it has run out (in the `stopTimer()` function), the most important step is to cancel the timeout running inside the browser. The `clearTimeout()` method uses the global `timerID` value to do that. Then the function turns off the running switch and zeros out the display.

When you run the timer, you may occasionally notice that the time skips a second. It's not cheating. It just takes slightly more than one second to wait for the timeout and then finish the calculations for the next second's display. What you're seeing is the display catching up with the real time left.

close()

	NN2	NN3	NN4	NN6	IE3/J1	IE3/J2	IE4	IE5	IE5.5
Compatibility	✓	✓	✓	✓	✓	✓	✓	✓	✓

Example

See Listing 16-4 (for the `window.closed` property), which provides an elaborate, cross-platform, bug-accommodating example of applying the `window.close()` method across multiple windows.

confirm("*message*")

	NN2	NN3	NN4	NN6	IE3/J1	IE3/J2	IE4	IE5	IE5.5
Compatibility	✓	✓	✓	✓	✓	✓	✓	✓	✓

Example

The example in Listing 16-23 shows the user interface part of how you can use a confirm dialog box to query a user before clearing a table full of user-entered data. The line in the title bar, as shown in Figure 2-7, or the "JavaScript Confirm" legend in earlier browser versions, cannot be removed from the dialog box.

Listing 16-23: **The Confirm Dialog Box**

```
<HTML>
<HEAD>
<TITLE>window.confirm() Method</TITLE>
<SCRIPT LANGUAGE="JavaScript">
function clearTable() {
    if (confirm("Are you sure you want to empty the table?")) {
        alert("Emptying the table...") // for demo purposes
        //statements that actually empty the fields
    }
}
</SCRIPT>
</HEAD>
<BODY>
<FORM>
<!-- other statements that display and populate a large table -->
<INPUT TYPE="button" NAME="clear" VALUE="Reset Table" onClick="clearTable()">
</FORM>
</BODY>
</HTML>
```

Figure 2-7: A JavaScript confirm dialog box (IE5/Windows format)

createPopup()

	NN2	NN3	NN4	NN6	IE3/J1	IE3/J2	IE4	IE5	IE5.5
Compatibility									✓

Example
See Listing 16-49 later in this chapter for an example of the `createPopup()` method.

disableExternalCapture()
enableExternalCapture()

	NN2	NN3	NN4	NN6	IE3/J1	IE3/J2	IE4	IE5	IE5.5
Compatibility			✓						

Example
As this was a little-used feature of NN4 even while the browser enjoyed a substantial installed base, it becomes less important as that browser version recedes into history. You can find an example of this feature at the Support Center for this book (`http://www.dannyg.com/update.html`) or on pp.213–214 of the *JavaScript Bible*, 3rd edition.

execScript("*exprList*"[, *language*])

	NN2	NN3	NN4	NN6	IE3/J1	IE3/J2	IE4	IE5	IE5.5
Compatibility							✓	✓	✓

Example
Use The Evaluator (Chapter 13 in the *JavaScript Bible*) to experiment with the `execScript()` method. The Evaluator has predeclared global variables for the lowercase letters a through z. Enter each of the following statements into the top text box and observe the results for each.

```
a
```

When first loaded, the variable is declared but assigned no value, so it is undefined.

```
window.execScript("a = 5")
```

The method returns no value, so the mechanism inside The Evaluator says that the statement is undefined.

a

The variable is now 5.

```
window.execScript("b = a * 50")
b
```

The b global variable has a value of 250. Continue exploring with additional script statements. Use semicolons to separate multiple statements within the string parameter.

find(["*searchString*" [, *matchCaseBoolean, searchUpBoolean*]])

	NN2	NN3	NN4	NN6	IE3/J1	IE3/J2	IE4	IE5	IE5.5
Compatibility			✓						

Example

A simple call to the window.find() method looks as follows:

```
var success = window.find("contract")
```

If you want the search to be case-sensitive, add at least one of the two optional parameters:

```
success = wind.find(matchString,caseSensitive,backward)
```

Because this method works only in NN4, refer to discussions of the TextRange and Range objects in Chapter 19 of the *JavaScript Bible* for more modern implementations of body text searching.

GetAttention()

	NN2	NN3	NN4	NN6	IE3/J1	IE3/J2	IE4	IE5	IE5.5
Compatibility				✓					

Example

Use The Evaluator (Chapter 13 in the *JavaScript Bible*) in NN6 to set a timer that gives you enough time to switch to another application and wait for the attention signal to fire. Enter the following statement into the top text box, click the Evaluate button, and then quickly switch to another program:

```
setTimeout("GetAttention()", 5000)
```

After a total of five seconds, the attention signal fires.

moveBy(*deltaX,deltaY*)
moveTo(*x,y*)

	NN2	NN3	NN4	NN6	IE3/J1	IE3/J2	IE4	IE5	IE5.5
Compatibility			✓	✓			✓	✓	✓

Example

Several examples of using the window.moveTo() and window.moveBy() methods are shown in Listing 16-24. The page presents four buttons, each of which performs a different kind of browser window movement.

Listing 16-24: **Window Boogie**

```
<HTML>
<HEAD>
<TITLE>Window Gymnastics</TITLE>
<SCRIPT LANGUAGE="JavaScript1.2">
var isNav4 = ((navigator.appName == "Netscape") &&
(parseInt(navigator.appVersion) >= 4))
// wait in onLoad for page to load and settle in IE
function init() {
    // fill missing IE properties
    if (!window.outerWidth) {
        window.outerWidth = document.body.clientWidth
        window.outerHeight = document.body.clientHeight + 30
    }
    // fill missing IE4 properties
    if (!screen.availWidth) {
        screen.availWidth = 640
        screen.availHeight = 480
    }
}
// function to run when window captures a click event
function moveOffScreen() {
    // branch for NN security
    if (isNav4) {
netscape.security.PrivilegeManager.enablePrivilege("UniversalBrowserWrite")
    }
    var maxX = screen.width
    var maxY = screen.height
    window.moveTo(maxX+1, maxY+1)
    setTimeout("window.moveTo(0,0)",500)
    if (isNav4) {
netscape.security.PrivilegeManager.disablePrivilege("UniversalBrowserWrite")
    }
```

Continued

Listing 16-24 *(continued)*

```
}
// moves window in a circular motion
function revolve() {
    var winX = (screen.availWidth - window.outerWidth) / 2
    var winY = 50
    window.resizeTo(400,300)
    window.moveTo(winX, winY)

    for (var i = 1; i < 36; i++) {
        winX += Math.cos(i * (Math.PI/18)) * 5
        winY += Math.sin(i * (Math.PI/18)) * 5
        window.moveTo(winX, winY)
    }
}
// moves window in a horizontal zig-zag pattern
function zigzag() {
    window.resizeTo(400,300)
    window.moveTo(0,80)
    var incrementX = 2
    var incrementY = 2
    var floor = screen.availHeight - window.outerHeight
    var rightEdge = screen.availWidth - window.outerWidth
    for (var i = 0; i < rightEdge; i += 2) {
        window.moveBy(incrementX, incrementY)
        if (i%60 == 0) {
            incrementY = -incrementY
        }
    }
}
// resizes window to occupy all available screen real estate
function maximize() {
    window.moveTo(0,0)
    window.resizeTo(screen.availWidth, screen.availHeight)
}
</SCRIPT>
</HEAD>
<BODY onLoad="init()">
<FORM NAME="buttons">
<B>Window Gymnastics</B><P>
<UL>
<LI><INPUT NAME="offscreen" TYPE="button" VALUE="Disappear a Second"
onClick="moveOffScreen()">
<LI><INPUT NAME="circles" TYPE="button" VALUE="Circular Motion"
onClick="revolve()">
<LI><INPUT NAME="bouncer" TYPE="button" VALUE="Zig Zag" onClick="zigzag()">
<LI><INPUT NAME="expander" TYPE="button" VALUE="Maximize" onClick="maximize()">
</UL>
</FORM>
</BODY>
</HTML>
```

To run successfully in NN, the first button requires that you have codebase principals turned on (see Chapter 46 of the *JavaScript Bible*) to take advantage of what would normally be a signed script. The `moveOffScreen()` function momentarily moves the window entirely out of view. Notice how the script determines the size of the screen before deciding where to move the window. After the journey off screen, the window comes back into view at the upper-left corner of the screen.

If using the Web sometimes seems like going around in circles, then the second function, `revolve()`, should feel just right. After reducing the size of the window and positioning it near the top center of the screen, the script uses a bit of math to position the window along 36 places around a perfect circle (at 10-degree increments). This is an example of how to control a window's position dynamically based on math calculations. IE complicates the job a bit by not providing properties that reveal the outside dimensions of the browser window.

To demonstrate the `moveBy()` method, the third function, `zigzag()`, uses a `for` loop to increment the coordinate points to make the window travel in a saw tooth pattern across the screen. The x coordinate continues to increment linearly until the window is at the edge of the screen (also calculated on the fly to accommodate any size monitor). The y coordinate must increase and decrease as that parameter changes direction at various times across the screen.

In the fourth function, you see some practical code (finally) that demonstrates how best to simulate maximizing the browser window to fill the entire available screen space on the visitor's monitor.

navigate("*URL*")

	NN2	NN3	NN4	NN6	IE3/J1	IE3/J2	IE4	IE5	IE5.5
Compatibility					✓	✓	✓	✓	✓

Example

Supply any valid URL as the parameter to the method, as in

```
window.navigate("http://www.dannyg.com")
```

open("*URL*", "*windowName*" [, "*windowFeatures*"][,*replaceFlag*])

	NN2	NN3	NN4	NN6	IE3/J1	IE3/J2	IE4	IE5	IE5.5
Compatibility	✓	✓	✓	✓	✓	✓	✓	✓	✓

Example

The page rendered by Listing 16-26 displays a single button that generates a new window of a specific size that has only the statusbar turned on. The script here shows all the elements necessary to create a new window that has all the right stuff on most platforms. The new window object reference is assigned to a global variable, `newWindow`. Before a new window is generated, the script looks to see if the window has never been generated before (in which case `newWindow` would be `null`) or, for newer browsers, the window is closed. If either condition is true, the window is created with the `open()` method. Otherwise, the existing window is brought forward with the `focus()` method (NN3+ and IE4+).

As a safeguard against older browsers, the script manually adds an `opener` property to the new window if one is not already assigned by the `open()` method. The current `window` object reference is assigned to that property.

Due to the timing problem that afflicts all IE generations, the HTML assembly and writing to the new window is separated into its own function that is invoked after a 50 millisecond delay (NN goes along for the ride, but it could accommodate the assembly and writing without the delay). To build the string that is eventually written to the document, I use the += (add-by-value) operator, which appends the string on the right side of the operator to the string stored in the variable on the left side. In this example, the new window is handed an <H1>-level line of text to display.

Listing 16-26: **Creating a New Window**

```
<HTML>
<HEAD>
<TITLE>New Window</TITLE>
<SCRIPT LANGUAGE="JavaScript">
var newWindow
function makeNewWindow() {
    if (!newWindow || newWindow.closed) {
        newWindow = window.open("","","status,height=200,width=300")
        if (!newWindow.opener) {
        newWindow.opener = window
        }
        // force small delay for IE to catch up
        setTimeout("writeToWindow()", 50)
    } else {
        // window's already open; bring to front
        newWindow.focus()
    }
}
function writeToWindow() {
    // assemble content for new window
    var newContent = "<HTML><HEAD><TITLE>One Sub Window</TITLE></HEAD>"
    newContent += "<BODY><H1>This window is brand new.</H1>"
    newContent += "</BODY></HTML>"
    // write HTML to new window document
    newWindow.document.write(newContent)
    newWindow.document.close() // close layout stream
}
</SCRIPT>
</HEAD>
<BODY>
<FORM>
```

```
<INPUT TYPE="button" NAME="newOne" VALUE="Create New Window"
 onClick="makeNewWindow()">
</FORM>
</BODY>
</HTML>
```

If you need to create a new window for the lowest common denominator of scriptable browser, you will have to omit the `focus()` method and the `window.closed` property from the script (as well as add the NN2 bug workaround described earlier). Or you may prefer to forego a subwindow for all browsers below a certain level. See Listing 16-3 (in the `window.closed` property discussion) for other ideas about cross-browser authoring for subwindows.

print()

	NN2	NN3	NN4	NN6	IE3/J1	IE3/J2	IE4	IE5	IE5.5
Compatibility			✓	✓				✓	✓

Example

Listing 16-27 is a frameset that loads Listing 16-28 into the top frame and a copy of the Bill of Rights into the bottom frame.

Listing 16-27: **Print Frameset**

```
<HTML>
<HEAD>
<TITLE>window.print() method</TITLE>
</HEAD>
<FRAMESET ROWS="25%,75%">
    <FRAME NAME="controls" SRC="lst16-28.htm">
    <FRAME NAME="display" SRC="bofright.htm">
</FRAMESET>
</HTML>
```

Two buttons in the top control panel (Listing 16-28) let you print the whole frameset (in those browsers and OSs that support it) or just the lower frame. To print the entire frameset, the reference includes the parent window; to print the lower frame, the reference is directed at the `parent.display` frame.

Listing 16-28: **Printing Control**

```
<HTML>
<HEAD>
<TITLE>Print()</TITLE>
</HEAD>
<BODY>
<FORM>
<INPUT TYPE="button" NAME="printWhole" VALUE="Print Entire Frameset"
onClick="parent.print()"><P>
<INPUT TYPE="button" NAME="printFrame" VALUE="Print Bottom Frame Only"
onClick="parent.display.print()"><P>
</FORM>
</BODY>
</HTML>
```

If you don't like some facet of the printed output, blame the browser's print engine, and not JavaScript. The print() method merely invokes the browser's regular printing routines. Pages whose content is generated entirely by JavaScript print only in NN3+ and IE4+.

prompt("*message*", "*defaultReply*")

	NN2	NN3	NN4	NN6	IE3/J1	IE3/J2	IE4	IE5	IE5.5
Compatibility	✓	✓	✓	✓	✓	✓	✓	✓	✓

Example

The function that receives values from the prompt dialog box in Listing 16-29 (see the dialog box in Figure 2-8) does some data-entry validation (but certainly not enough for a commercial site). The function first checks to make sure that the returned value is neither null (Cancel) nor an empty string (the user clicked OK without entering any values). See Chapter 43 of the *JavaScript Bible* for more about data-entry validation.

Listing 16-29: **The Prompt Dialog Box**

```
<HTML>
<HEAD>
<TITLE>window.prompt() Method</TITLE>
<SCRIPT LANGUAGE="JavaScript">
function populateTable() {
    var howMany = prompt("Fill in table for how many factors?","")
    if (howMany != null && howMany != "") {
```

```
        alert("Filling the table for " + howMany) // for demo
        //statements that validate the entry and
        //actually populate the fields of the table
    }
}
</SCRIPT>
</HEAD>
<BODY>
<FORM>
<!-- other statements that display and populate a large table -->
<INPUT TYPE="button" NAME="fill" VALUE="Fill Table..."
onClick="populateTable()">
</FORM>
</BODY>
</HTML>
```

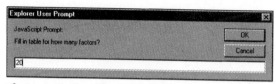

Figure 2-8: The prompt dialog box displayed from Listing 16-29 (Windows format)

Notice one important user interface element in Listing 16-29. Because clicking the button leads to a dialog box that requires more information from the user, the button's label ends in an ellipsis (or, rather, three periods acting as an ellipsis character). The ellipsis is a common courtesy to let users know that a user interface element leads to a dialog box of some sort. As in similar situations in Windows and Macintosh programs, the user should be able to cancel out of that dialog box and return to the same screen state that existed before the button was clicked.

resizeBy(*deltaX,deltaY*)
resizeTo(*outerwidth,outerheight*)

	NN2	NN3	NN4	NN6	IE3/J1	IE3/J2	IE4	IE5	IE5.5
Compatibility			✓	✓			✓	✓	✓

Example

You can experiment with the resize methods with the page in Listing 16-30. Two parts of a form let you enter values for each method. The one for `window.resize()` also lets you enter a number of repetitions to better see the impact of the values. Enter zero and negative values to see how those affect the method. Also test the limits of different browsers.

Listing 16-30: Window Resize Methods

```
<HTML>
<HEAD>
<TITLE>Window Resize Methods</TITLE>
<SCRIPT LANGUAGE="JavaScript">
function doResizeBy(form) {
    var x = parseInt(form.resizeByX.value)
    var y = parseInt(form.resizeByY.value)
    var count = parseInt(form.count.value)
    for (var i = 0; i < count; i++) {
        window.resizeBy(x, y)
    }
}
function doResizeTo(form) {
    var x = parseInt(form.resizeToX.value)
    var y = parseInt(form.resizeToY.value)
    window.resizeTo(x, y)
}
</SCRIPT>
</HEAD>
<BODY>
<FORM>
<B>Enter the x and y increment, plus how many times the window should be resized
by these increments:</B><BR>
Horiz:<INPUT TYPE="text" NAME="resizeByX" SIZE=4>
Vert:<INPUT TYPE="text" NAME="resizeByY" SIZE=4>
How Many:<INPUT TYPE="text" NAME="count" SIZE=4>
<INPUT TYPE="button" NAME="ResizeBy" VALUE="Show resizeBy()"
onClick="doResizeBy(this.form)">
<HR>
<B>Enter the desired width and height of the current window:</B><BR>
Width:<INPUT TYPE="text" NAME="resizeToX" SIZE=4>
Height:<INPUT TYPE="text" NAME="resizeToY" SIZE=4>
<INPUT TYPE="button" NAME="ResizeTo" VALUE="Show resizeTo()"
onClick="doResizeTo(this.form)">
</FORM>
</BODY>
</HTML>
```

routeEvent(*event*)

	NN2	NN3	NN4	NN6	IE3/J1	IE3/J2	IE4	IE5	IE5.5
Compatibility			✓						

Example

The `window.routeEvent()` method is used in the example for
`window.captureEvents()`, Listing 16-21.

scroll(*horizontalCoord, verticalCoord*)

	NN2	NN3	NN4	NN6	IE3/J1	IE3/J2	IE4	IE5	IE5.5
Compatibility		✓	✓	✓			✓	✓	✓

Example

To demonstrate the `scroll()` method, Listing 16-31 defines a frameset with a
document in the top frame (Listing 16-32) and a control panel in the bottom frame
(Listing 16-33). A series of buttons and text fields in the control panel frame directs
the scrolling of the document. I've selected an arbitrary, large GIF image to use in
the example. To see results of some horizontal scrolling values, you may need to
shrink the width of the browser window until a horizontal scrollbar appears in the
top frame. Figure 2-9 shows the results in a shrunken window with modest horizontal and vertical scroll values entered into the bottom text boxes. If you substitute
`scrollTo()` for the `scroll()` methods in Listing 16-33, the results will be the
same, but you will need version browsers at a minimum to run it.

Listing 16-31: **A Frameset for the scroll() Demonstration**

```
<HTML>
<HEAD>
<TITLE>window.scroll() Method</TITLE>
</HEAD>

<FRAMESET ROWS="50%,50%">
    <FRAME SRC="lst16-32.htm" NAME="display">
    <FRAME SRC="lst16-33.htm" NAME="control">
</FRAMESET>
</HTML>
```

Listing 16-32: **The Image to Be Scrolled**

```
<HTML>
<HEAD>
<TITLE>Arch</TITLE>
</HEAD>
```

Continued

Listing 16-32 *(continued)*

```
<BODY>
<H1>A Picture is Worth...</H1>
<HR>
<CENTER>
<TABLE BORDER=3>
<CAPTION ALIGN=bottom>A Splendid Arch</CAPTION>
<TD>
<IMG SRC="arch.gif">
</TD></TABLE></CENTER>
</BODY>
</HTML>
```

Listing 16-33: **Controls to Adjust Scrolling of the Upper Frame**

```
<HTML>
<HEAD>
<TITLE>Scroll Controller</TITLE>
<SCRIPT LANGUAGE="JavaScript1.1">
function scroll(x,y) {
    parent.frames[0].scroll(x,y)
}
function customScroll(form) {
    parent.frames[0].scroll(parseInt(form.x.value),parseInt(form.y.value))
}
</SCRIPT>
</HEAD>
<BODY>
<H2>Scroll Controller</H2>
<HR>
<FORM NAME="fixed">
Click on a scroll coordinate for the upper frame:<P>
<INPUT TYPE="button" VALUE="0,0" onClick="scroll(0,0)">
<INPUT TYPE="button" VALUE="0,100" onClick="scroll(0,100)">
<INPUT TYPE="button" VALUE="100,0" onClick="scroll(100,0)">
<P>
<INPUT TYPE="button" VALUE="-100,100" onClick="scroll(-100,100)">
<INPUT TYPE="button" VALUE="20,200" onClick="scroll(20,200)">
<INPUT TYPE="button" VALUE="1000,3000" onClick="scroll(1000,3000)">
</FORM>
<HR>
<FORM NAME="custom">
Enter a Horizontal
<INPUT TYPE="text" NAME="x" VALUE="0" SIZE=4>
and Vertical
<INPUT TYPE="text" NAME="y" VALUE="0" SIZE=4>
value.  Then
```

```
<INPUT TYPE="button" VALUE="click to scroll" onClick="customScroll(this.form)">
</FORM>
</BODY>
</HTML>
```

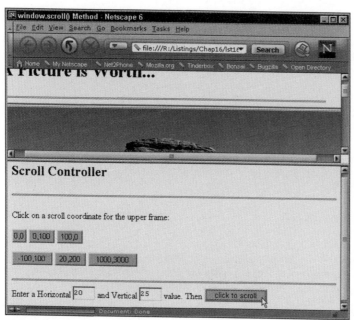

Figure 2-9: Scripts control the scrolling of the top frame

Notice that in the `customScroll()` function, JavaScript must convert the string values from the two text boxes to integers (with the `parseInt()` method) for the `scroll()` method to accept them. Nonnumeric data can produce very odd results. Also be aware that although this example shows how to adjust the scroll values in another frame, you can set such values in the same frame or window as the script, as well as in subwindows, provided that you use the correct object references to the window.

scrollBy(*deltaX,deltaY*)
scrollTo(*x,y*)

	NN2	NN3	NN4	NN6	IE3/J1	IE3/J2	IE4	IE5	IE5.5
Compatibility			✓	✓			✓	✓	✓

Example

To work with the `scrollTo()` method, you can use Listings 16-31 through 16-33 (the `window.scroll()` method) but substitute `window.scrollTo()` for `window.scroll()`. The results should be the same. For `scrollBy()`, the example starts with the frameset in Listing 16-34. It loads the same content document as the `window.scroll()` example (Listing 16-32), but the control panel (Listing 16-35) provides input to experiment with the `scrollBy()` method.

Listing 16-34: **Frameset for ScrollBy Controller**

```
<HTML>
<HEAD>
<TITLE>window.scrollBy() Method</TITLE>
</HEAD>

<FRAMESET ROWS="50%,50%">
    <FRAME SRC="1st16-32.htm" NAME="display">
    <FRAME SRC="1st16-35.htm" NAME="control">
</FRAMESET>
</HTML>
```

Notice in Listing 16-35 that all references to window properties and methods are directed to the `display` frame. String values retrieved from text fields are converted to number with the `parseInt()` global function.

Listing 16-35: **ScrollBy Controller**

```
<HTML>
<HEAD>
<TITLE>ScrollBy Controller</TITLE>
<SCRIPT LANGUAGE="JavaScript1.2">
function page(direction) {
    var pixFrame = parent.display
    var deltaY = (pixFrame.innerHeight) ? pixFrame.innerHeight :
        pixFrame.document.body.scrollHeight
    if (direction == "up") {
        deltaY = -deltaY
    }
    parent.display.scrollBy(0, deltaY)
}
function customScroll(form) {
    parent.display.scrollBy(parseInt(form.x.value), parseInt(form.y.value))
}
</SCRIPT>
</HEAD>
<BODY>
<B>ScrollBy Controller</B>
<FORM NAME="custom">
Enter an Horizontal increment
```

```
<INPUT TYPE="text" NAME="x" VALUE="0" SIZE=4>
and Vertical
<INPUT TYPE="text" NAME="y" VALUE="0" SIZE=4>
value.<BR>Then
<INPUT TYPE="button" VALUE="click to scrollBy()"
onClick="customScroll(this.form)">
<HR>
<INPUT TYPE="button" VALUE="PageDown" onClick="page('down')">
<INPUT TYPE="button" VALUE="PageUp" onClick="page('up')">

</FORM>
</BODY>
</HTML>
```

setCursor("*cursorType*")

	NN2	NN3	NN4	NN6	IE3/J1	IE3/J2	IE4	IE5	IE5.5
Compatibility				✓					

Example

Use The Evaluator (Chapter 13 in the *JavaScript Bible*) in NN6 to experiment with setting the cursor. After clicking the top text box in preparation for typing, roll the cursor to a location atop an empty spot on the page. Then enter the following statements one at a time into the top text box and press Enter/Return:

```
setCursor("wait")
setCursor("spinning"
setCursor("move")
```

After evaluating each statement, roll the cursor around the page, and notice where the cursor reverts to its normal appearance.

setInterval("*expr*", *msecDelay* [, *language*])
setInterval(*funcRef*, *msecDelay* [, *funcarg1*, ..., *funcargn*])

	NN2	NN3	NN4	NN6	IE3/J1	IE3/J2	IE4	IE5	IE5.5
Compatibility			✓	✓			✓	✓	✓

Example

The demonstration of the `setInterval()` method entails a two-framed environment. The framesetting document is shown in Listing 16-36.

Listing 16-36: setInterval() Demonstration Frameset

```
<HTML>
<HEAD>
<TITLE>setInterval() Method</TITLE>
</HEAD>

<FRAMESET ROWS="50%,50%">
    <FRAME SRC="1st16-37.htm" NAME="control">
    <FRAME SRC="bofright.htm" NAME="display">
</FRAMESET>
</HTML>
```

In the top frame is a control panel with several buttons that control the automatic scrolling of the Bill of Rights text document in the bottom frame. Listing 16-37 shows the control panel document. Many functions here control the interval, scrolling jump size, and direction, and they demonstrate several aspects of applying setInterval().

Notice that in the beginning the script establishes a number of global variables. Three of them are parameters that control the scrolling; the last one is for the ID value returned by the setInterval() method. The script needs that value to be a global value so that a separate function can halt the scrolling with the clearInterval() method.

All scrolling is performed by the autoScroll() function. For the sake of simplicity, all controlling parameters are global variables. In this application, placement of those values in global variables helps the page restart autoscrolling with the same parameters as it had when it last ran.

Listing 16-37: setInterval() Control Panel

```
<HTML>
<HEAD>
<TITLE>ScrollBy Controller</TITLE>
<SCRIPT LANGUAGE="JavaScript1.2">
var scrollSpeed = 500
var scrollJump = 1
var scrollDirection = "down"
var intervalID

function autoScroll() {
    if (scrollDirection == "down") {
        scrollJump = Math.abs(scrollJump)
    } else if (scrollDirection == "up" && scrollJump > 0) {
        scrollJump = -scrollJump
    }
    parent.display.scrollBy(0, scrollJump)
    if (parent.display.pageYOffset <= 0) {
```

```
                clearInterval(intervalID)
        }
}

function reduceInterval() {
    stopScroll()
    scrollSpeed -= 200
    startScroll()
}
function increaseInterval() {
    stopScroll()
    scrollSpeed += 200
    startScroll()
}
function reduceJump() {
    scrollJump -= 2
}
function increaseJump() {
    scrollJump += 2
}
function swapDirection() {
    scrollDirection = (scrollDirection == "down") ? "up" : "down"
}
function startScroll() {
    parent.display.scrollBy(0, scrollJump)
    if (intervalID) {
        clearInterval(intervalID)
    }
    intervalID = setInterval("autoScroll()",scrollSpeed)
}
function stopScroll() {
    clearInterval(intervalID)
}
</SCRIPT>
</HEAD>
<BODY onLoad="startScroll()">
<B>AutoScroll by setInterval() Controller</B>
<FORM NAME="custom">
<INPUT TYPE="button" VALUE="Start Scrolling" onClick="startScroll()">
<INPUT TYPE="button" VALUE="Stop Scrolling" onClick="stopScroll()"><P>
<INPUT TYPE="button" VALUE="Shorter Time Interval" onClick="reduceInterval()">
<INPUT TYPE="button" VALUE="Longer Time Interval"
onClick="increaseInterval()"><P>
<INPUT TYPE="button" VALUE="Bigger Scroll Jumps" onClick="increaseJump()">
<INPUT TYPE="button" VALUE="Smaller Scroll Jumps" onClick="reduceJump()"><P>
<INPUT TYPE="button" VALUE="Change Direction" onClick="swapDirection()">

</FORM>
</BODY>
</HTML>
```

The `setInterval()` method is invoked inside the `startScroll()` function. This function initially "burps" the page by one `scrollJump` interval so that the test in `autoScroll()` for the page being scrolled all the way to the top doesn't halt a page from scrolling before it gets started. Notice, too, that the function checks for the existence of an interval ID. If one is there, it is cleared before the new one is set. This is crucial within the design of the example page, because repeated clicking of the Start Scrolling button triggers multiple interval timers inside the browser. Only the most recent one's ID would be stored in `intervalID`, allowing no way to clear the older ones. But this little side trip makes sure that only one interval timer is running. One of the global variables, `scrollSpeed`, is used to fill the delay parameter for `setInterval()`. To change this value on the fly, the script must stop the current interval process, change the `scrollSpeed` value, and start a new process. The intensely repetitive nature of this application is nicely handled by the `setInterval()` method.

setTimeout("expr", msecDelay [, language])
setTimeout(functionRef, msecDelay [, funcarg1, ..., funcargn])

	NN2	NN3	NN4	NN6	IE3/J1	IE3/J2	IE4	IE5	IE5.5
Compatibility	✓	✓	✓	✓	✓	✓	✓	✓	✓

Example

When you load the HTML page in Listing 16-38, it triggers the `updateTime()` function, which displays the time (in hh:mm am/pm format) in the statusbar. Instead of showing the seconds incrementing one by one (which may be distracting to someone trying to read the page), this function alternates the last character of the display between an asterisk and nothing, like a visual "heartbeat."

Listing 16-38: **Display the Current Time**

```
<HTML>
<HEAD>
<TITLE>Status Bar Clock</TITLE>
<SCRIPT LANGUAGE="JavaScript">
<!--
var flasher = false
// calculate current time, determine flasher state,
// and insert time into status bar every second
function updateTime() {
    var now = new Date()
    var theHour = now.getHours()
    var theMin = now.getMinutes()
    var theTime = "" + ((theHour > 12) ? theHour - 12 : theHour)
    theTime += ((theMin < 10) ? ":0" : ":") + theMin
```

```
        theTime  += (theHour >= 12) ? " pm" : " am"
        theTime += ((flasher) ? " " : "*")
        flasher = !flasher
        window.status = theTime
        // recursively call this function every second to keep timer going
        timerID = setTimeout("updateTime()",1000)
}
//-->
</SCRIPT>
</HEAD>

<BODY onLoad="updateTime()">
</BODY>
</HTML>
```

In this function, the `setTimeout()` method works in the following way: Once the current time (including the flasher status) appears in the statusbar, the function waits approximately one second (1,000 milliseconds) before calling the same function again. You don't have to clear the `timerID` value in this application because JavaScript does it for you every time the 1,000 milliseconds elapse.

A logical question to ask is whether this application should be using `setInterval()` instead of `setTimeout()`. This is a case in which either one does the job. To use `setInterval()` here would require that the interval process start outside of the `updateTime()` function, because you need only one process running that repeatedly calls `updateTime()`. It would be a cleaner implementation in that regard, instead of the tons of timeout processes spawned by Listing 16-38. On the other hand, the application would not run in any browsers before NN4 or IE4, as Listing 16-38 does.

To demonstrate passing parameters, you can modify the `updateTime()` function to add the number of times it gets invoked to the display in the statusbar. For that to work, the function must have a parameter variable so that it can catch a new value each time it is invoked by `setTimeout()`'s expression. For all browsers, the function would be modified as follows (unchanged lines are represented by the ellipsis):

```
function updateTime(i) {
    ...
    window.status = theTime + "  (" + i + ")"
    // pass updated counter value with next call to this function
    timerID = setTimeout("updateTime(" + i+1 + ")",1000)
}
```

If you were running this exclusively in NN4+, you could use its more convenient way of passing parameters to the function:

```
timerID = setTimeout(updateTime,1000, i+1)
```

In either case, the `onLoad` event handler would also have to be modified to get the ball rolling with an initial parameter:

```
onLoad = "updateTime(0)"
```

Caution   One warning about `setTimeout()` functions that dive into themselves as frequently as this one does: Each call eats up a bit more memory for the browser
application in Navigator 2. If you let this clock run for a while, some browsers may
encounter memory difficulties, depending on which operating system they're
using. But considering the amount of time the typical user spends on Web pages
(even if only 10 or 15 minutes), the function shouldn't present a problem. And any
reloading invoked by the user (such as by resizing the window in Navigator 2)
frees up memory once again.

```
showModalDialog("URL"[, arguments]
[, features])
showModelessDialog("URL"[, arguments]
[, features])
```

	NN2	NN3	NN4	NN6	IE3/J1	IE3/J2	IE4	IE5	IE5.5
Compatibility							(✓)	✓	✓

Example

To demonstrate the two styles of dialog boxes, I have implemented the same
functionality (setting some session visual preferences) for both modal and modeless dialog boxes. This tactic shows you how to pass data back and forth between
the main page and both styles of dialog box windows.

The first example demonstrates how to use a modal dialog box. In the process,
data is passed into the dialog box window and values are returned. Listing 16-39 is
the HTML and scripting for the main page. A button's `onClick` event handler invokes
a function that opens the modal dialog box. The dialog box's document (Listing
16-40) contains several form elements for entering a user name and selecting a few
color styles for the main page. Data from the dialog is fashioned into an array to be
sent back to the main window. That array is initially assigned to a local variable,
`prefs`, as the dialog box closes. If the user cancels the dialog box, the returned value
is an empty string, so nothing more in `getPrefsData()` executes. But when the user
clicks OK, the array comes back. Each of the array items is read and assigned to its
respective form value or style property. These values are also preserved in the global
`currPrefs` array. This allows the settings to be sent to the modal dialog box (as the
second parameter to `showModalDialog()`) the next time the dialog box is opened.

Listing 16-39: **Main Page for showModalDialog()**

```
<HTML>
<HEAD>
<TITLE>window.setModalDialog() Method</TITLE>
<SCRIPT LANGUAGE="JavaScript">
var currPrefs = new Array()
```

```
function getPrefsData() {
    var prefs = showModalDialog("lst16-40.htm", currPrefs,
        "dialogWidth:400px; dialogHeight:300px")
    if (prefs) {
        if (prefs["name"]) {
            document.all.firstName.innerText = prefs["name"]
            currPrefs["name"] = prefs["name"]
        }
        if (prefs["bgColor"]) {
            document.body.style.backgroundColor = prefs["bgColor"]
            currPrefs["bgColor"] = prefs["bgColor"]
        }
        if (prefs["textColor"]) {
            document.body.style.color = prefs["textColor"]
            currPrefs["textColor"] = prefs["textColor"]
        }
        if (prefs["h1Size"]) {
            document.all.welcomeHeader.style.fontSize = prefs["h1Size"]
            currPrefs["h1Size"] = prefs["h1Size"]
        }
    }
}
function init() {
    document.all.firstName.innerText = "friend"
}
</SCRIPT>

</HEAD>
<BODY BGCOLOR="#eeeeee" STYLE="margin:20px" onLoad="init()">
<H1>window.setModalDialog() Method</H1>
<HR>
<H2 ID="welcomeHeader">Welcome, <SPAN ID="firstName"> </SPAN>!</H2>
<HR>
<P>Use this button to set style preferences for this page:
<BUTTON ID="prefsButton" onClick="getPrefsData()">
Preferences
</BUTTON>
</BODY>
</HTML>
```

The dialog box's document, shown in Listing 16-40, is responsible for reading the incoming data (and setting the form elements accordingly) and assembling form data for return to the main window's script. Notice when you load the example that the TITLE element of the dialog box's document appears in the dialog box window's title bar.

When the page loads into the dialog box window, the init() function examines the window.dialogArguments property. If it has any data, the data is used to preset the form elements to mirror the current settings of the main page. A utility function, setSelected(), pre-selects the option of a SELECT element to match the current settings.

Buttons at the bottom of the page are explicitly positioned to be at the lower-right corner of the window. Each button invokes a function to do what is needed to close the dialog box. In the case of the OK button, the `handleOK()` function sets the `window.returnValue` property to the data that come back from the `getFormData()` function. This latter function reads the form element values and packages them in an array using the form elements' names as array indices. This helps keep everything straight back in the main window's script, which uses the index names, and is therefore not dependent upon the precise sequence of the form elements in the dialog box window.

Listing 16-40: Document for the Modal Dialog

```
<HTML>
<HEAD>
<TITLE>User Preferences</TITLE>
<SCRIPT LANGUAGE="JavaScript">
// Close the dialog
function closeme() {
    window.close()
}

// Handle click of OK button
function handleOK() {
    window.returnValue = getFormData()
    closeme()
}

// Handle click of Cancel button
function handleCancel() {
    window.returnValue = ""
    closeme()
}
// Generic function converts form element name-value pairs
// into an array
function getFormData() {
    var form = document.prefs
    var returnedData = new Array()
    // Harvest values for each type of form element
    for (var i = 0; i < form.elements.length; i++) {
        if (form.elements[i].type == "text") {
            returnedData[form.elements[i].name] = form.elements[i].value
        } else if (form.elements[i].type.indexOf("select") != -1) {
            returnedData[form.elements[i].name] =
            form.elements[i].options[form.elements[i].selectedIndex].value
        } else if (form.elements[i].type == "radio") {
            returnedData[form.elements[i].name] = form.elements[i].value
        } else if (form.elements[i].type == "checkbox") {
            returnedData[form.elements[i].name] = form.elements[i].value
        } else continue
    }
    return returnedData
}
```

```
// Initialize by setting form elements from passed data
function init() {
    if (window.dialogArguments) {
        var args = window.dialogArguments
        var form = document.prefs
        if (args["name"]) {
            form.name.value = args["name"]
        }
        if (args["bgColor"]) {
            setSelected(form.bgColor, args["bgColor"])
        }
        if (args["textColor"]) {
            setSelected(form.textColor, args["textColor"])
        }
        if (args["h1Size"]) {
            setSelected(form.h1Size, args["h1Size"])
        }
    }
}
// Utility function to set a SELECT element to one value
function setSelected(select, value) {
    for (var i = 0; i < select.options.length; i++) {
        if (select.options[i].value == value) {
            select.selectedIndex = i
            break
        }
    }
    return
}
// Utility function to accept a press of the
// Enter key in the text field as a click of OK
function checkEnter() {
    if (window.event.keyCode == 13) {
        handleOK()
    }
}
</SCRIPT>
</HEAD>

<BODY BGCOLOR="#eeeeee" onLoad="init()">
<H2>Web Site Preferences</H2>
<HR>
<TABLE BORDER=0 CELLSPACING=2>
<FORM NAME="prefs" onSubmit="return false">
<TR>
<TD>Enter your first name:<INPUT NAME="name" TYPE="text" VALUE="" SIZE=20
onKeyDown="checkEnter()">
</TR>

<TR>
<TD>Select a background color:
<SELECT NAME="bgColor">
    <OPTION VALUE="beige">Beige
    <OPTION VALUE="antiquewhite">Antique White
```

Continued

Listing 16-40 *(continued)*

```
    <OPTION VALUE="goldenrod">Goldenrod
    <OPTION VALUE="lime">Lime
    <OPTION VALUE="powderblue">Powder Blue
    <OPTION VALUE="slategray">Slate Gray
</SELECT>
</TR>

<TR>
<TD>Select a text color:
<SELECT NAME="textColor">
    <OPTION VALUE="black">Black
    <OPTION VALUE="white">White
    <OPTION VALUE="navy">Navy Blue
    <OPTION VALUE="darkorange">Dark Orange
    <OPTION VALUE="seagreen">Sea Green
    <OPTION VALUE="teal">Teal
</SELECT>
</TR>

<TR>
<TD>Select "Welcome" heading font point size:
<SELECT NAME="h1Size">
    <OPTION VALUE="12">12
    <OPTION VALUE="14">14
    <OPTION VALUE="18">18
    <OPTION VALUE="24">24
    <OPTION VALUE="32">32
    <OPTION VALUE="48">48
</SELECT>
</TR>
</TABLE>
</FORM>
<DIV STYLE="position:absolute; left:200px; top:220px">
<BUTTON STYLE="width:80px" onClick="handleOK()">OK</BUTTON>  
<BUTTON STYLE="width:80px" onClick="handleCancel()">Cancel</BUTTON>
</DIV>
</BODY>
</HTML>
```

One last convenience feature of the dialog box window is the onKeyPress event handler in the text box. The function it invokes looks for the Enter key. If that key is pressed while the box has focus, the same handleOK() function is invoked, as if the user had clicked the OK button. This feature makes the dialog box behave as if the OK button is an automatic default, just as "real" dialog boxes.

You should observe several important structural changes that were made to turn the modal approach into a modeless one. Listing 16-41 shows the version of the main window modified for use with a modeless dialog box. Another global variable, prefsDlog, is initialized to eventually store the reference to the modeless window returned by the showModelessWindow() method. The variable gets used to invoke the init() function inside the modeless dialog box, but also as conditions in an if construction surrounding the generation of the dialog box. The reason this is needed is to prevent multiple instances of the dialog box being created (the button is still alive while the modeless window is showing). The dialog box won't be created again as long as there is a value in prefsDlog, and the dialog box window has not been closed (picking up the window.closed property of the dialog box window).

The showModelessDialog() method's second parameter is a reference to the function in the main window that updates the main document. As you see in a moment, that function is invoked from the dialog box when the user clicks the OK or Apply buttons.

Listing 16-41: **Main Page for showModelessDialog()**

```
<HTML>
<HEAD>
<TITLE>window.setModelessDialog() Method</TITLE>
<SCRIPT LANGUAGE="JavaScript">
var currPrefs = new Array()
var prefsDlog
function getPrefsData() {
    if (!prefsDlog || prefsDlog.closed) {
        prefsDlog = showModelessDialog("lst16-42.htm", setPrefs,
        "dialogWidth:400px; dialogHeight:300px")
        prefsDlog.init(currPrefs)
    }
}

function setPrefs(prefs) {
    if (prefs["bgColor"]) {
        document.body.style.backgroundColor = prefs["bgColor"]
        currPrefs["bgColor"] = prefs["bgColor"]
    }
    if (prefs["textColor"]) {
        document.body.style.color = prefs["textColor"]
        currPrefs["textColor"] = prefs["textColor"]
    }
    if (prefs["h1Size"]) {
        document.all.welcomeHeader.style.fontSize = prefs["h1Size"]
        currPrefs["h1Size"] = prefs["h1Size"]
    }
    if (prefs["name"]) {
        document.all.firstName.innerText = prefs["name"]
        currPrefs["name"] = prefs["name"]
    }
}

function init() {
    document.all.firstName.innerText = "friend"
}
</SCRIPT>
```

Continued

Listing 16-41 *(continued)*

```
</HEAD>
<BODY BGCOLOR="#eeeeee" STYLE="margin:20px" onLoad="init()">
<H1>window.setModelessDialog() Method</H1>
<HR>
<H2 ID="welcomeHeader">Welcome, <SPAN ID="firstName"> </SPAN>!</H2>
<HR>
<P>Use this button to set style preferences for this page:
<BUTTON ID="prefsButton" onClick="getPrefsData()">
Preferences
</BUTTON>
</BODY>
</HTML>
```

Changes to the dialog box window document for a modeless version (Listing 16-42) are rather limited. A new button is added to the bottom of the screen for an Apply button. As in many dialog box windows you see in Microsoft products, the Apply button lets current settings in dialog boxes be applied to the current document but without closing the dialog box. This approach makes experimenting with settings easier.

The Apply button invokes a handleApply() function, which works the same as handleOK(), except the dialog box is not closed. But these two functions communicate back to the main window differently than a modal dialog box. The main window's processing function is passed as the second parameter of showModelessDialog() and is available as the window.dialogArguments property in the dialog box window's script. That function reference is assigned to a local variable in both functions, and the remote function is invoked, passing the results of the getFormData() function as parameter values back to the main window.

Listing 16-42: **Document for the Modeless Dialog Box**

```
<HTML>
<HEAD>
<TITLE>User Preferences</TITLE>
<SCRIPT LANGUAGE="JavaScript">
// Close the dialog
function closeme() {
    window.close()
}

// Handle click of OK button
function handleOK() {
    var returnFunc = window.dialogArguments
    returnFunc(getFormData())
    closeme()
}
```

```
// Handle click of Apply button
function handleApply() {
    var returnFunc = window.dialogArguments
    returnFunc(getFormData())
}


// Handle click of Cancel button
function handleCancel() {
    window.returnValue = ""
    closeme()
}
// Generic function converts form element name-value pairs
// into an array
function getFormData() {
    var form = document.prefs
    var returnedData = new Array()
    // Harvest values for each type of form element
    for (var i = 0; i < form.elements.length; i++) {
        if (form.elements[i].type == "text") {
            returnedData[form.elements[i].name] = form.elements[i].value
        } else if (form.elements[i].type.indexOf("select") != -1) {
            returnedData[form.elements[i].name] =
            form.elements[i].options[form.elements[i].selectedIndex].value
        } else if (form.elements[i].type == "radio") {
            returnedData[form.elements[i].name] = form.elements[i].value
        } else if (form.elements[i].type == "checkbox") {
            returnedData[form.elements[i].name] = form.elements[i].value
        } else continue
    }
    return returnedData
}
// Initialize by setting form elements from passed data
function init(currPrefs) {
    if (currPrefs) {
        var form = document.prefs
        if (currPrefs["name"]) {
            form.name.value = currPrefs["name"]
        }
        if (currPrefs["bgColor"]) {
            setSelected(form.bgColor, currPrefs["bgColor"])
        }
        if (currPrefs["textColor"]) {
            setSelected(form.textCclor, currPrefs["textColor"])
        }
        if (currPrefs["h1Size"]) {
            setSelected(form.h1Size, currPrefs["h1Size"])
        }
    }
}
// Utility function to set a SELECT element to one value
function setSelected(select, value) {
    for (var i = 0; i < select.options.length; i++) {
        if (select.options[i].value == value) {
```

Continued

Listing 16-42 *(continued)*

```
            select.selectedIndex = i
            break
        }
    }
    return
}
// Utility function to accept a press of the
// Enter key in the text field as a click of OK
function checkEnter() {
    if (window.event.keyCode == 13) {
        handleOK()
    }
}
</SCRIPT>
</HEAD>

<BODY BGCOLOR="#eeeeee" onLoad="init()">
<H2>Web Site Preferences</H2>
<HR>
<TABLE BORDER=0 CELLSPACING=2>
<FORM NAME="prefs" onSubmit="return false">
<TR>
<TD>Enter your first name:<INPUT NAME="name" TYPE="text" VALUE="" SIZE=20
onKeyDown="checkEnter()">
</TR>

<TR>
<TD>Select a background color:
<SELECT NAME="bgColor">
    <OPTION VALUE="beige">Beige
    <OPTION VALUE="antiquewhite">Antique White
    <OPTION VALUE="goldenrod">Goldenrod
    <OPTION VALUE="lime">Lime
    <OPTION VALUE="powderblue">Powder Blue
    <OPTION VALUE="slategray">Slate Gray
</SELECT>
</TR>

<TR>
<TD>Select a text color:
<SELECT NAME="textColor">
    <OPTION VALUE="black">Black
    <OPTION VALUE="white">White
    <OPTION VALUE="navy">Navy Blue
    <OPTION VALUE="darkorange">Dark Orange
    <OPTION VALUE="seagreen">Sea Green
    <OPTION VALUE="teal">Teal
</SELECT>
</TR>
```

```
<TR>
<TD>Select "Welcome" heading font point size:
<SELECT NAME="h1Size">
    <OPTION VALUE="12">12
    <OPTION VALUE="14">14
    <OPTION VALUE="18">18
    <OPTION VALUE="24">24
    <OPTION VALUE="32">32
    <OPTION VALUE="48">48
</SELECT>
</TR>
</TABLE>
</FORM>
<DIV STYLE="position:absolute; left:120px; top:220px">
<BUTTON STYLE="width:80px" onClick="handleOK()">OK</BUTTON>  
<BUTTON STYLE="width:80px" onClick="handleCancel()">Cancel</BUTTON>  
<BUTTON STYLE="width:80px" onClick="handleApply()">Apply</BUTTON>
</DIV>
</BODY>
</HTML>
```

The biggest design challenge you probably face with respect to these windows is deciding between a modal and modeless dialog box style. Some designers insist that modality has no place in a graphical user interface; others say that there are times when you need to focus the user on a very specific task before any further processing can take place. That's where a modal dialog box makes perfect sense.

sizeToContent()

	NN2	NN3	NN4	NN6	IE3/J1	IE3/J2	IE4	IE5	IE5.5
Compatibility				✓					

Example

Use The Evaluator (Chapter 13 in the *JavaScript Bible*) in NN6 to try the sizeToContent() method. Assuming that you are running The Evaluator from the Chap13 directory on the CD-ROM (or the directory copied as-is to your hard disk), you can open a subwindow with one of the other files in the directory, and then size the subwindow. Enter the following statements into the top text box:

```
a = window.open("lst13-02.htm","")
a.sizeToContent()
```

The resized subwindow is at the minimum recommended width for a browser window, and at a height tall enough to display the little bit of content in the document.

Event handlers
onAfterPrint
onBeforePrint

	NN2	NN3	NN4	NN6	IE3/J1	IE3/J2	IE4	IE5	IE5.5
Compatibility								✓	✓

Example

The following script fragment assumes that the page includes a DIV element whose style sheet includes a setting of display:none as the page loads. Somewhere in the Head, the print-related event handlers are set as properties:

```
function showPrintCopyright() {
    document.all.printCopyright.style.display = "block"
}
function hidePrintCopyright() {
    document.all.printCopyright.style.display = "none"
}
window.onbeforeprint = showPrintCopyright
window.onafterprint = hidePrintCopyright
```

onBeforeUnload

	NN2	NN3	NN4	NN6	IE3/J1	IE3/J2	IE4	IE5	IE5.5
Compatibility							✓	✓	✓

Example

The simple page in Listing 16-43 shows you how to give the user a chance to stay on the page.

Listing 16-43: **Using the onBeforeUnload Event Handler**

```
<HTML>
<HEAD>
<TITLE>onBeforeUnload Event Handler</TITLE>
<SCRIPT LANGUAGE="JavaScript">
function verifyClose() {
    event.returnValue = "We really like you and hope you will stay longer."
}
```

```
window.onbeforeunload = verifyClose
</SCRIPT>

</HEAD>
<BODY>
<H1>onBeforeUnload Event Handler</H1>
<HR>
<P>Use this button to navigate to the previous page:
<BUTTON ID="go" onClick="history.back()">
Go Back
</BUTTON>
</BODY>
</HTML>
```

onHelp

	NN2	NN3	NN4	NN6	IE3/J1	IE3/J2	IE4	IE5	IE5.5
Compatibility							✓	✓	✓

Example

The following script fragment can be embedded in the IE5-only modeless dialog box code in Listing 16-44 to provide context-sensitive help within the dialog box. Help messages for only two of the form elements are shown here, but in a real application you add messages for the rest.

```
function showHelp() {
    switch (event.srcElement.name) {
        case "bgColor" :
            alert("Choose a color for the main window\'s background.")
            break
        case "name" :
            alert("Enter your first name for a friendly greeting.")
            break
        default :
            alert("Make preference settings for the main page styles.")
    }
    event.returnValue = false
}
window.onhelp = showHelp
```

Because this page's help focuses on form elements, the switch construction cases are based on the name properties of the form elements. For other kinds of pages, the id properties may be more appropriate.

FRAME Element Object

Properties

borderColor

	NN2	NN3	NN4	NN6	IE3/J1	IE3/J2	IE4	IE5	IE5.5
Compatibility							✓	✓	✓

Example

Although you may experience problems (especially in IE5) changing the color of a single frame border, the W3C DOM syntax would look like the following if the script were inside the framesetting document:

```
document.getElementById("contentsFrame").borderColor = "red"
```

The IE-only version would be:

```
document.all["contentsFrame"].borderColor = "red"
```

These examples assume the frame name arrives to a script function as a string. If the script is executing in one of the frames of the frameset, add a reference to parent in the preceding statements.

contentDocument

	NN2	NN3	NN4	NN6	IE3/J1	IE3/J2	IE4	IE5	IE5.5
Compatibility				✓					

Example

A framesetting document script might be using the ID of a FRAME element to read or adjust one of the element properties, and then need to perform some action on the content of the page through its document object. You can get the reference to the document object via a statement, such as the following:

```
var doc = document.getElementById("FRAME3").contentDocument
```

Then your script can, for example, dive into a form in the document:

```
var val = doc.mainForm.entry.value
```

Document

	NN2	NN3	NN4	NN6	IE3/J1	IE3/J2	IE4	IE5	IE5.5
Compatibility							✓	✓	✓

Example

While you have far easier ways to reach the document object of another frame (parent.*otherFrameName*.document), the following statement takes the long way to get there to retrieve the number of forms in the document of another frame:

```
var formCount = parent.document.all.contentsFrame.Document.forms.length
```

Using the Document property only truly makes sense when a function is passed a FRAME or IFRAME element object reference as a parameter, and the script must, among other things more related to those objects, access the document contained by those elements.

frameBorder

	NN2	NN3	NN4	NN6	IE3/J1	IE3/J2	IE4	IE5	IE5.5
Compatibility				✓			✓	✓	✓

Example

The default value for the frameBorder property is yes. You can use this setting to create a toggle script (which, unfortunately, does not change the appearance in IE). The W3C-compatible version looks like the following:

```
function toggleFrameScroll(frameID) {
    var theFrame = document.getElementById(frameID)
    if (theFrame.frameBorder == "yes") {
        theFrame.frameBorder = "no"
    } else {
        theFrame.frameBorder    = "yes"
    }
}
```

height
width

	NN2	NN3	NN4	NN6	IE3/J1	IE3/J2	IE4	IE5	IE5.5
Compatibility							✓	✓	✓

Example

The following fragment assumes a frameset defined with two frames set up as two columns within the frameset. The statements here live in the framesetting document. They retrieve the current width of the left frame and increase the width of that frame by ten percent. Syntax shown here is for the W3C DOM, but can be easily adapted to IE-only terminology.

```
var frameWidth = document.getElementById("leftFrame").width
document.getElementById("mainFrameset").cols = (Math.round(frameWidth * 1.1)) +
",*"
```

Notice how the numeric value of the existing frame width is first increased by ten percent and then concatenated to the rest of the string property assigned to the frameset's `cols` property. The asterisk after the comma means that the browser should figure out the remaining width and assign it to the right-hand frame.

noResize

	NN2	NN3	NN4	NN6	IE3/J1	IE3/J2	IE4	IE5	IE5.5
Compatibility				✓			✓	✓	✓

Example

The following statement turns off the ability for a frame to be resized:

```
parent.document.getElementById("myFrame1").noResize = true
```

Because of the negative nature of the property name, it may be difficult to keep the logic straight (setting `noResize` to `true` means that resizability is turned off). Keep a watchful eye on your Boolean values.

scrolling

	NN2	NN3	NN4	NN6	IE3/J1	IE3/J2	IE4	IE5	IE5.5
Compatibility				✓			✓	✓	✓

Example

Listing 16-45 produces a frameset consisting of eight frames. The content for the frames is generated by a script within the frameset (via the `fillFrame()` function). Event handlers in the Body of each frame invoke the `toggleFrameScroll()` function. Both ways of referencing the FRAME element object are shown, with the IE-only version commented out.

In the `toggleFrameScroll()` function, the `if` condition checks whether the property is set to something other than `no`. This allows the condition to evaluate to `true` if the property is set to either `auto` (the first time) or `yes` (as set by the function). Note that the scrollbars don't disappear from the frames in IE5.5 or NN6.

Listing 16-45: **Controlling the FRAME.scrolling Property**

```
<HTML>
<HEAD>
<TITLE>frame.scrolling Property</TITLE>
</HEAD>
<SCRIPT LANGUAGE="JavaScript">
function toggleFrameScroll(frameID) {
    // IE5 & NN6 version
    var theFrame = document.getElementById(frameID)
    // IE4+ version
    // var theFrame = document.all[frameID]

    if (theFrame.scrolling != "no") {
        theFrame.scrolling = "no"
    } else {
        theFrame.scrolling = "yes"
    }
}
// generate content for each frame
function fillFrame(frameID) {
    var page = "<HTML><BODY onClick='parent.toggleFrameScroll(\"" +
        frameID + "\")'><SPAN STYLE='font-size:24pt'>"
    page += "<P>This frame has the ID of:</P><P>" + frameID + ".</P>"
    page += "</SPAN></BODY></HTML>"
    return page
}
</SCRIPT>
<FRAMESET ID="outerFrameset" COLS="50%,50%">
    <FRAMESET ID="innerFrameset1" ROWS="25%,25%,25%,25%">
        <FRAME ID="myFrame1" SRC="javascript:parent.fillFrame('myFrame1')">
        <FRAME ID="myFrame2" SRC="javascript:parent.fillFrame('myFrame2')">
        <FRAME ID="myFrame3" SRC="javascript:parent.fillFrame('myFrame3')">
        <FRAME ID="myFrame4" SRC="javascript:parent.fillFrame('myFrame4')">
    </FRAMESET>
    <FRAMESET ID="innerFrameset2" ROWS="25%,25%,25%,25%">
        <FRAME ID="myFrame5" SRC="javascript:parent.fillFrame('myFrame5')">
        <FRAME ID="myFrame6" SRC="javascript:parent.fillFrame('myFrame6')">
        <FRAME ID="myFrame7" SRC="javascript:parent.fillFrame('myFrame7')">
        <FRAME ID="myFrame8" SRC="javascript:parent.fillFrame('myFrame8')">
    </FRAMESET>
</FRAMESET>
</HTML>
```

`src`

	NN2	NN3	NN4	NN6	IE3/J1	IE3/J2	IE4	IE5	IE5.5
Compatibility				✓			✓	✓	✓

Example

For best results, use fully formed URLs as value for the `src` property, as shown here:

```
parent.document.getElementById("mainFrame").src = "http://www.dannyg.com"
```

Relative URLs and `javascript:` pseudo-URLs will also work most of the time.

FRAMESET Element Object

Properties

`border`

	NN2	NN3	NN4	NN6	IE3/J1	IE3/J2	IE4	IE5	IE5.5
Compatibility							✓	✓	✓

Example

Even though the property is read/write in IE4+, changing the value does not change the thickness of the border you see in the browser. If you need to find the thickness of the border, a script reference from one of the frame's documents would look like the following:

```
var thickness = parent.document.all.outerFrameset.border
```

`borderColor`

	NN2	NN3	NN4	NN6	IE3/J1	IE3/J2	IE4	IE5	IE5.5
Compatibility							✓	✓	✓

Example

To retrieve the current color setting in a frameset, a script reference from one of the frame's documents would look like the following:

```
var borderColor = parent.document.all.outerFrameset.borderColor
```

```
cols
rows
```

	NN2	NN3	NN4	NN6	IE3/J1	IE3/J2	IE4	IE5	IE5.5
Compatibility				✓			✓	✓	✓

Example

Listings 16-46 through 16-48 show the HTML for a frameset and two of the three documents that go into the frameset. The final document is an HTML version of the U.S. Bill of Rights, which is serving here as a content frame for the demonstration.

The frameset listing (16-46) shows a three-frame setup. Down the left column is a table of contents (16-47). The right column is divided into two rows. In the top row is a simple control (16-48) that hides and shows the table of contents frame. As the user clicks the hot text of the control (located inside a SPAN element), the onClick event handler invokes the toggleTOC() function in the frameset. Figure 2-10 shows the frameset with the menu exposed.

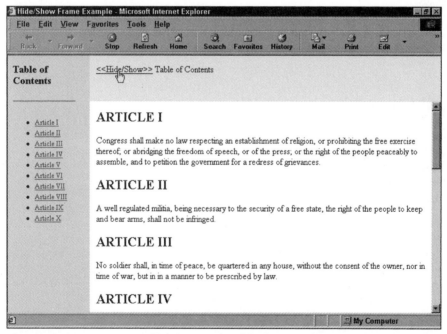

Figure 2-10: Frameset specifications are modified on the fly when you click on the top control link.

Syntax used in this example is W3C-compatible. To modify this for IE-only, you replace `document.getElementById("outerFrameset")` with `document.all.outerFrameset` and `elem.firstChild.nodeValue` to `elem.innerText`. You can also branch within the scripts to accommodate both styles.

> **Listing 16-46: Frameset and Script for Hiding/Showing a Frame**

```
<HTML>
<HEAD>
<TITLE>Hide/Show Frame Example</TITLE>
</HEAD>
<SCRIPT LANGUAGE="JavaScript">
var origCols
function toggleTOC(elem, frm) {
    if (origCols) {
        showTOC(elem)
    } else {
        hideTOC(elem, frm)
    }
}
function hideTOC(elem, frm) {
    var frameset = document.getElementById("outerFrameset")
    origCols = frameset.cols
    frameset.cols = "0,*"
}
function showTOC(elem) {
    if (origCols) {
        document.getElementById("outerFrameset").cols = origCols
        origCols = null
    }
}
</SCRIPT>
<FRAMESET ID="outerFrameset" FRAMEBORDER="no" COLS="150,*">
    <FRAME ID="TOC" NAME="TOCFrame" SRC="lst16-47.htm">
    <FRAMESET ID="innerFrameset1" ROWS="80,*">
        <FRAME ID="controls" NAME="controlsFrame" SRC="lst16-48.htm">
        <FRAME ID="content" NAME="contentFrame" SRC="bofright.htm">
    </FRAMESET>
</FRAMESET>
</HTML>
```

When a user clicks the hot spot to hide the frame, the script copies the original `cols` property settings to a global variable. The variable is used in `showTOC()` to restore the frameset to its original proportions. This allows a designer to modify the HTML for the frameset without also having to dig into scripts to hard-wire the restored size.

Listing 16-47: **Table of Contents Frame Content**

```
<HTML>
<HEAD>
<TITLE>Table of Contents</TITLE>
</HEAD>
<BODY BGCOLOR="#eeeeee">
<H3>Table of Contents</H3>
<HR>
<UL STYLE="font-size:10pt">
<LI><A HREF="bofright.htm#article1" TARGET="contentFrame">Article I</A></LI>
<LI><A HREF="bofright.htm#article2" TARGET="contentFrame">Article II</A></LI>
<LI><A HREF="bofright.htm#article3" TARGET="contentFrame">Article III</A></LI>
<LI><A HREF="bofright.htm#article4" TARGET="contentFrame">Article IV</A></LI>
<LI><A HREF="bofright.htm#article5" TARGET="contentFrame">Article V</A></LI>
<LI><A HREF="bofright.htm#article6" TARGET="contentFrame">Article VI</A></LI>
<LI><A HREF="bofright.htm#article7" TARGET="contentFrame">Article VII</A></LI>
<LI><A HREF="bofright.htm#article8" TARGET="contentFrame">Article VIII</A></LI>
<LI><A HREF="bofright.htm#article9" TARGET="contentFrame">Article IX</A></LI>
<LI><A HREF="bofright.htm#article10" TARGET="contentFrame">Article X</A></LI>
</UL>
</BODY>
</HTML>
```

Listing 16-48: **Control Panel Frame**

```
<HTML>
<HEAD>
<TITLE>Control Panel</TITLE>
</HEAD>
<BODY>
<P>
<SPAN ID="tocToggle"
     STYLE="text-decoration:underline; cursor:hand"
     onClick="parent.toggleTOC(this)"> &lt;&lt;Hide/Show&gt;&gt;</SPAN>
Table of Contents
</P>
</BODY>
</HTML>
```

frameBorder

	NN2	NN3	NN4	NN6	IE3/J1	IE3/J2	IE4	IE5	IE5.5
Compatibility							✓	✓	✓

Example

The default value for the `frameBorder` property is `yes`. You can use this setting to create a toggle script (which, unfortunately, does not change the appearance in IE). The IE4+-compatible version looks like the following:

```
function toggleFrameScroll(framesetID) {
    var theFrameset = document.all(framesetID)
    if (theFrameset.frameBorder == "yes") {
        theFrameset.frameBorder = "no"
    } else {
        theFrameset.frameBorder = "yes"
    }
}
```

frameSpacing

	NN2	NN3	NN4	NN6	IE3/J1	IE3/J2	IE4	IE5	IE5.5
Compatibility							✓	✓	✓

Example

Even though the property is read/write in IE4+, changing the value does not change the thickness of the frame spacing you see in the browser. If you need to find the spacing as set by the tag's attribute, a script reference from one of the frame's documents would look like the following:

```
var spacing = parent.document.all.outerFrameset.frameSpacing
```

IFRAME Element Object

Properties

align

	NN2	NN3	NN4	NN6	IE3/J1	IE3/J2	IE4	IE5	IE5.5
Compatibility				✓			✓	✓	✓

Example

The default setting for an IFRAME alignment is `baseline`. A script can shift the IFRAME to be flush with the right edge of the containing element as follows:

```
document.getElementById("iframe1").align = "right"
```

contentDocument

	NN2	NN3	NN4	NN6	IE3/J1	IE3/J2	IE4	IE5	IE5.5
Compatibility				✓					

Example

A document script might be using the ID of an IFRAME element to read or adjust one of the element properties; it then needs to perform some action on the content of the page through its document object. You can get the reference to the document object via a statement, such as the following:

```
var doc = document.getElementById("FRAME3").contentDocument
```

Then your script can, for example, dive into a form in the document:

```
var val = doc.mainForm.entry.value
```

frameBorder

	NN2	NN3	NN4	NN6	IE3/J1	IE3/J2	IE4	IE5	IE5.5
Compatibility				✓			✓	✓	✓

Example

See the example for the FRAME.frameBorder property earlier in this chapter.

hspace
vspace

	NN2	NN3	NN4	NN6	IE3/J1	IE3/J2	IE4	IE5	IE5.5
Compatibility							✓	✓	✓

Example

The following fragment sets the white space surrounding an IFRAME element to an equal amount:

```
document.all.myIframe.hspace = 20
document.all.myIframe.vspace = 20
```

Unfortunately these changes do not work for IE5/Windows.

scrolling

	NN2	NN3	NN4	NN6	IE3/J1	IE3/J2	IE4	IE5	IE5.5
Compatibility				✓			✓	✓	✓

Example

The following `toggleIFrameScroll()` function accepts a string of the IFRAME element's ID as a parameter and switches between on and off scroll bars in the IFRAME. The `if` condition checks whether the property is set to something other than `no`. This test allows the condition to evaluate to true `if` the property is set to either `auto` (the first time) or `yes` (as set by the function).

```
function toggleFrameScroll(frameID) {
    // IE5 & NN6 version
    var theFrame = document.getElementById(frameID)
    // IE4+ version
    // var theFrame = document.all[frameID]
    if (theFrame.scrolling != "no") {
        theFrame.scrolling = "no"
    } else {
        theFrame.scrolling = "yes"
    }
}
```

src

	NN2	NN3	NN4	NN6	IE3/J1	IE3/J2	IE4	IE5	IE5.5
Compatibility				✓			✓	✓	✓

Example

For best results, use fully formed URLs as value for the `src` property, as shown here:

```
document.getElementById("myIframe").src = "http://www.dannyg.com"
```

Relative URLs and `javascript:` pseudo-URLs also work most of the time.

popup Object

Properties

document

	NN2	NN3	NN4	NN6	IE3/J1	IE3/J2	IE4	IE5	IE5.5
Compatibility									✓

Example

Use The Evaluator (Chapter 13 in the *JavaScript Bible*) to experiment with the popup object and its properties. Enter the following statements into the top text box. The first statement creates a pop-up window, whose reference is assigned to the a global variable. Next, a reference to the body of the pop-up's document is preserved in the b variable for the sake of convenience. Further statements work with these two variables.

```
a = window.createPopup()
b = a.document.body
b.style.border = "solid 2px black"
b.style.padding = "5px"
b.innerHTML = "<P>Here is some text in a popup window</P>"
a.show(200,100, 200, 50, document.body)
```

See the description of the show() method for details on the parameters.

isOpen

	NN2	NN3	NN4	NN6	IE3/J1	IE3/J2	IE4	IE5	IE5.5
Compatibility									✓

Example

Use The Evaluator (Chapter 13 in the *JavaScript Bible*) to experiment with the isOpen property. Enter the following statements into the top text box. The sequence begins with a creation of a simple pop-up window, whose reference is assigned to the a global variable. Note that the final statement is actually two statements, which are designed so that the second statement executes while the pop-up window is still open.

```
a = window.createPopup()
a.document.body.innerHTML = "<P>Here is a popup window</P>"
a.show(200,100, 200, 50, document.body); alert("Popup is open:" + a.isOpen)
```

If you then click into the main window to hide the pop-up, you will see a different result if you enter the following statement into the top text box by itself:

```
alert("Popup is open:" + a.isOpen)
```

Methods

```
hide()
show(left, top, width, height[,
positioningElementRef])
```

	NN2	NN3	NN4	NN6	IE3/J1	IE3/J2	IE4	IE5	IE5.5
Compatibility									✓

Example

Listing 16-49 demonstrates both the show() and hide() methods for a popup object. A click of the button on the page invokes the selfTimer() function, which acts as the main routine for this page. The goal is to produce a pop-up window that "self-destructs" five seconds after it appears. Along the way, a message in the pop-up counts down the seconds.

A reference to the pop-up window is preserved as a global variable, called popup. After the popup object is created, the initContent() function stuffs the content into the pop-up by way of assigning style properties and some innerHTML for the body of the document that is automatically created when the pop-up is generated. A SPAN element is defined so that another function later on can modify the content of just that segment of text in the pop-up. Notice that the assignment of content to the pop-up is predicated on the pop-up window having been initialized (by virtue of the popup variable having a value assigned to it) and that the pop-up window is not showing. While invoking initContent() under any other circumstances is probably impossible, the validation of the desired conditions is good programming practice.

Back in selfTimer(), the popup object is displayed. Defining the desired size requires some trial and error to make sure the pop-up window comfortably accommodates the text that is put into the pop-up in the initContent() function.

With the pop-up window showing, now is the time to invoke the countDown() function. Before the function performs any action, it validates that the pop-up has been initialized and is still visible. If a user clicks the main window while the counter is counting down, this changes the value of the isOpen property to false, and nothing inside the if condition executes.

This countDown() function grabs the inner text of the SPAN and uses paresInt() to extract just the integer number (using base 10 numbering, because we're dealing with zero-leading numbers that can potentially be regarded as octal values). The condition of the if construction decreases the retrieved integer by one. If the decremented value is zero, then the time is up, and the pop-up window is hidden with the popup global variable returned to its original, null value. But if the value is other than zero, then the inner text of the SPAN is set to the decremented value (with a leading zero), and the setTimeout() method is called upon to reinvoke the countDown() function in one second (1000 milliseconds).

Listing 16-49: **Hiding and Showing a Pop-up**

```
<HTML>
<HEAD>
<TITLE>popup Object</TITLE>
<SCRIPT LANGUAGE="JavaScript">
var popup
function initContent() {
    if (popup && !popup.isOpen) {
        var popBody = popup.document.body
        popBody.style.border = "solid 3px red"
        popBody.style.padding = "10px"
        popBody.style.fontSize = "24pt"
        popBody.style.textAlign = "center"
        var bodyText = "<P>This popup will self-destruct in "
        bodyText += "<SPAN ID='counter'>05</SPAN>"
        bodyText += " seconds...</P>"
        popBody.innerHTML = bodyText
    }
}
function countDown() {
    if (popup && popup.isOpen) {
        var currCount = parseInt(popup.document.all.counter.innerText, 10)
        if (--currCount == 0) {
            popup.hide()
            popup = null
        } else {
            popup.document.all.counter.innerText = "0" + currCount
            setTimeout("countDown()", 1000)
        }
    }
}
function selfTimer() {
    popup = window.createPopup()
    initContent()
    popup.show(200,200,400,100,document.body)
    setTimeout("countDown()", 1000)
}
</SCRIPT>
</HEAD>
<BODY>
<FORM>
<INPUT TYPE="button" VALUE="Impossible Mission" onClick="selfTimer()">
</FORM>
</BODY>
</HTML>
```

The `hide()` method here is invoked by a script that is running while the pop-up window is showing. Because a pop-up window automatically goes away if a user clicks the main window, it is highly unlikely that the `hide()` method would ever be invoked by itself in response to user action in the main window. If you want a script in the pop-up window to close the pop-up, use `parentWindow.close()`.

✦   ✦   ✦

Location and History Objects (Chapter 17)

In This Chapter

Loading new pages
and other media
types via the
`location` object

Passing data between
pages via URLs

Navigating through
the browser history
under script control

While both the `location` and `history` objects contain
valuable information about the user's Web surfing
habits and even the content of forms, they could also be
abused by nefarious scripts that wish to invade the privacy of
unsuspecting site visitors. As a result, browsers do not
expose the private details to scripts (except in NN4+ via
signed scripts and the user's express permission).

The `location` object, however, is still an important object
to know and exploit. As shown in the examples here, you can
use it as one cookie-free way to pass text data from one page
to another. And the object remains the primary way scripts
load a new page into the browser.

Examples Highlights

✦ The frameset listing for the `location.host` property
demonstrates several `location` object properties. You
also find an example of how signed scripts can be used
in NN4+ to access `location` object properties for pages
served by a different domain.

✦ Listings for the `location.search` property pass data
from one page to another via a URL. In this case, a script
in a page not only makes sure that your site gets served
within the prescribed frameset, but the specific page
also gets loaded into one of the frames, even if it is not
the page specified in the frameset's definition.

✦ Observe the `location.replace()` method's example.
This method comes in handy when you don't want one
of your pages to become part of the browser's history:
Clicking the Back button skips over the replaced page.

✦ Run Listings 17-12 and 17-13 for the `history.back()`
method to see how the behavior of this method varies
among browsers. Consult the *JavaScript Bible* text for
details on the evolution of this method.

Location Object

Properties

hash

	NN2	NN3	NN4	NN6	IE3/J1	IE3/J2	IE4	IE5	IE5.5
Compatibility	✓	✓	✓	✓	✓	✓	✓	✓	✓

Example

When you load the script in Listing 17-1, adjust the size of the browser window so only one section is visible at a time. When you click a button, its script navigates to the next logical section in the progression and eventually takes you back to the top.

Listing 17-1: **A Document with Anchors**

```
<HTML>
<HEAD>
<TITLE>location.hash Property</TITLE>
<SCRIPT LANGUAGE="JavaScript">
function goNextAnchor(where) {
    window.location.hash = where
}
</SCRIPT>
</HEAD>

<BODY>

<A NAME="start"><H1>Top</H1></A>
<FORM>
<INPUT TYPE="button" NAME="next" VALUE="NEXT" onClick="goNextAnchor('sec1')">
</FORM>
<HR>
<A NAME="sec1"><H1>Section 1</H1></A>
<FORM>
<INPUT TYPE="button" NAME="next" VALUE="NEXT" onClick="goNextAnchor('sec2')">
</FORM>
<HR>
<A NAME="sec2"><H1>Section 2</H1></A>
<FORM>
<INPUT TYPE="button" NAME="next" VALUE="NEXT" onClick="goNextAnchor('sec3')">
</FORM>
<HR>
<A NAME="sec3"><H1>Section 3</H1></A>
<FORM>
```

```
<INPUT TYPE="button" NAME="next" VALUE="BACK TO TOP"
onClick="goNextAnchor('start')">
</FORM>

</BODY>
</HTML>
```

Anchor names are passed as parameters with each button's `onClick` event handler. Instead of going through the work of assembling a `window.location` value in the function by appending a literal hash mark and the value for the anchor, here I simply modify the `hash` property of the current window's location. This is the preferred, cleaner method.

If you attempt to read back the `window.location.hash` property in an added line of script, however, the window's actual URL probably will not have been updated yet, and the browser will appear to be giving your script false information. To prevent this problem in subsequent statements of the same function, construct the URLs of those statements from the same variable values you use to set the `window.location.hash` property—don't rely on the browser to give you the values you expect.

host

	NN2	NN3	NN4	NN6	IE3/J1	IE3/J2	IE4	IE5	IE5.5
Compatibility	✓	✓	✓	✓	✓	✓	✓	✓	✓

Example

Use the documents in Listings 17-2 through 17-4 as tools to help you learn the values that the various `window.location` properties return. In the browser, open the file for Listing 17-2. This file creates a two-frame window. The left frame contains a temporary placeholder (Listing 17-4) that displays some instructions. The right frame has a document (Listing 17-3) that enables you to load URLs into the left frame and get readings on three different windows available: the parent window (which creates the multiframe window), the left frame, and the right frame.

Listing 17-2: **Frameset for the Property Picker**

```
<HTML>
<HEAD>
<TITLE>window.location Properties</TITLE>
</HEAD>
<FRAMESET COLS="50%,50%" BORDER=1 BORDERCOLOR="black">
    <FRAME NAME="Frame1" SRC="lst17-04.htm">
    <FRAME NAME="Frame2" SRC="lst17-03.htm">
</FRAMESET>
</HTML>
```

Listing 17-3: **Property Picker**

```
<HTML>
<HEAD>
<TITLE>Property Picker</TITLE>
<SCRIPT LANGUAGE="JavaScript">
var isNav4 = (navigator.appName == "Netscape" &&
navigator.appVersion.charAt(0) >= 4) ? true : false

function fillLeftFrame() {
    newURL = prompt("Enter the URL of a document to show in the left frame:","")
    if (newURL != null && newURL != "") {
    parent.frames[0].location = newURL
    }
}

function showLocationData(form) {
    for (var i = 0; i <3; i++) {
        if (form.whichFrame[i].checked) {
            var windName = form.whichFrame[i].value
            break
        }
    }
    var theWind = "" + windName + ".location"
    if (isNav4) {
    netscape.security.PrivilegeManager.enablePrivilege("UniversalBrowserRead")
    }
    var theObj = eval(theWind)
    form.windName.value = windName
    form.windHash.value = theObj.hash
    form.windHost.value = theObj.host
    form.windHostname.value = theObj.hostname
    form.windHref.value = theObj.href
    form.windPath.value = theObj.pathname
    form.windPort.value = theObj.port
    form.windProtocol.value = theObj.protocol
    form.windSearch.value = theObj.search
    if (isNav4) {
    netscape.security.PrivilegeManager.disablePrivilege("UniversalBrowserRead")
    }
}
</SCRIPT>
</HEAD>
<BODY>
Click the "Open URL" button to enter the location of an HTML document to display
in the left frame of this window.
<FORM>
<INPUT TYPE="button" NAME="opener" VALUE="Open URL..."
onClick="fillLeftFrame()">
<HR>
<CENTER>
Select a window/frame. Then click the "Show Location Properties" button to view
each window.location property value for the desired window.<P>
```

```
<INPUT TYPE="radio" NAME="whichFrame" VALUE="parent" CHECKED>Parent window
<INPUT TYPE="radio" NAME="whichFrame" VALUE="parent.frames[0]">Left frame
<INPUT TYPE="radio" NAME="whichFrame" VALUE="parent.frames[1]">This frame
<P>
<INPUT TYPE="button" NAME="getProperties" VALUE="Show Location Properties"
onClick="showLocationData(this.form)">
<INPUT TYPE="reset" VALUE="Clear"><P>
<TABLE BORDER=2>
<TR><TD ALIGN=right>Window:</TD><TD><INPUT TYPE="text" NAME="windName"
SIZE=30></TD></TR>
<TR><TD ALIGN=right>hash:</TD>
<TD><INPUT TYPE="text" NAME="windHash" SIZE=30></TD></TR>

<TR><TD ALIGN=right>host:</TD>
<TD><INPUT TYPE="text" NAME="windHost" SIZE=30></TD></TR>

<TR><TD ALIGN=right>hostname:</TD>
<TD><INPUT TYPE="text" NAME="windHostname" SIZE=30></TD></TR>

<TR><TD ALIGN=right>href:</TD>
<TD><TEXTAREA NAME="windHref" ROWS=3 COLS=30 WRAP="soft">
</TEXTAREA></TD></TR>

<TR><TD ALIGN=right>pathname:</TD>
<TD><TEXTAREA NAME="windPath" ROWS=3 COLS=30 WRAP="soft">
</TEXTAREA></TD></TR>

<TR><TD ALIGN=right>port:</TD>
<TD><INPUT TYPE="text" NAME="windPort" SIZE=30></TD></TR>

<TR><TD ALIGN=right>protocol:</TD>
<TD><INPUT TYPE="text" NAME="windProtocol" SIZE=30></TD></TR>

<TR><TD ALIGN=right>search:</TD>
<TD><TEXTAREA NAME="windSearch" ROWS=3 COLS=30 WRAP="soft">
</TEXTAREA></TD></TR>
</TABLE>
</CENTER>
</FORM>
</BODY>
</HTML>
```

Listing 17-4: **Placeholder Document for Listing 17-2**

```
<HTML>
<HEAD>
<TITLE>Opening Placeholder</TITLE>
```

Continued

Listing 17-4 *(continued)*

```
</HEAD>
<BODY>
Initial placeholder. Experiment with other URLs for this frame (see right).
</BODY>
</HTML>
```

Figure 3-1 shows the dual-frame browser window with the left frame loaded with a page from my Web site.

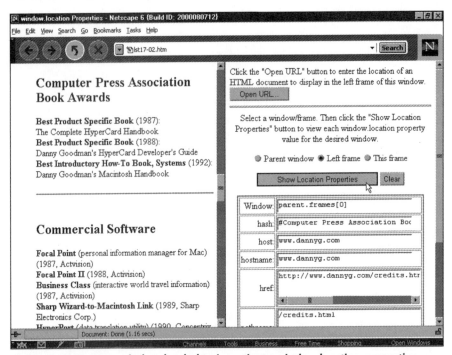

Figure 3-1: Browser window loaded to investigate window.location properties

For the best results, open a URL to a Web document on the network from the same domain and server from which you load the listings (perhaps your local hard disk). If possible, load a document that includes anchor points to navigate through a long document. Click the Left frame radio button, and then click the button that shows all properties. This action fills the table in the right frame with all the available `location` properties for the selected window. Figure 3-2 shows the complete results for a page from my Web site that is set to an anchor point.

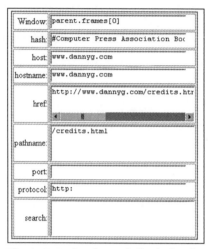

Window:	parent.frames[0]
hash:	#Computer Press Association Boo
host:	www.dannyg.com
hostname:	www.dannyg.com
href:	http://www.dannyg.com/credits.htr
pathname:	/credits.html
port:	
protocol:	http:
search:	

Figure 3-2: Readout of all window.location properties for the left frame

Attempts to retrieve these properties from URLs outside of your domain and server result in a variety of responses based on your browser and browser version. NN2 returns `null` values for all properties. NN3 presents an "access disallowed" security alert. With codebase principals turned on in NN4 (see Chapter 46 of the *JavaScript Bible*), the proper values appear in their fields. IE3 does not have the same security restrictions that Navigator does, so all values appear in their fields. But in IE4+, you get a "permission denied" error alert. See the following discussion for the meanings of the other listed properties and instructions on viewing their values.

hostname

	NN2	NN3	NN4	NN6	IE3/J1	IE3/J2	IE4	IE5	IE5.5
Compatibility	✓	✓	✓	✓	✓	✓	✓	✓	✓

Example

See Listings 17-2 through 17-4 for a set of related pages to help you view the hostname data for a variety of other pages.

href

	NN2	NN3	NN4	NN6	IE3/J1	IE3/J2	IE4	IE5	IE5.5
Compatibility	✓	✓	✓	✓	✓	✓	✓	✓	✓

Example

Listing 17-5 includes the `unescape()` function in front of the part of the script that captures the URL. This function serves cosmetic purposes by displaying the pathname in alert dialog boxes for browsers that normally display the ASCII-encoded version.

Listing 17-5: **Extracting the Directory of the Current Document**

```
<HTML>
<HEAD>
<TITLE>Extract pathname</TITLE>
<SCRIPT LANGUAGE="JavaScript">
// general purpose function to extract URL of current directory
function getDirPath(URL) {
    var result = unescape(URL.substring(0,(URL.lastIndexOf("/")) + 1))
    return result
}
// handle button event, passing work onto general purpose function
function showDirPath(URL) {
    alert(getDirPath(URL))
}
</SCRIPT>
</HEAD>

<BODY>
<FORM>
<INPUT TYPE="button" VALUE="View directory URL"
onClick="showDirPath(window.location.href)">
</FORM>
</BODY>
</HTML>
```

pathname

	NN2	NN3	NN4	NN6	IE3/J1	IE3/J2	IE4	IE5	IE5.5
Compatibility	✓	✓	✓	✓	✓	✓	✓	✓	✓

Example

See Listings 17-2 through 17-4 earlier in this chapter for a multiple-frame example you can use to view the `location.pathname` property for a variety of URLs of your choice.

port

	NN2	NN3	NN4	NN6	IE3/J1	IE3/J2	IE4	IE5	IE5.5
Compatibility	✓	✓	✓	✓	✓	✓	✓	✓	✓

Example

If you have access to URLs containing port numbers, use the documents in Listings 17-2 through 17-4 to experiment with the output of the `location.port` property.

protocol

	NN2	NN3	NN4	NN6	IE3/J1	IE3/J2	IE4	IE5	IE5.5
Compatibility	✓	✓	✓	✓	✓	✓	✓	✓	✓

Example

See Listings 17-2 through 17-4 for a multiple-frame example you can use to view the `location.protocol` property for a variety of URLs. Also try loading an FTP site to see the `location.protocol` value for that type of URL.

search

	NN2	NN3	NN4	NN6	IE3/J1	IE3/J2	IE4	IE5	IE5.5
Compatibility	✓	✓	✓	✓	✓	✓	✓	✓	✓

Example

As mentioned in the opening of Chapter 16 of the *JavaScript Bible* about frames, you can force a particular HTML page to open inside the frameset for which it is designed. But with the help of the search string, you can reuse the same framesetting document to accommodate any number of content pages that go into one of the frames (rather than specifying a separate frameset for each possible combination of pages in the frameset). The listings in this section create a simple example of how to force a page to load in a frameset by passing some information about the page to the frameset. Thus, if a user has a URL to one of the content frames (perhaps it has been bookmarked by right-clicking the frame or it comes up as a search engine result), the page appears in its designated frameset the next time the user visits the page.

The fundamental task going on in this scheme has two parts. The first is in each of the content pages where a script checks whether the page is loaded inside a frameset. If the frameset is missing, then a search string is composed and appended to the URL for the framesetting document. The framesetting document has its own short script that looks for the presence of the search string. If the string is there, then the script extracts the search string data and uses it to load that specific page into the content frame of the frameset.

Listing 17-6 is the framesetting document. The `getSearchAsArray()` function is more complete than necessary for this simple example, but you can use it in other instances to convert any number of name/value pairs passed in the search string (in traditional format of `name1=value1&name2=value2&etc.`) into an array whose indexes are the names (making it easier for scripts to extract a specific piece of passed data). Version branching takes place because, for convenience, the `getSearchAsArray()` function uses text and array methods that don't exist in browsers prior to NN3 or IE4.

Listing 17-6: **A Smart Frameset**

```
<HTML>
<HEAD>
<TITLE>Example Frameset</TITLE>
<SCRIPT LANGUAGE="JavaScript">
// Convert location.search into an array of values
// indexed by name.
function getSearchAsArray() {
    var minNav3 = (navigator.appName == "Netscape" &&
parseInt(navigator.appVersion) >= 3)
    var minIE4 = (navigator.appName.indexOf("Microsoft") >= 0 &&
parseInt(navigator.appVersion) >= 4)
    var minDOM = minNav3 || minIE4    // baseline DOM required for this function
    var results = new Array()
    if (minDOM) {
        var input = unescape(location.search.substr(1))
        if (input) {
            var srchArray = input.split("&")
            var tempArray = new Array()
            for (var i = 0; i < srchArray.length; i++) {
                tempArray = srchArray[i].split("=")
                results[tempArray[0]] = tempArray[1]
            }
        }
    }
    return results
}
function loadFrame() {
    if (location.search) {
        var srchArray = getSearchAsArray()
        if (srchArray["content"]) {
            self.content.location.href = srchArray["content"]
        }
    }
}
</SCRIPT>
</HEAD>
```

```
<FRAMESET COLS="250,*" onLoad="loadFrame()">
    <FRAME NAME="toc" SRC="lst17-07.htm">
    <FRAME NAME="content" SRC="lst17-08.htm">
</FRAMESET>
</HTML>
```

Listing 17-7 is the HTML for the table of contents frame. Nothing elaborate goes on here, but you can see how normal navigation works for this simplified frameset.

Listing 17-7: **The Table of Contents**

```
<HTML>
<HEAD>
<TITLE>Table of Contents</TITLE>
</HEAD>
<BODY BGCOLOR="#eeeeee">
<H3>Table of Contents</H3>
<HR>
<UL>
<LI><A HREF="lst17-08.htm" TARGET="content">Page 1</A></LI>
<LI><A HREF="lst17-08a.htm" TARGET="content">Page 2</A></LI>
<LI><A HREF="lst17-08b.htm" TARGET="content">Page 3</A></LI>
</UL>
</BODY>
</HTML>
```

Listing 17-8 shows one of the content pages. As the page loads, the `checkFrameset()` function is invoked. If the window does not load inside a frameset, then the script navigates to the framesetting page, passing the current content URL as a search string. Notice that for browsers that support the `location.replace()` method, the loading of this page on its own does not get recorded to the browser's history and isn't accessed if the user hits the Back button.

Listing 17-8: **A Content Page**

```
<HTML>
<HEAD>
<TITLE>Page 1</TITLE>
<SCRIPT LANGUAGE="JavaScript">
function checkFrameset() {
    var minNav3 = (navigator.appName == "Netscape" &&
parseInt(navigator.appVersion) >= 3)
    var minIE4 = (navigator.appName.indexOf("Microsoft") >= 0 &&
parseInt(navigator.appVersion) >= 4)
```

Continued

Listing 17-8 *(continued)*

```
    var minDOM = minNav3 || minIE4    // baseline DOM required for this function
    var isNav4 = (navigator.appName == "Netscape" &&
parseInt(navigator.appVersion) == 4)
    if (parent == window) {
        // Don't do anything if running NN4
        // so that the frame can be printed on its own
        if (isNav4 && window.innerWidth == 0) {
            return
        }
        if (minDOM) {
            // Use replace() to keep current page out of history
            location.replace("lst17-06.htm?content=" + escape(location.href))
        } else {
            location.href = " lst17-06.htm?content=" + escape(location.href)
        }
    }
}
// Invoke the function
checkFrameset()
</SCRIPT>
</HEAD>
<BODY>
<H1>Page 1</H1>
<HR>
</BODY>
</HTML>
```

In practice, I recommend placing the code for the checkFrameset() function and call to it inside an external .js library and linking that library into each content document of the frameset. That's why the function assigns the generic location.href property to the search string—you can use it on any content page.

Methods
reload(*unconditionalGETBoolean*)

	NN2	NN3	NN4	NN6	IE3/J1	IE3/J2	IE4	IE5	IE5.5
Compatibility		✓	✓	✓			✓	✓	✓

Example
To experience the difference between the two loading styles, load the document in Listing 17-9. Click a radio button, enter some new text, and make a choice in the SELECT object. Clicking the Soft Reload/Refresh button invokes a method that

reloads the document as if you had clicked the browser's Reload/Refresh button. It also preserves the visible properties of form elements. The Hard Reload button invokes the `location.reload()` method, which resets all objects to their default settings.

Listing 17-9: **Hard versus Soft Reloading**

```
<HTML>
<HEAD>
<TITLE>Reload Comparisons</TITLE>
<SCRIPT LANGUAGE="JavaScript1.1">
function hardReload() {
    location.reload(true)
}
function softReload() {
    history.go(0)
}
</SCRIPT>
</HEAD>
<BODY>
<FORM NAME="myForm">
<INPUT TYPE="radio" NAME="rad1" VALUE = 1>Radio 1<BR>
<INPUT TYPE="radio" NAME="rad1" VALUE = 2>Radio 2<BR>
<INPUT TYPE="radio" NAME="rad1" VALUE = 3>Radio 3<P>
<INPUT TYPE="text" NAME="entry" VALUE="Original"><P>
<SELECT NAME="theList">
<OPTION>Red
<OPTION>Green
<OPTION>Blue
</SELECT>
<HR>
<INPUT TYPE="button" VALUE="Soft Reload" onClick="softReload()">
<INPUT TYPE="button" VALUE="Hard Reload" onClick="hardReload()">
</FORM>
</BODY>
</HTML>
```

replace("*URL*")

	NN2	NN3	NN4	NN6	IE3/J1	IE3/J2	IE4	IE5	IE5.5
Compatibility		✓	✓	✓			✓	✓	✓

Example

Calling the `location.replace()` method navigates to another URL similarly to assigning a URL to the location. The difference is that the document doing the calling doesn't appear in the history list after the new document loads. Check the history listing (in your browser's usual spot for this information) before and after clicking Replace Me in Listing 17-10.

Listing 17-10: **Invoking the location.replace() Method**

```
<HTML>
<HEAD>
<TITLE>location.replace() Method</TITLE>
<SCRIPT LANGUAGE="JavaScript1.1">
function doReplace() {
    location.replace("lst17-01.htm")
}
</SCRIPT>
</HEAD>
<BODY>
<FORM NAME="myForm">
<INPUT TYPE="button" VALUE="Replace Me" onClick="doReplace()">
</FORM>
</BODY>
</HTML>
```

History Object

Properties

length

	NN2	NN3	NN4	NN6	IE3/J1	IE3/J2	IE4	IE5	IE5.5
Compatibility	✓	✓	✓	✓	✓	✓	✓	✓	✓

Example

The simple function in Listing 17-11 displays one of two alert messages based on the number of items in the browser's history.

Listing 17-11: **A Browser History Count**

```
<HTML>
<HEAD>
<TITLE>History Object</TITLE>
<SCRIPT LANGUAGE="JavaScript">
```

```
function showCount() {
    var histCount = window.history.length
    if (histCount > 5) {
        alert("My, my, you\'ve been busy. You have visited " + histCount +
        " pages so far.")
    } else {
        alert("You have been to " + histCount + " Web pages this session.")
    }
}
</SCRIPT>
</HEAD>

<BODY>
<FORM>
<INPUT TYPE="button" NAME="activity" VALUE="My Activity" onClick="showCount()">
</FORM>
</BODY>
</HTML>
```

Methods

back()

	NN2	NN3	NN4	NN6	IE3/J1	IE3/J2	IE4	IE5	IE5.5
Compatibility	✓	✓	✓	✓	✓	✓	✓	✓	✓

Example

Listings 17-12 and 17-13 provide a little workshop in which you can test the behavior of a variety of backward and forward navigation in different browsers. The frameset appears in Figure 3-3. Some features work only in NN4+.

Listing 17-12: **Navigation Lab Frameset**

```
<HTML>
<HEAD>
<TITLE>Back and Forward</TITLE>
</HEAD>
<FRAMESET COLS="45%,55%">
    <FRAME NAME="controller" SRC="lst17-13.htm">
    <FRAME NAME="display" SRC="lst17-01.htm">
</FRAMESET>
</HTML>
```

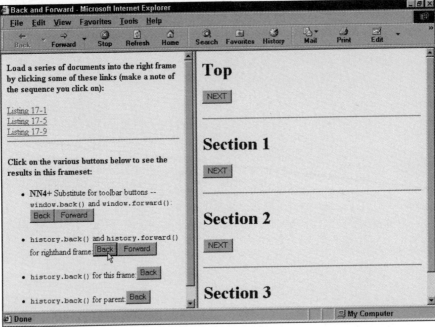

Figure 3-3: Experiment with back and forward behaviors in different browsers

The top portion of Listing 17-13 contains simple links to other example files from this chapter. A click of any link loads a different document into the right-hand frame to let you build some history inside the frame.

Listing 17-13: **Navigation Lab Control Panel**

```
<HTML>
<HEAD>
<TITLE>Lab Controls</TITLE>
</HEAD>
<BODY>
<B>Load a series of documents into the right frame by clicking some of these
links (make a note of the sequence you click on):</B><P>
<A HREF="lst17-01.htm" TARGET="display">Listing 17-1</A><BR>
<A HREF="lst17-05.htm" TARGET="display">Listing 17-5</A><BR>
<A HREF="lst17-09.htm" TARGET="display">Listing 17-9</A><BR>
<HR>
<FORM NAME="input">
<B>Click on the various buttons below to see the results in this
frameset:</B><P>
<UL>
<LI><B>NN4+</B> Substitute for toolbar buttons -- <TT>window.back()</TT> and
<TT>window.forward()</TT>:<INPUT TYPE="button" VALUE="Back"
onClick="window.back()"><INPUT TYPE="button" VALUE="Forward"
onClick="window.forward()"><P>
```

```
<LI><TT> history.back()</TT> and <TT>history.forward()</TT> for righthand frame:
<INPUT TYPE="button" VALUE="Back" onClick="parent.display.history.back()"><INPUT
TYPE="button" VALUE="Forward" onClick="parent.display.history.forward()"><P>

<LI><TT>history.back()</TT> for this frame:<INPUT TYPE="button" VALUE="Back"
onClick="history.back()"><P>

<LI><TT>history.back()</TT> for parent:<INPUT TYPE="button" VALUE="Back"
onClick="parent.history.back()"><P>
</UL>
</FORM>
</BODY>
</HTML>
```

go(*relativeNumber* | *"URLOrTitleSubstring"*)

	NN2	NN3	NN4	NN6	IE3/J1	IE3/J2	IE4	IE5	IE5.5
Compatibility	✓	✓	✓	✓	✓	✓	✓	✓	✓

Example

Fill in either the number or text field of the page in Listing 17-14 and then click the associated button. The script passes the appropriate kind of data to the go() method. Be sure to use negative numbers for visiting a page earlier in the history.

Listing 17-14: **Navigating to an Item in History**

```
<HTML>
<HEAD>
<TITLE>history.go() Method</TITLE>
<SCRIPT LANGUAGE="JavaScript">
function doGoNum(form) {
    window.history.go(parseInt(form.histNum.value))
}
function doGoTxt(form) {
    window.history.go(form.histWord.value)
}
</SCRIPT>
</HEAD>

<BODY>
<FORM>
<B>Calling the history.go() method:</B>
<HR>
```

Continued

Listing 17-14 *(continued)*

```
Enter a number (+/-):<INPUT TYPE="text" NAME="histNum" SIZE=3 VALUE="0">
<INPUT TYPE="button" VALUE="Go to Offset" onClick="doGoNum(this.form)"><P>
Enter a word in a title:<INPUT TYPE="text" NAME="histWord">
<INPUT TYPE="button" VALUE="Go to Match" onClick="doGoTxt(this.form)">
</FORM>
</BODY>
</HTML>
```

✦   ✦   ✦

The Document and Body Objects (Chapter 18)

◆ ◆ ◆ ◆

In This Chapter

Accessing arrays of
objects contained by
the document object

Writing new
document content to
a window or frame

Managing BODY
element scrolling in IE

◆ ◆ ◆ ◆

To include coverage of the document object and BODY element object in the same chapter is logical, provided you
don't fall into a conceptual trap that has been set during the
evolution of document object models. The document object
has been with us since the beginning. Even though it is an
abstract object (that is to say, the object exists simply by virtue
of a page loading into the browser, rather than associated with
any HTML tag), a number of its properties reflect attributes
that are defined in a page's <BODY> tag. For instance, the properties for link colors and background images, whose behaviors
are set in BODY element attributes, have been exposed via the
document object since the earliest days.

In more modern object models (IE4+ and W3C DOM), the
BODY element is its own object. The document object
strengthens its role as a "super-container" of all the HTML element objects in the page. Thus, the BODY element object is a
child element of the root document object (see Chapter 14 of
the *JavaScript Bible* for more details). But now that the BODY
element object can expose its own attributes as properties,
the document object no longer needs to play that role, except
for the sake of backward compatibility with scripts written for
older browsers. Instead, the document object assumes an
even greater role, especially in the W3C DOM, by providing
critical properties and methods of a global nature for the
entire document.

It is clear, of course, that the BODY element has an important role to play. Both the IE4+ and W3C DOMs expose the `document.body` property, which returns a reference to the BODY element of the current document. The IE4+ DOM, however, bestows even more importance to the BODY element, by forcing it to be the frame of reference for how much a document's content scrolls inside a window or frame. All other DOMs put that control into the hands of the window (that is, scrolling the window rather than the BODY element inside the window).

Examples Highlights

✦ Observe in Listing 18-1 how (backward-compatible) `document` object properties for various colors (`alinkColor` and the like) impact the look of the page. It may be even more important to experience the lack of dynamic control that these properties provide in a variety of browsers.

✦ See how IE4+/Windows exposes date information about the document in Listing 18-4.

✦ Listings 18-11 and 18-12 provide a workshop to let you test how well your target browsers support the `document.referrer` property. You may need to put them on your server for the real test. Unfortunately, IE/Windows doesn't always provide the desired information.

✦ If you script for W3C-DOM compatibility, be sure to grasp the `document.getElementById()` and `document.getElementsByName()` methods with the help of the example steps provided.

✦ The `document.write()` method is one of the most important ones in the vocabulary. Listings 18-16 through 18-18 demonstrate its power.

✦ See examples for `document.body.scrollLeft` and `document.body.doScroll()` to control document scrolling in IE, and the `onScroll` event handler example (Listing 18-21) to see how to keep a page scrolled at a fixed position.

Document Object

Properties
`activeElement`

	NN2	NN3	NN4	NN6	IE3/J1	IE3/J2	IE4	IE5	IE5.5
Compatibility							✓	✓	✓

Example

Use The Evaluator (Chapter 13 in the *JavaScript Bible*) with IE4+ to experiment with the `activeElement` property. Type the following statement into the top text box:

```
document.activeElement.value
```

After you press the Enter key, the Results box shows the value of the text box you just typed into (the very same expression you just typed). But if you then click the Evaluate button, you will see the `value` property of that button object appear in the Results box.

```
alinkColor
bgColor
fgColor
linkColor
vlinkColor
```

	NN2	NN3	NN4	NN6	IE3/J1	IE3/J2	IE4	IE5	IE5.5
Compatibility	✓	✓	✓	✓	✓	✓	✓	✓	✓

Example

I select some color values at random to plug into three settings of the ugly colors group for Listing 18-1. The smaller window displays a dummy button so that you can see how its display contrasts with color settings. Notice that the script sets the colors of the smaller window by rewriting the entire window's HTML code. After changing colors, the script displays the color values in the original window's textarea. Even though some colors are set with the color constant values, properties come back in the hexadecimal triplet values. You can experiment to your heart's content by changing color values in the listing. Every time you change the values in the script, save the HTML file and reload it in the browser.

Listing 18-1: **Color Sampler**

```
<HTML>
<HEAD>
<TITLE>Color Me</TITLE>
<SCRIPT LANGUAGE="JavaScript">
function defaultColors() {
    return "BGCOLOR='#c0c0c0' VLINK='#551a8b' LINK='#0000ff'"
}

function uglyColors() {
    return "BGCOLOR='yellow' VLINK='pink' LINK='lawngreen'"
}
```

Continued

Listing 18-1 *(continued)*

```
function showColorValues() {
    var result = ""
    result += "bgColor: " + newWindow.document.bgColor + "\n"
    result += "vlinkColor: " + newWindow.document.vlinkColor + "\n"
    result += "linkColor: " + newWindow.document.linkColor + "\n"
    document.forms[0].results.value = result
}
// dynamically writes contents of another window
function drawPage(colorStyle) {
    var thePage = ""
    thePage += "<HTML><HEAD><TITLE>Color Sampler</TITLE></HEAD><BODY "
    if (colorStyle == "default") {
        thePage += defaultColors()
    } else {
        thePage += uglyColors()
    }
    thePage += ">Just so you can see the variety of items and color, <A "
    thePage += "HREF='http://www.nowhere.com'>here\'s a link</A>, and " +
               "<A HREF='http://home.netscape.com'> here is another link </A> " +
               "you can use on-line to visit and see how its color differs " +
               "from the standard link."
    thePage += "<FORM>"
    thePage += "<INPUT TYPE='button' NAME='sample' VALUE='Just a Button'>"
    thePage += "</FORM></BODY></HTML>"
    newWindow.document.write(thePage)
    newWindow.document.close()
    showColorValues()
}
// the following works properly only in Windows Navigator
function setColors(colorStyle) {
    if (colorStyle == "default") {
        document.bgColor = "#c0c0c0"
    } else {
        document.bgColor = "yellow"
    }
}
var newWindow = window.open("","","height=150,width=300")
</SCRIPT>
</HEAD>

<BODY>
Try the two color schemes on the document in the small window.
<FORM>
<INPUT TYPE="button" NAME="default" VALUE='Default Colors'
    onClick="drawPage('default')">
<INPUT TYPE="button" NAME="weird" VALUE="Ugly Colors"
    onClick="drawPage('ugly')"><P>
<TEXTAREA NAME="results" ROWS=3 COLS=20></TEXTAREA><P><HR>
These buttons change the current document, but not correctly on all platforms<P>
```

```
<INPUT TYPE="button" NAME="default" VALUE='Default Colors'
    onClick="setColors('default')">
<INPUT TYPE="button" NAME="weird" VALUE="Ugly Colors"
    onClick="setColors('ugly')"><P>
</FORM>
<SCRIPT LANGUAGE="JavaScript">
drawPage("default")
</SCRIPT>
</BODY>
</HTML>
```

To satisfy the curiosity of those who want to change the color of a loaded document on the fly, the preceding example includes a pair of buttons that set the color properties of the current document. If you're running browsers and versions capable of this power (see Table 18-1), everything will look fine; but in other platforms or earlier versions, you may lose the buttons and other document content behind the color. You can still click and activate these items, but the color obscures them. Unless you know for sure that users of your Web page use only browsers and clients empowered for background color changes, do not change colors by setting properties of an existing document.

Note

If you are using Internet Explorer 3 for the Macintosh, you will experience some difficulties with Listing 18-1. The script in the main document loses its connection with the subwindow; it does not redraw the second window with other colors. You can, however, change the colors in the main document. The significant flicker you may experience is related to the way the Mac version redraws content after changing colors.

anchors

	NN2	NN3	NN4	NN6	IE3/J1	IE3/J2	IE4	IE5	IE5.5
Compatibility	✓	✓	✓	✓	✓	✓	✓	✓	✓

Example

In Listing 18-2, I append an extra script to Listing 17-1 (in Chapter 3 of this book) to demonstrate how to extract the number of anchors in the document. The document dynamically writes the number of anchors found in the document. You will not likely ever need to reveal such information to users of your page, and the document.anchors property is not one that you will call frequently. The object model defines it automatically as a document property while defining actual anchor objects.

Listing 18-2: **Reading the Number of Anchors**

```
<HTML>
<HEAD>
<TITLE>document.anchors Property</TITLE>
<SCRIPT LANGUAGE="JavaScript">
function goNextAnchor(where) {
    window.location.hash = where
}
</SCRIPT>
</HEAD>

<BODY>

<A NAME="start"><H1>Top</H1></A>
<FORM>
<INPUT TYPE="button" NAME="next" VALUE="NEXT" onClick="goNextAnchor('sec1')">
</FORM>
<HR>

<A NAME="sec1"><H1>Section 1</H1></A>
<FORM>
<INPUT TYPE="button" NAME="next" VALUE="NEXT" onClick="goNextAnchor('sec2')">
</FORM>
<HR>

<A NAME="sec2"><H1>Section 2</H1></A>
<FORM>
<INPUT TYPE="button" NAME="next" VALUE="NEXT" onClick="goNextAnchor('sec3')">
</FORM>
<HR>

<A NAME="sec3"><H1>Section 3</H1></A>
<FORM>
<INPUT TYPE="button" NAME="next" VALUE="BACK TO TOP"
onClick="goNextAnchor('start')">
</FORM>
<HR><P>
<SCRIPT LANGUAGE="JavaScript">
document.write("<I>There are " + document.anchors.length +
" anchors defined for this document</I>")
</SCRIPT>
</BODY>
</HTML>
```

applets

	NN2	NN3	NN4	NN6	IE3/J1	IE3/J2	IE4	IE5	IE5.5
Compatibility		✓	✓	✓			✓	✓	✓

Example

The `document.applets` property is defined automatically as the browser builds the object model for a document that contains applet objects. You will rarely access this property, except to determine how many applet objects a document has.

bgColor

See `alinkColor`.

body

	NN2	NN3	NN4	NN6	IE3/J1	IE3/J2	IE4	IE5	IE5.5
Compatibility				✓			✓	✓	✓

Example

Use The Evaluator (Chapter 13 in the *JavaScript Bible*) to examine properties of the BODY element object. First, to prove that the `document.body` is the same as the element object that comes back from longer references, enter the following statement into the top text box with either IE5 or NN6:

```
document.body == document.getElementsByTagName("BODY")[0]
```

Next, check out the BODY object's property listings later in this chapter and enter the listings into the top text box to review their results. For example:

```
document.body.bgColor
document.body.tagName
```

charset

	NN2	NN3	NN4	NN6	IE3/J1	IE3/J2	IE4	IE5	IE5.5
Compatibility							✓	✓	✓

Example

Use The Evaluator (Chapter 13 in the *JavaScript Bible*) to experiment with the
`charset` property. To see the default setting applied to the page, enter the following statement into the top text box:

```
document.charset
```

If you are running IE5+ for Windows 98 and you enter the following statement,
the browser will apply a different character set to the page:

```
document.charset = "iso-8859-2"
```

If your version of Windows does not have that character set installed in the system, the browser may ask permission to download and install the character set.

characterSet

	NN2	NN3	NN4	NN6	IE3/J1	IE3/J2	IE4	IE5	IE5.5
Compatibility				✓					

Example

Use The Evaluator (Chapter 13 in the *JavaScript Bible*) to experiment with the
`characterSet` property in NN6. To see the default setting applied to the page,
enter the following statement into the top text box:

```
document.characterSet
```

cookie

	NN2	NN3	NN4	NN6	IE3/J1	IE3/J2	IE4	IE5	IE5.5
Compatibility	✓	✓	✓	✓	✓	✓	✓	✓	✓

Example

Experiment with the last group of statements in Listing 18-3 to create, retrieve,
and delete cookies. You can also experiment with The Evaluator by assigning a
name/value pair string to `document.cookie`, and then examining the value of the
`cookie` property.

defaultCharset

	NN2	NN3	NN4	NN6	IE3/J1	IE3/J2	IE4	IE5	IE5.5
Compatibility							✓	✓	✓

Example

Use The Evaluator (Chapter 13 in the *JavaScript Bible*) to experiment with the defaultCharset property. To see the default setting applied to the page, enter the following statement into the top text box:

```
document.defaultCharset
```

documentElement

	NN2	NN3	NN4	NN6	IE3/J1	IE3/J2	IE4	IE5	IE5.5
Compatibility				✓				✓	✓

Example

Use The Evaluator (Chapter 13 in the *JavaScript Bible*) to examine the behavior of the documentElement property. In IE5+ or NN6, enter the following statement into the top text field:

```
document.documentElement.tagName
```

The result is HTML, as expected.

expando

	NN2	NN3	NN4	NN6	IE3/J1	IE3/J2	IE4	IE5	IE5.5
Compatibility							✓	✓	✓

Example

Use The Evaluator (Chapter 13 in the *JavaScript Bible*) to experiment with the document.expando property in IE4+. Begin by proving that the document object can normally accept custom properties. Type the following statement into the top text field:

```
document.spooky = "Boo!"
```

This property is now set and stays that way until the page is either reloaded or unloaded.

Now freeze the document object's properties with the following statement:

```
document.expando = false
```

If you try to add a new property, such as the following, you receive an error:

```
document.happy = "tra la"
```

Interestingly, even though document.expando is turned off, the first custom property is still accessible and modifiable.

fgColor

See alinkColor.

fileCreatedDate
fileModifiedDate
fileSize

	NN2	NN3	NN4	NN6	IE3/J1	IE3/J2	IE4	IE5	IE5.5
Compatibility							✓	✓	✓

Example

Listing 18-4 dynamically generates several pieces of content relating to the creation and modification dates of the file, as well as its size. More importantly, the listing demonstrates how to turn a value returned by the file date properties into a genuine date object that can be used for date calculations. In the case of Listing 18-4, the calculation is the number of full days between the creation date and the day someone views the file. Notice that the dynamically generated content is added very simply via the innerText properties of carefully-located SPAN elements in the body content.

Listing 18-4: **Viewing File Dates**

```
<HTML>
<HEAD>
<TITLE>fileCreatedDate and fileModifiedDate Properties</TITLE>
<SCRIPT LANGUAGE="JavaScript">
function fillInBlanks() {
    var created = document.fileCreatedDate
    var modified = document.fileModifiedDate
    document.all.created.innerText = created
    document.all.modified.innerText = modified
    var createdDate = new Date(created).getTime()
    var today = new Date().getTime()
    var diff = Math.floor((today - createdDate) / (1000*60*60*24))
    document.all.diff.innerText = diff
    document.all.size.innerText = document.fileSize
}
</SCRIPT>
</HEAD>

<BODY onLoad="fillInBlanks()">
<H1>fileCreatedDate and fileModifiedDate Properties</H1>
<HR>
```

```
<P>This file (<SPAN ID="size"> </SPAN> bytes) was created
on <SPAN ID="created"> </SPAN> and most
recently modified on <SPAN ID="modified"> </SPAN>.</P>
<P>It has been <SPAN ID="diff"> </SPAN> days since this file was
created.</P>
</BODY>
</HTML>
```

forms

	NN2	NN3	NN4	NN6	IE3/J1	IE3/J2	IE4	IE5	IE5.5
Compatibility	✓	✓	✓	✓	✓	✓	✓	✓	✓

Example

The document in Listing 18-5 is set up to display an alert dialog box that simulates navigation to a particular music site, based on the checked status of the "bluish" check box. The user input here is divided into two forms: one form with the check box and the other form with the button that does the navigation. A block of copy fills the space in between. Clicking the bottom button (in the second form) triggers the function that fetches the checked property of the "bluish" checkbox by using the document.forms[i] array as part of the address.

Listing 18-5: **Using the document.forms Property**

```
<HTML>
<HEAD>
<TITLE>document.forms example</TITLE>
<SCRIPT LANGUAGE="JavaScript">
function goMusic() {
    if (document.forms[0].bluish.checked) {
        alert("Now going to the Blues music area...")
    } else {
        alert("Now going to Rock music area...")
    }
}
</SCRIPT>
</HEAD>

<BODY>
<FORM NAME="theBlues">
<INPUT TYPE="checkbox" NAME="bluish">Check here if you've got the blues.
</FORM>
<HR>
```

Continued

Listing 18-5 *(continued)*

```
M<BR>
o<BR>
r<BR>
e<BR>
<BR>
C<BR>
o<BR>
p<BR>
y<BR>
<HR>
<FORM NAME="visit">
<INPUT TYPE="button" VALUE="Visit music site" onClick="goMusic()">
</FORM>
</BODY>
</HTML>
```

frames

	NN2	NN3	NN4	NN6	IE3/J1	IE3/J2	IE4	IE5	IE5.5
Compatibility							✓	✓	✓

Example

See Listings 16-7 and 16-8 (in Chapter 2 of this book) for examples of using the `frames` property with window objects. The listings work with IE4+ if you swap references to the `window` with `document`.

height
width

	NN2	NN3	NN4	NN6	IE3/J1	IE3/J2	IE4	IE5	IE5.5
Compatibility			✓	✓					

Example

Use The Evaluator (Chapter 13 in the *JavaScript Bible*) to examine the `height` and `width` properties of that document. Enter the following statement into the top text box and click the Evaluate button:

```
"height=" + document.height + "; width=" + document.width
```

Resize the window so that you see both vertical and horizontal scrollbars in the browser window and click the Evaluate button again. If either or both numbers get smaller, the values in the Results box are the exact size of the space occupied by the document. But if you expand the window to well beyond where the scrollbars are needed, the values extend to the number of pixels in each dimension of the window's content region.

images

	NN2	NN3	NN4	NN6	IE3/J1	IE3/J2	IE4	IE5	IE5.5
Compatibility		✓	✓	✓	(✓)		✓	✓	✓

Example

The `document.images` property is defined automatically as the browser builds the object model for a document that contains image objects. See the discussion about the `Image` object in Chapter 22 of the *JavaScript Bible* for reference examples.

implementation

	NN2	NN3	NN4	NN6	IE3/J1	IE3/J2	IE4	IE5	IE5.5
Compatibility				✓					

Example

Use The Evaluator (Chapter 13 in the *JavaScript Bible*) to experiment with the `document.implementation.hasFeature()` method in NN6. Enter the following statements one at a time into the top text field and examine the results:

```
document.implementation.hasFeature("HTML","1.0")
document.implementation.hasFeature("HTML","2.0")
document.implementation.hasFeature("HTML","3.0")
document.implementation.hasFeature("CSS","2.0")
document.implementation.hasFeature("CSS2","2.0")
```

Feel free to try other values.

lastModified

	NN2	NN3	NN4	NN6	IE3/J1	IE3/J2	IE4	IE5	IE5.5
Compatibility	✓	✓	✓	✓	✓	✓	✓	✓	✓

Example

Experiment with the document.lastModified property with Listing 18-6. But also be prepared for inaccurate readings if the file is located on some servers or local hard disks.

Listing 18-6: document.lastModified Property in Another Format

```
<HTML>
<HEAD>
<TITLE>Time Stamper</TITLE>
</HEAD>
<BODY>
<CENTER> <H1>GiantCo Home Page</H1></CENTER>
<SCRIPT LANGUAGE="JavaScript">
update = new Date(document.lastModified)
theMonth = update.getMonth() + 1
theDate = update.getDate()
theYear = update.getFullYear()
document.writeln("<I>Last updated:" + theMonth + "/" + theDate + "/" + theYear +
"</I>")
</SCRIPT>
<HR>
</BODY>
</HTML>
```

As noted at great length in the Date object discussion in Chapter 36 of the *JavaScript Bible*, you should be aware that date formats vary greatly from country to country. Some of these formats use a different order for date elements. When you hard-code a date format, it may take a form that is unfamiliar to other users of your page.

layers

	NN2	NN3	NN4	NN6	IE3/J1	IE3/J2	IE4	IE5	IE5.5
Compatibility			✓						

Example

Listing 18-7 demonstrates only for NN4 how to use the document.layers property to crawl through the entire set of nested layers in a document. Using reflexive calls to the crawlLayers() function, the script builds an indented list of layers in the same hierarchy as the objects themselves and displays the results in an alert dialog box. After you load this document (the script is triggered by the onLoad event handler), compare the alert dialog box contents against the structure of <LAYER> tags in the document.

Listing 18-7: **A Navigator 4 Layer Crawler**

```
<HTML>
<HEAD>
<SCRIPT LANGUAGE="JavaScript1.2">
var output = ""
function crawlLayers(layerArray, indent) {
    for (var i = 0; i < layerArray.length; i++) {
        output += indent + layerArray[i].name + "\n"
        if (layerArray[i].document.layers.length) {
            var newLayerArray = layerArray[i].document.layers
            crawlLayers(newLayerArray, indent + "  ")
        }
    }
    return output
}
function revealLayers() {
    alert(crawlLayers(document.layers, ""))
}
</SCRIPT>
</HEAD>
<BODY onLoad="revealLayers()">
<LAYER NAME="Europe">
    <LAYER NAME="Germany"></LAYER>
    <LAYER NAME="Netherlands">
        <LAYER NAME="Amsterdam"></LAYER>
        <LAYER NAME="Rotterdam"></LAYER>
    </LAYER>
    <LAYER NAME="France"></LAYER>
</LAYER>
<LAYER NAME="Africa">
    <LAYER NAME="South Africa"></LAYER>
    <LAYER NAME="Ivory Coast"></LAYER>
</LAYER>
</BODY>
</HTML>
```

linkColor

See alinkColor.

links

	NN2	NN3	NN4	NN6	IE3/J1	IE3/J2	IE4	IE5	IE5.5
Compatibility	✓	✓	✓	✓	✓	✓	✓	✓	✓

Example

The `document.links` property is defined automatically as the browser builds the object model for a document that contains link objects. You rarely access this property, except to determine the number of link objects in the document.

location
URL

	NN2	NN3	NN4	NN6	IE3/J1	IE3/J2	IE4	IE5	IE5.5
Compatibility	(✓)	✓	✓	✓	(✓)	(✓)	✓	✓	✓

Example

HTML documents in Listing 18-8 through 18-10 create a test lab that enables you to experiment with viewing the `document.URL` property for different windows and frames in a multiframe environment. Results are displayed in a table, with an additional listing of the `document.title` property to help you identify documents being referred to. The same security restrictions that apply to retrieving `window.location` object properties also apply to retrieving the `document.URL` property from another window or frame.

Listing 18-8: **Frameset for document.URL Property Reader**

```
<HTML>
<HEAD>
<TITLE>document.URL Reader</TITLE>
</HEAD>
<FRAMESET ROWS="60%,40%">
    <FRAME NAME="Frame1" SRC="lst18-10.htm">
    <FRAME NAME="Frame2" SRC="lst18-09.htm">
</FRAMESET>
</HTML>
```

Listing 18-9: **document.URL Property Reader**

```
<HTML>
<HEAD>
<TITLE>URL Property Reader</TITLE>
<SCRIPT LANGUAGE="JavaScript1.1">
function fillTopFrame() {
    newURL=prompt("Enter the URL of a document to show in the top frame:","")
    if (newURL != null && newURL != "") {
        top.frames[0].location = newURL
    }
}

function showLoc(form,item) {
    var windName = item.value
    var theRef = windName + ".document"
    form.dLoc.value = unescape(eval(theRef + ".URL"))
    form.dTitle.value = unescape(eval(theRef + ".title"))
}
</SCRIPT>
</HEAD>

<BODY>
Click the "Open URL" button to enter the location of an HTML document to display
in the upper frame of this window.
<FORM>
<INPUT TYPE="button" NAME="opener" VALUE="Open URL..." onClick="fillTopFrame()">
</FORM>
<HR>
<FORM>
Select a window or frame to view each document property values.<P>
<INPUT TYPE="radio" NAME="whichFrame" VALUE="parent"
onClick="showLoc(this.form,this)">Parent window
<INPUT TYPE="radio" NAME="whichFrame" VALUE="top.frames[0]"
onClick="showLoc(this.form,this)">Upper frame
<INPUT TYPE="radio" NAME="whichFrame" VALUE="top.frames[1]"
onClick="showLoc(this.form,this)">This frame<P>
<TABLE BORDER=2>
<TR><TD ALIGN=RIGHT>document.URL:</TD>
<TD><TEXTAREA NAME="dLoc" ROWS=3 COLS=30 WRAP="soft"></TEXTAREA></TD></TR>

<TR><TD ALIGN=RIGHT>document.title:</TD>
<TD><TEXTAREA NAME="dTitle" ROWS=3 COLS=30 WRAP="soft"></TEXTAREA></TD></TR>
</TABLE>
</FORM>
</BODY>
</HTML>
```

> ### Listing 18-10: **Placeholder for Listing 18-8**
>
> ```
> <HTML>
> <HEAD>
> <TITLE>Opening Placeholder</TITLE>
> </HEAD>
> <BODY>
> Initial place holder. Experiment with other URLs for this frame (see below).
> </BODY>
> </HTML>
> ```

parentWindow

	NN2	NN3	NN4	NN6	IE3/J1	IE3/J2	IE4	IE5	IE5.5
Compatibility							✓	✓	✓

Example

To prove the `parentWindow` property points to the document's window, you can enter the following statement into the top text field of The Evaluator (Chapter 13 in the *JavaScript Bible*):

```
document.parentWindow == self
```

This expression evaluates to `true` only if both references are of the same object.

protocol

	NN2	NN3	NN4	NN6	IE3/J1	IE3/J2	IE4	IE5	IE5.5
Compatibility							✓	✓	✓

Example

If you use The Evaluator (Chapter 13 in the *JavaScript Bible*) to test the `document.protocol` property, you will find that it displays `File Protocol` in the results because you are accessing the listing from a local hard disk or CD-ROM.

referrer

	NN2	NN3	NN4	NN6	IE3/J1	IE3/J2	IE4	IE5	IE5.5
Compatibility	✓	✓	✓	✓	✓	✓	✓	✓	✓

Example

This demonstration requires two documents (and for IE, you'll also need to access the documents from a Web server). The first document, in Listing 18-11, simply contains one line of text as a link to the second document. In the second document (Listing 18-12), a script verifies the document from which the user came via a link. If the script knows about that link, it displays a message relevant to the experience the user had at the first document. Also try opening Listing 18-12 in a new browser window from the Open File command in the File menu to see how the script won't recognize the referrer.

Listing 18-11: **A Source Document**

```
<HTML>
<HEAD>
<TITLE>document.referrer Property 1</TITLE>
</HEAD>

<BODY>
<H1><A HREF="lst18-12.htm">Visit my sister document</A>
</BODY>
</HTML>
```

Listing 18-12: **Checking document.referrer**

```
<HTML>
<HEAD>
<TITLE>document.referrer Property 2</TITLE>
</HEAD>

<BODY><H1>
<SCRIPT LANGUAGE="JavaScript">
if(document.referrer.length > 0 &&
document.referrer.indexOf("18-11.htm") != -1){
    document.write("How is my brother document?")
} else {
    document.write("Hello, and thank you for stopping by.")
}
</SCRIPT>
</H1></BODY>
</HTML>
```

scripts

	NN2	NN3	NN4	NN6	IE3/J1	IE3/J2	IE4	IE5	IE5.5
Compatibility							✓	✓	✓

Example

You can experiment with the `document.scripts` array in The Evaluator (Chapter 13 in the *JavaScript Bible*). For example, you can see that only one SCRIPT element object is in The Evaluator page if you enter the following statement into the top text field:

```
document.scripts.length
```

If you want to view all of the properties of that lone SCRIPT element object, enter the following statement into the bottom text field:

```
document.scripts[0]
```

Among the properties are both `innerText` and `text`. If you assign an empty string to either property, the scripts are wiped out from the object model, but not from the browser. The scripts disappear because after the scripts loaded, they were cached outside of the object model. Therefore, if you enter the following statement into the top field:

```
document.scripts[0].text = ""
```

the script contents are gone from the object model, yet subsequent clicks of the Evaluate and List Properties buttons (which invoke functions of the SCRIPT element object) still work.

selection

	NN2	NN3	NN4	NN6	IE3/J1	IE3/J2	IE4	IE5	IE5.5
Compatibility							✓	✓	✓

Example

See Listings 15-30 and 15-39 in Chapter 1 of this book to see the `document.selection` property in action for script-controlled copying and pasting (IE/Windows only).

URL

See `location`.

vlinkColor

See `alinkColor`.

width

See `height`.

Methods

captureEvents(*eventTypeList*)

	NN2	NN3	NN4	NN6	IE3/J1	IE3/J2	IE4	IE5	IE5.5
Compatibility			✓						

Example

See the example for the NN4 `window.captureEvents()` method (Listing 16-21 from Chapter 2 of this book) to see how to capture events on their way to other objects. In that example, you can substitute the `document` reference for the `window` reference to see how the document version of the method works just like the window version. If you understand the mechanism for windows, you understand it for documents. The same is true for the other NN4 event methods.

close()

NN2	NN3	NN4	NN6	IE3/J1	IE3/J2	IE4	IE5	IE5.5
Compatibility	✓	✓	✓	✓	✓	✓	✓	✓

Example

Before you experiment with the `document.close()` method, be sure you understand the `document.write()` method described later in this chapter. After that, make a separate set of the three documents for that method's example (Listings 18-16 through 18-18 in a different directory or folder). In the `takePulse()` function listing, comment out the `document.close()` statement, as shown here:

```
msg += "<P>Make it a great day!</BODY></HTML>"
parent.frames[1].document.write(msg)
//parent.frames[1].document.close()
```

Now try the pages on your browser. You see that each click of the upper button appends text to the bottom frame, without first removing the previous text. The reason is that the previous layout stream was never closed. The document thinks that you're still writing to it. Also, without properly closing the stream, the last line of text may not appear in the most recently written batch.

createAttribute("*attributeName*")

	NN2	NN3	NN4	NN6	IE3/J1	IE3/J2	IE4	IE5	IE5.5
Compatibility				✓					

Example

Unfortunately, the setAttributeNode() method in NN6 does not yet work with attributes generated by the createAttribute() method. This will be fixed eventually, and you can experiment adding attributes to sample elements in The Evaluator. In the meantime, you can still create an attribute and inspect its properties. Enter the following text into the top text box:

```
a = document.createAttribute("author")
```

Now enter a into the bottom text box to inspect the properties of an Attr object.

createElement("*tagName*")

	NN2	NN3	NN4	NN6	IE3/J1	IE3/J2	IE4	IE5	IE5.5
Compatibility				✓			✓	✓	✓

Example

Chapter 15 of the *JavaScript Bible* contains numerous examples of the document.createElement() method in concert with methods that add or replace content to a document. See Listings 15-10, 15-21, 15-22,15-28, 15-29, and 15-31 in Chapter 1 of this book.

createEventObject([*eventObject*])

	NN2	NN3	NN4	NN6	IE3/J1	IE3/J2	IE4	IE5	IE5.5
Compatibility									✓

Example

See the discussion of the `fireEvent()` method in Chapter 15 of the *JavaScript Bible* for an example of the sequence to follow when creating an event to fire on an element.

createStyleSheet(["*URL*"[, *index*]])

	NN2	NN3	NN4	NN6	IE3/J1	IE3/J2	IE4	IE5	IE5.5
Compatibility							✓	✓	✓

Example

Listing 18-13 demonstrates adding an internal and external style sheet to a document. For the internal addition, the `addStyle1()` function invokes `document.createStyleSheet()` and adds a rule governing the P elements of the page (not available for IE5/Mac). In the `addStyle2()` function, an external file is loaded. That file contains the following two style rules:

```
H2 {font-size:20pt; color:blue}
P  {color:blue}
```

Notice that by specifying a position of zero for the imported style sheet, the addition of the internal style sheet always comes afterward in `styleSheet` object sequence. Thus, except when you deploy only the external style sheet, the red text color of the P elements overrides the blue color of the external style sheet. If you remove the second parameter of the `createStyleSheet()` method in `addStyle2()`, the external style sheet is appended to the end of the list. If it is the last style sheet to be added, the blue color prevails. Repeatedly clicking the buttons in this example continues to add the style sheets to the document.

Listing 18-13: **Using document.createStyleSheet()**

```
<HTML>
<HEAD>
<TITLE>document.createStyleSheet() Method</TITLE>
<SCRIPT LANGUAGE="JavaScript">
function addStyle1() {
    var newStyle = document.createStyleSheet()
    newStyle.addRule("P", "font-size:16pt; color:red")
}

function addStyle2() {
    var newStyle = document.createStyleSheet("lst18-13.css",0)
}
```

Continued

Listing 18-13 *(continued)*

```
</SCRIPT>
</HEAD>

<BODY>
<H1>document.createStyleSheet() Method</H1>
<HR>
<FORM>
<INPUT TYPE="button" VALUE="Add Internal" onClick="addStyle1()"> 
<INPUT TYPE="button" VALUE="Add External" onClick="addStyle2()">
</FORM>
<H2>Section 1</H2>
<P>Lorem ipsum dolor sit amet, consectetaur adipisicing elit,
sed do eiusmod tempor incididunt ut labore et dolore magna aliqua.
Ut enim adminim veniam, quis nostrud exercitation ullamco laboris
nisi ut aliquip ex ea commodo consequat.</P>
<H2>Section 2</H2>
<P>Duis aute irure dolor in reprehenderit involuptate velit esse
cillum dolore eu fugiat nulla pariatur. Excepteur sint occaecat
cupidatat non proident, sunt in culpa qui officia deseruntmollit
anim id est laborum.</P>
</BODY>
</HTML>
```

createTextNode("*text*")

	NN2	NN3	NN4	NN6	IE3/J1	IE3/J2	IE4	IE5	IE5.5
Compatibility				✓				✓	✓

Example

While Chapter 14 and 15 of the *JavaScript Bible* (Listing 15-21 in Chapter 1, for instance) provide numerous examples of the createTextNode() method at work, using The Evaluator (Chapter 13 in the *JavaScript Bible*) is instructive to see just what the method generates in IE5+ and NN6. You can use one of the built-in global variables of The Evaluator to hold a reference to a newly generated text node by entering the following statement into the top text field:

```
a = document.createTextNode("Hello")
```

The Results box shows that an object was created. Now, look at the properties of the object by typing a into the bottom text field. The precise listings of properties varies between IE5+ and NN6, but the W3C DOM properties that they share in common indicate that the object is a node type 3 with a node name of #text. No parents, children, or siblings exist yet because the object created here is not part of the document hierarchy tree until it is explicitly added to the document.

To see how insertion works, enter the following statement into the top text field to append the text node to the myP paragraph:

```
document.getElementById("myP").appendChild(a)
```

The word "Hello" appears at the end of the simple paragraph lower on the page. Now you can modify the text of that node either via the reference from the point of view of the containing P element or via the global variable reference for the newly created node:

```
document.getElementById("myP").lastChild.nodeValue = "Howdy"
```

or

```
a.nodeValue = "Howdy"
```

elementFromPoint(x, y)

	NN2	NN3	NN4	NN6	IE3/J1	IE3/J2	IE4	IE5	IE5.5
Compatibility							✓	✓	✓

Example

Listing 18-14 is a document that contains many different types of elements, each of which has an ID attribute assigned to it. The onMouseOver event handler for the document object invokes a function that finds out which element the cursor is over when the event fires. Notice that the event coordinates are event.clientX and event.clientY, which use the same coordinate plane as the page for their point of reference. As you roll the mouse over every element, its ID appears on the page. In Figure 4-1, the pointer is inside a table cell, whose ID appears in bold at the end of the first paragraph. Some elements, such as BR and TR, occupy no space in the document, so you cannot get their IDs to appear. On a typical browser screen size, a positioned element rests atop one of the paragraph elements so that you can see how the elementFromPoint() method handles overlapping elements. If you scroll the page, the coordinates for the event and the page's elements stay in sync.

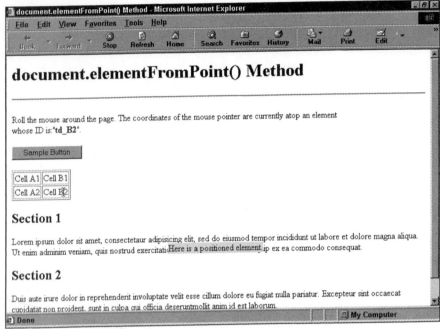

Figure 4-1: Revealing the object located at an event screen position

Listing 18-14: **Using the elementFromPoint() Method**

```
<HTML>
<HEAD>
<TITLE>document.elementFromPoint() Method</TITLE>
<SCRIPT LANGUAGE="JavaScript">
function showElemUnderneath() {
    var elem = document.elementFromPoint(event.clientX, event.clientY)
    document.all.mySpan.innerText = elem.id
}
document.onmouseover = showElemUnderneath
</SCRIPT>
</HEAD>


<BODY ID="myBody">
<H1 ID="header">document.elementFromPoint() Method</H1>
<HR ID="myHR">
<P ID="instructions">Roll the mouse around the page. The coordinates
of the mouse pointer are currently atop an element<BR ID="myBR">whose ID
is:"<SPAN ID="mySpan" STYLE="font-weight:bold"></SPAN>".</P>
<FORM ID="myForm">
<INPUT ID="myButton" TYPE="button" VALUE="Sample Button" onClick=""> 
</FORM>
<TABLE BORDER=1 ID="myTable">
```

```
<TR ID="tr1">
    <TD ID="td_A1">Cell A1</TD>
    <TD ID="td_B1">Cell B1</TD>
</TR>
<TR ID="tr2">
    <TD ID="td_A2">Cell A2</TD>
    <TD ID="td_B2">Cell B2</TD>
</TR>
</TABLE>
<H2 ID="sec1">Section 1</H2>
<P ID="p1">Lorem ipsum dolor sit amet, consectetaur adipisicing elit,
sed do eiusmod tempor incididunt ut labore et dolore magna aliqua.
Ut enim adminim veniam, quis nostrud exercitation ullamco laboris
nisi ut aliquip ex ea commodo consequat.</P>
<H2 ID="sec2">Section 2</H2>
<P ID="p2">Duis aute irure dolor in reprehenderit involuptate velit esse
cillum dolore eu fugiat nulla pariatur. Excepteur sint occaecat
cupidatat non proident, sunt in culpa qui officia deseruntmollit
anim id est laborum.</P>
<DIV ID="myDIV" STYLE="position:absolute; top:340; left:300; background-
color:yellow">
Here is a positioned element.</DIV>
</BODY>
</HTML>
```

execCommand("*commandName*"[, *UIFlag*] [, *param*])

	NN2	NN3	NN4	NN6	IE3/J1	IE3/J2	IE4	IE5	IE5.5
Compatibility							✓	✓	✓

Example

You can find many examples of the execCommand() method for the TextRange object in Chapter 19 of the *JavaScript Bible*. But you can try out the document-specific commands in The Evaluator (Chapter 13 in the *JavaScript Bible*) if you like. Try each of the following statements in the top text box and click the Evaluate button:

```
document.execCommand("Refresh")
document.execCommand("SelectAll")
document.execCommand("Unselect")
```

All methods return true in the Results box.

Because any way you can evaluate a statement in The Evaluator forces a body selection to become deselected before the evaluation takes place, you can't experiment this way with the selection-oriented commands.

getElementById("*elementID*")

	NN2	NN3	NN4	NN6	IE3/J1	IE3/J2	IE4	IE5	IE5.5
Compatibility				✓				✓	✓

Example

You can find many examples of this method in use throughout this book, but you can take a closer look at how it works by experimenting in The Evaluator (Chapter 13 in the *JavaScript Bible*). A number of elements in The Evaluator have IDs assigned to them, so that you can use the method to inspect the objects and their properties. Enter the following statements into both the top and bottom text fields of The Evaluator. Results from the top field are references to the objects; results from the bottom field are lists of properties for the particular object.

```
document.getElementById("myP")
document.getElementById("myEM")
document.getElementById("myTitle")
document.getElementById("myScript")
```

As you see in the Results field, NN6 is more explicit about the type of HTML element object being referenced in the top text field than IE5. But nevertheless, both browsers are pointing to the same objects.

getElementsByName("*elementName*")

	NN2	NN3	NN4	NN6	IE3/J1	IE3/J2	IE4	IE5	IE5.5
Compatibility				✓				✓	✓

Example

Use The Evaluator to test out the getElementsByName() method. All form elements in the upper part of the page have names associated with them. Enter the following statements into the top text field and observe the results:

```
document.getElementsByName("output")
document.getElementsByName("speed").length
document.getElementsByName("speed")[0].value
```

You can also explore all of the properties of the text field by typing the following expression into the bottom field:

```
document.getElementsByName("speed")[0]
```

getSelection()

	NN2	NN3	NN4	NN6	IE3/J1	IE3/J2	IE4	IE5	IE5.5
Compatibility			✓	✓					

Example

The document in Listing 18-15 provides a cross-browser (but not IE5/Mac) solution to capturing text that a user selects in the page. Selected text is displayed in the textarea. The script uses browser detection and branching to accommodate the diverse ways of recognizing the event and reading the selected text.

Listing 18-15: **Capturing a Text Selection**

```
<HTML>
<HEAD>
<TITLE>Getting Selected Text</TITLE>
<SCRIPT LANGUAGE="JavaScript">
var isNav4 = (navigator.appName == "Netscape"
    && parseInt(navigator.appVersion) == 4)
var isNav4Min = (navigator.appName == "Netscape" &&
    parseInt(navigator.appVersion) >= 4)
var isIE4Min = (navigator.appName.indexOf("Microsoft") != -1 &&
    parseInt(navigator.appVersion) >= 4)
function showSelection() {
    if (isNav4Min) {
        document.forms[0].selectedText.value = document.getSelection()
    } else if (isIE4Min) {
        if (document.selection) {
            document.forms[0].selectedText.value =
                document.selection.createRange().text
            event.cancelBubble = true
        }
    }
}
if (isNav4) {
    document.captureEvents(Event.MOUSEUP)
}
document.onmouseup = showSelection
</SCRIPT>
</HEAD>

<BODY>
<H1>Getting Selected Text</H1>
<HR>
<P>Select some text and see how JavaScript can capture the selection:</P>
<H2>ARTICLE I</H2>
<P>
```

Continued

document.getSelection()

Listing 18-15 *(continued)*

```
Congress shall make no law respecting an establishment of religion, or
prohibiting the
free exercise thereof; or abridging the freedom of speech, or of the press; or
the right of the people peaceably to assemble, and to petition the government
for a redress of grievances.
</P>
</HR>
<FORM>
<TEXTAREA NAME="selectedText" ROWS=3 COLS=40 WRAP="virtual"></TEXTAREA>
</FORM>
</BODY>
</HTML>
```

open(["*mimeType*"] [, *replace*])

	NN2	NN3	NN4	NN6	IE3/J1	IE3/J2	IE4	IE5	IE5.5
Compatibility	✓	✓	✓	✓	✓	✓	✓	✓	✓

Example

You can see an example of where the `document.open()` method fits in the scheme of dynamically creating content for another frame in the discussion of the `document.write()` method later in this chapter.

queryCommandEnabled("*commandName*")
queryCommandIndterm("*commandName*")
queryCommandCommandState("*commandName*")
queryCommandSupported("*commandName*")
queryCommandText("*commandName*")
queryCommandValue("*commandName*")

	NN2	NN3	NN4	NN6	IE3/J1	IE3/J2	IE4	IE5	IE5.5
Compatibility							✓	✓	✓

Example

See the examples for these methods covered under the `TextRange` object in Chapter 19 of the *JavaScript Bible*.

recalc([*allFlag*])

	NN2	NN3	NN4	NN6	IE3/J1	IE3/J2	IE4	IE5	IE5.5
Compatibility								✓	✓

Example

You can see an example of recalc() in Listing 15-32 (in Chapter 1 of this book) for the setExpression() method. In that example, the dependencies are between the current time and properties of standard element objects.

write("*string1*" [,"*string2*" ... [, "*stringn*"]])
writeln("*string1*" [,"*string2*" ... [, "*stringn*"]])

	NN2	NN3	NN4	NN6	IE3/J1	IE3/J2	IE4	IE5	IE5.5
Compatibility	✓	✓	✓	✓	✓	✓	✓	✓	✓

Example

The example in Listings 18-16 through 18-18 demonstrates several important points about using the document.write() or document.writeln() methods for writing to another frame. First is the fact that you can write any HTML code to a frame, and the browser accepts it as if the source code came from an HTML file somewhere. In the example, I assemble a complete HTML document, including basic HTML tags for completeness.

Listing 18-16: **Frameset for document.write() Example**

```
<HTML>
<HEAD>
<TITLE>Writin' to the doc</TITLE>
</HEAD>
<FRAMESET ROWS="50%,50%">
    <FRAME NAME="Frame1" SRC="lst18-17.htm">
    <FRAME NAME="Frame2" SRC="lst18-18.htm">
</FRAMESET>
</HTML>
```

Listing 18-17: **document.write() Example**

```
<HTML>
<HEAD>
<TITLE>Document Write Controller</TITLE>
<SCRIPT LANGUAGE="JavaScript">
function takePulse(form) {
    var msg = "<HTML><HEAD><TITLE>On The Fly with " + form.yourName.value +
        "</TITLE></HEAD>"
    msg += "<BODY BGCOLOR='salmon'><H1>Good Day " + form.yourName.value +
        "!</H1><HR>"
    for (var i = 0; i < form.how.length; i++) {
        if (form.how[i].checked) {
            msg += form.how[i].value
            break
        }
    }
    msg += "<P>Make it a great day!</BODY></HTML>"
    parent.Frame2.document.write(msg)
    parent.Frame2.document.close()
}
function getTitle() {
    alert("Lower frame document.title is now:" + parent.Frame2.document.title)
}
</SCRIPT>
</HEAD>

<BODY>
Fill in a name, and select how that person feels today. Then click "Write To
Below"
to see the results in the bottom frame.
<FORM>
Enter your first name:<INPUT TYPE="text" NAME="yourName" VALUE="Dave"><P>
How are you today? <INPUT TYPE="radio" NAME="how"
VALUE="I hope that feeling continues forever." CHECKED>Swell
<INPUT TYPE="radio" NAME="how" VALUE="You may be on your way to feeling Swell">
Pretty Good
<INPUT TYPE="radio" NAME="how" VALUE="Things can only get better from here.">
So-So<P>
<INPUT TYPE="button" NAME="enter" VALUE="Write To Below"
    onClick="takePulse(this.form)">
<HR>
<INPUT TYPE="button" NAME="peek" VALUE="Check Lower Frame Title"
    onClick="getTitle()">
</BODY>
</HTML>
```

Listing 18-18: **Placeholder for Listing 18-16**

```
<HTML>
<HEAD>
<TITLE>Placeholder</TITLE>
<BODY>
</BODY>
</HTML>
```

Figure 4-2 shows an example of the frame written by the script.

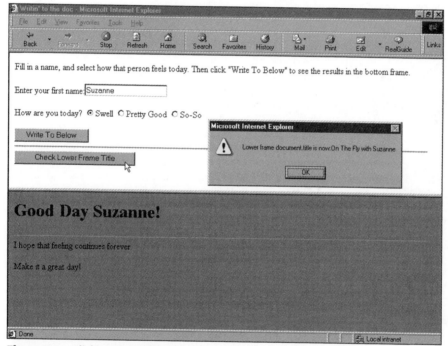

Figure 4-2: Clicking the Write To Below button in the upper frame causes a script to assemble and write HTML for the bottom frame.

A second point to note is that this example customizes the content of the document based on user input. This customization makes the experience of working with your Web page feel far more interactive to the user — yet you're doing it without any CGI programs running on the server.

The third point I want to bring home is that the document created in the separate frame by the `document.write()` method is a genuine `document` object. In this example, for instance, the `<TITLE>` tag of the written document changes if you redraw the lower frame after changing the entry of the name field in the upper frame. If you click the lower button after updating the bottom frame, you see that the `document.title` property has, indeed, changed to reflect the `<TITLE>` tag written to the browser in the course of displaying the frame's page (except in NN4/Mac, which exhibits a bug for this property in a dynamically written document). The fact that you can artificially create full-fledged JavaScript document objects on the fly represents one of the most important powers of serverless CGI scripting (for information delivery to the user) with JavaScript. You have much to take advantage of here if your imagination is up to the task.

Notice that except for NN2, you can easily modify Listing 18-17 to write the results to the same frame as the document containing the field and buttons. Instead of specifying the lower frame

```
parent.frames[1].document.open()
parent.frames[1].document.write(msg)
parent.frames[1].document.close()
```

the code simply can use

```
document.open()
document.write(msg)
document.close()
```

This code would replace the form document with the results and not require any frames in the first place. Because the code assembles all of the content for the new document into one variable value, that data survives the one document.write() method.

The frameset document (Listing 18-18) creates a blank frame by loading a blank document (Listing 18-18). An alternative I highly recommend is to have the frame-setting document fill the frame with a blank document of its own creation. See "Blank Frames" in Chapter 16 of the *JavaScript Bible* for further details about this technique for NN3+ and IE3+.

Event Handlers

onStop

	NN2	NN3	NN4	NN6	IE3/J1	IE3/J2	IE4	IE5	IE5.5
Compatibility								✓	✓

Example

Listing 18-19 provides a simple example of an intentional infinitely looping script. In case you load this page into a browser other than IE5, you can click the Halt Counter button to stop the looping. The Halt Counter button and the onStop event handler invoke the same function.

Listing 18-19: **Scripting the Browser Stop Button**

```
<HTML>
<HEAD>
```

```
<TITLE>onStop Event Handler</TITLE>
<SCRIPT LANGUAGE="JavaScript">
var counter = 0
var timerID
function startCounter() {
    document.forms[0].display.value = ++counter
    //clearTimeout(timerID)
    timerID = setTimeout("startCounter()", 10)
}
function haltCounter() {
    clearTimeout(timerID)
    counter = 0
}
document.onstop = haltCounter
</SCRIPT>
</HEAD>

<BODY>
<H1>onStop Event Handler</H1>
<HR>
<P>Click the browser's Stop button (in IE) to stop the script counter.</P>
<FORM>
<P><INPUT TYPE="text" NAME="display"></P>
<INPUT TYPE="button" VALUE="Start Counter" onClick="startCounter()">
<INPUT TYPE="button" VALUE="Halt Counter" onClick="haltCounter()">
</FORM>
</BODY>
</HTML>
```

BODY Element Object

Properties

aLink
bgColor
link
text
vLink

	NN2	NN3	NN4	NN6	IE3/J1	IE3/J2	IE4	IE5	IE5.5
Compatibility				✓			✓	✓	✓

Example

You can modify Listing 18-1 for use with IE4+ and NN6+ only by using the new property names instead. Replace all references to the document properties with their document.body equivalents. For example, the function would be reworked as the following (changes in boldface):

```
function showColorValues() {
    var result = ""
    result += "bgColor: " + newWindow.document.body.bgColor + "\n"
    result += "vLink: " + newWindow.document.body.vLink + "\n"
    result += "link: " + newWindow.document.body.link + "\n"
    document.forms[0].results.value = result
}
```

background

	NN2	NN3	NN4	NN6	IE3/J1	IE3/J2	IE4	IE5	IE5.5
Compatibility				✓			✓	✓	✓

Example

If you have a background image file named images/logoBG.gif, a script can set the background via the following statement:

```
document.body.background = "images/logoBG.gif"
```

To clear the background image:

```
document.body.background = ""
```

If a background color has been previously set, the color becomes visible after the image disappears.

bgColor

See aLink.

bgProperties

	NN2	NN3	NN4	NN6	IE3/J1	IE3/J2	IE4	IE5	IE5.5
Compatibility							✓	✓	✓

Example

Both of the following statements change the default behavior of background image scrolling in IE4+:

```
document.body.bgProperties = "fixed"
```

or

```
document.body.style.backgroundAttachment = "fixed"
```

The added benefit of using the style sheet version is that it also works in NN6.

bottomMargin
leftMargin
rightMargin
topMargin

	NN2	NN3	NN4	NN6	IE3/J1	IE3/J2	IE4	IE5	IE5.5
Compatibility							✓	✓	✓

Example

Both of the following statements change the default left margin in IE4+:

```
document.body.leftMargin = 30
```

or

```
document.body.style.marginLeft = 30
```

leftMargin

See bottomMargin.

link

See aLink.

noWrap

	NN2	NN3	NN4	NN6	IE3/J1	IE3/J2	IE4	IE5	IE5.5
Compatibility							✓	✓	✓

Example

To change the word wrapping behavior from the default, the statement is:

```
document.body.noWrap = true
```

rightMargin

See bottomMargin.

scroll

	NN2	NN3	NN4	NN6	IE3/J1	IE3/J2	IE4	IE5	IE5.5
Compatibility							✓	✓	✓

Example

To change the scrollbar appearance from the default, the statement is:

```
document.body.scroll = "no"
```

scrollLeft
scrollTop

	NN2	NN3	NN4	NN6	IE3/J1	IE3/J2	IE4	IE5	IE5.5
Compatibility							✓	✓	✓

Example

Listing 18-20 is the IE4+ version of the NN example for pageXOffset and pageYOffset properties (Listing 16-13 in Chapter 2). Everything about these two examples is the same except for the syntax that retrieves the values indicating how much the document is scrolled in a window.

Listing 18-20: **Viewing the scrollLeft and scrollTop Properties**

```
<HTML>
<HEAD>
<TITLE>Master of all Windows</TITLE>
<SCRIPT LANGUAGE="JavaScript">
function leftFrame() {
    var output = "<HTML><BODY><H3>Body Scroll Values</H3><HR>\n"
    output += "<FORM>body.scrollLeft:<INPUT TYPE='text' NAME='xOffset'
SIZE=4><BR>\n"
    output += "body.scrollTop:<INPUT TYPE='text' NAME='yOffset' SIZE=4><BR>\n"
    output += "</FORM></BODY></HTML>"
    return output
}
```

```
function rightFrame() {
    var output = "<HTML><HEAD><SCRIPT LANGUAGE='JavaScript'>\n"
    output += "function showOffsets() {\n"
    output += "parent.readout.document.forms[0].xOffset.value =  " +
        "document.body.scrollLeft\n"
    output += "parent.readout.document.forms[0].yOffset.value =  " +
        "document.body.scrollTop\n}\n"
    output += "document.onclick = showOffsets\n"
    output += "<\/SCRIPT></HEAD><BODY><H3>Content Page</H3>\n"
    output += "Scroll this frame and click on a table border to view " +
        "page offset values.<BR><HR>\n"
    output += "<TABLE BORDER=5 WIDTH=800>"
    var oneRow = "<TD>Cell 1</TD><TD>Cell 2</TD><TD>Cell 3</TD><TD>Cell 4</TD>" +
        "<TD>Cell 5</TD>"
    for (var i = 1; i <= 30; i++) {
        output += "<TR><TD><B>Row " + i + "</B></TD>" + oneRow + "</TR>"
    }
    output += "</TABLE></BODY></HTML>"
    return output
}
</SCRIPT>
</HEAD>
<FRAMESET COLS="30%,70%">
    <FRAME NAME="readout" SRC="javascript:parent.leftFrame()">
    <FRAME NAME="display" SRC="javascript:parent.rightFrame()">
</FRAMESET>
</HTML>
```

text

See aLink.

topMargin

See bottomMargin.

vLink

See aLink.

Methods

createTextRange()

	NN2	NN3	NN4	NN6	IE3/J1	IE3/J2	IE4	IE5	IE5.5
Compatibility							✓	✓	✓

Example

See Listing 19-8 (in Chapter 5 of this book) for an example of the `createTextRange()` method in action.

doScroll(["*scrollAction*"])

	NN2	NN3	NN4	NN6	IE3/J1	IE3/J2	IE4	IE5	IE5.5
Compatibility								✓	✓

Example

Use The Evaluator (Chapter 13 in the *JavaScript Bible*) to experiment with the `doScroll()` method in IE5+. Size the browser window so that at least the vertical scrollbar is active (meaning it has a thumb region). Enter the following statement into the top text field and press Enter a few times to simulate clicking the PgDn key:

```
document.body.doScroll()
```

Return to the top of the page and now do the same for scrolling by the increment of the scrollbar down arrow:

```
document.body.doScroll("down")
```

You can also experiment with upward scrolling. Enter the desired statement in the top text field and leave the text cursor in the field. Manually scroll to the bottom of the page and then press Enter to activate the command.

Event Handlers

onAfterPrint
onBeforePrint

See the `onAfterPrint` event handler for the `window` object, Chapter 16 of the *JavaScript Bible*.

onScroll

	NN2	NN3	NN4	NN6	IE3/J1	IE3/J2	IE4	IE5	IE5.5
Compatibility							✓	✓	✓

Example

Listing 18-21 is a highly artificial demonstration of what can be a useful tool for some page designs. Consider a document that occupies a window or frame, but one that you don't want scrolled, even by accident with one of the newer mouse wheels that are popular with Wintel PCs. If scrolling of the content would destroy the appearance or value of the content, then you want to make sure that the page always zips back to the top. The onScroll event handler in Listing 18-21 does just that. Notice that the event handler is set as a property of the document.body object after the page has loaded. While the event handler can also be set as an attribute of the <BODY> tag, to assign it as a property requires the page to load first. Until then, the document.body object does not yet officially exist in the object model for this page.

Listing 18-21: **Forcing Scrolling to Stay at the Page Top**

```
<HTML>
<HEAD>
<TITLE>onScroll Event Handler</TITLE>
<SCRIPT LANGUAGE="JavaScript">
function zipBack() {
    window.scroll(0,0)
}
function init() {
    document.body.onscroll = zipBack
}
</SCRIPT>
</HEAD>

<BODY onLoad="init()">
<H1>onScroll Event Handler</H1>
<HR>
This page always zips back to the top if you try to scroll it.
<P>
<IFRAME FRAMEBORDER=0 SCROLLING="no" HEIGHT=1000 SRC="bofright.htm"></IFRAME>
</P>
</BODY>
</HTML>
```

✦　　✦　　✦

Body Text Objects (Chapter 19)

The subject of body text objects encompasses both HTML element objects and several abstract DOM objects that make it easier for scripts to manipulate text-oriented body content that may not be contained within its own element tag. While the HTML element objects are easy to grasp, the abstract objects that work with stretches of visible body text have their own vocabularies and peculiarities.

Many HTML element objects in this category may become obsolete when the installed base of browsers capable of supporting Cascading Style Sheets reaches critical mass. CSS adherents would much rather use style sheets for font specifications in place of the old-fashioned <FONT> tag. But other elements in this group, such as the header elements (H1, H2, and so on), provide context for content that scripts may find useful for tasks such as creating a table of contents on the fly.

More intriguing is the concept of a text range, which is essentially an object that represents an arbitrary series of text characters within a document. A text ranges can work within an element (or text node) or extend beyond element borders, just as if a user selected a bunch of text that includes portions of what are HTML elements behind the scenes.

Unfortunately for scripters, the vocabulary for text range manipulation is very different for the IE4+/Windows and W3C object models. Moreover, the two objects do not always share the same functionality, making it even more difficult to program cross-browser implementations using text ranges. Be alert to the compatibility ratings for each example before trying out a listing or step-by-step sequence.

Examples Highlights

✦ Many site visitors (this author included) frown on the application of the scrolling MARQUEE element because it tends to distract visitors, rather than convey meaningful information. But if you insist on using it, Listing 19-3 demonstrates how scripts can control numerous behaviors.

✦ Listing 19-4 lets you examine how the NN6 (W3C DOM) `Range` object treats boundary points within the node hierarchy of a document.

✦ To insert a node into an arbitrary point within another, see Listing 19-5's application of the `Range.insertNode()` method.

✦ Walk through the steps for `Range.selectNode()` method to see how to set a range to encompass an entire node or its contents.

✦ Run Listing 19-8 to see how NN6 (W3C DOM) provides additional facilities for manipulating text content within a node. The listing also demonstrates `try-catch` error handling.

✦ Listing 19-10 shows the IE4+/Windows `TextRange` object's way of comparing range boundaries (the IE version of Listing 19-4).

✦ The `TextRange` object provides practical text search facilities, which are demonstrated in Listing 19-11. In the process, several `TextRange` properties and methods get a workout, including the use of bookmarks within a range. A simple undo buffer adds to the user friendliness of the application.

FONT Element Object

Properties

`color`

	NN2	NN3	NN4	NN6	IE3/J1	IE3/J2	IE4	IE5	IE5.5
Compatibility				✓			✓	✓	✓

Example

Listing 19-1 contains a page that demonstrates changes to the three FONT element object properties: `color`, `face`, and `size`. Along the way, you can see an economical use of the `setAttribute()` method to do the work for all of the property changes. This page loads successfully in all browsers, but the `SELECT` lists make changes to the text only in IE4+ and NN6+.

A P element contains a nested FONT element that encompasses three words whose appearance is controlled by three select lists. Each list controls one of the three FONT object properties, and their NAME attributes are strategically assigned the names of the properties (as you see in a moment). VALUE attributes for OPTION elements contain strings that are to be assigned to the various properties. Each SELECT element invokes the same setFontAttr() function, passing a reference to itself so that the function can inspect details of the element.

The first task of the setFontAttr() function is to make sure that only browsers capable of treating the FONT element as an object get to the meat of the function. The test for the existence of document.all and the myFONT element blocks all older browsers from changing the font characteristics. As the page loads, the document.all property is set for NN6 by using a variation of the normalization technique described in Chapter 14 of the *JavaScript Bible*.

For suitably equipped browsers, the function next extracts the string from the value property of the SELECT object that was passed to the function. If a selection is made (meaning other than the first, empty one), then the single nested statement uses the setAttribute() method to assign the value to the attribute whose name matches the name of the SELECT element.

Note An odd bug in IE5/Mac doesn't let the rendered color change when changing the color property. But the setting is valid, as proven by selecting any of the other two property choices.

Listing 19-1: Controlling FONT Object Properties

```
<HTML>
<HEAD>
<TITLE>FONT Object Properties</TITLE>
<SCRIPT LANGUAGE="JavaScript">
// document.all normalization trick for NN6
if (navigator.appName == "Netscape" && parseInt(navigator.appVersion) >= 5) {
    document.all = document.getElementsByTagName("*")
}

// one function does all!
function setFontAttr(select) {
    if (document.all && document.all.myFONT) {
        var choice = select.options[select.selectedIndex].value
        if (choice) {
            document.all.myFONT.setAttribute(select.name, choice)
        }
    }
}
</SCRIPT>
</HEAD>

<BODY>
<H1>Font Object Properties</H1>
<BR>
```

Continued

Listing 19-1 *(continued)*

```
<P>This may look like a simple sentence, but
<FONT ID="myFONT">THESE THREE WORDS</FONT>
are contained by a FONT element.</P>

<FORM>
Select a text color:
<SELECT NAME="color" onChange="setFontAttr(this)">
    <OPTION></OPTION>
    <OPTION VALUE="red">Red</OPTION>
    <OPTION VALUE="green">Green</OPTION>
    <OPTION VALUE="blue">Blue</OPTION>
    <OPTION VALUE="#FA8072">Some Hex Triplet Value</OPTION>
</SELECT>
<BR>
Select a font face:
<SELECT NAME="face" onChange="setFontAttr(this)">
    <OPTION></OPTION>
    <OPTION VALUE="Helvetica">Helvetica</OPTION>
    <OPTION VALUE="Times">Times</OPTION>
    <OPTION VALUE="Comic Sans MS, sans-serif">Comic Sans MS, sans-serif</OPTION>
    <OPTION VALUE="Courier, monospace">Courier, monospace</OPTION>
    <OPTION VALUE="Zapf Dingbats, serif">Zapf Dingbats, serif</OPTION>
</SELECT>
<BR>
Select a font size:
<SELECT NAME="size" onChange="setFontAttr(this)">
    <OPTION></OPTION>
    <OPTION VALUE="3">3 (Default)</OPTION>
    <OPTION VALUE="+1">Increase Default by 1</OPTION>
    <OPTION VALUE="-1">Decrease Default by 1</OPTION>
    <OPTION VALUE="1">Smallest</OPTION>
    <OPTION VALUE="7">Biggest</OPTION>
</SELECT>
</BODY>
</HTML>
```

face

	NN2	NN3	NN4	NN6	IE3/J1	IE3/J2	IE4	IE5	IE5.5
Compatibility				✓			✓	✓	✓

Example

See Listing 19-1 for an example of values that can be used to set the `face` property of a FONT element object. While you will notice visible changes to most choices on the page, the font face selections may not change from one choice to another; this all depends on the fonts that are installed on your PC.

size

	NN2	NN3	NN4	NN6	IE3/J1	IE3/J2	IE4	IE5	IE5.5
Compatibility				✓			✓	✓	✓

Example

See Listing 19-1 for an example of values that can be used to set the `size` property of a FONT element object. Notice that incrementing or decrementing the `size` property is applied only to the size assigned to the `SIZE` attribute of the element (or the default, if none is specified) and not the current setting adjusted by script.

HR Element Object

Properties

align

	NN2	NN3	NN4	NN6	IE3/J1	IE3/J2	IE4	IE5	IE5.5
Compatibility				✓			✓	✓	✓

Example

Listing 19-2 contains a page that demonstrates the changes to the five HR element object properties: `align`, `color`, `noShade`, `size`, and `width`. Along the way, you can see an economical use of the `setAttribute()` method to do the work for all of the property changes. This page loads successfully in all browsers, but the SELECT lists make changes to the text only in IE4+ and NN6+ (because they treat the element as an object).

An HR element (whose ID is `myHR`) is displayed with the browser default settings (100% width, centered, and its "magic" color). Each list controls one of the five HR object properties, and their `NAME` attributes are strategically assigned the names of the properties (as you see in a moment). `VALUE` attributes for OPTION elements contain strings that are to be assigned to the various properties. Each SELECT element invokes the same `setHRAttr()` function, passing a reference to itself so that the function can inspect details of the element. Figure 5-1 shows the page after several choices have modified the HR element.

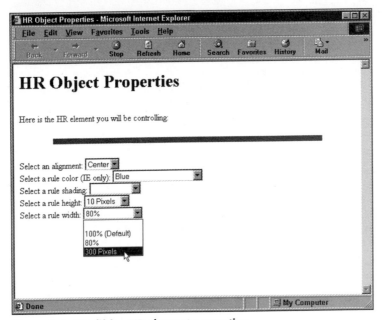

Figure 5-1: Modifying HR element properties

The first task of the `setHRAttr()` function is to make sure that only browsers capable of treating the HR element as an object get to the meat of the function. As the page loads, the `document.all` property is set for NN6 using a normalization technique described in Chapter 14 of the *JavaScript Bible*.

For suitably equipped browsers, the function next reads the string from the `value` property of the SELECT object that is passed to the function. If a selection is made (that is, other than the first, empty one), then the single, nested statement uses the `setAttribute()` method to assign the value to the attribute whose name matches the name of the SELECT element.

Listing 19-2: **Controlling HR Object Properties**

```
<HTML>
<HEAD>
<TITLE>HR Object Properties</TITLE>
<SCRIPT LANGUAGE="JavaScript">
// document.all normalization trick for NN6
if (navigator.appName == "Netscape" && parseInt(navigator.appVersion) >= 5) {
   document.all = document.getElementsByTagName("*")
}

// one function does all!
function setHRAttr(select) {
```

```
        if (document.all && document.all.myHR) {
            var choice = select.options[select.selectedIndex].value
            if (choice) {
                document.all.myHR.setAttribute(select.name, choice)
            }
        }
    }
}
</SCRIPT>
</HEAD>

<BODY>
<H1>HR Object Properties</H1>
<BR>
<P>Here is the HR element you will be controlling:</P>
<HR ID="myHR">
<FORM>
Select an alignment:
<SELECT NAME="align" onChange="setHRAttr(this)">
    <OPTION></OPTION>
    <OPTION VALUE="left">Left</OPTION>
    <OPTION VALUE="center">Center</OPTION>
    <OPTION VALUE="right">Right</OPTION>
</SELECT>
<BR>
Select a rule color (IE only):
<SELECT NAME="color" onChange="setHRAttr(this)">
    <OPTION></OPTION>
    <OPTION VALUE="red">Red</OPTION>
    <OPTION VALUE="green">Green</OPTION>
    <OPTION VALUE="blue">Blue</OPTION>
    <OPTION VALUE="#FA8072">Some Hex Triplet Value</OPTION>
</SELECT>
<BR>
Select a rule shading:
<SELECT NAME="noShade" onChange="setHRAttr(this)">
    <OPTION></OPTION>
    <OPTION VALUE=true>No Shading</OPTION>
    <OPTION VALUE=false>Shading</OPTION>
</SELECT>
<BR>
Select a rule height:
<SELECT NAME="size" onChange="setHRAttr(this)">
    <OPTION></OPTION>
    <OPTION VALUE=2>2 (Default)</OPTION>
    <OPTION VALUE=4>4 Pixels</OPTION>
    <OPTION VALUE=10>10 Pixels</OPTION>
</SELECT>
<BR>
Select a rule width:
<SELECT NAME="width" onChange="setHRAttr(this)">
    <OPTION></OPTION>
    <OPTION VALUE="100%">100% (Default)</OPTION>
```

Continued

HR.align

Listing 19-2 *(continued)*

```
    <OPTION VALUE="80%">80%</OPTION>
    <OPTION VALUE=300>300 Pixels </OPTION>
</SELECT>
</BODY>
</HTML>
```

color

	NN2	NN3	NN4	NN6	IE3/J1	IE3/J2	IE4	IE5	IE5.5
Compatibility				✓			✓	✓	✓

Example

See Listing 19-2 earlier in this chapter for an example of values that can be used to set the color property of an HR element object.

noShade

	NN2	NN3	NN4	NN6	IE3/J1	IE3/J2	IE4	IE5	IE5.5
Compatibility				✓			✓	✓	✓

Example

See Listing 19-2 earlier in this chapter for an example of values that can be used to set the noShade property of an HR element object. Because of the buggy behavior associated with setting this property, adjusting the property in the example has unexpected (and usually undesirable) consequences.

size

	NN2	NN3	NN4	NN6	IE3/J1	IE3/J2	IE4	IE5	IE5.5
Compatibility				✓			✓	✓	✓

Example

See Listing 19-2 earlier in this chapter for an example of values that can be used to set the size property of an HR element object.

`width`

	NN2	NN3	NN4	NN6	IE3/J1	IE3/J2	IE4	IE5	IE5.5
Compatibility				✓			✓	✓	✓

Example

See Listing 19-2 earlier in this chapter for an example of values that can be used to set the `width` property of an HR element object.

MARQUEE Element Object

Properties

`behavior`

	NN2	NN3	NN4	NN6	IE3/J1	IE3/J2	IE4	IE5	IE5.5
Compatibility							✓	✓	✓

Example

Listing 19-3 contains a page that demonstrates the changes to several MARQUEE element object properties: `behavior`, `bgColor`, `direction`, `scrollAmount`, and `scrollDelay`. This page and scripts are intended only for IE4+. See the description of Listing 19-1 for details on the attribute setting script.

Listing 19-3: **Controlling MARQUEE Object Properties**

```
<HTML>
<HEAD>
<TITLE>MARQUEE Object Properties</TITLE>
<SCRIPT LANGUAGE="JavaScript">
// one function does all!
function setMARQUEEAttr(select) {
    if (document.all && document.all.myMARQUEE) {
        var choice = select.options[select.selectedIndex].value
        if (choice) {
            document.all.myMARQUEE.setAttribute(select.name, choice)
        }
    }
}
```

Continued

Listing 19-3 *(continued)*

```
</SCRIPT>
</HEAD>

<BODY>
<H1>MARQUEE Object Properties</H1>
<BR>
<HR>
<MARQUEE ID="myMARQUEE" WIDTH=400 HEIGHT=24>This is the MARQUEE element object
you will be controlling.</MARQUEE>
<FORM>
<INPUT TYPE="button" VALUE="Start Marquee"
onClick="document.all.myMARQUEE.start()">
<INPUT TYPE="button" VALUE="Stop Marquee"
onClick="document.all.myMARQUEE.stop()">
<BR>
Select a behavior:
<SELECT NAME="behavior" onChange="setMARQUEEAttr(this)">
    <OPTION></OPTION>
    <OPTION VALUE="alternate">Alternate</OPTION>
    <OPTION VALUE="scroll">Scroll</OPTION>
    <OPTION VALUE="slide">Slide</OPTION>
</SELECT>
<BR>
Select a background color:
<SELECT NAME="bgColor" onChange="setMARQUEEAttr(this)">
    <OPTION></OPTION>
    <OPTION VALUE="red">Red</OPTION>
    <OPTION VALUE="green">Green</OPTION>
    <OPTION VALUE="blue">Blue</OPTION>
    <OPTION VALUE="#FA8072">Some Hex Triplet Value</OPTION>
</SELECT>
<BR>
Select a scrolling direction:
<SELECT NAME="direction" onChange="setMARQUEEAttr(this)">
    <OPTION></OPTION>
    <OPTION VALUE="left">Left</OPTION>
    <OPTION VALUE="right">Right</OPTION>
    <OPTION VALUE="up">Up</OPTION>
    <OPTION VALUE="down">Down</OPTION>
</SELECT>
<BR>
Select a scroll amount:
<SELECT NAME="scrollAmount" onChange="setMARQUEEAttr(this)">
    <OPTION></OPTION>
    <OPTION VALUE=4>4</OPTION>
    <OPTION VALUE=6>6 (Default)</OPTION>
    <OPTION VALUE=10>10</OPTION>
</SELECT>
<BR>
Select a scroll delay:
```

```
<SELECT NAME="scrollDelay" onChange="setMARQUEEAttr(this)">
    <OPTION></OPTION>
    <OPTION VALUE=50>Short</OPTION>
    <OPTION VALUE=85>Normal</OPTION>
    <OPTION VALUE=125>Long</OPTION>
</SELECT>
</BODY>
</HTML>
```

bgColor

	NN2	NN3	NN4	NN6	IE3/J1	IE3/J2	IE4	IE5	IE5.5
Compatibility							✓	✓	✓

Example

See Listing 19-3 earlier in this chapter for an example of how to apply values to the bgColor property.

direction

	NN2	NN3	NN4	NN6	IE3/J1	IE3/J2	IE4	IE5	IE5.5
Compatibility							✓	✓	✓

Example

See Listing 19-3 earlier in this chapter for an example of how to apply values to the direction property.

scrollAmount
scrollDelay

	NN2	NN3	NN4	NN6	IE3/J1	IE3/J2	IE4	IE5	IE5.5
Compatibility							✓	✓	✓

Example

See Listing 19-3 earlier in this chapter for an example of how to apply values to the scrollAmount and scrollDelay properties.

Methods

```
start()
stop()
```

	NN2	NN3	NN4	NN6	IE3/J1	IE3/J2	IE4	IE5	IE5.5
Compatibility							✓	✓	✓

Example

See Listing 19-3 earlier in this chapter for examples of both the `start()` and `stop()` methods, which are invoked in event handlers of separate controlling buttons on the page. Notice, too, that when you have the behavior set to `slide`, stopping and restarting the MARQUEE does not cause the scroll action to start from a blank region.

Range Object

Properties

```
collapsed
```

	NN2	NN3	NN4	NN6	IE3/J1	IE3/J2	IE4	IE5	IE5.5
Compatibility				✓					

Example

Use The Evaluator (Chapter 13 in the *JavaScript Bible*) to experiment with the `collapsed` property. Reload the page and assign a new range to the a global variable by typing the following statement into the top text box:

```
a = document.createRange()
```

Next, set the range to encompass a node:

```
a.selectNode(document.body)
```

Enter `a.collapsed` into the top text box . The expression returns `false` because the end points of the range are not the same.

commonAncestorContainer

	NN2	NN3	NN4	NN6	IE3/J1	IE3/J2	IE4	IE5	IE5.5
Compatibility				✓					

Example

Use The Evaluator (Chapter 13 in the *JavaScript Bible*) to experiment with the commonAncestorContainer property. Reload the page and assign a new range to the a global variable by typing the following statement into the top text box:

```
a = document.createRange()
```

Now set the start point to the beginning of the contents of the myEM element and set the end point to the end of the surrounding myP element:

```
a.setStartBefore(document.getElementById("myEM").firstChild)
a.setEndAfter(document.getElementById("myP").lastChild)
```

Verify that the text range is set to encompass content from the myEM node (the word "all") and end of myP nodes:

```
a.toString()
```

Verify, too, that the two end point containers are different nodes:

```
a.startContainer.tagName
a.endContainer.tagName
```

Finally, see what node contains both of these two end points:

```
a.commonAncestorContainer.id
```

The result is the myP element, which both the myP and myEM nodes have in common.

endContainer
startContainer

	NN2	NN3	NN4	NN6	IE3/J1	IE3/J2	IE4	IE5	IE5.5
Compatibility				✓					

Example

Use The Evaluator (Chapter 13 in the *JavaScript Bible*) to experiment with the endContainer and startContainer properties. Reload the page and assign a new range to the a global variable by typing the following statement into the top text box:

```
a = document.createRange()
```

Now set the range to encompass the myEM element:

```
a.selectNode(document.getElementById("myEM")
```

Inspect the containers for both the start and end points of the selection:

```
a.startContainer.id
a.endContainer.id
```

The range encompasses the entire myEM element, so the start and end points are outside of the element. Therefore, the container of both start and end points is the myP element that also surrounds the myEM element.

endOffset
startOffset

	NN2	NN3	NN4	NN6	IE3/J1	IE3/J2	IE4	IE5	IE5.5
Compatibility				✓					

Example

Use The Evaluator (Chapter 13 in the *JavaScript Bible*) to experiment with the endOffset and startOffset properties, following similar paths you just saw in the description. Reload the page and assign a new range to the a global variable by typing the following statement into the top text box:

```
a = document.createRange()
```

Now set the range to encompass the myEM element and then move the start point outward to a character within the myP element's text node:

```
a.selectNode(document.getElementById("myEM"))
a.setStart(document.getElementById("myP").firstChild, 7)
```

Inspect the node types of the containers for both the start and end points of the selection:

```
a.startContainer.nodeType
a.endContainer.nodeType
```

The startContainer node type is 3 (text node), while the endContainer node type is 1 (element). Now inspect the offsets for both the start and end points of the selection:

```
a.startOffset
a.endOffset
```

Methods

cloneContents()
cloneRange()

	NN2	NN3	NN4	NN6	IE3/J1	IE3/J2	IE4	IE5	IE5.5
Compatibility				✓					

Example

When Netscape outfits the NN6 browser with the cloneContents() method, use The Evaluator (Chapter 13 in the *JavaScript Bible*) to see the method in action. Begin by creating a new range object that contains the text of the myP paragraph element.

```
a = document.createRange()
a.selectNode(document.getElementById("myP")
```

Next, clone the original range and preserve the copy in variable b:

```
b = a.cloneContents()
```

Move the original range so that it is an insertion point at the end of the body by first expanding it to encompass the entire body and then collapse it to the end

```
a.selectNode(document.body)
a.collapse(false)
```

Now, insert the copy at the very end of the body:

```
a.insertNode(b)
```

If you scroll to the bottom of the page, you see a copy of the text.

See the description of the compareBoundaryPoints() method later in this chapter to see an example of the cloneRange() method.

collapse([startBoolean])

	NN2	NN3	NN4	NN6	IE3/J1	IE3/J2	IE4	IE5	IE5.5
Compatibility				✓					

Example

See Listings 19-11 (in this chapter) and 15-14 (in Chapter 1 of this book) to see the collapse() method at work (albeit with the IE TextRange object).

compareBoundaryPoints(*typeInteger, sourceRangeRef*)

	NN2	NN3	NN4	NN6	IE3/J1	IE3/J2	IE4	IE5	IE5.5
Compatibility				✓					

Example

The page rendered by Listing 19-4 lets you experiment with text range comparisons in NN6+. The bottom paragraph contains a SPAN element that has a `Range` object assigned to its nested text node after the page loads (in the `init()` function). That fixed range becomes a solid reference point for you to use while you select text in the paragraph.

Note Unfortunately, the `window` object method that converts a user selection into an object is not connected correctly in the first release of NN6. Even if it were, the inverted values returned by the `compareBoundaryPoints()` method would give you incorrect results. Try this example on subsequent versions of NN6.

After you make a selection, all four versions of the `compareBoundaryPoints()` method run to compare the start and end points of the fixed range against your selection. One column of the results table shows the raw value returned by the `compareBoundaryPoints()` method, while the third column puts the results into plain language.

To see how this page works, begin by selecting the first word of the fixed text range (carefully drag the selection from the first red character). You can see that the starting positions of both ranges are the same, because the returned value is 0. Because all of the invocations of the `compareBoundaryPoints()` method are on the fixed text range, all comparisons are from the point of view of that range. Thus, the first row of the table for the `START_TO_END` parameter indicates that the start point of the fixed range comes before the end point of the selection, yielding a return value of -1.

Other selections to make include:

✦ Text that starts before the fixed range and ends inside the range

✦ Text that starts inside the fixed range and ends beyond the range

✦ Text that starts and ends precisely at the fixed range boundaries

✦ Text that starts and ends before the fixed range

✦ Text that starts after the fixed range

Study the returned values and the plain language results and see how they align with the selection you made.

Listing 19-4: **Lab for NN6 compareBoundaryPoints() Method**

```
<HTML>
<HEAD>
<TITLE>TextRange.compareBoundaryPoints() Method</TITLE>
<STYLE TYPE="text/css">
TD {text-align:center}
.propName {font-family:Courier, monospace}
#fixedRangeElem {color:red; font-weight:bold}
</STYLE>
<SCRIPT LANGUAGE="JavaScript">
var fixedRange

function setAndShowRangeData() {
    try {
        var selectedRange = window.getSelection()
        selectedRange = selectedRange.getRangeAt(0)
        var result1 = fixedRange.compareBoundaryPoints(Range.START_TO_END,
            selectedRange)
        var result2 = fixedRange.compareBoundaryPoints(Range.START_TO_START,
            selectedRange)
        var result3 = fixedRange.compareBoundaryPoints(Range.END_TO_START,
            selectedRange)
        var result4 = fixedRange.compareBoundaryPoints(Range.END_TO_END,
            selectedRange)

        document.getElementById("B1").innerHTML = result1
        document.getElementById("compare1").innerHTML = getDescription(result1)
        document.getElementById("B2").innerHTML = result2
        document.getElementById("compare2").innerHTML = getDescription(result2)
        document.getElementById("B3").innerHTML = result3
        document.getElementById("compare3").innerHTML = getDescription(result3)
        document.getElementById("B4").innerHTML = result4
        document.getElementById("compare4").innerHTML = getDescription(result4)
    }
    catch(err) {
        alert("Vital Range object services are not yet implemented in this
browser.")
    }
}

function getDescription(comparisonValue) {
    switch (comparisonValue) {
        case -1 :
            return "comes before"
            break
        case 0 :
            return "is the same as"
            break
        case 1 :
```

Continued

Listing 19-4 *(continued)*

```
                return "comes after"
                break
        default :
                return "vs."
    }
}

function init() {
    fixedRange = document.createRange()
    fixedRange.selectNodeContents(document.getElementById("fixedRangeElem").
firstChild)
    fixedRange.setEnd(fixedRange.endContainer,
fixedRange.endContainer.nodeValue.length)
}
</SCRIPT>
</HEAD>

<BODY onLoad="init()">
<H1>TextRange.compareBoundaryPoints() Method</H1>
<HR>
<P>Select text in the paragraph in various places relative to
the fixed text range (shown in red). See the relations between
the fixed and selected ranges with respect to their start
and end points.</P>
<TABLE ID="results" BORDER=1 CELLSPACING=2 CELLPADDING=2>
<TR><TH>Property</TH><TH>Returned Value</TH><TH>Fixed Range vs. Selection</TR>
<TR>
    <TD CLASS="propName">StartToEnd</TD>
    <TD CLASS="count" ID="B1"> </TD>
    <TD CLASS="count" ID="C1">Start of Fixed <SPAN ID="compare1">vs.</SPAN>
    End of Selection</TD>
</TR>
<TR>
    <TD CLASS="propName">StartToStart</TD>
    <TD CLASS="count" ID="B2"> </TD>
    <TD CLASS="count" ID="C2">Start of Fixed <SPAN ID="compare2">vs.</SPAN>
    Start of Selection</TD>
</TR>
<TR>
    <TD CLASS="propName">EndToStart</TD>
    <TD CLASS="count" ID="B3"> </TD>
    <TD CLASS="count" ID="C3">End of Fixed <SPAN ID="compare3">vs.</SPAN>
    Start of Selection</TD>
</TR>
<TR>
    <TD CLASS="propName">EndToEnd</TD>
    <TD CLASS="count" ID="B4"> </TD>
    <TD CLASS="count" ID="C4">End of Fixed <SPAN ID="compare4">vs.</SPAN>
    End of Selection</TD>
</TR>
```

```
</TABLE>
<HR>
<P onMouseUp="setAndShowRangeData()">
Lorem ipsum dolor sit, <SPAN ID="fixedRangeElem">consectetaur adipisicing
elit</SPAN>,
sed do eiusmod tempor incididunt ut labore et dolore aliqua. Ut enim adminim
veniam,
quis nostrud exercitation ullamco laboris nisi ut aliquip ex ea commodo
consequat.</P>
</BODY>
</HTML>
```

createContextualFragment("*text*")

	NN2	NN3	NN4	NN6	IE3/J1	IE3/J2	IE4	IE5	IE5.5
Compatibility				✓					

Example

Use The Evaluator (Chapter 13 in the *JavaScript Bible*) to create a document fragment and replace an existing document tree node with the fragment. Begin by creating the range and fragment:

```
a = document.createRange()
a.selectNode(document.body)
b = a.createContextualFragment("<SPAN STYLE='font-size:22pt'>a bunch of
</SPAN>")
```

This fragment consists of a SPAN element node with a text node nested inside. At this point, you can inspect the properties of the document fragment by entering b into the bottom text box.

To replace the myEM element on the page with this new fragment, use the replaceChild() method on the enclosing myP element:

```
document.getElementById("myP").replaceChild(b, document.getElementById("myEM"))
```

The fragment now becomes a legitimate child node of the myP element and can be referenced like any node in the document tree. For example, if you enter the following statement into the top text box of The Evaluator, you can retrieve a copy of the text node inside the new SPAN element:

```
document.getElementById("myP").childNodes[1].firstChild.nodeValue
```

deleteContents()

	NN2	NN3	NN4	NN6	IE3/J1	IE3/J2	IE4	IE5	IE5.5
Compatibility				✓					

Example

Use The Evaluator (Chapter 13 in the *JavaScript Bible*) to experiment with deleting contents of both a text node and a complete element node. Begin by creating a text range for the text node inside the myEM element (enter the third statement, which wraps below, as one continuous expression):

```
a = document.createRange()
a.setStart(document.getElementById("myEM").firstChild, 0)
a.setEnd(document.getElementById("myEM").lastChild,
    document.getElementById("myEM").lastChild.length)
```

Verify the makeup of the range by entering a into the bottom text box and inspect its properties. Both containers are text nodes (they happen to be the same text node), and offsets are measured by character positions.

Now, delete the contents of the range:

```
a.deleteContents()
```

The italicized word "all" is gone from the tree, but the myEM element is still there. To prove it, put some new text inside the element:

```
document.getElementById("myEM").innerHTML = "a band of "
```

The italic style of the EM element applies to the text, as it should.

Next, adjust the range boundaries to include the myEM element tags, as well:

```
a.selectNode(document.getElementById("myEM"))
```

Inspect the Range object's properties again by entering a into the bottom text box. The container nodes are the P element that surrounds the EM element; the offset values are measured in nodes. Delete the range's contents:

```
a.deleteContents()
```

Not only is the italicized text gone, but the myEM element is gone, too. The myP element now has but one child node, the text node inside. The following entries into the top text box of The Evaluator verify this fact:

```
document.getElementById("myP").childNodes.length
document.getElementById("myP").childNodes[0].nodeValue
```

If you try this example in early versions of NN6, however, you see that the deleteContents() method also removes the text node following the myEM element. This is buggy behavior, demonstrating that the method works best on text nodes, rather than elements.

extractContents()

	NN2	NN3	NN4	NN6	IE3/J1	IE3/J2	IE4	IE5	IE5.5
Compatibility				✓					

Example

When Netscape outfits the NN6 browser with the extractContents() method, use The Evaluator (Chapter 13 in the *JavaScript Bible*) to see how the method works. Begin by creating a new range object that contains the text of the myP paragraph element.

```
a = document.createRange()
a.selectNode(document.getElementById("myP"))
```

Next, extract the original range's content and preserve the copy in variable b:

```
b = a.extractContents()
```

Move the original range so that it is an insertion point at the end of the body by first expanding it to encompass the entire body and then collapse it to the end

```
a.selectNode(document.body)
a.collapse(false)
```

Now, insert the extracted fragment at the very end of the body:

```
a.insertNode(b)
```

If you scroll to the bottom of the page, you see a copy of the text.

insertNode(*nodeReference*)

	NN2	NN3	NN4	NN6	IE3/J1	IE3/J2	IE4	IE5	IE5.5
Compatibility				✓					

Example

Listing 19-5, which relies on selection and Range object features not implemented in the first release of NN6, demonstrates the insertNode() method plus some additional items from the NN6 selection object. The example even includes a rudimentary undo buffer for scripted changes to a text range. In the page generated by this listing, users can select any text in a paragraph and have the script automatically convert the text to all uppercase characters. The task of replacing a selection with other text requires several steps, starting with the selection, which is retrieved via the window.getSelection() method. After making sure the selection contains some text (that is, the selection isn't collapsed), the selection is preserved as a range object so that the starting text can be stored in a global variable (as a property of the `undoBuffer` global variable object). After that, the selection is deleted from the document tree, leaving the selection as a collapsed insertion point. A copy of that selection in the form of a range object is preserved in the `undoBuffer` object so that the undo script knows where to reinsert the original text. A new text node is created with an uppercase version of the original text, and, finally, the `insertNode()` method is invoked to stick the converted text into the collapsed range.

Undoing this operation works in reverse. Original locations and strings are copied from the `undoBuffer` object. After creating the range with the old start and end points (which represent a collapsed insertion point), the resurrected text (converted to a text node) is inserted into the collapsed range. For good housekeeping, the `undoBuffer` object is restored to its unused form.

Listing 19-5: **Inserting a Node into a Range**

```
<HTML>
<HEAD>
<TITLE>NN Selection Object Replacement</TITLE>
<SCRIPT LANGUAGE="JavaScript">
var undoBuffer = {rng:null, txt:""}
function convertSelection() {
    var sel, grossRng, netRng, newText
    try {
        sel = window.getSelection()
        if (!sel.isCollapsed) {
            grossRng = sel.getRangeAt(0)
            undoBuffer.txt = grossRng.toString()
            sel.deleteFromDocument()
            netRng = sel.getRangeAt(0)
            undoBuffer.rng = netRng
            newText = document.createTextNode(undoBuffer.txt.toUpperCase())
            netRng.insertNode(newText)
        }
    }
    catch(err) {
        alert("Vital Range object services are not yet implemented in this
browser.")
    }
}
function undoConversion() {
    var rng, oldText
    if (undoBuffer.rng) {
        rng = document.createRange()
        rng.setStart(undoBuffer.rng.startParent, undoBuffer.rng.startOffset)
        rng.setEnd(undoBuffer.rng.endParent, undoBuffer.rng.endOffset)
        oldText = document.createTextNode(undoBuffer.txt)
        rng.insertNode(oldText)
        undoBuffer.rng = null
        undoBuffer.txt = ""
    }
}
```

```
</SCRIPT>
</HEAD>
<BODY>
<H1 ID="H1_1">NN6 Selection Object Replacement</H1>
<HR>
<P ID="P_1" onMouseUp="convertSelection()">This paragraph
contains text that you can select. Selections are deleted and
replaced by all uppercase versions of the selected text.</P>
<BUTTON onClick="undoConversion()">Undo Last</BUTTON>
<BUTTON onClick="location.reload(true)">Start Over</BUTTON>
</BODY>
</HTML>
```

isValidFragment("*HTMLText*")

	NN2	NN3	NN4	NN6	IE3/J1	IE3/J2	IE4	IE5	IE5.5
Compatibility				✓					

Example

You can try the validity of any strings that you like in The Evaluator (Chapter 13 in the *JavaScript Bible*). You will discover, however, that the object model can make a document fragment out of just about any string. For instance, if you attempt to create a document fragment out of some random text and an end tag, the document fragment will consist of a text node and an element node of the type indicated by the end tag.

selectNode(*nodeReference*)
selectNodeContents(*nodeReference*)

	NN2	NN3	NN4	NN6	IE3/J1	IE3/J2	IE4	IE5	IE5.5
Compatibility				✓					

Example

Use The Evaluator (Chapter 13 in the *JavaScript Bible*) to see the behavior of both the selectNode() and selectNodeContents() methods work. Begin by creating a new range object.

```
a = document.createRange()
```

Set the range boundaries to include the myP element node:

```
a.selectNode(document.getElementById("myP"))
```

Enter a into the bottom text box to view the properties of the range. Notice that because the range has selected the entire paragraph node, the container of the range's start and end points is the BODY element of the page (the parent element of the myP element).

Now change the range so that it encompasses only the contents of the myP element:

```
a.selectNodeContents(document.getElementById("myP"))
```

Click the List Properties button to view the current properties of the range. The container of the range's boundary points is the P element that holds the element's contents.

setEnd(*nodeReference, offset*)
setStart(*nodeReference, offset*)

	NN2	NN3	NN4	NN6	IE3/J1	IE3/J2	IE4	IE5	IE5.5
Compatibility				✓					

Example

Use The Evaluator (Chapter 13 in the *JavaScript Bible*) to experiment with both the setStart() and setEnd() methods. Begin by creating a new range object.

```
a = document.createRange()
```

For the first range, set the start and end points to encompass the second node (the myEM element) inside the myP element:

```
a.setStart(document.getElementById("myP"), 1)
a.setEnd(document.getElementById("myP"), 2)
```

The text encompassed by the range consists of the word "all" plus the trailing space that is contained by the myEM element. Prove this by entering the following statement into the top text box:

```
a.toString()
```

If you then click the Results box to the right of the word "all," you see that the results contain the trailing space. Yet, if you examine the properties of the range (enter a into the bottom text box), you see that the range is defined as actually starting before the myEM element and ending after it.

Next, adjust the start point of the range to a character position inside the first text node of the myP element:

```
a.setStart(document.getElementById("myP").firstChild, 11)
```

Click the List Properties button to see that the startContainer property of the range is the text node, and that the startOffset measures the character position. All end boundary properties, however, have not changed. Enter a.toString() in the top box again to see that the range now encompasses text from two of the nodes inside the myP element.

You can continue to experiment by setting the start and end points to other element and text nodes on the page. After each adjustment, verify the properties of the a range object and the text it encompasses (via `a.toString()`).

setEndAfter(*nodeReference*)
setEndBefore(*nodeReference*)
setStartAfter(*nodeReference*)
setStartBefore(*nodeReference*)

	NN2	NN3	NN4	NN6	IE3/J1	IE3/J2	IE4	IE5	IE5.5
Compatibility				✓					

Example

Use The Evaluator (Chapter 13 in the *JavaScript Bible*) to experiment with all four methods. Begin by creating a new range object.

```
a = document.createRange()
```

For the first range, set the start and end points to encompass the `myEM` element inside the `myP` element:

```
a.setStartBefore(document.getElementById("myEM"))
a.setEndAfter(document.getElementById("myEM"))
```

The text encompassed by the range consists of the word "all" plus the trailing space that is contained by the `myEM` element. Prove this by entering the following statement into the top text box:

```
a.toString()
```

Next, adjust the start point of the range to the beginning of the first text node of the `myP` element:

```
a.setStartBefore(document.getElementById("myP").firstChild)
```

Enter a into the bottom text box to see that the `startParent` property of the range is the P element node, while the `endParent` property points to the EM element.

You can continue to experiment by setting the start and end points to before and after other element and text nodes on the page. After each adjustment, verify the properties of the a range object and the text it encompasses (via `a.toString()`).

surroundContents(*nodeReference*)

	NN2	NN3	NN4	NN6	IE3/J1	IE3/J2	IE4	IE5	IE5.5
Compatibility				✓					

Example

Listing 19-6, which relies on `selection` and `Range` object features not implemented in the first release of NN6, demonstrates how the `surroundContents()` method wraps a range inside a new element. As the page loads, a global variable (`newSpan`) stores a SPAN element that is used as a prototype for elements to be used as new surrounding parent nodes. When you select text in either of the two paragraphs, the selection is converted to a range. The `surroundContents()` method then wraps the range with the `newSpan` element. Because that SPAN element has a class name of `hilite`, the element and its contents pick up the style sheet properties as defined for that class selector.

Listing 19-6: Using the Range.surroundContents() Method

```
<HTML>
<HEAD>
<TITLE>Range.surroundContents() Method</TITLE>
<STYLE TYPE="text/css">
.hilite {background-color:yellow; color:red; font-weight:bold}
</STYLE>
<SCRIPT LANGUAGE="JavaScript">
var newSpan = document.createElement("SPAN")
newSpan.className = "hilite"

function highlightSelection() {
    var sel, rng
    try {
        sel = window.getSelection()
        if (!sel.isCollapsed) {
            rng = sel.getRangeAt(0)
            rng.surroundContents(newSpan.cloneNode(false))
        }
    }
    catch(err) {
        alert("Vital Range object services are not yet implemented in this
browser.")
    }
}
</SCRIPT>
</HEAD>
<BODY>
<H1>Range.surroundContents() Method</H1>
<HR>
<P onMouseUp="highlightSelection()">These paragraphs
contain text that you can select. Selections are surrounded
by SPAN elements that share a stylesheet class selector
for special font and display characteristics.</P>

<P onMouseUp="highlightSelection()">Lorem ipsum dolor
sit amet, consectetaur adipisicing elit,
sed do eiusmod tempor incididunt ut labore et dolore magna
```

```
aliqua. Ut enim adminim veniam, quis nostrud exercitation
ullamco laboris nisi ut aliquip ex ea commodo consequat.</P>
</BODY>
</HTML>
```

toString()

	NN2	NN3	NN4	NN6	IE3/J1	IE3/J2	IE4	IE5	IE5.5
Compatibility				✓					

Example

Use The Evaluator (Chapter 13 in the *JavaScript Bible*) to see the results of the toString() method. Enter the following sequence of statements into the top text box:

```
a = document.createRange()
a.selectNode(document.getElementById("myP"))
a.toString()
```

If you type only a into the top text box, you see the text contents of the range, but don't be fooled. Internal workings of The Evaluator attempt to evaluate any expression entered into that text field. Assigning a range object to a text box forces an internal application of the toString() method (just as the Date object does when you create a new object instance in The Evaluator).

selection Object

Properties

type

	NN2	NN3	NN4	NN6	IE3/J1	IE3/J2	IE4	IE5	IE5.5
Compatibility							✓	✓	✓

Example

Listing 19-7 contains a page that demonstrates several features of the selection object. When you make a selection with the Deselect radio button selected, you see the value of the selection.type property (in the statusbar) before and after the selection is deselected. After the selection goes away, the type property returns None.

Listing 19-7: Using the document.selection Object

```
<HTML>
<HEAD>
<TITLE>selection Object</TITLE>
<SCRIPT LANGUAGE="JavaScript">
function processSelection() {
    if (document.choices.process[0].checked) {
        status = "Selection is type: " + document.selection.type
        setTimeout("emptySelection()", 2000)
    } else if (document.choices.process[1].checked) {
        var rng = document.selection.createRange()
        document.selection.clear()
    }
}
function emptySelection() {
    document.selection.empty()
    status = "Selection is type: " + document.selection.type
}
</SCRIPT>
</HEAD>
<BODY>
<H1>IE selection Object</H1>
<HR>
<FORM NAME="choices">
<INPUT TYPE="radio" NAME="process" CHECKED>De-select after two seconds<BR>
<INPUT TYPE="radio" NAME="process">Delete selected text.
</FORM>
<P onMouseUp="processSelection()">Lorem ipsum dolor sit amet, consectetaur
adipisicing elit, sed do eiusmod tempor incididunt ut labore et dolore magna
aliqua. Ut enim adminim veniam, quis nostrud exercitation ullamco laboris nisi
ut aliquip ex ea commodo consequat. Duis aute irure dolor in reprehenderit
involuptate velit esse cillum dolore eu fugiat nulla pariatur.
</BODY>
</HTML>
```

Methods

clear()

	NN2	NN3	NN4	NN6	IE3/J1	IE3/J2	IE4	IE5	IE5.5
Compatibility							✓	✓	✓

Example

See Listing 19-7 earlier in this chapter to see the `selection.clear()` method at work.

createRange()

	NN2	NN3	NN4	NN6	IE3/J1	IE3/J2	IE4	IE5	IE5.5
Compatibility							✓	✓	✓

Example

See Listings 15-36 and 15-45 to see the `selection.createRange()` method turn user selections into text ranges.

empty()

	NN2	NN3	NN4	NN6	IE3/J1	IE3/J2	IE4	IE5	IE5.5
Compatibility							✓	✓	✓

Example

See Listing 19-7 earlier in this chapter to view the `selection.empty()` method at work.

Text and TextNode Objects

Properties

data

	NN2	NN3	NN4	NN6	IE3/J1	IE3/J2	IE4	IE5	IE5.5
Compatibility				✓			✓	✓	✓

Example

In the example for the `nodeValue` property used in a text replacement script (in Chapter 1 of this book), you can substitute the `data` property for `nodeValue` to accomplish the same result.

Methods

```
appendData("text")
deleteData(offset, count)
insertData(offset, "text")
replaceData(offset, count, "text")
substringData(offset, count)
```

	NN2	NN3	NN4	NN6	IE3/J1	IE3/J2	IE4	IE5	IE5.5
Compatibility				✓					

Example

The page created by Listing 19-8 is a working laboratory that you can use to experiment with the five data-related methods in NN6+. The text node that invokes the methods is a simple sentence in a P element. Each method has its own clickable button, followed by two or three text boxes into which you enter values for method parameters. Don't be put off by the length of the listing. Each method's operation is confined to its own function and is fairly simple.

Each of the data-related methods throws exceptions of different kinds. To help handle these errors gracefully, the method calls are wrapped inside a try/catch construction. All caught exceptions are routed to the handleError() function where details of the error are inspected and friendly alert messages are displayed to the user. See Chapter 39 of the *JavaScript Bible* for details on the try/catch approach to error handling in W3C DOM-capable browsers.

Listing 19-8: **Text object Data Method Laboratory**

```
<HTML>
<HEAD>
<TITLE>Data Methods of a W3C Text Object</TITLE>
<SCRIPT LANGUAGE="JavaScript">
function doAppend(form) {
    var node = document.getElementById("myP").firstChild
    var newString = form.appendStr.value
    try {
        node.appendData(newString)
    }
    catch(err) {
        handleError(err)
    }
}
function doDelete(form) {
    var node = document.getElementById("myP").firstChild
    var offset = form.deleteOffset.value
```

```
        var count = form.deleteCount.value
        try {
            node.deleteData(offset, count)
        }
        catch(err) {
            handleError(err)
        }
    }
    function doInsert(form) {
        var node = document.getElementById("myP").firstChild
        var offset = form.insertOffset.value
        var newString = form.insertStr.value
        try {
            node.insertData(offset, newString)
        }
        catch(err) {
            handleError(err)
        }

    }

    function doReplace(form) {
        var node = document.getElementById("myP").firstChild
        var offset = form.replaceOffset.value
        var count = form.replaceCount.value
        var newString = form.replaceStr.value
        try {
            node.replaceData(offset, count, newString)
        }
        catch(err) {
            handleError(err)
        }
    }
    function showSubstring(form) {
        var node = document.getElementById("myP").firstChild
        var offset = form.substrOffset.value
        var count = form.substrCount.value
        try {
            alert(node.substringData(offset, count))
        }
        catch(err) {
            handleError(err)
        }
    }
    // error handler for these methods
    function handleError(err) {
        switch (err.name) {
            case "NS_ERROR_DOM_INDEX_SIZE_ERR":
                alert("The offset number is outside the allowable range.")
                break
            case "NS_ERROR_DOM_NOT_NUMBER_ERR":
                alert("Make sure each numeric entry is a valid number.")
```

Continued

Listing 19-8 *(continued)*

```
            break
        default:
            alert("Double-check your text box entries.")
    }
}
</SCRIPT>
</HEAD>
<BODY>
<H1>Data Methods of a W3C Text Object</H1>
<HR>
<P ID="myP" STYLE="font-weight:bold; text-align:center">
So I called myself Pip, and became to be called Pip.</P>
<FORM NAME="choices">
<P><INPUT TYPE="button" onClick="doAppend(this.form)" VALUE="appendData()">
String:<INPUT TYPE="text" NAME="appendStr" SIZE=30></P>

<P><INPUT TYPE="button" onClick="doDelete(this.form)" VALUE="deleteData()">
Offset:<INPUT TYPE="text" NAME="deleteOffset" SIZE=3>
Count:<INPUT TYPE="text" NAME="deleteCount" SIZE=3></P>

<P><INPUT TYPE="button" onClick="doInsert(this.form)" VALUE="insertData()">
Offset:<INPUT TYPE="text" NAME="insertOffset" SIZE=3>
String:<INPUT TYPE="text" NAME="insertStr" SIZE=30></P>

<P><INPUT TYPE="button" onClick="doReplace(this.form)" VALUE="replaceData()">
Offset:<INPUT TYPE="text" NAME="replaceOffset" SIZE=3>
Count:<INPUT TYPE="text" NAME="replaceCount" SIZE=3>
String:<INPUT TYPE="text" NAME="replaceStr" SIZE=30></P>

<P><INPUT TYPE="button" onClick="showSubstring(this.form)"
VALUE="substringData()">
Offset:<INPUT TYPE="text" NAME="substrOffset" SIZE=3>
Count:<INPUT TYPE="text" NAME="substrCount" SIZE=3></P>

</FORM>
</BODY>
</HTML>
```

splitText(*offset*)

	NN2	NN3	NN4	NN6	IE3/J1	IE3/J2	IE4	IE5	IE5.5
Compatibility				✓				✓	✓

Example

Use The Evaluator (Chapter 13 in the *JavaScript Bible*) to see the `splitText()` method in action. Begin by verifying that the `myEM` element has but one child node, and that its `nodeValue` is the string "all":

```
document.getElementById("myEM").childNodes.length
document.getElementById("myEM").firstChild.nodeValue
```

Next, split the text node into two pieces after the first character:

```
document.getElementById("myEM").firstChild.splitText(1)
```

Two text nodes are now inside the element:

```
document.getElementById("myEM").childNodes.length
```

Each text node contains its respective portion of the original text:

```
document.getElementById("myEM").firstChild.nodeValue
document.getElementById("myEM").lastChild.nodeValue
```

If you are using NN6, now bring the text nodes back together:

```
document.getElementById("myEM").normalize()
document.getElementById("myEM").childNodes.length
```

At no time during these statement executions does the rendered text change.

TextRange Object

Properties

```
boundingHeight
boundingLeft
boundingTop
boundingWidth
```

	NN2	NN3	NN4	NN6	IE3/J1	IE3/J2	IE4	IE5	IE5.5
Compatibility							✓	✓	✓

Example

Listing 19-9 provides a simple playground to explore the four bounding properties (and two offset properties) of a `TextRange` object. As you select text in the big paragraph, the values of all six properties are displayed in the table. Values are also updated if you resize the window via an `onResize` event handler.

Notice, for example, if you simply click in the paragraph without dragging a selection, the `boundingWidth` property shows up as zero. This action is the equivalent of a `TextRange` acting as an insertion point.

Listing 19-9: **Exploring the Bounding TextRange Properties**

```
<HTML>
<HEAD>
<TITLE>TextRange Object Dimension Properties</TITLE>
<STYLE TYPE="text/css">
TD {text-align:center}
.propName {font-family: Courier, monospace}
</STYLE>
<SCRIPT LANGUAGE="JavaScript">
function setAndShowRangeData() {
    var range = document.selection.createRange()
    B1.innerText = range.boundingHeight
    B2.innerText = range.boundingWidth
    B3.innerText = range.boundingTop
    B4.innerText = range.boundingLeft
    B5.innerText = range.offsetTop
    B6.innerText = range.offsetLeft
}
</SCRIPT>
</HEAD>

<BODY onResize="setAndShowRangeData()">
<H1>TextRange Object Dimension Properties</H1>
<HR>
<P>Select text in the paragraph below and observe the "bounding"
property values for the TextRange object created for that selection.</P>
<TABLE ID="results" BORDER=1 CELLSPACING=2 CELLPADDING=2>
<TR><TH>Property</TH><TH>Pixel Value</TH></TR>
<TR>
    <TD CLASS="propName">boundingHeight</TD>
    <TD CLASS="count" ID="B1"> </TD>
</TR>
<TR>
    <TD CLASS="propName">boundingWidth</TD>
    <TD CLASS="count" ID="B2"> </TD>
</TR>
<TR>
    <TD CLASS="propName">boundingTop</TD>
    <TD CLASS="count" ID="B3"> </TD>
</TR>
<TR>
    <TD CLASS="propName">boundingLeft</TD>
    <TD CLASS="count" ID="B4"> </TD>
</TR>
<TR>
    <TD CLASS="propName">offsetTop</TD>
    <TD CLASS="count" ID="B5"> </TD>
</TR>
<TR>
    <TD CLASS="propName">offsetLeft</TD>
    <TD CLASS="count" ID="B6"> </TD>
```

```
</TR>
</TABLE>
<HR>
<P onMouseUp="setAndShowRangeData()">
Lorem ipsum dolor sit amet, consectetaur adipisicing elit, sed do eiusmod
tempor incididunt ut labore et dolore magna aliqua. Ut enim adminim veniam,
quis nostrud exercitation ullamco laboris nisi ut aliquip ex ea commodo
consequat. Duis aute irure dolor in reprehenderit involuptate velit esse
cillum dolore eu fugiat nulla pariatur. Excepteur sint occaecat cupidatat
non proident, sunt in culpa qui officia deseruntmollit anim id est laborum
Et harumd und lookum like Greek to me, dereud facilis est er expedit.
</P>
</BODY>
</HTML>
```

htmlText

	NN2	NN3	NN4	NN6	IE3/J1	IE3/J2	IE4	IE5	IE5.5
Compatibility							✓	✓	✓

Example

Use The Evaluator (Chapter 13 in the *JavaScript Bible*) to investigate values returned by the `htmlText` property. Use the top text box to enter the following statements and see the values in the Results box.

Begin by creating a `TextRange` object for the entire body and store the range in local variable `a`:

```
a = document.body.createTextRange()
```

Next, use the `findText()` method to set the start and end points of the text range around the word "all," which is an EM element inside the `myP` paragraph:

```
a.findText("all")
```

The method returns `true` (see the `findText()` method) if the text is found and the text range adjusts to surround it. To prove that the text of the text range is what you think it is, examine the `text` property of the range:

```
a.text
```

Because the text range encompasses all of the text of the element, the `htmlText` property contains the tags for the element as well:

```
a.htmlText
```

If you want to experiment by finding other chunks of text and looking at both the `text` and `htmlText` properties, first restore the text range to encompass the entire body with the following statement:

```
a.expand("textEdit")
```

You can read about the `expand()` method later in this chapter. In other tests, use `findText()` to set the range to "for all" and just "for al." Then, see how the `htmlText` property exposes the EM element's tags.

text

	NN2	NN3	NN4	NN6	IE3/J1	IE3/J2	IE4	IE5	IE5.5
Compatibility							✓	✓	✓

Example

See Listing 19-11 later in this chapter for the `findText()` method to see the `text` property used to perform the replace action of a search-and-replace function.

Methods

collapse([*startBoolean*])

	NN2	NN3	NN4	NN6	IE3/J1	IE3/J2	IE4	IE5	IE5.5
Compatibility							✓	✓	✓

Example

See Listings 19-11 (in this chapter) and 15-14 (in Chapter 1 of this book) to see the `collapse()` method at work.

compareEndPoints("*type*", *rangeRef*)

	NN2	NN3	NN4	NN6	IE3/J1	IE3/J2	IE4	IE5	IE5.5
Compatibility							✓	✓	✓

Example

The page rendered by Listing 19-10 lets you experiment with text range comparisons. The bottom paragraph contains a SPAN element that has a `TextRange` object assigned to its text after the page loads (in the `init()` function). That fixed range becomes a solid reference point for you to use while you select text in the paragraph. After you make a selection, all four versions of the `compareEndPoints()` method run to compare the start and end points of the fixed range against your selection. One column of the results table shows the raw value returned by the `compareEndPoints()` method, while the third column puts the results into plain language.

To see how this page works, begin by selecting the first word of the fixed text range (double-click the word). You can see that the starting positions of both ranges are the same, because the returned value is 0. Because all of the invocations of the `compareEndPoints()` method are on the fixed text range, all comparisons are from the point of view of that range. Thus, the first row of the table for the `StartToEnd` parameter indicates that the start point of the fixed range comes before the end point of the selection, yielding a return value of -1.

Other selections to make include:

✦ Text that starts before the fixed range and ends inside the range

✦ Text that starts inside the fixed range and ends beyond the range

✦ Text that starts and ends precisely at the fixed range boundaries

✦ Text that starts and ends before the fixed range

✦ Text that starts after the fixed range

Study the returned values and the plain language results and see how they align with the selection you make.

Listing 19-10: **Lab for compareEndPoints() Method**

```
<HTML>
<HEAD>
<TITLE>TextRange.compareEndPoints() Method</TITLE>
<STYLE TYPE="text/css">
TD {text-align:center}
.propName {font-family:Courier, monospace}
#fixedRangeElem {color:red; font-weight:bold}
</STYLE>
<SCRIPT LANGUAGE="JavaScript">
var fixedRange

function setAndShowRangeData() {
    var selectedRange = document.selection.createRange()
    var result1 = fixedRange.compareEndPoints("StartToEnd", selectedRange)
    var result2 = fixedRange.compareEndPoints("StartToStart", selectedRange)
    var result3 = fixedRange.compareEndPoints("EndToStart", selectedRange)
    var result4 = fixedRange.compareEndPoints("EndToEnd", selectedRange)

    B1.innerText = result1
    compare1.innerText = getDescription(result1)
    B2.innerText = result2
    compare2.innerText = getDescription(result2)
```

Continued

Listing 19-10 *(continued)*

```
    B3.innerText = result3
    compare3.innerText = getDescription(result3)
    B4.innerText = result4
    compare4.innerText = getDescription(result4)
}

function getDescription(comparisonValue) {
    switch (comparisonValue) {
        case -1 :
            return "comes before"
            break
        case 0 :
            return "is the same as"
            break
        case 1 :
            return "comes after"
            break
        default :
            return "vs."
    }
}

function init() {
    fixedRange = document.body.createTextRange()
    fixedRange.moveToElementText(fixedRangeElem)
}
</SCRIPT>
</HEAD>

<BODY onLoad="init()">
<H1>TextRange.compareEndPoints() Method</H1>
<HR>
<P>Select text in the paragraph in various places relative to
the fixed text range (shown in red). See the relations between
the fixed and selected ranges with respect to their start
and end points.</P>
<TABLE ID="results" BORDER=1 CELLSPACING=2 CELLPADDING=2>
<TR><TH>Property</TH><TH>Returned Value</TH><TH>Fixed Range vs. Selection</TH></TR>
<TR>
    <TD CLASS="propName">StartToEnd</TD>
    <TD CLASS="count" ID="B1"> </TD>
    <TD CLASS="count" ID="C1">Start of Fixed
    <SPAN ID="compare1">vs.</SPAN> End of Selection</TD>
</TR>
<TR>
    <TD CLASS="propName">StartToStart</TD>
    <TD CLASS="count" ID="B2"> </TD>
    <TD CLASS="count" ID="C2">Start of Fixed
    <SPAN ID="compare2">vs.</SPAN> Start of Selection</TD>
</TR>
```

```
<TR>
    <TD CLASS="propName">EndToStart</TD>
    <TD CLASS="count" ID="B3"> </TD>
    <TD CLASS="count" ID="C3">End of Fixed
    <SPAN ID="compare3">vs.</SPAN> Start of Selection</TD>
</TR>
<TR>
    <TD CLASS="propName">EndToEnd</TD>
    <TD CLASS="count" ID="B4"> </TD>
    <TD CLASS="count" ID="C4">End of Fixed
    <SPAN ID="compare4">vs.</SPAN> End of Selection</TD>
</TR>
</TABLE>
<HR>
<P onMouseUp="setAndShowRangeData()">
Lorem ipsum dolor sit, <SPAN ID="fixedRangeElem">consectetaur adipisicing
elit</SPAN>,
sed do eiusmod tempor incididunt ut labore et dolore aliqua. Ut enim adminim
veniam,
quis nostrud exercitation ullamco laboris nisi ut aliquip ex ea commodo
consequat.</P>
</BODY>
</HTML>
```

duplicate()

	NN2	NN3	NN4	NN6	IE3/J1	IE3/J2	IE4	IE5	IE5.5
Compatibility							✓	✓	✓

Example

Use The Evaluator (Chapter 13 in the *JavaScript Bible*) to see how the `duplicate()` method works. Begin by creating a new `TextRange` object that contains the text of the `myP` paragraph element.

```
a = document.body.createTextRange()
a.moveToElementText(myP)
```

Next, clone the original range and preserve the copy in variable b:

```
b = a.duplicate()
```

The method returns no value, so don't be alarmed by the "undefined" that appears in the Results box. Move the original range so that it is an insertion point at the end of the body by first expanding it to encompass the entire body, and then collapse it to the end:

```
a.expand("textedit")
a.collapse(false)
```

Now, insert the copy at the very end of the body:

```
a.text = b.text
```

If you scroll to the bottom of the page, you'll see a copy of the text.

execCommand("*commandName*"[, *UIFlag*[, *value*]])

	NN2	NN3	NN4	NN6	IE3/J1	IE3/J2	IE4	IE5	IE5.5
Compatibility							✓	✓	✓

Example

Use The Evaluator (Chapter 13 in the *JavaScript Bible*) to see how to copy a text range's text into the client computer's Clipboard. Begin by setting the text range to the myP element:

```
a = document.body.createTextRange()
a.moveToElementText(myP)
```

Now use execCommand() to copy the range into the Clipboard:

```
a.execCommand("Copy")
```

To prove that the text is in the Clipboard, click the bottom text field and choose Paste from the Edit menu (or press Ctrl+V).

expand("*unit*")

	NN2	NN3	NN4	NN6	IE3/J1	IE3/J2	IE4	IE5	IE5.5
Compatibility							✓	✓	✓

Example

You can find examples of the expand() method in Listing 15-14.

findText("*searchString*"[, *searchScope*, *flags*])

	NN2	NN3	NN4	NN6	IE3/J1	IE3/J2	IE4	IE5	IE5.5
Compatibility							✓	✓	✓

Example

Listing 19-11 implements two varieties of a text search-and-replace operation, while showing you how to include extra parameters for case-sensitive and whole word searches. Both approaches begin by creating a TextRange for the entire body, but they immediately shift the starting point to the beginning of the DIV element that contains the text to search.

One search-and-replace function prompts the user to accept or decline replacement for each instance of a found string. The select() and scrollIntoView() methods are invoked to help the user see what is about to be replaced. Notice that even when the user declines to accept the replacement, the text range is collapsed to the end of the found range so that the next search can begin after the previously found text. Without the collapse() method, the search can get caught in an infinite loop as it keeps finding the same text over and over (with no replacement made). Because no counting is required, this search-and-replace operation is implemented inside a while repeat loop.

The other search-and-replace function goes ahead and replaces every match and then displays the number of replacements made. After the loop exits (because there are no more matches), the loop counter is used to display the number of replacements made.

Listing 19-11: **Two Search and Replace Approaches (with Undo)**

```
<HTML>
<HEAD>
<TITLE>TextRange.findText() Method</TITLE>
<SCRIPT LANGUAGE="JavaScript">
// global range var for use with Undo
var rng

// return findText() third parameter arguments
function getArgs(form) {
    var isCaseSensitive = (form.caseSensitive.checked) ? 4 : 0
    var isWholeWord = (form.wholeWord.checked) ? 2 : 0
    return isCaseSensitive ^ isWholeWord
}

// prompted search and replace
function sAndR(form) {
    var srchString = form.searchString.value
    var replString = form.replaceString.value
    if (srchString) {
        var args = getArgs(form)
        rng = document.body.createTextRange()
        rng.moveToElementText(rights)
        clearUndoBuffer()
        while (rng.findText(srchString, 10000, args)) {
            rng.select()
```

Continued

Listing 19-11 *(continued)*

```
            rng.scrollIntoView()
            if (confirm("Replace?")) {
                rng.text = replString
                pushUndoNew(rng, srchString, replString)
            }
            rng.collapse(false)
        }
    }
}

// unprompted search and replace with counter
function sAndRCount(form) {
    var srchString = form.searchString.value
    var replString = form.replaceString.value
    var i
    if (srchString) {
        var args = getArgs(form)
        rng = document.body.createTextRange()
        rng.moveToElementText(rights)
        for (i = 0; rng.findText(srchString, 10000, args); i++) {
            rng.text = replString
            pushUndoNew(rng, srchString, replString)
            rng.collapse(false)
        }
        if (i > 1) {
            clearUndoBuffer()
        }
    }
    document.all.counter.innerText = i
}

// BEGIN UNDO BUFFER CODE
// buffer global variables
var newRanges = new Array()
var origSearchString

// store original search string and bookmarks of each replaced range
function pushUndoNew(rng, srchString, replString) {
    origSearchString = srchString
    rng.moveStart("character", -replString.length)
    newRanges[newRanges.length] = rng.getBookmark()
}

// empty array and search string global
function clearUndoBuffer() {
    document.all.counter.innerText = "0"
    origSearchString = ""
    newRanges.length = 0
}
```

```
// perform the undo
function undoReplace() {
    if (newRanges.length && origSearchString) {
        for (var i = 0; i < newRanges.length; i++) {
            rng.moveToBookmark(newRanges[i])
            rng.text = origSearchString
        }
        document.all.counter.innerText = i
        clearUndoBuffer()
    }
}
</SCRIPT>
</HEAD>
<BODY>
<H1>TextRange.findText() Method</H1>
<HR>
<FORM>
<P>Enter a string to search for in the following text:
<INPUT TYPE="text" NAME="searchString" SIZE=20 VALUE="Law">  
<INPUT TYPE="checkbox" NAME="caseSensitive">Case-sensitive  
<INPUT TYPE="checkbox" NAME="wholeWord">Whole words only</P>
<P>Enter a string with which to replace found text:
<INPUT TYPE="text" NAME="replaceString" SIZE=20 VALUE="legislation"></P>
<P><INPUT TYPE="button" VALUE="Search and Replace (with prompt)"
onClick="sAndR(this.form)"></P>
<P><INPUT TYPE="button" VALUE="Search, Replace, and Count (no prompt)"
onClick="sAndRCount(this.form)">
<SPAN ID="counter">0</SPAN> items found and replaced.</P>
<P><INPUT TYPE="button" VALUE="Undo Search and Replace"
onClick="undoReplace()"></P>
</FORM>

<DIV ID="rights">
<A NAME="article1">
<H2>ARTICLE I</H2>
</A>
<P>
Congress shall make no law respecting an establishment of religion, or
prohibiting the free exercise thereof; or abridging the freedom of speech, or of
the press; or the right of the people peaceably to assemble, and to petition the
government for a redress of grievances.
</P>
[The rest of the text is snipped for printing here, but it is on the CD-ROM
version.]
</DIV>
</BODY>
</HTML>
```

Having a search-and-replace function available in a document is only one-half of the battle. The other half is offering the facilities to undo the changes. To that end,

Listing 19-11 includes an undo buffer that accurately undoes only the changes made in the initial replacement actions.

The undo buffer stores its data in two global variables. The first, origSearchString, is simply the string used to perform the original search. This variable is the string that has to be put back in the places where it had been replaced. The second global variable is an array that stores TextRange bookmarks (see getBookmark() later in this chapter). These references are string values that don't mean much to humans, but the browser can use them to recreate a range with its desired start and end points. Values for both the global search string and bookmark specifications are stored in calls to the pushUndoNew() method each time text is replaced.

A perhaps unexpected action of setting the text property of a text range is that the start and end points collapse to the end of the new text. Because the stored bookmark must include the replaced text as part of its specification, the start point of the current range must be adjusted back to the beginning of the replacement text before the bookmark can be saved. Thus, the pushUndoNew() function receives the replacement text string so that the moveStart() method can be adjusted by the number of characters matching the length of the replacement string.

After all of the bookmarks are stored in the array, the undo action can do its job in a rather simple for loop inside the undoReplace() function. After verifying that the undo buffer has data stored in it, the function loops through the array of bookmarks and replaces the bookmarked text with the old string. The benefit of using the bookmarks rather than using the replacement function again is that only those ranges originally affected by the search-and-replace operation are touched in the undo operation. For example, in this document if you replace a case-sensitive "states" with "States" two replacements are performed. At that point, however, the document has four instances of "States," two of which existed before. Redoing the replacement function by inverting the search-and-replace strings would convert all four back to the lowercase version — not the desired effect.

getBookmark()

	NN2	NN3	NN4	NN6	IE3/J1	IE3/J2	IE4	IE5	IE5.5
Compatibility							✓	✓	✓

Example

Listing 19-11 earlier in this chapter shows how the getBookmark() method is used to preserve specifications for text ranges so that they can be called upon again to be used to undo changes made to the text range. The getBookmark() method is used to save the snapshots, while the moveToBookmark() method is used during the undo process.

inRange(*otherRangeRef*)

	NN2	NN3	NN4	NN6	IE3/J1	IE3/J2	IE4	IE5	IE5.5
Compatibility							✓	✓	✓

Example

Use The Evaluator (Chapter 13 in the *JavaScript Bible*) to see the inRange() method in action. The following statements generate two distinct text ranges, one for the myP paragraph element and the other for the myEM element nested within.

```
a = document.body.createTextRange()
a.moveToElementText(myP)
b = document.body.createTextRange()
b.moveToElementText(myEM)
```

Because the myP text range is larger than the other, invoke the inRange() method on it, fully expecting the return value of true

```
a.inRange(b)
```

But if you switch the references, you see that the larger text range is not "in" the smaller one:

```
b.inRange(a)
```

isEqual(*otherRangeRef*)

	NN2	NN3	NN4	NN6	IE3/J1	IE3/J2	IE4	IE5	IE5.5
Compatibility							✓	✓	✓

Example

Use The Evaluator (Chapter 13 in the *JavaScript Bible*) to try the isEqual() method. Begin by creating two separate TextRange objects, one for the myP element and one for myEM.

```
a = document.body.createTextRange()
a.moveToElement(myP)
b = document.body.createTextRange()
b.moveToElement(myEM)
```

Because these two ranges encompass different sets of text, they are not equal, as the results show from the following statement:

```
a.isEqual(b)
```

But if you now adjust the first range boundaries to surround the myEM element, both ranges are the same values:

```
a.moveToElement(myEM)
a.isEqual(b)
```

move("*unit*"[, *count*])

	NN2	NN3	NN4	NN6	IE3/J1	IE3/J2	IE4	IE5	IE5.5
Compatibility							✓	✓	✓

Example

Use The Evaluator (Chapter 13 in the *JavaScript Bible*) to experiment with the move() method. To see how the method returns just the number of units it moves the pointer, begin by creating a text range and set it to enclose the myP element:

```
a = document.body.createTextRange()
a.moveToElementText(myP)
```

Now enter the following statement to collapse and move the range backward by 20 words.

```
a.move("word", -20)
```

Continue to click the Evaluate button and watch the returned value in the Results box. The value shows 20 while it can still move backward by 20 words. But eventually the last movement will be some other value closer to zero. And after the range is at the beginning of the BODY element, the range can move no more in that direction, so the result is zero.

moveEnd("*unit*"[, *count*])
moveStart("*unit*"[, *count*])

	NN2	NN3	NN4	NN6	IE3/J1	IE3/J2	IE4	IE5	IE5.5
Compatibility							✓	✓	✓

Example

Use The Evaluator (Chapter 13 in the *JavaScript Bible*) to experiment with the moveEnd() and moveStart() methods. Begin by creating a text range and set it to enclose the myEM element:

```
a = document.body.createTextRange()
a.moveToElementText(myEM)
```

To help you see how movements of the pointers affect the text enclosed by the range, type a into the bottom text box and view all the properties of the text range. Note especially the `htmlText` and `text` properties. Now enter the following statement to move the end of the range forward by one word.

```
a.moveEnd("word")
```

Click on the List Properties button to see that the text of the range now includes the word following the EM element. Try each of the following statements in the top text box and examine both the integer results and (by clicking the List Properties button) the properties of the range after each statement:

```
a.moveStart("word", -1)
a.moveEnd("sentence")
```

Notice that for a sentence, a default unit of 1 expands to the end of the current sentence. And if you move the start point backward by one sentence, you'll see that the lack of a period-ending sentence prior to the `myP` element causes strange results.

Finally, force the start point backward in increments of 20 words and watch the results as the starting point nears and reaches the start of the BODY:

```
a.moveStart("word", -20)
```

Eventually the last movement will be some other value closer to zero. And as soon as the range is at the beginning of the BODY element, the range can move no more in that direction, so the result is zero.

moveToBookmark("*bookmarkString*")

	NN2	NN3	NN4	NN6	IE3/J1	IE3/J2	IE4	IE5	IE5.5
Compatibility							✓	✓	✓

Example

Listing 19-11 earlier in this chapter shows how to use the `moveToBookmark()` method to restore a text range so that changes that created the state saved by the bookmark can be undone. The `getBookmark()` method is used to save the snapshots, while the `moveToBookmark()` method is used during the undo process.

moveToElementText(*elemObjRef*)

	NN2	NN3	NN4	NN6	IE3/J1	IE3/J2	IE4	IE5	IE5.5
Compatibility							✓	✓	✓

Example

A majority of examples for other `TextRange` object methods in this chapter use the `moveToElementText()` method. Listings 19-10 and 19-11 earlier in this chapter show the method within an application context.

moveToPoint(x, y)

	NN2	NN3	NN4	NN6	IE3/J1	IE3/J2	IE4	IE5	IE5.5
Compatibility							✓	✓	✓

Example

Use The Evaluator to see the `moveToPoint()` method in action. Begin by creating a text range for the entire BODY element:

```
a = document.body.createTextRange()
```

Now, invoke the `moveToPoint()` method to a location 100, 100, which turns out to be in the rectangle space of the Results textarea:

```
a.moveToPoint(100,100)
```

If you type `a` into the bottom text box and view the properties, both the `htmlText` and `text` properties are empty because the insertion point represents no visible text content. But if you gradually move, for example, the start point backward one character at a time, you will see the `htmlText` and `text` properties begin to fill in with the body text that comes before the TEXTAREA element, namely the "Results:" label and the `<BR>` tag between it and the TEXTAREA element. Enter the following statement into the top text box and click the Evaluate button several times.

```
a.moveStart("character", -1)
```

Enter `a` into the bottom text box after each evaluation to list the properties of the range.

parentElement()

	NN2	NN3	NN4	NN6	IE3/J1	IE3/J2	IE4	IE5	IE5.5
Compatibility							✓	✓	✓

Example

Use The Evaluator (Chapter 13 in the *JavaScript Bible*) to experiment with the `parentElement()` method. Begin by setting the text range to the `myEM` element:

```
a = document.body.createTextRange()
a.moveToElementText(myEM)
```

To inspect the object returned by the `parentElement()` method, enter the following statement in the lower text box:

```
a.parentElement()
```

If you scroll down to the `outerHTML` property, you see that the parent of the text range is the `myEM` element, tag and all.

Next, extend the end point of the text range by one word:

```
a.moveEnd("word")
```

Because part of the text range now contains text of the `myP` object, the `outerHTML` property of `a.parentElement()` shows the entire `myP` element and tags.

pasteHTML("*HTMLText*")

	NN2	NN3	NN4	NN6	IE3/J1	IE3/J2	IE4	IE5	IE5.5
Compatibility							✓	✓	✓

Example

Use The Evaluator (Chapter 13 in the *JavaScript Bible*) to experiment with the `pasteHTML()` method. The goal of the following sequence is to change the `<EM>` tag to a `<SPAN>` tag whose `STYLE` attribute sets the color of the original text that was in the EM element.

Begin by creating the text range and setting the boundaries to the `myEM` element:

```
a = document.body.createTextRange()
a.moveToElementText(myEM)
```

While you can pass the HTML string directly as a parameter to `pasteHTML()`, storing the HTML string in its own temporary variable may be more convenient (and more easily testable), such as:

```
b = "<SPAN STYLE='color:red'>" + a.text + "</SPAN>"
```

Notice that we concatenate the text of the current text range, because it has not yet been modified. Now we can paste the new HTML string into the current text range

```
a.pasteHTML(b)
```

At this point the EM element is gone from the object model, and the SPAN element is in its place. Prove it to yourself by looking at the HTML for the `myP` element:

```
myP.innerHTML
```

As noted earlier, the `pasteHTML()` method is not the only way to insert or replace HTML in a document. This method makes excellent sense when the user selects some text in the document to be replaced, because you can use the `document.selection.createRange()` method to get the text range for the selection. But if you're not using text ranges for other related operations, consider the other generic object properties and methods available to you.

select()

	NN2	NN3	NN4	NN6	IE3/J1	IE3/J2	IE4	IE5	IE5.5
Compatibility							✓	✓	✓

Example

See Listing 19-11 earlier in this chapter for an example of the `select()` method in use.

setEndPoint("*type*", *otherRangeRef*)

	NN2	NN3	NN4	NN6	IE3/J1	IE3/J2	IE4	IE5	IE5.5
Compatibility							✓	✓	✓

Example

Use The Evaluator to experiment with the `setEndPoint()` method. Begin by creating two independent text ranges, one for the `myP` element and one for `myEM`:

```
a = document.body.createTextRange()
a.moveToElementText(myP)
b = document.body.createTextRange()
b.moveToElementText(myEM)
```

Before moving any end points, compare the HTML for each of those ranges:

```
a.htmlText
b.htmlText
```

Now, move the start point of the `a` text range to the end point of the `b` text range:

```
a.setEndPoint("StartToEnd", b)
```

If you now view the HTML for the a range,

```
a.htmlText
```

you see that the `<P>` tag of the original `a` text range is nowhere to be found. This demonstration is a good lesson to use the `setEndPoint()` method primarily if you are concerned only with visible body text being inside ranges, rather than an element with its tags.

TextRectangle Object

Properties

```
bottom
left
right
top
```

	NN2	NN3	NN4	NN6	IE3/J1	IE3/J2	IE4	IE5	IE5.5
Compatibility								✓	✓

Example

Listing 19-12 lets you click one of four nested elements to see how the TextRectangle is treated. When you click one of the elements, that element's TextRectangle dimension properties are used to set the size of a positioned element that highlights the space of the rectangle. Be careful not to confuse the visible rectangle object that you see on the page with the abstract TextRectangle object that is associated with each of the clicked elements.

An important part of the listing is the way the action of sizing and showing the positioned element is broken out as a separate function (setHiliter()) from the one that is the onClick event handler function (handleClick()). This is done so that the onResize event handler can trigger a script that gets the current rectangle for the last element clicked, and the positioned element can be sized and moved to maintain the highlight of the same text. As an experiment, try removing the onResize event handler from the <BODY> tag and watch what happens to the highlighted rectangle after you resize the browser window: the rectangle that represents the TextRectangle remains unchanged and loses track of the abstract TextRectangle associated with the actual element object.

Listing 19-12: **Using the TextRectangle Object Properties**

```
<HTML>
<HEAD>
<TITLE>TextRectangle Object</TITLE>
<SCRIPT LANGUAGE="JavaScript">
// preserve reference to last clicked elem so resize can re-use it
var lastElem
// TextRectangle left tends to be out of registration by a couple of pixels
var rectLeftCorrection = 2
```

Continued

Listing 19-12 *(continued)*

```
// process mouse click
function handleClick() {
    var elem = event.srcElement
    if (elem.className && elem.className == "sample") {
        // set hiliter element only on a subset of elements
        lastElem = elem
        setHiliter()
    } else {
        // otherwise, hide the hiliter
        hideHiliter()
    }
}
function setHiliter() {
    if (lastElem) {
        var textRect = lastElem.getBoundingClientRect()
        hiliter.style.pixelTop = textRect.top + document.body.scrollTop
        hiliter.style.pixelLeft = textRect.left + document.body.scrollLeft -
            rectLeftCorrection
        hiliter.style.pixelHeight = textRect.bottom - textRect.top
        hiliter.style.pixelWidth = textRect.right - textRect.left
        hiliter.style.visibility = "visible"
    }
}
function hideHiliter() {
    hiliter.style.visibility = "hidden"
    lastElem = null
}
</SCRIPT>
</HEAD>
<BODY onClick="handleClick()" onResize="setHiliter()">
<H1>TextRectangle Object</H1>
<HR>
<P>Click on any of the four colored elements in the paragraph below and watch
the highlight rectangle adjust itself to the element's TextRectangle object.

<P CLASS="sample">Lorem ipsum dolor sit amet, <SPAN CLASS="sample"
STYLE="color:red">consectetaur adipisicing elit</SPAN>, sed do eiusmod tempor
<SPAN CLASS="sample" STYLE="color:green">incididunt ut labore et dolore <SPAN
CLASS="sample" STYLE="color:blue">magna aliqua</SPAN>. Ut enim adminim veniam,
quis nostrud exercitation ullamco</SPAN> laboris nisi ut aliquip ex ea commodo
consequat. Duis aute irure dolor in reprehenderit involuptate velit esse cillum
dolore eu fugiat nulla pariatur.</P>
<DIV ID="hiliter" STYLE="position:absolute; background-color:salmon; z-index:-1;
visibility:hidden"></DIV>
</BODY>
</HTML>
```

◆   ◆   ◆

Image, Area, and Map Objects (Chapter 22)

✦ ✦ ✦ ✦

In This Chapter

How to precache and swap images

Invoking action immediately after an image loads

Creating interactive, client-side image maps

✦ ✦ ✦ ✦

The IMG element object is a popular scripting target, largely because it is easy to script it for effects such as mouse rollovers. Moreover, the element's scriptability extends backward in time to all but the very first generation of script-able browsers. Playing a supporting role in image rollovers is the abstract `Image` object, which scripts use to pre-load images into the browser's cache for instantaneous image swapping. Even though the two objects manifest themselves differently within script operations, they share properties and methods, making it easy to learn their capabilities side by side.

AREA and MAP element objects work closely with each other. In practice, an AREA element resembles an A element that is set to work as a link. Both elements create clickable "hot spots" on the page that typically lead the user to other locations within the site or elsewhere on the Web. They also share a number of URL-related properties.

Examples Highlights

✦ Most IE browsers can load both still and motion images (such as MPEG movies) into an IMG element. Listing 22-3 shows how to swap between still and motion images via the `dynsrc` property.

✦ The page created from Listing 22-4 lets you compare the performance of swapping images with and without pre-caching. You also see how to have scripts rotate images on a timed schedule.

✦ Watch how the IMG element's `onLoad` event handler can trigger actions in Listing 22-5.

✦ A powerful Listing 22-7 demonstrates how scripts can fashion new client-side area maps when a different pic-ture file loads into an IMG element.

Image and IMG Element Objects

Properties

`align`

	NN2	NN3	NN4	NN6	IE3/J1	IE3/J2	IE4	IE5	IE5.5
Compatibility				✓			✓	✓	✓

Example

Listing 22-1 enables you to choose from the different `align` property values as they influence the layout of an image whose HTML is embedded inline with some other text. Resize the window to see different perspectives on word-wrapping on a page and their effects on the alignment choices. Not all browsers provide distinctive alignments for each choice, so experiment in multiple supported browsers.

Listing 22-1: **Testing an Image's align Property**

```
<HTML>
<HEAD>
<TITLE>IMG align Property</TITLE>
<SCRIPT LANGUAGE="JavaScript">

function setAlignment(sel) {
    document.myIMG.align = sel.options[sel.selectedIndex].text
}
</SCRIPT>
</HEAD>
<BODY>
<H1>IMG align Property</H1>
<HR>
<FORM>
Choose the image alignment:
<SELECT onChange="setAlignment(this)">
    <OPTION>absbottom
    <OPTION>absmiddle
    <OPTION>baseline
    <OPTION SELECTED >bottom
    <OPTION >left
    <OPTION>middle
    <OPTION>right
    <OPTION>texttop
    <OPTION>top

</SELECT>
</FORM>
```

```
<HR>
<P>Lorem ipsum dolor sit amet, consectetaur adipisicing elit,
sed do eiusmod tempor incididunt ut labore et dolore magna
aliqua. <IMG NAME="myIMG" SRC="desk1.gif" HEIGHT=90 WIDTH=120>
Ut enim adminim veniam, quis nostrud exercitation
ullamco laboris nisi ut aliquip ex ea commodo consequat.</P>
</BODY>
</HTML>
```

alt

	NN2	NN3	NN4	NN6	IE3/J1	IE3/J2	IE4	IE5	IE5.5
Compatibility				✓			✓	✓	✓

Example

Use The Evaluator (Chapter 13 in *JavaScript Bible*) to assign a string to the alt property of the document.myIMG image on the page. First, assign a nonexistent image to the src property to remove the existing image:

```
document.myIMG.src = "fred.gif"
```

Scroll down to the image, and you can see a space for the image. Now, assign a string to the alt property:

```
document.myIMG.src = "Fred\'s face"
```

The extra backslash is required to escape the apostrophe inside the string. Scroll down to see the new alt text in the image space.

border

	NN2	NN3	NN4	NN6	IE3/J1	IE3/J2	IE4	IE5	IE5.5
Compatibility		✓	✓	✓			✓	✓	✓

Example

Feel free to experiment with the document.myIMG.border property for the image in The Evaluator (Chapter 13 in *JavaScript Bible*) by assigning different integer values to the property.

complete

	NN2	NN3	NN4	NN6	IE3/J1	IE3/J2	IE4	IE5	IE5.5
Compatibility	✓	✓	✓				✓	✓	✓

Example

To experiment with the image.complete property, quit and relaunch your browser before loading Listing 22-2 (in case the images are in memory cache). As each image loads, click the "Is it loaded yet?" button to see the status of the complete property for the image object. The value is false until the loading finishes; then, the value becomes true. The arch image is the bigger of the two image files. You may have to quit and relaunch your browser between trials to clear the arch image from the cache (or empty the browser's memory cache). If you experience difficulty with this property in your scripts, try adding an onLoad event handler (even if it is empty, as in Listing 22-2) to your <IMG> tag.

Listing 22-2: **Scripting image.complete**

```
<HTML>
<HEAD>
<SCRIPT LANGUAGE="JavaScript1.1">
function loadIt(theImage,form) {
    form.result.value = ""
    document.images[0].src = theImage
}
function checkLoad(form) {
    form.result.value = document.images[0].complete
}
</SCRIPT>
</HEAD>
<BODY>
<IMG SRC="cpu2.gif" WIDTH=120 HEIGHT=90 onLoad="">
<FORM>
<INPUT TYPE="button" VALUE="Load keyboard"
onClick="loadIt('cpu2.gif',this.form)">
<INPUT TYPE="button" VALUE="Load arch"
onClick="loadIt('arch.gif',this.form)"><P>
<INPUT TYPE="button" VALUE="Is it loaded yet?" onClick="checkLoad(this.form)">
<INPUT TYPE="text" NAME="result">
</FORM>
</BODY>
</HTML>
```

dynsrc

	NN2	NN3	NN4	NN6	IE3/J1	IE3/J2	IE4	IE5	IE5.5
Compatibility							✓	✓	✓

Example

To swap between still and video sources, simply empty the opposite property. Listing 22-3 shows a simplified example that swaps between one fixed image and one video image. This listing exhibits most of the bugs associated with changing between static image and video sources described in the text.

Listing 22-3: **Changing Between Still and Motion Images**

```
<HTML>
<HEAD>
<TITLE>IMG dynsrc Property</TITLE>
<SCRIPT LANGUAGE="JavaScript">

var trainImg = new Image(160,120)
trainImg.src = "amtrak.jpg"
trainImg.dynsrc = "amtrak.mpg"

function setLoop() {
    var selector = document.forms[0].looper
    document.myIMG.loop = selector.options[selector.selectedIndex].value
}

function setImage(type) {
    if (type == "jpg") {
        document.myIMG.dynsrc = ""
        document.myIMG.src = trainImg.src
    } else {
        document.myIMG.src = ""
        document.myIMG.start = "fileopen"
        setLoop()
        document.myIMG.dynsrc = trainImg.dynsrc
    }
}
</SCRIPT>
</HEAD>
<BODY>
<H1>IMG dynsrc Property</H1>
<HR>
<FORM>
Choose image type:
<INPUT TYPE="radio" NAME="imgGroup" CHECKED onClick="setImage('jpg')">Still
```

Continued

Listing 22-3 *(continued)*

```
<INPUT TYPE="radio" NAME="imgGroup" onClick="setImage('mpg')">Video
<P>Play video how many times after loading:
<SELECT NAME="looper" onChange="setLoop()">
    <OPTION VALUE=1 SELECTED>Once
    <OPTION VALUE=2>Twice
    <OPTION VALUE=-1>Continuously
</SELECT></P>
</FORM>
<HR>
<IMG NAME="myIMG" SRC="amtrak.jpg" HEIGHT=120 WIDTH=160>
</BODY>
</HTML>
```

If you don't explicitly set the start property to fileopen (as shown in Listing 22-3), users of IE for the Macintosh have to double-click (IE4) or click (IE5) the movie image to make it run.

fileCreatedDate
fileModifiedDate
fileSize

	NN2	NN3	NN4	NN6	IE3/J1	IE3/J2	IE4	IE5	IE5.5
Compatibility							✓	✓	✓

Example

These properties are similar to the same-named properties of the document object. You can see these properties in action in Listing 18-4. Make a copy of that listing, and supply an image before modifying the references from the document object to the image object to see how these properties work with the IMG element object.

height
width

	NN2	NN3	NN4	NN6	IE3/J1	IE3/J2	IE4	IE5	IE5.5
Compatibility		✓	✓	✓			✓	✓	✓

Example

Use The Evaluator (Chapter 13 in *JavaScript Bible*) to experiment with the `height` and `width` properties. Begin retrieving the default values by entering the following two statements into the top text box:

```
document.myIMG.height
document.myIMG.width
```

Increase the height of the image from its default 90 to 180:

```
document.myIMG.height = 180
```

If you scroll down to the image, you see that the image has scaled in proportion. Next, exaggerate the width:

```
document.myIMG.width = 400
```

View the resulting image.

hspace
vspace

	NN2	NN3	NN4	NN6	IE3/J1	IE3/J2	IE4	IE5	IE5.5
Compatibility		✓	✓	✓			✓	✓	✓

Example

Use The Evaluator (Chapter 13 in *JavaScript Bible*) to experiment with the `hspace` and `vspace` properties. Begin by noticing that the image near the bottom of the page has no margins specified for it and is flush left with the page. Now assign a horizontal margin spacing of 30 pixels:

```
document.myIMG.hspace = 30
```

The image has shifted to the right by 30 pixels. An invisible margin also exists to the right of the image.

isMap

	NN2	NN3	NN4	NN6	IE3/J1	IE3/J2	IE4	IE5	IE5.5
Compatibility				✓			✓	✓	✓

Example

The image in The Evaluator page is not defined as an image map. Thus, if you type the following statement into the top text box, the property returns `false`:

```
document.myIMG.isMap
```

loop

	NN2	NN3	NN4	NN6	IE3/J1	IE3/J2	IE4	IE5	IE5.5
Compatibility							✓	✓	✓

Example

See Listing 22-3 for the `dynsrc` property to see the `loop` property in action.

lowsrc
lowSrc

	NN2	NN3	NN4	NN6	IE3/J1	IE3/J2	IE4	IE5	IE5.5
Compatibility		✓	✓	✓			✓	✓	✓

Example

See Listing 22-5 for the image object's `onLoad` event handler to see how the source-related properties affect event processing.

name

	NN2	NN3	NN4	NN6	IE3/J1	IE3/J2	IE4	IE5	IE5.5
Compatibility	✓	✓	✓	✓	(✓)		✓	✓	✓

Example

You can use The Evaluator to examine the value returned by the `name` property of the image on that page. Enter the following statement into the top text box:

```
document.myIMG.name
```

Of course, this is redundant because the name is part of the reference to the object.

nameProp

	NN2	NN3	NN4	NN6	IE3/J1	IE3/J2	IE4	IE5	IE5.5
Compatibility								✓	✓

Example

You can use The Evaluator to compare the results of the `src` and `nameProp` properties in IE5+/Windows. Enter each of the following statements into the top text box:

```
document.myIMG.src
document.myIMG.nameProp
```

protocol

	NN2	NN3	NN4	NN6	IE3/J1	IE3/J2	IE4	IE5	IE5.5
Compatibility							✓	✓	✓

Example

You can use The Evaluator to examine the `protocol` property of the image on the page. Enter the following statement into the top text box:

```
document.myIMG.protocol
```

src

	NN2	NN3	NN4	NN6	IE3/J1	IE3/J2	IE4	IE5	IE5.5
Compatibility	✓	✓	✓	(✓)			✓	✓	✓

Example

In the following example (Listing 22-4), you see a few applications of image objects. Of prime importance is a comparison of how precached and regular images feel to the user. As a bonus, you see an example of how to set a timer to automatically change the images displayed in an image object. This feature is a popular request among sites that display advertising banners.

As the page loads, a global variable is handed an array of image objects. Entries of the array are assigned string names as index values (`"desk1"`, `"desk2"`, and so on). The intention is that these names ultimately will be used as addresses to the array entries. Each image object in the array has a URL assigned to it, which precaches the image.

The page (see Figure 6-1) includes two IMG elements: one that displays non-cached images and one that displays cached images. Under each image is a SELECT element that you can use to select one of four possible image files for each element. The onChange event handler for each SELECT list invokes a different function to change the noncached (loadIndividual()) or cached (loadCached()) images. Both of these functions take as their single parameter a reference to the form that contains the SELECT elements.

To cycle through images at five-second intervals, the checkTimer() function looks to see if the timer check box is checked. If so, the selectedIndex property of the cached image SELECT control is copied and incremented (or reset to zero if the index is at the maximum value). The SELECT element is adjusted, so you can now invoke the loadCached() function to read the currently selected item and set the image accordingly.

For some extra style points, the <BODY> tag includes an onUnload event handler that invokes the resetSelects() function. This general-purpose function loops through all forms on the page and all elements within each form. For every SELECT element, the selectedIndex property is reset to zero. Thus, if a user reloads the page, or returns to the page via the Back button, the images start in their original sequence. An onLoad event handler makes sure that the images are in sync with the SELECT choices and the checkTimer() function is invoked with a five-second delay. Unless the timer check box is checked, however, the cached images don't cycle.

Listing 22-4: **A Scripted Image Object and Rotating Images**

```
<HTML>
<HEAD>
<TITLE>Image Object</TITLE>
<SCRIPT LANGUAGE="JavaScript">
// global declaration for 'desk' images array
var imageDB
// pre-cache the 'desk' images
if (document.images) {
    // list array index names for convenience
    var deskImages = new Array("desk1", "desk2", "desk3", "desk4")
    // build image array and pre-cache them
    imageDB = new Array(4)
    for (var i = 0; i < imageDB.length ; i++) {
        imageDB[deskImages[i]] = new Image(120,90)
        imageDB[deskImages[i]].src = deskImages[i] + ".gif"
    }
}
// change image of 'individual' image
function loadIndividual(form) {
    if (document.images) {
        var gifName = form.individual.options[form.individual.selectedIndex].value
        document.thumbnail1.src = gifName + ".gif"
    }
}
// change image of 'cached' image
function loadCached(form) {
    if (document.images) {
```

```
            var gifIndex = form.cached.options[form.cached.selectedIndex].value
            document.thumbnail2.src = imageDB[gifIndex].src
        }
    }
    // if switched on, cycle 'cached' image to next in queue
    function checkTimer() {
        if (document.images && document.Timer.timerBox.checked) {
            var gifIndex = document.selections.cached.selectedIndex
            if (++gifIndex > imageDB.length - 1) {
                gifIndex = 0
            }
            document.selections.cached.selectedIndex = gifIndex
            loadCached(document.selections)
            var timeoutID = setTimeout("checkTimer()",5000)
        }
    }
    // reset form controls to defaults on unload
    function resetSelects() {
        for (var i = 0; i < document.forms.length; i++) {
            for (var j = 0; j < document.forms[i].elements.length; j++) {
                if (document.forms[i].elements[j].type == "select-one") {
                    document.forms[i].elements[j].selectedIndex = 0
                }
            }
        }
    }
    // get things rolling
    function init() {
        loadIndividual(document.selections)
        loadCached(document.selections)
        setTimeout("checkTimer()",5000)
    }
    </SCRIPT>
    </HEAD>

    <BODY onLoad="init()" onUnload="resetSelects ()">
    <H1>Image Object</H1>
    <HR>
    <CENTER>
    <TABLE BORDER=3 CELLPADDING=3>
    <TR><TH></TH><TH>Individually Loaded</TH><TH>Pre-cached</TH></TR>
    <TR><TD ALIGN=RIGHT><B>Image:</B></TD>
    <TD><IMG SRC="cpu1.gif" NAME="thumbnail1" HEIGHT=90 WIDTH=120></TD>
    <TD><IMG SRC="desk1.gif" NAME="thumbnail2" HEIGHT=90 WIDTH=120></TD>
    </TR>
    <TR><TD ALIGN=RIGHT><B>Select image:</B></TD>
    <FORM NAME="selections">
    <TD>
    <SELECT NAME="individual" onChange="loadIndividual(this.form)">
    <OPTION VALUE="cpu1">Wires
    <OPTION VALUE="cpu2">Keyboard
```

Continued

Listing 22-4 *(continued)*

```
<OPTION VALUE="cpu3">Desks
<OPTION VALUE="cpu4">Cables
</SELECT>
</TD>
<TD>
<SELECT NAME="cached" onChange="loadCached(this.form)">
<OPTION VALUE="desk1">Bands
<OPTION VALUE="desk2">Clips
<OPTION VALUE="desk3">Lamp
<OPTION VALUE="desk4">Erasers
</SELECT></TD>
</FORM>
</TR></TABLE>
<FORM NAME="Timer">
<INPUT TYPE="checkbox" NAME="timerBox" onClick="checkTimer()">Auto-cycle through
pre-cached images
</FORM>
</CENTER>
</BODY>
</HTML>
```

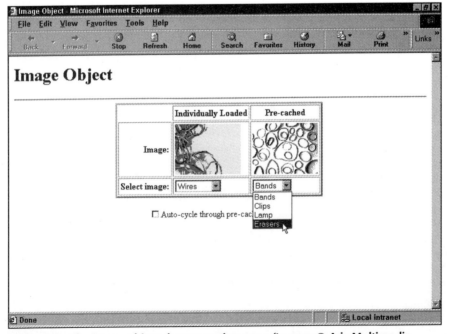

Figure 6-1: The image object demonstration page (Images © Aris Multimedia Entertainment, Inc., 1994)

start

	NN2	NN3	NN4	NN6	IE3/J1	IE3/J2	IE4	IE5	IE5.5
Compatibility							✓	✓	✓

Example

See Listing 22-3 earlier in this chapter for an example of how you can use the start property with a page that loads a movie clip into an IMG element object.

x
y

	NN2	NN3	NN4	NN6	IE3/J1	IE3/J2	IE4	IE5	IE5.5
Compatibility			✓						

Example

If you want to scroll the document so that the link is a few pixels below the top of the window, use a statement such as this:

```
window.scrollTo(document.images[0].x, (document.images[0].y - 3))
```

Event handlers
onAbort
onError

	NN2	NN3	NN4	NN6	IE3/J1	IE3/J2	IE4	IE5	IE5.5
Compatibility		✓	✓	✓			✓	✓	✓

Example

Listing 22-5 includes an onAbort event handler. If the images already exist in the cache, you must quit and relaunch the browser to try to stop the image from loading. In that example, I provide a reload option for the entire page. How you handle the exception depends a great deal on your page design. Do your best to smooth over any difficulties that users may encounter.

onLoad

	NN2	NN3	NN4	NN6	IE3/J1	IE3/J2	IE4	IE5	IE5.5
Compatibility		✓	✓	✓			✓	✓	✓

Example

Quit and restart your browser to get the most from Listing 22-5. As the document first loads, the LOWSRC image file (the picture of pencil erasers) loads ahead of the computer keyboard image. When the erasers are loaded, the onLoad event handler writes "done" to the text field even though the main image is not loaded yet. You can experiment further by loading the arch image. This image takes longer to load, so the LOWSRC image (set on the fly, in this case) loads way ahead of it.

Listing 22-5: **The Image onLoad Event Handler**

```
<HTML>
<HEAD>
<SCRIPT LANGUAGE="JavaScript">
function loadIt(theImage,form) {
    if (document.images) {
        form.result.value = ""
        document.images[0].lowsrc = "desk1.gif"
        document.images[0].src = theImage
    }
}
function checkLoad(form) {
    if (document.images) {
        form.result.value = document.images[0].complete
    }
}
function signal() {
    if(confirm("You have stopped the image from loading. Do you want to try
again?")) {
        location.reload()
    }
}
</SCRIPT>
</HEAD>
<BODY>
<IMG SRC="cpu2.gif" LOWSRC="desk4.gif" WIDTH=120 HEIGHT=90
onLoad="if (document.forms[0].result) document.forms[0].result.value='done'"
onAbort="signal()">
<FORM>
<INPUT TYPE="button" VALUE="Load keyboard"
onClick="loadIt('cpu2.gif',this.form)">
<INPUT TYPE="button" VALUE="Load arch"
onClick="loadIt('arch.gif',this.form)"><P>
```

```
<INPUT TYPE="button" VALUE="Is it loaded yet?" onClick="checkLoad(this.form)">
<INPUT TYPE="text" NAME="result">
</FORM>
</BODY>
</HTML>
```

AREA Element Object

Properties

```
coords
shape
```

	NN2	NN3	NN4	NN6	IE3/J1	IE3/J2	IE4	IE5	IE5.5
Compatibility				✓			✓	✓	✓

Example

See Listing 22-7 for a demonstration of the `coords` and `shape` properties in the context of scripting MAP element objects.

MAP Element Object

Property

```
areas
```

	NN2	NN3	NN4	NN6	IE3/J1	IE3/J2	IE4	IE5	IE5.5
Compatibility				✓			✓	✓	✓

Example

Listing 22-7 demonstrates how to use scripting to replace the AREA element objects inside a MAP element. The scenario is that the page loads with one image of a computer keyboard. This image is linked to the `keyboardMap` client-side image map, which specifies details for three hot spots on the image. If you then switch the image displayed in that IMG element, scripts change the useMap property of the IMG element object to point to a second MAP that has specifications more suited to the desk lamp in the second image. Roll the mouse pointer atop the images, and view the URLs associated with each area in the statusbar (for this example, the URLs do not lead to other pages).

Another button on the page, however, invokes the makeAreas() function (not working in IE5/Mac), which creates four new AREA element objects and (through DOM-specific pathways) adds those new area specifications to the image. If you roll the mouse atop the image after the function executes, you can see that the URLs now reflect those of the new areas. Also note the addition of a fourth area, whose status bar message appears in Figure 6-2.

Listing 22-7: **Modifying AREA Elements on the Fly**

```
<HTML>
<HEAD>
<TITLE>MAP Element Object</TITLE>
<SCRIPT LANGUAGE="JavaScript">
// generate area elements on the fly
function makeAreas() {
    document.myIMG.src = "desk3.gif"
    // build area element objects
    var area1 = document.createElement("AREA")
    area1.href = "Script-Made-Shade.html"
    area1.shape = "polygon"
    area1.coords = "52,28,108,35,119,29,119,8,63,0,52,28"
    var area2 = document.createElement("AREA")
    area2.href = "Script-Made-Base.html"
    area2.shape = "rect"
    area2.coords = "75,65,117,87"
    var area3 = document.createElement("AREA")
    area3.href = "Script-Made-Chain.html"
    area3.shape = "polygon"
    area3.coords = "68,51,73,51,69,32,68,51"
    var area4 = document.createElement("AREA")
    area4.href = "Script-Made-Emptyness.html"
    area4.shape = "rect"
    area4.coords = "0,0,50,120"
    // stuff new elements into MAP child nodes
    if (document.all) {
        // works for IE4+
        document.all.lampMap.areas.length = 0
        document.all.lampMap.areas[0] = area1
        document.all.lampMap.areas[1] = area2
        document.all.lampMap.areas[2] = area3
        document.all.lampMap.areas[3] = area4
```

```
      } else if (document.getElementById) {
          // NN6 adheres to node model
          var mapObj = document.getElementById("lamp_map")
          while (mapObj.childNodes.length) {
              mapObj.removeChild(mapObj.firstChild)
          }
          mapObj.appendChild(area1)
          mapObj.appendChild(area2)
          mapObj.appendChild(area3)
          mapObj.appendChild(area4)
          // workaround NN6 display bug
          document.myIMG.style.display = "inline"
      }
}

function changeToKeyboard() {
    document.myIMG.src = "cpu2.gif"
    document.myIMG.useMap = "#keyboardMap"
}

function changeToLamp() {
    document.myIMG.src = "desk3.gif"
    document.myIMG.useMap = "#lampMap"
}
</SCRIPT>
</HEAD>
<BODY>
<H1>MAP Element Object</H1>
<HR>
<IMG NAME="myIMG" SRC="cpu2.gif" WIDTH=120 HEIGHT=90 USEMAP="#keyboardMap">
<FORM>
<P><INPUT TYPE="button" VALUE="Load Lamp Image" onClick="changeToLamp()">
<INPUT TYPE="button" VALUE="Write Map on the Fly" onClick="makeAreas()"></P>
<P>
<INPUT TYPE="button" VALUE="Load Keyboard Image"
onClick="changeToKeyboard()"></P>
</FORM>
<MAP NAME="keyboardMap">
<AREA HREF="AlpaKeys.htm" SHAPE="rect" COORDS="0,0,26,42">
<AREA HREF="ArrowKeys.htm" SHAPE="polygon"
COORDS="48,89,57,77,69,82,77,70,89,78,84,89,48,89">
<AREA HREF="PageKeys.htm" SHAPE="circle" COORDS="104,51,14">
</MAP>
<MAP NAME="lampMap">
<AREA HREF="Shade.htm" SHAPE="polygon"
COORDS="52,28,108,35,119,29,119,8,63,0,52,28">
<AREA HREF="Base.htm" SHAPE="rect" COORDS="75,65,117,87">
<AREA HREF="Chain.htm" SHAPE="polygon" COORDS="68,51,73,51,69,32,68,51">
</MAP>
</BODY>
</HTML>
```

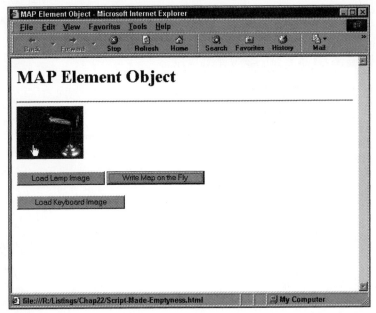

Figure 6-2: Scripts created a special client-side image map for the image.

✦   ✦   ✦

The Form and Related Objects (Chapter 23)

◆ ◆ ◆ ◆

In This Chapter

Customizing FORM object behavior prior to submission

Preventing accidental form submissions or resets

Using images for Reset and Submit buttons

Processing form validations

◆ ◆ ◆ ◆

Because HTML forms have been scriptable since the earliest days of scriptable browsers, they tend to attract the attention of a lot of page and site designers. Even though the FORM element is primarily the container of the interactive form controls (covered in succeeding chapters), it's not uncommon to find scripts modifying the `action` property (corresponding to the ACTION attribute) based on user input. Moreover, the `onSubmit` event handler is a vital trigger for batch validation just before the form data goes up to the server.

The other HTML element for which this chapter contains an example is the LABEL element object. A LABEL element is a container of text that is associated with a form control. This is a practical user interface enhancement in modern browsers in that such labels can essentially forward mouse events to their controls, thus widening the physical target for mouse clicks of radio buttons and checkboxes, much like "real" applications. The value of scriptability for this element, however, accrues predominantly when scripts dynamically modify page content.

Examples Highlights

✦ Listing 23-2 puts the `form.elements` array to work in a generic function that resets all text fields in a form to empty, without touching the settings of other types of controls.

✦ If you prefer to use images for your form's reset and submit actions, Listing 22-3 shows you how to do just that with the `form.reset()` and `form.submit()` methods.

✦ While batch form validations are shown in several places throughout the *JavaScript Bible*, Listing 23-4 demonstrates how both the onReset and onSubmit event handlers, in concert with the window.confirm() method, let scripts permit or prevent a form from being reset or submitted.

FORM Object

Properties

action

	NN2	NN3	NN4	NN6	IE3/J1	IE3/J2	IE4	IE5	IE5.5
Compatibility	✓	✓	✓	✓	✓	✓	✓	✓	✓

Example

The following statement assigns a mailto: URL to the first form of a page:

```
document.forms[0].action = "mailto:jdoe@giantco.com"
```

elements

	NN2	NN3	NN4	NN6	IE3/J1	IE3/J2	IE4	IE5	IE5.5
Compatibility	✓	✓	✓	✓	✓	✓	✓	✓	✓

Example

The document in Listing 23-2 demonstrates a practical use of the elements property. A form contains four fields and some other elements mixed in between (see Figure 7-1). The first part of the function that acts on these items repeats through all the elements in the form to find out which ones are text box objects and which text box objects are empty. Notice how I use the type property to separate text box objects from the rest, even when radio buttons appear amid the fields. If one field has nothing in it, I alert the user and use that same index value to place the insertion point at the field with the field's focus() method.

Listing 23-2: **Using the form.elements Array**

```
<HTML>
<HEAD>
<TITLE>Elements Array</TITLE>
<SCRIPT LANGUAGE="JavaScript">
function verifyIt() {
    var form = document.forms[0]
    for (i = 0; i < form.elements.length; i++) {
        if (form.elements[i].type == "text" && form.elements[i].value == ""){
            alert("Please fill out all fields.")
            form.elements[i].focus()
            break
        }
        // more tests
    }
    // more statements
}
</SCRIPT>
</HEAD>
<BODY>
<FORM>
Enter your first name:<INPUT TYPE="text" NAME="firstName"><P>
Enter your last name:<INPUT TYPE="text" NAME="lastName"><P>
<INPUT TYPE="radio" NAME="gender">Male
<INPUT TYPE="radio" NAME="gender">Female <P>
Enter your address:<INPUT TYPE="text" NAME="address"><P>
Enter your city:<INPUT TYPE="text" NAME="city"><P>
<INPUT TYPE="checkbox" NAME="retired">I am retired
</FORM>
<FORM>
<INPUT TYPE="button" NAME="act" VALUE="Verify" onClick="verifyIt()">
</FORM>
</BODY>
</HTML>
```

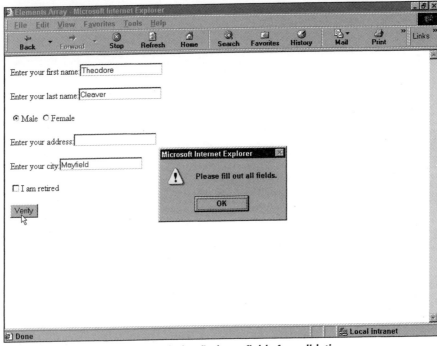

Figure 7-1: The elements array helps find text fields for validation.

encoding
enctype

	NN2	NN3	NN4	NN6	IE3/J1	IE3/J2	IE4	IE5	IE5.5
Compatibility	✓	✓	✓	✓	✓	✓	✓	✓	✓

Example

If you need to modify the first form in a document so that the content is sent in non-URL-encoded text at the user's request, the statement is:

```
document.forms[0].encoding = "text/plain"
```

length

	NN2	NN3	NN4	NN6	IE3/J1	IE3/J2	IE4	IE5	IE5.5
Compatibility	✓	✓	✓	✓	✓	✓	✓	✓	✓

Example

Use The Evaluator (Chapter 13 in the *JavaScript Bible*) to determine the number of form controls in the first form of the page. Enter the following statement into the top text box:

```
document.forms[0].length
```

method

	NN2	NN3	NN4	NN6	IE3/J1	IE3/J2	IE4	IE5	IE5.5
Compatibility	✓	✓	✓	✓	✓	✓	✓	✓	✓

Example

If you need to modify the first form in a document so that the content is sent via the POST method, the statement is:

```
document.forms[0].method = "POST"
```

target

	NN2	NN3	NN4	NN6	IE3/J1	IE3/J2	IE4	IE5	IE5.5
Compatibility	✓	✓	✓	✓	✓	✓	✓	✓	✓

Example

If you want to direct the response from the first form's CGI to a new window (rather than the target specified in the form's tag), use this statement:

```
document.forms[0].target = "_blank"
```

Methods

reset()

	NN2	NN3	NN4	NN6	IE3/J1	IE3/J2	IE4	IE5	IE5.5
Compatibility		✓	✓	✓			✓	✓	✓

Example

In Listing 23-3, I assign the act of resetting the form to the HREF attribute of a link object (that is attached to a graphic called reset.jpg). I use the javascript: URL to invoke the reset() method for the form directly (in other words, without doing it via function). Note that the form's action in this example is to a nonexistent URL. If you click the Submit icon, you receive an "unable to locate" error from the browser.

Listing 23-3: **form.reset() and form.submit() Methods**

```
<HTML>
<HEAD>
<TITLE>Registration Form</TITLE>
</HEAD>
<BODY>
<FORM NAME="entries" METHOD=POST ACTION="http://www.u.edu/pub/cgi-bin/register">
Enter your first name:<INPUT TYPE="text" NAME="firstName"><P>
Enter your last name:<INPUT TYPE="text" NAME="lastName"><P>
Enter your address:<INPUT TYPE="text" NAME="address"><P>
Enter your city:<INPUT TYPE="text" NAME="city"><P>
<INPUT TYPE="radio" NAME="gender" CHECKED>Male
<INPUT TYPE="radio" NAME="gender">Female <P>
<INPUT TYPE="checkbox" NAME="retired">I am retired
</FORM>
<P>
<A HREF="javascript:document.forms[0].submit()"><IMG SRC="submit.jpg" HEIGHT=25
WIDTH=100 BORDER=0></A>
<A HREF="javascript:document.forms[0].reset()"><IMG SRC="reset.jpg" HEIGHT=25
WIDTH=100 BORDER=0></A>
</BODY>
</HTML>
```

submit()

	NN2	NN3	NN4	NN6	IE3/J1	IE3/J2	IE4	IE5	IE5.5
Compatibility	✓	✓	✓	✓	✓	✓	✓	✓	✓

Example

Consult Listing 23-3 for an example of using the submit() method from outside of a form.

Event handlers

onReset

	NN2	NN3	NN4	NN6	IE3/J1	IE3/J2	IE4	IE5	IE5.5
Compatibility		✓	✓	✓			✓	✓	✓

Example

Listing 23-4 demonstrates one way to prevent accidental form resets or submissions. Using standard Reset and Submit buttons as interface elements, the <FORM> object definition includes both event handlers. Each event handler calls its own function that offers a choice for users. Notice how each event handler includes the word return and takes advantage of the Boolean values that come back from the confirm() method dialog boxes in both functions.

Listing 23-4: **The onReset and onSubmit Event Handlers**

```
<HTML>
<HEAD>
<TITLE>Submit and Reset Confirmation</TITLE>
<SCRIPT LANGUAGE="JavaScript">
function allowReset() {
    return window.confirm("Go ahead and clear the form?")
}
function allowSend() {
    return window.confirm("Go ahead and mail this info?")
}
</SCRIPT>
</HEAD>
<BODY>
<FORM METHOD=POST ENCTYPE="text/plain" ACTION="mailto:trash4@dannyg.com"
onReset="return allowReset()" onSubmit="return allowSend()">
```

Continued

Listing 23-4 *(continued)*

```
Enter your first name:<INPUT TYPE="text" NAME="firstName"><P>
Enter your last name:<INPUT TYPE="text" NAME="lastName"><P>
Enter your address:<INPUT TYPE="text" NAME="address"><P>
Enter your city:<INPUT TYPE="text" NAME="city"><P>
<INPUT TYPE="radio" NAME="gender" CHECKED>Male
<INPUT TYPE="radio" NAME="gender">Female <P>
<INPUT TYPE="checkbox" NAME="retired">I am retired<P>
<INPUT TYPE="reset">
<INPUT TYPE="submit">
</FORM>
</BODY>
</HTML>
```

onSubmit

	NN2	NN3	NN4	NN6	IE3/J1	IE3/J2	IE4	IE5	IE5.5
Compatibility	✓	✓	✓	✓	✓	✓	✓	✓	✓

Example

See Listing 23-4 for an example of trapping a submission via the onSubmit event handler.

LABEL Element Object

Property

htmlFor

	NN2	NN3	NN4	NN6	IE3/J1	IE3/J2	IE4	IE5	IE5.5
Compatibility				✓			✓	✓	✓

Example

The following statement uses W3C DOM-compatible syntax (IE5+ and NN6) to assign a form control reference to the htmlFor property of a label:

```
document.getElementById("myLabel").htmlFor = document.getElementById("myField")
```

◆   ◆   ◆

Button Objects (Chapter 24)

◆ ◆ ◆ ◆

In This Chapter

Triggering action
from a user's click of
a button

Using checkboxes to
control display of
other form controls

Distinguishing
between radio button
families and their
individual buttons

◆ ◆ ◆ ◆

The topic of button form controls encompasses clickable user interface elements that have a variety of applications, some of which are quite specific. For example, radio buttons should be presented in groups offering two or more mutually exclusive choices. A checkbox, on the other hand, is used to signify an "on" or "off" setting related to whatever label is associated with the button. The only tricky part of these special behaviors is that radio buttons assigned to a single group must share the same name, and the document object model provides access to single buttons within the group by way of an array of objects that share the name. For a script to determine which radio button is currently selected, a `for` loop through the array then allows the script to inspect the `checked` property of each button to find the one whose value is `true`.

Then there are what appear to be plain old rounded rectangle buttons. Two versions — the INPUT element of type button and the newer BUTTON element — work very much alike, although the latter is not obligated to appear nested inside a FORM element. A common mistake among newcomers, however, is to use the INPUT element of type `submit` to behave as a button whose sole job is to trigger some script function without any form submission. Genuine submit buttons force the form to submit itself, even if the button's `onClick` event handler invokes a script function. If the form has no ACTION attribute assigned to it, then the default action of the submission causes the page to reload, probably destroying whatever tentative script variable values and other data have been gathered on the page.

Examples Highlights

◆ If a button's event handler passes that button object's reference to the handler function, the object's `form` property provides the function with a valid reference to the containing form, allowing the script an easy way to access information about the form or create references to other form controls.

✦ Of course, the `onClick` event handler is the most important for button controls. Listing 24-1 demonstrates passing button references to event handler functions.

✦ Listing 24-4 shows how a checkbox setting can influence the URL of the form's action.

✦ Sometimes a complex form requires that checking a checkbox makes other items in the form visible. Listing 24-5 employs scriptable style sheets to assist in the job.

✦ Use Listing 24-6 as a model for how to find which radio button among those of a single group is checked.

The BUTTON Element Object and the Button, Submit, and Reset Input Objects

Properties

form

	NN2	NN3	NN4	NN6	IE3/J1	IE3/J2	IE4	IE5	IE5.5
Compatibility	✓	✓	✓	✓	✓	✓	✓	✓	✓

Example

The following function fragment receives a reference to a button element as the parameter. The button reference is needed to decide which branch to follow; then the form is submitted.

```
function setAction(btn) {
    if (btn.name == "normal") {
        btn.form.action = "cgi-bin/normal.pl"
    } else if (btn.name == "special") {
        btn.form.action = "cgi-bin/specialHandling.pl"
    }
    btn.form.submit()
}
```

Notice how this function doesn't have to worry about the form reference, because its job is to work with whatever form encloses the button that triggers this function. Down in the form, two buttons invoke the same function. Only their names ultimately determine the precise processing of the button click:

```
<FORM>
...
<INPUT TYPE="button" NAME="normal" VALUE="Regular Handling"
onClick="setAction(this)">
```

```
<INPUT TYPE="button" NAME="special" VALUE="Special Handling"
onClick="setAction(this)">
</FORM>
```

name

	NN2	NN3	NN4	NN6	IE3/J1	IE3/J2	IE4	IE5	IE5.5
Compatibility	✓	✓	✓	✓	✓	✓	✓	✓	✓

Example

See the example for the `form` property earlier in this chapter for a practical application of the `name` property.

value

	NN2	NN3	NN4	NN6	IE3/J1	IE3/J2	IE4	IE5	IE5.5
Compatibility	✓	✓	✓	✓	✓	✓	✓	✓	✓

Example

In the following excerpt, the statement toggles the label of a button from "Play" to "Stop" (except in NN/Mac through version 4):

```
var btn = document.forms[0].controlButton
btn.value = (btn.value == "Play") ? "Stop" : "Play"
```

Methods

click()

	NN2	NN3	NN4	NN6	IE3/J1	IE3/J2	IE4	IE5	IE5.5
Compatibility	✓	✓	✓	✓	✓	✓	✓	✓	✓

Example

The following statement demonstrates how to script a click action on a button form control named `sender`:

```
document.forms[0].sender.click()
```

Event handlers
onClick

	NN2	NN3	NN4	NN6	IE3/J1	IE3/J2	IE4	IE5	IE5.5
Compatibility	✓	✓	✓	✓	✓	✓	✓	✓	✓

Example

Listing 24-1 demonstrates not only the onClick event handler of a button but also how you may need to extract a particular button's name or value properties from a general-purpose function that services multiple buttons. In this case, each button passes its own object as a parameter to the displayTeam() function. The function then displays the results in an alert dialog box. A real-world application would probably use a more complex if...else decision tree to perform more sophisticated actions based on the button clicked (or use a switch construction on the btn.value expression for NN4+ and IE4+).

Listing 24-1: **Three Buttons Sharing One Function**

```
<HTML>
<HEAD>
<TITLE>Button Click</TITLE>
<SCRIPT LANGUAGE="JavaScript">
function displayTeam(btn) {
    if (btn.value == "Abbott") {alert("Abbott & Costello")}
    if (btn.value == "Rowan") {alert("Rowan & Martin")}
    if (btn.value == "Martin") {alert("Martin & Lewis")}
}
</SCRIPT>
</HEAD>

<BODY>
Click on your favorite half of a popular comedy team:<P>
<FORM>
<INPUT TYPE="button" VALUE="Abbott" onClick="displayTeam(this)">
<INPUT TYPE="button" VALUE="Rowan" onClick="displayTeam(this)">
<INPUT TYPE="button" VALUE="Martin" onClick="displayTeam(this)">
</FORM>
</BODY>
</HTML>
```

Checkbox Input Object

Properties

checked

	NN2	NN3	NN4	NN6	IE3/J1	IE3/J2	IE4	IE5	IE5.5
Compatibility	✓	✓	✓	✓	✓	✓	✓	✓	✓

Example

The simple example in Listing 24-2 passes a form object reference to the JavaScript function. The function, in turn, reads the checked value of the form's checkbox object (checkThis.checked) and uses its Boolean value as the test result for the if...else construction.

Listing 24-2: **The checked Property as a Conditional**

```
<HTML>
<HEAD>
<TITLE>Checkbox Inspector</TITLE>
<SCRIPT LANGUAGE="JavaScript">
function inspectBox(form) {
    if (form.checkThis.checked) {
        alert("The box is checked.")
    } else {
        alert("The box is not checked at the moment.")
    }
}
</SCRIPT>
</HEAD>

<BODY>
<FORM>
<INPUT TYPE="checkbox" NAME="checkThis">Check here<P>
<INPUT TYPE="button" NAME="boxChecker" VALUE="Inspect Box"
onClick="inspectBox(this.form)">
</FORM>
</BODY>
</HTML>
```

defaultChecked

	NN2	NN3	NN4	NN6	IE3/J1	IE3/J2	IE4	IE5	IE5.5
Compatibility	✓	✓	✓	✓	✓	✓	✓	✓	✓

Example

The function in Listing 24-3 (this fragment is not in the CD-ROM listings) is designed to compare the current setting of a checkbox against its default value. The `if` construction compares the current status of the box against its default status. Both are Boolean values, so they can be compared against each other. If the current and default settings don't match, the function goes on to handle the case in which the current setting is other than the default.

Listing 24-3: Examining the defaultChecked Property

```
function compareBrowser(thisBox) {
    if (thisBox.checked != thisBox.defaultChecked) {
        // statements about using a different set of HTML pages
    }
}
```

value

	NN2	NN3	NN4	NN6	IE3/J1	IE3/J2	IE4	IE5	IE5.5
Compatibility	✓	✓	✓	✓	✓	✓	✓	✓	✓

Example

The scenario for the skeleton HTML page in Listing 24-4 is a form with a checkbox whose selection determines which of two actions to follow for submission to the server. After the user clicks the Submit button, a JavaScript function examines the checkbox's `checked` property. If the property is `true` (the button is checked), the script sets the `action` property for the entire form to the content of the value property—thus influencing where the form goes on the server side. If you try this listing on your computer, the result you see varies widely with the browser version you use. For most browsers, you see some indication (an error alert or other screen notation) that a file with the name `primaryURL` or `alternateURL` doesn't exist. Unfortunately, IE5.5/Windows does not display the name of the file that can't be opened. Try the example in another browser if you have one. The names and the error message come from the submission process for this demonstration.

Listing 24-4: Adjusting a CGI Submission Action

```
<HTML>
<HEAD>
<TITLE>Checkbox Submission</TITLE>
<SCRIPT LANGUAGE="JavaScript">
function setAction(form) {
    if (form.checkThis.checked) {
        form.action = form.checkThis.value
    } else {
        form.action = "file://primaryURL"
    }
    return true
}
</SCRIPT>
</HEAD>
<BODY>
<FORM METHOD="POST" ACTION="">
<INPUT TYPE="checkbox" NAME="checkThis" VALUE="file://alternateURL">Use
alternate<P>
<INPUT TYPE="submit" NAME="boxChecker" onClick="return setAction(this.form)">
</FORM>
</BODY>
</HTML>
```

Event handlers

onClick

	NN2	NN3	NN4	NN6	IE3/J1	IE3/J2	IE4	IE5	IE5.5
Compatibility	✓	✓	✓	✓	✓	✓	✓	✓	✓

Example

The page in Listing 24-5 shows how to trap the click event in one checkbox to influence the visibility and display of other form controls. After you turn on the Monitor checkbox, a list of radio buttons for monitor sizes appears. Similarly, engaging the Communications checkbox makes two radio buttons visible. Your choice of radio button brings up one of two further choices within the same table cell (see Figure 8-1).

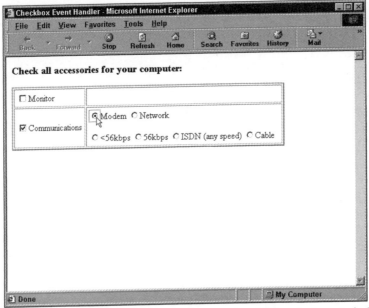

Figure 8-1: Clicking on button choices reveals additional relevant choices

Notice how the `toggle()` function was written as a generalizable function. This function can accept a reference to any checkbox object and any related span. If five more groups like this were added to the table, no additional functions would be needed.

In the `swap()` function, an application of a nested `if...else` shortcut construction is used to convert the Boolean values of the `checked` property to the strings needed for the `display` style property. The nesting is used to allow a single statement to take care of two conditions: the group of buttons to be controlled and the `checked` property of the button invoking the function. This function is not generalizable, because it contains explicit references to objects in the document. The `swap()` function can be made generalizable, but due to the special relationships between pairs of span elements (meaning one has to be hidden while the other displayed in its place), the function would require more parameters to fill in the blanks where explicit references are needed.

Note A rendering bug in NN6 causes the form controls in the lower right frame to lose their settings when the elements have their `display` style property set to `none`. The problem is related to the inclusion of P or similar block elements inside a table cell that contains controls. Therefore, if you uncheck and recheck the Communications checkbox in the example page, the previously displayed subgroup shows up even though no radio buttons are selected. You can script around this bug by preserving radio button settings in a global variable as you hide the group, and restoring the settings when you show the group again.

Syntax used to address elements here is the W3C DOM-compatible form, so this listing runs as is with IE5+ and NN6+. You can modify the listing to run in IE4 by adapting references to the document.all format.

Listing 24-5: **A Checkbox and an onClick event Handler**

```
<HTML>
<HEAD>
<TITLE>Checkbox Event Handler</TITLE>
<STYLE TYPE="text/css">
#monGroup {visibility:hidden}
#comGroup {visibility:hidden}
</STYLE>
<SCRIPT LANGUAGE="JavaScript">
// toggle visibility of a main group spans
function toggle(chkbox, group) {
    var visSetting = (chkbox.checked) ? "visible" : "hidden"
    document.getElementById(group).style.visibility = visSetting
}
// swap display of communications sub group spans
function swap(radBtn, group) {
    var modemsVisSetting = (group == "modems") ?
        ((radBtn.checked) ? "" : "none") : "none"
    var netwksVisSetting = (group == "netwks") ?
        ((radBtn.checked) ? "" : "none") : "none"
    document.getElementById("modems").style.display = modemsVisSetting
    document.getElementById("netwks").style.display = netwksVisSetting
}
</SCRIPT>
</HEAD>

<BODY>
<FORM>
<H3>Check all accessories for your computer:</H3>
<TABLE BORDER=2 CELLPADDING=5>
<TR>
    <TD>
    <INPUT TYPE="checkbox" NAME="monitor"
    onClick="toggle(this, 'monGroup')">Monitor
    </TD>
    <TD>
    <SPAN ID="monGroup">
        <INPUT TYPE="radio" NAME="monitorType">15"
        <INPUT TYPE="radio" NAME="monitorType">17"
        <INPUT TYPE="radio" NAME="monitorType">21"
        <INPUT TYPE="radio" NAME="monitorType">>21"
    </SPAN>
    </TD>
</TR>
<TR>
    <TD>
```

Continued

Listing 24-5 *(continued)*

```
<INPUT TYPE="checkbox" NAME="comms"
    onClick="toggle(this, 'comGroup')">Communications
</TD>
<TD>
<SPAN ID="comGroup">
    <P><INPUT TYPE="radio" NAME="commType"
        onClick="swap(this, 'modems')">Modem
    <INPUT TYPE="radio" NAME="commType"
        onClick="swap(this, 'netwks')">Network</P>
        <P><SPAN ID="modems" STYLE="display:none">
            <INPUT TYPE="radio" NAME="modemType"><56kbps
            <INPUT TYPE="radio" NAME="modemType">56kbps
            <INPUT TYPE="radio" NAME="modemType">ISDN (any speed)
            <INPUT TYPE="radio" NAME="modemType">Cable
        </SPAN>
        <SPAN ID="netwks" STYLE="display:none">
            <INPUT TYPE="radio" NAME="netwkType">Ethernet 10Mbps (10-Base T)
            <INPUT TYPE="radio" NAME="netwkType">Ethernet 100Mbps (10/100)
            <INPUT TYPE="radio" NAME="netwkType">T1 or greater
        </SPAN> </P>
</SPAN>
</TD>
</TR>

</TABLE>
</FORM>
</BODY>
</HTML>
```

Radio Input Object

Properties

checked

	NN2	NN3	NN4	NN6	IE3/J1	IE3/J2	IE4	IE5	IE5.5
Compatibility	✓	✓	✓	✓	✓	✓	✓	✓	✓

Example

Listing 24-6 uses a repeat loop in a function to look through all buttons in the Stooges group in search of the checked button. After the loop finds the one whose checked property is `true`, it returns the value of the index. In one instance, that index value is used to extract the `value` property for display in the alert dialog box; in the other instance, the value helps determine which button in the group is next in line to have its checked property set to `true`.

Listing 24-6: Finding the Selected Button in a Radio Group

```
<HTML>
<HEAD>
<TITLE>Extracting Highlighted Radio Button</TITLE>
<SCRIPT LANGUAGE="JavaScript">
function getSelectedButton(buttonGroup){
    for (var i = 0; i < buttonGroup.length; i++) {
        if (buttonGroup[i].checked) {
            return i
        }
    }
    return 0
}
function fullName(form) {
    var i = getSelectedButton(form.stooges)
    alert("You chose " + form.stooges[i].value + ".")
}
function cycle(form) {
    var i = getSelectedButton(form.stooges)
    if (i+1 == form.stooges.length) {
        form.stooges[0].checked = true
    } else {
        form.stooges[i+1].checked = true
    }
}
</SCRIPT>
</HEAD>

<BODY>
<FORM>
<B>Select your favorite Stooge:</B>
<P><INPUT TYPE="radio" NAME="stooges" VALUE="Moe Howard" CHECKED>Moe
<INPUT TYPE="radio" NAME="stooges" VALUE="Larry Fine" >Larry
<INPUT TYPE="radio" NAME="stooges" VALUE="Curly Howard" >Curly
<INPUT TYPE="radio" NAME="stooges" VALUE="Shemp Howard" >Shemp</P>
<P><INPUT TYPE="button" NAME="Viewer" VALUE="View Full Name..."
onClick="fullName(this.form)"></P>
<P><INPUT TYPE="button" NAME="Cycler" VALUE="Cycle Buttons"
onClick="cycle(this.form)"> </P>
</FORM>
</BODY>
</HTML>
```

defaultChecked

	NN2	NN3	NN4	NN6	IE3/J1	IE3/J2	IE4	IE5	IE5.5
Compatibility	✓	✓	✓	✓	✓	✓	✓	✓	✓

Example

In the script fragment of Listing 24-7 (not among the CD-ROM files), a function is passed a reference to a form containing the Stooges radio buttons. The goal is to see, in as general a way as possible (supplying the radio group name where needed), if the user changed the default setting. Looping through each of the radio buttons, you look for the one whose CHECKED attribute is set in the <INPUT> definition. With that index value (i) in hand, you then look to see if that entry is still checked. If not (notice the ! negation operator), you display an alert dialog box about the change.

Listing 24-7: **Has a Radio Button Changed?**

```
function groupChanged(form) {
    for (var i = 0; i < form.stooges.length; i++) {
        if (form.stooges[i].defaultChecked) {
            if (!form.stooges[i].checked) {
                alert("This radio group has been changed.")
            }
        }
    }
}
```

length

	NN2	NN3	NN4	NN6	IE3/J1	IE3/J2	IE4	IE5	IE5.5
Compatibility	✓	✓	✓	✓	✓	✓	✓	✓	✓

Example

See the loop construction within the function of Listing 24-7 for one way to apply the length property.

value

	NN2	NN3	NN4	NN6	IE3/J1	IE3/J2	IE4	IE5	IE5.5
Compatibility	✓	✓	✓	✓	✓	✓	✓	✓	✓

Example

Listing 24-6 (earlier in this chapter) demonstrates how a function extracts the `value` property of a radio button to display otherwise hidden information stored with a button. In this case, it lets the alert dialog box show the full name of the selected Stooge.

Event handlers
onClick

	NN2	NN3	NN4	NN6	IE3/J1	IE3/J2	IE4	IE5	IE5.5
Compatibility	✓	✓	✓	✓	✓	✓	✓	✓	✓

Example

Every time a user clicks one of the radio buttons in Listing 24-8, he or she sets a global variable to `true` or `false`, depending on whether the person is a Shemp lover. This action is independent of the action that is taking place if the user clicks on the View Full Name button. An `onUnload` event handler in the `<BODY>` definition triggers a function that displays a message to Shemp lovers just before the page clears (click the browser's Reload button to leave the current page prior to reloading). Here I use an initialize function triggered by `onLoad` so that the current radio button selection sets the global value upon a reload.

Listing 24-8: **An onClick event Handler for Radio Buttons**

```
<HTML>
<HEAD>
<TITLE>Radio Button onClick Handler</TITLE>
<SCRIPT LANGUAGE="JavaScript">
var ShempOPhile = false
function initValue() {
    ShempOPhile = document.forms[0].stooges[3].checked
}
 function fullName(form) {
    for (var i = 0; i < form.stooges.length; i++) {
        if (form.stooges[i].checked) {
            break
```

Continued

Listing 24-8 *(continued)*

```
        }
    }
    alert("You chose " + form.stooges[i].value + ".")
}
function setShemp(setting) {
    ShempOPhile = setting
}
function exitMsg() {
    if (ShempOPhile) {
        alert("You like SHEMP?")
    }
}
</SCRIPT>
</HEAD>

<BODY onLoad="initValue()" onUnload="exitMsg()">
<FORM>
<B>Select your favorite Stooge:</B><P>
<INPUT TYPE="radio" NAME="stooges" VALUE="Moe Howard" CHECKED
onClick="setShemp(false)">Moe
<INPUT TYPE="radio" NAME="stooges" VALUE="Larry Fine"
onClick="setShemp(false)">Larry
<INPUT TYPE="radio" NAME="stooges" VALUE="Curly Howard"
onClick="setShemp(false)">Curly
<INPUT TYPE="radio" NAME="stooges" VALUE="Shemp Howard"
onClick="setShemp(true)">Shemp<P>
<INPUT TYPE="button" NAME="Viewer" VALUE="View Full Name..."
onClick="fullName(this.form)">
</FORM>
</BODY>
</HTML>
```

See also Listing 24-5 for further examples of scripting onClick event handlers for radio buttons — this time to hide and show related items in a form.

✦   ✦   ✦

Text-Related Form Objects (Chapter 25)

◆ ◆ ◆ ◆

In This Chapter

Capturing and
modifying text field
contents

Triggering action and
entering text

Giving focus to a text
field and selecting its
contents

◆ ◆ ◆ ◆

When your page needs input from visitors beyond
"yes" or "no" answers, text fields are the interface
elements that provide the blank spaces. Whether you specify
the one-line INPUT element or the multi-line TEXTAREA element, this is where visitors can not only express themselves,
but also enter information in formats that might cause your
carefully constructed back-end database to go haywire. More
often than not, it is the text box that benefits most from client-
side form validation.

Despite the fact that the primary user action in a text box
is typing, keyboard events became available to scripters only
starting with the version 4 browsers from both Microsoft and
Netscape. But they arrived fully formed, with a suite of events
for the downstroke, upstroke, and complete press-and-release
action of typing a character. From there, the event object
takes over to help scripts uncover the character code and
whether the user held down any modifier keys while typing
the character. You can find examples of this kind of event handling in the examples for Chapters 1 and 13 of this book.

Text boxes are not always as scriptable as you might like
them to be. Modern browsers can apply style sheets to adjust
font characteristics of the complete text box, but you cannot,
say, set some of the words inside a text box to bold. Even
something as common (in other programs) as having the text
insertion pointer automatically plant itself at the end of existing text is possible so far only in IE4+/Windows via the
TEXTAREA's `createTextRange()` method and associated
`TextRange` object methods (see `TextRange` object examples
in Chapter 5 of this book). The moral of the story is to keep
your expectations for the powers of text fields at moderate
levels.

Examples Highlights

✦ Because the `value` property holds the string value of the text box, it is also the property you use to dump new text into a box. Listings 25-2 and 25-3 read from and write to a text box, transforming the entered contents along the way. You see three different approaches to the task.

✦ During client-side validation, you help the visitor by directing the text insertion pointer to the text field that failed a validation. Listing 25-4 shows how to use the `focus()` and `select()` methods along with a workaround for an IE/Windows timing problem that normally gets in the way.

✦ Use the `onChange` event handler (not `onBlur`) as a trigger for real-time data validation, as demonstrated in Listing 25-6. You also see the syntax that prevents form submission when validation fails.

✦ In IE4+ and NN6, you can adjust the size of a TEXTAREA element after the page has loaded. The example for the `cols` and `rows` properties lets you see the results in The Evaluator.

Text Input Object

Properties

defaultValue

	NN2	NN3	NN4	NN6	IE3/J1	IE3/J2	IE4	IE5	IE5.5
Compatibility	✓	✓	✓	✓	✓	✓	✓	✓	✓

Example

Important: Listings 25-1, 25-2, and 25-3 feature a form with only one text INPUT element. The rules of HTML forms say that such a form submits itself if the user presses the Enter key whenever the field has focus. Such a submission to a form whose action is undefined causes the page to reload, thus stopping any scripts that are running at the time. FORM elements for of these example listings contain an `onSubmit` event handler that both blocks the submission and attempts to trigger the text box `onChange` event handler to run the demonstration script. In some browsers, such as IE5/Mac, you may have to press the Tab key or click outside of the text box to trigger the `onChange` event handler after you enter a new value.

Listing 25-1 has a simple form with a single field that has a default value set in its tag. A function (`resetField()`) restores the contents of the page's lone field to the value assigned to it in the `<INPUT>` definition. For a single-field page such as this, defining a `TYPE="reset"` button or calling `form.reset()` works the same way because such buttons reestablish default values of all elements of a form. But if you want to reset only a subset of fields in a form, follow the example button and function in Listing 25-1.

Listing 25-1: Resetting a Text Object to Default Value

```
<HTML>
<HEAD>
<TITLE>Text Object DefaultValue</TITLE>
<SCRIPT LANGUAGE="JavaScript">
function upperMe(field) {
    field.value = field.value.toUpperCase()
}
function resetField(form) {
    form.converter.value = form.converter.defaultValue
}
</SCRIPT>
</HEAD>

<BODY>
<FORM onSubmit="window.focus(); return false">
Enter lowercase letters for conversion to uppercase: <INPUT TYPE="text"
NAME="converter" VALUE="sample" onChange="upperMe(this)">
<INPUT TYPE="button" VALUE="Reset Field"
onClick="resetField(this.form)">
</FORM>
</BODY>
</HTML>
```

---

form

	NN2	NN3	NN4	NN6	IE3/J1	IE3/J2	IE4	IE5	IE5.5
Compatibility	✓	✓	✓	✓	✓	✓	✓	✓	✓

Example

The following function fragment receives a reference to a text element as the parameter. The text element reference is needed to decide which branch to follow; then the form is submitted.

```
function setAction(fld) {
    if (fld.value.indexOf("@") != -1) {
        fld.form.action = "mailto:" + fld.value
    } else {
        fld.form.action = "cgi-bin/normal.pl"
    }
    fld.form.submit()
}
```

Notice how this function doesn't have to worry about the form reference, because its job is to work with whatever form encloses the text field that triggers this function.

maxLength

	NN2	NN3	NN4	NN6	IE3/J1	IE3/J2	IE4	IE5	IE5.5
Compatibility				✓			✓	✓	✓

Example

Use The Evaluator (Chapter 13 in *JavaScript Bible*) to experiment with the maxLength property. The top text field has no default value, but you can temporarily set it to only a few characters and see how it affects entering new values:

```
document.forms[0].input.maxLength = 3
```

Try typing into the field to see the results of the change. To restore the default value, reload the page.

name

	NN2	NN3	NN4	NN6	IE3/J1	IE3/J2	IE4	IE5	IE5.5
Compatibility	✓	✓	✓	✓	✓	✓	✓	✓	✓

Example

Consult Listing 25-2 later in this chapter, where I use the text object's name, convertor, as part of the reference when assigning a value to the field. To extract the name of a text object, you can use the property reference. Therefore, assuming that your script doesn't know the name of the first object in the first form of a document, the statement is

```
var objectName = document.forms[0].elements[0].name
```

readOnly

	NN2	NN3	NN4	NN6	IE3/J1	IE3/J2	IE4	IE5	IE5.5
Compatibility				✓			✓	✓	✓

Example

Use The Evaluator (Chapter 13 in *JavaScript Bible*) to set the bottom text box to be read-only. Begin by typing anything you want in the bottom text box. Then enter the following statement into the top text box:

```
document.forms[0].inspector.readOnly = true
```

While existing text in the box is selectable (and therefore can be copied into the clipboard), it cannot be modified or removed.

size

	NN2	NN3	NN4	NN6	IE3/J1	IE3/J2	IE4	IE5	IE5.5
Compatibility				✓			✓	✓	✓

Example

Resize the bottom text box of The Evaluator (Chapter 13 in *JavaScript Bible*) by entering the following statements into the top text box:

```
document.forms[0].inspector.size = 20
document.forms[0].inspector.size = 400
```

Reload the page to return the size back to normal (or set the value to 80).

value

	NN2	NN3	NN4	NN6	IE3/J1	IE3/J2	IE4	IE5	IE5.5
Compatibility	✓	✓	✓	✓	✓	✓	✓	✓	✓

Example

As a demonstration of how to retrieve and assign values to a text object, Listing 25-2 shows how the action in an `onChange` event handler is triggered. Enter any lowercase letters into the field and click out of the field. I pass a reference to the entire form object as a parameter to the event handler. The function extracts the value, converts it to uppercase (using one of the JavaScript string object methods), and assigns it back to the same field in that form.

Listing 25-2: **Getting and Setting a Text Object's Value**

```
<HTML>
<HEAD>
<TITLE>Text Object Value</TITLE>
<SCRIPT LANGUAGE="JavaScript">
function upperMe(form) {
    inputStr = form.converter.value
    form.converter.value = inputStr.toUpperCase()
}
</SCRIPT>
</HEAD>
```

Continued

Listing 25-2 *(continued)*

```
<BODY>
<FORM onSubmit="window.focus(); return false">
Enter lowercase letters for conversion to uppercase: <INPUT TYPE="text"
NAME="converter" VALUE="sample" onChange="upperMe(this.form)">
</FORM>
</BODY>
</HTML>
```

I also show two other ways to accomplish the same task, each one more efficient than the previous example. Both utilize the shortcut object reference to get at the heart of the text object. Listing 25-3 passes the text object — contained in the `this` reference — to the function handler. Because that text object contains a complete reference to it (out of sight, but there just the same), you can access the `value` property of that object and assign a string to that object's `value` property in a simple assignment statement.

Listing 25-3: **Passing a Text Object (as this) to the Function**

```
<HTML>
<HEAD>
<TITLE>Text Object Value</TITLE>
<SCRIPT LANGUAGE="JavaScript">
function upperMe(field) {
    field.value = field.value.toUpperCase()
}
</SCRIPT>
</HEAD>

<BODY>
<FORM onSubmit="window.focus(); return false">
Enter lowercase letters for conversion to uppercase: <INPUT TYPE="text"
NAME="converter" VALUE="sample" onChange="upperMe(this)">
</FORM>
</BODY>
</HTML>
```

Yet another way is to deal with the field values directly in an embedded event handler — instead of calling an external function (which is easier to maintain because all scripts are grouped together in the Head). With the function removed from the document, the event handler attribute of the `<INPUT>` tag changes to do all the work:

```
<INPUT TYPE="text" NAME="converter" VALUE="sample"
onChange="this.value = this.value.toUpperCase()">
```

The right-hand side of the assignment expression extracts the current contents of the field and (with the help of the `toUpperCase()` method of the string object) converts the original string to all uppercase letters. The result of this operation is assigned to the `value` property of the field.

The application of the this keyword in the previous examples may be confusing at first, but these examples represent the range of ways in which you can use such references effectively. Using this by itself as a parameter to an object's event handler refers only to that single object — a text object in Listing 25-3. If you want to pass along a broader scope of objects that contain the current object, use the `this` keyword along with the outer object layer that you want. In Listing 25-2, I sent a reference to the entire form along by specifying `this.form` — meaning the form that contains "this" object, which is being defined in the line of HTML code.

At the other end of the scale, you can use similar-looking syntax to specify a particular property of the `this` object. Thus, in the last example, I zeroed in on just the `value` property of the current object being defined — `this.value`. Although the formats of `this.form` and `this.value` appear the same, the fact that one is a reference to an object and the other just a value can influence the way your functions work. When you pass a reference to an object, the function can read and modify properties of that object (as well as invoke its functions); but when the parameter passed to a function is just a property value, you cannot modify that value without building a complete reference to the object and its value.

Methods

blur()

	NN2	NN3	NN4	NN6	IE3/J1	IE3/J2	IE4	IE5	IE5.5
Compatibility	✓	✓	✓	✓	✓	✓	✓	✓	✓

Example

The following statement invokes the `blur()` method on a text box named `vanishText`:

```
document.forms[0].vanishText.blur()
```

focus()

	NN2	NN3	NN4	NN6	IE3/J1	IE3/J2	IE4	IE5	IE5.5
Compatibility	✓	✓	✓	✓	✓	✓	✓	✓	✓

Example

See Listing 25-4 for an example of an application of the `focus()` method in concert with the `select()` method.

select()

	NN2	NN3	NN4	NN6	IE3/J1	IE3/J2	IE4	IE5	IE5.5
Compatibility	✓	✓	✓	✓	✓	✓	✓	✓	✓

Example

A click of the Verify button in Listing 25-4 performs a validation on the contents of the text box, making sure the entry consists of all numbers. All work is controlled by the checkNumeric() function, which receives a reference to the field needing inspection as a parameter. Because of the way the delayed call to the doSelection() function has to be configured, various parts of what will become a valid reference to the form are extracted from the field's and form's properties. If the validation (performed in the isNumber() function) fails, the setSelection() method is invoked after an artificial delay of zero milliseconds. As goofy as this sounds, this method is all that IE needs to recover from the display and closure of the alert dialog box. Because the first parameter of the setTimeout() method must be a string, the example assembles a string invocation of the setSelection() function via string versions of the form and field names. All that the setSelection() function does is focus and select the field whose reference is passed as a parameter. This function is now generalizable to work with multiple text boxes in a more complex form.

Listing 25-4: **Selecting a Field**

```
<HTML>
<HEAD>
<TITLE>Text Object Select/Focus</TITLE>
<SCRIPT LANGUAGE="JavaScript">
// general purpose function to see if a suspected numeric input is a number
function isNumber(inputStr) {
    for (var i = 0; i < inputStr.length; i++) {
        var oneChar = inputStr.charAt(i)
        if (oneChar < "0" || oneChar > "9") {
            alert("Please make sure entries are integers only.")
            return false
        }
    }
    return true
}
function checkNumeric(fld) {
    var inputStr = fld.value
    var fldName = fld.name
    var formName = fld.form.name
    if (isNumber(inputStr)) {
        // statements if true
    } else {
```

```
            setTimeout("doSelection(document." + formName + ". " + fldName + ")", 0)
    }
}

function doSelection(fld) {
    fld.focus()
    fld.select()
}
</SCRIPT>
</HEAD>

<BODY>
<FORM NAME="entryForm" onSubmit="return false">
Enter any positive integer: <INPUT TYPE="text" NAME="numeric"><P>
<INPUT TYPE="button" VALUE="Verify" onClick="checkNumeric(this.form.numeric)">
</FORM>
</BODY>
</HTML>
```

Event handlers

```
onBlur
onFocus
onSelect
```

	NN2	NN3	NN4	NN6	IE3/J1	IE3/J2	IE4	IE5	IE5.5
Compatibility	✓	✓	✓	✓	✓	✓	✓	✓	✓

Example

To demonstrate one of these event handlers, Listing 25-5 shows how you may use the window's statusbar as a prompt message area after a user activates any field of a form. When the user tabs to or clicks on a field, the prompt message associated with that field appears in the statusbar. In Figure 9-1, the user has tabbed to the second text box, which caused the statusbar message to display a prompt for the field.

Listing 25-5: **The onFocus event Handler**

```
<HTML>
<HEAD>
<TITLE>Elements Array</TITLE>
<SCRIPT LANGUAGE="JavaScript">
```

Continued

document.*formObject*.*textObject*.onBlur

Listing 25-5 *(continued)*

```
function prompt(msg) {
    window.status = "Please enter your " + msg + "."
}
</SCRIPT>
</HEAD>

<BODY>
<FORM>
Enter your first name:<INPUT TYPE="text" NAME="firstName"
onFocus="prompt('first name')"><P>
Enter your last name:<INPUT TYPE="text" NAME="lastName"
onFocus="prompt('last name')"><P>
Enter your address:<INPUT TYPE="text" NAME="address"
onFocus="prompt('address')"><P>
Enter your city:<INPUT TYPE="text" NAME="city" onFocus="prompt('city')"><P>
</FORM>
</BODY>
</HTML>
```

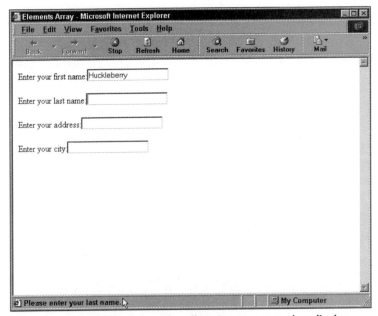

Figure 9-1: An onFocus event handler triggers a statusbar display.

onChange

	NN2	NN3	NN4	NN6	IE3/J1	IE3/J2	IE4	IE5	IE5.5
Compatibility	✓	✓	✓	✓	✓	✓	✓	✓	✓

Example

Whenever a user makes a change to the text in a field in Listing 25-6 and then either tabs or clicks out of the field, the change event is sent to that field, triggering the onChange event handler.

Because the form in Listing 25-6 has only one field, the example demonstrates a technique you can use that prevents a form from being "submitted" if the user accidentally presses the Enter key. The technique is as simple as defeating the submission via the onSubmit event handler of the form. At the same time, the onSubmit event handler invokes the checkIt() function, so that pressing the Enter key (as well as pressing Tab or clicking outside the field) triggers the function.

Listing 25-6: **Data Validation via an onChange event Handler**

```
<HTML>
<HEAD>
<TITLE>Text Object Select/Focus</TITLE>
<SCRIPT LANGUAGE="JavaScript">
// general purpose function to see if a suspected numeric input is a number
function isNumber(inputStr) {
    for (var i = 0; i < inputStr.length; i++) {
        var oneChar = inputStr.substring(i, i + 1)
        if (oneChar < "0" || oneChar > "9") {
            alert("Please make sure entries are numbers only.")
            return false
        }
    }
    return true
}
function checkIt(form) {
    inputStr = form.numeric.value
    if (isNumber(inputStr)) {
        // statements if true
    } else {
        form.numeric.focus()
        form.numeric.select()
    }
}
</SCRIPT>
</HEAD>

<BODY onSubmit="checkIt(this); return false">
```

Continued

Listing 25-6 *(continued)*

```
<FORM>
Enter any positive integer: <INPUT TYPE="text" NAME="numeric"
onChange="checkIt(this.form)"><P>
</FORM>
</BODY>
</HTML>
```

TEXTAREA Element Object

Properties

`cols`
`rows`

	NN2	NN3	NN4	NN6	IE3/J1	IE3/J2	IE4	IE5	IE5.5
Compatibility				✓			✓	✓	✓

Example

Use The Evaluator to play with the `cols` and `rows` property settings for the Results textarea on that page. Shrink the width of the textarea by entering the following statement into the top text box:

```
document.forms[0].output.cols = 30
```

And make the textarea one row deeper:

```
document.forms[0].output.rows++
```

Methods

`createTextRange()`

	NN2	NN3	NN4	NN6	IE3/J1	IE3/J2	IE4	IE5	IE5.5
Compatibility							✓	✓	✓

Example

See the example for the `TextRange.move()` method in Chapter 5 of this book to see how to control the text insertion pointer inside a TEXTAREA element.

✦   ✦   ✦

Select, Option, and Optgroup Objects (Chapter 26)

The SELECT element is the best space-saving device in the HTML form repertoire. Whether you choose the pop-up menu or scrolling list display style, your page can provide visitors with a visually compact list of literally hundreds of items from which to choose. From a scripter's point of view, however, it is a complex item to manage, especially in older browsers.

In truth, the SELECT element is an outer wrapper for the OPTION element items nested within. Each OPTION element contains the text that the user sees in the list, as well as a hidden value that may be more meaningful to a server database or client script. The difficulty with browsers prior to IE4 and NN6 is that reading the hidden value of the currently chosen item in the list requires an extensive reference to not only the SELECT element, but to the item in the array of OPTION element objects. To reach that specific item, the script uses a reference to the SELECT object's `selectedIndex` property as the `options` array index. Newer browsers simplify the matter by providing a single `value` property for the SELECT object that returns the value of the currently selected item (or of the first item when multiple choices are allowed).

Many browser versions provide script facilities for modifying the content of a SELECT list. But the effect is not perfect in browsers that don't also reflow the page to reflect the potentially resized width of the list.

A user interface debate rages about whether a SELECT list, whose purpose is obviously intended to direct site navigation, should navigate immediately upon making a choice or if the user should also click on an explicit "Go" button next to the list. The former is faster for the impatient visitor, but the latter doesn't shoot off to an undesired page when the user makes a wrong selection. Good luck with that decision.

Examples Highlights

✦ To harvest the values of all selected items in a multiple list, your script needs to cycle through the SELECT element's `options` array and inspect the `selected` property of each, as shown in Listing 26-4.

✦ Scripts can also retrieve the text of the selected item, instead of the hidden value. Compare two similar applications that work with the `text` (Listing 26-5) and `value` (Listing 26-6) properties.

✦ Listings 26-5 and 26-6 show the backward-compatible, long reference to retrieve a chosen option's details. The modern alternative accompanies the example for the `SELECT.value` property.

✦ See Listing 26-8 for another example of triggering a script via the `onChange` event handler of a SELECT object.

✦ Implementations of the OPTGROUP element object may need improvement before Listing 26-9 behaves as it should to modify hierarchical labels within a SELECT list.

SELECT Element Object

Properties

length

	NN2	NN3	NN4	NN6	IE3/J1	IE3/J2	IE4	IE5	IE5.5
Compatibility	✓	✓	✓	✓	✓	✓	✓	✓	✓

Example

See Listing 26-1 in Chapter 26 of the *JavaScript Bible* for an illustration of the way you use the `length` property to help determine how often to cycle through the repeat loop in search of selected items. Because the loop counter, i, must start at 0, the counting continues until the loop counter is one less than the actual length value (which starts its count with 1).

multiple

	NN2	NN3	NN4	NN6	IE3/J1	IE3/J2	IE4	IE5	IE5.5
Compatibility				✓			✓	✓	✓

Example

The following statement toggles between single and multiple selections on a SELECT element object whose `SIZE` attribute is set to a value greater than 1:

```
document.forms[0].mySelect.multiple = !document.forms[0].mySelect.multiple
```

options[*index*]

	NN2	NN3	NN4	NN6	IE3/J1	IE3/J2	IE4	IE5	IE5.5
Compatibility	✓	✓	✓	✓	✓	✓	✓	✓	✓

Example

See Listings 26-1 through 26-3 in Chapter 26 of the *JavaScript Bible* for examples of how the options array references information about the options inside a SELECT element.

options[*index*].defaultSelected

	NN2	NN3	NN4	NN6	IE3/J1	IE3/J2	IE4	IE5	IE5.5
Compatibility	✓	✓	✓	✓	✓	✓	✓	✓	✓

Example

The following statement preserves a Boolean value if the first option of the SELECT list is the default selected item:

```
var zeroIsDefault = document.forms[0].listName.options[0].defaultSelected
```

options[*index*].index

	NN2	NN3	NN4	NN6	IE3/J1	IE3/J2	IE4	IE5	IE5.5
Compatibility	✓	✓	✓	✓	✓	✓	✓	✓	✓

Example

The following statement assigns the index integer of the first option of a SELECT element named listName to a variable named itemIndex.

```
var itemIndex = document.forms[0].listName.options[0].index
```

options[*index*].selected

	NN2	NN3	NN4	NN6	IE3/J1	IE3/J2	IE4	IE5	IE5.5
Compatibility	✓	✓	✓	✓	✓	✓	✓	✓	✓

Example

To accumulate a list of all items selected by the user, the `seeList()` function in Listing 26-4 systematically examines the `options[index].selected` property of each item in the list. The text of each item whose `selected` property is `true` is appended to the list. I add the `"\n "` inline carriage returns and spaces to make the list in the alert dialog box look nice and indented. If you assign other values to the `VALUE` attributes of each option, the script can extract the `options[index].value` property to collect those values instead.

Listing 26-4: **Cycling through a Multiple-Selection List**

```
<HTML>
<HEAD>
<TITLE>Accessories List</TITLE>
<SCRIPT LANGUAGE="JavaScript">
function seeList(form) {
    var result = ""
    for (var i = 0; i < form.accList.length; i++) {
        if (form.accList.options[i].selected) {
            result += "\n   " + form.accList.options[i].text
        }
}
    alert("You have selected:" + result)
}
</SCRIPT>
</HEAD>

<BODY>
<FORM>
<P>Control/Command-click on all accessories you use:
<SELECT NAME="accList" SIZE=9 MULTIPLE>
    <OPTION SELECTED>Color Monitor
    <OPTION>Modem
    <OPTION>Scanner
    <OPTION>Laser Printer
    <OPTION>Tape Backup
    <OPTION>MO Drive
    <OPTION>Video Camera
</SELECT> </P>
<P><INPUT TYPE="button" VALUE="View Summary..."
onClick="seeList(this.form)"></P>
</FORM>
</BODY>
</HTML>
```

options[*index*].text

	NN2	NN3	NN4	NN6	IE3/J1	IE3/J2	IE4	IE5	IE5.5
Compatibility	✓	✓	✓	✓	✓	✓	✓	✓	✓

Example

To demonstrate the text property of an option, Listing 26-5 applies the text from a selected option to the document.bgColor property of a document in the current window. The color names are part of the collection built into all scriptable browsers; fortunately, the values are case-insensitive so that you can capitalize the color names displayed and assign them to the property.

Listing 26-5: **Using the options[index].text Property**

```
<HTML>
<HEAD>
<TITLE>Color Changer 1</TITLE>
<SCRIPT LANGUAGE="JavaScript">
function seeColor(form) {
    var newColor = (form.colorsList.options[form.colorsList.selectedIndex].text)
    document.bgColor = newColor
}
</SCRIPT>
</HEAD>

<BODY>
<FORM>
<P>Choose a background color:
<SELECT NAME="colorsList">
    <OPTION SELECTED>Gray
    <OPTION>Lime
    <OPTION>Ivory
    <OPTION>Red
</SELECT></P>
<P><INPUT TYPE="button" VALUE="Change It" onClick="seeColor(this.form)"></P>
</FORM>
</BODY>
</HTML>
```

`options[index].value`

	NN2	NN3	NN4	NN6	IE3/J1	IE3/J2	IE4	IE5	IE5.5
Compatibility	✓	✓	✓	✓	✓	✓	✓	✓	✓

Example

Listing 26-6 requires the option text that the user sees to be in familiar, multiple-word form. But to set the color using the browser's built-in color palette, you must use the one-word form. Those one-word values are stored in the VALUE attributes of each <OPTION> definition. The function then reads the value property, assigning it to the bgColor of the current document. If you prefer to use the hexadecimal triplet form of color specifications, those values are assigned to the VALUE attributes (<OPTION VALUE="#e9967a">Dark Salmon).

Listing 26-6: **Using the options[index].value Property**

```
<HTML>
<HEAD>
<TITLE>Color Changer 2</TITLE>
<SCRIPT LANGUAGE="JavaScript">
function seeColor(form) {
    var newColor =
(form.colorsList.options[form.colorsList.selectedIndex].value)
    document.bgColor = newColor
}
</SCRIPT>
</HEAD>

<BODY>
<FORM>
<P>Choose a background color:
<SELECT NAME="colorsList">
    <OPTION SELECTED VALUE="cornflowerblue">Cornflower Blue
    <OPTION VALUE="darksalmon">Dark Salmon
    <OPTION VALUE="lightgoldenrodyellow">Light Goldenrod Yellow
    <OPTION VALUE="seagreen">Sea Green
</SELECT></P>
<P><INPUT TYPE="button" VALUE="Change It" onClick="seeColor(this.form)"></P>
</FORM>
</BODY>
</HTML>
```

selectedIndex

	NN2	NN3	NN4	NN6	IE3/J1	IE3/J2	IE4	IE5	IE5.5
Compatibility	✓	✓	✓	✓	✓	✓	✓	✓	✓

Example

In the `inspect()` function of Listing 26-7, notice that the value inside the `options` property index brackets is a reference to the object's `selectedIndex` property. Because this property always returns an integer value, it fulfills the needs of the index value for the `options` property. Therefore, if you select Green in the pop-up menu, `form.colorsList.selectedIndex` returns a value of 1; that reduces the rest of the reference to `form.colorsList.options[1].text`, which equals "Green."

Listing 26-7: **Using the selectedIndex Property**

```
<HTML>
<HEAD>
<TITLE>Select Inspector</TITLE>
<SCRIPT LANGUAGE="JavaScript">
function inspect(form) {
    alert(form.colorsList.options[form.colorsList.selectedIndex].text)
}
</SCRIPT>
</HEAD>

<BODY>
<FORM>
<P><SELECT NAME="colorsList">
    <OPTION SELECTED>Red
    <OPTION VALUE="Plants"><I>Green</I>
    <OPTION>Blue
</SELECT></P>
<P><INPUT TYPE="button" VALUE="Show Selection" onClick="inspect(this.form)"></P>
</FORM>
</BODY>
</HTML>
```

size

	NN2	NN3	NN4	NN6	IE3/J1	IE3/J2	IE4	IE5	IE5.5
Compatibility				✓			✓	✓	✓

Example

The following statement sets the number of visible items to 5:

```
document.forms[0].mySelect.size = 5
```

value

	NN2	NN3	NN4	NN6	IE3/J1	IE3/J2	IE4	IE5	IE5.5
Compatibility				✓			✓	✓	✓

Example

The function in Listing 26-6 that accesses the chosen value the long way can be simplified for newer browsers only with the following construction:

```
function seeColor(form) {
    document.bgColor = form.colorsList.value
}
```

Methods

item(*index*)
namedItem("*optionID*")

	NN2	NN3	NN4	NN6	IE3/J1	IE3/J2	IE4	IE5	IE5.5
Compatibility				✓					

Example

The following statement assigns an OPTION element reference to a variable:

```
var oneOption = document.forms[0].mySelect.namedItem("option3_2")
```

Event handlers

onChange

	NN2	NN3	NN4	NN6	IE3/J1	IE3/J2	IE4	IE5	IE5.5
Compatibility	✓	✓	✓	✓	✓	✓	✓	✓	✓

Example

Listing 26-8 is a version of Listing 26-6 that invokes all action as the result of a user making a selection from the pop-up menu. The onChange event handler in the <SELECT> tag replaces the action button. For this application—when you desire a direct response to user input—an appropriate method is to have the action triggered from the pop-up menu rather than by a separate action button.

Notice two other important changes. First, the SELECT element now contains a blank first option. When a user visits the page, nothing is selected yet, so you should present a blank option to encourage the user to make a selection. The function also makes sure that the user selects one of the color-valued items before it attempts to change the background color.

Second, the BODY element contains an onUnload event handler that resets the form. The purpose behind this is that if the user navigates to another page and uses the Back button to return to the page, the script-adjusted background color does not persist. I recommend you return the SELECT element to its original setting. Unfortunately, the reset does not stick to the form in IE4 and IE5 for Windows (although this problem appears to be repaired in IE5.5). Another way to approach this issue is to use the onLoad event handler to invoke seeColor(), passing as a parameter a reference to the SELECT element. Thus, if the SELECT element choice persists, the background color is adjusted accordingly after the page loads.

Listing 26-8: **Triggering a Color Change from a Pop-Up Menu**

```
<HTML>
<HEAD>
<TITLE>Color Changer 2</TITLE>
<SCRIPT LANGUAGE="JavaScript">
function seeColor(list) {
    var newColor = (list.options[list.selectedIndex].value)
    if (newColor) {
        document.bgColor = newColor
    }
}
</SCRIPT>
</HEAD>

<BODY onUnload="document.forms[0].reset()">
<FORM>
```

Continued

Listing 26-8 *(continued)*

```
<P>Choose a background color:
<SELECT NAME="colorsList" onChange="seeColor(this)">
    <OPTION SELECTED VALUE="">
    <OPTION VALUE="cornflowerblue">Cornflower Blue
    <OPTION VALUE="darksalmon">Dark Salmon
    <OPTION VALUE="lightgoldenrodyellow">Light Goldenrod Yellow
    <OPTION VALUE="seagreen">Sea Green
</SELECT></P>
</FORM>
</BODY>
</HTML>
```

OPTION Element Object

Properties
label

	NN2	NN3	NN4	NN6	IE3/J1	IE3/J2	IE4	IE5	IE5.5
Compatibility				✓				✓	

Example
The following statement modifies the text that appears as the selected text in a pop-up list:

```
document.forms[0].mySelect.options[3].label = "Widget 9000"
```

If this option is the currently selected one, the text on the pop-up list at rest changes to the new label.

OPTGROUP Element Object

Properties
label

	NN2	NN3	NN4	NN6	IE3/J1	IE3/J2	IE4	IE5	IE5.5
Compatibility				✓				✓	

Example

I present Listing 26-9 in the hope that Microsoft and Netscape will eventually eradicate the bugs that afflict their current implementations of the label property. When the feature works as intended, Listing 26-9 demonstrates how a script can alter the text of option group labels. This page is an enhanced version of the background color setters used in other examples of this chapter. Be aware that IE5/Mac does not alter the last OPTGROUP element's label, and NN6 achieves only a partial change to the text displayed in the SELECT element.

Listing 26-9: **Modifying OPTGROUP Element Labels**

```
<HTML>
<HEAD>
<TITLE>Color Changer 3</TITLE>
<SCRIPT LANGUAGE="JavaScript">
var regularLabels = ["Reds","Greens","Blues"]
var naturalLabels = ["Apples","Leaves","Sea"]
function setRegularLabels(list) {
    var optGrps = list.getElementsByTagName("OPTGROUP")
    for (var i = 0; i < optGrps.length; i++) {
        optGrps[i].label = regularLabels[i]
    }
}
function setNaturalLabels(list) {
    var optGrps = list.getElementsByTagName("OPTGROUP")
    for (var i = 0; i < optGrps.length; i++) {
        optGrps[i].label = naturalLabels[i]
    }
}
function seeColor(list) {
    var newColor = (list.options[list.selectedIndex].value)
    if (newColor) {
        document.bgColor = newColor
    }
}
</SCRIPT>
</HEAD>

<BODY onUnload="document.forms[0].reset()">
<FORM>
<P>Choose a background color:
<SELECT name="colorsList" onChange="seeColor(this)">
    <OPTGROUP ID="optGrp1" label="Reds">
        <OPTION value="#ff9999">Light Red
        <OPTION value="#ff3366">Medium Red
        <OPTION value="#ff0000">Bright Red
        <OPTION value="#660000">Dark Red
    </OPTGROUP>
    <OPTGROUP ID="optGrp2" label="Greens">
        <OPTION value="#ccff66">Light Green
```

Continued

Listing 26-9 *(continued)*

```
        <OPTION value="#99ff33">Medium Green
        <OPTION value="#00ff00">Bright Green
        <OPTION value="#006600">Dark Green
    </OPTGROUP>
    <OPTGROUP ID="optGrp3" label="Blues">
        <OPTION value="#ccffff">Light Blue
        <OPTION value="#66ccff">Medium Blue
        <OPTION value="#0000ff">Bright Blue
        <OPTION value="#000066">Dark Blue
    </OPTGROUP>
</SELECT></P>
<P>
<INPUT TYPE="radio" NAME="labels" CHECKED
onClick="setRegularLabels(this.form.colorsList)">Regular Label Names
<INPUT TYPE="radio" NAME="labels"
onClick="setNaturalLabels(this.form.colorsList)">Label Names from Nature</P>
</FORM>
</BODY>
</HTML>
```

✦   ✦   ✦

Table and List Objects (Chapter 27)

C H A P T E R

◆ ◆ ◆ ◆

In This Chapter

Modifying table cell content

Adding and deleting table rows

Modifying table dimensions, colors, and borders

Changing numbering sequences and bullet symbols for LI element objects

◆ ◆ ◆ ◆

Dynamic object models that take advantage of automatic page reflow create huge opportunities for creative Web designers. Nowhere is that more apparent than in the TABLE element object and all the other objects that nest within (TR, TH, TD, and so on). Not only is it possible to swap the content of a table cell at any time, but the object models provide powerful methods for completely remolding the composition of a table on the fly.

HTML tables are at once elegant because they provide a lot of pleasing organization to a page with little code, and also complex due to the large number of related elements and substantial list of attributes for each element. Those attributes become object properties in the modern object model, so it means that scripters have much to choose from (and be confused by) when bringing tables to life.

Using the special-purpose methods that insert rows and cells also takes some initial adjustment for many scripters. For example, inserting a row has almost no visual effect on an existing table until you not only insert cells into the row, but also plant content in the cells. Code examples for these operations are part of the general discussion of the TABLE object in the *JavaScript Bible*.

Designers whose browser targets are IE4+/Windows can also take advantage of Microsoft's data binding technology. Data from external sources can fill tables with only the slightest bit of HTML markup. Chapter 15 contains examples of this in its discussion of the `dataFld` and related properties.

This chapter also includes objects for ordered and unordered lists (and list items nested within). In concert with style sheets that can include or exclude elements from page rendering, these objects provide additional layout opportunities for clever designers.

Examples Highlights

✦ Scripts can adjust the value of a TABLE object's `width` property, including switching between a fixed pixel size and a percentage of the table container's width.

✦ Compare the examples for the IE5/Windows `TABLE.cells` property and the `TR.cells` property for IE4+ and NN6.

✦ Follow the example for the `TD.colSpan` property to observe how a table responds to such changes in real time.

✦ Examples for list-related elements show how to set the list types for script-generated lists.

TABLE Element Object

Properties

align

	NN2	NN3	NN4	NN6	IE3/J1	IE3/J2	IE4	IE5	IE5.5
Compatibility				✓			✓	✓	✓

Example

Use The Evaluator (Chapter 13 in the *JavaScript Bible*) to see the `align` property at work. The default value (`left`) is in force when the page loads. But you can shift the table to right-align with the body by entering the following statement into the top text box for IE5+ and NN6+:

```
document.getElementById("myTable").align = "right"
```

background

	NN2	NN3	NN4	NN6	IE3/J1	IE3/J2	IE4	IE5	IE5.5
Compatibility							✓	✓	✓

Example

Treat the `background` property of a table like you do the `src` property of an IMG element object. If you precache an image, you can assign the `src` property of the precached `image` object to the `background` property of the table for quick image changing. Such an assignment statement looks like the following:

```
document.all.myTable.background = imgArray["myTableAlternate"].src
```

bgColor

	NN2	NN3	NN4	NN6	IE3/J1	IE3/J2	IE4	IE5	IE5.5
Compatibility				✓			✓	✓	✓

Example

Use The Evaluator (Chapter 13 in the *JavaScript Bible*) to assign a color to the table. After looking at the table to see its initial state, enter the following IE5+/NN6+ statement into the top text box:

```
document.getElementById("myTable").bgColor = "lightgreen"
```

When you look at the table again, you see that only some of the cells turned to green. This is because colors also are assigned to table elements nested inside the outermost table element, and the color specification closest to the actual element wins the contest.

border

	NN2	NN3	NN4	NN6	IE3/J1	IE3/J2	IE4	IE5	IE5.5
Compatibility				✓			✓	✓	✓

Example

To remove all traces of an outside border of a table (and, in some combinations of attributes of other table elements, borders between cells), use the following statement (in IE5+/NN6+ syntax):

```
document.getElementById("myTable").border = 0
```

borderColor
borderColorDark
borderColorLight

	NN2	NN3	NN4	NN6	IE3/J1	IE3/J2	IE4	IE5	IE5.5
Compatibility							✓	✓	✓

Example

Assuming that you have set the initial light and dark color attributes of a table, the following function swaps the light and dark colors to shift the light source to the opposite corner:

```
function swapColors(tableRef) {
    var oldLight = tableRef.borderColorLight
    tableRef.borderColorLight = tableRef.borderColorDark
    tableRef.borderColorDark = oldLight
}
```

While you can easily invoke this function over and over by ending it with a
`setTimeout()` method that calls this function after a fraction of a second, the
results are very distracting to the person trying to read your page. Please don't do it.

caption

	NN2	NN3	NN4	NN6	IE3/J1	IE3/J2	IE4	IE5	IE5.5
Compatibility				✓			✓	✓	✓

Example

The following example, for use with The Evaluator (Chapter 13 in the *JavaScript
Bible*) in NN6+, demonstrates the sequence of assigning a new CAPTION element
object to a table. While the table in The Evaluator already has a CAPTION element,
the following statements replace it with an entirely new one. Enter each of the
following statements into the top text box, starting with the one that saves a long
reference into a variable for multiple uses at the end:

```
t = document.getElementById("myTable")
a = document.createElement("CAPTION")
b = document.createTextNode("A Brand New Caption")
a.appendChild(b)
t.replaceChild(a, t.caption)
```

A view of the table shows that the new caption has replaced the old one because a
table can have only one CAPTION element.

cellPadding
cellSpacing

	NN2	NN3	NN4	NN6	IE3/J1	IE3/J2	IE4	IE5	IE5.5
Compatibility				✓			✓	✓	✓

Example

Use The Evaluator (Chapter 13 in the *JavaScript Bible*) to adjust the
`cellPadding` and `cellSpacing` properties of the demonstrator table. First, adjust
the padding (IE5+/NN6 syntax):

```
document.getElementById("myTable").cellPadding = 50
```

Now, adjust the cell spacing:

```
document.getElementById("myTable").cellSpacing = 15
```

Notice how `cellSpacing` affected the thickness of inter-cell borders.

cells

	NN2	NN3	NN4	NN6	IE3/J1	IE3/J2	IE4	IE5	IE5.5
Compatibility								✓	✓

Example

Use The Evaluator with IE5+ for Windows to have JavaScript calculate the number of columns in the demonstrator table with the help of the `cells` and `rows` properties. Enter the following statement into the top text box:

```
document.all.myTable.cells.length/document.all.myTable.rows.length
```

The result is the number of columns in the table.

dataPageSize

	NN2	NN3	NN4	NN6	IE3/J1	IE3/J2	IE4	IE5	IE5.5
Compatibility							✓	✓	✓

Example

If you want to change the number of visible rows of linked data in the table to 15, use the following statement:

```
document.all.myTable.dataPageSize = 15
```

frame

	NN2	NN3	NN4	NN6	IE3/J1	IE3/J2	IE4	IE5	IE5.5
Compatibility				✓			✓	✓	✓

Example

Listing 27-4 presents a page that cycles through all possible settings for the `frame` property. The `frame` property value is displayed in the table's caption. (Early versions of NN6 might fail to refresh part of the page after adjusting the `frame` property.)

Listing 27-4: **Cycling Through Table frame Property Values**

```
<HTML>
<HEAD>
<TITLE>TABLE.frame Property</TITLE>

<SCRIPT LANGUAGE="JavaScript">
var timeoutID
var frameValues = ["box", "above", "rhs", "below", "lhs", "hsides", "vsides",
                   "border", "void"]
function rotateBorder(i) {
    document.getElementById("myTABLE").frame = frameValues[i]
    document.getElementById("myCAPTION").innerHTML = frameValues[i]
    i = (++i == frameValues.length) ? 0 : i
    timeoutID = setTimeout("rotateBorder(" + i + ")", 2000)
}
function stopRotate() {
    clearTimeout(timeoutID)
    document.getElementById("myTABLE").frame = "box"
    document.getElementById("myCAPTION").innerHTML = "box"
}
</SCRIPT>
</HEAD>

<BODY>
<H1>TABLE.frame Property</H1>
<HR>
<FORM NAME="controls">
<FIELDSET>
<LEGEND>Cycle Table Edge Visibility</LEGEND>
<TABLE WIDTH="100%" CELLSPACING=20><TR>
<TD><INPUT TYPE="button" VALUE="Cycle" onClick="rotateBorder(0)"></TD>
<TD><INPUT TYPE="button" VALUE="Stop" onClick="stopRotate()"></TD>
</TR>
</TABLE>
</FIELDSET>
</TABLE>
</FIELDSET>
</FORM>
<HR>
<TABLE ID="myTABLE" CELLPADDING=5 BORDER=3 ALIGN="center">
<CAPTION ID="myCAPTION">Default</CAPTION>
<THEAD ID="myTHEAD">
<TR>
    <TH>River<TH>Outflow<TH>Miles<TH>Kilometers
</TR>
</THEAD>
<TBODY>
<TR>
    <TD>Nile<TD>Mediterranean<TD>4160<TD>6700
</TR>
<TR>
    <TD>Congo<TD>Atlantic Ocean<TD>2900<TD>4670
```

```
</TR>
<TR>
    <TD>Niger<TD>Atlantic Ocean<TD>2600<TD>4180
</TR>
<TR>
    <TD>Zambezi<TD>Indian Ocean<TD>1700<TD>2740
</TR>
</TABLE>
</BODY>
</HTML>
```

height
width

	NN2	NN3	NN4	NN6	IE3/J1	IE3/J2	IE4	IE5	IE5.5
Compatibility				✓			✓	✓	✓

Example

Use The Evaluator (Chapter 13 in the *JavaScript Bible*) to adjust the width of the demonstrator table. Begin by increasing the width to the full width of the page:

```
document.getElementById("myTable").width = "100%"
```

To restore the table to its minimum width, assign a very small value to the property:

```
document.getElementById("myTable").width = 50
```

If you have IE4+, you can perform similar experiments with the height property of the table.

rows

	NN2	NN3	NN4	NN6	IE3/J1	IE3/J2	IE4	IE5	IE5.5
Compatibility				✓			✓	✓	✓

Example

Use The Evaluator to examine the number of rows in the demonstrator table. Enter the following statement into the top text box:

```
document.getElementById("myTable").rows.length
```

In contrast, notice how the rows property sees only the rows within the demonstrator table's TBODY element:

```
document.getElementById("myTbody").rows.length
```

rules

	NN2	NN3	NN4	NN6	IE3/J1	IE3/J2	IE4	IE5	IE5.5
Compatibility				✓			✓	✓	✓

Example

Listing 27-5 presents a page that cycles through all possible settings for the rules property. The rules property value is displayed in the table's caption. When you run this script, notice the nice border display for this table's combination of COLGROUP and table row segment elements. Figure 11-1 shows the IE/Windows rendition for the groups type of table rules. Early versions of NN6 may not render the altered table correctly, and scripted changes won't appear on the page.

Listing 27-5: **Cycling Through Table rules Property Values**

```
<HTML>
<HEAD>
<TITLE>TABLE.rules Property</TITLE>

<SCRIPT LANGUAGE="JavaScript">
var timeoutID
var rulesValues = ["all", "cols", "groups", "none", "rows"]
function rotateBorder(i) {
    document.getElementById("myTABLE").rules = rulesValues[i]
    document.getElementById("myCAPTION").innerHTML = rulesValues[i]
    i = (++i == rulesValues.length) ? 0 : i
    timeoutID = setTimeout("rotateBorder(" + i + ")", 2000)
}
function stopRotate() {
    clearTimeout(timeoutID)
    document.getElementById("myTABLE").rules = "all"
    document.getElementById("myCAPTION").innerHTML = "all"
}
</SCRIPT>
</HEAD>

<BODY>
<H1>TABLE.rules Property</H1>
<HR>
<FORM NAME="controls">
<FIELDSET>
<LEGEND>Cycle Table Rule Visibility</LEGEND>
<TABLE WIDTH="100%" CELLSPACING=20><TR>
<TD><INPUT TYPE="button" VALUE="Cycle" onClick="rotateBorder(0)"></TD>
<TD><INPUT TYPE="button" VALUE="Stop" onClick="stopRotate()"></TD>
</TR>
</TABLE>
</FIELDSET>
</TABLE>
</FIELDSET>
</FORM>
```

```
<HR>
<TABLE ID="myTABLE" CELLPADDING=5 BORDER=3 ALIGN="center">
<CAPTION ID="myCAPTION">Default</CAPTION>
<COLGROUP SPAN=1>
<COLGROUP SPAN=3>
<THEAD ID="myTHEAD">
<TR>
    <TH>River<TH>Outflow<TH>Miles<TH>Kilometers
</TR>
</THEAD>
<TBODY>
<TR>
    <TD>Nile<TD>Mediterranean<TD>4160<TD>6700
</TR>
<TR>
    <TD>Congo<TD>Atlantic Ocean<TD>2900<TD>4670
</TR>
<TR>
    <TD>Niger<TD>Atlantic Ocean<TD>2600<TD>4180
</TR>
<TR>
    <TD>Zambezi<TD>Indian Ocean<TD>1700<TD>2740
</TR>
</TABLE>
</BODY>
</HTML>
```

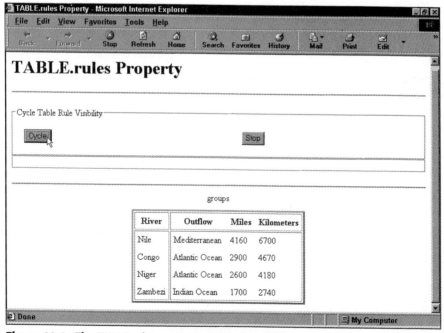

Figure 11-1: The TABLE.rules property set to "groups"

tBodies

	NN2	NN3	NN4	NN6	IE3/J1	IE3/J2	IE4	IE5	IE5.5
Compatibility				✓			✓	✓	✓

Example

Use The Evaluator (Chapter 13 in the *JavaScript Bible*) to access the tBodies array and reveal the number of rows in the one TBODY segment of the demonstrator table. Enter the following statement into the top text box:

```
document.getElementById("myTable").tBodies[0].rows.length
```

Methods

moveRow(*sourceRowIndex, destinationRowIndex*)

	NN2	NN3	NN4	NN6	IE3/J1	IE3/J2	IE4	IE5	IE5.5
Compatibility								✓	✓

Example

If you want to shift the bottom row of a table to the top, you can use the shortcut reference to the last item's index value (-1) for the first parameter:

```
var movedRow = document.all.someTable.moveRow(-1, 0)
```

TBODY, TFOOT, and THEAD Element Objects

Properties

vAlign

	NN2	NN3	NN4	NN6	IE3/J1	IE3/J2	IE4	IE5	IE5.5
Compatibility				✓			✓	✓	✓

Example

Use The Evaluator (Chapter 13 in the *JavaScript Bible*) to modify the vertical alignment of the content of the TBODY element in the demonstrator table. Enter the following statement in the top text box to shift the content to the bottom of the cells:

```
document.getElementById("myTBody").vAlign = "bottom"
```

Notice that the cells of the THEAD element are untouched by the action imposed on the TBODY element.

COL and COLGROUP Element Objects

Properties

span

	NN2	NN3	NN4	NN6	IE3/J1	IE3/J2	IE4	IE5	IE5.5
Compatibility				✓			✓	✓	✓

Example

The following statement assigns a span of 3 to a newly created COLGROUP element stored in the variable colGroupA:

```
colGroupA.span = 3
```

TR Element Object

Properties

cells

	NN2	NN3	NN4	NN6	IE3/J1	IE3/J2	IE4	IE5	IE5.5
Compatibility				✓			✓	✓	✓

Example

Use The Evaluator (Chapter 13 in the *JavaScript Bible*) to retrieve the number of TD elements in the second row of the demonstrator table. Enter the following statement into the top text box (W3C DOM syntax shown here):

```
document.getElementById("myTable").rows[1].cells.length
```

height

	NN2	NN3	NN4	NN6	IE3/J1	IE3/J2	IE4	IE5	IE5.5
Compatibility							✓	✓	✓

Example

Use The Evaluator (Chapter 13 in the *JavaScript Bible*) in IE4+ to expand the height of the second row of the demonstrator table. Enter the following statement into the top text box:

```
document.all.myTable.rows[1].height = 300
```

If you attempt to set the value very low, the rendered height goes no smaller than the default height.

rowIndex
sectionRowIndex

	NN2	NN3	NN4	NN6	IE3/J1	IE3/J2	IE4	IE5	IE5.5
Compatibility				✓			✓	✓	✓

Example

Use The Evaluator (Chapter 13 in the *JavaScript Bible*) to explore the rowIndex and sectionRowIndex property values for the second physical row in the demonstrator table. Enter each of the following statements into the top text box (W3C DOM syntax shown here):

```
document.getElementById("myTable").rows[1].rowIndex
document.getElementById("myTable").rows[1].sectionRowIndex
```

The result of the first statement is 1 because the second row is the second row of the entire table. But the sectionRowIndex property returns 0 because this row is the first row of the TBODY element in this particular table.

TD and TH Element Objects

Properties

cellIndex

	NN2	NN3	NN4	NN6	IE3/J1	IE3/J2	IE4	IE5	IE5.5
Compatibility				✓			✓	✓	✓

Example

You can rewrite the cell addition portion of Listing 27-2 (in Chapter 27 in the *JavaScript Bible*) to utilize the cellIndex property. The process entails modifying the insertTableRow() function so that it uses a do...while construction to keep adding cells to match the number of data slots. The function looks like the following (changes shown in boldface):

```
function insertTableRow(form, where) {
    var now = new Date()
    var nowData = [now.getHours(), now.getMinutes(), now.getSeconds(),
        now.getMilliseconds()]
    clearBGColors()
    var newCell
    var newRow = theTableBody.insertRow(where)
    var i = 0
    do {
        newCell = newRow.insertCell(i)
        newCell.innerHTML = nowData[i++]
        newCell.style.backgroundColor = "salmon"
    } while (newCell.cellIndex < nowData.length)
    updateRowCounters(form)
}
```

This version is merely for demonstration purposes and is not as efficient as the sequence shown in Listing 27-2. But the cellIndex property version can give you some implementation ideas for the property. It also shows how dynamic the property is, even for brand new cells.

colSpan
rowSpan

	NN2	NN3	NN4	NN6	IE3/J1	IE3/J2	IE4	IE5	IE5.5
Compatibility				✓			✓	✓	✓

Example

Use The Evaluator (Chapter 13 in the *JavaScript Bible*) to witness how modifying either of these properties in an existing table can destroy the table. Enter the following statement into the top text box:

```
document.getElementById("myTable").rows[1].cells[0].colSpan = 3
```

Now that the first cell of the second row occupies the space of three columns, the browser has no choice but to shift the two other defined cells for that row out beyond the original boundary of the table. Experiment with the rowSpan property the same way. To restore the original settings, assign 1 to each property.

height
width

	NN2	NN3	NN4	NN6	IE3/J1	IE3/J2	IE4	IE5	IE5.5
Compatibility				✓			✓	✓	✓

Example

Use The Evaluator (Chapter 13 in the *JavaScript Bible*) to see the results of setting the `height` and `width` properties of an existing table cell. Enter each of the following statements into the top text box and study the results in the demonstrator table (W3C DOM syntax used here):

```
document.getElementById("myTable").rows[1].cell[1].height = 100
document.getElementById("myTable").rows[2].cell[0].width = 300
```

You can restore both cells to their original sizes by assigning very small values, such as 1 or 0, to the properties. The browser prevents the cells from rendering any smaller than is necessary to show the content.

noWrap

	NN2	NN3	NN4	NN6	IE3/J1	IE3/J2	IE4	IE5	IE5.5
Compatibility				✓			✓	✓	✓

Example

The following statement creates a new cell in a row and sets its `noWrap` property to prevent text from word-wrapping inside the cell:

```
newCell = newRow.insertCell(-1)
newCell.noWrap = true
```

You need to set this property only if the cell must behave differently than the default, word-wrapping style.

OL Element Object

Properties

start

	NN2	NN3	NN4	NN6	IE3/J1	IE3/J2	IE4	IE5	IE5.5
Compatibility				✓			✓	✓	✓

Example

The following statements generate a new OL element and assign a value to the `start` property:

```
var newOL = document.createElement("OL")
newOL.start = 5
```

`type`

	NN2	NN3	NN4	NN6	IE3/J1	IE3/J2	IE4	IE5	IE5.5
Compatibility				✓			✓	✓	✓

Example

The following statements generate a new OL element and assign a value to the `type` property so that the sequence letters are uppercase Roman numerals:

```
var newOL = document.createElement("OL")
newOL.type = "I"
```

UL Element Object
Properties
`type`

	NN2	NN3	NN4	NN6	IE3/J1	IE3/J2	IE4	IE5	IE5.5
Compatibility				✓			✓	✓	✓

Example

The following statements generate a new UL element and assign a value to the `type` property so that the bullet characters are empty circles:

```
var newUL = document.createElement("UL")
newUL.type = "circle"
```

LI Element Object
Properties
`type`

	NN2	NN3	NN4	NN6	IE3/J1	IE3/J2	IE4	IE5	IE5.5
Compatibility				✓			✓	✓	✓

Example

See the examples for the `OL.type` and `UL.type` properties earlier in this chapter.

value

	NN2	NN3	NN4	NN6	IE3/J1	IE3/J2	IE4	IE5	IE5.5
Compatibility				✓			✓	✓	✓

Example

The following statements generate a new LI element and assign a value to the `start` property:

```
var newLI = document.createElement("LI")
newLI.start = 5
```

◆   ◆   ◆

Navigator and Other Environment Objects (Chapter 28)

Objects covered in this chapter are somewhat distant from the document and its content, but they are no less important to scripters. Any script branching that relies on knowing details about the browser version or other aspects of the environment running the browser calls upon the navigator object. Properties of the navigator object (also named the clientInformation object in IE4+), reveal browser brand and version information, as well as operating system and, in some cases, encryption powers of the browser. Using signed scripts with NN4+, you can even script modification to browser preferences.

Avoid using navigator object properties for browser version branching when more sophisticated techniques — notably object detection as described in Chapter 14 of the *JavaScript Bible* — are less dependent upon future quirks in object model developments. But version detection is perfect when you know that a special workaround is needed for some glitch in a specific version or class of browser. For example, NN4/Windows can exhibit some strange behavior when attempting to print a page whose content relies on script execution. Provided you have a code workaround for the problem, you can divert script execution for just that version of NN in just the Windows version.

Examples in this chapter also touch upon the screen object and the IE/Windows userProfile object. The screen object is useful in determining the size of a new window, but there is little need to script the userProfile object.

Examples Highlights

◆ Listing 28-1 provides numerous functions that examine `navigator` object properties. The functions examples are provided more as demonstrations of specific values your scripts may need to look for, rather than as some super "browser sniffer." Determining specific IE versions is a bit tricky, so observe how to go about it by way of the `navigator.appVersion` property.

◆ NN4+ provides access to browser preferences via the `navigator.preference()` method, as shown in Listing 28-2. To implement this feature in a production page, you'll need to use signed scripts.

◆ Experiment with the `screen.availLeft` and `screen.availTop` properties in NN4+, especially in the Windows environment to see how the taskbar affects these property values.

◆ For IE4+/Windows, follow the sequence of examples for the `userProfile` object's methods to see how scripts can read user profile fields.

clientInformation Object (IE4+) and navigator Object (All)

Properties

```
appCodeName
appName
appVersion
userAgent
```

	NN2	NN3	NN4	NN6	IE3/J1	IE3/J2	IE4	IE5	IE5.5
Compatibility	✓	✓	✓	✓	✓	✓	✓	✓	✓

Example

Listing 28-1 provides a number of reusable functions that your scripts can employ to determine a variety of information about the currently running browser. This is not intended in any way to be an all-inclusive browser-sniffing routine; instead, I offer samples of how to extract information from the key navigator properties to determine various browser conditions.

All functions in Listing 28-1 return a Boolean value inline with the pseudo-question presented in the function's name. For example, the `isWindows()` function returns `true` if the browser is any type of Windows browser; otherwise, it returns `false`. (In Internet Explorer 3, the values are 0 for `false` and -1 for `true`, but those values are perfectly usable in if conditional phrases). If this kind of browser detection occurs frequently in your pages, consider moving these functions into an external .js source library for inclusion in your pages (see Chapter 13 of the *JavaScript Bible* for tips on creating .js libraries). When you load this page, it presents fields that display the results of each function depending on the type of browser and client operating system you use.

Listing 28-1: **Functions to Examine Browsers**

```
<HTML>
<HEAD>
<TITLE>UserAgent Property Library</TITLE>
<SCRIPT LANGUAGE="JavaScript">
// basic brand determination
function isNav() {
    return (navigator.appName == "Netscape")
}

function isIE() {
    return (navigator.appName == "Microsoft Internet Explorer")
}

// operating system platforms
function isWindows() {
    return (navigator.appVersion.indexOf("Win") != -1)
}

function isWin95NT() {
    return (isWindows() && (navigator.appVersion.indexOf("Win16") == -1 &&
        navigator.appVersion.indexOf("Windows 3.1") == -1))
}

function isMac() {
    return (navigator.appVersion.indexOf("Mac") != -1)
}

function isMacPPC() {
    return (isMac() && (navigator.appVersion.indexOf("PPC") != -1 ||
        navigator.appVersion.indexOf("PowerPC") != -1))
}

function isUnix() {
    return (navigator.appVersion.indexOf("X11") != -1)
}

// browser versions
function isGeneration2() {
    return (parseInt(navigator.appVersion) == 2)
}
```

Continued

Listing 28-1 *(continued)*

```
function isGeneration3() {
    return (parseInt(navigator.appVersion) == 3)
}

function isGeneration3Min() {
    return (parseInt(navigator.appVersion.charAt(0)) >= 3)
}
function isNav4_7() {
    return (isNav() && parseFloat(navigator.appVersion) == 4.7)
}

function isMSIE4Min() {
    return (isIE() && navigator.appVersion.indexOf("MSIE") != -1)
}

function isMSIE5_5() {
    return (navigator.appVersion.indexOf("MSIE 5.5") != -1)
}

function isNN6Min() {
    return (isNav() && parseInt(navigator.appVersion) >= 5)
}

// element referencing syntax
function isDocAll() {
    return (document.all) ? true : false
}

function isDocW3C() {
    return (document.getElementById) ? true : false
}

// fill in the blanks
function checkBrowser() {
    var form = document.forms[0]
    form.brandNN.value = isNav()
    form.brandIE.value = isIE()
    form.win.value = isWindows()
    form.win32.value = isWin95NT()
    form.mac.value = isMac()
    form.ppc.value = isMacPPC()
    form.unix.value = isUnix()
    form.ver3Only.value = isGeneration3()
    form.ver3Up.value = isGeneration3Min()
    form.Nav4_7.value = isNav4_7()
    form.Nav6Up.value = isNN6Min()
    form.MSIE4.value = isMSIE4Min()
    form.MSIE5_5.value = isMSIE5_5()
```

```
      form.doc_all.value = isDocAll()
      form.doc_w3c.value = isDocW3C()
}
</SCRIPT>
</HEAD>

<BODY onLoad="checkBrowser()">
<H1>About This Browser</H1>
<FORM>
<H2>Brand</H2>
Netscape Navigator:<INPUT TYPE="text" NAME="brandNN" SIZE=5>
Internet Explorer:<INPUT TYPE="text" NAME="brandIE" SIZE=5>
<HR>
<H2>Browser Version</H2>
3.0x Only (any brand):<INPUT TYPE="text" NAME="ver30nly" SIZE=5><P>
3 or Later (any brand): <INPUT TYPE="text" NAME="ver3Up" SIZE=5><P>
Navigator 4.7: <INPUT TYPE="text" NAME="Nav4_7" SIZE=5><P>
Navigator 6+: <INPUT TYPE="text" NAME="Nav6Up" SIZE=5><P>
MSIE 4+: <INPUT TYPE="text" NAME="MSIE4" SIZE=5><P>
MSIE 5.5:<INPUT TYPE="text" NAME="MSIE5_5" SIZE=5><P>
<HR>
<H2>OS Platform</H2>
Windows: <INPUT TYPE="text" NAME="win" SIZE=5>
Windows 95/98/2000/NT: <INPUT TYPE="text" NAME="win32" SIZE=5><P>
Macintosh: <INPUT TYPE="text" NAME="mac" SIZE=5>
Mac PowerPC: <INPUT TYPE="text" NAME="ppc" SIZE=5><P>
Unix: <INPUT TYPE="text" NAME="unix" SIZE=5><P>
<HR>
<H2>Element Referencing Style</H2>
Use <TT>document.all</TT>: <INPUT TYPE="text" NAME="doc_all" SIZE=5><P>
Use <TT>document.getElementById()</TT>: <INPUT TYPE="text" NAME="doc_w3c"
SIZE=5><P>
</FORM>
</BODY>
</HTML>
```

Sometimes you may need to use more than one of these functions together. For example, if you want to create a special situation for the `window.open()` bug that afflicts UNIX and Macintosh versions of Navigator 2, then you have to put your Boolean operator logic powers to work to construct a fuller examination of the browser:

```
function isWindowBuggy() {
    return (isGeneration2() && (isMac() || isUnix()))
}
```

You can see many more examples of browser sniffing, including more details about handling AOL browsers, in an article by Eric Krock at: `http://developer.netscape.com:80/docs/examples/javascript/browser_type.html`.

appMinorVersion

	NN2	NN3	NN4	NN6	IE3/J1	IE3/J2	IE4	IE5	IE5.5
Compatibility							✓	✓	✓

Example

Use The Evaluator (Chapter 13 in the *JavaScript Bible*) to examine the two related version properties of your IE browser(s). Type the following two statements into the top text box and observe the results:

```
navigator.appVersion
navigator.minorAppVersion
```

There is a good chance that the values returned are not related to the browser version number shown after MSIE in the appVersion value.

cookieEnabled

	NN2	NN3	NN4	NN6	IE3/J1	IE3/J2	IE4	IE5	IE5.5
Compatibility				✓			✓	✓	✓

Example

Use The Evaluator to see the value of the navigator.cookieEnabled property on your browsers. Enter the following statement into the top text box:

```
navigator.cookieEnabled
```

Feel free to change the cookie preferences setting temporarily to see the new value of the property. You do not have to relaunch the browser for the new setting to take effect.

cpuClass

	NN2	NN3	NN4	NN6	IE3/J1	IE3/J2	IE4	IE5	IE5.5
Compatibility							✓	✓	✓

Example

Use The Evaluator (Chapter 13 in the *JavaScript Bible*) to see how IE reports the cpuClass of your PC. Enter the following statement into the top text box:

```
navigator.cpuClass
```

mimeTypes

	NN2	NN3	NN4	NN6	IE3/J1	IE3/J2	IE4	IE5	IE5.5
Compatibility		✓	✓	✓			(✓)	(✓)	(✓)

Example

For examples of the `mimeTypes` property and details about using the mimeType object, see the discussion of this object later in the chapter. A number of simple examples showing how to use this property to see whether the `navigator` object has a particular MIME type do not go far enough in determining whether a plug-in is installed and enabled to play the incoming data.

onLine

	NN2	NN3	NN4	NN6	IE3/J1	IE3/J2	IE4	IE5	IE5.5
Compatibility							✓	✓	✓

Example

Use The Evaluator (Chapter 13 in the *JavaScript Bible*) to see the online state of your IE browsers. Enter the following statement into the top text box:

```
navigator.onLine
```

Verify your browsing mode by checking the Work Offline choice in the File menu. If it is checked, the `onLine` property should return `false`.

oscpu

	NN2	NN3	NN4	NN6	IE3/J1	IE3/J2	IE4	IE5	IE5.5
Compatibility				✓					

Example

Use The Evaluator (Chapter 13 in the *JavaScript Bible*) with NN6 to see what your client machine reports to you by entering the following statement into the top text box:

```
navigator.oscpu
```

platform

	NN2	NN3	NN4	NN6	IE3/J1	IE3/J2	IE4	IE5	IE5.5
Compatibility			✓	✓			✓	✓	✓

Example

Use The Evaluator (Chapter 13 in the *JavaScript Bible*) to see what your computer reports as its operating system. Enter the following statement into the top text box:

```
navigator.platform
```

product
productSub
vendor
vendorSub

	NN2	NN3	NN4	NN6	IE3/J1	IE3/J2	IE4	IE5	IE5.5
Compatibility				✓					

Example

Use The Evaluator (Chapter 13 in the *JavaScript Bible*) on your copy of NN6 to see the values returned for these four properties. Enter each of the following statements into the top text box of the page and see the values for each in the Results box:

```
navigator.product
navigator.productSub
navigator.vendor
navigator.vendorSub
```

Also check the value of the `navigator.userAgent` property to see how many of these four property values are revealed in the `userAgent` property.

systemLanguage
userLanguage

	NN2	NN3	NN4	NN6	IE3/J1	IE3/J2	IE4	IE5	IE5.5
Compatibility							✓	✓	✓

Example

Use The Evaluator (Chapter 13 in the *JavaScript Bible*) with your IE4+ browser to compare the values of the three language-related properties running on your computer. Enter each of the following statements into the top text box:

```
navigator.browserLanguage
navigator.systemLanguage
navigator.userLanguage
```

Don't be surprised if all three properties return the same value.

Methods

preference(*name* [, *val*])

	NN2	NN3	NN4	NN6	IE3/J1	IE3/J2	IE4	IE5	IE5.5
Compatibility			✓	✓					

Example

The page in Listing 28-2 displays checkboxes for several preference settings, plus one text box to show a preference setting value for the size of the browser's disk cache. To run this script without signing the scripts, turn on codebase principals as directed in Chapter 46 of the *JavaScript Bible*. (The listing file on the CD-ROM does not employ signed scripts.)

One function reads all the preferences and sets the form control values accordingly. Another function sets a preference when you click its checkbox. Because of the interaction among three of the cookie settings, it is easier to have the script rerun the showPreferences() function after each setting rather than you trying to manually control the properties of the three checkboxes. Rerunning that function also helps verify that you set the preference.

Listing 28-2: **Reading and Writing Browser Preferences**

```
<HTML>
<HEAD>
<TITLE>Reading/Writing Browser Preferences</TITLE>
<SCRIPT LANGUAGE="JavaScript1.2">
function setPreference(pref, value) {
    netscape.security.PrivilegeManager.enablePrivilege(
        "UniversalPreferencesWrite")
    navigator.preference(pref, value)
    netscape.security.PrivilegeManager.revertPrivilege(
        "UniversalPreferencesWrite")
    showPreferences()
}
```

Continued

Listing 28-2 *(continued)*

```
function showPreferences() {
    var form = document.forms[0]
    netscape.security.PrivilegeManager.enablePrivilege(
        "UniversalPreferencesRead")
    form.imgLoad.checked = navigator.preference("general.always_load_images")
    form.cacheSize.value = navigator.preference("browser.cache.disk_cache_size")
    form.ssEnable.checked = navigator.preference("browser.enable_style_sheets")
    form.autoIEnable.checked = navigator.preference("autoupdate.enabled")
    var cookieSetting = navigator.preference("network.cookie.cookieBehavior")
    for (var i = 0; i < 3; i++) {
        form.elements["cookie" + i].checked = (i == cookieSetting) ? true :
false
    }
    form.cookieWarn.checked =
navigator.preference("network.cookie.warnAboutCookies")
    netscape.security.PrivilegeManager.revertPrivilege(
        "UniversalPreferencesRead")
}
</SCRIPT>
</HEAD>

<BODY onLoad="showPreferences()">
<H1>Browser Preferences Settings Sampler</H1>
<HR>
<FORM>
<INPUT TYPE="checkbox" NAME="imgLoad"
onClick="setPreference('general.always_load_images',this.checked)">
Automatically Load Images<BR>
<INPUT TYPE="checkbox" NAME="ssEnable"
onClick="setPreference('browser.enable_style_sheets',this.checked)">
Style Sheets Enabled<BR>
<INPUT TYPE="checkbox" NAME="autoIEnable"
onClick="setPreference('autoupdate.enabled',this.checked)">
AutoInstall Enabled<BR>
<INPUT TYPE="checkbox" NAME="cookie0"
onClick="setPreference('network.cookie.cookieBehavior',0)">
Accept All Cookies<BR>
<INPUT TYPE="checkbox" NAME="cookie1"
onClick="setPreference('network.cookie.cookieBehavior',1)">
Accept Only Cookies Sent Back to Server<BR>
<INPUT TYPE="checkbox" NAME="cookie2"
onClick="setPreference('network.cookie.cookieBehavior',2)">
Disable Cookies<BR>
<INPUT TYPE="checkbox" NAME="cookieWarn"
onClick="setPreference('network.cookie.warnAboutCookies',this.checked)">
Warn Before Accepting Cookies<BR>
Disk cache is <INPUT TYPE="text" NAME="cacheSize" SIZE=10> KB <BR>
</FORM>
</BODY>
</HTML>
```

screen Object

Properties

```
availLeft
availTop
```

	NN2	NN3	NN4	NN6	IE3/J1	IE3/J2	IE4	IE5	IE5.5
Compatibility			✓	✓					

Example

If you are a Windows user, you can experiment with these NN4+ properties via The Evaluator (Chapter 13 in the *JavaScript Bible*). With the taskbar at the bottom of the screen, enter these two statements into the top text box:

```
screen.availLeft
screen.availTop
```

Next, drag the taskbar to the top of the screen and try both statements again. Now, drag the taskbar to the left edge of the screen and try the statements once more.

userProfile Object

Methods

```
addReadRequest("attributeName")
```

	NN2	NN3	NN4	NN6	IE3/J1	IE3/J2	IE4	IE5	IE5.5
Compatibility							✓	✓	✓

Example

See Listing 28-4 in Chapter 28 in the *JavaScript Bible* for an example of the addReadRequest() method in action. You can also invoke it from the top text box in The Evaluator (Chapter 13 in the *JavaScript Bible*). For example, enter the following statement to queue one request:

```
navigator.userProfile.addReadRequest("vCard.LastName")
```

To continue the process, see examples for doReadRequest() and getAttribute() later in this chapter.

doReadRequest(*reasonCode, identification*[, *domain*[, *path*[, *expiration*]]])

	NN2	NN3	NN4	NN6	IE3/J1	IE3/J2	IE4	IE5	IE5.5
Compatibility							✓	✓	✓

Example

See Listing 28-4 in the *JavaScript Bible* for an example of the doReadRequest() method in action. If you entered the addReadRequest() example for The Evaluator earlier in this chapter, you can now bring up the permissions dialog box (if you have a user profile for your version of Windows) by entering the following statement into the top text box:

```
navigator.userProfile.doReadRequest(1, "Just me!")
```

getAttribute("*attributeName*")

	NN2	NN3	NN4	NN6	IE3/J1	IE3/J2	IE4	IE5	IE5.5
Compatibility							✓	✓	✓

Example

See Listing 28-4 in Chapter 28 in the *JavaScript Bible* for an example of the getAttribute() method in action. Also, if you followed The Evaluator examples for this object, you can now extract the desired information (provided it is in your user profile). Enter the following statement into the top text box:

```
navigator.userProfile.getAttribute("vCard.LastName")
```

✦   ✦   ✦

Event Objects (Chapter 29)

♦ ♦ ♦ ♦

In This Chapter

Uncovering the
coordinates and
target element of a
mouse event

Intercepting keyboard
events

Observing event
propagation in
different event object
models

♦ ♦ ♦ ♦

As earlier generations of scriptable browsers fade from the installed base, the event models of newer browsers become that much more important to scripters. Although cross-browser developers must concern themselves with the incompatibilities of as many as three distinct event models (NN4, IE4+, and W3C DOM used in NN6), scripts increasingly rely on information conveyed by the event object to know where the event came from.

The importance of event object properties is clear when you see how modern DOMs bind events to objects. Although the "old-fashioned" event handler attribute inside an element tag still works, the prescribed ways to bind events to elements simply assign a function reference to an event type belonging to the event. The significance of this approach is that event handlers no longer receive custom parameters, such as references to the element that used to be passed via the `this` operator. It becomes the job of the function to inspect the event object property that contains a reference to the target of the event.

Fortunately for scripters, the event object model (regardless of which ones you need to support) endows each event object with a list of valuable properties that enhance what event handler functions can do. In addition to character key and mouse button data, you can uncover the coordinates of a mouse event, the condition of modifier keys, and even a reference to the object from which the cursor has just rolled (or where it went after leaving the bounds of the current object).

The code examples in this chapter are grouped by the event object model family. This means that the examples are written to work only within the associated DOM. For cross-browser handling of event objects, see the rest of the discussion in Chapter 29 of the *JavaScript Bible*. But use the examples here to fully understand the meaning of each event object's properties and (in NN6) methods. Where possible, the listings that demonstrate parallel properties in multiple object models look and behave the same to the user; the differences are in the code. As an exercise for the inquisitive, you could write a single-page version that combines syntax from multiple event objects models. Listings 29-17 and 29-22 would be good places to start.

Examples Highlights

✦ No fewer than four pairs of coordinate value properties arrive with the IE4+ event object. Listing 29-14 helps you understand what each pair of values represent with respect to regular body elements as well as positioned elements. Follow the suggested steps to experience the meaning of the properties in a variety of contexts.

✦ Load Listing 29-16 to see keyboard character data for all three keyboard events. Again, follow the suggested steps to understand important differences among keyboard event types and also different kinds of keys (characters versus non-characters).

✦ Listing 29-17 demonstrates how to derive a reference to the element that receives the event in the IE4+ event model.

✦ NN6 keyboard events get a workout in Listing 29-18, particularly the way the character and key codes reveal important details for different keyboard event types.

✦ All four pairs of event coordinate properties for NN6 are reported when you run Listing 29-19 and click on different elements.

✦ The important concepts associated with the NN6 event object's `currentTarget` and `eventPhase` properties are demonstrated in Listing 29-20. Be prepared to spend time with the page and the source code to understand how events propagate through the element hierarchy.

✦ Listing 29-23 uses the NN6 `event.timeStamp` property to calculate the instantaneous typing speed within a text field.

NN4 event Object

Properties

`data`

	NN2	NN3	NN4	NN6	IE3/J1	IE3/J2	IE4	IE5	IE5.5
Compatibility			✓						

Example

The page in Listing 29-12 contains little more than a TEXTAREA in which the URLs of dragged items are listed. To run this script without signing the scripts, turn on codebase principals, as directed in Chapter 46 of the *JavaScript Bible*.

To experiment with this listing, load the page and drag any desktop icons that represent files, applications, or folders to the window. Select multiple items and drag them all at once. Because the `onDragDrop` event handler evaluates to `return false`, the files are not loaded into the window. If you want merely to look at the

URL and allow only some to process, you would generate an if...else construction to return true or false to the event handler as needed. A value of return true allows the normal processing of the DragDrop event to take place after your event handler function has completed its processing.

Listing 29-12: Obtaining URLs of a DragDrop Event's data Property

```
<HTML>
<HEAD>
<TITLE>Drag and Drop</TITLE>
<SCRIPT LANGUAGE="JavaScript1.2">
function handleDrag(evt) {
    netscape.security.PrivilegeManager.enablePrivilege("UniversalBrowserRead")
    var URLArray = evt.data
    netscape.security.PrivilegeManager.disablePrivilege("UniversalBrowserRead")
    if (URLArray) {
        document.forms[0].output.value = URLArray.join("\n")
    } else {
        document.forms[0].output.value = "Nothing found."
    }
    return false
}
</SCRIPT>
</HEAD>
<BODY onDragDrop="return handleDrag(event)">
<B>Drag a URL to this window (NN4 only).</B>
<HR>
<FORM>
URLs:<BR>
<TEXTAREA NAME="output" COLS=70 ROWS=4></TEXTAREA><BR>
<INPUT TYPE="reset">
</FORM>
</BODY>
</HTML>
```

---

layerX
layerY
pageX
pageY
screenX
screenY

	NN2	NN3	NN4	NN6	IE3/J1	IE3/J2	IE4	IE5	IE5.5
Compatibility			✓						

Example

You can see the effects of the coordinate systems and associated properties with the page in Listing 29-13. Part of the page contains a three-field readout of the layer-, page-, and screen-level properties. Two clickable objects are provided so that you can see the differences between an object not in any layer and an object residing within a layer. The object not confined by a layer has its layer and page coordinates the same in the event object properties.

Additional readouts display the event object coordinates for resizing and moving a window. If you maximize the window under Windows, the Navigator browser's top-left corner is actually out of sight, four pixels up and to the left. That's why the screenX and screenY values are both -4.

Listing 29-13: **NN4 Event Coordinate Properties**

```
<HTML>
<HEAD>
<TITLE>X and Y Event Properties</TITLE>
<SCRIPT LANGUAGE="JavaScript">
function checkCoords(evt) {
    var form = document.forms[0]
    form.layerCoords.value = evt.layerX + "," + evt.layerY
    form.pageCoords.value = evt.pageX + "," + evt.pageY
    form.screenCoords.value = evt.screenX + "," + evt.screenY
    return false
}
function checkSize(evt) {
    document.forms[0].resizeCoords.value = evt.layerX + "," + evt.layerY
}
function checkLoc(evt) {
    document.forms[0].moveCoords.value = evt.screenX + "," + evt.screenY
}
</SCRIPT>
</HEAD>
<BODY onResize="checkSize(event)" onMove="checkLoc(event)">
<H1>X and Y Event Properties (NN4)</H1>
<HR>
<P>Click on the button and in the layer/image to see the coordinate values for
the event object.</P>
<FORM NAME="output">
<TABLE>
<TR><TD COLSPAN=2>Mouse Event Coordinates:</TD></TR>
<TR><TD ALIGN="right">layerX, layerY:</TD><TD><INPUT TYPE="text"
NAME="layerCoords" SIZE=10></TD></TR>
<TR><TD ALIGN="right">pageX, pageY:</TD><TD><INPUT TYPE="text" NAME="pageCoords"
SIZE=10></TD></TR>
<TR><TD ALIGN="right">screenX, screenY:</TD><TD><INPUT TYPE="text"
NAME="screenCoords" SIZE=10></TD></TR>
<TR><TD ALIGN="right"><INPUT TYPE="button" VALUE="Click Here"
onMouseDown="checkCoords(event)"></TD></TR>
<TR><TD COLSPAN=2><HR></TD></TR>
```

```
<TR><TD COLSPAN=2>Window Resize Coordinates:</TD></TR>
<TR><TD ALIGN="right">layerX, layerY:</TD><TD><INPUT TYPE="text"
NAME="resizeCoords" SIZE=10></TD></TR>
<TR><TD COLSPAN=2><HR></TD></TR>
<TR><TD COLSPAN=2>Window Move Coordinates:</TD></TR>
<TR><TD ALIGN="right">screenX, screenY:</TD><TD><INPUT TYPE="text"
NAME="moveCoords" SIZE=10></TD></TR>
</TABLE>
</FORM>
<LAYER NAME="display" BGCOLOR="coral" TOP=140 LEFT=300  HEIGHT=250 WIDTH=330>
<A HREF="javascript:void(0)" onClick="return checkCoords(event)">
<IMG SRC="nile.gif" WIDTH=320 HEIGHT=240" BORDER=0></A>
</LAYER>
</BODY>
</HTML>
```

IE4+ event Object

Properties

clientX
clientY
offsetX
offsetY
screenX
screenY
x
y

	NN2	NN3	NN4	NN6	IE3/J1	IE3/J2	IE4	IE5	IE5.5
Compatibility							✓	✓	✓

Example

Listing 29-14 provides readings of all event coordinate properties in an interactive way. An onMouseDown event handler triggers all event handling, and you can click the mouse anywhere on the page to see what happens. You see the tag of the element targeted by the mouse event to help you visualize how some of the coordinate properties are determined. An image is encased inside a positioned DIV element to help you see what happens to some of the properties when the event is targeted inside a positioned element.

Listing 29-14: IE4+ Event Coordinate Properties

```
<HTML>
<HEAD>
<TITLE>X and Y Event Properties (IE4+)</TITLE>
<SCRIPT LANGUAGE="JavaScript">
function checkCoords() {
    var form = document.forms[0]
    form.srcElemTag.value = "<" + event.srcElement.tagName + ">"
    form.clientCoords.value = event.clientX + "," + event.clientY
    form.pageCoords.value = (event.clientX + document.body.scrollLeft) +
        "," + (event.clientY + document.body.scrollTop)
    form.offsetCoords.value = event.offsetX + "," + event.offsetY
    form.screenCoords.value = event.screenX + "," + event.screenY
    form.xyCoords.value = event.x + "," + event.y
    form.parElem.value = "<" + event.srcElement.offsetParent.tagName + ">"
    return false
}
function handleSize() {
    document.forms[0].resizeCoords.value = event.clientX + "," + event.clientY
}
</SCRIPT>
</HEAD>
<BODY onMouseDown="checkCoords()" onResize="handleSize()">
<H1>X and Y Event Properties (IE4+)</H1>
<HR>
<P>Click on the button and in the DIV/image to see the coordinate values for the
event object.</P>
<FORM NAME="output">
<TABLE>
<TR><TD COLSPAN=2>IE Mouse Event Coordinates:</TD></TR>
<TR><TD ALIGN="right">srcElement:</TD><TD><INPUT TYPE="text" NAME="srcElemTag"
SIZE=10></TD></TR>
<TR><TD ALIGN="right">clientX, clientY:</TD><TD><INPUT TYPE="text"
NAME="clientCoords" SIZE=10></TD>
<TD ALIGN="right">...With scrolling:</TD><TD><INPUT TYPE="text"
NAME="pageCoords" SIZE=10></TD></TR>
<TR><TD ALIGN="right">offsetX, offsetY:</TD><TD><INPUT TYPE="text"
NAME="offsetCoords" SIZE=10></TD></TR>
<TR><TD ALIGN="right">screenX, screenY:</TD><TD><INPUT TYPE="text"
NAME="screenCoords" SIZE=10></TD></TR>
<TR><TD ALIGN="right">x, y:</TD><TD><INPUT TYPE="text" NAME="xyCoords"
SIZE=10></TD>
<TD ALIGN="right">...Relative to:</TD><TD><INPUT TYPE="text" NAME="parElem"
SIZE=10></TD></TR>
<TR><TD ALIGN="right"><INPUT TYPE="button" VALUE="Click Here"></TD></TR>
<TR><TD COLSPAN=2><HR></TD></TR>
<TR><TD COLSPAN=2>Window Resize Coordinates:</TD></TR>
<TR><TD ALIGN="right">clientX, clientY:</TD><TD><INPUT TYPE="text"
NAME="resizeCoords" SIZE=10></TD></TR>
</TABLE>
```

```
</FORM>
<DIV ID="display" STYLE="position:relative; left:100">
<IMG SRC="nile.gif" WIDTH=320 HEIGHT=240" BORDER=0>
</DIV>
</BODY>
</HTML>
```

Here are some tasks to try with the page that loads from Listing 29-14 to help you understand the relationships among the various pairs of coordinate properties:

1. Click the dot above the "i" on the "Click Here" button label. The target element is the button (INPUT) element, whose offsetParent is a table cell element. The offsetY value is very low because you are near the top of the element's own coordinate space. The client coordinates (and x and y), however, are relative to the viewable area in the window. If your browser window is maximized in Windows, the screenX and clientX values will be the same; the difference between screenY and clientY is the height of all the window chrome above the content region. With the window not scrolled at all, the client coordinates are the same with and without scrolling taken into account.

2. Jot down the various coordinate values and then scroll the page down slightly (clicking the scrollbar fires an event) and click the dot on the button again. The clientY value shrinks because the page has moved upward relative to the viewable area, making the measure between the top of the area smaller with respect to the button. The Windows version does the right thing with the offset properties, by continuing to return values relative to the element's own coordinate space; the Mac, unfortunately, subtracts the scrolled amount from the offset properties.

3. Click the large image. The client properties perform as expected for both Windows and Mac, as do the screen properties. For Windows, the x and y properties correctly return the event coordinates relative to the IMG element's offsetParent, which is the DIV element that surrounds it. Note, however, that the browser "sees" the DIV as starting 10 pixels to the left of the image. In IE5.5/Windows, you can click within those ten transparent pixels to the left of the image to click the DIV element. This padding is inserted automatically and impacts the coordinates of the x and y properties. A more reliable measure of the event inside the image is the offset properties. The same is true in the Macintosh version, as long as the page isn't scrolled, in which case the scroll, just as in Step 2, affects the values above.

4. Click the top HR element under the heading. It may take a couple of tries to actually hit the element (you've made it when the HR element shows up in the srcElement box). This is to reinforce the way the client properties provide coordinates within the element itself (again, accept on the Mac when the page is scrolled). Clicking at the very left end of the rule, you eventually find the 0,0 coordinate.

Finally, if you are a Windows user, here are two examples to try to see some of the unexpected behavior of coordinate properties.

1. With the page not scrolled, click anywhere along the right side of the page, away from any text so that the BODY element is `srcElement`. Because the BODY element theoretically fills the entire content region of the browser window, all coordinate pairs except for the screen coordinates should be the same. But offset properties are two pixels less than all the others. By and large, this difference won't matter in your scripts, but you should be aware of this potential discrepancy if precise positioning is important. For inexplicable reasons, the offset properties are measured in a space that is inset two pixels from the left and top of the window. This is not the case in the Macintosh version, where all value pairs are the same from the BODY perspective.

2. Click the text of the H1 or P elements (just above and below the long horizontal rule at the top of the page). In theory, the offset properties should be relative to the rectangles occupied by these elements (they're block elements, after all). But instead, they're measured in the same space as the client properties (plus the two pixels). This unexpected behavior doesn't have anything to do with the cursor being a text cursor, because if you click inside any of the text box elements, their offset properties are properly relative to their own rectangles. This problem does not afflict the Macintosh version.

You can see further examples of important event coordinate properties in action in the discussion of dragging elements around the IE page in Chapter 31 of the *JavaScript Bible*.

fromElement
toElement

	NN2	NN3	NN4	NN6	IE3/J1	IE3/J2	IE4	IE5	IE5.5
Compatibility							✓	✓	✓

Example

Listing 29-15 provides an example of how the `fromElement` and `toElement` properties can reveal the life of the cursor action before and after it rolls into an element. When you roll the cursor to the center box (a table cell), its `onMouseOver` event handler displays the text from the table cell from which the cursor arrived. In Figure 13-1, for example, the user has just rolled the cursor into the center box from the West box. If the cursor comes in from one of the corners (not easy to do), a different message is displayed.

Listing 29-15: **Using the toElement and fromElement Properties**

```
<HTML>
<HEAD>
<TITLE>fromElement and toElement Properties</TITLE>
<STYLE TYPE="text/CSS">
.direction {background-color:#00FFFF; width:100; height:50; text-align:center}
#main {background-color:#FF6666; text-align:center}
</STYLE>
<SCRIPT LANGUAGE="JavaScript">
function showArrival() {
    var direction = (event.fromElement.innerText) ? event.fromElement.innerText
:
    "parts unknown"
    status = "Arrived from: " + direction
}
function showDeparture() {
    var direction = (event.toElement.innerText) ? event.toElement.innerText :
    "parts unknown"
    status = "Departed to: " + direction
}
</SCRIPT>
</HEAD>
<BODY>
<H1>fromElement and toElement Properties</H1>
<HR>
<P>Roll the mouse to the center box and look for arrival information
in the status bar. Roll the mouse away from the center box and look for
departure information in the status bar.</P>

<TABLE CELLSPACING=0 CELLPADDING=5>
<TR><TD></TD><TD CLASS="direction">North</TD><TD></TD></TR>
<TR><TD CLASS="direction">West</TD>
<TD ID="main" onMouseOver="showArrival()" onMouseOut="showDeparture()">Roll</TD>
<TD CLASS="direction">East</TD></TR>
<TR><TD></TD><TD CLASS="direction">South</TD><TD></TD></TR>
</TABLE>
</BODY>
</HTML>
```

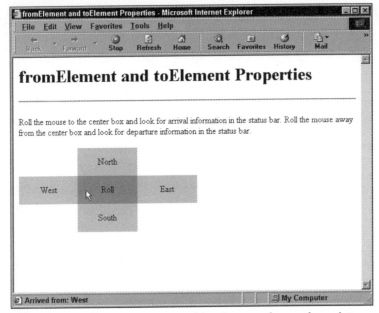

Figure 13-1: onMouseOver event object knows whence the pointer came.

This is a good example to experiment with in the browser, because it also reveals a potential limitation. The element registered as the `toElement` or `fromElement` must fire a mouse event to register itself with the browser. If not, the next element in the sequence that registers itself is the one acknowledged by these properties. For example, if you roll the mouse into the center box and then extremely quickly roll the cursor to the bottom of the page, you may bypass the South box entirely. The text that appears in the statusbar is actually the inner text of the BODY element, which is the element that caught the first mouse event to register itself as the `toElement` for the center table cell.

keyCode

	NN2	NN3	NN4	NN6	IE3/J1	IE3/J2	IE4	IE5	IE5.5
Compatibility							✓	✓	✓

Example

Listing 29-16 provides an additional play area to view the `keyCode` property for all three keyboard events while you type into a TEXTAREA. You can use this page later as an authoring tool to grab the precise codes for keyboard keys you may not be familiar with.

Listing 29-16: **Displaying keyCode Property Values**

```
<HTML>
<HEAD>
<TITLE>keyCode Property</TITLE>
<STYLE TYPE="text/css">
TD {text-align:center}
</STYLE>
<SCRIPT LANGUAGE="JavaScript">
function showCode(which) {
    document.forms[0].elements[which].value = event.keyCode
}
function clearEm() {
    for (var i = 1; i < document.forms[0].elements.length; i++) {
        document.forms[0].elements[i].value = ""
    }
}
</SCRIPT>
</HEAD>
<BODY>
<H1>keyCode Property</H1>
<HR>
<P></P>
<FORM>
<P>
<TEXTAREA NAME="scratchpad" COLS="40" ROWS="5" WRAP="hard"
onKeyDown="clearEm(); showCode('down')" onKeyUp="showCode('up')"
onKeyPress="showCode('press')"></TEXTAREA>
</P>
<TABLE CELLPADDING="5">
<TR><TH>Event</TH><TH>event.keyCode</TH></TR>
<TR><TD>onKeyDown:</TD><TD><INPUT TYPE="text" NAME="down" SIZE="3"></TD></TR>
<TR><TD>onKeyPress:</TD><TD><INPUT TYPE="text" NAME="press" SIZE="3"></TD></TR>
<TR><TD>onKeyUp:</TD><TD><INPUT TYPE="text" NAME="up" SIZE="3"></TD></TR>
</TABLE>
</FORM>
</BODY>
</HTML>
```

The following are some specific tasks to try with the page to examine key codes (if you are not using a browser set for English and a Latin-based keyboard, your results may vary):

1. Enter a lowercase letter "a". Notice how the onKeyPress event handler shows the code to be 97, which is the Unicode (and ASCII) value for the first of the lowercase letters of the Latin alphabet. But the other two events record just the key's code: 65.

2. Type an uppercase "A" via the Shift key. If you watch closely, you see that the Shift key, itself, generates the code 16 for the onKeyDown and onKeyUp events.

But the character key then shows the value 65 for all three events, because the ASCII value of the uppercase letter happens to match the keyboard key code for that letter.

3. Press and release the Down Arrow key (be sure the cursor still flashes in the TEXTAREA, because that's where the keyboard events are being monitored). As a non-character key, it does not fire an `onKeyPress` event. But it does fire the other events, and assigns 40 as the code for this key.

4. Poke around with other non-character keys. Some may produce dialog boxes or menus, but their key codes are recorded nonetheless. Note that not all keys on a Macintosh keyboard register with IE/Mac.

returnValue

	NN2	NN3	NN4	NN6	IE3/J1	IE3/J2	IE4	IE5	IE5.5
Compatibility							✓	✓	✓

Example

You can find several examples of the `returnValue` property at work in Chapter 15 of the *JavaScript Bible* and in Listings 15-30, 33, 36, 37, 38, and 45 in Chapter 1 of this book. Moreover, many of the other examples in Chapter 15 of the *JavaScript Bible* can substitute the `returnValue` property way of canceling the default action if the scripts were to be run exclusively on IE4+.

srcElement

	NN2	NN3	NN4	NN6	IE3/J1	IE3/J2	IE4	IE5	IE5.5
Compatibility							✓	✓	✓

Example

As a simplified demonstration of the power of the `srcElement` property, Listing 29-17 has but two event handlers defined for the BODY element, each invoking a single function. The idea is that the `onMouseDown` and `onMouseUp` events will bubble up from whatever their targets are, and the event handler functions will find out which element is the target and modify the color style of that element.

An extra flair is added to the script in that each function also checks the `className` property of the target element. If the `className` is `bold`—a class name shared by three SPAN elements in the paragraph—the style sheet rule for that class is modified so that all items share the same color (see Figure 13-2). Your scripts can do even more in the way of filtering objects that arrive at the functions to perform special operations on certain objects or groups of objects.

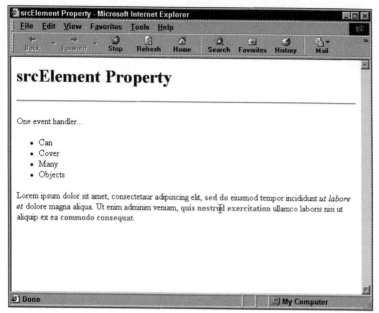

Figure 13-2: Clicking on one SPAN element highlights fellow class members.

Notice that the scripts don't have to know anything about the objects on the page to address each clicked one individually. That's because the srcElement property provides all of the specificity needed for acting on the target element.

Listing 29-17: **Using the srcElement property**

```
<HTML>
<HEAD>
<TITLE>srcElement Property</TITLE>
<STYLE TYPE="text/css">
.bold {font-weight:bold}
.ital {font-style:italic}
</STYLE>
<SCRIPT LANGUAGE="JavaScript">
function highlight() {
    var elem = event.srcElement
    if (elem.className == "bold") {
        document.styleSheets[0].rules[0].style.color = "red"
    } else {
        elem.style.color = "#FFCC00"
    }
}
function restore() {
    var elem = event.srcElement
    if (elem.className == "bold") {
```

Continued

Listing 29-17 *(continued)*

```
        document.styleSheets[0].rules[0].style.color = ""
    } else {
        elem.style.color = ""
    }
}
</SCRIPT>
</HEAD>
<BODY onMouseDown="highlight()" onMouseUp="restore()">
<H1>srcElement Property</H1>
<HR>
<P>One event handler...</P>
<UL>
<LI>Can
<LI>Cover
<LI>Many
<LI>Objects
</UL>
<P>
Lorem ipsum dolor sit amet, consectetaur adipisicing elit,
<SPAN CLASS="bold">sed do </SPAN>eiusmod tempor incididunt
<SPAN CLASS="ital">ut labore et </SPAN>dolore magna aliqua.
Ut enim adminim veniam, <SPAN CLASS="bold">quis nostrud
exercitation </SPAN>ullamco laboris nisi ut aliquip ex ea
<SPAN CLASS="bold">commodo consequat</SPAN>.
</P>
</BODY>
</HTML>
```

type

	NN2	NN3	NN4	NN6	IE3/J1	IE3/J2	IE4	IE5	IE5.5
Compatibility							✓	✓	✓

Example

Use The Evaluator (Chapter 13 in the *JavaScript Bible*) to see values returned by the type property. Enter the following object name into the bottom text box and press Enter/Return:

event

If necessary, scroll the Results box to view the type property, which should read keypress. Now click the List Properties button. The type changes to click. The reason for these types is that the event object whose properties are being shown here is the event that triggers the function to show the properties. From the text box, an onKeyPress event handler triggers that process; from the button, an onClick event handler does the job.

NN6+ event Object

```
charCode
keyCode
```

	NN2	NN3	NN4	NN6	IE3/J1	IE3/J2	IE4	IE5	IE5.5
Compatibility				✓					

Example

Listing 29-18 provides a play area to view the charCode and keyCode properties for all three keyboard events while you type into a TEXTAREA. You can use this later as an authoring tool to grab the precise codes for keyboard keys you may not be familiar with.

Listing 29-18: **Displaying charCode and keyCode Property Values**

```
<HTML>
<HEAD>
<TITLE>charCode and keyCode Properties</TITLE>
<STYLE TYPE="text/css">
TD {text-align:center}
</STYLE>
<SCRIPT LANGUAGE="JavaScript">
function showCode(which, evt) {
    document.forms[0].elements[which + "Char"].value = evt.charCode
    document.forms[0].elements[which + "Key"].value = evt.keyCode
}
function clearEm() {
    for (var i = 1; i < document.forms[0].elements.length; i++) {
        document.forms[0].elements[i].value = ""
    }
}
</SCRIPT>
</HEAD>
<BODY>
<H1>charCode and keyCode Properties</H1>
<HR>
<P></P>
<FORM>
<P>
```

Continued

Listing 29-18 *(continued)*

```
<TEXTAREA NAME="scratchpad" COLS="40" ROWS="5" WRAP="hard"
onKeyDown="clearEm(); showCode('down', event)" onKeyUp="showCode('up', event)"
onKeyPress="showCode('press', event)"></TEXTAREA>
</P>
<TABLE CELLPADDING="5">
<TR><TH>Event</TH><TH>event.charCode</TH><TH>event.keyCode</TH></TR>
<TR><TD>onKeyDown:</TD><TD><INPUT TYPE="text" NAME="downChar" SIZE="3"></TD>
<TD><INPUT TYPE="text" NAME="downKey" SIZE="3"></TD></TR>
<TR><TD>onKeyPress:</TD><TD><INPUT TYPE="text" NAME="pressChar" SIZE="3"></TD>
<TD><INPUT TYPE="text" NAME="pressKey" SIZE="3"></TD></TR>
<TR><TD>onKeyUp:</TD><TD><INPUT TYPE="text" NAME="upChar" SIZE="3"></TD>
<TD><INPUT TYPE="text" NAME="upKey" SIZE="3"></TD></TR>
</TABLE>
</FORM>
</BODY>
</HTML>
```

Here are some specific tasks to try with the page to examine key codes (if you are not using a browser set for English and a Latin-based keyboard, your results may vary):

1. Enter a lowercase letter "a". Notice how the onKeyPress event handler shows the charCode to be 97, which is the Unicode (and ASCII) value for the first of the lowercase letters of the Latin alphabet. But the other two event types record just the key's code: 65.

2. Type an uppercase "A" via the Shift key. If you watch closely, you see that the Shift key, itself, generates the key code 16 for the onKeyDown and onKeyUp events. But the character key then shows the value 65 for all three events (until you release the Shift key), because the ASCII value of the uppercase letter happens to match the keyboard key code for that letter.

3. Press and release the Down Arrow key (be sure the cursor still flashes in the TEXTAREA, because that's where the keyboard events are being monitored). As a non-character key, all three events stuff a value into the keyCode property, but zero into charCode. The keyCode value for this key is 40.

4. Poke around with other non-character keys. Some may produce dialog boxes or menus, but their key codes are recorded nonetheless.

```
clientX
clientY
layerX
layerY
pageX
pageY
screenX
screenY
```

	NN2	NN3	NN4	NN6	IE3/J1	IE3/J2	IE4	IE5	IE5.5
Compatibility				✓					

Example

You can see the effects of the coordinate systems and associated NN6 properties with the page in Listing 29-19. You can view coordinate values for all four measuring systems, as well as some calculated value. Two clickable objects are provided so that you can see the differences between an object not in any layer and an object residing within a layer (although anything you see is clickable, including text nodes). Figure 13-3 shows the results of a click inside the positioned layer.

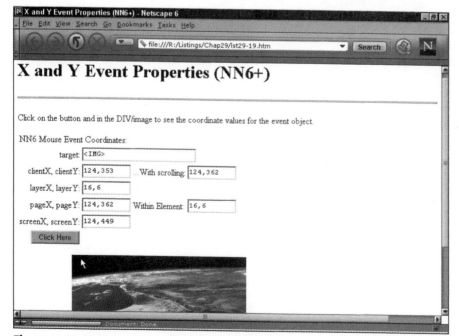

Figure 13-3: NN6 event coordinates for a click inside a positioned element

One of the calculated fields applies window scrolling values to the client coordinates. But, as you will see, these calculated values are the same as the more convenient page coordinates. The other calculated field shows the coordinates relative to the rectangular space of the target element. Notice in the code that if the nodeType of the target indicates a text node, that node's parent node (an element) is used for the calculation.

Listing 29-19: **NN6 Event Coordinate Properties**

```
<HTML>
<HEAD>
<TITLE>X and Y Event Properties (NN6+)</TITLE>
<SCRIPT LANGUAGE="JavaScript">
function checkCoords(evt) {
    var form = document.forms["output"]
    var targText, targElem
    if (evt.target.nodeType == 3) {
        targText = "[textnode] inside <" + evt.target.parentNode.tagName + ">"
        targElem = evt.target.parentNode
    } else {
        targText = "<" + evt.target.tagName + ">"
        targElem = evt.target
    }
    form.srcElemTag.value = targText
    form.clientCoords.value = evt.clientX + "," + evt.clientY
    form.clientScrollCoords.value = (evt.clientX + window.scrollX) +
        "," + (evt.clientY + window.scrollY)
    form.layerCoords.value = evt.layerX + "," + evt.layerY
    form.pageCoords.value = evt.pageX + "," + evt.pageY
    form.inElemCoords.value =
    (evt.pageX - targElem.offsetLeft - document.body.offsetLeft) +
        "," + (evt.pageY - targElem.offsetTop - document.body.offsetTop)
    form.screenCoords.value = evt.screenX + "," + evt.screenY
    return false
}
</SCRIPT>
</HEAD>
<BODY onMouseDown="checkCoords(event)">
<H1>X and Y Event Properties (NN6+)</H1>
<HR>
<P>Click on the button and in the DIV/image to see the coordinate values for the
event object.</P>
<FORM NAME="output">
<TABLE>
<TR><TD COLSPAN=2>NN6 Mouse Event Coordinates:</TD></TR>
<TR><TD ALIGN="right">target:</TD>
    <TD COLSPAN=3><INPUT TYPE="text" NAME="srcElemTag" SIZE=25></TD></TR>
<TR><TD ALIGN="right">clientX, clientY:</TD>
    <TD><INPUT TYPE="text" NAME="clientCoords" SIZE=10></TD>
        <TD ALIGN="right">...With scrolling:</TD>
        <TD><INPUT TYPE="text" NAME="clientScrollCoords" SIZE=10></TD></TR>
```

```
<TR><TD ALIGN="right">layerX, layerY:</TD>
    <TD><INPUT TYPE="text" NAME="layerCoords" SIZE=10></TD></TR>
<TR><TD ALIGN="right">pageX, pageY:</TD>
    <TD><INPUT TYPE="text" NAME="pageCoords" SIZE=10></TD>
    <TD ALIGH="right">Within Element:</TD>
    <TD><INPUT TYPE="text" NAME="inElemCoords" SIZE=10></TR>
<TR><TD ALIGN="right">screenX, screenY:</TD>
    <TD><INPUT TYPE="text" NAME="screenCoords" SIZE=10></TD></TR>
<TR><TD ALIGN="right"><INPUT TYPE="button" VALUE="Click Here"></TD></TR>
</TABLE>
</FORM>
<DIV ID="display" STYLE="position:relative; left:100">
<IMG SRC="nile.gif" WIDTH=320 HEIGHT=240" BORDER=0>
</DIV>
</BODY>
</HTML>
```

currentTarget

	NN2	NN3	NN4	NN6	IE3/J1	IE3/J2	IE4	IE5	IE5.5
Compatibility				✓					

Example

Listing 29-20 shows the power of the currentTarget property to reveal the element that is processing an event during event propagation. Similar to the code in Listing 29-7, this example is made simpler because it lets the event object's properties do more of the work to reveal the identity of each element that processes the event. Event listeners assigned for various propagation modes are assigned to a variety of nodes in the document. After you click the button, each listener in the propagation chain fires in sequence. The alert dialog shows which node is processing the event. And, as in Listing 29-7, the eventPhase property is used to help display the propagation mode in force at the time the event is processed by each node.

Listing 29-20: **currentTarget and eventPhase Properties**

```
<HTML>
<HEAD>
<TITLE>currentTarget and eventPhase Properties</TITLE>
<SCRIPT LANGUAGE="JavaScript">
function init() {
    // using old syntax to assign bubble-type event handlers
    document.onclick = processEvent
    document.body.onclick = processEvent
```

Continued

Listing 29-20 *(continued)*

```
        // turn on click event capture for document and form
        document.addEventListener("click", processEvent, true)
        document.forms[0].addEventListener("click", processEvent, true)
        // set bubble event listener for form
        document.forms[0].addEventListener("click", processEvent, false)
}
function processEvent(evt) {
        var currTargTag, msg
        if (evt.currentTarget.nodeType == 1) {
            currTargTag = "<" + evt.currentTarget.tagName + ">"
        } else {
            currTargTag = evt.currentTarget.nodeName
        }
        msg = "Event is now at the " + currTargTag + " level "
        msg += "(" + getPhase(evt) + ")."
        alert(msg)
}
// reveal event phase of current event object
function getPhase(evt) {
        switch (evt.eventPhase) {
            case 1:
                return "CAPTURING"
                break
            case 2:
                return "AT TARGET"
                break
            case 3:
                return "BUBBLING"
                break
            default:
                return ""
        }
}
</SCRIPT>
</HEAD>
<BODY onLoad="init()">
<H1>currentTarget and eventPhase Properties</H1>
<HR>
<FORM>
<INPUT TYPE="button" VALUE="A Button" NAME="main1"
    onClick="processEvent(event)">
</FORM>
</BODY>
</HTML>
```

You can also click other places on the page. For example, if you click to the right of the button, you will be clicking the FORM element. Event propagation and processing adjusts accordingly. Similarly, if you click the header text, the only event listeners that see the event are in the document and BODY levels.

eventPhase

	NN2	NN3	NN4	NN6	IE3/J1	IE3/J2	IE4	IE5	IE5.5
Compatibility				✓					

Example

See Listing 29-20 earlier in this chapter for an example of how you can use a `switch` construction to branch function processing based on the event phase of the current event object.

relatedTarget

	NN2	NN3	NN4	NN6	IE3/J1	IE3/J2	IE4	IE5	IE5.5
Compatibility				✓					

Example

Listing 29-21 provides an example of how the `relatedTarget` property can reveal the life of the cursor action before and after it rolls into an element. When you roll the cursor to the center box (a table cell), its `onMouseOver` event handler displays the text from the table cell from which the cursor arrived (the `nodeValue` of the text node inside the table cell). If the cursor comes in from one of the corners (not easy to do), a different message is displayed.

The two functions that report the results employ a bit of filtering to make sure that they process the event object only if the event occurs on an element and if the `relatedTarget` element is anything other than a nested text node of the central table cell element. Because nodes respond to events in NN6, this extra filtering prevents processing whenever the cursor makes the transition from the central TD element to its nested text node.

Listing 29-21: **Using the relatedTarget Property**

```
<HTML>
<HEAD>
<TITLE>relatedTarget Properties</TITLE>
<STYLE TYPE="text/CSS">
.direction {background-color:#00FFFF; width:100; height:50; text-align:center}
#main {background-color:#FF6666; text-align:center}
</STYLE>
<SCRIPT LANGUAGE="JavaScript">
function showArrival(evt) {
    if (evt.target.nodeType == 1) {
        if (evt.relatedTarget != evt.target.firstChild) {
```

Continued

Listing 29-21 *(continued)*

```
                var direction = (evt.relatedTarget.firstChild) ?
                evt.relatedTarget.firstChild.nodeValue : "parts unknown"
                status = "Arrived from: " + direction
        }
    }
}
function showDeparture(evt) {
    if (evt.target.nodeType == 1) {
        if (evt.relatedTarget != evt.target.firstChild) {
            var direction = (evt.relatedTarget.firstChild) ?
            evt.relatedTarget.firstChild.nodeValue : "parts unknown"
            status = "Departed to: " + direction
        }
    }
}
</SCRIPT>
</HEAD>
<BODY>
<H1>relatedTarget Properties</H1>
<HR>
<P>Roll the mouse to the center box and look for arrival information
in the status bar. Roll the mouse away from the center box and look for
departure information in the status bar.</P>

<TABLE CELLSPACING=0 CELLPADDING=5>
<TR><TD></TD><TD CLASS="direction">North</TD><TD></TD></TR>
<TR><TD CLASS="direction">West</TD>
<TD ID="main" onMouseOver="showArrival(event)"
            onMouseOut="showDeparture(event)">Roll</TD>
<TD CLASS="direction">East</TD></TR>
<TR><TD></TD><TD CLASS="direction">South</TD><TD></TD></TR>
</TABLE>
</BODY>
</HTML>
```

target

	NN2	NN3	NN4	NN6	IE3/J1	IE3/J2	IE4	IE5	IE5.5
Compatibility				✓					

Example

As a simplified demonstration of the power of the target property, Listing 29-22 has but two event handlers defined for the BODY element, each invoking a single function. The idea is that the onMouseDown and onMouseUp events will bubble up from whatever their targets are, and the event handler functions will find out which element is the target and modify the color style of that element.

An extra flair is added to the script in that each function also checks the className property of the target element. If the className is bold — a class name shared by three SPAN elements in the paragraph — the style sheet rule for that class is modified so that all items share the same color. Your scripts can do even more in the way of filtering objects that arrive at the functions to perform special operations on certain objects or groups of objects.

Notice that the scripts don't have to know anything about the objects on the page to address each clicked one individually. That's because the target property provides all of the specificity needed for acting on the target element.

Listing 29-22: **Using the target Property**

```
<HTML>
<HEAD>
<TITLE>target Property</TITLE>
<STYLE TYPE="text/css">
.bold {font-weight:bold}
.ital {font-style:italic}
</STYLE>
<SCRIPT LANGUAGE="JavaScript">
function highlight(evt) {
    var elem = (evt.target.nodeType == 3) ? evt.target.parentNode : evt.target
    if (elem.className == "bold") {
        document.styleSheets[0].cssRules[0].style.color = "red"
    } else {
        elem.style.color = "#FFCC00"
    }
}
function restore(evt) {
    var elem = (evt.target.nodeType == 3) ? evt.target.parentNode : evt.target
    if (elem.className == "bold") {
        document.styleSheets[0].cssRules[0].style.color = "black"
    } else {
        elem.style.color = "black"
    }
}
</SCRIPT>
</HEAD>
<BODY onMouseDown="highlight(event)" onMouseUp="restore(event)">
<H1>target Property</H1>
<HR>
<P>One event handler...</P>
<UL>
<LI>Can
<LI>Cover
<LI>Many
<LI>Objects
```

Continued

Listing 29-22 *(continued)*

```
</UL>
<P>
Lorem ipsum dolor sit amet, consectetaur adipisicing elit,
<SPAN CLASS="bold">sed do </SPAN>eiusmod tempor incididunt
<SPAN CLASS="ital">ut labore et </SPAN>dolore magna aliqua.
Ut enim adminim veniam, <SPAN CLASS="bold">quis nostrud
exercitation </SPAN>ullamco laboris nisi ut aliquip ex ea
<SPAN CLASS="bold">commodo consequat</SPAN>.
</P>
</BODY>
</HTML>
```

timeStamp

	NN2	NN3	NN4	NN6	IE3/J1	IE3/J2	IE4	IE5	IE5.5
Compatibility				✓					

Example

Listing 29-23 uses the `timeStamp` property to calculate the instantaneous typing speed when you type into a TEXTAREA (see Figure 13-4). The calculations are pretty raw and work only on intra-keystroke times without any averaging or smoothing that a more sophisticated typing tutor might perform. Calculated values are rounded to the nearest integer.

Listing 29-23: **Using the timeStamp property**

```
<HTML>
<HEAD>
<TITLE>timeStamp Property</TITLE>
<SCRIPT LANGUAGE="JavaScript">
var stamp
function calcSpeed(evt) {
    if (stamp) {
        var gross = evt.timeStamp - stamp
        var wpm = Math.round(6000/gross)
        document.getElementById("wpm").firstChild.nodeValue = wpm + " wpm."
    }
    stamp = evt.timeStamp

}
</SCRIPT>
</HEAD>
```

```
<BODY>
<H1>timeStamp Property</H1>
<HR>
<P>Start typing, and watch your instantaneous typing speed below:</P>
<P>
<TEXTAREA COLS=60 ROWS=10 WRAP="hard" onKeyPress="calcSpeed(event)"></TEXTAREA>
</P>
<P>Typing Speed: <SPAN ID="wpm"> </SPAN></P>
</BODY>
</HTML>
```

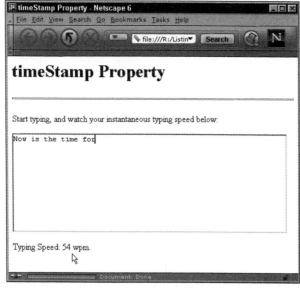

Figure 13-4: The timeStamp property helps calculate typing speed.

✦   ✦   ✦

Style Sheet Objects (Chapter 30)

Examples in this chapter focus on the properties and methods of the `styleSheet` object. As described in Chapter 30 of the *JavaScript Bible*, object models that support scriptable style sheets define both the STYLE element object (representing the element created with a `<STYLE>` tag pair) and the more abstract `styleSheet` object. The latter may be created by virtue of a STYLE element or perhaps imported from an external style sheet definition file.

Use the `styleSheet` object to gain access to the details of the rules defined for a given style sheet. Methods of the `styleSheet` object (different syntax for IE4+ and W3C object models) allow dynamic creation or deletion of rules within a style sheet. Properties of the `styleSheet` object (again, different syntax) return arrays of objects representing the style rules contained by the style sheet. The rule objects themselves have properties allowing reading and writing of rule selectors and even individual style attributes within that rule (since a single rule can list multiple style attributes).

Examples Highlights

+ Compare examples for the `styleSheet.cssRules` and `styleSheet.rules` properties to see how different browsers provide access to arrays of rule objects.

+ You can observe in The Evaluator (Chapter 13 in the *JavaScript Bible*) how the `styleSheet.disabled` property can switch a style sheet on and off dynamically.

+ Compare the `styleSheet` object method pairs for inserting and deleting rules to an existing style sheet. The walk-through examples let you follow the same steps for both the IE4+ and NN6 syntaxes.

+ The final example in this chapter demonstrates how scripts can modify a single attribute of a style sheet rule.

The syntax in the demonstration is for NN6 and IE5/Mac, but referencing the `cssRules` property provides the same access for the IE4+ object model.

styleSheet Object

Properties

cssRules

	NN2	NN3	NN4	NN6	IE3/J1	IE3/J2	IE4	IE5	IE5.5
Compatibility				✓				(✓)	(✓)

Example

Use The Evaluator (Chapter 13 in the *JavaScript Bible*) to look at the `cssRules` property in NN6+ or IE5+/Mac. First, view how many rules are in the first styleSheet object of the page by entering the following statement into the top text box:

```
document.styleSheets[0].cssRules.length
```

Now use the array with an index value to access one of the rule objects to view the rule object's properties list. Enter the following statement into the bottom text box:

```
document.styleSheets[0].cssRules[1]
```

You use this syntax to modify the style details of an individual rule belonging to the styleSheet object.

cssText

	NN2	NN3	NN4	NN6	IE3/J1	IE3/J2	IE4	IE5	IE5.5
Compatibility								✓	✓

Example

Use The Evaluator (Chapter 13) to replace the style rules in one blast via the `cssText` property. Begin by examining the value returned from the property for the initially disabled style sheet by entering the following statement into the top text box:

```
document.styleSheets[0].cssText
```

Next, enable the style sheet so that its rules are applied to the document:

```
document.styleSheets[0].disabled = false
```

Finally, enter the following statement into the top text box to overwrite the style sheet with entirely new rules.

```
document.styleSheets[0].cssText = "P {color:red}"
```

Reload the page after you are finished to restore the original state.

disabled

	NN2	NN3	NN4	NN6	IE3/J1	IE3/J2	IE4	IE5	IE5.5
Compatibility				✓			✓	✓	✓

Example

Use The Evaluator (Chapter 13 in the *JavaScript Bible*) to toggle between the enabled and disabled state of the first styleSheet object on the page. Enter the following statement into the top text box:

```
document.styleSheets[0].disabled = (!document.styleSheets[0].disabled)
```

The inclusion of the NOT operator (!) forces the state to change from true to false or false to true with each click of the Evaluate button.

ownerNode

	NN2	NN3	NN4	NN6	IE3/J1	IE3/J2	IE4	IE5	IE5.5
Compatibility				✓					

Example

Use The Evaluator (Chapter 13 in the *JavaScript Bible*) with NN6 to inspect the ownerNode of the first styleSheet object in the document. Enter the following statement into the top text box:

```
document.styleSheets[0].ownerNode.tagName
```

The returned value is the STYLE element tag name.

owningElement

	NN2	NN3	NN4	NN6	IE3/J1	IE3/J2	IE4	IE5	IE5.5
Compatibility							✓	✓	✓

Example

Use The Evaluator (Chapter 13 in *JavaScript Bible*) with IE4+ to inspect the owningElement of the first styleSheet object in the document. Enter the following statement into the top text box:

```
document.styleSheets[0].owningElement.tagName
```

The returned value is the STYLE element tag name.

rules

	NN2	NN3	NN4	NN6	IE3/J1	IE3/J2	IE4	IE5	IE5.5
Compatibility							✓	✓	✓

Example

Use The Evaluator (Chapter 13 in the *JavaScript Bible*) with IE4+ to examine the rules property of the first styleSheet object in the page. First, find out how many rules are in the first styleSheet object by entering the following statement into the top text box:

```
document.styleSheets[0].rules.length
```

Next, examine the properties of one of the rules by entering the following statement into the bottom text box:

```
document.styleSheets[0].rules[1]
```

You now see the all the properties that IE4+ exposes for a rule object.

Methods

```
addRule("selector", "styleSpec"[, index])
removeRule(index)
```

	NN2	NN3	NN4	NN6	IE3/J1	IE3/J2	IE4	IE5	IE5.5
Compatibility							✓	✓	✓

Example

Use The Evaluator (Chapter 13 in the *JavaScript Bible*) with IE4+ to add a style sheet rule to the first styleSheet object of the page. First, make sure the style sheet is enabled by entering the following statement into the top text box:

```
document.styleSheets[0].disabled = false
```

Next, append a style that sets the color of the TEXTAREA element:

```
document.styleSheets[0].addRule("TEXTAREA", "color:red")
```

Enter any valid object (such as `document.body`) into the bottom text box to see how the style has been applied to the TEXTAREA element on the page.

Now remove the style, using the index of the last item of the `rules` collection as the index:

```
document.styleSheets[0].removeRule(document.styleSheets[0].rules.length - 1)
```

The text in the TEXTAREA returns to its default color.

deleteRule(*index*)
insertRule("*rule*", *index*)

	NN2	NN3	NN4	NN6	IE3/J1	IE3/J2	IE4	IE5	IE5.5
Compatibility				✓					

Example

Use The Evaluator (Chapter 13 in the *JavaScript Bible*) with NN6+ to add a style sheet rule to the first styleSheet object of the page. First, make sure the style sheet is enabled by entering the following statement into the top text box:

```
document.styleSheets[0].disabled = false
```

Next, append a style that sets the color of the TEXTAREA element:

```
document.styleSheets[0].insertRule("TEXTAREA {color:red}",
document.styleSheets[0].cssRules.length)
```

Enter any valid object (such as `document.body`) into the bottom text box to see how the style has been applied to the TEXTAREA element on the page.

Now remove the style, using the index of the last item of the rules collection as the index:

```
document.styleSheets[0].deleteRule(document.styleSheets[0].cssRules.length - 1)
```

The first release of NN6 processes most, but not all, of the internal actions in response to the `deleteRule()` method. The method returns no value, so the Results box correctly reports `undefined` after evaluating the `deleteRule()` example statement. At the same time, the method has genuinely removed the rule from the styleSheet object (as proven by inspecting the `length` property of the `document.styleSheets[0].cssRules` array). But the browser does not refresh the page display to reflect the removal of the rule.

cssRule and rule Objects

Properties

selectorText

	NN2	NN3	NN4	NN6	IE3/J1	IE3/J2	IE4	IE5	IE5.5
Compatibility				✓			✓	✓	✓

Example

Use The Evaluator (Chapter 13 in the *JavaScript Bible*) to examine the selectorText property of rules in the first styleSheet object of the page. Enter each of the following statements in the top text box:

```
document.styleSheets[0].rules[0].selectorText
document.styleSheets[0].rules[1].selectorText
```

Compare these values against the source code view for the STYLE element in the page.

style

	NN2	NN3	NN4	NN6	IE3/J1	IE3/J2	IE4	IE5	IE5.5
Compatibility				✓			✓	✓	✓

Example

Use The Evaluator (Chapter 13 in the *JavaScript Bible*) to modify a style property of one of the styleSheet rules in the page. The syntax shown here is for IE4+, but you can substitute the cssRules reference for the rules collection reference in NN6 (and IE5/Mac) if you like.

Begin by reloading the page and making sure the style sheet is enabled. Enter the following statement into the top text box:

```
document.styleSheets[0].disabled = false
```

The first rule is for the myP element on the page. Change the rule's font-size style:

```
document.styleSheets[0].rules[0].style.fontSize = "20pt"
```

Look over the style object properties in the discussion of the style object later in this chapter and have fun experimenting with different style properties. After you are finished, reload the page to restore the styles to their default states.

✦　　✦　　✦

The NN4 Layer Object (Chapter 31)

◆ ◆ ◆ ◆

In This Chapter

Using NN4-specific
syntax for positioned
elements

How to move, hide,
and show positioned
content in NN4

Setting the clipping
rectangle of a layer
in NN4

◆ ◆ ◆ ◆

Chapter 31 of the *JavaScript Bible* is devoted to positioned objects in all object models. Only Navigator 4 has its own set of dedicated positionable objects: the LAYER and ILAYER element objects. In the IE4+ and W3C DOMs, virtually any renderable element is positionable, although it is common practice to restrict such activity to SPAN and DIV elements. Because properties of the SPAN, DIV, and other HTML element objects are covered in detail in other chapters, Chapter 31 provides the details of the NN4 layer object.

Examples shown here support NN4 layer object details, but the rest of the discussion and code listings in *JavaScript Bible* Chapter 31 go to great lengths to recreate the same behaviors in both the IE4+ and W3C (NN6) object models. This will help those scripters who developed extensively for NN4's Dynamic HTML make the transition to NN6 and its support for Dynamic HTML (which is not much different from that in the IE4+ object model). Obviously, all examples shown below require NN4.

Examples Highlights

✦ Clipping of layer rectangles is not an easy concept to grasp at first (in any object model). Listing 31-2 provides a workbench to explore the various properties associated with the clipping rectangle. Listing 31-5 demonstrates the relationship between moving a layer and adjusting its clipping rectangle.

✦ Listing 31-6 is an extensive demonstration of a variety of layer coordinate system properties.

✦ Most layer object properties are handled in later object models through style sheet property manipulation. Listing 31-8 shows the NN4 layer way of handling a layer's visibility, while Listing 31-9 demonstrates adjusting the stacking order of layers.

✦ Scripts for dragging a layer (with the help of the layer object's move methods) appear in Listing 31-11. Another type of dragging—dragging a corner to resize a layer—takes center stage in Listing 31-12a.

NN4 Layer Object

Properties

```
above
below
siblingAbove
siblingBelow
```

	NN2	NN3	NN4	NN6	IE3/J1	IE3/J2	IE4	IE5	IE5.5
Compatibility			✓						

Example

Listing 31-1 enables you to experiment with just one set of these properties: *layerObject*.above and *layerObject*.below. The page is almost in the form of a laboratory/quiz that enables you to query yourself about the values of these properties for two swappable layers.

Listing 31-1: **A Layer Quiz**

```
<HTML>
<HEAD>
<SCRIPT LANGUAGE="JavaScript">
function checkAbove(oneLayer) {
    document.forms[0].errors.value = ""
    document.forms[0].output.value = oneLayer.above.name
}
function checkBelow(oneLayer) {
    document.forms[0].errors.value = ""
    document.forms[0].output.value = oneLayer.below.name
}
function swapLayers() {
    if (document.yeller.above) {
        document.yeller.moveAbove(document.greeny)
    } else {
        document.greeny.moveAbove(document.yeller)
    }
}
```

```
function onerror(msg) {
    document.forms[0].output.value = ""
    document.forms[0].errors.value = msg
    return true
}
</SCRIPT>
</HEAD>
<BODY>
<H1>Layer Ordering</H1>
<HR>
<FORM>
Results:<INPUT TYPE="text" NAME="output"><P>
<INPUT TYPE="button" VALUE="Who's ABOVE the Yellow layer?"
onClick="checkAbove(document.yeller)"><BR>
<INPUT TYPE="button" VALUE="Who's BELOW the Yellow layer?"
onClick="checkBelow(document.yeller)"><P>
<INPUT TYPE="button" VALUE="Who's ABOVE the Green layer?"
onClick="checkAbove(document.greeny)"><BR>
<INPUT TYPE="button" VALUE="Who's BELOW the Green layer?"
onClick="checkBelow(document.greeny)"><P>
<INPUT TYPE="button" VALUE="Swap Layers" onCLick="swapLayers()"><P>
If there are any errors caused by missing <BR>
properties, they will appear below:<BR>
<TEXTAREA NAME="errors" COLS=30 ROWS=3 WRAP="virtual"></TEXTAREA>
</FORM>
<LAYER NAME="yeller" BGCOLOR="yellow" TOP=110 LEFT=300 WIDTH=200 HEIGHT=200>
<B>This is just a yellow layer.</B>
</LAYER>
<LAYER NAME="greeny" BGCOLOR="lightgreen" TOP=150 LEFT=340 WIDTH=200 HEIGHT=200>
<B>This is just a green layer.</B>
</LAYER>
</BODY>
</HTML>
```

The page contains two layers: one colored yellow and the other light green. Legends on four buttons ask you to guess whether one layer is above or below the other. For example, if you click the button labeled "Who's ABOVE the Yellow layer?" and the green layer is above it, the name of that green layer appears in the Results field. But if layers are oriented such that the returned value is null, the error message (indicating that the nonexistent object doesn't have a name property) appears in the error field at the bottom. Another button enables you to swap the order of the layers so you can try your hand at predicting the results based on your knowledge of layers and the above and below properties. Positioned objects in IE4+ and NN6 have no comparable properties to the four described in this section.

background

	NN2	NN3	NN4	NN6	IE3/J1	IE3/J2	IE4	IE5	IE5.5
Compatibility			✓						

Example

A simple example (Listing 31-2) defines one layer that features five buttons to change the background image of a second layer. I put the buttons in a layer because I want to make sure the buttons and background layer rectangles align themselves along their top edges on all platforms.

As the second layer loads, I merely assign a gray background color to it and write some reverse (white) text. Most of the images are of the small variety that repeat in the layer. One is a large photograph to demonstrate how images are clipped to the layer's rectangle. Along the way, I hope you also heed the lesson of readability demonstrated by the difficulty of reading text on a wild-looking background. For an example compatible with IE5+ and NN6+, see Listing 31-13.

Listing 31-2: **Setting Layer Backgrounds**

```
<HTML>
<HEAD>
<SCRIPT LANGUAGE="JavaScript">
function setBg(URL) {
    document.bgExpo.background.src = URL
}
</SCRIPT>
</HEAD>
<BODY>
<H1>Layer Backgrounds</H1>
<HR>
<LAYER NAME="buttons" TOP=100>
    <FORM>
        <INPUT TYPE="button" VALUE="The Usual"
onClick="setBg('cr_kraft.gif')"><BR>
        <INPUT TYPE="button" VALUE="A Big One" onClick="setBg('arch.gif')"><BR>
        <INPUT TYPE="button" VALUE="Not So Usual"
onClick="setBg('wh86.gif')"><BR>
        <INPUT TYPE="button" VALUE="Decidedly Unusual"
onClick="setBg('sb23.gif')"><BR>
        <INPUT TYPE="button" VALUE="Quick as..."
onClick="setBg('lightnin.gif')"><BR>
    </FORM>
</LAYER>
<LAYER NAME="bgExpo" BGCOLOR="gray" TOP=100 LEFT=250 WIDTH=300 HEIGHT=260>
<B><FONT COLOR="white">Some text, which may or may not read well with the
various backgrounds.</FONT></B>
```

```
</LAYER>
</BODY>
</HTML>
```

bgColor

	NN2	NN3	NN4	NN6	IE3/J1	IE3/J2	IE4	IE5	IE5.5
Compatibility			✓						

Example

You can have some fun with Listing 31-3, which uses a number of layer scripting techniques. The page presents a kind of palette of eight colors, each one created as a small layer (see Figure 15-1). Another, larger layer's bgColor property changes as you roll the mouse over any color in the palette.

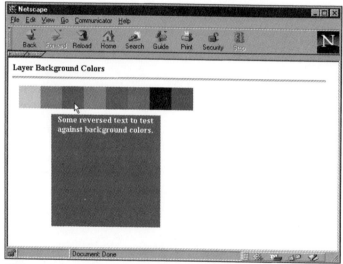

Figure 15-1: Drag the mouse across the palette to change the layer's background color.

To save HTML lines to create those eight color palette layers, I use a script to establish an array of colors and then document.write() the <LAYER> tags with appropriate attribute settings so the layers all line up in a contiguous row. By pre-defining a number of variable values for the size of the color layers, I can make all of them larger or smaller with the change of only a few script characters.

The document object handles the job of capturing the mouseOver events. I turn on the document's captureEvents() method such that it traps all mouseOver events and hands them to the `setColor()` function. The `setColor()` function reads the target object's `bgColor` and sets the larger layer's `bgColor` property to the same. If this page had other objects that could receive `mouseOver` events for other purposes, I would use `routeEvents()` to let those events pass on to their intended targets. For the purposes of this example, however, the events need to go no further. Listing 31-14 in the *JavaScript Bible* shows the same functionality working in IE5+ and NN6+.

Listing 31-3: **Layer Background Colors**

```
<HTML>
<HEAD>
<SCRIPT LANGUAGE="JavaScript">
function setColor(e) {
    document.display.bgColor = e.target.bgColor
}
document.captureEvents(Event.MOUSEOVER)
document.onmouseover = setColor
</SCRIPT>
</HEAD>
<BODY>
<H1>Layer Background Colors</H1>
<HR>
<SCRIPT LANGUAGE="JavaScript">
var oneLayer
var colorTop = 100
var colorLeft = 20
var colorWidth = 40
var colorHeight = 40
var colorPalette = new
Array("aquamarine","coral","forestgreen","goldenrod","red",
                     "magenta","navy","teal")
for (var i = 0; i < colorPalette.length; i++) {
    oneLayer = "<LAYER NAME=swatch" + i + " TOP=" + colorTop
    oneLayer += " LEFT=" + ((colorWidth * i) + colorLeft)
    oneLayer += " WIDTH=" + colorWidth + " HEIGHT=" + colorHeight
    oneLayer += " BGCOLOR=" + colorPalette[i] + "></LAYER>\n"
    document.write(oneLayer)
}
</SCRIPT>
<LAYER NAME="display" BGCOLOR="gray" TOP=150 LEFT=80 WIDTH=200 HEIGHT=200>
<B><FONT COLOR="white"><CENTER>Some reversed text to test against background
colors.</CENTER></FONT></B>
</LAYER>
</BODY>
</HTML>
```

clip

	NN2	NN3	NN4	NN6	IE3/J1	IE3/J2	IE4	IE5	IE5.5
Compatibility			✓						

Example

Because of the edge movement behavior of adjustments to *layerObject*.clip properties, Listing 31-4 enables you to experiment with adjustments to each of the six properties. The document loads one layer that you can adjust by entering alternative values into six text fields — one per property. Figure 15-2 shows the page.

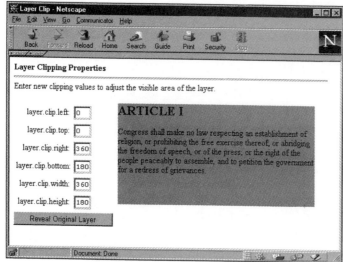

Figure 15-2: Experiment with layer.clip properties.

As you enter values, all properties are updated to show their current values (via the showValues() function). Pay particular attention to the apparent motion of the edge and the effect the change has on at least one other property. For example, a change to the *layerObject*.clip.left value also affects the *layerObject*.clip.width property value.

Listing 31-4: **Adjusting layer.clip Properties**

```
<HTML>
<HEAD>
<TITLE>Layer Clip</TITLE>
<SCRIPT LANGUAGE="JavaScript">
var origLayerWidth = 0
var origLayerHeight = 0
```

Continued

Listing 31-4 *(continued)*

```javascript
function initializeXY() {
    origLayerWidth = document.display.clip.width
    origLayerHeight = document.display.clip.height
    showValues()
}

function setClip(field) {
    var clipVal = parseInt(field.value)
    document.display.clip[field.name] = clipVal
    showValues()
}
function showValues() {
    var form = document.layers[0].document.forms[0]
    var propName
    for (var i = 0; i < form.elements.length; i++) {
        propName = form.elements[i].name
        if (form.elements[i].type == "text") {
            form.elements[i].value = document.display.clip[propName]
        }
    }
}
var intervalID
function revealClip() {
    var midWidth = Math.round(origLayerWidth /2)
    var midHeight = Math.round(origLayerHeight /2)
    document.display.clip.left = midWidth
    document.display.clip.top = midHeight
    document.display.clip.right = midWidth
    document.display.clip.bottom = midHeight
    intervalID = setInterval("stepClip()",1)
}
function stepClip() {
    var widthDone = false
    var heightDone = false
    if (document.display.clip.left > 0) {
        document.display.clip.left += -2
        document.display.clip.right += 2
    } else {
        widthDone = true
    }
    if (document.display.clip.top > 0) {
        document.display.clip.top += -1
        document.display.clip.bottom += 1
    } else {
        heightDone = true
    }
    showValues()
    if (widthDone && heightDone) {
        clearInterval(intervalID)
```

```
      }
}
</SCRIPT>
</HEAD>
<BODY onLoad="initializeXY()">
<H1>Layer Clipping Properties</H1>
<HR>
Enter new clipping values to adjust the visible area of the layer.<P>
<LAYER TOP=130>
<FORM>
<TABLE>
<TR>
    <TD ALIGN="right">layer.clip.left:</TD>
    <TD><INPUT TYPE="text" NAME="left" SIZE=3 onChange="setClip(this)"></TD>
</TR>
<TR>
    <TD ALIGN="right">layer.clip.top:</TD>
    <TD><INPUT TYPE="text" NAME="top" SIZE=3 onChange="setClip(this)"></TD>
</TR>
<TR>
    <TD ALIGN="right">layer.clip.right:</TD>
    <TD><INPUT TYPE="text" NAME="right" SIZE=3 onChange="setClip(this)"></TD>
</TR>
<TR>
    <TD ALIGN="right">layer.clip.bottom:</TD>
    <TD><INPUT TYPE="text" NAME="bottom" SIZE=3 onChange="setClip(this)"></TD>
</TR>
<TR>
    <TD ALIGN="right">layer.clip.width:</TD>
    <TD><INPUT TYPE="text" NAME="width" SIZE=3 onChange="setClip(this)"></TD>
</TR>
<TR>
    <TD ALIGN="right">layer.clip.height:</TD>
    <TD><INPUT TYPE="text" NAME="height" SIZE=3 onChange="setClip(this)"></TD>
</TR>
</TABLE>
<INPUT TYPE="button" VALUE="Reveal Original Layer" onClick="revealClip()">
</FORM>
</LAYER>
<LAYER NAME="display" BGCOLOR="coral" TOP=130 LEFT=200 WIDTH=360 HEIGHT=180>
<H2>ARTICLE I</H2>
<P>
Congress shall make no law respecting an establishment of religion, or
prohibiting the free exercise thereof; or abridging the freedom of speech, or of
the press; or the right of the people peaceably to assemble, and to petition the
government for a redress of grievances.
</P>
</LAYER>
</BODY>
</HTML>
```

Listing 31-4 has a lot of other scripting in it to demonstrate a couple of other clip area techniques. After the document loads, the `onLoad` event handler initializes two global variables that represent the starting height and width of the layer as determined by the `clip.height` and `clip.width` properties. Because the `<LAYER>` tag does not specify any `CLIP` attributes, the `layerObject.clip` region is ensured of being the same as the layer's dimensions at load time.

I preserve the initial values for a somewhat advanced set of functions that act in response to the Reveal Original Layer button. The goal of this button is to temporarily shrink the clipping area to nothing and then expand the clip rectangle gradually from the very center of the layer. The effect is analogous to a zoom-out visual effect.

The clip region shrinks to practically nothing by setting all four edges to the same point midway along the height and width of the layer. The script then uses `setInterval()` to control the animation in `setClip()`. To make the zoom even on both axes, I first make sure that the initial size of the layer is an even ratio: twice as wide as it is tall. Each time through the `setClip()` function, the `clip.left` and `clip.right` values are adjusted in their respective directions by two pixels and `clip.top` and `clip.bottom` are adjusted by one pixel.

To make sure the animation stops when the layer is at its original size, I check whether the `clip.top` and `clip.left` values are their original zero values. If they are, I set a Boolean variable for each side. When both variables indicate that the clip rectangle is its original size, the script cancels the `setInterval()` action. Listing 31-15 in the *JavaScript Bible* demonstrates how to adjust clipping in IE5+ and NN6+ syntax.

left
top

	NN2	NN3	NN4	NN6	IE3/J1	IE3/J2	IE4	IE5	IE5.5
Compatibility			✓						

Example

To enable you to experiment with manually setting *layerObject*`.top` and *layerObject*`.left` properties, Listing 31-5 is a modified version of the `layer.clip` example (Listing 31-4). The current example again has the one modifiable layer, but it has only four text fields in which you can enter values. Two fields are for the *layerObject*`.left` and *layerObject*`.top` properties; the other two are for the *layerObject*`.clip.left` and *layerObject*`.clip.top` properties. I present both sets of values here to help reinforce the lack of connection between layer and clip location properties in the same layer object. You can find the corresponding syntax for IE5+ and NN6+ in Listing 31-16 of the *JavaScript Bible*.

Listing 31-5: **Comparison of Layer and Clip Location Properties**

```
<HTML>
<HEAD>
<TITLE>Layer vs. Clip</TITLE>
<SCRIPT LANGUAGE="JavaScript">
function setClip(field) {
    var clipVal = parseInt(field.value)
    document.display.clip[field.name] = clipVal
    showValues()
}
function setLayer(field) {
    var layerVal = parseInt(field.value)
    document.display[field.name] = layerVal
    showValues()
}
function showValues() {
    var form = document.layers[0].document.forms[0]
    form.elements[0].value = document.display.left
    form.elements[1].value = document.display.top
    form.elements[2].value = document.display.clip.left
    form.elements[3].value = document.display.clip.top
}
</SCRIPT>
</HEAD>
<BODY onLoad="showValues()">
<B>Layer vs. Clip Location Properties</B>
<HR>
Enter new layer and clipping values to adjust the layer.<P>
<LAYER TOP=80>
<FORM>
<TABLE>
<TR>
    <TD ALIGN="right">layer.left:</TD>
    <TD><INPUT TYPE="text" NAME="left" SIZE=3 onChange="setLayer(this)"></TD>
</TR>
<TR>
    <TD ALIGN="right">layer.top:</TD>
    <TD><INPUT TYPE="text" NAME="top" SIZE=3 onChange="setLayer(this)"></TD>
</TR>
<TR>
    <TD ALIGN="right">layer.clip.left:</TD>
    <TD><INPUT TYPE="text" NAME="left" SIZE=3 onChange="setClip(this)"></TD>
</TR>
<TR>
    <TD ALIGN="right">layer.clip.top:</TD>
    <TD><INPUT TYPE="text" NAME="top" SIZE=3 onChange="setClip(this)"></TD>
</TR>
</TABLE>
</FORM>
```

Continued

Listing 31-5 *(continued)*

```
</LAYER>
<LAYER NAME="display" BGCOLOR="coral" TOP=80 LEFT=200 WIDTH=360 HEIGHT=180>
<H2>ARTICLE I</H2>
<P>
Congress shall make no law respecting an establishment of religion, or
prohibiting the free exercise thereof; or abridging the freedom of speech, or of
the press; or the right of the people peaceably to assemble, and to petition the
government for a redress of grievances.
</P>
</LAYER>
</BODY>
</HTML>
```

pageX
pageY

	NN2	NN3	NN4	NN6	IE3/J1	IE3/J2	IE4	IE5	IE5.5
Compatibility			✓						

Example

Listing 31-6 defines one outer layer and one nested inner layer of different colors (see Figure 15-3). The inner layer contains some text content; the outer layer is sized initially to present a colorful border by being below the inner layer and 10 pixels wider and taller.

Two sets of fields display (and enable you to change) the *layerObject*.pageX, *layerObject*.pageY, *layerObject*.left, and *layerObject*.top properties for each of the nested layers. Each set of fields is color-coded to its corresponding layer.

When you change any value, all values are recalculated and displayed in the other fields. For example, the initial pageX position for the outer layer is 200 pixels; for the inner layer, the pageX value is 205 pixels (accounting for the 5-pixel "border" around the inner layer). If you change the outer layer's pageX value to 220, the outer layer moves to the right by 20 pixels, taking the inner layer along for the ride. The layer.pageX value for the inner layer after the move is 225 pixels.

The outer layer values for the pairs of values are always the same no matter what. But for the inner layer, the page values are significantly different from the layer.left and layer.top values because these latter values are measured relative to their containing layer — the outer layer. If you move the outer layer, the inner layer values for *layerObject*.left and *layerObject*.top don't change one iota. Listing 31-17 in the *JavaScript Bible* shows the comparable syntax for IE5+ and NN6+.

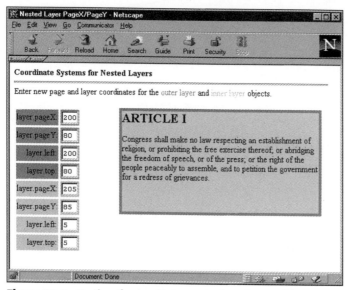

Figure 15-3: Testing the position properties of nested layers

Listing 31-6: **Testing Nested Layer Coordinate Systems**

```
<HTML>
<HEAD>
<TITLE>Nested Layer PageX/PageY</TITLE>
<SCRIPT LANGUAGE="JavaScript">
function setOuterPage(field) {
    var layerVal = parseInt(field.value)
    document.outerDisplay[field.name] = layerVal
    showValues()
}
function setOuterLayer(field) {
    var layerVal = parseInt(field.value)
    document.outerDisplay[field.name] = layerVal
    showValues()
}
function setInnerPage(field) {
    var layerVal = parseInt(field.value)
    document.outerDisplay.document.innerDisplay[field.name] = layerVal
    showValues()
}
function setInnerLayer(field) {
    var layerVal = parseInt(field.value)
    document.outerDisplay.document.innerDisplay[field.name] = layerVal
    showValues()
}
```

Continued

Listing 31-6 *(continued)*

```
function showValues() {
    var form = document.layers[0].document.forms[0]
    form.elements[0].value = document.outerDisplay.pageX
    form.elements[1].value = document.outerDisplay.pageY
    form.elements[2].value = document.outerDisplay.left
    form.elements[3].value = document.outerDisplay.top
    form.elements[4].value = document.outerDisplay.document.innerDisplay.pageX
    form.elements[5].value = document.outerDisplay.document.innerDisplay.pageY
    form.elements[6].value = document.outerDisplay.document.innerDisplay.left
    form.elements[7].value = document.outerDisplay.document.innerDisplay.top
}
</SCRIPT>
</HEAD>
<BODY onLoad="showValues()">
<B>Coordinate Systems for Nested Layers</B>
<HR>
Enter new page and layer coordinates for the <FONT COLOR="coral">outer
layer</FONT> and <FONT COLOR="aquamarine">inner layer</FONT> objects.<P>
<LAYER TOP=80>
<FORM>
<TABLE>
<TR>
    <TD ALIGN="right" BGCOLOR="coral">layer.pageX:</TD>
    <TD BGCOLOR="coral"><INPUT TYPE="text" NAME="pageX" SIZE=3
        onChange="setOuterPage(this)"></TD>
</TR>
<TR>
    <TD ALIGN="right" BGCOLOR="coral">layer.pageY:</TD>
    <TD BGCOLOR="coral"><INPUT TYPE="text" NAME="pageY" SIZE=3
        onChange="setOuterPage(this)"></TD>
</TR>
<TR>
    <TD ALIGN="right" BGCOLOR="coral">layer.left:</TD>
    <TD BGCOLOR="coral"><INPUT TYPE="text" NAME="left" SIZE=3
        onChange="setOuterLayer(this)"></TD>
</TR>
<TR>
    <TD ALIGN="right" BGCOLOR="coral">layer.top:</TD>
    <TD BGCOLOR="coral"><INPUT TYPE="text" NAME="top" SIZE=3
        onChange="setOuterLayer(this)"></TD>
</TR>
<TR>
    <TD ALIGN="right" BGCOLOR="aquamarine">layer.pageX:</TD>
    <TD BGCOLOR="aquamarine"><INPUT TYPE="text" NAME="pageX" SIZE=3
        onChange="setInnerPage(this)"></TD>
</TR>
<TR>
    <TD ALIGN="right" BGCOLOR="aquamarine">layer.pageY:</TD>
    <TD BGCOLOR="aquamarine"><INPUT TYPE="text" NAME="pageY" SIZE=3
        onChange="setInnerPage(this)"></TD>
</TR>
```

```
<TR>
    <TD ALIGN="right" BGCOLOR="aquamarine">layer.left:</TD>
    <TD BGCOLOR="aquamarine"><INPUT TYPE="text" NAME="left" SIZE=3
        onChange="setInnerLayer(this)"></TD>
</TR>
<TR>
    <TD ALIGN="right" BGCOLOR="aquamarine">layer.top:</TD>
    <TD BGCOLOR="aquamarine"><INPUT TYPE="text" NAME="top" SIZE=3
        onChange="setInnerLayer(this)"></TD>
</TR>
</TABLE>
</FORM>
</LAYER>
<LAYER NAME="outerDisplay" BGCOLOR="coral" TOP=80 LEFT=200 WIDTH=370 HEIGHT=190>
<LAYER NAME="innerDisplay" BGCOLOR="aquamarine" TOP=5 LEFT=5 WIDTH=360
HEIGHT=180>
<H2>ARTICLE I</H2>
<P>
Congress shall make no law respecting an establishment of religion, or
prohibiting the free exercise thereof; or abridging the freedom of speech, or of
the press; or the right of the people peaceably to assemble, and to petition the
government for a redress of grievances.
</P>
</LAYER>
</LAYER>
</BODY>
</HTML>
```

src

	NN2	NN3	NN4	NN6	IE3/J1	IE3/J2	IE4	IE5	IE5.5
Compatibility			✓						

Example

Setting the *layerObject*.src property of a layer that is a member of a layer family (that is, a family with at least one parent and one child) can be tricky business if you're not careful. Listing 31-7 presents a workspace for you to see how changing the src property of outer and inner layers affects the scenery.

When you first load the document, one outer layer contains one inner layer (each with a different background color). Control buttons on the page enable you to set the *layerObject*.src property of each layer independently. Changes to the inner layer content affect only that layer. Long content forces the inner layer to expand its depth, but the inner layer's view is automatically clipped by its parent layer.

Changing the outer layer content, however, removes the inner layer completely. Code in the following listing shows one way to examine for the presence of a particular layer before attempting to load new content in it. If the inner layer doesn't exist, the script creates a new layer on the fly to replace the original inner layer.

Listing 31-7: **Setting Nested Layer Source Content**

```
<HTML>
<HEAD>
<TITLE>Layer Source</TITLE>
<SCRIPT LANGUAGE="JavaScript">
function loadOuter(doc) {
    document.outerDisplay.src = doc
}
function loadInner(doc) {
    var nested = document.outerDisplay.document.layers
    if (nested.length > 0) {
        // inner layer exists, so load content or restore
        if (doc) {
            nested[0].src = doc
        } else {
            restoreInner(nested[0])
        }
    } else {
        // prompt user about restoring inner layer
        if (confirm("The inner layer has been removed by loading an " +
        "outer document. Restore the original layers?")) {
            restoreLayers(doc)
        }
    }
}
function restoreLayers(doc) {
    // reset appearance of outer layer
    document.outerDisplay.bgColor = "coral"
    document.outerDisplay.resizeTo(370,190) // sets clip
    document.outerDisplay.document.write("")
    document.outerDisplay.document.close()
    // generate new inner layer
    var newInner = new Layer(360, document.layers["outerDisplay"])
    newInner.bgColor = "aquamarine"
    newInner.moveTo(5,5)
    if (doc) {
        // user clicked an inner content button
        newInner.src = doc
    } else {
        // return to pristine look
        restoreInner(newInner)
    }
    newInner.visibility = "show"
}
function restoreInner(inner) {
    inner.document.write("<HTML><BODY><P><B>Placeholder text for raw inner " +
    "layer.</B></P></BODY></HTML>")
    inner.document.close()
    inner.resizeTo(360,180) // sets clip
}
</SCRIPT>
```

```
</HEAD>
<BODY>
<B>Setting the <TT>layer.src</TT> Property of Nested Layers</B>
<HR>
Click the buttons to see what happens when you load new source documents into
the <FONT COLOR="coral">outer layer</FONT> and <FONT COLOR="aquamarine">inner
layer</FONT> objects.<P>
<LAYER TOP=100 BGCOLOR="coral">
<FORM>
Load into outer layer:<BR>
<INPUT TYPE="button" VALUE="Article I" onClick="loadOuter('article1.htm')"><BR>
<INPUT TYPE="button" VALUE="Entire Bill of Rights"
onClick="loadOuter('bofright.htm')"><BR>
</FORM>
</LAYER>
<LAYER TOP=220 BGCOLOR="aquamarine">
<FORM>
Load into inner layer:<BR>
<INPUT TYPE="button" VALUE="Article I" onClick="loadInner('article1.htm')"><BR>
<INPUT TYPE="button" VALUE="Entire Bill of Rights"
onClick="loadInner('bofright.htm')"><BR>
<INPUT TYPE="button" VALUE="Restore Original" onClick="loadInner()"><BR>
</FORM>
</LAYER>
<LAYER NAME="outerDisplay" BGCOLOR="coral" TOP=100 LEFT=200 WIDTH=370
HEIGHT=190>
    <LAYER NAME="innerDisplay" BGCOLOR="aquamarine" TOP=5 LEFT=5 WIDTH=360
HEIGHT=180>
    <P><B>Placeholder text for raw inner layer.</B></P>
    </LAYER>
</LAYER>
</BODY>
</HTML>
```

Restoring the original layers via script (as opposed to reloading the document) does not perform a perfect restoration. The key difference is that the scripts use the *layerObject*.resizeTo() method to set the layers to the height and width established by the <LAYER> tags that create the layers in the first place. This method, however, sets the clipping rectangle of the layer—not the layer's size. Therefore, if you use the script to restore the layers, loading the longer text file into either layer does not force the layer to expand to display all the content; the clipping region governs the view.

visibility

	NN2	NN3	NN4	NN6	IE3/J1	IE3/J2	IE4	IE5	IE5.5
Compatibility			✓						

Example

Use the page in Listing 31-8 to see how the `layerObject`.visibility property settings affect a pair of nested layers. When the page first loads, the default inherit setting is in effect. Changes you make to the outer layer by clicking the outer layer buttons affect the inner layer, but setting the inner layer's properties to hide or show severs the visibility relationship between parent and child. Listing 31-19 in the *JavaScript Bible* shows this example with IE5+ and NN6+ syntax.

Listing 31-8: **Nested Layer Visibility Relationships**

```
<HTML>
<HEAD>
<TITLE>Layer Source</TITLE>
<SCRIPT LANGUAGE="JavaScript">
function setOuterVis(type) {
    document.outerDisplay.visibility = type
}
function setInnerVis(type) {
    document.outerDisplay.document.innerDisplay.visibility = type
}
</SCRIPT>
</HEAD>
<BODY>
<B>Setting the <TT>layer.visibility</TT> Property of Nested Layers</B>
<HR>
Click the buttons to see what happens when you change the visibility of the
<FONT COLOR="coral">outer layer</FONT> and <FONT COLOR="aquamarine">inner
layer</FONT> objects.<P>
<LAYER TOP=100 BGCOLOR="coral">
<FORM>
Control outer layer property:<BR>
<INPUT TYPE="button" VALUE="Hide Outer Layer" onClick="setOuterVis('hide')"><BR>
<INPUT TYPE="button" VALUE="Show Outer Layer" onClick="setOuterVis('show')"><BR>
</FORM>
</LAYER>
<LAYER TOP=220 BGCOLOR="aquamarine">
<FORM>
Control inner layer property:<BR>
<INPUT TYPE="button" VALUE="Hide Inner Layer" onClick="setInnerVis('hide')"><BR>
<INPUT TYPE="button" VALUE="Show Inner Layer" onClick="setInnerVis('show')"><BR>
<INPUT TYPE="button" VALUE="Inherit Outer Layer"
onClick="setInnerVis('inherit')"><BR>
</FORM>
</LAYER>
<LAYER NAME="outerDisplay" BGCOLOR="coral" TOP=100 LEFT=200 WIDTH=370
HEIGHT=190>
    <LAYER NAME="innerDisplay" BGCOLOR="aquamarine" TOP=5 LEFT=5 WIDTH=360
HEIGHT=180>
    <P><B>Placeholder text for raw inner layer.</B></P>
    </LAYER>
</LAYER>
</BODY>
</HTML>
```

zIndex

	NN2	NN3	NN4	NN6	IE3/J1	IE3/J2	IE4	IE5	IE5.5
Compatibility			✓						

Example

The relationships among the three stacking property values can be difficult to visualize. Listing 31-9 offers a way to see the results of changing the *layerObject*.zIndex properties of three overlapping sibling layers. Figure 15-4 shows the beginning organization of layers after the page loads.

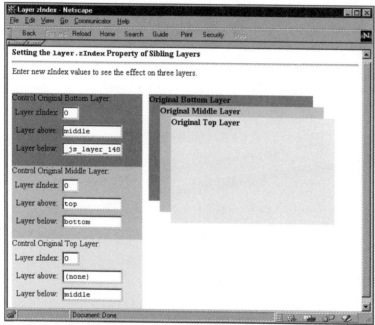

Figure 15-4: A place to play with zIndex property settings

The sequence of the <LAYER> tags in the document governs the original stacking order. Because the attribute is not set in the HTML, the initial values appear as zero for all three layers. But, as the page reveals, the *layerObject*.above and *layerObject*.below properties are automatically established. When a layer has no other layer object above it, the page shows (none). Also, if the layer below the bottom of the stack is the main window, a strange inner layer name is assigned (something like _js_layer_21).

To experiment with this page, first make sure you understand the *layerObject*.above and *layerObject*.below readings for the default order of the layers. Then, assign different orders to the layers with value sequences such as

3-2-1, 1-3-2, 2-2-2, and so on. Each time you enter one new value, check the actual layers to see if their stacking order changed and how that affected the other properties of all layers. Listing 31-20 in the *JavaScript Bible* shows how to achieve the same action with IE5+ and NN6+ syntax.

Listing 31-9: **Relationships Among zIndex, above, and below**

```
<HTML>
<HEAD>
<TITLE>Layer zIndex</TITLE>
<SCRIPT LANGUAGE="JavaScript">
function setZ(field) {
    switch (field.name) {
        case "top" :
            document.top.zIndex = parseInt(field.value)
            break
        case "mid" :
            document.middle.zIndex = parseInt(field.value)
            break
        case "bot" :
            document.bottom.zIndex = parseInt(field.value)
    }
    showValues()
}
function showValues() {
    document.layers[0].document.forms[0].bot.value = document.bottom.zIndex
    document.layers[1].document.forms[0].mid.value = document.middle.zIndex
    document.layers[2].document.forms[0].top.value = document.top.zIndex

    document.layers[0].document.forms[0].above.value = (document.bottom.above) ?
        document.bottom.above.name : "(none)"
    document.layers[1].document.forms[0].above.value = (document.middle.above) ?
        document.middle.above.name : "(none)"
    document.layers[2].document.forms[0].above.value = (document.top.above) ?
        document.top.above.name : "(none)"

    document.layers[0].document.forms[0].below.value = (document.bottom.below) ?
        document.bottom.below.name : "(none)"
    document.layers[1].document.forms[0].below.value = (document.middle.below) ?
        document.middle.below.name : "(none)"
    document.layers[2].document.forms[0].below.value = (document.top.below) ?
        document.top.below.name : "(none)"
}
</SCRIPT>
</HEAD>
<BODY onLoad="showValues()">
<B>Setting the <TT>layer.zIndex</TT> Property of Sibling Layers</B>
<HR>
Enter new zIndex values to see the effect on three layers.<P>
<LAYER TOP=90 WIDTH=240 BGCOLOR="coral">
```

```
<FORM>
Control Original Bottom Layer:<BR>
<TABLE>
<TR><TD ALIGN="right">Layer zIndex:</TD><TD><INPUT TYPE="text" NAME="bot" SIZE=3
onChange="setZ(this)"></TD></TR>
<TR><TD ALIGN="right">Layer above:</TD><TD><INPUT TYPE="text" NAME="above"
SIZE=13></TD></TR>
<TR><TD ALIGN="right">Layer below:</TD><TD><INPUT TYPE="text" NAME="below"
SIZE=13></TD></TR>
</TABLE>
</FORM>
</LAYER>
<LAYER TOP=220 WIDTH=240 BGCOLOR="aquamarine">
<FORM>
Control Original Middle Layer:<BR>
<TABLE>
<TR><TD ALIGN="right">Layer zIndex:</TD><TD><INPUT TYPE="text" NAME="mid" SIZE=3
onChange="setZ(this)"></TD></TR>
<TR><TD ALIGN="right">Layer above:</TD><TD><INPUT TYPE="text" NAME="above"
SIZE=13></TD></TR>
<TR><TD ALIGN="right">Layer below:</TD><TD><INPUT TYPE="text" NAME="below"
SIZE=13></TD></TR>
</TABLE></FORM>
</LAYER>
<LAYER TOP=350 WIDTH=240 BGCOLOR="yellow">
<FORM>
Control Original Top Layer:<BR>
<TABLE><TR><TD ALIGN="right">Layer zIndex:</TD><TD><INPUT TYPE="text" NAME="top"
SIZE=3 onChange="setZ(this)"></TD></TR>
<TR><TD ALIGN="right">Layer above:</TD><TD><INPUT TYPE="text" NAME="above"
SIZE=13></TD></TR>
<TR><TD ALIGN="right">Layer below:</TD><TD><INPUT TYPE="text" NAME="below"
SIZE=13></TD></TR>
</TABLE>
</FORM>
</LAYER>
<LAYER NAME="bottom" BGCOLOR="coral" TOP=90 LEFT=260 WIDTH=300 HEIGHT=190>
    <P><B>Original Bottom Layer</B></P>
</LAYER>
    <LAYER NAME="middle" BGCOLOR="aquamarine" TOP=110 LEFT=280 WIDTH=300
    HEIGHT=190>
    <P><B>Original Middle Layer</B></P>
</LAYER>
<LAYER NAME="top" BGCOLOR="yellow" TOP=130 LEFT=300 WIDTH=300 HEIGHT=190>
    <P><B>Original Top Layer</B></P>
</LAYER>
</LAYER>
</BODY>
</HTML>
```

Methods

load("*URL*", *newLayerWidth*)

	NN2	NN3	NN4	NN6	IE3/J1	IE3/J2	IE4	IE5	IE5.5
Compatibility			✓						

Example

Buttons in Listing 31-10 enable you to load short and long documents into a layer. The first two buttons don't change the width (in fact, the second parameter to *layerObject*.load() is the *layerObject*.clip.left value). For the second two buttons, a narrower width than the original is specified. Click the Restore button frequently to return to a known state.

Listing 31-10: **Loading Documents into Layers**

```
<HTML>
<HEAD>
<TITLE>Layer Loading</TITLE>
<SCRIPT LANGUAGE="JavaScript">
function loadDoc(URL,width) {
    if (!width) {
        width = document.myLayer.clip.width
    }
    document.myLayer.load(URL, width)
}
</SCRIPT>
</HEAD>
<BODY>
<B>Loading New Documents</B>
<HR>
<LAYER TOP=90 WIDTH=240 BGCOLOR="yellow">
<FORM>
Loading new documents:<BR>
<INPUT TYPE="button" VALUE="Small Doc/Existing Width"
onClick="loadDoc('article1.htm')"><BR>
<INPUT TYPE="button" VALUE="Large Doc/Existing Width"
onClick="loadDoc('bofright.htm')"><P>
<INPUT TYPE="button" VALUE="Small Doc/Narrower Width"
onClick="loadDoc('article1.htm',200)"><BR>
<INPUT TYPE="button" VALUE="Large Doc/Narrower Width"
onClick="loadDoc('bofright.htm',200)"><P>
<INPUT TYPE="button" VALUE="Restore" onClick="location.reload()"></FORM>
</LAYER>
<LAYER NAME="myLayer" BGCOLOR="yellow" TOP=90 LEFT=300 WIDTH=300 HEIGHT=190>
    <P><B>Text loaded in original document.</B></P>
```

```
</LAYER>
</BODY>
</HTML>
```

---

moveAbove(*layerObject*)
moveBelow(*layerObject*)

	NN2	NN3	NN4	NN6	IE3/J1	IE3/J2	IE4	IE5	IE5.5
Compatibility			✓						

Example

You can see the *layerObject*.moveAbove() method at work in Listing 31-1.

moveBy(*deltaX,deltaY*)
moveTo(*x,y*)
moveToAbsolute(*x,y*)

	NN2	NN3	NN4	NN6	IE3/J1	IE3/J2	IE4	IE5	IE5.5
Compatibility			✓						

Example

Listing 31-11 shows a demonstration of the *layerObject*.moveTo() method. It is a simple script that enables you to click and drag a layer around the screen. The script employs the coordinate values of the mouseMove event; after compensating for the offset within the layer at which the click occurs, the script moves the layer to track the mouse action.

I want to present this example for an additional reason: to explain an important user interface difference between Windows and Macintosh versions of NN4. In Windows versions, you can click and hold the mouse button down on an object and let the object receive all the mouseMove events as you drag the cursor around the screen. On the Macintosh, however, NN4 tries to compensate for the lack of a second mouse button by popping up a context-sensitive menu at the cursor position when the user holds the mouse button down for more than just a click. To prevent the pop-up menu from appearing, the engage() method invoked by the onMouseDown event handler ends with return false.

Notice in the following listing how the layer captures a number of mouse events. Each one plays an important role in creating a mode that is essentially like a mouseStillDown event (which doesn't exist in NN4's event model). The mouseDown event sets a Boolean flag (engaged) indicating that the user clicked down in the layer. At the same time, the script records how far away from the layer's top-left corner the `mouseDown` event occurred. This offset information is needed so that any setting of the layer's location takes this offset into account (otherwise, the top-left corner of the layer would jump to the cursor position and be dragged from there).

During the drag (`mouseDown` events firing with each mouse movement), the `dragIt()` function checks whether the drag mode is engaged. If so, the layer is moved to the page location calculated by subtracting the original downstroke offset from the `mouseMove` event location on the page. When the user releases the mouse button, the `mouseUp` event turns off the drag mode Boolean value. Listing 31-21 in the *JavaScript Bible* shows a version of this example for IE5+ and NN6.

Listing 31-11: **Dragging a Layer**

```
<HTML>
<HEAD>
<TITLE>Layer Dragging</TITLE>
<SCRIPT LANGUAGE="JavaScript">
var engaged = false
var offsetX = 0
var offsetY = 0
function dragIt(e) {
    if (engaged) {
        document.myLayer.moveTo(e.pageX - offsetX, e.pageY - offsetY)
    }
}
function engage(e) {
    engaged = true
    offsetX = e.pageX - document.myLayer.left
    offsetY = e.pageY - document.myLayer.top
    return false
}
function release() {
    engaged = false
}
</SCRIPT>
</HEAD>
<BODY>
<B>Dragging a Layer</B>
<HR>
<LAYER NAME="myLayer" BGCOLOR="lightgreen" TOP=90 LEFT=100 WIDTH=300 HEIGHT=190>
    <P><B>Drag me around the window.</B></P>
</LAYER>
<SCRIPT LANGUAGE="JavaScript">
document.myLayer.captureEvents(Event.MOUSEDOWN | Event.MOUSEUP |
Event.MOUSEMOVE)
document.myLayer.onMouseDown = engage
document.myLayer.onMouseUp = release
document.myLayer.onMouseMove = dragIt
</SCRIPT>
</BODY>
</HTML> .
```

resizeBy(*deltaX,deltaY*)
resizeTo(*width,height*)

	NN2	NN3	NN4	NN6	IE3/J1	IE3/J2	IE4	IE5	IE5.5
Compatibility			✓						

Example

It is important to understand the ramifications of content flow when these two methods resize a layer. Listing 31-12a (and the companion document Listing 31-12b) shows you how to set the lower-right corner of a layer to be dragged by a user for resizing the layer (much like grabbing the resize corner of a document window). Three radio buttons enable you to choose whether and when the content should be redrawn to the layer — never, after resizing, or during resizing.

Event capture is very much like that in Listing 31-11 for layer dragging. The primary difference is that drag mode is engaged only when the mouse event takes place in the region of the lower-right corner. A different kind of offset value is saved here because, for resizing, the script needs to know the mouse event offset from the right and bottom edges of the layer.

Condition statements in the resizeIt() and release() functions verify whether a specific radio button is checked to determine when (or if) the content should be redrawn. I designed this page with the knowledge that its content might be redrawn. Therefore, I built the content of the layer as a separate HTML document that loads in the <LAYER> tag.

Redrawing the content requires reloading the document into the layer. I use the *layerObject*.load() method because I want to send the current *layerObject*.clip.width as a parameter for the width of the clip region to accommodate the content as it loads.

An important point to know about reloading content into a layer is that all property settings for the layer's event capture are erased when the document loads. Overcoming this behavior requires setting the layer's onLoad event handler to set the layer's event capture mechanism. If the layer event capturing is specified as part of the statements at the end of the document, the layer ignores some important events needed for the dynamic resizing after the document reloads the first time.

As you experiment with the different ways to resize and redraw, you see that redrawing during resizing is a slow process because of the repetitive loading (from cache) needed each time. On slower client machines, it is easy for the cursor to outrun the layer region, causing the layer to not get mouseOver events at all. It may not be the best-looking solution, but I prefer to redraw after resizing the layer.

Listing 31-22 in the *JavaScript Bible* shows a version designed for the IE5+ and NN6 object models. Because content automatically reflows in those browsers, you do not have to load the content of the positioned element from an external document.

Listing 31-12a: **Resizing a Layer**

```
<HTML>
<HEAD>
<TITLE>Layer Resizing</TITLE>
<SCRIPT LANGUAGE="JavaScript">
var engaged = false
var offsetX = 0
var offsetY = 0
function resizeIt(e) {
    if (engaged) {
        document.myLayer.resizeTo(e.pageX + offsetX, e.pageY + offsetY)
        if (document.forms[0].redraw[2].checked) {
            document.myLayer.load("lst31-12b.htm", document.myLayer.clip.width)
        }
    }
}
function engage(e) {
    if (e.pageX > (document.myLayer.clip.right - 10) &&
        e.pageY > (document.myLayer.clip.bottom - 10)) {
        engaged = true
        offsetX = document.myLayer.clip.right - e.pageX
        offsetY = document.myLayer.clip.bottom - e.pageY
    }
}
function release() {
    if (engaged && document.forms[0].redraw[1].checked) {
        document.myLayer.load("lst31-12b.htm", document.myLayer.clip.width)
    }
    engaged = false
}
function grabEvents() {
    document.myLayer.captureEvents(Event.MOUSEDOWN | Event.MOUSEUP |
Event.MOUSEMOVE)
}
</SCRIPT>
</HEAD>
<BODY>
<B>Resizing a Layer</B>
<HR>
<FORM>
Redraw layer content:<BR>
<INPUT TYPE="radio" NAME="redraw" CHECKED>Never
<INPUT TYPE="radio" NAME="redraw">After resize
<INPUT TYPE="radio" NAME="redraw">During resize
</FORM>
<LAYER NAME="myLayer" SRC="lst31-12b.htm" BGCOLOR="lightblue" TOP=120 LEFT=100
WIDTH=300 HEIGHT=190 onLoad="grabEvents()">
</LAYER>
<SCRIPT LANGUAGE="JavaScript">
```

```
document.myLayer.onMouseDown = engage
document.myLayer.onMouseUp = release
document.myLayer.onMouseMove = resizeIt
</SCRIPT>
</BODY>
</HTML>
```

Listing 31-12b: **Content for the Resizable Layer**

```
<HTML>
<BODY>
    <P><B>Resize me by dragging the lower-right corner.</B></P>
    <SCRIPT LANGUAGE="JavaScript">
    if (navigator.userAgent.indexOf("Mac") != -1) {
        document.write("(Mac users: Ctrl-Click me first; then Click to stop
dragging.)")
    }
    </SCRIPT>
</BODY>
</HTML>
```

✦   ✦   ✦

String and Number Objects (Chapters 34 and 35)

CHAPTER 16

♦ ♦ ♦ ♦

In This Chapter

Parsing text at the character level

Performing search-and-replace operations with regular expressions

Converting between character codes and text

Setting number format and precision

♦ ♦ ♦ ♦

Knowing how to manipulate strings of text characters is a vital programming skill. You may not have to do it all the time, but you should be fully aware of the possibilities for this manipulation that are built into whatever programming language you use. In JavaScript (as in any object-based or object-oriented language), strings are objects that have numerous properties and methods to assist in assembling, tearing apart, extracting, and copying chunks of strings.

Any characters that users enter into text boxes become parts of string objects. In IE4+ and NN6, text inside HTML element tags can be treated as strings. In IE4+, you can even work with the HTML tags as strings. Therefore, of all the core language objects to implant in your scripting consciousness, the string object is it (arrays, whose examples come in the next chapter of this book, rank Number Two on the list).

Numbers are much less frequently thought of as objects because they tend to be used as-is for calculations. JavaScript 1.5 in recent browsers, however, endows the number object with practical methods, especially one that (finally) offers built-in control over the number of digits displayed to the right of the decimal point for floating-point numbers.

When examples in this chapter encourage you to enter a sequence of expressions in The Evaluator, be sure to follow through with every step. But also make sure you understand the results of each expression in order to visualize the particular method operates.

Examples Highlights

✦ Study the code and operation of Listing 34-2 to see how to use JavaScript to convert characters to character codes and vice versa. Converting ASCII or Unicode numeric values to their corresponding characters requires the `String.fromCharCode()` method of the static `String` object.

✦ Compare the sequence of steps for the *string*`.indexOf()` and *string*`.lastIndexOf()` methods to grasp fully the behavior of each and the differences between them.

✦ Listing 34-4 lets you experiment with the *string*`.replace()` and *string*`.search()` methods, both of which utilize regular expression powers available in JavaScript 1.2 of NN4+ and IE4+. Notice how the script functions assemble the regular expression objects with global modifiers.

✦ Walk through the steps of the *string*`.split()` method example to convert a string to an array.

✦ Compare the behaviors and coding of Listings 34-6 and 34-7 to distinguish the subtle differences between the *string*`.substr()` and *string*`.substring()` methods.

✦ Study the example for *string*`.toLowerCase()` and *string*`.toUpperCase()` to see how to remove case sensitivity issues for some operations.

✦ Convert a long floating-point number to a dollars-and-cents string by following the steps for the *number*`.toFixed()` method.

String Object

Properties

constructor

	NN2	NN3	NN4	NN6	IE3/J1	IE3/J2	IE4	IE5	IE5.5
Compatibility			✓	✓			✓	✓	✓

Example

Use The Evaluator (Chapter 13 in the *JavaScript Bible*) to test the value of the `constructor` property. Enter the following statements into the top text box:

```
a = new String("abcd")
a.constructor == String
a.constructor == Number
```

Parsing methods

string.charAt(*index*)

	NN2	NN3	NN4	NN6	IE3/J1	IE3/J2	IE4	IE5	IE5.5
Compatibility	✓	✓	✓	✓	✓	✓	✓	✓	✓

Example

Enter each of the following statements into the top text box of The Evaluator:

```
a = "banana daiquiri"
a.charAt(0)
a.charAt(5)
a.charAt(6)
a.charAt(20)
```

Results from each of the charAt() methods should be b, a (the third "a" in "banana"), a space character, and an empty string, respectively.

string.charCodeAt([*index*])
String.fromCharCode(*num1* [, *num2* [, ... numn]])

	NN2	NN3	NN4	NN6	IE3/J1	IE3/J2	IE4	IE5	IE5.5
Compatibility			✓	✓			✓	✓	✓

Example

Listing 34-2 provides examples of both methods on one page. Moreover, because one of the demonstrations relies on the automatic capture of selected text on the page, the scripts include code to accommodate the different handling of selection events and capture of the selected text in Navigator and Internet Explorer 4.

After you load the page, select part of the body text anywhere on the page. If you start the selection with the lowercase letter "a," the character code displays as 97. If you select no text, the result is NaN.

Try entering numeric values in the three fields at the bottom of the page. Values below 32 are ASCII control characters that most fonts represent as hollow squares. But try all other values to see what you get. Notice that the script passes all three values as a group to the String.fromCharCode() method, and the result is a combined string. Thus, Figure 16-1 shows what happens when you enter the uppercase ASCII values for a three-letter animal name.

Listing 34-2: **Character Conversions**

```
<HTML>
<HEAD>
<TITLE>Character Codes</TITLE>
<SCRIPT LANGUAGE="JavaScript">
var isNav = (navigator.appName == "Netscape")
var isNav4 = (isNav && parseInt(navigator.appVersion == 4))
function showCharCode() {
    if (isNav) {
        var theText = document.getSelection()
    } else {
        var theText = document.selection.createRange().text
    }
    if (theText) {
        document.forms[0].charCodeDisplay.value = theText.charCodeAt()
    } else {
        document.forms[0].charCodeDisplay.value = " "
    }
}
function showString(form) {
    form.result.value =
String.fromCharCode(form.entry1.value,form.entry2.value,form.entry3.value)
}
if (isNav4) {
    document.captureEvents(Event.MOUSEUP)
}
document.onmouseup = showCharCode
</SCRIPT>
</HEAD>
<BODY>
<B>Capturing Character Codes</B>
<FORM>
Select any of this text, and see the character code of the first character.<P>
Character Code:<INPUT TYPE="text" NAME="charCodeDisplay" SIZE=3><BR>
<HR>
<B>Converting Codes to Characters</B><BR>
Enter a value  0-255:<INPUT TYPE="text" NAME="entry1" SIZE=4><BR>
Enter a value  0-255:<INPUT TYPE="text" NAME="entry2" SIZE=4><BR>
Enter a value  0-255:<INPUT TYPE="text" NAME="entry3" SIZE=4><BR>
<INPUT TYPE="button" VALUE="Show String" onClick="showString(this.form)">
Result:<INPUT TYPE="text" NAME="result" SIZE=5>
</FORM>
</BODY>
</HTML>
```

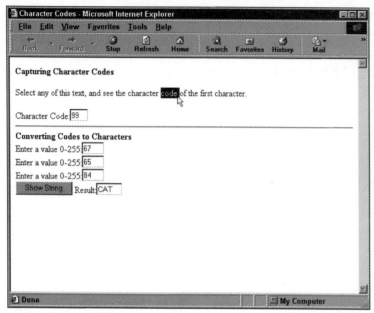

Figure 16-1: Conversions from text characters to ASCII values and vice versa

string.indexOf(searchString [, startIndex])

	NN2	NN3	NN4	NN6	IE3/J1	IE3/J2	IE4	IE5	IE5.5
Compatibility	✓	✓	✓	✓	✓	✓	✓	✓	✓

Example

Enter each of the following statements (up to, but not including the "//" comment symbols) into the top text box of The Evaluator (you can simply replace the parameters of the indexOf() method for each statement after the first one). Compare your results with the results shown below.

```
a = "bananas"
a.indexOf("b")      // result = 0 (index of 1st letter is zero)
a.indexOf("a")      // result = 1
a.indexOf("a",1)    // result = 1 (start from 2nd letter)
a.indexOf("a",2)    // result = 3 (start from 3rd letter)
a.indexOf("a",4)    // result = 5 (start from 5th letter)
a.indexOf("nan")    // result = 2
a.indexOf("nas")    // result = 4
a.indexOf("s")      // result = 6
a.indexOf("z")      // result = -1 (no "z" in string)
```

string.`lastIndexOf(`*searchString*`[,` *startIndex*`])`

	NN2	NN3	NN4	NN6	IE3/J1	IE3/J2	IE4	IE5	IE5.5
Compatibility	✓	✓	✓	✓	✓	✓	✓	✓	✓

Example

Enter each of the following statements (up to, but not including the "//" comment symbols) into the top text box of The Evaluator (you can simply replace the parameters of the `lastIndexOf()` method for each statement after the first one). Compare your results with the results shown below.

```
a = "bananas"
a.lastIndexOf("b")      // result = 0 (index of 1st letter is zero)
a.lastIndexOf("a")      // result = 5
a.lastIndexOf("a",1)    // result = 1 (from 2nd letter toward the front)
a.lastIndexOf("a",2)    // result = 1 (start from 3rd letter working toward front)
a.lastIndexOf("a",4)    // result = 3 (start from 5th letter)
a.lastIndexOf("nan")    // result = 2 [except for -1 Nav 2.0 bug]
a.lastIndexOf("nas")    // result = 4
a.lastIndexOf("s")      // result = 6
a.lastIndexOf("z")      // result = -1 (no "z" in string)
```

string.`match(`*regExpression*`)`

	NN2	NN3	NN4	NN6	IE3/J1	IE3/J2	IE4	IE5	IE5.5
Compatibility			✓	✓			✓	✓	✓

Example

To help you understand the *string*.`match()` method, Listing 34-3 provides a workshop area for experimentation. Two fields occur for data entry: the first is for the long string to be examined by the method; the second is for a regular expression. Some default values are provided in case you're not yet familiar with the syntax of regular expressions (see Chapter 38 of the *JavaScript Bible*). A check box lets you specify whether the search through the string for matches should be case-sensitive. After you click the "Execute match()" button, the script creates a regular expression object out of your input, performs the *string*.`match()` method on the big string, and reports two kinds of results to the page. The primary result is a string version of the array returned by the method; the other is a count of items returned.

Listing 34-3: **Regular Expression Match Workshop**

```
<HTML>
<HEAD>
<TITLE>Regular Expression Match</TITLE>
<SCRIPT LANGUAGE="JavaScript">
function doMatch(form) {
    var str = form.entry.value
    var delim = (form.caseSens.checked) ? "/g" : "/gi"
    var regexp = eval("/" + form.regexp.value + delim)
    var resultArray = str.match(regexp)
    if (resultArray) {
        form.result.value = resultArray.toString()
        form.count.value = resultArray.length
    } else {
        form.result.value = "<no matches>"
        form.count.value = ""
    }
}
</SCRIPT>
</HEAD>
<BODY>
<B>String Match with Regular Expressions</B>
<HR>
<FORM>
Enter a main string:<INPUT TYPE="text" NAME="entry" SIZE=60
  VALUE="Many a maN and womAN have meant to visit GerMAny."><BR>
Enter a regular expression to match:<INPUT TYPE="text" NAME="regexp" SIZE=25
  VALUE="\wa\w">
<INPUT TYPE="checkbox" NAME="caseSens">Case-sensitive<P>
<INPUT TYPE="button" VALUE="Execute match()" onClick="doMatch(this.form)">
<INPUT TYPE="reset"><P>
Result:<INPUT TYPE="text" NAME="result" SIZE=40><BR>
Count:<INPUT TYPE="text" NAME="count" SIZE=3><BR>
</FORM>
</BODY>
</HTML>
```

The default value for the main string has unusual capitalization intentionally. The capitalization lets you see more clearly where some of the matches come from. For example, the default regular expression looks for any three-character string that has the letter "a" in the middle. Six string segments match that expression. With the help of capitalization, you can see where each of the four strings containing "man" are extracted from the main string. The following table lists some other regular expressions to try with the default main string.

RegExp	Description
man	Both case-sensitive and not
man\b	Where "man" is at the end of a word
\bman	Where "man" is at the start of a word
me*an	Where zero or more "e" letters occur between "m" and "a"
.a.	Where "a" is surrounded by any one character (including space)
\sa\s	Where "a" is surrounded by a space on both sides
z	Where a "z" occurs (none in the default string)

In the scripts for Listing 34-3, if the `string.match()` method returns `null`, you are informed politely, and the count field is emptied.

string.replace(*regExpression, replaceString*)

	NN2	NN3	NN4	NN6	IE3/J1	IE3/J2	IE4	IE5	IE5.5
Compatibility			✓	✓			✓	✓	✓

Example

The page in Listing 34-4 lets you practice with the *string*.replace() and *string*.search() methods and regular expressions in a friendly environment. The source text is a five-line excerpt from *Hamlet*. You can enter the regular expression to search for, and the replacement text as well. Note that the script completes the job of creating the regular expression object, so that you can focus on the other special characters used to define the matching string. All replacement activities act globally, because the g parameter is automatically appended to any expression you enter.

Default values in the fields replace the contraction 'tis with "it is" after you click the "Execute replace()" button (see Figure 16-2). Notice that the backslash character in front of the apostrophe of 'tis (in the string assembled in mainString) makes the apostophe a non-word boundary, and thus allows the \B't regular expression to find a match there. As described in the section on the *string*.search() method, the button connected to that method returns the offset character number of the matching string (or -1 if no match occurs).

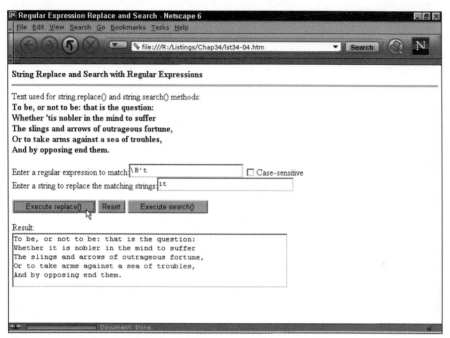

Figure 16-2: Using the default replacement regular expression

You could modify the listing so that it actually replaces text in the HTML paragraph for IE4+ and NN6. The steps include wrapping the paragraph in its own element (for example, a SPAN), and invoking the `replace()` method on the `innerHTML` of that element. Assign the results to the `innerHTML` property of that element to complete the job.

Listing 34-4: **Lab for string.replace() and string.search()**

```
<HTML>
<HEAD>
<TITLE>Regular Expression Replace and Search</TITLE>
<SCRIPT LANGUAGE="JavaScript">
var mainString = "To be, or not to be: that is the question:\n"
mainString += "Whether \'tis nobler in the mind to suffer\n"
mainString += "The slings and arrows of outrageous fortune,\n"
mainString += "Or to take arms against a sea of troubles,\n"
mainString += "And by opposing end them."

function doReplace(form) {
    var replaceStr = form.replaceEntry.value
    var delim = (form.caseSens.checked) ? "/g" : "/gi"
    var regexp = eval("/" + form.regexp.value + delim)
    form.result.value = mainString.replace(regexp, replaceStr)
}
```

Continued

Listing 34-4 *(continued)*

```
function doSearch(form) {
    var replaceStr = form.replaceEntry.value
    var delim = (form.caseSens.checked) ? "/g" : "/gi"
    var regexp = eval("/" + form.regexp.value + delim)
    form.result.value = mainString.search(regexp)
}
</SCRIPT>
</HEAD>
<BODY>
<B>String Replace and Search with Regular Expressions</B>
<HR>
Text used for string.replace() and string.search() methods:<BR>
<B>To be, or not to be: that is the question:<BR>
Whether 'tis nobler in the mind to suffer<BR>
The slings and arrows of outrageous fortune,<BR>
Or to take arms against a sea of troubles,<BR>
And by opposing end them.</B>

<FORM>
Enter a regular expression to match:<INPUT TYPE="text" NAME="regexp" SIZE=25
VALUE="\B't">
<INPUT TYPE="checkbox" NAME="caseSens">Case-sensitive<BR>
Enter a string to replace the matching strings:<INPUT TYPE="text"
NAME="replaceEntry" SIZE=30 VALUE="it "><P>
<INPUT TYPE="button" VALUE="Execute replace()" onClick="doReplace(this.form)">
<INPUT TYPE="reset">
<INPUT TYPE="button" VALUE="Execute search()" onClick="doSearch(this.form)"><P>
Result:<BR>
<TEXTAREA NAME="result" COLS=60 ROWS=5 WRAP="virtual"></TEXTAREA>
</FORM>
</BODY>
</HTML>
```

string.search(*regExpression*)

	NN2	NN3	NN4	NN6	IE3/J1	IE3/J2	IE4	IE5	IE5.5
Compatibility			✓	✓			✓	✓	✓

Example

Listing 34-4, for the *string*.replace() method, also provides a laboratory to experiment with the *string*.search() method.

string.slice(startIndex [, endIndex])

	NN2	NN3	NN4	NN6	IE3/J1	IE3/J2	IE4	IE5	IE5.5
Compatibility			✓	✓			✓	✓	✓

Example

With Listing 34-5, you can try several combinations of parameters with the *string*.slice() method (see Figure 16-3). A base string is provided (along with character measurements). Select from the different choices available for parameters and study the outcome of the slice.

Listing 34-5: **Slicing a String**

```
<HTML>
<HEAD>
<TITLE>String Slicing and Dicing, Part I</TITLE>
<SCRIPT LANGUAGE="JavaScript">
var mainString = "Electroencephalograph"
function showResults() {
    var form = document.forms[0]
    var param1 = parseInt(form.param1.options[form.param1.selectedIndex].value)
    var param2 = parseInt(form.param2.options[form.param2.selectedIndex].value)
    if (!param2) {
        form.result1.value = mainString.slice(param1)
    } else {
        form.result1.value = mainString.slice(param1, param2)
    }
}
</SCRIPT>
</HEAD>
<BODY onLoad="showResults()">
<B>String slice() Method</B>
<HR>
Text used for the methods:<BR>
<FONT SIZE=+1><TT><B>Electroencephalograph<BR>
----5----5----5----5-</B></TT></FONT>
<TABLE BORDER=1>
<FORM>
<TR><TH>String Method</TH><TH>Method Parameters</TH><TH>Results</TH></TR>
<TR>
<TD>string.slice()</TD><TD ROWSPAN=3 VALIGN=middle>
( <SELECT NAME="param1" onChange="showResults()">
    <OPTION VALUE=0>0
    <OPTION VALUE=1>1
    <OPTION VALUE=2>2
    <OPTION VALUE=3>3
    <OPTION VALUE=5>5
```

Continued

Listing 34-5 *(continued)*

```
</SELECT>,
<SELECT NAME="param2" onChange="showResults()">
    <OPTION >(None)
    <OPTION VALUE=5>5
    <OPTION VALUE=10>10
    <OPTION VALUE=-1>-1
    <OPTION VALUE=-5>-5
    <OPTION VALUE=-10>-10
</SELECT> ) </TD>
<TD><INPUT TYPE="text" NAME="result1" SIZE=25></TD>
</TR>
</FORM>
</TABLE>
</BODY>
</HTML>
```

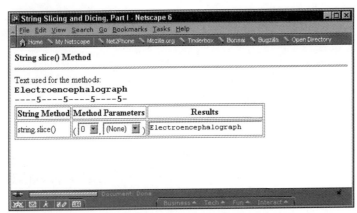

Figure 16-3: Lab for exploring the string.slice() method

string.split("*delimiterCharacter*" [, *limitInteger*])

	NN2	NN3	NN4	NN6	IE3/J1	IE3/J2	IE4	IE5	IE5.5
Compatibility		✓	✓	✓			✓	✓	✓

Example

Use The Evaluator (Chapter 13 in the *JavaScript Bible*) to see how the string.split() method works. Begin by assigning a comma-delimited string to a variable:

```
a = "Anderson,Smith,Johnson,Washington"
```

Now split the string at comma positions so that the string pieces become items in an array, saved as b:

```
b = a.split(",")
```

To prove that the array contains four items, inspect the array's length property:

```
b.length      // result: 4
```

string.substr(*start* [, *length*])

	NN2	NN3	NN4	NN6	IE3/J1	IE3/J2	IE4	IE5	IE5.5
Compatibility			✓	✓			✓	✓	✓

Example

Listing 34-6 lets you experiment with a variety of values to see how the *string*.substr() method works.

Listing 34-6: **Reading a Portion of a String**

```
<HTML>
<HEAD>
<TITLE>String Slicing and Dicing, Part II</TITLE>
<SCRIPT LANGUAGE="JavaScript">
var mainString = "Electroencephalograph"
function showResults() {
    var form = document.forms[0]
    var param1 = parseInt(form.param1.options[form.param1.selectedIndex].value)
    var param2 = parseInt(form.param2.options[form.param2.selectedIndex].value)
    if (!param2) {
        form.result1.value = mainString.substr(param1)
    } else {
        form.result1.value = mainString.substr(param1, param2)
    }
}
</SCRIPT>
</HEAD>
<BODY onLoad="showResults()">
<B>String substr() Method</B>
<HR>
Text used for the methods:<BR>
<FONT SIZE=+1><TT><B>Electroencephalograph<BR>
----5----5----5----5-</B></TT></FONT>
<TABLE BORDER=1>
<FORM>
<TR><TH>String Method</TH><TH>Method Parameters</TH><TH>Results</TH></TR>
<TR>
```

Continued

Listing 34-6 *(continued)*

```
<TD>string.substr()</TD><TD ROWSPAN=3 VALIGN=middle>
( <SELECT NAME="param1" onChange="showResults()">
    <OPTION VALUE=0>0
    <OPTION VALUE=1>1
    <OPTION VALUE=2>2
    <OPTION VALUE=3>3
    <OPTION VALUE=5>5
</SELECT>,
<SELECT NAME="param2" onChange="showResults()">
    <OPTION >(None)
    <OPTION VALUE=5>5
    <OPTION VALUE=10>10
    <OPTION VALUE=20>20
</SELECT> ) </TD>
<TD><INPUT TYPE="text" NAME="result1" SIZE=25></TD>
</TR>
</FORM>
</TABLE>
</BODY>
</HTML>
```

string.substring(*indexA, indexB*)

	NN2	NN3	NN4	NN6	IE3/J1	IE3/J2	IE4	IE5	IE5.5
Compatibility	✓	✓	✓	✓	✓	✓	✓	✓	✓

Example

Listing 34-7 lets you experiment with a variety of values to see how the `string.substring()` method works. If you are using Navigator 4, try changing the LANGUAGE attribute of the script to `JavaScript1.2` and see the different behavior when you set the parameters to 5 and 3. The parameters switch themselves, essentially letting the second index value become the beginning of the extracted substring.

Listing 34-7: **Reading a Portion of a String**

```
<HTML>
<HEAD>
<TITLE>String Slicing and Dicing, Part III</TITLE>
<SCRIPT LANGUAGE="JavaScript">
var mainString = "Electroencephalograph"
function showResults() {
```

```
    var form = document.forms[0]
    var param1 = parseInt(form.param1.options[form.param1.selectedIndex].value)
    var param2 = parseInt(form.param2.options[form.param2.selectedIndex].value)
    if (!param2) {
        form.result1.value = mainString.substring(param1)
    } else {
        form.result1.value = mainString.substring(param1, param2)
    }
}
</SCRIPT>
</HEAD>
<BODY onLoad="showResults()">
<B>String substr() Method</B>
<HR>
Text used for the methods:<BR>
<FONT SIZE=+1><TT><B>Electroencephalograph<BR>
----5----5----5----5-</B></TT></FONT>
<TABLE BORDER=1>
<FORM>
<TR><TH>String Method</TH><TH>Method Parameters</TH><TH>Results</TH></TR>
<TR>
<TD>string.substring()</TD><TD>
( <SELECT NAME="param1" onChange="showResults()">
    <OPTION VALUE=0>0
    <OPTION VALUE=1>1
    <OPTION VALUE=2>2
    <OPTION VALUE=3>3
    <OPTION VALUE=5>5
</SELECT>,
<SELECT NAME="param2" onChange="showResults()">
    <OPTION >(None)
    <OPTION VALUE=3>3
    <OPTION VALUE=5>5
    <OPTION VALUE=10>10
</SELECT> ) </TD>
<TD><INPUT TYPE="text" NAME="result1" SIZE=25></TD>
</TR>
</FORM>
</TABLE>
</BODY>
</HTML>
```

string.toLowerCase()
string.toUpperCase()

	NN2	NN3	NN4	NN6	IE3/J1	IE3/J2	IE4	IE5	IE5.5
Compatibility	✓	✓	✓	✓	✓	✓	✓	✓	✓

Example

You can use the `toLowerCase()` and `toUpperCase()` methods on literal strings, as follows:

```
var newString = "HTTP://www.Netscape.COM".toLowerCase()
    // result = "http://www.netscape.com"
```

The methods are also helpful in comparing strings when case is not important, as follows:

```
if (guess.toUpperCase() == answer.toUpperCase()) {...}
    // comparing strings without case sensitivity
```

*string.*toString()
*string.*valueOf()

	NN2	NN3	NN4	NN6	IE3/J1	IE3/J2	IE4	IE5	IE5.5
Compatibility			✓	✓			✓	✓	✓

Examples

Use The Evaluator to test the `valueOf()` method. Enter the following statements into the top text box and examine the values that appear in the Results field:

```
a = new String("hello")
typeof a
b = a.valueOf()
typeof b
```

Because all other JavaScript core objects also have the `valueOf()` method, you can build generic functions that receive a variety of object types as parameters, and the script can branch its code based on the type of value that is stored in the object.

Number Object

Properties

```
MAX_VALUE
MIN_VALUE
NEGATIVE_INFINITY
POSITIVE_INFINITY
```

	NN2	NN3	NN4	NN6	IE3/J1	IE3/J2	IE4	IE5	IE5.5
Compatibility		✓	✓	✓		✓	✓	✓	✓

Example

Enter each of the four Number object expressions into the top text field of The Evaluator to see how the browser reports each value.

```
Number.MAX_VALUE
Number.MIN_VALUE
Number.NEGATIVE_INFINITY
Number.POSITIVE_INFINITY
```

Methods

number.toExponential(fractionDigits)
number.toFixed(fractionDigits)
number.toPrecision(precisionDigits)

	NN2	NN3	NN4	NN6	IE3/J1	IE3/J2	IE4	IE5	IE5.5
Compatibility				✓					✓

Example

You can use The Evaluator to experiment with all three of these methods with a variety of parameter values. Before invoking any method, be sure to assign a numeric value to one of the built-in global variables in The Evaluator (a through z).

```
a = 10/3
a.toFixed(4)
"$" + a.toFixed(2)
```

None of these methods works with number literals (for example, 123.toExponential(2) does not work).

number.toString([radix])

	NN2	NN3	NN4	NN6	IE3/J1	IE3/J2	IE4	IE5	IE5.5
Compatibility	✓	✓	✓			✓	✓	✓	✓

Example

Use The Evaluator to experiment with the toString() method. Assign the number 12 to the variable a and see how the number is converted to strings in a variety of number bases:

```
a = 12
a.toString()     // base 10
a.toString(2)
a.toString(16)
```

✦   ✦   ✦

The Array Object (Chapter 37)

Whenever you are faced with having to manage any kind of list or series of related data chunks, the first technique to turn to is stuffing those chunks into an array. Once the data is inside an array, your scripts can then perform quick and easy lookups, based on for loops through numerically indexed arrays, or via instant searching with the help of string indexes (à la Java hash tables).

As the examples in this chapter demonstrate, the JavaScript array object features numerous methods to facilitate managing the data inside an array. It also helps that JavaScript is loose enough to allow arrays to grow or shrink as their data requires.

Perhaps the two most important features of JavaScript arrays to have in your hip pocket are converting arrays to delimited string objects and sorting. Conversion to strings is important when you wish to transport data from an array to another venue that passes only strings, such as passing data to another page via the URL search string. At the receiving end, a script converts the search string to an array through the inverse operation provided by the *string*.split() method.

JavaScript's array sorting feature is remarkably powerful and flexible. Even if the array consists of objects, you can sort the array based on values assigned to properties of those objects.

Examples Highlights

+ Convert an array into a delimited string via the code shown in Listing 37-7.

+ To flip the order of an array without resorting to sorting, see Example 37-8 for the *array*.reverse() method.

+ Listing 37-9 demonstrates a few important aspects of the *array*.sort() method. In addition to the traditional alphabetical sorting, one of the sorting functions operates on the length property of the string object stored in each entry of the array. Powerful stuff with very little code.

✦ Walk through the steps for the *array*.splice() method to observe how JavaScript in NN4+ and IE5.5+ can replace entries inside an array. One example replaces three items with one, indicating that you are not bound to maintaining the same array length.

Array Object Methods

array.concat(*array2*)

	NN2	NN3	NN4	NN6	IE3/J1	IE3/J2	IE4	IE5	IE5.5
Compatibility			✓	✓			✓	✓	✓

Example

Listing 37-6 is a bit complex, but it demonstrates both how arrays can be joined with the *array*.concat() method and how values and objects in the source arrays do or do not propagate based on their data type. The page is shown in Figure 17-1.

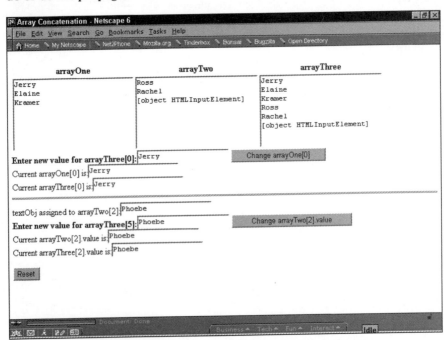

Figure 17-1: Object references remain "alive" in a concatenated array.

After you load the page, you see readouts of three arrays. The first array consists of all string values; the second array has two string values and a reference to a form object on the page (a textbox named "original" in the HTML). In the initialization routine of this page, not only are the two source arrays created, but they are joined with the *array*.concat() method, and the result is shown in the third box. To show the contents of these arrays in columns, I use the *array*.join() method, which brings the elements of an array together as a string delimited in this case by a return character—giving us an instant column of data.

Two series of fields and buttons let you experiment with the way values and object references are linked across concatenated arrays. In the first group, if you enter a new value to be assigned to arrayThree[0], the new value replaces the string value in the combined array. Because regular values do not maintain a link back to the original array, only the entry in the combined array is changed. A call to showArrays() proves that only the third array is affected by the change.

More complex is the object relationship for this demonstration. A reference to the first text box of the second grouping has been assigned to the third entry of arrayTwo. After concatenation, the same reference is now in the last entry of the combined array. If you enter a new value for a property of the object in the last slot of arrayThree, the change goes all the way back to the original object—the first text box in the lower grouping. Thus, the text of the original field changes in response to the change of arrayThree[5]. And because all references to that object yield the same result, the reference in arrayTwo[2] points to the same text object, yielding the same new answer. The display of the array contents doesn't change, because both arrays still contain a reference to the same object (and the VALUE attribute showing in the <INPUT> tag of the column listings refers to the default value of the tag, not to its current algorithmically retrievable value shown in the last two fields of the page).

Listing 37-6: **Array Concatenation**

```
<HTML>
<HEAD>
<TITLE>Array Concatenation</TITLE>
<SCRIPT LANGUAGE="JavaScript1.1">
// global variables
var arrayOne, arrayTwo, arrayThree, textObj
// initialize after load to access text object in form
function initialize() {
    var form = document.forms[0]
    textObj = form.original
    arrayOne = new Array("Jerry", "Elaine","Kramer")
    arrayTwo = new Array("Ross", "Rachel",textObj)
    arrayThree = arrayOne.concat(arrayTwo)
    update1(form)
    update2(form)
    showArrays()
}
// display current values of all three arrays
function showArrays() {
    var form = document.forms[0]
    form.array1.value = arrayOne.join("\n")
    form.array2.value = arrayTwo.join("\n")
```

Continued

Listing 37-6 *(continued)*

```
    form.array3.value = arrayThree.join("\n")
}
// change the value of first item in Array Three
function update1(form) {
    arrayThree[0] = form.source1.value
    form.result1.value = arrayOne[0]
    form.result2.value = arrayThree[0]
    showArrays()
}
// change value of object property pointed to in Array Three
function update2(form) {
    arrayThree[5].value = form.source2.value
    form.result3.value = arrayTwo[2].value
    form.result4.value = arrayThree[5].value
    showArrays()
}
</SCRIPT>
</HEAD>
<BODY onLoad="initialize()">
<FORM>
<TABLE>
<TR><TH>arrayOne</TH><TH>arrayTwo</TH><TH>arrayThree</TH></TR>
<TR>
<TD><TEXTAREA NAME="array1" COLS=25 ROWS=6></TEXTAREA></TD>
<TD><TEXTAREA NAME="array2" COLS=25 ROWS=6></TEXTAREA></TD>
<TD><TEXTAREA NAME="array3" COLS=25 ROWS=6></TEXTAREA></TD>
</TR>
</TABLE>
<B>Enter new value for arrayThree[0]:</B><INPUT TYPE="text" NAME="source1"
VALUE="Jerry">
<INPUT TYPE="button" VALUE="Change arrayThree[0]"
onClick="update1(this.form)"><BR>
Current arrayOne[0] is:<INPUT TYPE="text" NAME="result1"><BR>
Current arrayThree[0] is:<INPUT TYPE="text" NAME="result2"><BR>
<HR>

textObj assigned to arrayTwo[2]:<INPUT TYPE="text" NAME="original"
onFocus="this.blur()"></BR>
<B>Enter new value for arrayThree[5]:</B><INPUT TYPE="text" NAME="source2"
VALUE="Phoebe">
<INPUT TYPE="button" VALUE="Change arrayThree[5].value"
onClick="update2(this.form)"><BR>
Current arrayTwo[2].value is:<INPUT TYPE="text" NAME="result3"><BR>
Current arrayThree[5].value is:<INPUT TYPE="text" NAME="result4"><P>

<INPUT TYPE="button" VALUE="Reset" onClick="location.reload()">
</FORM>
</BODY>
</HTML>
```

array.join(*separatorString*)

	NN2	NN3	NN4	NN6	IE3/J1	IE3/J2	IE4	IE5	IE5.5
Compatibility		✓	✓	✓		✓	✓	✓	✓

Example

The script in Listing 37-7 converts an array of planet names into a text string. The page provides you with a field to enter the delimiter string of your choice and shows the results in a textarea.

Listing 37-7: **Using the Array.join() Method**

```
<HTML>
<HEAD>
<TITLE>Array.join()</TITLE>
<SCRIPT LANGUAGE="JavaScript1.1">
solarSys = new Array(9)
solarSys[0] = "Mercury"
solarSys[1] = "Venus"
solarSys[2] = "Earth"
solarSys[3] = "Mars"
solarSys[4] = "Jupiter"
solarSys[5] = "Saturn"
solarSys[6] = "Uranus"
solarSys[7] = "Neptune"
solarSys[8] = "Pluto"

// join array elements into a string
function convert(form) {
    var delimiter = form.delim.value
    form.output.value = unescape(solarSys.join(delimiter))
}
</SCRIPT>
<BODY>
<H2>Converting arrays to strings</H2>
This document contains an array of planets in our solar system.<HR>
<FORM>
Enter a string to act as a delimiter between entries:
<INPUT TYPE="text" NAME="delim" VALUE="," SIZE=5><P>
<INPUT TYPE="button" VALUE="Display as String" onClick="convert(this.form)">
<INPUT TYPE="reset">
<TEXTAREA NAME="output" ROWS=4 COLS=40 WRAP="virtual">
</TEXTAREA>
</FORM>
</BODY>
</HTML>
```

Notice that this method takes the parameter very literally. If you want to include nonalphanumeric characters, such as a newline or tab, do so with URL-encoded characters (%0D for a carriage return; %09 for a tab) instead of inline string literals. In Listing 37-7, the results of the *array*.join() method are subjected to the unescape() function in order to display them in the TEXTAREA.

array.reverse()

	NN2	NN3	NN4	NN6	IE3/J1	IE3/J2	IE4	IE5	IE5.5
Compatibility		✓	✓	✓		✓	✓	✓	✓

Example

Listing 37-8 is an enhanced version of Listing 37-7, which includes another button and function that reverse the array and display it as a string in a text area.

Listing 37-8: **Array.reverse() Method**

```
<HTML>
<HEAD>
<TITLE>Array.reverse()</TITLE>
<SCRIPT LANGUAGE="JavaScript1.1">
solarSys = new Array(9)
solarSys[0] = "Mercury"
solarSys[1] = "Venus"
solarSys[2] = "Earth"
solarSys[3] = "Mars"
solarSys[4] = "Jupiter"
solarSys[5] = "Saturn"
solarSys[6] = "Uranus"
solarSys[7] = "Neptune"
solarSys[8] = "Pluto"

// show array as currently in memory
function showAsIs(form) {
    var delimiter = form.delim.value
    form.output.value = unescape(solarSys.join(delimiter))
}
// reverse array order, then display as string
function reverseIt(form) {
    var delimiter = form.delim.value
    solarSys.reverse()    // reverses original array
    form.output.value = unescape(solarSys.join(delimiter))
}
</SCRIPT>
<BODY>
<H2>Reversing array element order</H2>
This document contains an array of planets in our solar system.<HR>
<FORM>
```

```
Enter a string to act as a delimiter between entries:
<INPUT TYPE="text" NAME="delim" VALUE="," SIZE=5><P>
<INPUT TYPE="button" VALUE="Array as-is" onClick="showAsIs(this.form)">
<INPUT TYPE="button" VALUE="Reverse the array" onClick="reverseIt(this.form)">
<INPUT TYPE="reset">
<INPUT TYPE="button" VALUE="Reload" onClick="self.location.reload()">
<TEXTAREA NAME="output" ROWS=4 COLS=60>
</TEXTAREA>
</FORM>
</BODY>
</HTML>
```

Notice that the `solarSys.reverse()` method stands by itself (meaning, nothing captures the returned value) because the method modifies the `solarSys` array. You then run the now inverted `solarSys` array through the *array*.`join()` method for your text display.

array.sort([*compareFunction*])

	NN2	NN3	NN4	NN6	IE3/J1	IE3/J2	IE4	IE5	IE5.5
Compatibility		✓	✓	✓		✓	✓	✓	✓

Example

You can look to Listing 37-9 for a few examples of sorting an array of string values (see Figure 17-2). Four buttons summon different sorting routines, three of which invoke comparison functions. This listing sorts the planet array alphabetically (forward and backward) by the last character of the planet name and also by the length of the planet name. Each comparison function demonstrates different ways of comparing data sent during a sort.

Listing 37-9: **Array.sort() Possibilities**

```
<HTML>
<HEAD>
<TITLE>Array.sort()</TITLE>
<SCRIPT LANGUAGE="JavaScript1.1">
solarSys = new Array(9)
solarSys[0] = "Mercury"
solarSys[1] = "Venus"
solarSys[2] = "Earth"
solarSys[3] = "Mars"
solarSys[4] = "Jupiter"
solarSys[5] = "Saturn"
solarSys[6] = "Uranus"
```

Continued

Listing 37-9 *(continued)*

```
solarSys[7] = "Neptune"
solarSys[8] = "Pluto"
// comparison functions
function compare1(a,b) {
    // reverse alphabetical order
    if (a > b) {return -1}
    if (b > a) {return 1}
    return 0
}
function compare2(a,b) {
    // last character of planet names
    var aComp = a.charAt(a.length - 1)
    var bComp = b.charAt(b.length - 1)
    if (aComp < bComp) {return -1}
    if (aComp > bComp) {return 1}
    return 0
}
function compare3(a,b) {
    // length of planet names
    return a.length - b.length
}
// sort and display array
function sortIt(form, compFunc) {
    var delimiter = ";"
    if (compFunc == null) {
        solarSys.sort()
    } else {
        solarSys.sort(compFunc)
    }
    // display results in field
    form.output.value = unescape(solarSys.join(delimiter))
}
</SCRIPT>
<BODY onLoad="document.forms[0].output.value = unescape(solarSys.join(';'))">
<H2>Sorting array elements</H2>
This document contains an array of planets in our solar system.<HR>
<FORM>
Click on a button to sort the array:<P>
<INPUT TYPE="button" VALUE="Alphabetical A-Z" onClick="sortIt(this.form)">
<INPUT TYPE="button" VALUE="Alphabetical Z-A"
onClick="sortIt(this.form,compare1)">
<INPUT TYPE="button" VALUE="Last Character"
onClick="sortIt(this.form,compare2)">
<INPUT TYPE="button" VALUE="Name Length" onClick="sortIt(this.form,compare3)">
<INPUT TYPE="button" VALUE="Reload Original" onClick="self.location.reload()">
<INPUT TYPE="text" NAME="output" SIZE=62>
</TEXTAREA>
</FORM>
</BODY>
</HTML>
```

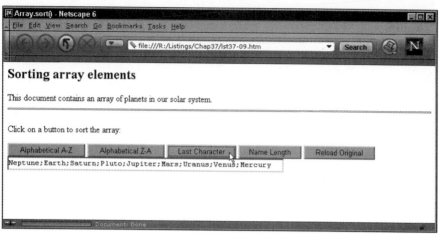

Figure 17-2: Sorting an array of planet names alphabetically by last character

```
array.splice(startIndex , deleteCount[,
item1[, item2[,...itemN]]])
```

	NN2	NN3	NN4	NN6	IE3/J1	IE3/J2	IE4	IE5	IE5.5
Compatibility			✓	✓					✓

Example

Use The Evaluator (Chapter 13 in the *JavaScript Bible*) to experiment with the splice() method. Begin by creating an array with a sequence of numbers:

```
a = new Array(1,2,3,4,5)
```

Next, remove the center three items, and replace them with one string item:

```
a.splice(1, 3, "two/three/four")
```

The Results box shows a string version of the three-item array returned by the method. To view the current contents of the array, enter a into the top text box.

To put the original numbers back into the array, swap the string item with three numeric items:

```
a.splice(1, 1, 2, 3, 4)
```

The method returns the single string, and the a array now has five items in it again.

✦   ✦   ✦

What's on the CD-ROM

The accompanying Windows–Macintosh CD-ROM contains a complete set of HTML document listings and an electronic version of this book, plus additional listings and the full text of the *JavaScript Bible, Gold Edition*. You also receive Adobe Acrobat Reader software to view and search the electronic versions of the books.

System Requirements

To derive the most benefit from the example listings, you should have both Netscape Navigator 6 (or later) and Internet Explorer 5 (or later) installed on your computer. While many scripts run in both browsers, several scripts demonstrate features that are available on only one browser or the other. To write scripts, you can use a simple text editor, word processor, or dedicated HTML editor.

To use the Adobe Acrobat Reader, you need the following:

✦ For Windows 95, Windows 98, or Windows NT 4.0 (with SP3 or later), you should be using a 486 or Pentium computer with 16MB of RAM and 10MB of hard disk space.

✦ Macintosh users require a PowerPC, System 7.1,2 or later, at least 8MB of RAM, and 8MB of disk space.

Disc Contents

Platform-specific software is located in the appropriate Windows and Macintosh directories on the CD-ROM. The contents include the following items.

JavaScript listings for Windows and Macintosh text editors

Almost all example listings from this book and the *JavaScript Bible, Gold Edition* are on the CD-ROM in the form of complete HTML files, which you can load into a browser to see the language item in operation (a few others are plain text files, which you can view in your browser or text editor). A directory called Listings contains the example files, with nested folders named for each chapter of the *JavaScript Bible*. Each HTML file's name is keyed to the Listing number in the book. For example, the file for Listing 15-1 is named `lst15-01.htm`. Note that the first part of each listing number is keyed to a *JavaScript Bible* chapter number. Thus, Listing 15-1 demonstrates a term discussed in Chapter 15 of the *JavaScript Bible* (both editions), although the printed listing and discussion about the listing appears in Chapter 1 of this book because Chapter 1 contains examples for *JavaScript Bible* Chapter 15.

For your convenience, an `index.html` file in the Listings folder provides a front-end table of contents to the HTML files for the book's program listings. Open that file from your browser whenever you want to access the program listing files. If you intend to access that index page frequently, you can bookmark it in your browser(s). Using the index file to access the listing files can be very important in some cases, because several individual files must be opened within their associated framesets to work properly. Accessing the files through the `index.html` file assures that you open the frameset. The `index.html` file also shows browser compatibility ratings for all the listings. This saves you time from opening listings that are not intended to run on your browser. To examine and modify the HTML source files, open them from your favorite text editor program (for Windows editors, be sure to specify the `.htm` file extension in the Open File dialog box).

You can open all example files directly from the CD-ROM, but if you copy them to your hard drive, access is faster and you will be able to experiment with modifying the files more readily. Copy the folder named Listings from the CD-ROM to any location on your hard drive.

Electronic versions of the books

These are complete, searchable versions of both this book and the *JavaScript Bible, Gold Edition*, provided in Adobe Acrobat `.pdf` format. The Acrobat text for this book is in the folder named JSExamples PDF, while the *JavaScript Bible* text is in the JSBGold PDF folder.

Adobe Acrobat Reader

The Adobe Acrobat Reader is a helpful program that enables you to view the entire contents of both this book and the *JavaScript Bible, Gold Edition*, which are in `.pdf` format on the CD-ROM. To install and run Adobe Acrobat Reader, follow these steps:

For Windows

1. Start Windows Explorer or Windows NT Explorer and then open the Acrobat folder on the CD-ROM.

2. In the Acrobat folder, double-click the rs405eng.exe icon and follow the instructions presented on-screen for installing Adobe Acrobat Reader.

For Macintosh

1. Open the Acrobat folder on the CD-ROM.

2. In the Acrobat folder, double-click the Adobe Acrobat Installer icon and follow the instructions presented on-screen for installing Adobe Acrobat Reader.

✦   ✦   ✦

Index

Continued

Continued

Continued

Continued

Continued

Hungry Minds, Inc.
End-User License Agreement

4. Restrictions on Use of Individual Programs. You must follow the individual requirements and restrictions detailed for each individual program in the Appendix of this Book. These limitations are also contained in the individual license agreements recorded on the Software Media. These limitations may include a requirement that after using the program for a specified period of time, the user must pay a registration fee or discontinue use. By opening the Software packet(s), you will be agreeing to abide by the licenses and restrictions for these individual programs that are detailed in the Appendix and on the Software Media. None of the material on this Software Media or listed in this Book may ever be redistributed, in original or modified form, for commercial purposes.

5. Limited Warranty.

(a) HMI warrants that the Software and Software Media are free from defects in materials and workmanship under normal use for a period of sixty (60) days from the date of purchase of this Book. If HMI receives notification within the warranty period of defects in materials or workmanship, HMI will replace the defective Software Media.

(b) HMI AND THE AUTHOR OF THE BOOK DISCLAIM ALL OTHER WARRANTIES, EXPRESS OR IMPLIED, INCLUDING WITHOUT LIMITATION IMPLIED WARRANTIES OF MERCHANTABILITY AND FITNESS FOR A PARTICULAR PURPOSE, WITH RESPECT TO THE SOFTWARE, THE PROGRAMS, THE SOURCE CODE CONTAINED THEREIN, AND/OR THE TECHNIQUES DESCRIBED IN THIS BOOK. HMI DOES NOT WARRANT THAT THE FUNCTIONS CONTAINED IN THE SOFTWARE WILL MEET YOUR REQUIREMENTS OR THAT THE OPERATION OF THE SOFTWARE WILL BE ERROR FREE.

(c) This limited warranty gives you specific legal rights, and you may have other rights that vary from jurisdiction to jurisdiction.

6. Remedies.

(a) HMI's entire liability and your exclusive remedy for defects in materials and workmanship shall be limited to replacement of the Software Media, which may be returned to HMI with a copy of your receipt at the following address: Software Media Fulfillment Department, Attn.: *JavaScript Examples Bible: The Essential Companion to JavaScript Bible*, Hungry Minds, Inc., 10475 Crosspoint Blvd., Indianapolis, IN 46256, or call 1-800-762-2974. Please allow four to six weeks for delivery. This Limited Warranty is void if failure of the Software Media has resulted from accident, abuse, or misapplication. Any replacement Software Media will be warranted for the remainder of the original warranty period or thirty (30) days, whichever is longer.

(b) In no event shall HMI or the author be liable for any damages whatsoever (including without limitation damages for loss of business profits, business interruption, loss of business information, or any other pecuniary loss) arising from the use of or inability to use the Book or the Software, even if HMI has been advised of the possibility of such damages.

(c) Because some jurisdictions do not allow the exclusion or limitation of liability for consequential or incidental damages, the above limitation or exclusion may not apply to you.

7. U.S. Government Restricted Rights. Use, duplication, or disclosure of the Software for or on behalf of the United States of America, its agencies and/or instrumentalities (the "U.S. Government") is subject to restrictions as stated in paragraph (c)(1)(ii) of the Rights in Technical Data and Computer Software clause of DFARS 252.227-7013, or subparagraphs (c) (1) and (2) of the Commercial Computer Software - Restricted Rights clause at FAR 52.227-19, and in similar clauses in the NASA FAR supplement, as applicable.

8. General. This Agreement constitutes the entire understanding of the parties and revokes and supersedes all prior agreements, oral or written, between them and may not be modified or amended except in a writing signed by both parties hereto that specifically refers to this Agreement. This Agreement shall take precedence over any other documents that may be in conflict herewith. If any one or more provisions contained in this Agreement are held by any court or tribunal to be invalid, illegal, or otherwise unenforceable, each and every other provision shall remain in full force and effect.

CD-ROM Installation Instructions

The files on this CD-ROM can be accessed and used from both Windows 95 (or later) and Macintosh environments. Some Macintosh program files require MacOS 8.6 or later, but program listing text files can be opened with any MacOS version. For Windows, access the software with My Computer or Windows Explorer. Macintosh users can access files by using the Finder.

You can open all of the example file listings directly from the CD-ROM, but access will be faster — and you will be able to experiment with modifying the files more readily — if you copy the listings to your hard drive. Copy the folder named Listings from the CD-ROM to any location on your hard drive.

To open the listing scripts on this CD-ROM, you should have a copy of Microsoft Internet Explorer 5 (or later), Netscape Navigator 6 (or later), or both browsers installed on your computer.

To run the listing scripts from your browser, open the file named index.html in the Listings folder. This page provides a table of contents consisting of direct links to the listings, showing which browsers are compatible with each listing.

Access the Adobe Acrobat (PDF) files for the book's contents from the CD-ROM. Be sure to install the index files into your copy of Acrobat to take advantage of full-text search.

For more details on installing and running the CD-ROM contents, see the Appendix.

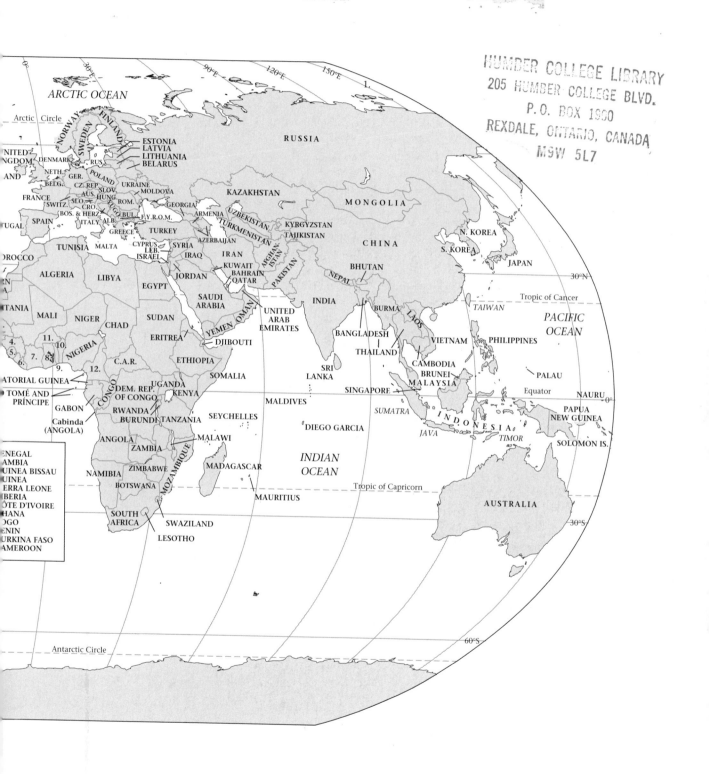

Anthropology

A Global Perspective
Fifth Edition

160101

Raymond Scupin
Lindenwood University

Christopher R. DeCorse
Syracuse University

Upper Saddle River, New Jersey 07458

Library of Congress Cataloging-in-Publication Data

Scupin, Raymond.
  Anthropology: a global perspective / Raymond Scupin, Christopher R. DeCorse.—5th ed.
    p. cm.
  Includes bibliographical references and index.
  ISBN 0-13-111470-0
  1. Anthropology. I. DeCorse, Christopher R. II. Title.

GN25.S393 2004
301—dc21
                                                                    2003042910

AVP/Publisher: Nancy Roberts
Managing Editor: Sharon Chambliss
VP, Director of Production and Manufacturing: Barbara Kittle
Editorial/Production Supervision: Barbara Reilly
Copyeditor: Serena Hoffman
Prepress and Manufacturing Manager: Nick Sklitsis
Prepress and Manufacturing Buyer: Ben Smith
Creative Design Director: Leslie Osher
Art Director: Nancy Wells
Interior Design: Bruce Killmer
Cover Design: Jill Lehan
AVP/Director of Marketing: Beth Mejia
Senior Marketing Manager: Amy Speckman
Marketing Assistant: Adam Laitman
Editorial Assistant: Lee Peterson
Photo Researcher: Beaura Kathy Ringrose
Image Permission Coordinator: Nancy Seise
Cover Image Specialist: Karen Sanatar
Interior Image Specialist: Beth Boyd-Brenzel
Manager, Rights and Permissions: Zina Arabia
Director, Image Resource Center: Melinda Reo
Cover Art: Stéphan Daigle/SIS

This book was set in 10/12 Garamond by Interactive Composition Corp. and
was printed and bound by Courier Companies, Inc. The cover was printed by Coral Graphics.

© 2004, 2001, 1998, 1995, 1992 by Pearson Education, Inc.
Upper Saddle River, New Jersey 07458

Printed in the United States of America

10 9 8 7 6 5 4 3 2 1

ISBN 0-13-111470-0

Pearson Education LTD., London
Pearson Education Australia PTY, Limited, Sydney
Pearson Education Singapore, Pte. Ltd
Pearson Education North Asia Ltd, Hong Kong
Pearson Education Canada, Ltd., Toronto
Pearson Educación de Mexico, S.A. de C.V.
Pearson Education—Japan, Tokyo
Pearson Education Malaysia, Pte. Ltd
Pearson Education, Upper Saddle River, New Jersey

Brief Contents

v

Contents

PART V
PRESTATE SOCIETIES

PART VI
STATE SOCIETIES

Boxes

Preface

◆ EDUCATIONAL GOALS AND ORIENTATION OF THIS TEXT

We all recognize that the world is getting smaller. Instantaneous global communications, trade among far-flung nations, geopolitical events affecting countries and hemispheres, and the ease of international travel are bringing people and cultures into more intimate contact with one another than ever before, forcing this generation of students to become more knowledgeable about societies other than their own. With that in mind, this textbook is grounded in the belief that an enhanced global awareness is essential for people preparing to take their place in the fast-paced, increasingly interconnected world of the twenty-first century. Anthropology is ideally suited to introduce students to a global perspective. Each of the subfields of anthropology has a broad focus on humanity; this helps liberate students from a narrow, parochial view and enables them to see and understand the full sweep of the human condition.

The anthropological perspective, which stresses critical-thinking processes, the evaluation of competing hypotheses, and the skills to generalize from specific data and assumptions, contributes significantly to a well-rounded education. This text engages readers in the varied intellectual activities underlying the anthropological approach by delving into both classic and recent research in the fields that make up anthropology.

This text reflects a strong commitment to anthropology's traditional holistic and integrative approach. It spells out how the four basic subfields of anthropology—physical anthropology, archaeology, linguistics, and ethnology—together yield a comprehensive understanding of humanity. Because the subfields tend to overlap, insights from all of them are woven together to reveal the holistic fabric of a particular society or the threads uniting all of humanity.

An interdisciplinary outlook resonates throughout this book. All contemporary anthropologists draw on the findings of biologists, paleontologists, geologists, economists, historians, psychologists, sociologists, political scientists, religious studies specialists, philosophers, and researchers in other fields whose work sheds light on anthropological inquiry. In probing various anthropological topics, this text often refers to research conducted in these other fields. In addition to enlarging the scope and reach of the text, exploring interactions between anthropology and other fields sparks the critical imagination that brings the learning process to life.

The comparative approach, another traditional cornerstone of the anthropological perspective, is spotlighted in this text as well. When anthropologists assess fossil evidence, artifacts, languages, or cultural beliefs and values, they weigh comparative evidence, while acknowledging the unique elements of each society and culture. This text casts an inquiring eye on materials from numerous geographical regions and historical eras to enrich student understanding.

A diachronic approach also characterizes this book. In evaluating human evolution, prehistoric events, language divergence, or developments in social structure, anthropologists must rely on models that reflect changes through time, so this diachronic orientation suffuses the text.

◆ THREE UNIFYING THEMES OF THIS TEXT

In prior editions of this textbook, we emphasized two unifying themes that structured the material in the text. We wanted to introduce students to the *diversity of human societies* and cultural patterns the world over and to the *similarities that make all humans fundamentally alike*. To achieve these two parallel goals, we paid as much attention to universal human characteristics as we did to particular cultural characteristics of local regions. We emphasized the growing interconnectedness of humans throughout the world and the positive and negative consequences of this reality. Contacts and interactions among people in different societies have occurred throughout history. However, modern advances in communication and transportation have accelerated the process of globalization in recent decades. One goal of this text is to call on anthropological studies of various societies to discover how people are responding to the process of globalization. We continue with this approach with this fifth edition of this textbook.

However, we also want to make a third theme more prominent in this edition. This third theme focuses on the fundamental bridge between the sciences and humanities within anthropology. We call this the *synthetic-complementary approach,* which views the scientific method and the methods in the humanities as complementary and suggests that one is incomplete without the other. This theme had been mentioned in previous editions of this textbook, but we make it much more explicit in this fifth edition.

In another, earlier anthropology textbook published by Prentice Hall (1964), the late Eric Wolf emphasized that anthropology has always had one foot in the sciences and one foot in the humanities. Wolf said, "Anthropology is both the most scientific of the humanities and the most humanistic of the sciences (1964:88). However, many textbooks in anthropology offer either a complete scientific orientation or a total humanistic approach. We would like to carry on the tradition that Eric Wolf accentuated in his book. One of the important goals in the revision of this textbook is to highlight the fundamental importance of the synthetic-complementary approach to science and the humanities in anthropology.

Some anthropologists have concluded that the scientific approach is not suitable for assessing and interpreting human behavior and culture, whereas others believe that the humanistic approach is not appropriate for developing general cross-cultural and causal explanations about human behavior and culture. This has led to textbooks that focus either on one or the other approach. In this textbook, we highlight how the interpretive-humanistic perspective is complementary to the scientific method, which seeks general cross-cultural and causal explanations for human behavior and culture. This third important theme will dovetail with the two

other themes, demonstrating how human behavior is both culturally unique and particular to a specific culture, and how it is also universal. The interpretive-humanistic perspective provides insight into the specifics of human behavior within different cultures, whereas the scientific approach offers a method to test causal explanations that allow for insight into universal aspects of human behavior.

◆ ORGANIZATION OF THE BOOK

The arrangement and treatment of topics in this text differ from that of other texts. In Part I, we introduce the basic concepts of the four fields of anthropology. Chapter 1 introduces the field of anthropology and explains how it relates to the sciences and humanities. This lead-in chapter also examines how anthropologists use the scientific method. Chapter 2 examines how paleoanthropologists and archaeologists locate and interpret fossils and the record of past human behavior. This chapter is intended to provide background information on topics such as dating techniques and excavation methods, which will be mentioned in later chapters. Chapter 3 presents basic evolutionary concepts, focusing on evolutionary processes and the origins of life on earth. Principles of heredity and molecular genetics are also briefly introduced.

In Part II we focus on research done in physical anthropology. Chapter 4 focuses on the primates, discussing taxonomy and the fossil finds that allow researchers to trace primate ancestry. It also includes a discussion of living nonhuman primates and the primate features found in humans. This background in primate evolution provides an introduction to hominid evolution, the focus of Chapter 5. Trends in hominid evolution and some of the more important hominid fossil finds are examined. The chapter then discusses different interpretations of the evolution of the hominids and the origins of *Homo sapiens*. This section concludes with the study of modern human variation in Chapter 6. This chapter explores the different sources of human variation—genetic, environmental, and cultural—and how physical anthropologists examine this variation.

Part III concentrates on the research done by archaeologists. Chapters 7, 8, and 9 present archaeological perspectives on human culture, spanning the earliest tool traditions through the appearance of complex societies and the state. Chapter 7 opens with an expanded discussion of Paleolithic cultures. This chapter presents the archaeological evidence for early hominid and human behavior, dealing with the stone tools and technological developments of the Lower, Middle, and Upper Paleolithic. Chapter 8 concentrates on the origins of domestication and settled life. It includes a discussion of how archaeologists study the origins of domestication, as well as developments in different world areas. Chapter 9 presents a discussion of the rise of the state and complex societies. As in the preceding chapters, this discussion includes a substantive presentation of developments in different world areas, as well as the archaeological evidence that archaeologists use to evaluate the growth of political and social complexity in ancient societies.

In Part IV, Chapters 10, 11, 12, and 13 reinforce one another. Chapter 10 examines the concept of culture as it is understood in anthropology. Beginning with the notions of material and nonmaterial culture, this chapter goes on to cite examples of cultural diversity found throughout the world. Here we also stress cultural universals and similarities that unify all of humanity. We also integrate the discussion of the concept of culture with the process of enculturation in order to bridge Chapters 10 on culture with Chapter 11 on the enculturation process. To refine our discussion of culture and enculturation, we develop some new materials on recent research in cognitive anthropology.

In Chapter 11, we emphasize how anthropologists bridge the gap between biology and culture as they gain a greater understanding of enculturation and personality development in unfamiliar societies. To explore this topic, we turn to the classic studies conducted by Ruth Benedict and Margaret Mead, as well as the most recent research in psychoanalytic anthropology, childhood training in societies around the world, incest, sexuality, cognition, emotions, and the cross-cultural research on personality disorders. In addition, we also discuss the fields of cognitive anthropology and evolutionary psychology. Many psychological anthropologists have been attempting to incorporate the findings from this new field into their hypotheses.

Chapter 12, on language, dovetails with the previous chapter in several key ways. We have refined our discussion of the differences between ape communication and human language. New conclusions have been reached recently in laboratory research and primatological fieldwork comparing ape communication with human languages. Following up on these studies, we have revised our section on Chomsky's transformational model and other related anthropological findings that suggest interactive relationships between biology and culture. We have expanded our discussion of the Sapir–Whorf hypothesis. Other research findings in linguistic anthropology, including historical linguistics, complement material in the emerging field of sociolinguistics and introduce students to the most recent developments in the field.

Theory—classic and contemporary—frames Chapter 13, which offers a critical evaluation of the strengths and weaknesses of each theoretical paradigm. This chapter also amplifies the earlier treatment of the material-nonmaterial aspects of culture by comparing theories highlighting material culture with those placing greater emphasis on nonmaterial, symbolic culture. We have added new sections on both feminist anthropology and postmodern anthropology, which include criticisms of extreme views in those areas of research.

In Part V, beginning with Chapter 14, this text presents a much different organizational scheme compared with that of other texts. Instead of structuring the book according to specific topics in anthropology such as subsistence, economy, family, kinship, political organization, and religion, this text organizes the material based on levels of societal organization and regional topics.

In this fifth edition of *Anthropology: A Global Perspective,* Chapter 14 walks students through the methods, research strategies, and ethical dilemmas that confront cultural anthropologists. Then readers learn about the major variables cultural anthropologists analyze to gain insight into different types of societies: environment and subsistence, demography, technology, economy, social structure, family, kinship, gender, age, political systems, law, and religion. With this background, students are ready to understand subsequent chapters.

Chapter 14 also presents the multidimensional approach, which most contemporary anthropologists use to analyze the elements of society and culture. Rather than grounding an understanding of society and culture in a single factor, this orientation taps into both material and nonmaterial aspects of culture to view the full spectrum of society holistically and to produce a balanced treatment of key issues that are aspects of anthropological analysis. Again, we integrate the scientific and humanistic approaches in this chapter.

In Chapters 15, 16, and 17, the text reports the major anthropological findings related to prestate societies (bands, tribes, and chiefdoms). Because these classifications have been open to interpretation among anthropologists, these labels are used with extreme caution. Even though many anthropologists either shun these terms or seriously question their utility in describing complex, changing societies, we believe that these classifications give students who are first exposed to the discipline a good grasp of the fundamentals of prestate societies.

In Part VI, Chapters 18 and 19 move on to agricultural and industrial state societies, whose key characteristics emerge in the interconnections among variables such as political economy and social stratification. Chapter 18 features the basic elements of agricultural societies as revealed by archaeologists, historians, and anthropologists. Chapter 19 opens with a new look at the Industrial Revolution and the process of modernization, segueing into comparative research conducted in England, Western Europe, the United States, the former Soviet Union, and Japan to illustrate the dynamics of industrial states.

Sound pedagogical logic underlies this approach. Instead of presenting important anthropological research on demography, gender, economy, kinship, ethnicity, political systems, and religion as single chapters (usually corresponding to single lectures), this organizational scheme spotlights how these variables permeate the entire spectrum of human experience in different types of societies. While the single-chapter format tends to marginalize these topics, this text's approach—based on different levels of societal organization—allows students to focus on the interconnections between the political economy and gender, age, family, kinship, religion, demography, technology, environment, and other variables. As a result, students gain a holistic understanding of human societies.

Organizing material according to levels of societal organization in no way implies or endorses a simplistic, unilineal view of sociocultural evolution. In fact, the ladderlike evolutionary perspective on society comes in for criticism throughout the text. While recognizing the inherent weaknesses of

using such classifications as "tribes" and "chiefdoms"—including the parallel tendencies to lump diverse societies into narrow categories and create artificial boundaries among societies—we believe that these groupings nonetheless serve the valuable purpose of introducing beginning students to the sweeping concepts that make anthropology distinctive. Generalizations about tribes and chiefdoms help students unfamiliar with anthropology's underpinnings to absorb basic concepts and data; the complexities and theoretical controversies within the discipline can always be addressed in more specialized advanced courses.

In Part VII, we include a discussion in Chapter 20 of modernization theory, with a critique of the terminology of First, Second, Third, and Fourth Worlds as being too simplistic to apply to what anthropological data demonstrate. This Cold War terminology is outdated from today's standpoint, especially based on ethnographic data regarding the complex levels of development and diversity found in the so-called Third World—and the formerly industrial socialist societies of the Second World that have mostly dissipated.

In Chapter 20, we delve into the theoretical paradigms that anthropologists have modified to understand the interrelationships among various societies of the world. Modernization, dependency, and world-systems theories (and criticisms of them) are introduced to develop the global perspective. We emphasize that societies cannot be understood as independent, isolated units. This global perspective informs all the subsequent chapters, reinforcing a sense of global awareness among students. Chapter 20 also considers the problems generated by contact between the industrial states and prestate aboriginal societies. It goes on to address a number of salient questions raised by these contacts: How are these prestate societies becoming absorbed into global economic and political networks? How are prestate peoples responding to this situation? And what are anthropologists doing to enhance the coping strategies of these native peoples?

Another significant change that we adopted from the fourth edition is the development of two new chapters that focus on Latin America, Africa, and the Caribbean (Chapter 21) and the Middle East and Asia (Chapter 22). These two chapters emphasize the globalization process in these regions and reveal what anthropologists are finding in their local studies related to the overall trend of globalization. We emphasize how all of these cultural regions are becoming more interconnected. These two chapters document the evolving interrelationships between Western countries and non-Western regions by drawing on historical research. In addition to probing classic ethnographic research, contemporary issues in each region are placed within a broad historical context, offering readers finely honed diachronic insights into social and political developments in each of these non-Western areas.

In Part VIII, we develop a new chapter on race and ethnicity (Chapter 23). This chapter reviews the extensive research that anthropologists have been doing since the beginning of the twentieth century. We cover the material related to the development of racism in Western society, with an anthropological critique of racism based on scientific evidence. We also provide perspectives on ethnicity that anthropologists have developed for understanding race and ethnic relations. Examples of this research are provided by a review of race and ethnic relations in U.S. society from an anthropological perspective. We believe that the placement of this chapter within the globalization section reinforces how the process of globalization has had broad consequences for race and ethnicity issues worldwide.

Chapter 24 highlights contemporary global trends that are changing our world. Anthropological research is brought to bear on the environmental, demographic, economic, political, ethnic, and religious trends that are shaking the foundations of many societies. Among the topics addressed in this context are global warming, the Green Revolution, the increasing consumption of nonrenewable energy by industrial societies, the impact of multinational corporations, the demise of socialist regimes, and the rise of new ethnic and religious movements.

Chapter 25 sheds light on the fifth subfield of anthropology: applied anthropology. Here we consider key issues in applied anthropology, including applied physical anthropology and forensic anthropology, medical anthropology, cultural resource management, and recent research aimed at solving practical problems in societies the world over. One of the goals of this chapter is to introduce students to new career possibilities in the field of anthropology.

FEATURES OF THIS TEXT

BOXES

In **Critical Perspectives** boxes, designed to stimulate independent reasoning and judgment, students take the role of anthropologist by engaging in the critical analysis of specific problems and issues that arise in anthropological research. A successful holdover from the first edition, these Critical Perspectives boxes encourage students to use rigorous standards of evidence when evaluating assumptions and hypotheses regarding scientific and philosophical issues that have no easy answers. We have added several new Critical Perspective boxes for this fifth edition. By probing beneath the surface of various assumptions and hypotheses in these exercises, students stand to discover the excitement and challenge of anthropological investigation.

Anthropologists at Work boxes, profiling prominent anthropologists, humanize many of the issues covered in the chapters. These boxes—another carryover from the first edition—go behind the scenes to trace the personal and professional development of some of today's leading anthropologists.

Finally, **Applying Anthropology** boxes—new to the previous edition—show students how research in anthropology can help solve practical problems confronting contemporary societies. Students often ask: What relevance does anthropology have to the problems we face in our generation? These Applying Anthropology boxes answer the relevance question head on. For example, one box notes that anthropologists unearth research data to help ease tensions in multicultural relations in U.S. society. Another box describes how linguistic anthropologists work with indigenous peoples to preserve their languages as the indigenous peoples adjust to the modern world. The concluding chapter of the text ties together many of these Applying Anthropology boxes by placing in perspective the full panoply of issues addressed in applied anthropology.

PEDAGOGICAL AIDS

For sound pedagogical reasons, we have retained some features in this fifth edition of *Anthropology:*

A Global Perspective. Each chapter opens with a Chapter Outline and Chapter Questions that will help guide students to the most important issues addressed in the chapter. And each chapter ends with Questions to Think About that address issues covered in the chapter that students can use to help comprehend the material in the chapter. In addition, each chapter ends with a Summary and a list of Key Terms that will help students focus on important concepts introduced in the chapter. Finally, Internet Exercises help students use the World Wide Web to explore various topics and issues addressed in the chapters.

◈ SUPPLEMENTS

This carefully prepared supplements package is intended to give the instructor the resources needed to teach the course and the student the tools needed to successfully complete the course.

FOR THE INSTRUCTOR

Instructor's Resource and Testing Manual This essential instructor's tool includes chapter overviews, chapter objectives, lecture and discussion topics, classroom activities, research and writing topics, print and non-print resources, and over 1,600 questions in multiple-choice, true/false, and essay formats. All test questions are page-referenced to the text.

TestGEN This computerized software allows instructors to create their own personalized exams, to edit any or all test questions, and to add new questions. Other special features of this program, which is available for Windows and Macintosh, include random generation of an item set, creation of alternate versions of the same test, scrambling question sequence, and test preview before printing.

Videos Prentice Hall is pleased to offer two video series: *The Changing American Indian in a Changing America: Videocases of American Indian Peoples,* and *Rites of Passage: Videocases of Traditional African Peoples.* In addition, a selection of high quality, award-winning videos from the Filmmakers Library collection is available upon adoption. Please see your Prentice Hall sales representative for more information.

Anthropology Transparencies, Series IV Taken from graphs, diagrams, and tables in this text and other sources, more than 50 full-color transparencies offer an effective means of amplifying lecture topics.

Anthropology Central Available to users of *Anthropology, Fifth Edition,* this passcode-protected online resource allows instructors to download the complete instructor's manual, lecture and graphics PowerPoint slides, and *Strategies in Teaching Anthropology, First Edition.* See your Prentice Hall sales representative for more information.

FOR THE STUDENT

Study Guide Designed to reinforce information in the text, the study guide includes chapter outlines and summaries, key concepts, critical thinking questions, student self-tests, and suggested readings.

Companion Website™ In tandem with the text, students can now take full advantage of the World Wide Web to enrich their study of anthropology through the Scupin website. This resource correlates the text with related material available on the Internet. Features of the website include chapter objectives, study questions, and links to interesting material and information from other sites on the Web that can reinforce and enhance the content of each chapter. *Address:* **www.prenhall.com/scupin**

The Prentice Hall Guide to Evaluating Online Resources with Research Navigator™, Anthropology, 2004 This guide provides you access to Prentice Hall's new Research Navigator™, your one-stop research solution complete with extensive help on the research process and three exclusive databases full of relevant and reliable source material including EBSCO's **ContentSelect**™ Academic Journal Database, *The New York* **Times** Search-by-Subject Archive, and **Best of the Web** Link Library. It is free to students when packaged with *Anthropology, Fifth Edition.*

The New York Times*/Prentice Hall *Themes of the Times *The New York Times* and Prentice Hall are sponsoring *Themes of the Times,* a program designed to enhance student access to current information relevant to the classroom. Through this program, the core subject matter provided in the text is supplemented by a collection of timely articles from one of the world's most distinguished newspapers, *The New York Times*. These articles demonstrate the vital, ongoing connection between what is learned in the classroom and what is happening in the world around us. To enjoy a wealth of information provided by *The New York Times* daily, a reduced subscription rate is available. For information, call toll-free: 1-800-631-1222.

Prentice Hall and *The New York Times* are proud to co-sponsor *Themes of the Times*. We hope it will make the reading of both textbooks and newspapers a more dynamic, involving process.

ACKNOWLEDGMENTS

A textbook like this one requires the enormous effort of many people. We would like to thank the following reviewers for their valuable comments on the various editions of this textbook:

Susan Abbott-Jamieson, University of Kentucky; Kelly D. Alley, Auburn University; Barbara Gallatin Anderson, Southern Methodist University; Robert Bee, University of Connecticut; Harumi Befu, Stanford University; John E. Blank, Cleveland State University; Barry Bogin, University of Michigan–Dearborn; Donald E. Brown, University of California–Santa Barbara; Robert Carmack, SUNY–Albany; A. H. Peter Castro, Syracuse University; Miriam S. Chaiken, Indiana University of Pennsylvania; Gail W. Cromack, Onondaga Community College; James Duvall, Contra Costa College; Allen S. Ehrlich, Eastern Michigan University; Michele Ruth Gamburd, Portland State University; Josef Gamper, Monterey Peninsula College; Alan Goodman, Hampshire College; Leonard Greenfield, Temple University; Joan Gross, Oregon State University; Raymond Hames, University of Nebraska; W. Penn Handwerker, Humbolt State University; Elvin Hatch, University of California–Santa Barbara; Richard D. Harris, University of Portland; Robert W. Hefner, Boston University; Benita J. Howell, University of Tennessee–Knoxville; Arian Ishaya, DeAnza Community College; Norris Johnson, University of North Carolina–Chapel Hill; Rita S. Kipp, Kenyon College; Nancy B. Leis, Central Michigan University; William Leons, University of Toledo; James Lett, Indian River Community College; Kenneth E. Lewis, Michigan State University; Ann P. McElroy, SUNY–Buffalo; Robert R. McIrvin, University of North Carolina–Greensboro; Nancy P. McKee, Washington State University; Ester Maring, Southern Illinois University–Carbondale; Barry H. Michie, Kansas State University; David Minderhout, Bloomsburg University; Katherine Moore, Bentley College; Robert Moorman, Miami-Dade Community College–North; James Myers, CSU–Chico; Tim O'Meara, Melbourne University; John W. Page, Kirkland, Washington; Curt Peterson, Elgin Community College; Leonard Plotnicov, University of Pittsburgh; D. Tab Rasmussen, Washington University–St. Louis; James L. Ross, University of Akron; Susan D. Russell, Northern Illinois University; Michael Salovesh, Northern Illinois University; L. Schell, SUNY–Albany; Edwin S. Segal, University of Louisville; David H. Spain, University of Washington; John Townsend, Syracuse University; Robert B. Townsend, College of Lake County; Trudy Turner, University of Wisconsin at Milwaukee; Stephen A. Tyler, Rice University; Virginia J. Vitzthum, University of California–Riverside; Alaka Wali, University of Maryland; William Wedenoja, Southwest Missouri State University; Ronald K. Wetherington, Southern Methodist University; Aubrey Williams, University of Maryland; Pamela Willoughby, University of Alberta; and Larry Zimmerman, University of South Dakota. We also extend thanks to all colleagues who sent us photos and information for use in the biography boxes.

We are grateful for the unwavering support given to this project by Prentice Hall. Without the moral support and encouragement of publisher Nancy Roberts and managing editor Sharon Chambliss, we would have never been able to complete it. We would like to thank Barbara Reilly, our production editor, who kept us on deadline.

Our warmest appreciation goes to our families, whose emotional support and patience throughout the publication of the five editions of this text truly made this book possible.

Anyone with comments, suggestions, or recommendations regarding this text is welcome to send e-mail (Internet) messages to the following addresses: **rscupin@lindenwood.edu** or **crdecorse@maxwell.syr.edu.**

Raymond Scupin
Christopher R. DeCorse

About the Authors

Raymond Scupin is professor of anthropology at Lindenwood University. He received his B.A. degree in history and Asian studies, with a minor in anthropology, from the University of California–Los Angeles. He completed his M.A. and Ph.D. degrees in anthropology at the University of California–Santa Barbara. Dr. Scupin is truly a four-field anthropologist. During graduate school, Dr. Scupin did archaeological and ethnohistorical research on Native Americans in the Santa Barbara region. He did extensive ethnographic fieldwork in Thailand with a focus on understanding the ethnic and religious movements among the Muslim minority. In addition, he taught linguistics and conducted linguistic research while based at a Thai university.

Dr. Scupin has been teaching undergraduate courses in anthropology for over twenty years at a variety of academic institutions, including community colleges, research universities, and a four-year liberal arts university. Thus, he has taught a very broad spectrum of undergraduate students. Through his teaching experience, Dr. Scupin was prompted to write this textbook, which would allow a wide range of undergraduate students to understand the holistic and global perspectives of the four-field approach in anthropology. In 1999 Dr. Scupin received the Missouri Governor's Award for Teaching Excellence.

Dr. Scupin has published many studies based on his ethnographic research in Thailand. He recently returned to Thailand and other countries of Southeast Asia to update his ethnographic data. He is a member of many professional associations, including the American Anthropological Association, the Asian Studies Association, and the Council of Thai Studies. Dr. Scupin has recently authored *Religion and Culture: An Anthropological Focus* and *Race and Ethnicity: An Anthropological Focus on the U.S. and the World,* both published by Prentice Hall Press.

Christopher R. DeCorse received his bachelor of arts and master's degrees in anthropology and archaeology, completing his doctorate in archaeology at the University of California–Los Angeles. His theoretical interests include the interpretation of ethnicity, culture change, and variability in the archaeological record. Dr. DeCorse has excavated a variety of prehistoric and historic period sites in the United States, the Caribbean, and Africa, but his primary area of research has been in the archaeology, ethnohistory, and ethnography of Sierra Leone and Ghana. His most recent research has focused on culture contact and change at the African settlement of Elmina, Ghana, the site of the first European trade-post in sub-Saharan Africa. He is currently collaborating on several projects that examine connections between Africa and the Americas.

Dr. DeCorse has taught archaeology and general anthropology in various undergraduate and graduate programs, including the University of Ghana, Indiana University of Pennsylvania, and Syracuse University, where he is currently an associate professor in the Department of Anthropology. In addition to *The Record of the Past,* he has co-authored *Worldviews in Human Expression,* an introduction to the humanities from an anthropological perspective. He also serves on the advisory or editorial boards of *Annual Editions* in physical anthropology and archaeology, *International Journal of Historical Archaeology,* and *Beads: Journal of the Society of Bead Researchers.* He has participated on a number of committees and panels, including work as a consultant on human evolution and agricultural origins for the National Center for History in the Schools.

Dr. DeCorse has received several academic honors and awards, including Fulbright and Smithsonian fellowships. He has published more than thirty articles, reviews, and research notes in a variety of publications, including *The African Archaeological Review, Historical New Hampshire, Historical Archaeology,* and *Slavery and Abolition.* A volume on his work at Elmina, *Under the Castle Cannon,* and an edited volume, *West Africa during the Atlantic Slave Trade,* were published in 2001.

1

Introduction
to Anthropology

CHAPTER QUESTIONS

- What is unique about the field of anthropology as compared with other disciplines?

- How does the field of anthropology bridge both the sciences and the humanities?

- Why should any student study anthropology?

Anthropologist Morton Fried once pointed out the similarities among space travel, science fiction, and the field of anthropology (1977). He noted that when Neil Armstrong became the first human to set foot on the moon in July 1969, his step constituted first contact. To space travelers and science fiction writers, *first contact* refers to the first meeting between humans and extraterrestrial beings. To anthropologists, the phrase refers to initial encounters between peoples of different societies. For thousands of years, peoples throughout the world have had first contacts with each other. Perhaps in the future, through further exploration in space, there may be initial encounters between humans and creatures from other worlds.

Imagine the year 2100, when space travelers from earth have these first contacts with extraterrestrials in far-off galaxies. Undoubtedly, the travelers from Earth will want to grasp the nature of these beings. Because the extraterrestrial beings will certainly differ physically from humans, the space travelers will attempt to investigate their physical characteristics. For this investigation, they will examine the environmental conditions of the distant planet to determine how these creatures originated and why they developed specific physical traits. They will also look closely at physical variations within the extraterrestrial population.

Beyond individual physical characteristics of the extraterrestrial beings, the space explorers will wonder how the extraterrestrial society developed, so they will try to study the technology and other aspects of the alien society that would indicate patterns of change over time. In the year 2100, space scientists may be able to conduct this analysis with sophisticated equipment and methods that allow them to examine the layers of the newly discovered planet's crust to locate different inventions, buildings, or art forms that have emerged in specific time periods.

One of the first problems the space travelers will almost surely encounter is communicating with the extraterrestrials. They will need to determine the form of communication used by these creatures and attempt to distinguish patterns of sounds or other methods used to transmit information. The space travelers may discover that different forms of communication are used in different places on the

1

Neil Armstrong on the moon.

over the past hundred years to conduct their investigations. There are two major goals of anthropology: to understand the *uniqueness and diversity* of human behavior and human societies around the world, and to discover the *fundamental similarities* that link human beings the world over both in the past and the present. To accomplish these goals, anthropologists undertake systematic case studies of people living in particular locations, in the past and present, and use comparative techniques to assess the similarities and differences among societies.

Using these goals as a springboard, anthropology has forged distinctive objectives and propelled research that has broadened our understanding of humanity, from the beginnings of human societies to the present. This chapter introduces the distinctive approaches used in anthropology to achieve these goals.

Anthropology: The Four Subfields

The word *anthropology* stems from the Greek words *anthropo,* meaning human beings or humankind, and *logia,* translated as knowledge of or the study of. Thus, we can define **anthropology** as the systematic study of humankind. This definition in itself, however, does not distinguish anthropology from other disciplines. After all, historians, psychologists, economists, sociologists, and scholars in many other fields systematically study humankind in one way or another. Anthropology stands apart because it combines four subdisciplines, or subfields, that bridge the natural sciences, the social sciences, and the humanities. These four subdisciplines—physical anthropology, archaeology, linguistic anthropology, and ethnology or cultural anthropology—give anthropologists a broad approach to the study of humanity the world over, both past and present. Figure 1.1 shows these subfields and the various specializations that make up each one. A discussion of these subdisciplines and some of the key specializations in each follows.

These subfields of anthropology emerged in Western society in an attempt to understand non-Western peoples. Europeans, including Christopher Columbus, had been exploring and colonizing the world since the fifteenth century. These Western peoples had encounters with non-Western native peoples in the Americas, Africa, the Middle East, and

planet, prompting the human visitors to compare these disparate communication patterns to understand the different language groupings found on the planet.

The space scientists could also gain an understanding of the extraterrestrials by living in their communities and observing their behavior. In addition to recording these behaviors as accurately as possible, the space travelers might have to participate in the extraterrestrials' rituals and daily activities to gain an insider's perspective.

The space travelers would strive to determine in what ways these extraterrestrials resemble and differ from human beings on Earth. Drawing on all of their findings, they would compare the extraterrestrials' physical characteristics, the development of their society over time, their forms of communication, and their overall behavior and thought with that of humans.

As we shall see in this chapter, the field of anthropology seeks to understand humanity in much the same way that future space travelers would investigate the lifestyles of extraterrestrials. Anthropologists have developed specialized procedures

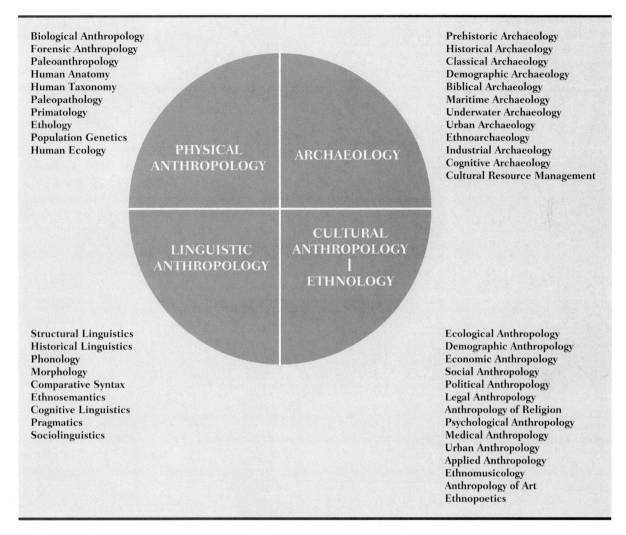

Biological Anthropology
Forensic Anthropology
Paleoanthropology
Human Anatomy
Human Taxonomy
Paleopathology
Primatology
Ethology
Population Genetics
Human Ecology

Prehistoric Archaeology
Historical Archaeology
Classical Archaeology
Demographic Archaeology
Biblical Archaeology
Maritime Archaeology
Underwater Archaeology
Urban Archaeology
Ethnoarchaeology
Industrial Archaeology
Cognitive Archaeology
Cultural Resource Management

PHYSICAL
ANTHROPOLOGY

ARCHAEOLOGY

LINGUISTIC
ANTHROPOLOGY

CULTURAL
ANTHROPOLOGY
|
ETHNOLOGY

Structural Linguistics
Historical Linguistics
Phonology
Morphology
Comparative Syntax
Ethnosemantics
Cognitive Linguistics
Pragmatics
Sociolinguistics

Ecological Anthropology
Demographic Anthropology
Economic Anthropology
Social Anthropology
Political Anthropology
Legal Anthropology
Anthropology of Religion
Psychological Anthropology
Medical Anthropology
Urban Anthropology
Applied Anthropology
Ethnomusicology
Anthropology of Art
Ethnopoetics

FIGURE 1.1 This figure shows the four core subfields of anthropology. It also includes some of the various specializations that have developed within each of the subfields, which will be introduced in this text. Many of these specializations overlap with one another in the actual studies carried out by anthropologists.

Asia. Various European travelers, missionaries, and government officials had described some of these non-Western societies, cultures, and races. By the nineteenth century, anthropology had developed into the primary discipline and science for understanding these non-Western societies and cultures. The major questions that these early nineteenth-century anthropologists grappled with had to do with the basic differences and similarities of human societies, cultures, and the physical variations of people throughout the world. Anthropologists have continued to answer these basic questions

through systematic research efforts within the four fields described below.

Physical Anthropology

Physical anthropology is the branch of anthropology concerned with humans as a biological species. As such, it is the subdiscipline most closely related to the natural sciences. Physical anthropologists conduct research in two major areas: human evolution and modern human variation. The investigation of human evolution presents one of the most

Although anthropologists study the distinctive features of different cultures, they also recognize the fundamental similarities among people throughout the world.

tantalizing areas of anthropological study. Research has now traced the African origins of humanity back over six million years. Fieldwork in other world areas has traced the expansion of early human ancestors throughout the world. Much of the evidence for human origins consists of **fossils,** the fragmentary remains of bones and living materials preserved from earlier periods. The study of human evolution through analysis of fossils is called **paleoanthropology** (the prefix *paleo* means "old" or "prehistoric"). Paleoanthropologists use a

variety of sophisticated scientific techniques to date, classify, and compare fossil bones to determine the links between modern humans and their biological ancestors. They may work closely with archaeologists when studying ancient tools and activity areas to learn about the behavior of early human ancestors.

Other physical anthropologists explore human evolution through **primatology,** the study of primates. **Primates** are mammals that belong to the same overall biological classification as humans

ANTHROPOLOGISTS AT WORK

C. LORING BRACE: PHYSICAL ANTHROPOLOGIST

C. Loring Brace was an under-graduate at Williams College, where he pursued a major in geology with a strong dose of biology. His family roots go back to early migrants from southern England who settled in Massachusetts and Connecticut, one of whom helped bring Charles Darwin's ideas to the attention of the U.S. public. After being drafted into the military from graduate school to serve in the Korean War, Brace returned to graduate school at Harvard University in the mid-1950s to focus on the field of physical anthropology, or paleoanthropology. He worked under all the leading evolutionary biologists and anthropologists of that time. In the summer of 1959, Brace had the opportunity to work at a French Paleolithic site with one of his teachers from Harvard, Hallam L. Movius. This field experience taught him that excavation is an extremely important element in paleoanthropology; however, he recognized that the skeletal data and artifacts had to be synthesized carefully to tell a coherent story about human evolution.

After this fieldwork experience, Brace traveled and visited prehistoric skeletal collections in Monaco, Italy, Switzerland, Paris, Croatia, and London to study the chronological sequence of human evolution and the relationship of the various finds. He carefully studied the evolution of teeth in the fossilized remains of many human ancestors. In particular, he

was interested in how culture might have effected physical evolution. Brace developed the unique hypothesis that the cultural innovation of cooking by Neandertals was important in the reduction in the size of their teeth. He continued to pursue the ideas of linking cultural artifacts with physical evolution, such as the use of dinnerware and its effects on the evolution of jaws and teeth. He has proposed many theories that have been evaluated by other physical anthropologists.

Brace began teaching and building a physical anthropology component of the anthropology department at the University of California at Santa Barbara in the early 1960s. From Santa Barbara he moved to the University of Michigan, where he has become the curator of the Physical Anthropology Unit in the Museum of Anthropology. He has an extensive fossil collection from all over the world, which he continues to analyze to develop fruitful hypotheses. He has traveled around the world to do research in his chosen field. Brace's students include many of the leading physical anthropologists today, such as Dean D. Falk, Carol J. Lauer, Frank Spencer, and Robert Hinton.

One of the most important issues in which Loring Brace has been involved is the study of race within anthropology. He has criticized the American cultural tendency to classify different

C. Loring Brace

peoples into distinctive racial categories, which has had negative effects on society and the field of physical anthropology. He collaborated with the senior physical anthropologist Ashley Montagu, who wrote the definitive treatise on the myth of race entitled *Man's Most Dangerous Myth: The Fallacy of Race*. This book was first published in 1942 during the Nazi period and represented the first systematic attempt to debunk the racist thinking of scientists and lay people on this subject. A new 1997 edition of Montagu's critical work was published, for which Brace wrote the foreword, emphasizing the importance of anthropological research in this area. C. Loring Brace has been working on a new book called *Race Is a Four Letter Word*, which criticizes the racial thinking of many social scientists. Known as a maverick to many of his colleagues, Brace continues to stimulate new ideas and hypotheses in the field of physical anthropology.

and therefore share similar physical characteristics and a close evolutionary relationship with us. Many primatologists observe primates such as chimpanzees, gorillas, gibbons, and orangutans in their natural habitats to ascertain the similarities and differences between these other primates and humans. These observations of living primates may provide insight into the behaviors of early human ancestors.

Another group of physical anthropologists focuses their research on the range of physical variation within and among different "modern" human populations. These anthropologists study human variation by measuring physical characteristics, such as body size, variation in blood types, differences in skin color, or various genetic traits. Human *osteology* is the particular area of specialization within physical anthropology dealing with the study of the human skeleton. Such studies have wide-ranging applications, including the identification of murder victims from fragmentary skeletal remains to the design of ergonomic airplane cockpits. Physical anthropologists are also interested in evaluating how disparate physical characteristics reflect evolutionary adaptations to different environmental conditions, thus shedding light on why human populations vary.

An increasingly important area of research for some physical anthropologists is *genetics,* the study of the biological "blueprints" that dictate the inheritance of physical characteristics. Research on genetics examines a wide variety of questions. It has, for example, been important in identifying the genetic sources of some diseases, such as sickle cell anemia, cystic fibrosis, and Tay-Sachs disease. Genetics has also become an increasingly important complement to paleoanthropological research. Through the study of the genetic makeup of modern humans, physical anthropologists have been working on calculating the genetic distance among modern humans, thus providing a means of inferring rates of evolution and the evolutionary relationships within the species. These data have helped provide independent evidence for the African origins of the modern human species and human ancestors. These genetic studies have also been used to determine the physical and evolutionary connections between Native Americans and Asiatic peoples.

Archaeology

Through **archaeology,** the branch of anthropology that seeks out and examines the artifacts of past societies, we learn about the culture of those societies—the shared way of life of a group of people that includes their values, beliefs, and norms. **Artifacts,** the material products of former societies, provide clues to the past. Some archaeological sites reveal spectacular jewelry like that found by the movie character Indiana Jones or the treasures of a pharaoh's tomb. Most artifacts are not so glamorous, however. Despite the popular image of archaeology as an adventurous, even romantic pursuit, it usually consists of methodical, rigorous scientific research (see the box "Patty Jo Watson: Archaeologist"). Archaeologists often spend hours sorting through ancient trash piles, or **middens,** to discover how members of past societies ate their meals, what tools they used in their household and in their work, and what beliefs gave meaning to their lives. The broken fragments of pottery, stone, glass, and other materials are collected and carefully analyzed in a laboratory setting. It may take months or even years to fully complete the study of an excavation. Unlike the glorified adventures of fictional archaeologists, the real-world field of archaeology thrives on the intellectually challenging adventure of systematic, scientific research that enlarges our understanding of the past.

Archaeologists have examined sites the world over, from campsites of the earliest humans to modern landfills. Some archaeologists investigate past societies whose history is primarily told by the archaeological record. Known as *prehistoric archaeologists,* they study the artifacts of groups such as the ancient inhabitants of Europe or the first humans to arrive in the Americas. Because these researchers have no written documents or oral traditions to help interpret the sites and artifacts that they recover, the archaeological record provides the primary source of information for their interpretations about the past. *Historical archaeologists,* on the other hand, work with historians in investigating the artifacts of societies of the more recent past. For example, some historical archaeologists have probed the remains of plantations in the southern United States to gain an understanding of the lifestyles of enslaved Africans and slave owners during the nineteenth century.

ANTHROPOLOGISTS AT WORK

PATTY JO WATSON: ARCHAEOLOGIST

After two years of studies in zoology at Iowa State College, Patty Jo Watson changed course and decided to pursue graduate study in archaeology at the University of Chicago. Working with Robert Braidwood, Watson became adept at using precise scientific methods to assess artifacts left behind by past societies. Early in her career, Watson participated in the excavation of a prehistoric society in the Middle East. Later, after marrying philosopher and geologist Richard (Red) Watson, professor of philosophy at Washington University in St. Louis, who introduced her to cave exploration, she focused her energies on investigating the prehistory of caves.

Watson took a keen interest in Native American cave explorers in Kentucky, especially in the Mammoth Cave system, the longest network of caves in the world, with approximately three hundred and fifty miles of interconnected passageways. The

system includes Salts Cave, Colossal Cave, Unknown Cave, Crystal Cave, and many others. For more than twenty years, Watson and her colleagues surveyed, mapped, and explored the prehistoric artifacts of the Mammoth Cave system. They uncovered evidence that Native American cavers, thought to be purely hunter-gatherers, actually cultivated plants to supplement their diet of game animals and wild plants. This discovery has yielded major insights concerning the development of agriculture in Native North American societies.

Watson, the Edward Mallinckrodt Distinguished University Professor of Anthropology at Washington University, and two of her colleagues have written two major books on the philosophy of archaeology: *Explanation in Archaeology: An Explicitly Scientific Approach* (1971) and *Archaeological Explanation: The Scientific Method in Archaeology*

Patty Jo Watson

(1984). As a result of her contributions to cave archaeology and the prehistory of Native American culture made over a thirty-five-year career, Watson was inducted into the National Academy of Sciences, an honor *The New York Times* described as "second only to the Nobel Prize." She is one of a small number of American women selected for membership in this prestigious organization.

Other archaeologists, called *classical archaeologists,* conduct research on ancient civilizations such as in Egypt, Greece, and Rome.

There are many more areas of specialization within archaeology that reflect area or topical specializations, or the time period on which the archaeologist works (see Figure 1.1). There are, for example, industrial archaeologists, biblical archaeologists, medieval and postmedieval archaeologists, and Islamic archaeologists. Underwater archaeologists work on a variety of places and time periods the world over; they are distinguished from other

archaeologists by the distinctive equipment, methods, and procedures needed to excavate under water.

In a novel approach, still other archaeologists have turned their attention to the very recent past. For example, in 1972 William L. Rathje began a study of modern garbage as an assignment for the students in his introductory anthropology class. Even he was surprised at the number of people who took an interest in the findings. A careful study of garbage reveals insights about modern society that cannot be ferreted out in any other way. Whereas

ANTHROPOLOGISTS AT WORK

BAMBI B. SCHIEFFELIN: LINGUISTIC ANTHROPOLOGIST

As an undergraduate at Columbia University, Bambi Schieffelin was drawn to two fields: anthropology and comparative literature. After spending a summer on a field trip to rural Bolivia and a year in the southern highlands of Papua New Guinea, Schieffelin decided to pursue a doctorate in anthropology, with a specialty in linguistic anthropology. She combined the fields of developmental psychology, linguistics, and anthropology, which prepared her for fieldwork among the Kaluli people in Papua New Guinea. After completing her Ph.D. degree, Schieffelin spent a year teaching at the University of California at Berkeley and also teaching linguistics at Stanford University. Since 1986 she has been teaching at New York University in the department of anthropology.

Schieffelin's work focuses on language use and socialization. She studies how language is learned and acquired by children, and how it is used in various social contexts. She has collaborated with Elinor Ochs to develop innovative approaches to understanding how language use is influenced by socialization. Together they have edited several volumes, including *Language Socialization across Cultures* (1987). In addition, Schieffelin has developed these topics in her own book, *The Give and Take of Everyday Life: Language Socialization of Kaluli Children* (1990).

Through their research on children's language socialization,

Schieffelin and Ochs contributed to a cross-cultural understanding of this process. Until the early 1970s, most of the theories on language and socialization had been drawn from psychological research on middle-class Americans. Schieffelin and Ochs focused instead on language and socialization among many different societies. They emphasized the importance of cultural practices in shaping verbal activities. For example, prior to their research, it was assumed that "baby talk" was the same all over the world. They found, however, that "baby talk" is not universal and is linked to ideas that people have about children.

In her ethnographic research, Schieffelin tape-records and transcribes everyday social interactions in different speech communities. She has carried out research in Papua New Guinea since 1967, focusing not only on language socialization, but on language change and the introduction of literacy into a nonliterate society. In addition to this work in a relatively traditional society, Schieffelin has worked in a number of urban speech communities in the United States, where linguistic diversity is apparent on every street corner. Her research in Philadelphia among Sino-Vietnamese people focused on language socialization and literacy, and her studies of Haitians in New York analyzed language socialization and code-switching practices.

As a linguistic anthropologist, Schieffelin tries to integrate two

Bambi Schieffelin

perspectives. First, she focuses on how the study of language use can lead to insights into how culture is transmitted from generation to generation in everyday social interactions. Second, she analyzes the ways in which language expresses social relationships and cultural meanings across different social and political contexts. Her work represents the most current developments in linguistic anthropology today.

Linguistic anthropologists have broadened their vision of places in which to investigate language use—including legal, medical, scientific, educational, and political arenas—as these contexts are critical to understanding how power is acquired and distributed. They are also studying all varieties of literacy, including television and radio, providing new perspectives on these new forms of global communication.

questionnaires and interviews depend on the cooperation and interpretation of respondents, garbage provides an unbiased physical record of human activity. Rathje's "garbology project" is still in progress and, combined with information from respondents, offers a unique look at patterns of waste management, consumption, and alcohol use in contemporary U.S. society (Rathje & Ritenbaugh, 1984 and the discussion of Rathje's project in Ch. 25).

Linguistic Anthropology

Linguistics, the study of language, has a long history that dovetails with the discipline of philosophy but is also one of the integral subfields of anthropology. **Linguistic anthropology** focuses on the relationship between language and culture, how language is used within society, and how the human brain acquires and uses language. As do other types of anthropologists, linguistic anthropologists seek to discover the ways in which languages are different from one another as well as how they are similar to one another. Two wide-ranging areas of research in linguistic anthropology are structural linguistics and historical linguistics.

Structural linguistics explores how language works. Structural linguists compare grammatical patterns or other linguistic elements to learn how contemporary languages mirror and differ from one another. Structural linguistics has also uncovered some intriguing relationships between language and thought patterns among different groups of people. Do people who speak different languages with different grammatical structures think and perceive the world differently from each other? Do native Chinese speakers think or view the world and life experiences differently from native English speakers? These are some of the questions that structural linguists attempt to answer.

Linguistic anthropologists also examine the connections between language and social behavior in different cultures. This specialty is called **sociolinguistics.** Sociolinguists are interested both in how language is used to define social groups and how belonging to particular groups leads to specialized kinds of language use. In Thailand, for example, there are thirteen forms of the pronoun *I*. One form is used with equals, other forms come into play with people of higher status, and some forms are used when males address females (Scupin, 1988).

Another area of research that has interested linguistic anthropologists is historical linguistics. **Historical linguistics** concentrates on the comparison and classification of different languages to discern the historical links among languages. By examining and analyzing grammatical structures and sounds of languages, researchers are able to discover rules for how languages change over time, as well as which languages are related to one another historically. This type of historical linguistic research is particularly useful in tracing the migration routes of various societies through time, confirming archaeological and paleoanthropological data gathered independently. For example, through historical linguistic research, anthropologists have corroborated the Asian origins of many Native American populations.

Cultural Anthropology or Ethnology

Cultural anthropology, sometimes also known as **ethnology,** is the subfield of anthropology that examines various contemporary societies and cultures throughout the world. Cultural anthropologists do research in all parts of the world, from the tropical rainforests of the Democratic Republic of the Congo and Brazil to the arctic regions of Canada, from the deserts of the Middle East to the urban areas of China. Until recently, most cultural anthropologists conducted research on non-Western or remote cultures in Africa, Asia, the Middle East, Latin America, the Pacific Islands, and on the Native American populations in the United States. Today, however, many cultural anthropologists have turned to research on their own cultures to gain a better understanding of its institutions and cultural values.

Cultural anthropologists or ethnologists (sometimes the terms *sociocultural anthropologist* or *ethnographer* are used interchangeably with *cultural anthropologist* or *ethnologist*) use a unique research strategy in conducting their fieldwork in different settings. This research strategy is referred to as **participant observation,** which involves learning the language and culture of the group being studied by participating in the group's daily activities. Through this intensive participation, the cultural anthropologist becomes deeply familiar with the group and can understand and explain the society and culture of the group as an insider. We

ANTHROPOLOGISTS AT WORK

BRUCE KNAUFT: CULTURAL ANTHROPOLOGIST

Though he planned to major in philosophy as an undergraduate at Yale University, Bruce Knauft took an anthropology course and became fascinated by the idea of living and working in a different cultural environment. He explored this idea by living in an inner-city ghetto in New Haven, Connecticut, and then by working and traveling in southern France. Following graduate work at the University of Michigan, Knauft and his wife, Eileen Cantrell, conducted two years of field research among the Gebusi people of Papua New Guinea from 1980 to 1982. Gebusi lived in a remote lowland rainforest and continued to practice customs such as male initiation, spirit mediumship, sorcery divination, festive dancing in elaborate costume, and ritual homosexuality. Since Gebusi did not speak an outside language, Knauft had to learn the vernacular without the aid of translators. His work focused on symbolism, religion, and politics.

While collecting genealogies and analyzing kinship, Knauft found that a large number of Gebusi had been executed by other Gebusi as sorcerers. Elaborate beliefs in sorcery alternately masked and revealed important causes of violence in Gebusi society. Knauft documented that

Bruce Knauft with Gebusi man

Gebusi had one of the highest rates of homicide documented in the cross-cultural record. His first book, *Good Company and Violence*, explored the tension between spiritual beliefs, social organization, and violence among Gebusi. His second book, *South Coast New Guinea Cultures*, considered the relation between religious beliefs and political systems comparatively across a wide range of so-called "flamboyant" cultures in southern New Guinea.

More generally, Knauft's work combines the interpretive study of symbols and meanings with political patterns of coercion, inequality, or domination by some groups or types of people over others. He has explored this issue in a number of different contexts—including gender, sexuality, ethnicity, state organization, and, at the other end of the spectrum, the origin of language and the development of social organization in early human evolution. On one hand, cultural anthropologists such as Knauft try to appreciate cultures by "getting inside" their worldview and empathizing with it as much as possible. On the other hand, they use a broader explanatory framework to understand how local cultures interact with political and economic

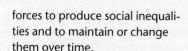

forces to produce social inequalities and to maintain or change them over time.

These issues have deepened in cultural anthropology in recent years. Critics have questioned how anthropologists represent the people they study: What biases and political effects do anthropologists themselves produce or perpetuate? Are anthropologists effectively representing the concerns of local people in a contemporary world? These questions were taken up by Dr. Knauft in his third book, *Genealogies for the Present in Cultural Anthropology*. In this work, Knauft addressed a wide range of critical issues that had intensified since he had himself been a graduate student during the late 1970s. As he consulted a range of recent ethnographies and theories, he developed a new concept of "critical humanism." This notion retains anthropology's long-standing commitment to appreciating cultural diversity but combines it with deeper understanding of social and cultural inequalities—including their relation to anthropologists' own research and writing.

Relatedly, Knauft suggests that anthropology needs stronger representation from different vantage points and especially from larger numbers of minority scholars, women, and researchers born or raised in different countries or world areas. His perspective emphasizes the importance of social and cultural change in a contemporary world. This is especially true in regions, such as New Guinea, which were the focus of classic anthropological fieldwork but have since undergone major changes. These themes are considered in Dr. Knauft's fourth book, a regional study entitled *From Primitive to Post-colonial in Melanesia and Anthropology*.

Applying these themes in his own fieldwork, Knauft went back for a six-month restudy of the Gebusi in 1998. He found that the Gebusi he had previously lived with had relocated next to the government station and had transformed their way of life. Gebusi are now converts to Christianity; they go to church and to the market; their children go to school; and they even have their own community soccer and rugby teams, who play in a local sports league against their erstwhile tribal enemies. Having documented these changes, Knauft is now finishing his latest monograph, *Exchanging the Past*, as well as an edited volume, *Critically Modern*. These works document and put in broader perspective aspects of culture change in relation to inequality in a contemporary world. Along with most cultural anthropologists, Knauft wants to keep cultural anthropology in tune with the changes of a modern world, while appreciating how current developments are influenced by long-standing local beliefs and practices. He remains highly committed to cultural anthropology as a process of rich personal engagement, interpretive understanding, and critical analysis based on empirical documentation.

Since 1985, Dr. Knauft has been a faculty member of Emory University in Atlanta, where he is Samuel C. Dobbs Professor of Anthropology. Emory's Department of Anthropology maintains an active dialogue between the humanistic and the scientific sides of the field. Likewise, Dr. Knauft pursues an interdisciplinary approach to anthropology that encourages ongoing conversation between interpretive and explanatory points of view. He enjoys teaching and has mentored undergraduate and graduate students who have gone on to conduct their own ethnographic research in a number of world areas, including Melanesia, Australia, South Asia, the Middle East, Africa, South America, Eastern Europe, and the United States.

discuss the methods and techniques of cultural anthropologists at greater length in Chapter 14.

The results of the fieldwork of the cultural anthropologist are written up as an **ethnography,** a description of a society. A typical ethnography reports on the environmental setting, economic patterns, social organization, political system, and religious rituals and beliefs of the society under study. This description of a society is based on what anthropologists call *ethnographic data*. The gathering of ethnographic data in a systematic manner is the specific research goal of the cultural anthropologist. Technically, the term *ethnologist* refers to anthropologists who focus on the cross-cultural aspects of the various ethnographic studies done by the cultural anthropologists. Ethnologists take the data that are produced by the individual ethnographic studies and analyze this data to produce cross-cultural generalizations about humanity and cultures everywhere.

Holistic Anthropology, Interdisciplinary Research, and the Global Perspective

Most anthropologists are trained in all four subfields of anthropology. Because of all the research being done in these different fields (more than three hundred journals and hundreds of books are published every year dealing with anthropological research), no one individual can keep abreast of all the developments across the discipline's full spectrum. Consequently, anthropologists usually specialize in one of the four subfields. Nevertheless, most anthropologists are firmly committed to a **holistic** approach to understanding humankind— a broad, comprehensive account that draws on all four subfields under the umbrella of anthropology. This holistic approach involves the analysis of biological, environmental, psychological, economic, historical, social, and cultural conditions of humanity. In other words, anthropologists study the physical characteristics of humans, including their genetic endowment, as well as their prehistoric, historical, and social and cultural environments. Through collaborative studies among the various specialists in the four subfields, anthropologists can ask broadly framed questions about humanity.

Anthropology does not limit itself to its own four subfields to realize its research agenda. Although it stands as a distinct discipline, anthropology has strong links to other social sciences. Cultural anthropology or ethnology, for instance, is closely related to sociology. In the past, cultural anthropologists examined the traditional societies of the world, whereas sociologists focused on modern societies. Today cultural anthropologists and sociologists explore many of the same societies using similar research approaches. For example, both rely on statistical and nonstatistical data whenever appropriate in their studies of different types of societies.

As we shall discover in later chapters, cultural anthropology also overlaps the fields of psychology, economics, and political science. Cultural anthropologists draw on psychology when they assess the behavior of people in other societies. Psychological questions bearing on perception, learning, and motivation all figure in ethnographic fieldwork. Additionally, cultural anthropologists or ethnologists probe the economic and political behavior and thought of people in various societies, using these data for comparative purposes.

Finally, anthropology dovetails considerably with the field of history, which, like anthropology, encompasses a broad range of events. Every human event that has ever taken place in the world is a potential topic for both historians and anthropologists. Historians describe and explain human events that have occurred throughout the world; anthropologists place their biological, archaeological, linguistic, and ethnographic data in the context of these historical developments.

Through the four subfields and the interdisciplinary approach, anthropologists have emphasized a *global perspective*. The global perspective enables anthropologists to consider the biological, environmental, psychological, economic, historical, social, and cultural conditions of humans at all times and in all places. Anthropologists do not limit themselves to understanding a particular society or set of societies but rather attempt to go beyond specific or local conditions and demonstrate the interconnections among societies throughout the world. This global perspective is used throughout this text to show how anthropologists place their findings in the interconnecting worldwide community of humanity.

Applied Anthropology

Although the four major subfields of anthropology (physical anthropology, archaeology, linguistic anthropology, and cultural anthropology) are well established, a fifth major subfield has in recent years come to be recognized. **Applied anthropology** is the use of data gathered from the other subfields of anthropology in an effort to offer practical solutions to problems within modern societies. These problems may be environmental, technological, economic, social, political, or cultural. Many anthropologists are at work attempting to solve different types of problems through the use of anthropological data, as is discussed more thoroughly in Chapter 25.

Anthropological Explanations

A fundamental question faced by all anthropologists is how to evaluate the data that they gather from the particular social, cultural, or biological phenomena they study. Human knowledge is rooted in personal experience, as well as in the beliefs, traditions, and norms maintained by the society people live in. This includes such knowledge as assumptions about putting on warm clothing in cold weather and bringing an umbrella if it is going to rain, for example. Yet it also includes notions about how food should be prepared, what constitutes "appropriate" behavior, and perceptions about the social and cultural roles of men and women.

Religion constitutes another source of human knowledge. Religious beliefs and faith are most often derived from sacred texts, such as the Bible, Qu'ran, and Talmud, but they are also based on intuitions, dreams, visions, and extrasensory perceptions. Most religious beliefs are cast in highly personal terms and, like personal knowledge, span a wide and diverse range. People who do not accept these culturally coded assumptions may be perceived as different, abnormal, or nonconformist by other members of their society. Yet ethnographic and cross-cultural research in anthropology demonstrates that such culturally constituted knowledge is not as general as we might think. This research indicates that as humans, we are not born with this knowledge. Such knowledge tends to vary both among different societies and among different groups within the same society.

Popular perceptions about other cultures have often been based on ethnocentric attitudes. **Ethnocentrism** is the practice of judging another society by the values and standards of one's own society. To some degree, ethnocentrism is a universal phenomenon. As humans learn the basic values, beliefs, and norms of their society, they tend to think of their own culture as preferable, ranking other cultures as less desirable. Members of a society may be so committed to their own cultural traditions that they cannot conceive of any other way of life. They often view other cultural traditions as strange or alien, perhaps even inferior, crazy, or immoral.

Such deeply ingrained perceptions are difficult to escape, even for anthropologists. Nineteenth-century anthropologists, for example, often reinforced ethnocentric beliefs about other societies. The twentieth century saw the co-opting of anthropological data to serve specific political and social ends. In the twentieth century, however, anthropologists increasingly began to recognize the biases that prevented the interpretation of other cultures in more valid, systematic ways.

The Scientific Method

Given the preceding concerns, it is critical to understand how anthropological interpretations are evaluated. In contrast to personal knowledge and religious faith, anthropological knowledge is not based on traditional wisdom or revelations. Rather, anthropologists employ the **scientific method,** a logical system used to evaluate data derived from systematic observation. Researchers rely on the scientific method to investigate both the natural and the social worlds because the approach allows them to make claims about knowledge and to verify those claims with systematic, logical reasoning. Through critical thinking and skeptical thought, scientists strive to suspend judgment about any claim for knowledge until it has been verified.

Testability and *verifiability* lie at the core of the scientific method. There are two ways of developing testable propositions: the inductive method and the deductive method. In the **inductive method,** the scientist first makes observations and collects

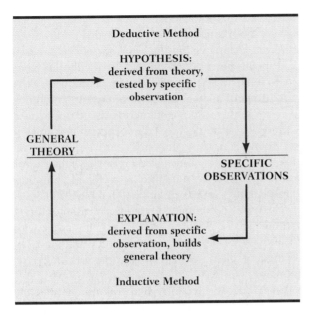

Deductive Method

HYPOTHESIS:
derived from theory,
tested by specific
observation

**GENERAL
THEORY**

**SPECIFIC
OBSERVATIONS**

EXPLANATION:
derived from specific
observation, builds
general theory

Inductive Method

FIGURE 1.2   Deductive and inductive research methods.

data (see Figure 1.2). Many of the data collected are referred to as variables. A **variable** is any piece of data that changes from case to case. For example, a person's height, weight, age, and sex all constitute variables. Researchers use the observations about different variables to develop hypotheses about the data. A **hypothesis** is a testable proposition concerning the relationship between particular sets of variables in the collected data. The practice of testing hypotheses is the major focus of the scientific method, as scientists test one another's hypotheses to confirm or refute them. If a hypothesis is found to be valid, it may be woven together with other hypotheses into a more general theory. **Theories** are statements that explain hypotheses and observations about natural or social phenomena. Because of their explanatory nature, theories often encompass a variety of hypotheses and observations. One of the most comprehensive theories in anthropology is the theory of evolution (see Chapter 3). This theory helps explain a diversity of hypotheses about biological and natural phenomena, as well as discoveries by paleoanthropologists and geneticists.

In contrast to the inductive method, the **deductive method** of scientific research begins with a general theory from which scientists develop testable hypotheses. Data are then collected to evaluate these hypotheses. Initial hypotheses are sometimes referred to as "guesstimates" because they may be based on guesswork by the scientist. These hypotheses are tested through experimentation and replication. As with the inductive method, the testing and retesting of hypotheses and theories is used to ensure the reliability of observations made.

Through these methods researchers do not arrive at absolute truths. Theories may be invalidated or falsified by contradictory observations. Yet even if numerous observations and hypotheses suggest a particular theory is true, the theory always remains open to further testing and evaluation. The systematic evaluation of hypotheses and theories enables scientists to state their conclusions with a certainty that cannot be applied to personal and culturally construed knowledge.

Despite the thoroughness and verification that characterize the research, anthropological explanations have limitations. Unlike conclusions drawn in the natural sciences, anthropological knowledge is frequently presented as tentative and hypothetical because the conclusions are based on assumptions and presuppositions about the myriad variables that affect human thought and behavior. The complexities of the phenomena being studied make it difficult to assess all of the potential variables, and disagreements about interpretations are common. The point here, however, is not that progress is impossible. Anthropological evidence can be verified or discarded by making assumptions explicit and weeding out contradictory, subjective knowledge. Poor hypotheses are rejected and replaced by better explanations. Explanations can be made stronger by drawing on independent lines of evidence to support and evaluate theories. This process makes the scientific method much more effective than other means of acquiring knowledge.

Anthropology and the Humanities

The scientific method, however, is not the only means used by anthropologists to study different societies and cultures. Anthropologists also employ a more humanistic-interpretive approach as they study specific cultures in different regions of the world. Think of this analogy. When botanists examine a flower, they attempt to understand the different components of the plant within a scientific framework; they analyze the biochemistry and physical aspects of the flower. However, when painters, poets, or novelists perceive a flower, they understand the plant from an aesthetic standpoint. They might interpret the flower as a symbolic phenomenon that represents nature. The scientist and the humanist use different approaches and perspectives when examining the natural world. Anthropologists employ a humanistic-interpretive approach in many circumstances.

James Peacock uses another type of analogy to discuss the difference between the scientific and humanistic-interpretive approach in anthropology (1986). Peacock draws from the field of photography to construct his analogy. He discusses the "harsh light" of the rigor of scientific analysis, including the study of biological and material conditions of a society, versus the "soft focus" used when interpreting the symbols, art, literature, religion, or music of different societies. Peacock concludes that both the "harsh light" and "soft focus" are vital ingredients of the anthropological perspective.

Cultural anthropologists utilize the humanistic-interpretive method as they conduct ethnographic research. However, archaeologists also try to employ these same methods when examining artifacts from ancient societies. When cultural anthropologists or archaeologists examine various practices and institutions in different societies, they often find that an outsider cannot easily comprehend these phenomena. In order to comprehend these different practices and institutions, the cultural anthropologist or archaeologist often has to interpret these phenomena, just as one might interpret a literary, poetic, or religious text. Cultural beliefs and practices may not be easily translatable from one society to another. Cultural anthropologists or archaeologists frequently find practices and institutions that have meaning and significance only within a specific language and culture. The cultural anthropologist or archaeologist endeavors to understand a cultural practice or institution that may have a rich, deep, localized meaning within the society being examined but is not easily converted into a transcultural or cross-cultural meaning. We focus more thoroughly on this humanistic-interpretive approach in Chapter 13 on anthropological explanations.

Thus, in addition to its interconnections with the natural and social sciences, the discipline of

Ethnomusicologists study the musical traditions of different societies. This photo shows music being played in Mongolia.

anthropology is also aligned with the humanistic fields of inquiry. This is particularly true with respect to the field of cultural anthropology, as these researchers are involved in the study of different contemporary cultures. When participating in the life and experience of people in various societies, ethnologists must confront a multitude of different behaviors and values that may have to be translated and interpreted. As mentioned above, the archaeologist also confronts this type of problem when studying past cultures and civilizations from different regions of the world. Similar issues confront linguistic anthropologists as they translate and understand various languages.

Many anthropologists explore the creative cultural dimensions of humanity, such as myth, folklore, poetry, art, music, and mythology. **Ethnopoetics** is the study of poetry and how it relates to the experiences of people in different societies; for example, a provocative study of the poetry of a nomadic tribe of Bedouins in the Middle East has yielded new insights into the concepts of honor and shame in these societies (Abu-Lughod, 1987). Another related field, **ethnomusicology,** is devoted to the study of musical traditions in various societies throughout the world. Ethnomusicologists record and analyze music and the traditions that give rise to musical expressions, exploring similarities and differences in musical performance and composition. Other anthropologists study the art of particular societies, such as pottery styles among Native American groups.

Studies of fine art conducted by anthropologists have contributed to a more richly hued, global portrait of humankind. Artistic traditions spring up in all societies, and anthropologists have shed light on the music, myths, poetry, literature, and art of non-Western and other remote peoples. As a result, we now have a keener appreciation of the diverse creative abilities exhibited by humans throughout the world. As anthropologists analyze these humanistic and artistic traditions, they broaden our understanding of the economic, social, political, and religious conditions that prevail within these societies.

One fundamental difference exists between the scientific aspect of anthropology and the humanistic-interpretive side. This difference pertains to the amount of progress one can achieve within these two different but complementary enterprises. Science has produced a cumulative increase in its knowledge base through its methodology. Thus, in the fields of astronomy, physics, chemistry, biology, and anthropology there has been significant progress in the accumulation of knowledge. We know much more about these fields of science than our ancestors knew in the fifteenth or nineteenth centuries. As we shall see in Chapter 13 on anthropological explanations, anthropologists today have a much better understanding of human behavior and culture than did anthropologists in the nineteenth century. Through the use of the scientific method, anthropology has been able to make strides in assessing human behavior and cultural developments. In contrast, one cannot discuss the progress in the humanities in the same manner. Myth, literature, music, and poetry have not progressed in the way that scientific explanations have. One certainly cannot say that the literature or music of the twenty-first century has progressed beyond that of Sophocles', Shakespeare's, Dante's, Bach's, or Beethoven's time period. As we shall see, the various humanistic endeavors involving beliefs, myths, and artistic expression in small-scale and ancient civilizations are extremely sophisticated and symbolically complex, and one cannot

assess modern societies as "superior" or more "progressive" in those domains. The same thing, however, cannot be said for the scientific discoveries and developments in such areas as astronomy, physics, chemistry, biology, geology, or anthropology. The scientific knowledge in these areas has definitely become more effective in offering explanations regarding the natural and social world.

Why Study Anthropology?

Many students today question the practical benefits of their educational experience. Hence, you might ask, "Why study anthropology?" First, anthropology contributes to a general liberal arts education, which helps students develop intellectually and personally, as well as professionally. Numerous studies indicate that a well-rounded education contributes to a person's success in any chosen career, and because of its broad interdisciplinary nature, anthropology is especially well suited to this purpose.

Critical Thinking and Global Awareness

In the context of a liberal arts education, anthropology and anthropological research cultivate critical thinking skills. As we noted earlier, the scientific method relies on constant evaluation of, and critical thinking about, data collected in the field. By being exposed to the cultures and lifestyles of unfamiliar societies, students may adopt a more critical and analytical stance toward conditions in their own society. Critical thinking skills enhance the reasoning abilities of students wherever life takes them.

Anthropology also creates an expanding global awareness and an appreciation for cultures other than our own. In this age of rapid communication, worldwide travel, and increasing economic interconnections, young people preparing for careers in the twenty-first century must recognize and show sensitivity toward the cultural differences among peoples, while understanding the fundamental similarities that make us all distinctly human. In this age of cultural diversity and increasing internationalization, sustaining this dual perception of underlying similar human characteristics and outward cultural differences has both practical and moral benefits. Nationalistic, ethnic, and racial bigotry are rife today in many parts of the world, yet our continuing survival and happiness depend on greater mutual understanding. Anthropology promotes a cross-cultural perspective that allows us to see ourselves as part of one human family in the midst of tremendous diversity. Our society needs citizens not just of some local region or group but also, and more importantly, we need world citizens who can work cooperatively in an inescapably multicultural and multinational world to solve our most pressing problems of bigotry, poverty, and violence.

In addition, an anthropology course gives students a chance to delve into a discipline whose roots lie in both science and the humanities. As we have seen, anthropology brings to bear rigorous scientific methods and models in examining the causes of human evolution, behavior, and social relationships. But anthropologists also try to achieve a humanistic understanding of other societies in all their rich cultural complexity. Anthropology casts a wide net, seeking an understanding of ancient and contemporary peoples, biological and societal developments, and human diversity and similarities throughout the world.

Viewing life from the anthropological perspective, students will also gain a greater understanding of their personal lives in the context of the long period of human evolution and development. In learning about behavior patterns and cultural values in distant societies, students question and acquire new insights into their own behavior. Thus, anthropology nurtures personal enlightenment and self-awareness, which are fundamental goals of education.

While these general goals are laudable, the study of anthropology also offers more pragmatic applications (Omohundro, 1998). As seen in the discussion of applied anthropology, all of the traditional subfields of anthropology have areas of study with direct relevance to modern life. Many students have found it useful to combine an anthropology minor or major with another degree. For example, given the increasingly multicultural and international focus of today's world, students preparing for careers in business, management, marketing, or public service may find it advantageous to have some anthropology courses on their résumés. The concepts and knowledge gleaned from anthropology may enable students to find practical applications in dealing with issues of cultural and ethnic diversity and multiculturalism on a daily basis. Similarly, policy makers in federal, state, and local governments may find it useful to have an understanding of historic preservation issues and cultural resource management concerns. In education, various aspects of anthropology—including evolution, study of the human past, non-European cultures, and the interpretation of cultural and social phenomena—are increasingly being integrated into elementary and secondary school curricula. Education majors preparing for the classroom can draw on their background in anthropology to provide a more insightful context for some of these issues.

SUMMARY

Anthropology consists of four subfields: physical anthropology, archaeology, linguistic anthropology, and cultural anthropology or ethnology. Each of these subfields uses distinctive methods for examining humanity in the past and in all areas of the world today. Physical anthropologists investigate human evolution and the physical variation of human populations across many geographical regions. Archaeologists study the past by analyzing artifacts (material remains) of past societies. Linguistic anthropologists focus their studies on languages, seeking out historical relationships among languages, pursuing clues to the evolution of particular languages and comparing one language with another to determine differences and similarities.

Cultural anthropologists conduct fieldwork in various societies to examine people's lifestyles. They describe these societies in written studies, called ethnographies, that highlight behavior and thought patterns characteristic of the people studied. In examining societies, cultural anthropologists use systematic research methods and strategies, primarily participant observation, which involves participating in the daily activities of the people they are studying.

Anthropologists draw on the scientific method to investigate humanity, while recognizing the limitations of science in grasping the subtleties of human affairs. Yet anthropology is also a humanistic discipline that focuses on such cultural elements as art, music, and religion. By bridging science and the humanities, anthropology enables us to look at humanity's biological and cultural heritage with a broad perspective.

For students, anthropology creates a global awareness and a deep appreciation of humanity past and present. By evaluating anthropological data, students develop critical thinking skills. And the process of anthropological inquiry—exploring other cultures and comparing them to one's own—sheds light on one's personal situation as a human being in a particular time and place.

QUESTIONS TO THINK ABOUT

1. As an anthropologist on a starship in the twenty-first century, you are a specialist in "first contact" situations. Briefly describe your goals and methods.

2. As an anthropologist, you find out about the existence of a group of humans in the Amazon rainforest that has never been contacted. How would you use the four subfields of anthropology to investigate this human community?

3. How do anthropologists utilize the scientific method in their studies? What are the limitations of the scientific method in anthropological studies?

4. You are talking with a friend who asks, "Why would anyone want to study anthropology? What practical benefits may be gained from taking a course in anthropology?" How would you answer your friend?

5. What is the holistic approach, and how is it related to anthropology, the four subfields, and other disciplines?

KEY TERMS

anthropology
applied anthropology
archaeology
artifacts
cultural anthropology
deductive method
ethnocentrism
ethnography
ethnology
ethnomusicology

ethnopoetics
fossils
historical linguistics
holistic
hypothesis
inductive method
linguistic anthropology
linguistics
middens
paleoanthropology

participant observation
primates
primatology
scientific method
sociolinguistics
structural linguistics
theories
variable

INTERNET EXERCISES

1. Peruse **http://www.wsu.edu:8001/vcwsu/ commons/topics/culture/culture-index. html**. How do the twelve definitions of culture presented by Clyde Kluckhohn compare to the field of anthropology explained in this chapter?

2. After reading the section about archaeology in Chapter 1, look at the following website: **http: //www.pbs.org/wgbh/nova/ubar/tools/**. How does modern high technology help archaeologists do their jobs? Why is remote sensing so valuable a tool?

SUGGESTED READINGS

AGAR, MICHAEL H. 1980. *The Professional Stranger: An Informal Introduction to Ethnography*. New York: Academic Press. This excellent introduction to how ethnologists prepare for fieldwork also presents an insightful autobiographical account of fieldwork conducted in various locations across the United States.

BARFIELD, THOMAS (Ed.). 1997. *The Dictionary of Anthropology*. Oxford: Blackwell. This is a useful source for looking up any of the topics addressed in cultural anthropology. It contains the most current references for most research areas in cultural anthropology.

BOYD, ROBERT, and JOAN B. SILK. 1997. *How Humans Evolved*. New York: W. W. Norton. One of a number of introductory textbooks in physical anthropology. Various sections deal with the fossil record, genetics, primates, and human evolutionary trends.

CHAGNON, NAPOLEON A. 1974. *Studying the Yanomamö*. New York: Holt, Rinehart & Winston. A renowned anthropologist's thorough introduction to ethnological fieldwork. It includes many classic examples of "culture shock" experienced by ethnologists in the course of fieldwork.

DeCORSE, CHRISTOPHER. 2000. *The Record of the Past: An Introduction to Physical Anthropology and Archaeology*. Upper Saddle River, NJ: Prentice Hall. A new, readable introduction to the fields of physical anthropology and archaeology.

DEETZ, JAMES. 1996. *In Small Things Forgotten: The Archaeology of Early American Life*. New York: Bantam, Doubleday Dell. A popular, highly readable overview of historical archaeology in the United States by one of the leading scholars in the field. It discusses the sources of information and special dating methods that can be used by archaeologists studying the recent past, as well as how archaeologists have addressed specific research questions.

FAGAN, BRIAN M. 2003. *Archaeology: A Brief Introduction*, 8th ed. Upper Saddle River, NJ: Prentice Hall. A concise introduction to the field of archaeology. The sophisticated techniques and procedures used by contemporary archaeologists are highlighted.

FEDER, KENNETH L. 2002. *Frauds, Myths and Mysteries: Science and Pseudoscience in Archaeology*, 4th ed. Mountain View, CA: Mayfield. An excellent introduction to how archaeologists evaluate their findings, highlighted with entertaining discussions of several frauds and myths, as well as genuine mysteries about the past.

HICKERSON, NANCY P. 1980. *Linguistic Anthropology*. New York: Holt, Rinehart & Winston. A succinct examination of anthropological linguistics, focusing on the most important topics in this subfield of anthropology.

LETT, JAMES. 1997. *Science, Reason and Anthropology*. Lanham, MD: Rowman and Littlefield. An overview of the scientific and humanistic emphases within anthropology. Lett encourages the use of the scientific method as the most appropriate means of explaining culture and human behavior.

LEVINSON, DAVID, and MELVIN EMBER (Eds.). 1996. *Encyclopedia of Cultural Anthropology*. New York: Henry Holt and Company. This four-volume encyclopedia has extensive essays on the most important research topics in cultural anthropology written by the leading researchers in the discipline.

PEACOCK, JAMES L. 1986. *The Anthropological Lens: Harsh Light, Soft Focus*. Cambridge: Cambridge University Press. In this well-written work, James Peacock introduces the importance of anthropology as a discipline that deepens our understanding of humanity. He demonstrates how the study of anthropology contributes to self-understanding.

POWDERMAKER, HORTENSE. 1966. *Stranger and Friend: The Way of an Anthropologist*. New York: W. W. Norton. A classic autobiographical account chronicling ethnological fieldwork in Africa and the United States. The unique problems and challenges confronting a female ethnologist are addressed in this volume.

SCHICK, KATHY D., and NICHOLAS TOTH. 1993. *Making Silent Stones Speak: Human Evolution and the Dawn of Technology*. New York: Simon & Schuster. An interesting and readable account of more than two decades of research on the origins of human tool manufacture and use, the volume provides a clear illustration of the interdisciplinary, collaborative nature of paleoanthropological research. A book that can be read by both the novice and experienced researcher.

SPERBER, DAN. 1998. *Explaining Culture: A Naturalistic Approach*. Oxford: Blackwell. This text offers a synthetic means of combining a humanistic-interpretive approach and a scientific perspective in the study of culture and the human mind.

2

The Record
of the Past

CHAPTER QUESTIONS

- How can we learn from the past from fossil evidence?

- What is the archaeological record?

- What does the archaeological record tell us about past societies?

- How does historical archaeology differ from ethnoarchaeology?

- What are some of the basic techniques of locating archaeological sites?

- What are the basic techniques of excavation?

- How do archaeologists date their artifacts?

Why study the human past? During the early history of anthropology, the answer to this question was straightforward. The study of fossils and artifacts of the past sprang out of a curiosity about the world and the desire to collect and organize objects. This curiosity was, in part, a reflection of the increasing interest in the natural world that arose with the scientific revolution in the Western world beginning in the fifteenth century (see Chapter 3). For early collectors, however, the object was often an end in itself. Items were placed on shelves to look at, with little or no interest expressed in where the fossils might have come from or what the artifact and associated materials might tell about the people that produced them. Collectors of this kind are called **antiquaries.**

Early antiquarian collections often incorporated many different items in addition to fossils and archaeological materials. For example, the museum of Olaus Wormius, a seventeenth-century Danish scholar, included uniquely shaped stones, seashells, ethnographic objects, and curiosities from around the world, in addition to fossils and ancient stone tools (Daniel, 1981). While these objects were sometimes described and illustrated with great care, they were not analyzed or interpreted to shed light on the evolution of life or the lifeways of ancient humans. Of course, ancient coins, metal artifacts, and jewelry were recognized for what they were, but stone tools and even ancient pottery were generally regarded as naturally occurring objects or the work of trolls, elves, and fairies.

By the late eighteenth century, scholars started to move beyond the simple description of objects to an increasing appreciation of the significance of fossil remains and the material traces of ancient human societies. This appreciation fell within the context of a host of new observations in the natural sciences, including many about the geological record and the age of the earth. In 1797, an English country gentleman named John Frere published an account of some stone tools he had found in a gravel quarry in Suffolk. Although brief, the

CRITICAL PERSPECTIVES

ENGENDERING ARCHAEOLOGY: THE ROLE OF WOMEN IN AZTEC MEXICO

The interpretation of the material record poses a challenge to archaeologists. It provides excellent evidence on some subjects—researchers can readily discuss ancient technology, diet, hunting techniques, and the plan of an ancient settlement—but some topics are more difficult to address. What were the marriage customs, the political system, or the religious beliefs of the ancient inhabitants of a site? These factors are by nature nonmaterial and are not preserved archaeologically. Even documentary records may offer only limited insight on some topics.

In a fascinating study of gender among the Aztec of ancient Mexico, archaeologist Elizabeth Brumfiel utilized both the archaeological and the documentary record to provide new insights into the past (Brumfiel, 1983, 1991). The Aztec civilization was flourishing in central Mexico when the Spanish reached the Americas. It had emerged as the principal state in the region by the fifteenth century, eventually dominating an area stretching from the Valley of Mexico to modern-day Guatemala, some 500 miles to the southwest. The capital, Tenochtitlán, was an impressive

religious center built on an island in Lake Texcoco. The city's population numbered tens of thousands when the Aztec leader, Montezuma, was killed during fighting with Spanish conquistadors led by Hernán Cortés in 1520. Within decades of the first Spanish contact, the traces of the Aztec Empire had crumbled and been swept aside by European colonization.

Records of the Aztec civilization survive in documentary accounts recorded by the Spanish. The most comprehensive is a monumental treatise on Aztec life, from the raising of children to religious beliefs, written by Fray Bernardino de Sahagun. It is the most exhaustive record of a Native American culture from the earliest years of European contact. For this reason it has been a primary source of information about Aztec life and culture.

Sahagun's description of the role of women in Aztec society focuses on weaving and food preparation. Regrettably, as Brumfiel points out, his work offers little insight into how these endeavors were tied to other economic, political, and religious activities. In addition, Sahagun does not comment on some of

his own illustrations, which show women involved in such undertakings as healing and marketing. Interpretations based solely on Sahagun's descriptions marginalize women's roles in production as nondynamic and of no importance in the study of culture change.

To obtain a more holistic view of women in Aztec society, Brumfiel turned to other sources. The Aztecs also possessed their own records. Although most of them were sought out and burned by the zealous Spanish priests, some Aztec codices survive. These sources indicate that textiles were essential as tribute, religious offerings, and exchange. Many illustrations also depict women in food production activities. In addition to various categories of food, the codices show the griddles, pots, and implements used in food preparation.

Independent information on these activities is provided by the archaeological record. For example, the relative importance of weaving can be assessed by the number and types of spindle whorls, the perforated ceramic disks used to weight the spindle during spinning, found on sites. Archaeological indications of

description is tantalizing in terms of the changing attitude toward traces of the past. The stone tools—actually Paleolithic hand axes—were found at a depth of more than twelve feet in association with the bones of extinct animals, in a layer of soil that appeared undisturbed by more recent materials. Frere correctly surmised that the tools were "from a very remote period indeed, even beyond that of the present world" (Daniel, 1981:39). This was a recognition of prehistoric archaeology.

Aztec codex showing women weaving.

dietary practices can be inferred from ceramic griddles, cooking pots, jars, and stone tools used in the gathering and preparation of food.

Brumfiel notes that the most interesting aspect of archaeological data on both weaving and food preparation is the variation. Given the static model of women's roles seen in the documentary records, a uniform pattern might be expected in the archaeological data. In fact, precisely the opposite is true. Evidence for weaving and cooking activities varies in different sites and over time. Brumfiel suggests that the performance of these activities was influenced by a number of variables, including environmental zones, proximity to urban markets, social status, and intensified agricultural production.

Food preparation, essential to the household, was also integral to the tenfold increase in the population of the Valley of Mexico during the four centuries preceding Spanish rule. As population expanded during the later Aztec period, archaeological evidence indicates that there was intensified food production in the immediate hinterland of Tenochtitlán. Conversely, the evidence for weaving decreases, indicating that women shifted from weaving to market-oriented food production. These observations are not borne out at sites further away from the Aztec capital. In more distant sites, women intensified the production of tribute cloth with which the Aztec empire transacted business.

This model provides a much more dynamic view of women's roles in Aztec society. The observations are consistent with the identification of the household as a flexible social institution that varies with the presented opportunities and constraints. It also underscores the importance of considering both women's and men's roles as part of an interconnected, dynamic system.

Brumfiel's research provides insights into the past that neither archaeological nor documentary information can supply on its own. She was fortunate to have independent sources of information that she could draw on to interpret and evaluate her conclusions.

POINTS TO PONDER

1. In the absence of any documentary or ethnographic information, how can archaeologists examine the gender of past societies?

2. Can we automatically associate some artifacts with men or with women?

3. Would interpretations vary in different cultural settings?

The nineteenth century saw the first fossil finds of ancient human ancestors. They included the bones found in the Neander Valley of Germany in 1857, now recognized as an archaic human species, *Homo neanderthalensis*, or Neandertal man (see Chapter 5). Although this was a historic discovery, the significance of the fossil was not realized at the time. Interpretations were diverse. Some scholars correctly interpreted the finds as an early human ancestor, but others variously dismissed the bones

CRITICAL PERSPECTIVES

HISTORICAL ARCHAEOLOGY

Some archaeologists have the luxury of written records and oral histories to help them locate and interpret their finds. Researchers delving into ancient Egyptian sites, the ancient Near East, Greek and Roman sites, Chinese civilization, Mayan temples, Aztec cities, Islamic sites, biblical archaeology, and the settlements of medieval Europe can all refer to written sources, ranging from religious texts to explorers' accounts and tax records.

Why dig for archaeological materials if written records or oral traditions can tell the story? Although such sources may provide a tremendous amount of information, they do not furnish a complete record (Beaudry, 1988; Deetz, 1996). Whereas the life story of a head of state, records of trade contacts, or the date of a

temple's construction may be preserved, the lives of many people and the minutia of everyday life were seldom noted. In addition, the written record was often biased by the writer's personal or cultural perspective. For example, much of the written history of Native Americans, sub-Saharan Africans, Australian Aborigines, and many other indigenous peoples were recorded by European missionaries, traders, and administrators, who frequently provided only incomplete accounts viewed in terms of their own interests and beliefs.

Information from living informants may also provide important information about some populations, particularly societies with limited written records. In recognizing the significance of such nonwritten sources, however,

it is also necessary to recognize their distinct limitations. The specific roles oral traditions played (and continue to play) varied in different cultural settings. Just as early European chroniclers viewed events with reference to their own cultures' traditions, so oral histories are shaped by the worldviews, histories, and beliefs of the various cultures that employ them. Interpreting such material may be challenging for individuals outside the originating cultures. Study of the archaeological record may provide a great deal of information not found in other sources and provide an independent means of evaluating conclusions drawn on the basis of other sources of information (see the box "Engendering Archaeology: The Role of Women in Aztec Mexico"). For example, it has proven particularly useful in

as those of a Cossack soldier, an elderly Dutchman, a powerfully built Celt, or a pathological idiot (Johanson & Edey, 1981:28–29). Information continued to accumulate, however, and by the end of the century, the roots of modern archaeological and paleoanthropological study were well established.

Answering Questions

Few modern archaeologists or paleoanthropologists would deny the thrill of finding a well-preserved fossil, an intact arrow point, or the sealed tomb of a king, but the romance of discovery is not the primary driving force for these scientists. In contrast to popular movie images, modern researchers are

likely to spend more time in a laboratory or in front of a word processor than looking for fossils or exploring lost cities. Perhaps their most fundamental desire is to reach back in time to understand more fully our past. This book deals with some of the major questions that have been addressed by paleoanthropologists and archaeologists: the evolution of the human species, the human settlement of the world, the origins of agriculture, and the rise of complex societies and the state.

Although anthropologists make an effort to document the record of bygone ages as fully as possible, they clearly cannot locate every fossil, document every archaeological site, or even record every piece of information about each artifact recovered. Despite decades of research, only a

assessing change and continuity in indigenous populations during the past 500 years (Rogers & Wilson, 1988; DeCorse, 1998, 2001).

In North America, during the past several decades, an increasing amount of work has concentrated on the history of immigrants from Europe, Asia, Africa, and other world areas who arrived in the last 500 years. Archaeological studies have proven of great help in interpreting historical sites and past lifeways, as well as culture change, sociopolitical developments, and past economic systems (Noel Hume, 1983; Leone & Potter, 1988). Among the most significant areas of study is the archaeology of slavery (Singleton, 1985, 1999). Although living in literate societies, slaves were prohibited from writing and left a very limited documentary record of their own. Archaeological data have been used to provide a much more complete picture of plantation life and slave society.

Archaeologist Merrick Posnansky interviewing the chief of the town of Hani, Ghana in 1983. Researchers can use knowledge gathered from living informants to help interpret archaeologoical finds.

Source: Courtesy of Merrick Posnansky, UCLA.

POINTS TO PONDER

1. What are some different sources of "historical" information—written and orally preserved accounts—that you can think of? How are these different from one another in terms of the details they might provide?

2. Consider a particular activity or behavior important to you (for example, going to school, participating in a sport, or pursuing a hobby). How would evidence of the activity be presented in written accounts, oral histories, and the archaeological record?

minute portion of such important fossil localities as those in the Fayum Depression in Egypt and Olduvai Gorge in Tanzania have been studied. In examining an archaeological site or even a particular artifact, many different avenues of research might be pursued (see the box "Engendering Archaeology: The Role of Women in Aztec Mexico" on pages 22–23). For example, when investigating pottery from a particular archaeological site, some archaeologists might concentrate on the technical attributes of the clay and the manufacturing process (Rice, 1987). Others might focus on the decorative motifs on the pottery and how they relate to the myths and religious beliefs of the people who created them. Still other researchers might be most interested in the pottery's distribution (where it was found) and what this conveys about ancient trade patterns.

Research is guided by the questions about the past that the anthropologist wants to answer. To ensure that appropriate data are recovered to address these questions, the paleoanthropologist or archaeologist begins a project by preparing a **research design,** in which the objectives of the project are set out and the strategy for recovering the relevant data is outlined. The research design must take into account the types of data that will be collected and how those data relate to existing anthropological knowledge. Within the research design, the anthropologist specifies what types of methods will be used for the investigation. Different topical or area specializations require specific background

APPLYING ANTHROPOLOGY

UNDERWATER ARCHAEOLOGY

Sunken ships, submerged settlements, and flooded towns: This wide variety of sites of different time periods, in different world areas, shares the need for specialized techniques to locate, excavate, and study them (Throckmorton, 1987; Greene, 1990). Although efforts were occasionally made in the past to recover cargoes from sunken ships, it was only with the invention and increasing accessibility of underwater breathing equipment during the twentieth century that the systematic investigation of underwater sites became feasible.

A tantalizing example of an underwater archaeological project is the excavation and raising of the preserved remains of the *Mary Rose,* the pride of the young English navy and the flower of King Henry VIII's fleet. The 700-ton warship, which was probably the first English warship designed to carry a battery of guns between its decks, foundered and sank in Portsmouth harbor on a warm July afternoon in 1545. Henry VIII, camped with his army at Southsea Castle, is said to have witnessed the disaster and heard the cries of the crew. In the 1970s, the site of the Mary Rose was rediscovered and was systematically explored by volunteer divers from around the world. The ship produced a spectacular array of over 14,000 artifacts, ranging from massive cannon to musical instruments, famed English longbows, and navigational equipment. Finds from the Mary Rose and the preserved portions of the hull can be seen at the Mary Rose Ship Hall and Exhibition at the H. M. Naval Base, Portsmouth, England.

Most people associate underwater archaeology with sunken ships, and this in fact represents an important part of the subdiscipline. However, natural disasters may also submerge cities and towns. Such was the case of Port Royal, Jamaica, a flourishing trade center and gathering place for pirates during the seventeenth century. In 1692, a violent earthquake and tidal wave submerged or buried portions of the city, preserving a record for future archaeologists. Excavations at the site spanning the last three decades have recovered a wealth of materials from seventeenth-century life (Hamilton & Woodward, 1984).

Finds from beneath the waves have a great deal of relevance for archaeological interpretation. They may provide a record of human settlement during periods of lower sea level. Often artifacts from underwater sites are better preserved and so present a wider range of materials than those from land. Even more important, underwater sites are immune to the continued disturbances associated with human activity that are typical of most land sites. Shipwrecks and sunken cities like Port Royal can be compared to time capsules, containing a selection of artifacts that were in use in a certain context at a specific time. Archaeologists working on land seldom have such clearly sealed archaeological deposits.

POINTS TO PONDER

1. Archaeological excavation on land is a meticulous and careful process. Discuss how excavation and recording methods would have to be modified to conduct archaeological research underneath the water.

2. Given the unique location and preservation found at underwater sites, why might they be more appropriate or important for considering certain types of research questions than land sites?

knowledge or familiarity with specialized techniques (see the boxes "Historical Archaeology" and "Underwater Archaeology"). The anthropologist must also be well grounded in the different theoretical perspectives of anthropology relevant to the research questions. Before going into the field, the researcher must also analyze the existing data, which might include geological surveys, archaeological research reports, descriptions by travelers to the region, and interviews with local inhabitants. These data may provide details about the research site and also help place the fossils or the archaeological sites to be studied in a broad context. Generally, the research design is then reviewed by other anthropologists, who recommend it for funding by various government or private research foundations.

Although this book attempts to provide an overview of some of the techniques used and some current interpretations, new finds and improved methods are constantly changing the amount and kind of information available. New fossils are constantly uncovered and archaeological sites exposed. Each of these discoveries adds to the amount of information available to interpret the past—and to evaluate and revise existing interpretations.

Paleoanthropological Study

Paleoanthropologists study the traces of ancient humans and human ancestors to comprehend the biological evolution of the human species and to understand the lifestyles of these distant relations. As will be discussed in Chapter 5, the behavior, diet, and activities of these early humans were very different from those of modern humans. Determining their behavior, as well as the age of the finds and the environment in which early humans lived, is dependent on an array of specialized skills and techniques. Understanding depends on the holistic, interdisciplinary approach that characterizes anthropology.

As in all anthropological research, a paleoanthropological project begins with a research design outlining the objectives of the project and the methodology to be employed. This would include a description of the region and the time period to be examined, the data that will be recovered, and an explanation of how the proposed research would contribute to existing knowledge. For example, researchers might target geological deposits of a specific location and age for examination because of the potential to discover the origins of the common ancestors of humans and apes (see Chapter 4), the earliest branches on the human lineage, or the fossil record of the first modern humans (see Chapter 5).

The initial survey work for a paleoanthropological project often relies on paleontologists and geologists, who provide an assessment of the age of the deposits within the region to be studied and the likely conditions that contributed to their formation. Clues about the age may be determined through the identification of distinctive geological deposits and associated floral and faunal remains (see the discussion of dating methods and faunal correlation later in the chapter). Such information also helps in the reconstruction of the paleoecology of the region and, hence, the environment in which early human ancestors lived. **Paleoecology** (*paleo,* from the Greek, meaning "old," and *ecology,* meaning "study of environment") is the study of ancient environments.

Based on the information provided by paleontologists and geologists, more detailed survey work is undertaken to locate traces of early humans. Looking for such traces has been likened to looking for a needle in a haystack, except in this case the "looking" involves the scrutiny of geological deposits and the careful excavation of buried skeletal remains and associated material. This stage of the research may draw on the skills of the archaeologist, who is trained to examine the material remains of past societies (see discussion of "Archaeological Excavation" below).

Fossils and Fossil Localities

Much of paleoanthropological research focuses on the locating and study of fossil remains. **Fossils** are the preserved remains, impressions, or traces of living creatures from past ages. They form when an organism dies and is buried by soft mud, sand, or silt (Figure 2.1). Over time this sediment hardens, preserving the remains of the creature within. Occasionally, conditions may be such that actual portions of an organism are preserved—fragments of shell, teeth, or bone. But most fossils have been altered in some way, the decayed parts of bone or shell having been replaced by minerals or surrounding sediment. Even in cases in which fragments of bone or shell are present, they have often been broken or deformed and need to be carefully reconstructed.

FIGURE 2.1   Only a small number of the creatures that have lived are preserved as fossils. After death, predators, scavengers, and natural processes destroy many remains, frequently leaving only fragmentary traces for researchers to uncover.

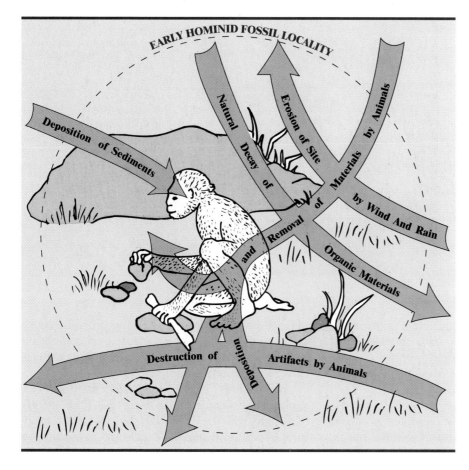

FIGURE 2.2 A variety of different activities and events contributes to the formation of an individual fossil locality. These include activities by the early human ancestors, but also such natural processes as decomposition and decay, erosion by wind and rain, and movement of bones and artifacts by animals. Paleoanthropologists must try to decipher these different factors in interpreting the behavior of early human ancestors.

Despite the imperfection of the fossil record, a striking history of life on earth has survived. Careful study of fine-grained sediments sometimes reveals the preservation of minute fossils of shellfish, algae, and pollen. Improved techniques, such as computer and electronic scanning equipment, have revealed that images of the delicate structure in bones or the interior of a skull may be preserved in a fossil (see the box, "New Perspectives on the Taung Child," in Chapter 5). Scientists have identified some early human ancestors on the basis of very fragmentary remains. Paleoanthropologists working with these finds may report the discovery of a new fossil species, describing the fossils and noting the tenuous nature of their conclusions. As more evidence is uncovered, the original interpretation may be confirmed, reinterpreted, or declared false in light of the new findings.

Paleoanthropologists refer to places where fossils are found as **fossil localities.** These are spots where predators dropped animals they had killed, places where creatures were naturally covered by sediments, or sites where early humans actually lived. Of particular importance in interpreting fossil localities is the **taphonomy** of the site—the study of the variety of natural and behavioral processes that led to the formation of the deposits uncovered. As seen in Figure 2.2, the taphonomy of an individual fossil locality may be complex, and the unraveling of the history that contributed to its formation very challenging indeed. The fossil locality may include traces of the activities of early humans—the artifacts resulting from their behavior, tool manufacture, and discarded food remains, as well as the remains of the early humans themselves. On the other hand, these traces may have been altered by a

Bones and other archaeological remains are often fragmentary and must be excavated with great care. Here, an archaeologist works on one of the approximately 200 bodies—thought to date to pre-Columbian times—found at the construction site for a subway in Mexico City.

host of disturbances, including erosion by wind and rain and destruction and movement by wild animals.

Only a small number of the once-living creatures are preserved in the fossil record. After death, few animals are left to lie peacefully, waiting to be covered by layers of sediment and preserved as fossils. Many are killed by predators that scatter the bones. Scavengers may carry away parts of the carcass, and insects, bacteria, and weather quickly destroy many of the remains that are left. As a result, individual fossil finds are often very incomplete. Some areas might not have had the right conditions to fossilize and preserve remains, or the remains of early human ancestors that may be present might be so fragmentary and mixed with deposits of other ages to be of limited use. Another consideration is the accessibility of fossil deposits. Fossils may be found in many areas, but they often lie buried under deep deposits that make it impossible for researchers to study them and assess their age and condition. In other instances, however, erosion by wind or water exposes underlying layers of rock that contain fossils, thus providing the paleoanthropologist the chance to discover them— even as they are weathering away.

Once a fossil locality is found, systematic excavations are undertaken to reveal buried deposits. In excavating, paleoanthropologists take great pains to record a fossil's exact position in relation to the surrounding sediments; only if the precise location is known can a fossil be accurately dated and any associated archaeological and paleontological materials be accurately interpreted.

After fossils have been removed from the ground, the detailed analysis of the finds begins. This starts with the careful cleaning of fossil remains and associated materials. Fossils are generally preserved in a hardened mineralized deposit, and cleaning may be tedious and time-consuming. Artifacts and faunal remains from the excavations will be labeled and carefully described, and any fossil remains of early humans reconstructed. Drawing on all of the geological, paleontological, archaeological, and physical anthropological information, the paleoanthropologist then attempts to place the discoveries in the context of other discoveries and interpretations. The anatomical characteristics of the fossils of the early humans will be compared to other fossils to try and assess their evolutionary relationship, and the other data will be brought to bear on the reconstruction of the ancient environment and models of the way they lived.

Archaeological Research

Culture is a fundamental concept in the discipline of anthropology. In popular use, most people use the word *culture* to refer to "high culture": Shakespeare's works, Beethoven's symphonies, Michelangelo's sculptures, gourmet cooking, imported wines, and so on. Anthropologists, however, use the term in a much broader sense to refer to a shared way of life that includes values, beliefs, and norms transmitted within a particular society from generation to generation. This view of culture includes agricultural practices, social organization, religion, political systems, science, and sports. **Culture** thus encompasses all aspects of human activity, from the fine arts to popular entertainment, from everyday behavior to the most deeply rooted religious beliefs. It contains the plans, rules, techniques, and designs for living.

Archaeologists are concerned with the interpretation of the cultures of past human societies through examination of the physical traces these societies left behind. The objectives of archaeological research vary tremendously in terms of the time periods, geographical areas, and research questions considered. Many researchers have examined the themes dealt with in this book: the lifestyles of early human ancestors, the initial settlement of the Americas, the origins of agriculture, and the emergence of complex political systems. However, other archaeologists have turned their attention to the more recent past and have examined the archaeological record of European colonization over the past five hundred years and nineteenth-century American society; they have even shed light on modern society by sifting through garbage bags and landfills.

In seeking to understand past cultures through their physical traces, archaeologists face an inherent difficulty. By its very nature, culture is *nonmaterial*—that is, it refers to intangible products of human society (such as values, beliefs, religion, and norms), which are not preserved archaeologically. Hence, archaeologists must rely on the **artifacts**—the physical remains of past societies. This residue of the past is called material culture. **Material culture** consists of the physical products of human society (ranging from weapons to clothing). The earliest traces of material culture are stone tools dating back more than two and a half million years: simple choppers, scrapers, and flakes. Modern material culture consists of all the physical objects that a contemporary society produces or retains from the past, such as tools, streets, buildings, homes, toys, medicines, and automobiles. Archaeologists investigate these material traces of

societies to examine the values, beliefs, and norms that represent the patterned ways of thinking and acting within past societies.

Archaeological interpretation has historically been strongly influenced by cultural anthropology theory (Lamberg-Karlovsky, 1989; Trigger, 1989). *Cultural anthropology*—the study of modern human populations—helps archaeologists understand how cultural systems work and how the archaeological record might reflect portions of these systems. On the other hand, archaeology offers cultural anthropology a time depth that cannot be obtained through observations of living populations. The archaeological record provides a record of past human behavior. Clearly, it furnishes important insights into past technology, providing answers to such questions as "When did people learn to make pottery?" and "How was iron smelted?" However, artifacts also offer clues to past ideals and belief systems. Consider, for example, what meanings and beliefs are conveyed by such artifacts as a Christian cross, a Jewish menorah, or a Hopi kachina figure. Other artifacts convey cultural beliefs in more subtle ways. Everyday items such as the knife, fork, spoon, and plate used in Americans' meals are not the only utensils suitable for the task; indeed, food preference itself is a culturally influenced choice.

The Archaeological Record

The preservation of archaeological materials varies (Schiffer, 1987). Look at the objects that surround you. How long would these artifacts survive if left uncared for and exposed to the elements? As is the case with the fossil record, the archaeological past is a well-worn and fragmentary cloth rather than a complete tapestry. Stone artifacts endure very well, and thus it is not surprising that much of our knowledge of early human lifeways is based on stone tools. Ceramics and glass may also survive very well; but iron and copper corrode, and organic materials, such as bone, cloth, paper, and wood, generally disappear quickly.

In some cases environmental conditions that limit insect and microbial action and protect a site from exposure to the elements may allow for the striking preservation of archaeological materials. Some of the most amazing cases are those in which items have been rapidly frozen. An illustration of this kind of preservation is provided by the discovery in 1991 of the 5,300-year-old frozen remains of a Bronze Age man by hikers in Italy's Tyrol mountains (Fowler, 2000). With the body were a wooden backpack, a wooden bow, fourteen bone-tipped arrows, and fragments of clothing. In other instances, a waterlogged environment, very dry climate, or rapid burial may create conditions for excellent preservation. Such unique instances provide archaeologists with a much more complete record than is usually found.

Places of past human activity that are preserved in the ground are called **archaeological sites.** Sites reflect the breadth of human endeavor. Some are settlements that may have been occupied for a considerable time, for example, a Native American village or an abandoned gold-mining town in the American West. Other sites reflect specialized activities; for instance, a ceremonial center, a burial ground, or a place where ancient hunters killed and butchered an animal.

Much of the archaeologist's time is devoted to the study of artifacts, any objects made or modified by humans. They include everything from chipped stone tools and pottery to plastic bottles and computers. Nonmovable artifacts, such as an ancient fire hearth, a pit dug in the ground, or a wall, are called **features.** In addition to artifacts and features, archaeologists examine items recovered from archaeological sites that were not produced by humans but nevertheless provide important insights into the past. Animal bones, shells, and plant remains recovered from an archaeological site furnish information on both the past climatic conditions and the diet of the early inhabitants. The soil of a site is also an important record of past activities and the natural processes that affected a site's formation. Fires, floods, and erosion all leave traces in the earth for the archaeologist to discover. All of these data may yield important information about the age, organization, and function of the site being examined. These nonartifactual organic and environmental remains are referred to as **ecofacts.**

Of crucial importance to the archaeologist is the context in which archaeological materials are found. An artifact's **context** is its specific location in the ground and associated archaeological materials. Without a context, an artifact offers only a limited amount of potential information. By itself, a pot may be identified as something similar to other finds from a specific area and time period, but it provides no new information. If, however, it and similar pots are found to contain offerings of a particular kind and are associated with female burials, a whole range of other inferences may be made about the past. By removing artifacts from sites, laypersons unwittingly cause irreparable damage to the archaeological record.

Locating Sites

In 1940, schoolboys retrieving their dog from a hole in a hillside near Montignac, France, found themselves in an underground cavern. The walls were covered with delicate black and red paintings of bison, horses, and deer. The boys had discovered Lascaux Cave, one of the finest known examples of Paleolithic cave art.

Chance findings such as this sometimes play a role in the discovery of archaeological remains, but researchers generally have to undertake a systematic examination, or **survey,** of a particular area, region, or country to locate sites. They will usually begin by examining previous descriptions, maps, and reports of the area for references to archaeological sites. Informants who live and work in the area may also be of great help in directing archaeologists to discoveries.

Of course, some archaeological sites are more easily located than others; the great pyramids near Cairo, Egypt; Stonehenge in southern England; and the Parthenon of Athens have never been lost. Though interpretations of their precise use may differ, their impressive remains are difficult to miss. Unfortunately, many sites, particularly some of the more ancient, are more difficult to locate. The settlements occupied by early humans were usually small, and only ephemeral traces are preserved in the ground. In many instances they may be covered under many feet of sediment. Examination of the ground surface may reveal scatters of artifacts or discolorations in the soil, which provide clues to buried deposits. Sometimes nature inadvertently helps archaeologists, as erosion may expose sites. Archaeologists can also examine road cuts, building projects, and freshly plowed land for archaeological materials.

In the field, an archaeologist defines what areas will be targeted for survey. These areas will be determined by the research design but also by

 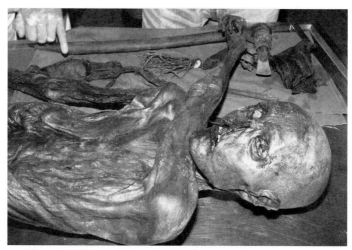

In some cases, environmental conditions may allow for amazing preservation, as illustrated by the 4,000-year-old naturally mummified remains of a woman from arid hills near the Chinese city of Urumqi (left), and the 5,300-year-old frozen remains of a man found in Italy's Tyrol mountains (above).

environmental and topographical considerations, as well as the practical constraints of time and money. Archaeological surveys can be divided into *systematic* and *unsystematic* approaches (Renfrew & Bahn, 1996). The latter is simpler, the researcher simply walking over trails, riverbanks, and plowed fields in the survey area and making notes of any archaeological material observed. This approach avoids the problem of climbing through thick vegetation or rugged terrain. Unfortunately, it may also produce a biased sample of the archaeological remains present; ancient land uses might have little correspondence with modern trails or plowed fields.

Researchers use many different methods to ensure more systematic results. In some instances, a region, valley, or site is divided into a *grid,* which is then walked systematically. In other instances, transects may provide useful information, particularly where vegetation is very thick. In this case, a straight line, or *transect,* is laid out through the area to be surveyed. Fieldworkers then walk along this line, noting changes in topography, vegetation, and artifacts.

Subsurface Testing and Survey Because many archaeological sites are buried in the ground, many surveys incorporate some kind of subsurface testing. This may involve digging auger holes or shovel test pits at regular intervals in the survey, the soil from which is examined for any traces of archaeological material. This technique may provide important information on the location of an archaeological site, its extent, and the type of material represented.

Today many different technological innovations allow the archaeologist to prospect for buried sites without lifting a spade. The utility of these tools can be illustrated by the magnetometer and resistivity meter. The **proton magnetometer** is a sensor that can detect differences in the soil's magnetic field caused by buried features and artifacts. A buried foundation will give a different reading than an ancient road, both being different from the surrounding undisturbed soil. As the magnetometer is systematically moved over an area, a plan of buried features can be created.

Electrical **resistivity** provides similar information, though it is based on a different concept. A resistivity meter is used to measure the electrical current passing between electrodes that are placed in the ground. Variation in electrical current indicates differences in the soil's moisture content, which in turn reflects buried ditches, foundations, or walls, which retain moisture to varying degrees.

Although at times yielding spectacular results, techniques such as magnetometer and resistivity surveys are not without their limitations. Buried metal at a site may confuse the magnetic readings of other materials, and a leaking hose wreaks havoc with a resistivity meter. Both techniques may produce confusing patterns as a result of shallowly buried geological features such as bedrock.

Remote Sensing   An archaeologist was once heard to say that "one ought to be a bird to be a field archaeologist," and indeed, the perspective provided by **aerial photography** is a boon to archaeologists (Daniel, 1981:165). Experiments with aerial photography occurred prior to World War I, but it was during the war that its potential importance to archaeological surveys was recognized. Pilots noticed that some sites, invisible on the ground, were dramatically illustrated from the air. The rich organic soils found in archaeological sites, subtle depressions in the ground surface, or slight differences in vegetation resulting from buried features may be dramatically illustrated in aerial photographs. More recent technological innovations, such as the use of infrared, false color photography, help identify differences in vegetation and make abandoned settlements and patterns of past land use more apparent. Aerial photography has proven very important in locating sites, but it is also of particular use in mapping and interpretation (Kruckman, 1987).

Of less use to archaeologists are photographs taken from extremely high altitudes by satellites or space shuttles (Ebert, 1984). Often the scale of these pictures and their cost make them of limited immediate use. A striking application of such sophisticated techniques, however, is illustrated by some of the research in Mesoamerica. In 1983, National Aeronautics and Space Administration scientists, working with archaeologists, were able to identify ancient Mesopotamian and Mayan settlements and farmlands that had not been located with other techniques. *Space imaging radar,* which can detect features buried under six feet of sand, proved helpful in identifying ancient caravan routes on the Arabian Peninsula. These routes enabled researchers to locate the lost city of Ubar, a trade center that was destroyed around A.D. 100, and the city of Saffara on the Indian Ocean. As space age technology becomes both more refined and more affordable, it may provide an increasingly important resource for archaeologists.

Archaeological Excavation

Archaeological surveys provide invaluable information about the past. The distribution of sites on the landscape offers knowledge about the use of natural resources, trade patterns, and political organization. Surveys also help define the extent of specific sites and allow for a preliminary assessment of their age and function. These data are invaluable in interpreting regional developments and how individual sites form part of a larger picture. However, depending on the project's research objectives, an archaeologist may want more detailed information about individual sites. Once an archaeological site has been located, it may be targeted for systematic archaeological excavation (Figure 2.3).

Excavation is costly, time-consuming, and also destructive. Once dug up, an archaeological site is gone forever; it can be "reassembled" only through the notes kept by the archaeologist. For this reason, archaeological excavation is undertaken with great care. Although picks and shovels may occasionally come into play, the tools used most commonly are the trowel, whisk broom, and dustpan. Different techniques may be required for different kinds of sites. For example, more care might be taken in

Satellite photo of the Nile River in Egypt illustrates the stark contrast between the river's floodplain and the surrounding desert. At the southern edge of the image is Luxor, which includes the ruins of the ancient Egyptian city of Thebes. Archaeologists are increasingly able to use space-age technology to locate archaeological features.

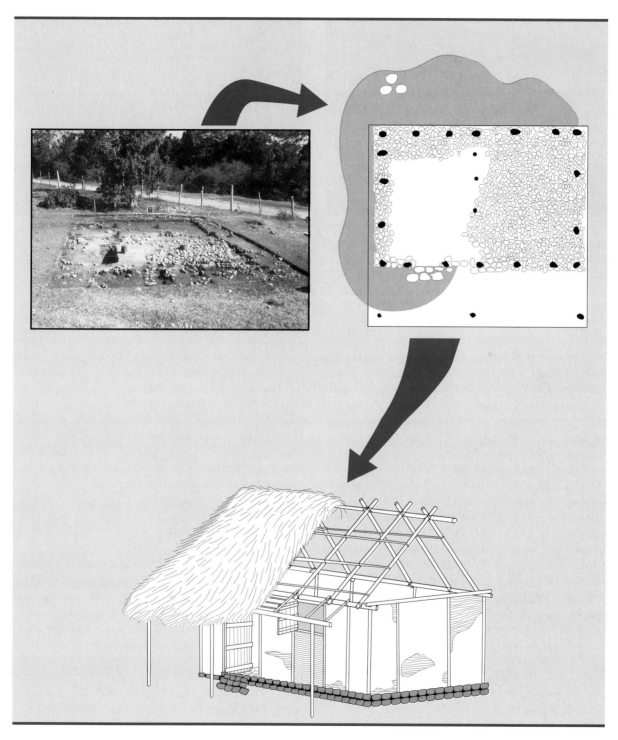

FIGURE 2.3 Excavation, archeological plan, and artist's reconstruction of an eighteenth-century slave cabin at Seville Plantation, St. Anne's, Jamaica. The meticulous recording of excavated artifacts and features allows archaeologists to reconstruct the appearance of past settlements. In this case, eighteenth-century illustrations and written descriptions helped the artist add features, such as the roof, that were not preserved archeologically.

Source: Courtesy of Douglas V. Armstrong, Syracuse University.

Aerial photography often allows the identification of archaeological sites that may be invisible on the ground. This aerial photograph of a recently plowed cornfield in Perry County, southern Illinois, led to the discovery of the Grier Site. Subsequent excavation revealed that the site had been occupied from the Archaic to the Mississippian; the burials date to about 1000 B.C.

Source: Courtesy of Larry Kruckman, Indiana University, Pennsylvania.

excavating the remains of a small hunting camp than a nineteenth-century house in an urban setting covered with tons of fill. On underwater sites, researchers must contend with recording finds using specialized techniques, while wearing special breathing apparatus (see the boxes "Underwater Archaeology" and "George Fletcher Bass: Underwater Archaeologist"). Nevertheless, whatever the site, the archaeologist carefully records the context of each artifact uncovered, each feature exposed, and any changes in surrounding soil.

Work usually begins with the clearing of the site and the preparation of a detailed site plan. A grid is placed over the site. This is usually fixed to a **datum point,** some permanent feature or marker that can be used as a reference point and will allow the excavation's exact position to be relocated. As in the case of other facets of the research project, the research design determines the areas to be excavated. Excavations of *midden* deposits, or ancient trash piles, often provide insights into the range of artifacts at a site, but excavation of dwellings might provide more information into past social organization, political organization, and socioeconomic status.

A question often asked archaeologists is how deep they have to dig to "find something." The answer is, "Well, that depends." The depth of any given archaeological deposit is contingent on a wide range of variables, including the type of site,

how long it was occupied, the types of soil represented, and the environmental history of the area. In some cases artifacts thousands or even hundreds of thousands of years old may lie exposed on the surface. In other cases, flooding, burial, or cultural activities may cover sites with thick layers of soil. A clear illustration of this is seen in *tells* (settlement mounds) in the Near East, which sometimes consist of archaeological deposits covering more than 100 square acres many feet deep.

Dating Methods

How old is it? This simple question is fundamental to the study of the past. Without the ability to order temporally the developments and events that occurred in the past, there is no way to assess evolutionary change, cultural developments, or technological innovations. Paleoanthropologists and archaeologists employ many different dating techniques. Some of these are basic to the interpretation of both the fossil record and archaeological sites. Others are more appropriate for objects of certain ages or for particular kinds of materials (for example, volcanic stone, as opposed to organic material). Hence, certain techniques are more typically associated with archaeological research than paleoanthropological research, and vice versa.

ANTHROPOLOGISTS AT WORK

GEORGE FLETCHER BASS: UNDERWATER ARCHAEOLOGIST

George Fletcher Bass is one of the pioneers of underwater archaeology—a field that he actually didn't set out to study and, indeed, a field that was virtually unrecognized as a discipline when he entered it. Bass began his career with a master's degree in Near Eastern archaeology at Johns Hopkins University, which he completed in 1955. He then attended the American School of Classical Studies at Athens and excavated at the sites of Lerna, Greece, and Gordion, Turkey. Following military service in Korea, Bass began his doctoral studies in classical archaeology at the University of Pennsylvania. It was there, in 1960, that he was asked by Professor Rodney S. Young if he would learn to scuba dive in order to direct the excavation of a Bronze Age shipwreck discovered off Cape Geldonya, Turkey. Bass's excavations of this site were the first time an ancient shipwreck was excavated in its entirety under the water.

During the 1960s, Bass went on to excavate two Byzantine shipwrecks off Yassi Ada, Turkey. At these sites he developed a variety of specialized methods for underwater excavation, including new mapping techniques, a submersible decompression chamber,

and a two-person submarine. In 1967, his team was the first to locate an ancient shipwreck using side-scanning sonar. In addition to setting standards for underwater archaeological research, these excavations captured popular imagination and revealed shipwrecks as time capsules containing a spectacular array of artifacts, many unrecovered from terrestrial sites (Throckmorton, 1962; Bass, 1963, 1973).

After completing his doctorate in 1964, Bass joined the faculty at the University of Pennsylvania. He remained there until 1973, when he left to found the Institute of Nautical Archaeology (INA), which has been affiliated with Texas A&M University since 1976. Under his guidance, the INA has become one of the world's premier programs in underwater archaeology. The institute has conducted research throughout the world on shipwrecks and sites of a diversity of time periods. Bass has continued to focus on shipwrecks in Turkey, where he is an honorary citizen of the town of Bodrum. Some of his more recent projects include a fourteenth-century B.C. wreck with a cargo of copper, ivory, tin, glass, and ebony, and a medieval ship with a large cargo of Islamic glass.

Dr. George Bass, after a dive.

George Bass is currently the George T. and Gladys H. Abell Distinguished Professor of Nautical Archaeology and holder of the George O. Yamini Family Chair in Nautical Archaeology at Texas A&M University. He has written or edited seven books and is the author of more than one hundred articles. Because of his unique contribution to underwater archaeology, Bass has been widely recognized and has received awards from the National Geographic Society, the Archaeological Institute of America, and the Society for Historical Archaeology.

In any given project, several different dating techniques are used in conjunction with one another to independently validate the age of the materials being examined. Dating methods can be divided into two broad categories that incorporate a variety of specific dating techniques: relative and absolute dating. Accurate dating of discoveries depends on both methods.

Relative Dating

Relative dating refers to dating methods that determine whether one particular fossil, artifact, fossil locality, or site dates before or after another. The most basic relative dating method is **stratigraphic dating,** a technique pioneered by the seventeenth-century Danish scientist Niels Stensen (1638–1687). Today Stensen is better known by the latinized version of his name, Nicholas Steno. Steno was the first person to suggest that the hard rock where fossils are found had once been soft sediments that had gradually solidified. Because sediments had been deposited in layers, or *strata,* Steno argued that each successive layer was younger than the layers underneath. Steno's **law of supraposition** states that in any succession of rock layers, the lowest rocks have been there the longest and the upper rocks have been in place for progressively shorter periods. This assumption forms the basis of stratigraphic dating.

Steno was concerned with the study of geological deposits, but stratigraphic dating is also of key importance in dating archaeological materials (Figure 2.4). An archaeological site presents a complex layer cake of stratigraphic levels representing the accumulation of cultural material, such as trash and housing debris, as well as natural strata resulting from flooding, the decomposition of organic material, and the like. Layers associated with human occupation often accumulate to striking depths.

Like all relative dating methods, stratigraphic dating does not allow researchers to assign an actual numerical age to a fossil or artifact. Rather, it indicates only whether one fossil is older or younger than another within the same stratigraphic sequence. This technique is essential to paleoanthropological and archaeological interpretation because it allows researchers to evaluate *change through time.* However, researchers must take notice of any disturbances that may have destroyed the order of geological or archaeological deposits.

Disturbances in the earth's crust, such as earthquakes and volcanoes, can shift or disrupt stratigraphic layers. Archaeological sites may be ravaged by erosion, burrowing animals, and human activity.

Faunal Succession   One of the first people to record the location of fossils systematically was William Smith (1769–1839), the "father" of English geology. An engineer at a time when England was being transformed by the construction of railway lines and canals, Smith noticed that as rock layers were exposed by the construction, distinct fossils occurred in the same relative order again and again. He soon found that he could arrange rock samples from different areas in the correct stratigraphic order solely on the basis of the fossils they contained. Smith had discovered the principle of **faunal succession** (literally, "animal" succession). A significant scientific milestone, Smith's observations were made sixty years before Darwin proposed his evolutionary theories to explain how and why life forms changed through time.

Since Smith's era, paleontologists have studied thousands of fossil localities around the world. Information on the relative ages of fossils from these sites provides a means of correlating the relative ages of different fossil localities and also casts light on the relative ages of fossils that are not found in stratigraphic context. Placing fossils in a relative time frame in this way is known as **faunal correlation.**

Palynology   Remains of plant species, which have also evolved over time, can be used for relative dating as well. **Palynology** is the study of pollen grains, the minute male reproductive parts of plants. By examining preserved pollen grains, we can trace the adaptations vegetation underwent in a region from one period to another. In addition to helping scientists establish the relative ages of strata, studies of both plant and animal fossils offer crucial clues to the reconstruction of the environments where humans and human ancestors lived.

The FUN Trio   Scientists can determine the relative age of bones by measuring the elements of fluorine, uranium, and nitrogen in the fossil specimens. These tests, which can be used together, make up the *FUN* trio. Fluorine and uranium occur naturally in groundwater and gradually collect in bones after they are buried. Once absorbed, the fluorine and uranium remain in the bones, steadily accumulating

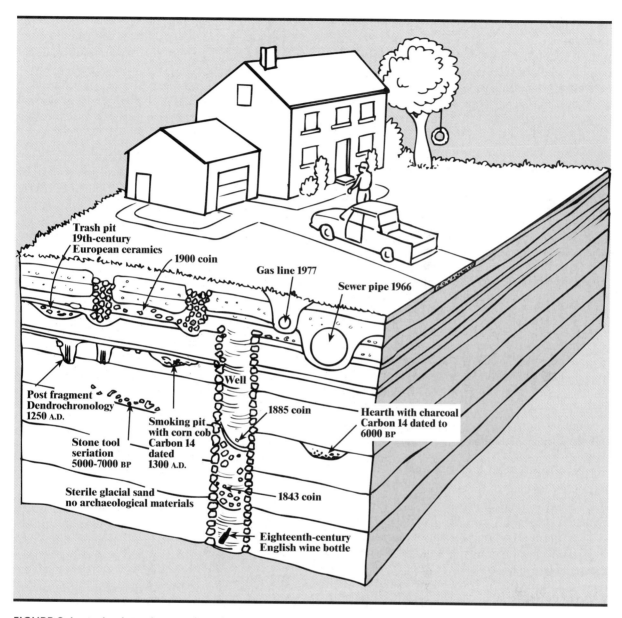

FIGURE 2.4 Archeological materials and the remnants of human occupation often accumulate to striking depth. This hypothetical profile illustrates the potentially complex nature of the archeological record and how different techniques might be combined to date discoveries.

over time. By measuring the amounts of these absorbed elements, scientists can estimate the length of time the bones have been buried. Nitrogen works in the opposite way. The bones of living animals contain approximately 4 percent nitrogen, and when the bones start to decay, the concentration of nitrogen steadily decreases. By calculating the percentage of nitrogen remaining in a fossilized bone, scientists can calculate its approximate age.

The FUN trio techniques all constitute relative dating methods because they are influenced by local environmental factors. The amounts of fluorine and uranium in groundwater differ from region to region, and variables such as temperature and the chemicals present in the surrounding soil affect the rate at which nitrogen dissipates. Because of this variation, relative concentrations of fluorine, uranium, and nitrogen in two fossils from different areas of the world may be similar despite the fact that they differ significantly in age. The techniques are thus of greatest value in establishing the relative age of fossils from the same deposit. To some extent, these methods have been supplanted by more modern, numerical dating methods (see below), but they nevertheless present an important alternative means of validating the relative ages of fossil finds (see "The Piltdown Fraud" in Chapter 5).

Numerical, or Absolute, Dating

During the nineteenth century, scientists experimented with many methods designed to pinpoint the numerical age of the earth itself and the geological epochs. Many of these methods were based on observations of the physical world. Studies of erosion rates, for example, indicated that it had taken millions of years to cut clefts in the earth like the Grand Canyon in the United States. Other strategies were based on the rates at which salt had accumulated in the oceans, the earth had cooled, and geological sediments had formed (Prothero, 1989).

These early approaches were flawed by a limited understanding of the complexity of such natural processes, and therefore they greatly underestimated the earth's age. For example, Sir Arthur Keith, a prominent English paleoanthropologist of the early twentieth century, posited that the Eocene epoch began approximately 2 million years ago. Yet modern estimates place the Eocene between 55 million and 34 million years ago. In contrast to these early researchers, today's scientists have a wide variety of highly precise methods of dating paleontological and archaeological finds.

Several of the most important numerical dating techniques used today are based on *radioactive decay,* a process in which *radioisotopes,* unstable atoms of certain elements, break down, or decay, by throwing off subatomic particles and energy over time. These changes can produce either a different isotope of the same element or another element entirely. In terms of dating, the significance of radioactive decay is that it occurs at a set rate

regardless of environmental conditions, such as temperature fluctuations, amount of ground water, or the depth below surface. The amount of decay that has taken place can be measured with a device called a *mass spectrometer.* Hence, by calculating how much decay has occurred in a geological specimen or an artifact, scientists can assign to it a numerical age.

Radiocarbon Dating   The technique of using radioactive decay as a dating tool was pioneered by Willard Libby, who received the 1960 Nobel Prize in chemistry for his work on radiocarbon dating. **Radiocarbon dating,** as its name implies, is based on the decay of carbon 14 ($_{14}$C), a radioactive (unstable) isotope of carbon that eventually decays into nitrogen. The concentration of carbon 14 in a living organism is comparable to that of the surrounding atmosphere and is absorbed by the organism as carbon dioxide (CO_2). When the organism dies, the intake of CO_2 ends. Thus, as the carbon 14 in the organism begins to decay, it is not replaced by additional radiocarbon from the atmosphere.

Like other radioisotopes, carbon 14 decays at a known rate that can be expressed in terms of its *half-life,* the interval of time required for half of the radioisotope to decay. The half-life of carbon 14 is 5,730 years. By measuring the quantity of carbon 14 in a specimen, scientists can determine the amount of time that has elapsed since the organism died.

Radiocarbon dating is of particular importance to archaeologists because it can be used to date organic matter, including fragments of ancient wooden tools, charcoal from ancient fires, and skeletal material. The technique has generally been used to date materials less than 50,000 years old. The minuscule amounts of radiocarbon remaining in materials older than this make measurement difficult. However, refined techniques have produced dates of up to 80,000 years old (Prothero, 1989). Because of the time period represented, radiocarbon is of limited use to paleoanthroplogists who may be dealing with fossil finds millions of years old. However, radiocarbon dating has become of great importance to archaeologists who deal with materials of more recent age.

Potassium-Argon and Fission-Track Dating   Several isotopes that exhibit radioactive decay are present in rocks of volcanic origin. Some of these isotopes decay at very slow rates over billions of years. Two radiometric techniques that have proven of particular help to paleoanthropologists and archaeologists studying early human ancestors are potassium-argon and fission-track dating. These methods do not date fossil material itself. Rather, they can be used to date volcanic ash and lava flows, which are associated with fossil finds. Fortunately, many areas that have produced fossil discoveries were volcanically active in the past and can be dated by using these techniques. These methods have been employed at such fossil localities as the Fayum Depression in Egypt (see Chapter 4) and Olduvai Gorge in Tanzania (see Chapter 5).

In **potassium-argon dating,** scientists measure the decay of a radioisotope of potassium, known as potassium 40 ($_{40}K$), into an inert gas, argon (Ar). During the intense heat of a volcanic eruption, any argon present in a mineral is released, leaving only the potassium. As the rock cools, the potassium 40 begins to decay into argon. Because the half-life of $_{40}K$ is 1.3 billion years, the potassium-argon method can be used to date very ancient finds as well as more recent deposits. Although this technique has been used successfully to date rocks as young as 10,000 years old, it is most effective on samples dating between 1 million and 4.5 billion years old (Prothero, 1989).

Fission-track dating is based on the decay of a radioactive isotope of uranium ($_{238}U$), which releases energy at a regular rate. In certain minerals, microscopic scars, or tracks, from the decay process are produced. By counting the number of tracks in a sample, scientists can estimate fairly accurately when the rocks were formed. Fission-track dating is used to determine the age of geological samples between 300,000 and 4.5 billion years old, and thus it can provide independent confirmation on the age of strata dated using potassium-argon dating. Although this is generally a technique of more use to paleoanthropologists, dates have been obtained on glass and pottery glazes less than 2,000 years old, and so presents a technique of potential help to archaeologists studying the more recent past (Brill, 1964).

Dendrochronology Dendrochronology is a unique type of numerical dating based on the annual growth rings found in some species of trees (Figure 2.5). Because a ring corresponds to a single year, the age of a tree can be determined by counting the number of rings. This principle was recognized as early as the late eighteenth century by the Reverend Manasseh Cutler, who used it to infer that a Native American mound site in Ohio was at least 463 years old. The modern science of dendrochronology was pioneered in the early twentieth century by A. E. Douglass using well-preserved wood from the American Southwest.

Today tree-ring dating is a great deal more sophisticated than counting tree rings. In addition to recording annual growth, tree rings also preserve a record of environmental history: thick rings represent years when the tree received ample rain; thin rings denote dry spells. In more temperate regions, the temperature and the amount of sunlight may affect the thickness of the rings. Trees of the same species in a localized area will generally show a similar pattern of thick and thin rings. This pattern can then be overlapped with patterns from successively older trees to build up a master dendrochronology sequence. In the American Southwest, a sequence using the bristlecone pine has now been extended to almost 9,000 years ago. Work on oak sequences in Ireland and Germany has been used to create a master dendrochronology sequence dating back over 10,000 years.

The importance of this method is manifest. Dendrochronology has proven of great significance in areas such as the American Southwest, where the dry conditions often preserve wood. The growth rings in fragments of wood from archaeological sites can be compared to the master dendrochronology sequence, and the date the tree was cut down can be calculated. Even more important, dendrochronology provides an independent means of evaluating radiocarbon dating. Fragments dated by both techniques confirm the importance of radiocarbon as a dating method. However, wood dated by both techniques indicates that carbon 14 dates more than 3,000 years old are increasingly younger than their actual age. The reason for this lies in the amount of carbon 14 in the earth's atmosphere. Libby's initial calculations were based on the assumption that the concentration was constant over time, but we now know that it has varied. Dendrochronologies have allowed scientists to correct, or calibrate, radiocarbon dates, rendering them more accurate.

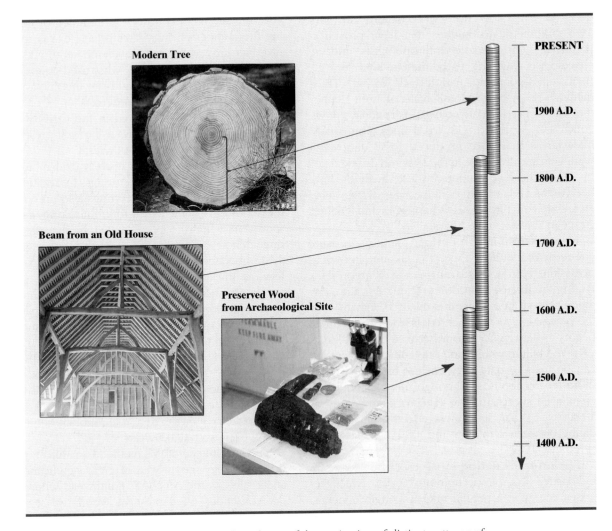

FIGURE 2.5 Dendrochronology is based on the careful examination of distinct patterns of thin and thick growth rings, which preserve a record of a region's environmental history. As illustrated here, samples of wood from different contexts may be pieced together to provide a master dendrochronology. Fragments of wood from archeological sites can then be compared to this dendrochronology to determine the period in which the tree lived.

Seriation

Unlike the dating techniques discussed thus far, which utilize geological, chemical, or paleontological principles, seriation is based on the study of archaeological materials. Simply stated, **seriation** is a dating technique based on the assumption that any particular artifact, attribute, or style will appear, gradually increase in popularity until it reaches a peak, and then progressively decrease. Archaeologists measure these changes by comparing the relative percentages of certain attributes or styles in different stratigraphic levels in a site or in different sites. Using the principle of increasing and decreasing popularity of attributes, archaeologists are able to place categories of artifacts in a relative chronological order.

The principles of seriation can be illustrated by examining stylistic changes in New England gravestones of the seventeenth, eighteenth, and nineteenth centuries. Unlike many artifacts, gravestones can be closely dated. To validate the principle of

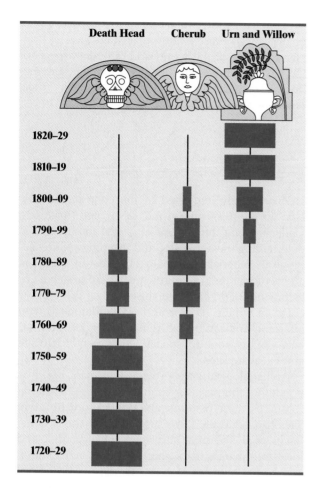

FIGURE 2.6   The seriation of gravestones in a New England cemetery by archeologist James Deetz illustrates the growth and gradual decline in popularity of a closely dated series of decorative motifs.

Source: From *In Small Things Forgotten* by James Deetz. Copyright © 1996 by James Deetz. Used by permission of Doubleday, a division of Random House, Inc.

seriation, archaeologist James Deetz charted how colonial gravestone designs changed through time. His study of gravestones in Stoneham Cemetery, Massachusetts, as illustrated in Figure 2.6, demonstrates the validity of the method. In the course of a century, death's-head motifs were gradually replaced by cherub designs, which in turn were replaced by urn and willow decorations. The study also illustrates how local variation in beliefs and trade patterns may influence the popularity of an attribute.

Interpretations about the Past

Views of the past are, unavoidably, tied to the present. As we discussed in Chapter 1, anthropologists try to validate their observations by being explicit about their assumptions. Prevailing social and economic conditions, political pressures, and theoretical perspectives all may affect interpretation. During the early twentieth century, bits and pieces of physical anthropology, archaeology, and linguistic information were muddled together to support the myth of a superior German race (Daniel, 1981). Gustav Kossina, initially trained as a philologist, distorted archaeological interpretations to bolster chronologies that showed development starting in Germany and spreading outward to other parts of Europe.

Archaeological and historical information was also used to validate racist apartheid rule in South Africa. South African textbooks often proffered the idea that black, Bantu-speaking farmers migrating from the north and white and Dutch-speaking settlers coming from the southwest arrived in the South African hinterland at the same time. This interpretation had clear relevance to the present: Both groups had equal claim to the land. However, over the past two decades, a new generation of archaeologists has knocked the underpinning from this contrived history (Hall, 1988). Archaeological evidence indicates that the ancestors of the black South Africans had moved into the region by A.D. 200, 1,500 years before the initial European settlement.

In these cases, versions of the past were constructed with dangerous effects on the present. More commonly, errors in interpretation are less intentional and more subtle. All researchers carry their own personal and cultural bias with them. Human societies are complex, and how this complexity is manifested archaeologically varies. These factors make the evaluation of interpretations challenging, and differences of opinion frequently occur.

Although there is no formula that can be used to evaluate all paleoanthropological and archaeological materials, there are useful guidelines. As seen in the preceding chapter, a key aspect of anthropological research is a systematic, scientific approach to data. Outmoded, incorrect interpretations can be revealed through the testing of hypotheses and replaced by more convincing observations. The validity of a particular interpretation can be strengthened by the use of independent lines of evidence; if they lead to similar conclusions, the validity of the interpretation is strengthened. Academic books and articles submitted for publication are reviewed by other researchers, and authors are challenged to clarify points and strengthen observations.

In many cases the evaluation of a particular theory or hypothesis must await the accumulation of data. Many regions of the world and different aspects of the past are virtually unstudied. Therefore, any theories about these areas or developments must remain tentative and subject to reevaluation.

SUMMARY

Paleoanthropologists and archaeologists examine different aspects of the human past. Paleoanthropologists concentrate on the evolution of humans as a biological species and the behavior of early human ancestors, whereas archaeologists are concerned with past human cultures—their lifestyles, technology, and social systems—through the material remains they left behind. Researchers examine many different aspects of the past. To ensure that data relevant to the paleoanthropologists' and archaeologists' questions are recovered, projects begin with a research design, which sets out the objectives and formulates the strategy for recovering the pertinent information. Both subdisciplines overlap and utilize experts from other fields to provide a holistic interpretation of the past.

Paleoanthropologists work with fossils, the preserved traces of past life. Places where fossils are found are termed fossil localities. The fossil record is far from complete; only a small portion of the creatures that have lived are preserved. Nevertheless, an impressive record of past life has survived. Careful study and improved technology reveal minute fossils of shellfish, algae, and pollen and images of the delicate structure in bones. Paleoanthropology integrates the fields of geology, paleontology, and archaeology, as well as physical anthropology, to provide a more holistic interpretation of the emergence and the behavior of early human ancestors.

The archaeological record encompasses all the material traces of past cultures. Places of past human activity that are preserved in the ground are called archaeological sites. Sites contain artifacts (objects made or modified by humans) as well as other traces of past human activity and a record of the environmental conditions that affected the site. In studying archaeological materials, archaeologists are particularly interested in the context, the specific location of finds and associated materials. Understanding the context is of key importance in determining the age, uses, and meanings of archaeological materials. Specialized fields of study in archaeology may require special approaches or techniques. For example, historical archaeologists draw on written records and oral traditions to help interpret archaeological remains. Underwater archaeologists require special equipment to locate and excavate sites.

Archaeological sites provide important information about the past: for example, the use of natural resources, trade patterns, and political organization. Sites can be located in many different ways. Often traces of a site may survive on the ground, and local informants, maps, and previous archaeological reports may be of help. To discover sites, archaeologists may survey areas, looking for any indications of archaeological remains. Surface examinations may be supplemented by subsurface testing to identify buried deposits. Technological aids such as the magnetometer or resistivity meter may also help archaeologists identify artifacts and features beneath the ground.

Depending on a project's objectives, archaeological sites may be targeted for excavation. Digging is always undertaken with great care, and information about the work is carefully recorded. Before excavation, a site is divided into a grid, which allows each artifact to be carefully located. The depth of an excavation depends on a number of variables, including the type of site, the length of occupation, the soils present, and the area's environmental history.

Dating of fossils and archaeological materials is of key importance in the interpretation of the past. Without the ability to order finds temporally, there is no way of assessing evolutionary change, technological innovations, or cultural developments. Paleoanthropologists and archaeologists use many different dating techniques, which can be classified as either relative or absolute dating methods. Methods such as stratigraphic dating, faunal succession, and fluorine, uranium, and nitrogen analyses provide only relative ages for finds in the same deposits. Absolute techniques like radiocarbon dating, potassium-argon dating, and dendrochronology can be used to assign actual numerical ages to finds.

Interpretations of the past are inevitably influenced by the present. At times theories have been used to support political ends, as seen in Nazi Germany and the apartheid policies of South Africa. Researchers try to avoid bias by employing systematic, scientific methodology. Theories can be revealed as false through testing and replaced by more convincing arguments. These, in turn, can be negated or strengthened by exploring new lines of evidence. Archaeological theories, often derived from cultural anthropology, help archaeologists conceptualize how cultures work and what aspects of a past culture might be preserved archaeologically. Ultimately, this reflection provides a more complete explanation of the dynamics of past cultures and culture change.

QUESTIONS TO THINK ABOUT

1. What are the distinct issues, concerns, and methods that distinguish paleoanthropology and archaeology?

2. How do the archaeological and fossil records differ in terms of their content?

3. What is meant by the term *historical archaeology*? What are some ways in which archaeological research can improve our understanding of history?

4. What are the principal issues that you would address in preparing a research design for an archaeological or paleoanthropological project? What concepts, activities, and logistics would you consider?

5. A great deal of archaeological information can be obtained without moving a single shovelful of dirt. Describe three different methods used by archaeologists to explore sites in the field that are not dependent upon excavation.

6. What are the principal differences between relative and absolute dating? Discuss two methods each of relative dating and absolute dating, describing the advantages and limitations of each.

KEY TERMS

aerial photography
antiquaries
archaeological sites
artifacts
context
culture
datum point
dendrochronology
ecofacts
faunal correlation

faunal succession
features
fission-track dating
fossil localities
fossils
law of supraposition
material culture
paleoecology
palynology
potassium-argon dating

proton magnetometer
radiocarbon dating
relative dating
research design
resistivity
seriation
stratigraphic dating
survey
taphonomy

INTERNET EXERCISES

1. Underwater archaeology as described in the Applying Anthropology box on page 26 is a unique field. Take a look at these two related websites:

   http://www.adp.fsu.edu/ADPMain.html

   http://www.adp.fsu.edu/summer2000/ uwfieldschl.html

   List the requirements to be an underwater archaeologist. What personality traits might be important for this type of work? What are the rewards of underwater archaeology?

2. **http://spirit.lib.uconn.edu/ArchNet**   This site provides a number of hotlinks to other interesting archaeological sites as well as copious information on regional archaeology and access to archaeological data. Here you can find a list of museums around the world that feature new world archaeology, old world archaeology, or exhibits on culture.

SUGGESTED READINGS

DANIEL, GLYN. 1981. *A Short History of Archaeology.* New York: Thames & Hudson. A brief introduction to the history of archaeology by one of the leading scholars on the subject. This volume concentrates on developments in Europe, Africa, and Asia and makes a nice contrast with the Willey and Sabloff volume also listed here.

FERGUSON, LELAND. 1992. *Uncommon Ground: Archaeology and Early African America, 1650–1800.* Washington, DC: Smithsonian Institution Press. A highly readable and interesting account synthesizing archaeological and documentary sources to provide a fuller account of the early history of enslaved Africans in the Americas.

PROTHERO, DONALD R. 1989. *Interpreting the Stratigraphic Record.* New York: W. H. Freeman. An authoritative work on the principal techniques and methods used in dating and interpreting the geological record.

RENFREW, COLIN, and PAUL BAHN. 2000. *Archaeology: Theories, Methods and Practice,* 3rd ed. New York: Thames & Hudson. An introductory text that provides a brief overview of the history of archaeology and a first-rate, understandable survey of the methods and techniques archaeologists use in the field and in the laboratory.

THROCKMORTON, PETER (Ed.). 1987. *The Sea Remembers: Shipwrecks and Archaeology from Homer's Greece to the Rediscovery of the Titanic.* New York: Weidenfeld & Nicholson. A compilation on nautical archaeology by one of the pioneers in the field. It provides an enjoyable, broad survey of the variety of shipwreck sites and discoveries that have been recovered from them.

WILLEY, GORDON R., and JEREMY A. SABLOFF. 1993. *A History of American Archaeology,* 3rd ed. New York: W. H. Freeman. A comprehensive and very readable overview of the origins and development of American archaeology, from the first descriptions of monuments by European explorers to the present theoretical approaches.

CHAPTER

3

Evolution

CHAPTER OUTLINE

CHAPTER QUESTIONS

- How do other cosmologies of human origins differ from the scientific view of evolution?

- In what ways does Darwin's view of evolution differ from Lamarck's?

- How does natural selection work?

- What were Mendel's contributions to our understanding of heredity?

- In what ways has molecular genetics broadened our insights into evolution?

- How do mutations affect the evolutionary process?

- How does the new view of punctuated equilibrium help us understand evolution?

- What is the basic weakness of the so-called scientific creationist approach?

One of the challenges of physical anthropology is to provide insights into the origins of humankind. The fossil record preserves traces of past life on earth, clearly charting a progression of simple one-celled organisms to increasingly diverse forms. A small portion of the fossil evidence relevant to human evolution is presented in Chapters 4 and 5. How did different forms of life appear and new species arise? The biological explanations for this change are the focus of this chapter.

Theories concerning the evolution of life date back to the ancient Greeks, but it was only during the nineteenth century that the first comprehensive theories of evolution were developed. They were made possible through discoveries in many different areas. The acceptance of evolutionary theory is based on research in many fields. Indeed, the value of evolutionary theory is its utility as a consistent explanation for a wide variety of phenomena. Before examining the scientific basis for our understanding of evolution, it is useful to consider other explanations of human origins.

Cosmologies and Human Origins

The most profound human questions are the ones that perplex us the most. Who are we? Where did we come from? Why are we here? What is our place in the universe? These questions have been shared by all peoples throughout history. Most cultures have developed sophisticated explanations that provide answers to these fundamental questions. **Cosmologies** are conceptual frameworks that present the universe (the *cosmos*) as an orderly system. They often include answers to these basic questions about the place of humankind in the universe and about human origins, usually considered the most sacred of all cosmological conceptions.

Cosmologies account for the ways in which supernatural beings or forces formed the earth and people. They are transmitted from generation to generation through ritual, education, laws, art, and language. For example, the Navajo Indians believe that the Holy People, supernatural and sacred, lived below ground in twelve lower worlds. A massive underground flood forced the Holy People to crawl through a hollow reed to the surface of the earth, where they created the universe. A deity named Changing Woman gave birth to the Hero Twins, called Monster Slayer and Child of the Waters. Human mortals, called Earth Surface People, emerged, and First Man and First Woman were formed from the ears of white and yellow corn.

In the tradition of Taoism, male and female principles known as *yin* and *yang* are the spiritual and material sources for the origins of humans and other living forms. Yin is considered the passive, negative, feminine force or principle in the universe, the source of cold and darkness, whereas yang is the active, positive, masculine force or principle, the source of heat and light. Taoists believe that the interaction of these two opposite principles brought forth the universe and all living forms out of chaos. These examples illustrate just two of the highly varied origin traditions held by different people around the world.

Western Traditions of Origin

In the Western tradition, the ancient Greeks had various mythological explanations for the origin of humans. One early view was that Prometheus fashioned humans out of water and earth. Another had Zeus ordering Pyrrha, the inventor of fire, to throw stones behind his back; these stones became men and women. Later Greek cosmological views

This painting by Michelangelo in the Sistine Chapel represents the idea of spiritual creation, which was the dominant worldview in Western cosmology for centuries.

considered biological evolution. Thales of Miletus (c. 636–546 B.C.) argued that life originated in the sea and that humans initially were fishlike, eventually moving onto dry land and evolving into mammals. A few hundred years later, Aristotle (384–322 B.C.) suggested another theory of creation through evolution. Based on comparative physiology and anatomy, his argument stated that life had evolved from simple lower forms to complex higher forms, such as humans.

The most important cosmological tradition affecting Western views of creation is recounted in the biblical Book of Genesis, which is found in Greek texts dating back to the third century B.C. This Judaic tradition describes how God created the cosmos. It begins with "In the beginning God created the heaven and the earth" and describes how Creation took six days, during which light, heaven, earth, vegetation, sun, moon, stars, birds, fish, animals, and humans originated. Yahweh, the Creator, made man, Adam, from "dust" and placed him in the Garden of Eden. Woman, Eve, was created from Adam's rib. Later, as Christianity spread throughout Europe, this tradition became the dominant cosmological explanation of human origins.

The Scientific Revolution

In the Western world following the medieval period (c. A.D. 1450), scientific discoveries began to influence conceptions about humanity's relationship to the rest of the universe. Copernicus and Galileo presented the novel idea that the earth is just one of many planets revolving around the sun. As this idea became accepted, humans could no longer view themselves and their planet as the center of the universe, as had been the traditional belief. This shift in cosmological thinking set the stage for entirely new views of humanity's links to the rest of the natural world. New developments in the geological sciences began to revise the estimates of the age of the earth radically. These and other scientific discoveries in astronomy, biology, chemistry, mathematics, and other disciplines dramatically transformed Western thought, including ideas about humankind.

The scientific theory of evolution, which sees plant and animal species originating through a gradual process of development from earlier forms,

provides an explanation of human origin. Although it is not intended to contradict cosmologies, it is based on a different kind of knowledge. Cosmological explanations frequently involve divine or supernatural forces that are, by their nature, impossible for human beings to observe. We accept them, believe them, on the basis of faith. Scientific theories of evolution, in contrast, are derived from the belief that the universe operates according to regular processes that can be observed. The scientific method is not a rigid framework that provides indisputable answers. Instead, scientific theories are propositions that can be evaluated by future testing and observation. Acceptance of the theory of evolution is based on observations in many areas of geology, paleontology, and biology.

Catastrophism versus Uniformitarianism

In the Western world before the Renaissance, the Judeo-Christian view of Creation provided the only framework for understanding humanity's position in the universe. The versions of Creation discussed in the biblical text fostered a specific concept of time: a linear, nonrepetitive, unique historical framework that began with divine Creation. These events were chronicled in the Bible; there was no concept of an ancient past stretching far back in time before human memory. In the seventeenth century, this view of Creation led Archbishop James Ussher of Ireland (1581–1665) to calculate the "precise" age of the earth. By calculating the number of generations mentioned in the Bible, Ussher dated the beginning of the universe to the year 4004 B.C. Thus, according to Bishop Ussher's estimate, the earth was approximately 6,000 years old.

The biblical account of Creation led to a particular view of the existence of plants and animals on earth. Because the Bible recounted the creation of the world and everything on it in six days, medieval theologians reasoned that the various species of plants and animals must be fixed in nature. In other words, they had not changed since the time of divine Creation. God had created plants and animals to fit in perfectly with specific environments and did not intend for them to change. This idea regarding the permanence of species influenced the thinking of many early scientists. The view of a static universe with unchanging species posed problems for early geologists and naturalists (a term used at that time to refer to biologists), who were beginning to study thick layers of stone and gravel deposits containing the fossilized remains of forms of life not represented in living species. They also documented the systematic change in the types of fossil species represented (see discussion of faunal succession Chapter 2).

Catastrophism Scientists proposed a variety of theories to explain the evidence presented in the geological and fossil records. One interpretation was presented by Georges Cuvier (1769–1832), who is sometimes called the father of zoology. Cuvier studied the fossil record, including the remains of prehistoric elephantlike animals called *mammoths* in the vicinity of Paris, and noted the successive replacement of fossil species through time. He proposed the geological theory known as **catastrophism,** which reasoned that many species had disappeared since Creation through catastrophes such as floods, earthquakes, and other major geological disasters. Some species of animals might survive these events, just as the animals collected by Noah survived the biblical flood. The new species of animals that appeared in the following layers represented a new creation event. Catastrophism became the best-known geological explanation consistent with the literal interpretation of the biblical account of Creation.

Uniformitarianism Other geologists challenged catastrophism and the rigidity of nature through scientific studies. One of the first critics was the French naturalist Comte Georges Louis Leclerc de Buffon, who in 1774 theorized that the earth changed through gradual, natural processes that were still observable. He proposed that rivers had created canyons, waves had changed shorelines, and other forces had transformed different features of the earth. After being criticized by theologians, Buffon attempted to coordinate his views with biblical beliefs. He suggested that the six days of Creation described in the Bible should not be interpreted literally. Buffon suggested that these passages actually refer to six *epochs* of gradual Creation rather than to 24-hour days. Each epoch consisted of thousands of years in which the earth and different species of life were transformed. Although Buffon's interpretation allowed more time for geological changes in the earth's past, there was no evidence for the six epochs of gradual creation.

As information on the geological record accumulated, the uniformitarian view eventually became the mainstream position in geology. In 1795, James Hutton, in his landmark book *Theory of the Earth,* explained how natural processes of erosion and deposition of sediments had formed the various geological strata of the earth. Hutton indicated that these natural processes must have taken thousands of years. In his book, he estimated that the earth was at least several million years old. In 1833, Charles Lyell, the father of modern geology, reinforced the uniformitarian view. In *Principles of Geology,* he argued that scientists could deduce the age of the earth from the rate at which sediments are deposited and by measuring the thickness of rocks. Through these measurements, Lyell also concluded that the earth was millions of years old. This view of gradual change, which provided the basis for later geological interpretations, was referred to as **uniformitarianism.**

Modern geologists have a much better understanding of geological processes and more sophisticated means of dating the earth. As will be discussed later, the age of the earth is now estimated to be billions, rather than millions, of years, divided into five major ages and many other periods and epochs (see Table 3.1 on page 52). In addition, recent evidence suggests that during some periods, violent changes affected the earth's geological conditions. Although the views of Hutton and Lyell have been superseded, they were historically important in challenging the traditional views of a static universe with fixed species. The uniformitarian view thus set the stage for an entirely new way of envisioning the universe, the earth, and the living forms on the planet.

Theories of Evolution

Evolution refers to the process of change in species over time. Evolutionary theory holds that existing species of plants and animals have emerged over millions of years from simple organisms. Before the mid-1800s, many thinkers had suggested evolutionary theories, but because they lacked an understanding of how old the earth really was, and because no reasonable explanation for the evolutionary process had been formulated, most people could not accept these theories.

Table 3.1	A Record of Geological Time			
Era	**Period**	**Epoch**	**Millions of Years Ago**	**Geological Conditions and Evolutionary Development**
Cenozoic (Age of Mammals)	Quaternary	Recent	0.01	End of last Ice Age; warmer climate. Decline of woody plants; rise of herbaceous plants. Age of *Homo sapiens*.
		Pleistocene	2.0	Four Ice Ages; glaciers in Northern Hemisphere; uplift of Sierras. Extinction of many large mammals and other species.
	Tertiary	Pliocene	5	Uplift and mountain building; volcanoes; climate much cooler. Development of grasslands; flowering plants; decline of forests. Large carnivores; many grazing mammals; first humanlike primates.
		Miocene	25	Climate drier, cooler; mountain formation. Flowering plants continue to diversify. Many forms of mammals.
		Oligocene	38	Rise of Alps and Himalayas; most land low; volcanic activity in Rockies. Spread of forests; flowering plants; rise of monocotyledons. Apes evolve; all present mammal families represented.
		Eocene	55	Climate warmer. Gymnosperms and flowering plants dominant. Age of Mammals begins; modern birds.
		Paleocene	65	Climate mild to cool; continental seas disappear. Evolution of primate mammals.
Mesozoic (Age of Reptiles)	Cretaceous		144	Continents separated; formation of Rockies; other continents low; large inland seas and swamps. Rise of flowering plants; gymnosperms decline. Dinosaurs peak, then become extinct; toothed birds become extinct; first modern birds; primitive mammals.
	Jurassic		213	Climate mild; continents low; inland seas; mountains form; continental drift continues. Gymnosperms common. Large, specialized dinosaurs; first toothed birds; insectovorous marsupials.
	Triassic		248	Many mountains and deserts form; continental drift begins. Gymnosperms dominant. First dinosaurs; egg-laying mammals.
Paleozoic (Age of Ancient Life)	Permian		286	Continents merge as Pangaea; glaciers; formation of Appalachians. Conifers diversify; cycads evolve. Modern insects appear; mammal-like reptiles; extinction of many Paleozoic invertebrates.
	Carboniferous		360	Lands low; great coal swamps; climate warm and humid, then cooler. Forests of ferns, club mosses, horsetails, and gymnosperms. First reptiles; spread of ancient amphibians; many insect forms; ancient sharks abundant.

Era	Period	Epoch	Millions of Years Ago	Geological Conditions and Evolutionary Development
	Devonian		408	Glaciers; inland seas. Terrestrial plants well established; first forests; gymnosperms and bryophytes appear. Age of Fishes; amphibians and wingless insects appear; many trilobites.
	Silurian		438	Continents mainly flat; flooding. Vascular plants appear; algae dominant in aquatic environment. Fish evolve; terrestrial arthropods.
	Ordovician		505	Sea covers continents; climate warm. Marine algae dominant; terrestrial plants appear. Invertebrates dominant; fish appear.
	Cambrian		570	Climate mild; lands low; oldest rocks with abundant fossils. Algae dominant in aquatic environment. Age of Marine Invertebrates; most modern phyla represented.
(Precambrian) Proterozoic			1,500	Planet cooled; glaciers; earth's crust forms; mountains form. Primitive algae and fungi, marine protozoans. Toward end, marine invertebrates.
Archean			3.5 billion	Evidence of first prokaryotic cells.
Origin of the Earth			4.6 billion	
Origin of the Universe			15–20 billion	

One such early theory of evolution was posited by the French chemist and biologist, Jean Baptiste de Lamarck (1744–1829). Lamarck proposed that species change and adapt to their environment through physical characteristics acquired in the course of their lifetime. He thought that when the environment changed, *besoin* (the will or desire for change within organisms) would enable them to adapt to their new circumstances. In other words, if a particular animal needed specialized organs to help in adaptation, these organs would evolve accordingly. In turn, the animals would pass on these new organs to their offspring.

The most famous example used by Lamarck was the long necks of giraffes. He suggested that the long neck of the giraffe evolved when a short-necked ancestor took to browsing on the leaves of trees instead of on grass. Lamarck speculated that the ancestral giraffe, in reaching up, stretched and elongated its neck. The offspring of this ancestral giraffe stretched still further. As this process repeated itself from generation to generation, the present long neck of the giraffe was eventually achieved.

Variations of Lamarck's view of inheritance are sometimes known as the *inheritance of acquired characteristics.* Many nineteenth-century scientists used this concept to explain how physical characteristics originated and were passed on to successive offspring. Today, however, this theory is rejected for several reasons. First, Lamarck overestimated the ability of a plant or an animal to "will" a trait or physical characteristic into being to adapt to an environment. In addition, we now know that physical traits acquired during an organism's lifetime cannot be inherited by the organism's offspring. For example, a weightlifter's musculature, an acquired characteristic, will not be passed on to his or her children. Nevertheless, Lamarck's ideas were historically important as an early theory attempting to explain evolutionary change.

Darwin, Wallace, and Natural Selection

Two individuals affected strongly by the scientific revolution were Charles Darwin and Alfred Wallace, nineteenth-century British naturalists. Through their

The photos of different dogs exhibit the wide variation in physical characteristics found within the same species.

Source: Courtesy of (from left) C. R. DeCorse, Margaret Antonini, Joyce Perkins.

careful observations and their identification of a plausible mechanism for evolutionary change, they transformed perspectives of the origin of species. Impressed by the enormous variation present in living species, Darwin and Wallace independently developed an explanation of the basic mechanism of evolution. This mechanism is known as **natural selection.**

Beginning in 1831, Darwin traveled for five years on a British ship, the HMS *Beagle,* on a voyage around the world. During this journey, he collected numerous species of plants and animals from many different environments. Meanwhile, Wallace was observing different species of plants and animals on the islands off Malaysia. Although both Darwin and Wallace arrived at the theory of natural selection simultaneously and independently, Darwin went on to present a thorough and completely documented statement of the theory in his book *On the Origin of Species,* published in 1859.

In their theory of natural selection, Darwin and Wallace emphasized the enormous variation that exists in all plant and animal species. They combined this observation with those of Thomas Malthus, a nineteenth-century clergyman and political economist whose work focused on human populations. The relevance of Malthus's work was his observation that it is a basic principle of nature that living creatures produce more offspring than can generally be expected to survive and reproduce. For the thousands of tadpoles that hatch from eggs, few live to maturity. Similarly, only a small number of the seeds from a maple tree germinate and grow into trees. In recognizing the validity of this fact, Darwin and Wallace realized that there would be *selection* in which organisms survived.

Variation within species and reproductive success are the basis of natural selection. Darwin and Wallace reasoned that certain individuals in a species may be born with particular characteristics or traits that make them better able to survive. For example, certain individuals in a plant species may naturally produce more seeds than others, or some frogs in a single population may have coloring that blends in with the environment better than others, making them less likely to be eaten by predators. Individuals with these advantageous characteristics are more likely to reproduce and, subsequently, pass on these traits to their offspring. Darwin and Wallace called this process *natural selection* because nature, or the demands of the environment, actually determines which individuals (or which traits) survive. This process, repeated countless times over millions of years, is the means by which species change or evolve over time.

Examples of Natural Selection

One problem Darwin faced in writing *On the Origin of Species* was a lack of well-documented examples of natural selection at work. Most major changes in nature take place over thousands or millions of years. As a result, the process of natural selection is often too slow to be documented in a researcher's lifetime. However, when animals or plants are exposed to rapid changes in their environment, we can actually observe natural selection in action.

A classic case of natural selection is illustrated by the finches of the Galapagos Islands, located about 500 miles off the coast of South America. These birds were studied by Charles Darwin when he visited the islands during his travels on the HMS *Beagle*. Volcanic in origin and cut off from the South American mainland, the Galapagos have a diversity of species related to, but distinct from, those of South America. Darwin was struck by how the geographic isolation of a small population could expose its members to new environmental conditions where different adaptive features might be favored. Darwin described the variation in the Islands' finches: In general, the birds have rather dull plumage and are quite similar, except in the size and shape of their beaks—a feature that is closely related to the ways in which the birds obtain their food. Some species of finch, for example, have short thick beaks that they use to eat seeds, buds, and fruits, while others have long, straight beaks and subsist primarily on nectar from flowers.

The finches of the island of Daphne Major in Galapagos were the focus of a long-term research project by Peter and Rosemary Grant, beginning in 1973 (Grant, 1986; Weiner, 1994). The island is small enough to allow researchers to intensively study the island's flora and fauna, and provide an unambiguous demonstration of natural selection in operation. The Grants and their students focused on two species of finch—the medium ground finch and the cactus finch. Over time, every finch on the island was captured, carefully measured and weighed, and also tagged, so that each bird could be identified in the field. The diet of the birds was documented and the availability of food resources charted. A dramatic change in the finches' food resources occurred between mid-1976 and early 1978 as a result of a drought. The lack of rainfall led to a decrease in the food supplies favored by smaller-beaked finches because the remaining food consisted of larger, harder seeds that were difficult for finches with small beaks to break open. On the other hand, finches with larger, heavier beaks were able to more easily crack and extract food from hard-shelled seeds. Not surprisingly, many of the finches with smaller beaks died of starvation during the drought.

The finches of the Galapagos Islands provide an excellent example of natural selection at work. The beaks of the various species of finch are used for exploiting different kinds of foods. If environmental conditions suddenly change, some characteristics may be more favored than others.

The variation in beak size is a good illustration of how natural selection may act on different species, but it also illustrates the significance of variation within individual species. Of the more than 1,000 medium ground finches found on the island at the beginning of the Grant's study, only 180 remained after the drought. Notably, the finches that survived had a larger average beak size than that of the population prior to the drought. As beak size is an inherited characteristic, the new generations of birds born after the drought also had a larger average beak size. This case study illustrates how natural selection can eliminate maladaptive traits from a population and select for features that help ensure survival and, ultimately, reproductive success for some members of a species. Many modern scientists believe that new species emerge when small populations become isolated from the parent group and encounter new selective pressures that may favor different characteristics.

Natural selection is currently viewed as one of four major guiding forces in the evolution of species. It enabled Darwin to explain the mechanisms of biological evolution, and it remains a powerful explanation for the development of living species of plants and animals. Before turning to the other three processes that guide evolution, we will consider the way traits are passed on from one generation to the next.

Principles of Inheritance

Darwin contributed to the modern understanding of biological evolution by thoroughly documenting the *variation* of living forms and by identifying the key process of natural selection. Like most nineteenth-century scientists, however, he did not understand *heredity,* or how specific traits are passed on from one generation to the next. Darwin reasoned that during the reproductive process, the parental substances mix to produce new traits in the parents' offspring. These conclusions were based in part on his experiments with plants and animals, in which he had observed that the offspring often had characteristics from both parents. Darwin was unclear about how these traits were transmitted, but he thought that, as with an alloy such as bronze, which is a mixture of tin and copper, the traits of an offspring represented a blending of parental substances.

Mendel and Modern Genetics

Modern understanding of heredity emerged through the studies by an Austrian monk named Gregor Mendel (1822–1884). During the 1860s, Mendel began a series of breeding experiments with pea plants, experiments that revolutionized biological thought. Although his findings were not recognized until the twentieth century, Mendel laid the groundwork for what is today known as the science of *genetics,* the biological subfield that deals with heredity.

In compiling his rules of genetics, Mendel discredited earlier theories of inheritance. He demonstrated conclusively that traits are inherited in a particulate manner. In other words, individuals do not inherit traits through a blending of parental substances, such as fluids or metal alloys, as Darwin had believed. Rather, traits are passed from parents to offspring in individual "particles," or packages.

Mendel's Experiments   Some of Mendel's most important experiments involved the crossbreeding of pea plants that differed in certain key characteristics. For example, he carefully cross-pollinated purebred plants that produced only yellow peas with purebred plants that produced only green peas. By following the results of cross-pollination through several generations, Mendel discovered a distinct pattern of reproduction. The first generation of hybrid plants—that is, plants produced by parents having different purebred characteristics—were all yellow. However, when he crossbred these hybrid plants, the second generation contained both yellow and green plants. Thus, the green color that seemed to disappear in the first generation of hybrids reappeared in the second generation. Significantly, the ratio of yellow to green plants in the second generation was always approximately three-to-one (3:1).

Dominant and Recessive Traits   Mendel drew several important conclusions from these experiments. First, he rejected the earlier notions of inheritance, such as blending. None of the pea plants exhibited a mixed color; all were either yellow or green. In addition, he concluded that certain traits, like yellow color, prevailed over other traits, such as green color. The prevailing traits he termed **dominant.** In contrast, he labeled as **recessive** those traits that were unexpressed in one generation but expressed in subsequent generations. In pea plants, he found that yellow was dominant and green was recessive.

Mendel repeated these experiments focusing on size (tall versus dwarf plants), shape (round versus wrinkled peas), and other characteristics. In each case, he arrived at the same results. The crossbreeding of purebred plants with dominant and recessive traits produced only offspring that exhibited the dominant characteristics. However, the offspring of these hybrid plants exhibited dominant and recessive traits in the 3:1 ratio. The fact that this ratio reappeared consistently convinced Mendel that the key to heredity lay deep within the pea plant seeds. Mendel concluded that the particles responsible for passing traits from parents to offspring occurred in pairs, the individual receiving one from each parent. Purebred parents could pass on only the dominant or recessive trait, whereas hybrid parents could pass on either one. Mendel labeled the dominant traits *A* and the recessive ones *a.* Purebreds thus contain either *AA* (pure dominant) or *aa* (pure recessive); hybrids contain *Aa.* Individuals with *Aa,* of course, exhibit the dominant trait.

Genes and Heredity   From Mendel's work and that of other biologists, we now know that traits are determined by genes. A **gene** is a discrete unit of hereditary information that determines specific physical characteristics of organisms. Most sexually reproducing plants and animals have two genes for every physical trait, one gene inherited from each parent. The alternate forms of the same genes, such as "tall" or "dwarf," are referred to as **alleles.** When an organism has two of the same kinds of alleles, it is **homozygous** for that gene. Thus, homozygous tall plants are *TT* (purebred dominant for tallness), whereas homozygous dwarf plants are *tt* (purebred recessive for shortness). In contrast, when an organism has two different alleles, it is **heterozygous** for that gene. Thus, the *Tt* hybrids are heterozygous plants, possessing both tall and dwarf alleles.

When a heterozygous plant expresses only characteristics of one allele such as tallness, that allele is dominant. The allele whose expression is masked in a heterozygote (for example, shortness) is a recessive allele. Thus, two organisms with different allele combinations for a particular trait may have the same outward appearance: *TT* and *Tt* pea plants will appear the same.

Biologists distinguish between the genetic constitution and the outward appearance of an organism. The specific genetic constitution of an organism is referred to as its **genotype;** the external, observable characteristics of that organism, which are shaped in part by both the organism's genetic makeup and unique life history, are called its **phenotype.** Genotype and phenotype are illustrated in Figure 3.1.

Principle of Segregation Mendel's theory explained how hybrid parents expressing only the dominant trait could produce offspring exhibiting the recessive trait. As Figure 3.2 illustrates, the mixing of two *Tt* configurations produces four combinations: one *TT*, two *Tt*, and one *tt*. This accounts for the 3:1 ratio that Mendel observed. From this calculation, Mendel concluded that the particle containing the recessive trait, which is masked by the dominant trait in one generation, can separate, or *segregate,* from that trait during reproduction. If this occurs in both parents, the offspring can inherit two

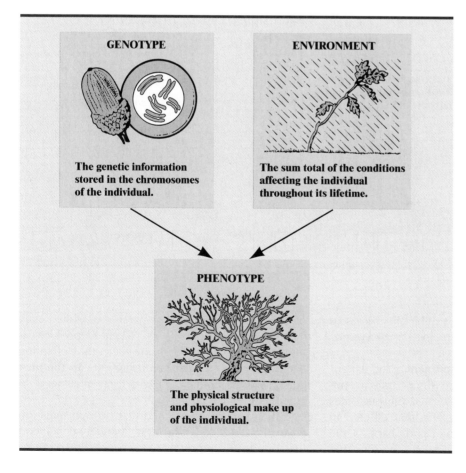

FIGURE 3.1 The genotype interacts with the external environment to produce the phenotype.

Source: From The *Illustrated Origin of Species* by Charles Darwin, abridged by Richard Leakey (Rainbird/Faber & Faber, 1979). Reprinted by permission of the Robert Harding Picture Library.

GENOTYPE

The genetic information stored in the chromosomes of the individual.

ENVIRONMENT

The sum total of the conditions affecting the individual throughout its lifetime.

PHENOTYPE

The physical structure and physiological make up of the individual.

FIGURE 3.2 In one of his experiments, Mendel crossbred plants that were purebred (homozygous) for particular traits, as illustrated here by the tall and dwarf pea plants. As tallness is a dominant trait, all the offspring of this cross were tall. In the third generation, however, the recessive traits reappear, or segregate.

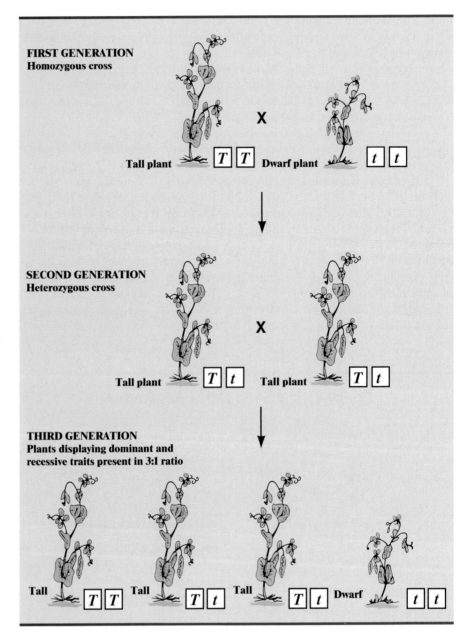

FIRST GENERATION
Homozygous cross

Tall plant T T Dwarf plant t t

SECOND GENERATION
Heterozygous cross

Tall plant T t Tall plant T t

THIRD GENERATION
Plants displaying dominant and recessive traits present in 3:1 ratio

Tall T T Tall T t Tall T t Dwarf t t

recessive particles and thus exhibit the recessive trait. Mendel called this the *principle of segregation*.

Principle of Independent Assortment The experiments just discussed all focused on one trait. In subsequent studies, Mendel investigated the outcomes of fertilization between pea plants that differed in two ways, such as in both color and shape of the pea. As in the previous experiments, the offspring

of purebred (homozygous) parents exhibited only the dominant characteristics. When Mendel crossfertilized these hybrids, however, the offspring displayed the characteristics present in the first generation in a ratio of 9:3:3:1, as illustrated in Figure 3.3.

This experiment indicated that no two traits are always passed on together. Mendel concluded that during the reproductive process, the particles

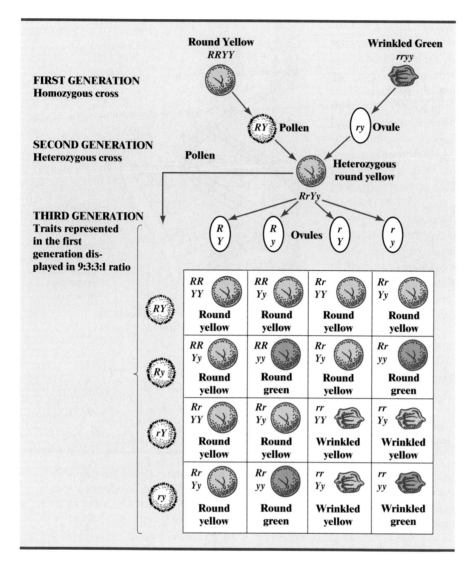

FIRST GENERATION
Homozygous cross

SECOND GENERATION
Heterozygous cross

THIRD GENERATION
Traits represented
in the first
generation dis-
played in 9:3:3:1 ratio

FIGURE 3.3 This diagram, referred to as an extended Punnett square, demonstrates the principle of independent assortment discovered by Mendel. When two heterozygous pea plants are cross-fertilized, the alleles that determine two different traits sort independently of each other, ceating the phenotypic ratio of 9:3:3:1.

determining different traits separate from one another and then *recombine* to create variation in the next generation. Thus, in the experiment cited above, Mendel's plants produced peas that were yellow and round, yellow and wrinkled, green and wrinkled, and green and round. Mendel referred to this result as the *principle of independent assortment.*

Because Mendel did not have the advanced technology to investigate cellular biology, he did not know the inner workings of the units of inheritance. But his principles of segregation and independent assortment are still viewed as key operative mechanisms in the transmission of traits from one generation to another.

Molecular Genetics

Modern scientists have a better understanding than did Mendel of the dynamics of heredity at the cellular level. They have discovered that, like other animals, humans have two different forms of cells: **somatic cells** (body cells) and **gametes** (sex cells: eggs and sperm). Within the nucleus of the somatic cells are pairs of **chromosomes,** which contain the hereditary units. Humans have twenty-three pairs of chromosomes, or forty-six chromosomes in all. When these somatic cells divide in the natural process of fissioning to produce new cells—a process biologists call **mitosis**—they replicate themselves to produce cells having forty-six chromosomes. Mitosis is simply a process for making identical cells within a single living individual.

In contrast, human sex cells, or gametes, are produced through the process of **meiosis**—two successive cell divisions that produce cells with only *half* the number of chromosomes (twenty-three). Meiosis reduces the amount of genetic material to half to prepare for sexual reproduction. During fertilization, when the two sex cells are joined together, they reproduce a new organism with forty-six chromosomes. It is during meiosis and sexual reproduction that Mendel's principles of segregation and independent assortment operate. This reshuffling, or recombination, of genetic material does not change allele frequencies by itself. It ensures, however, that the entire range of traits present in a species is produced and can subsequently be acted on by evolutionary forces.

The Role of DNA   How are hereditary units contained in chromosomes? Biologists have discovered that each chromosome contains the genetic material that determines the physical characteristics of an organism.

The secret of this genetic blueprint is a large molecule of **deoxyribonucleic acid** (DNA) in each chromosome. The DNA molecule looks like a spiral ladder, or more poetically, like a *double helix* (Figure 3.4). The sides of the ladder consist of sugar (deoxyribose) and phosphate, and the rungs are made up of four nitrogen bases: adenine, thymine, guanine, and cytosine.

The DNA bases are arranged in sequences of three, called *codons*. These sequences determine the assembly of different amino acids. For example, the combination and arrangement of the bases guanine, thymine, and cytosine encode the amino acid glutamine. **Amino acids** are chemicals joined together in chains to produce different proteins—chemical compounds that are fundamental to the makeup and running of the body's cells. There are twenty different kinds of amino acids that can, in differing combinations and amounts, produce millions of different proteins basic to life. The arrangement of bases in the DNA strands is copied by similar molecules, which enables the transfer of the pattern from the chromosomes to other parts of the cell where the production of proteins actually takes place. For the purposes of this discussion, a gene can be

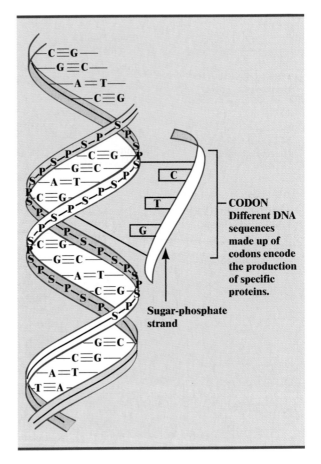

FIGURE 3.4   This illustration shows the chemical structure of DNA. The DNA molecule forms a spiral ladder of sugar (S) and phosphate (P) linked by four nitrogen bases: adenine (A), guanine (G), thymine (T), and cytosine (C).

considered a DNA sequence, divided into codons, that encodes the production of a particular protein chain. Different DNA sequences made up of codons encode the production of specific proteins.

Population Genetics and Evolution

To understand the process of evolution fully, we cannot focus on individuals. A person's genetic makeup, fixed during conception, remains with that individual throughout his or her lifetime. Although people mature and may change in appearance, they do not *evolve* in a biological sense.

Evolution refers to change in the genetic makeup of a *population* of organisms. A **population** here refers to a group of individuals who can potentially interbreed. To understand evolution, a scientist must consider all the genes in a population. This assortment of genes is known as the **gene pool.** Any particular gene pool consists of different allele frequencies, the relative amounts of the alternate forms of genes that are present.

In terms of genetics, evolution can be defined as the process of change in allele frequencies between one generation and the next. Alternation of the gene pool of a population is influenced by four evolutionary processes, one of which, natural selection, has already been discussed in relation to the work of Charles Darwin and Alfred Wallace. The other three processes are mutation, gene flow, and genetic drift.

Mutations

Mutations are alterations of genetic material at the cellular level. They can occur spontaneously during the cell replication process, or they can be induced by environmental factors such as radiation. Although we frequently think of mutations as harmful, they introduce variation into the gene pool and may create new, advantageous characteristics. Mutation serves as the primary force behind evolution because it is the *only* source of new genetic variation. The other evolutionary processes act on the genetic variation introduced through mutation. The role of mutation was only recognized during this century with better understanding of molecular genetics.

Most mutations occur in the somatic cells of organisms. These types of mutations are not heritable. When the organism dies, the mutation dies with it. Some mutations, however, alter the DNA in reproductive cells. In this case, even change in a single DNA base, or a *point mutation,* may produce observable phenotypic change; for example, differences in blood chemistry. A mutation occurring in this instance will be passed on to the offspring.

Generally, the rates of mutations are relatively stable. But if we make the conservative estimate that humans have two copies of each of one hundred thousand genes and the average rate of mutations is 3×10^{-5}, then each of us on average carries six new mutant genes. When the size of the human population is considered, it is evident that the mutation process provides a large source of variability. It would, however, be unlikely for evolution to occur solely as a result of mutation. The rate of mutation of a particular trait within a specific population is likely to be relatively low—perhaps present only in one individual out of 10,000. Hence, mutation alone would be unlikely to effect great change in allele frequencies within the population. Yet if mutations are acted on by natural selection, they become a potentially important source of evolutionary change.

Gene Flow

Gene flow is the exchange of alleles between populations as a result of interbreeding. When this exchange occurs, new genetic material may be introduced, changing the allele frequencies in a population. The process of gene flow has affected most human societies. Migrants from one society enter a new region and intermarry with the local population. Through reproduction, they transmit new genes into the population. In this way, new mutations arising in one population can be transmitted to other members of the species.

In addition to providing a mechanism for introducing new genetic material, gene flow can act to decrease variation between populations. If two distinct populations continue to interbreed, they will become progressively similar genetically. Migration and connections between different populations have long been a feature of human societies and among early human ancestors. This genetic interconnectedness explains why new human species have not emerged: There has been sufficient gene flow between populations to prevent the creation of substantial genetic distance.

With the development of modern transportation, gene flow occurs on a worldwide scale. In this context, however, it is useful to remember that many cultural or social factors play a role in gene flow in human populations. Religious practices, socioeconomic status, and ethnicity may all influence the selection of mates (see Chapter 6).

Genetic Drift

Genetic drift is evolutionary change resulting from random sampling phenomena that eliminate or maintain certain alleles in a gene pool. It includes the influence of chance events that may affect evolutionary change that are in no way influenced by individuals' genetic makeup. For example, in any population, only a small sample of the potential array of genetic material is passed on from one generation to the next. Every human being produces hundreds of thousands of gametes, each representing a different genetic combination, yet people produce only a few offspring. The chance selection of genetic material that occurs during reproduction results in minor changes in allele frequencies from one generation to the next. Chance events, such as death by disease or accident, also bring about change in allele frequencies. For example, if only ten individuals within a population carry a particular genetic trait and all of them die as a result of accident or disease, this genetic characteristic will not be passed on to the next generation.

Because evolution occurs in populations, change resulting from genetic drift is influenced by the size of the population as well as the relative allele frequencies represented. In larger populations, random events such as accidental deaths are unlikely to have as significant an effect on the population's gene pool. In smaller populations, however, such events can substantially alter the genetic variation present. A particular kind of genetic drift, known as the **founder effect,** results when only a small number of individuals in a population pass on their genes to the following generation. Such a situation might result when a famine decimates a large group, or when a small migrant population moves away and establishes a new settlement in an isolated area. In these instances, the founding members of the succeeding generation will have only a portion—a sample—of the full range of the genetic material that was present in the original population. Because early human ancestors and human populations lived in small bands of people perhaps consisting of family groups, genetic drift was likely an important evolutionary force.

Natural Selection

Natural selection provides the key to evolution. It can be defined as change resulting from differential reproductive success in the allele frequencies of a population. The other evolutionary forces already discussed are important in creating variation in allele frequencies within and between populations, but they provide no direction—no means for a population to adapt to changing conditions. This direction is provided by natural selection.

As illustrated in the case of Darwin's finches on the Galapagos Islands, certain alleles (as expressed in particular physical traits such as long or short beaks) may be selected for by environmental factors. They may enable an organism to resist disease better, obtain food more efficiently, or avoid predators more effectively. Individuals with such advantages will, on average, be more successful in reproducing and thereby pass on their genes to the next generation at higher rates.

Evolutionary "success" can be evaluated only in relative terms; if the environment changes, selection pressures also change. In the case of the finches, the larger- and smaller-beaked varieties were initially equally successful (or "fit"), but as food resources were depleted by drought, the individuals with heavier beaks were favored. This shift in allele frequencies in response to changing environmental conditions is called **adaptation.** Through evolution, species develop characteristics that allow them to survive and reproduce successfully in particular environmental settings. The specific environmental conditions to which a species is adapted is referred to as its **ecological niche.**

How Does Evolution Occur?

Although it is useful to discuss mutation, gene flow, genetic drift, and natural selection as distinct processes, they all interact to affect evolutionary change. Mutation provides the ultimate source of new genetic variants, whereas gene flow, genetic drift, and natural selection alter the frequency of the new allele. The key consideration is change in the genetic characteristics of a population from one generation to the next. Over time, this change may produce major differences among populations that were originally very similar.

To measure evolutionary change, researchers find it useful to evaluate evolutionary processes operating on a population by comparing allele frequencies for a particular trait to an idealized, mathematical model known as the **Hardy-Weinberg theory of genetic equilibrium.** This model, developed independently by G. H. Hardy and W. Weinberg, sets hypothetical conditions under which none of the evolutionary processes is acting and no evolution is taking place. The model makes several important assumptions. It presumes that no mutation is taking place (there are no new alleles); there is no gene flow (no migration or movement in or out of the population); no genetic drift (a large enough population is represented that there is no variation in allele frequencies due to sampling); and that natural selection is not operating on any of the alleles represented. The model also assumes that mating is randomized within the population so that all individuals have equal potential of mating with all other individuals of the opposite sex.

Given these assumptions, there will be no change in allele frequencies from one generation to the next. If examination of genotype frequencies within a population matches the idealized model, no evolution is taking place, and the population is said to be in Hardy-Weinberg equilibrium. If study suggests the genotype frequencies are not the same as the predicted model, then we know that at least one of the assumptions must be incorrect. Further research can then be undertaken to identify what the source of evolutionary change is. In practice, determining which evolutionary populations are acting on a population is challenging. Different evolutionary processes may act against one another, giving the appearance that none is operating. Small amounts of change may also go unrecognized. Nevertheless, the Hardy-Weinberg theory provides a starting point for evaluating evolutionary change.

Speciation

One of the most interesting areas of research in evolutionary theory is how, why, and when new species arise. This is known as the study of **speciation.** Generally, biologists define a **species** as a group of organisms that have similar physical characteristics and can potentially interbreed with one another to produce fertile offspring, and who are reproductively isolated from other populations.

Gradualism According to evolutionary theory, speciation occurs when there is an interruption in gene flow between populations that formerly were one species but became isolated by geographic barriers. In geographic isolation, these populations may reside in different types of environments, and natural selection, mutation, or genetic drift may lead to increasingly different allele frequencies. Eventually, through evolutionary change, these two populations become so different genetically that

A characteristic of a species is that its members can successfully interbreed only with one another. The mule is the offspring of a female horse and a male donkey, two clearly distinct species. As mules are always sterile, however, the reproductive isolation of the two species is maintained.

they are no longer the same species. Darwin hypothesized that speciation was a gradual process of evolution occurring very slowly as different populations became isolated. This view is called *gradualism,* or the **gradualistic theory of speciation.**

Punctuated Equilibrium Beginning in the early twentieth century, some scientists challenged the gradualistic interpretation of speciation, arguing that new species might appear rapidly. *Paleontologists* (fossil specialists) Stephen Jay Gould and Niles Eldredge (1972) proposed a theory known as **punctuated equilibrium.** When examining ancient fossil beds, paleontologists discovered that some plants or animals seemed to exhibit little change over millions of years. These creatures appeared to remain in a state of equilibrium with their habitats for long geological periods. However, the fossil record indicates that major changes, or punctuations, appear to have occurred every so often, leading to rapid speciation.

Punctuated equilibrium and gradualism (see Figure 3.5) present extreme perspectives of the rate at which evolution occurs, but the two views are not incompatible. The fossil record provides examples of both cases (Brown & Rose, 1987; Levinton, 1988). The particular rate of change in a particular species depends on its specific adaptive features and the surrounding environmental conditions. Most paleontologists, biologists, and anthropologists hypothesize that both types of evolution have occurred under

FIGURE 3.5 An illustration of two models of evolution. Gradualism implies a gradual, steady rate of speciation, while punctuated equilibrium suggests evolutionary change as a series of steps and starts. The fossil record provides evidence of both views.

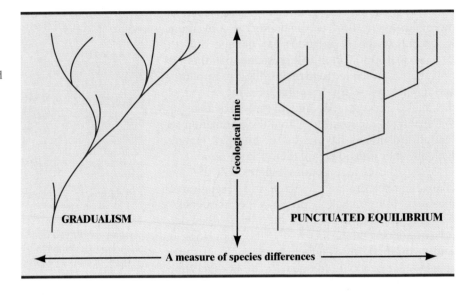

different circumstances during different geological epochs. As our understanding of the fossil record increases, we will be better able to specify when and where speciation and evolution occurred rapidly and when and where they occurred gradually.

Adaptive Radiation

Adaptive radiation provides a useful illustration of the evolutionary process and the factors that influence rates of evolutionary change. **Adaptive radiation** is the rapid diversification and adaptation of an evolving population into new ecological niches.

As we have seen, organisms have tremendous reproductive potential, yet this potential is generally limited by the availability of food, shelter, and space in the environment. Competition with other organisms and natural selection limit the number of offspring that live. Eventually, organisms may utilize all the resources available in a particular ecological niche. This compels some individuals in a population to exploit new niches where resources are more available and chances for survival greater. Evolutionary change may allow for rapid expansion into new environments. For example, when reptiles first adapted to land environments, they were able to expand into a vast array of ecological niches with little competition.

Sometimes environmental change creates conditions favorable for the adaptive radiation of some species. Natural disasters may lead to the extinction of many forms of life, as described in the box "The Nemesis Theory." Such conditions favor species that have the ability to exploit the changing conditions. Evolutionary processes acting on the expanding population may produce many new varieties and species adapted to ecological niches different from the parent population. The adaptive radiation of many species is recorded in the fossil record.

The Evolution of Life

Modern scientific findings indicate that the universe as we know it began to develop between 15 billion and 20 billion years ago. At approximately 4.6 billion years ago, the sun and the earth formed, and about a billion years later, the first life appeared in the sea. Through evolution, living forms developed adaptive characteristics, survived, and reproduced. Geological forces and environmental changes, bringing about both gradual and rapid changes, led to new forms of life.

From studying the fossilized bones and teeth of different creatures, paleontologists have tracked the evolution of living forms throughout the world. They document the fossil record according to geological time, which is divided into *eras,* which are subdivided into *periods,* which in turn are composed of *epochs* (look back to Table 3.1 on pages 52–53).

CRITICAL PERSPECTIVES

THE NEMESIS THEORY

Most scientists today accept some form of punctuated equilibrium, the idea that dramatic changes, or punctuations, have occurred periodically in the evolution of life. One possible explanation for some of these punctuations is a hypothesis known as the *Nemesis theory*. This theory suggests that extraterrestrial forces are partly responsible for the pace and direction of the evolution of life. It argues that mass extinctions were caused by collisions of the earth and gigantic comets more than 6 miles in diameter and weighing a trillion tons.

The name *Nemesis* refers to a "death star," a hypothetical companion star to the sun, 2 light-years away and not yet seen by any astronomer. According to the Nemesis theory, this star has an eccentric orbit that periodically passes through the Oort Cloud, an envelope of billions of comets surrounding the solar system, deflecting comets randomly into space, some of which strike the earth. Paleontologist David Raup suggests that this Nemesis orbit occurs at a regular pattern every 26 million years (Raup, 1986).

It is hypothesized that the explosions produced by these collisions—millions of times greater than the largest nuclear bomb ever tested—threw dust and debris into the atmosphere, shutting out the sun's radiation and warmth for more than two years. These months of darkness, similar to a "nuclear winter," were followed by soaring temperatures, polluted air, and dead seas. With the blockage of sunlight, photosynthesis was suppressed, thereby choking off plant life, interrupting most of the earth's food chains, and ultimately causing mass extinctions of millions of plant and animal species (Alvarez et al., 1980). Some paleontologists think that these mass extinctions, occurring at intervals of 26 million years, help explain the patterns of evolution found on the earth. They believe, for example, that the extinction of the dinosaurs may have resulted from an extraterrestrial collision. Though many unsubstantiated hypotheses remain, this interpretation has been lent some support by increasing geological evidence for meteor strikes at critical periods in the earth's evolutionary past. The stories of science fiction novels and film thus may have some basis in reality.

As Stephen Jay Gould (1985) has pointed out, however, the disastrous conditions caused by the death star would also have created conditions conducive to new forms of life. Thus, although the destruction caused by Nemesis may have resulted in the demise of the dinosaurs, it produced new environmental conditions that favored the adaptive radiation of creatures such as mammals. In other words, it set the stage for an explosion of new life forms.

The Nemesis theory is just that—a testable proposition that must be evaluated by many scientists from different disciplines. As with any theory, scientists have raised significant questions regarding this interpretation. While rapid extinctions of species are well documented in the fossil record, many scientists offer alternative explanations for these extinctions, for example, large-scale volcanic activity (Signor & Lipps, 1982; Benton, 1986; Officer, 1990). In any case, the Nemesis theory continues to be one contending explanation for the extinction and development of different forms of life.

Analogy and Homology

How do paleontologists determine evolutionary relationships? Two useful concepts in discussing the divergence and differentiation of living forms are analogy and homology. **Analogy** refers to similarities in organisms that have no genetic relationship.

Analogous forms result from *convergent evolution*, the process by which two unrelated types of organisms develop similar physical characteristics. These resemblances emerge when unrelated organisms adapt to similar environmental niches. For example, hummingbirds and hummingmoths resemble each other physically and have common behavioral

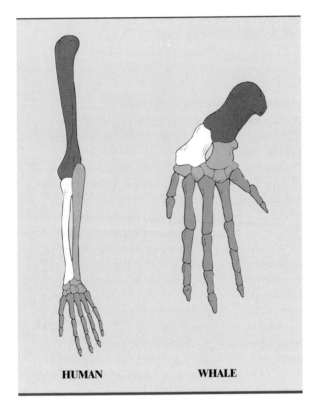

HUMAN   **WHALE**

FIGURE 3.6 The structural similarities between the human hand and the whale's fin are an example of homology: features that share a common evolutionary origin but which may differ in form and function.

characteristics. However, they share no direct evolutionary descent.

In contrast, **homology** refers to traits that have a common genetic origin but may differ greatly in form and function. For example, a human hand bears little resemblance to a whale's fin. Humans and whales live in very different environments, and the hand and fin perform in very different ways. Careful examination of human and whale skeletons, however, reveals many structural similarities (see Figure 3.6). These similarities indicate a common genetic ancestry. Thus, the hand and the fin are homologous.

Plate Tectonics and Continental Drift

In examining the evolution and distribution of living forms, it is important to consider the role of geological processes. The formation of natural features such as continents, mountains, and oceans provides an important mechanism for restricting or encouraging gene flow. **Plate tectonics** is the complex geological process that brings about the drift of continents. The outer shell of the earth is made up of plates that are in constant motion caused by the movement of molten rocks deep within the earth. According to scientific investigation, the continents move a few centimeters a year (Tarling, 1985). Over millions of years, the continents have sometimes drifted together and then separated, a process known as **continental drift.**

Determining the precise location of different continents at specific geological time periods has helped scientists to understand evolutionary connections among different species of plants and animals. Scientists hypothesize that until about 200 million years ago, the earth's landmass was one gigantic, interconnected continent, which is referred to as *Pangaea.* During the Mesozoic era, Pangaea began to break apart, forming two supercontinents. The southern supercontinent, known as *Gondwana,* consisted of what are now South America, Africa, Antarctica, Australia, and India. The northern continent, consisting of North America, Greenland, Europe, and Asia, is known as *Laurasia* (see Figure 3.7).

Throughout the Mesozoic and Cenozoic eras, the supercontinents continued to move. South America separated from Africa; North America, Greenland, and Europe divided; and Africa joined with Eurasia. Forty million years ago, North America separated from Europe. By 20 million years ago, the continued fracturing and movements of the geological plates resulted in the gradual migration of the continents to their present locations.

Examination of continental drift has helped paleontologists and other scientists understand the distribution of different plant and animal species. For example, the same types of fossil reptiles have been recovered from Mesozoic deposits in North America and the Gobi Desert in Asia, a good indication that these landmasses were connected at that time. In contrast, the separation of South America from other continents during the Cenozoic supports the fossil and biological evidence for the divergence of primates from Africa, Asia, and Europe and primates from the Americas (see Chapter 4).

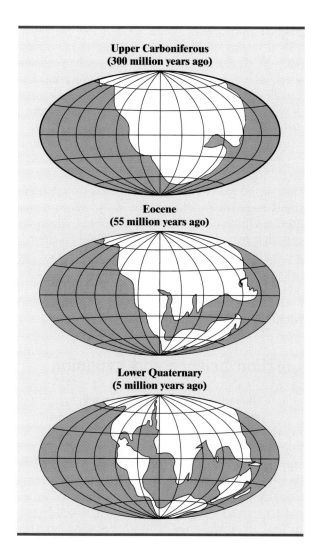

Upper Carboniferous
(300 million years ago)

Eocene
(55 million years ago)

Lower Quaternary
(5 million years ago)

FIGURE 3.7 Understanding the geological process of continental drift—the movement of continents as a result of plate tectonics—helps paleontologists understand the distribution of fossil species.

Blood Chemistry and DNA

The majority of information on the evolution of life and human origin is provided by the fossil record. In recent years, however, studies of the genetic makeup of living organisms have received increasing attention. It is striking to note that despite the tremendous diversity of life, the DNA codes for the production of proteins—with few exceptions— dictate the joining of the same amino acids in all organisms, from the simplest one-celled plants and

animals to humans. This semblance of genetic building blocks provides additional evidence for the common origin of all life.

Study of the differences and similarities in the arrangement of genetic material for living animals provides important insights into evolutionary relationships. Similarities in the DNA of different species indicate that they inherited genetic blueprints (with minor modifications) from a common ancestor. In most instances this information has provided independent confirmation of conclusions about evolutionary relationships based on the study of skeletal characteristics and fossil remains. In some instances, however, physical characteristics may be confused because of convergent evolution. Study of genetic information and blood chemistry helps to avoid this confusion.

Genetic material of living animals has also been used to estimate when different species diverged. A technique known as *molecular dating* was developed by Vincent Sarich and Allan Wilson of the University of California, Berkeley (1967). The technique involves comparing amino acid sequences or, more recently, using what is called *DNA hybridization* to compare DNA material itself. As a result, Sarich and Wilson provided useful insights into the genetic relationship of humans to other species and estimates regarding when species may have separated.

Molecular dating is based on two key assumptions: (1) that molecular evolution proceeds at a fairly constant rate over time, and (2) that the greater the similarity between animals in biochemical terms, the more likely it is that they share a close evolutionary relationship. Research based on these concepts has been applied to the interpretation of human evolution (see Chapters 4 and 5).

The reliability of this technique as a dating tool has been hotly debated. Many scientists challenge the assumption that molecular evolution is constant over time. Rather, they believe that variation in mutation rates and the disparate generation lengths of different species skew the measurements of the "molecular clock" (Lovejoy & Meindl, 1972; Goodman, Baba, & Darga, 1983; Li & Tanimura, 1987). Other researchers feel that the technique remains useful if the potential limitations are taken into consideration. Future work may help to resolve these issues.

The Paleontological Record

The Precambrian and Paleozoic Eras The fossil evidence shows that during the Precambrian, simple forms of life resembling modern bacteria, including some species that may have been able to *photosynthesize,* had emerged. Apparently, the predominant organisms during this era were various kinds of algae. Beginning with the Paleozoic, which dates from 570 million to 248 million years ago, deposits of fossils became more abundant, enabling paleontologists to follow the adaptive radiation of jellyfish, worms, fish, amphibians, and early reptiles.

The Mesozoic Era The Mesozoic (248 million to 65 million years ago) marks the adaptive radiation of reptiles. This era is divided into the Triassic, Jurassic, and Cretaceous periods. The Mesozoic is known as the Age of Reptiles. Unlike earlier forms of life, reptiles could exist entirely outside the water. They were the first successful land animals and reigned as the dominant species in this new environment. Many of the snakes, lizards, and turtles found in Mesozoic formations are similar to contemporary species. Of all the reptiles that lived during the Mesozoic, the dinosaurs are the most well known today. They included the giant carnivore (meat eater) *Tyrannosaurus;* larger, plant-eating creatures such as the *Brachiosaurus;* and numerous other species, both large and small.

Although reptiles were the dominant animals of the Mesozoic, paleontologists have found fossils of many other organisms from this same era. For example, bird fossils, some even showing the outlines of feathers, have been preserved from the Jurassic period. The paleontological record demonstrates beyond a doubt that a direct evolutionary relationship exists between reptiles and birds. One classic fossil example is *Archaeopteryx,* an animal about the size of a crow, with small wings, teeth, and a long, reptilian tail.

Near the end of the Cretaceous period, many animals became extinct. Changing climatic conditions, competition from newly evolving mammals, and, possibly, extraterrestrial episodes led to the demise of many reptile species, including the dinosaurs, as well as many other organisms.

The Cenozoic Era The Cenozoic (65 million years ago to the present), or the Age of Mammals, was characterized by the dominance and adaptive radiation of mammals. This era is divided into two periods, the Tertiary, which encompassed 63 million years, and the Quaternary, which covers the last 2 million years. During the Cenozoic, various species of mammals came to occupy every environmental niche. Some, such as whales and dolphins, adapted to the sea. Others, such as bats, took to the air. Most mammals, however, are land animals, including dogs, horses, rats, bears, rabbits, apes, and humans. One of the major evolutionary advantages that enabled mammals to radiate so rapidly was their reproductive efficiency. In contrast to reptiles, which lay eggs that are vulnerable to predators, most mammals retain their eggs internally within the female. The eggs are thus protected and nourished until they reach an advanced stage of growth. Consequently, a much higher percentage of the young survive into adulthood, when they can reproduce.

Creation Science and Evolution

One of the striking things about Darwin's theory of evolution through natural selection is its resiliency. Although some aspects of his work, such as his interpretations of heredity, have been modified, the validity and importance of the basic tenets of the theory as a means of explaining changes in species through time have been largely reaffirmed by almost a century and a half of scientific study. Nevertheless, some segments of Western society have not accepted evolutionary theory. Evolution offers a view of the origins and development of life that contradicts literal interpretations of the Bible. Although evolutionary theory does not implicitly preclude the possibility of a supernatural deity, it does not require divine intervention to explain the origins of life. For this reason, some people continue to reject evolutionary theory.

Currently in U.S. society, some religious fundamentalists, who call themselves *creation scientists,* are attempting to refute evolutionary explanations. These people propose a biblically based explanation of the origins of the universe and of life. Creation scientists argue that the universe was created by divine fiat within a period of six days. They further argue that Creation occurred about 10,000 years ago, challenging modern scientific evidence that indicates billions of years of geological history and dismissing the evidence of the fossil record. According to the creationists, all the evidence collected by modern biologists, anthropologists, and geologists is biased in favor of an evolutionary position. They claim that scientific estimates of the age of the earth—approximately 4.6 billion years—are based on inaccurate dating methods. Creationists explain the existence of fossilized remains of ancient and prehistoric life by referring to a universal flood that covered the entire earth for forty days. Surviving creatures were saved by being taken aboard a wooden ship, or ark, constructed by Noah. Creatures that did not survive this flood, such as dinosaurs, became extinct. Creationists present the divine origin of life as a scientific theory and, further, argue that this view should taught in public schools along with evolution.

The Shortcomings of Creation Science

Creation scientists read the texts and theories presented by anthropologists, biologists, geologists, and paleontologists and then present their arguments against evolutionary views. They do very little, if any, direct research to refute evolutionary hypotheses. Consequently, their arguments are derived from biblical sources, mixed with misunderstandings of evolutionary hypotheses (Kitcher, 1982; Harrold & Eve, 1987; Futuyma, 1995).

The cosmological framework espoused by the scientific creationists is not buttressed by the systematic testing of hypotheses that is required by the scientific method. Creationist ideas regarding physical laws, geological findings, and biological processes are unsupported by any empirical observations. For example, scientists around the world find no physical evidence of a universal flood. Local floods did occur, and they may be related to the story of Noah that appears in the Bible (and in earlier Babylonian texts). But to date, no evidence exists suggesting any type of global flood that had the potential to wipe out all human life and other creatures such as dinosaurs (Stiebing, 1984).

Thus, creation scientists are not scientific at all. The basis for their model of Creation is a literal interpretation of biblical sources—a view that weighs each biblical passage as equally literal and the absolute authority on all matters, whether religious, political, historical, or scientific. Creation scientists argue that no evidence for geological events or

physical laws can take precedence over Scripture. This is an argument based on faith rather than on testable, verifiable hypotheses. Therefore, this creationist scenario is neither correctable nor falsifiable. The model proposed by the creation scientists has not offered a challenge to evolutionary theory, which many theologians and major religions accept as a valid scientific theory. Theologian Langdon Gilkey, who has written extensively about the creationist-evolutionist controversy, states:

> First, "creation science" is not a scientific model, and therefore it is not at all a direct alternative to the scientific theory of evolution. On the contrary, it represents a religious or theological model of the explanation of origins which neither conflicts with nor excludes scientific theories of origins. (Gilkey, 1986:174)

The perception of creation science as a religious interpretation is shared by the vast majority of the scientific community, as well as most mainstream Protestant, Catholic, and Judaic scholars and theologians. Efforts to require the teaching of creation science or, alternatively, to ban the teaching of evolution in public schools have been consistently defeated on the basis of the constitutional guarantee of the separation of church and state. Yet attempts to incorporate creation science into school curricula continue to occur.

A more recent clash over supernatural, rather than scientific, perceptions of the origins of life is represented by *intelligent design theory,* which also purports to offer a scientific alternative to evolution. Proponents of this view appear to accept the geological and fossil evidence for the antiquity of the earth and also the evidence for some evolutionary processes. However, they argue that evolutionary theory cannot explain the complexity of life on earth. Rather, the core of this theory rests on the acceptance of a supernatural deity, or intelligent designer, who is responsible for the purposeful complexity of nature, either through creation or divine plan. While appearing superficially more scientific than creation scientists, proponents of this theory fail to bolster their interpretations with scientific research. As in all religious belief, the strength of this view does not depend on observable or verifiable phenomena, but rather faith in a supernatural being, which by nature is unobservable.

SUMMARY

Following the scientific revolutions in the West, various developments in the natural sciences, including geology and biology, led to new perspectives on the age of the earth and humankind's origins. Geologists began to discover that the earth had an ancient history, much longer than the few thousand years allowed by a literal reading of biblical chronology. In the nineteenth century, these new ideas influenced biologists Charles Darwin and Alfred Wallace, who were documenting the tremendous variation of plants and animals around the world. From their observations, they developed the theory of natural selection to explain how organisms evolved over time, adapting and reproducing successfully in particular environments.

Although Darwin and Wallace recognized the vast amount of variation in organisms in different environments, they lacked an adequate understanding of how characteristics were passed on from one generation to the next or, in other words, the principles of heredity. Through his experiments on pea plants, an Austrian monk, Gregor Mendel, discovered the essential principles of heredity. Mendel's insights regarding the transmission of dominant and recessive traits, segregation, and independent assortment have remained basic to our understanding of heredity.

Modern scientists have refined Mendel's insights on the study of inheritance. Today, biologists have a better understanding of cell biology and what is known as molecular genetics. Through studies of cells, biologists have unraveled some of the processes of inheritance. The DNA molecule found in the cell is the key factor in determining the traits that organisms inherit from their parents. It contains the chemical information that provides the coding for specific proteins that determine the physical characteristics of organisms.

Modern biologists study evolution in populations of organisms. They identify changes that mutation, gene flow, genetic drift, and natural selection create in the allele frequencies of populations. Changes in allele frequencies may enhance or limit the abilities of a population to adjust successfully to a specific environment.

Recently, paleontologists have challenged the gradualist form of evolution as proposed by early thinkers such as Darwin. They have found that species of organisms sometimes remain unchanged for millions of years, and then new species suddenly develop successfully in varied environments. Today this punctuated equilibrium model of evolution complements the earlier gradualist model in explaining the proliferation of different species of organisms on the earth.

Some people have not accepted the modern scientific theories regarding the development of the universe and living organisms. In particular, creation scientists have rejected the evolutionary concepts of modern biology. They propose that the earth has a recent history dating back about 10,000 years, and they believe that different species of life were created spontaneously by divine fiat. The creationists do not conduct scientific studies to refute the modern explanations of evolution. Instead, they criticize scientific findings based on a distorted understanding of evolutionary processes and of the scientific enterprise itself. Scientific creationists do not offer scientific explanations but rather base their views on religious faith. As emphasized in Chapter 1, scientific knowledge takes a distinctively different form from that of religious knowledge. Hypothesis testing and acts of faith are radically different means of acquiring knowledge of the universe. To mix one form of knowledge with another, as the creationist scientists do, is to misunderstand this fundamental difference.

QUESTIONS TO THINK ABOUT

1. Compare the scientific contributions of Buffon, Cuvier, and Lyell. How did each attempt to provide a more scientific understanding of the past?

2. In your own words, explain what is meant by the terms *natural selection, adaptation,* and *evolution*. Create examples to illustrate the concepts.

3. What are the four mechanisms of evolution, and how do they operate to change gene frequencies in a population?

4. Is gene flow influenced by cultural factors such as religion, kinship, language, socioeconomic status, and ethnicity? If so, how? Give some examples.

5. Should contemporary models of human evolution be classified as "origin myths"? Why or why not?

6. What is creation science? How is it different from science? Should creation science be taught alongside the theory of evolution in public school science classrooms? Why or why not?

KEY TERMS

adaptation

adaptive radiation

alleles

amino acids

analogy

catastrophism

chromosomes

continental drift

cosmologies

deoxyribonucleic acid (DNA)

dominant

ecological niche

evolution

founder effect

gametes

gene

gene flow

gene pool

genetic drift

genotype

gradualistic theory of speciation

Hardy-Weinberg theory of
    genetic equilibrium

heterozygous

homology

homozygous

meiosis

mitosis

mutation

natural selection

phenotype

plate tectonics

population

punctuated equilibrium

recessive

somatic cells

speciation

species

uniformitarianism

INTERNET EXERCISES

1. Review the Critical Perspectives box "The Nemesis Theory." How does this theory relate to the extinction of the dinosaurs? Look over the description of this theory at **http://stommel.tamu.edu/~baum/paleo/paleogloss/node30.html**. What is an Oort cloud? Why is a 26-million-year cycle predicted? What are the drawbacks to this theory?

2. Plate tectonics and the concept of continental drift have explained much geological phenomenon. Look at the map of the plates at **http://volcano.und.nodak.edu/vwdocs/volc_images/tectonic_plates.html**. How can an understanding of the movement of the various plates lead to an understanding of how geological processes have an impact on biological evolution?

3. Look at the information on embryonic development at **http://www.ultranet.com/~jkimball/BiologyPages/T/Taxonomy.html#EmbryonicDevelopment**. What is the meaning of the phrase "ontogeny recapitulates phylogeny?" Why is this statement an oversimplification of the process of embryonic development?

SUGGESTED READINGS

DARWIN, C. R. 1975. *On the Origin of Species by Means of Natural Selection or the Preservation of the Favored Races in the Struggle for Life.* New York: W. W. Norton.

A reprint of one of the most important books of all time. This long essay by Darwin is still of great significance to modern readers.

FUTUYMA, DOUGLAS J. 1995. *Science on Trial: The Case for Evolution*. Fitchburg, MA: Sinauer. A concise summary of the evidence for biological evolution, it provides a point-by-point refutation of pseudoscientific creationist claims and is an excellent survey of the major issues and sources of debate involved.

GOULD, STEPHEN JAY. 1989. *Wonderful Life: The Burgess Shale and the Nature of History*. New York: W. W. Norton. This fascinating work by North America's most famous biologist and paleontologist presents the most recent thinking on evolutionary processes, including punctuated equilibrium and related issues. Gould's earlier collection of essays from the magazine *Natural History*—published under such titles as *An Urchin in the Storm, Ever Since Darwin, The Panda's Thumb,* and *The Flamingo's Smile*—are also recommended for understanding the most important issues in modern evolutionary thought.

RAUP, DAVID M. 1986. *The Nemesis Affair: A Story of the Death of the Dinosaurs and the Ways of Science*. New York: W. W. Norton. The Nemesis theory proposes that "Nemesis," a companion star to our sun, circles in an orbit that brings it close to earth every 26 million years. Theorists propose that comets generated by the passage of this "death star" caused dramatic changes in the direction of life on earth. David Raup, a noted paleontologist, provides a stimulating and entertaining discussion of the origin of the Nemesis theory and the how and why of scientific inquiry.

SPROUL, BARBARA. 1979. *Primal Myths: Creating the World*. New York: Harper & Row. A superb collection of origin myths found throughout the world. It demonstrates the range of the human creative imagination in constructing cosmologies.

CHAPTER

4

The Primates

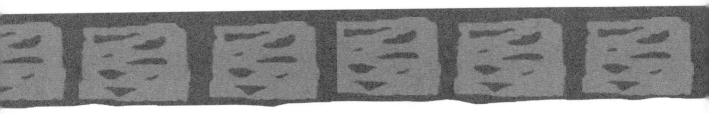

CHAPTER OUTLINE

PRIMATE CHARACTERISTICS

Dentition, Eyesight, and Brain Size / Reproduction and Maturation

CLASSIFICATION OF PRIMATES

Primate Subdivisions / Classification of Fossil Primates

THE EVOLUTION OF THE PRIMATE ORDER

Primate Origins / Fossil Prosimians / Modern Prosimians / Evolution of the Anthropoids / Emergence of the Hominoids / Modern Apes

PRIMATE BEHAVIOR

Primate Social Groups / Sociobiology

THE HUMAN PRIMATE

CHAPTER QUESTIONS

- What are the basic characteristics of primates?

- What are the basic subdivisions of primates?

- What does the fossil evidence tell us about primate evolution?

- How do the anthropoids differ from the hominoids?

- What are some of the characteristics of the modern apes?

- What are some of the basic behaviors associated with the primates?

- How does the human primate differ from other primates?

Members of the mammalian order **primates** are a diverse group of animals, including humans, monkeys, prosimians, and apes. They share certain characteristics such as large brain size, keen vision, dexterous hands, and a generalized skeleton that allows for great physical agility. Primates also tend to have smaller litters than other animals, devoting more care and attention to the rearing of their offspring. Certain traits are prominent in some primates and hardly evident in others. Similar features can be found in many nonprimates. For example, the lion has very efficient eyesight, and the tree squirrel is exceedingly agile. However, the unique *combination* of traits found in the primates distinguishes them from other animals.

We can trace the striking similarities among primates to a series of shared evolutionary relationships. Many people hold a common misconception about human evolution—the mistaken belief that humans descended from modern apes such as the gorilla and chimpanzee. This is a highly inaccurate interpretation of both Charles Darwin's thesis and contemporary scientific theories of human evolution, which suggest that millions of years ago some animals developed certain characteristics through evolutionary processes that made them precursors of later primates, including humans. Darwin posited that humans share a common ancestor (now extinct) with living apes but evolved along lines completely different from modern gorillas and chimpanzees.

Primate *paleontologists* and *paleoanthropologists* study fossil bones and teeth of early primates to trace lines of human evolution dating back millions of years. Meanwhile, *primatologists* concentrate on living, nonhuman primates, working to discover subtle similarities and differences among these creatures. As researchers weave together the fossil record and conclusions from primatological observations, they discern the outlines of a vivid tapestry of human evolution—how it occurred and what makes humans physically and behaviorally distinct from other primate species.

Primate Characteristics

Primate evolution has produced some key physical and anatomical traits that represent adaptations to **arboreal** conditions—that is, life in trees (LeGros Clark, 1962; Richard, 1985). Among the most important physical characteristics of primates is their generalized skeletal structure, which allows for a great deal of flexibility in movement. Consider, for example, the *clavicle*, or collarbone, a feature found in early mammals. This skeletal element has been lost in faster, more specialized land animals, such as the dog and the horse, which have more rigid skeletons. In primates, the clavicle provides both support and flexibility, enabling them to rotate their shoulders and arms to perform a range of movements. In the wild, this skeletal structure gives primates the ability to reach for branches and food while roaming through treetops. Humans, of course, do not live in trees. However, their generalized primate skeleton greatly enhances their ability to drive cars, catch baseballs, and throw spears.

Dexterity in the digits (fingers and toes) of the feet and hands, another key primate trait, makes it easy for primates to grasp and manipulate objects. All primates (except for the callitrichids) have sensitive pads on their fingertips rather than claws, and many have five digits on their hands and feet, which can be used for grasping objects. Unlike cats or rodents, with claws, primates climb by wrapping their hands and feet around branches. An important distinguishing element of the primate hand is the **opposable thumb,** found in humans and many other primates (Figure 4.1). Humans can touch the tips of each of their fingers with the thumb, an ability that makes them adept at manipulating small objects. Some primates do not have opposable thumbs, but all members of the Primate order share a high degree of digit mobility.

Dentition, Eyesight, and Brain Size

Dentition, the number, form, and arrangement of teeth, serves as a distinguishing characteristic of many types of animals. Because they are strong

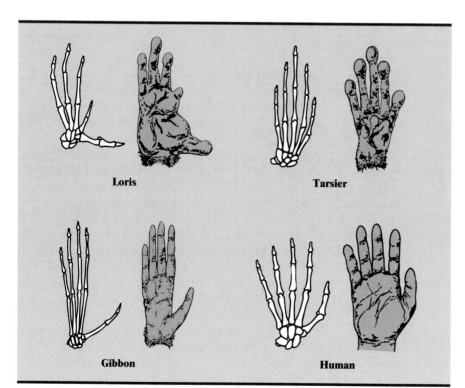

Loris

Tarsier

Gibbon

Human

FIGURE 4.1 Examples of primate hands. Although they vary in form, they share a high degree of manual dexterity.

Source: Adapted from Fig. 2.20, p. 31 in *Primate Adaptation and Evolution* by John G. Fleagle. Copyright © 1988 by Academic Press, reproduced by permission of the publisher. All rights reserved.

and are often better preserved in the fossil record than other parts of the skeleton, teeth are particularly valuable evidence for paleontologists, who use them to identify extinct primates. Compared to other mammals, primates have multipurpose teeth that can be used for either cutting or crushing foods. The dental structure of primates is consistent with an **omnivorous** diet, made up of a variety of foods, from plants, fruits, nuts, and seeds to insects and other animals.

Different teeth perform different functions. The anterior (front) teeth, including the incisors and canines, are used to transfer food into the mouth. They are designed for cutting, tearing, and biting. Their shape varies from one primate species to another as a result of evolutionary adaptations to particular food-processing situations. The posterior (back) teeth, or molars, are less specialized. They simply break down food by crushing or grinding.

Refined vision also sets primates apart. Whereas many animals are highly dependent on *olfaction,* the sense of smell, primates, having large eyes oriented to the front and protected by bony structures, rely heavily on vision. This visual orientation favors *binocular* and *stereoscopic vision,* in which the visual fields of the eyes overlap, transmitting images to both sides of the brain. Primates benefit from enhanced depth perception as a result. Evolution has also made the retina of primates' eyes sensitive to different wavelengths of light, producing color vision in most primates. Primates depend on their highly developed visual sense to identify food and coordinate grasping and leaping.

Distinguishing primates even more are the size and complexity of the brain. Relative to body size, primates have larger brains than any land animal; only the brains of marine mammals are of comparable relative size (Fleagle, 1988). In primates, the *neocortex,* the surface portion of the brain associated with sensory messages and voluntary control of movement, features a large number of convolutions, or folds, which maximize the surface area. As they evolved, these larger brains undoubtedly helped primates to locate and extract food and to avoid predators (Jolly, 1985).

Reproduction and Maturation

In contrast to most other animals, primates reproduce few offspring, and these undergo long periods of growth and development. The **gestation period** for primates—that is, the length of time the young spend in the mother's womb—is longer than that of nonprimate animals of comparable size. Primate offspring are born helpless and unable to survive on their own. For this reason, they have long periods of maturation, during which they remain highly dependent on their parents and other adults. As an example, a kitten reaches full adulthood at one year, whereas a baboon takes seven or eight years to reach maturity. Humans, in contrast, have a period of infancy that lasts six years. Full adulthood, characterized by the appearance of the third molars, or "wisdom teeth," is reached at 20 years of age.

During this protracted maturation process, primates learn complex adaptive tasks from other members of their species, primarily by observing their mothers, fathers, and others in their social group. Through this *social learning,* primates gain the skills needed to locate food and shelter and to elude predators.

All these evolutionary trends can be traced through the lines of primates from the Eocene to the present day. Enhanced locomotion, refinements in vision and brain functions, an extended period of offspring dependency, and increased life span all combined to make primates adaptable to a variety of environmental niches.

Classification of Primates

Taxonomy, the science of classification, gives scientists a convenient way of referring to, and comparing, living and extinct organisms. Modern taxonomy is based on the work of the Swedish scientist Carl von Linnace, also known as Carolus Linnaeus (1707–1778). Linnaeus created a system of Latin names to categorize plants and animals based on their similarities. The Linnaean system follows a hierarchical pattern (see Table 4.1), ranging from large categories such as *kingdoms,* which encompass creatures sharing overarching characteristics, to small groups, or *species,* whose members can all potentially interbreed.

Human beings belong to the kingdom Animalia, one of the several major divisions of nature. Members of this kingdom are mobile, complex organisms that sustain themselves by eating plants and other animals. Other categories, or *taxa,* are based

Table 4.1	Classification Relevant to Human Ancestry

The classification of living organisms is hierarchical. Membership in a kingdom is determined by very basic characteristics. Classification into other categories is based on increasingly specific criteria. The words *primate, anthropoid, hominoid,* and *hominid* are used to refer to members of the categories Primates, Anthropoidea, Hominoidea, and Hominidae. Superfamily names generally end in *oidea,* family names in *idae,* and subfamily names in *inae.*

Category	Taxon	Common Description
Kingdom	Animalia	Animals
Phylum	Chordata	Animals with notochords
Subphylum	Vertebrata	Animals with backbones
Superclass	Tetrapoda	Four-footed vertebrates
Class	Mammalia	Vertebrates with body hair and mammary glands
Order	Primates	All prosimians, monkeys, apes, and humans
Suborder	Anthropoidea	All monkeys, apes, and humans
Infraorder	Catarrhini	Old World anthropoids
Superfamily	Hominoidea	Apes and humans
Family	Hominidae	Bipedal apes
Genus	*Homo*	Humans and their immediate ancestors
Species	*Homo Sapiens*	Modern human species

Source: From Marvin Harris, *Culture, People, Nature: An Introduction to General Anthropology.* Copyright ©1988. All rights reserved. Reprinted by permission of Allyn and Bacon.

on more specific criteria (see Table 4.1). For example, humans have backbones, a feature that places them in the subphylum Vertebrata, while the presence of body hair and mammary glands further identifies them as members of the class Mammalia (mammals). Classes are subdivided into a number of orders; humans belong to the order Primates. Like other mammals, primates are warm-blooded animals that possess hair for insulation and nourish their young with milk from mammary glands. However, primates' refined visual sense, manual dexterity, distinctive skeletal structure, and large brain size differentiate them from other mammals.

Although all primates share certain basic characteristics, we do see a great deal of variation among species. There is some disagreement among primatologists about how particular species are related to one another and how the order should be divided. When Linnaeus developed his classification system to facilitate the comparison of organisms, Darwin had not yet introduced his theory of evolution. However, after Darwin's publication of *On the Origin of Species* in 1859, biologists increasingly applied theories of evolution to systems of classification, giving

rise to a number of scientific disputes about the basis of classification. Some scientists focus on physical similarities among species, traits that most likely emerged as evolutionary adaptations to specific environments. Other scientists stress actual genetic links, determined through the study of DNA.

How do scientists distinguish between genetic links and adaptive characteristics? Consider the classification of humans, chimpanzees, gorillas, and orangutans. On the one hand, African apes and orangutans, which have certain physical traits in common, have traditionally been placed in their own family, Pongidae. Humans, on the other hand, followed another evolutionary line entirely, making them distinct in appearance. In contrast to other primates, humans have developed a complex culture—material objects and nonmaterial concepts—that they use to interact with the environment. They have a much larger brain than the other primates and lack the others' thick covering of body hair. For this reason, scientists place humans and their immediate ancestors in the family Hominidea. However, careful study of ape and human anatomy and molecular studies of genetic material indicate that in actuality humans and the African apes are more closely related than either group is to the orang-utans (Andrews & Martin, 1987). Today, in classifying species, many scientists try to bear in mind both the genetic relatedness of species and the characteristics produced by specialized adaptations.

Primate Subdivisions

The order Primates is divided into two suborders: *Prosimii,* or prosimians, and *Anthropoidea,* or anthropoids. The prosimians include modern lemurs, lorises, and tarsiers, all of which are found exclusively in Asia and Africa. The modern anthropoids, comprising all monkeys, apes, and humans, can be separated into two smaller divisions, or infraorders: *Platyrrhini,* referring to all monkeys found in the Americas, and *Catarrhini,* or anthropoids found in Europe, Asia, and Africa. The catarrhines are subdivided into the superfamilies *Cercopithecoidea,* monkeys, and *Hominoidea,* including apes and humans. Paleoanthropologists take a particular interest in members of the superfamily *Hominoidea* because these are the primates most closely related to humans. The **hominoids** fall into three families: *Hylobatidae* (lesser apes), *Pongidae* (great apes), and *Hominidae* (hominids).

Classification of Fossil Primates

Biologists and primatologists sometimes disagree about the classification of living organisms. However, paleontologists and paleoanthropologists face even more daunting challenges in their attempts to classify extinct species because they must base their conclusions solely on characteristics preserved in the fossil record, such as skeletal structure and dentition. Natural variations within populations, the vagaries of climatic and geological changes, and the ravages of time all make identifying species on this basis exceedingly difficult (Conroy, 1990; Hartwig, 2002).

In the past, scientists have placed great emphasis on the skull, or *cranium,* in distinguishing fossil primates from one another. The cranium provides clues to an extinct animal's vision, diet, cognitive abilities, and posture. However, as increasing numbers of fossils have been recovered, paleontologists are now looking more closely at the *postcranial skeleton,* all the bones of the body excluding the skull (Strasser & Dagosto, 1988). By examining the postcranial skeleton, we can determine a great deal

about a primate's posture and locomotion, which in turn tell us a great deal about the animal's adaptations to disparate environments. As we bring together all this information, we can discern much more clearly how fossil primates looked and functioned in their environments.

The fossil record for certain periods is sketchy, at best. For example, we know that the period spanning 4 million to 8 million years ago was very important in terms of primate evolution and the adaptations that led to the human lineage. Unfortunately, fossils from that age are not well preserved. Because of the fragmentary nature of the fossil record, we may never know precisely how primate evolution proceeded.

The Evolution of the Primate Order

The 200 species of modern primates represent the products of millions of years of adaptation. Primates evolved during the Tertiary and Quaternary periods in the Cenozoic era (see Table 3.1, pages 52–53). The Tertiary period is subdivided into five successive epochs: Paleocene, Eocene, Oligocene, Miocene, and Pliocene. The Quaternary period comprises the Pleistocene and Holocene epochs.

Scientists speculate that the first mammals related to the primates appeared during the Paleocene, approximately 65 million years ago (Figure 4.2). Although not true primates, these early mammals resembled primates in some respects, particularly in the shape and arrangement of their teeth. The oldest recognizable primates emerged in the Eocene, bearing some resemblance to modern primates, yet identical to no species alive today.

Because many living primates inhabit environments similar to those occupied by extinct species, the study of these modern-day primates casts light on the adaptive characteristics of earlier primate species. In some ways, modern nonhuman primates embody the evolutionary phases through which the primates passed over millions of years. According to the fossil record, the prosimians developed as the earliest forms of primates, followed by the anthropoids.

Primate Origins

The ancestors of modern prosimians and anthropoids evolved during the late Cretaceous and early

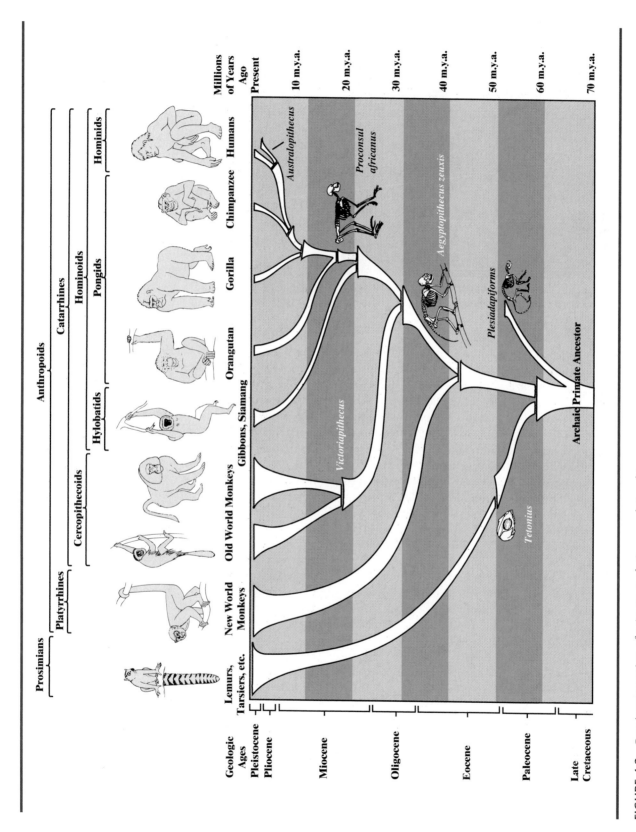

FIGURE 4.2 One interpretation of primate evolutionary relationships.

Source: From *Biology* Fifth Edition by Helena Curtis and N. Sue Barnes, © 1989 by Worth Publishers. Used with permission.

Primates most likely evolved from creatures similar in appearance to modern tree shrews.

Tertiary epochs (70 million to 55 million years ago). These creatures resembled modern squirrels or tree shrews in size and appearance and were well adapted to an arboreal lifestyle. Fossil remains of these ancestral primates have been unearthed in Asia, Europe, Africa, and America. Many primate-like animals appeared during the middle Paleocene, and a number of different genera—collectively referred to as *plesiadapiforms*—were among the most successful. Sometimes classified as a distinct suborder of archaic Primates, plesiadapiforms have no modern representatives. Plesiadapiform fossils have been unearthed in Europe and North America; the genus *Plesiadapis*, perhaps the best known, was described on the basis of fossil finds in the western United States and France (Gingerich, 1986). *Plesiadapis* had a long snout and a squat, stocky body, similar to the modern groundhog. A delicate impression in limestone indicates that these creatures had long, bushy tails.

Certain aspects of plesiadapiform dentition distinguish these creatures from earlier animals. These basic features, which are retained as *primitive characteristics* in later primates, suggest that the plesiadapiforms are related to later primates. However, the plesiadapiforms also exhibit selected adaptations to particular environmental niches. These distinctive adaptations, or *derived characteristics,* include specialized teeth, cranial structure, and limb bones unlike those of any later primates. Many of the plesiadapiforms' specialized, derived nature indicates that they are not precursors of any later primate groups.

For 30 million to 35 million years, these early creatures thrived in the forest areas of the world. Presumably, they fed on insects, seeds, bird eggs, and other small life forms. At the end of the Eocene, many of these early animals became extinct for reasons that are unclear. Some scientists speculate that changing climatic conditions modified the animals' environments, making survival impossible. Others conjecture that these creatures could not compete effectively with more successful animals such as rodents and prosimian primates.

The Earliest Primates?   One of the earliest primate ancestors, a tiny animal, *Purgatorius,* has been described on the basis of finds at a number of sites in North America (Clemens, 1974). Paleontologists who have found *Purgatorius* jaw fragments and many isolated teeth conjecture that this creature subsisted primarily on a diet of insects. The dentition of *Purgatorius* barely resembles that of later primates, but its primatelike molars indicate that this diminutive creature had a more omnivorous diet than that of other insectivores. These molars distinguish *Purgatorius* from other early mammals and suggest an ancestral relationship between this creature and more recent primates. Of the plesiadapiforms, only *Purgatorius* has enough of an unspecialized nature to be considered ancestral to modern primates.

Although the remains of *Purgatorius* have been uncovered only in North America, we cannot assume that primates first evolved there. It's important to note that North America was still attached to Europe when *Purgatorius* thrived, and primates could have moved easily between the continents. The discovery of *Purgatorius* on this continent may reflect the limited number of finds from this period in other areas. The earliest primates may have evolved in other parts of the world, including Africa and Asia. The discovery of 60-million-year-old fossil teeth near the Atlas mountains of Morocco lends support to the theory that early primates emerged in Africa (Gingerich, 1990). These teeth define a previously unknown species, *Altialasius koulchii,* tiny creatures probably weighing no more than 3.5 ounces. Given the fragmentary nature of the finds, the precise relationship of this species to primates is uncertain. These creatures may be precursors of anthropoid primates, or they may represent a side branch, such as the plesiadapiforms.

Fossil Prosimians

The prosimians, which appeared at the beginning of the Eocene, were the first true primates, and, like the earlier plesiadapiforms, early prosimian primates flourished. Researchers have located the most complete prosimian fossil finds in North America and Europe, but more fragmentary examples of prosimian fossils have been discovered in Asia and Africa (Fleagle, 1988).

In examining the cranial structure of the Eocene prosimians, scientists have found striking evidence to indicate that these animals relied much more on vision than on their sense of smell. Consider the *endocast*—a cast of the brain—of *Tetonius,* a 50-million-year-old prosimian found in Wyoming (Radinsky, 1967). Although the olfactory portions of the brain are small compared to earlier creatures, the occipital and temporal lobes—the sections of the cerebrum associated with vision—are relatively large. From its large eyes, researchers deduce that *Tetonius* was **nocturnal**—that is, it searched for food at night when other animals were sleeping. Present-day (extant) nocturnal animals have large eyes to take in the greater amounts of light needed for night vision. A nocturnal orientation can be inferred in extinct animals whose crania reveal large orbits (spaces in the skull for eyes).

Scientists have unearthed few postcranial skeletons of the early prosimians, but the available finds suggest that these creatures were evolving toward the more generalized skeletal structure that characterizes later primates. With slender limbs and modified hands and feet, these primates most likely had some of the locomotor and grasping abilities of modern species. And in some species, nails were replacing claws (Dagosto, 1988). These characteristics prefigure modern families of prosimians.

Interestingly, some fossil prosimians also exhibit features that resemble the most primitive characteristics in the anthropoid primates, such as the orbits of the eye and the structure of foot and leg bones. Paleoanthropologist Elwyn Simons (1972) has described these early prosimians as "the first primates of modern aspect," signaling their important place in primate evolution.

Modern Prosimians

Modern prosimians have changed relatively little from their ancestors and reside in small, isolated populations. They include the lemurs and indris of Madagascar (an island off the east coast of Africa), the lorises of tropical southeast Asia and Africa, and the tarsiers of southeast Asia.

A heightened visual sense makes most of the living prosimians nocturnal, although they do not have color vision. Like their fellow primates, however, they possess stereoscopic vision and enlarged brains relative to other animals, which help them to coordinate leaping and food gathering in their arboreal environment. A keen sense of smell, more highly developed than that of the anthropoid primates, helps them to seek out food and shelter at night.

Like other primates, the prosimians use the five dexterous digits on their hands and feet to grasp objects and to move easily through trees. Some *prosimii,* such as the indris, move by vertical clinging and leaping from branch to branch in an upright position, springing with their hind legs and landing with their arms and legs. All of the living prosimians have nails instead of claws on their digits, but some have retained grooming claws on their hind feet, which are used to clean their fur. Because of the extensive destruction of the tropical rain forests in which the prosimians live, all are endangered animals.

Evolution of the Anthropoids

As many of the early prosimians gradually became extinct at the end of the Eocene epoch, new types of primates emerged in tropical forest environments. Among these new primates were creatures ancestral to modern anthropoids, including humans. Scientists divide the anthropoids into three groups based on their distinct ecological niches (Fleagle, 1988). The three categories are the platyrrhines (all monkeys from the Americas, or New World monkeys) and the two superfamilies of catarrhines (monkeys, or cercopithecoids, from Europe, Asia, and Africa, also called Old World monkeys, and the hominoids, including apes and humans).

The divergent evolution of the higher primates is closely tied to plate tectonics and continental drift, examined in Chapter 3. During the late Cretaceous period, approximately 65 million years ago, North America and Europe were joined, allowing free migration of primates between what later became the European, African, and Asian continents and the Americas. About 40 million years ago, the Americas separated from Europe, Asia, and Africa, ending contact between primates from the Eastern and Western Hemispheres. This geological development resulted in disparate lines of primate evolution. Platyrrhines evolved in southern Mexico and Central and South America, and cercopithecoids developed in Africa and Asia. We shall first examine the monkeys in the Americas and then delve into the evolution of monkeys and hominoids in Europe, Asia, and Africa.

Evolution of the Platyrrhines The fossil record for the evolution of the monkeys in the Americas (platyrrhines) is sparse and consists only of fragmentary fossil evidence from Bolivia, Colombia, Argentina, and Jamaica. Indeed, all of the primate fossils found in South America would fill no more than a shoe box (Fleagle, 1988). Paleontologists, therefore, have not been able to reconstruct a detailed account of how anthropoid evolution proceeded in the Americas. Current interpretations favor the theory that the platyrrhines evolved from African anthropoid primates, a theory consistent with the limited fossil evidence and shared similarities in dentition and biochemical characteristics.

Although African origins for the platyrrhines present the most likely interpretation of the available fossil evidence, scientists remain puzzled about how ancestral anthropoids may have arrived in South America from Africa. Uncertainty surrounds much of our understanding of continental drift during this period, making it difficult to date precisely when various landmasses separated. South America is believed to have been an island continent during most of the early Cenozoic era.

Although periods of low sea levels during the Oligocene (38 million to 25 million years ago) may have exposed landmasses and created areas of relatively shallow water in the South Atlantic, movement between the continents would still have involved crossing open water. Transportation over large expanses of water on floating masses of vegetation has been used to explain the movement of some species; and, in fact, ocean currents would have been favorable to an African–South American

crossing. Yet it has been questioned whether this method of dispersal is consistent with primate dietary and climatic requirements.

North and Central America have also been suggested as the home of the ancestral platyrrhines, but there is no fossil evidence to bolster such an interpretation (Fleagle, 1988). Paleogeographical reconstructions would also seem to confound this theory, as they suggest that during the Oligocene the distance between South America and landmasses to the north was even greater than that between South America and Africa. However, the geological history of the Caribbean is poorly known. Another candidate for the platyrrhine origins is Antarctica. Though it was joined to South America during the appropriate time period, the absence of any information on the evolution of mammalian species on Antarctica makes this scenario impossible to evaluate.

Modern Monkeys of the Americas The monkeys of the Americas encompass fifty-two different species—including the marmosets, the tamarins, the sakis, and the squirrel, howler, spider, and wooly monkeys—having a tremendous range in physical appearance and adaptations (Jolly, 1985). One feature that distinguishes anthropoids from the Americas from those from Europe, Asia, or Africa is the shape of the nose. The former monkeys have broad, widely flaring noses with nostrils facing outward. The latter anthropoids have narrow noses with the nostrils facing downward.

Monkeys from the Americas spend their days in trees, coming to the ground only to move from one tree to another. Their elongated limbs are ideal for grasping tree branches. As **quadrupeds,** they use all four limbs for locomotion. In addition, many of these monkeys have developed a unique grasping, or *prehensile,* tail. Prehensile tails serve as a fifth limb, enabling some platyrrhines to hang from branches and feed with their other limbs. This unusual tail also gives the monkeys greater coordination and balance as they move through trees. Most monkeys from the Americas eat a varied, omnivorous diet that includes fruits, insects, and small animals.

Evolution of the Catarrhines Compared to the meager fossil findings of monkeys from the Americas, paleontologists have unearthed extensive anthropoids from Europe, Asia, and Africa. Specimens have been recovered from all over these continents,

A spider monkey hanging from its prehensile tail. Primates with prehensile tails are found only in the Americas.

including many regions that primates no longer inhabit. Among the most significant fossil localities are those in the Fayum Depression in Egypt, an extremely arid region rich in fossil-bearing strata dating from 45 million to 31 million years ago (see Figure 4.3). Anthropoid fossils abound in the upper part of the formation, dating back about 37 million years ago. During this period, the Fayum was a lush tropical forest, ideal for primates, and an amazing variety of plant and animal fossils have been unearthed in this once-fertile region (Simons & Rasmussen, 1990).

Parapithecids   Among the most interesting of the early anthropoid primates are representatives of the family Parapithecidae. However, scientists have not determined the precise relationship of these animals to later primates. Skeletal and dental structures of certain parapithecids resemble those of platyrrhines. Discovering these features in African

fossils, researchers conjectured that parapithecids may have emerged sometime near the divergence of the anthropoids from the Americas and those from Europe, Asia, and Africa. However, the parapithecids exhibit many specialized, derived dental traits that suggest evolutionary adaptations leading away from the lines of later anthropoids. One theory holds that these early anthropoid primates may represent a distinct branch early in the anthropoid line (Fleagle & Kay, 1987; Fleagle, 1988).

Apidium, one particularly well-known parapithecid identified in hundreds of fossil finds, was a small, quadrupedal primate with a short snout. It had thirty-six teeth, the same number found in modern monkeys from the Americas. Its comparatively small orbits indicate that *Apidium* was **diurnal,** that is, active during the day. Postcranial bones, such as the long hind legs and flexible ankles, lead researchers to believe that *Apidium* was an effective leaper.

Cercopithecoids   In tracing the earliest potential ancestors of monkeys (cercopithecoids) of Europe, Asia, and Africa, paleontologists cite the Miocene deposits in northern and eastern Africa, pegged at 26 million to 5 million years old. *Victoriapithecus,* one of these fossil monkeys, thrived near Lake Victoria in Kenya (Fleagle, 1988). A small to medium-sized monkey, weighing between 10 and 55 pounds, *Victoriapithecus* was quadrupedal and appears to have been equally well suited for an arboreal or **terrestrial** (ground-dwelling) life. Such adaptable capabilities would have been useful in the middle Miocene environment of Kenya, which scientists believe was an open woodland.

Victoriapithecus and related genera had a number of characteristics of modern cercopithecoid species. For example, the chewing surfaces of *Victoriapithecus* molars had distinctive patterns of cusps and ridges that are found in extant species. In addition, males and females had different-sized canine teeth, a feature *Victoriapithecus* had in common with all monkeys of Europe, Asia, and Africa. However, some of the more derived features found in later monkeys were absent from *Victoriapithecus.* Thus, these primates cannot be placed in any modern subfamily. Rather, because they represent a transitional form between earlier catarrhines and modern monkeys, they make up their own subfamily of extinct primitive monkeys, the *Victoriapithecinae.*

FIGURE 4.3   A stratigraphic profile of fossil-bearing deposits in the Fayum Depression in Egypt.

Source: Adapted from Fig. 12.4, p. 328 in *Primate Adaptation and Evolution* by John G. Fleagle. Copyright © 1988 by Academic Press, reproduced by permission of the publisher. All rights reserved.

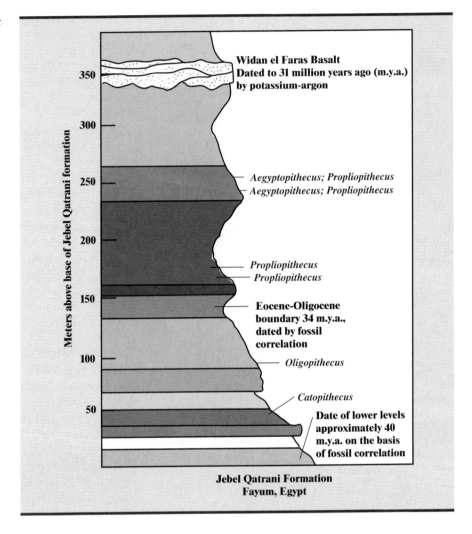

Meters above base of Jebel Qatrani formation

**Widan el Faras Basalt
Dated to 31 million years ago (m.y.a.)
by potassium-argon**

Aegyptopithecus; Propliopithecus
Aegyptopithecus; Propliopithecus

Propliopithecus
Propliopithecus

**Eocene-Oligocene
boundary 34 m.y.a.,
dated by fossil
correlation**

Oligopithecus

Catopithecus

**Date of lower levels
approximately 40
m.y.a. on the basis
of fossil correlation**

**Jebel Qatrani Formation
Fayum, Egypt**

Remains of many other species of monkeys have been found in fossil beds of Pliocene and Pleistocene age (6 million years of age up to the recent past). The majority of these extinct species can be conveniently organized into the same subfamilies as living monkeys, providing a neat link between *Victoriapithecus* and the present.

Modern Monkeys of Europe, Asia, and Africa

Modern-day cercopithecoids encompass an extremely diverse group, consisting of seventy-eight different species scattered throughout sub-Saharan Africa, southern Asia, and northern Japan. Next to humans, they are the most widely distributed primate group. These monkeys include different species of macaques, langurs, savanna and hamadryas baboons, geladas, colobus monkeys, and proboscis monkeys. Like the anthropoids of the Americas, these monkeys are quadrupedal. Although primarily arboreal, some, such as the savanna baboons, are terrestrial. Unlike their American counterparts, these monkeys do not have prehensile tails; however, some do use their tails as aids in communication and balance.

These monkeys break down into two subfamilies: Cercopithecinea and Colobinea. Most of the cercopithecines live in Africa, but some, such as the macaques, are also found in Asia. The colobines include the langurs of Asia and the African colobus monkeys. The two subfamilies differ most with respect to nutrition. The cercopithecines have a slightly more varied diet, feeding on many types of

The gibbon's long arms and powerful shoulder muscles allow it to negotiate its arboreal environment by brachiating, an arm-over-arm suspensory locomotion used to move from branch to branch. Many primates can easily hang from tree branches with one hand while feeding or wrestling with a playmate with the other. However, brachiating primates such as the gibbon swing through the trees like acrobats, covering up to 30 feet in a single motion.

vegetation and fruit. Their cheek pouches act like storage bins; these pouches can be filled with food intended to be eaten in another place. In contrast, the colobines subsist primarily on leaves; often referred to as "leaf-eating monkeys," they have specialized teeth, stomachs, and intestines that enable them to digest the woody, cellulose parts of plants. Compared to the cercopithecines, the colobines are less mobile, often residing in the trees where they feed.

Pronounced **sexual dimorphism,** in which males and females of the same species exhibit separate characteristics, distinguishes many cercopithecine monkeys. The male baboon, for example, has a much larger body and larger canine teeth than the female. These differences arise as a result of rivalry among males for females. Species in which competition for sexual mates is limited exhibit little sexual dimorphism, whereas species characterized by intense competition display the most dramatic dimorphism (Kay et al., 1988). Other features, including relative differences in the size of the testes and sexual swelling in females during ovulation, also correlate with mating rivalry and patterns of social organization.

Emergence of the Hominoids

The evolution of the anthropoids set the stage for the appearance of the first hominoids and, consequently, the emergence of more immediate human ancestors. Consider representatives of the genus *Aegyptopithecus,* discovered in the Fayum region in Egypt and dating from approximately 33 million years ago (see the box "Interpreting the Fayum Fossils"). The fossil evidence for *Aegyptopithecus* includes a skull, numerous jaw fragments, and several limb bones. *Aegyptopithecus* is believed to have been comparable in size to a modern howler monkey, which weighs only 13 to 18 pounds

Skull of Aegyptopithecus zeuxis, *an Oligocene anthropoid, excavated from the Fayum Depression in Egypt.*

Source: Courtesy of D. Tab Rasmussen.

CRITICAL PERSPECTIVES

INTERPRETING THE FAYUM FOSSILS

Popular magazines and museum displays tend to arrange information into neat packages. Sophisticated illustrations present the viewer with a concise graphic summary of millions of years of human or primate evolution. Yet these sharply drawn illustrations and explanations belie the tenuous nature of many interpretations of the age, environment, and relationship among different fossil species. Consider the challenges faced by primate paleontologists conducting research in the Fayum Depression, located 100 miles southwest of Cairo, Egypt, along the northwestern margin of the Sahara Desert. Here researchers have made some of the most exciting discoveries of early primate fossils, gaining insights into the ancient environment of the region and piecing together pictures of extinct primates that were ancestral to modern monkeys, apes, and humans.

Paleontologists confront an apparent contradiction in tracing the roots of modern primates: The living catarrhines thrive in the tropical forests of Africa and Southeast Asia, yet fossil specimens come primarily from desert regions like the Fayum. This disparity stems from the incomplete nature of the fossil record. Fossil strata are not exposed in tropical forest regions, and the lush vegetation makes the identification of sites difficult. In contrast, the Jebel Qatrani Formation at the Fayum constitutes a geological "layer cake," hundreds of feet thick, that spans the Eocene and Oligocene epochs (see Figure 4.3). Over millions of years of wind and water erosion, these early deposits have been exposed for scientists to examine. Larger fossils and resistant pieces of stone lie in scattered gravel patches called "desert pavement"; lighter fossils have disappeared, carried away by desert winds.

Uniquely accessible and fossil-rich, the Fayum has attracted researchers for more than a century, most prominently Elwyn Simons of Duke University, who has spent thirty years piecing together the region's past (Simons & Rasmussen, 1990). Like most paleontologists, scientists working in the Fayum sometimes expose fossils by carefully digging away hard, overlying sediments with hammers, chisels, and brushes. However, nature has been enlisted as an ally in the Fayum excavations as well. To expose new fossil-bearing deposits, researchers sweep away hardened layers of desert pavement, revealing unweathered layers of sediment. Within a year the harsh winds may scour away as much as six inches of loose, underlying sand, uncovering new fossils. This technique works especially well when it comes to more delicate fossil remains.

In dating the Fayum fossils, various methods have come into play. Through faunal correlation with dated fossils from other areas, the earliest marine sediments at the Fayum can be traced to the middle Eocene (less than 45 million years ago), whereas the earliest primates in the region most likely emerged in the late Eocene (around 37 million years ago). The fossil-bearing deposits are capped by layers of basalt, a rock of volcanic origin that dates from 31 million years ago, as determined by potassium-argon dating (Fleagle et al., 1986). Scientists have assessed the relative ages of fossils in the deposit by carefully plotting their stratigraphic position in the formation.

Dry, bleak, and inhospitable today, the Fayum underwent major environmental changes over millions of years. Originally covered by the ancient Mediterranean Sea—the earliest layers in the Fayum are marine sediments—the Fayum experienced a gradual geological shift to a terrestrial environment. Fossils recovered from the terrestrial deposits of the Eocene and Oligocene number in the tens of thousands, including a wide array of extinct rodents, water birds, bats, snakes, and turtles (Simons & Rasmussen, 1990). All of the Fayum finds clearly indicate that the late Eocene and Oligocene environment was wet and tropical. The bones of paleomastodons, the oldest-known elephants, have also been unearthed at the Fayum, as well as insects, tropical plants, and fossilized trees of various kinds. In fact, new species are constantly being discovered. Here we can see the importance of long-term research at individual fossil sites.

The ample supplies of fresh water and food in the Oligocene tropical forest of the Fayum provided an ideal environment for early primates. Almost a thousand primate fossils have been found there, representing eleven species (Rasmussen & Simons, 1988; Simons, 1989a, 1990; Simons & Rasmussen, 1990). Among the most interesting of these finds are the remains of *Aegyptopithecus* (Simons, 1984). A number of other early hominoids have also been identified, including *Catopithecus, Oligopithecus,* and *Propliopithecus.* How are all these different species related? Undoubtedly, some of these creatures contributed to the evolution of modern anthropoids. Yet determining how evolution actually proceeded—which forms of life preceded others and how and when successful adaptations emerged—remains a daunting task.

To establish evolutionary relationships, scientists scrutinize fossil remains for key identifying features. Basic characteristics shared by all members of a family, such as similarities in dentition and the structure of the skull, are called primitive characteristics, and they are helpful in grouping the animals together as early anthropoids. However, because

Egypt's Fayum Depression is desert today, but fossils of fruit, nuts, and vines indicate that a tropical forest covered that region 33 million years ago.

the same primitive characteristics are found in all the early anthropoids, they are of no help in determining the relationships within the group. To track down these relationships, scientists examine derived characteristics, the more distinct or specialized traits in individual fossil species that evolved as adaptations to particular environments. More closely related animals will have more of these characteristics in common.

Primate paleontologists cite the physical features of some of the Fayum anthropoids as evidence that these creatures are part of the same lineage—that is, a group of animals sharing an evolutionary

relationship that makes up a branch in the order Primates. Animals with a common lineage can be arranged in a ladderlike progression. For example, *Catopithecus* may have given rise to *Oligopithecus,* which eventually evolved into the characteristics seen in *Aegyptopithecus.* Some species of *Propliopithecus* may represent either intermediary stages in this progression or members of a related lineage.

Even though work at a fossil locality as fruitful as the Fayum Depression may raise more questions for paleontologists than it answers, little by little the fossil finds help fill in gaps about primate and human evolution. And as these finds flesh out the picture of primate evolution, they shed light on how primates developed, how they negotiated their early environments, and perhaps how thinking, sentient beings emerged on the planet.

POINTS TO PONDER

1. How does the fragmentary nature of the fossil evidence affect the validity of anthropological interpretations and hypotheses?

2. What types of evidence are missing from the fossil record that would contribute to our understanding of extinct species?

3. When, if ever, do you think our understanding of the evolutionary process will be "complete"?

(Fleagle, 1983). The postcranial bones reflect the skeletal structure of an arboreal quadruped.

The dentition of *Aegyptopithecus* offers several useful insights. Dental structure, for example, indicates that this early ape subsisted on a diet of fruit and leaves. Researchers have also noted a great deal of variation in the size of canine teeth, which may indicate that the species was sexually dimorphic. Building on this hypothesis, scientists make the theoretical leap that *Aegyptopithecus* lived in social groups in which competition over females was intense.

Aegyptopithecus resembles primitive monkeys and prosimians in several key respects, including its small brain and diminutive skeletal structure. However, other features, such as its thirty-two teeth—the same number found in humans and apes—suggest that *Aegyptopithecus* may represent an ancestor of later hominoids.

Hominoid Evolution   The fossil record sheds little light on the period spanning the time when *Aegyptopithecus* flourished through the early Miocene, some 10 million years later. However, we can state with certainty that the Miocene (24 million to 5 million years ago) brought apes to the fore. According to the fossil evidence, the earliest forms of protoapes evolved in Africa before 18 million years ago. After that, Africa was connected to Europe and Asia through the Arabian peninsula, enabling hominoids to migrate to these other continents. The fossil evidence indicates that the late Miocene apes made remarkable adaptations to all sorts of geographic and climatic conditions in Europe, the Middle East, Asia, and Africa.

A study of various Miocene fossil species spotlights the intermediate stages through which modern hominoids passed. However, determining the exact lineages leading to specific living species is complicated.

Scientists attempting to classify Miocene apes are hampered by two problems: the vast number of species and fragmentary fossil evidence. They categorize these apes primarily on the basis of their teeth, which prompted some imaginative researchers to dub them the "dental apes." This method of identification has one major weakness, however; convergent evolution in similar environmental settings (say, the tropical forests of present-day Africa and the tropical forests of contemporary South Asia) may

have produced nearly identical dentition in primates of markedly different ancestry. The postcranial bones of Miocene apes and protoapes reveal a number of apelike and monkeylike trait combinations dissimilar from any found in living hominoids. This leads researchers to speculate that these fossil species engaged in locomotive and behavior patterns unlike any exhibited by modern species (Fleagle, 1983).

Proconsul   The best-known early Miocene protoape, *Proconsul africanus* (Figure 4.4), has been reconstructed, offering a good illustration of the mix of features found in some of the Miocene primates. This protoape's pronounced snout, or muzzle, contrasted significantly with the more diminutive snout in the majority of later monkeys and apes. Yet the auditory region of the brain in this protoape was indistinguishable from that of living apes and monkeys from Eurasia and Africa. Other regions of the brain also mirrored those of living monkeys, but much of the sensory and mental development seen in living apes was absent (Falk, 1983). Examining the postcranial skeleton of

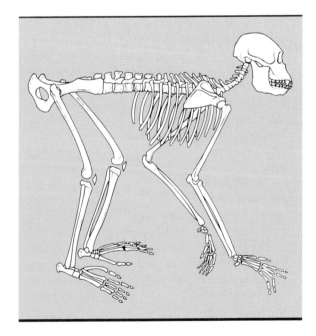

FIGURE 4.4   A reconstructed skeleton of *Proconsul africanus* based on finds from East Africa.

Source: Adapted from Roger Lewin, *Human Evolution: An Illustrated Introduction,* Blackwell Scientific Publications, 1989, p. 58. Used by permission of Blackwell Science Ltd.

P. africanus, researchers have noted similarities to both apes and monkeys (Walker & Pickford, 1983; Beard et al., 1986). Moreover, the size and structure of the leg bones (especially the fibula) and the configuration of the foot resembled those of apes. Like living apes, *P. africanus* lacked a tail. However, the arrangements of the arm and hand bones had more in common with some monkeys than with apes. Despite these similarities, *P. africanus* lacked many of the more specialized features of modern apes or monkeys. A quadrupedal creature, adapted to an arboreal environment, *P. africanus* nonetheless lacked the swinging and leaping capabilities of apes and monkeys. Although *Proconsul* stands as an ancestor of later hominoids, the precise relationship between these primates has yet to be specified.

Ancestors of Modern Hominoids　Early researchers studying the middle and late Miocene apes attempted to trace clear ancestral lines back in time to specific species. But the evolutionary status of these various species has become increasingly complicated as new finds are made. Current research casts doubt on the hope that any such neat and tidy picture will ever emerge.

Hylobatids　Modern representatives of the family Hylobatidae, including the siamang and the gibbon, are the most specialized and the smallest of the living apes. Various fossil specimens dating back as far as the Oligocene and Miocene have occasionally been classified as ancestral gibbons (Fleagle, 1988). However, these identifications are based on very superficial similarities between fossil and extant species. Looking closely at specific features, we see that these extinct creatures were far more primitive, lacking a number of refined cranial and postcranial skeletal developments found in all the living catarrhines. These discrepancies, combined with the fragmentary nature of the fossil finds, make interpretations of early hylobatid ancestry extremely tenuous (Fleagle, 1988). The earliest definitive examples of gibbon species date from the Pleistocene (less than 2 million years ago) in China and Indonesia.

The Orangutan　The only existing hominoid whose evolutionary history is comparatively well understood is the Asian member of the family Pongidae, the orangutan (genus *Pongo*). Fossil ancestors of the orangutan fall into two subgroups of Miocene hominoids, *Ramapithecus* and *Sivapithecus,* dating

to about 16 million to 8 million years ago. These hominoids thrived in a variety of environments, including tropical forests as well as drier, open bushlands. Although *Sivapithecus* and *Ramapithecus* were long regarded as distinct groups, they are closely related, and today's researchers tend to combine them into the same genus.

The dentition and facial anatomy of the sivapithecines resemble those of modern apes and humans more than those of earlier hominoids. For this reason, some paleoanthropologists previously viewed these creatures as ancestors of human beings. However, because the more specific features of the lower face of some sivapithecines bear remarkable similarity to those of the modern orangutan, paleoanthropologists now agree that the sivapithecines were ancient relatives of modern orangutans, although they were not actual orangutans. Recent finds in Turkey, India, and Pakistan suggest that sivapithecines may have moved on all fours, like modern chimpanzees and gorillas, rather than spending a great deal of time climbing trees, as do orangutans.

Gigantopithecus　Some Miocene apes were enormous, including an extinct group of hominoids related to the Asian sivapithecines (Ciochon et al., 1990). Classified as *Gigantopithecus* (Figure 4.5), these massive creatures were first identified on the basis of their teeth, which were being sold in Chinese shops as "dragon bones." Very fragmentary gigantopithecine fossils have been found in China, Vietnam, Pakistan, and northern India. The earliest gigantopithecine are from late Miocene fossil localities (dating from approximately 5 million years ago), and the most recent are from Pleistocene caves dating from less than 1 million years ago. Judging from the fossil remains, the gigantopithecines towered over other primates; no doubt, their huge teeth and jaws presented an intimidating sight. The larger of the two species, *G. blacki,* may have reached a height of 6 to 9 feet and weighed up to 600 pounds.

The dentition of *Gigantopithecus* resembles that of *Sivapithecus;* both share such features as thick enamel and low, flat cusps. These similarities suggest that the gigantopithecines descended from the earlier apes. Judging from the large teeth and thick, heavy mandibles, paleontologists theorize that *Gigantopithecus* subsisted on a diet of hard, fibrous plants such as bamboo. This hypothesis gained

FIGURE 4.5 Drawing on fossils of extinct species and associated remains of other plants and animals, researchers are able to reconstruct the appearance and behavior of ancient primates, as in this illustration of *Gigantopithecus.*

Source: Adapted from Fig. 13.20, p. 386 in *Primate Adaptation and Evolution* by John G. Fleagle. Copyright © 1988 by Academic Press, reproduced by permission of the publisher.

support recently when scientists discovered microscopic traces of plant residue called *phytoliths* on fossil teeth. These deposits may be consistent with a diet of bamboo.

The oversized features of *Gigantopithecus* have prompted speculation that this creature may be an ancestor of an as-yet-undiscovered Abominable Snowman residing in the frozen heights of the Himalayas. Most primatologists believe, however, that *Gigantopithecus* represents a highly specialized form of hominoid that diverged from the other lines and became extinct about 1 million years ago.

African Pongids and Hominids   Like detectives who follow all sorts of trails—some fruitful, some dead ends—to reconstruct the sequence of events leading to a particular incident, paleontologists work doggedly to trace ape and human origins. Unfortunately, the trail has gone cold in the search for the Miocene and Pliocene ancestors of the African pongids and hominids. One line of Miocene apes that probably prefigures modern pongids and hominids are members of the genus *Proconsul.* For several decades two *Proconsul* species (africanus and major) were thought to be ancestral to modern chimps and gorillas (see Figure 4.4). This relationship to a modern species, however, was

based on size and geographic distribution, not shared morphological characteristics (Fleagle, 1988: 391). Further studies demonstrate that *Proconsul* and other Miocene apes were far more primitive in structure than living species. Furthermore, relatively recent molecular dating studies lead experts to believe that *Proconsul* lived long before the divergence of the pongid and hominid lines (Ciochon & Corruccini, 1983). Moreover, scientists have come upon almost no hominoid fossils from the period between 8 million and 4 million years ago, which appears to have been a key time in the emergence of the hominids (see Chapter 5).

Recent discoveries indicate that the radiation of the Miocene hominoids was far more complex than previously thought, including as many as twelve genera—providing many more clues but no solutions to the question of hominoid origins. Other representatives of the genus *Proconsul*—mostly teeth but a few fragments of skulls, limb bones, and vertebra—show considerable variation. Weight estimates range from 10 to 150 pounds. Available evidence also suggests varying environmental adaptations and locomotive patterns. Although none of these species can be pointed to as the specific ancestor of modern hominoids, *Proconsul* species likely represent hominoid ancestors near the divergence of hylobatids, pongids, and hominids (see Figure 4.2).

The Extinction of Most Miocene Apes During the early Miocene, ape species proliferated, but most became extinct for reasons that still elude scientists (Conroy, 1990). By the middle Miocene (approximately 16 million to 10 million years ago), ape species became dramatically less common compared to monkeys, reversing the earlier trend. Apes all but disappeared from the fossil assemblages of the late Miocene (10 million to 5 million years ago), and, as yet, there have not been any fossil finds of apes in Eurasia and Africa after the Miocene. In contrast, the middle Miocene fossil record provides evidence of abundant and diverse species of monkeys and the radiation of African monkeys into Eurasia. At the end of the Miocene, the specialized bipedal apes, the hominids, made their appearance (see Chapter 5).

Global climatic and ecological changes undoubtedly played a role in the extinction of the Miocene apes. Although it is difficult to generalize about a time period spanning 20 million years, the trend in continental climates was toward drier and cooler conditions (Conroy, 1990). Sixteen million years ago, the tropical rain forests of Africa were replaced by more open woodlands and savannahs. In the circum-Mediterranean region, the climate became more temperate and seasonal.

Many of the Miocene apes probably had difficulty adjusting to the cooler, drier climates. It is only in the less temperate, more tropical regions of Asia and Africa that apes continue to survive. However, some of the hominoids became more terrestrial, successfully adjusting to the new, open environments. It is these species that became the precursors of modern apes and humans.

Modern Apes

The modern apes, descendants of the Miocene hominoids, are found only in Asia and Africa (Richard, 1985). In Asia, the surviving species include the gibbon, the siamang, and the orangutan. The African hominoids are the chimpanzee and the gorilla.

The Gibbon and Siamang The gibbon and siamang are the most numerous of the living apes, inhabiting evergreen forests throughout southeast Asia. There are several species of gibbon, which weigh between 11 and 14 pounds. The siamang is larger, weighing up to 25 pounds. The hylobatids savor a diverse diet, ranging from fruits and leaves to spiders and termites, although the choice of food depends on local environments and the time of year.

All the hylobatids have relatively short trunks; extremely long, slender arms; curved fingers (see Figure 4.1); and powerful shoulder muscles. These characteristics enable them to negotiate their arboreal environment through brachiation. **Brachiation** refers to arm-over-arm suspensory locomotion used to move from branch to branch. Many primates can easily hang from tree branches with one hand while feeding or wrestling with a playmate with the other. However, brachiating primates such as the gibbon swing through the trees like acrobats, covering up to 30 feet in a single motion.

The gibbons and siamangs live in monogamous family groups consisting of male-female pairs and as many as four immature offspring. These young may stay in the family group for up to ten years. Foraging for food together or individually, families sometimes range over large areas and fiercely defend their territories. The hylobatids are noisy, often calling and vocalizing to signal their presence to other groups.

The Orangutan The orangutan, the only Asian pongid alive today, lives exclusively in the heavily forested regions of the Indonesian islands of Borneo and Sumatra. Orangs are large, sexually dimorphic apes. Males weigh about 150 pounds, whereas females reach about half that size. Because of their large size, orangs are not as agile as the lesser apes. Nevertheless, their long arms and fingers allow them to move quite efficiently through the trees. When traveling long distances, they occasionally drop to the ground and move in a quadrupedal fashion. The orangutan has a distinctive *noyau* social organization, in which adult males and females do not live in large social groups or pairs. Instead, adult females, together with their immature offspring, range over comparatively small areas searching for leaves, fruits, and seeds. Adult males, in contrast, cover larger areas, often encountering several females with whom they may mate.

Increasingly, these shy, mostly solitary creatures are facing extinction in many areas as development eliminates their ranges and the depletion of the tropical rain forests continues apace. At one time, more than 500,000 orangutans inhabited the tropics of Asia, but today the orangutan has become an endangered species. A total of perhaps 30,000 survive in Borneo and Sumatra.

The Gorilla   The best-known apes still roaming the earth are the gorilla and the chimpanzee. As with the orangutan, the habitats of these great apes are being threatened by humans. Today these apes—all confined to restricted areas in Africa—are listed as endangered species. About 40,000 lowland gorillas (the type usually seen in zoos) live in the forests of western and central Africa. In the lake areas of East Africa, only 400 mountain gorillas remain.

The gorilla is the largest living primate (Richards, 1985; Schaller, 1976). The adult male weighs up to 400 pounds; the female grows to about 200 pounds. Although they can climb, gorillas are the most terrestrial of all primates, besides humans, because of their great size. On the ground, they use an unusual quadrupedal form of locomotion called **knuckle walking.** Rather than supporting their forelimbs with the palms of their hands (as do most other primates), knuckle walkers rest their hands on the ground in a curled position, with the tops of their curled middle and index fingers bearing their weight. Big-boned creatures, gorillas also have large, powerful jaws and chewing muscles for eating a wide variety of terrestrial vegetation such as roots, shoots, and bark. Yet despite their tremendous size and strength, they are shy, gentle creatures.

Gorillas thrive in social groups of about twelve animals, although the group's size may range from two to twenty, and lone males are occasionally seen. Groups are dominated by an older male, or silverback. Observing mountain gorillas over a long period, Dian Fossey discovered that their groups consist of unrelated females and immature males (see the box "Primatologists in the Field: Jane Goodall and Dian Fossey" on pages 94–95). Female gorillas may transfer from one group to another once or many times during their lives. This pattern differs markedly from other primate groups, which are made up of related individuals. Males appear to transfer less frequently than females, and when leaving a group they generally do not join another. New groups may form when females join a lone male.

The Chimpanzee   Chimpanzees inhabit a broad belt across equatorial Africa from the west coast to Lake Tanganyika in the east. Two species of chimpanzees have been identified in Africa: the "common" chimpanzee (*Pan troglodytes*) and the "pygmy" chimpanzee (*Pan paniscus*). At present, pygmy chimpanzees are found only in a small forested area of central Africa, whereas the common chimp inhabits both rain forests and mountain forests as well as dry woodland regions. Like gorillas, chimpanzees are knuckle walkers whose anatomy suits this form of locomotion. However, chimps also spend a good deal of time swinging in the trees and feeding on all sorts of fruit and vegetation. In addition, primatologists have discovered that chimps occasionally hunt, eating birds and small mammals (Goodall, 1986). Chimps and gorillas

An infant chimpanzee (Pan troglodytes) *in northeastern Sierra Leone. Genetically, the chimpanzee and the gorilla are almost identical to humans.*

are recognized as the most intelligent of all the apes. Recent studies indicate that from a genetic standpoint, chimpanzees and humans are over 95 percent identical (Goodman & Lasker, 1975).

Chimpanzees band together in less structured social organizations than those of other anthropoid primates. A chimpanzee community may number from fifteen individuals to several dozen, but adults of both sexes sometimes forage alone and sometimes band together into groups of between four and ten. There is no overall leader, and the makeup of the smaller feeding groups is constantly changing. Chimpanzee communities are defined by groups of males that generally maintain friendly relations and utilize the same range.

Primatologist Jane Goodall (1986) has observed that male-female sexual bonding among chimpanzees is extremely fluid. One female may mate with a number of males in the group. In other cases, a male and a receptive female may form a temporary sexual bond, or *consortship,* and travel together for several days. As Goodall has also noted (1986), the fluid nature of chimpanzee social life makes the day-to-day experiences of a chimpanzee far more varied than those of most other primates.

Primate Behavior

Modern primates have complex learning abilities and engage in multifaceted social activities. Some primates of the same species exhibit disparate forms of social organization and behavior because of differing ecological circumstances. The behavior of other primates varies within the species, even when they live in similar environmental conditions. Despite this diversity, primatologists studying these creatures in their natural habitats have identified some common primate behaviors.

A cornerstone of primate life is the relationship between mothers and infants. Many animals virtually ignore their offspring after birth. However, as mentioned earlier, primates tend to have longer periods of maturation than other animals. During infancy, primates are cared for by their mothers, often forming a lasting bond (Harlow & Harlow, 1961). This mother-infant attachment is particularly strong among the anthropoid apes, and it may continue throughout a primate's lifetime. We find poignant examples of chimps tenderly caring for an injured infant or mother in Jane Goodall's studies of chimpanzees in the wild. These close attachments undergird primate social organization.

Primate Social Groups

Most primates congregate in social groups, or communities, sometimes known as *troops.* Living in groups confers many advantages, including a more effective defense against predators, enhanced food gathering, more intensive social learning, greater assistance in rearing offspring, and increased reproductive opportunities. By ensuring these things, primates make sure that infants receive adequate care, nourishment, and protection, and bolster their reproductive success.

As part of group living, primates engage in various kinds of affiliative behavior that help resolve conflicts and promote group cohesion. This conduct, which may involve interpersonal behavior such as hugging, kissing, and sex, can be illustrated by **social grooming.** Whereas other animals groom themselves, social grooming is unique to primates. Chimpanzees will sit quietly as other members of the troop carefully pick through their hair, removing ticks, fleas, dirt, and other debris. Social grooming not only promotes hygiene but also reduces conflict and friction between males and females and between young and old in the troop. Grooming works like a "social cement," bonding together members of the troop by maintaining social interaction, organization, and order among them all (Jolly, 1985; Falk, 2000; Strier, 2003).

Primates also use a wide variety of *displays*— including body movements, vocalizations, olfactory (odor-related) signals, and facial gestures—to communicate with one another. In making these displays, primates express basic emotions such as fear and affection, as well as convey threats, greetings, courtship signals, and warnings of impending danger. The primates communicate through grunts, hoots, ground slapping, head bobbing, screams, scent marking (among prosimians), and facial gestures (among anthropoids of Eurasia and Africa). The more intelligent apes, especially the gorillas and chimpanzees, draw on a more highly developed repertoire of communication tools.

Dominance Hierarchy A social order known as **dominance hierarchy** characterizes the group

ANTHROPOLOGISTS AT WORK

PRIMATOLOGISTS IN THE FIELD: JANE GOODALL AND DIAN FOSSEY

For many years, our ideas about the behaviors of nonhuman primates came from observations of animals in captivity. Removed from their natural environments and often secluded from other animals, these primates did not exhibit normal behavior patterns. By observing primates in the wild, we can sketch a much more accurate picture of their activities and responses. Such studies, though, pose special problems. Animals like chimpanzees and gorillas live in areas that are heavily forested and difficult to reach. They keep their distance from humans, making close observation challenging. In addition, primates are long-lived (great apes may reach an age of 50 years), which makes it difficult for researchers to draw conclusions about maturation and long-term social relations. Today we know a great deal about the behavior of chimpanzees, gorillas, and other primates in their natural habitats. This information was gathered through the persistence of many primatologists, but the pioneering work of two researchers—Jane van Lawick Goodall and Dian Fossey— deserves special note.

Jane Goodall was born in Bournemouth, England, in 1934. As a child, she was always fascinated by living creatures. In one of her books, *In the Shadow of Man*, she recounts how at age 4 she crept into a henhouse and patiently waited five hours to see how a chicken laid an egg. At age 8, Goodall decided that when she grew up she would go to Africa and live with wild animals. This long-standing desire took her to Kenya in the late 1950s, where she met Louis Leakey, noted for his research on human origins (see Chapter 5). Leakey encouraged Goodall's interest in African wildlife, suggesting that she study chimpanzees. At that time, almost nothing was known about the behavior of wild chimpanzees. Only one study had been carried out, and that had lasted less than three months, far too short a period to gather much meaningful information. Leakey secured funding for Goodall to study chimpanzees in an isolated area near Lake Tanganyika in East Africa.

Arriving in Gombe National Park in 1960, Goodall found the chimpanzees frustratingly uncooperative. It took her more than six months to overcome their deeply rooted fear of humans. Goodall's work (1971, 1990) on the Gombe chimps has now spanned more than thirty years, providing invaluable insight into chimpanzee behavior. She was the first to observe chimpanzees manufacturing simple tools to extract termites—a favorite food—from their nests.

She has documented the long-term bonds between mother and child and the complexity of social relations. Goodall was also the first to spot the darker side of chimpanzee behavior, including occasional instances of cannibalism, murder, and warfare. We owe these important observations about the social behavior of chimps to Goodall's extraordinary commitment. Hers is the longest ongoing study of any primate group. She continues her work today at the Gombe Stream Research Center, which she established.

Another key contributor to primate studies was Dian Fossey, who spent eighteen years documenting the life of the mountain gorillas of Parc des Virungas, Zaire, and Parc des Volcans, Rwanda (Fossey, 1983). Dian Fossey was born in 1936 in San Francisco. She had always dreamed of visiting Africa to study the wildlife, a dream she fulfilled in 1963 when she borrowed enough money for a seven-week safari to observe the mountain gorillas of Mount Mikeno, Zaire. While in East Africa, Fossey sought out Louis Leakey, who was then supporting Jane Goodall's work. Convinced of Fossey's commitment, Leakey was instrumental in obtaining funding for her to initiate research for a long-term study of the mountain gorilla.

Fossey faced particularly difficult problems in her studies. The habitat of the mountain gorilla is threatened by the extension of cultivation and herd lands. In addition, the area is hunted by people from nearby African settlements, who often use snares to capture animals like the antelope; tragically, gorillas are sometimes caught in these traps. In other cases, gorillas themselves have been the target of poachers who have cultivated a thriving market in gorilla body parts. Some tribes use gorilla ears, tongues, testicles, and small fingers to make a virility potion. Gorilla heads and hands have sometimes been sold as gruesome souvenirs to European tourists for about twenty dollars apiece. Fossey estimated that two-thirds of gorilla deaths were the result of poaching.

Fossey adopted a strong stand against poachers, practicing what she called "active conservation." She destroyed traps, raided temporary shelters used by poachers, and herded gorillas away from areas where hunters proliferated. In 1985, she was brutally murdered in her cabin at the Karisoke Research Center in Rwanda. Some

Dian Fossey's patience eventually allowed her to make careful observations of mountain gorillas. Her tragic death in the field has been recounted in the film Gorillas in the Mist.

of her experiences are recounted in the book *Gorillas in the Mist,* published shortly before her death and subsequently made into a movie.

Significantly, Goodall and Fossey had received no formal training in primatology before beginning their fieldwork. Although later granted a doctorate from Cambridge University, Goodall had only a secondary school education and experience in business when she first went to Kenya. Fossey had been an occupational therapist before going to Africa, and she garnered official recognition for her work only after years of field experience. With their

extraordinary courage and commitment, these women overcame tremendous obstacles to undertake their research.

The work of researchers like Goodall and Fossey has greatly broadened our knowledge of the behavior of living primates, but this knowledge is accumulating far too slowly. The fossil record indicates that primates once ranged over a much wider portion of the globe than they do today. Many species that are now extinct suffered from environmental changes over the past 30 million years; however, the perilous position of some modern primates can be laid directly at the doorstep of humans. In many areas, primates are still hunted for food. Expanding human settlements and the destruction of forests directly endanger nonhuman primates, threatening the very survival of animals like the mountain gorilla of central Africa, the lion-tail macaque of India, the golden-lion tamarin of Brazil, and many others. The work of researchers like Goodall and Fossey highlights the plight of humankind's closest living relatives and may awaken people to the myriad preventable threats these creatures face.

living arrangements among primates (Fedigan, 1983). Dominance refers to the relative social status or rank of a primate, which is determined by its ability to compete successfully with its peers for objects of value such as food and sexual partners. In most primate groups, a specific dominance or rank hierarchy is based on size, strength, and age. In general, males dominate females of the same age, and older, stronger individuals acquire a higher rank than younger and weaker ones. Certain females may dominate others because they are better able to compete for food, thus enhancing their reproductive success. Each member of the group must learn its rank in the hierarchy and act accordingly. Even species like the chimpanzee, which do not have single, dominant group leaders, are organized into a dominance hierarchy. Once the order of dominance is established in the group, this hierarchical structure serves to head off conflict and socially disruptive activities. In some ecological circumstances, such as a harsh savannah, the dominance hierarchy is extremely rigid. Under more forgiving conditions, such as a forested region, the hierarchy is more loosely structured. In either case, the dominance hierarchy reduces chaotic behaviors and promotes orderly, adaptive conduct.

Primate Aggression   Primatologists have observed that dominance hierarchies inhibit outright aggression and conflict (Richards, 1985; Goodall, 1986). Goodall describes some circumstances in which violence and aggression erupt in chimpanzee communities. Adult males patrol the perimeters of their home range, looking for trespassers. Though chimpanzee males rarely cross into the home ranges of other communities, when trespassing does occur, the patrol party viciously attacks the outsider.

In one incident witnessed by Goodall, a number of adult males split off from their community and moved from one area of their home range in Gombe National Park to another area. During a three-year period, the original group attacked and killed most of the members of this renegade community. Goodall concludes that when a dominance hierarchy is disrupted or when dominance hierarchies are not well developed (as, for instance, when chimps break away from one community to form another), violence and warfare may result.

Primate Sexual Behavior   Male-female sexual behavior among primates does not follow a single pattern; rather, it varies according to environmental circumstances and the particular species of primate. As in the case of the gibbon, there may be monogamous sexual bonds between one male and one female. However, most of the higher primates do not form a close, singular sexual bond. Primatologists usually find in a group a single dominant adult male that has exclusive access to females. Sexual relations in all primate groups depend on many complex social factors. Friendships and alliances with other individuals underlie access to mates. Sometimes female gorillas side with a young dominant male against an older one (Fossey, 1983; Campbell, 1987). Such social subtleties and nuances, especially pronounced among the anthropoid primates, distinguish primate behavior from that of other species.

Sociobiology

Sociobiology provides an important theoretical perspective on primate behavior. Sociobiologists begin with the assumption that natural selection has acted on behavior in the same way it has acted on physical characteristics (Wilson, 1975, 1978). Thus some behaviors survive over others on the basis of how well they contribute to survival and reproductive success. Sociobiologists are not concerned with how specific genes may lead to specific forms of behavior; rather, they are interested in general strategies of behavior and how these might be adaptive in contributing to the reproductive success of a species or individual. According to this approach, successful reproductive strategies have led to innate predispositions that influence behavior. Sociobiology has provided an important explanatory mechanism for many primatologists.

It has been demonstrated that some of the behavior seen in social insects, invertebrates, and some lower vertebrates is genetically controlled. These organisms will exhibit certain patterns of behavior, even if they have never been exposed to any other members of their species and, thus, never had the opportunity to learn their behavior. Such behavior patterns are termed *innate*. On the other hand, *learned* behavior is clearly of great importance in other vertebrates, and including primates. The challenge is to decipher which aspects of the behavior in a particular animal or individual are genetically influenced and which are learned.

In light of this, consider, for example, how sociobiologists view sexual reproductive strategies in primates. Sociobiologists observe that nature has assigned females and males very different parts to play in the reproductive process. Whereas males release millions of sperm in a single ejaculation, females produce only a relatively few eggs, perhaps hundreds over a lifetime. Furthermore, females are pregnant for months and cannot become pregnant again for a period of time. Thus, in principle at least, males are biologically capable of fathering thousands of offspring, whereas females are able to bear a much smaller number of offspring.

From these biological givens, sociobiologists argue that, from an adaptive viewpoint, males may reproduce their genes most efficiently through a strategy of sexual promiscuity that maximizes their number of offspring. This strategy does not, however, serve the reproductive interests of females. Each pregnancy demands great expenditures of energy. Thus, the efficient female strategy is to choose carefully a male whose qualities will contribute to her offspring's ability to survive and reproduce most successfully (Symons, 1979). Sociobiologists do not argue that such male and female reproductive strategies are conscious processes, just that in the course of evolution animals who did not practice these behaviors have been gradually eliminated. Thus, over a long period of time, certain innate predispositions survived.

Some sociobiologists have suggested that such innate predispositions influence a wide variety of human behaviors, including economic practices, kinship relations, aggression, the presence or absence of warfare in small-scale societies, and male–female relationships (Barash, 1987) (see the box on "Human Aggression," in Chapter 16). Many anthropologists have found such suggestions problematic and controversial. They instead underscore the role of learned behavior and human culture. Anthropologist Marshall Sahlins (1976), for example, views this approach as an abuse of evolutionary theory in explaining cultural phenomena. Focusing on kin selection, he cites cases in which human kinship systems are organized by cultural rather than by biological categories. For example, he notes that in some societies there are kinship categories for "brothers," "aunts," "uncles," and so on that have little relationship to actual genealogical relationships. Sahlins concludes that human kinship is not always organized according to degree of genetic relatedness, as sociobiology predicts, and he dismisses sociobiology as a valid theory. In a different vein, biologists Stephen Jay Gould and Richard Lewontin (1979) have critiqued sociobiology as a circular reasoned argument that presents simplistic, idealized situations rarely found in nature.

Sociobiologists have generally responded to such critiques by emphasizing that their hypotheses are tentative and need to be evaluated and tested through empirical research. They argue that to dismiss the entire field of sociobiology through examples of ethnographic data that do not appear to support the theory is extreme. Furthermore, sociobiologists doubt that biological forces will ever be shown to "determine" human behavior, and that human behavior is always a result of both biological and cultural factors. Still, they underscore that some biological tendencies may make some cultural patterns easier to learn than others.

The Human Primate

As members of the order Primates, humans share many physical and anatomical similarities, as well as some behavioral characteristics, with other species of primates. Like other primates, modern humans can rotate their arms fully, grasp branches, and stand erect. The striking resemblance between the skeletons of a chimpanzee and a human being clearly identifies humans as primates. Yet humans possess certain novel capacities and abilities that make them unique.

For example, humans alone walk upright on two legs. Chimps, gorillas, and orangutans may stand upright for short periods, but only humans maintain a completely erect posture and consistently walk upright on two legs. The human pelvis, legs, and feet provide the balance and coordination that make this type of movement possible. Because human hands are not needed for locomotion, they have evolved into highly precise organs for the manipulation of objects. Human hands have short finger bones (or phalanges) compared to other primates (see Figure 4.1). This trait further enhances humans' manual dexterity. We examine in Chapter 5 the adaptive aspects of *bipedalism* (walking on two legs) and the consequences of this evolutionary advance for early hominid behavior.

Humans' sensory organs bear a striking similarity to those of some of the other primates. For example, humans, as well as apes and monkeys, have keen visual acuity, including stereoscopic, binocular, and color vision. They also have diminished olfactory abilities compared to other animals. Thus, humans, apes, and monkeys all appear to perceive the external world in much the same way.

Although all primates have large brains relative to body size, the human brain is three times as large as we would expect for a primate of this size and build (Passingham, 1982). The human cerebrum, referred to in common usage as the "gray matter," and its outer covering, the neocortex (the section that controls higher brain functions), are far more highly developed than those of other primates, allowing humans to engage in complex learning, abstract thought, and the storing and processing of vast amounts of information. The size and complexity of the human brain, together with the protracted period of dependence and maturation characteristic of young humans, stand as the most significant differences between humans and other primates and give rise to the former's extraordinary capacity to learn; to their imaginative social interactions; and to their facility—unique among all life forms—to use and produce symbols, language, and culture.

SUMMARY

Members of the order Primates are a diverse group of animals, classified together on the basis of certain shared characteristics that include a high degree of manual dexterity, keen eyesight, complexity of the brain, prolonged periods of maturation, sophisticated social learning, and a generalized skeleton that allows a great deal of versatility in movement.

Although all primates share certain fundamental characteristics, they also exhibit a great deal of variation. The order Primates is divided into smaller categories—families, genera, and species—based on more specific criteria. This classification scheme reflects the evolutionary relationship of primates to one another. Although scientists essentially agree on these divisions, there are differences of opinion concerning which criteria should be used to define how one species relates to another.

Problems faced in classifying fossil organisms are especially complicated. Primate paleontologists excavate fossil localities to uncover the remains of early primates, and thousands of fossil primates have been unearthed. However, only a small percentage of the organisms that have lived are preserved in the fossil record. Remains are often very fragmentary, making the identification of fossil species difficult. As researchers accumulate more information, they revise or modify earlier interpretations.

The evolution of modern primates, including humans, can be traced back in time through the fossil record. Fossil primates resemble modern species, but none was identical to any creature living today. Modern primates represent the culmination of millions of years of adaptation to particular environmental niches. Nevertheless, modern primates embody some attributes found in ancestral forms. Many living primates occupy environments similar to those inhabited by extinct species. Thus, by studying modern primates, paleontologists gain insight into the abilities and adaptive qualities of species that are no longer extant. Studies of primate fossils, combined with observations of the behavior of living primates, suggest that primates evolved in a forest environment.

Modern primates display a wide variety of behavioral patterns. Nevertheless, some generalized observations can be made. Many primate species congregate in social groups, sometimes referred to as troops, which afford increased protection from predators, more reproductive opportunities, and more opportunities for social learning. Within groups, members are often organized into a social order, or dominance hierarchy. Often this order is based on age, size, and strength. In general, males dominate females of the same species, and larger, stronger individuals acquire more status than younger and weaker individuals. Primates often engage in various kinds of affiliative behavior, such as kissing, hugging, and social grooming. This friendly behavior is coupled with a variety of displays of emotions, from greetings to warnings.

An important theoretical perspective of primate behavior is presented by sociobiology. This interpretation is based on the premise that natural selection has acted upon behavior patterns in the same way that it has acted upon physical characteristics. This does not presume a genetic basis for certain behaviors, but rather that certain behaviors might lead to reproductive success. Some researchers have challenged this theory, yet many primatologists, as well as some anthropologists, see it as a potential explanatory mechanism for some aspects of both primate and human behavior.

Even though humans have many unique abilities, they are still a primate species. Their ability to perform physical tasks, ranging from grasping a doorknob to driving a car, depends on physical abilities that evolved in earlier primates. Insight into the origins of human social behavior, too, can be gleaned from observations of nonhuman primates.

QUESTIONS TO THINK ABOUT

1. Primate evolution has produced some physical and anatomical traits that are related to an arboreal adaptation. What are some of these characteristics? Do all primates share these features?

2. How are fossil primates classified? Is it easier to classify a living species or one that is extinct? What is the definition of a species?

3. What is the difference between derived and primitive traits? How are these characteristics used to classify fossil primates?

4. Discuss the characteristics unique to the hominoids. When did the hominoid radiation take place? How is hominoid evolution relevant to human evolution?

5. Consider the distinctive aspects of primate behavior. How do you think this might provide clues to the behavior of early human ancestors?

6. How does the human primate differ from other primates?

KEY TERMS

arboreal
brachiation
dentition
diurnal
dominance hierarchy
gestation period

hominoids
knuckle walking
nocturnal
omnivorous
opposable thumb
primates

quadrupeds
sexual dimorphism
social grooming
taxonomy
terrestrial

INTERNET EXERCISES

1. Read the article "The Primates of Myanmar" at **http://www.myanmar-embassy-islamabad. net/Article2001/Sept/Sept15.html**. What are Elwyn Simons's conclusions about *Aegyptopithecus zeuxis,* according to this article?

2. The Anthropologists at Work box "Primatologists in the Field: Jane Goodall and Dian Fossey" describes the rigors of fieldwork in Africa. Review the following sites and then describe what it takes to be a field primatologist. What personal traits might be necessary for success

in this field? **http://www.anthro.mankato. msus.edu/information/biography/fghij/ fossey_dian.html** and **http://www.wic.org/ bio/jgoodall.htm**.

3. Review the following website: **http://www. ship.edu/~cgboeree/sociobiology.html**. How does Edwin O. Wilson define sociobiology? Why did his original proposal become so controversial? What are the major conclusions of sociobiology?

SUGGESTED READINGS _____

CONROY, GLEN C. 1990. *Primate Evolution*. New York: W. W. Norton. A detailed but readable synthesis of current scholarship on primate evolution. Contains excellent introductory sections that examine evolutionary change, paleontological methods, and the ways scientists grapple with disparate interpretations of the fossil record.

FLEAGLE, JOHN G. 1988. *Primate Adaptation and Evolution*. New York: Academic Press. A survey of the fossil evidence on primate evolution, interspersed with information on the adaptive strategies of modern primates. A richly detailed and comprehensive work.

FOSSEY, DIAN. 1983. *Gorillas in the Mist*. Boston: Houghton Mifflin. A personal account of Fossey's research on the mountain gorilla in Zaire and Rwanda, and her struggle to preserve the gorilla against human encroachments.

GOODALL, JANE. 1990. *Through a Window: Thirty Years Observing the Chimpanzees of Gombe*. Boston: Houghton Mifflin. An extremely readable account by a leading primatologist of fieldwork among chimpanzees in their natural environment in Africa.

JOLLY, ALISON. 1985. *The Evolution of Primate Behavior*. New York: Macmillan. A comprehensive summary of existing knowledge on primate behavior. This revised edition incorporates much new information culled from contemporary primate studies.

Hominid Evolution

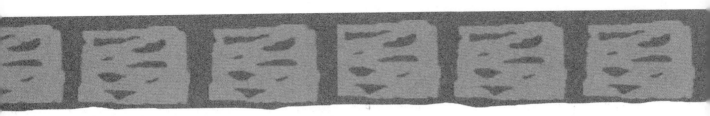

CHAPTER OUTLINE

TRENDS IN HOMINID EVOLUTION

Bipedalism / Reduction of the Face, Teeth, and Jaws / Increase in Cranial Capacity / Other Physical Changes

FOSSIL EVIDENCE FOR HOMINID EVOLUTION

The Oldest Hominids / Early Hominids from Kanapoi and East Turkana / Australopithecus afarensis / The Laetoli Footprints / Taung Child: Australopithecus africanus / Australopithecus aethiopicus: The "Black Skull" / Robust Australopithecines from South Africa / Australopithecus boisei: The "Nutcracker Man"/ Homo habilis: The "Handyman" / Java Man: The "First" Homo erectus / Peking Man and Other Homo erectus

INTERPRETING THE FOSSIL RECORD

Australopithecus africanus as Ancestor / Australopithecus afarensis as Ancestor / Revised Models / Missing Pieces in the Fossil Record? / Genetic Differences and Hominid Evolution

FROM HOMO ERECTUS TO HOMO SAPIENS

Transitional Forms

THE EVOLUTION OF HOMO SAPIENS

Multiregional Evolutionary Model / Replacement Model / Partial Replacement? / Mitochondrial DNA Research

ARCHAIC HOMO SAPIENS

Homo sapiens neanderthalensis

CHAPTER QUESTIONS

- What are the principal trends in hominid evolution? Within genus *Homo?*

- What special problems do paleoanthropologists face in interpreting the fossil record?

- What are the basic differences between Australopithecines and *Homo habilis?*

- How does *Homo erectus* differ from *Homo habilis?*

- In what ways do the new developments in molecular dating help anthropologists interpret hominid evolution?

- What are the basic differences between the multiregional and replacement hypotheses regarding the evolution of modern *Homo sapiens?*

- What are some of the different theories regarding the evolution of *Homo neanderthalensis?*

The evolution of the primates in the Eocene, Oligocene, and Miocene epochs serves as a backdrop for the emergence of early human ancestors. By the Miocene epoch (25 million to 5 million years ago), primates in various forms—the precursors of modern prosimians, monkeys, and apes—proliferated in many geographic regions. Some time in the late Miocene or early Pliocene, new and distinct forms of primates emerged. Classified as the family Hominidae, or **hominids,** these different primate species present a range of distinctive features in their teeth, jaws, and brains that represent adaptations to varying environments. However, they all share the structural anatomy needed for **bipedalism**—the ability to walk upright on two legs. It is this characteristic that separates them from other primates and identifies them as a distinct family. Although a variety of branches and limbs are represented, as a group the hominids are the closest fossil relatives of modern humans.

Paleoanthropologists have advanced and discounted numerous interpretations of hominid evolution over the past century. Initially, few fossils had been located, making it difficult for researchers to evaluate the diversity, distribution, and longevity of different hominid species. New discoveries were at times assigned genus and species names, only to be reclassified as additional finds were made. There are also many ongoing debates about which skeletal features are of principal importance in classifying fossil species. Although opinions diverge on the proper naming and classification of individual fossil specimens, paleoanthropologists are in broad agreement about the evolution of the human species from a small-brained bipedal ape, the hominid lineage branching off from the other primates approximately 6 million years ago. For the purposes of this discussion, we focus on two overarching genuses of hominid: *Australopithecus,* which emerged first, and genus *Homo.* Each of these groups includes a number of different species. Going back over 4 million years, the australopithecines are the older group, and they are only known from African fossil finds. The earliest representatives of the species are *A. anamensis* and *A. afarensis.* The australopithecines evolved from roughly 4 million to 1 million years ago. After that, there is no trace of this genus in the fossil record, leading paleoanthropologists to conclude that they became extinct at about that time.

Some of the australopithecines gave rise to genus *Homo* and, eventually, modern humans. Interestingly, early representatives of genus *Homo,* which bear some resemblance to the australopithecines, coexisted with the later australopithecines between 2 million and 1 million years ago. What distinguishes the first representatives of genus *Homo* from the australopithecine line is a trend toward larger brain size. The earliest member of the *Homo* line to be identified in the fossil record is *H. habilis,* dating between 2.2 million and 1.6 million years ago, followed by *H. erectus,* whose oldest specimens are pegged at over a million and a half years ago. *Homo*

erectus, in turn, evolved into *H. sapiens,* the species that encompasses modern humans, during the past 400,000 years.

Trends in Hominid Evolution

The hominids are members of the order Primates. As such, they share the basic primate characteristics discussed in Chapter 4, including a generalized skeleton, a high degree of manual dexterity, and prolonged infant dependency. But the hominids evolved with distinctive characteristics. As noted, the first and most significant of these is bipedalism, a feature found in all hominids. Other distinctive features include the reduction of face, jaw, and anterior teeth, and a trend toward increasing cranial capacity in genus *Homo.* Changes in these attributes are preserved in the fossil remains of early hominids, and the evolutionary relationships of different species are traced on the basis of the similarities and differences present in individual finds. These characteristics are least pronounced in the earliest hominids, while modern humans exemplify their full development. Other trends, such as degrees of social complexity and the origins of human culture, are also of great importance, but such features cannot be directly inferred from fossil remains. Rather, they are inferred on the basis of early hominid tools, food remains, and living sites, topics examined in Chapter 7.

Bipedalism

Hominids are the only primates that are fully bipedal. Although gorillas, chimpanzees, and orangutans can stand upright, they are primarily knuckle walkers that spend most of their time on all fours. As with other types of locomotion, bipedalism is reflected in skeletal structure. For example, the hips and knees of humans differ markedly from those of knuckle walkers like the chimpanzee (Lovejoy, 1981, 1988). Paleoanthropologists also focus a great deal of attention on the **foramen magnum,** the opening in the base of the skull through which the spinal cord passes. In quadrupedal animals, this aperture is located at the back of the skull, which causes the head to extend out in front of the body. In contrast, the foramen magnum in bipedal creatures is located on the bottom of the skull, sitting squarely

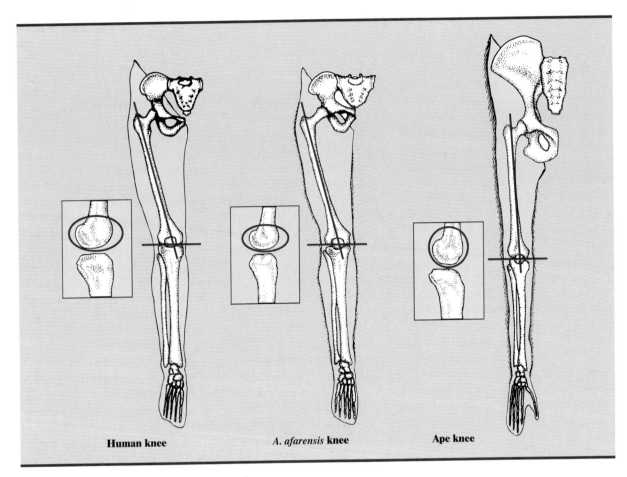

Human knee   *A. afarensis* **knee**   **Ape knee**

FIGURE 5.1   Drawing of Lucy's knee bones and hips compared with those of humans and apes (Lucy's skeletal structure is almost identical to that of modern humans indicating that, like humans, *A. afarensis* was fully bipedal.

Source: Adapted from Donald Johanson and Maitland Edey, *Lucy: The Beginnings of Humankind,* Simon & Schuster, 1981, p. 157. Copyright © 1981 Luba Dmytryk Gudz/Brill Atlanta.

above the body. Structures of the skull associated with bipedalism are especially important because the postcranial bones of many fossil hominids have not been preserved.

Bipedalism stands as the earliest and the most important trend in hominid evolution. Initially, many paleoanthropologists believed that the first known hominids were not proficient at bipedalism, perhaps moving with a swinging, slouched gait like that of chimpanzees or gorillas. These interpretations were based on limited fossil finds and have not been supported by more recent studies. Fossil remains of the oldest known hominids indicate that these creatures walked as well as modern humans

(Figure 5.1). Our best scientific guess places the appearance of bipedalism in hominids sometime between 6 million and 10 million years ago, a period of time poorly represented in the fossil record.

Adaptive Aspects of Bipedalism   Scientists have advanced a number of intriguing but unsubstantiated theories to explain the evolution of bipedalism in early hominids. It is important to recognize that whereas bipedalism is very efficient in terms of energy expenditure, it is a relatively slow means of locomotion—clearly, a disadvantage in avoiding predators. How was this feature adaptive, and why was it selected for? Although bipedal posture can be clearly inferred on the basis of skeletal remains, it is more difficult to reconstruct the behavior of early hominids and how upright posture may have been beneficial.

One possible advantage of upright posture may have been that it allowed ancestral hominids to see over the high grass of Miocene savannas to identify both predators and food sources. Such behavior has been observed among modern ground-dwelling primates such as baboons and chimpanzees, which adopt upright postures to survey their surroundings (Oakley, 1964). Other theories on the origins of bipedalism underscore that this type of locomotion served early hominids by freeing the hands to perform such tasks as transporting food, carrying infants, and using tools. These activities, in turn, would have resulted in a number of important social and cultural innovations.

Tool Use Because early hominids lacked sharp teeth and strong jaws, the ability to use tools would have given them the option of choosing from a greater variety of food sources, thus ensuring increased survival and ultimate reproductive success (Washburn, 1960; Pilbeam, 1972; Shipman, 1984). In fact, some anthropologists attribute the emergence of bipedalism in hominids exclusively to the need to use tools; unfortunately, the existing evidence does not support this hypothesis. The earliest tools, simple stone choppers, date only to 2.5 million years ago, whereas the origin of bipedalism can be traced back 3 or 4 million years earlier.

Nevertheless, advocates of the argument that the need to use tools gave rise to bipedalism discount this evidence as inconclusive. As they correctly point out, tools made of other materials, such as wood, plants, or bone, may have been used much earlier but are not identifiable in the archaeological record. Tools of these materials are unlikely to be preserved or even recognized as tools if they are recovered (Wolpoff, 1983). Modern nonhuman primates such as chimpanzees make simple tools of twigs and grass to extract food from tight spots, and similar improvised tools may have been made by early hominids.

Transport of Food and Offspring Consider, too, the ability to transport food and offspring—important activities among the hominids. Yet how these abilities relate to the selective pressures that initially prompted the evolution of bipedalism is

unclear (Lovejoy, 1981, 1984). Paleoanthropologists conjecture that, as with other primates, the offspring of early hominids clung firmly to the mother. This allowed the female to move freely in search of food or to find safety. Although bipedalism allows for infants to be carried, that advantage would seem to be greatly outweighed by the inability to move quickly through the trees to elude predators. Likewise, food carrying would seem to have limited adaptive significance because animals tend to consume food where it is found.

Paleoanthropologist Owen Lovejoy has suggested that the evolution of bipedalism turned on much more than merely the ability to carry objects. Because it involved the modification of a wide range of biological and behavioral traits, it must have conferred some adaptive advantage on early hominids, even before they had fully developed the physical capabilities for bipedalism. Lovejoy posits that the crucial advantage may have been the ability to transport food back to a mate by walking upright and using simple implements such as broad leaves to maximize the amount of food that could be carried. Provisioning by the male would have allowed the female to increase the quality and quantity of time devoted to infant care. This intensification of parental attention, in turn, would have promoted the survival of infants and, therefore, the species. Taking the theory a step further, Lovejoy asserts that food sharing and the cooperation that underlies this behavior may have produced a reproductive strategy that favored sexual fidelity and close, long-term relations between a male and a female.

Assessing Lovejoy's interpretations concerning early hominid behavior on the basis of fragmentary fossils remains is very difficult indeed, and many researchers have critiqued his suggestions. Nevertheless, the overarching point that bipedalism had important social, as well as behavioral, consequences is likely a reasonable assumption. This trait probably evolved as a result of a confluence of factors. Sorting out which ones played the most prominent roles in the development of this adaptation continues to challenge anthropologists.

Reduction of the Face, Teeth, and Jaws

We also see in hominid evolution a series of interrelated changes primarily associated with diet and food-processing requirements. The oldest fossil hominids have a protruding, or *prognathic,* face. In addition, their incisor and canine teeth are large compared to those of modern humans. To accommodate the larger canines, which extend beyond the other teeth, there are gaps between the teeth of the opposing jaw. Finally, the teeth of early hominids are arranged in a U-shaped pattern, and the teeth on opposite sides of the mouth are parallel. All these characteristics are similar to features found in modern pongids, including modern gorillas, orangutans, and chimps.

Approximately 2 million years ago, these characteristics started to become less pronounced in hominids. As noted in Chapter 4, primate teeth can handle an omnivorous diet with ease. However, hominid teeth, with flat molar crowns and thick tooth enamel, are highly specialized for grinding. Early primates, as well as living prosimians and anthropoids, had large canine and incisor teeth, which are well suited to cutting and slicing. In contrast, the size of these teeth is greatly reduced in later hominids. Early representatives of the genus *Homo* have smaller canines, and the gaps associated with larger teeth disappear. In humans, the canine teeth retain a distinctive shape, but they are almost the same size as the other teeth. Of all the hominids, the faces of modern humans are the least protruding.

Some australopithecines developed massive chewing muscles and extremely large molars compared to those of modern humans. This strong dentition earned one species, *Australopithecus boisei,* the nickname "nutcracker man." Scientists believe that these features most likely evolved in response to a diet of coarse, fibrous vegetation. Paleoanthropologists cite several key skeletal structures in the jaw and the cranium as evidence of this creature's powerful chewing capacity. Thick, enlarged jaws and cheekbones provided attachments for these huge muscles. Some australopithecine fossil specimens have a **sagittal crest,** a bony ridge along the top of the skull, which grows larger as more chewing muscles reach up along the midline of the cranium.

In contrast to the australopithecines, evolving *Homo* species may have consumed a more varied diet based on gathering vegetation, hunting animals, and scavenging. This theory corresponds with the size and contour of their molars—similar to those of modern humans—and the absence of such features as sagittal crests, which accompany specialized chewing muscles.

Increase in Cranial Capacity

In the genus *Homo,* a distinctive characteristic is a tendency toward increased cranial capacity and the complexity of the brain. Like the changes in dentition, growth in cranial capacity first appears in hominids dating from less than 2 million years ago. Before that, the size of the hominid brain underwent comparatively little change. Early australopithecines such as *A. afarensis* (which lived some 3 million to 4 million years ago) had a cranium about the size of a softball, barely surpassing that of a modern chimpanzee. Hominid cranial capacity remained fairly constant at this size for 2 million years, averaging just over 400 cubic centimeters (cc). Then, some time after 2 million years ago, members of the genus *Homo* began to show a steady increase in cranial size. The brain in *Homo erectus* averaged 1,000 cc, and the modern human brain measures, on average, 1,350 cc, a threefold increase from the australopithecines. Significantly, this constitutes an increase in both *relative* and *absolute* size. Even taking into account that modern humans are substantially larger than australopithecines, the relative size of the hominid brain more than doubled in the last 2 million years (McHenry, 1982).

Changes in the cranial capacity of early hominids undoubtedly influenced physical and social developments, which are less easily studied through fossil remains. For instance, increasing brain size almost certainly prompted numerous modifications in hominid diet, the use of tools, the evolution of language, and the intricacies of social organization. Greater sophistication in any of these areas may have improved early hominids' chances of survival.

Other Physical Changes

The evolution of certain physical characteristics of hominids is difficult to trace because the characteristics are not preserved in the fossil record. For example, unlike other surviving primates, modern humans are not completely covered with hair. Presumably, there was a tendency toward less body hair during hominid evolution, but we can find no indication of this in the fossilized remains. Loss of body hair, as well as characteristics such as skin color, might be a relatively recent phenomenon (see discussion in Chapter 6).

Fossil Evidence for Hominid Evolution

In *On the Origin of Species,* Charles Darwin devoted relatively little attention to human evolution, noting simply, "Much light will be thrown on the origin of man and his history" (Darwin, 1979:222). In the mid-nineteenth century, when Darwin was writing his treatise, scientists had scant fossil evidence for hominid origins. Since Darwin's time, however, thousands of hominid fossils have been recovered, most of them in Africa. The Hominid Vault of the Kenya National Museum alone contains hundreds of hominid specimens from Kenya and Tanzania, and more than 1,500 specimens have been recovered from South African sites. Specimens range from isolated teeth to nearly complete skeletons. Although paleoanthropologists have uncovered many spectacular finds, some discoveries merit special attention because they prompted anthropologists to modify theories of human evolution. In this section, we examine several of the most important fossil finds, beginning with the oldest. The locations of some of these key discoveries are illustrated in Figure 5.2.

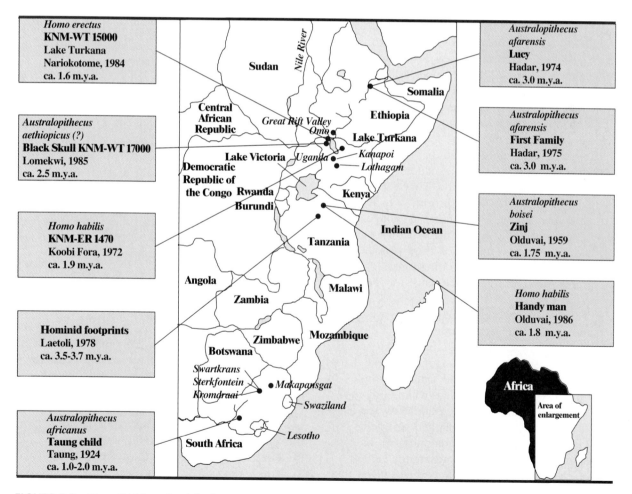

FIGURE 5.2   Map of African fossil finds.

Source: Figure, "Map of African fossil finds," from Roger Lewin, *In the Age of Mankind: A Smithsonian Book of Human Evolution,* Smithsonian Books, 1988, p. 71. (Art by Phil Jordan and Julie Scheiber). Reprinted by permission of Phil Jordan and Associates, Inc.

The Oldest Hominids

Fossil evidence for the evolution of the first hominids remains very incomplete. Finds predating
4.5 million years ago are limited and, for the most
part, fragmentary. The classification of these discoveries and the relationship of these creatures to
later species are uncertain, though some intriguing
finds have been discovered. Among the most
promising locales are a series of sites in Kenya,
particularly the areas around Lake Turkana, Lake
Baringo, and the Tugen Hills in the Rift Valley region of northern and western Kenya. The Middle
Awash area of Ethiopia also has great potential.
Geological deposits in each of these areas span the
relevant time periods, and well-preserved fossil deposits are represented.

Among the candidates for traces of the oldest
hominids are a series of fossilized teeth and a
few pieces of postcranial bone found in 2000 in
the Lukeino Formation in the Tugen Hills (Senut et
al., 2001), designated *Orrorin tugenensis*. The researchers who discovered the finds have suggested
that this species is an ancestor of later hominids.
This is very significant, as the fossil locality where
the remains were discovered has been securely
dated to between 5.6 and 6.2 million years ago. If
recognized as a hominid, the Tugen Hills finds
would indeed be those of "orrorin," which means
"original man" in the local African language. However, because of the fragmentary nature of these
fossils and the uncertainty of their classification,
their hominid status has been questioned.

More widely accepted candidates for the oldest
hominids come from a series of fossil localities in
the Middle Awash area of Ethiopia. This region,
located at the intersection of the Rift Valley, the
Red Sea, and the Gulf of Aden, has produced some
of the most spectacular and earliest hominid fossil finds, including Lucy and other examples of
Australopithecus afarensis that will be discussed
below. Fossil localities in the Middle Awash excavated by a number of researchers over the past
decade have produced a large number of fossil
fragments that collectively represent the earliest hominids yet recovered. They have been given their
own genus and species designation: *Ardipithecus
ramidus*. The oldest of these discoveries, recovered
from several different sites representing different
time periods, have been dated to between 5.8 and

5.2 million years old (Halle-Selassie, 2001). The site
of Aramis, also in the Middle Awash, was explored
in a series of expeditions beginning in 1992 (White
et al., 1995). This research produced the remains
of several dozen individuals dated to less than
4.4 million years ago.

Although the Middle Awash discoveries are
likely hominid, they are very primitive compared to
later australopithecines, such as *A. afarensis* and
A. africanus (discussed below). The cranial capacity of the Middle Awash creatures is quite small—at
least as small as that of other early hominids—but
the form of the cranium is also more apelike, and
the canine teeth are larger. Despite these distinctive
features, the placement of the cranium over the
spinal column, the shape of the pelvis, and the
structure of the limb bones are consistent with
bipedal locomotion—the hallmark of the hominids.
Because of the distinctive, primitive aspects of
the Aramis finds, researchers have argued that the
Aramis discoveries represent the earliest and most
primitive hominids yet found, but that they are not
directly ancestral to later hominids (White et al.,
1995). The earlier of the finds, those dating to between 5.8 and 5.2 million years old, have distinctive features, as well as some similarities to the
younger finds from Aramis. For this reason they
have been given a different subspecies designation:
Ardipithecus ramidus kadabba. Their age and
primitive features suggest that these creatures may
represent an evolutionary position very close to the
last common ancestor of humans and chimps.

Early Hominids from Kanapoi and East Turkana

The region around Lake Turkana in northern
Kenya has also yielded a host of important fossil
finds, including the discoveries of *Australopithecus
aethiopicus, Homo habilis,* and *Homo erectus* (discussed subsequently). The earliest hominid remains
are represented by a number of finds made over
the past 30 years at Kanapoi, southwest of Lake
Turkana, and Allia Bay, on the eastern side of Lake
Turkana. Some of the most recent discoveries and
assessments of the finds have been made by Meave
Leakey (Leakey et al., 1995).

The fossils are fragmentary, including teeth and
jaw fragments and some postcranial bones. The

age of the finds is placed between 3.9 million and 4.2 million years ago. The leg bones are consistent with bipedal—hominid—posture, but the finds also present some distinctive attributes. Like *Ardipithecus,* the skull and the teeth are quite primitive. The external ear openings are also unlike more recent hominids. However, in contrast to the *Ardipithecus* remains, the molar enamel on the teeth of these specimens is thick, and thus more analogous to more recent hominids. Hence, the finds may represent a transitional link between species such as *Ardipithecus* and the australopithecines. Because of their similarity to later finds, Meave Leakey and her colleagues have placed the discoveries in genus *Australopithecus* but assigned them a new species designation, *anamensis,* in recognition of their distinctive attributes. The relationship of these finds to *Australopithecus afarensis* is still being evaluated, but most researchers place them at the base of the australopithecine branch.

Among the most intriguing of the Turkana finds are a group of fossils from sediments dating between 3.2 and 3.5 million years old uncovered by Meave Leakey (2001). In many respects, the species represented is comparable to other early hominids in terms of its small cranial capacity and bipedal capabilities. Its most distinguishing feature, and the characteristic from which it draws its name, is a comparatively flat face beneath the nose. The genus and species name assigned, *Kenyanthropus platyops,* means "flat-faced man of Kenya." The most interesting aspect of this discovery is the fact that its age is comparable to that of *Australopithecus afarensis.* As discussed below, in interpreting the relationship of different fossil finds many researchers have viewed *A. afarensis* as ancestral to all later hominids. The presence of the *Kenyanthropus* provides an alternative candidate for the ancestor of later hominids.

Australopithecus afarensis

During the 1970s, a joint American–French team of paleoanthropologists led by Donald Johanson and Maurice Taieb made several exciting finds in the well-preserved geological beds near the Great Rift Valley in the Hadar area of the Afar region of Ethiopia (Johanson et al., 1982; see the box "Donald Johanson: Paleoanthropologist"). This valley has

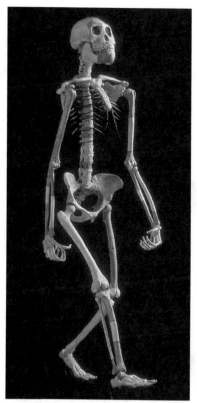

Reconstruction of skeletal remains of Australopithecus afarensis, *recovered by Donald Johanson at Hadar, Ethiopia, in 1974.*

experienced extensive mountain-building and volcanic activity over the last several million years, which brought many fossils to the surface, where they await discovery by researchers.

Because many subtle differences distinguish the dentition of the various Hadar hominids, Johanson initially believed that more than one species was represented. After subsequent study of the remains, however, Johanson and his colleagues concluded that the hominids all belong to a single species, which they designated *Australopithecus afarensis* (Johanson, White, & Coppens, 1978; Bower, 1991). The researchers argue that the differences they discerned are the result of natural variation and sexual dimorphism within the species. Other scholars, however, still maintain that more than one species is represented.

Lucy   Among the most spectacular finds made by Johanson's team at Hadar was a fossilized skeleton

ANTHROPOLOGISTS AT WORK

DONALD JOHANSON: PALEOANTHROPOLOGIST

Born in Illinois in 1943, Donald Johanson is one of the world's most influential and best-known paleoanthropologists. His first-hand accounts of research in Ethiopia (Johanson & Edey, 1981) and Olduvai Gorge (Johanson & Shreeve, 1989) have earned popular acclaim for their readable and thought-provoking insights into the field of paleoanthropology.

In 1973, Johanson, in conjunction with French geologist Maurice Taieb, began research in an area known as Hadar in the Afar triangle of northeastern Ethiopia. At that time the region had been largely unexplored by paleoanthropologists. Although the present climate is arid and inhospitable, the fossil record indicates that the region supported a variety of life forms 4 million to 3 million years ago. In Hadar, Johanson and his fellow researchers uncovered many finds that cast light on early hominids and their environment.

Two spectacular finds in Hadar have received particular attention. The first, uncovered in 1974, was a strikingly complete (40 percent) skeleton of an early hominid affectionately referred to as "Lucy." The second find, unearthed in 1975 at a site designated AL 333, consisted of a remarkable

collection of hundreds of hominid bones, representing at least thirteen individuals. Johanson believes that all the creatures at AL 333 may have died at the same time in a sudden catastrophic event like a flash flood. Both discoveries were representative of a previously undescribed species, which Johanson named *Australopithecus*.

In 1978, Johanson, in conjunction with paleoanthropologist Timothy White, reinterpreted the prevailing notions about hominid ancestry. They surveyed existing information and integrated it with Johanson's finds from Hadar. Then they restructured the hominid family tree, placing *A. afarensis* at the base, with two branches, one sprouting toward the genus *Australopithecus* and the other giving rise to the genus *Homo*. Although more recent discoveries lead to the conclusion that the hominids may be divided into more than two branches, the majority of paleoanthropologists accept *A. afarensis* as the earliest known hominid.

Some of Johanson's interpretations have been called into question. Other researchers have challenged his classification of *A. afarensis*, arguing that the fossils represent more than one species.

Donald Johanson (far left) with other paleoanthropologists analyzing hominid fossils from the Afar region of Ethiopia.

His major critics include paleoanthropologists Mary and Richard Leakey, known for their own research at Olduvai Gorge, Laetoli, Koobi Fora, and Lake Turkana. Johanson has observed: "Frustrating as it is, the distantly tantalizing truths about our origins will probably not be revealed before we ourselves are buried under the earth. But that will not stop me from testing and retesting new hypotheses, exploring further possibilities" (Johanson & Shreeve, 1989:133).

of an ancient hominid that was almost 40 percent intact, making it among the earliest and most complete fossil hominids recovered. This find, scientifically designated *Australopithecus afarensis*, became popularly known as "Lucy" (named after a Beatles song, "Lucy in the Sky with Diamonds"). Initial discussions of the discovery concluded that Lucy was a female, but some more recent analyses have suggested the remains are actually those of a male. Such interpretive disagreements underscore the challenges researchers face in analyzing fragmentary remains of nonliving species. Lucy had a small cranium (440 cc) and large canine teeth. In fact, Lucy's skull resembles that of a modern chimpanzee. However, below the neck the anatomy of the spine, pelvis, hips, thigh bones, and feet clearly shows that Lucy walked on two feet (Lovejoy, 1988). Lucy was a fairly small creature, weighing approximately 75 pounds, and she stood about 3.5 to 4 feet tall.

The First Family Another important discovery at Hadar came in 1975 at a fossil locality known as site 333. Johanson and his crew found many hominid bones scattered along a hillside. Painstakingly piecing them together, the researchers reconstructed thirteen individuals, including both adults and infants, with anatomical characteristics similar to those of Lucy. Experts hypothesize that these finds may represent one social group that died at the same time, perhaps during a flash flood. The group has, in fact, been referred to as the "First Family of Humankind" (Johanson & Edey, 1981). However, as the precise conditions that produced the site remain uncertain, this interpretation must be regarded as tentative.

The *Australopithecus afarensis* fossils discovered at Hadar have been dated between 3 million and 4 million years ago, making these some of the earliest well-described hominid remains. The fossils are remarkably primitive in comparison to other australopithecines; from the neck up, including the teeth, cranium, and jaw, *A. afarensis* is definitely apelike. However, the abundant limb bones and anatomical structures indicating pelvic orientation, as well as the position of the hips and knees, indicate that *A. afarensis* was a fully erect, bipedal creature (Lovejoy, 1988). Other finds, comparable to those from Hadar, have been reported from Laetoli, in eastern Africa.

The Laetoli Footprints

The site of Laetoli, some 30 miles south of Olduvai Gorge in northern Tanzania, has produced a number of fossil finds, including possible examples of *Australopithecus afarensis,* the fossil species described at Hadar. However, the site is best known for the remarkable discovery of fossilized footprints. Thousands of footprints of various species of ancient animals are preserved in an ancient layer of mud covered with volcanic ash. A finding by Mary Leakey in 1978 confirms that fully bipedal creatures roamed the earth approximately 3.5 million years ago (Leakey and Hay, 1979). The evidence consists of a trail more than 75 feet long made by at least two hominids, maybe three. Intensive studies of these footprints revealed that the mode of locomotion for these early hominids was fully bipedal and was similar to that of modern humans.

A hominid footprint fossilized in volcanic ash at Laetoli, Tanzania is shown next to a modern foot. Dated at over 3.5 million years, the trail of footprints at the site provides dramatic evidence that early hominids such as Australopithecus afarensis *were fully bipedal.*

CRITICAL PERSPECTIVES

NEW PERSPECTIVES ON THE TAUNG CHILD

Since the days of Raymond Dart, paleoanthropologists have been using advanced scientific techniques to analyze ancient hominids. In one of the newest technological advances, scientists Glenn C. Conroy and Michael Vanier (1990) of Washington University in St. Louis peered inside the fossilized skull of the Taung child by means of computer image-enhancing techniques and sophisticated electronic scanning equipment. Scientists had previously been unable to examine the inside of the skull because it was packed tightly with ancient sediment. Conventional X-rays could not penetrate the dense mineral deposits, and attempts to remove the sediment risked damaging the fossil itself.

Conroy and Vanier combined more than forty computerized tomography (CT) pictures into a single three-dimensional image, modeling the inside and outside of the Taung child's skull. Tomography is a medical procedure that doctors normally use to probe the inside of a solid object, such as an arm or a leg, by sweeping an X-ray over an electronically predetermined cross section, yielding a two-dimensional likeness. Once Conroy and Vanier produced the image of the Taung fossil, they electronically sliced, dissected,

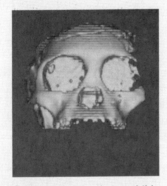

A CT scan of the Taung child.

Source: Courtesy of Glenn C. Conroy, Washington University.

and scanned the skull without damaging it. They detected thin bones and patterns of dentition no paleoanthropologist had seen before.

These tomographic pictures have led to the conclusion that *Australopithecus africanus* is much more primitive than had previously been thought. Looking at the outer portions of the fossil, some researchers, including Dart, had concluded that *A. africanus* was ancestral to the genus *Homo*. The new information may spur a reevaluation of this interpretation.

Imaging procedures and computer modeling give paleoanthropologists important new tools in their search into human origins. Using these techniques, scientists are now able to scan dense material without damaging it. These approaches should help paleoanthropologists refine their hypotheses, leading to a clearer picture of humankind's roots.

Taung Child: *Australopithecus africanus*

The Taung child is memorable as the first example of the genus *Australopithecus* described. The find was named *Australopithecus africanus*, the "southern ape of Africa," by its discoverer (see the box "New Perspectives on the Taung Child"). Dated between 2 million and 3 million years old, it represents a species of hominid that lived after the species discussed in the preceding sections. However, it possessed smaller cranial capacity than more recent examples of genus *Homo*. *A. africanus* is primarily known from sites in South Africa.

The discovery of the Taung child stemmed from a remarkable combination of coincidence and luck. The man responsible for the find was Raymond Dart, an Australian-born anatomist living in South Africa. In 1924, in a box of fossils from the rubble of a limestone quarry near the town of Taung, South Africa, Dart found the front of a skull, a jaw, and an endocranial cast of a previously unknown hominid. On the basis of the teeth, Dart judged the creature to have been quite young at death, and he called his discovery the "Taung child" (Dart 1925, 1967). Today the individual is estimated to have been between 3 and 4 years old at the time of death.

Although the Taung child had certain apelike features, it also exhibited a number of unique characteristics. For example, the foramen magnum was further forward in the Taung child than in modern apes, indicating that this creature's head was balanced above the spine. In other words, it moved with the upright posture characteristic of a biped. The brain of the Taung child was very small, hardly larger than that of a chimpanzee. Its structure, however, differed from that of apes and was more highly developed in some regions. The teeth were much closer in size to a human child's than to an infant ape's. Dart astounded the scientific world by announcing that the Taung child was a hominid, an intermediate link between humans and earlier primates.

At the time of its discovery, many paleoanthropologists challenged Dart's conclusion, arguing that the Taung child was really an ape. Contemporary evolutionary theories suggested that large cranial capacity was the critical characteristic of hominid evolution, and critics pointed out that the cranial capacity of Dart's find was too small for it to have been ancestral to humans (see the box "The Piltdown Fraud"). But Dart's critics were proven wrong. In the decades following the discovery of the Taung child, a number of similar finds were made in South Africa. During the 1940s, Dart excavated additional fossils from Makapansgat Cave. Scottish paleontologist Robert Broom (1938) also came upon a number of similar fossils at Sterkfontein. Some of these new finds were adult specimens of creatures like the Taung child. With their humanlike dentition, bipedal capabilities, and small cranial capacity, they were unquestionably hominids. These discoveries clearly established the Taung child as a hominid and *Australopithecus* as a valid genus.

Adult specimens of *A. africanus* probably weighed between 40 and 60 pounds and were between 3.5 and 4.75 feet tall; their cranial capacity averaged around 450 cc. Although the age of the South African finds is still uncertain, the gracile australopithecines seem to date to between 3 million and 2 million years ago, a conclusion based on study of the fossils of extinct animals of known age found in the same deposits.

Australopithecus aethiopicus: The "Black Skull"

The incomplete puzzle of hominid ancestry was filled in with one more piece in 1985, this one dug out of the fossil beds west of Lake Turkana, at a fossil locality known as Lomekwi I. Discovered by English paleoanthropologist Alan Walker, the find consists of the fragments of an australopithecine but of a type far more robust than *A. africanus*. Because the fossil had been stained blue-black by manganese in the soil, it became known as the "Black Skull," or, by its Kenya National Museum catalogue number, KNM-WT 17000 (Walker et al., 1986). Possibly another member of the same species is represented by more incomplete remains found earlier in the Omo River valley of Ethiopia. These have been designated *Australopithecus aethiopicus* by some researchers.

The Black Skull allows us to sketch a more complex, intricate picture of the hominid family tree. Found in sediments dating to approximately 2.5 million years ago, the fossil's cranium is small, comparable in size and shape to that of the *A. afarensis* fossils from Hadar. The movement of the *A. aethiopicus* jaw is also similar to that of *A. afarensis*. Yet the face is large, prognathic, and very robust, boasting massive teeth and a pronounced sagittal crest. In these respects the Black Skull resembles finds such as *Australopithecus boisei*, and other robust australopithecines that date somewhat later. We can, therefore, venture a reasonable guess that the age and structure of *Australopithecus aethiopicus* place it between *A. afarensis* and *A. boisei*.

Robust Australopithecines from South Africa

In addition to remains of *Australopithecus africanus*, South African sites have produced remains of other fossil hominids more recent in age than *A. africanus* (Broom 1938, 1949). Because of this variation, Dart, Broom, and other researchers gave these discoveries a number of new genus and species designations. Although differences of opinion still exist about their exact relationship to other species, for convenience they are generally designated *Australopithecus robustus* to distinguish them from the more delicate, or gracile, *A. africanus*.

CRITICAL PERSPECTIVES

THE PILTDOWN FRAUD

One of the most bizarre stories in the history of paleoanthropology involves the fossil known as "Piltdown man." Widely discussed and debated for several decades, this discovery was eventually exposed as an elaborate fraud. Although it does not figure in current theories of hominid evolution, we examine the Piltdown man controversy because the alleged specimen was accepted as a legitimate human ancestor during the early decades of the twentieth century and influenced interpretations of human evolution (Weiner, 1955; Blinderman, 1986). This cautionary tale illustrates the efficiency of modern scientific techniques but also serves as a warning about how scientists can be swayed by their own preconceived ideas.

Piltdown man was "discovered" in 1912 in a gravel quarry near Sussex, England, by a lawyer and amateur geologist named Charles Dawson. The quarry had previously produced the bones of extinct animals dating to the early Pleistocene (approximately 1.8 million years ago). The supposed hominid remains uncovered there consisted of the upper portion of the cranium and jaw. The skull was very large, with a cranial capacity of about 1,400 cc, which placed it within the range of modern humans. However, the lower jaw was apelike, the canine teeth large and pointed. This picture of early hominids mirrored popular early-twentieth-century notions of the unique intellectual capabilities of humanity. Humans,

so the interpretation went, evolved their large brains first, with other characteristics appearing later. In fact, a great deal of evidence points to just the opposite evolutionary pattern.

Piltdown man was officially classified as *Eoanthropus dawsoni* ("Dawson's dawn man") and accepted by the scientific community as the earliest known representative of humans found in western Europe. A number of paleoanthropologists in France, Germany, and the United States remained skeptical about the findings, but they were unable to disprove the consensus of the English scientific community. As time went by, however, more hominid fossils were discovered, and none of them exhibited the

Australopithecine skulls from the limestone deposits of South Africa. The example at lower left is a robust form; a gracile form is at top right.

South African examples of *A. robustus* are poorly dated, but available evidence suggests that they are more recent than *A. africanus*, perhaps dating between 2 million and 1 million years ago. Scientists have posited that *A. robustus* was larger than *A. africanus*, weighing more than 200 pounds. We can only venture educated guesses about the height and weight of these creatures, however, because of the relatively small pieces of postcranial bone that have been recovered. In fact, the body sizes of the gracile and robust forms may have been comparable (McHenry, 1988), although the skull and dentition of *A. robustus* clearly distinguish it. Specimens have a large, broad face and enormous teeth and jaws. Another feature found in *A. robustus* but absent in *A. africanus* is a sagittal crest. All of these features indicate that *A. robustus* could chew tough, fibrous foods.

combination of an apelike jaw and a large, humanlike cranium.

With contradictory evidence mounting, skepticism grew in the paleoanthropological community concerning the legitimacy of the Piltdown fossils. Finally, in the early 1950s, scientists completed a detailed reexamination of the Piltdown material. Using fluorine analysis (see Chapter 2) they discovered that the skull and jaw were of relatively recent vintage; the jaw, in fact, was younger than the skull. In reality, the Piltdown fossil consisted of a human skull from a grave a few thousand years old attached to the jaw of a recently deceased adolescent orangutan. The apelike teeth embedded in the jaw had been filed down to resemble human teeth, and the place where the jaw joined the skull had been broken away. The jaw was stained with a chemical to match the color of the skull.

Clearly, whoever perpetrated the Piltdown hoax had some knowledge of paleoanthropology. By the time the hoax was unmasked, most of the people who could have been implicated had died (Blinderman, 1986). Putting aside the question of who was responsible for the hoax, we now recognize that paleoanthropological research between 1912 and the 1950s was definitely harmed by the Piltdown find, because the scientific community pursued a false path in hominid research. The initial acceptance of the Piltdown fraud as legitimate may partially explain why one of the most startling hominid fossil discoveries of the early twentieth century was relegated to relative obscurity for so many years. This discovery was the Taung child.

POINTS TO PONDER

1. What lessons does the Piltdown fraud provide for the way paleoanthropological research should proceed and how findings should be validated?

2. The recovery methods and the limited information on the context of the find clearly contributed to the success of the Piltdown fraud. Contrast the details of the Piltdown discovery with more recent finds at Olduvai Gorge, Tanzania, or Hadar, Ethiopia.

3. Can you think of other cases in which researchers' theoretical perspectives have affected their interpretation of the evidence?

Australopithecus boisei: The "Nutcracker Man"

Following the initial discoveries in South Africa, many additional australopithecine fossils have come to light. One of the most exciting finds, called *Australopithecus boisei*, was the first of many discoveries made in eastern Africa by paleoanthropologists Louis and Mary Leakey. *Australopithecus boisei* was found in the Olduvai Gorge, a 30-mile canyon stretching across the Serengeti Plain of Tanzania. In 1959, Mary Leakey recovered an almost complete fossil skull from the gorge. The find was a robust australopithecine but was even more robust than the examples known from South Africa. The teeth of *A. boisei* were distinctly hominid in form but were much larger than those of any other australopithecines, a feature that earned *A. boisei* the nickname "Nutcracker Man." Louis Leakey (1959) formally dubbed it *Zinjanthropus boisei*, but similarities with the robust forms from South Africa led to its eventual inclusion in the genus *Australopithecus*. Today it is formally referred to as *Australopithecus boisei* and less formally as "Zinj." What makes the find particularly notable is that it was the first early hominid find to be dated using a numerical dating technique.

Dating *Australopithecus boisei*   Because of the vagaries of nature, the australopithecine finds of South Africa have been difficult to date. Scientists cannot precisely determine the conditions that formed the fossil localities where they were found. However, researchers know with certainty that the deposits have been eroded and disturbed by nature, and that fossils of varying ages have been mixed together. In contrast, the fossil deposits at Olduvai Gorge lie in undisturbed strata, occupying the same relative positions in which they were originally deposited. In addition, the area around Olduvai Gorge was volcanically active in the past. As a result, deposits of *tuff*, a porous rock formed from volcanic ash, created distinct layers within the Olduvai deposits, and these layers can be dated by using the potassium-argon method (see Chapter 2). Potassium-argon dates on tuffs above and below Zinj placed the fossil's age at approximately 1.75 million years old. This date, and later estimates on other fossil finds, revolutionized paleoanthropology by finally providing numerical ages for specific fossil specimens.

Homo habilis: The "Handyman"

The discovery of Zinj in 1959, and it subsequent dating by potassium argon dating, sparked a flurry of activity at Olduvai Gorge. Between 1960 and 1964, the Leakeys and their colleagues excavated the fragmentary remains of approximately twenty fossil hominids (Leakey, 1961). Some were clearly *Homo erectus;* others appeared comparable to the Zinj find. However, still other fossils pointed to the existence of a creature unlike any of the known australopithecines or *H. erectus*. The distinguishing characteristic of the new species was its cranial capacity, which Louis Leakey estimated at close to 640 cc, significantly larger than that of any australopithecine but still substantially smaller than that of *Homo erectus*. The Leakeys named the creature *Homo habilis,* or "handyman."

For years, many critics challenged this conclusion, maintaining that the fossils fell within the normal cranial range of australopithecines. Eventually, the Leakeys' son, Richard, confirmed his father's interpretations through discoveries from the fossil deposits of Koobi Fora on the eastern shores of Lake Turkana, Kenya. Excavations by Richard Leakey and his coworkers produced several specimens that have been classified as *Homo habilis*. The most complete of these, found in 1972, is known by its Kenya National Museum catalogue number, KNM-ER 1470. Unlike the fragmentary remains of the Olduvai specimens, the 1470 skull is relatively complete and has a cranial capacity of 775 cc. The various *H. habilis* remains from Olduvai and Koobi Fora date from between 2.2 million and 1.6 million years ago (Simons, 1989b). Hence, the range of these hominids overlaps those of the robust australopithecines and, perhaps, the later range of *Australopithecus aethiopicus* and *africanus*.

Java Man: The "First" Homo erectus

Many fossil specimens dating between *Homo habilis* and *Homo sapiens* are designated *Homo erectus*, which is transitional in terms of the cranial features present. The first discovery of a *Homo erectus* was made in 1891 by the Dutch doctor Eugene Dubois. At the time, this was the first bona fide discovery of a pre-*Homo sapiens* hominid. Digging near Trinil on the Solo River in northern Java (an Indonesian island), Dubois found a leg bone, two molars, and the top of a hominid cranium. The leg was indistinguishable from that of a modern human, but the cranium, small and flat compared to those of modern humans, had heavy browridges. Dubois named his find *Pithecanthropus erectus* ("erect ape-man"), but today the species is classified as *Homo erectus*.

Dubois (1894) viewed his find as a missing link between humans and modern apes, but this view betrayed faulty understanding of Darwin's theory of evolution. Darwin's "missing link" referred to a common ancestor of the human and ape lineages; he never proposed a direct link between modern humans and apes, which represent the end points of distinct evolutionary lines. Other scientists correctly placed *Pithecanthropus* as an intermediary form on the evolutionary track between *Homo sapiens* and an earlier hominid ancestor.

Peking Man and Other Homo erectus

Following the discovery of "Java man," scientists started gathering information about similar creatures at a rapid pace in the first decades of the twentieth century. Many of the most important finds came from Zhoukoudian, about 30 miles southwest of Beijing (then spelled Peking in English transliteration), China. In 1929, a team of researchers led by Chinese geologist W. C. Pei found a skull embedded in limestone during an excavation. Pei showed the skull to Davidson Black, a Canadian anatomist who was teaching at Peking Union Medical College. Concluding from his analysis that this skull represented a form of early human, Black labeled the creature *Sinanthropus pekinensis,* commonly known as "Peking man."

His curiosity piqued, Black undertook additional work at the site, which eventually produced 6 skulls, 12 skull fragments, 15 pieces of lower jaw, 157 teeth, and miscellaneous pieces of postcranial skeleton (Rukang, Wu, & Lin, 1983). Also unearthed at the site were traces of charcoal (possibly the remains of cooking fires) and stone tools. Anatomist Franz Weidenreich succeeded Black at the medical college and prepared casts, photos, and drawings of the Zhoukoudian fossils. Before the Japanese invasion during World War II, Weidenreich fled China with these reproductions—a fortuitous move for science, because the actual fossils were lost during the war and have never been recovered. Recent dating of the stratum where the Zhoukoudian fossils were recovered suggests that Peking man lived between 460,000 and 230,000 years ago.

In addition to more finds in China, discoveries were made in other areas. Forty years after Dubois's excavations in Java, anthropologist G. H. R. Koenigswald uncovered the remains of comparable early hominids in the same area. Initially, scientists, working with few finds and lacking comparative specimens, speculated that each of these discoveries constituted a new evolutionary branch. We now know that, despite their disparate locations, these early discoveries are all representatives of a single genus and species, today classified as *Homo erectus.* In many respects, *Homo erectus* is identical to modern humans, although the postcranial skeleton is generally heavier and more robust. What most sets this species apart from *Homo sapiens* is the cranium, which lacks the high, vaulted appearance of that of modern humans and has a smaller average brain capacity.

Homo erectus was a highly successful and widely dispersed species. Well-dated fossil finds date between 1.6 million and 400,000 years ago. Recent dating of animal bones associated with *Homo erectus* fossils from the sites of Ngandong and Sambungmacan, Java, suggest that pockets of *Homo erectus* populations may have existed as recently as 50,000 years ago. With the exception of *Homo sapiens,* this species had the widest distribution of any hominid. Fossil finds bearing *H. erectus* features have been recovered from Kenya, Tanzania, Zambia, Algeria, Morocco, China, and Java (Day, 1986).

One of the oldest and most complete finds, known as "Turkana boy," was recovered at the Nariokotome site near Lake Turkana in Kenya. Recently, finds that may date from the same period as Nariokotome have been found outside Africa. Though still being evaluated, a possible *H. erectus* mandible from the Republic of Georgia in eastern Europe has been provisionally dated to 1.5 million years ago. The redating of finds from fossil localities in Sangriran and Mojokerto in Java to 1.6 million years ago has also raised questions about both the distribution and the evolution of *H. erectus* (Swisher et al., 1994). Some of the more recent examples of *Homo erectus* share many similarities with modern humans, perhaps illustrating both the interrelatedness of the species with *H. sapiens* and the arbitrary nature of classification. Some researchers have argued that the finds possessing the more modern characteristics should be designated by a separate species name, *H. ergaster.*

Interpreting the Fossil Record

Several sources of evidence indicate that the earliest human ancestors evolved in Africa. The oldest hominids, as well as the earliest fossil evidence for anatomically modern humans, are from Africa. Climatic conditions on the African continent during the Pliocene and Pleistocene were warm, and they would have been well suited to evolving hominids. Our closest genetic relatives, the chimpanzee and gorilla, also emerged there, suggesting a large primate genetic pool. Finally, the earliest stone tools, represented by the Oldowan tradition, are also known from Africa. Although the recent discovery and dating of early representatives of genus *Homo* from Asia have raised questions concerning when hominids migrated out of Asia, the prevailing consensus for hominid origins remains Africa.

While the geographical origins of the hominids may be somewhat clear, it is more challenging to chart the hominid family tree. As paleoanthropologists unearthed increasing numbers of early hominid fossils, their interpretations of hominid evolution have become increasingly complex. Initially, scientists drew a straight evolutionary line from *Australopithecus africanus* to *Homo erectus* and on to *Homo sapiens.* But recent finds clearly demonstrate that in several instances more than one species of hominid roamed the earth at the same time. How were these different species related, and how do they relate to the evolution of *Homo sapiens?*

Fundamental to the study of hominid evolution is the question of which features should be used to classify genuses and species. Because the size and complexity of the brain are the most distinctive physical characteristics of modern humans, increasing cranial capacity is clearly an important feature of the *Homo* line. Yet the range of cranial capacities overlaps among hominids, making it difficult to use this as the basis for distinguishing discrete species (Tattersall, 1986). Study of modern species demonstrates that there is, in fact, a great deal of variation within species in features such as cranial capacity, body size, and skeletal structure. For example, chimps from Tanzania's Gombe National Park display an astonishing degree of variation in size and skeletal structure (Bower, 1990). In interpreting fragmentary hominid fossils from widely separated localities, we must take into account such natural variation within species.

In the preceding discussion of the fossil evidence for hominid evolution, the names designating specific genuses and species are intended to provide a simplified overview of some of the principal discoveries. The names used here are among the most widely accepted appellations used by paleoanthropologists, but they are not universally agreed on. Perspectives of hominid classification lie between two extremes. Some scientists, who can be called *splitters,* argue that some species designations do not reflect all the species represented. For instance, some researchers have argued that the *A. afarensis* finds from Hadar do not constitute a single, sexually dimorphic species but rather at least two distinct species. Others in this camp contend that further divisions are called for within the gracile and robust australopithecines (Tattersall, 1986). In fact, many researchers place the majority of the robust australopithecines (including *A. aethiopicus, A. robustus,* and *A. boisei*) into a separate genus from *Australopithecus,* called *Paranthropus.* Concerns about the differences between the early and late examples of *H. erectus* have led to the reclassification

of some of the former as *H. ergaster,* and some researchers have called for further divisions.

At the opposite extreme from the splitters are the *lumpers,* who maintain that current taxonomic designations place too much emphasis on differences among individuals and do not sufficiently consider variations within species. This position is best advocated by C. Loring Brace (Brace & Montagu, 1965; Brace, 1967, 1989). Brace asserts that the information available on *Homo habilis, A. afarensis,* and *A. aethiopicus* is insufficient to categorize each as a distinct species and advocates including them with other genus and species. For example, *H. habilis, H. ergaster,* and other finds might be included with *Homo erectus.*

At this point it is useful to underscore that the different perspectives presented by lumpers and splitters include a great deal of consensus about the differences in the individual fossil finds. The divergence in opinion is about what the differences in the fossil finds imply about taxonomic classification and the process of speciation.

Many interpretations of hominid evolution have been advanced through the years. Some of these, explored in the following section, are illustrated in Figure 5.3. When they were proposed, they represented valid attempts to explain the available fossil evidence. Like all sciences, paleoanthropology proceeds by formulating hypotheses and then testing them against empirical data. In contrast to most sciences, however, the data from the fossil record cannot be obtained by laboratory experiments. Rather, paleoanthropologists must await the next unpredictable fossil find. As new evidence is uncovered, new hypotheses are developed, and old ones are modified or discarded. As the number of fossil species represented has increased and our understanding of the fossil record has become more refined, the interpretations have had to account for more variation and thus have become increasingly complex (see Figure 5.4 on page 120).

Australopithecus africanus as Ancestor

A number of theories propounded in the 1960s and 1970s placed *A. africanus* at the base of the hominid family tree, as illustrated in Figure 5.3(a). These interpretations of evolution basically held that hominids developed along two main branches.

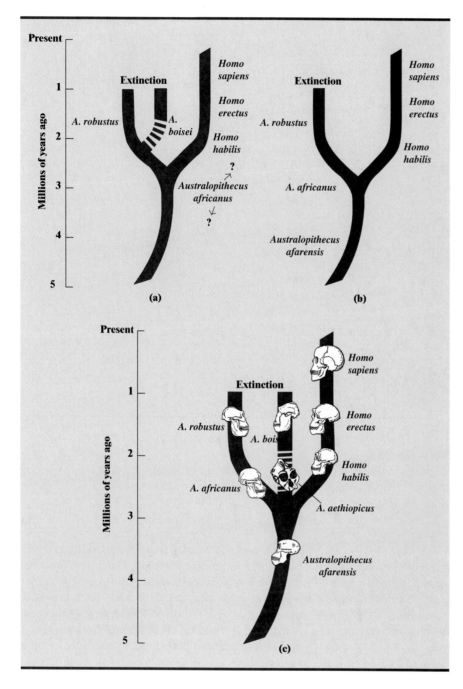

FIGURE 5.3 Different interpretations of hominid evolution: (a) Various theories have placed *A. africanus* in a position ancestral to *Homo* or to both *Homo* and later australopithecines. The robust australopithecines are placed on their own side branch. (b) In 1979, Johanson and White named a new species, *A. afarensis,* which they placed at the base of the hominid family tree leading to both *Australopithecus* and *Homo.* *A. africanus* was moved to a side branch leading to the robust australopithecines. (c) In 1985, the discovery of *A. aethiopicus* made the picture more complex, suggesting that all of the australopithecines cannot be located on a single side branch. More recent discoveries have led to further revision (see Figure 5.4).

As the most sophisticated of the australopithecines, *A. africanus* was considered the most likely to have given rise to the genus *Homo* and was therefore placed at the bottom of the branch leading to *Homo habilis, H. erectus,* and ultimately *H. sapiens.* The robust australopithecines occupied their own branch, eventually becoming extinct around 1 million years ago. Because of their large teeth and specialized chewing apparatus, the robust australopithecines were not viewed as directly ancestral to *Homo.* In some interpretations, *A. africanus* was located at the base of the hominid tree, suspected of

FIGURE 5.4 Revised models: More recent discoveries have extended the hominid family tree further back in time. New branches have also been added, making the hominid family tree look more like a bush.

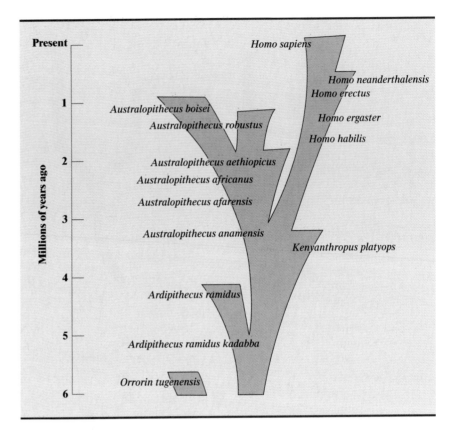

being ancestral to both the later australopithecines and genus *Homo.* Other variations saw *A. boisei* and *A. robustus* on separate branches entirely.

Australopithecus afarensis as Ancestor

Following the discovery of Lucy and the First Family at Hadar in the 1970s, Donald Johanson and Timothy White proposed a new interpretation of hominid evolution, which is illustrated in Figure 5.3(b). Variations of this interpretation were incorporated into many models in the following decade. Johanson and White hypothesized that the genus *Australopithecus* began with *A. afarensis,* dated at about 4 million to 3 million years ago. They contended that *A. afarensis* was the common ancestor of all subsequent hominids. In their scheme, one of the branches from *A. afarensis* leads to *A. africanus* and *A. robustus.* The other major branch leads toward the evolution of *Homo habilis* and succeeding species of *Homo,* culminating in modern *Homo sapiens* (Johanson & White, 1979).

Many paleoanthropologists concurred with this model of hominid evolution until the mid-1980s.

Revised Models

More recent discoveries have extended the hominid family tree further back in time. Many new branches have also been added, making the hominid family tree look more like a bush. Models must now take into account older and more primitive species like *Ardipithecus ramidus, Australopithecus anamensis,* and *Kenyanthropus platyops.* The recovery of finds such as these leads researchers to question whether *Australopithecus afarensis* or, indeed, any of the australopithecines are ancestral to genus *Homo.*

Interpretations must also grapple with the relationships of more recent hominids. With the discovery of the Black Skull in 1985, a comparatively neat picture of human evolution suddenly grew clouded and more complex. Johanson and White had placed *A. boisei* at the end of the extinct line of australopithecines, a sort of hyper-robust form of

A. robustus (Figure 5.3b). This was a logical conclusion, given the available fossil evidence at the time. Unfortunately, *A. aethiopicus* doesn't fit into this crisp picture. It has certain characteristics found in *A. boisei* but not in *A. africanus* and *A. robustus,* yet *A. aethiopicus* is as old as *A. africanus*. Scientists wishing to insert the Black Skull into the Johanson and White evolutionary tree would be hard pressed to explain how certain features appeared in *A. aethiopicus,* disappeared in *A. africanus* and *A. robustus,* and then reappeared in *A. boisei* (Johanson & Shreeve, 1989). A more logical and workable interpretation places *A. boisei* and *A. robustus* on branches of their own. Other limbs would lead to *A. africanus* and genus *Homo,* as pictured in Figure 5.3(c).

Acceptance of new species and a more branching view of hominid evolution have led to the reanalysis and reinterpretation of earlier finds (Figure 5.4). Some researchers have underscored variation within fossils formerly recognized as single species. Hence splitting has become somewhat more fashionable than lumping. This is particularly true within genus *Homo*. Fossils commonly designated *H. erectus* span from 1.6 million years ago to less than 400,000 years old. Although some differences in the structure of the cranium are present, *H. erectus* had been generally seen as an extremely well-adapted and long-lived species. However, some scientists have argued that some of the earliest *H. erectus* finds from Africa, as well as more recent finds from other world areas, should be assigned to a separate species: *Homo ergaster*. They see these fossils as having characteristics more transitional to *H. sapiens*. Consequently, they would place *H. ergaster* more directly ancestral to *Homo sapiens* than other *H. erectus* finds, which would be placed in a separate lineage. Similarly, fossils formerly categorized as *H. habilis* are now classified by some researchers as *H. rudolfensis*.

Missing Pieces in the Fossil Record?

All of the preceding views of hominid evolution are based on excavated fossils. Part of the problem with these interpretations—and the continuing need for revision—lies in the fact that that our perception of the fossil record is woefully incomplete. The currently known fossils do not represent the extent and diversity of extinct species. Some scholars have long contended that australopithecines

like Lucy emerged after the split between the *Australopithecus* and *Homo* lineages. In other words, the australopithecines represent a separate hominid branch, and the early part of the *Homo* lineage is still unknown (Shipman, 1986a). Given the fact that fossils of hominids dating earlier than 4 million years ago are fragmentary and their ancestry uncertain, any number of scenarios might be posited but cannot be evaluated because of the lack of fossil remains.

A tantalizing illustration of our inadequate knowledge of the fossil record is underscored by recent finds from West Africa. All of the early hominids discussed thus far were recovered from sites in the eastern and southern parts of the continent, ranging from South Africa to Ethiopia. Consequently, models of hominid evolution have focused on these finds and generally assumed that the hominids evolved in these areas. However, fossils found at a site near Koro Toro in Chad in 1995 have necessitated a reassessment of this view. The distribution of hominids in West Africa is poorly known. The region lacks the extensive, and more thoroughly explored, exposures of Pliocene and Pleistocene deposits that have been studied in other parts of Africa. The Chad find consists of a fossilized jaw and seven teeth from deposits dating between 3 and 3.5 million years old. The fragmentary finds share some similarity to eastern African finds such as *A. afarensis,* but the specimen has been placed in the new species, *Australopithecus bahrelghazali*. The presence of this find, far beyond what had been considered the geographic distribution of early hominids, raises questions about how much we don't know. It is possible that further research will lead the search for human ancestry in entirely new directions.

This perspective recognizes the inadequacy of the fossil record and the incomplete nature of the available data. Of course it also lacks explanatory value and, as a result, is a pretty unsatisfactory conclusion. Despite the limited information, the majority of paleoanthropologists prefer to speculate on the potential relationships of the known fossil species. These reconstructions allow us to think about how the human species may have emerged. It is likely that future discoveries will extend the human lineage further back in time and produce an increasingly "bushy" hominid family tree, and models of hominid lineages will continue to be revised.

Genetic Differences and Hominid Evolution

All of the previous interpretations are rooted in studies of the fossil record—actual traces of early hominids recovered from the ground. During the past several decades, some researchers have approached the study of human evolution from a completely different direction. As noted in Chapter 3, scientists have studied the genetic differences of living animals and attempted to time the divergence of different species. This is done by studying the similarities and differences in their chromosomes and DNA sequencing, which vary in different species. Comparing data from modern prosimians, monkeys, and apes, researchers have demonstrated that chimpanzees and humans are identical in many respects and evince differences of less than 5 percent at the biochemical-genetic level. There is slightly more distance between humans and gorillas, but genetically the similarities still approach 100 percent. This similarly in genetic code suggests a closer evolutionary relationship among the hominoids than with the hominoids and other primates. The genetic data are, therefore, consistent with similarities in anatomy and skeletal structure, and the hominoids are appropriately placed in the superfamily Hominoidea (see Table 4.1 and Figure 4.2).

Drawing on these data, some researchers have gone a step further and attempted to infer the amount of time it took for evolution to produce the amount of genetic distance between various species. This is based on determining the rate at which mutation, and ultimately the process of speciation, takes place. Surveying genetic information, some researchers have suggested that the separation of the pongids and hominids occurred between 10 million and 4 million years ago (Silby & Alquist, 1984; Brown, 1990). The genetic information, therefore, would appear to complement the australopithecine fossil evidence, which suggests that the divergence had occurred prior to 4 million years ago.

When cautiously applied, genetic information facilitates classification and aids in formulating workable hypotheses concerning human evolution. However, conclusions about the rates at which genetic change takes place are not universally accepted. In actuality, the rate of change may differ in different species, making the purported "molecular clock" unreliable. Molecular dating at best provides only a rough approximation of the relative genetic distance between different species and the possible time of divergence. It provides no clues to how ancestral hominids adapted to different environments, to their feeding habits, to their geographic range, to their lifeways, or to any of the myriad other questions that concern paleoanthropology. Clues to human origins continue to depend on discoveries pried from the fossil record.

From *Homo erectus* to *Homo sapiens*

Scientists cannot pinpoint which selective pressures prompted *H. erectus* to evolve into *H. sapiens*. Fossils of *H. erectus* range in age from 1.6 million to 400,000 years old. The longevity of the species is a testament to how well *H. erectus* adapted to different environmental conditions, having ranged across the diverse climates from Africa and southern Europe to Asia. Presumably, *H. sapiens* must have had some adaptive advantage over earlier hominids, but no consensus has emerged about what specific selective pressures were involved. Among the physical changes found in *H. sapiens* are a larger brain and full speech capabilities, which undoubtedly sparked concomitant behavioral consequences. Many of the distinctive characteristics seen in *H. sapiens* stem from cultural factors as well. As will be seen in Chapter 7, *H. erectus* made increasing use of socially learned technology to interact with and control the environment. This trend intensifies in later human populations.

Many hominid remains from the period between 400,000 and 200,000 years ago are difficult to classify because they exhibit physical traits characteristic of both *H. erectus* and *H. sapiens*. These hominids, which can be alternately viewed as either advanced *H. erectus* or early *H. sapiens,* can be referred to as **transitional forms.** The discovery of finds that do not fit neatly into taxonomic categories is not surprising. As we saw in Chapter 4, related species have many similar characteristics that reflect their evolutionary relationships. Transitional forms illustrate these relationships and offer physical evidence of the process of speciation.

Transitional Forms

In examining the transition from *H. erectus* to *H. sapiens,* we need to cast a critical eye on the physical characteristics that distinguish the two species. *Homo erectus* shares many physical features with modern humans; in fact, the postcranial skeletons are essentially the same, except for the generally heavier, more massive structure of *H. erectus* bones. The major differences between the two species appear in the skull. *Homo sapiens* skulls are high and vaulted, providing a large cranial capacity. In contrast, the skulls of *H. erectus* feature a **postorbital constriction,** meaning that the front portion of the skull is narrow and the high forehead of *H. sapiens* is absent. Lacking the high, vaulted cranium of *H. sapiens*, the skull of *H. erectus* is widest toward the base.

Homo erectus also exhibits a prognathic face, an attribute of early hominids that is absent in *H. sapiens*. The anterior teeth of *H. erectus* are relatively small compared to those of earlier *Homo* species but large in comparison to those of modern humans. Other distinctive characteristics of *H. erectus* make scientists believe that these creatures had strong jaw and neck muscles. These traits include a slight ridge at the back of the skull and heavy eyebrow ridges, structural features that have disappeared in modern humans.

Transitional forms bearing various combinations of *H. erectus* and *H. sapiens* features have been discovered in Europe, Asia, and Africa. The mosaic of physical characteristics found in some specimens has sparked debate over how to designate species most appropriately. This debate can be illustrated by the Petralona cranium, uncovered in eastern Greece in 1960 (Day, 1986). Scientists dispute the age of the find (claims of 1 million years old have been made), yet the consensus among paleoanthropologists leans toward an age of between 400,000 and 350,000 years. The species designation of this fossil has also been contested. The Petralona cranium exhibits certain *H. erectus* characteristics, including thick bones, pronounced brow ridges, and a low cranial vault. However, the cranial capacity is estimated at approximately 1,200 cc, placing it at the uppermost limits of *H. erectus* and the lower range of *H. sapiens*.

The Evolution of *Homo sapiens*

Although paleoanthropologists generally agree that *H. erectus* evolved into *H. sapiens*, they disagree about how, where, and when this transition

occurred. Early interpretations were based on limited information and often emphasized the uniqueness of individual finds. Recent researchers have offered a number of different theories (Howells, 1976; Mellars, 1988, 1989; Sussman, 1993). They fall into two overarching models representing opposing perspectives: the multiregional evolutionary model and the replacement model.

Multiregional Evolutionary Model

According to the **multiregional evolutionary model,** the gradual evolution of *H. erectus* into modern *H. sapiens* took place in many regions of Asia, Africa, and Europe at the same time, as illustrated in Figure 5.5(a). Through natural selective pressures and genetic difference, local *H. erectus* populations developed particular traits that varied from region to region. However, as characteristics of *H. sapiens* appeared in certain areas, *gene flow*—the widespread sharing of genes—between populations prevented the evolution of distinct species. The emergence of *H. sapiens* was, therefore, a widespread phenomenon, although different regional populations continued to exhibit distinctive features.

Working from the multiregional evolutionary model, we would expect to see a great deal of regional genetic continuity, meaning that the fossil finds from a particular geographic area should display similarities from the first *H. erectus* to those of modern populations. Supporters of this model argue that such continuities do indeed exist. For example, skeletal remains of early *H. sapiens* from different regions of China, North Africa, and Europe resemble modern populations in those areas in some respects (Smith, 1984; Thorne & Wolpoff, 1992). Certain distinctive features can be identified in the cranium, dentition, jaws, and particular features of the postcranial skeleton.

Replacement Model

The second major paradigm to explain the evolution of modern humans is the **replacement model,** or the single-source model (Stringer, 1985). This model holds that *H. sapiens* evolved in one area of the world first and migrated to other regions, as illustrated in Figure 5.5(b). It is called a replacement model because it assumes that *H. sapiens* were contemporaries of the earlier *H. erectus* but eventually replaced them. Thus, although the modern and

FIGURE 5.5 Two different interpretations of the emergence of *H. sapiens.* The multiregional evolutionary model (a) suggests regional continuity and the gradual evolution of all *H. erectus* and archaic *H. sapiens* populations into modern humans. In contrast, supporters of the replacement model (b) see modern humans as evolving in one world area and spreading out, replacing earlier hominid populations. Some researchers have drawn on both models.

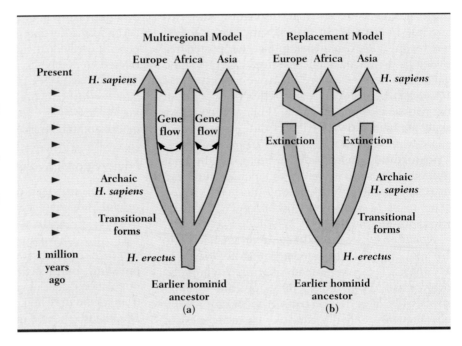

archaic species overlapped in their spans on earth, they were highly distinctive, genetically different evolutionary lineages. According to the replacement hypothesis, *H. sapiens* populations all descended from a single common ancestral group. Consequently, there is minimal diversity among modern humans.

Some researchers believe that fossil evidence supporting the replacement hypothesis may be found in the homeland of all hominids, Africa. Fossils of anatomically modern *H. sapiens,* provisionally dated to between 130,000 and 70,000 years ago, have been found in eastern and southern Africa (Stringer & Andrews, 1988). In Omo, Ethiopia, hominid remains consisting of a mandible and postcranial bones have been classified as *H. sapiens.* In addition, some intermediate fossils with both archaic and modern traits have been found in North Africa. These African fossil finds may represent the earliest examples of modern humans found anywhere in the world. Some advocates of the replacement model contend that after evolving in Africa, early *H. sapiens* migrated to other regions, replacing earlier hominid populations that had arrived in those same regions hundreds of thousands of years before.

However, the fossil evidence from Africa has a number of limitations. Scientists cannot pinpoint

the precise stratigraphic position of some of the finds, and the ages of the sites where the remains were located pose problems as well (Mellars, 1989; Deacon, 1992; Klein, 1992). The finds may be younger than present dating indicates. If so, they would not predate finds from other areas, thereby providing no support for the hypothesis that all humans diffused from Africa. Other researchers have postulated that *H. sapiens* may have originated in southwest or East Asia. But these hypotheses, too, cannot be confirmed through available fossil evidence.

Partial Replacement?

It is possible that neither of the preceding models for the emergence of anatomically modern humans is completely correct. The process may have been more complex and encompassed more variables than can be neatly wrapped up in either of the two overarching models (Lahr & Foley, 1994). Emergent human populations may have incorporated a great deal of physical diversity—as well as behavioral, social, and linguistic differences. It is unlikely that migrations ("Out of Africa" and elsewhere) were nice unidirectional affairs involving the movement of homogeneous populations. Many different migrations via different routes, recolonization of previously occupied territories, and gene flow with other populations were more probable. Understanding of such variables may provide insight into not only the emergence of modern humans, but also the source of the diversity underlying present-day populations.

In one partial replacement scenario, anatomically modern *H. sapiens* may have emerged in southern Africa first, over 100,000 years ago, and then migrated outward. In the Near East, they met and, to some extent, interbred with earlier archaic populations. In fact, fossil evidence from the Near East, as well as Europe and East Asia, indicates that different hominid species overlapped in time and space. As a result of interbreeding, anatomically modern humans hybridized with earlier archaic populations, eventually replacing them. This interpretation, and ones like it, underscores elements of both the multiregional and replacement models, with an emphasis on the latter. It may more correctly represent the complex and gradual nature of the processes represented.

Mitochondrial DNA Research

Researchers have also brought biochemical techniques to bear on the question of the origins of modern humans. Working at the University of California, Berkeley, in the 1980s, a team of researchers studied the mitochondrial DNA of modern women (Cann et al., 1987; Stoneking et al., 1987). On the basis of the studies, which were widely publicized, they argued that modern humanity could be traced back to a single African female who lived between 200,000 and 130,000 years ago (referred to as Eve). Although seemingly providing an important means of validating fossil evidence, the technique proved to be fraught with problems.

The apparent strength of the technique lies in the distinctive characteristics of mitochondrial DNA (mtDNA). This type of DNA is located in the portion of the cell that helps convert cellular material into the energy needed for cellular activity. In contrast to nuclear DNA (see Chapter 3), mtDNA is not carried by the sperm when it fertilizes the egg. The genetic code embedded in mtDNA, therefore, is passed on only through the female. Thus, each of us inherits this type of DNA from our mother, our mother's mother, and so on, along a single, maternal genealogical line.

The study by the Berkeley team focused on the mtDNA of 147 women from Africa, Asia, Europe, Australia, and New Guinea (Cann et al., 1987). The accumulation of random mutations in the different populations displayed distinctive patterns. The mtDNA of the African women tended to be more diverse, or heterogeneous, suggesting that mutations present had a long time to accumulate. In other populations, the mtDNA was more uniform, or homogeneous, a sign that they had not had as much time to accumulate mutations. Assuming a constant mutation rate, the researchers inferred a maternal line in Africa dating back to between 200,000 and 130,000 years ago. This interpretation of the mtDNA data favored a replacement model, with Africa as the ultimate place of origin of all later anatomically human populations.

Although mitochondrial dating initially received a great deal of media attention, aspects of the research were soon challenged by other researchers. Some researchers have noted that mtDNA may mutate rapidly and at irregular rates, not at the constant rate the researchers presumed. If so, studies of mtDNA could not yield any precise dates for the separation of different human populations. The theory is also problematic in that it assumes that none of Eve's descendents interbred with any individuals outside of Eve's maternal line. Any exchange of genes with a different gene pool would create an additional source of variation unaccounted for. Even more problematic is the computer program that was used to create the model. The computer created a human family "tree" by making the fewest number of branches that could be used to explain the genetic relatedness of the individuals studied. Unfortunately, the computer could produce millions of equally simple trees, with no guarantee that it had identified the correct model. Other computer runs produced trees that supported Asian or European origins.

Although more recent studies have addressed some of these issues, the debate over the validity of the technique continues (Vigilant et al., 1991; Wilson & Cann, 1992; Frayer et al., 1993; Sussman, 1993; Templeton, 1993; Mountain, 1998). Research on mtDNA did yield useful information. By demonstrating the greater amount of genetic variation present in African populations, it provided further support for other types of evidence that suggest that the human lineage evolved in Africa. It stands as a good example of the degree of scrutiny—and debate—that new theories attract.

Archaic *Homo sapiens*

Although debate still rages over the classification of certain hominids dating between 200,000 and 400,000 years ago, there is much more agreement over later finds. For the most part, all hominid fossils dating to the last 200,000 years are classified as *H. sapiens.*

This is not to say that *H. sapiens* populations of 200,000 years ago were identical to modern humans. Anatomically modern humans did not appear until between 130,000 and 40,000 years ago, earlier in some regions than others. Even these fossils do not have all the characteristics of modern populations. However, the distinctive features noted in these early *H. sapiens* populations are all considered within the range of variation found in a single species. Individual fossil finds are sometimes given subspecies names to signal a particular distinction, as, for example, *Homo sapiens steinheimensis,* found in a gravel pit in Steinheim, Germany, on the River Murr in 1933. To simplify our discussion, hominids of the last 200,000 years can be divided into two categories: **archaic *Homo sapiens*** and **anatomically modern *Homo sapiens.***

Archaic *H. sapiens* follow the evolutionary path leading through transitional forms of *H. erectus* to modern *H. sapiens.* Indeed, some finds dating before 200,000 years ago, including the Petralona cranium, have been labeled archaic *H. sapiens.* At the other extreme, hominid fossils with archaic *H. sapiens* features overlap with clearly modern humans.

The mosaic of features that characterizes archaic *H. sapiens* takes clear shape in remains unearthed at the Broken Hill Mine in Kabwe, Zambia. These finds consist of a cranium and the postcranial bones of three or four individuals, dated to at least 125,000 years ago (Day, 1986). On the one hand, the thickness of the bone, heavy browridges, and sloping forehead of the cranium are characteristic of *H. erectus.* Also like *H. erectus,* the Kabwe skull is widest at the base. On the other hand, the cranial capacity is large (1,280 cc), and the postcranial skeleton bears a strong resemblance to *H. sapiens* (Kennedy, 1984). The Kabwe find once again raises the question of which features best differentiate species.

Homo sapiens neanderthalensis

One of the best-known examples of archaic *H. sapiens* is *H. sapiens neanderthalensis,* also known popularly as "Neandertal man." Neandertal fossils dating between 130,000 and 35,000 years ago have been discovered in Europe and the Middle East. In the past, climatic conditions in this area spanned a more extreme range than they do today. The southern regions had warmer, milder

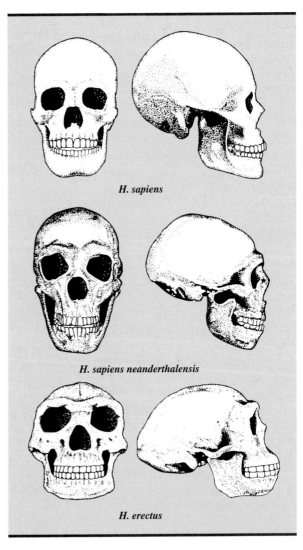

H. sapiens

H. sapiens neanderthalensis

H. erectus

FIGURE 5.6   A comparison of the skulls of *H. erectus,* *H. sapiens neanderthalensis,* and modern *H. sapiens.* The most distinctive feature of the latter is the high, vaulted forehead and the prominent chin.

climates, and the northern regions were partially glaciated and extremely cold.

The Neandertal physique has become the model for the "cave men" portrayed in the media. They have often been portrayed as second-rate hominids, swept to extinction by quicker-thinking modern humans (Brace, 1964; for readable, fictional portrayals, see Auel, 1981; Golding, 1981). This depiction stems, in part, from an early find of a skeleton of an elderly individual whom scientists later determined had suffered from arthritis. In fact, Neandertals were quite literally thick-skulled and had the heavy browridges seen in *H. erectus.* In the classic Neandertal, the midportion of the face protruded as if the nose and surrounding features were pulled forward (Figure 5.6). The front teeth of Neandertals were larger than those of modern humans. Often, Neandertal teeth bear evidence of heavy wear (some were actually worn down to stubs), which leads researchers to believe that the teeth may have been used by Neandertals in much the same way as tools.

The image of the Neandertal as an entirely brutish creature is misleading. The large Neandertal cranial capacity ranged from 1,200 to 2,000 cc and could accommodate a brain as large as, or even larger than, that of a modern human. Moreover, relatively recent studies of Neandertal endocasts indicate that the structure and intellectual capacities of the Neandertal brain mirrored those of modern

humans (Holloway, 1985). Artifacts used by these populations reflect a much more complex range of adaptive skills than do those of pre-*H. sapiens* hominids (see Chapter 7).

Neandertals and Modern Humans   Ever since the first Neandertal skulls were found in the nineteenth century, scientists have pondered the links between Neandertals and modern humans (Figure 5.7). Early interpretations that viewed Neandertals as an intermediate ancestor between *Homo erectus* and anatomically modern humans have been discarded. Their restricted geographic range and distinctive physical characteristics make this scenario unlikely. Neandertals also appear to have co-existed with anatomically modern humans until the relatively recent past, perhaps as little as 30,000 years ago. A growing consensus among anthropologists holds that Neandertals had distinctive physical features that separate them from anatomically modern *H. sapiens,* but no one has come up with a cogent, widely accepted theory to explain which selective pressures produced these features.

Paleoanthropologists tend to favor the hypothesis that a "pre-Neandertal" population, possibly originating in another region and migrating to the classic Neandertal area, underwent severe natural selection in response to the cold environment of Europe. In this view, natural selection and lack of gene flow with other *H. sapiens* populations produced the

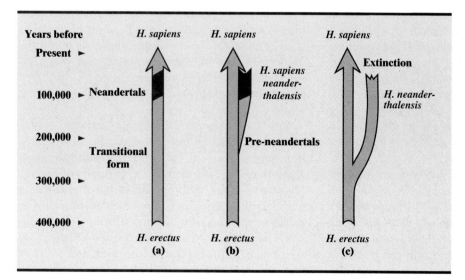

FIGURE 5.7 Three interpretations of the evolutionary relationships between Neandertals and modern humans: (a) unilinear evolution, (b) pre-neandertals, (c) separate lineages.

distinctive Neandertal characteristics. Such an interpretation might be consistent with recent molecular testing of genetic material extracted from Neandertal bones. These data suggest that Neandertals did not contribute to the mitochondrial DNA pool of modern populations (Krings et al., 1997).

SUMMARY

The hominids, a distinct family in the order Primates, include modern humans and their immediate ancestors. Although hominids share certain general features with all primates, they also evince a number of distinct characteristics. These include a fully bipedal posture; reduction of the face, jaw, and anterior teeth; and (in the genus *Homo*) increasing cranial capacity. Fossil evidence indicates that bipedalism stands as the earliest hominid trait, evolving some time between 6 million and 10 million years ago. Changes in other features appear more recently, primarily during the past 2 million years.

As the number of fossil discoveries has increased, the interpretations of the hominid family tree have become increasingly complex. For simplicity, this discussion focuses on two genera: *Australopithecus*, which includes species that may be ancestral to humans as well as extinct side branches, and *Homo*, the genus that includes modern humans. Paleoanthropologists believe that *A. anamensis* is at the base of the hominid family tree, with at least two branches that lead to later australopithecines on one side and the genus *Homo* and modern humans on the other.

Homo sapiens, the species that includes modern humans, evolved from *H. erectus* populations between 400,000 and 200,000 years ago. Skeletal remains from this time span often reveal a mix of characteristics from both species. These transitional hominid forms, which are difficult to classify, can be viewed as either advanced *H. erectus* or early *H. sapiens*. Anthropologists point to these transitional forms as physical evidence of the process of speciation.

A general consensus holds that *H. erectus* populations gave rise to *H. sapiens* by 200,000 years ago; yet how, when, and where this transition occurred are topics of heated debate. The opposing perspectives fall into two overarching models. Advocates of the multiregional evolutionary model believe that *H. sapiens* emerged in Asia, Africa, and Europe more or less concurrently. According to this theory, a high degree of regional continuity marks the evolution of humans from the first arrival of *H. erectus* up to the present. In contrast to the multiregional perspective are several theories united in their view of a replacement, or single-source, model of *H. sapiens* origins. These theories argue that *H. sapiens* evolved first in one region of the world, later diffusing into other regions and replacing earlier hominid populations. Some researchers have concluded that Africa was the point of origin of *H. sapiens*, with expansion outward from there. Although this theory may hold a great deal of promise, fossil evidence and genetic studies must be evaluated cautiously. In fact, an interpretation incorporating some elements of both the multiregional and replacement models may better represent the complexity of the actual situation.

Hominid skeletons from throughout the world dating to the last 200,000 years are generally classified as *H. sapiens*. Yet we find in these forms a great deal of variation, prompting archaeologists to identify them by a number of subspecies names. For convenience, *H. sapiens* can be divided into two categories: archaic and anatomically modern forms. Archaic *H. sapiens* retain some of the traits seen in earlier *H. erectus* populations. Anatomically modern *H. sapiens*, showing most of the characteristics associated with modern humans, appeared approximately 130,000 to 40,000 years ago in different world areas.

The best-known archaic *H. sapiens* forms, *H. sapiens neanderthalensis*, have been identified through hundreds of finds in Europe and the Near East. Because Neandertals have many distinctive physical features, anthropologists have advanced a number of theories regarding their relationship to anatomically modern humans. Current consensus tends to regard Neandertals as an archaic subspecies of *H. sapiens* that disappeared as a result of intensive selective pressures and genetic drift.

QUESTIONS TO THINK ABOUT

1. What are the critical evolutionary trends that differentiated the hominids from other primates?

2. Controversy surrounds the issue of how many genuses and species of hominid are present in the fossil record. On what basis are these distinctions made? How many genuses and species do you think there are?

3. Several different lines of evidence suggest that the hominids evolved in Africa. Discuss these different sources of information.

4. Many interpretations of hominid evolution (phylogenetic or family trees) have been advanced through the years. Which of the scenarios given in the text do you think makes the most sense? Why?

5. Fossils are not the only evidence used to provide information on hominid evolution. What are some of the other sources of information and data that are used to reconstruct the phylogeny of the hominids?

6. Contrast the multiregional evolutionary model with the replacement model for the emergence of anatomically modern humans. Can you think of a "critical test" that would allow you to evaluate the validity of these theories?

KEY TERMS

anatomically modern *Homo sapiens*
archaic *Homo sapiens*
bipedalism

foramen magnum
hominids
multiregional evolutionary model

postorbital constriction
replacement model
sagittal crest
transitional forms

INTERNET EXERCISES

1. Refer to the Anthropologists at Work box "Donald Johanson: Paleoanthropologist." What do paleoanthropologists do? Look at the following website: **http://www.talkorigins.org/faqs/homs/djohanson.html**. What background does Dr. Johanson have? How does it relate to what he does?

2. Read the account at **http://faculty.vassar.edu/piketay/evolution/Taung.html**. How does it differ from the findings revealed in the Critical Perspectives box "New Perspectives on the Taung Child"? Could the same technique discussed here be used on other human fossils?

3. The Piltdown Fraud, explained in the Critical Perspectives box on pages 114–15, derailed physical anthropology for nearly thirty-one years. Look over the following websites and then propose a method or methods that would allow us to avoid this type of fakery again.
http://www.talkorigins.org/faqs/piltdown/drawhorn.html

http://www1.umn.edu/scitech/piltdown.htm

http://www.cs.colorado.edu/~lindsay/creation/piltdown.html

4. Investigate the interactive Skull Module on the CSU Chico anthropology department's website at **http://www.csuchico.edu/anth/Module/skull.html**. How can anthropology students use this site? How does this site relate to the chapter? Does it help in understanding the anatomy of the skull described in the chapter? Why or why not?

5. Explore the Center for the Study of Chinese Prehistory website at **http://www.cruzio.com/~cscp/index.htm**. How does the fossil skull on the first page compare to a modern human skull! (compare to the skull used in the first Internet exercise of this chapter)? What type of skull is it? What is the evidence for human evolution in China?

SUGGESTED READINGS

BLINDERMAN, C. 1986. *The Piltdown Inquest*. Buffalo, NY: Prometheus Books. An account of the "discovery" and uncovering of the Piltdown man fraud. Although it does not conclusively solve the mystery, the book discusses all the possible suspects in this scientific whodunit. Now more than four decades old, J. S. Weiner's *The Piltdown Forgery,* published in 1955, still conveys some of the excitement and speculation that surrounded the unmasking of the forgery.

JANUS, CHRISTOPHER J., and WILLIAM BRASHER. 1975. *The Search for Peking Man*. A gripping tale of the discovery, disappearance, and search for the still missing remains of Peking man.

JOHANSON, DONALD C., and MAITLAND A. EDEY. 1981. *Lucy: The Beginnings of Humankind*. New York: Simon & Schuster. An exciting, firsthand account of Johanson's discovery of "Lucy" (*Australopithecus afarensis*) in Hadar, Ethiopia, and the role of this discovery in restructuring interpretations of human origins. The book also includes an excellent overview of the history and development of the field of paleoanthropology.

LEWIN, ROGER. 1993. *The Origin of Modern Humans*. New York: Scientific American Library. This volume provides a highly readable introduction to the questions of when and where modern humans originated. It is well illustrated and also includes a glossary of key terms.

TRINKAUS, ERIK, and PAT SHIPMAN. 1994. *The Neandertals: Of Skeletons, Scientists, and Scandal*. New York: Vintage Books. A gripping look at the discovery and interpretation of the Neandertals, presented in historical perspective from the first finds of the nineteenth century to today.

CHAPTER

6

Human Variation

CHAPTER QUESTIONS

- What are the basic sources of variation of human physical characteristics?

- What are the hypotheses regarding the variation of skin color among human populations?

- How does natural selection influence body build?

- What do studies suggest regarding the heritability of intelligence differences among various human populations?

- What were some of the early folk and scientific ideas regarding race?

- How do modern anthropologists treat the concept of race?

As we noted in Chapter 5, *Homo sapiens* populations migrated throughout the world, settling in all sorts of climatic and environmental settings. Even though modern humans live in more diverse environmental conditions than does any other primate group, we all bear a striking genetic similarity. Recent scientific assessments of population genetics and human variation confirm that although humans are widely distributed and have experienced a degree of reproductive isolation, no human population has become so genetically isolated as to constitute a separate species. Rather, all modern humans are the product of a tremendous amount of gene exchange.

Although modern humans represent a single species, we clearly are not all alike. As a species, humans exhibit a great deal of *phenotypic variation*—individuals' external, observable characteristics, which are shaped in part by both their genetic makeup and unique life history (see Chapter 3). Differences in many physical characteristics, such as height, skin color, hair texture, and facial features, are readily discernible. While some of this variation stems from heredity, many differences among human populations are the result of human culture—how we dress, the kinds of houses we live in, our marriage customs—and are not genetically determined. Physical anthropologists study humans as a biological species, whereas cultural anthropologists attempt to unravel the myriad elements of cultural diversity. As we shall see, however, cultural practices also affect genetic and physical variation by influencing gene flow or altering the environment. The challenge of identifying the sources of human diversity and how this diversity should be viewed are the focus of this chapter.

Sources of Human Variation

To understand variation among human populations, we must consider three primary causes: (1) *evolutionary processes,* which affect genetic diversity within and between populations; (2) *environment*—the variation among individuals that springs from their unique life experiences in specific environments; and (3) *culture*—the variation stemming from disparate cultural beliefs and practices inculcated during the formative years and reinforced throughout life. These sources of variation will be discussed in turn.

Genetics and Evolution

As discussed in Chapter 3, a population's total complement of genes is referred to as a *gene pool.* In *Homo sapiens,* as well as in many animal populations, genes may have two or more alternate forms (or *alleles*)—a phenomenon called **polymorphism** (literally, "many forms"). These differences are expressed in various physical characteristics, ranging from hair and eye color to less visible differences in blood chemistry. Many of these traits vary in their expression in different world areas. For example, we associate certain hair texture and skin color with populations in specific geographic areas. Species made up of populations that can be distinguished regionally on the basis of discrete physical traits are called **polytypic.**

The genetic variation present in the human species is the product of the four fundamental processes of evolution that were examined in Chapter 3: mutations, natural selection, gene flow, and genetic drift. *Mutations,* which are random changes in the genetic code, bring about changes in alleles. Mutations may result in evolutionary change only if they occur in the sex cells of individuals, enabling this change to be passed on to succeeding generations. Mutations are important in explaining human variation because they are ultimately the source of all genetic variation. They may be beneficial, detrimental, or neutral in terms of an organism's reproductive success. The evolutionary process that determines which new mutations will enter a population is *natural selection.* Through this evolutionary process, traits that diminish reproductive success will be eliminated, whereas traits enhancing the ability to reproduce will become more widespread.

Although natural selection has favored certain traits in human populations, it does not explain all genetic variation. Some physical characteristics, such as eye color, confer no discernible reproductive advantages. We might expect such neutral traits to be evenly distributed throughout human populations as a result of gene flow, yet this is not the case. The *nonrandom distribution* of neutral traits illustrates *genetic drift,* the processes of selection that alter allele frequencies. Genetic drift is particularly useful in explaining differences among genetically isolated populations.

Consider the physical differences that distinguish the people of central Africa from those living in northern Arctic regions. Gene flow, or the introduction of new genes into a population's gene pool through interbreeding with another population, is highly unlikely for these geographically distant peoples. In addition, most human cultures maintain rules of *endogamy*—that is, marriage to someone within one's own group—thereby further restricting gene flow. Scientists speculate that Paleolithic populations consisted of small bands of between thirty and one hundred individuals in which genetic drift may have been an important factor.

The Physical Environment

The physical environment influences human variation by promoting or restricting growth and development. Physical differences among humans may arise as a result of how well requirements for growth are met. **Acclimatization** is the physiological process of becoming accustomed to a new environment. We can examine the effects of the physical environment by studying how individuals with similar genetic makeup develop in different environmental settings. If, for example, identical twins were separated at birth and reared far apart in different regions of the world, any physical variation between them could be attributed to their disparate physical environments. In fact, studies have demonstrated that humans are highly sensitive to changes in their physical surroundings.

Culture

Many of the features that distinguish human populations stem from culture. People differ in the customs and beliefs that guide the way they eat, dress, and build their homes. Such differences are primarily superficial. If a child born in one region of the world is raised in another culture, he or she will learn and embrace the customs and beliefs of the adopted culture. Culture may influence human genetic variation through religious beliefs, social organization, marriage practices, or prejudices that restrict intermarriage among different groups and thus inhibit gene flow. Cultural beliefs also determine diet, living conditions, and the environment in which people work; these effects, in turn, either promote or hamper human growth and development.

Evaluating Reasons for Variation

Although we know that genetic, environmental, and cultural factors all contribute to human variation, it is often difficult to assess the relative importance of each. All three influences, in combination, yield the characteristics found in an individual. We can see the intertwined nature of these sources of variation by examining body height. How tall a person grows clearly stems, in part, from his or her genetic makeup. This can be illustrated by certain African, Philippine, and New Guinean populations that have mean heights of less than 5 feet. This average is much lower than that of most other human populations. Studies indicate that the relatively short stature in these populations is caused by a deficiency in a hormone that stimulates growth, a genetic trend (Shea & Gomez, 1988).

At the same time, however, height varies significantly even among populations that are genetically similar. One way to account for this is to examine variation in environmental factors, such as the amount of sunlight a person is exposed to, the average daily temperature, differences in health and nutrition, and rates of exposure to disease. Consider seasonal changes in growth rates: Children living in temperate climates grow more quickly during the spring and summer than during the fall and winter, and children in tropical climates experience growth spurts during the dry season rather than during the rainy season (Bogin, 1978). In both instances, scientists conjecture that more rapid growth correlates with greater exposure to sunlight, although precisely how this works remains unclear. One theory holds that the increased sunlight in certain seasons stimulates the body's production of vitamin D, which promotes bone growth.

Finally, cultural factors can also affect people's health and, as a consequence, their growth. In certain cultures, for example, some social groups have greater access than others to food, shelter, and protection against childhood diseases, all of which affect growth rates. Underprivileged children whose basic nutritional needs are often unsatisfied will not grow as tall as those born into a society with material abundance.

Because of the complex interrelationships among genetic, environmental, and cultural influences, the relative importance of each of these elements can be deciphered only through detailed analysis of specific human populations.

Adaptive Aspects of Human Variation

Natural selection has played a key role in the evolution of the human species, but what role has it played in variation among modern humans? As scientists probe human variation, they have posited a variety of ways in which natural selection may have contributed to some of the differences observed in modern human populations. If natural selection promoted these differences, there should be evidence to substantiate this assertion. Unfortunately, since soft tissues are not preserved in the fossil record, the validity of these theories can only be evaluated indirectly. How do we assess the effects of natural selection? One way is to look at how different physical characteristics enable modern humans to adapt to disparate environmental conditions.

Skin Color

Human skin color varies tremendously among both individuals and groups, and multiple shades of skin color are found in different world areas. The basis for this variation is complex. The current consensus among researchers is that skin color is a *polygenic* trait that is a consequence of variation in the alleles of more than one gene. However, the specific genetic loci involved, the precise manner of inheritance, and the evolutionary factors that may have contributed to variation in skin color are the focus of continuing research (Byard, 1981; Jablonsky & Chaplin, 2000). Another striking physical difference between humans and other primates is our lack of body hair. Our relatively hairless skin is covered with sweat glands, which other primates lack. Why do humans differ so markedly in appearance from nonhuman primates?

It is likely that our early hominid ancestors had relatively light-colored skin and bodies covered with hair, much like the chimpanzee and gorilla, our closest living biological relatives. Light skin color and thick body hair are well suited to forest and wooded environments; however, as early hominids moved out into more open savannas, this would have been a disadvantage. Here human ancestors would have faced higher temperatures, greater energy expenditure to obtain food, and, subsequently, increased risk of heat stroke and heat exhaustion. The solution was to sweat more, which cools the body through evaporation. Unfortunately, early hominids were likely poor at sweating. Again, as is the case with modern chimpanzees and gorillas, they probably had relatively few sweat glands, which were primarily located on the palms of their hands and the soles of their feet. In some cases, however, individuals may have been born with more than the typical number of sweat glands. These individuals would have been able to sweat more and thus maximize the time they could spend foraging for food and, ultimately, better ensure their reproductive success. Modern humans, with some two million sweat glands spread across their bodies, are formidable at sweating.

Differences in Skin Color   Three substances combine to give human skin its color: melanin, hemoglobin, and carotene (Poirer, Stini, & Wreden, 1990). Most important of these is *melanin,* the dark pigment that primarily determines the lightness or darkness of skin and which is responsible for variations of tan, brown, and black skin color. Melanin is produced by cells known as *melanocytes,* in the bottom layers of the skin. Interestingly, all modern humans have about the same number of melanocytes. However, their arrangement and the amount of melanin they produce underlie variation in skin color. These factors are, to some extent, genetically controlled (Szabo, 1967).

Hemoglobin, a protein that contains iron, gives red blood cells their color. In people with less melanin in their skin, this red color shows through more strongly, tinting their skin pink. *Carotene,* an orange-yellow pigment that confers a yellowish tinge, is contained in certain foods, so people with a large amount of carotene in their diet may have an orange tone in their skin. However, the presence of carotene does not impart a yellowish cast to the skin of individuals of Asian descent. Rather, this skin tone is the result of a thickening of the exterior layers of skin.

Skin color is also directly influenced by the environment. Exposure to the ultraviolet radiation in sunlight stimulates the production of melanin, yielding what we call a tan. Thus, variation in individuals' skin color stems from the interaction of both genetic and environmental factors (Williams-Blangero & Blangero, 1992).

The Geographic Distribution of Skin Color   Analysis of the distribution of skin pigmentation reveals a distinctive pattern. In most world areas, skin color is generally darker in populations closer to the equator (Birdsell, 1981). Further north and south of the equatorial zone, skin coloration is lighter. This observation was particularly true before the large population migrations of the last 500 years.

Scientists who have studied the distribution patterns of skin pigmentation hypothesize that natural selection played a decisive role in producing varying shades of skin color. Although interpretation remains open to question, several adaptive aspects of pigmentation suggest reasons why skin color may have been favored by natural selection. First, darker skin confers advantages in a tropical environment. Of the different pigments noted, only melanin provides protection from ultraviolet (UV) radiation in sunlight, which has been shown to have a number of detrimental effects. Prolonged exposure to the sun can cause sunburn, sunstroke, skin cancer, and most important, significantly decrease folate levels (Jablonsky & Chaplin, 2000). Folate, a member of the vitamin B complex, is essential for normal fetal development. Low folate levels in mothers have been correlated with embryonic defects such as spina bifida and anencephaly (the absence of a full brain or spinal cord). Even an hour of exposure to intense sunlight is sufficient to reduce folate levels by half in light-skinned individuals. Originally, as *Homo sapiens* evolved in the tropical equatorial zones, a darker skin pigmentation most likely proved highly adaptive.

If the adaptive advantages of darker skin are clear cut, why do some human populations have light-colored skin? Research suggests that darker skin is not necessarily advantageous in all environmental settings. As people moved into more temperate regions with less sunlight, other selective pressures, primarily the need for vitamin D, conferred an adaptive advantage on light pigmentations. We know today that when human skin is exposed to UV radiation in sunlight, the UV rays stimulate the synthesis of vitamin D. Insufficient levels of vitamin D can cause deficiency diseases like rickets, which makes the bones soft and ultimately deformed. The fossil record indicates that some *Homo neanderthalensis* individuals from northern Europe suffered from rickets (Boaz & Almquist, 1997). With this in mind, physical anthropologists conjecture that the production of optimal levels of vitamin D may have had a hand in the distribution of light skin. Lower UV levels closely correspond with fairer skin coloration (Jablonsky & Chaplin, 2000).

People who inhabited equatorial regions with ample exposure to sunlight evolved darker skin pigmentation to avoid the deleterious effects of UV radiation. In contrast, people who lived in cold, cloudy climates and consequently wore heavy clothing much of the time improved their chances of survival if they had lighter skin, which absorbed higher levels of UV radiation and, thus, synthesized more vitamin D. Over time, natural selection favored darker skin in the tropics and lighter skin in regions with lower levels of sunlight and the associated UV radiation.

In addition, light skin may increase resistance to frostbite—another reason why lighter-skinned populations predominated in the colder northern regions. Studies of U.S. soldiers during the Korean War revealed that people with darker skin were more prone to frostbite (Post et al., 1975). Further studies have tentatively linked darker skin color with genetic resistance to certain tropical diseases as well (Wasserman, 1965; Polednak, 1974). These selective pressures may have variously favored lighter or darker skin in different environmental settings.

Body Build

The influence of natural selection and environment on human body and limb forms is especially pronounced. These interrelationships were first noted by the nineteenth-century English zoologist Carl Bergmann. He observed that in mammal and bird populations, the larger members of the species predominate in the colder parts of the species range, whereas the smaller representatives are more common in warmer areas. This pattern also holds true for human populations.

Bergmann explained these findings in reference to the ways birds and mammals dissipate heat. Bergmann's rule states that smaller animals, which have larger surface areas relative to their body weights, lose excess heat efficiently and therefore function better at higher temperatures. Larger animals, which have a smaller surface area relative to their body weight, dissipate heat more slowly and are therefore better adapted to cold climates. The same applies to humans: People living in cold climates tend to have stocky torsos and heavier average body weights, whereas people in warmer regions have more slender frames on average.

Building on Bergmann's observations about heat loss, the American zoologist J. A. Allen did research on protruding parts of the body, particularly arms and legs. Allen's rule maintains that individuals living in colder areas generally have shorter, stockier limbs. Longer limbs, which lose heat more quickly, typify populations in warmer climates. Bergmann's and Allen's rules are illustrated by the contrasting body builds of a Masai warrior from Tanzania and an American Eskimo (see photographs on p. 137).

Bergmann's and Allen's observations can be partially explained by natural selection. However, acclimatization also affects body and limb size, according to studies conducted among modern U.S. groups descended from recent migrants from Asia,

A Masai warrior from Tanzania in East Africa (left) and a Native American Eskimo (right), illustrating how body weight and shape vary according to both Bergmann's rule and Allen's rule.

Africa, and, primarily, Europe (Newman & Munroe, 1955). Researchers discovered that individuals born in warmer states generally developed longer limbs and more slender body types than did those from colder states. Because these developments occurred within such a short time (a few generations at most), they could not be attributed to evolutionary processes. Laboratory experiments with animals produced similar findings. Mice raised in cold conditions developed shorter, stouter limbs than did mice growing up in warmer settings (Riesenfeld, 1973).

Cranial and Facial Features

Because the human skull and facial features vary tremendously in shape, numerous theories explaining this variation have been advanced over the centuries. In the nineteenth century, many people embraced *phrenology*, the belief that a careful study of the bumps of the cranium could be used to "read" an individual's personality or mental

abilities or even the future. Other nineteenth-century theories posited a relationship among race, cranial shape, and facial features. None of these beliefs has withstood scientific scrutiny.

Why, then, do skull shapes vary? As with body build, the shape of the skull and face may represent adaptations to the physical environment. By examining hundreds of populations, researchers have found a close correlation between skull shapes and climate. People living in colder climates tend to have rounded heads, which conserve heat better, whereas people in warmer climates tend to have narrow skulls (Beals, 1972). Other studies have considered the environmental factors that may have favored specific nose types. Studies indicate that higher, narrower nasal openings have more mucous membranes, surfaces that moisten inhaled air. People living in drier climates tend to have more mucous membranes, regardless of whether the environment is hot or cold. Of course, these observations are generalizations; many individual exceptions can also be cited.

Biochemical Characteristics

Research on human variation has revealed less obvious differences among populations than skin color, body build, and facial appearance. Variation occurring in dozens of less visible features—such as blood type, the consistency of earwax, and other subtle biochemical traits—also illustrates evolutionary processes at work. It is easy to imagine how natural selection may have affected the distribution of some of these features. Consider, for example, resistance to disease. If a lethal illness were introduced into a population, individuals with a natural genetic resistance would have an enhanced chance of survival. With increased odds of reproducing, these individuals' genetic blueprints would quickly spread throughout the population (Motulsky, 1971).

History offers many tragic examples of one population inflicting disease on another that had no natural immunity. For example, when Europeans first came in contact with indigenous peoples of the Americas and the South Pacific, they carried with them the germs that cause measles and smallpox. Because these diseases had afflicted European populations for centuries, most Europeans had adapted natural immunities to them. When the diseases were introduced into populations that had never been exposed to them, however, plagues of catastrophic proportions ensued. Many Native American and Polynesian populations were decimated by the spread of diseases brought to their lands by Europeans.

Blood Types   Among the most studied biochemical characteristics are blood types. They are the phenotypic expression of three alleles—A, B, and O. A and B are both dominant, whereas O is recessive. These different alleles are a good illustration of polymorphism in a simple genetic trait. They are expressed in four phenotypes: type A (genotypes AA and AO); type B (genotypes BB and BO); type AB (genotype AB); and type O (genotype OO).

The three blood-group alleles are found throughout the world in varying frequencies from population to population. Type O is by far the most common, ranging from over 50 percent in areas of Asia, Australia, Africa, and Europe to 100 percent among some Native American groups. Type A occurs throughout the world but generally

in smaller percentages than does type O. Type B has the lowest frequency. Believed to have been totally absent from native South American groups, type B is most common in Eurasia and can be tracked in a clinal distribution outward into Europe in the west, and Asia in the east.

Anthropologists, citing the nonrandom distribution of blood types, conclude that natural selection may have favored certain gene frequencies, keeping the percentage of individual alleles stable in particular populations. This natural selection might have something to do with resistance to disease. Each blood type constitutes a different antigen on the surface of red blood cells. An *antigen* is any substance that produces *antibodies,* proteins that combat foreign substances entering the body. The presence of these different antigens and antibodies is the reason doctors need to know a person's blood type before giving a blood transfusion. Type A blood has anti-B antibodies, and vice versa. Type O incorporates antibodies that fight against proteins in both type A and type B. People with blood type B (with anti-A antibodies) are better able to fight off diseases such as syphilis, which resemble type A antigens on a biochemical level. Similarly, scientists have posited links between blood types and resistance to many infectious diseases, including bubonic plague, smallpox, and typhoid fever. Before the advent of modern medical technology, natural resistance to these diseases would have conferred critical adaptive advantages.

Sickle-Cell Anemia

By studying population genetics and evolutionary change within populations, scientists have gained important insights into certain genetic diseases, that is, those brought on by lethal genes that result in severe disabilities. One such disease, sickle-cell anemia, produces an abnormal form of *hemoglobin,* the blood molecule that carries oxygen in the bloodstream. In individuals with sickle-cell anemia, the abnormal hemoglobin molecules rupture and collapse into a sicklelike shape, inhibiting the distribution of oxygen. Individuals afflicted with sickle-cell anemia often die in childhood.

Why did natural selection fail to eliminate such a lethal gene? Geneticists and physical anthropologists investigating this question discovered that

A scanning electron micrograph of a deformed red blood cell (left) in sickle-cell anemia, a hereditary blood disease. To the right of the sickle cell is a normal, biconcave red blood cell.

sickle-cell anemia affects up to 40 percent of the population in regions where *malaria,* an infectious disease spread by mosquitoes, is prevalent. These regions include portions of Africa, the Mediterranean, the Arabian peninsula, and India. Investigators found that the blood of those who carry the sickle-cell gene is sufficiently inhospitable to the malaria parasite to confer on sickle-cell carriers an important genetic resistance over noncarriers in regions where malaria is rampant. Thus, although carriers may contract malaria, they are less likely to die from it.

It works like this: Recalling from Chapter 3 Mendel's *principle of segregation,* we note that there are three genotypes—homozygous dominant (AA), heterozygous (Aa), and homozygous recessive (aa). Because people who are homozygous for sickle-cell anemia usually die within the first year of life (Motulsky, 1971), only individuals who are heterozygous for the trait can transmit the disease to the next generation. Two heterozygous parents have a 25 percent chance of having a child who manifests the disease. Although these individuals may suffer from anemia, they are better suited to survive the threat of malaria than are individuals who do not carry the sickle-cell gene. Studies confirm that heterozygous carriers of sickle-cell anemia have higher fertility rates than noncarriers in regions where malaria is common (Livingston, 1971). Consequently, the survival of those with heterozy-

gous genotypes balances the deaths of those that are homozygous recessive for the trait. The sickle-cell gene, therefore, is transmitted from generation to generation as an evolutionary adaptation in areas where malaria is prevalent.

Balanced Polymorphism   In the case of sickle-cell anemia, a lethal recessive gene confers partial protection against malaria. When homozygous and heterozygous genes exist in a state of relative stability, or equilibrium, within a population, this is known as **balanced polymorphism.** In equatorial Africa, 40 percent of the population carries the sickle-cell gene, constituting an evolutionary trade-off. Natural selection has created this balanced polymorphism to protect the African populations, but at a high cost: the deaths of some people.

By examining the sickle-cell gene, we also see an example of how natural selection acts against a harmful genetic trait. Approximately 2 to 6 percent of African Americans carry the sickle-cell gene— a greater percentage than that found in individuals of non-African origin in the United States but far lower than incidences of sickle-cell anemia among African populations (Workman et al., 1963). In part, this can be explained by gene flow between African Americans and other populations not affected by the sickle-cell gene. However, statistical studies point to another reason. Unlike Africa, the United States does not have high levels of malarial infection; therefore, the gene represents a severe liability. It is no longer favored by natural selection and is therefore gradually being eliminated from the gene pool.

Lactase Deficiency

Humans also vary in how well they digest particular foods. Most extensively studied is variation in the production of a digestive enzyme called *lactase,* which is responsible for the digestion of *lactose,* the sugar found in milk. All human infants can digest milk. However, the majority of humans lack the genetic coding that continues to produce lactase after about 4 years of age, a tendency also seen in other mammals. Without lactase, milk ferments in the intestine, causing diarrhea and cramps. This condition is referred to as **lactase deficiency.** As one researcher has noted, "Contrary to popular advertising, everybody does not need milk, at least not as adults. In fact, for millions of human beings, milk consumption leads to severe discomfort" (Nelson & Jurmain, 1988:166). The majority of adults in Asian and African populations do not drink milk because they are not able to digest it properly.

Reasons for variation in lactase production among human populations are difficult to confirm, but researchers believe that certain conditions favor the ability to digest lactose. The capability is especially common among populations that have a history of *pastoralism,* the reliance on domesticated animals such as cows, sheep, and goats. Such animals provide plenty of milk to drink. In this cultural environment, natural selection favors individuals best able to make use of all available sources of nutrition. European populations, among the most lactose-tolerant, are partly descended from Middle Eastern pastoralists. African pastoralists such as the Fulani also produce significantly more lactase than do Africans who do not raise dairy animals (Relethford, 1997).

Effects of the Physical Environment

We have highlighted the role of evolutionary processes in human variation, but we have also noted how differences in physical surroundings affect human variation. Think back to the differences between genotype and phenotype. The environment may produce vastly different appearances (*phenotypes*) in organisms of very similar genotypes. For example, if we take two plants with identical genetic makeup (*genotypes*) and plant one in a fertile, well-irrigated field and the other in a stony, poorly watered area, the resulting plants will look completely different despite their genetic similarity. Humans have settled in an amazing range of environmental zones, and the physical environment plays a comparable role in causing differences in human populations.

High-Altitude Adaptations

Consider people living in high-altitude environments such as the Himalaya or Andes mountains. Because of the lower barometric pressure at high altitude, people take in less oxygen, making the air feel "thinner." So at high elevations, most humans experience dizziness and breathing difficulties, which are symptoms of *hypoxia,* or oxygen deficiency. People raised in high-altitude environments, however, do not have these reactions. They have adapted to lower amounts of oxygen in different ways, including higher breathing rates, greater lung capacity, larger hearts, and more red cells in their blood, all of which promote greater oxygen exchange (Stini, 1975). We attribute this adaptation to high altitudes to acclimatization, because children born in lowland environments who are raised at higher elevations develop many of the same physical characteristics as those born in the latter environment (Frisancho, 1979).

Cultural Diversity in Human Populations

As noted in Chapter 5, culture and society play key roles in our interaction with the environment. It is not surprising, therefore, that culture also influences human—and sometimes genetic—variation. Although humans can theoretically choose a mate from among any potential spouses within geographic limits, culture often circumscribes those choices. In the Middle East, for example, Christians,

Members of an Amish community. The Amish, a religious community in Pennsylvania and the Midwest, severely restrict interaction with other cultures. Religion, ethnicity, and perceived cultural differences can curb gene flow among human populations.

Jews, and Muslims live in close proximity to one another, yet most marry within their own religious group. Sometimes these cultural sanctions take on the force of law. For example, at one time both South Africa and certain regions of the United States had laws prohibiting marriage between whites and blacks. Such cultural practices inhibit gene flow and contribute to genetic drift within a population. Other cultural practices actually alter the environment and can affect the allocation of resources. Nowhere is the impact of culture more pronounced than in modern urban societies.

The Impact of Modern Urban Life

Urbanization—the concentration of populations into large urban centers—has altered human lifestyles in dramatic and significant ways. Certain issues must be addressed whenever large numbers of people live together in a small area: How will they be supplied with food and water? How will sanitation needs be met? Will crowded living conditions enhance life or make it barely tolerable? Different cultures have worked through these issues with varying degrees of success. In some cities, overcrowding, combined with poor knowledge of sanitation, food storage, and personal hygiene, has contributed to nutritional deficiencies and the spread of infectious disease and reduced growth rates. Daily life in modern American cities exposes

people to air pollution, contaminated water, high noise levels, and other environmental hazards, all of which aggravate physiological stress.

Toxic waste, brought on by the improper disposal of hazardous chemicals, poses a problem of immense proportions in the United States. An example of the threat to human health and development is Love Canal, near Niagara Falls, New York, which was used as a dumping ground for chemical waste between 1940 and 1953 (Vianna & Polan, 1984; Paigen et al., 1987). Studies have shown that women who lived close to the dump site gave birth to infants with lower average weights than women in other areas. Further research demonstrated that children raised near Love Canal were shorter than children of the same age raised elsewhere. This tendency was most pronounced in children who lived near Love Canal for the longest period of time.

Lower birth rates and reduced growth rates may be just the tip of the iceberg. As awareness of the threat of toxic waste increases, links to a host of other health hazards, neurological disorders, and cancer rates are being identified.

The Concept of Race

Physical characteristics such as skin pigmentation, nose shape, and hair texture have prompted people

An Ainu elder male. The Ainu, an ethnic group in northern Japan, are generally distinguished from other Japanese by such physical features as lighter skin and higher-bridged noses—attributes frequently associated with European populations. The distribution of characteristics like these confounds attempts at racial classification.

throughout history to classify humans into different "races." To modern biologists, **races** constitute divisions within humankind based on identifiable hereditary traits (Brues, 1977). These divisions are an attempt to categorize the great variation among humans. Biologists recognize these divisions for what they are: crude and roughly drawn boundaries, at best.

Although the diversity of human populations is undeniable, delineating specific races has little practical or scientific value in studying human variation (Gould, 1977). As we shall see, physical characteristics do not divide humans into readily discernible groups or races. Furthermore, classification of physical characteristics serves only to label particular categories of phenomena arbitrarily selected by the researcher. It does not explain the *reason* for the observed variation. Despite the scientific limitations of the concept of race, we examine early racial classifications because incorrect and faulty ideas stemming from some classifications are

still widespread. Table 6.1 summarizes racial classification systems.

Ancient Classification Systems

Early racial classifications were *folk taxonomies,* informal and unscientific classifications based on skin color. In the fourteenth century B.C., the ancient Egyptians divided all human populations into one of four categories: red for Egyptians, yellow for people to the east, white for people to the north, and black for Africans to the south (Gossett, 1963). Later, in the biblical book of Genesis, a similar classification scheme appears in a tale chronicling the distribution of the human population: "And the sons of Noah that went forth from the ark were Shem, Ham and Japheth: . . . these are the three sons of Noah: and of them was the whole earth overspread" (Genesis 9:18–19).

The descendants of Shem (the Semites) were the ancient Israelites. The descendants of Ham ventured to the south and the east, and the descendants of Japheth moved north. The word *Ham* originally meant "black" and referred to the black soil of the Nile delta, but its meaning was eventually changed to describe the skin color of Ham's descendants. At the end of Genesis, the descendants of Ham are condemned to be "servants of servants unto [their] brethren" (Genesis 9:25). Many Westerners subsequently cited this passage as the justification for an entrenched system of racial discrimination (Leach, 1988).

By correlating physical characteristics with cultural differences, classification systems such as these assumed erroneously that populations that shared certain physical traits, especially skin color, also exhibited similar behaviors. These beliefs gave rise to many popular misconceptions and generalizations concerning the values, traditions, and behaviors of non-Western peoples.

Early "Scientific" Studies of Race

During the eighteenth and nineteenth centuries, the body of scientific knowledge expanded, and scientific methodologies became more sophisticated in the West; scientists and philosophers thus began to apply scientific principles to the question of race. In one of the earliest scientific efforts to organize human variation into racial categories, the

| Table 6.1 | **How Many Races Are There?** |

Examples of different racial classifications, and their basis, are contained in the table. Other researchers have suggested completely different races and definitions. The great disagreement among scientists over the number and characteristics of different races is a good indication of the limited usefulness of the concept. Most modern researchers focus their efforts on explaining why there is variation in particular traits.

Origin of Theory	Number of Races	Description	Basis of Classification
Ancient Egyptians, 14th century B.C.	4	Egyptians (red), Easterners (yellow), people from the north (white), and people to the south (black)	Skin color
Carolus Linnaeus, 1735	4	Europeans (white), North American Indians (red), Asiatics (yellow), Africans (black)	Skin color
Johann Blumenbach, 1775	5	Caucasian, Ethiopian, Mongolian, Malay, Native American	Skin color, hair color, facial features, and other physical traits
J. Deniker, 1900	29	Adriatic, Ainu, Assyroid, Australian, Berber, Bushman, Dravidian, Ethiopian, Littoral-European, Western-European, Northern-European, Eastern-European, Ibero-Insular, Indo-Afghan, Indonesian, Melanesian, Negrito, Negro, Polynesian, Semite, South American, North American, Central American, Patagonian, Eskimo, Lapp, Ugrian, Turkish, Mongol	Hair color and texture, eye color
William Boyd, 1950	6	European, African, Asiatic, American Indian, Australoid, Early European	Blood groups
Carleton Coon, Stanley Garn, & Joseph Birdsell, 1950	30	Murrayian, Ainu, Alpine, N.W. European, N.E. European, Lapp, Forest Negro, Melanesian, Negrito, Bushman Bantu, Sudanese, Carpentarian, Dravidian, Hamite, Hindu, Mediterranean, Nordic, N. American Colored, S. African Colored, Classic Mongoloid, N. Chinese, S.E. Asiatic, Tibeto-Indonesian, Mongoloid, Turkic, Am. Indian Marginal, Am. Indian Central, Ladino, Polynesian, Neo-Hawaiian	Evolutionary trends, body build, and special surface features such as skin color and facial structure
Stanley Garn, 1961	9	Africans, Amerindian (Native Americans), Asiatics, Australians, Europeans, Indians, Melanesian-Papuans, Micronesians, Polynesians	Geographic boundaries restricting gene flow
Walter Bodmer, 1976	3	Africans, Caucasians, Easterners (including Australians and Pacific Islanders)	Major geographical groups

Swiss scientist Carolus Linnaeus constructed a taxonomy in 1758 that divided *H. sapiens* into four races based on skin color: Europeans (white), North American Indians (red), Asiatics (yellow), and Africans (black). (Linnaeus is discussed in Chapter 4 for his systematic classification of all living creatures.)

In 1781, a German scientist, Johann Blumenbach, devised a racial classification system that is still sometimes used in popular, unscientific discussions of race. He divided humans into five distinct groups—Caucasian, Mongolian, Malay, Ethiopian, and Native American—corresponding to the colors white, yellow, brown, black, and red, respectively. Blumenbach based his racial typology primarily on skin color, but he considered other traits as well, including facial features, chin form, and hair color.

Limitations of Classification Systems

Because these typologies were created before Darwin and Mendel had published their findings, they did not incorporate the modern principles of natural selection, heredity, and population genetics. For example, Mendel's principle of independent assortment holds that physical traits are not linked together in the process of reproduction and transmission of genetic material. In other words, there is no "package" of characteristics that is passed on to members of different "races." Thus, blond hair and blue eyes are not consistently found in tandem, just as a specific skin color and hair texture are not linked to each other. Rather, these traits are independent of one another, leading to varying combinations in different individuals. Variation in the combination of traits makes it impossible to classify races according to well-defined criteria that hold for entire populations.

Continuous Variation   Scientists encounter another fundamental problem in distinguishing races. Instead of falling into discrete divisions, many characteristics exhibit a spectrum from one extreme to another, a phenomenon called **continuous variation.** Figure 6.1 illustrates this concept by showing the overlap of different skin colors, as measured by reflected light. If skin color is to be used as the primary criterion for determining race, how, then, do we divide the races? Inevitably, any boundaries we draw are entirely arbitrary.

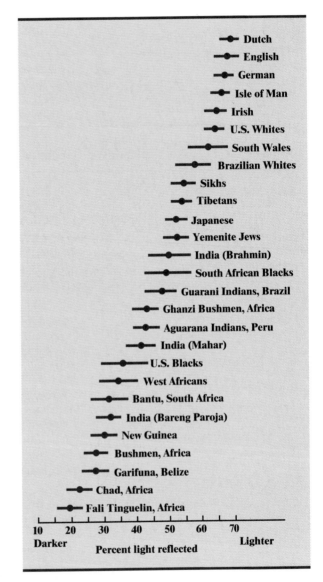

FIGURE 6.1   Variation in skin color, as measured by the amount of reflected light. The measurements cannot be divided into natural divisions, thus illustrating the arbitrary nature of racial classification.

Source: From *The Human Species: An Introduction to Biological Anthropology* by John Relethford. Copyright © 1990 by Mayfield Publishing Company. Reprinted by permission of the publisher.

If races constituted fundamental divisions within the human species, such differences would be readily measurable; in fact, they are not. As scientific information has accumulated, the picture has become increasingly complicated and the boundaries more obscure. This is clearly illustrated

The extermination of millions of Jews by the Nazis before and during World War II was justified by unscientific theories of race that had no basis in empirical fact.

by the disagreement among researchers over the number and characteristics of different races. Some people have attempted to explain continuous variation as a function of *mongrelization,* or interbreeding. This notion follows the logic that at some point in the past, the races were "pure," but the lines separating one race from another have become blurred by recent interbreeding. Such ideas reveal a naive understanding of the human past. Although gene flow may have been more restricted in some groups than in others, human populations have always interbred, so different races would have been impossible to distinguish during any time period.

Racism   At times, racial classifications have been used to justify **racism,** an ideology that advocates the superiority of certain races and the inferiority of others, and leads to prejudice and discrimination against particular populations. In many societies, including our own, racist beliefs were used to rationalize slavery and the political oppression of minority groups. Such racist views justified the African slave trade, which provided labor for plantations in the Americas until the Civil War. In the 1930s, the Nazi racist ideology, based on the presumed superiority of a pure "Aryan race," was used to justify the annihilation of millions of Jews and other "non-Aryan" peoples in Europe.

Racist beliefs have no basis in fact. Human groups never fit into such neat categories. Many Jewish people living in Europe during the Holocaust possessed the same physical features as those associated with Aryans. Even staunch advocates of Nazi ideology found it difficult to define precisely which physical characteristics supposedly distinguished one "race" from another.

Geographical Races

Stanley Garn (1971) took a different tack in classifying modern humans into races. Unlike earlier theorists, Garn did not rely on single, arbitrary characteristics such as skin pigmentation in developing his classification system. Instead, he focused on the impact evolutionary forces may have had on geographically isolated human populations. Garn divided modern humans into what he called *geographical races,* populations isolated from one another by natural barriers such as oceans, mountains, and deserts. He reasoned that because of these barriers most people in each population married within their own gene pool. Garn's taxonomy divided humans into nine geographical races: Amerindian, Polynesian, Micronesian, Melanesian-Papuan, Australian, Asiatic, Indian, European, and African. These were further divided into smaller local races and microraces that reflected restricted gene flow among smaller populations.

In an innovative and substantial shift, Garn's approach sought to frame the classification of human races in evolutionary terms. However, critics have pointed out that even these divisions imply stronger differences among races than actually exist. In addition, some of Garn's designated races exhibit an enormous amount of variation. Consider, for example, the Mediterranean race, which extends, according to Garn, from Morocco in the far western Mediterranean to the Saudi Arabian peninsula thousands of miles to the east. It is difficult to imagine the culturally diverse groups included in this vast area as a discrete breeding population. Even more important, the degree of difference between this group and others is no greater than the variation within the group itself (Lewontin, 1972).

Alternative Approaches to Human Variation

Taxonomies that classify humans into separate races, even those based on modern scientific evolutionary theories, fall short because they are too static to encompass the dynamic nature of human interaction and the consequences of varying environmental and evolutionary forces. Any criterion selected as the basis for classification is necessarily arbitrary. The physical characteristics that have historically been used to distinguish one race from another form an extremely small part of a human's total genetic makeup. There are so many variations among individuals within populations that the classification schemes tend either to break down or to become extremely blurred. For these reasons, the majority of physical anthropologists currently studying human variation steer clear of defining race. Instead, they focus on explaining variation in specific traits.

Clinal Distribution

Because many physical traits vary independently of one another, some researchers have found it useful to examine single traits, or unitary variables. In many contemporary studies of biological variation scientists plot the distribution of individual traits on maps by zones known as **clines.** A **clinal distribution** map can be likened to a weather map. Rather than simply stating whether it is going to be hot or cold, weather maps detail the temperatures in different parts of the country. Lines tracing temperatures identify approaching storm fronts, and special designations indicate areas experiencing heat waves. These graphic weather maps reflect the intersection of a range of variables and aim at explaining weather patterns beyond the local level. Similarly, plotting the distribution of individual traits may shed light on the genetic, environmental, and cultural factors that influenced their distribution. Using mathematical models to analyze evolutionary processes in a gene pool, scientists have tracked specific physical traits within a population.

Anthropologist Joseph Birdsell (1981) conducted a clinal distribution study of blond, or tawny, hair among Australian Aborigines. While conducting fieldwork, Birdsell noted that the majority of Aborigines had dark brown hair, but some had tawny hair. Significantly, the tawny hair trait was not evenly distributed throughout the Aborigine population, but was concentrated in certain areas. A map of the percentages of tawny-haired individuals in each region revealed the spread of the trait (Figure 6.2). In some areas of the western desert, 100 percent of the people had tawny hair. Farther away from the western desert, fewer tawny-haired people were to be found. Birdsell speculated that a mutation or, more likely, repeated mutations produced light-colored hair in some individuals. In certain areas the light-colored hair replaced the original dark brown hair color, for reasons that are unclear. Over time, through gene flow with surrounding groups, the new trait spread outward. The clinal distribution of tawny hair offers a graphic illustration of microevolutionary change over time within one human population.

This approach can be used to examine other differences in human populations, but it also further underscores the problems inherent in attempts at racial classification. When plotted individually, the varying distribution of physical traits is made more apparent. Clinal distributions of other physical characteristics in Australian Aborigines differ from that for tawny hair color. In light of this complexity, it is not surprising that modern researchers describe variation within species in terms of clinal distributions, rather than trying to delineate distinctive subspecies or races.

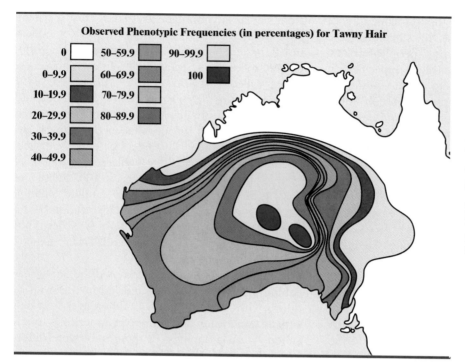

Observed Phenotypic Frequencies (in percentages) for Tawny Hair

0
0–9.9
10–19.9
20–29.9
30–39.9
40–49.9
50–59.9
60–69.9
70–79.9
80–89.9
90–99.9
100

FIGURE 6.2 A clinal distribution map of tawny hair color in Australia. The trait probably originated in the western desert, where it is most common. The percentage of tawny hair decreases in waves spreading out from this area. This is an example of a study focusing on one genetic trait.

Source: From *Human Evolution* by Joseph B. Birdsell. Copyright © 1975, 1981 by Harper & Row, Inc. Reprinted by permission of Addison-Wesley Educational Publishers, Inc.

Multivariate Analysis

In contrast to univariate approaches that focus on a single trait, **multivariate analysis** examines the interrelationships among a number of different traits. Such studies are extremely complex, and scientists using this approach must decide which physical traits and which variables should be examined. Anthropologist R. C. Lewontin adopted a multivariate approach in his study of human variation. Lewontin (1972) probed the distribution of physical traits that vary in human populations, including those that have been considered distinctive to certain races, such as skin color and hair texture. In focusing on how the distribution of these traits compares to common divisions by race, he noted that traits used to identify races do not accurately reflect human variation. Observed differences among Africans, Caucasians, Mongoloids, South Asians, Oceanians, Australian Aborigines, and Native Americans (divisions that approximate Garn's geographical races) account for only about 6 percent of the total amount of variation in human populations. Almost 94 percent of human variation of physical traits occurs *within* each of these different

"races." Lewontin's findings further underscore the highly limited usefulness of the concept of race.

Heredity and Intelligence

Intelligence is the capacity to process and evaluate information for problem solving. It can be contrasted with *knowledge,* which is the storage and recall of learned information. Heredity undoubtedly plays a role in intelligence. This is confirmed by the fact that the intelligence of genetically related individuals (for example, parents and their biological children) display the closest correlation. Yet other factors also come into play. In no area of study have the varying effects of genes, environment, and culture been more confused than in the interpretation of intelligence.

Following Darwin's publications on human evolution, many writers grounded allegedly "scientific" racist philosophies on misinterpretations of his theory. In nineteenth-century England, thinkers such as Herbert Spencer and Francis Galton believed that social evolution worked by allowing superior members of society to rise to the top while inferior ones sank to the bottom. These views reinforced the false belief that particular groups of people, or races, had quantifiably different intellectual capacities. In 1853 similar ideas coalesced into a four-volume scientific treatise by the French aristocrat Joseph Arthur de Gobineau entitled *Essai sur l'inégalité des races humaines* (*Essay on the Inequality of the Races of Humanity*). In this work, Gobineau described the whole of human history as a struggle among the various "races" of humanity. He argued that each race had its own intellectual capacity, either high or low, and that there were stronger and weaker races. Gobineau promoted the conquest of so-called "weaker races" by allegedly stronger ones. He opens the book with the statement that everything great, noble, and fruitful in the works of humanity springs from the Aryan family, the so-called "super race." The Aryans spread out to create, first, the Hindu civilization, then the Egyptian, Assyrian, Greek, Chinese, Roman, German, Mexican, and Peruvian civilizations (Montagu, 1997; Banton, 1998). Gobineau argued that these civilizations declined because of "racial mixing." These "scientific" views of racism were later taken up by writers such as Houston Stewart Chamberlain in twentieth-century Europe, whose writings in turn influenced Adolph Hitler. Gobineau's ideas were the philosophical progenitors of Hitler's *Mein Kampf,* which promoted the notions of racial superiority and inferiority. In the 1930s, the Nazi "scientific" racist ideology, based on the presumed superiority of a pure "Aryan race," was used to justify the annihilation of millions of Jews and other "non-Aryan" peoples, such as Slavs and Gypsies in Europe.

Measuring Intelligence

Most scientists agree that intelligence varies among individuals. Yet it has been difficult to measure intelligence objectively because tests inevitably reflect the beliefs and values of a particular cultural group. Nevertheless, a number of devices have been developed to measure intelligence, most prominent among them the *intelligence quotient (IQ)* test devised by French psychologist Alfred Binet in 1905. Binet's test was brought to the United States and modified to become the Stanford-Binet test. The inventors warned that the test was valid only when the children tested came

from similar environments; yet the IQ test is widely used today for tracking students in the U.S. educational system, sparking controversy among educators and social scientists alike. In a controversial book called *The Bell Curve: Intelligence and Class Structure in American Life* (1994), Richard Herrnstein and Charles Murray argue that research evidence supports the conclusion that race is related to intelligence. Utilizing a bell curve statistical distribution, they place the intelligence quotient of people with European ancestry at 100. People of East Asian ancestry exceed that standard slightly, averaging 103; people of African descent fall below that standard, with an average IQ of 90. Their findings imply that IQ scores are related to genetic differences among races.

A number of scientists have noted the faulty reasoning used by Herrnstein and Murray, as well as others who have attributed IQ differences between African Americans and European Americans to so-called "racial groupings." If there truly were differences between African Americans and European Americans for IQ scores, then African Americans with more European ancestry ought to have higher IQ scores than those with less European ancestry. In a major IQ study of hundreds of African Americans based on blood testing to determine European ancestry, Scarr and Weinberg (1978) found no significant differences between IQ scores and the degree of European admixture.

In more recent studies of ethnic groups around the world, Thomas Sowell (1994, 1995), an African American social scientist, has demonstrated that most of the documented racial differences in intelligence are due to environmental factors. Sowell tracked IQ scores in various racial and ethnic categories from early in the twentieth century. He found that, on average, immigrants to the United States from European nations such as Poland, Italy, and Greece, as well as from Asian countries including China and Japan, scored ten to fifteen points below longtime U.S. citizens. However, people in these same ethnic categories today—Asian Americans, Polish Americans, Italian Americans, or Greek Americans—have IQ scores that are average or above average. Among Italian Americans, for example, average IQ rose by almost ten points in fifty years; among Polish and Chinese Americans, the rise was almost twenty points. It is obvious that as immigrants settled in the United States, their new cultural and environmental surroundings affected them in ways that improved their measured intelligence.

Among African Americans, Sowell noted, northerners have historically scored higher than southerners on IQ tests, by about ten points. Moreover, the IQ scores of African Americans who migrated from the south to the north after 1940 rose in the same way as they did among immigrants from abroad. Other studies indicate that middle-class African Americans score higher on IQ tests than do lower-class white Americans.

These test-score disparities indicate that cultural patterns matter. African Americans are no less intelligent than other groups, but, carrying a legacy of disadvantage, many contend with a cultural environment that discourages self-confidence and achievement. Most anthropological research on this topic indicates that when differences in socioeconomic status and other factors were controlled for, the difference between African Americans and European Americans was insignificant (Molnar, 1983, 1992). Additional studies show that educational enrichment programs boost IQ scores (Loehlin, Lindzey, & Spuhler, 1975; Jensen, 1980; Molnar, 1997). In Japan, a group of people known as the *burakumin* (see Chapter 19), who exhibit no major physical differences between themselves and other Japanese people but have been subject to prejudice and discrimination for centuries in their society, tend to score lower on IQ tests than other Japanese (Molnar, 1983, 1992). This indicates the strong influence of socioeconomic factors in measuring IQ tests. Additional studies show that educational enrichment programs boost IQ scores (Loehlin, Lindzey, & Spuhler, 1975; Molnar, 1997). Much research has determined that IQ scores increase within every generation of every population by 3 to 5 points, indicating the profound influence of social and educational conditions on IQ scores. The other major criticism of Herrnstein and Murray and likeminded theorists is that they reify "race" as if races were based on clear-cut and distinct genetic groups, ignoring the enormous variation within these so-called races.

What Do Intelligence Tests Measure?

Most psychologists agree that intelligence is not a readily definable characteristic like height or hair color. Psychologists view intelligence as a general capacity for "goal-directed adaptive behavior," that is, behavior based on learning from experience, problem solving, and reasoning (Myers, 1998). Though this definition of intelligence would be acceptable to most social scientists, we now recognize that some people are talented in mathematics, others in writing, and still others in aesthetic pursuits such as music, art, and dance. Because abilities vary from individual to individual, psychologists such as Howard Gardner question the view of intelligence as a single factor in human makeup. Based on cross-cultural research, Gardner (1983) has concluded that intelligence does not constitute a single characteristic but rather amounts to a mix of many differing faculties. According to Gardner, each of us has distinct aptitudes for making music, for spatially analyzing the visual world, for mastering athletic skills, and for understanding ourselves and others—a type of social intelligence. Not surprisingly, Gardner concludes that no single test can possibly measure what he refers to as these "multiple intelligences."

The majority of psychologists and other scientists concur with Gardner's findings that intelligence spans a wide and diverse range. The IQ test ranks people according to their performance of various cognitive tasks, especially those that relate to scholastic or academic problem solving. Yet it cannot predict how successfully a person will adapt to specific environmental situations or even handle a particular job. Throughout the world people draw on various forms of intelligence to perform inventive and creative tasks, ranging from composing music to developing efficient hunting strategies. Before we call someone "intelligent," we have to know what qualities and abilities are important in that person's environment. Different sorts of cognitive abilities lead to success in a hunting-and-gathering society, an agricultural society, or an industrial society.

SUMMARY

Human beings throughout the world constitute a single species, *Homo sapiens*. Nevertheless, humans vary in specific physical traits, such as skin color,

body build, cranial shape, facial features, and a variety of biochemical characteristics. These characteristics are the products of the dynamic interaction of evolutionary forces, the environment, and cultural variables. Although we know that all of these factors contribute to human variation, it is often difficult to assess the relative importance of each. All three influences, in combination, yield the characteristics found in an individual.

Natural selection has played a key role in the evolution of the human species, but what role has it played in variation among modern humans? As scientists probe human variation, they have posited a variety of ways in which natural selection may have contributed to some of the differences observed in modern human populations. If natural selection promoted these differences, there should be evidence to substantiate this assertion. Unfortunately, since soft tissues are not preserved in the fossil record, the validity of these theories can only be evaluated indirectly. How do we assess its effects? One way is to look at how different physical characteristics enable modern humans to adapt to disparate environmental conditions.

Studies suggest that many genetically controlled traits may be the result of natural selection. For example, the protection against ultraviolet radiation afforded by the melanin in dark skin would be adaptive in tropical environments. Alternatively, light skin may increase resistance to frostbite—a feature that may have favored fairer skin in the colder northern regions. Other studies have tentatively linked darker skin color with genetic resistance to certain tropical diseases. These selective pressures may have variously favored lighter or darker skin in different environmental settings. Other advantageous characteristics seem to be associated with body build, cranial and facial features, and biochemical characteristics such as blood groups.

Physical characteristics such as skin pigmentation, nose shape, and hair texture have prompted people throughout history to classify humans into different "races." To modern biologists, races constitute divisions within humankind based on identifiable hereditary traits. These divisions are an attempt to categorize the great variation among humans. Biologists recognize these divisions for what they are: roughly drawn, arbitrary boundaries, at best. Physical characteristics do not divide humans into readily discernible groups or races. Furthermore, classification of physical characteristics serves only to label particular categories of phenomena arbitrarily selected by the researcher. It does not explain the reason for the observed variation.

Rather than attempting to delineate major races, recent research has focused on the distribution and study of specific traits and the explanation of the processes that may have produced them. In many contemporary studies of biological variation, scientists plot the distribution of individual traits on maps by zones known as clines. Plotting the distribution of individual traits may shed light on the genetic, environmental, and cultural factors that influenced their distribution. Using mathematical models to analyze evolutionary processes in a gene pool, scientists have tracked specific physical traits within populations.

Human beings also display variation in intelligence, which can be defined as the capacity to process and evaluate information for problem solving. Although individuals vary in their intelligence, researchers generally agree that environmental and cultural factors influence intelligence much more than hereditary or genetic factors. A consensus among educators and social scientists holds that rather than being a singular trait, intelligence is actually a mix of all sorts of different faculties, which cannot be measured by one culturally coded test.

QUESTIONS TO THINK ABOUT

1. What are the basic sources of variation of human physical characteristics?

2. Consider different sources of variation in humans. What evolutionary factors explain these differences? Do the same evolutionary processes act on all characteristics?

3. What factors must be considered when studying the relationship between race and intelligence?

4. Why have racial classifications proven of little explanatory value to physical anthropologists?

5. Comment on this statement: "There are no races, just clines."

KEY TERMS

acclimatization

balanced polymorphism

clinal distribution

clines

continuous variation

lactase deficiency

multivariate analysis

polymorphism

polytypic

races

racism

INTERNET EXERCISES

1. Read the statement of the American Association of Physical Anthropologists at **http://www.physanth.org/positions/race.html**. How does this compare to the discussion of race in the chapter? Why are scientific studies of race so difficult? What are the limits to distinguishing groups of people using the concept of race?

2. Clinal variation is another model of understanding human variation. Read about the models of classification at **http://anthro.palomar.edu/vary/vary_2.htm** and compare the typological model, the populational model, and the clinal model. What is a clinal distribution? How does the clinal model fare compared to the others?

SUGGESTED READINGS

BOAZ, NOEL T., and ALAN J. ALMQUIST. 1997. *Biological Anthropology: A Synthetic Approach to Human Evolution.* Upper Saddle River, NJ: Prentice Hall. An excellent introduction to most of the important topics on human variation explored by biological and physical anthropologists.

BRUES, ALICE M. 1977. *People and Races.* New York: Macmillan. Brues examines physical variation in human populations living in different geographic regions. Though somewhat dated, this introductory work contains a great deal of useful information about human variation.

GOULD, STEPHEN JAY. 1981. *The Mismeasure of Man.* New York: W. W. Norton. Highly readable, this book spotlights the limitations of several attempts to correlate race with intelligence. The author looks at each theory and its flaws.

HARRISON, G. A., J. M. TANNER, D. R. PILBEAM, and P. T. BAKER. 1988. *Human Biology: An Introduction to Human Evolution, Variation, Growth, and Adaptability.* Oxford: Oxford University Press. A thorough overview of human variation.

RELETHFORD, JOHN. 1997. *The Human Species: An Introduction to Biological Anthropology.* Mountain View, CA: Mayfield. This well-written and well-organized textbook on biological anthropology offers a good introduction to human evolution, microevolution, and variation.

CHAPTER

7

Paleolithic Cultures

CHAPTER QUESTIONS

- What challenges do archaeologists face when interpreting the lifestyles of the early hominids at Olduvai Gorge?

- How did *Homo erectus* culture differ from that of the earlier hominids?

- What were some of the technological and cultural developments of the Neandertals?

- In what ways did modern *Homo sapiens* cultures of the Upper Paleolithic represent advancements in comparison with Neandertals?

- What have archaeologists concluded regarding the peopling of the Americas?

- What is the archaeological consensus regarding the migration of modern *Homo sapiens* in Asia, Australia, and the Pacific islands?

In the preceding chapters we saw how physical anthropologists have used fossils and biochemical characteristics to trace the evolution of humans as a biological species over the past 10 million years. During this period a number of hominid species evolved, including some ancestral to modern humans. In addition to changes in physical characteristics, there were also changes in how these early human ancestors lived: What did they eat? What tools did they use? What was their social organization and culture like? It is the archaeologist's job to interpret the record of these aspects of humans and of human ancestors.

In studying the archaeological record, researchers face a daunting task. Early hominid behavior and the roots of human culture can be inferred only indirectly from the living areas, food remains, and tools that early human ancestors left behind. Although useful insights have been gleaned, the material record presents only a shaded view of the dynamic behaviors they represent. Thus archaeologists and other anthropologists must bring to the field a keen sense of imagination, a detective's acuity, and boundless patience to piece together the lifeways of our long-dead hominid ancestors.

Lifestyles of the Earliest Hominids

Much of what we know about the lifestyles of the earliest hominids is based on the tools they left behind. As noted in Chapter 5, bipedalism freed hominids' hands for such tasks as food gathering, infant care, and tool use. There is no question that tools had important consequences for early hominids, allowing them to exploit a wider range of food, defend themselves more effectively, and generally perform many tasks that they would not have been able to do otherwise. For example, tools allowed early hominids to cut through the tough hides of other animals, which could then be used as food.

The first tools were very likely *unmodified* pieces of wood, stone, bone, or horn that were picked up to perform a specific task and then discarded. Observations indicate that chimpanzees use tools such as sticks or folded blades of grass to extract termites from their nests (Goodall, 1986). Early hominids probably used similar tools. Unfortunately, as noted in Chapter 5, artifacts of this kind are unlikely to be preserved or identified in archaeological contexts.

Archaeologists have studied stone tools extensively because they survive very well, even after being buried in the ground for millions of years. Researchers refer to the earliest stone tools produced by pre-*Homo sapiens* hominids as **Lower Paleolithic** implements, referring to the earliest part of the Old Stone Age (roughly between 2.5 million and 200,000 years ago).

The First Tools

The oldest known stone tools, dating back 2.5 million years ago in Africa, were first identified by Louis and Mary Leakey at Olduvai Gorge in Tanzania, East Africa. They called this technology **Oldowan,** another version of the name *Olduvai*. Oldowan

tools are basically river cobbles with sharpened edges. The cobbles, perhaps measuring as much as 4 inches across, were sharpened by using a hammer stone to break off chips, or flakes, in a process called **percussion flaking** (Figure 7.1a). As flakes were removed, they left behind a sharp edge that could be used for cutting, producing a crude pebble tool or chopper (Figure 7.1b). The flakes themselves had sharp edges that could also be used for cutting. Smaller tools like these were likely well suited for cutting and scraping (Potts 1991, 1993). Tools with flaking on one side are termed *unifacial;* those with flaking on two sides, *bifacial.*

Pebble tools and flakes are the most distinctive Oldowan implements, but other artifacts have also been found. Some of these implements required little or no modification. For example, the hammer stones used to manufacture stone tools and possibly to crack bones to extract the nutritious marrow from inside bones are no more than natural stones of convenient size and shape. Their battered surfaces are the only indication of their use. Some stones recovered from archaeological sites bear no obvious evidence of use. Called *manuports,* archaeologists know that they were handled by early hominids because they are found together with other artifacts in places where such stones do not naturally occur.

How Tools Were Used   Because the Oldowan tools are highly primitive, even trained researchers often find it difficult to tell which stones were manufactured by early hominids and which were broken by natural forces. In general, archaeologists note that

FIGURE 7.1 Oldowan technology: (a) The percussion flaking method, in which a hammer stone is used to remove flakes from a stone to produce a chopper tool; (b) an Oldowan chopper.

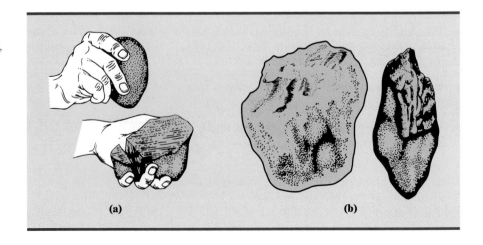

(a)   (b)

the flaking in manufactured tools follows a more regular, consistent pattern than in stones in which a sharp edge is produced by natural processes. Through **experimental studies,** paleoanthropologists may actually duplicate the process used by these protohumans to create their tools, striking flakes off a cobble to produce a chopper, for example. Experimenting with these replica tools, researchers have discovered that they can be used for a variety of tasks, including cutting through hides, dismembering animals, and whittling wood (Isaac, 1984).

Researchers also conduct **use-wear and residue studies** to help decipher how early tools were used. When a person cuts or shaves something with a stone tool, the tool's edge becomes nicked and dull. These use-wear patterns may be the result of specific activities such as cutting, scraping, or chopping, and thus provide clues to how a tool was used. In addition, the material the flake or pebble tool has cut may leave a distinctive polish or residue on certain types of stone. In examining fifty-six stone artifacts from Koobi Fora, dating to 1.5 million years ago, Lawrence Keeley and Nicholas Toth (1981) determined that four of these tools had been used to cut meat and five others bore residues of plant matter.

Indirect evidence of tool use comes from the remains of butchered animals (Potts, 1988). By analyzing cut marks on animal remains, researchers have determined how tools were used to cut and scrape soft flesh off the bone. Chopping marks, resulting from the splitting of bones or the separating of joints, are rare. However, paleoanthropologists suspect that hominids, presumably with the help of stone tools, did break open bones to expose the marrow.

Early Hominid Behavior

The Oldowan tools convey valuable information about the lifestyles of early hominids, particularly when they are found in an archaeological context and associated with other artifacts (see Chapter 2). At Olduvai Gorge, tools have been found in clusters along with discarded animal bones and flakes cast off from tool manufacture. In one case more than 40,000 bones and 2,600 stones were found together. In another instance, researchers came upon a ring of stone 14 feet in diameter, a feature that

some experts have interpreted as evidence of a foundation for a simple structure or shelter (M. D. Leakey, 1971). These archaeological sites have been interpreted as living floors or occupation areas, where early hominids lived, prepared food, ate, and slept. However, while they can undoubtedly be seen as places of early hominid activity, most researchers are reluctant to make the theoretical leap from a circle of stone to an actual shelter.

Deciphering the Archaeological Record Piecing together the artifacts from the Olduvai sites, researchers have advanced various theories to explain the origins of human culture. These interpretations have often prompted a great deal of debate, and views of early hominid behavior have dramatically changed over the past fifty years. During the 1960s and 1970s, Glynn Isaac (1978) and Louis Leakey developed a model that focused on "man the hunter" (Lee & Devore, 1968). According to this perspective, hunting—facilitated by bipedalism, increased cranial capacity, and tool use—was the key to early hominid life. In a model that assumed a great deal of social complexity, Isaac and Leakey conjectured that the Olduvai sites served as **home bases,** locations where hominids lived. They argued that males brought back meat, particularly from large animals, to the home base to be shared with other adults (especially females) and children who had remained in camp. In this view, food sharing, prolonged infant care, and the social interaction that occurred at the home base prefigured the kind of social arrangements that characterize modern human societies. Drawing an analogy to contemporary human hunting-and-gathering populations, such as the Ju/hoansi or !Kung San of southern Africa, this model provides an idealized interpretation of human lifestyles stretching back 2 million years.

Many researchers viewed the man-the-hunter model as problematic, however. Critics pointed out that its idealized version of the hominid past puts far too much emphasis on the role of the male and too little on that of the female (Dahlberg, 1981; Tanner, 1981; Fedigan, 1986). Drawing on observations of modern hunter-gatherers, they argued that plants—fruits, seeds, and vegetables—and not meat were the major food source for early hominids. Because women generally gathered plants, they played the key role in providing food. In addition, use of the hands was as important to females (who cared for infants) as to males (who made tools and hunted). Because hominid infants had lost the ability to cling to the mother with their hands and feet, the mother's hands had to be free to carry her offspring. Recent scholarship has criticized the preceding theories for assuming that early hominid behavior paralleled that of modern humans (Gould, 1980; Binford, 1985; Potts, 1988).

Primate Models of Human Behavior   Another frustrating aspect of each of the preceding scenarios about hominid behavior was the limited amount of information afforded by the archaeological record. To obtain insights into what the social life of early hominids may have been like, some researchers have turned to the study of living nonhuman primates. Although the behavior of human ancestors did not mirror that of modern chimpanzees or baboons—or any living primate—studies of modern primates shed light on how environmental factors shape social behavior, leading researchers to develop models of early hominid behavior (Kinsey, 1987). The research has been made possible by long-term studies of nonhuman primates such as those conducted by Jane Goodall and Dian Fossey, noted in Chapter 4. The mother-infant bonds, friendships, and complex patterns of social interaction found in higher primates offer useful insights into early hominid behavior. Of the living nonhuman primates, two groups—the baboons and the chimpanzees—have received particular attention.

Although baboons constitute a distinct evolutionary branch within the primates, they resemble hominids because they evolved in an arboreal environment, but today they are primarily terrestrial. Many preliminary generalizations about primate social interaction were based on observations of baboon behavior simply because they were among the earliest primate groups to be studied (Strum & Mitchell, 1987). Baboons exhibit clear patterns of competition, dominance, and aggression, so these features figured prominently in hypotheses about early hominid behavior (Ardrey, 1961; Morris, 1967), with scientific speculations stressing the adaptive role of aggression as a defense against predators and as a mechanism for mate selection. These initial conjectures also portrayed hominid society as male dominated. In recent years, however, more complete information on baboons, as well as

descriptions of the behavior of other primate species, have prompted researchers to conclude that primate behavior varies considerably, even within species. For example, baboons forge cooperative ties and friendships as well as acting out aggressive tendencies (Smuts, 1987; Strum & Mitchell, 1987).

Fieldwork by Jane Goodall inspired several models of hominid behavior based on the activities of wild chimpanzees. According to one model, proposed by Nancy Tanner (1987), chimpanzee behavior supports the argument that females played a key role in obtaining plant foods among early hominids. Chimpanzees are the only apes that regularly use tools to crack nuts and to extract insects from nests. Field observations have shown females to be more consistent and more proficient tool users than males. The interactions between mothers and their offspring have piqued scientists' curiosity as well. Female chimps commonly share food with their young, and mothers have been observed rewarding their daughters for learning how to use tools. Tanner suggests that early hominids may have engaged in similar dynamics in tool use and strategies for the acquisition of food and the feeding of young.

Current Perspectives   Reanalyzing the data from early hominid localities and using innovative analytical techniques, researchers produced very different and more nuanced interpretations of early hominid life. Current theories do not assume the high degree of social complexity posited by the home-base model. Rather, archaeological evidence indicates that many fossil localities were visited by large predatory animals and probably were not safe for early hominids. Consequently, it is unlikely that they can be interpreted as evidence of campsites or the location of dwellings.

Lewis Binford (1985) has further suggested that much of the bone found at hominid sites is not the product of hunting forays but rather the remains of animals killed by other predators, which were then scavenged by hominids. The bones include the ends of leg bones, horn, and crania—not the choice cuts of meat one would expect a hunter to bring home, but very consistent with the remains that might be scavenged from a kill site. Binford's interpretation gains additional support from microscopic studies of bones showing that, at least in some cases, cut marks from tools overlie

A young female chimpanzee uses a stick to dig insects out of a fallen tree. Study of nonhuman primate behavior may provide clues to the behavior of early hominids.

carnivore tooth marks (Potts & Shipman, 1981; Shipman, 1986b). In addition, studies of wear patterns on hominids' teeth indicate that fruit was integral to their diet. At this point it is impossible to state with any degree of certainty the relative importance of gathered plant foods and scavenging, but these activities were likely more important to early hominids than hunting.

In all likelihood, the diet, behavior and social organization of early hominids was unlike that of either humans or modern primates. Indeed, the distinctive adaptive strategies of these early human ancestors were probably the very features that distinguished them from other primate species. Richard Potts (1988) notes three key factors suggesting that early hominids lived in social groups of some kind: "(1) Social groups are a general part of higher primate life; (2) tool use and manufacture were undoubtedly learned in a social setting; and (3) the feasibility of site production would seem to depend on communal use of stone materials at sites" (p. 304). While less evocative than earlier models, these observations are a more realistic assessment of creatures whose behavior was likely dramatically different from our own.

Homo erectus Culture

In contrast to the scant traces of earlier hominid species, the archaeological record of *Homo erectus* is more substantial and the tools more readily recognizable. Physically, *H. erectus* resembled modern humans, with a cranial capacity less than that of today's humans but greater than that of earlier hominids. In addition, the shape of *H. erectus* skulls leads researchers to believe that these protohumans may have been the first hominids with both the physical and mental capacities for speech. These changes in physical characteristics undoubtedly underlie a myriad of behavioral, social, and cultural developments, which are only hinted at in the archaeological record. The success of *H. erectus* is perhaps best illustrated by the fact that they had the widest distribution of any hominid aside from *Homo sapiens*.

The Acheulian

Lower Paleolithic tool traditions changed very slowly. The simple Oldowan pebble tools and flakes remained the characteristic artifacts 1 million years after their first appearance. Approximately 1.5 million years ago, some changes began to appear, including tools with more advanced flaking that may have served as drills and protobifaces. These increasingly sophisticated implements are referred to as signs of the Developed Oldowan. Also during this period a new tool tradition emerged, the **Acheulian** (Figure 7.2). Acheulian tools have been found in sites dating between 800,000 and 200,000 years ago. They have been found with the remains of *H. erectus,* the hominid generally credited with producing them. However, this time period includes fossil evidence for transitional or archaic examples of *H. sapiens* and other finds

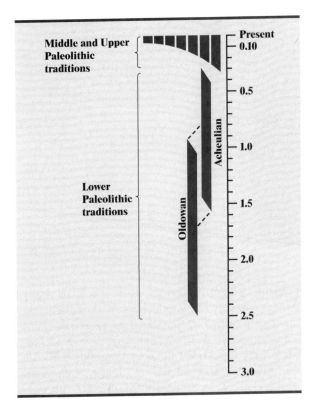

FIGURE 7.2 A chart giving historical dates for the Oldowan and Acheulian technologies. The Lower Paleolithic traditions were relatively simple and long-lasting. They were followed by Middle and Upper Paleolithic industries, which were more complex and varied.

that some researchers believe should be designated *H. ergaster* (see Chapter 5). Depending on the resolution of these debates, the question of who made the tools remains somewhat open.

The Acheulian is named after the town of St. Acheul, France, where some of the first finds were made. Like the Oldowan choppers, Acheulian tools were produced by percussion flaking, but exhibit more complexity. Most characteristic of the Acheulian is the *hand ax,* a sharp, bifacially flaked stone tool shaped like a large almond, which would have been effective for a variety of chopping and cutting tasks (Figure 7.3a). Unlike Oldowan pebble tools and flakes, which consisted of irregularly flaked natural cobbles, the hand ax was fashioned by removing many flakes to produce a specific form. In other words, the toolmaker had to be able to picture a specific shape in a stone. Late Acheulian tools were produced through a more refined brand of percussion flaking, the **baton method,** pictured in Figure 7.3b. In this technique a hammer, or baton, of bone or antler was used to strike off flakes. The baton allowed for more accurate flaking and produced shallower, more delicate flakes than a hammer stone. As in the case of the Oldowan, many Acheulian flakes bear evidence of further modification.

Living Sites

Archaeological sites bearing signs of *H. erectus* life have produced large numbers of hand axes,

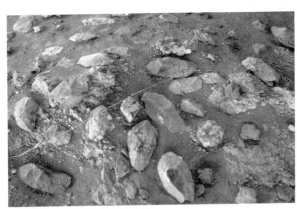

The archaeological site of Olorgesailie, Kenya, one of the most informative Acheulian sites in Africa, dates to approximately 700,000–900,000 years ago. A walkway at the site allows visitors to view Paleolithic tools exposed on the surface. A cleaver or cutting tool is shown on the right.

Source: Courtesy of Pamela Willoughby, University of Alberta.

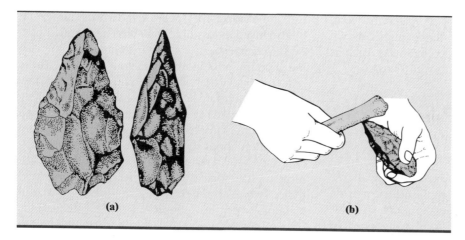

FIGURE 7.3 In later Acheulian technology, the characteristic hand axes (a) were made by the baton method (b).

FIGURE 7.4 A hypothetical reconstruction of a shelter of stones and saplings as it may have appeared approximately 300,000 years ago at Terra Amata, France.

Source: Adapted from Henry de Lumley, "A Paleolithic Camp at Nice." Copyright © 1969 by Scientific American, Inc. Illustration by Eric Mose. Reprinted by permission of the artist, Eric Mose.

flakes, and other stone tools. Cave sites such as Zhoukoudian, China, which yielded the remains of Peking man, also preserved an array of animal bones and possibly traces of fire hearths (Binford & Ho, 1985; Clark & Harris, 1985). Fire hearths are particularly significant as they would have provided a source of heat for both cooking and warmth. As in the case of early hominid fossil localities, however, the interpretation of many of the *H. erectus* sites is challenging. Supposed hearths have been shown to be natural features, and ash deposits actually natural organic layers, not traces of fires. Studies showing bite marks on some hominid fossils indicate that predators also frequented these sites,

raising questions about how the cave deposits were formed and about hominid activities at the site.

In southern Europe, open-air sites such as Torralba and Ambrona in Spain and Terra Amata on the French Riviera have produced large assemblages of tools, as well as possible evidence for structures that may shed light on the behaviors of the more recent *H. erectus* populations (de Lumley, 1969; Laville et al., 1980; Villa, 1983). Interpreting the Terra Amata finds, Henri de Lumley suggested they may include evidence of simple shelters constructed over a framework of posts braced with rocks (see Figure 7.4). The occupants of Terra Amata enjoyed a varied diet, consuming such large animals as extinct species of deer, elephant, boar, rhinoceros, and wild ox. Other food sources, drawn from the Mediterranean, included mollusks, such as oysters, mussels, and limpets, as well as fish.

Middle and Upper Paleolithic Industries

The archaeological record associated with *H. sapiens* becomes increasingly sophisticated and diverse. Tools and dwellings become more complex and display a wide array of local variation. The time span associated with European and Southwest Asian archaic *H. sapiens* (beginning approximately 200,000 years ago) is called the **Middle Paleolithic.** The term *Middle Stone Age* is used to refer to the Middle Paleolithic in Africa and Eurasia. The time roughly associated with modern *H. sapiens* (after 40,000 years ago) is called the **Upper Paleolithic,** or *Late Stone Age.* Note, however, that these periods are separated on the basis of variations in tool types and manufacturing techniques, and the chronological divisions are intended to provide only the crudest of guidelines. The actual appearance of characteristic Middle or Upper Paleolithic tools varies in different world areas, some of the earliest dated finds coming from southern Africa.

The association of specific tool traditions with individual hominid species has proven problematic. Exemplifying the Lower Paleolithic are the Oldowan and Acheulian traditions; the Middle and Upper Paleolithic periods saw a burst of creative energy and technological innovations that distinguish them from the Lower Paleolithic.

Technological Advances

Percussion flaking gained some refinement in the Middle Paleolithic with the **Levalloisian technique.** Using this method, the toolmaker first shaped a stone into a regular form by striking flakes off the exterior. Additional pieces were then struck off from one side to form a flat striking platform. From this prepared core the toolmaker struck the edge to produce flakes that were fashioned into scrapers, points, and knives. The Levalloisian technique created longer cutting edges relative to the size of the stone, allowing for a more economical use of the stone. Tools were standardized and could be produced in less time than with earlier methods.

The archaeological record points to an increasing amount of regional variation in tools. These reflect subtle variation in techniques and the raw material used to make the tools, but they also likely indicate the varying needs of individuals adapting to different environments. There is somewhat more information about the Middle Paleolithic in Europe and the Near East than in other areas because more archaeological research has been conducted there. However, regional innovations in stone tool technology can be seen in Middle Paleolithic finds throughout the world. In Africa, for example, rapid innovation in tool technology occurred during this period. J. Desmond Clark (1970), who devoted years of study to the prehistory of Africa, notes that this change "is in marked contrast to the very slow development of the Acheulian tool tradition during the preceding half a million years, or more" (p. 108).

Some of the most sophisticated Middle Stone Age percussion-flaking techniques from Africa can be seen in the Howieson's Poort industry tools from southern Africa, tentatively dated between 90,000 and 50,000 years ago (Phillipson, 1993). These tools reveal a trend away from larger, cruder forms to smaller, more carefully flaked implements—such as small scrapers and shaped flakes—made of finer-grained lithic materials. Some archaeological evidence indicates that more refined toolkits may have facilitated the first settlement of portions of Africa that had not been extensively occupied earlier, including the arid regions of northeastern Africa (Clark, 1970:107; Bailey et al., 1989).

The Neandertals

Neandertals, the archaic *H. sapiens* who inhabited Europe and the Middle East between 130,000 and 35,000 years ago, also fashioned implements whose versatility far surpassed earlier technologies. The Middle Paleolithic stone tool industry associated with Neandertal populations is known as the **Mousterian,** which is named after a rock shelter at Le Moustier, France, where it was first described. Produced by the Levalloisian technique, Mousterian implements could have been used for cutting, leather working, piercing, food processing, woodworking, hunting, and producing weapons (Binford & Binford, 1966; Bordes, 1968).

Shanidar Cave in northern Iraq is the site of some of the most fascinating discoveries of Neandertal remains.

The Neandertals were probably the first humans to adapt fully to the cold climates of northern Europe. Their technology must have included the manufacture of cloth; otherwise they would not have survived the cold winters. Clues to Neandertal life have come from the archaeological record. Scientists have discovered substantial evidence that Neandertals occupied caves and rock shelters, as well as open-air sites that may have served as temporary camps during the summer months. Archaeologists cite remains of charcoal deposits and charred bones as indications that Neandertals utilized fire not only for warmth but also for cooking and, perhaps, for protection against dangerous animals.

There is evidence that the scavenging of carcasses killed by predators and the gathering of plant resources continued. But there is evidence that the Neandertals were efficient hunters who stalked both small and large game, including such extinct creatures as European elephants, elk, bison, and huge bears that stood between 9 and 12 feet tall and weighed up to 1,500 pounds. Their lifestyle must have been carefully attuned to the seasonal resources available. In the cold climate of Ice Age Europe, the storage of food for the winter months was probably of great importance.

Neandertal Ritual Beliefs Study of Neandertal sites has also given archaeologists the first hints of activities beyond hunting-and-gathering and the struggle for subsistence—possible evidence that

Neandertals practiced rituals. Regrettably, much of this evidence, portrayed in countless movies, novels, and caricatures, is far more circumstantial than archaeologists would like. Finds that have been examined include both bear bones and Neandertal artifacts. From Drachenlock Cave in Switzerland, it was even reported that twenty bear skulls had been found in an arrangement of stone slabs—a discovery interpreted as a crude shrine. Some writers have used these discoveries to paint a complex picture of Neandertal ritual.

Despite the romantic appeal of a Neandertal "cave bear cult," however, these interpretations lack the most important thing archaeologists need to glean insights into such complex issues as prehistoric ritual beliefs: clearly documented *archaeological context* (Chase & Dibble, 1987; Trinkaus & Shipman, 1994). In the absence of clear associations between the bear bones and the tools, this evidence suggests only that Neandertals visited a cave in which bears may have hibernated and occasionally died. The Drachenlock Cave finds were not excavated by trained archaeologists, and no plans or photographs of the discovery were made at the time of excavation (Rowley-Conwy, 1993). Without this information, interpretation of a Neandertal shrine remains entirely speculative.

More convincing than the evidence for a bear cult are discoveries suggesting that Neandertals were the first hominids to intentionally bury their dead. Finds at a number of sites—including Shanidar, Iraq;

Teshik-Tash, Uzbekistan; La Chapelle-aux-Saints, France; and Kebara, Israel (Solecki, 1971; Rowley-Conwy, 1993)—have been interpreted as intentional burials. Of these finds, the evidence for burial is most compelling at the French and Israeli sites. In both instances, the skeleton of a Neandertal man was found in a pit that seems to be too regular in shape to have been formed naturally.

Other skeletal evidence suggests that Neandertals may have cared for individuals with disabilities. At the Shanidar site, for example, archaeologists identified the remains of one individual who had the use of only one arm—the result of an accident or a birth defect. Despite that disability, this individual lived a relatively long life. Although no set of ritual beliefs or social altruism can be definitely inferred on the basis of these finds, they do indicate the growing group communication, social complexity, and awareness that distinguish humans.

Modern *Homo sapiens* and Their Cultures

The hominid fossil record of the last 40,000 years consists exclusively of anatomically modern *H. sapiens*. Between 40,000 and 10,000 years ago, these populations migrated throughout the globe, adapting both physically and culturally to conditions in disparate regions.

Physically, these populations resembled modern humans in most respects. Their fossilized skeletons do not have the heavy, thick bones, large teeth, and prominent brow ridges seen in the Neandertals and other archaic forms. The high, vaulted shape of the cranium is modern, too, with dimensions similar to those of present-day humans. From the cold climates of northern Asia to the deserts of Africa, groups of *H. sapiens* shared similar characteristics as part of one species. Like modern populations, however, these early groups likely exhibited variation in physical traits, such as skin color, body build, and facial features, that represent adaptations to local environmental conditions and selective pressures (see Chapter 6). Archaeological sites associated with anatomically modern *H. sapiens* display a flowering of cultural expression in everything from toolmaking to home building, social arrangements, and subsistence strategies.

The Technology of *Homo sapiens*

Modern *H. sapiens* populations crafted increasingly complex tools and developed strategies to deal with their varied environments. These innovations are reflected in an array of different stone tool traditions. Upper Paleolithic peoples produced a number of specialized stone tools as well, including *borers* (drills) and *burins* (chisel-like tools for working bone or ivory). Tools like these facilitated the manufacture of the bone, antler, and ivory artifacts that became increasingly common during the Upper Paleolithic. European archaeologists divide the Upper Paleolithic period into the Chatelperronian, Aurignacian, Gravettian, Solutrean, and Magdalenian stone industries, which encompass tremendous variation in stone tool types. Stone tool production made a major technological advance with increasingly fine techniques of producing *blades* (long, narrow flakes that had all sorts of uses as knives, harpoons, and spear points). Among the most striking examples of Upper Paleolithic percussion flaking are Solutrean projectile points, dated to 20,000 years ago. These implements, often measuring several inches long, probably functioned as spear points. Yet the flaking is so delicate and the points so sharp that it is difficult to imagine them fastened to the end of a spear. Some researchers have ventured a guess that they may have been made as works of art, not tools for everyday use.

Spear throwers (Figure 7.5)—long, thin pieces of wood or ivory that extended the reach of the hunter's arm—were invented during this period, too. A particularly important innovation, spear throwers enabled Upper Paleolithic hunters to hurl projectiles much faster than they could by hand.

This period also marked the debut of **composite tools,** implements fashioned from several pieces. For example, consider the harpoon, which might consist of a wooden shaft that is slotted for the insertion of sharp stone flakes. Additional signs of technological progress at Upper Paleolithic sites ranged from needles for sewing clothing and fibers for making rope to evidence of nets and trapping equipment.

Like Lower Paleolithic groups, Upper Paleolithic technology indicates that early *H. sapiens* were efficient hunters. Many archaeological sites contain bones from mammoths, giant deer, musk ox, reindeer, steppe bison, and other animals. In

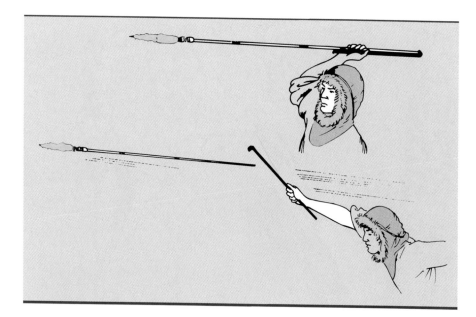

FIGURE 7.5 An innovation of the Upper Paleolithic was the spear thrower, a device that extended the hunter's arm, enabling him to make a more powerful throw.

addition, piles of animal bones have been discovered at the bottom of high cliffs. In reconstructing the meaning of these finds, archaeologists conjecture that *H. sapiens* hunters stampeded the animals off cliffs to be killed and butchered by waiting hunters below. Archaeologists have also found the remains of traps that Upper Paleolithic hunters used to snare animals. Upper Paleolithic people gathered plants to supplement their diet and probably for medicinal purposes. However, because of the small size of Upper Paleolithic living areas and the limited amount of plant remains recovered from archaeological sites, we can sketch only an incomplete picture of the diet during that period.

Shelters In the Upper Paleolithic period, technology advanced to the point where people were proficient at building shelters, some quite elaborate. Among the more spectacular are five shelters from a 15,000-year-old site at Mezhirich in Ukraine, constructed from bones of mammoths, an extinct species of elephant (Gladkih et al., 1984). The mammoths' jaws formed the shelter's base, and ribs, tusks, and other bones were used for the sides. Inside, archaeologists discovered work areas, hearths, and accumulations of artifacts. Storage pits were located between the structures—indications that the shelters were inhabited for long periods.

Scientists speculate that the settlement may have been occupied by more than fifty people.

To accomplish the technological and social innovations of the Upper Paleolithic, *H. sapiens* had by this time fully acquired the skills needed to accumulate and transmit knowledge—that is, the rudiments of language. In addition, the inhabitants of these settlements had developed highly efficient subsistence strategies that gave them free time for experimentation and innovation (Figure 7.6).

Reconstruction of an Upper Paleolithic dwelling made with mammoth bones, such as those found at the 15,000-year-old site of Mezhirich in Ukraine.

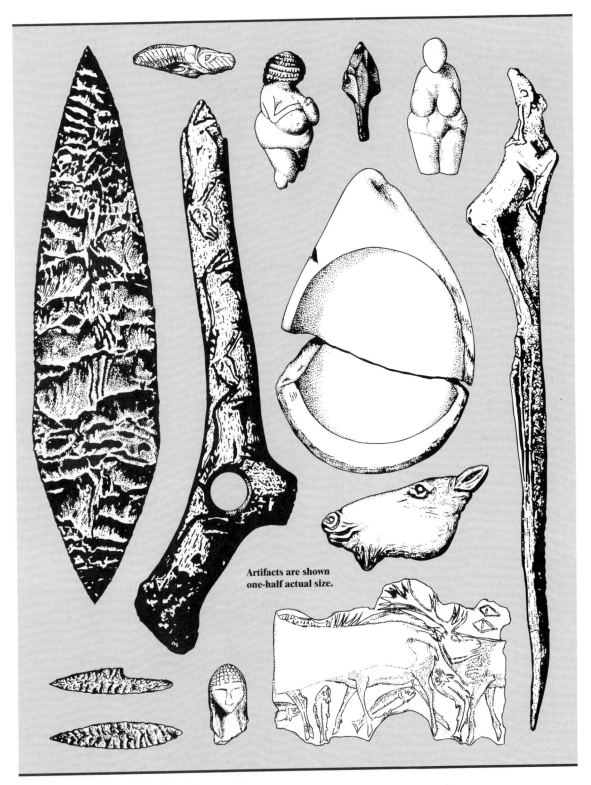

Artifacts are shown
one-half actual size.

FIGURE 7.6 The archeological record of the Upper Paleolithic becomes progressively more elaborate, including more sophisticated stone tools and nonutilitarian items such as those pictured here.

Source: W. J. Sollas, *Ancient Hunters and Their Modern Representatives*, Macmillan, 1911.

Ethnicity and Social Organization

Advances in toolmaking took different forms around the world. Some of this regional variation stemmed from specialized technologies suited to particular environments; in other cases, toolmaking technology was driven by the specific types of stone available in a region. Regional differences may also reflect patterns of culture, ethnicity, and individual expression. Archaeologist James Sackett (1982), who has studied the classic Middle and Upper Paleolithic finds in France, notes that tools serving the same function seem to exhibit a great deal of variation. Many Upper Paleolithic artisans fashioned their stone tools in distinctive styles that vary from region to region, possibly signaling the first traces of ethnic and cultural divisions in human populations. Just as we often associate particular styles in dress, decoration, and housing with specific ethnic groups, archaeologists rely on expressions of ethnic identity preserved in material remains to piece together the lifestyles of earlier peoples. A sense of imagination comes through in Upper Paleolithic artifacts as well. Compared to the Middle Paleolithic, there are more nonutilitarian objects, including items for personal adornment (White, 1982). In addition, because some of these artifacts were obtained from distant sources, archaeologists believe that trade networks had arisen by this time. The term *archaeological cultures* refers to the lifeways of past peoples reconstructed from the distinctive artifacts these cultures left behind.

To glean insights into the culture and social organization of Paleolithic peoples, researchers have looked at modern hunter-gatherers. Contemporary hunter-gatherer societies—with their relatively small groups, low population density, highly nomadic subsistence strategies, and loosely defined territorial boundaries—have social organizations that tie kin (related individuals) together and foster unity within and among groups. Constant circulation of material goods in such societies not only enhances and maintains kin ties through mutual obligations but also inhibits the accumulation of wealth by any individuals in the society. This enables these societies to remain *egalitarian*—societies that have very small differences in wealth among individuals. There are no rich or poor in these types of societies.

The most common form of political organization among ethnographically documented hunter-gatherer societies is the **band,** a fairly small group of people tied together by close kinship relations. A band is the least complex form of political system—and most likely the oldest. Each band is politically independent of the others and has its own internal leadership. Most of the leaders in the bands are males, but females also take on some important leadership roles. Leaders are chosen because of their skills in hunting, food collecting, communication, decision making, or other personal abilities. Political leaders, however, generally do not control the group's economic resources or exercise political power as they do in other societies, and there is little, if any, social stratification between political leaders and others in the band. Because band societies are highly egalitarian, with no fundamental differences between those with and those without wealth or political power, leaders of bands must lead by persuasion and personal influence rather than by coercion or withholding resources. Leaders do not maintain a military or police force and thus have no definitive authority.

Although it is tempting to draw a similar picture of Paleolithic hunters, the analogy is not without limitations. The archaeological record of the Paleolithic is consistent with small kin-based groups. Yet archaeological information on Paleolithic hunter-gatherers suggests that their subsistence strategies varied substantially and probably included the beginnings of some of the complexity, socioeconomic inequality, and more sedentary lifestyle that characterize more recent periods (Price & Brown, 1985).

The Upper Paleolithic in Europe

In Europe, the Upper Paleolithic marked changes that mirrored developments in much of the rest of the world. Best known among the European *H. sapiens* of the Upper Paleolithic are the *Cro-Magnon,* dated at about 40,000 years ago, whose name comes from the Cro-Magnon site in Dordogne, France. The fragmentary remains of five or six individuals, recovered from a rock shelter in 1868, provided the first evidence for the entry of anatomically modern *H. sapiens* into Europe. At the various Cro-Magnon sites, artifacts reveal an elaborate technology. Cro-Magnon stone workers were particularly adept at producing blades, which varied

Upper Paleolithic painting of bison and other animals from a cave in France. Although interpretations of the meanings vary, paintings such as these convey the changing nature of the Paleolithic.

according to the different activities they were used for, the region, and possibly the social group.

By 17,000 years ago, some Cro-Magnon groups had specialized in procuring game from migrating herds of reindeer. In the summer, these bands established encampments on rises that offered a clear view of the herds. For shelter in the warm weather, scientists speculate that they may have used lightweight tents. As the weather turned cold, they would relocate in smaller groups back to the warmth and shelter of the caves. In a major technological advance, Cro-Magnons completely harnessed fire, using such materials as iron pyrite to make sparks to ignite dry tinder. Archaeologists have found evidence for this mastery of fire in sites as widespread as Belgium and the former Soviet Union. Hearths have been uncovered in caves and in open-air locations bearing remnants of shelters. Charred wood and large quantities of bone ash at these sites indicate that Cro-Magnons used fire for cooking as well as for heat.

Paleolithic Art

In addition to their other technological accomplishments, the Upper Paleolithic peoples of Europe created an impressive array of artwork. Sculptures in bone, ivory, and stone, found throughout Europe, depict human figures, including some speculatively dubbed "Venus" fertility goddesses. Magnificent abstract and naturalistic renderings of animals and humans dressed in the hides of animals decorate the walls of caves in Spain and France, including the Lascaux caves. These murals, or cave paintings, may have been drawn to celebrate a successful hunt or to ensure a better future. Because some of them are located deep in underground caves, researchers have speculated that this art held profound spiritual and religious significance for the Cro-Magnons. Imagine how awe-inspiring a religious celebration or initiation ceremony would have been in a dark underground chamber adorned with beautiful paintings. Still, these evocative cave murals could have been painted solely as an expression of the artist's view of life (Halverson, 1987).

The Migration of Upper Paleolithic Humans

Upper Paleolithic hunter-gatherers developed a number of specialized technologies that allowed them to adapt to diverse environments in ways their precursors could not have imagined. By harnessing fire to cook and heat shelters, they could eat a greater variety of foods and live in all sorts of climates, including the frigid north. In addition, their technology allowed them to produce simple watercraft. At home in such a wide variety of environments, *H. sapiens* increased their populations and settled in all parts of the globe, including North and South America and Australia, continents that had previously been unoccupied by hominids.

Changes in world climatic conditions during the past 100,000 years allowed the movement of modern *H. sapiens* populations into new areas. During the latter part of the Pleistocene, or Ice Age, when climatic conditions were much cooler and wetter than they are now, Asia, North America, and the northern regions of Europe were covered by huge sheets of ice, or glaciers, which extended from the polar ice caps. The vast amount of water frozen in these glaciers lowered sea levels around the world by hundreds of feet, exposing vast tracts of land, known as *continental shelves,* that were previously (and are at present) beneath the sea. Many regions of the world surrounded by water today were connected to other land areas when these low-lying landmasses were exposed by lower water levels. These "land bridges" allowed *H. sapiens* to migrate from one region to another over land that is now covered by seawater.

Upper Paleolithic Hunters in the Americas

Archaeologists believe that the first humans came to the Americas from Siberia into modern Alaska over a low-lying land bridge that is now the Bering Strait. Following herds of large game animals, these people migrated southward into North and South America. Today the Bering Strait is a frigid body of water connecting the Pacific and Arctic oceans. Between 75,000 and 10,000 years ago, however, glaciers that lowered sea levels transformed this region into a landmass, known as Beringia, that was more than 1,000 miles wide (Hopkins, 1982). A natural land bridge, Beringia linked Europe and Asia to the Americas.

Physical similarities between Asians and Native Americans, bolstered by historical linguistic analyses, clearly establish the Asian origin of Native American populations. Historical linguistic studies by Joseph Greenberg of Stanford University divide Native American languages into three broad groups: Aleut-Eskimo, Na-Dene, and Amerind. Greenberg (1986) argues that these different linguistic groups represent three migrations from Asia. Because Amerind is the most widespread and diversified, the linguist

contends that it has had more time to evolve. Aleut-Eskimo, in contrast, is confined to a comparatively small number of Native American groups, an indication that these are the most recent arrivals.

Although most anthropologists agree that Native Americans migrated from Asia, they disagree about when this migration took place. Contemporary scholars embrace one of two major perspectives concerning the peopling of the Americas: the Clovis-first hypothesis and the pre-Clovis hypothesis. The **Clovis-first hypothesis** holds that the first humans arrived in the Americas about 12,000 years ago. The **pre-Clovis hypothesis** pegs this migration at a much earlier date, perhaps 30,000 to 40,000 years ago.

The Clovis-First Hypothesis   The term *Clovis* refers to a distinctive type of stone spear point first found at Blackwater Draw, near Clovis, New Mexico. Clovis spear points, measuring several inches long, have flaked channels, or *flutes,* down the middle, which may have made them easier to attach to the spear shaft. Clovis points have been recovered from a number of North American sites and are closely dated to between about 11,200 and 10,900 years ago (Haynes, 1991). In the Clovis-first hypothesis, these tools are interpreted as the work of Paleo-Indians— the first migrants to enter North America from Asia. They are presumed to have arrived in the Canadian Yukon approximately 12,000 years ago, a figure based on estimates of how long it would have taken migratory hunters to reach the Clovis sites identified

Clovis spear points found at various sites in North America. First described at a site near Clovis, New Mexico, these spear points are characteristic of New World Paleo-Indian cultures.

in the United States. The Clovis people, in turn, gave rise to later Native American cultures.

Clovis spear points and associated artifacts clearly establish that human settlements dotted America after 12,000 years ago. Yet archaeologists are puzzled by the rapid spread of early Paleo-Indian cultures throughout the Americas. Could humans have migrated from Alaska and put down roots in such disparate areas as Maine and the southernmost tip of South America in a mere 1,000 or 2,000 years? Recent studies indicate that the rate of migration proposed by Clovis-first proponents is unrealistically fast (Whitley & Dorn, 1993). Questioning this accelerated time frame, some scientists believe that humans must have arrived in the Americas before 12,000 years ago in order to have settled throughout the Americas by 10,000 to 11,000 years ago.

The Pre-Clovis Hypothesis   Advocates of the hypothesis that humans inhabited the Americas earlier than 12,000 years ago are building a strong but still controversial case. Some archaeologists have dated sites in North and South America to between 12,000 and 40,000 years ago, but because dating these sites is extremely difficult, many archaeologists do not accept them as evidence of pre-Clovis settlement. Most of the artifacts found at these sites fail to meet one of two key criteria: (1) They do not demonstrate conclusively that humans lived at these sites,

or (2) they cannot be accurately dated to a period before 12,000 years ago (Carlisle, 1988; Dillehay & Meltzer, 1991; Meltzer, 1993; Taylor, 1995). Two pre-Clovis sites serve to illustrate the types of finds represented: the Meadowcroft Rock Shelter, near Pittsburgh, Pennsylvania, and Monte Verde in Chile.

Meadowcroft Rock Shelter   Excavations at Meadowcroft were undertaken by archaeologist James Adavasio over a period of six years (Carlisle & Adavasio, 1982). Artifacts uncovered here provide evidence of early human occupation, including Paleo-Indian tools dated to 15,000 years ago. Deeper levels of the excavation produced dates of 19,000 years ago, but artifacts pegged to those dates are limited; the earliest is a fragment of bark that the excavators believe was trimmed to make a basket. Critics also say that the flora and fauna remains represented are not consistent with the supposedly late Pleistocene age of the early levels.

Monte Verde   A pre-Clovis site has been identified in the Monte Verde forests of Chile, where, beginning in 1976, archaeologist Tom Dillehay (1989) has conducted research and excavations. Because of the moist soil in the area, preservation is much better than is generally seen at other Paleo-Indian sites. Dillehay found the remains of forty-two plants and the bones of rodents, fish, and larger animals that had been hunted by human settlers, as well as

Paleo-Indian bison kill in the western United States. Early humans in North America probably depended on a wide variety of plants and animals. Kill sites such as these, however, suggest a heavy reliance on large animals.

flaked stone tools. There were also traces of a row of huts, built of wooden frames with hide coverings, which may have housed between thirty and fifty people. Some of the stone tools had been brought from 60 miles away. Most significant of all, radiocarbon dating has established the age of the Monte Verde artifacts at between 12,000 and 13,000 years ago. Subsequent excavations of simpler stone tools from earlier strata may yet push this date back beyond 30,000 years ago.

Both North and South America have yielded other archaeological signs of pre-Clovis human settlements. Through recent experimental dating techniques on rock art and artifacts from the western United States, archaeologists have also pegged as pre-Clovis a number of these items (Dorn et al., 1986; Dorn & Whitley, 1988). Finds such as these have cast increasing doubt on the Clovis-first scenario. Settlement by small migratory groups before 30,000 years ago is more likely (Adovasio and Page, 2002; Dillehay, 2000).

A Water Route to the Americas? In addition to earlier dates for the initial settlement of the Americas, archaeologists have also explored other possible models for the means of migration. Land migration via the Bering Land Bridge has long been favored, but did the first Americans necessarily walk? Movement along the Pacific Rim and down the western coast of North and South America using simple watercraft is being increasingly considered as a means of population movement. Of course, this theory is constrained by the fact that the archaeological evidence for the first watercraft dates tens of thousands of years after the oldest American sites. Yet water migration remains a very plausible, and perhaps even probable, means of initial human settlement. We can say this with confidence because we have evidence dating back more than 40,000 for the settlement of areas that could not have been reached by land. This brings us to the discussion of the arrival of the first humans on the island continent of Australia.

Homo sapiens in Asia, Australia, and Oceania

The occupation of Asia by hominids extends back several hundred thousand years, as we saw with the discoveries of *H. erectus* in Java and China. But this settlement did not spread to Japan or the island continent of Australia; instead, these two areas began to be populated only in the Upper Paleolithic with the advent of *H. sapiens*.

Like the settlement of the Americas, the date of the first arrival of human populations in Japan is still an open question. Lower sea levels during the Pleistocene produced expanses of dry land linking Japan to the Asian mainland and allowed migration. Yet few early sites have been located. Archaeologists excavating at Fukui Cave in northern Kyushu have discovered several stone tools and flakes dated to more than 31,000 years ago (Aikens & Higuchi, 1981).

The Initial Settlement of New Guinea and Australia

Archaeological research pins the earliest human settlement in Australia to 50,000 years ago, perhaps somewhat earlier. At that time, Australia was connected by a continental shelf to New Guinea, but there were no land bridges between the Australia–New Guinea landmass and the Southeast Asia mainland. Scientists therefore speculate that the first humans arrived in Australia by simple rafts or boats, but to date no evidence of these vessels has been uncovered. There are signs of human occupation by 35,000 to 40,000 years ago over most of the continent, with the possible exception of Australia's central desert (White & O'Connell, 1982; White, 1993). The earliest finds from the island of Tasmania, located south of Australia, are somewhat more recent, dating to between 30,000 and 35,000 years ago.

On the basis of stone tool industries and skeletal remains, some Australian archaeologists have postulated that the continent was settled by two waves of immigrants. The earliest of the arrivals are represented by the finds at Bobongara on New Guinea's Huon Peninsula, dated to about 45,000 years ago. The diagnostic stone tools at this site consist of crude axes, weighing 4 to 5 pounds, that were made by striking large, irregular flakes off river cobbles (White, 1993).

The Bobongara finds can be contrasted with later tools (dated after about 26,000 years ago) from sites such as Nawamoyn and Malangangerr in northern Australia and Nombe in the New Guinea highlands. Some of the stone tools from these sites were partly shaped by grinding the edges against other stones. As will be seen in Chapter 8, this *ground stone technique* does not become common in other world areas for another 10,000 years. Citing these discoveries, some researchers have argued that these different stone tool technologies might represent different immigrant populations.

Searching for support of this theory, researchers have turned to physical anthropology and skeletons of early Australians. The earliest human remains in Australia, dating back some 20,000 years, come from Lake Mungo in the southeastern interior of the continent. The skulls of the two individuals represented are described as delicate. They have frequently been contrasted with finds at another site, Kow Swamp, which dates somewhat later. Scientists have identified more than forty burials at Kow Swamp, and compared to the Lake Mungo remains, the skulls are generally heavier and have sloping foreheads.

On the basis of these differences, some researchers postulate that these remains reflect two different migratory populations. This view can only be classified as highly speculative, however, since the Lake Mungo remains represent only two individuals. The two collections do share many similarities, and perhaps if more individuals had been found at Lake Mungo, the two populations might appear to be closer in heritage (Habgood, 1985).

Pacific Frontiers   The Pacific islands, or Oceania, were the last great frontier of human habitation. The Pacific Ocean covers one-third of the earth's surface, broken only occasionally by islands and coral reefs. The islands, spread over thousands of miles, are usually divided into three groups: Melanesia, which includes the smaller islands immediately north and east of Australia; Micronesia, which is farther north and includes the islands of Guam, Naura, Marshall, and Gilbert; and Polynesia, which includes widely scattered islands such as Tahiti and Hawaii east of the preceding groups. The achievements of the early settlers of these regions are all the more remarkable when it is realized that many of the islands are not visible from other bodies of land. Nevertheless, humans had settled hundreds of the islands long before the arrival of the first European mariners in the sixteenth century.

Not surprisingly, the earliest evidence for human settlement comes from the larger islands of Melanesia, closer to New Guinea. Archaeological evidence from the Bismarck and Solomon islands places the first evidence for human occupation at about 30,000 years ago. Like the early settlements of New Guinea and Australia, this evidence consists of stone tools associated with hunting-and-gathering adaptations. The settlement of the smaller islands of Melanesia, as well as those of Micronesia and Polynesia, was substantially later, perhaps beginning no more than 3,000 or 4,000 years ago (Irwin, 1993). These settlers were farmers, who brought domesticated animals and root crops with them (see Chapter 8). They also brought a pottery and shell tool technology.

SUMMARY

The lifestyles of the earliest hominids remain an enigma. Much of the insight we have gleaned comes from the study of the stone tools and butchered animal bones they left behind. Interpretations of these finds vary considerably. Some models liken hominid behavior to that of human hunter-gatherers. Other hypotheses stress the importance of females in child rearing, social learning, and food gathering. Still other studies draw parallels between early hominids and the behaviors of modern primates. Although early hominids undoubtedly lived in social groups and learned how to make tools in a social setting, the growing consensus among researchers is that they exhibited distinctive behavior patterns unlike any modern primates, including humans.

In contrast to earlier hominids, the activities and tools of *H. erectus*—the species that precedes *H. sapiens*—are more readily identifiable. The Acheulian tool technology is characterized by the hand ax, a bifacially flaked tool that could be used for a variety of cutting and chopping tasks. Technological innovations, including the development of more elaborate stone tools and probably the use of fire and the ability to make simple shelters, may have prompted the movement of *H. erectus* out of Africa into cooler climates.

Homo sapiens created stone tools in the Middle and Upper Paleolithic. Stone tools and other elements of technology became increasingly more complex, particularly during the Upper Paleolithic, when all sorts of new stone tools were added to the material inventory. These implements helped in the manufacture of ivory, bone, and horn artifacts. The Upper Paleolithic also saw the debut of artistic expression in cave painting, sculpture, and engraving.

Regional stone tool industries reflect increasingly specialized adaptations to local environmental conditions. Learning how to make use of more varied resources allowed Upper Paleolithic populations to expand into world regions that had previously been unoccupied by hominids. Areas first settled during the last 50,000 years include Japan, Australia, and the Americas. Migrations into these areas were facilitated by lower sea levels, which exposed land that had been, or is currently, under water.

A great deal of evidence indicates that the Americas were settled by people migrating from Asia. Yet archaeological information on these migrations remains scanty, leading to disagreements about precisely when and how they occurred. Substantial evidence confirms human settlement from 12,000 years ago on, represented by the Clovis tradition, but increasing evidence has pushed the arrival date back to more than 30,000 years ago. Land migration via a land bridge in the area of the modern-day Bering Sea has long been favored, but movement along the Pacific Rim and down the western coast of North and South America using simple watercraft is being increasingly considered as a means of population movement.

Archaeologists have also dated the sequence of migrations of *Homo sapiens* into Asia, Australia, and Oceania. These world areas were never joined to the Asian mainland by land bridges and so must have been settled using watercraft. Archaeological research pins the earliest human settlement in Australia to 50,000 years ago, perhaps somewhat earlier. There are signs of human occupation by 35,000 to 40,000 years ago over most of the continent, with the possible exception of Australia's central desert. The earliest finds from the island of Tasmania, located south of Australia, are somewhat more recent, dating to between 30,000 and 35,000 years ago.

The Pacific Islands, or Oceania, were the last great frontier of human habitation. The achievements of the early settlers of these regions are all the more remarkable when it is realized that many of the islands are not visible from other bodies of land. Nevertheless, humans had settled hundreds of the islands long before the arrival of the first European mariners in the sixteenth century. The earliest evidence for human settlement comes from the larger islands of Melanesia, closer to New Guinea. Archaeological evidence from the Bismarck and Solomon islands places the first evidence for human occupation at about 30,000 years ago. The settlement of the smaller islands of Melanesia, as well as those of Micronesia and Polynesia, was substantially later, perhaps beginning no more than 3,000 or 4,000 years ago.

QUESTIONS TO THINK ABOUT

1. Given the information we have available, describe what might have been a typical day in the life of an early hominid family. Where did they live? What kind of society did they have? What did they eat? What tools did they use?

2. Describe the specific changes in chipped stone tools that characterized the evolution of technology from the Oldowan to the Acheulian, Mousterian, and Upper Paleolithic periods. What do you think were the consequences of these technological changes?

3. What do the changes in stone tools over time reveal about changes in the humans who were making them? How were the styles of tools and their methods of manufacture affected by changes in human behavior?

4. What are the principal arguments for and against the idea of a pre-Clovis migration to the Americas? What is the nature of the archaeological evidence that supports or refutes the pre-Clovis hypothesis?

5. When was the continent of Australia first populated and by whom? What kind of archaeological evidence do we have for the first native Australians?

KEY TERMS

Acheulian

band

baton method

Clovis-first hypothesis

composite tools

experimental studies

home bases

Levalloisian technique

Lower Paleolithic

Middle Paleolithic

Mousterian

Oldowan

percussion flaking

pre-Clovis hypothesis

Upper Paleolithic

use-wear and residue studies

INTERNET EXERCISES

1. Review the following sites on flint knapping. Notice the attention to detail that modern people pay to this old technology. Considering that many old technologies are now forgotten, why does flint knapping seems to keep its allure? What do you think the motivation is for this pursuit into ancient technology? What artistic expression might be possible here? Do anthropologists look at projectile points of the past as artwork?

    http://www.woodlandoriginals.com/products/

    http://www.greatlakeslithics.com/

    http://www.geocities.com/Yosemite/Trails/5685/

    http://www.eskimo.com/~knapper/

    http://www.hf.uio.no/iakk/roger/lithic/sarc.html

2. Examine the photos at **http://www.settheory.com/paleolithic_implements/paleolithic_dates_eras.html**. What special feature of the displayed tool makes it an Oldowan tool? Describe the process of manufacture of this tool.

3. Take a look at the cave painting displayed on the following website: **http://www-sor.inria.fr/~pierre/lascaux/**. Do you feel that this is truly artwork (remember when it was painted) or is it religious symbolism, or even, perhaps, an inventory of animals and a recording of hunts of the past? Explain your answers.

SUGGESTED READINGS

GAMBLE, CLIVE. 1986. *The Paleolithic Settlement of Europe.* Cambridge: Cambridge University Press. This book surveys issues in the interpretation of the European archaeological record, including the first evidence of *H. erectus* through the appearance of *H. sapiens.*

KINSEY, WARREN G. (Ed.). 1987. *The Evolution of Human Behavior: Primate Models.* Albany: State University of New York Press. A collection of scholarly essays illustrating the relevance of modern, nonhuman primate behavior to interpretations of early hominid activities. The text includes useful overviews, as well as case studies of particular primate groups.

LEAKEY, RICHARD, and RICHARD LEWIN. 1992. *Origins Reconsidered: In Search of What Makes Us Human.* New York: Doubleday. In this volume, internationally known paleoanthropologist Richard Leakey attempts to reach beyond the fossil remains to the origins of mental and cognitive abilities that distinguish human beings. Touching on philosophy, anthropology, biology, and linguistics, above all the book provides a personal narrative of some of the major hominid discoveries of all time.

PHILLIPSON, DAVID W. 1993. *African Archaeology,* 2nd ed. New York: Cambridge University Press. A survey of African archaeology ranging from an overview of human origins up to the late prehistoric period. The text includes an excellent overview of developments during the Middle and Late Stone Ages.

WHITE, J. PETER, and JAMES O'CONNELL. 1982. *A Prehistory of Australia, New Guinea and Sahul.* Sydney: Academic Press. A definitive and well-written presentation of the information available on the settlement of Australia and New Guinea.

8

The Origins of Domestication and Settled Life

CHAPTER OUTLINE

CHAPTER QUESTIONS

- How can Mesolithic and Archaic developments be seen as the further elaboration of trends that started in the Upper Paleolithic?

- What are the transformations in human subsistence, technology, and lifestyle implied by the term *Neolithic*?

- How did the origins of food production differ in different world areas?

- What are some artifacts that represent the early Neolithic period in the Americas?

- What were the major consequences of the domestication for prehistoric peoples?

In the past 15,000 years, humans have undergone minimal changes in physical characteristics; in contrast, human cultural adaptations have grown substantially more sophisticated. The most significant of these cultural shifts relates to *subsistence,* the manner in which humans obtain food and nourishment.

As seen in Chapter 7, Upper Paleolithic populations were probably relatively mobile, *nomadic* people who hunted migratory herd animals and gathered naturally occurring plant and animal resources. These hunter-gatherers drew extensively from their environment but likely made no conscious effort to alter or modify it intentionally.

Beginning late in the Pleistocene epoch, approximately 15,000 years ago, this pattern gradually began to change in some parts of the world. Rather than moving around in pursuit of large animals, humans started to make more intensive use of smaller game animals and wild plants within localized areas. Fishing and gathering marine resources also yielded valuable food sources as people became less mobile and increasingly focused their energies on the exploitation of plants and animals within particular regional environments. In time, they also started to experiment with planting crops and raising wild animals in captivity, practices that set the stage for one of the most dramatic changes in human history: the beginning of *food production*. This chapter explores the how and why of this exciting transformation.

The Late Pleistocene: Changes in Climate and Culture

Between the late Pleistocene and the early Holocene (the current geologic epoch), a gradual warming of the earth's temperature caused the great glaciers of the Pleistocene to melt. Sea levels rose in coastal areas, and lands that had been compressed under the glaciers rose. As the earth's climate changed, many species of plants and animals became extinct. For example, Pleistocene megafauna like the mammoth disappeared. Yet many others adapted to the new conditions and even expanded in the new environments. In both North America and Europe, as the ice sheets melted, thick forests replaced the *tundra,* the vast treeless plains of the Arctic regions. These climatic changes enabled human populations to migrate to northern areas that previously had been uninhabitable.

The reshaping of the earth's environments prompted new patterns of technological development. As large game became extinct in Europe and North America, for example, humans increasingly relied on smaller game, learned how to fish, and gathered plants to satisfy nutritional needs in a strategy that represented a subtle change, one to **broad-spectrum collecting.** Because of variation in local environments, many specialized regional patterns and technologies developed, making it increasingly difficult to generalize about developments worldwide. These new subsistence strategies have been referred to as the **Mesolithic** in Europe, Asia, and Africa and the **Archaic** in the Americas.

Mesolithic and Archaic Technology

The transition to broad-spectrum collecting began in different regions at different times and had varying consequences. In some areas relatively permanent settlements emerged, whereas in other regions people maintained mobile, nomadic lifestyles. In general, however, percussion-flaked Mesolithic and Archaic tools differ markedly from those of the Paleolithic; typically they are much smaller and more specialized than Paleolithic implements. Some of the most common Mesolithic tools are known as **microliths,** small flakes of stone that were used for a variety of purposes, including harpoon barbs and specialized cutting tools. The bow

and arrow appeared in the Upper Paleolithic, and both Mesolithic and Archaic peoples made extensive use of this technological innovation, which allowed hunters to kill game from a greater distance and with more accuracy than did spears.

A new type of stone tool, *ground stone,* also became common in many societies. Some of these implements were probably unintentional products of food processing. To make seeds and nuts more palatable, people pulverized them between a hand-held grinding stone and a larger stone slab or even a large rock. This activity shaped the hand stones and wore depressions, or grooves, into the stone slabs. Using a similar grinding process, Mesolithic peoples intentionally made some stones into axes, gouges, and *adzes* (specialized tools to shape wood). Tools with similar functions had been produced by percussion flaking during the Paleolithic, but ground-stone tools tended to be much stronger.

The increasingly sophisticated stone-working technology that characterized the Mesolithic and Archaic periods allowed for a great many innovations in such activities as the harvesting of resources and the shaping of wood for building. Although watercraft were developed during the Upper Paleolithic (as indicated by the human settlement of Australia), ground-stone tools would have made it easier to cut down logs and hollow out the inside to make dugout canoes. Vessels of this type would have improved mobility and enabled people to exploit more diverse ocean, lake, and river resources. Ground-stone sinkers and fishhooks made from shell, bone, or stone attest to the development and importance of tools specifically used to exploit aquatic resources.

The European Mesolithic European Mesolithic sites display a variety of subsistence strategies, reflecting a range of adaptations to various local conditions. Northern European sites such as Meiendorf and Stellmoor in northern Germany include extensive evidence of reindeer kills. On the other hand, sites in France, Britain, and Ireland display reliance on a greater diversity of animals (Price & Brown, 1985). Archaeological evidence for Mesolithic subsistence strategies and how archaeologists interpret this information can be illustrated by the well-studied British site of Star Carr, dating to about 10,000 years ago. Meticulous excavation by archaeologist J. G. D. Clark between 1949 and 1951

ANTHROPOLOGISTS AT WORK

GRAHAME CLARK AND THE MESOLITHIC

Grahame Clark (1907–1995) was one of the most influential archaeologists of the twentieth century. Drawing on his exhaustive knowledge of the archaeological record, he placed the British Mesolithic in a wider context and effectively created a view of a world prehistory. Also an active and inspiring teacher, Clark invigorated the Cambridge University archaeology department and made it one of the leading programs in the world. His research set a standard for fieldwork that pioneered interdisciplinary, collaborative research, now taken for granted. His life's work illustrates the changing views and archaeological perceptions of the Mesolithic, as well as the emergence of archaeology in the twentieth century as the scientific study of the past (Fagan, 2001).

Clark's interest in archaeology began when he was a boy in

Grahame Clark (right) in the field.

Sussex Downs, England, where prehistoric archaeological sites abound. There he roamed the hills looking for artifacts. As an adolescent at Marlborough College (what in the United States would be called a private preparatory school), he continued his collecting and also visited archaeological excavations, including the famous Windmill Hill Neolithic site. This informal education

served him well. Clark wrote papers and gave lectures on archaeology, developing a lifelong curiosity about the ancient world. When he was still at Marlborough he published four papers in the Natural History Society *Reports*. The first dealt with the classification and description of the artifacts he collected on his field trips. The young Clark was determined to become a professional archaeologist.

The period between the World Wars was a time of changing perspectives. The field of prehistoric archaeology was still a relatively new discipline. Much of the work that had been undertaken in the preceding century had focused on the description, classification, and dating of archaeological finds. There were still relatively few professional archaeologists, and much of the work on British

produced traces of many different activities (Clark, 1979; Fagan, 2001). Large piles of refuse, or *middens,* contained bones of wild game such as elk, pig, bear, and especially red deer. Discovered tools included projectile points fashioned from elk and red deer antlers and stone microliths, which may have been used for scraping hides or shaping antlers. The careful excavations also produced a host of *organic remains,* such as plant remains and smaller fragments of bone, that provide further insight into the resources utilized at the site.

Though researchers agree that Star Carr was a small, intermittently occupied camp, opinions about its precise function have varied. Clark saw it as a winter settlement of several families of men, women,

and children, who used a period of semisettled existence to replace equipment expended during other, more mobile seasons. More recent evidence supports the view that the site had a more specialized function, perhaps serving as a hunting camp or butchering station used for very short periods at different times of the year (Andresen et al., 1981). The camp may have been optimally located to exploit game trails. Such seasonal occupation may be characteristic of other Mesolithic sites. In either scenario, Star Carr demonstrates the intensive exploitation of local resources and the associated technologies.

The Archaic in the Americas   The changes and diversity in adaptations noted at European Mesolithic

and European Paleolithic, Mesolithic, and Neolithic sites was done by amateur archaeologists. As Clark was developing his interests, a new generation of archaeologists was starting to synthesize the information from sites and to interpret, rather than simply describe, their finds.

Grahame Clark entered Cambridge University in 1926, which at the time was one of the few places one could go for undergraduate training in archaeology. He studied history during his first two years, but retained his resolve to be an archaeologist. He subsequently studied cultural anthropology, physical anthropology, and archaeology, three of the four major subdisciplines of anthropology covered in this book. This breadth of background is reflected in the holistic perspective he later brought to his research. While an undergraduate, he published several papers, including detailed artifact studies. His knowledge, scholarly abilities, and tenacity were recognized, and Clark became the first candidate to be registered for a doctorate in archaeology at Cambridge University. His doctoral dissertation topic was the British Mesolithic.

At the time, the Mesolithic was ill defined archaeologically. The prevailing view saw the classic Upper Paleolithic peoples disappearing and eventually being replaced by Neolithic farmers, with the two archaeological periods separated by a hiatus. The simple archaeological artifacts placed chronologically in between were seen by some as degraded examples of the classic Upper Paleolithic industries. Clark undertook a systematic study of all the Mesolithic artifacts he could find, including materials from all over Britain and Europe. He recognized the Mesolithic's unique characteristics and the role of environmental change. He interpreted the Mesolithic toolkit as an innovation designed to exploit new subsistence strategies at the end of the Pleistocene, developments that, in turn, set the stage for food production.

Although Clark's view of the Mesolithic has been enhanced by more recent research, his view of the Mesolithic as a transitional period of experimentation and intensive exploitation of local resources remains central to our understanding of Mesolithic life.

---

sites also characterize Archaic sites in the Americas. The specific technologies and resources involved are different, but the experimentation and intensive exploitation of local resources are similar. American Archaic sites are usually categorized on the basis of geographic divisions, such as the Western Archaic, the Great Lakes Archaic, and the Northern Archaic (Jennings, 1989). In turn, these categories are subdivided into regional traditions (distinguished by different tool complexes) and temporal periods (that is, Early, Middle, and Late).

The Koster site in the Illinois River valley illustrates Archaic traditions. The Early Archaic remains found at this site, dating from about 9,500 years ago, indicate that the occupants of the site ate fish, freshwater mussels, and nuts, and hunted white-tailed deer and a variety of smaller animals. These remains likely indicate there were seasonal camps at the site, repeatedly occupied by small bands of hunter-gatherers over several centuries. The Early Archaic finds contrast dramatically with the Middle Archaic finds, which date from around 7,000 years ago, also discovered at Koster. This period is characterized by larger and much more permanent settlements, including sturdy houses made of log supports covered with branches and clay. The occupants subsisted on many of the same foods as in the preceding period, but they concentrated more on easily obtainable resources found within a few miles of their settlement. The

Antler mask from the British Mesolithic settlement of Star Carr, dating to approximately 10,000 years ago. Careful excavation also produced a host of other remains that aided the interpretation of the activities and diet of the inhabitants of the site.

site may have been occupied for most, if not all, of the year.

Some North American Archaic sites seem to prefigure the technological and social complexity typical of later food-producing societies. For example, the Poverty Point sites in the lower Mississippi Valley, which are dated to between 3,300 and 2,200 years ago, include the remains of naturally available foods and stone tools typical of other Archaic sites, but also include fired clay balls. These clay balls were likely used as *cooking stones* that could be heated in a fire and dropped into wooden bowls or baskets to cook food. These balls provide the earliest evidence of fired clay in North America. Even more striking are the vast earthworks of five concentric octagonal ridges and mounds found at the Poverty Point site in Louisiana. The earthworks provide evidence of organizational capabilities and ritual expression more typical of later food-producing societies.

Origins of Food Production: The Neolithic Period

The **Neolithic,** or New Stone Age, beginning before 10,000 years ago in some world areas, marks one of the most pivotal changes in human history: the shift from food gathering to food production. Like the change from the Paleolithic to the Mesolithic, the transition to the New Stone Age occurred gradually. During the Mesolithic period, human populations experimented with new types of subsistence activities, including the practice of growing plants, known as **cultivation.** Some groups deliberately collected seeds for planting, not just for consumption. In addition, certain populations began to tame animals like wild dogs or wolves to have as companions and to help in hunting. Other groups sought to capture wild varieties of sheep, goats, cattle, and horses and to travel with these animals to suitable pastures as the seasons changed.

Eventually, some populations came to rely on certain cultivated plants more than on others. They also concentrated their energies on raising particular animals. In other words, some of these groups engaged in **artificial selection,** a process similar to natural selection in which people encourage the reproduction of certain plants or animals and prevent others from breeding. In effect, these human populations were modifying the reproductive patterns of certain plants and animals to propagate characteristics better suited to their own needs. Gradually, this process yielded plants and animals that were distinct from wild species and dependent on humans. This process is referred to as **domestication.**

To some extent, the domestication of plants and animals may have occurred in an unplanned way. When people gathered wild seeds, the larger seeds on the stem were easier to pick. Similarly, people likely kept more docile, easily tamed animals rather than the more aggressive members of the species. In some world areas about 10,000 years ago, these processes of artificial selection promoted societies that placed great emphasis on domesticated plants and animals. Because people had to remain in certain areas to tend their crops, they began to put down roots for a more permanent home.

Plant and Animal Domestication

Much of what we know about domestication comes from the archaeological record. Because wild and domesticated species differ physically, researchers can trace the transition to domestication by examining plant and animal remains (Ucko & Dimbleby, 1969; Struever, 1970; Cowan & Watson, 1992; Smith, 1995). For example, wild species of grains such as wheat and barley have fragile *rachis,* the portion of the stem where the seeds are attached. This feature is advantageous in the wild because the seeds easily fall to the ground, where they can germinate and reproduce. In contrast, on domesticated plants, seeds tend to cling to the stems, attached with firm rachis. This would not enhance the plants' reproductive success in the wild but it does facilitate harvesting by humans. Domesticated plants also have larger edible parts, as a rule, something early farmers would have favored.

Increasing knowledge about both plant domestication and the exploitation of wild species is a result of intensifying awareness among researchers of the need to recover plant remains from excavations through more refined recovery techniques. A great deal of information has been obtained by the use of a technique known as **flotation.** When placed in water, soil from an excavation sinks, whereas organic materials, including plant remains, float to the surface. These can then be skimmed off and examined for identifiable fragments. Other information may be obtained by studying the stomach contents of well-preserved bodies and *coprolites,* or fossilized feces.

Although archaeologists can easily distinguish plant species in the wild from those that were domesticated, the domestication of animals is more difficult to discern from archaeological evidence, even though many features distinguish wild from domesticated animals. Unlike their wild counterparts, domesticated cattle and goats produce more milk than their offspring need; this excess is used by humans. Wild sheep do not produce wool, and undomesticated chickens do not lay extra eggs. Unfortunately, however, the animal remains—primarily skeletons—found at archaeological sites often exhibit only subtle differences between wild and domesticated species. Researchers have traditionally considered reduction in jaw or tooth size as an indication of domestication in some species, for example, the pig. Other studies have attempted to identify changes in bone shape and internal structure. Although providing possible insights, such approaches are problematic when the diversity within animal species is considered because the particular characteristics used to identify "domesticated" stock may fall within the range found in wild herds.

A different approach to the study of animal domestication is to look for possible human influence on the makeup and distribution of wild animal populations, for example, changing ratios in the ages and sexes of the animals killed by humans. Archaeological evidence from Southwest Asia shows that Paleolithic hunters, who killed wild goats and sheep as a staple of their lifestyle, initially killed animals of both sexes and of any age. However, as time went on, older males were targeted, whereas females and their young were spared. This has been interpreted as an intentional move to maximize yield. Some sheep bones dating back 9,000 years have been found in Southwest Asian sites far away from the animals' natural habitat, suggesting that animals were captured to be killed when needed (Perkins, 1964).

Observations such as these may suggest human intervention and incipient domestication, but conclusions need to be carefully assessed (Wilson et al., 1982). Recent research has pointed out that sex ratios and percentages of juvenile individuals vary substantially in wild populations. Moreover, all predators, not just humans, hunt selectively. Finally, information on the ancient distribution of animal species is unknown.

Other Archaeological Evidence   In the absence of direct evidence from plant and animal remains, archaeologists attempting to examine the origins of food production at times indirectly infer a shift to domestication. For example, because the food-processing requirements associated with food production, as opposed to hunting and gathering, necessitated specific technological innovations, food-processing artifacts such as grinding stones are found more frequently at Neolithic sites. In addition, Neolithic peoples had to figure out ways to store food crops, because agricultural production is seasonal. Thus, during the Neolithic, structures

Jomon pottery from Japan. Pottery, produced from fired clay, is generally associated with the Neolithic period. However, in the case of the Jomon culture, it was initially developed by sedentary hunter-gatherers.

used as granaries became increasingly common, allowing for the stockpiling of large food supplies against periods of famine. Agricultural peoples constructed large and small granaries or storage bins and pits out of such diverse materials as wood, stone, brick, and clay. Remnants of these storage structures are found archaeologically.

Sherds of pottery, too, often give clues to Neolithic communities. Whereas nomadic hunter-gatherers could not easily carry heavy clay pots in their search for new herds and food sources, the settled agrarian lifestyle encouraged the development of pottery, which makes it easier to cook and store food.

Generalizations about farming cannot be made solely on the basis of indirect evidence such as pottery, however, as the same artifact inventory is not associated with the transition to domestication in all cultural settings. In many instances, evidence for domestication precedes the use of pottery. For example, in some sites in Southwest Asia, domesticated barley appears before the use of pottery (Miller, 1992). Conversely, some of the earliest pottery yet discovered, some 10,500 years old, was produced by the Jomon culture of Japan, a sedentary hunting-and-gathering society (Aikens & Higuchi, 1981).

Distribution of Wild Species Archaeology does not provide all of the answers. Plant and animal remains are often poorly preserved or nonexistent. Furthermore, finding early plant or animal remains at a particular site does not necessarily mean that the plant was domesticated there. The species may have originally been domesticated elsewhere and introduced to the area where the remains were discovered. One way researchers trace the provenance of a domesticated species is to pinpoint the areas where related wild species are currently found. Because wild species served as the breeding stock for domesticated varieties, domestication probably occurred in these areas. For example, wild species of tomato have been identified in South America, making that a prime candidate as the site of initial cultivation. Domesticated lettuce, which is presently grown in many regions of the world, probably derived from prickly lettuce, a wild species of the same genus that is native to Asia Minor. The origin of domesticated cattle has been traced to *Bos primigenius,* the wild ox, an animal native to Europe, Asia, and Africa that became extinct in Europe in the early seventeenth century (Fagan, 1998).

Ethnographic Studies We can also discover clues to domestication in ethnographic data. Modern cultures make varying use of wild, as well as domesticated, plants and animals.

The cross-cultural study of plant use in modern populations is termed *ethnobotany;* the study of the interrelationship between ancient plants and human populations is called **paleoethnobotany.** In one example of this kind of approach, archaeologist Merrick Posnansky (1984) examined what he refers to as "the past in the present." He observes that in addition to domesticates, modern farmers in Ghana, West Africa, harvest more than 200 species of wild plants on a seasonal basis. The farmers also trap wild animals such as the grass cutter, or cane rat, to supplement their diet. Posnansky draws a parallel between these practices and similar activities by early farmers, based on finds at nearby archaeological sites some 3,500 years old.

As the early inhabitants of the region faced similar subsistence challenges in a comparable environmental setting, Posnansky speculates that studies of modern farmers may provide insights into the options available to ancient farmers and the mechanisms that eventually led to domestication.

Why Did Domestication Occur?

Today we take food production for granted. The vast majority of the world's population depends for sustenance on crops and animals domesticated and cared for by humans. In contrast, hunting and gathering accounts for a comparatively small part of our diet. However, scientists have not determined conclusively why domestication initially took place.

Although the benefits of food producing may seem obvious from a modern perspective, the transition to a reliance on domesticated foods was not necessarily an obvious choice for Paleolithic and Mesolithic hunter-gatherers. In contrast to hunting and gathering, agriculture takes much more time and energy. The soil has to be tilled, seeds must be planted, and the crops need protection from weeds and pests. Moreover, agriculture demands patience. Several months may elapse from the time a crop is planted until it can be harvested. Tree crops like bananas and plantains may not bear fruit until almost a year after planting. In addition, agricultural production is a risky enterprise. Despite the considerable effort that people invest in planting, weeding, and protecting crops, the harvest may still fail, producing enormous hardships for the entire society.

Hunting-and-gathering, in comparison, represents a highly successful subsistence strategy. Compared to the farmers' investment in labor, hunter-gatherers spend a comparatively limited amount of time procuring food. Ethnographic studies of groups like the Bushmen and San of southern Africa indicate that they may invest only between twelve and nineteen hours a week in the search for food (Diamond, 1987; Lee, 1969). Although figures may vary, this method clearly affords them a great deal more leisure time than their agrarian neighbors. Undoubtedly, as seen in Chapter 7, humans were hunter-gatherers for the vast majority of their history; as recently as 500 years ago, 15 percent of the world's populations still subsisted by that means (Murdock, 1968).

The disadvantages of agricultural production, then, would appear to outweigh the benefits, yet most of our hunting-and-gathering ancestors made the transition to agriculture. Diverse explanations have been posited, but no consensus has emerged. An early theory of the nineteenth century credited a solitary, unknown genius with suddenly coming up with the idea of planting seeds; this innovation, then, led to agricultural civilizations. Such a simplistic scenario is clearly unlikely. Gathering information from a number of world regions, archaeologists have formulated several provocative theories to explain the transition to agriculture.

The Oasis Theory

In the 1930s, V. Gordon Childe (1936, 1952) advanced one of the first scientific theories concerning the move to domestication. Childe suggested that at the end of the Pleistocene a major climatic change transformed the environment in regions like Southwest Asia and made new subsistence strategies necessary. Severe droughts, he argued, forced humans to concentrate their settlements around fertile oases and to explore new subsistence strategies. This, in turn, led to agriculture. According to Childe, who called this presumed period of dramatic change the Neolithic "revolution," agriculture enabled humans to maintain a reliable food supply in extreme conditions. Once invented, the concept of food production spread rapidly to other regions.

Popularly known as the *oasis theory,* Childe's theory was seen as a plausible interpretation by the archaeological community for a number of years. However, data to support Childe's supposition was lacking, and subsequent archaeological and geological research has failed to confirm his interpretations. There is no evidence for the dramatic changes in the late Pleistocene environment of Southwest Asia along the lines Childe suggested, or for the clustering of populations around fertile oases.

The Readiness Hypothesis

A different theory, developed by archaeologist Robert Braidwood (1960), was based on finds excavated in Southwest Asia during the 1940s and 1950s. Braidwood undertook fieldwork specifically to evaluate Childe's theory and to examine the origins of agriculture. He observed that climatic conditions comparable to those at the end of the Pleistocene had existed in this region at several time periods dating back at least 75,000 years. If agriculture was developed in response to environmental pressures as Childe suggested, why hadn't domestication occurred earlier? Braidwood (1960) hypothesized that after a long period, human populations became increasingly familiar with the plants and animals around them:

> Around 8000 B.C. the inhabitants of the hills around the fertile crescent had come to know their habitat so well that they were beginning to domesticate the plants and animals they had been collecting and hunting. At slightly later times human cultures reached the corresponding level in Central America and perhaps in the Andes, in southeastern Asia, and in China. From these "nuclear" zones cultural diffusion spread the new way of life to the rest of the world. (p. 6)

Braidwood's statement may present a plausible description of agricultural origins, but like Childe's theory, Braidwood's hypothesis does not really explain what prompted hunter-gatherers to adopt agriculture as a way of life. Underlying his model is a sweeping assumption about human nature or psychology—that earlier peoples were not ready to innovate or develop agriculture for some unexplained reason. This theory, sometimes referred to as the *readiness hypothesis,* does not answer two key questions: how and why domestication originated when it did.

Population Models

More recent models of the origins of agriculture have been influenced by economist Ester Boserup's (1965) theories about the relationships among population, labor, and resources. Although Boserup initially set out to explain changes in complex agricultural practices, her ideas can be applied equally well to the origins of domestication. She speculated that societies will intensify their cultivation practices only when they are forced to by rising population pressure on the available resources. Making the transition from simple to intensive agriculture requires such a substantial increase in labor that the results may not warrant the effort. History attests to this statement. Many hunting-and-gathering societies were familiar with intensive agriculture but did not adopt these practices because of the vast increase in labor needed to succeed. In this view, then, agricultural production would not make sense for populations who enjoy reliable food resources and experience limited population growth. At some point, however, population pressures may force people to adopt food-production techniques. Researchers differ in their interpretations of what factors may have caused these pressures.

Demographic Stress   Archaeologist Lewis Binford (1968) linked increasing population pressure to environmental change. Binford noted that at the end of the Pleistocene period, sea levels began to rise with the melting of the world's glaciers in the temperate regions. He reasoned that rising sea levels would have forced coastal peoples to migrate into interior regions, where other populations had already settled. In Binford's view, this movement would lead to population increases and demographic stress. In response to these demographic and environmental shifts, populations would begin systematically to cultivate the land so there would be adequate food supplies for the expanding population. Thus, Binford contended, population pressure prompted the development of agriculture.

Population Growth   Archaeologist Mark Cohen (1977) formulated another hypothesis that attributes domestication to population growth. Cohen pointed out that by the end of the Paleolithic era, hunting-and-gathering societies had spread to all parts of the world. During their migrations they gradually expanded the amount and variety of wild food resources they could draw on for sustenance. Eventually, these populations were using nearly all of the naturally available food. As populations continued to grow and territorial expansion left very few unpopulated areas for nomadic hunter-gatherers to explore, the need to feed greater numbers of people gave rise to agrarianism.

Recent archaeological research delving into the origins of agriculture has unearthed more controversy than consensus. Some researchers, including Fekri Hassan (1981), have criticized the population-pressure models proposed by Boserup, Binford, and Cohen, arguing that population pressures alone would not make people abandon hunting and gathering in favor of intensive agriculture. Furthermore, although most archaeologists would agree that population densities did increase at the end of the Pleistocene, they have no clear sense of whether this population surge occurred before or after the transition to food production.

Human Selection and the Environment

Many researchers have focused on particular local conditions and cultural settings that may have precipitated or affected different patterns of domestication. Carl O. Sauer (1952) was among the first researchers to stress how human adaptations may have paved the way for domestication. His research on the early cultivation of root crops in East Asia yielded the conclusion that plants were first domesticated by successful, sedentary food collectors who had the opportunity to observe the plants' growth cycle. Sauer considered Southeast Asia to be a major center of domestication, and he suggested that domestication spread outward from there, thus underscoring diffusion as a source of agricultural origins.

Studying data from Mesoamerica and Southwest Asia, archaeologist Kent Flannery (1965, 1973) approached the question from a different perspective. He argued that an important push for domestication came when humans introduced plants to environmental zones *outside* the areas where the plants normally flourished. Why did they do this? According to Flannery's hypothesis, transplantation might have stemmed from population growth or from a human desire to exploit certain resources on a more permanent basis. Under these circumstances, humans would have had to invest extra time to nurture plants removed from their natural environment. This, then, eventually resulted in domestication.

Coevolution

One archaeologist, David Rindos (1984), examines the question of domestication in a biological evolutionary framework. Rindos criticizes other interpretations of the origins of domestication for placing too much emphasis on conscious or intentional human selection. He argues that humans *unintentionally* promoted the survival and dispersal of certain types of plants through such activities as weeding, storing, irrigating, and burning fields. As particular species of plants became more common because of these practices, human reliance on them increased. This, in turn, led to further changes in plant distribution and morphology. According to Rindos, human agricultural practices and biological changes in cultivated plants evolved simultaneously. Human agents unintentionally selected and germinated specific varieties of plants and adopted certain behaviors that created a link between agricultural yields and population growth.

Rindos's research underscores the role of unconscious human choice in the process of domestication. However, other archaeologists emphasize that learning, cognition, culture, and conscious processes are as crucial in explaining the origins of agriculture as are unconscious choices. For example, Michael Rosenberg (1990) points out that cultural norms regarding property and territorial arrangements in hunter-gatherer populations were a conscious societal development. Similarly, he believes that such deliberate cultural choices affected the transition to agriculture.

Agricultural Origins in Perspective

Contemporary anthropologists tend to credit a complex interplay of factors for the transition from food gathering to food production as human populations evolved. Some schools of thought hold that our predecessors consciously decided to gamble on food production after considering the advantages and drawbacks of agricultural enterprise. According to this view, early humans weighed population pressures and the need for reliable food sources against the intense labor and the uncertainties of growing their own food plus the likelihood that naturally occurring resources would meet all their needs.

Other theoretical approaches suggest that a less intentional process was at work. These models hold that particular plants took well to the soil in areas where humans had settled, and people just followed their instincts, making the shift from hunting-and-gathering to agriculture with little thought of the consequences.

Although archaeologists have reached no consensus concerning the exact reasons for domestication, many of the details of where and when domestication occurred have been revealed by ongoing research. With these data in hand, researchers all agree that the process was much more intricate, gradual, and varied than the "revolution" envisioned by early theorists.

Domestication in Different Regions of the World

Researchers looking into the Neolithic have traditionally spotlighted Southwest Asia and, to a lesser extent, China and Mesoamerica (Harlan, 1971; Smith 1995). This is understandable, as these are areas where some of the first archaeological evidence pertaining to domestication was recovered, and they still represent some of the earliest examples of the transition to food production. However, the origins and diffusion of domestication are complex and worldwide in scope. Although domestication occurred earlier in some areas than in others, it took place independently in many regions and it involved a vast number of species (Figure 8.1). We now turn to how the transition was made from hunting-and-gathering to food production in different areas of the world.

Southwest Asia

In Israel, Jordan, Syria, Turkey, Iraq, and Iran—the area known as the *Fertile Crescent*—scientists have chronicled a gradual trend toward the exploitation of a variety of resources. This area extends along a curve from the Red Sea, north along the eastern edge of the Mediterranean Sea, then southeast through the Zagros mountains of Iran and Iraq, down to the Persian Gulf (Figure 8.2). It includes a number of distinct environmental zones, ranging from high mountains to the fertile Tigris and Euphrates River valleys. Here, early hunter-gatherers found a wide range of natural resources.

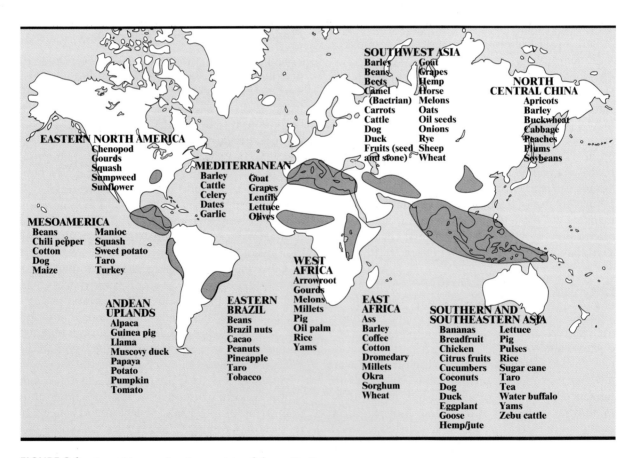

FIGURE 8.1   A world map showing centers of domestication.

Source: Adapted from Arthur Gettis, et al., *Introduction to Geography*, 5th ed. Copyright © 1995 The McGraw-Hill Companies. Used by permission of the McGraw-Hill Companies.

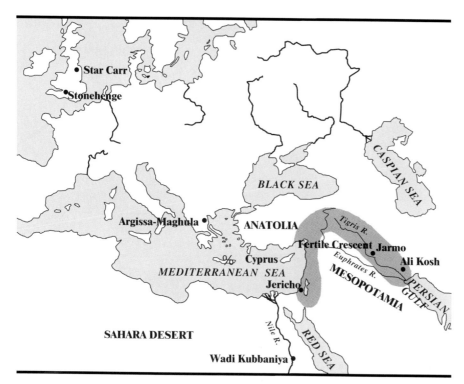

FIGURE 8.2 Sites of domestication in Southwest Asia, Europe, and the Nile Valley.

The Natufians The best-known Mesolithic people of Southwest Asia are the Natufians, who lived in the eastern portion of the Fertile Crescent in what is today part of Israel and Jordan, subsisting on wild animals and wild plants (Mellaart, 1975; Henry, 1984). Approximately 13,000 to 11,400 years ago, the Natufians settled in villages, where they cultivated wild grains and cereal grasses. Archaeologists have discovered a number of items that confirm these new dietary practices, from mortars, pestles, and ground-stone bowls to sharp flint blades that were inserted into bone handles and used to cut grains (Figure 8.3). Archaeologists know how these blades were used because a distinctive residue, called **silica gloss,** was left by the plant stalks. Among the plants exploited by the Natufians were wild barley and various species of legumes, which provided a rich source of protein (Miller, 1992).

Natufian society also demonstrates the increasing elaboration associated with more permanent settlement. Whereas early Natufian sites were established in natural rock shelters, some later settlements were quite substantial, incorporating houses with stone foundations, paved floors, and storage chambers. Variation in the material wealth found in

graves suggests that there was some differentiation in social status. Imported items such as seashells, salt, and obsidian (a volcanic glass) attest to the Natufians' expanding trade contacts as well. These data suggest greater social complexity than that of earlier societies.

The manipulation of wild plants by the Natufians and other Mesolithic populations paved the way for later farming communities, which emerged more than 11,000 years ago, and display a reliance on various combinations of domesticated plants and animals. After several thousand years, a distinct pattern of village life—based on wheat, barley, peas, beans and lentils, sheep, goats, pigs, and cattle—appeared. These Neolithic societies continued the elaboration of material culture initiated in earlier periods.

One of the most famous of these Neolithic settlements was Jericho, which was flourishing long before the time of Joshua and the Israelites as described in the Bible (Kenyon, 1972). The earliest settlement at Jericho was most likely a temporary seasonal camp that gradually became a more permanent settlement. By 10,000 years ago Jericho was a sizable town with permanent mud-brick structures containing finely plastered floors and walls.

FIGURE 8.3 A hypothetical reconstruction of a Natufian sickle, showing stone blades set in a bone handle. Traces of silica gloss, a distinctive polish resulting from cutting plant stems, have been found on stone blades, suggesting how they were used.

Source: Adapted from D. A. E. Garrod and D. M. A. Bate, *The Stone Age of Mount Carmel* (New York: Oxford University Press, 1937); and James Mellaart, *The Earliest Civilizations of the Near East* (London: Thames and Hudson, 1975). Reprinted by permission of Oxford University Press.

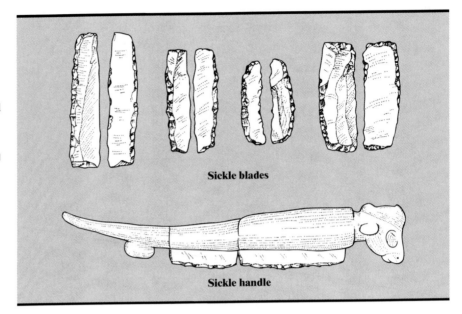

Sickle blades

Sickle handle

A massive stone wall with towers and a defensive ditch were built around the settlement. The long occupation at Jericho, consisting of substantial villages built on the same spot over thousands of years, provides an excellent illustration of a *tell*, a type of archaeological site that became increasingly common during the Neolithic.

The Eastern Fertile Crescent Remnants of the Neolithic transition have been found in other parts of the Fertile Crescent as well. In the valley steppeland areas of the Zagros Mountains and surrounding hills, archaeologists have uncovered extensive evidence of a way of life based on cultivation and *pastoralism,* a subsistence strategy that has as its core the rearing of domesticated animals. By 10,000 years ago, Neolithic farming villages dotted the entire region.

Agriculture spread rapidly to the lowland area of the Mesopotamian plain, which was flooded each spring by the Tigris and Euphrates rivers. The annual flooding enabled crops to mature before the soil was completely dried out, and it gave rise to one of humankind's most important innovations— *irrigation systems* to maintain crop growth from season to season. At Ali Kosh, one of the earliest farming sites in this region, archaeologists have discovered sequential phases of human occupation dating back 9,500 years. The earliest settlements

may have been seasonal, the people relying for sustenance on wild animals, fish, and waterfowl. Over time, however, the region's inhabitants gradually began cultivating or domesticating plants and animals, including sheep, emmer wheat, and barley. Signs of irrigation and domesticated cattle appeared about 7,500 years ago.

Europe

Although considered a discrete area here, Europe actually comprises a variety of different climatic, topographical, and cultural regions, ranging from the mild Mediterranean climates in the south to the frigid areas of Sweden, northwestern Russia, and northern Poland. Mesolithic hunting-and-gathering populations exploiting resources in these varied climes probably initially used crop agriculture only as a minor adjunct.

Traditional views held that early farmers expanded in a wave from Southwestern Asia and Anatolia, displacing earlier Mesolithic populations (Dennell, 1992; Evans & Rasson, 1984). Although current evidence suggests that most crops, including barley, peas, lentils, vetch, and rye, were introduced, there was a great deal of variation in the timing and manner of adoption. In addition, the local domestication of some crops, such as oats and peas, cannot be ruled out.

Surveying the available data, we can discern three different patterns of agricultural adoption (Dennell, 1992). First, in some areas such as southeastern and central Europe, evidence for domestication appears suddenly and is frequently associated with village settlement and pottery. In the second pattern, the evidence for farming appears gradually; there is no clear distinction between Mesolithic and Neolithic settlements. This pattern holds true for western Europe, the British Isles, and much of the Mediterranean coast. Domesticated grains, legumes, and livestock turn up in different combinations and at different times, eventually giving rise to true farming communities only after hundreds of years. Third, in some areas such as Sweden and Finland, a shift to agriculture occurs gradually, but the evidence for Mesolithic subsistence patterns continues, suggesting that the agricultural practices were not initially successful in the northern climates.

Megaliths   By 6,000 years ago, agriculture was thriving throughout most of Europe. One of the most interesting and enigmatic developments of Neolithic Europe was the appearance of large stone structures, or **megaliths** (Greek for "large stones"). Archaeological sites dating to the period show traces of large houses, fragments of well-made pottery, and evidence of trade contacts with other regions. Distinctive burial complexes also characterize this period. Elaborate tombs with chambers for several bodies were constructed from large stone slabs and boulders. These structures were the earliest megaliths. Later megaliths were much more intricately designed, consisting of circular patterns of huge, upright stones.

The most famous megalithic structure is Stonehenge, located on Salisbury Plain in southern England. Popular wisdom credits the massive stone monuments to the Druids, a religious sect in Britain during the first century B.C. In fact, Stonehenge far predates the Druids. Archaeological research reveals that work on Stonehenge first began around 3000 B.C. and spanned the next 2,000 years. As illustrated in the chapter-opening photo, a circle of thirty vertical stones, each weighing more than 25 tons, marks the center of the site. Running across the tops of these stones is a series of thirty stones, each weighing about 6 tons.

Excavated remains of the great tower of early Jericho, a thriving Neolithic settlement that developed from a temporary camp used by Mesolithic hunter-gatherers.

No one has yet pinpointed why Stonehenge and other megaliths were constructed, but studies over the past several decades have indicated that many of the stone structures mark astronomical observations (Hawkins, 1965; Hoyle, 1977). For example, viewed from the center of Stonehenge, outlying stones indicate the summer and winter solstices; other alignments point to positions of the moon and possibly other celestial bodies. The knowledge of the heavens expressed in Stonehenge may indicate the importance of the stars in interpreting the seasons of the year. These imposing monuments also clearly indicate a growing social complexity in Neolithic Europe. They may have served to reinforce the social, economic, and religious authority of the people who directed their construction.

East Asia

Agricultural practices unrelated to those in Southwest Asia emerged in the far eastern part of the continent. As in other world areas, the advent of domestication was preceded by a period of ambitious experimentation with naturally occurring plants and animals (Gorman, 1969, 1977). Researchers disagree about when people in the Asian region initially domesticated plants. Some, citing evidence from Thailand, argue that root crops, particularly various species of yams, were domesticated very early, perhaps as far back as 11,000 years ago (Solheim, 1971). Crops like these are propagated by dividing and replanting living plants, an activity referred to as **vegiculture.** Unfortunately, however, it is very difficult to distinguish domesticated from wild root crops, as Carl Sauer (1952), an early researcher on the origins of Asian domestication, has noted. In addition, archaeological remains needed to clear up this mystery are fragmentary. So whereas experts agree that root crops were exploited very early in Southeast Asia, no one can specify with certainty the precise time period of domestication.

The earliest evidence for the domestication of rice, too, is uncertain, but archaeologists believe it occurred somewhat later than the domestication of root crops. Yet many areas have not been studied in detail, and much of the available information is inconclusive. In one major site in northeastern Thailand known as Spirit Cave, archaeologist Chester Gorman identified artifacts that hint at rice cultivation by 9,000 years ago, but no actual grains were found. Rice husks dating back 7,000 years have been found at Khok Phanon Di, Thailand. Other sites in the region have yielded evidence of domestication that may date even earlier (Fagan, 1998).

China The origins of domestication in China remain sketchy. Some researchers have asserted that Chinese agricultural beginnings date to some time before 9,000 years ago (Chang, 1970, 1975; Crawford, 1992). Sites with pottery dating before 8,500 years ago are generally assumed by archaeologists to be early Neolithic, although actual plant remains are absent. The earliest direct evidence for domestication comes from northern China between 8,500 and 7,000 years ago. Villages of this period supported a mixed economy dependent on hunting-gathering, fishing, and plant and animal husbandry.

Domesticates include foxtail millet, broomcorn millet, and Chinese cabbage. Domesticated animals are represented by the pig, the dog, and possibly the chicken.

These early societies were the forerunners of later cultures such as Yang-shao, which flourished throughout much of the Yellow River valley between 5000 and 3000 B.C. Yang-shao sites are typically more than five times the size of those of the preceding period (Crawford, 1992). In addition to earlier domesticates, domesticated animals such as cattle, sheep, and goats were raised. Significantly, these societies were not entirely dependent on domestication; hunting, gathering, and fishing continued to supplement their diet. Rice, an important staple today, did not become important in northern China until much more recently. Yang-shao farming villages comprised fairly substantial dwellings that were built partly below ground. Special areas were designated for the manufacture of pottery, and cemeteries were located outside the village. Many characteristics of modern Chinese culture can be identified in these communities.

From these early centers of domestication in China and Southeast Asia, archaeologists have documented the spread of agriculture from the Asian mainland into Korea, through Japan, and into the islands of Southeast Asia and the Pacific.

In contrast to developments in China, broad-spectrum collecting continued in Korea until 4,000 years ago and even later, after 2,400 years ago, in Japan. Subsequently, rice cultivation predominated in these regions, culminating in the evolution of complex agricultural societies.

The peoples of Southeast Asia also concentrated on intensive rice growing, which propelled the development of societies throughout Malaysia and the Indonesian Islands. The Pacific islands (Melanesia, Micronesia, and Polynesia) staked their agricultural claims on taro, yams, and tree crops like breadfruit, coconut, and banana.

Africa

Archaeological information on the growth of agriculture in Africa is not as well documented as it is for other regions of the world. Only limited research has been undertaken there, and the tropical climates that predominate on the continent do not preserve plant and animal remains well over time.

Archaeologists working at Wadi Kubbaniya used fine screens to sift excavated soil for plant and animal remains. Improved recovery techniques such as this one have dramatically increased available information on ancient diet and the origins of domestication.

This is unfortunate because modern African societies maintain a wide variety of agricultural practices, making the region a key area of study for researchers probing the transition to food production (Clark & Brandt, 1984). More than forty genera of domesticated plants have been identified, including many crops that are still of considerable importance in Africa. Based on these findings, researchers believe that several centers of domestication developed independently.

Changes in subsistence strategies similar to those that heralded the advent of the Mesolithic and the Neolithic in the Near East and Asia took place very early in Africa. Upper Paleolithic populations in Egypt's Upper Nile Valley were harvesting, and perhaps cultivating, grains 18,000 years ago (Wendorf & Schild, 1981). Evidence for these activities comes from excavations at such sites as Wadi Kubbaniya on the Nile River, where archaeologist Fred Wendorf recovered grinding stones and sickle blades with silica gloss. By 8,000 years ago, wetter environmental conditions had allowed the expansion of people into the Sahara, and semipermanent and permanent settlements dating to this period have been identified in Egypt's western desert (Wendorf & Schild, 1984). Excavations at these sites have yielded remains of domesticated cattle, barley, well-made pottery, and storage pits. Other sites in Egypt, of more recent age, have produced emmer wheat, flax, lentils, chickpeas, sheep, and goats.

Whereas the domesticates represented suggest a Southwestern Asian origin, the associated toolkits are distinctly African (Harlan, 1992).

Archaeological finds in sub-Saharan Africa reveal many regional traditions that effectively made use of a host of wild plant and animal resources. In contrast to northern Africa, however, the transition to food production seems to have occurred more slowly. The thick tropical rain forests of western and central Africa impeded the diffusion of agricultural technology to this region. Furthermore, the plethora of naturally occurring animal and plant resources was more than sufficient to meet the subsistence needs of the indigenous hunting-and-gathering populations.

Some 4,500 years ago, climatic conditions in the Sahara desert were less arid and more suitable for human settlement than they are today. The primacy of pastoralism in this region is confirmed by archaeological evidence that domesticated cattle, goats, and sheep spread southward from northern Africa beginning about 7,000 years ago and expanded into eastern and western Africa about 4,000 years ago (A. Smith, 1984). At the earliest sites, artifacts such as grinding stones suggest that plant foods were being processed, even though few actual plant remains or residue have been recovered. In the western Sahara, the earliest trace of the extensive use of domesticated plants dates after 3,200 years ago. The most telling evidence comes

CRITICAL PERSPECTIVES

THE ORIGINS OF MAIZE

One of the most important domesticated plants from the Americas is maize *(Zea mays)*. After originating in Mesoamerica, maize cultivation spread throughout much of North and South America, where it became a principal staple of many Native American populations. Following the arrival of the Europeans in the fifteenth century, the plant was taken from the Americas and introduced throughout the world, and it is now an important food crop in Europe, Asia, and Africa. The origins of the plant and its evolutionary ancestry have long been the focus of a great deal of research and debate. The identification of the wild ancestor of maize provides a good illustration of the kind of evidence researchers must draw on to trace the evolutionary history of a plant (Smith, 1995).

Archaeological data have provided a record of the origins and spread of maize. The evidence from the Tehuacan Valley, Mexico, now includes almost 21,000 cobs and cob fragments, 797 kernels, and many fragments of husks, leaves, tassel fragments, and roots that present a remarkable record

Domesticated species of plants and animals differ physically from wild varieties. In this photograph, the oldest maize cobs can be readily distinguished from the larger, more recent examples.

of the plants' evolution spanning almost 7,000 years. The earliest finds come from the lowest levels of the San Marcos and Coxcatlán caves located in the Tehuacan Valley. These early plants are quite unlike modern varieties. Their cobs are less than two inches long, and they characteristically have eight rows of six to nine kernels, each partially enclosed by soft husklike sheaths. More recent cobs are successively larger, with increasing numbers of kernels that lack the husklike coverings.

Although the evolutionary history of maize might seem very well documented, the archaeological evidence failed to conclusively reveal the wild ancestor from which domesticated maize originated. Some researchers initially believed that the early cobs from the San Marcos and Coxcatlán

from Dhar Tichett, an archaeological site where impressions of bulrush millet and sorghum were preserved in pottery sherds.

Plant remains of probable African domesticates such as sorghum, pearl millet, African rice, and yams do not appear until much later. However, it is likely that domestication had occurred earlier; vegiculture based on the cultivation of indigenous yam species may have begun in sub-Saharan West Africa between 7,000 and 6,000 years ago (Phillipson, 1993). Yet speculation stems entirely from circumstantial evidence; pottery and ground stone appear in the archaeological record of this time period. More intensive agricultural practices in forest regions, beginning approximately 2,000 years ago, may have been facilitated by the advent of ironworking, when iron tools made clearing land more labor efficient (Fagan, 1998).

caves actually predated the domestication of *Zea mays* and, in fact, represented the plant's wild, now extinct ancestor. Other scientists disagreed and proposed that a variety of a wild grass, called *teosinte*, was the progenitor of domestic maize. Teosinte is an annual grass that still grows in Mexico.

We now know that teosinte is the wild ancestor of maize. The conclusive evidence was provided by several lines of research. Careful reanalysis of the cobs recovered archaeologically from San Marcos Cave revealed that the cobs clearly had features of a domesticated plant. In particular, the plants lacked any means of dispersing their seeds and, consequently, no means of reproducing naturally. Humans would have had to strip the kernels from the cobs and plant them. Hence, the plants were completely dependent on humans to propagate and were domesticated in the fullest sense.

In addition, researchers located a modern variety of maize, called Argentine popcorn, which shares many of the features found in the early cobs from the San Marcos and Coxcatlán caves. This domesticated plant is still grown in limited quantities in Argentina. Unlike modern maize, the plant is relatively short, 3 to 4 feet high, with one to five branches. Ears occur at the ends of the branches and along their length, each plant producing ten to fifteen small ears, hardly larger than those found on teosinte. Researchers believe that this plant may be a relic of the initial dispersal of domesticated maize into South America from Mesoamerica.

Finally, to identify the ancestor of maize, botanists traced the distribution of modern species of teosinte in Mexico and Central America, some of which occur only in remote and inaccessible areas. Several of these varieties were found to have morphological and physical similarities in common with the early maize plants, suggesting a closer ancestral relationship. Analysis of the genetic material of one of these varieties, *Zea mays parviglumis*, showed it to be indistinguishable from domesticated maize. The modern distribution of parviglumis varieties most like maize are limited to upper slopes of the Balsas River drainage, more than 100 miles west of the Tehaucan Valley. The morphological and genetic similarities of these plants to domestic *Zea mays* conclusively demonstrate that this variety of teosinte is the progenitor of maize and, thus, the likely geographical region where initial domestication took place.

POINTS TO PONDER

1. What are the different lines of evidence that allowed the ancestor of domesticated maize to be identified? What are the strengths and limitations of each of these explanations?

2. What factors might make the discovery of the evolutionary history of other plant species more difficult to determine?

3. If you were designing a research project to examine the origins of domesticated wheat, what are some of the methlological concerns you would consider?

The Origins of Domestication in the Americas

In the Americas, the transition from the Paleolithic to the Archaic began around 7000 B.C. This shift in subsistence strategies encompasses a wide range of cultures and tool technologies. Many American cultures—reflecting numerous regional variations and spanning a great many environmental zones— developed subsistence strategies based on domesticated crops that flourished locally. In describing these adaptations, archaeologists generally use specific names rather than the generic *Neolithic*.

Mesoamerica

Mesoamerica extends from the northern boundary of present-day Mexico to the southern borders of Nicaragua and Costa Rica. As in the past, the region today encompasses a great deal of environmental and cultural diversity. Early cultivation techniques and domesticates also varied, a factor that needs to be considered when reaching general conclusions about the advent of agriculture in the region. At present, all of the early evidence for plant cultivation and domestication comes from Mexico, much of it from dry cave sites; these data, then, can represent only a small portion of the variation probably present (Flannery, 1985; McClung de Tapia, 1992).

One of the major archaeological studies of this region was carried out by archaeologist Richard MacNeish, who examined the sequence of agricultural developments in the Tehuacan Valley in Mexico. Through the excavation of twelve sites, MacNeish found traces of human occupation extending back 12,000 years, with early settlers subsisting on the meat of wild animals. Beginning around 10,000 years ago, however, the population increasingly turned to wild plants as a source of food, eventually cultivating wild species. After about 7,000 years ago, these native peoples had domesticated maize (see the box "The Origins of Maize" on page 190), chiles, avocados, and gourds (MacNeish, 1970). Gradually, the population of the Tehuacan Valley came to rely almost exclusively on

domesticated crops, particularly maize (Figure 8.4). Similar sequential developments—from hunting to cultivating plants and, finally, a complete reliance on domesticates—have been documented in other areas.

Archaeologists have tracked changes in Mesoamerican subsistence strategies by examining artifacts such as stone-grinding slabs, locally called *metates,* and hand-grinding stones, known as *manos.* They have also noted the construction of food storage facilities and the permanent settlement of large populations in village farming communities. This pattern of intensive agriculture eventually took hold in various regions of Mesoamerica and spread to North America.

South America

As in Mesoamerica, South America encompassed a number of diverse cultural and ecological settings for early agriculture (Pearsall, 1992). These included at least three distinct systems: first, a suite of practices adapted to the low-altitude cultivation of manioc (a root crop), maize, and beans; second, a mid-altitude system focused on maize, peanuts, and beans; and third, a high-altitude Andean system

FIGURE 8.4 A graph illustrating changes in the relative importance of wild and domesticated food resources exploited by the people of the Tehuacan Valley, Mexico, as determined from archaeological remains. The figure traces the gradual transition from an almost exclusive reliance on natural resources to dependence on domesticated crops. Graphs of other world areas would follow a similar pattern.

Source: Adapted from R. S. MacNeish, Q. Nelken-Turner, and I. W. Johnson, *The Prehistory of the Tehuacan Valley*, Vol. 2 (University of Texas Press, 1967). Copyright ©1967 Robert S. Peabody Museum of Archaeology, Phillips Academy, Andover, Mass. Reprinted by permission. All rights reserved.

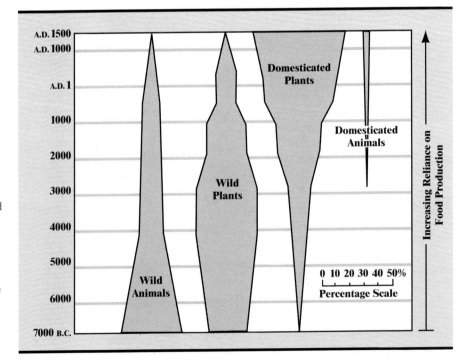

involving a number of minor tubers and cereals but dominated by the potato. There is no complete picture for the domestication of any one crop.

Indications of early agricultural developments in South America have been found in a number of areas, but many of the better-known sites are located in Peru. Near the foothills of the Andes on the Peruvian coast are fertile river valleys that are ideal for the cultivation of food. Following the Pleistocene, people congregated in coastal regions, finding sustenance in fish and other marine resources. By about 10,000 years ago, these sedentary communities were experimenting with a variety of wild plant species. The earliest cultivated species—including the bottle gourd, manioc, chiles, beans, squash, and potatoes—appeared before 4500 B.C. Evidence for peanuts, jack beans, and *achira* (a starchy root) dates slightly later. Notably, the evidence for the use of many crops precedes the presence of ceramics. In fact, the abundant remains of cotton dating between 2000 B.C. and 1500 B.C. has given this period the name the "Cotton Preceramic."

Because the highland terrain includes steep mountain slopes that cut through a variety of microenvironments, the subsistence strategies of the early inhabitants of the Peruvian highlands differed markedly from those of coastal people (Fagan, 1998). Here the transition to agriculture is documented by archaeological finds at such sites as the Guitarrero and Pikimachay caves, which preserve a record extending back about 12,000 years. Early highland hunting-and-gathering populations first subsisted on animals like the giant sloth and smaller species of wild game, plus a variety of wild plants. Finds of more recent age from a number of sites indicate an Archaic subsistence based on the hunting of camelids and deer and the gathering of wild plants (Pearsall, 1992). The earliest evidence for plant cultivation dates to 10,000 years ago. Many of the earliest finds of cultivated plants are from the highlands, supporting interpretations that many of the crops involved may have originated there.

Species of maize, squash, potatoes, beans, gourds, and other crops became common between 8,000 and 5,000 years ago. Archaeologists believe that the llama, a South American pack animal, and the guinea pig had been domesticated by 5,500 years ago.

North America

Researchers long viewed North America as peripheral to the domestication center located in Mesoamerica. Although knowledge about important plant crops such as corn, squash, and beans appears to have filtered northward from Mesoamerica, inhabitants of North America also domesticated other plants and animals on their own long before the arrival of introduced domesticates (Smith, 1989; 1995). Archaeologists have uncovered evidence from archaeological sites in Alabama, Arkansas, Illinois, Kentucky, Missouri, Ohio, and Tennessee that various starchy and oily seeds were domesticated in what has been termed the *Eastern Agricultural Complex* (Ford, 1985; Keegan, 1987).

Species of plants that appear to have been independently domesticated in North America include goosefoot (*Chenopodium berlandieri*), marsh elder (*Iva annua*), and sunflower (*Helianthus annus*), as well as a potentially indigenous variety of squash (*Cucurbita pepo*). As in other areas, the manipulation of wild plants likely began in the Archaic, with some domesticated species recovered from sites dating between 4,000 and 5,000 years ago. Although the importance of these local species was overshadowed by maize and other introduced domesticates, a description of lower Mississippi in the 1720s makes it clear that Chenopodium was still grown by the Native Americans in the 1720s. Unfortunately, this domesticated plant is now extinct.

The cultivation of Mesoamerican domesticates such as maize and beans spread into North America during the period between A.D. 800 and 1100 (Smith, 1989). Gradually, maize became the most important crop in farming communities throughout North America. In what is now the southwestern United States, maize cultivation led to specialized dry-land farming practices in Pueblo cultures such as the Hohokam, the Anasazi, and the Mogollon. These practices included irrigation methods and precise planting and harvesting schedules organized around rainy seasons.

An array of agricultural technologies, which promoted the cultivation of maize, beans, and squash, diffused throughout the midwest, the southeast, and eventually the northeast, culminating in the Adena and Hopewell cultures (in the eastern United States) and the immense Mississippian cultural complex with its center at Cahokia, now in Illinois. Artwork

Native American cultures developed a wide variety of agricultural practices suitable for many different environments. Farming communities, such as those at the Cliff Palace ruins in Colorado, flourished for hundreds of years by making effective use of the limited water available.

and other artifacts generated by these societies indicate contacts with Mesoamerica across the Gulf of Mexico and through the river systems connecting the Mississippi with the Ohio, Missouri, and Illinois rivers.

Consequences of Domestication

Although no one can pinpoint the precise reasons for the domestication of plants and animals, these activities clearly had far-reaching consequences, especially on the environment. All farming involves modification of the natural environment by clearing the land of naturally occurring vegetation. Some agriculturalists do periodically allow the land to lie fallow (uncultivated), but it is eventually cleared again, preventing the regrowth of wild plants. Domesticated animals also alter the environment by grazing and preventing the natural regrowth of plants. Larger settlements and more intensive land use by humans frequently contribute to soil erosion and a decline in soil fertility.

Population Growth

As agriculture transforms the landscape, it also gives rise to increases in human populations by making

food supplies more stable and reliable. Even more significant, agriculture yields more food per acre of land, which allows a given region to support a larger population. The surge in world population during the Neolithic period constituted a major demographic shift in human history. The annual population growth rate rose dramatically, leading to a tenfold population increase from the end of the Paleolithic, when scientists estimate the total world population at 30 million. By the year A.D. 1, some researchers conclude that the world population stood at approximately 300 million (Hassan, 1981).

Health and Nutrition

Although agricultural developments promoted population growth, they did not necessarily improve the quality of life in agricultural societies. In fact, in a number of areas, the advent of domesticated crops actually contributed to a decline in human health (Cohen & Armelagos, 1984; Larsen, 1995). The larger settlements of the Neolithic increasingly brought people into contact with one another, facilitating the spread of infectious disease. In some cases people also became dependent on particular domesticated plants like corn, to the exclusion of most other foodstuffs. This restricted diet did not fulfill nutritional requirements as well as that of hunter-gatherers, which encompassed a wide variety of both plants and animals. Reliance on one crop rather than on a variety of wild resources also boosted the risk of famine.

Archaeologists can study the impact of Neolithic life by studying human skeletons (Goodman et al., 1984). Poor nutrition, which causes arrested growth and disease, leaves identifiable traces on the bone. Signs of physiological stress brought on by food shortages show up in *Harris lines,* lines in long bones indicating periods of arrested growth, and in *enamel hypoplasias,* deficiency in tooth enamel. Calculations of prehistoric people's average height and age of death also shed light on changes in general health.

In a survey of worldwide data, Anna Curtenius Roosevelt (1984) concluded that Paleolithic and Mesolithic populations did experience food stress. However, she found more signs of stress and other health and nutritional problems in sedentary Neolithic communities:

> It seems that a large proportion of most sedentary prehistoric populations under intensive agriculture underwent chronic and life-threatening malnutrition and disease, especially during infancy and childhood. The causes of the nutritional stress are likely to have been the poverty of the staple crops in most nutrients except calories, periodic famines caused by the instability of the agricultural system, and chronic lack of food due to both population growth and economic expropriation by elites. The increases in infectious disease probably reflect both a poorer diet and increased interpersonal contact in crowded settlements, and it [infectious disease] is, in turn, likely to have aggravated nutritional problems. (pp. 573–574)

Increasing Material Complexity

Technological advances during the Neolithic brought about dramatic changes in food production and other economic and cultural activities. Archaeologically, the Neolithic takes shape through an explosion of artifacts. Most Neolithic settlement sites have huge trash mounds, or middens, containing food remains, broken tools, and other garbage. Sorting through these artifacts and the detritus of these societies reveals an increasingly sophisticated material culture. Clay was shaped into vessels of

many forms and was also used to make smoking pipes, lamps, and sculptures. Plants cultivated by humans included cotton and flax, which were then woven into cloth. Interestingly, many Neolithic artifacts resemble material goods familiar to modern-day humans. For example, some sites contained the remains of chairs, tables, and beds similar to those used today (Clark & Piggott, 1965). Ritual structures and ornamentation also became more elaborate.

Innovations in transportation technology also occurred in the Neolithic. In Southwest Asia, people used the wheel to construct transportation vehicles. American civilizations knew how to make wheels (they were found on toys in Mesoamerica), but they did not use the wheel in any vehicles, most likely because, unlike peoples in Europe, Asia, and Africa, they had not domesticated oxen or cattle to pull vehicles. Moreover, in the mountainous regions of the Andes where the llama was domesticated, wheeled transportation was inefficient.

As populations settled permanently in villages and urban areas, they built durable dwellings of mud, brick, stone, and mortar, depending on locally available materials. As a sign of growing divisions on the basis of wealth, prestige, and status in these societies, some houses had many rooms with private courtyards and rich furnishings, whereas others were very modest.

Increasing Social Stratification and Political Complexity

As the preceding discussion of the Neolithic illustrates, during the past 10,000 years human societies became more and more individualized. Some populations successfully pursued hunting-and-gathering subsistence strategies up through modern times. For others, relatively simple agricultural methods sufficed. Looking at how human societies evolved through history, however, we see a gradual but unmistakable progression from egalitarian social arrangements in which all members of a society have roughly equal access to power and prestige, to more stratified societies. Paleolithic cultures, with their emphasis on hunting-and-gathering by small bands, accorded people of the same sex and capabilities more or less equal shares in the benefits of social living, even as they acknowledged that some

CRITICAL PERSPECTIVES

WAR BEFORE CIVILIZATION?

As we consider life during the Neolithic, the images that most commonly come to mind are of a peaceful people who lived a rugged lifestyle, exploited natural resources, and were united in a shared goal of survival. Although hunting large game animals would have required both courage and implements capable of inflicting fatal wounds, we seldom consider that these weapons were turned against other human beings. In a book entitled *War before Civilization*, archaeologist Lawrence H. Keeley (1996) questions this pacifist view. In a far-ranging study that moves from the archaeological record of the Mesolithic and Archaic to the complex societies of Mesoamerica and the Nile Valley, Keeley convincingly demonstrates that archaeological evidence on early human societies provides ample demonstration of warfare, murder, and mayhem.

Keeley's own experience as an archaeologist began as a college freshman excavating a prehistoric Native American village site on San Francisco Bay, California. The site contained many burials of individuals who had met violent deaths, as evidenced by the stone projectile points embedded in their skeletons. This evidence suggests that the violent deaths in the population were at least four times the percentage of violent deaths in the United States and Europe during the war-filled twentieth century. Despite this fact, the general view at the time was that the Native peoples of California were exceptionally peaceable.

The situation in coastal California was not unique. Keeley examined archaeological data and descriptions of conflicts in non-Western societies and found that the circumstances in other world areas and other time periods were equally, if not more, violent. Early farming communities and early agricultural states provide numerous illustrations of conflict and warfare. Excavations of a fortification ditch at Crow Creek, South Dakota (A.D. 1325) revealed the skeletal remains of nearly 500 men, women, and children who had been scalped, mutilated, and left exposed to scavengers before being interred. Studies of early Neolithic settlements (6,000 to 7,000 years old) in Europe and Britain, including sites excavated by Keeley, show that the first farmers to colonize central and northwestern Europe built villages fortified with palisades and ditches. Some of these settlements bear clear evidence of archery attacks, destruction by fire, and violent deaths. The defensive sites seem to have been located along the margins of territories, possibly as protection against earlier hunting-and-gathering Mesolithic populations. The early Maya civilizations of Mesoamerica were frequently at war, as evidenced by fortifications and numerous murals showing warriors and captives. Some of the earliest written records include chronicles of conquests and military victories.

If evidence for conflict and warfare is so prevalent in early societies, why have archaeologists generally failed to discuss this aspect of our past? The explanation provides a good illustration of how research objectives and designs shape the interpretations we reach. Keeley

were better hunters or more gifted leaders than others. In contrast, during the Mesolithic and the Neolithic, there was a clear trend toward greater social stratification all over the world. Certain members of these societies acquired more influence than others in societal decision making, such as how to allocate agricultural surpluses, and were thus able to accumulate more wealth. Another marked change was the emergence of full-time craft specialists, individuals who concentrated on the manufacture of tools and other goods. These developments set the stage for all sorts of momentous changes in human social and political life, as we shall see in the next chapter.

argues that archaeologists have essentially "pacified the past" and "shared a pervasive bias against the possibility of prehistoric warfare" (Keeley, 1996:vii). Preconceived perceptions and methodologies aimed at answering other questions prohibited researchers from looking for evidence of conflict or recognizing relevant data that were uncovered. Given his own grounding in traditional views of the past, Keeley himself was actually surprised when his research on early European Neolithic sites revealed evidence of fortifications. His work at the site of Darion had earlier revealed defensive features, yet he noted that subconsciously he had not really believed his own arguments concerning the evidence for fortifications, and he assumed that Darion's fortifications were an aberration (Keeley, 1996, viii). With a particular view of the past in mind, defensive sites have often been described by the more neutral terms *enclosures* or *symbolic features*, and the significance of violent death in pre-Columbian Native American populations left unexplored.

Keeley further points out that anthropological views of non-Western, pre-industrial societies, which serve as analogies for the behavior of prehistoric peoples, were similarly biased. Ethnographic descriptions of conflicts were colored by views of modern warfare. Because battles involving multiple combatants are the characteristic events and primary goals of contemporary conflicts, it was these features that ethnographers recorded. Of course, battles in tribal societies involved far fewer people, and they often stopped after a relatively small number of casualties. While these observations may seem to support a more peaceful view of nonindustrialized societies and less violent images of prehistoric peoples, they fail to take into account the numbers of people killed in raids, ambushes, and surprise attacks on villages that represent the major component of tribal warfare. Keeley concludes:

Primitive war was not a puerile or deficient form of warfare, but war reduced to its essentials: killing enemies with a minimum risk, denying them the means of life via vandalism and theft (even the means of reproduction by the kidnapping of their women and children), terrorizing them into either yielding territory or desisting from their encroachments and aggressions (Keeley, 1996:175).

Popular imagery of the peaceful, noble savage fails to recognize in prehistoric societies the same rapaciousness that characterizes our own, and thus robs them of some of their humanity. Sadly, the evidence from the past holds the same catalog of deaths, violence, and destruction.

POINTS TO PONDER

1. Discuss Keeley's ideas. What other interpretations might explain the archaeological evidence he discusses other than warfare and conflict?

2. Think about your own images of Paleolithic hunter-gatherers and views of ethnographically known hunter-gatherers. How are these views different from the ones presented by Keeley?

3. Do you think Keeley makes his case?

SUMMARY

The transition from a reliance on naturally occurring plants and animals to food production occurred in many world areas at different times. This shift took place gradually, beginning with the more intensive exploitation of local plant and animal resources in the period known as the Mesolithic or Archaic. In some cases, permanent or semipermanent settlements were built around these resources, and specialized tool technologies appeared for processing plant foods, for hunting, and for fishing.

Many Mesolithic and Archaic populations also started to plant wild seeds and capture wild animals. The manipulation of wild species was the first stage in the transition to food production. After a period of human selection, some plants and animals became domesticated—physically distinct from wild varieties and dependent on humans for reproduction.

The change in subsistence to domesticated species marks the beginning of the Neolithic period. Yet why domestication took place at all remains speculative. On the one hand, domestication provides more regular food supplies, allowing for growth in human populations. On the other hand, hunter-gatherers actually invest much less time in subsistence activities than do food producers. Domesticated crops must be planted, weeded, and watered for several months before they can be harvested, and the chance of crop failure makes agriculture a risky and time consuming investment.

Archaeologists have offered many hypotheses to explain the origins of food production. Some cite climatic changes at the end of the Pleistocene and population growth as key elements. Others tend to view the shift to food production as a complex process involving fundamental changes in the way humans interacted with the environment. Archaeological evidence indicates a great deal of regional and local variation in the plant and animal species involved and in the specific subsistence practices.

Researchers looking into the Neolithic have often highlighted the evidence for early domestication in Southwest Asia and, to a lesser extent, China and Mesoamerica. In fact, these areas did produce some of the first archaeological evidence pertaining to domestication, and they still represent some of the earliest examples of the transition to food production. However, the origins and diffusion of domestication are complex and worldwide in scope. Although domestication occurred earlier in some areas than in others, it took place independently in many regions, and it involved a vast number of species. Areas of Southeast Asia, Africa, Europe, North America, and South America also witnessed indigenous domestication.

Food production clearly had important consequences for human history. Because people had to stay near their crops, Neolithic people became more sedentary than earlier hunting-and-gathering populations. This transition, however, was not without disadvantages. Diseases associated with larger population concentrations and the tendency to concentrate on growing one crop gave rise to poorer health and deficiency diseases.

In addition to a dramatic increase in population, the Neolithic period is also marked by increasingly sophisticated material culture, social stratification, and political complexity. These trends set the stage for the emergence of states in many world areas.

QUESTIONS TO THINK ABOUT

1. What were the principal effects of climatic change on human populations at the end of the Pleistocene period? What aspects of human existence would likely have been affected by climate change?

2. Discuss what is meant by the terms Archaic and Mesolithic. In what ways are they both different from and similar to the periods that preceded and followed them?

3. Childe, Braidwood, Binford, Cohen, and Rindos provide very different models for the origins of domestication. What are the strengths and weaknesses of each? Based on what you have learned, which theory do you favor?

4. Why is information about the size and density of human populations relevant to studies of the domestication of plants and animals?

5. Compare and contrast the origins of agriculture in Asia, Mesoamerica, and the Fertile Crescent. When and where does the first evidence for agriculture appear? What were the most important agricultural crops, and where were they domesticated?

6. In what ways have the ability to produce food through agriculture and the adoption of a sedentary lifestyle affected the human experience? Discuss specific ways that these changes affected human health and reproduction.

KEY TERMS

Archaic

artificial selection

broad-spectrum collecting

cultivation

domestication

flotation

megaliths

Mesolithic

microliths

Neolithic

paleoethnobotany

silica gloss

vegiculture

INTERNET EXERCISES

1. Read about early farming in China at the following website: **http://www.britannica.com/ eb/article?eu=127720&tocid=71748&query= early%20farming%20in%20china&ct=**. What types of soil were present, what types of tools were used, and what crops were grown? How does the environment affect the selection of crop types?

2. What environmental changes happened during the Mesolithic? Refer to the following website to

investigate this question: **http://www.tundria. com/Linguistics/EurMesol.htm#Changes% 20in%20the%20Environment**.

3. What is plant and animal domestication? Where did these processes occur first? What types of plants and animals were selected for this? Why? Answers to these questions can be found at **http://www.ag.usask.ca/exhibits/walkway/ what/plantdom.html**.

SUGGESTED READINGS

COHEN, MARK, and GEORGE J. ARMELAGOS (Eds.). 1984. *Paleopathology at the Origins of Agriculture.* New York: Academic Press. This volume focuses on the consequences of domestication for human nutrition and health in different parts of the world.

COWAN, C. WESLEY, and PATTY JO WATSON. 1992. *The Origins of Agriculture: An International Perspective.* Washington, DC: Smithsonian Institution Press. This edited volume provides detailed case studies of the evidence for domestication in many world areas, including Far East Asia, Southwest Asia, Africa, and the Americas.

FAGAN, BRIAN M. 1998. *Peoples of the Earth: An Introduction to World Prehistory,* 9th ed. New York: HarperCollins. A broad introductory survey that spans human evolution through the origins of agriculture, placing developments in different regions of the world in perspective.

FAGAN, BRIAN M. 2001. *Grahame Clark: An Intellectual Life of an Archaeologist.* Cambridge, MA: Westview. This well-written and engaging volume is a biography of John Grahame Douglas Clark, one of the major figures in the study and interpretation of the Mesolithic and excavator of the famous Mesolithic site, Star Carr.

RINDOS, DAVID. 1984. *The Origins of Agriculture: An Evolutionary Perspective.* New York: Academic Press. An in-depth look at the origins of agriculture from an evolutionary viewpoint. Also included are brief critiques of other theoretical approaches.

SMITH, BRUCE D. 1995. *The Emergence of Agriculture.* New York: Scientific American Library. This well-presented volume surveys the origins of agriculture in global perspective and provides one of the most comprehensive and readable syntheses currently available.

9

The Rise of the State and Complex Society

CHAPTER OUTLINE

THE STATE AND CIVILIZATION

Types of Political Systems / Early States

STUDYING COMPLEX SOCIETIES

*Written Language / Defining States
Archaeologically / Monumental Architecture /
Specialization / Status and Social Ranking /
Trade and Exchange / The Archaeology
of Religion*

THEORIES ABOUT STATE FORMATION

*Integrationist Perspectives / Conflict Theories /
Perspectives on State Formation*

STATES IN DIFFERENT WORLD AREAS

*Civilizations in Southwest Asia / Agricultural
Civilizations in Africa / Early Asian Civilizations /
Empires of the Americas / Andean Civilizations*

THE COLLAPSE OF STATE SOCIETIES

Reasons for Collapse

CHAPTER QUESTIONS

- What are the basic characteristics of civilization, as defined by archaeologists?

- What criteria do anthropologists use to define the state?

- What are the basic theories about state formation, and what evidence do archaeologists draw on to substantiate these theories?

- Where are some of the major state civilizations located?

As we saw in Chapter 8, the advent of domestication during the Neolithic brought many changes to human societies, including more settled communities, population growth, increased social stratification, and growing political complexity. Gradually, as permanent settlements expanded, people in many regions of the world developed techniques such as irrigation, plow cultivation, and the use of fertilizers, which allowed fields to be cultivated year after year. These intensive agricultural practices produced food surpluses, which contributed to further changes in human subsistence and political organization. Beginning approximately 5,500 years ago in some areas, these developments coalesced in the appearance of complex societies commonly called *civilizations*.

One aspect of the growing social complexity was institutionalized government, or the **state**, run by full-time officials. The intensification of agriculture was accompanied by the rise of agrarian states in Southwest Asia, Egypt, India, China, and later in Greece, Rome, Byzantium, Southeast Asia, sub-Saharan Africa, and feudal Europe. The agrarian states in the Americas included the Teotihuacán, Mayan, and Aztec empires of Mesoamerica and the Incan Empire of Peru. The location of some of these states is highlighted in Figure 9.1. In this chapter we examine how archaeologists study the development of social and cultural complexity in early societies and some of the theories that explain why states formed initially.

The State and Civilization

V. Gordon Childe, whose theories on domestication were discussed in Chapter 8, also wrote on the origin of complex societies. He believed that the rise of civilization could be easily defined by the appearance of a specific combination of features,

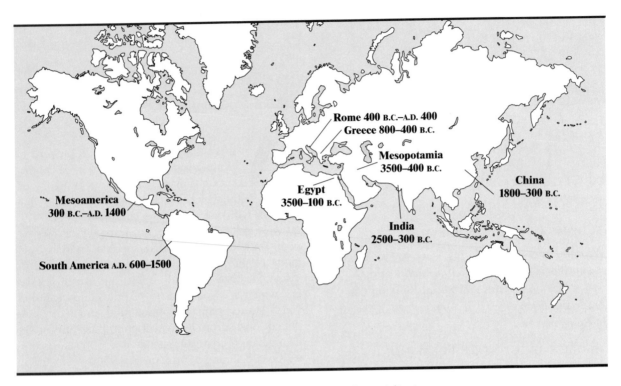

FIGURE 9.1 Early states present an abundance of technology, craft specialization, and artistic achievement. The states shown here represent some of the earliest states in the world.

including urban centers of between 7,000 and 20,000 inhabitants; a highly specialized division of labor, with economic roles other than those pertaining to agricultural production; a ruling class of religious, civil, and military leaders; extensive food surpluses; monumental architecture; the use of numbers and writing systems for record keeping; developments in arithmetic, geometry, and astronomy; sophisticated art expressed in a variety of materials; long-distance trade; and an institutionalized form of political organization based on force—the state (Childe, 1950).

Although definitions such as Childe's incorporate many of the features that are popularly used to characterize civilization, such definitions have little use for anthropologists. A survey of the archaeological and historical information that is now available reveals that such neat definitions as Childe's are too rigid to define the diversity in the societies under study. In fact, all of the features noted by Childe are rarely present in the earliest societies that have been termed civilizations. Different interpretations

of what characteristics are the key ingredients of civilization create more problems than they solve. In this text, the term *civilization* is used in a general way to indicate a complex society with some of the features noted by Childe.

Types of Political Systems

In studying the development of early societies, today's anthropologists generally focus on specific features rather than all-encompassing definitions. One of the most important distinctions researchers make concerns different kinds of political organization. Many anthropologists use variations of a fourfold classification system first developed by anthropologist Elman Service (1971), which divides societies into bands, tribes, chiefdoms, and states. As we saw in Chapter 7, a *band* is the least complex—and, most likely, the oldest—form of political system. It is the most common form among hunter-gatherer societies and is based on close kinship relations within a fairly small group of people. **Tribes** are more complex societies with political institutions that unite larger groupings of people into a political system. Tribes do not have centralized, formal political institutions, but they do have *sodalities*, groups based on kinship, age, or gender that provide for a more complex political organization. **Chiefdom** political systems are more complex than tribal societies in that they are formalized and centralized. Chiefdoms establish centralized authority over many communities through a variety of complex economic, social, and religious institutions. Despite their size and complexity, however, chiefdoms are still fundamentally organized by kinship principles. Although chiefdoms have different levels of status and political authority, the people within these levels are related to one another through kinship ties. Eric Wolf (1982) has referred to bands, tribes, and chiefdoms as *kin-ordered societies.*

The state is structurally distinguished from other societies on the basis of an institutionalized bureaucracy or government. States are political systems with centralized bureaucratic institutions to establish power and authority over large populations in different territories. While the ruler of a state may be an inherited position, state systems are not based on kinship. Because early states were more complex and highly organized than prestate societies, they could not rely solely on kinship to define different status positions. Land ownership and occupation became more important than kinship in organizing society. In the highly centralized agricultural societies, the state itself replaced kin groups as the major integrating principle. State bureaucracies govern society on behalf of ruling authorities through procedures that plan, direct, and coordinate highly political processes.

This classification system, too, is not without some of the problems faced in Childe's definition of civilization; political organizations form more of a continuum than four neat divisions, and some societies do not fit into an individual category (Cohen & Service, 1978; Johnson & Earle, 2000; McIntosh, 1999). From an archaeological perspective, it may also be especially challenging to assess, for example, whether a particular society had the characteristics of a chiefdom or a state, let alone more nuanced variation in sociopolitical structures. The classification serves, like any classification scheme, to facilitate comparison and organize information,

but it should be used flexibly, with the dynamic nature of human societies in mind.

Early States

Early states were typically characterized by a high degree of social inequality. The creation of substantial food surpluses, along with better food-storage technologies, led to new forms of economic relations. Mastery was based primarily on the control of agricultural surpluses, often administered by a complex administrative system. For this reason the term **agricultural states** is often used to describe these early societies. Many people were freed from working in the fields to pursue other specialized functions. Hundreds of new occupations developed in the urban centers. Craftsworkers produced tools, clothing, jewelry, pottery, and other accessories. Other workers engaged in commerce, government, religion, education, the military, and other sectors of the economy.

This new division of labor influenced both rural and urban areas. Farm laborers were not only involved in essential food production, they also turned to crafts production to supplement their income. Over time, some agricultural villages began to produce crafts and commodities not just for their own consumption but for trade with other villages and with the urban centers. With increasing long-distance trade, regional and local marketplaces, as well as marketplaces in the urban areas, began to emerge. Foodstuffs and other commodities produced by peasants, artisans, and craftsworkers were bought and sold in these marketplaces. Through these activities, rural villages became involved in widespread trading alliances and marketing activities. In early cities such as Ur, Memphis, Teotihuacán, and Tikal, markets were centrally located, offering both imported and domestically manufactured items as well as food. In addition, marketplaces arose throughout the countryside. A steady flow of goods developed from villages to towns to regional and national capitals.

The power of the rulers in agricultural states was often expressed in sumptuous palaces, monumental architecture, and a luxuriant lifestyle. The opulent lifestyle of the leaders could be contrasted with that of the other classes. It was in early states that slavery and the state-sanctioned use of force to enforce laws became common. The leaders of the state often sanctioned their positions through the manipulation of religious institutions and symbols. The division between the supernatural and social institutions that we make today had little meaning in these cultural settings (Trigger, 1993).

One major factor that contributed to the evolution of agricultural states was the development of a more sophisticated technology. To some extent, it represented modifications of existing technologies. For example, stone tools such as axes, hammers, knives, and scrapers were refined for more prolonged use. Increased knowledge of metallurgy enabled some agricultural peoples to create more durable tools. For example, copper, tin, and iron ores were smelted and cast into weapons, armor, ornaments, and other tools. Many technological innovations were dramatically expressed in myriad artwork and monumental construction, illustrated by such massive structures as the Pyramid of the Sun at Teotihuacán in Mexico, which rises more than 200 feet and covers some 650 square feet.

Agricultural states emerged in many parts of the world. Six of the earliest were in Mesopotamia (3500 B.C.); the Egyptian Old Kingdom (3500 B.C.); China (2500 B.C.); the Indus River valley, India (2500 B.C.); and Mexico and Peru (300 B.C.). Other agricultural states flourished in many other areas, including Greece and Rome, tropical Africa, Southeast Asia, and, to a lesser extent, North America. These societies exhibited many of the signs of complexity, social stratification, and specialization that Childe used to define civilization (Service, 1975; Connah, 1987; Tainter, 1990; Trigger, 1993).

Studying Complex Societies

Archaeologists draw on many sources of information to reconstruct the nature of early agricultural states. Variations in such features as settlement patterns and site characteristics, for example, can be associated with different forms of political organization or social stratification. Depending on a researcher's theoretical orientation and research design, a project may focus on certain aspects of a prehistoric state, perhaps on the link between the control of agricultural land and status differentiation or the expression of religious beliefs in art and architecture.

Written Language

The advent of state-level organization gives archaeologists a source of information not available to researchers working on earlier periods: written sources (Daniels & Bright, 1995). As noted, Childe considered writing to be fundamental to the definition of civilization. However, surveying early states, archaeologist Bruce Trigger (1993) notes that there are no obvious differences in social, political, and economic organization between societies that had writing and those that did not. In the absence of writing, important events and records were remembered by special historians, at times with the use of memory aids such as the knotted strings utilized by the Inca of South America.

Anthropologists have explored the origins of writing and its effects on society. Writing systems may have originated in agricultural states in response to commercial and political needs; for example, as a means of keeping accounts for taxation. But as complex civilizations developed, writing systems became linked with historical, literary, and religious expression. Often their specific function varied in different cultural settings. Undoubtedly, literacy gives great social and economic power to the official bureaucrats, lawyers, and priests of large-scale political states (Goody, 1987).

Written records may provide information on administration, ruling dynasties, political divisions, trade contacts, and locations of settlements. Because of the amount of information such sources provide, archaeologists working in some regions may gear their work toward locating and interpreting early libraries or archives. This is particularly true of research in Southwest Asia, where many records are preserved on clay tablets. Apart from the information preserved in the records themselves, repositories such as libraries indicate the degree of centralized authority and bureaucratic organization that was present.

Writing Systems   Many agricultural states developed writing systems that enabled people to keep records, document their history, and produce religious texts. Early pictures, sometimes referred to as *pictographs,* may have been the precursors of early writing systems. **Ideographic writing systems,** one early form of writing, use simple pictures to communicate ideas; each picture represents an idea.

Egyptian hieroglyphics are one of the world's oldest forms of writing.

Source: © Copyright The British Museum.

Other forms of writing emerged in different regions. **Hieroglyphic writing** evolved from an ideographic type of picture writing. Hieroglyphic writing simplifies a picture into a symbol, which has a direct relationship to the sound of a word. People in different parts of the world, like the Egyptians and Mayas, developed hieroglyphic systems independently of one another.

In another form of writing, called *syllabic writing,* the characters themselves express nothing but a sequence of sounds. These sounds make up the syllables of the language. Syllabic writing is much more efficient than ideographic or hieroglyphic writing because it uses a smaller number of characters. The ancient Semitic writing systems such as Arabic and Hebrew were syllabic systems. One modern language that still involves a mostly syllabic writing system is Japanese (although Japanese writing also includes Chinese characters).

Eventually, in the Mediterranean region, *alphabetic writing systems* evolved from syllabic forms. In alphabetic writing there is a sign for each sound (technically each phoneme) of the language rather than one for each word or for each syllable. This is the most efficient writing system because most languages have only twelve to sixty total sounds. Hence, an alphabetic writing system can, with the fewest possible units, record every possible utterance in the language. The Greek writing system is the first to be considered fully alphabetic because it has a separate written symbol for each vowel and consonant. From the Greek system, the Romans adapted the Latin alphabet, which became the basis of the writing system of Western Europe and, eventually, of English.

In actuality, this system involves neither language nor writing. Most likely it was independent of the language spoken by the people, and the meaning of the pictures can be read by anyone.

The Chinese writing system developed from an ideographic pictorial system. The Chinese characters, estimated to number between 70,000 and 125,000, have been conventionalized, but it is still easy to recognize their ideographic origin. In the Chinese system, the individual symbols are whole units that have meaning (one picture stands for one morpheme). There is no connection between sounds (phonemes) and the writing. This means that the Chinese who speak different dialects, such as Mandarin, Cantonese, or Hakka, can read the same text without difficulty. Thus, writing has been one of the strongest cultural forces in unifying Chinese culture.

Defining States Archaeologically

Important clues about the scale and complexity of an ancient society can be gleaned by studying the size and distribution of settlements. The world's first cities developed from Neolithic villages. With the emergence of state societies, larger urban settlements, or *cities,* became focal points of government, trade, and religious life. The first states were linked to the control or dominance of particular territories, which often incorporated settlements of different size and function. Archaeologists can use this information to locate the centers of ancient states, infer political divisions, and define sites with specialized functions.

In Chapter 2 we saw how archaeologists gather information on past settlements through ground surveys, remote sensing techniques like aerial photography, and excavation. Drawing on these resources, an archaeologist can produce a map of early settlements. In addition to locating sites accurately, determining their age is of great importance; without this information, developments at a particular time cannot be evaluated.

Central Place Theory A concept archaeologists find useful in considering the implications of past settlement patterns is **central place theory,** developed by the German geographer Walter Christaller (1933). Surveying the contemporary distribution of towns in southern Germany in the 1930s, Christaller hypothesized that given uniform topography, resources, and opportunities, the distribution of sites in a region would be perfectly regular. Political and economic centers would be located an equal distance from one another; each in turn would be surrounded by a hierarchical arrangement of smaller settlements, all evenly spaced. The archaeological implications of the theory are clear: The largest archaeological site in a region might be assumed to be the capital; regional centers would be represented by slightly smaller sites; and village sites would be even smaller.

Central place theory is not without its limitations. Natural resources and topography are not uniform. In addition, the size of sites of the same level or function may vary. Nevertheless, the study of modern and ancient settlements confirms the basic premise of central place theory: Major centers are located some distance from one another and surrounded by sites in a hierarchically nested pattern. Mathematical models based on this premise have provided more sophisticated ways of modeling ancient states (Renfrew & Cooke, 1979).

Evidence for Administration In addition to size, archaeologists use a host of other indicators to determine the position of sites in a settlement hierarchy. The primary center of the state can be expected to have more indications of administration, higher status, and more centralized authority than other settlements in the region. These features might be represented by monumental architecture,

Clay sealings, such as these recovered at the site of Askut in the Sudan, provide clues about administration and state organization.

Source: Courtesy of Stuart Tyson Smith, University of California, Santa Barbara.

administrative buildings, archives, and storage facilities. In many societies people used seals to impress clay sealings with marks of ownership and authority (see the photo above). Such artifacts might be expected to be particularly prevalent in political, economic, or religious centers (Smith, 1990). Features such as these may suggest a site's role as a primary center even if it is smaller in size than other settlements.

The archaeological record also provides indications of administration outside of the primary center. There may be evidence of centralized administration such as that just noted, but to a lesser extent. Road systems and carefully maintained pathways might link settlements within a state. A feature that seems associated with many early states is the establishment of outposts in key locations along their margins (Algaze, 1993). Such outposts may have served to defend territory, secure access to resources, gain influence in peripheral areas, or to facilitate trade.

Monumental Architecture

No archaeological discoveries captivate popular imagination more than the temples, palaces, and tombs of past civilizations. Aside from the obvious advantage of helping archaeologists locate sites, monumental architecture preserves information about the political organization, ritual beliefs, and lifeways of ancient people. As seen in Chapter 8, megalithic monuments such as Stonehenge were erected by prestate societies. However, the surplus of wealth, high-density populations, and organization harnessed by states made monumental architecture one of the most striking legacies of state societies. The great temples, pyramids, and palaces of ancient civilizations were the work of thousands of skilled artisans, laborers, and slaves, who quarried and transported huge stones and sculpted numerous artworks. Although some buildings had civil functions, the purpose of most monumental constructions in agricultural states was intertwined with religious conceptions and beliefs.

Monumental architecture served different functions in different cultural settings. For example, the 5,000-year-old ziggurats of the Sumerian state in Mesopotamia were both places of worship and centers of food distribution. The massive ziggurat at the Sumerian city of Warka (Uruk) had two flights of steps leading to a temple or shrine. The structure had extensive mosaic decorations and the earliest known use of columns in building con-

struction. This temple, as well as other buildings, represents the product of hundreds of craftsworkers such as stonemasons and architects.

The pyramids, which are characteristic of the Egyptian Old Kingdom, are an example of a very different type of monumental construction. Based on beliefs of resurrection and life in an afterworld, the Egyptian pyramids, constructed as burial chambers for the pharaohs, contained many material items for use in the afterworld. The first pyramid was built under the direction of Pharaoh Djoser approximately 4,680 years ago. It is the smallest of the royal pyramids constructed at the capital at Memphis, near modern Cairo. The pyramid of Djoser was followed by more complex structures, culminating with the Great Pyramid at Giza, which is 481 feet tall and covers 13 acres at its base. The Great Pyramid dates to the reign of Pharaoh Khufu, or Cheops, approximately 4,600 years ago. Next to the Great Pyramid, two smaller pyramids made of quarried limestone blocks were built by later pharaohs.

Monuments in the Americas Monument construction was also prevalent among civilizations in the Americas. For example, the Maya built many palaces, temples, and pyramid complexes. One of the Mayan centers in Guatemala, Tikal, which had a population of about 50,000 inhabitants, contained 300 large ceremonial and civic buildings dominated by large temple pyramids that were almost 200 feet high. At the top of these structures were temples decorated with carvings made from a plaster or cement called *stucco*. These carvings represented Mayan religious beliefs in half-human–half-jaguar figures, snakes, eagles, alligators, and other spirit beings. The Maya believed in the *nagual,* an animal spirit that lived apart from humans but could at certain times merge with the human soul. Thus, many Mayan religious carvings expressed the concept of the nagual.

Sumerian ziggurats, such as the one shown here, served as places of worship and centers of food distribution.

Specialization

We have already discussed the growth of administration and bureaucracy and the intensification of agricultural practices in state-level societies. Similarly, the artwork and monument construction of the agricultural civilizations represents a dramatic shift in the scale of technology and the organization of production compared with that of small-scale societies. During the Neolithic, few people were able to devote themselves full time to nonagricultural pursuits; potters, metalworkers, and weavers also farmed the land. In state societies, more people were able to concentrate on a variety of specialized tasks full time, supported by the food surplus made available by intensive agriculture.

Many of the agricultural civilizations produced brilliantly painted pottery, sculpture, and other artwork. Often enormous ovens, called *kilns*, were used to produce pottery bowls, flasks, and dishes, which were decorated with geometric designs and representations of animals and people. Elaborate watercolors painted on plaster walls called *frescoes*, as well as statues, intricate stone carvings, and beautiful murals, testify to the impressive development of the arts in agricultural civilizations. Sophisticated and elaborate metal objects also characterized many agricultural states.

In settlements of state societies, craft specialists were often concentrated in particular areas. Because each craft frequently had its own distinctive technology, these areas can be readily identified archaeologically. For example, in Mesoamerica, excavations have uncovered extensive areas associated with the flaking of *obsidian*, a volcanic glass. In other settings, special tools and work areas for weaving, sewing, leather working, potting, metalworking, and even beer brewing have been identified. In some societies, one's craft specialization and one's profession were linked to social position and status.

Status and Social Ranking

Written accounts and illustrations, often depicting the wealth and power of rulers, underscore the disparities that existed between the rich and the poor in state societies. The kind of housing, clothing, and material goods people had access to was rigidly controlled. Many of these distinctions are recognizable archaeologically in palace complexes, exotic trade items, and greater-than-average concentrations of wealth. For example, Teotihuacán, which flourished in Mexico between A.D. 150 and 750, was a planned city with perhaps as many as 120,000 inhabitants at its peak (Millon et al., 1974; Millon, 1976). Neither the houses nor their furnishings were uniform; larger compounds with lavish interior decoration suggest a great deal of variation in wealth and status.

The power of the rulers of early states was often expressed in art and architecture, here illustrated by a brass plaque depicting the Oba (king) of Benin (now in modern Nigeria) flanked by retainers.

Important indications of status differences were also expressed in burials (Brown, 1971; Chapman et al., 1981). Through the study of skeletal remains, physical anthropologists are often able to determine the age, sex, and health of an individual. Surveying materials associated with the burial and its archaeological context, researchers gain insights into the deceased's social standing. For example, the amount of labor invested in the Egyptian pyramids indicates the importance of the pharaoh as well as the organizational power of the state. In some instances, servants were put to death and buried with a ruler.

Archaeologists often study *grave goods,* artifacts associated with a body, to evaluate status. It is logical to assume that the grave of an individual of higher status will have a larger number and more valuable array of goods than that of a commoner. However, it is important to recognize the extensive variation between and within cultural groups because of other variables, such as age, occupation, and gender.

Trade and Exchange

Trade—the exchange of goods and services—has long been a feature of human societies. However, with growing social and political complexity, some individuals began to concentrate on trade full time, and exchange networks extended over ever-growing areas. Expanded mercantile exchange may be indicated by the appearance of standardized weights and measures as well as monetary systems, including coinage. Documentary records may also list trade contacts and the costs and amounts of materials exchanged. More information comes from the trade materials themselves. Resources were not evenly distributed throughout the landscape, and items such as precious stones, metals, and amber were frequently traded over long distances. Raw materials might have been exchanged for finished products like pottery, hides, beads, and cloth. As some of these items have survived, they provide an archaeological record of past exchange (Adams, 1974; Earle & Ericson, 1977).

Certain kinds of raw materials, or *artifacts,* may be characteristic of a particular region. By plotting the distribution of these commodities, an archaeologist may be able to trace past trade networks. Typically, the availability a trade material decreases as distance from the source increases. Hence, it is logical to assume that as one moves away from a resource or production center, archaeological sites will contain fewer examples of that particular type of trade material. Yet interpretation of this information is less straightforward than one might think. Simply counting the instances of a particular artifact at sites fails to consider the site size or function, the variation in preservation, and the amount of archaeological work that has been undertaken (Renfrew & Bahn, 1996). To assess this trade successfully, archaeologists need to consider these variables.

Some trade materials can be readily recognized as exotic imports. At times, coins, sealings, or manufacturers' marks on such artifacts as pottery may even indicate specific sources. But the origin of some artifacts is less clear. Pottery styles can be copied, and stones of diverse origin can look quite similar. To identify an artifact's origins, archaeologists use a number of techniques of varying sophistication. The simplest method is to examine an object such as a stone or potsherd under low magnification for rocks, minerals, or other inclusions that can be linked to a particular location.

A much more sophisticated technique, referred to as **trace element analysis,** involves the study of the elements found in artifacts (Tite, 1972). The basic chemical configuration of certain kinds of stones is broadly similar—all obsidian, for example, contains silicon, oxygen, and calcium—but certain elements may be present in very small quantities. These trace elements may occur in quite different concentrations in materials from different sources. Their presence in artifacts can be plotted, providing a means of assessing distribution patterns.

The Archaeology of Religion

Allusion to the importance of religion in early states has pervaded the preceding discussion. Ritual structures such as temples and pyramids and the status afforded to religious leaders are potent testaments to religious beliefs. However, real understanding of the workings of ancient religions remains elusive. Aside from the obvious recourse to written texts, which when available offer a great deal of information, archaeologists must infer religious beliefs from material culture. A standard joke among archaeologists when confronting any artifact whose function is unknown is to describe it as a "ritual object," an explanation that serves to underscore the challenge of inferring the complex, nonmaterial aspects of past cultures.

Although the study of past religions is difficult, insights may be drawn from a number of different sources. Often religious beliefs are given physical expression in places of worship. These locations may have artifacts, spatial arrangements, architectural features, and decorative elements distinct from other buildings at a site. In many cultures, worship involved offerings or animal and human sacrifices, traces of which may be preserved. Archaeological finds may also include representations of deities, ritual figures, or symbols that convey religious beliefs. At times an individual artifact may provide important clues. Surveying traces of the Moche, a small state in the valleys of coastal Peru that reached its zenith between about A.D. 100 and 600, archaeologists used detailed depictions of rituals on pottery and murals to interpret material recovered archaeologically (Donnan & Castillo, 1992). Finally, some of the most tantalizing indications of past belief systems are provided by burials. The manner of interment, grave goods, and funerary objects provides insight into mortuary rituals and, ultimately, some of the most important of human belief systems.

Reconstructions of ancient rituals and religious beliefs are presented in research from around the world. Indeed, it would be impossible to interpret monuments like the pyramids or Egypt or the temples of the Moche without examining the unique belief systems of which they were a part. Consequently, the study of past religions, although challenging, remains an important focus of anthropological research.

Theories about State Formation

One of the major questions that anthropologists have attempted to answer is: Why did state societies emerge? Agricultural states arose independently in different world areas at different times and not at all in some regions. To explain state formation, researchers have posited an array of theories, which can be divided into two overarching perspectives: integrationist (or functionalist) theories and conflict theories (Lenski, 1966; Service, 1975; Cohen & Service, 1978; Haas, 1982).

Integrationist theories of state formation assume that society as a whole benefited from state organization, or in other words, the state was a positive, integrative response to conditions that a society faced. The benefits that certain individuals or groups in a society may have obtained were balanced by the key organizational or managerial functions they performed, which enabled the society to survive and prosper.

In contrast, **conflict theories** emphasize domination and exploitation. It is thought that state organization arose out of the ability of certain individuals or subgroups in a society to monopolize or control resources. State organization, therefore, has been advantageous only to the dominant elite in a society and, in general, very costly to subordinate groups like the peasantry (Fried, 1967).

Integrationist Perspectives

An early integrationist view of state formation was proposed independently by Julian Steward (1955)

and Karl Wittfogel (1957), who linked the development of the state to the construction and maintenance of irrigation projects needed in intensive agriculture. This view, sometimes known as the *hydraulic hypothesis,* suggests that the expansion of intensive agriculture created problems such as disputes among landowners and the need to build and operate irrigation canals, dikes, and other technology. To resolve these problems, labor had to be recruited, mobilized, fed, and organized. To fulfill all these functions, people developed centralized bureaucracies.

Archaeologists have challenged the hydraulic hypothesis on a number of points. One criticism is that many of the irrigation projects associated with agricultural civilizations were organized locally in communities without centralized governments. This appears to be the case in early Mesopotamia,

In areas such as the Nile Valley, the shaduf, *a bucket on a long weighted pole, was used to bring water to irrigation channels. The construction and control of water resources may have played an important role in the origin of early states.*

Mesoamerica, South America, and China (Adams, 1966; Chang, 1986). For example, in Tiahuanaca, Peru, the archaeological research demonstrates that individuals constructed their own canals to irrigate their crops long before evidence for any administrative hierarchy or state system appeared.

Another problem with the hydraulic thesis is that in such areas as Egypt and India, the state bureaucracy had developed prior to the initiation of large-scale irrigation. Therefore, instead of large-scale irrigation contributing to the rise of the state, it was actually a later consequence of state development.

Trade and Exchange   Other integrationist perspectives are illustrated by several theories that emphasize the role of trade in the emergence of the state (Rathje, 1971; Wright & Johnson, 1975). In these scenarios, the organizational requirements needed to produce trade items and to manage trade were a major driving force. Increased labor specialization associated with the production of trade items led to a concomitant rise in administrative specialization.

Although it seems clear that trade was important in many early states, to characterize its role as a primary cause in the rise of state society is probably simplistic. Increased understanding of prestate exchange systems and techniques such as trace element analysis have made the picture of early exchange far more complex than was previously thought (Sabloff & Lamberg-Karlovsky, 1975). Inter- and intraregional trade probably predates state formation in many instances, and increased trade may be a consequence of state society in some world areas. However, this is a theory that can be evaluated more thoroughly as techniques for attributing sources of trade items become more available.

Warfare and Circumscription   Anthropologist Robert Carneiro (1970) concentrates on the role of warfare in the formation of early states. Carneiro hypothesizes that population growth in a region with clearly defined boundaries, such as a narrow valley surrounded by high mountains, leads to land shortages, resulting in increased competition and warfare among villages. In this context, efficient military organization is advantageous. Eventually one group becomes powerful enough to dominate. Members of this group become the state administrators, who rule over the less powerful groups. Thus, the state emerges in regions where land is in short supply and competition for scarce resources exists.

Although Carneiro's focus on warfare might make this theory seem more like a conflict theory (see following discussion), it is integrationist in that the state ensures its members both land and security.

Carneiro (1970) suggests that population centers can be confined, or *circumscribed,* by factors other than geography. Circumscription can also occur when an expanding population is surrounded by other powerful societies. This "social circumscription" may prevent weaker groups from migrating into surrounding regions where they can enjoy greater autonomy.

Systems Models   Other integrationist hypotheses are based on *systems model* approaches, which emphasize the requirements of agricultural states to organize large populations; to produce, extract, and exchange economic resources; to maintain military organizations; and to manage information (Flannery, 1972; Wright, 1977). Instead of emphasizing one variable such as irrigation or trade, these theorists attempt to understand the links among agriculture, technology, economy, and other specialized functions in an overall state system. In addition, systems theorists also consider the importance of centralized organization in long-distance trade and the value of a state bureaucracy in mobilizing the military to protect trade routes.

Conflict Theories

Conflict theories of state formation include various formulations, all of which stress the need to protect the interests of the dominant elite from other members of the society. Morton Fried (1967) developed a conflict model that focuses on population growth. According to Fried, as populations grew, vital resources such as land became increasingly scarce, causing various groups to compete for these resources. Ultimately, this competition led to domination by a particular group, which then enjoyed privileged access to land and other economic resources. This dominant group constructed the state to maintain its privileged position. To accomplish this, the state, backed by the ruling elite, used force and repression against subordinate groups. Thus, in Fried's view, the state is coercive and utilizes force to perpetuate the economic and political inequalities in a society. This conflict model is closely related to the Marxist anthropological approaches.

Other researchers have underscored the evidence for stratification and domination by a ruling elite during the earliest phases of state formation. For example, Jonathan Haas (1982) uses data from various world areas to validate conflict theory. Though Haas concedes that the process of state formation included some integrative functions, he concludes that the elites dominated economic resources to the point that they could exert repressive and coercive power over the rest of the population. For example, Haas maintains that the large-scale monument construction of state societies required a ruling elite that coerced peasants to pay tribute and provide labor to the state. The ruling elite could use its control over economic resources to mobilize large-scale labor projects. Haas does not believe that chiefdoms could extract this labor and tribute from their populations.

Archaeologist Elizabeth Brumfiel (1983) approaches conflict from another direction. Drawing on evidence from the Aztec state, she hypothesizes that coercion and repression evolve from political rather than from the economic determinants proposed by Fried and Haas. Brumfiel focuses on the political networks and the elimination of competition utilized by various Aztec leaders to consolidate the authority of one ruling group. During one phase of political competition, the rulers centralized their authority through organizational reforms that reduced the power of subordinate rulers and

nobles. Brumfiel maintains that these manipulations are important preconditions for state formation and coercion.

Criticisms of the Conflict Approach   Some theorists are critical of the different conflict models. Using various archaeological data, Elman Service (1975) and other researchers concede that inequality and conflict are basic aspects of state development, but they emphasize the enormous conflict-reducing capacities of state systems that coordinate and organize diverse groups of people. Service argues that the archaeological record does not indicate any class-based conflict that results in state formation. Following theorists such as Max Weber, the integrationists further argue that state systems become coercive or repressive only when they are weak. Service argues that strong centralized state systems provide benefits to all social groups and thereby gain political legitimacy and authority, which reduce the degree of repression and coercion needed to maintain order. In this sense, Service views state societies as differing only in degree from chiefdom societies.

Some writers have questioned the theoretical underpinning of conflict theories, which assumes that human ambition, greed, and exploitation are universal motivating factors (Tainter, 1990). If such characteristics are common to all societies, why didn't food surpluses, status differentiation, and class conflict appear in all societies? Hunting-and-gathering populations have social mechanisms that maintain egalitarian relationships and hinder individual ambition. If class conflict is a universal explanation of state formation, "How did the human species survive roughly 99 percent of its history without the state?" (Tainter, 1990:35). These factors suggest that the causal reasons for state formation are more complex than intragroup conflict.

Perspectives on State Formation

The reasons for state formation are clearly complex, involving demographic, social, political, economic, environmental, and cultural factors. Certain theories seem to fit conditions in particular world areas but not others. Empirical evaluation of causal factors on the basis of archaeological information is challenging. Not surprisingly, many researchers have called for the combination of integrationist and conflict

The Inca fortress of Sacsahuaman, Peru. Conflict theorists point to the massive labor requirements used to construct monumental structures to underscore the exploitive nature of state societies.

theories to reach a full understanding of the dynamics of state formation. Indeed, the theories surveyed are not, in truth, as simple as they have been presented, and many theorists recognize the importance of other causal factors. On the one hand, it is clear that the organizational and managerial capabilities of state society are worthwhile; on the other, it may be noted that the benefits of stratification are not as advantageous to all members of a population as some integrationist theories hypothesize. It is likely, as Ronald Cohen (1978) has suggested, that multiple roads to statehood exist.

States in Different World Areas

As in the case of agricultural origins, early research on the emergence of state-level societies and civilizations concentrated on a few world areas such as Southwest Asia and Egypt. More recent work, however, has provided insight into a variety of societies throughout the world. It is not possible to survey all of them, but the following discussion provides some idea of the diversity of the civilizations represented.

Civilizations in Southwest Asia

Some of the earliest agricultural civilizations in the world emerged in Southwest Asia. Both the Neolithic revolution and the development of intensive agriculture in the area have been well documented, with evidence dating to about 6,000 years ago. Extensive civilizations arose at the base of the Zagros Mountains in the Mesopotamian valley near the Tigris and Euphrates rivers. One of the earliest civilizations, known as the Sumerian Empire, contained twenty urban centers, such as Uruk, Ur, Ubaid, and Eridu, dating back to 2500 B.C. Some of these cities had populations of more than 10,000 people, covering areas of 6 square kilometers. The rulers of these cities tried to maintain political stability by building walled fortresses for protection from nomadic invaders.

By 2100 B.C., the city of Ur in southern Mesopotamia had become the center of an extensive empire that established a large-scale regional bureaucracy to collect taxes and tribute. The breadth of political control and organization of labor in the Ur Empire is manifested in the *ziggurat,* a large cere-monial center with a monumental structure made up of a series of platforms with a small temple at the top where the priests conducted rituals. In time, however, the costs of maintaining political domination over a vast region, coupled with large-scale population growth, overtaxed Ur's economic and physical resources. In 2000 B.C., the empire collapsed. Archaeologists have concluded that in the 1,000 years following the fall of Ur, the number of settlements in Mesopotamia declined by 40 percent (Tainter, 1990).

Other major empires in northern Mesopotamia included Babylon (2000–323 B.C.) and Assyria (1920–1780 B.C.). These empires established widespread trade routes throughout the Middle East. They maintained political control over extensive rural regions, requiring peasants to provide surplus food and labor for monument construction. Babylon's ruler, Hammurabi, developed the first written legal codes to maintain a standardized system of political rules for the Babylonian Empire.

Other agricultural peoples of Southwest Asia were the Phoenicians, the Arameans, and the Hebrews, who settled the kingdom of Israel in about 1000 B.C. In addition, in the country now known as Iran, the Persian civilization rose to conquer much of the Middle East in the sixth century B.C.

The agricultural civilizations of the Middle East influenced one another through the rapid spread of technology and culture. Contacts among the civilizations were enhanced by the movement of trading ships in the Mediterranean. In addition, long-distance trade by land was conducted throughout the region. For example, via extensive caravan routes the Bedouins carried goods from port cities in the Arabian peninsula across the desert to cities such as Damascus, Jerusalem, and Cairo. Because of these economic and cultural connections, all these civilizations had broad knowledge of metallurgy, highly developed writing and coinage systems, and an extensive network of roads, as well as sophisticated ecclesiastical religions with full-time priests.

Agricultural Civilizations in Africa

When people think of African civilization, they likely think of Egypt. The pyramids, tombs, and temples of ancient Egypt have captured our imagination. The treasures of the pharaohs, such as those of Tutankhamun (fourteenth century B.C.), are spectacular by any standard. State-level society in Egypt can be traced back to the unification of Upper and Lower Egypt in about 3100 B.C. This empire, known as the Old Kingdom, maintained a highly centralized bureaucracy headed by monarchs, called pharaohs, who were believed to possess supernatural authority. Urban areas such as Memphis and Thebes, with populations of more than 100,000, sprang up next to the Nile River, where agricultural production exceeded that of Mesopotamia. In contrast to the Sumerian cities, urban centers such as Thebes and Memphis were cut off from surrounding nomadic tribes by desert regions; thus, they did not have to construct walled fortresses to maintain security. Various Egyptian states continued to exist until the Persians conquered the region in 525 B.C.

Nubia Farther south, the fertile flood plain of the Nile, which was so important to the people of ancient Egypt, was also invaluable to people living to the south in an area traditionally known as Nubia, which today is part of the country of Sudan. Evidence of one of Nubia's earliest civilizations is provided by the site of Kerma, located 500 kilometers north of Khartoum. Kerma may have been the capital of the Nubian state of Kush that is referred to in Egyptian texts of the Middle Kingdom. The town's ruins include a spectacular monumental mud-brick structure called a *deffufa*. Large tumuli (mounds), containing hundreds of human sacrificial victims, and associated settlement areas are also indicative of the town's importance. Although some Egyptian influences are evident at Kerma, it was clearly an indigenous state, the origins of which can be traced back to the second or third millennium B.C.

A number of other civilizations are associated with Nubia, among the best known being Meroe, which flourished between 500 B.C. and A.D. 300. Meroe is located south and east of Kerma, above the fifth cataract of the Nile. Unique characteristics of Meroitic civilization include temples to the lion-god Apedemek, a distinct system of kingship, and a unique form of writing. Used from about the second century B.C. to the fourth century A.D., the Meroitic script remains undeciphered today. Meroe reached its peak after 300 B.C., when trade connections were made with Egypt and the classical Graeco-Roman world. The civilization declined rapidly during the third century A.D.

The East African Coast Coastal East Africa was linked with other areas by an extensive sea trade. Settlements had developed in coastal Kenya and Tanzania by the first century A.D. Arabic and classical Greek references indicate a long period of contact with peoples to the north and east. The arrival of Persian Gulf settlers may date back to the ninth century A.D., with Indian colonists arriving five centuries later. The remains of some of these settlements are quite impressive. Gedi, on the Kenyan coast, covers approximately 45 acres and probably flourished between the thirteenth and the sixteenth centuries A.D. The ruins of the town include impressive stone-walled structures, mosques, and Islamic tombs. Examples of other coastal settlements can be seen at Kilwa and Lamu. These are only a few examples, however; an estimated 173 towns on the coast have stone ruins (Connah, 1987). Studies of these communities have traditionally focused on external trade, but more recent work is stressing the importance of indigenous populations.

Great Zimbabwe One of the best-known states of southeastern Africa is known as Great Zimbabwe (1250–1450). The central city, also known as Great Zimbabwe, was situated near the Zambezi River and contained more than 200 large stone buildings in its center. A temple or ritual enclosure within the city is the largest prehistoric structure found in sub-Saharan Africa. It consists of a great circular building surrounded by walls 24 feet high. These imposing remains were surrounded by less permanent structures made of timber and clay, which archaeologists believe may have housed 18,000 people.

Archaeologist Graham Connah (1987) has described Great Zimbabwe as "the best-known and most ill-used archaeological site in Africa." Early ethnocentric European theories suggested that the site was a copy of the Queen of Sheba's palace, perhaps built by a group of lost white settlers. Poor archaeological work destroyed much of the information that could have been obtained by excavation. More recent work indicates that Great Zimbabwe can best be understood as a continuation of indigenous African cultural traditions. The origins of Great Zimbabwe begin with twelfth-century A.D. Iron Age sites, and the settlement itself gained prominence between the thirteenth and fifteenth centuries. Archaeological data suggest continuities with the Bantu-speaking Shona people, who still occupy the area.

Great Zimbabwe was a center of an extensive empire. Sites with similar wall construction, ceremonial structures, and artifacts are found throughout the modern nations of Zimbabwe and South Africa. The most important economic activities included cultivation of cereal crops, cattle raising, gold mining, and long-distance trade along the East African coast. The artistic achievements of this civilization can be seen in magnificent soapstone sculptures of crocodiles, birds, and other animals.

West Africa   West Africa includes a large area of great environmental and cultural diversity. Many sections have not been well studied by archaeologists. Generally, the region seems to have developed larger and more nucleated settlements than the eastern part of the continent. Increasing trade contacts and political organization in the Senegambia are evidenced by the appearance of *tumuli* (large burial mounds with exotic grave goods) and megaliths. Examples of the latter are the sites of Kerbach and Wasu, which have circles of carefully dressed stones. Unfortunately, many of these sites remain largely unexamined, and no associated living areas have been excavated.

The Yoruba people of southwestern Nigeria developed large urban centers in both the savannas and the rain forest. One forest city, known as Ife, contained a large palace complex and many other monuments with stone and terra cotta sculptures (Connah, 1987). Ife was a major political and ceremonial center where artisans produced bronze castings of religious figures. The artwork suggests a high degree of technological sophistication and craft specialization.

Much more is known about the later West African states of ancient Ghana and Mali, which flourished in the western Sudan. Both of these states are known from Arabic accounts, in which Ghana is mentioned from the eighth to tenth centuries A.D. The origins of Mali may date back almost as far, but Mali reached its apogee much later. It is described by Ibn Battuta in A.D. 1352. The wealth of ancient Mali was well known, and Malian cities such as Timbuktu were familiar to European writers of the period. Unfortunately, although the capitals of ancient Mali and Ghana have tentatively been located, excavation has not yet provided a clear picture of their origins.

A great deal of information has appeared about African states in the past few decades. However, much more work needs to be undertaken. Evidence indicates that trade was an important factor in many areas, but lack of archaeological work in associated settlements and surrounding areas makes it difficult to evaluate what resources may have been important. Many parts of Africa have not been studied at all. For example, very little is known about the culture that produced the spectacular tenth-century A.D. metalworking at Igbo Ukwu, Nigeria. Other regions, such as central Africa, are virtually unknown.

Early Asian Civilizations

Major agricultural states emerged in Asia following the Neolithic period. One developed in the Indus River valley in southern Asia. Two of Asia's largest cities, Harappa and Mohenjo-Daro, developed on the Indus River in what is today the country of Pakistan. Mohenjo-Daro developed about 2,500 years ago and had a population of nearly 35,000. The city was well planned and laid out in a grid, with single-room apartments, multi-room houses, courtyards, and the ancient world's most sophisticated sewer and plumbing system. In the center of the city stood an enormous mound constructed of mud brick, which was protected by fortifications. Close to this ceremonial and political center were a large public bathhouse and a bathing pool that may have been used for ritual purposes (Fagan, 1998).

China   Independent urban centers also developed in China. Beginning about 2,500 years ago, during the Shang dynasty, intensive agricultural production culminated in the emergence of the earliest major urban areas of China, which were situated near the Yellow River. One ancient Shang city, known as Yin, which had large structures such as palaces and platform altars, appears to have been the center of this civilization (Chang, 1975, 1976, 1986). These urban centers were divided into residential, craft production, and royal neighborhoods, each with appropriate structures. The cities had

CRITICAL PERSPECTIVES

CONTACTS BETWEEN TWO WORLDS?

The structural similarities of Egyptian pyramids to those of Native American civilizations have fostered theories about contact between the Near East and the Americas. For example, one idea promoted in the sixteenth century was that the indigenous peoples of the Americas were the descendants of the so-called "Lost Tribes of Israel." Another theory proposed that the ancient continents of Atlantis and Mu connected the continents of America and Europe, enabling people to migrate between the two.

In a speculative book entitled *American Genesis* (1981), Jeffrey Goodman proposes that all populations throughout the world are related to an original population located in California, which

he asserts was the original Garden of Eden. Goodman contends that from this location, humans inhabited the Americas and crossed the continents of Atlantis and Mu to enter Europe and Asia. Zoologist Barry Fell (1980) has proposed that America was settled by colonists from Europe and North Africa some time between 3000 and 1000 B.C. In an even more radical vein, popular writer Erich Von Daniken (1970) has argued that extraterrestrial beings colonized the Americas and left behind ideas for the development of civilization.

Archaeologists and physical anthropologists who have analyzed the question of early contacts between continents are skeptical of these theories. As we saw in

Chapter 7, the consensus regarding the peopling of the Americas is that migrations occurred across the Bering Strait from Asia. All of the dental evidence and skeletal remains indicate that Native Americans have the same physical characteristics as Asians. There have been no archaeological discoveries connecting ancient Israelites or any other societies with those of the Americas. In addition, geologists have not found any evidence of lost continents such as Atlantis and Mu. Certainly, archaeologists have not identified any evidence of spaceships.

The similar pyramid construction in the Near East and the Americas, in addition to other evidence, has led to some interesting hypotheses regarding

walled fortresses designed to keep out nomadic invaders such as Mongol pastoralists from regions farther north. From these early cities, China developed an increasingly large agricultural state incorporating millions of people.

Southeast Asia   A number of agricultural states also emerged in Southeast Asia. Wet-rice cultivation and extensive irrigation projects provided the basis for large state societies such as the Pagan dynasty of Burma (1044–1287), the Ayudhyan dynasty of Thailand (1350–1760), the Khmer Empire of Cambodia (802–1431), and the Majapahit kingdom of Indonesia (1350–1425).

The Khmer civilization was typical of the Southeast Asian empires. It had a large urban center that contained more than 20,000 temples, including the

enormous temple of Angkor Wat. The Khmer rulers, who were considered semidivine, had a bureaucratic staff of 300,000 priests, supported by the tribute of millions of peasants (Sardesai, 1989).

Empires of the Americas

Following the emergence of an agricultural system based on the production of maize, beans, and squash, a series of indigenous complex societies developed in Mesoamerica and South America (see the box "Contacts between Two Worlds?"). In lowland Mesoamerica, a sedentary farming civilization known as the Olmec developed at about 1500 B.C. The Olmec civilization is regarded as the "mother civilization" of Mesoamerica, because many of the features represented provided a template for later

transoceanic contacts. A number of serious scholars of diffusionism have offered hypotheses that are still being evaluated by archaeologists. Anthropologist George Carter (1988) has suggested that plants and animals spread from Asia to America before the age of Columbus. Evidence such as pottery design, artwork, and plants has led some archaeologists to hypothesize pre-Columbian diffusion across the Pacific (Jett, 1978).

Most archaeologists have not collected enough convincing data to confirm these hypotheses. Although similarities exist between the Near East and Native American pyramids, they appear to be based on the universal and practical means of monument construction. There are a finite number of ways to construct a high tower with stone blocks. For this reason, children from widely different cultural settings often construct pyramids when playing with blocks.

Archaeologist Kenneth Feder (1999) reviewed many of the myths, mysteries, and frauds that have been perpetrated about the past. He thinks that many people are prone to believe these speculations rather than accept the scientifically verified evidence. Because the past cannot be experienced directly, people are drawn to speculative accounts of what occurred. This does not mean that anthropologists have absolutely disproved their findings about such phenomena as connections between the two worlds. Anthropologists, however, must rely on the precise evaluation of hypotheses to substantiate their explanations of whether there were any contacts between these areas.

POINTS TO PONDER

1. What ideas have you heard regarding connections between distant civilizations?

2. What types of evidence would convince you of connections between civilizations? How would you go about assessing information about these ideas?

3. What would it take to convince you that extraterrestrial creatures brought civilization to earth?

4. What does an extraterrestrial origin imply about the abilities of humans to develop their own civilizations?

---

societies. Olmec achievements include large-scale monument construction, hieroglyphic writing, and a calendar system. These cultural accomplishments indicate that the Olmec society was highly organized; yet whether it represents state- or chiefdom-level organization is uncertain (Coe, 1977; Service, 1978).

Another major civilization, known as the Maya, arose in lowland Mesoamerica around 300 B.C. After several centuries, the Maya developed a diversified agricultural system that was a combination of slash-and-burn horticulture, intensive horticulture based on hillside terracing, and large-scale irrigation agriculture. The Mayan population has been estimated at 3 million (Coe, Snow, & Benson, 1986). From large ceremonial centers such as Tikal in northern Guatemala and Palenque in Mexico, the Maya maintained extensive trade networks with peoples throughout the region. In these centers an elite class emerged that traced its royal lineages back to various deities. Archaeologists agree that the Mayan centers, with hieroglyphic writing, knowledge of astronomy, calendars, priests, and large monuments, were states.

In the central highland area of Mexico, known as the Valley of Mexico, a major city emerged that became the center of an agricultural empire of perhaps 1 million inhabitants. Most archaeologists believe that this empire eventually incorporated both Mayan lowland and highland ceremonial centers. Known as Teotihuacán, it is estimated to have had a population of more than 150,000 by about A.D. 200 (Sanders & Price, 1968). By A.D. 600, it was the sixth-largest city in the world. Its boundaries extended over an area of about 8 square miles. Teotihuacán

The Pyramid of the Moon looms over the ancient city of Teotihuacán in central Mexico. The city, which may have had a population of 150,000 by A.D. 600, included residential complexes and craft centers, as well as dozens of temples and religious structures.

was divided into quarters and district neighborhoods, with as many as 2,200 apartment houses and 400 crafts workshops. It had more than seventy-five temples, including the Pyramid of the Sun and the Pyramid of the Moon. The Pyramid of the Sun is the largest monument in pre-Columbian America.

The inhabitants of the Valley of Mexico developed a highly effective pattern of cultivation known as *chinampas*. The valley contained many lakes and swamps that were used as gardens. In chinampas cultivation, farmers dug up the muddy bottom from lakes and swamps and planted maize, beans, and squash in this rich soil. This system of cultivation was extremely productive and allowed farmers to plant and harvest several times a year to support dense populations.

The decline of the Teotihuacán civilization, which occurred about A.D. 700, is still being investigated by archaeologists. The evidence from artifacts suggests that the flow of goods into the city from outlying regions was abruptly reduced. The city and its monuments were systematically burned. The population dropped within fifty years to one-fourth its former size (Tainter, 1990). This decline was followed by a period of political fragmentation that enabled other groups, such as the Toltec and eventually the Aztec, to dominate the region politically. The Aztec settled in the city of Tenochtitlán, located at the current site of Mexico City. By 1400, they had established political control over an empire of 25 million people.

Andean Civilizations

The Andean civilizations of Peru—including Moche and Huari (200 B.C.–A.D. 600) in the north, Tiahuanaco (A.D. 200–1100) in the south near Lake Titicaca, and the Incan Empire (1476–1534)—developed intensive agriculture based on elaborate systems of irrigation and canals. The Andean peoples, like the Mesoamericans, relied on mixed patterns of agriculture, involving slash-and-burn cultivation in some areas and more intensive agriculture in others, to support large urban centers. The major food crops were maize, potatoes, and a plant called quinoa, the seeds of which are ground for flour. The most important domesticated animals were the llama, which provided both meat and transportation, and the alpaca, which produced wool for textile production.

As with Teotihuacán, Andean cities became the centers of regional states. The empire of Huari dominated almost the entire central Andean region and developed locally based urban centers to control outlying provinces. In addition, vast trading links produced interconnections with many regions. Tiahuanaco controlled a large rural area characterized by massive construction and irrigation projects that required large amounts of state-recruited labor. These empires collapsed by A.D. 1100 (Tainter, 1990). Later, the Inca settled in the urban capital of Cuzco and consolidated imperial domain over all of modern-day Peru and adjacent areas. Supported by a well-organized militia and an efficient state organization dominated by a divine emperor, the Inca ruled over a population of 6 million.

The Collapse of State Societies

Perhaps no aspect of early agricultural states is more intriguing than the question of why they ceased to function. As discussed in the chapter opening, no agricultural states exist today. Lost ruins, palaces hidden in tropical forests, and temples buried beneath shifting sand captivate the attention of archaeologists and the public alike. These images grip our attention all the more because of the lusterless prospect that the downfall of these ancient societies offers insight into the limitations of our own civilization. As Joseph Tainter (1990:2) notes: "Whether or not collapse was the most outstanding event of ancient history, few would care for it to become the most significant event of the present era."

In looking at their demise, it is important to note that many early agricultural states were exceedingly successful. They flourished in many different world areas for hundreds of years. The ancient Egyptian Old Kingdom, which spanned a period of almost 1,000 years, is particularly notable, but many lasted longer than the 200-odd years the United States has been in existence. The apparent success of these states makes the reasons for their collapse all the more enigmatic. What accounts for the loss of centralized authority; the decline in stratification and social differentiation; the interruption of trade; and the fragmentation of large political units that seem to document the end of many different civilizations? These features extend beyond the end of specific governments or political systems; rather, they seem to reflect the breakdown of entire cultural systems.

Reasons for Collapse

In examining the downfall of complex societies, writers have posited many different theories. Among the earliest were notions that collapse was somehow an innate, inevitable aspect of society, to be likened to the aging of a biological organism. Plato, for example, wrote that "since all created things must decay, even a social order . . . cannot last forever, but will decline" (quoted in Tainter, 1990:74). Although romantically appealing, such interpretations lack explanatory value and cannot be evaluated by empirical observation.

More recent scholars have sought a more precise understanding of the factors that contributed to collapse. Many theories have focused on the depletion of key resources as a result of human mismanagement or climatic change. In an agricultural state, conditions that interfered with or destroyed the society's ability to produce agriculture surplus would have had serious consequences. If the society was unable to overcome this depletion, collapse would result. Reasons such as this have been posited as contributing to the collapse of complex societies such as Mesopotamia (Adams, 1981), Egypt (Butzer, 1984), and Mesoamerica (Haas, 1982). (The role of environmental degradation in the collapse of one society is examined in more detail in the box "The Downfall of the Moche.")

In some cases, researchers have suggested that resource depletion may be the result of sudden catastrophic events such as earthquakes, volcanic eruptions, or floods, which have an impact on agricultural lands as well as other resources. One of the most well-known theories of this kind links the destruction of Minoan civilization in the Mediterranean to the eruption of the Santorini volcano on the island of Thera (Marinatos, 1939).

Other theories have suggested that conditions within societies have led to collapse. Many of these theories stress the tension or conflict resulting from social stratification. For example, mismanagement, excessive taxes, demands for food and labor, or other forms of exploitation by a ruling class are seen as instigating revolts or uprisings by the disaffected peasant class. Without the support of the peasants, the political system cannot function and the state collapses (Yoffe, 1979; Guha, 1981; Lowe, 1985).

Alternatively, some researchers have viewed collapse as the result of the societies' failure to respond to changing conditions. For example, Elman Service (1960:97) argued: "The more specialized and adapted a form in a given evolutionary stage, the smaller its potential for passing to the next stage." Underlying this interpretation is the assumption that successful adaptation to a particular environmental or cultural setting renders a society inflexible and unable to adapt to changing conditions.

CRITICAL PERSPECTIVES

THE DOWNFALL OF THE MOCHE

By 200 B.C. a number of small state-level societies had emerged in northwestern South America along the coast and hinterland of present-day Peru. The best known is that of the Moche, which was centered in the Moche and nearby Chicama valleys. At its peak the state controlled satellite communities in a number of neighboring valleys, eventually extending its influence hundreds of miles to the north and south (Donnan & McClelland, 1979).

The archaeological record provides a rich testament to the wealth and power of the Moche. Ceremonial complexes, such as those near the modern city of Trujillo, include adobe-brick temple platforms, pyramids, and associated room complexes that may have served as palaces. In 1987, the riches found in an undisturbed tomb of a Moche warrior-priest near the modern village of Sipán led some to dub

the discovery "a King Tut of the New World." Although the Moche possessed no writing system, the interpretation of the Sipán tomb and other Moche sites is aided by exquisite depictions of Moche life on pottery vessels.

The Moche kingdom flourished for almost 800 years. However, by 600 A.D., the classic Moche ceremonial centers were abandoned, and power shifted to other areas. Archaeological excavations and recent photographs taken by the space shuttle *Challenger* have provided insights into what may have caused this collapse (Moseley & Richardson, 1992). Excavations during the 1970s provided part of the answer to the Moche mystery. Prior to that time Moche ceremonial structures were known, but no one had found any settlements, leading archaeologists to believe that the populations that had built the monumental structures had lived

elsewhere. Deep excavations at Moche sites during 1972, however, revealed residences, civic buildings, and high-status cemeteries buried under almost 30 feet of sand—evidence that the Moche centers had been destroyed at their peak of prosperity.

Interpretations of the archaeological findings have been aided by recent insights into the environmental conditions that may have ravaged the Moche sites and buried them with sand. Between A.D. 500 and 600, the Moche region experienced devastating rainfall and large-scale flooding characteristic of a climatic phenomenon today known as *El Niño*. During normal climatic conditions, a cold stream of water known as the Humboldt or Peru Current flows through the Pacific Ocean along the west coast of South America. This cold water limits rainfall along the coast, producing the New World's driest

In this setting, less complex societies with greater flexibility overthrew older states.

Anthropologist Joseph Tainter notes in a survey that most of the models that have been presented focus on specific case studies, not on the understanding of collapse as a general phenomenon. He points out that most researchers assume that the decline in complexity associated with collapse is a catastrophe: "An end to the artistic and literary features of civilization, and the umbrella of service and protection that an administration provides, are seen as fearful events, truly paradise lost" (Tainter, 1990:197). Tainter argues that, in reality,

collapse represents a logical choice in the face of declining returns. When people's investment in complexity fails to produce benefits, they opt for disintegration.

Theories concerning the collapse of states can be evaluated in light of ethnographic, historical, and archaeological evidence. Upon surveying information from different states, it appears that reasons for collapse are exceedingly complex. The specific manifestation varies in individual settings, just as the specific features that define states differ. Adequate appraisal is dependent on the existence of a great deal of information about the society under study,

desert in northern Chile and Peru. During an *El Niño* event, which may last 18 months, this pattern suddenly changes, with disastrous consequences. Warm water flows along the coast, and the normally arid coastland is beset with torrential rains and flooding, while severe droughts plague the usually wetter highlands of Peru and Bolivia. Archaeological evidence indicates that flood waters, possibly from one or more *El Niño* events, destroyed Moche settlements and stripped as much as 15 feet from some sites. Although the Moche survived the flooding, by A.D. 600 sand dunes engulfed irrigation canals, fields, and architecture.

Recent studies of photographs taken by the space shuttle *Challenger* in 1983 and earlier satellite photos have helped explain the dune encroachment (Moseley & Richardson, 1992). The high-altitude photographs of the Peruvian coast link the formation of new beach ridges and

dune systems to earthquakes and *El Niño*. The *Challenger* photographs indicate that a new beach ridge formed between 1970 and 1975. The ridge's appearance was linked to the Rio Santa earthquake of 1970, which caused massive landslides that dumped huge amounts of earth into the dry river valleys. The torrential rains of the *El Niño* event of 1972–1973 carried this debris into the ocean, where strong currents deposited it in a new beach ridge. The ridge, in turn, provided the sand for the dunes that swept inland.

The available evidence seems to support the theory that *El Niño* events, possibly exacerbated by earthquakes, may have contributed to the downfall of the Moche state. Additional evidence suggests that there may have been periods of extreme drought prior to A.D. 600. The combination of these environmental disasters beyond human control could have seriously undermined

the state's ability to produce the agricultural surplus it needed to survive. In the absence of any means of overcoming these problems, the downfall of the Moche state may have been inevitable.

POINTS TO PONDER

1. What other evidence could be used to evaluate this interpretation of the collapse of the Moche state?

2. Even if excellent evidence for environmental disasters is uncovered, can other reasons for the collapse of the Moche be ruled out?

3. Is it likely that it will be possible to create general models that will explain the collapse of societies in all cultural and environmental settings?

4. Do you think that study of ancient states offers any insights into problems facing modern societies?

including its technological capabilities, population, agricultural yields, and climatic conditions in the region. The difficulty involved in assessing competing models is perhaps best illustrated by the fact that very different theories have often been used to explain the decline of the same society.

SUMMARY

During the Neolithic, people in many regions of the world developed techniques such as irrigation, plow cultivation, and the use of fertilizers, which allowed fields to be cultivated year after year. These intensive agricultural practices produced food surpluses, which contributed to further changes in human subsistence and political organization. Approximately 5,500 years ago in some world areas, these developments led to the appearance of complex societies frequently called civilizations—a term that V. Gordon Childe used to indicate the presence of a complex set of traits, including population concentration in cities, agricultural surpluses, monumental architecture, craft specialization, stratified social organization, and institutionalized political authority. Today, anthropologists generally focus on the role and function of specific features and are less concerned with overarching definitions.

One aspect of early societies that interests anthropologists is the appearance of an institutionalized form of government, the state, run by full-time officials. Early states were characterized by a great deal of social inequality. The ruler's position was based on the control of agricultural surpluses and was sanctioned by religious institutions and symbols.

Archaeologists can draw on many sources of information to reconstruct the nature of early agricultural states. They may be able to use written records, a source of information that researchers working on earlier periods did not have. Many different kinds of archaeological information, including settlement patterns, site features, and artifacts, are also available. Differences in these variables may provide clues to the origins, extent, and structure of early state systems.

A question of interest to many anthropologists has been the origin of political complexity and the rise of agricultural states. The many different theories that have been proposed can be divided into two major positions: the integrationist and the conflict perspectives. Integrationist theorists view the early state as having functioned to provide benefits to all members of a society. The conflict theorists believe that the state was created to enforce status divisions and primarily benefited the ruling class. Reasons for state formation probably varied in different cultural settings and incorporated elements of both integrationist and conflict theories.

Archaeologists have been conducting research in different areas of the world, including the Americas, Africa, and Asia, in order to test their models of state formation. These studies have provided many examples of the origins of the state and revealed a variety of differences in their timing, characteristics, and cultural expressions.

QUESTIONS TO THINK ABOUT

1. Examine the criteria that were used by V. Gordon Childe to define civilization. What are the problems with his definition?

2. What is meant by central place theory? Using specific examples, discuss how this concept is useful for understanding the nature of ancient agricultural states.

3. Why is the presence of monumental architecture considered to be a good indication of the presence of a stratified society?

4. What techniques can archaeologists use to recognize evidence of trade and exchange in ancient civilizations? What role did long-distance exchange play in the emergence of social status and social complexity?

5. Using specific examples, explain the differences between integrationist and conflict theories of the origins of state formation. Which of these perspectives do you feel provides a more realistic interpretation, and why?

6. Define specialization as it applies to the evolution of ancient states. When does specialization first appear, and how can it be recognized archaeologically? Discuss the difference between specialization as seen in state societies and specialization in Neolithic societies.

KEY TERMS

agricultural states
central place theory
chiefdom
conflict theories

hieroglyphic writing
ideographic writing
  systems
integrationist theories

state
trace element analysis
tribes

INTERNET EXERCISES

1. Look at the article titled "Empires in the Dust" (Collapse of Bronze Age Cultures in 2,200 B.C.) **http://www.worldagesarchive.com/Referen ce_Links/Empires_in_the_Dust.htm**. What conclusions about environmental change are reviewed here and what possible implications may they have for our current civilizations?

2. Look at the following websites:

   http://www.bealenet.com/~bluesart/ marx/conflict.html

   http://www.umsl.edu/~rkeel/280/ critical.html

http://www.libstudy.hawaii.edu/ manicas/pdf_files/new%20courses/ ConflictTheory.pdf.

How is Marxism related to conflict theory as related in this chapter?

3. Read the article "Patterns of State Collapse and Reconstruction in Central Africa: Reflections on the Crisis in the Great Lakes" from the African Studies Quarterly. It can be found at **http://web.africa.ufl.edu/asq/v1/3/2.htm**. How does the explanation it offers compare to the reasons for state collapse proposed in this chapter?

SUGGESTED READINGS

CONNAH, GRAHAM. 1987. *African Civilizations: Precolonial Cities and States in Tropical Africa: An Archaeological Perspective*. Cambridge: Cambridge University Press. A survey of complex societies in sub-Saharan Africa by one of the leading Africanists, this volume provides a survey of the limited archaeological information available about this large, diverse world area.

DAVIES, W. V. 1987. *Egyptian Hieroglyphs*. Berkeley: University of California Press. A basic introduction to one of the world's oldest writing systems, this volume provides a brief, readable introduction to the concepts of hieroglyphic writing, its development, its cultural setting, and its translation by archaeologists. This book is one of a series of volumes by the University of California Press surveying early writing systems.

SASSON, JACK M. (Ed.). 1994. *Civilizations of the Ancient Near East*. New York: Charles Scribner's. This authoritative compendium, including chapters by 189 contributors, surveys many of the key discoveries and interpretations that have refined our understanding of some of the world's earliest civilizations.

TAINTER, JOSEPH A. 1990. *The Collapse of Complex Societies*. New York: Cambridge University Press. A seminal attempt to provide a general model of collapse in complex societies. Although Tainter aimed at addressing his own theoretical position, the volume provides an excellent survey and critique of previous work on the subject.

TRIGGER, BRUCE. 1993. *Early Civilizations: Ancient Egypt in Context*. Cairo: American University in Cairo Press. A very readable survey of early states; broader in scope than the title suggests.

CHAPTER

10

Culture

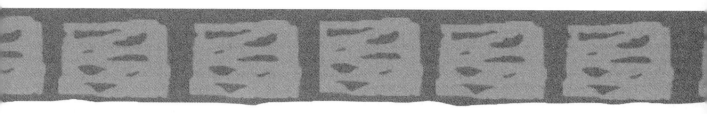

CHAPTER QUESTIONS

- What are the basic characteristics of the term *culture* as discussed by anthropologists?

- What are the basic components of culture?

- How does culture lead to both differences and similarities among people in widely separated societies?

The Characteristics of Culture

As we stated in Chapter 2, culture is a fundamental element within the discipline of anthropology. We noted that, in everyday use, most people in this country use the word culture to refer to "high culture"—Shakespeare's works, Beethoven's symphonies, Michelangelo's sculptures, gourmet cooking, imported wines, and so on. E. B. Tylor, the first

professional anthropologist, proposed a definition of culture that includes all of human experience:

> *Culture . . . is that complex whole which includes knowledge, belief, arts, morals, law, custom, and any other capabilities and habits acquired by man as a member of society. (1871)*

This view suggests that culture includes tools, weapons, fire, agriculture, animal domestication, metallurgy, writing, the steam engine, glasses, airplanes, computers, penicillin, nuclear power, rock-and-roll, video games, designer jeans, religion, political systems, subsistence patterns, science, sports, and social organizations. In Tylor's view, culture includes all aspects of human activity, from the fine arts to popular entertainment, from everyday behavior to the development of sophisticated technology. It contains the plans, rules, techniques, designs, and policies for living.

This nineteenth-century definition of culture has some terminology that would not be acceptable to modern anthropologists. For example, it relies on the word "man" to refer to what we currently would refer to as "humanity." Most anthropologists today would accept a broad conception of **culture** as a shared way of life that includes values, beliefs, and norms transmitted within a particular society from generation to generation.

Notice that this definition includes the term *society*. In general terms, **society** refers to a particular group of animals within a specific territory. In particular, it refers to the patterns of relationships among the animals within this definite territory. Biologists often refer to certain types of insects, herd animals, and social animals such as monkeys and apes as living in societies.

In the past, anthropologists attempted to make a simple distinction between culture and society. Society was said to consist of the patterns of relationships among people within a specified territory, and culture was viewed as the byproducts of those relationships. This view of society as distinguishable from culture was derived from ethnographic studies of small-scale societies. In such societies, people within a specific territory were believed to share a common culture. However, contemporary anthropologists have found this notion of shared culture to be too simplistic and crude. For example, in most countries where modern anthropologists conduct ethnographic research, the societies are extremely complex and consist of distinctive groups that maintain different cultural traditions. Thus, this simple distinction between society and culture is too artificial for modern anthropologists. And even in small-scale societies, the conception that all of these people share a collective "culture" is also too simplistic. As we shall see in the next chapter, this crude conception of a collectively shared culture often resulted in gross stereotypes and vulgar generalizations of groups of people and their behavior.

Many anthropologists have adopted the hybrid term *sociocultural system*—a combination of the terms society (or social) and culture—to refer to what used to be called "society" or "culture." As we shall see in later chapters, many anthropologists use the term sociocultural system as the basic conceptual framework for analyzing ethnographic research.

Culture Is Learned

The unique capacity for culture in the human species depends on learning. We do not inherit our culture through our genes in the way we inherit our physical characteristics, as we discussed in Chapter 2. Instead, we obtain our culture through the process of enculturation. **Enculturation** is the process of social interaction through which people learn and acquire their culture. We will study this process in more detail in the next chapter. Humans acquire their culture both consciously, through formal learning, and unconsciously, through informal interaction. Anthropologists distinguish among several types of learning. One type is known as **situational learning,** or trial-and-error learning, in which an organism adjusts its behavior on the basis of direct experience. In other words, a stimulus is presented in the environment, and the animal

responds and receives reinforcement or feedback from the response, either in the form of a reward (pleasure) or punishment (pain). Psychologists refer to this type of learning as *conditioning.*

Humans and many other animals, even single-celled organisms, learn situationally and modify their behavior in different situations. For example, dogs can learn a variety of tricks through rewards such as treats given after the completion of the trick. In some cases, human behavior can be modified through conditioning. Overeating, gambling, and smoking can sometimes be reduced through psychological techniques involving rewarding new forms of behavior.

Another form of learning, called **social learning,** occurs when one organism observes another organism respond to a stimulus and then adds that response to its own collection of behaviors. Thus, the organism need not have the direct experience; it can observe how others behave and then imitate or avoid these behaviors. Obviously, humans learn by observing classmates, teachers, parents, friends, and the media. Other social animals also learn in this manner. For example, wolves learn hunting strategies by observing pack members. Similarly, chimpanzees observe other chimps fashioning twigs with which to hunt termites and then imitate these behaviors.

Symbols and Symbolic Learning

The form of learning that is uniquely human and that provides the basis for the capacity for culture is known as **symbolic learning.** Symbolic learning is based on our linguistic capacity and ability to use and understand **symbols**—arbitrary meaningful units or models we use to represent reality. Symbols are the conceptual devices that we use to communicate abstract ideas to one another. We communicate these symbols to one another through language. For example, children can learn to distinguish and name coins such as pennies, nickels, and quarters and use this money as a symbolic medium of exchange. The linguistic capacity that we are born with gives us the unique ability to make and use symbolic distinctions.

Humans learn most of their behaviors and concepts through symbolic learning. We do not have to

These photos illustrate three types of learning: The pigeon (above left) is being conditioned to behave in a specific manner, an example of situational learning. The chimpanzee (above right) is using a tool—a crumbled leaf—as a sponge for drinking water; the chimp learned this behavior by observing other chimps, an example of social learning. The teacher (left) is communicating ideas to a child, an example of symbolic learning.

depend on situational learning or observations of others to perceive and understand the world and one another. We have the uniquely human ability to abstract the essence of complex events and patterns, creating images through symbols and bestowing meaning on them.

Through the ability to symbolize, humans can learn and create meanings and transmit these meanings to one another effectively. Parents do not have to depend on direct experience to teach children. As children mature, they can learn abstract rules and concepts involving symbolic communication. When we study mathematics, we learn to manipulate abstract symbols. As you read this textbook, you are learning new ideas based on symbols transmitted to you through English words in ink on a page. Symbolic learning has almost infinite possibilities in terms of absorbing and using information in creative ways. Most of our learning as humans is based on this symbolic-learning process.

Symbols and Signs Symbols are arbitrary units of meaning, in contrast to **signs,** which are directly associated with concrete physical items or activities. Many nonhuman animals can learn signs. For example, a dog can learn to associate the ringing of a bell (a physical activity) with drinking water. Hence, both humans and other animals can learn signs and apply them to different sorts of activities or to concrete items.

Symbols are different from signs in that they are not associated with any direct, concrete item or physical activity; they are much more abstract. A symbol's meaning is not always obvious. (See the box "Key National Symbols.") However, many symbols are powerful and often trigger unconscious

CRITICAL PERSPECTIVES

KEY NATIONAL SYMBOLS

Societies throughout the world have drawn upon important cultural symbols as a means of distinguishing their community from others. Some of these cultural symbols are secular or nonreligious in meaning, whereas others have religious connotations. Anthropologist Victor Turner (1967) described symbols as "multivocal," suggesting that they have multiple meanings for people within a society. He also said that symbols have the characteristic of "condensation"—the ability to unify many things and actions into a single formation.

National symbols such as flags have the potential for expressing deep-felt emotions in condensed forms. Flags, with their great public visibility, have been an extremely important symbolic medium of political communication throughout the centuries. In U.S. society, the flag is a key secular symbol reflecting deeply felt community ties. A number of legal battles have been waged over the so-called "desecration" of the U.S. flag. For example, members of the Jehovah's Witnesses religious sect refuse on principle to salute the flag, for which they have been prosecuted. Political protesters, such as those opposed to the Vietnam War in the 1960s, tried to dramatize their cause by burning the flag or otherwise defacing it. In the late 1980s, the issue found its way to the Supreme Court, which ruled that a protester who had burned the flag at the 1988 Republican National Convention

was merely expressing free speech. The Court later ruled that a law protecting the flag from desecration was unconstitutional. This issue remains controversial for many U.S. citizens, and there is a political movement to amend the Constitution to protect the flag.

The recent controversy over the flying of the Confederate flag over the South Carolina state house also demonstrates the potency of symbols and the different meanings evoked by symbols for different peoples. Some white southerners view the Confederate flag as part of their cultural heritage, while many African Americans understand the flag as a symbol of slavery.

Various religious symbols have produced fundamental meanings and metaphors for many countries throughout the world. For example, the symbols associated with the Virgin Mary in Roman Catholicism have developed into national symbols of unity for some countries.

In Mexico, the symbolism associated with the Virgin of Guadalupe has served to unify different ethnic communities (Wolf, 1958; Kurtz, 1982; Ingham, 1986). After Spain had colonized the indigenous Indian communities of Mexico beginning in the sixteenth century, many of the Indians, such as the Aztecs, were converted to Roman Catholicism. According to Mexican tradition, the Virgin Mary appeared before a Christianized Indian, Juan Diego,

A portrait of the Madonna. Murillo, Bartolomeo Esteban. "The Immaculate Conception of Excorial." Museo del Prado, Madrid, Spain. Scala/Art Resource. N.Y.

in 1531, in the form of a brown-skinned Indian woman.

Tepeyac, the place where the apparition appeared, was the sacred site of an Aztec fertility goddess, Tonantzin, known as Our Lady Mother. Aztec cosmology contained many notions regarding the virgin births of deities. For example, Huitzilopochtli, the deity believed to have led the Aztecs to their home in Tenochtitlán, had been miraculously conceived by the Aztec mother goddess. Thus, Aztec religious beliefs regarding Tonantzin somewhat paralleled Catholic teachings about Mary.

During the Virgin's appearance, she commanded Juan Diego to inform the bishop of Mexico that a shrine should be built at the spot. The Shrine of the Virgin of Guadalupe is today a huge church, or basilica. Over the altar, Juan Diego's cloak hangs, embossed with the image of a young, dark-skinned woman wearing an open crown and flowing gown, standing on a half-moon that symbolizes the Immaculate Conception.

The Virgin of Guadalupe became a potent symbol that has endured throughout generations, assuming different meanings for different social groups. To the Indians of Mexico, the Virgin embodies both Tonantzin and the newer Catholic beliefs and aspirations concerning eternal salvation. To the *mestizos*—people with mixed Spanish and Indian ancestry—she represents the supernatural mother who gave them a place in both the indigenous and colonial worlds. To Mexicans in general, the Virgin represents the symbolic resolution of the many conflicts and problems that resulted from violent encounters between the Europeans and the local population (Kurtz, 1982). The Guadalupe shrine has become one of the most important pilgrimage sites in Mexico.

The Virgin Mary has also played an important symbolic role in a European country that has undergone major political and social transformations. Until recently Poland was a socialist country under the indirect control of the former Soviet Union. Beginning in the 1980s, however, the Polish people, who were organized through a union-based political party known as Solidarity, began to challenge the Communist Party that ruled Poland. During Communist Party rule in Poland, religious symbolism and Roman Catholicism, deeply rooted in Polish history, were to some degree repressed by the government.

One of the most important symbols of Polish Catholicism is a famous picture of the Virgin Mary in a Paulite monastery. According to Polish tradition, the picture, known as the Black Madonna of Czestochowa, was painted by St. Luke the Evangelist, one of the authors of the Christian New Testament, on a piece of cypress wood from the table used by Mary. After the picture was placed in the monastery, where it was revered by many Polish Catholics, a party of robbers raided the monastery for treasures in 1430 and slashed the image of the Madonna with a sword. Although painstakingly restored, the picture still bears the scars of that destruction, with sword slashes on the cheek of the Black Madonna.

As Poland was divided among different countries such as Sweden, Germany, Turkey, and Russia during various periods, the image of the Black Madonna served as a symbol of Polish religious and national unity. It became one of the most important pilgrimage sites for Polish Catholicism. Millions of pilgrims from Poland and other European countries made their way to the Czestochowa shrine every year to take part in various religious rites. When the Solidarity movement in Poland challenged the Communist Party during the 1980s, leaders such as Lech Walesa wore an image of the Black Madonna on their suit lapels. Pope John Paul II visited the Black Madonna shrine and placed a golden rose there to help resuscitate religiosity in Poland. Thus, the Black Madonna image served to unify Polish Catholics in their struggle against the antireligious stance of the communist authorities.

National symbols, whether religious or secular, have played extremely important roles in mobilizing people and countries in times of transition and struggle. These national symbols reflect the deep feelings that tie peoples together in what some scholars have referred to as "imagined communities" (Anderson, 1983). Regardless of whether these communities are imagined or not, such symbols are key aspects of culture that are likely to be retained by societies worldwide in the twenty-first century.

POINTS TO PONDER

1. What kinds of feelings and emotions do you have when you hear your national anthem played as you watch your flag?

2. Can you think of any other examples of national symbols that have played a role in world history or politics?

3. Are there any disadvantages of national symbols that have influenced various societies?

4. Could international symbols be developed that would draw all of humanity together?

stimuli of behaviors or emotional states. For example, the designs and colors of the flags of different countries represent symbolic associations with abstract ideas and concepts. In some flags the color red may refer to blood, whereas in others it may symbolize revolution. In many countries, the desecration of the national flag, itself a symbol, is considered a crime. When the symbols associated with particular abstract ideas and concepts that are related to the national destiny of a society are violated, powerful emotions may be aroused.

The ability of symbolization, creating symbols and bestowing meaning on them, enhances our learning capacities as humans in comparison with other types of animals. Anthropologist Leslie White maintained that the most distinctive feature of being human is the ability to create symbols:

> It is impossible for a dog, horse, or even an ape, to have any understanding of the meaning of the sign of the cross to a Christian, or of the fact that black (white among the Chinese) is the color of mourning. No chimpanzee or laboratory rat can appreciate the difference between Holy water and distilled water, or grasp the meaning of Tuesday, 3, or sin. (1971:23–24)

Symbols and Culture   The human capacity for culture is based on our linguistic and cognitive ability to symbolize. Culture is transmitted from generation to generation through symbolic learning and language. (In Chapter 12 we discuss the relationship between language and culture.) Through the transmission of culture, we learn how to subsist, how to socialize, how to govern our society, and what gods to worship. Culture is the historical accumulation of symbolic knowledge that is shared by a society. This symbolic knowledge is transmitted through learning, and it can change rapidly from parents to children and from one generation to the next. Generally, however, people in societies go to great lengths to conserve their culture and symbolic traditions. The persistence of cultural and symbolic traditions is as widespread as cultural change.

Culture Is Shared

Culture consists of the shared practices and understandings within a society. To some degree, culture is based on shared meanings that are to some extent "public" and thus beyond the mind of any individual (Geertz, 1973). Some of this culture exists before the birth of an individual into the society, and it may continue (in some form) beyond the death of any particular individual. These publicly shared meanings provide designs or recipes for surviving and contributing to the society. On the other hand, culture is also *within the mind* of individuals. For example, we mentioned that children learn the symbolic meanings of money in coins of different denominations and bills. The children figure out the meanings of money by observing practices and learning the various symbols that are public. However, the child is not just a passive assimilator of that cultural knowledge. Cognitive anthropologists such as Roy D'Andrade and Naomi Quinn emphasize **schemas,** or cultural models that are internalized by individuals and have an influence on decision making and behavior. They emphasize how culture is acquired by and modeled as schemas within individual minds and can motivate, shape, and transform the symbols and meanings (Quinn & Holland, 1987; D'Andrade, 1989, 1995).

It is apparent that cultural understandings are not shared equally by all members of a society. Even in small-scale societies, culture is shared differently by males and females or by young and old. Some individuals in these societies have a great deal of knowledge regarding agriculture, medical practices, or religious beliefs; those beliefs and knowledge are not equally distributed. In our complex industrialized society, culture consists of a tremendous amount of information and knowledge regarding technology and other aspects of society. Different people learn different aspects of culture, such as repairing cars or television sets, understanding nuclear physics or federal tax regulations, or composing music. Hence, to some extent culture varies from person to person, from subgroup to subgroup, from region to region, from age group to age group, and from gender to gender. Anthropologists today note how culture is "contested," referring to how people question and may fundamentally disagree and struggle over the specifics of culture. Yet despite this variation, some common cultural understandings allow members of society to adapt, to communicate, and to interact with one another. Without some of these common understandings, a society could not exist.

The Components of Culture

At the beginning of the chapter we defined culture as a shared way of life. Within this broad definition, anthropologists have tried to isolate the key elements that constitute culture. Two of the most basic components are material and nonmaterial culture.

Material culture consists of the physical products of human society (ranging from weapons to clothing styles), whereas **nonmaterial culture** refers to the intangible products of human society (values, beliefs, and norms). As we discussed in Chapter 2, the earliest traces of material culture are stone tools associated with early hominids. They consist of a collection of very simple choppers, scrapers, and flakes. Modern material culture consists of all the physical objects that a contemporary society produces or retains from the past, such as tools, streets, buildings, homes, toys, medicines, and automobiles. Cultural anthropologists investigate the material culture of the societies they study, and they also examine the relationship between the material culture and the nonmaterial culture: the values, beliefs, and norms that represent the patterned ways of thinking and acting within a society. Archaeologists, meanwhile, are primarily concerned with interpreting past societies by studying their material remains.

Values

Values are the standards by which members of a society define what is good or bad, holy or unholy, beautiful or ugly. They are assumptions that are widely shared within the society. Values are a central aspect of the nonmaterial culture of a society and are important because they influence the behavior of the members of a society. The predominant values in the United States include individual achievement and success, efficiency, progress, material comfort, equality, freedom, science, rationality, nationalism, and democracy, along with many other assumptions (Williams, 1970; Bellah et al., 1985). Although these values might seem normal to Americans, they are not accepted values in all societies. For instance, just as American society tends to emphasize individualism and self-reliance, other societies, such as Japan, stress cooperation and community interest instead.

Beliefs

Beliefs held by the members of a society are another aspect of nonmaterial culture. **Beliefs** are cultural conventions that concern true or false assumptions, specific descriptions of the nature of the universe and humanity's place in it. Values are generalized notions of what is good and bad; beliefs are more specific and, in form at least, have more content. "Education is good" is a fundamental value in American society, whereas "Grading is the best way to evaluate students" is a belief that reflects assumptions about the most appropriate way to determine educational achievement.

Most people in a given society assume that their beliefs are rational and firmly grounded in common sense. As we saw in Chapter 1, however, some beliefs may not necessarily be scientifically valid. For example, our commonsense understandings may lead us to conclude that the earth is flat and stationary. When we look around us, the plane of the earth looks flat, and we don't feel as if the earth is rotating around the sun. Yet our commonsense beliefs about these notions are contradicted by the knowledge gained by the scientific method.

Many anthropologists refer to the worldview of a particular society. A **worldview** consists of various beliefs about the nature of reality and provides people with a more or less consistent orientation toward the world. Worldviews help people interpret and understand the reality surrounding them. In some societies, such as the traditional Azande of East Africa or the traditional Navajos of the southwest region of the United States, witchcraft is believed to cause illnesses in some unfortunate individuals. In other societies, such as that of Canada, medical doctors diagnose illness by using the scientific method, and the causes of illness are attributed to viruses, bacteria, or other material forces. Anthropologists might say that this is a result of different worldviews among these different societies.

Some beliefs may be combined into an ideology. An **ideology** consists of cultural symbols and beliefs that reflect and support the interests of specific groups within society (Yengoyan, 1986). Particular groups promote ideologies for their own ends as a means of maintaining and justifying economic and political authority. Different economic and political systems—capitalism, socialism, communism, democratic institutions, and totalitarian governments—are based on differing ideologies. For example, leaders in capitalist societies maintain the ideology that individuals should be rewarded monetarily based on their own self-interest. In contrast, leaders in socialist societies use the ideology that emphasizes the well-being of the community or society over individual self-interest.

In some societies, especially complex societies with many different groups, an ideology may produce **cultural hegemony,** the ideological control by one dominant group over beliefs and values. For example, one dominant ethnic group may impose its cultural beliefs on subordinate groups. In the United States, the dominant ethnic group in the eighteenth and nineteenth centuries, white Anglo-Saxon Protestants, was able to impose its language, cultural beliefs, and practices on the Native Americans in U.S. society. In many areas of the world, minority groups are often forced to accept the ideologies of the economically and politically dominant groups through the process of cultural hegemony.

Norms

Norms—a society's rules of right and wrong behavior—are another aspect of nonmaterial culture. Norms are shared rules or guidelines that define how people "ought" to behave under certain circumstances. Norms are generally connected to the values, beliefs, worldviews, and ideologies of a society. For example, we have seen that in American culture individualism is a basic value that is reflected in the prevailing worldview. Not surprisingly, then, American society has many norms based on the notion of individual initiative and responsibility. Individuals are admonished to work for their own self-interest and not to become a burden to their families or community. Older Americans, if self-sufficient, are not supposed to live with their children. Likewise, self-sufficient young adults beyond a certain age are not supposed to live with their parents. These individualistic norms reflect the values of U.S. society and contrast with norms existing in many other societies. In many agricultural societies, it

would be considered immoral to allow aging parents to live outside the family. In these societies, the family is a moral community that should not be separated. Rather than individualism, these norms emphasize communal responsibility within the family unit. Some anthropologists use the term *ethos* to refer to the socially acceptable norms within a society (Geertz, 1973).

Folkways   Norms guiding ordinary usages and conventions of everyday life are known as **folkways.** Members of a society frequently conform to folkways so readily that they are hardly aware these norms exist. For example, if a Chinese anthropologist were to ask an American why Americans eat with knives and forks, why Americans allow dating between single men and women without chaperones, or why American schoolchildren are not allowed to help one another on exams, he or she might get vague and uninformative answers, such as "Because that's the way it is done," or "It's the custom," or even "I don't know." Cultural anthropologists are accustomed to receiving these kinds of answers from the members of the society they are studying. These folkway norms or standards of etiquette are so embedded in the society that they are not noticeable unless they are openly violated.

Folkways help ensure that social life proceeds smoothly by providing guidelines for an individual's behavior and expectations of other people's behavior. At the same time, folkways allow for some flexibility. Although most people conform to folkways most of the time, folkways are sometimes violated, but these violations are not severely punished. Thus, in American society people who eat with chopsticks rather than with a knife and fork or who do not keep their lawns neatly mowed are not considered immoral or depraved, nor are they treated as criminals.

Mores   **Mores** (pronounced MOR-ays) are much stronger norms than are folkways. Members of society believe that their mores are crucial for the maintenance of a decent and orderly way of life. People who violate mores are usually severely punished, though punishment for the violation of mores varies from society to society. It may take the form of ostracism, vicious gossip, public ridicule, exile, losing one's job, physical beating, imprisonment, commitment to a mental asylum, or even execution.

Afghan women in burqas.

For example, in some Islamic societies such as Iran and Saudi Arabia, the manner in which a woman dresses in public is considered morally significant. If a woman violates the dress code in these societies, she may be arrested and imprisoned. As we shall see later in the text, in hunting-and-gathering societies, individuals who do not share goods or resources with others are often punished by gossip, ridicule, and occasionally ostracism.

Not all norms can be neatly categorized as either folkways or mores. Distinguishing between the two is especially difficult when dealing with societies other than our own. In reality, norms fall at various points on a continuum, depending on the particular circumstances and the society under consideration. The prohibition of public nudity may be a strong norm in some societies, but it may be only a folkway or pattern of etiquette in another society. Even within a society, rules of etiquette may come to have moral significance. For example, as already discussed, the proper form of dress for women in some societies is not just a matter of etiquette but has moral or religious connotations.

Values, beliefs, norms, and worldviews are used by many social scientists when referring to nonmaterial culture. However, not all anthropologists agree with concise, clear-cut distinctions among these terms. The terms are used only to help us understand the complex symbolic aspects of nonmaterial culture.

Ideal versus Real Culture

When discussing values, beliefs, and norms, cultural anthropologists often distinguish between ideal culture and real culture. **Ideal culture** consists of what people say they do or should do, whereas **real culture** refers to their actual behaviors. Cultural anthropologists have discovered that the ideal culture frequently contrasts with people's actual behavior. For instance, a foreign anthropologist may learn that Americans cherish the value of equal opportunity, yet in observing Americans, the anthropologist might encounter many cases in which people from different economic, class, racial, ethnic, and religious backgrounds are treated in a highly unequal manner. In later chapters, we discuss how some societies are structured around kinship ties and principles of lineage such as patrilineal and matrilineal descent. Anthropologists often discover, however, that these kinship and descent principles are violated by the actual practices of people (Kuper, 1988). Thus, in all societies anthropologists find that there are differences between the ideal and real cultural practices of individuals.

Cultural Diversity

Throughout history, humans have expressed an interest in cultural diversity. People have recognized differences in values, norms, beliefs, and practices everywhere. Whenever different groups have come into contact with one another, people have compared and contrasted their respective cultural traditions. Societies often differentiated themselves from one another based on these variant cultural patterns. For example, one of the first Western historians, Herodotus, a Greek scholar of the fifth century B.C., wrote about the different forms of behavior and belief in societies such as Egypt. He described how the Egyptians behaved and thought differently from the Greeks.

Writings on the diversity of cultures have often been based on ethnocentric attitudes. As we saw in Chapter 1, *ethnocentrism* is the practice of judging another society by the values and standards of one's own society. It appears that ethnocentrism is a universal phenomenon (Brown, 2003). As humans learn the basic values, beliefs, and norms of their society, they tend to think of their own group and culture as preferable, ranking other cultures as less desirable. In fact, members of a society become so committed to particular cultural traditions that they cannot conceive of any other way of life. They often view other cultural traditions as strange, alien, inferior, crazy, or immoral.

The study of cultural diversity became one of the principal objectives of anthropology as it developed as a profession in the nineteenth century. But like earlier writers, nineteenth-century anthropologists often reinforced ethnocentric beliefs about other societies (see Chapter 13). In the twentieth century, however, anthropologists began to recognize that ethnocentrism prevents them from viewing other cultures in a scientific manner.

To combat the problem of ethnocentrism, twentieth-century anthropologists developed the concept of cultural relativism. **Cultural relativism** is the view that cultural traditions must be understood within the context of a particular society's solutions to problems and opportunities. Cultural relativism is a method or procedure for explaining and interpreting other people's cultures. Because cultural traditions represent unique adaptations and symbolic systems for different societies, these traditions must be understood by anthropologists as objectively as possible. In order to do an ethnographic study, anthropologists must suspend their own judgments to examine another society in terms of its history and culture. Cultural relativism

offers anthropologists a means of investigating other societies without imposing ethnocentric assumptions. The cultural anthropologist attempts to understand the logic of the people she or he is studying. Perhaps that logic does not make sense from the anthropologist's perspective, but the task is to understand and explain the reasoning of the people studied.

Although cultural relativism provides a sound methodological basis for ethnographic research, it may involve some serious ethical problems. For example, many cultural anthropologists have found themselves in societies in which cultural practices may produce physical harm for people. How does the cultural anthropologist refrain from making a value judgment about such cultural practices as infanticide or child or spousal abuse, torture, murder, or other harmful practices? This issue is an ever-present problem for anthropologists and deserves careful thought. Anthropologists don't argue that any practice or culture is as good or worthy as another. In fact, one of the major goals in anthropology is to improve conditions and enhance human rights for all people. After learning about different practices and traditions in other societies throughout this text, the moral problems raised by cultural relativism are discussed in Chapter 25.

Food and Diversity

To understand the difference between human biological and cultural behaviors, we may simply observe the variety of ways in which different societies satisfy a basic biological drive such as hunger. Although humans are omnivorous animals with the ability to digest many types of plants and animals for nutrition, there are many differences in eating behaviors and food preferences throughout the world.

In general, American culture labels animals as either edible or inedible. Most Americans would be repulsed by the thought of eating insects and insect larvae, but many societies consider them to be delicacies. American culture also distinguishes between "pets," which are not eaten, and "farm animals" such as chickens, cows, and pigs, which can be eaten. In the United States, horses are considered pets, and there are no industries for raising them for human consumption. Yet horsemeat is a regular part of the continental European diet. The French, Belgians, Dutch, Germans, Italians, Poles, and other

Europeans consume significant quantities of horse-meat each year (Harris, 1985).

Anthropologists explain differences in dietary preferences in different ways. For example, Mary Douglas offers an explanation of why the Jewish people have prohibitions about eating pork. She describes this prohibition in her book *Purity and Danger: An Analysis of the Concepts of Pollution and Taboo* (1966) by suggesting that all societies have symbolic classifications of certain objects or foods that are unclean, tabooed, polluted, or dirty, as well as what is clean, pure, or undefiled. To illustrate her ideas regarding the classification of matter or foods, Douglas examined the ancient Israelites' classification of animals and taboos against eating certain animals such as pigs and shellfish, as described in Leviticus in the Bible. Douglas argues that, like other humans, the ancient Israelites classify reality by placing things into distinguishable "mental boxes." However, some things don't fit neatly into distinguishable mental boxes. Some items are anomalous and ambiguous and fall between the basic categories that are used to define cultural reality. These anomalous items are usually treated as unclean, impure, unholy, polluting, or defiling. Douglas refers to how these processes influenced the classification of animals among the ancient Israelites. She alludes to the descriptions in the first chapter of the Bible, Genesis, where God creates the animals with specific characteristics: birds with feathers are soaring in the sky; fish with scales and fins are swimming in the water; and creatures with four feet are walking, hopping, or jumping on the land. However, some animals did not easily fit into the cultural categories used for the classification of animals. Animals that combined elements of different realms were considered ambiguous, and therefore unclean or unholy. For example, terrestrial animals that moved by "swarming upon the earth" were declared unclean and were prohibited from eating. Pigs were also unclean and prohibited in the ancient Israelite diet. Clean edible animals such as sheep, goats, and cattle had cloven hoofs and chewed cud. These animals were considered clean and could be eaten. However, pigs had cloven hoofs but did not chew cud. Consequently, the pig was unclean, polluting, and tabooed because it failed to fit into the cultural classification of reality accepted by the ancient Israelites. Shellfish and eels are also unclean

animals because they swim in the water but lack fins and scales. These anomalous creatures fall outside of the systematic classification of animals. Douglas maintains that the dietary laws of Leviticus represented an ideal construction of reality that represented God's plan of creation, which was based on perfection, order, and holiness. This became integral to the worldview of the ancient Israelites and affected their dietary preferences.

Anthropologist Marvin Harris has shown that cultural dietary preferences frequently have an adaptive significance (1977, 1985). For example, he explains the origins of the pig taboo in Judaism (and later in Islam) by analyzing the ecological conditions of the ancient Middle East. Like Douglas, he emphasizes that among the ancient Israelites, pigs were viewed as abominable animals not suited for human consumption. Yet pigs have been a primary source of protein and fat throughout China and Europe. In some societies in the Pacific Islands, pigs are so highly regarded they are treated as members of the family (but they are also eaten). Because so many societies show no aversion to the consumption of pork, Harris has tried to explain the prohibitions in Judaism and Islam. One medical explanation is that the pig is an unclean animal and that it carries diseases such as trichinosis, which is caused by a type of tapeworm. Harris, however, considers these explanations unsatisfactory. Regarding cleanliness, Harris acknowledges that because pigs cannot sweat, in hot, dry climates such as the Middle East they wallow in their excrement to keep cool. He points out, however, that other animals, such as goats and chickens, can also be dirty, but they are eaten. Similarly with disease, Harris notes that many other animals, such as cows, which are widely consumed, also carry diseases.

Harris explains the pig taboo with reference to the ecological conditions of the Middle East. He maintains that the restrictions represented a cultural innovation that helped the societies of this region to adapt. About 1200 B.C., the ancient Israelites had settled in a woodland area that had not been cultivated. As they rapidly cut down trees to convert areas to irrigated agricultural land, they also severely restricted areas suitable for raising pigs on natural forage. Eventually, pigs had to be fed grains as supplements, which made them extremely costly and direct competitors with humans. Moreover, they required artificial shade and moisture to keep cool.

In some areas of the world, pigs are prized as food; in other cultures, it is forbidden to eat pork.

In addition, pigs were not useful for pulling plows or producing milk, hides, or wool for clothing.

According to Harris, despite the increasing costs associated with pig raising, people were still tempted to raise them for nutritional reasons. He hypothesizes that the pig taboo was established through religious authorities and texts to inhibit this practice. Therefore, the pig was redefined as an unclean animal. Neighbors of the ancient Israelites, such as the Egyptians, began to share the abhorrence of the pig. The pig taboo was later incorporated into the Islamic religious text, the Qur'an, so that today both Muslims and Jews are forbidden to eat pork.

Thus, in Harris's hypothesis, in the hot, dry regions of the world where pigs were poorly adapted and extremely costly to raise, the meat of the pig came to be forbidden. He emphasizes the practical considerations of pig raising, including the fact that they are hard to herd and are not grazing animals like goats, sheep, or cattle. In contrast, in the cooler, wetter areas of the world that are more appropriate for pig raising, such as China or New Guinea, pig taboos were unknown, and pigs are the prized foods in these regions.

Both Douglas and Harris offer insights into the development of dietary preferences for Jews and Christians. While Douglas explores the important symbolic significance of these preferences, Harris examines the cost effectiveness and practical aspects of these food taboos. Anthropologists such as Harris and others have been studying dietary diversity, such as why some people prohibit the eating of beef, whereas other people have adopted it as an integral aspect of their diet. Food preferences illustrate how humans the world over have universal needs for protein, carbohydrates, minerals, and vitamins but obtain these nutrients in different ways, depending on the dietary preferences established within their culture.

Dress Codes and Symbolism

Although some cultural differences may relate to the environmental adaptations of societies emphasized by anthropologists such as Harris, much more of our cultural diversity is a consequence of symbolic creations. Symbols provide the basis of meaningful shared beliefs and worldviews within a society. Because of our inherent cultural capacity, we tend to be meaning-seeking creatures. In addition to the satisfaction of biological needs, we have needs for meaning and significance in our personal and social lives.

The importance of symbols as a source of cultural diversity can be seen in the dress codes and hairstyles of different societies. In most situations, the symbolism of clothing and hairstyles communicates different messages, ranging from political beliefs to identification with specific ethnic or religious groups. The tartan of a Scottish clan, the Mao jacket of a Chinese revolutionary, the black leather jacket and long hair of a motorcycle gang member in the United States, and the veil of an Islamic woman in Saudi Arabia provide a symbolic vocabulary that creates cultural diversity.

Many examples of clothing styles could be used to illustrate how symbols contribute to cultural diversity. Consider, for instance, changing dress codes in the United States. During the 1960s, many young people wore jeans, sandals, and beads to symbolize their rebellion against what they conceived as the conformist inclinations of American society. By the 1980s, many of the same people were wearing three-piece "power suits" as they sought to advance up the corporate ladder.

An example of how hairstyles can create meaningful symbolic codes can be seen in a group known as the Rastafarians (sometimes known as Rastas or Rastaman) of Jamaica. The majority of the people of Jamaica are of African descent. During the eighteenth and nineteenth centuries, they were brought to Jamaica by European slave traders to work on plantations. The Rastafarians are a specific religious group within Jamaica who believe that Haile Selassie (1892–1975), the former emperor of Ethiopia whose original name was Ras Tafari, was the black Messiah who appeared in the flesh for the redemption of all blacks exiled in the world of white oppression. Rastafarian religion fuses Old Testament teachings, Christian mysticism, and Afro-Jamaican religious beliefs. The Rastafarian movement originated as a consequence of harsh economic, political, and living conditions in the slums of Jamaica.

In the 1950s, during the early phase of the Rastafarian movement, some male members began to grow their hair in "locks" or "dreadlocks" to symbolize their religious and political commitments. This hairstyle became well known in Western society through reggae music and Rasta musicians such as the late Bob Marley. Rastafarians derive the symbolism of their dreadlock hairstyle from the Bible. They view the unshaven man as the natural man and invoke Samson as one of the most important figures in the Bible. Dreadlocks also reflect a dominant symbol in the Rastafarian movement—the lion—which is associated with Haile Selassie, one of whose titles was the "Conquering Lion of Judah." To simulate the spirit of the lion, some Rastas do not cut their hair, sometimes growing their locks 20 inches or more.

In addition, the dreadlock hairstyle has a deeper symbolic significance in Jamaican society, where hair was often referred to as an index of racial and social inequality. Fine, silky hair was considered "good," whereas woolly, kinky hair was frowned on (Barrett, 1977). The white person with fine, silky hair was considered higher on the social ladder than was the typical African descendant in Jamaica. Thus, the Rastafarian hairstyle was a defiant symbol of resistance to the cultural values and norms of Jamaican society.

The cultural symbolism of the Rastafarian dreadlocks and long beards represents savagery, wildness, danger, disorder, and degeneration. It sends the message that Rastafarians are outside of Jamaican society. Many Jamaicans view the dreadlocks as unkempt, dangerous, and dirty, yet to the Rastafarians, dreadlocks symbolize power, liberation, and defiance. Through their hairstyle, they announce to society that they do not accept the values, beliefs, and norms of the majority of the people.

Thus, to a great extent, culture consists of a network of symbolic codes that enhance values, beliefs, worldviews, and ideologies within a society. Humans go to great lengths to create symbols that provide meaning for individuals and groups. These

The late Bob Marley, a Rastafarian musician.

symbolic meanings are a powerful source of cultural diversity. When anthropologists study these symbolic codes and meanings, they often draw on the humanistic-interpretive approach to comprehend these phenomena.

Ethnicity

One important aspect of culture is the recognition of one's own group as distinct from another based on different values, beliefs, norms, and other characteristics. When referring to these differences, anthropologists use the terms *ethnic group* and *ethnicity*. **Ethnicity** is based on perceived differences in ancestral origins or descent and shared historical and cultural heritage. An **ethnic group** is a collectivity of people who believe they share a common history, culture, or ancestry. For example, a small ethnic group known as the Old Order Amish maintain very strong ethnic boundary markers in U.S. society (Hostetler, 1980; Kephart & Zellner, 1994). Amish ethnicity originated in Switzerland during the sixteenth century. The Amish descended from a group of Anabaptists who split off with their own leadership during the Protestant Reformation. After this split, the Amish began to define themselves as different from other Anabaptists, Protestants, and Catholics, and they faced a great deal of persecution from the religious authorities (Kephart & Zellner,

1994). Eventually, the Amish fled to the United States in the 1700s, settling first in Lancaster, Pennsylvania. From there, they have grown in size and live in twenty different states in the United States. The Amish population is about 100,000. There are no longer any Amish in Europe.

The Amish in the United States emphasize their ethnic difference through language by speaking a German dialect within their communities. The Amish dress in a traditional manner similar to the cultural codes of the 1600s. Men wear hats and long beards; women wear long hair, which is always covered by a hat in public. Based on their interpretation of the Bible, the Amish strive to maintain a conservative, traditional way of life that does not allow the adoption of modern technology such as electricity, automobiles, or television. They do not allow their children to be educated beyond the eighth grade so that they will not be exposed to modern U.S. culture. The Amish have a deeply emotional attachment to their ethnicity and culture. These sentiments are deeply rooted within Amish culture and are evident in their language, dress, and a traditional style of life, which distinguish them from other North Americans.

We discuss many different ethnic groups throughout the various chapters in this text, and in Chapter 23, we will elaborate on how anthropologists have developed methods to investigate the

An Amish family with their horse and carriage in the United States.

complexities of ethnicity, ethnic groups, and ethnic movements around the world.

Cultural Universals

As previously discussed, early anthropologists emphasized cultural diversity in their research and writings. Some anthropologists, however, began to recognize that humans throughout the world share some fundamental behavioral characteristics. George Murdock, an anthropologist who devoted himself to cross-cultural analysis, compiled a lengthy list of cultural universals from hundreds of societies. **Cultural universals** are essential behavioral characteristics of societies, and they are found all over the world. Murdock's list of cultural universals can be seen in Table 10.1; it includes such basics as language, cooking, family, folklore, games, community organizations, decorative art, education, ethics, myths, food taboos, numbers, personal names, magic, religion, puberty customs, toolmaking, and sexual restrictions. Although the specific content and practices of these universals may vary from society to society, the fact that these cultural universals exist underlies the essential reality that

modern humans are of one biological family and one species.

In an influential book entitled *Human Universals* (1991), anthropologist Donald E. Brown suggests that in their quest for describing cultural diversity, many anthropologists overlooked basic similarities in human behavior and culture. This emphasis led to stereotypes and distortions about people in other societies, who were viewed as "exotic," "inscrutable," and "alien."

Following in Murdock's footsteps, Brown describes many human universals. In one imaginative chapter, Brown creates a group of people he refers to as the "Universal People," who have all of the traits of any people in any society throughout the world. The Universal People have language with a complex grammar to communicate and think abstractly; kinship terms and categories for distinguishing relatives and age groupings; gender terms for male and female; facial expressions to show basic emotions; a concept of the self as subject and object; tools, shelter, and fire; patterns for childbirth and training; families and political groupings; conflict; etiquette; morality, religious beliefs, and worldviews; and dance, music, art, and other aesthetic standards. Brown's depiction of the Universal People clearly

Table 10.1	A List of Some Cultural Universals Described by Murdock		
age grading	faith healing	joking	pregnancy usages
athletics	family	kin groups	property rights
bodily adornments	feasting	kin terminology	propitiation of
calendar	fire making	language	supernatural beings
community organization	folklore	magic	puberty customs
cooking	food taboos	marriage	religious rituals
cooperative labor	funeral rites	mealtimes	residence rules
cosmology	games	medicine	sexual restrictions
courtship	gestures	modesty	soul concepts
dancing	gift giving	mourning	status differentiation
decorative art	greetings	music	tool making
division of labor	hair styles	mythology	trade
dream interpretation	hospitality	numerals	visiting
education	housing	obstetrics	weaning
ethics	hygiene	personal names	weather control
ethnobotany	incest taboos	population policy	
etiquette	inheritance rules	postnatal care	

Source: Adapted from George Peter Murdock, "The Common Denominator of Cultures." In *The Science of Man in the World Crisis* by Ralph Linten. Copyright © 1945 by Columbia University Press. Reproduced with permission of Columbia University Press in the format textbook via Copyright Clearance Center.

suggests that many behaviors and other aspects of human behavior result from certain problems that all societies face to maintain their physical and social survival. For a society to survive, it must have mechanisms to care for children, adapt to the physical environment, produce and distribute goods and services, maintain order, and provide explanations of the natural and social environment. In addition, many universal behaviors result from fundamental biological characteristics common to all people.

Anthropologists have discovered that culture can be both diverse and universal. The challenge for anthropology is to understand the basis of both this diversity and this universality. To paraphrase a saying of the late anthropologist Clyde Kluckhohn: Every human is like all other humans, some other humans, and no other human. The major objective of cultural anthropology is to investigate the validity of this statement.

SUMMARY

Culture is a key concept in anthropology. Culture is the learned, shared way of life that is transmitted from generation to generation in a society. Humans learn through direct experience (situational learning), observation (social learning), and symbols (symbolic learning). Symbols are arbitrary meanings that vary from society to society. Many anthropologists view symbolic learning as the major distinction between human and nonhuman animals.

Culture includes material and nonmaterial components. The material aspect of culture consists of tools, clothing, shelter, armaments, and other innovations that enable humans to adapt to their environments. The nonmaterial components of culture are values, beliefs, norms, worldviews, and ideologies.

Different societies maintain different cultural and symbolic structures, creating the great variety and diversity of norms, values, worldviews, and behaviors. Cultural anthropologists have discovered that cultural items—ranging from dress to technology to sexual practices to dietary habits—are enormously diverse.

Anthropologists also recognize that many patterns of human behavior are universal. The universal distribution of certain cultural traits suggests that humans everywhere have similar biological requirements and tendencies that influence behavior. Thus, anthropologists have been engaged in exploring both the diversity and the similarity of human cultures throughout the world.

QUESTIONS TO THINK ABOUT

1. How do anthropologists differentiate culture from nonhuman animal behavior?

2. As a college student, you have probably heard quite a bit about "cultural diversity" or "multiculturalism" and the changing demographics in the United States. What is multiculturalism? Why is it important to understand this concept? Are there any dangers in implementing multicultural education programs?

3. Using an anthropological perspective, explain the statement, "You are what you eat."

4. After reading the section on dress codes and symbolism, pick another example of dress codes and hairstyles and explain what they symbolize to the individuals involved.

5. Can you distinguish ethnic groups from one another in your own society? How do you make that distinction?

6. If you were to create the "Universal People" (see page 239), how would they behave and organize themselves? What would they believe? And how might they act? After you have constructed these imaginary people, read Donald E. Brown's chapter on "Universal People" in *Human Universals* (1991) for comparison.

7. Interpret the statement, "Every human is like all other humans, some other humans, and no other human."

KEY TERMS

beliefs
cultural hegemony
cultural relativism
cultural universals
culture
enculturation
ethnic group
ethnicity
folkways

ideal culture
ideology
material culture
mores
nonmaterial culture
norms
real culture
schemas
signs

situational learning
social learning
society
symbolic learning
symbols
values
worldview

INTERNET EXERCISES

1. Refer to **http://www.sociology.org.uk/ p2d2n2.htm**. Determine the categories that Murdock created when identifying his seventy or so universals. What do Keesing's observations (*Cultural Anthropology,* 1976) on the Lakker of Burma have to do with cultural universals? What possible explanation can there be for the behavior of the Lakker as described by Keesing?

2. What is the premise of relativism as explained by the article at the following website? **http:// www.wsu.edu:8001/vcwsu/commons/ topics/culture/culture-definitions/ shweder.html.** How does this compare to this chapter's section on the components of culture?

SUGGESTED READINGS

ANGELINO, E. (Ed.). 2002. *Annual Editions: Anthropology,* February 2003. Guilford, CT: Dushkin. A good selection of brief essays by many anthropologists, introducing material based on ethnographic findings from other societies.

BARRETT, RICHARD A. 1984. *Culture and Conduct,* 2nd ed. Belmont, CA: Wadsworth. A concise text that presents both the adaptive and symbolic aspects of culture studied by anthropologists.

BELLAH, ROBERT N., ET AL. 1986. *Habits of the Heart: Individualism and Commitment in American Life.* New York: Harper & Row. An analysis of American culture, emphasizing the conflict in values between a deeply rooted individualism and a sense of community interests.

CRONK, LEE. 1999. *That Complex Whole: Culture and the Evolution of Human Behavior.* Boulder, CO: Westview Press. This book treats the concept of culture within the fields of behavioral ecology and evolutionary psychology, which has had an influence on contemporary anthropology.

DEMUNCK, VICTOR. 2000. *Culture, Self, and Meaning.* Prospect Heights, IL: Waveland Press. An excellent discussion of how anthropologists have refined the notion of culture and its relationship to ideas of self and meaning.

GEERTZ, CLIFFORD. 1973. *The Interpretation of Cultures.* New York: Basic Books. A selection of essays by one of the most prominent contemporary anthropologists, who emphasizes a symbolic approach to the analysis of culture.

KUPER, ADAM. 1999. *Culture: The Anthropologists' Account.* Cambridge: Harvard University Press. An elegant historical and contemporary review of the concept of culture for advanced students.

11

The Process
of Enculturation

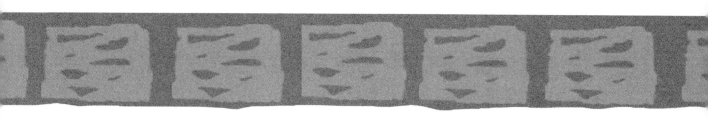

CHAPTER QUESTIONS

- What is the relationship between individuals and culture as studied by psychological anthropologists?

- How does nonhuman animal behavior differ from human behavior?

- How have anthropologists studied enculturation and its relationship to personality formation, sexual behavior, cognition, emotions, and mental disorders?

- In what way are the studies of enculturation limited?

In the previous chapter, we explored the concept of culture as it reflects the differences and similarities in human behavior and thought around the world. This chapter focuses on how anthropologists study the relationship between the individual and culture, or the process of *enculturation.* Anthropologists who focus on the process of enculturation are known as **psychological anthropologists.** Recall from Chapter 10 that enculturation is the process of social interaction through which people learn their culture. Unlike psychologists, who tend to study people within the psychologists' own societies, psychological anthropologists observe people and the process of enculturation in many different types of societies. Their research findings are then used as the basis of cross-cultural studies to determine how and why behavior, thoughts, and feelings differ and are similar from society to society.

Psychological anthropologists study the development of personality characteristics and individual behaviors in a given society and how they are influenced by enculturation. In their studies, anthropologists need to question basic assumptions regarding human nature. Is human nature primarily a matter of *biological influences* or of *cultural factors?* In order to study this question, psychological anthropologists focus on the enculturation process and precisely how this process influences personality characteristics, sexual behavior, thinking and cognition, emotional development, and particular abnormal behaviors in different societies. This chapter considers some of the major research by psychological anthropologists on the process of enculturation.

Biology versus Culture

Before we explore the specific aspects of psychological anthropology, we need to consider some questions. One fundamental concept that anthropologists reflect on is what is frequently referred to as "human nature." Two questions immediately arise when discussing this concept. If there are basic similarities or universal patterns of human behavior, does that mean that human nature is biologically transmitted through heredity? If this is the case, to what extent can culture or learning change human nature to produce variation in behavior within different societies? These questions have led to a controversy in anthropology, with some anthropologists emphasizing biological influences on human behavior and others emphasizing the social or cultural influences that affect behavior.

Today, however, most anthropologists realize that neither of these influences exists in absolute, pure form. Modern anthropologists are therefore adopting an *interactionist perspective,* which combines the effects of biology and culture to explain human behavior. Anthropologists recognize that human behavior depends on both our biological endowment and what we learn from our society or culture. What interactionists care about is the interrelationship between the biologically based and learned factors in any behavior.

Instincts and Human Nature

Another fundamental question addressed by anthropologists is to what extent human nature is

similar to that of other animals. For example, according to the traditional view of humans, the human body is "animal-like" or "machinelike," and the human mind is separate from the body. For many Westerners, this image of humans was used to distinguish humans from other types of animals.

Human Beings as Animals

What do we mean when we say that humans are animal-like? This statement can create misunderstandings because of the different meanings we give to the word "animal." On the one hand, we distinguish animals scientifically from plants and minerals. This system of classification places humans in the animal category. On the other hand, "animal" is sometimes used in a derogatory or pejorative sense. For example, in one of the earliest uses of the word in written English, Shakespeare wrote:

His intellect is not replenished, bee is only an animal, onely sensible in the duller parts. (Love's Labour's Lost, *IV. ii*)

This is the negative meaning of the term that we associate with films such as *Animal House,* referring to "uncivilized," "irrational," "unthinking," and "brutish" behaviors. In attempting to understand humans fully, anthropologists emphasize only the scientific meaning of the word animal. Anthropologists maintain that humans are partly like all animals, partly like certain types of animals, and partly like no other animal.

Because we are part of the animal kingdom, humans share certain characteristics with all animals. We have to consume certain amounts of carbohydrates, proteins, and minerals to survive, just as other animals do. We cannot photosynthesize and process our own foods from within, as plants do. In addition, we share certain characteristics with particular types of animals. For example, like other mammals, we have body hair, and human mothers have the capacity to suckle their offspring with milk produced after birth. Similarly, like other primates such as chimpanzees and gorillas, we have stereoscopic, color vision; we have nails instead of claws; we are extremely sociable; and our infants experience a long period of dependence on adults.

Despite these similarities with other animals, humans are unquestionably the most complex, intelligent, and resourceful creatures on the planet.

Humans have spread and adapted to every continent, becoming the most widely dispersed animal on the earth. We have been the most creative species in respect to our abilities to adjust to different conditions, ranging from tropical rainforests to deserts to rural agricultural areas to urban environments.

Instincts in Animals

Anthropologists have asked the question: What gives the human species its tremendous flexibility in adjusting to these different environments? One way of answering this question is to compare the fundamental behaviors of human and nonhuman animals. Many animals inherit instincts that allow them to take advantage of the specific conditions of their environment. Some of these instincts are called **closed instincts,** which are fixed, complex, genetically based, unlearned, species-specific behaviors that promote the survival of different species. Instinctive behaviors occur widely within the animal kingdom. For example, certain species of birds migrate during the winter season. Temperature changes or differences in ultraviolet radiation from the sun trigger biochemically based, inborn hormonal reactions that act on neurological mechanisms, stimulating all normal individuals within a particular species of bird to fly in a certain direction. This behavior enables the birds to find sufficient feeding grounds for survival during the winter season.

Another example of these species-specific instincts is the nest-building behavior of certain bird populations. In an experiment, scientists isolated as many as five generations of weaver finches and did not supply them with nest-building materials. (Weaver finches are small, brightly colored, seed-eating birds that construct complicated nests with side entrances.) When the scientists released the sixth generation of birds, however, these birds automatically built nests identical to those of their ancestors.

Bears hibernating, salmon swimming upstream to lay eggs during a specific season, spiders spinning perfect webs, and infant turtles and alligators walking unaided toward the water after hatching from eggs are other examples of instinctive behaviors. These behaviors can be thought of as a kind of innate knowledge with which these animals are born. This does not mean that nonhuman animals do not learn complex behaviors, however. In fact, many of them do learn many types of behaviors, but some of their behaviors are rigid and genetically based.

Instincts and Learned Behaviors

The fact that some animal behaviors are instinctive does not mean that environment has nothing to do with these behaviors. Although some animal behavior is near-perfect when it first appears, typically the development of most animal behavior involves a continuous interaction between the organism and the environment.

For example, song learning by birds varies from species to species. Some species do not need to be exposed to the specific vocalizations to reproduce them in near-perfect form. A particular species of dove sings a species-specific type of "coo" in perfect form even when reared with other species of doves. In contrast, parrots can learn to imitate any song they hear. But generally, many other birds, such as chaffinches, need to be exposed to the adult song during their early months to acquire the specific vocalization for their particular species (Hinde & Stevenson-Hinde, 1987).

A weaver finch building a nest—an example of instinctive behavior.

Most *ethologists* (scientists who study animal behavior) agree that complex instincts in different types of animals can be classified as exhibiting a closed or a more open type of genetic program. Closed types of instincts remain fairly stable, even when environmental conditions change, whereas open types respond more sensitively to changing circumstances. For example, many species of birds that migrate, such as geese, have changed their migratory behavior in response to environmental changes. Thus, this would be an example of **open instincts,** behaviors that are innate but are modifiable by learning and by environmental conditions. In some of the other cases described above, the song patterns of the dove represent a closed instinct, whereas the parrot's song imitations represent an open instinct.

Do Humans Possess Instincts?

Because humans are part of the animal kingdom, the question arises: Do we have any instinctive behaviors? This question is difficult to answer because we use the word "instinct" in different contexts. Sometimes we refer to athletes as having the right kind of instincts in going toward the basket or goal line. Upon further reflection, however, it is obvious that basketball or football players who respond in an automatic way to a play situation do so only after practicing for long hours and developing the coordination and skillful moves necessary for competitive sports. Because athletic skills are learned, they are not comparable to the instinctive behaviors of animals. We also use the term to refer to some intuitive processes. For example, we have all heard about relying on our instincts in making difficult decisions. Usually, when we refer to our "gut instincts," what we really mean are our "intuitions." Some intuitions may very well be based on innate predispositions, as we shall discuss in the section on the findings of anthropologists who use evolutionary psychological approaches. However, as mentioned above, closed instincts are genetically prescribed behaviors that rigidly determine behavior, whereas our intuitions are internal feelings and cognitive states that tend to motivate us in certain directions. It appears that some of our intuitions are more like open instincts, which involve a great deal of learning from the environment. As Matt Ridley, a

well-known biologist, states, "Instincts, in a species like the human one, are not immutable genetic programmers; they are predispositions to learn" (1996).

Thus, we can ask: Do humans, then, have any closed instincts like those of other nonhuman animals? Do we have any automatic, biologically controlled behaviors? Because of the wide range of behaviors shown by humans, most anthropologists and other social scientists agree that humans do not have any closed instincts.

We do have some genetically determined behaviors called *simple reflexes,* or involuntary responses, such as being startled by a loud noise, blinking our eyes, breathing, or throwing out our arms when we lose our balance. These reflexive behaviors are automatic responses to environmental conditions, and we do them unconsciously. But they are not comparable to the complex behaviors related to the closed instincts of some other species. Some anthropologists, however, influenced by evolutionary psychology, hypothesize that humans also have some genetically prepared behaviors that have enabled us to adapt to varying conditions in our evolutionary history. As mentioned above, evolutionary psychologists do think that humans have built-in "intuitions" that predispose certain forms of thinking and perhaps action. Yet evolutionary psychologists see the prepared behaviors as unlike the closed instincts of some other animals, because they can definitely be shaped by environmental conditions. We discuss the views of evolutionary psychologists further in a subsequent section of this chapter.

Drives

We humans also have basic, inborn **drives**—biological urges such as hunger, thirst, and sex—that need satisfaction. These drives are important for the survival of the species. Yet, again, these drives are not comparable to the closed instincts of nonhuman animals. We are not programmed to satisfy them in a rigid, mechanical manner. Rather, the ways in which we satisfy such drives are learned through experience. We do not automatically build a spider's web to capture our food; we have to learn to find food in ways that vary widely in many different types of environments. And, unlike some other animals, we may choose to override rather than to satisfy these drives. For example, people can ignore the hunger drive by going on hunger strikes as a political protest.

If we do not have closed instincts that rigidly prescribe our behavior, what do we have that makes us so successful and creative? The answer is that we have the capacity for flexibility in creating conditions and providing solutions for human survival. Some animals have a *closed biogram,* a genetically closed behavioral complex that is related to their specific environment. In contrast, humans have an *open biogram,* an extremely flexible genetic program that is shaped by learning experiences.

Culture versus Instinct

In addition to open biograms, our unprecedented success in adapting to different conditions reflects the influence of human culture. Our capacity for culture, an inherent aspect of the human mind, has enabled us to modify our behaviors and to shape and adjust to our natural environment. The capacity for culture is genetically programmed through the human brain and nervous system. To some degree, culture has replaced the closed instincts of nonhuman animals. But culture is not transmitted biologically through genetic programming. Instead, it is learned through the enculturation process and is passed on from generation to generation. Culture frees us from relying on the slow process of natural selection to adapt to specific environments.

Most genes (see Chapter 3) do not specifically encode for narrowly defined types of human behavior. We are not genetically programmed to build shelters in a certain manner, to devise patterns of economic distribution, to get married, to vote for a president, to carry out a revolution, or to believe in a particular religion. These are learned behaviors based on the enculturation processes that make up the economic, social, political, and religious practices and concepts of a particular society. Without culture, we would not be able to adjust to the tremendous range of environments throughout the world. We would not be able to adapt to Arctic conditions, hunt animals and collect plants, herd cattle, plant crops, or drive a car. The development of the human mind, with the capacity for culture, represents the greatest revolutionary breakthrough in the evolution of life.

Enculturation: Culture and Personality

Enculturation is a lifelong process, and it links the individual, the society, and the culture. Immediately after they are born, people begin to absorb through unconscious and conscious learning—situational, social, and symbolic—the etiquette, mores, values, beliefs, and practices of their society. Enculturation is, therefore, the process through which culture is transmitted from generation to generation.

Enculturation is a vital foundation of our humanity. Virtually helpless at birth, an infant needs care and is completely dependent on others for survival. Through the interaction of enculturation with biologically based predispositions, a person acquires his or her **personality,** the fairly stable patterns of thought, feeling, and action associated with a specific person. Personality includes several components: the cognitive, emotional, and behavioral. The *cognitive* component of personality consists of thought patterns, memory, belief, perception, and other intellectual capacities. The *emotional* component includes emotions such as love, hate, envy, jealousy, sympathy, anger, and pride. The *behavioral* component consists of the skills, aptitudes, competence, and other abilities or potentials that are developed throughout the course of a person's life.

Early Studies of Enculturation

During the 1930s and 1940s, a number of anthropologists began to research enculturation to learn about the influence of culture on personality development. At this time, some social scientists suggested that biology and race are the most influential determinants of human behavior (see Chapter 23). In Germany, for example, social scientists who were members of the Nazi Party promoted the idea that because of biological characteristics, some races are superior to others in respect to behavior and thought. Cultural anthropologists in the United States began to challenge this view of biological or racial determinism through research on enculturation (Degler, 1991). In particular, two women anthropologists, Ruth Benedict and Margaret Mead, became pioneers in early psychological anthropology. They published extensively and became prominent in this area of research. Both of these anthropologists maintained that each society and culture has a unique history. After studying processes such as child rearing and enculturation, they proposed that every culture is characterized by a dominant personality type. Culture, they argued, is essentially "personality writ large." The field studies they did became the basis of what was then called *culture-and-personality theory.*

Benedict and Culture Types   One classic example of the application of culture-and-personality theory is Benedict's analysis of the Plains and Pueblo Native American societies. In an essay titled "Psychological Types in the Cultures of the Southwest" (1928) and in a classic book, *Patterns of Culture* (1934), Benedict classified Pueblo societies as having an *Apollonian* (named for the Greek god Apollo) culture. The Pueblo cultural ethos stressed gentleness, cooperation, harmony, tranquility, and peacefulness. According to Benedict, these values explain why members of Pueblo societies were

Ruth Benedict portrayed the Plains Indians such as those with her in this photo as "Dionysian," or excessive in their behavior.

"moderate." The Pueblo rarely indulged in violence, and they avoided the use of drugs and alcohol to transcend their senses.

In contrast, Benedict characterized the Plains societies as *Dionysian* (after the Greek god Dionysius). She described how the values and ethos of the Plains groups were almost the direct opposite of those of the Pueblo. The Plains Indians were involved in warfare and violence, and their ritual behavior included the use of drugs, alcohol, fasting, and bodily self-torture to induce religious ecstasy. Benedict extended her analysis to such groups as the Kwakiutl Native American peoples and the Dobu of Melanesia. She referred to the Kwakiutl as "megalomaniacs" and the Dobuans as "paranoid," fearing and hating one another. In each case, she claimed that the group's values and ethos had created a distinctive cultural personality. In Benedict's analysis, the culture of a particular society can be studied by studying the personality of its bearers. The patterning or configuration of a particular culture is simply reflected in an individual's personality.

Mead in Samoa   Margaret Mead was one of the most influential contributors to the field of culture and personality. Although most of her ethnographic reports focused on fairly isolated, small-scale societies located in the Pacific islands, she addressed issues that concerned U.S. society, particularly adolescence, child care, and relationships between males and females. At the age of 23, Mead went to the Pacific island of Samoa to study adolescent development. In the United States and other societies, adolescence was usually identified with emotional conflict and rebellion against parental authority. Her mentor, Franz Boas (see Chapter 13), wanted her to investigate this aspect of life in Samoa to determine whether this pattern of adolescent development is universal. The central research question that Mead was to investigate was whether adolescent problems are the product of physiological changes occurring at puberty or the result of cultural factors.

Mead resided in Samoa for nine months and interviewed fifty Samoan girls in three villages. She concluded that, in contrast to U.S. society, adolescence in Samoa was not characterized by problems between the young and the old. She attributed the difference between the two societies to different sets of values, which produced different cultural personalities. In her book *Coming of Age in Samoa* (1928), she argued that Samoan society emphasized group harmony and cooperation. These values arose, according to Mead, from Samoan child-rearing practices. Samoan children were raised in family units that included many adults. Therefore, youngsters did not develop strong emotional ties to any one adult. Consequently, she argued, emotional bonds were relatively shallow.

For this reason, Mead continued, Samoan society was more casual than U.S. society. Children openly learned about sexuality, and adolescents freely engaged in premarital sex. In addition, Mead contended that Samoan society shared a common set of values and standards. Therefore, Samoan children were not exposed to conflicting values and political and religious beliefs, as were U.S. adolescents. For these reasons, Mead concluded, Samoan children experienced a much easier transition from adolescence into adulthood than did their counterparts in the United States.

The Culture-and-Personality School: An Evaluation

The anthropological tradition represented by Mead and Benedict stimulated more careful research regarding personality and culture. Much of the data provided by these early psychological anthropologists were important in understanding the enculturation process. As a result of these early studies, we now have a better understanding of personality formation, thought, behavior, and emotional development within different human societies.

Despite these accomplishments, the culture-and-personality school has been criticized on many fronts. One major shortcoming cited is the practice of characterizing an entire society in terms of one dominant personality. Culture-and-personality theorists assume that all members of a given society share the same cultural knowledge. This assumption produced highly stereotyped presentations of various cultures and peoples. In fact, culture and knowledge are distributed differently and unequally within society. Some people have a knowledge of values, beliefs, and ideologies that others do not have. As discussed in Chapter 10, people do not all share the same culture. Culture is variously distributed among different individuals. Thus, defining an entire society as a single personality creates cultural stereotypes rather than a realistic portrait of a people. Benedict, for example, neglected many

Margaret Mead with Samoan girl.

data that suggested that both the Plains and Pueblo societies exhibited Apollonian and Dionysian behaviors.

The culture-and-personality school has also been criticized for focusing entirely on the nonmaterial aspects of culture. Theorists such as Benedict went so far as to argue that cultural values are completely autonomous from material conditions (Hatch, 1973). Therefore, they did not include such factors as technology or the physical environment in their explanations of human behavior. Again using Benedict as an example, the fact that traditional Plains Indians were primarily bison-hunting groups, whereas the Pueblo peoples were agriculturalists in a semiarid desert, was not included in her analysis, yet this fact was obviously important in their societies.

A final criticism of the culture-and-personality theorists is their tendency to attribute human behavior entirely to cultural factors. Of course, their emphasis on cultural determinants rather than biological determinants reflects the attempt to criticize the biological and racist determinism prevalent during that period. However, in their descriptions they tended to dismiss any biological basis of behavior. This extreme culturalist perspective has since come under attack by a number of critics, most notably Australian anthropologist Derek Freeman.

The Freeman-Mead Controversy　In 1983 Freeman attracted a great deal of attention when he published a controversial book titled *Margaret Mead and Samoa: The Making and Unmaking of an Anthropological Myth*. Having conducted fieldwork in Samoa intermittently since 1940, Freeman concluded that Mead's findings were largely erroneous. Whereas Mead had portrayed the Samoan people as lacking strong passions, aggression, warfare, a sense of sin or guilt, rape, suicide, and other behaviors associated with intense emotions, Freeman claimed to find all of these behaviors.

Freeman challenged Mead by asserting that strong emotional ties did exist between parents and children in Samoan society. He also challenged Mead's conclusions concerning casual attitudes toward sexuality. Pointing out that Samoa had converted to Christianity during the 1830s, Freeman asserted that most Samoans had puritanical views toward sexuality. He found that virginity for girls was highly valued, casual sexual liaisons were prohibited, and adultery was severely punished. Government records indicated that the incidence of rape in Samoa (proportionate to population size) was twice as high as that in the United States.

Freeman also rejected Mead's claims for an easy transition from adolescence to adulthood. He noted that adolescents were severely punished by their parents for any transgressions. He presented charts illustrating that offenses and delinquent behaviors among Samoans peaked at the age of 16, especially for males. Thus, Freeman concluded that adolescents in Samoa go through a period of deviance and rebellion against their elders in the same way that other adolescents around the world do. Freeman asserted that hormonal changes as well as cultural influences have consequences for adolescent behavior everywhere. Samoan adolescents are not much different from adolescents elsewhere.

How could two anthropologists studying the same people arrive at such radically different conclusions? Freeman insisted that Mead's fieldwork was marked by many methodological shortcomings. He pointed out, for example, that Mead had studied the Samoan language for only six weeks prior to her fieldwork. Thus, her language skills were too limited for her to communicate accurately with the Samoans. Moreover, instead of residing with a Samoan family, she lived with an American family and conducted interviews intermittently from her household. Because she was a young female, she was not invited to important ceremonies. Of the fifty females she interviewed, half were not past puberty and therefore could not serve as models of the transition from adolescence to adulthood.

Freeman argued that the major reason for Mead's misinterpretation of Samoan society was her extreme reliance on the model of cultural determinism of theorists such as Benedict. Thus, Mead's portrayal of Samoa as a society without adolescent problems supported the claims of her close colleagues at that time, who maintained that biology has little influence on behavior. In contrast, Freeman emphasized an interactionist approach, which focuses on both biological and cultural influences. He argued that the biological changes that accompany adolescence inevitably affect adolescent behavior.

The Freeman-Mead debate remains a major controversy in anthropology. Supporters of Mead point out that Freeman studied Samoa years and even decades after Mead did. Because societies are not static, it is possible that Samoan values and lifestyles had changed by the time of Freeman's work. Freeman has two more recent books, *Margaret Mead and the Heretic: The Making and Unmaking of an Anthropological Myth* (1997) and *The Fateful Hoaxing of Margaret Mead* (1999), in which he emphasizes how Mead was strongly influenced by the ideas of cultural determinism. He indicates that Mead overlooked any type of biological influences on behavior. However, others note that Mead did not discount biology entirely; she merely rejected the extreme biological deterministic views of the time (Shankman, 1998, 2000). The Mead-Freeman controversy resulted in a complex debate that fueled a lot of controversy within anthropology. As the controversy matured, a number of anthropologists refined their understanding of both the realities and myths about Samoan culture and gained more insight of the interactionist approach in assessing enculturation issues (Shankman, 2001).

Childhood Training

Despite limitations of early research on enculturation and culture and personality, pioneering women anthropologists such as Margaret Mead, Ruth Benedict, and others were the first to systematically examine the effects of childhood training on personality development. Male ethnographers had not paid much attention to this subject. This innovative research has resulted in a much improved understanding of the techniques of childhood training and enculturation throughout the world. Since then, a number of studies of childhood training by psychological anthropologists have contributed to this area of research.

Japanese Childhood Training   Some contemporary ethnographic research projects focus on the type of childhood training and enculturation that influences the learning of basic concepts of a particular culture. One study, conducted by Joy Hendry (1992), focused on how children in Japan become enculturated. According to the Western stereotype, Japanese society is characterized as *collectivistic* rather than *individualistic*. A related stereotype is that Japanese

A Japanese mother with her baby.

society is a *consensus,* or *conformist,* society, with everyone submitting to the norms of the group. Hendry's ethnographic research on whether these stereotypes are correct focused on how children learn their initial concepts of Japanese culture and adjust to group behaviors.

Hendry found that small children are extremely important in Japanese culture. Babies are afforded every possible individual attention. For example, many highly educated mothers give up their careers to dedicate themselves to full-time nurturing once a child is born. The child is to be kept in a secure, harmonious household. A tiny child is often strapped to a mother's back or front while the mother works, shops, and performs daily routines. Also, an adult will lie down with a child at bedtime until he or she falls asleep, or in some cases sleeps all night with the child. From an American perspective, it appears that the child is totally indulged, but the child learns a great many routine tasks such as eating, washing, dressing, and toilet training through repetition until the child can do these tasks on his or her own.

During this early phase of enculturation, the child learns two basic cultural concepts: *uchi,* or inside of the house, including the people inside, and *soto,* the outside world. Human beings are categorized by these concepts, and various behaviors in a Japanese household, such as removing shoes before entering the house, reinforce the inside/outside dichotomy. *Uchi* is associated with safety, security, and cleanliness. *Soto* is where danger may lurk; big dogs, strangers, or even demons and ghosts may be outside. For the first few years of their lives, children play with siblings, cousins, and gradually with close neighbors. They are allowed to play in the immediate neighborhood from as early as 2 years of age if it is a safe environment, and the child begins to build up a new set of "inside" personal relations with neighbors who live nearby.

At the age of 4 or 5, the child is introduced to group life with outsiders in a kindergarten or day nursery. At first the children cry for a while and refuse to join in, but eventually they become involved with the new group of fellow kindergartners, and this becomes a new *uchi* group for them. They learn to cooperate with one another in the group and begin to develop an identity appropriate for group life. However, Hendry emphasizes that the children do not lose their individuality. Each child is treated as an individual by the teacher, who obtains a great deal of background knowledge about the child. (Parents fill out forms regarding their child's strengths and weaknesses, likes and dislikes, siblings, and other details.) In addition, teachers visit the child's home at least once during the academic year. Thus, along with learning to cooperate with their new *uchi* group, these children also become familiar with their own individuality and the individual characteristics of their peers. When engaging in group activities, whether in games, sports, learning activities, or other responsibilities, the children teach each other personal skills and abilities so that the entire group will benefit.

Hendry concludes that even though Japanese children learn to participate in many group-oriented activities, they do not completely lose their sense of individuality. Although Japanese society does not emphasize individualism in the same way U.S. society does, with its connotations of self-assertion and individual rights, Japanese children develop their own sense of self in respect to their individual talents and abilities.

Two-Way Enculturation One of the conclusions based on the new types of psychological anthropology studies such as Joy Hendry's is that children are not just passive recipients in the enculturation process. Instead, they are active contributors to the meaning and outcome of interactions with other members of society. As an example, in another ethnographic study, Bambi Schieffelin analyzed how Kaluli children in Papua New Guinea learn to decipher particular concepts and relationships for different social settings (1990). Kaluli children learn about the relationship *ade. Ade* behavior is a unique relationship between older sisters and younger brothers encouraged by mothers in early childhood. The younger brothers are socialized to appeal to an older sister for goods, services, and attention. The older sister "feels sorry for" her younger brother and shares food and nurtures him affectionately. Later, as children become older, they may use *ade* as a device to get something from someone or when they want to gain sympathy from someone. In other words, they learn to use the *ade* relationship in various contexts in which there are expectations of nurturing, sharing, and giving out feelings of compassion (Schieffelin, 1990). Thus, Kaluli children learn the content and

meaning of this *ade* relationship in the course of specific interactions with other people as they grow older. They learn to apply this cultural concept in many different social contexts with people outside the family. Caregivers may give verbal instruction and enforce other norms of the culture, but the contributions of the children themselves in this process are extremely important.

This new perspective in psychological anthropology moves away from a "one-way" conception of enculturation, which tended to emphasize children as passive recipients of culture. Modern psychological anthropologists emphasize a "two-way" conception that focuses on the interactive relationships between child and caregiver, child and siblings, child and peers, or child and outsiders. The child is viewed as an active agent in this new conception of enculturation. Children learn to design appropriate responses to specific social situations and contexts as they are exposed to them. Psychological anthropologists are contributing to a better understanding of how children acquire cultural knowledge through exposure and active participation in everyday social interaction.

Psychoanalytic Approaches in Anthropology

Sigmund Freud

A number of psychological anthropologists have been influenced by the concepts and ideas of Sigmund Freud, the founder of psychoanalysis and psychiatry. Freud (1856–1939), a Viennese physician trained in the natural sciences, viewed human behavior as a reflection of innate emotional factors. His theory of human behavior emphasizes the importance of emotions in the development of an individual's personality. He tried to demonstrate that a great deal of emotional life is unconscious; that is, people are often unaware of the real reasons for their feelings and actions. Freud postulated that the personality is made up of three sectors: the *id, ego,* and *superego.*

Freud believed that all humans are born with unconscious, innate drives for sex and aggression. These unconscious desires are part of the *id.* According to Freud, these drives promote the seeking of immediate pleasure and the avoidance of pain. The *id* represents the basic needs of humans, needs that exist in the unconscious. Freud maintained that the *id* is rooted in the biological organism and is present at birth; the newborn is basically a bundle of needs. But the sexual and aggressive drives are often frustrated by society. This frustration often results in what Freud termed *repression,* wherein the energy based on these sexual and aggressive drives of the *id* is redirected into socially approved forms of expression.

Eventually, the second part of the personality, the *ego,* becomes differentiated from the *id.* The *ego* represents the conscious attempt to balance the innate pleasure-seeking drives of the human organism with the demands and realities of the society. The *ego* is the "conscious" part of the personality and is sometimes referred to as the "reality part" of the personality.

Finally, the human personality develops the *superego,* which is the presence of culture within the individual. The *superego* is based on the internalized values and norms of society, which create the individual's conscience. The *superego* develops first in response to parental demands, but gradually the child learns that he or she has to respond to the society and culture at large. For example, Freud hypothesized that all male children are driven by an unconscious desire to have an affectionate and sexual relationship with their mother. This unconscious desire leads to hostility toward their natural father, the authority figure within the family. Freud called this the *Oedipus complex.* This desire is frustrated by the morality and norms of society, the *superego,* and the enculturation process. These emotional feelings become repressed, and the mature *ego* of the individual emerges to intervene between these desires and the dictates of society.

Freud's hypotheses were highly controversial in his own lifetime and remain so today. Although his theories are based on limited examples from his European medical and psychoanalytic practice, he extended his conclusions to include all of humanity. Freud's conceptions regarding enculturation have been modified by some modern anthropologists who study the role of childhood experiences in the formation of personality. However, his theories of emotional development and the role of the unconscious in personality represent significant contributions to anthropological research on enculturation.

Modern Psychoanalytic Anthropology

One of the most prominent contemporary anthropologists who uses a neo-Freudian approach in understanding human behavior is Melford Spiro. During his career, Spiro, a prodigious fieldworker, has done ethnographic research on the Ojibwa Indians, the Ifaluk people of Micronesia, the Israelis, and Burmese Buddhists. In all of his fieldwork, he states that his principal objective has been to illuminate "the universal through an examination of the particular" (Spiro, 1971).

Spiro maintains that human behavior cannot be adequately explained solely by environmental circumstances. He adopts some of Freud's concepts to explain such universal phenomena as aggression, sexuality, competition, and cooperation within society. In some of his early studies of the Ifaluk, he underscored the relationship among basic needs, cultural beliefs, and societal demands. For example, Spiro analyzed the Ifaluk belief in malevolent ghosts as a means of reducing interpersonal aggression and stimulating cooperation. Thus, according to Spiro (1952), the belief in harmful ghosts, an aspect of the *superego* that influences personality development, inhibits the expression of innate aggressive desires of the *id.*

Spiro's most recent work (1982) is a restudy of a classic ethnographic study by Bronislaw Malinowski of the Trobriand Islands (see Chapter 13). Malinowski did his study in the 1920s, a time in which Freud's ideas were becoming popular. Malinowski discovered that in Trobriand society, the natural, or biological, father plays a minor role in the family. The mother's brother is the principal authority within the Trobriand family. Malinowski reported that tension exists between the male children and their maternal uncle, rather than between natural father and son. From this data, Malinowski claimed that the Trobrianders do not have the Oedipus complex. In other words, he challenged Freud's claims about the universal occurrence of this phenomenon.

Relying on Malinowski's data on Trobriand society, Spiro concluded that Malinowski ignored much evidence bearing on the relationships within the Trobriand family. One problem was that Malinowski focused on adolescent males, whereas Freud maintained that the Oedipus complex develops during the infantile stage of development. Furthermore, as

CRITICAL PERSPECTIVES

THE ANTHROPOLOGY OF THE "SELF"

One topic that is currently inspiring a great deal of cross-cultural research is the issue of the individual, or the concept of the "person" within society. More specifically, many anthropologists are addressing these questions: Do people in different societies view themselves as "individuals," "selves," or "persons" who are separate from their social group? If not, can we assume that people in these societies are "self-motivated" or "self-interested" in pursuing various goals? We usually make this assumption to explain our own behaviors and those of other people in our own society. Can we use this assumption to explain the behavior of people in other societies?

In the West, we tend to regard people as individuals who feel free to pursue their self-interests, to marry or not to marry, and to do what they want with their private property. Individualism is stressed through cultural beliefs and ideologies that serve as a basis for our economic, social, political, legal, and religious institutions. But is this sense of individualism a "natural" condition, or is it a byproduct of our distinctive social and historical development? One way of answering this question is through cross-cultural research. If

we find that other people do not think in these terms, then we can assume that our thoughts about the self, mind, and individual are conditioned by our historical and cultural circumstances.

One early theorist who influenced modern anthropological research on these questions was Marcel Mauss, a French sociologist who argued that the concept of the "self" or "person" as separate from the "role" and "status" within society arose in relationship to modern capitalist society ([1938] 1985). Relying on the ethnographic research of anthropologists such as Franz Boas, he theorized that the concept of the individual person had developed uniquely in the West through the evolution of Roman law, Christian ideas of morality, and modern philosophical thought.

For example, according to Mauss, during the medieval period in Europe it would have been unheard of to think of an individual as completely separate from the larger social group. Medieval Christianity portrayed the individual as merely an element in God's creation, which was referred to as the "great chain of being." All elements in the universe were arranged in a hierarchy from God to angels, humans, animals, trees,

rocks, and other inorganic materials. All of these elements had a distinct value, depending on their distance from God. To modern Westerners, these views may appear strange and outmoded. However, according to some anthropologists, our view of ourselves as independent from groups and environments may be just as strange.

Influenced by Mauss, French anthropologist Louis Dumont (1970) argued that modern Western notions of individualism differ from those of other societies such as India. In his book *Homo Hierarchicus,* he contrasted Western individualism with Indian Hindu conceptions that value social hierarchy. He pointed out that Hindu philosophy treats individuals as members of caste groups, which are linked to one another in a social hierarchy. Thus, from the Hindu vantage point, individuals cannot be thought of as separate from their social environment.

Francis Hsu, a Chinese-American anthropologist, maintained that the Chinese concept of self is radically different from that of the West (1981). Hsu argued that whereas individualism permeates all U.S. values and institutions, in China the individual is inclined to be socially and

Spiro indicated, Malinowski overlooked the continuing sexual relationship between the biological father and mother. Spiro suggested that this does create sexual jealousy and tension between a son and his

natural father. From his neo-Freudian psychoanalytic perspective, Spiro hypothesized that Trobriand male children develop an Oedipus complex, just as do all male children throughout the world.

psychologically dependent on others. He contrasted the individual-centeredness of American society with the situation-centeredness of Chinese society. He concluded that the individual in China is strongly encouraged to conform to familistic and group norms.

Hsu argued that the situation-centeredness of Chinese society is partly responsible for its lack of economic and political development. In contrast, he believed that the individualism of American society has encouraged capitalist enterprise and democratic institutions. However, he also believed that the American concern for self and individualism has led to rampant materialism and consumerism and a lack of concern for the overall good of society.

Dorinne Kondo makes a similar argument regarding the Western notion of the self in comparison to the Japanese conception of the self (1990). Kondo refers to the Western notion of the autonomous, private self that moves across different social contexts, whereas the Japanese self is always viewed in a relational, socially bounded context. When the Japanese participate in workplace and neighborhood activities embedded within networks and hierarchies, they cannot conceive of their private "self." Even within

their households, individuals are constrained by their neighbors. On the other hand, do Westerners or Americans, as students or workers, feel they have complete control of their own "self" and their destiny (De Munck, 2000)?

These descriptions of different concepts of "self" may be exaggerations by anthropologists working in various societies. Perhaps all humans everywhere have similar concepts regarding the self.

POINTS TO PONDER

1. To what extent are your views of yourself as a distinct individual influenced by prevailing social norms?

2. Do you think that people throughout the world hold similar views? Why or why not?

3. Do you agree with Hsu's analysis of the benefits and shortcomings of widespread individualism?

4. What would be the advantages and disadvantages of a system that emphasizes the overall society rather than the individual?

Spiro's psychoanalytic view does not represent the only view of enculturation in anthropology. Yet his use of psychoanalytic models in combination with ethnographic field methods to offer compre- hensive hypotheses on the relationship among society, culture, and personality formation has been significant. Anthropologists inspired by the Freudian approach attempt to study the relationship among the unconscious thoughts, emotions, and motives of humans. In some cases they collaborate with psychiatrists to study dreams, symbols, fantasy life, interrelations among family members, and sexual relations (Paul, 1989; Herdt & Stoller, 1990).

Understanding Incest Avoidance and the Incest Taboo

One of the topics addressed by psychological anthropologists is incest. During their studies of interrelationships among family members and sexual relations in various societies, psychological anthropologists noted the widespread avoidance of incestuous behavior. They have developed various hypotheses to understand what are referred to as *incest avoidance* and the *incest taboo*. **Incest** involves sexual relations or marriage between certain relatives. **Incest avoidance** refers to the shunning of sexual relations and marriage between certain relatives. Incest avoidance is a universal phenomenon (Brown, 1991). It appears to be valid not only for humans, but also is widely found throughout the animal kingdom (Bischof, 1972; Murray & Smith, 1983). The **incest taboo** is based on strong cultural norms that prohibit sexual relations or marriage between certain relatives. Although incest avoidance is found universally, incest taboos are not. Anthropologists find that some societies view incest with disgust and revulsion; these societies have strong prohibitions or taboos against incest. Yet in other societies, people view incest as such an incredulous and even laughable behavior that no taboo is called for (Van den Berghe, 1979).

Freud offered a mythical explanation for the origins of the incest taboo in his book *Totem and Taboo* (1913). In this book Freud proposed that the incest taboo is a result of the Oedipus complex and the rivalry between fathers and sons. According to Freud, in the earliest family the sons rebelled against their fathers, resulting in what he referred to as "Primal Patricide." Having killed their fathers, the sons felt a sense of guilt, so they developed the incest taboo prohibiting sexual relations within the family.

Although anthropologists no longer take Freud's myth of Primal Patricide seriously, a recent book by Robert Paul, *Moses and Civilization: The Meaning Behind Freud's Myth* (1996), indicates that Freud was struggling to understand the relationships between fathers and sons, and men and women, and the family in modern Western civilization. There is no question that Freud's notions have had an enormous influence on thinking about the problems of incest avoidance and the incest taboo. Anthropologists have been studying these issues regarding incest and the family for a long period of time and have developed a number of different hypotheses to explain the worldwide prevalence of the incest taboo.

Although marriage and sex between parent and child or brother and sister are forbidden in almost all societies, certain exceptions do exist. Ancient Egyptians, Hawaiians, and Incas institutionalized incestuous brother-sister marriages within their ruling classes. This phenomenon is known as *royal incest*. The purpose of these practices was to maintain the ruling family's economic wealth and political power. For most people in most societies, however, marriages within the immediate family are forbidden.

Biological Explanations of Incest Avoidance

One ancient and widely held view of incest avoidance is that inbreeding within the immediate family causes genetic defects. This view is connected with the observation that abnormal or defective negative traits that are carried within the family would be accentuated by inbreeding.

The problem here is that inbreeding itself does not cause harmful genes to exist; it only perpetuates these harmful genes in a rapid fashion if they already exist within the immediate family. Little evidence exists suggesting that in Hawaiian, Egyptian, or Incan cultures, incestuous marriages resulted in any harmful, long-term genetic consequences. Populations apparently can be highly inbred for many generations and survive quite well. Thus, anthropologists must seek alternative explanations of the universality of incest avoidance.

Marital Alliance and the Incest Taboo

Rather than focus on biological tendencies, some anthropologists have concentrated on the social consequences of inbreeding. In an early explanation, E. B. Tylor (1889) hypothesized that incest taboos originated as a means to create alliances among different small-scale societies. Marriages outside of one's group create kinship alliances that encourage cooperation and improve chances for survival. Tylor coined the phrase "Marry out or be killed out" to summarize his argument that if people did not create these social alliances, dire consequences would follow, including warfare among the different groups. Anthropologists Leslie White and Claude Levi-Strauss have presented variations of this functionalist hypothesis (White, 1959; Levi-Strauss, 1969). The problem with these hypotheses is that they explain the origins of marrying outside of one's group rather than incest taboos (Van den Berghe, 1980).

Another type of explanation was proposed by Malinowski, who viewed the incest taboo as a mechanism that functions to sustain the family as an institution (1927). Malinowski argued that brother-sister, father-daughter, or mother-son marriages or sexual relations would generate status-role conflict and rivalry within the family, leading to dysfunctions and possible dissolution. The incest taboo thus serves to reduce family friction and conflict and to maintain harmony within the family. Obviously, this view is closest to the traditional Freudian perspective on the incest taboo.

Childhood Familiarity Hypothesis

Another explanation of the origin and perpetuation of incest avoidance is known as the *childhood familiarity hypothesis,* which proposes that siblings raised together in the family do not become erotically involved or sexually attracted to one another because of a biological tendency. Children living in close association with one another, however, would develop mutual sexual aversion and avoid incest.

A number of psychological anthropological studies appear to support this hypothesis. Arthur Wolf studied a marriage pattern in Taiwan called "minor marriage" (known locally as *sim-pua* marriage), in which a very young girl was adopted into the family of her future husband. The boy and the future bride were then raised in a sibling type of relationship. The purpose of this system was to allow the girl to adjust to her new family through a long association with her husband's kin. Wolf (1970) interviewed many people who were involved in these arranged relationships and found that most of them were dissatisfied both sexually and romantically with their

spouses. Both males and females were inclined to have extramarital relations, and divorce rates were higher than normal. These conclusions appear to support the childhood familiarity hypothesis.

Another study, conducted in Israel, also presented evidence to support this hypothesis. When European Jews first settled in what was then known as Palestine in the early twentieth century, they established collective communities known as *kibbutzim.* Within these *kibbutzim,* children were separated from the family into peer groups of six to eight children to be raised and socialized together. Children in these peer-group settings had sibling-like relationships with one another.

To examine the childhood familiarity hypothesis, Israeli anthropologist Yonina Talmon (1964) studied the second generation of three *kibbutzim.* She discovered that there were no married couples who had known each other from peer groups in the *kibbutzim.* Although as small children these individuals may have shown a sexual interest in members of the opposite sex within their peer groups, this interest diminished after maturity. A later comprehensive study of 211 *kibbutzim* by anthropologist Joseph Shepher (1983) found that of 2,769 married couples, only 14 marriages were from the

These Israeli children are eating lunch on a kibbutz. Anthropologists find that children who are raised together on a kibbutz usually do not marry one another.

ranks of the peer groups. Moreover, every one of these 14 marriages had been dissolved through separation or divorce.

Incest Avoidance: Interactionist Perspectives

Today, most anthropologists agree that incest avoidance likely occurs for a variety of reasons. From an evolutionary perspective, the rule of marrying outside one's family would help to create alliances. It would also induce greater genetic diversity, thereby enhancing the adaptation and survival of different populations. In an extensive cross-cultural analysis of mating systems, Melvin Ember (1975) hypothesized that populations expanding as a result of agricultural development began to notice the spread of (not the creation of) harmful genes as a result of inbreeding and therefore created incest prohibitions. And, additionally, as Malinowski had suggested, incest avoidance would support family roles and functions.

The fact that incest does occur, coupled with the existence of institutionalized incestuous marriage practices in the royal families of some societies, indicates that incest avoidance cannot be reduced to a biological instinct. Humans are not biologically programmed to avoid incest in any mechanistic fashion. The most comprehensive explanation of incest has to take into account generalized biological tendencies along with sociocultural factors.

In a new refinement of the childhood familiarity hypothesis, Paul Roscoe (1994) offers an interactionist explanation of incest avoidance. He suggests that relatives who are raised in close association with one another develop strong emotional bonds, or *kinship amity*—culturally based values that lead to a sense of mutual support and intense feelings of affection. In contrast, sexual arousal and sexual relations are connected to some degree with aggressive impulses, which have a physiological and neurological basis. Thus, sexual-aggressive impulses are depressed between close kin, who have developed kinship amity. In addition, according to Roscoe's hypothesis, kinship amity can be extended to distant kin through enculturation, resulting in an incest taboo that prohibits sex between more distant relatives. Interactionist explanations such as Roscoe's, combining both biological and cultural factors, are producing insightful hypotheses regarding incest avoidance.

Despite the fact that incest avoidance is found universally and is likely tied to biological processes, many social workers and psychologists note that we appear to be in the midst of an epidemic of incest. By one estimate, 1 in 20 women may be victims of father-daughter sexual abuse (Russell, 1986). Anthropologist Mark T. Erickson has been exploring this incidence of incest using a model based on evolutionary psychology and medicine (1999). He suggests that in contemporary societies, as the family unit has become more fragile with weaker kinship attachments, incest is likely to occur more frequently. In the cases of incest that do occur between father and daughter, the father is usually a person who has been sexually abused himself and has not developed close kinship and familial attachments with his children. An extreme lack of nurturance and mutual bonding between family members increases the likelihood of incest arising within families. Erickson's findings suggest that the incest avoidance biological processes can be stunted and distorted, leading to tragic results in contemporary societies.

Enculturation and the Sex Drive

Human sexuality is a subject that connects the biological and cultural aspects of the individual and society. The sex drive, sexual maturation, and sexual activity have different meanings for individuals depending on societal and cultural context. What are considered "normal" or "abnormal" or "deviant" patterns of sexuality differ from one society to another.

Anthropologists have studied enculturation and its consequences for sexual practices in varying societies. Like our biological drive of hunger, sex is a natural biological drive or urge for humans universally. However, this drive is channeled into certain directions through the process of enculturation.

Codes of Sexual Behavior

Societies differ with respect to how permissive or restrictive their codes or norms regarding sexuality are. Some societies approve of premarital and extramarital sexual relations, whereas others strictly segregate males from females to prohibit such relations. In some societies, sexual activity begins very early for both males and females to prepare for marriage. For example, with the Lepcha of Sikkim (a small kingdom north of India in the Himalayan Mountains), girls have their first sexual experience before puberty. In Lepcha society, sexual activity is considered as much a necessity as food or drink, and like food or drink, for the most part it does not matter from whom one receives it, though one is naturally grateful to those who provide it (Lindholm & Lindholm, 1980). The Lepcha have a great deal of sexual freedom and appear to have very little sexual jealousy.

The antithesis of this permissive pattern of sexuality is found in some Arab societies of the Middle East. In Saudi Arabia, girls and women are strictly segregated from boys and men. Young girls begin wearing a cloak and veil at the age of puberty. Saudi Arabian society prohibits the mixing of males and females, and to this end provides separate institutions for education, work, and other public facilities. In Saudi society, a family's honor is judged by its control over the sexuality of its daughters. Brides are expected to be virgins, and to guarantee this, families prevent daughters from interacting with boys. Sexual segregation and the dress code are strongly enforced by religious police in Saudi society.

Other highly restrictive attitudes and patterns of sexuality are found in societies such as the Inis Beag Islanders of Ireland, studied by anthropologist John Messenger (1971). Sex is never discussed openly at home or near children. Parents give no sexual instruction to children. Messenger reported that the Inis Beag people lack basic knowledge regarding sexual matters: for example, there seems to be a general ignorance of the ability of females to have orgasms; any expression of male or female sexuality is considered deviant; and it is believed that sexual activity weakens men. Females and males are separated from an early age. Dancing is permitted, but there is no touching or contact between males and females. Dirty jokes and nudity are strongly frowned upon. Messenger reports that there is little evidence of any premarital sex or any sexual foreplay between married people. Generally people marry very late in life, and there is a high percentage of celibate males in the population.

Homosexual Behavior

In exploring sexuality in other societies, psychological anthropologists have examined homosexuality by using a comparative, cross-cultural approach.

Homosexuality in ancient societies such as that of the Greeks and Romans was a well-accepted pattern of behavior. Many societies have had institutionalized cultural roles for people who are not classified as either male or female. In the country of Oman, anthropologist Unni Wikan (1991) describes individuals known as *xaniths,* who are transsexuals and represent a third gender. In some islands of Southeast Asia such as Bali and Java, third-gender individuals are not only accepted but have important roles to play in the society (Brown, 1976). In Thailand a third gender is represented by what are known as *kathoeys* (Nanda, 2000). *Kathoeys* are primarily transsexual males who dress in women's clothes and take on a feminine role in Thai society. Many Buddhists in Thailand believe that one becomes a *kathoey* as a result of a *karmic destiny* influenced by one's reincarnation. This karmic destiny is inherited and is unalterable.

In some Native American societies, certain males wore female clothing, and some devoted themselves to offering sexual services to male warriors. These individuals were referred to as *berdaches* by Europeans and were regarded as different from both males and females. These individuals, many of whom were homosexuals, also provided resources and took care of other subsistence activities for their neighbors and relatives in the society (Callender & Kochems, 1983). Within these Native American societies, the distinction between homosexuals and heterosexuals did not exist in the same way it does in Western European and U.S. culture. The sexuality of this third gender was not central to their identity or role within society. Instead, the central characteristic of this third gender was the occupational role. Traditionally, these individuals did not face prejudice and discrimination and were accepted as a natural third gender in their society.

Anthropologist Serena Nanda (1990, 2000) has done an extensive ethnographic study of the *hijras* of India, who are viewed as neither men nor women. They are born as males but undergo an operation in which their genitals are surgically removed. This operation transforms them, not into females (because they cannot give birth), but into *hijras,* a third gender. The *hijras* are followers of a particular Hindu deity and earn their living by performing at various types of religious ceremonies. They dress like females and to some extent exaggerate feminine behavior, but they also indulge in certain male-only behaviors, such as smoking a hookah (water pipe) and cigarettes. Within the cultural context of Indian society, the *hijras* are considered neither deviant nor unnatural but rather simply an additional form of gender.

Anthropologists have described a variety of male homosexual practices among the highland societies of Papua New Guinea. Among peoples such as the Etoro and the Sambia, male homosexuality is incorporated into initiation rituals. In these societies there appear to be no distinctions among heterosexual, homosexual, or bisexual individuals. Gilbert Herdt (1987) describes how prepubescent Sambian males are initiated into male secret societies and engage in strictly homosexual activities with the older males of these societies. They are obligated to perform regular oral intercourse on the older males and believe that obtaining the gift of semen from their seniors will enable them to become strong, vigorous warriors. These boys are forbidden to engage in any heterosexual relationships for about ten years. Following this lengthy period, they marry and, from that time onward, take up heterosexual relationships with their wives.

U.S. society has gone through different cycles of restrictiveness and permissiveness regarding cultural norms influencing sexual practices (D'Emilio, 1988). In the early history of the United States, Puritan norms equated sexuality with sinful behavior. Later, in the nineteenth century, American society reinforced restrictive Puritan attitudes. But in the 1920s, a more liberal, permissive era of sexual attitudes developed. The 1950s proved to be once again a more restrictive period, but this was followed by the sexual revolution of the 1960s. U.S. society is extremely complex, and many different norms and attitudes are represented in respect to sexuality. The restrictive legacy of Puritanism still exists in some groups, as evidenced by the various legal statutes in some states regarding homosexual practices. The attempt to regulate sexual behavior by government is a U.S. practice that has been abandoned by most other Western governments.

Enculturation and Cognition

Psychological anthropologists have been exploring thinking processes, or *cognition,* among different peoples in various societies. One assumption held widely by nineteenth-century and early twentieth-century social scientists was that people in small-scale or so-called "primitive" societies have different forms of cognition from people in civilized societies. This assumption was challenged by a number of anthropologists, who focused on cognitive development from a cross-cultural perspective.

Structuralism

Following World War II, French anthropologist Claude Levi-Strauss founded a field of study known as *structuralism.* The primary goal of structuralism is to investigate the thought processes of the human mind in a universal context; consequently, it is a field that overlaps psychological anthropology. Structuralists are interested in the unconscious and conscious patterns of human thinking. In one of his first major books, *The Savage Mind* (1966), Levi-Strauss discussed how peoples living in small-scale societies use the same unconscious thinking and reasoning processes that peoples in large-scale, complex societies do. He proposed that there is a universal logical form in human thought and cognition around the world.

Drawing on the field of linguistics, Levi-Strauss argued that thinking is based on *binary oppositions*. In other words, humans classify the natural and social world into polar types (binary oppositions) as a stage of reasoning. For example, foods are classified as raw versus cooked, or hot versus cold. From these binary contrasts, coherent patterns of thought are developed. In addition, he suggests that the fundamental binary structural distinctions between "nature" and "culture" are found in all societies. He demonstrated how religious mythologies universally invoke symbols that have a dualistic aspect between that of nature and culture. Levi-Strauss focused on such diverse phenomena as kinship, mythology, cuisine, and table manners to discover the hidden structural logic underlying these diverse cultural ideas and practices. Within all of these practices and beliefs, Levi-Strauss maintains that there are important logical and deep structural distinctions between nature and culture. Even though the rules and norms that structure these ideas and practices may appear arbitrary, Levi-Strauss believed that this "deep universal structure" underlies these cultural phenomena. Thus, this universal structure of the mind produces similar thinking and cognition throughout the world.

Jean Piaget

Jean Piaget (1896–1980), a Swiss psychologist, spent more than a half-century studying the ways in which children think, perceive, and learn. His research has influenced the anthropological perspective on cognition and enculturation. Piaget focused not only on what children learn but also on how they understand the world. He identified four major stages of cognitive development: sensorimotor, preoperational, concrete-operational, and formal-operational. Piaget hypothesized that these stages reflect biological maturation as well as enculturation. As each child progresses through these stages, he or she acquires more information and begins to organize and perceive reality in new and different ways.

Piaget's Four Stages of Human Development   The first stage of human development in Piaget's scheme is the *sensorimotor stage,* in which a child experiences the world only through the senses in terms of physical contact. In this stage, which corresponds to approximately the first two years of life, the infant explores the world through touching, sucking, listening, and other direct contact. According to Piaget, at this first stage children may imitate the sounds of others, but they do not have the capacity to use symbols.

The second stage, the *preoperational stage,* refers to the level of cognitive development in which symbols, including language, are first used. During this stage, roughly ages 2 to 7, children begin to experience the world abstractly. This symbolic learning enables children to conceive of something without having direct contact with it. Children gain the ability to distinguish among their ideas of the world, dreams, fantasies, and objective reality. Yet at this second stage, children do not use symbols as adults do. They learn to attach meanings and names to objects in their specific environment, but they do not conceptualize the world in general terms.

In the third stage, the *concrete-operational stage,* children between ages 7 and 11 begin to use logic, connecting events in terms of cause and effect, and

they learn to manipulate symbols in a more sophisticated manner. At this stage children are also able to put themselves in the position of another person and perceive a situation from another's point of view. This allows them to engage in complex activities such as games that involve a number of participants (including most team sports).

The fourth stage, known as the *formal-operational stage,* is the level of cognitive development characterized by highly abstract concepts and formal reasoning processes. At about age 12, children develop the capacity to think of themselves and the world in highly abstract terms rather than only in terms of concrete situations. They can envision alternatives to reality by proposing differing hypotheses for evaluation. In this final stage of cognitive development, which continues throughout adult life, children begin to use reasoning processes and abstract symbols to interpret and understand the world.

Psychological anthropologists are studying the cognitive development of children everywhere in the world.

Piaget suggested that certain innate categories regulate and order our experience of the world. Although he was certainly aware that the learning of values, norms, and beliefs is not the same from society to society, he believed that humans everywhere progress in the same sequence through the various stages described above. He also recognized that the precise age at which each stage of cognitive development is reached varies from individual to individual, depending on innate mental capacities and the nature of the enculturation experience.

Applying Piaget's Four Stages A number of anthropologists have been influenced by Piaget's model of enculturation and cognitive development. British anthropologist Maurice Bloch (1977, 1985) has suggested that many cultural universals are the result of bio-psychological factors shared by all humans that interact with the practical conditions of the world. For example, Bloch postulates that all humans have intuitive capabilities to perceive time and space in the same way. Time and space are fundamental concepts that enable humans to adapt to the practical conditions of the world. These practical conditions include changes in seasons, climatic and environmental characteristics, and the overall effects of natural aging processes. In Bloch's view, people can learn to conceptualize time and space in radically different ways, depending on religious beliefs and worldviews. For example, in the Hindu tradition, people perceive time cyclically in relationship to the creation and destruction of the universe that takes place over millions of years. In the Judeo-Christian tradition, people perceive time in a more linear fashion from the time of creation to the present. However, in both the Hindu and Judeo-Christian cultures, in everyday, practical circumstances, people perceive time both cyclically and linearly in relation to the cycle of seasonal changes or the life cycle of an individual through biological aging.

Other anthropologists have been testing Piaget's theories throughout the world to determine whether his stages are indeed universal. One noted psychological anthropologist, Michael Cole, has surveyed the field of cross-cultural Piagetian-based studies and concluded that the basic thinking processes are similar among all humans everywhere. All people use similar patterns of logic and develop an understanding of cause and effect relationships. People everywhere develop classification systems through similar processes of abstraction and generalization. The differences among cultural groups lie in the content of the values, beliefs, and norms of society (Cole & Scribner, 1974).

Cognitive Anthropology and Evolutionary Psychology

A number of anthropologists have been pursuing the understanding of human psychology through the fields of cognitive anthropology and evolutionary psychology. **Cognitive anthropology** is the study of cognition and cultural meanings through specific methodologies to elicit underlying unconscious *schemas* or *taxonomies* that structure human thinking processes. Cognitive anthropology developed in the 1950s and '60s through the systematic investigation of kinship terminologies within different cultures. However, more recently, cognitive anthropology has drawn upon the findings in the field of *cognitive science,* the study of the human mind based on computer modeling (D'Andrade, 1995; de Munck, 2000). Cognitive anthropologists have developed experimental methods and various cognitive tasks to use among people they study in their fieldwork to better comprehend human psychological processes and their relationship to culture. Through cognitive anthropology we have learned that the human mind organizes and structures the natural and social world in distinctive ways.

For example, cognitive anthropologists have been doing research on how humans classify and perceive colors in the natural world. The question that was asked was: Do people classify and categorize colors in an arbitrary manner based on their language and culture? Or do people classify, categorize, and perceive colors in similar ways throughout the world? Cognitive anthropologists Brent Berlin and Paul Kay have been studying the basic color terms of different societies since the 1960s. They analyzed the color-naming practices of informants from ninety-eight globally distributed language groups and found that societies differ dramatically in the number of basic color terms they possess, from two in some New Guinea tribes to eleven in English. They showed, however, that despite this difference, all color terms used by diverse societies follow a systematic pattern (1969).

A language with only two color terms will divide the color spectrum between white and black. If a language contains three terms, the spectrum will be black, red, and white. A language with four terms will have black, red, white, and either green, yellow, or blue. A language with six terms will have black, white, red, yellow, green, and blue. Language systems add basic color terms in a systematic progression until a maximum of eleven terms is reached.

Berlin and Kay suggest that this pattern indicates an evolutionary sequence common to all languages. Red is adopted after white and black. In general, a language does not adopt a term for brown unless it already has six color terms. English, most Western European languages, Russian, Japanese, and several others add four color terms: gray, pink, orange, and purple, after brown is classified. Berlin and Kay correlate the evolution of color terms with the evolution of society. Societies with only two color terms have a simple level of technology, whereas societies with eleven basic color terms have a complex technology.

The evidence from Berlin and Kay's study suggests that color naming is not at all arbitrary. If color terms were selected randomly, there would be thousands of possible color systems. In fact, there are only thirty-three possible color-naming systems. This study demonstrates the existence of *linguistic universals*—language features found universally.

In a more recent cognitive anthropological study, James Boster concluded that, as with colors, people from different societies classify birds in similar ways. Boster (1987) found that the South American Jivaro Indian population classified species of native birds in a manner corresponding to the way scientists classify these birds. To discover whether this pattern of classification was random, Boster had University of Kentucky students with no scientific training and no familiarity with South American birds classify these birds. The students did so with the exact criteria used by both the Jivaro Indians and the Western scientists. Most recently, two cognitive anthropologists working in Honduras found that insects were classified by Honduran farmers in the same way that scientists do worldwide (Bentley & Rodriguez, 2001). Cognitive anthropologists such as Scott Atran (1990, 1998) and Cecil Brown (1984) have shown that plants and animals are categorized and classified in universally similar taxonomies. These taxonomies are ordered according to the distinctive morphological features of the various plants and animals in nature. Despite variant cultures in different regions of the world, the human mind appears to organize the natural world in nonarbitrary ways.

These findings in cognitive anthropology suggest that the human mind organizes reality in terms of *prototypes,* distinctive classifications that help us map and comprehend the world. If reality was inherently unorganized and could be perceived in any way, then color naming and animal and plant classification would be completely arbitrary. The results of this research support the notion that people the world over share certain cognitive abilities, and language and culture is as likely to reflect human cognition as it is to shape it. It suggests that evolution selected certain fundamental visual-processing and category-building abilities for humans everywhere (Lakoff, 1987; Lakoff & Johnson, 2000; D'Andrade, 1995).

Cognitive anthropologists have discovered that not only do humans think in prototypes, but we also use *schemas* to help us understand, organize, and interpret reality. The concept of schemas was introduced by Jean Piaget to discuss a particular "cognitive structure which has reference to a class of similar action sequences" (de Munck, 2000). Schemas are constructed out of language, images, and logical operations of the human mind in order to mediate and provide meaning to social and cultural reality. Thus, schemas are more complex than prototypes or taxonomic categories. And schemas may vary from one culture to the next. For example, the schema "writing" in English and *kaku* in Japanese have some similarities, and these terms are usually translatable between the languages. They both refer to making some marks with an implement across a surface. The schema "writing" in English, however, always entails the act of writing in a language, whereas *kaku* can refer to writing or doodling or drawing a picture (D'Andrade, 1995). Cognitive anthropologists find that, like taxonomies, schemas are also organized into *hierarchies* and aid in our adapting and coping with cognitive and cultural complexities. Claudia Strauss is investigating how schemas are organized hierarchically in an analogous manner to how computers process data and information (1992). She has been investigating the interconnection of schemas within the individual mind and comparing them with how data are arranged, interconnected, and sorted within computers. These models from cognitive science and computer modeling are employed to gain insight into cultural values and beliefs within the mind.

In addition to prototypes, taxonomies, and schemas, cognitive anthropologists also investigate how narratives are used to coordinate thought processes. **Narratives** are stories or events that are represented within specific cultures. There are certain types of narratives, such as the story of "Little Red Riding Hood," that are easily retained by an individual's memory and told over and over again in a society. Thus, certain forms of narrative have easily recognizable plots and can be distributed widely through a society (Sperber, 1996). Other forms of narratives, such as a formal proof in mathematics or logic, are much more difficult to distribute widely. Cognitive anthropologists are studying religious mythologies, folktales, and other types of narratives to determine why some spread quickly and are effortlessly transmitted and used to produce cultural representations that endure for generations. Cognitive anthropological research has been fruitful in providing interactionist models of the ways in which humans everywhere classify, organize, understand, interpret, and narrate their natural social and cultural environment.

A recent development that draws upon cognitive anthropology and attempts to emphasize the interaction of nature (biology) and nurture (learning and culture) in understanding and explaining enculturation, human cognition, and human behavior is the field known as evolutionary psychology. This field includes anthropologists such as John Tooby, Daniel Sperber, Pascal Boyer, Donald Symons, Mark Flinn, and a number of psychologists, including Leda Cosmides and Paul Rozin. **Evolutionary psychology** is a field that draws on ethnographic research, psychological experiments, and evolutionary theory to demonstrate how the human brain developed and how it influences thinking processes and behavior. These anthropologists question the traditional premise that the human mind is a passive instrument that soaks up the cultural environment like a sponge. Instead, they view the human mind as designed by evolution to actively adjust to the culture and environment.

They begin with the understanding of the effects of evolution during the long period of the Paleolithic that caused the emergence of a specific form of human brain. Evolutionary psychologists suggest that the mind and culture coevolved. They believe that natural selective forces must have shaped the mind and behavior. Consequently, since natural selective forces are highly specific, they hypothesize that the human brain is divided into specialized *modules,* or independent units, which contain various functions that enabled our ancestral humans to adapt to Paleolithic conditions. These specific modules within the brain predispose humans to perceive, think, and behave in certain ways to allow for adaptation. In other words, there are genetically induced "evolved predispositions" that have consequences for human perception, thinking, emotions, and behavior today. For example, in the next chapter we review the research indicating that the human brain has a language-learning module enabling children to learn their language without learning the specific complex rules of grammar for communication.

Aside from the language-learning module, evolutionary psychologists, in a book entitled *The Adapted Mind* (1992) edited by Jerome Barkow, John Tooby, and L. Cosmides, have hypothesized that modules in the brain enable humans to understand intuitively the workings of nature, including motion, force, and how plants and animals function. The authors refer to psychological research that demonstrates how infants distinguish objects that move around (such as balls) from living organisms (such as people and animals) that are self-propelled. These anthropologists theorize that innate, specialized modules in the human brain help develop an intuitive understanding of biology and physics. Just as children learn their language without learning the formal grammatical rules, humans can perceive, organize, and understand basic biological and physical principles without learning formal scientific views. Children at very early ages have intuitive notions or "theories" about persons, animals, plants, or artifacts. They have an intuitive understanding of the underlying properties and behavioral expectations of these phenomena from early stages of infancy. In addition, young children at about 2 years old have the ability to comprehend how other people have intentions. In other words, these young children have an intuitive "theory of mind" and can determine how other people have thoughts and intend to use them in communication or behavior (Boyer, 1998).

Evolutionary psychologists further contend that the mind uses different rules to process different types of information. For example, they suggest there are innate modules that help interpret and predict other people's behavior and modules that enable humans to understand basic emotions such as happiness, sadness, anger, jealousy, and love. In addition, these specialized modules influence male-female relationships, mate choice, and cooperation or competition among individuals.

In *The Adapted Mind,* anthropologist Jerome Barkow (1992) asks why people like to watch soap operas. He answers that the human mind is designed by evolution to be interested in the social lives of others—rivals, mates, relatives, offspring, and acquaintances. To be successful in life requires knowledge of many different phenomena and social situations, evolutionary psychologists argue, and innate predispositions influence how we sense, interpret, think, perceive, communicate, and imagine to adapt and survive in the world.

Evolutionary psychologists tend to emphasize the commonalities and similarities in culture and behavior found among people in different parts of the world. Thus, they are interested in the types of human universals described by anthropologist Donald Brown (see Chapter 10). Although evolutionary psychologists do not ignore learning or culture, they hypothesize that innate modules or mechanisms in the brain make learning and enculturation happen.

Many evolutionary psychologists believe that some of the evolved predispositions that are inherited may not be as adaptive today as they were during the time of the Paleolithic. For example, humans during that period had to worry more about danger from wild animals and about getting enough salt and sugar to eat for survival, but such evolved predispositions may not help humans adapt to modern society.

Some anthropologists have criticized evolutionary psychology for not emphasizing the richness and complexity of cultural environments. At present, however, many anthropologists are using the methods of cognitive anthropology and evolutionary psychology to understand human nature and culture. The field of evolutionary psychology is in its infancy and will most likely grow to offer another interactionist perspective on human thought and behavior.

Enculturation and Emotions

One significant question asked by psychological anthropologists is to what degree enculturation influences emotions. Obviously, different language groups have different terms for emotions, but do the feelings of anger, happiness, grief, and jealousy vary from society to society? Do some societies have unique emotions? For example, Catherine Lutz, in her book *Unnatural Emotions: Everyday Sentiments on a Micronesian Atoll and their Challenge to Western Theory* (1988) suggests that many of the emotions exhibited by the Ifaluk people in the Pacific islands are not comparable to American or Western emotions. She notes that the Ifaluk emotion words *song* (justifiable anger) and *fago* (compassion/love/sadness) have no equivalent in English emotion terms, and that anthropologists need to examine the linguistic and cultural context to interpret what emotions mean from culture to culture. Lutz argues that emotions cannot be understood universally based on biological factors. Or are, as some anthropologists maintain, human emotions the same throughout the world?

Psychological anthropologists have been conducting research on the topic of emotions since the early research of Benedict and Mead. As discussed earlier in the chapter, Benedict and Mead argued that each culture is unique, and that people in various societies have different personalities and, consequently, different types of emotions. These different emotions are a result of the unique kind of enculturation that has shaped the individual's personality. In their view, the enculturation process is predominant in creating varying emotions among different societies. In other words, culture determines not only how people think and behave but also how they feel emotionally.

In contrast, other early psychological anthropologists focused on universal biological processes that produce similar emotional developments and feelings in people throughout the world. According to this perspective, emotions are seen as instinctive behaviors that stimulate physiological processes involving hormones and other chemicals in the brain. In other words, if an individual feels "anger," this automatically raises his or her blood pressure and stimulates specific muscle movements. In this view, emotional developments are part of the biology of humans universally, and thus emotions are experienced the same everywhere.

More recently, anthropologists have emphasized an interactionist approach, taking both biology and culture into account in their studies of emotions (Hinton, 1999). A study conducted by Karl Heider (1991) focused on three different ethnic groups in Indonesia: the Minangkabau in West Sumatra, the Minangkabau Indonesians, and the Javanese. Heider systematically described the vocabulary of emotions that each of these groups used to classify their feelings of sadness, anger, happiness, fear, surprise, love, contempt, shame, and disgust, along with other feelings. Through intensive interviews and observations, Heider proceeded to determine whether the vocabulary of emotions is directly related to specific emotional behaviors.

Following his ethnographic study, Heider concluded that four of the emotions—sadness, anger, happiness, and surprise—tend to be what he classifies as *basic cross-cultural emotions*. In other words, these emotions appear to be universally understood and stable across cultures. Other emotions, however, such as love, fear, and disgust, appear to vary among these societies. For example, love among the Minangkabau and Minangkabau Indonesians is mixed with the feeling of pity and is close to sadness. Fear is also mixed with guilt, and feelings of disgust are difficult to translate across cultural boundaries. Heider emphasizes that his study is preliminary and needs much more analysis and reanalysis; nevertheless, it is an interesting use of the interactionist approach to the study of emotions.

Daniel Fessler also explored how both biology and culture contribute to the development of human emotions (1999). Fessler did ethnographic work among the Bengkulu, an ethnic group in Sumatra, a major island in Indonesia. He discusses the importance of two emotions, *malu* and *bangga*, exhibited in many situations by the Bengkulu. *Malu* appears to be quite similar to "shame" in English. Bengkulu who feel *malu* withdraw from social interaction, stoop, avert their gaze. People who feel *malu* are described as those who have missed religious services, didn't attend to the sick, didn't send their children to school, drank alcohol, ate during times of fasting, or violated other norms. *Bangga* is the linguistic expression of the emotion that people feel when they do something well and have had success, such as doing well in baking cakes, winning an election, hosting a large feast, being skilled in oratory, or feeling good about one's physical appearance or one's house and furnishings. *Bangga* seems to be most similar to the emotion term "pride" in English. Fessler notes that *malu* and *bangga* appear to be exact opposites of one another, and both emotions provide individuals with an assessment of their relationship to the rest of the group. He suggests that these two emotions are universal and are found in all societies, and that they have evolved in connection with attempts to coordinate one's mind and behavior for cooperation and competition within groups of people. Fessler emphasizes that these emotions may be displayed and elaborated in different ways in various cultures; they reflect a universal, panhuman experience.

In *Thinking through Cultures: Expeditions in Cultural Psychology* (1991), psychological anthropologist Richard Shweder emphasizes that ethnographic research on emotions has demonstrated the existence of both universals and culturally specific aspects of emotional functioning among people in different societies. He uses a piano keyboard as an analogy to discuss emotional development in children. Children have something like an emotional keyboard, with each key being a separate emotion: disgust, interest, distress, anger, fear, contempt, shame, shyness, guilt, and so forth. A key is struck whenever a situation such as loss, frustration, or novelty develops. All children recognize and can discriminate among basic emotions by a young age. However, as adults, the tunes that are played on the keyboard vary with experience. Some keys are not struck at all, whereas others are played extensively. Shweder concludes, "It is ludicrous to imagine that the emotional functioning of people in different cultures is basically the same. It is just as ludicrous to imagine that each culture's emotional life is unique" (1991:252). Anthropologists recognize that an interactionist approach that takes into account human universals and cultural variation is necessary to comprehend the enculturation process and emotional development.

Culture and Mental Illness

Another area of interest for psychological anthropology is the study of mental illness in different societies. The major concerns of these studies revolve around two questions: Is there a universal concept of "normal" and "abnormal" behavior? and Do mental illnesses differ in their symptoms or patterns in different societies? These questions serve as the basis for many ethnographic projects in different societies.

What Is Abnormal?

In the early twentieth century, one of the assumptions in the fields of psychiatry and psychology was that mental illness and abnormal behavior are universal. In other words, depression, schizophrenia, psychoses, and other mental disorders are essentially the same for all humans. For example, in the field of psychiatry, particular types of mental disorders were classified by specific symptoms. Thus, a *psychosis* was classified as a type of mental disturbance characterized by personality disorganization, disturbed emotional responses, and a loss of contact with reality. A *neurosis* was characterized as a nonpsychotic disorder marked by considerable anxiety for individuals, especially when they are involved in social interaction.

Psychological anthropologists such as Ruth Benedict challenged these classifications of mental illness in the 1930s. Benedict argued that all criteria of abnormality reflect the particular culture of the individual and must be understood within the context of that culture. In her classic book *Patterns of Culture* (1934), Benedict remarked:

> It does not matter what kind of "abnormality" we choose for illustration, those which indicate extreme instability, or those which are more in the nature of character traits like sadism or delusions of grandeur or of persecution, there are well described cultures in which these abnormals function with ease and with honor and apparently without danger of difficulty to the society. ([1934] 1959:263)

In other words, Benedict questioned whether any type of absolute standards of "normalcy" as defined by Western preoccupations and categories were satisfactory criteria for mental health. Benedict described a situation in which an individual heard very loud voices, was plagued by dreams of falling off cliffs, and feared being devoured by swarms of yellow jackets. This individual went into a trance state, lay rigid on the ground, and shortly thereafter recovered and danced for three nights in a row. Although in Western society this individual would be

treated as "abnormal," Benedict suggested that this behavior and thought was not unusual in some societies. The individual described was a type of medicine man or woman and was not only accorded respect but enjoyed tremendous prestige within the particular Native American tribe to which he or she belonged.

Ethnographic descriptions such as these demonstrate the difficulties of classifying mental illness across cultural boundaries. When the concept of abnormality is applied cross-culturally, it becomes an extremely vague concept. Behavior that is considered deviant in one society may represent a culturally acceptable form of behavior in another. The fields of modern psychiatry and psychology have been attempting to revise their classification of mental illnesses and often work with anthropologists on joint research projects to refine understandings of psychological disorders.

Culture-Specific Disorders

A number of ethnographic studies have focused on mental disorders that are unique to certain cultural settings. These culture-specific disorders include *latah, amok, windigo,* and *pibloktoq. Latah* has been described as a mental disorder in areas of Southeast and East Asia. In Southeast Asia, *latah* appears as a type of hysteria or fear reaction that afflicts women who become easily startled, resulting in compulsively imitating behaviors or shouting repetitive phrases that they have heard (echolalia). Sometimes this disorder is triggered by the word "snake" or by tickling. In the East Asian area of Mongolia, however, David Aberle (1961) described a form of *latah* that affects men. These men may be startled suddenly and put their hands into a fire, jump into a river, or begin to scream obscenities wildly.

Amok is a culture-specific disorder that is described in Malaysia, Indonesia, and parts of the Philippines. It is a disorder of middle-aged males following a period of withdrawal marked by brooding over a perceived insult. During this period, in which the individual loses contact with reality, he may suffer from stress and sleep deprivation and consume large quantities of alcohol. Then a wild outburst marked by rage occurs, with the individual attempting a violent series of murderous attacks. The man may pick up a weapon such as a machete and attack any person or animal in his path. These aggressive, homicidal attacks will be followed by prolonged exhaustion and amnesia (Bourguignon, 1979). *Amok* appears to be a culturally sanctioned form of violent behavior viewed as an appropriate response to a specific situation in these Southeast Asian regions. (The Malay term *amok* has entered the English language, referring to wild, aggressive behavior, as in someone "running amok.")

Another culture-specific disorder, formerly found among the males of the Chippewa, Cree, and Montagnais-Naskapi Indians in Canada, is referred to as the *windigo psychosis*. It is described as a disorder in which the affected individual becomes deeply depressed and begins to believe that he has been possessed or bewitched by the spirit of a *windigo,* a cannibal giant with a heart or entrails of ice. The individual may have symptoms of nausea, anorexia, and insomnia and may see other humans being transformed into beavers or other animals. As these hallucinations occur, the individual begins to have an overwhelming desire to kill and eat these humans (Barnouw, 1985). This insatiable craving for human flesh has resulted in documented cases of homicide and cannibalism among some of these people (Marano, 1982; Barnouw, 1985).

The disorder *pibloktoq,* also referred to as Arctic hysteria, is found among Eskimo adults in Greenland and other Arctic regions. It may affect both men and women but has been described more frequently among women. The subject is initially irritable or withdrawn, then becomes violently emotional. The victim may scream as if terrified, tear off her clothes, run out into the snow, jump into fire, throw things around, and begin to "speak in tongues." After this period of excitement, the woman sometimes has convulsive seizures and then may fall asleep. On awakening she may be perfectly calm and have no memory of the incident. *Pibloktoq* usually has a high frequency in the winter, and a number of persons living in a small community may be afflicted with it during the cold months (Wallace, 1972). Thus, it may be a more extreme form of what Americans sometimes call "cabin fever."

A number of explanations have been put forth to explain these culture-specific mental disorders. For example, the *windigo* disorder has been attributed to the experience of starvation and famine conditions that can occur in the wintertime. Anthony Wallace (1972) suggests that a lack of calcium in the diet of Eskimos may partially explain the occurrence of *pibloktoq*. In these areas, the drastic annual variation in daylight may be partially responsible for these behavioral and emotional disturbances (Bourguignon, 1979).

Some critics believe that these culture-specific disorders may just be different expressions of certain illnesses such as paranoid schizophrenia or other types of psychoses. Persecution ideas, hysteria, panic disorders, and other bizarre behaviors occur in all societies to one degree or another. There is a substantial body of evidence from various sources that certain types of depression and schizophrenia are caused by biochemical disorders that are genetically inherited (McMahon & McMahon, 1983). International surveys by the World Health Organization have examined disorders such as schizophrenia around the world and have found some basic similarities in the symptom profiles (Marsella, 1979). Psychological anthropologists have found, however, that the cultural beliefs and worldviews, family communication patterns, early childhood training, and particular life stresses of certain societies influence the content of these mental disorders. The delusions, hallucinations, and other symptoms that occur with these disorders reflect wide-ranging cultural variations throughout the world. Psychological anthropologists are beginning to combine biological explanations with cultural variables to arrive at more comprehensive, interactionist explanations of mental illness and personality disorders.

The Limits of Enculturation

When we consider enculturation or socialization, we are confronted with this question: Are humans only robots who respond rigidly to the demands of their innate drives and the norms of their culture? If our behavior depends so much on the enculturation process, what becomes of human concepts such as freedom and free will? Do people in our society or other societies have any personal choice over their behavior, or is all behavior and thought shaped by innate drives and the norms of these societies?

Unique Biological Tendencies

In actuality, although enculturation plays a major role in producing personality and behavioral strategies within society, there are a number of reasons why enculturation is not completely determinative. First, people are born with different innate tendencies (not closed instincts) for responding to the environment in a variety of ways. Our individual behavior is partially a result of our biological constitution, which influences our hormones, metabolism, and other aspects of our physiology. All societies have people who differ with respect to temperament because of these innate tendencies. Enculturation cannot produce people who respond only to environmental or cultural pressures in a uniform manner.

Individual Variation

Second, enculturation is never a completely uniform process. Enculturation experiences are blended and synthesized in unique ways by individuals. Even in the most isolated, small-scale societies, young people behave differently from their parents. Furthermore, not all people in a particular society are socialized or enculturated in exactly the same manner. The vast amounts of information transmitted through enculturation often lead to variations in what children are taught in different families and institutions.

In addition, norms do not dictate behavior in any rigid manner. People in any society are always confronted with contradictory norms, and society is always changing, affecting the process of enculturation. Enculturation rarely provides people with a precise blueprint for the behavioral responses needed in the many situations they face.

Thus, enculturation is an imprecise process. People may internalize the general program for behavior—a series of ideal norms, rules, and cultural guidelines for action—but how these general principles apply in any specific set of concrete circumstances is difficult or impossible to specify. In some cases, people obey social and cultural rules completely, whereas in others they violate or ignore them. Enculturation provides the historically developed cultural forms through which the members of society share meanings and symbols and relate to one another. But in reality, people maneuver within these cultural forms, choosing their actions to fulfill both their own needs and the demands of their society.

SUMMARY

Psychological anthropologists attempt to understand similarities and differences in behavior, thought, and feelings among societies by focusing on the relationship between the individual and culture, or the process of enculturation. One question that psychological anthropologists focus on is the degree to which human behavior is influenced by biological tendencies versus learning. Today, most anthropologists have adopted an interactionist approach that emphasizes both biology and culture as influences on enculturation and human behavior.

Another related question is whether humans, as part of the animal kingdom, have instincts or genetically programmed behaviors that nonhuman animals have. Many nonhuman animals have closed instincts that rigidly structure their behavior patterns, allowing for survival and adaptation in specific environmental conditions. These closed instincts have been selected by environmental factors over millions of years of evolution.

It does not appear that humans have closed instincts. Instead, humans have the unique capacity for culture, which enables them to modify and shape their behavior to adapt to different environmental conditions. Without enculturation, humans are unable to think, behave, and develop emotionally in order to function in society.

The early studies of enculturation, called culture-and-personality studies, focused on culture as if it were an integrated type of personality. These early studies by pioneers such as Ruth Benedict and Margaret Mead provided some important data regarding enculturation processes, but they often exaggerated the significance of cultural determinants of human behavior. However, these efforts led to a more systematic examination of enculturation and childhood training. These studies have refined our understanding of childhood training in many different types of societies.

The theories of Sigmund Freud have had an influence on psychological anthropology. His model of enculturation and personality development has been used by a number of psychological anthropologists to investigate human behavior. In some cases, anthropologists collaborate with psychoanalysts to study dreams, sexual fantasies, family relations, and topics such as incest. Incest, incest avoidance, and the incest taboo have been studied thoroughly within anthropology, leading to insightful explanations for these phenomena.

Enculturation's relationship to sexual practices and norms has been a topic of research in psychological anthropology. A wide variation of sexual practices and norms in different parts of the world has been described. These practices and norms, including widely distributed patterns of homosexual behavior and acceptance of a third gender beyond male and female, indicate how enculturation influences the sex drive in human communities.

The relationship between enculturation and cognition has also been a field of study within psychological anthropology. Structuralist anthropology, developed by Claude Levi-Strauss, focuses on the relationship between culture and thought processes. Levi-Strauss hypothesized that the human mind is structured to produce underlying patterns of thinking that are universally based.

Psychologist Jean Piaget's studies on the development of cognitive processes have also influenced psychological anthropology. Many researchers are actively engaged in testing Piaget's stage model of cognitive development in different societies. Cognitive anthropologists have been drawing from the fields of computer modeling and psychological experimentation in laboratories to examine cognition. Evolutionary psychologists have hypothesized that humans have some genetically prepared predispositions that have a wide-ranging influence on enculturation, cognition, and human behavior. Their research has been a leading example of interactionist research in psychological anthropology.

Emotional development is another area of study in psychological anthropology. Researchers are trying to understand how emotions such as sadness, happiness, fear, anger, and contempt are similar and different from one society to another. Their findings indicate that there are both universal and specific cultural variations with respect to emotional development in different societies.

Psychological anthropologists have been exploring different forms of mental disorders in various societies. This type of research has led anthropology to challenge some of the typical classifications used in Western psychiatry and psychology to define mental disorders.

QUESTIONS TO THINK ABOUT

1. Discuss the differences between closed and open instincts. In your opinion, do humans have instincts?

2. What are some of the methods of enculturation used in your society? Give an example of how your own personality has been affected by enculturation.

3. Can anthropologists classify various cultures by identifying certain personality characteristics found among certain individuals, as did Ruth Benedict? Discuss the limitations of this approach.

4. Are emotional expressions universal? To what extent are human emotions such as anger or jealousy similar or different around the world?

5. Describe a pattern of human behavior that you believe to be "normal" for your society but that might be considered "abnormal" in another society.

KEY TERMS

closed instincts

cognitive anthropology

drives

evolutionary psychology

incest

incest avoidance

incest taboo

narratives

open instincts

personality

psychological
anthropologists

INTERNET EXERCISES

1. Explore **http://www.indiana.edu/~wanthro/URBAN.htm**. Look at section 3.1 of this website, "Early Urban Sociology." How do the concepts of *Gemeinschaft* and *Gesellschaft* relate to the concept of enculturation?

2. Play Lacan's Imaginary Prisoner Game at **http://enculturation.gmu.edu/1_2/heinemann/index.html**. How does playing the game create enculturation?   Compare your ideas to the text definition of enculturation.

SUGGESTED READINGS

BARNOUW, VICTOR. 1985. *Culture and Personality.* Homewood, IL: Dorsey Press. An excellent account of the whole field of psychological anthropology. It includes many of the classic studies as well as an evaluation of the overall field and data collected by psychological anthropologists.

BOURGUIGNON, ERIKA. 1979. *Psychological Anthropology: An Introduction to Human Nature and Cultural Differences.* New York: Holt, Rinehart & Winston. This book is another thorough introduction to the field of psychological anthropology. Bourguignon includes discussion of the classics and takes up topics such as the studies of altered states of consciousness and mental illness.

D'ANDRADE, ROY. 1995. *The Development of Cognitive Anthropology.* Cambridge: Cambridge University Press. This is the best overview of the field of cognitive anthropology. It summarizes the research that began in the early 1950s up through the modern day.

HINTON, ALEXANDER LABAN (Ed.). 1999. *Biocultural Approaches to the Emotions.* Cambridge: Cambridge University Press. A state-of-the-art overview of the most recent studies of human emotions by anthropologists who employ an interactionist understanding of biology and culture.

SHORE, BRADD. 1996. *Culture in Mind: Cognition, Culture, and the Problem of Meaning.* New York: Oxford University Press. A recently published book that criticizes many of the early approaches to combining culture and psychology in explaining human thought and behavior. Shore advocates a psychological anthropology approach that draws on recent trends in cognitive science and structuralism.

SHWEDER, RICHARD. 1991. *Thinking through Cultures: Expeditions in Cultural Psychology.* Cambridge, MA: Harvard University Press. A state-of-the-art introduction to major questions addressed by psychological anthropologists. This book includes many findings by psychologists and how those findings bear on anthropological studies.

WHITE, GEOFFREY M., and JOHN KIRKPATRICK (Eds.). 1985. *Person, Self, and Experience: Exploring Pacific Ethnopsychologies.* Berkeley: University of California Press. This anthology contains a series of essays by psychological anthropologists who focus on the Pacific islands. They describe how enculturation influences emotions, cognition, and behavior in various ways throughout the Pacific region. These researchers tend to emphasize the cultural perspective, viewing psychological development as primarily induced by cultural processes.

12

Language

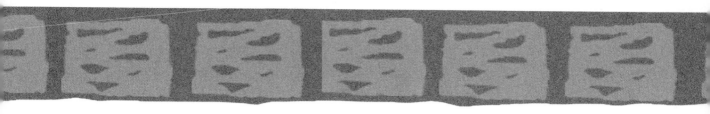

CHAPTER OUTLINE

CHAPTER QUESTIONS

- What is it that makes human languages unique in comparison with nonhuman animal communication?

- What does the research indicate about nonhuman animal communication?

- What do anthropologists conclude about the evolution of language?

- How do linguistic anthropologists study language?

- What have anthropologists learned about how children acquire their languages?

- What is the relationship between language and culture?

- How do anthropologists study the history of languages?

- What does the field of sociolinguistics tell us about language use?

- What other forms of communication do humans use aside from language?

In Chapter 10 we discussed how the capacity for culture enables humans to learn symbolically and to transmit symbols from generation to generation. **Language** is a system of symbols with standard meanings. Through language, members of a society are able to communicate with one another. It is an integral aspect of culture. Language allows humans to communicate with one another about what they are experiencing at any given moment, what they have experienced in the past, and what they are planning for the future. Like culture, the language of any particular individual exists before the birth of the individual and is publicly shared by the members of a society. People born in the United States are exposed to an English-speaking language community, whereas people in Russia learn the Russian language. These languages provide the context for symbolic understanding within these different societies. In this sense, language, as part of culture, transcends the individual. Without language, humans would have difficulty transmitting culture. Without culture, humans would lose their unique "humanity."

When linguists refer to language, they usually mean spoken language. Yet spoken language is only one form of communication. **Communication** is the act of transferring information to others. As we will discover in this chapter, many nonhuman animals have basic communication skills. We will also discover that humans communicate with one another in ways other than through language.

Nonhuman Communication

Teaching Apes to Sign

Psychologists and other scientists have conducted a considerable amount of research on animal communication. Some of the most interesting and controversial research on animal communication has been done on chimpanzees and gorillas, animals that are close physiologically and developmentally to humans. In 1966 psychologists Allen and Beatrice Gardner adopted a female chimpanzee named Washoe and began teaching her the American Sign Language (ASL, or Ameslan), a nonvocal form of communication used by the deaf. After several years, Washoe was able to master hundreds of signs. This was truly a remarkable feat for a chimpanzee, and it challenged the traditional assumption that only humans have the capacity for using symbols (Gardner & Gardner, 1969).

At the Yerkes Regional Primate Research Center at Emory University in Atlanta, Georgia, in the 1970s a chimpanzee named Lana was taught to communicate through a color-coded computer keyboard. Researchers concluded that Lana was able to use and combine signs in the computer language. For example, she referred to a cucumber as a "green banana" and to an orange as an "apple that is orange" (Rumbaugh, 1977). Primatologist Roger Fouts, who took over Washoe and three other survivors of the Gardners' project, found that these chimps could produce category words for certain types of foods: celery was "pipe food"; watermelon was "candy drink"; and radish, a food first tasted by Washoe, was "hurt cry food" (Fouts & Budd, 1979).

In a widely publicized study in the 1970s, Francine Patterson taught Koko, a female gorilla, to use 170 ASL words. Koko was billed as the world's first "talking" gorilla (Patterson & Cohn, 1978; Patterson & Linden, 1981). At the age of 4, Koko was given an intelligence test based on the Stanford-Binet Intelligence Scale and scored an 85, only slightly below the score of an average human child. Patterson contends that Koko even told stories about her violent capture in Africa. In addition, according to Patterson, Koko demostrated the capacity to lie, deceive, swear, joke, and combine signs in new and creative ways.

Ape Sign Language Reexamined

These studies of language use by apes have challenged traditional ideas regarding the gap between humans and other types of animals. They are not, however, without their critics. One source of criticism is based on work done at Columbia University by psychologist Herbert Terrace (1986). Terrace began examining the previous ape language studies by training a chimpanzee named Nim Chimpsky. Videotapes of the learning sessions were used to observe carefully the cues that may have been emitted by the trainers. Terrace also viewed the videotapes of the other studies on chimpanzee communication.

Terrace's conclusions challenged some of the earlier studies. Videotape analysis revealed that Nim rarely initiated signing behaviors, signing only in response to gestures by the instructors, and that 50 percent of his signs were simply imitative.

Researcher Joyce Butler showing Nim the chimpanzee the sign for drink.

Unlike humans, Nim did not learn the two-way nature of conversation. Nim also never signed without expecting some reward. In addition, Nim's phrases were random combinations of signs. And Nim never signed to another chimpanzee who knew ASL unless a teacher coached him. Finally, the videotapes of the other projects showed that prompters gave unconscious signals to the chimpanzees through their body gestures.

Terrace's overall conclusions indicate that chimpanzees are highly intelligent animals who can learn many signs. They cannot, however, understand *syntax,* the set of grammatical rules governing the way words combine to form sentences. An English-speaking child can systematically place a noun before a verb followed by an object without difficulty. A chimpanzee cannot use these types of grammatical rules to structure sentences. Terrace concludes that although chimpanzees have remarkable intellectual capacities and excellent memories, they do not have the syntactical abilities of humans to form sentences.

Terrace's work has not ended the ape language debate. In her book *Ape Language: From Conditioned Response to Symbol* (1986), Sue Savage-Rumbaugh reports on a ten-year-old chimpanzee named Kanzi who, she believes, communicates at the level of a two-year-old child. Kanzi has learned to communicate with *lexigrams,* geometric word-symbols that act as substitutes for human speech. Two hundred and fifty lexigrams are displayed on a large keyboard. At the age of two-and-a-half, Kanzi spontaneously reached for the keyboard, pointed to the lexigram for "chase," and ran away. Savage-Rumbaugh observed him repeatedly touch the lexigram for "chase" and scamper off. By age six, Kanzi had mastered a vocabulary of ninety symbols.

In addition, Savage-Rumbaugh notes that Kanzi indicated that he understood spoken English words. She observed Kanzi listening to spoken words like a human child does. The preliminary research indicates that Kanzi could understand English words, even when produced by a speech synthesizer. Another astonishing revelation reported by Savage-Rumbaugh is that Kanzi appeared to have a crude command of syntax. He seemed to be able to use word order to convey meaning. On his own initiative, Kanzi requested activities in the order he desired them. For example, if he wanted to be chased and play-bitten, he first pressed the lexigram

for "chase," then "bite." Savage-Rumbaugh reports that Kanzi could understand some 650 sentences.

These more recent research results are impressive, but whether they indicate that apes can use true language remains unclear. Most anthropologists have concluded that apes show the ability to manipulate linguistic symbols when the symbols are hand gestures or plastic symbols. That they cannot transmit language beyond the level of a two-year-old human child does not mean that they are failed humans. Chimps are perfectly good at being chimps. It would appear that humans have much different sorts of linguistic capacities.

Ethological Research on Ape Communication

In addition to laboratory research on animal communication, **ethologists,** scientists who study the behavior of animals in their natural environment, have conducted a number of impressive field studies. Ethologists find that many types of animals have *call systems*—certain sounds or vocalizations that produce specific meanings—which are used to communicate for adaptive purposes. Animals such as prairie dogs, chickens, various types of monkeys, and chimpanzees have call systems.

In an ethological study of gorillas in central Africa, George Schaller isolated twenty-two vocalizations used by these primates. This number compares with twenty vocalizations used by howler monkeys, thirty used by Japanese macaque monkeys, and nine used by gibbons (Schaller, 1976). Like these other vocalizations, the gorilla sounds are associated with specific behaviors or emotional states, such as restful feeding states, sexual behavior, play, anger, and warnings of approaching threats. Infant gorillas also emit certain sounds when their mothers venture off. Schaller admits that some vocalizations were not accompanied by any specific type of behavior or stimulus.

Chimpanzee Communication: Jane Goodall The most impressive long-term investigation of chimpanzees in their natural environment was carried out by Jane Goodall, a primatologist who has been studying the chimpanzees of the Gombe Game Reserve in Africa since 1960. Goodall has gathered a great deal of information on the vocalizations used by these chimps. Her observations have shown that the chimpanzees use a great variety of

Jane Goodall with chimpanzees.

calls, which are tied directly to emotional states such as fear, annoyance, and sexual excitement. She concludes that "the production of a sound in the absence of the appropriate emotional state seems to be an almost impossible task for the chimpanzee" (Goodall, 1986:125).

Goodall found that the chimps use *intraparty calls,* communication within the group, and *distance calls,* communication to other groups. Intraparty calls include pant-grunts directed to a higher-ranking individual within the group as a token of respect, and barks, whimpers, squeaks, screams, coughs, and other sounds directed toward other chimps in the immediate group. Distance calls serve a wider range of functions, including drawing attention to local food sources, announcing the precise location of individuals in the home territory, and, in times of distress, bringing help from distant allies. Further research is needed to discover whether the chimps use these vocalizations to distinguish among different types of foods and dangers in the environment.

Animal Communication and Human Language

Both laboratory and field studies of animal communication offer fascinating insights into the question of what distinguishes human communication from animal communication. Many Western philosophers have identified speech as the major distinction between humans and other animals. Modern studies on animal communication, however, suggest that the language gap separating humans from other animals is not as wide as it once appeared. These studies also indicate that fundamental differences exist between animal communication and human languages. The question is not whether animals can communicate, because we know that almost every animal can. The real question is: How does animal communication differ from human communication? In searching for an answer to this question, linguistic anthropologists have identified a number of distinctive characteristics of human languages. The four most important features are productivity, displacement, arbitrariness, and combining sounds (Hockett & Ascher, 1964).

Productivity

Human languages are inherently flexible and creative. Users of human languages, even small children, can create sentences never heard before by anyone. There are no limits to our capability to produce messages that refer to the past, present, or future. We can express different thoughts, meanings, and experiences in infinite ways. In contrast, animal communication systems in natural settings are rigid and fixed. The sounds of animal communications do not vary and cannot be modified. The offspring of chimpanzees will always use the same pattern of vocalization as the parents. In contrast, the highly flexible nature of human languages allows for efficient and creative uses of symbolic communication. William von Humboldt, a nineteenth-century linguist, used the phrase "the infinite use of finite media" to suggest the idea of linguistic productivity (von Humboldt, [1836] 1972; Pinker, 1994).

Displacement

It is clear from field studies, and to some extent from laboratory studies, that the meaning of a sound or vocalization of a nonhuman animal is closely tied to a specific type of stimulus. For example, the chimpanzee's vocalization is associated with a particular emotional state and stimulus. Thus, a growl or scream as a warning to the group cannot be made in the absence of some perceived threat. Similarly, animals such as parrots and mynah birds can learn to imitate a wide variety of words, but they cannot substitute or displace one word for another. In contrast, the meanings of sounds in human languages can refer to people, things, or events that are not present, a feature called *displacement*. We can discuss things that are not in front of our visual or auditory capacities.

This capacity for displacement enables humans to communicate with one another using highly abstract concepts. Humans can express their objectives in reference to the past, present, and future. They can discuss spiritual or hypothetical phenomena that do not exist concretely. They can discuss past history through myth or specific genealogical relations. Humans can refer to what will happen after death through myth or theological concepts such as heaven or spiritual enlightenment. Displacement allows humans to plan for the future through the use of foresight. Obviously, this linguistic ability for displacement is interrelated with the general symbolic capacities that are shared by humanity, providing the basis of culture as discussed in Chapter 10. Symbolic capacities allow humans to manipulate abstract concepts to develop complex beliefs and worldviews.

Arbitrariness

The arbitrariness of sounds in a communication system is another distinctive feature of human languages. Words seldom have any necessary connection with the concrete objects or abstract symbols they represent. In English we say one, two, and three to refer to the numbers, whereas the Chinese say *yi, er,* and *san.* Neither language has the "correct" word for the numbers, because there is no correct word. "Ouch" is pronounced "ay" in Spanish and "ishkatak" in the Nootkan Indian language. A German shepherd dog does not have any difficulty understanding the bark of a French poodle. An English speaker, however, will have trouble understanding a Chinese speaker.

Combining Sounds to Produce Meanings

We have mentioned that various animals have sounds that indicate different meanings in specific contexts. Human languages, in addition, have units of sound that cannot be correlated with units of meaning. Every human language has between twelve and sixty of these sound units, called *phonemes.* A **phoneme** is a unit of sound that distinguishes meaning in a particular language. For example, in English the difference between *dime* and *dine* is distinguished by the sound difference or phonemic difference between /m/ and /n/. English has forty-five phonemes, Italian has twenty-seven, and Hawaiian has thirteen (Farb, 1974).

Nonhuman animals cannot combine their sound units to communicate new meanings; one vocalization is given to indicate a specific response. In contrast, in human languages the same sounds can be combined and recombined to form different meanings. As an illustration, the sounds usually represented by the English letters *p, t, c,* and *a* (the vowel sound in the word *bat*) have no meaning on their own. But they can be used to form words like *pat, tap, cat, apt, act, tact, pact,* and so on, which do have meanings. The Hawaiian language, with only thirteen sound units, has almost three thousand words consisting of different combinations of three sounds, and more than five million words formed by combinations of six sounds. Phonemes that may have no meaning can be combined and recombined to form literally as many meaningful units (words) as people need or want. Primates and other animals do not have this ability.

Having defined these features of human language, we can discern fundamental differences between human and animal communication. However, some researchers working with chimpanzees in laboratories are still not willing to label human languages as "true languages," as distinguished from "animal communication systems." They criticize what they refer to as the "anthropocentric" view of language—the view that takes human language as its standard. Because chimpanzees do not have the physical ability to form the sounds made by humans, it may be unfair to compare their language strictly in terms of vocal communication.

The Evolution of Language

Throughout the centuries, linguists, philosophers, and physical anthropologists have developed theories concerning the origins of human language. One early theory, known as the "bowwow" theory, maintains that language arose when humans imitated the sounds of nature by the use of onomatopoeic words, such as "cock-a-doodle-do," or "sneeze," or "mumble." Another theory argues that language evolved as humans detected the natural sounds of objects in nature. Known as the "dingdong" theory, this argument assumed that a relationship exists between a word and its meaning because nature gives off a harmonic ring. For example, all of nature, including rocks, streams, plants, and animals, was thought to emit a ringing sound that could be detected by humans. The harmonic ring of a rock supposedly sounded like "rock". Both theories have been discredited, replaced by other hypotheses concerning the evolution of language.

The Anatomy of Language

As discussed earlier in the text, the evolution of hominids was accompanied by increases in brain size. The expansion of the hominid brain reflects the increasing size of the cerebral cortex, the part related to all of the higher functions of the brain, such as memory and, most likely, symbolic and cultural capacities. Although many capacities of the human brain—including memory, learning, and other functions—are not completely understood by modern science, we do know that the cerebral cortex contains the billions of nerve cells needed for receiving, storing, and processing information.

The Human Brain and Speech   Other centers of the brain play important roles in the human capacity for language. The human brain is divided into two hemispheres. Although neither hemisphere is dominant, and both play important roles in all functions, most human linguistic skills are more closely identified with one hemisphere. In general, the left hemisphere controls specialized functions related to linguistic abilities, and the right hemisphere controls functions related to spatial orientation and proportion. One area of the brain that is located in the left hemisphere and that especially influences human language abilities is known as *Broca's area;* it is associated with the production of sound or pronunciation and with grammatical abilities.

Another area related to linguistic abilities is *Wernicke's area,* also located in the left hemisphere of the brain. Wernicke's area is associated with the ability to understand the meanings of words and sentences, or the semantics of language. This center of the brain is important for listening and reading.

Human Anatomy and Speech   Other anatomical and physiological features contribute to human language abilities. No animal other than the human being has the anatomy for sustaining speech production. Human vocal organs form an irregular tube connecting the lungs, windpipe, and *larynx,* the voice box containing the vocal cords. Another vocal organ is the *pharynx,* the part of the vocal tract between the back of the tongue and the larynx extending into the nasal cavity. The larynx serves to hold air in the lungs and to control its release. These vocal organs work in conjunction with our tongue, lips, and nose to produce speech. The lungs force air through the pharynx, which changes shape to control the column of air. The nasal cavity, lips, and tongue can constrict or stop the flow of air at any point, enabling us to make vowel or consonant sounds. The organs involved in producing speech are illustrated in Figure 12.1.

The major difference between the anatomical structure of chimpanzees and that of modern humans in relation to speech is the lower position of the larynx and the consequent lengthening of the upper vocal tract in humans. Although this reconfiguration of the vocal tract makes breathing more difficult, increases the risk of death from choking, and crowds the teeth, which can lead to impacted wisdom teeth, the advantages of having language must

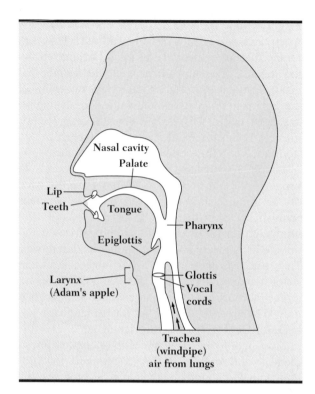

FIGURE 12.1 The physiology of speech-making, which is unique to humans.

have outweighed the disadvantages caused by the change in anatomy. Nonhuman primates such as chimps cannot speak; their vocal anatomy does not enable them to produce the sounds necessary for human speech, and in addition, their vocalizations do not appear to be under voluntary control.

Could Early Hominids Speak? Some physical anthropologists are using complex computer programs to compare the anatomy of primates, early hominids, and modern humans. Through this method, Philip Lieberman and Jeffrey Laitman have proposed a hypothesis regarding the evolution of language. They suggest that australopithecines did not have the vocal tract needed to produce the range of vowels found in human language. They also conclude that Neandertals, archaic *Homo sapiens,* could not produce vowels such as *a, i,* and *u,* thus limiting their linguistic abilities (Laitman, 1984; Lieberman, 1984). However, if Neandertals could have produced and combined phonemes into meaningful units, they may have had language. But

most researchers conclude that language, as we know it, appeared only within the last 100,000 years or so and is associated with the development of the vocal tract and other characteristics of modern *Homo sapiens.*

This analysis has given rise to a popular hypothesis regarding the evolution of language that suggests that australopithecines probably communicated through sign communication, vocal calls, and gestures. These communication abilities developed gradually with the evolution of *H. habilis, H. erectus,* and archaic *H. sapiens.* Eventually, these developments led to the increased symbolizing power of language that is associated with modern humans. Without more evidence, however, these hypotheses remain controversial.

Whatever the precise determinants of the evolution of language, it is difficult to identify the critical stage in the evolution from a simple, sign-based communication system to a more advanced symbolic form of language. It is, however, recognized that this capacity broadly expanded human capabilities for adaptation and creativity. The capacity for language was probably the last major step in our biological evolution. Since that time, human history has been dominated by cultural rather than biological evolution. This cultural evolution and the subsequent developments in adaptation and creativity could not have occurred before a fully evolved language ability.

The Structure of Language

Linguistic anthropologists compare the structure of different languages. To do so, they study the *sounds* of a language (phonology), the *words* of a language (morphology), the *sentence structure* of a language (syntax), the *meaning* of a language (semantics), and the *rules* for the appropriate use of language (pragmatics). More than six thousand languages have existed throughout history, all of which have contained these five components, although the components vary considerably from one language to another.

Phonology

Phonology is the study of the sounds used in language. Although all human languages have both vowel and consonant sounds, no language makes use of all the sounds humans can make. To study phonetic differences among languages, linguists have developed the International Phonetic Alphabet (IPA), which enables linguists to transcribe all the sounds produced in the world's languages. Each sound is used somewhere in the world, although no single language contains all of them. Each language has its own *phonetic inventory,* consisting of all the sounds normally produced by its speakers, and also a *phonemic inventory,* consisting of the sound units that can produce word contrasts in the language. As we have already seen, human languages, which have only a limited number of sounds, can combine these sounds to produce complex meanings.

Linguists attempt to discover the phonemes, or contrasting sound-units of a language, by looking for what are called *minimal pairs*—words that are identical except for one difference in sound. For example, the English words *lot* and *rot* form a minimal pair; they are identical except for their beginning sounds, spelled *l* and *r*. The fact that English speakers recognize *lot* and *rot* as different words establishes that /l/ and /r/ are contrasting sound-units, or phonemes, in English.

When linguistic anthropologists analyze the phonological system of a language, they attempt to organize the sounds, or **phones,** of the language into a system of contrasting phonemes. For example, English speakers produce both a /p/ sound and the same sound accompanied by aspiration, a light puff of air, symbolized in the IPA as /pʰ/; compare the difference between the *p* sounds in *spy* and *pie*. Since in English the sounds /p/ and /pʰ/ never form a minimal pair, and their pronunciation depends on their position in a word, these sounds are *allophones* of the same phoneme in English. In other languages, such as Aymara (spoken in Bolivia, Perú, and Chile), aspiration of consonants produces a phonemic contrast; compare Aymara /*hupa*/, which means they, with /*hupʰa*/, a kind of cereal. In Aymara, then, the sounds /p/ and /pʰ/ belong to separate phonemes, just as /l/ and /r/ do in English, as we saw above. This illustrates the fact that the "same" sounds may be contrastive in one language and not contrastive in another.

In addition to aspiration, sounds may be modified in other ways, including nasality, pitch, stress, length of time the sound is held, and so on. Many Asian languages, such as Chinese and Thai, are *tonal;* that is, a word's meaning is affected by the tones (contrasting pitches) of the sounds that make up the word. Put another way, the tones of the language have phonemic value. To an English speaker's ear, a Chinese or Thai speaker sounds musical. For example, in Thai *may* can mean "new," "to burn," or "silk," depending on the tone used.

Pueblo Indians use many nasalized sounds to produce phonemic differences. Arabs use the back of the tongue and the throat muscles, whereas Spanish speakers use the tip of the tongue. The !Kung San, or Ju/'hoansi, of southern Africa have a unique manner of producing phonemic differences. They use a sharp intake of air to make clicks that shape meaning for them. Their language also requires more use of the lips to produce smacks than most other languages. The Ju/'hoansi language has been referred to as a "clicking language."

Most people are unaware of the complex physiological and mental processes required for pronouncing the sounds of their native tongue. Only through extensive phonetic and phonological analysis by linguists and anthropologists is this component of language understood.

Morphology

To study the words of human languages, anthropologists isolate the **morphemes,** the smallest units of a language that convey meaning. The study of morphemes is called **morphology.** Morphemes may be short, only a single phoneme; or they may be a combination of phonemes. They are the minimal building blocks of meaning and cannot be reduced further. *Bound morphemes* are those morphemes that cannot stand alone, such as suffixes and prefixes. For example, in English *s* is a bound morpheme that indicates the plural, and the prefix *un* is a bound morpheme meaning not. *Free morphemes,* in contrast, are independent units of meaning; they can stand alone as nouns, verbs, adjectives, or adverbs. For example, words such as *boy, girl, happy,* and *close* are free morphemes.

In any language, morphemes are limited in number, and languages differ in how these morphemes are used and combined. In contrast to many languages, English has complex rules governing the formation of plurals of certain words (for example, *geese, mice, children,* and *shrimp*). Some languages, such as Chinese, generally use one morpheme for each word. Other languages, such as the Eskimo language, combine a large number of affixes to form words.

An important way that languages differ is the extent to which they use morphology to convey meaning. For example, in English we can say "the girl sees the dog" or "the dog sees the girl". The nouns *girl* and *dog* do not change form, and only their position in the sentence indicates which is subject and which is object. But in Russian, *dyevushka videt sobaku* means that the girl sees the dog; the dog sees the girl is *sobaka videt dyevushku*. Note that the endings on the nouns show which is subject and object, even if the word order is changed: *Sobaku videt dyevushka* still means that the girl sees the dog.

Syntax

The **syntax** of a language is the rules for the way phrases and sentences are made up out of words. For example, these rules determine whether a subject comes before or after a verb, or whether an object follows a verb. Linguistic anthropologist Joseph Greenberg (1990) classified languages based on word order within sentences—that is, the location of the subject (S), the verb (V), and the object (O). He demonstrated that these components occur in six possible orders: VSO, SVO, SOV, VOS, OSV, and OVS. But, in fact, what Greenberg found in his cross-linguistic comparison is that usually just three patterns of word order occur: VSO, SVO, SOV. Since his study, other languages have been discovered with the VOS, OVS, and OSV forms, though the last two are extremely rare (Smith, 1999).

Although most languages permit variation in syntax to allow for emphasis in expression, most linguists suggest that some innate universal capacities may influence word order. For example, the expression for the English sentence "The boy drank the water" can be found in all languages. Notice the variations in syntactical order among six different languages:

        S   V   O

English: the bóy dránk the wáter

       S   V   O

Russian: mál'c_ik vy´pil vódu

       V   S   O

Arabic: s_áraba lwáladu lma-?a

       S   V   O

Hausa: ya-ro- yás_a- ruwa-

       S   V   O

Thai: dègchaaj dyym nàam

       S   O   V

Quechua: wámbra yakúta upiárqan

(Hausa is a West African language. Quechua is a language of the ancient Incas and their modern descendants.)

The syntax of a language also includes rules for transforming one kind of sentence into another, for example, forming questions from statements. To form questions from statements, English has a rule that moves the auxiliary verb from its normal position in the sentence to a position at the front of the sentence. This rule allows us to take the statement "Mary will study for the exam," and by moving *will* to the front, transform it into the question "Will Mary study for the exam?"

Semantics

Semantics is the study of the meaning of symbols, words, phrases, and sentences of a language. The field of semantics has led to important developments in linguistic anthropology. Linguistic anthropologists focus on the meaning of language as it relates to beliefs, concepts, and patterns of thought in different societies. A specialty has developed to account for the meaning of concepts and terms with respect to kinship terms and other cultural phenomena. This specialty, sometimes referred to as *ethnosemantics,* overlaps the field of cognitive anthropology introduced in Chapter 11.

Kinship Terms The goal of ethnosemantics is to understand the meanings of words, phrases, and sentences, and how members of other societies use language to organize things, events, and behaviors.

For example, this type of analysis has been applied to kinship terminologies of many societies. It became increasingly clear to many anthropologists that they could not understand the kinship terms of other societies by simply translating them into English. English terms such as *mother, father, brother, brother-in-law, cousin, aunt,* and *uncle* treat the meaning of kinship terms differently from the kinship terms of other societies.

Some groups classify their kin with very precise terms for individuals, no matter how distantly they are related. English kin terms are fairly precise and distinct with respect to genealogical relatedness, yet English does not specify every kin relationship precisely. For example, English speakers do not distinguish between maternal and paternal uncles or aunts. Chinese kinship terminology, on the other hand, includes different terms for one's mother's brother and one's father's brother. There are separate terms for every sibling as well as for different cousins. This is an example of a highly descriptive kinship terminology. Other forms of kinship terminologies are highly generalized. In the Hawaiian kinship system, there is no specific term to parallel the English term *father.* Instead, the Hawaiians use one general term to classify their father and all male relatives in their father's generation. Some kinship terminologies, such as those of the Iroquois Indians, are intermediate between the descriptive and the generalized forms. The Iroquois have one single term for one's father and father's brother but two separate terms for one's mother and one's mother's brother.

Ethnosemanticists or cognitive anthropologists worked out systematic methods to understand the kinship terminologies of many different societies by focusing on the distinctive common features of these terminologies (D'Andrade, 1995). For example, in English there is a male and female contrast with every kin term except *cousin.* In addition, the feature of generation is designated in terms such as *uncle* and *nephew, aunt* and *niece,* and in these same terms we distinguish between ascending and descending generations. There is also a contrast between *direct* (same generation) and *collateral* (different generation) relatives. Great uncles and great aunts are collateral relatives, whereas brothers and sisters are direct relatives. Ethnosemanticists use these methods to analyze other forms of kinship terminologies in various societies.

Recently, a fascinating study by Larry Hirschfeld suggests that there are some universal aspects regarding the meaning of kinship terminology (1986, 1989). Hirschfeld found that children and adults assume that kinship terms refer to a "natural affinity" for their own genealogical relatives and families. Children appear to have an intuitive understanding of the relationship between kin terms and their relatives and family. Kinship terms are used to refer to people who share a common descent and an internal "essence." The family is based on a particular group of people and is different from a group of students in a class or other types of groups. Cognitive anthropologists continue to investigate kin terminologies and other cultural phenomena to seek out both similarities and differences among human groups.

Language Acquisition

Although human infants are born with the ability to speak a language, they are not born preprogrammed to speak a particular language such as English. Just as infants are exposed to enculturation to absorb and learn about their culture, they must be exposed to the phonemes, morphemes, syntax, and semantics of the language within their culture. Linguistic anthropologists have examined this process, drawing on different hypotheses regarding language acquisition.

Children learning language on a computer.

The empiricist philosopher John Locke (1632–1704) suggested that the human mind at birth is like a blank tablet, a *tabula rasa,* and that infants learn language through habit formation. This hypothesis was further developed by behavioral psychologists such as B. F. Skinner, who maintained that infants learn language through conditioned responses and feedback from their environment. An infant might babble a sound that resembles an acceptable word like "Daddy" and would then be rewarded for that response. Thus rewarded, the child would use the word "Daddy" in certain contexts. According to Skinner, children learn their entire language through this type of social conditioning.

The Enlightenment French philosopher René Descartes (1596–1650) advocated a contrasting view of language learning. He argued that innate ideas or structures in the human mind provide the basis for learning language. Until the late 1950s, most linguists and anthropologists working on language assumed that Locke's model, and by extension Skinner's, was correct. However, by about 1960 evidence began to accumulate that suggested that, in fact, humans come into the world especially equipped not only to learn language, but to learn any human language.

Chomsky on Language Acquisition

The most influential modern proponent of Descartes's hypothesis is linguist Noam Chomsky. Chomsky is interested in how people learn grammar, the set of rules that determine how sentences are constructed to produce meaningful statements. Most people cannot actually state the rules of their grammar, but they do use the rules to form understandable sentences. For example, in English we can transform the active sentence "Bill loves Mary" into a passive sentence, "Mary is loved by Bill." This change requires much grammatical knowledge, but most English speakers carry out this operation without thinking about it. According to Chomsky, all children learn these complex rules readily and do not seem to have difficulty producing meaningful statements, even when they have not been exposed to linguistic data that illustrate the rules in question. Furthermore, children are able to both produce and understand sentences they have never heard before. All this would be impossible, Chomsky claims, if learning language

Noam Chomsky

depended on trial-and-error learning and reinforcement, as Skinner had thought. In other words, Chomsky suggests that we are born with a brain prewired to enable us to acquire language easily; Chomsky often refers to this prewiring as *universal grammar.*

Universal grammar serves as a template, or model, against which a child matches and sorts out the patterns of morphemes and phonemes and the subtle distinctions that are needed to communicate in any language. According to Chomsky, a behavioristic understanding of language learning is too simplistic to account for the creativity and productivity of any human language. In his view, the universal structure of the human mind enables the child to acquire language and produce sentences never heard before. In addition, Chomsky and others who study language acquisition propose a *critical period,* between birth and roughly the onset of puberty, during which language acquisition must take place. If children are not exposed to language during that period, they may never be able to learn it, or they may learn it only in a very rudimentary fashion. Chomsky believes that the human brain contains genetically programmed blueprints or modules for language learning, and he often refers to language acquisition as a part of children's

APPLYING ANTHROPOLOGY

SAVING LANGUAGES

There are more than five thousand languages distributed throughout a population of over six billion people in the world. As many linguistic anthropologists have noted, however, tens of thousands of languages have become extinct through the years. In Western Europe, hundreds of languages disappeared with the expansion of agricultural empires that imposed their languages on conquered peoples. For example, during the expansion of the Roman Empire for approximately a thousand years, many tribal languages disappeared as they were replaced by Latin. Currently, only forty-five native languages still exist in Western Europe.

When Columbus discovered the Americas, more than two thousand languages existed among different Native American peoples. Yet even in pre-Columbian America, before A.D. 1500, native languages were displaced by the expansion of peoples such as the Aztecs and Incas in Central and South America. As the Spanish and British empires expanded into these regions, the indigenous languages began to disappear even more rapidly. A similar process has been ongoing throughout Asia, Africa, and the Middle East.

The majority of people in the world speak one of the "large" groups of languages, such as Mandarin Chinese (with more than one billion speakers), Spanish, or English. Most of the more than four thousand languages that exist are spoken in small-scale societies that have an average of five thousand people or so. For example, Papua New Guinea alone has perhaps as many as a thousand different languages distributed among various ethnic groups (Diamond, 1993). Other islands in countries such as Indonesia may have as many as four hundred different languages. Yet in all the areas of the Pacific and Asia, the "larger" languages are beginning to replace the "small" ones.

Some linguists estimate that if the present rate of the disappearance of languages remains constant, within a century or two our four thousand languages could be reduced to just a few hundred. For example, as young people in the Pacific islands begin to move from rural to urban regions, they usually abandon their traditional language and learn a majority tongue to be able to take advantage of educational and economic opportunities. As the media—television, radio, and newspapers—opt for a majority language, more people will elect to abandon their native languages. These are global processes that have resulted in linguistic homogeneity and the loss of traditional languages.

In North America and Alaska, there are some two hundred languages, ranging from Inuit and Yupik among the native Alaskans to Navajo, Hopi, Choctaw, Creek, Seminole, Chickasaw, and Cherokee in other areas. However, most of these languages are now on the verge of extinction. As Europeans began to expand and control North America and Alaska, they forced Native American children to speak the English language as a means of "civilizing" them. In many cases, Native American children were removed from their families and were forbidden to speak their native languages. In addition, most Native American peoples have had to learn English to adjust to circumstances in an English-language-dominated society. Thus, very few of the Native American languages are actively spoken.

Some people say that this process of global and linguistic homogenization and the loss of traditional languages is a positive development. As people begin to speak a common language, communication is increased, leading to improvements in societies that formerly could not unify through language. For example, in India, hundreds of languages existed before the British colonized the area. As the educated class in India (a small minority) began to learn and speak English, it helped provide a means of unifying India as a country. Many people say that for the purpose of developing commerce and political relationships, the abandonment of native languages is a good thing. Many businesspeople and politicians argue that multiple languages inhibit economic and political progress, and the elites of many countries have directly encouraged language loss.

A number of linguistic anthropologists, however, disagree with these policies. They may agree that people ought to have some common language to understand one another, to conduct business, and to have common political goals. But, they argue, this does not have to mean eliminating minority languages. It only requires that people become bilingual or multilingual. In most societies throughout the world, including Western Europe, people routinely learn two or more languages as children. The United States and Japan are exceptional in being monolingual societies.

Linguistic anthropologists find from their studies that people who are forced to abandon their native languages and cultures begin to lose their self-esteem. Bilingualism would permit these people to retain their own language while simultaneously learning the majority language to be able to share in a common national culture.

The U.S. government is beginning to realize that bilingualism has a positive influence on community development among minority populations such as Native Americans. Recently, a number of educational programs have been funded under the U.S. Bilingual Education Act. This act encourages the development of English-speaking skills; however, it also

Anthropologists are assisting people such as these Crow Indians in learning and thus saving their native languages.

offers instruction in the native languages. During the 1980s there were more than twenty Title VII projects serving Native American students from sixteen different language backgrounds.

Through these government-sponsored programs, linguistic anthropologists have been actively engaged in both research and language-renewal activities among the Native American population (Leap, 1988). These activities have led many younger Native Americans to become interested in studying their traditional languages, which may lead to improvements in classroom learning and inhibit high dropout rates among young students.

Anthropologist Russell Bernard has promoted the value of maintaining the native languages of people through the use of microcomputers (1992). Anthropologists use computers to help

develop writing systems and literature for native languages. Through this computer technology, anthropologists can help native peoples to produce literature in their own languages for future generations. Bernard emphasizes that this will enable all of humanity to profit from the ideas of these people. Bernard was able to establish a center in Mexico where the Indian population could learn to use computers to write in their native languages. Sixty Indian people have learned to write directly in languages such as Mixtec, Zapotec, Chatino, Amuzgo, Chinantec, and Mazataec. These native authors will use these texts to teach adults and children of their home regions to read. Projects such as these represent opportunities for anthropologists to apply their knowledge in solving important problems in U.S. society and beyond.

"growth," not something they do but rather something that happens to them.

Another important contribution of Chomsky's is the realization that human languages, despite their apparently great diversity, are really more alike than they are different. Anthropologists had previously assumed that languages could vary infinitely, and there was no limit to what could be found in a human language. Chomsky and the researchers that followed him, in contrast, have catalogued many basic, underlying ways in which all languages are really the same. In this view, a hypothetical Martian linguist visiting Earth would probably decide that all humans speak dialects of human language. Note that this is somewhat parallel to the search for cultural universals described in Chapter 10.

Chomsky's model is referred to as *generative grammar*. In this view, speakers of a language generate their sentences from a set of rules, some of which we have discussed above. This model is extremely powerful, because many sentences can be generated with a relatively small number of rules operating on the *lexicon*, or vocabulary, of the language. For example, a very simple generative grammar for English might include the following rules:

S —> NP VP (a sentence consists of a noun phrase plus a verb phrase)

VP —> V (NP) (a verb phrase consists of a verb plus an optional noun phrase)

NP —> Art N (a noun phrase consists of an article plus a noun)

N —> girl, dog

Art —> the, a

V —> sees

With this simple set of rules we can generate sentences like the girl sees the dog, a girl sees a dog, a dog sees the girl, the girl sees, and so on. Each time we add a noun or verb, we increase exponentially the number of sentences we can generate.

In the early years of generative grammar, Chomsky and others proposed an enormous number of complicated grammatical rules, including transformational rules, which had to be learned by children. But it soon became apparent that children could not, in the short time they take to acquire language, learn so many complex rules, and there has been a push more recently to simplify the generative model as much as possible. One of the more elegant outcomes of this trend has been the principles and parameters approach. One example of this is the head parameter, which determines whether the head of a phrase precedes or follows its complement (the only two possibilities). In English, for example, heads precede their complements, as illustrated below with the complements in brackets:

Verb + object	*sees [the dog]*
Preposition + object	*over [the rainbow]*
Noun + complement	*President [of Mexico]*
Adjective + complement	*afraid [of spiders]*

In other languages, like Japanese and Aymara, heads follow their complements (the rainbow + over; the dog + sees). Chomsky and others noticed that, as with the English examples above, this parameter tends to apply across all the possible phrase types in a language. In other words, English-speaking children don't have to learn, separately, that verbs precede their objects and prepositions precede theirs. They only need to learn one fact: The setting of the head parameter for English is head-initial. Once they know that, a number of apparently disparate facts about English fall into place. There is some evidence that children begin "setting" their head parameter very early, at around 2 years of age (Goodluck, 1991).

Recently, there has been a push toward what Chomsky and some other linguists call *minimalism,* a search for ways to further simplify the model of universal grammar, and many of the former generative rules have disappeared completely. One that remains is the *merge* rule, which allows for constituents such as words to be joined together (for example, forming the noun phrase *the dog* from the separate article *the* and noun *dog*). Another rule that continues to be useful is the *move* rule mentioned earlier. In keeping with minimalism, these rules are very general; what can be joined together, and what can be moved and to where, are determined by properties of the constituents involved (Chomsky, 1995).

Creole Languages One source of evidence for Chomsky's model of innate universal grammar is research on specific types of languages known as *creole* and *pidgin* languages. Linguist Derek Bickerton has compared these two types of languages from different areas of the world. Pidgin and creole languages develop from cross-cultural contact between speakers of mutually unintelligible languages. A pidgin language emerges when people combine terms from at least two different languages and develop a simple grammatical structure to communicate with one another. For example, in the New Guinea highlands, where many different languages were spoken, a pidgin language developed between the indigenous peoples and the Westerners.

In some cases, the children of the pidgin speakers begin to speak a creole language. The vocabulary of the creole language is similar to that of the pidgin, but the grammar is much more complex. There are more than a hundred known creole languages. Among them are the creole languages developed between African slaves and Europeans, leading to languages such as Haitian creole. A Hawaiian creole language emerged after contact between English-speaking Westerners and native Hawaiians.

What is remarkable, according to Bickerton, is that all these languages share similar grammatical patterns, despite the lack of contact among these diverse peoples. For example, Hawaiian creole uses the English word *walk* in a very different manner from standard English. The phrase "bin walk" means "had walked"; "stay walk" is continuing action, as in "I am walking" or "I was walking"; and "I bin stay walk" means "I had been walking." Although this phrasing might sound unusual to a person from England or the United States, it does conform to a clear set of grammatical rules. Very similar tense systems are found in all other creole languages, whatever their vocabularies or geographic origins.

Bickerton suggests that the development of creole languages may parallel the evolution of early human languages. Because of an innate universal grammatical component of the human mind, languages emerged in uniform ways. The prehistoric languages would have had structures similar to that of the creole languages. As languages developed in various types of environments with different characteristics, people evolved different vocabularies and sentence structures. Yet when societies are uprooted by cultural contact, the innate rules for ordering language remain intact. Bickerton's thesis suggests that humans do have some sort of universal linguistic acquisition device, as hypothesized by Chomsky (Bickerton, 1985, 1999).

Ebonics as a Creole Language A number of linguists have been doing research on Ebonics, a distinctive variety of American English spoken by some African Americans. The term *Ebonics* is derived from the words *ebony* and *phonics,* meaning "black sounds" (Rickford, 1997). Ebonics is also known as Black English Vernacular (BEV), Black English (BE), African American Vernacular English (AAVE), and African American English (AAE). The majority of African Americans do not speak Ebonics; however, it is commonly spoken among working-class and, in particular, among adolescent African Americans. Linguistic anthropologists have suggested that Ebonics may have emerged as a creole language under the conditions of slavery in the United States. As slaves from Africa, captured from different areas and speaking an enormous variety of languages, were placed together on plantations in the American South, they developed a pidgin language to communicate. From this pidgin, the children may have created a systematic syntax and grammar, as they were at the critical stage of language learning. Just as Jamaican or Haitian creole emerged in the Caribbean under the conditions of slavery, a variety of creoles may have evolved in the United States. One form of an early creole still exists among African Americans off the coast of South Carolina and Georgia on the Sea Islands. This creole is known as Gullah. Other forms of creole speech may have been introduced by the large numbers of slaves coming from Jamaica or Barbados into the American South, or could have emerged within early communities of slaves in the United States. Ebonics may very well be a product of this early creolization.

Linguist John Rickford notes that Ebonics is not just the use of slang. There are some slang terms in

Ebonics, such as "chillin" (relaxing) or "homey" (close friend), but there is a systematic grammar and pronunciation in the language. There are standard usages of sentences in Ebonics, such as "He runnin" ("He is running") or "He be running" ("He is usually running"), or "He bin runnin" ("He has been running for a long time and still is"). Other rules, such as dropping consonants at the end of words such as tes(*t*) and han(*d*), are evident in Ebonics. Rickford emphasizes that Ebonics is not just a lazy form of English. Ebonics is no more lazy English than Italian is a lazy form of Latin. These are different languages with systematically ordered grammar and pronunciation usages.

A controversy regarding Ebonics developed in Oakland, California, when the school board announced that they were going to recognize Ebonics as a separate language. The school board was committed to teaching American Standard English to the African American students. However, because of the prejudices and misunderstandings regarding Ebonics as "a lazy form of English," the Oakland school board set off a controversy all over the United States. Linguistic anthropologist Ronald Kephart has commented on this Ebonics controversy based on his extensive research on the study of creoles in the Caribbean (Monaghan, Hinton, & Kephart, 1997). Kephart studied creole English on the islands of Carriacou and Grenada. He did research on young students who were reading in the creole language as well as learning standard forms of English. The children who read in the creole language were able to learn the standard forms of English more readily, and they enjoyed the process. Kephart suggests that the recognition of Ebonics by the school board in Oakland would help children learn American Standard English. These children would appreciate the fact that the language they brought with them into the school was to be respected as another form of English, and they would develop more positive attitudes about themselves, and not be treated as "illiterate" or "lazy" children. This would help promote more effective learning strategies and enable the students to master American Standard English in a more humane manner.

It appears that language acquisition depends on both biological readiness and learning. The ability to speak seems to be biologically programmed, whereas a specific language is learned from the society the child grows up in. Children who are not exposed to language during their "critical period" may not be able to learn to use language properly. Research such as Chomsky's provides for further advances in an interactionist approach to test hypotheses regarding language, biology, mind, and thought.

Language, Thought, and Culture

In the early part of the twentieth century, Edward Sapir and Benjamin Whorf carried out studies of language and culture. Sapir was a prodigious fieldworker who described many Native American languages and provided the basis for the comparative method in anthropological linguistics. Whorf, an insurance inspector by profession and a linguist and anthropologist by calling, conducted comparative research on a wide variety of languages. Sapir and Whorf's research led their students to formulate a highly controversial hypothesis that differs dramatically from the theories of Chomsky and the ethnosemanticists.

The Sapir–Whorf Hypothesis

The **Sapir–Whorf hypothesis** assumes that a close relationship exists between language and culture, and that language defines experiences for us. In other words, although humans everywhere have approximately the same set of physical organs for perceiving reality—eyes to see, ears to hear, noses to smell—the human nervous system is bombarded with sensations of all kinds, intensities, and durations. These sensations do not all reach our consciousness. Rather, humans have a filtering device that classifies reality. This filtering device, according to the Sapir–Whorf hypothesis, is language. In this view, language, in effect, provides us with a special pair of glasses that heighten certain perceptions and dim others, determining what we perceive as reality.

A Case Study: The Hopi Language To understand this hypothesis, we look at some examples given by Whorf. Whorf compared the grammar of English with that of the Native American Hopi language of the southwestern part of the United States. He found that the verb forms indicating tense differ in

Hopi Indians in traditional dress. The Hopi language has been the subject of controversy within linguistic anthropology.

these two languages. English contains past, present, and future verb forms; the Hopi language does not. In English we can say, "I came home," "I am coming home," or "I will come home." The Hopi do not have the verb corresponding to the use of *come* (Whorf, 1956). From this type of example, Whorf inferred that Hopi and English speakers think about time in fundamentally different ways. English speakers conceptualize time in a measurable, linear form, speaking of a length of time or a point in time. We say that time is short, long, or great. We can save time, squander it, or spend it.

To the Hopi, in contrast, time is connected to the cycles of nature. Because they were farmers, their lives revolved around the different seasons for planting and harvesting. The Hopi, Whorf argued, did not see time as a motion upon space (that is, as time passing) but as a getting later of everything that has ever been done. Whorf concluded that the Hopi did not share the Western emphasis on history, calendars, and clocks. From evidence such as this, Sapir and Whorf developed their hypothesis that the language of a speaker provides a grid, or structure, that categorizes space, time, and other aspects of reality into a worldview. The Sapir–Whorf hypothesis is thus an example of linguistic relativism because it maintains that the world is experienced differently among different language communities.

Universals of Time Expression Anthropological linguist Ekkehart Malotki (1983) investigated the Sapir–Whorf hypothesis by reexamining the Hopi language. His research, based on many interviews with Hopi speakers, showed that, in fact, the Hopi calculate time in units very similar to those of native English speakers. He concluded that Whorf had exaggerated the extent to which language determines people's perceptions of time and demonstrated that the Hopi make linguistic distinctions between the past and the present based on tense form. In the Hopi language, tense is distinguished between future and nonfuture, instead of between past and present.

Anthropologist Hoyt Alverson (1994) investigated four different unrelated languages to determine how time is conceptualized. Alverson studied the metaphors and symbolic usages of time in the Mandarin language of the Chinese, the Hindi language of India, the Sesotho language of Africa, and English. He looked at 150 different linguistic usages of time from native speakers and showed that each language uses essentially the same types of metaphors and categories to express time. For example, time is always conceptualized as partible and divisible, and it can be expressed as either linear or circular. This study, along with Malotki's, suggests that all humans share a common cognitive framework when conceptualizing time. These findings undoubtedly have implications for humanity's genetic heritage, a universal cognitive evolution, and a common identity as a species.

Although these studies appear to have refuted the Sapir–Whorf hypothesis, most linguistic anthropologists agree that a relationship exists between language and thought. Rather than assert that language determines thought, they maintain that language influences the speaker's thinking and worldview. Some experts refer to this approach as a "weak" version of the linguistic relativity hypothesis.

Some contemporary researchers have looked for ways to reformulate the Sapir–Whorf hypothesis in the form of a more precise, testable hypothesis about the relationship between language, thought, and behavior. For example, John Lucy (1992) compared speakers of English and Yucatec Mayan to see if their languages led them to perform differently on tasks involving remembering and sorting objects. As predicted from the grammar of the languages, English speakers appeared to attend more closely to the number and also to the shape of the objects, while Mayan speakers paid less attention to number and more attention to the material from which the objects were made.

It is also true that specific languages contain the vocabulary needed to cope in particular environments. The need for a specific vocabulary in a society does not necessarily mean that language determines our perception of reality. After all, when a need to express some unlabeled phenomenon arises, speakers easily manufacture new words. English-speaking skiers, like Eskimos, distinguish among several types of snow, speaking of *powder, corn,* and so on.

Language may also influence social perception. For example, many women in English-speaking societies have long objected to the use of *man, men,* or *mankind* to refer to humanity and *he* to refer to any person, male or female. They argue that the use of these masculine terms reinforces the idea that humanity is male, and women are outsiders, the "second sex." Other gender-biased language occurs when words such as *lady* and *girl* are used in a demeaning manner to refer to women. In addition, the tradition of addressing females by the title *Mrs.* or *Miss* also reflects gender bias in English-speaking countries.

To help explain this presumed bias, another linguistic anthropologist, M. J. Hardman-de-Bautista (1978), has formulated the notion of *linguistic postulates,* distinctions that are made obligatorily in language and that also reflect distinctions central to culture. For example, in English, biological sex is marked on the third person singular pronouns (*she, he*). This distinction between female and male permeates English-speaking culture in important ways; for example, in how children are socialized into appropriate behavior ("be a nice little girl," "act like a lady," "be a man."). In the Aymara language of Peru and Bolivia, in contrast, the third person pronoun is not marked for sex or number, so that Aymara *jupa* means "she/he/they." Instead, for Aymara, the relevant contrast is human versus nonhuman, and *jupa* cannot be used to refer to an animal, such as a dog or llama; instead, a different pronoun must be used. Aymara children are not taught to behave like "nice girls" or "good boys" but rather to behave "like human beings, not like animals."

To remedy gender biases, some people have tried to change their linguistic habits. They have adopted terms such as *humankind, person,* and *Ms.* Terms such as *policeman* and *fireman* have been changed to *police officer* and *firefighter.* The adoption of more neutral ways of expressing gender may affect perceptions of gender relations in these societies.

Historical Linguistics

Historical linguistics is the study of language change and the historical relationships among different languages. The research in historical linguistics tries to discover what kinds of changes occur in languages and why. Research on this subject began in the late eighteenth century when Sir William Jones, a British legal scholar, suggested that the linguistic similarities of Sanskrit, an ancient Indian tongue, to ancient Greek, Latin, German, and English indicate that all these languages were descended from a common ancestral language. It was discovered that all these languages are part of one family, the Indo-European family, and share certain words and grammar. For example, the English word *three* is *trayas* in Sanskrit, *tres* in Latin, *treis* in Greek, and *drei* in German (see Table 12.1). The

Table 12.1	Comparative Word Chart of Indo-European Languages				
English	**Sanskrit**	**Latin**	**Greek**	**German**	**Old English**
To bear	Bhar	Ferre	Fero	Gebären	Beran
Father	Pitar	Pater	Patir	Vater	Fæder
Mother	Matar	Mater	Mitir	Mutter	Modor
Brother	Bhratar	Frater	Frater	Bruder	Brodor
Three	Trayas	Tres	Treis	Drei	Brie
Hundred	Sata	Centum	Ekaton	Hundert	Hund
Night	Nisitha	Noctis	Nikta	Nacht	Niht
Red	Rudhira	Ruber	Erithros	Rot	Read
Foot	Pada	Pedis	Podos	Fuss	Fot
Fish	Piska	Piscis	Ikhthis	Fisch	Fisc
Goose	Hamsa	Anser	Khin	Gans	Gos
What	Kwo	Quod	Ti	Was	Hwæt
Where	Kva	Quo	Pou	Wo	Hwær

Source: The Way of Language: An Introduction by Fred West. Copyright © 1975. Reproduced by permission of Heinle & Heinle, a division of Thomson Learning. Fax 800-730-2215.

similarity in Indo-European languages led some early anthropologists to conclude that all current languages could be traced to a single language family.

The Family-Tree Model

Modern historical linguists agree that they probably can never reconstruct the original language, but they still may be able to reach far back into history to reconstruct an early **protolanguage,** a parent language for many ancient and modern languages. Many linguists hold the view that all languages change in a regular, recognizable way, and that similarities among languages are due to a historical relationship among these languages. In other words, people living in adjacent areas of the world would tend to share similar phonological, syntactical, and semantic features of their languages. For example, the Romance languages of French, Spanish, Portuguese, Italian, and Romanian developed from Latin because of the historic relationship with one another through the influence of the Roman Empire. This view is known as the *family-tree theory of language change* (see Figure 12.2).

Most recently, historical linguists have been working with archaeologists to reconstruct the Proto-Indo-European language. They have found that the Indo-European languages did spread throughout distinctive regions for certain societies. British archaeologist Colin Renfrew (1989) hypothesizes that the spread of the Indo-European languages was linked to the spread of a particular technology and material culture. He suggests that the Indo-European languages spread throughout Europe from an original homeland in Anatolia, today part of Turkey, as early cultures adopted intensive agriculture. Similarly, English is currently promoted throughout the world as the language of television, computers, and other features of Western technology.

Assessing Language Change

To reconstruct a family tree of languages, the linguist compares the phonological (sounds) and morphological (words) characteristics of different languages. Linguistic anthropologist Morris Swadesh (1964) developed a systematic method of assessing historical language change. His goal was to date the separation of languages from one another using a statistical technique known as *glottochronology* (from the Greek *glotta,* meaning "tongue," and *chronos,* meaning "time"). Swadesh reasoned that the vocabulary of a language would remain stable at some

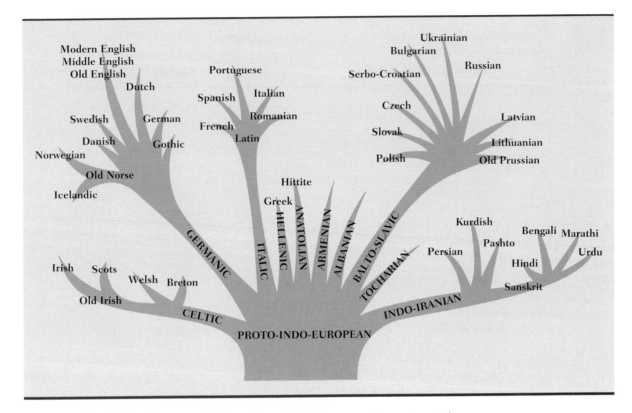

FIGURE 12.2   This family-tree model shows the relationships among the various Indo-European languages.

times but would change rapidly at others. Words for plants, animals, or technology would change quickly if the speakers migrated or came into contact with other groups. Swadesh thought, however, that a *core vocabulary* (words for pronouns and numbers, or for the body, earth, wood, and stone) would remain immune to cultural change. He thought that if we could measure the rate of retention of this core vocabulary, then we could measure the separation of one language from another.

By comparing core vocabularies from different languages, linguists found that on the average, 19 percent of this core vocabulary would change in a language in approximately 1,000 years. In other words, about 81 percent of the core vocabulary would be retained. From this formula, linguistic anthropologists have reconstructed languages and produced "family trees" of languages from around the world.

Through the study of language change, linguistic anthropologists have put to rest the idea that all current languages in the world can be traced to a single language family. Language change has been swift in some circumstances and gradual in others. Multiple borrowings, or the spread of vocabulary and grammar throughout the world, have affected most languages. Two linguistic researchers emphasize that many of the world's languages, including Russian, French, and English, have in their past development undergone radical change through language mixing (Thomason & Kaufman, 1988). In their book, the researchers claim that in the same way that many creole languages have emerged (discussed earlier in the chapter), other languages have developed through intensive culture contact. Instead of development of language from one source, there apparently are different centers and regions of language change.

Sociolinguistics

Linguistic anthropologists have researched the use of language in different social contexts, a field known as sociolinguistics. The sociolinguist takes the speech community as the framework for understanding the variation of speech in different social contexts. In general, linguistic anthropologists refer to this as the study of *pragmatics,* the rules for using language within speech communities.

The speech community is a social unit within which speakers share various ways of speaking. For example, in American society certain patterns of English syntax and pronunciation are acceptable in specific contexts (American Standard English), whereas others are considered unacceptable. An American child may sometimes learn nonstandard words in the family environment, and if the family considers them cute, the child may continue to use them. Eventually, however, the child moves out of the family into the larger speech community, encountering speech habits that differ from those of the home. If the child uses those words in school or with others, he or she will be reprimanded or laughed at.

Through a process of enculturation and socialization into the speech community, the child learns the language used in a variety of social contexts. Language plays a prominent role in the process of enculturation. American children learn the regional pronunciation and grammatical usages within their speech community.

Dialectal Differences in Spoken Language

A speech community may consist of subgroups that share specific linguistic usages within a larger common language family. If the linguistic usages of these subgroups are different but mutually intelligible, their language variations are called dialects. **Dialects** are linguistic differences in pronunciation, vocabulary, or syntax that may differ within a single language. For example, dialectal differences in American Standard English exist in the northeast, midwest, south, and southwest of the United States. In the southern United States, one might hear such grammatical items as "It wan't (or weren't) me," or pronunciation characteristics such as *Miz* for *Mrs.* and the frequent loss of *r* except before vowels:

foah for *four,* *heah* for *hear,* and *sulfuh* for *sulfur* (West, 1975).

Certain dialects of English are looked on as more prestigious than others, reflecting educational, class, ethnic, race, and regional differences. When viewing language as a global phenomenon, however, all languages are dialects that have emerged in different locales and regions of the world. In actuality, the English language is not one standard language but consists of many different dialects. To say that British English is more "correct" than American Standard English simply because England is the homeland of English does not make sense to a linguist. The forms of English spoken in England, Australia, Canada, the United States, India, South Africa, or the West Indies have distinctive differences in pronunciation and vocabulary. The same generalization can be applied to many languages and dialects.

Some linguists studying speech communities in the United States have concluded that specific regional dialects are gradually disappearing. As people move from one region to another for jobs and education, and as television and movies influence speech patterns, Americans are beginning to sound more alike (West, 1975). Through similar changes, many of the same processes are influencing different dialects and languages the world over.

Honorifics in Language

Sociolinguists have found that a number of languages contain honorific forms that determine the use of grammar, syntax, and other word usage. *Honorific* forms of language are used to express differences in social levels among speakers and are common in societies that maintain social inequality and hierarchy. Honorific forms can apply to the interaction between males and females, kin and nonkin, and higher- and lower-status individuals. For example, in many of the Pacific island societies such as Hawaii, a completely separate honorific vocabulary was used when addressing a person who was part of the royal family. People of lower rank were not allowed to use these forms of language among themselves.

In the Thai language, a number of different types of honorific pronouns are used in various social contexts. Factors such as age, social rank, gender, education, officialdom, and royal title influence which pronouns are used. For example, the first person pronoun *I* for a male is *phom,* a polite form of address between equals. The pronoun for *I* shifts to *kraphom* if a male is addressing a higher-ranking government official or a Buddhist monk. It shifts to *klaawkramom* when a male is addressing the prince of the royal family. All together, there are thirteen different forms of the pronoun *I.* Similar differences exist for the other pronouns in Thai to express deference, politeness, and respect (Palakornkul, 1972; Scupin, 1988).

In the Japanese and Korean languages, honorific forms require speakers to distinguish among several different verb forms and address terms that indicate deference, politeness, or everyday speech. Different speech levels reflect age, gender, social position, and out-groupness (the degree to which a person is considered outside a particular social group) (Martin, 1964). Specifically, the Japanese distinguish between *tatemae* and *honne* in all of their linguistic expressions: *Tatemae* is a very polite form of expression used with strangers; *honne* is the expression of "real" feelings and can be used only with close friends and family.

Greeting Behaviors

The exchange of greetings is the most ordinary, everyday use of language and gesture found universally. Yet sociolinguistic studies indicate that these routine greeting behaviors are considerably complex and produce different meanings in various social and cultural contexts. In many contexts, English speakers in the United States greet one another with the word "Hi" or "Hello." (The word *hello* originated from the English phrase *healthy be thou.*) Members of U.S. society also greet one another with questions such as "How are you?" or "How's it going?" or "What do you know?" In most contexts, these questions are not considered serious questions, and these exchanges of greetings are accompanied by a wave or a nod, a smile, or other gesture of recognition. They are familiar phrases that are used as exchanges in greetings. These greetings require little thought and seem almost mechanical.

Among Muslim populations around the world, the typical greeting between two males is the shaking of hands accompanied by the Arab utterance *As-salam ale-kum,* "May the peace of [Allah] be with you." This is the phrase used by Muslims even in non-Arabic-speaking societies. The *Qur'an,* the sacred religious text of Muslims, has an explicit injunction regarding this mode of greeting for the male Muslim community (Caton, 1986). A similar greeting of *Scholem aleicham,* "May peace be with you," is found among the Jewish populace throughout the world. In some Southeast Asian societies such as Vietnam, the typical greeting translates into English as "Have you eaten rice?"

Ethiopian Jewish males greeting each other. In many societies, males often greet each other with a kiss on the cheek.

All of the above greetings express a concern for another person's well-being. Although the English and Vietnamese greetings appear to be concerned with the physical condition of the person, whereas the Arab and Jewish phrases have a more spiritual connotation, they all essentially serve the same social purpose: They enable humans to interact in harmonious ways.

Yet there is a great deal more social information contained in these brief greeting exchanges than appears on the surface. For example, an English-speaking person in the United States can usually identify the different types of social contexts for the following greeting exchanges:

1. "Hi, Mr. Thomas!"
   "Hello, Johnny. How are you?"
2. "Good morning, Monica."
   "Good morning, sir."
3. "Sarah! How are you? You look great!"
   "Bill! It's so good to see you!"
4. "Good evening, Congressman."
   "Hello there. Nice to see you."

In greeting 1, the speakers are an adult and child; in 2, there is a difference in status, and the speakers may be an employee and employer; in 3, these speakers are close acquaintances; in 4, the second speaker does not remember or know the other person very well (Hickerson, 1980).

One author of this text did a systematic sociolinguistic study of greeting behaviors found among different ethnic and religious groups in Thailand (Scupin, 1988). Precise cultural norms determine the forms of greetings given to people of different status levels and ethnic groups. The traditional greeting of Thai Buddhists on meeting one another is expressed by each raising both hands, palm to palm, and lightly touching the body between the face and chest. Simultaneously, the person utters a polite verbal phrase. This salutation, known as the *waaj* (pronounced "why"), varies in different social contexts. The person who is inferior in social status (determined by age and social class) initiates the *waaj,* and the higher the hands are raised, the greater the deference and politeness expressed. For example, a young child will *waaj* a superior by placing the fingertips above the eyebrows, whereas a superior returning a *waaj* will raise the fingertips only

to the chest. A superior seldom performs a *waaj* when greeting someone of an inferior status. Other ethnic and religious groups, such as the Muslims in Thailand, use the *waaj* in formal interactions with Thai Buddhists, but among themselves they use the traditional Muslim greeting described previously.

Another form of Thai greeting found among Buddhists includes the *kraab,* which involves kneeling down and bowing to the floor in conjunction with the *waaj* in expressing respect to a superior political or religious official. The *kraab* is used to greet a high-ranking member of the royal family, a Buddhist monk, respected officials, and, traditionally, one's parents (Anuman-Rajadhon, 1961). These deferential forms of greetings are found in other societies that maintain social hierarchies based on royal authority or political or religious principles.

Though greeting behaviors differ from one society to another, anthropologists find that all peoples throughout the world have a means to greet one another to establish a basis for social interaction and demonstrate their concern for one another's welfare.

Nonverbal Communication

In interacting with other people, we use nonverbal cues as well as speech. As with language, nonverbal communication varies in human populations, in contrast to the nonverbal communication of nonhuman animals. Dogs, cats, and other animals have no difficulty communicating with one another in nonverbal ways. Human nonverbal communication, however, is extremely varied. It is often said that humans are the only creatures who can misunderstand one another.

Kinesics

Some anthropological linguists study gestures and other forms of body language. The study of **kinesics** is concerned with body motion and gestures used in nonverbal communication. Researchers estimate that humans use more than 250,000 facial expressions. Many of these expressions have different meanings in different circumstances. For example, the smile indicates pleasure, happiness, or friendliness in all parts of the world.

Some human facial expressions are based on universally recognized emotions.

Yet in certain contexts, a smile may signify an insult (Birdwhistle, 1970). Thus, the movement of the head, eyes, eyebrows, and hands or the posture of the body may be associated with specific symbolic meanings that are culturally defined.

Many types of nonverbal communication differ from society to society. Americans point to things with their fingers, whereas other peoples point with only their eyes, their chin, or their head. Shaking our head up and down means "yes" and from side to side means "no," but in parts of India, Greece, and Turkey the opposite is true. An "A-OK" sign in the United States or England means "you are all right," but it means "you are worth zero" in France or Belgium, and it is a very vulgar sign in Greece and Turkey (Ekman et al., 1984). Pointing to your head means "he or she is smart" in the United States, whereas it means "stupid" in Europe. The "V" sign of the 1960s meant "peace"; in contrast, in World War II England it meant "victory"; in Greece it is an insult. Obviously, humans can easily mis-understand each other because of the specific cultural meanings of nonverbal gestures.

Despite all these differences, however, research has revealed certain universal features associated with some facial expressions. For example, research by psychologist Paul Ekman and his colleagues suggests that there are some basic uniformities regarding certain facial expressions. Peoples from various societies recognize facial expressions indicating emotional states such as happiness, grief, disgust, fear, surprise, and anger. Ekman studied peoples recently contacted by Western society, such as the Fore people of Papua New Guinea (Ekman, 1973). When shown photos of facial expressions, the Fore had no difficulty determining the basic emotions that were being expressed. This research overlaps the psychological anthropology studies of emotions discussed in the previous chapter. Ekman has concluded that some universal emotional expressions are evident in certain facial displays of humans throughout the world.

Proxemics

Another nonverbal aspect of communication involves the use of space. **Proxemics** is the study of how people in different societies perceive and use space. Studies by Edward T. Hall (1981) indicate that no universal rules apply to the use of space. In American society, people maintain a different amount of "personal space" in different situations. We communicate with intimate acquaintances at a range of about 18 inches; however, with non-intimates, our space expands according to how well we know the person. In some other societies, people communicate at very close distances irrespective of the relationship among them.

Nonverbal communication is an important aspect of social interaction. Obvious gestural movements, such as bowing in Japan and shaking hands in the United States, may have a deep symbolic significance in certain contexts. The study of nonverbal communication will enrich our understanding of human behavior and might even improve communication among different societies.

When communicating, Arab males stand at a closer distance to each other than do U.S. males.

SUMMARY

Language is a vital component of human cultural knowledge. It is the most important means of expressing and transmitting symbols and culture from one person to another. Language is the major means of communication for humans. A great deal of laboratory and field research is shedding light on how the closest related species to humans, the apes, can learn sophisticated sign communication.

Linguists have focused on some specific criteria that distinguish human languages from animal communication. All human languages have certain features such as productivity, displacement, arbitrariness, and combining sounds that set them apart from animal communication systems.

Linguistic anthropologists study the structure of language by studying sound patterns (phonology), the meaning of words (morphology), and how these meaningful units are put together in phrases and sentences (syntax). They also focus on the meaning (semantics) of different terms used to classify reality. Although there are many differences in how people in various societies use terms to describe kinship

relations and physical phenomena, cognitive anthropologists have found some universals, such as the way people classify relatives. This suggests that humans have common biological capacities that determine how they perceive certain aspects of reality.

Linguistic anthropologists are interested in how language is acquired as an aspect of the enculturation process. The behaviorist model suggests that language is learned through positive and negative conditioning. In contrast, linguist Noam Chomsky suggests that all humans use an innate, or genetically encoded, capability for learning complicated syntax and grammar. Chomsky's model has led to research on languages such as creole languages.

Another topic explored in linguistic anthropology is the relationship among language, thought, and culture. An early hypothesis, known as the Sapir–Whorf hypothesis, suggested that language acts as a filter for the classification and perception of reality. This is known as linguistic relativism.

In reexamining the Sapir–Whorf hypothesis, anthropologists have concluded that the hypothesis exaggerates the extent to which language determines the perception of time, space, and other aspects of reality. Most modern anthropologists do not accept an extreme form of linguistic relativism as proposed by Sapir and Whorf's students.

Historical linguistics is the study of how languages are related to one another and how they have diverged from one another. Linguistic anthropologists have examined the historical relationships among languages. This research has helped understand the process of language change.

Sociolinguistics focuses on the relationship between language and society. Sociolinguists examine social interactions and the ways in which people use certain linguistic expressions that reflect the dialect patterns of their speech community. Researchers have found that many languages have nuances in linguistic usage such as greeting patterns or speech differences that vary according to age, gender, and status.

The study of nonverbal communication is also a rich field for linguistic anthropology. Although much nonverbal communication varies around the world, some forms can be understood universally. Anthropologists focus on the use of body language (kinesics) and the use of space (proxemics) to understand better how people supplement their spoken-language skills with nonverbal communication.

QUESTIONS TO THINK ABOUT

1. Suppose you are studying chimp communication. What limitations will you have in teaching the chimps a human language?
2. Give some examples of unique human linguistic abilities.
3. Provide some examples of phonemes, morphemes, syntax, and semantic aspects of language.
4. Do you agree with Skinner's or Chomsky's view of language learning? Why?
5. Can you think of any ways in which language influences culture, or vice versa?
6. What types of body language or gestures are universally understood?

KEY TERMS

communication
dialects
ethologists
historical linguistics
kinesics
language

morphemes
morphology
phonemes
phones
phonology
protolanguage

proxemics
Sapir–Whorf hypothesis
semantics
syntax

INTERNET EXERCISES

1. Explore the Ethnologue website found at **http://www.ethnologue.com/country_index.asp**. Click on the Ethnologue Country Index. How many living languages are there? Why do you think that there is such an unequal distribution of languages? What historical and geographical factors may have led to this modern distribution?
2. Refer to the Ethnologue site at **http://www.ethnologue.com/show_language.asp?code=ENG**. Click on the three-letter code for English [ENG]. How many countries speak English? Why so many?

SUGGESTED READINGS

CAVILLI-SFORZA, LUIGI LUCA, and FRANCESCO CAVILLI-SFORZA. 1995. *The Great Human Diasporas: The History and Evolution*. New York: Addison-Wesley. A broad overview of the migrations of peoples and languages since the beginnings of humankind. This book combines genetic research and biology with historical linguistics to examine human migrations up to the present.

CHOMSKY, NOAM. 1968. *Language and Mind*. New York: Harcourt, Brace & World. One of the primary texts by this innovative thinker, who changed the direction of linguistic research. This text is a highly philosophical critique of behaviorist approaches to understanding language.

CLARK, VIRGINIA P., PAUL A. ESCHHOLZ, and ALFRED F. ROSA (Eds.). 1981. *Language: Introductory Readings,* 3d ed. New York: St. Martin's Press. A comprehensive collection of useful contemporary essays based on research by linguists in many fields.

FARB, PETER. 1975. *Word Play: What Happens When People Talk*. New York: Bantam Books. A highly entertaining book on language by the late Peter Farb, a writer by profession and an anthropologist and linguist by avocation.

HYMES, DELL (Ed.). 1964. *Language in Culture and Society: A Reader in Linguistics and Anthropology*. New York: Harper & Row. The standard anthology of essays containing classic articles in the field of linguistic anthropology.

PINKER, STEVEN. 1994. *The Language Instinct: How the Mind Creates Language*. New York: HarperCollins. A highly readable account of the latest research in linguistic research.

TRUDGILL, PETER. 1983. *Sociolinguistics: An Introduction to Language and Society*. New York: Penguin Books. A popular introduction to the field of sociolinguistics by a British linguist.

WEST, FRED. 1975. *The Way of Language: An Introduction*. New York: Harcourt Brace Jovanovich. A concise introduction to linguistics for the general reader. It covers all of the major topics that linguists study, ranging from the evolution of language to sociolinguistics.

13

Anthropological Explanations

CHAPTER OUTLINE

NINETEENTH-CENTURY EVOLUTIONISM

Unilineal Evolution: Tylor / Unilineal Evolution: Morgan / Unilineal Evolution: A Critique

DIFFUSIONISM

British Diffusionism / German Diffusionism / The Limitations and Strengths of Diffusionism

HISTORICAL PARTICULARISM

Boas versus the Unilineal Evolutionists

FUNCTIONALISM: BRITISH ANTHROPOLOGY

Structural Functionalism: Radcliffe-Brown / Psychological Functionalism: Malinowski / The Limitations of Functionalism

TWENTIETH-CENTURY EVOLUTIONISM

Steward and Cultural Ecology / The Strengths of Neoevolutionism / Criticisms of Cultural Ecology

CULTURAL MATERIALISM

Criticisms of Cultural Materialism

MARXIST ANTHROPOLOGY

Evaluation of Marxist Anthropology

SYMBOLIC ANTHROPOLOGY: A HUMANISTIC METHOD OF INQUIRY

Criticisms of Symbolic Anthropology

MATERIALISM VERSUS CULTURALISM

FEMINIST ANTHROPOLOGY

Criticisms of Feminist Anthropology

POSTMODERNISM AND ANTHROPOLOGY

Postmodernists and Contemporary Research

SHIFTS IN ANTHROPOLOGICAL EXPLANATIONS

CHAPTER QUESTIONS

- What are the basic differences between the nineteenth-century and twentieth-century theoretical approaches in anthropology?

- What are the basic strengths and weaknesses of the various theories in anthropology?

In his conclusion in an excellent book entitled *Culture, Self, and Meaning* (2000), anthropologist Victor de Munck writes about how anthropology needs to engage itself in an interdisciplinary effort to understand human behavior and culture. He refers to the ancient Hindu-Buddhist story regarding the blind men and the elephant. This story was popularized by the nineteenth-century poet John Godfrey Saxe in 1900 and begins:

It was six men of Indostan
*   To learning much inclined*
Who went to see the Elephant
*   (Though all of them were blind),*
That each by observation
*   Might satisfy his mind.*
The First approached the Elephant,
*   And happening to fall*
Against his broad and sturdy side,
*   At once began to bawl:*
"God bless me! but the Elephant
*   Is very like a wall!"*

In the poem each of the blind men steps forward to examine the elephant. One feels the tusk and says the elephant is like a spear. Another grabs the trunk and likens the elephant to a snake. The poet concludes:

And so these men of Indostan
*   Disputed loud and long,*
Each in his own opinion
*   Exceeding stiff and strong,*
Though each was partly in the right
*   And all were in the wrong!*

This photo of a Japanese wood-block print illustrates the story of the "Blind Men and the Elephant."

Thus, each of the blind men was mistaking his own limited understanding of the part of the elephant for the fuller reality of the whole. In this chapter on anthropological explanation, we need to keep this legendary fable in mind. Anthropologists in every age have been attempting to understand humanity as a whole, but in reality they had only partial understandings. Yet each of these types of explanations has provided some limited perspectives on human behavior and culture. And, eventually, the knowledge accumulated from these partial perspectives has been probed and evaluated by anthropologists to offer a far more comprehensive picture of humanity in the twenty-first century than what we had in earlier centuries.

Another thing we need to keep in mind in this chapter is how anthropology is comprised of both the scientific and humanistic orientations. In Chapter 1 we discussed the scientific method and its application to anthropology. In that discussion we noted how anthropologists collect and classify data and then develop and test hypotheses. In the physical sciences, scientists use hypotheses to formulate theories from which they make predictions about natural phenomena. Chemists can rely on precise mathematical laws to help them deduce and predict what will happen when two chemical elements interact with one another. Physicists can predict from laws of gravity and motion what will happen when a spherical object is dropped from a building at a certain speed. These types of predictions allow engineers to produce aircraft that use certain fuels and withstand certain physical pressures, enabling them to fly long distances.

Although anthropology relies on the scientific method, its major objective is to provide explanations of human society and behavior. Human behavior is extremely complicated. The product of many different, interacting variables, it can seldom, if ever, be predicted. Anthropologists cannot predict the outcome of interactions between two individuals or among small groups, let alone among large groups at the societal level. Consequently, anthropology as a discipline does not have any specific theories and laws that can be used to predict human action or thought. For the most part, anthropologists restrict their efforts to testing hypotheses and improving their explanations of human society and behavior.

We need to remember that anthropology also employs methods in the humanities to interpret human endeavors such as religious, artistic, folklore, oral and written poetry, and other complex symbolic activities. This chapter will examine both the scientific and humanistic attempts to comprehend the differences and similarities of human behavior and cultures.

Nineteenth-Century Evolutionism

Modern anthropology emerged from the intellectual atmosphere of the Enlightenment, an eighteenth-century philosophical movement that stressed social progress based on human reason, and Darwin's theory of evolution. The first professional anthropologist—that is, an individual appointed to an academic position of anthropology—was a nineteenth-century British scholar, Edward B. Tylor. In 1871 Tylor published a major work titled *Primitive Culture*. At that time, Great Britain was involved in imperialistic expansion all over the world. Tylor thus had access to descriptions of non-Western societies through his contacts with travelers, explorers, missionaries, traders, and government officials. He combined these descriptions with nineteenth-century philosophy and Charles Darwin's ideas to develop a theory of societal evolution.

Unilineal Evolution: Tylor

The major question addressed by early anthropologists was: Why are societies at similar or different levels of evolution and development? Many people ask the same kinds of questions today. Tylor tried to answer that question through an explanation known as unilineal evolution. **Unilineal evolution** is the view that societies evolve in a single direction toward complexity, progress, and civilization. Tylor's basic argument was that because all humans are bestowed with innate rational faculties, they are continuously improving their societies. Through this process of evolution, societies move toward "progress" and "civilization."

In arriving at this conclusion, Tylor used accounts from Western observers to compare certain cultural elements from different societies, including technology, family, economy, political organization, art, religion, and philosophy. He then organized this evidence into categories or stages, ranging from what he termed "savagery" to "barbarism" to "civilization." Theorists like Tylor assumed that

hunter-gatherers and other non-Western societies were living at a lower level of existence than were the "civilized" societies of Europe. This was an ethnocentric view of societal development based on the belief that Western society is the center of the civilized world, and that non-Western societies are inherently inferior.

Tylor and other nineteenth-century thinkers also claimed that "primitives" would eventually evolve through the stages of barbarism to become civilized like British gentlemen and ladies. However, Tylor believed that these societies would need some assistance from the civilized world to reach this stage.

Unilineal Evolution: Morgan

Another nineteenth-century anthropologist who developed a unilineal scheme of evolution was an American, Lewis Henry Morgan (1818–1881). Morgan was a lawyer and banker who became fascinated with Native American societies. He gathered information on the customs, language, and other aspects of the culture of the Iroquois-speaking peoples of upstate New York. Eventually, under the auspices of the Smithsonian Institution, he distributed questionnaires to missionaries and travelers to collect information about many other non-Western societies.

Morgan and Kinship Theories Morgan was particularly interested in kinship terms used in different parts of the world. He observed that the Iroquois kinship terms were very different from those of English, Latin, Greek, and other European societies. He also noticed that these kinship terms were similar to those of the Ojibwa Indians, a group living in the midwestern United States. This led him to explore the relationship between the Iroquois and other peoples. Using the aforementioned questionnaires, he requested specific information on kinship terms from people all over the world.

From these data, Morgan began to conceive of the evolution of the family in a worldwide sense. He speculated that humans originally lived in "primitive hordes," in which sexual behavior was not regulated and individuals didn't know who their fathers were. He based this assumption on the discovery that certain peoples, such as Hawaiians, use one general term to classify their father and all male relatives in their father's generation (see Chapter 12). He postulated that brother-sister marriage then developed, followed by group marriage, and eventually a matriarchal family structure in which women held economic and political power. Morgan believed that the final stage of the evolution of the family began when males took control of the economy and politics, instituting a patriarchal system.

In addition to exploring the evolution of the family, Morgan, like Tylor, surveyed technological, economic, political, and religious conditions throughout the world. He compiled this evidence in his book *Ancient Society* ([1877] 1964), which presented his overall scheme of the evolution of society. Paralleling Tylor's views, Morgan believed in a hierarchy of evolutionary development from "savagery" to "civilization."

According to Morgan, one crucial distinction between civilized society and earlier societies is private property. He described the "savage" societies as "communistic," in contrast to "civilized" societies, whose institutions are based on private property.

Unilineal Evolution: A Critique

Although these nineteenth-century thinkers shared the view that humanity was progressing through various stages of development, their views were ethnocentric, contradictory, and speculative, and their evidence secondhand, based on the accounts of biased Europeans. The unilineal scheme of evolution was much too simplistic to account for the development of different societies.

In general, the unilineal evolutionists relied on nineteenth-century racist views of human development and misunderstandings of biological evolution to explain societal differences. For example, both Morgan and Tylor believed that people in various societies have different levels of intelligence. They believed that the people in so-called "savage societies" have less intelligence than those in "civilized societies." As discussed in Chapter 6, this view of different levels of intelligence among different groups is no longer accepted by the scientific community or modern anthropologists. Nevertheless, despite their inadequate theories and speculations regarding the evolution of society, these early anthropologists provided the first systematic methods for thinking about and explaining

the similarities and diversity of human societies. Like the blind men and the elephant, these anthropologists had only a limited perception and understanding of human behavior and culture.

Diffusionism

Another school of thought that used the comparative method to explain why different societies are at different levels of development was diffusionism. **Diffusionism,** which developed in the early part of the twentieth century, maintains that societal change occurs when societies *borrow* cultural traits from one another. Cultural knowledge regarding technology, economic ideas, religious views, or art forms spreads, or diffuses, from one society to another. There were two major schools of diffusionism: the British version associated with G. Elliot Smith and William J. Perry, and the German version associated with Father Wilhelm Schmidt.

British Diffusionism

The British school of diffusionism derived its theory from research on ancient Egypt. Smith and Perry were specialists in Egyptian culture and had carried out research in Egyptology for a number of years. From this experience they concluded that all aspects of civilizations, from technology to religion, originated in Egypt and diffused to other cultural areas. To explain the fact that some cultures no longer had cultural traits from Egypt, they resorted to an ethnocentric view, maintaining that some cultures had simply become "degenerate." That is, in contrast to the civilized world, the lesser developed peoples had simply forgotten the original ideas borrowed from Egypt.

German Diffusionism

The German school of diffusionism differed somewhat from that of the British. Schmidt and his followers argued that several early centers of civilization had existed, and that from these early centers cultural traits diffused outward in circles to other regions and peoples. In German this view is referred to as the *Kulturkreise* (culture circles) school of thought. In explaining why some primitive societies did not have the characteristics of civilization, the

Great Giza pyramid of Egypt. Some early anthropologists believed that all civilizations stemmed from ancient Egypt.

German school, like the British diffusionists, argued that these peoples had simply degenerated. Thus, diffusionist views, like the unilineal evolutionary views, represent ethnocentric perspectives of human societies outside the mainstream of Western civilization.

The Limitations and Strengths of Diffusionism

Early diffusionist views were based on erroneous assumptions regarding humankind's innovative capacities. Like the unilineal theorists, they maintained racist assumptions about the inherent inferiority of different non-Western peoples. The diffusionists assumed that some people were not sufficiently innovative to develop their own cultural traits.

Another limitation of the diffusionist approach is its assumption that cultural traits in the same geographical vicinity will inevitably spread from one society to another. Anthropologists find that diffusion is not an inevitable process. Societies can adjoin one another without exchanging cultural traits. For example, as we saw in Chapter 10, generations of Amish people in the United States have deliberately maintained their traditional ways despite being part of a nation in which modern technology is predominant.

However, diffusionism as a means of understanding societal development does have some validity. For example, diffusionism helps explain the emergence of the classical civilizations of Egypt, Greece, Phoenicia, and Rome. These peoples maintained continuous contact through trade and travel, borrowing many cultural traits from one another, such as writing systems. Thus, these anthropologists, again like the blind men and the elephant, had some partial explanations to offer on human behavior and society.

Historical Particularism

An early twentieth-century movement that developed in response to the unilineal evolutionary theory was led by the U.S. anthropologist Franz Boas, whom we discussed in Chapter 10. This movement proposed an alternative answer to why societal similarities and differences exist. Boas was educated in Germany as a natural scientist. Eventually he conducted fieldwork among the Eskimo in northern Canada and a Native American people known as the Kwakiutl, who lived on the northwest coast. He later solidified his position as the nation's foremost leader in anthropology at Columbia University in New York, where he trained many pioneers in the field until his retirement in 1937. Boas had a tremendous impact on the development of anthropology in the United States and internationally.

Boas versus the Unilineal Evolutionists

Boas became a vigorous opponent of the unilineal evolutionists. He criticized their attempts to propose stages of evolution through which all societies evolve. He also criticized their use of the comparative method and the haphazard manner in which they organized the data to fit their theories of evolutionary stages. He maintained that these nineteenth-century schemes of evolution were based on insufficient empirical evidence. Boas called for an end to "armchair anthropology," in which scholars took data from travelers, traders, and missionaries and plugged these data into a speculative model of evolution. He proposed that all anthropologists do rigorous, scientifically based fieldwork to collect basic ethnographic data.

Boas's fieldwork experience and his intellectual training in Germany led him to conclude that each society has its own unique historical development. This theory, known as **historical particularism,** maintains that each society must be understood as a product of its own history. This view led Boas to adopt the notion of **cultural relativism,** the belief that each society should be understood in terms of its own cultural practices and values (see Chapter 10). One aspect of this view is that no society evolved higher or lower than another. Thus, we

cannot rank any particular society above another in terms of degree of savagery, barbarity, or civility. Boas called for an end to the use of these derogatory, ethnocentric terms.

The Boasian view became the dominant theoretical trend in anthropology during the first half of the twentieth century. Anthropologists began to do rigorous ethnographic fieldwork in different societies to gather sound empirical evidence. Boas instituted the *participant-observer method* as a basic research strategy of ethnographic fieldwork (see Chapter 1). This strategy enabled ethnographers to gather valid empirical data to explain human behavior. Boas also encouraged his students to develop their linguistic skills so that they could learn the languages of the peoples they studied.

Boas worked in all four subfields of anthropology: physical anthropology, archaeology, ethnology, and linguistics. Some of his most important work involved taking precise assessments of the physical characteristics, including brain size and cranial capacity, of people in different societies. Boas was one of the first scientists in the United States to demonstrate that brain size and cranial capacities of modern humans are not linked directly to intelligence. His research indicated that brain size and cranial capacity differ widely within all races. Boas's findings challenged the racist assumptions put forward by the unilineal evolutionists. They also repudiated the type of racism that characterized black-white relations in the United States, as well as Nazi theories of racial superiority.

A direct outgrowth of the Boasian approach was the emergence of *culture-and-personality theory* in American anthropology. Boas trained two particularly noteworthy students, Ruth Benedict and Margaret Mead, pioneering anthropologists whose research is described in Chapter 11. The anthropological school represented by Benedict and Mead led to the development of more careful research regarding personality and culture. The methods used in this field have been refined and tested by many anthropologists (Barnouw, 1985). As a result, we now have a better understanding of enculturation and personality formation in human societies. Boas's efforts set the stage for a sound scientific approach in anthropology that led to definite progress in our comprehension of race and other issues in explaining human behavior and culture. Additionally, Boas pioneered the study of art, religion, folklore, music,

Portrait of Franz Boas

dance, and oral literature, providing the humanistic aspect of the anthropological enterprise.

Functionalism: British Anthropology

At approximately the same time that Boas and his U.S. students were questioning the claims of the unilineal evolutionists, British anthropologists were developing their own criticisms through the school of thought known as functionalism. **Functionalism** is the view that society consists of institutions that serve vital purposes for people. Instead of focusing on the origins and evolution of society, as the unilineal theorists did, the British functionalists explored the relationships among different institutions and how these institutions function to serve society or the individual. The question of whether these institutions serve the interests of society at large or the interests of the individual person divided the school of functionalism into two camps, each associated with a prominent figure in British anthropology. The two figures were A. R. Radcliffe-Brown and Bronislaw Malinowski.

Structural Functionalism: Radcliffe-Brown

The type of functionalism associated with Radcliffe-Brown is sometimes referred to as *structural functionalism*. Radcliffe-Brown had done research in Africa and on the Andaman Islands in southeastern Asia. He focused on the structure of society as reflected in the differing institutions that function to perpetuate the survival of *society*. He argued that a society's economic, social, political, and religious institutions serve to integrate the society as a whole. For example, he studied the social institutions that function to enhance group solidarity in small-scale societies. In some of his studies he emphasized how males had to marry outside their particular group into another group. Once the male marries, he establishes an important relationship with his wife's kin. Because he is an outsider, he has to show extreme respect to his new in-laws, so that he does not produce hostility. He may also establish a "joking relationship" with them, whereby hostility is reduced by playful teasing. Radcliffe-Brown suggested that all norms for specific behaviors and

obligations among different people in kinship relationships promote order and stability. Thus, to Radcliffe-Brown, these social institutions serve society's needs.

Psychological Functionalism: Malinowski

Malinowski's functionalism differed from that of Radcliffe-Brown in that it focused on how society functions to serve the *individual's* interests or needs. This view is known as *psychological functionalism*. Malinowski did his major ethnographic study in the Trobriand Islands off the coast of Papua New Guinea. He tried to demonstrate how individuals use cultural norms to satisfy certain needs.

Malinowski's analysis of magic among the Trobriand islanders illustrates his psychological functionalism. He observed that when the islanders went fishing in enclosed lagoons where fishing was reliable and safe, they depended on their technical knowledge and skill alone. When they went fishing on the open sea, however, which was more dangerous and highly unpredictable, they employed extensive magical beliefs and techniques. Thus, Malinowski argued that the use of magic arises in situations in which humans have no control over circumstances, such as weather conditions. Magical

Bronislaw Malinowski

techniques are used to reduce internal anxieties and tensions for these individuals. In addition to magic, the Trobrianders have an elaborate system of beliefs concerning death, the afterlife, sickness, and health. These beliefs aid in serving the needs of individuals as they adapt to the circumstances and exigencies of life. In other words, the individual has needs, both physiological and psychological, and cultural institutions, customs, and traditions exist to satisfy them.

The Limitations of Functionalism

Like the other early developments in anthropology, functionalism has its theoretical weaknesses. It fails to explain why societies are different or similar. Why do some societies have different types of institutions when similar ones might be able to fill the same function? This weakness arose from the tendency of functionalists to ignore historical processes. They were not concerned with the historical development of differing institutions but rather focused exclusively on how these institutions serve society and the individual. They could not explain, for example, why British society experienced rapid technological change whereas other societies did not, when all of these societies had similar needs.

Functionalists were also unable to explain social and cultural change very well, because they tended to view societies as static and unchanging. They could not explain why, if all institutions perform a particular function, these institutions would need to change.

Functionalism as a school of thought has influenced a great deal of research in anthropology. By focusing on the detailed, specific functions of institutions within existing societies, it encouraged the collection of valuable ethnographic data. As with Boas in U.S. anthropology, Radcliffe-Brown and Malinowski moved their field beyond the speculative theories of the "armchair anthropologists."

Twentieth-Century Evolutionism

After World War II some anthropologists renewed their interest in evolutionary explanations of societal and cultural phenomena. Up until that time, most anthropologists had devoted themselves to criticizing the unilineal evolutionists. But some anthropologists, led by Leslie White of the University of Michigan, suggested a new twentieth-century perspective on the evolution of society, which is sometimes referred to as *neoevolutionism*.

White treated societies, or *sociocultural systems*, as entities that evolved in relation to the amount of energy captured and used by each member of society. This energy is directed toward the production of resources for their survival. In White's words, "Culture evolves as the amount of energy harnessed per capita per year is increased, or as the efficiency of the instrumental means of putting the energy to work is increased" ([1949] 1971:368). In other words, the degree of societal development is measured by the amount of energy harnessed by these sociocultural systems. The greater the energy, the more highly evolved the sociocultural system.

White's hypothesis of cultural evolution explained the differences in levels of societal development by examining differences in technology and energy production. For example, he hypothesized that small-scale hunting-and-gathering societies had not developed complex sociocultural systems because they depended primarily on human energy for production. Because of a limited energy source for producing resources, their societies were simple, meager, and undeveloped. But following the agricultural revolution and the capture of energy through the domestication of plants and animals, sociocultural systems changed dramatically. The agricultural revolution represented an efficient use of human energy in harnessing new energy reserves, such as using draft animals to pull plows. In turn, these technological changes led to the emergence of cities, complex states, powerful political and religious elites, and new ideologies.

According to White, tracing the modern industrial age, as fossil-fuel technology developed, new forms of energy such as coal, oil, and natural gas were used, and sociocultural changes accelerated. Up until the Industrial Revolution, the changes in agricultural societies had been gradual, taking several thousand years. In contrast, the Industrial Revolution has taken less than five hundred years to produce widespread global transformations. Because White focused on sociocultural change on the global level rather than on particular societies, his approach has been called *general evolution*.

Steward and Cultural Ecology

At about the same period of time, anthropologist Julian Steward turned his attention to the evolution of society. Steward was instrumental in establishing the field of cultural ecology. Also called *ecological anthropology,* **cultural ecology** stresses the interrelationship among the natural conditions in the environment—rainfall, temperature, soils—and technology, social organization, and attitudes within a particular sociocultural system. Steward focused on how specific sociocultural systems adapt to environmental conditions.

Steward's cultural-ecology framework divides sociocultural systems into two different spheres: the culture core and secondary features. The *culture core* consists of those elements most closely related to subsistence: the environment, technology, and economic arrangements. The other characteristics, such as social organization, politics, and religion, constitute *secondary features* of society. Because Steward investigated the detailed characteristics of different environments, his approach is referred to as *specific evolution,* as opposed to White's general evolution. One of his most illustrative case studies involved the Shoshone Indians of the Great Basin of the western United States.

A Case Study: The Shoshone The Shoshone were hunter-gatherer groups whose society revolved around gathering seeds, pine nuts, roots, and berries, and hunting rabbits and antelopes. Steward discovered that these subsistence activities had definite effects on the organization of Shoshone kinship groups. Like all hunter-gatherer societies, the Shoshone were nomadic, moving from one location to another based on the availability of food. The Shoshone lived in a hot and dry desert environment that supported meager supplies of plants and animals. These people were forced to live in small, elementary family units and travel frequently in search of food. For a few months in the winter, however, they could live in larger social groups among interrelated family units because of the supply of pine nuts in the mountains. Thus, the environment and the availability of resources had a definite influence on the form of social organization during different seasons for these hunter-gatherer societies.

Through cases like this, Steward demonstrated how environmental influences (part of the culture core) affect the cultural developments in a sociocultural system. Steward used this approach to examine the agricultural civilizations of South America, Mesoamerica, the Near East, and the Far East. He found remarkable parallels in the evolution of these different civilizations. They all had irrigation systems, specialized occupations, centralized governments, and formalized state religions. Steward emphasized that many of these parallels were the result of similar environmental conditions, such as river valleys and alluvial plains that offered opportunities for the emergence of agricultural civilizations.

The Strengths of Neoevolutionism

The twentieth-century evolutionists differed from the earlier nineteenth-century evolutionists in several ways. First, they did not assume a unilineal direction of society through formalized stages such as savagery, barbarism, and civilization. Second, they were not ethnocentrically biased or racist when it came to understanding why different societies are at various levels of development. They abandoned crude terms such as "savagery" and explored environment, technology, and energy resources in assessing levels of sociocultural development. Third, they did not assume that sociocultural evolution toward complexity (or "civilization") is always equated with "progress," as did the nineteenth-century theorists. The neoevolutionists held that some aspects of small-scale societies are, in fact, better than those of complex societies. For example, in some respects family and social relationships tend to be more stable in small-scale societies than in large, complex societies.

Cultural ecology has become an extremely sophisticated area of research. It has been influenced by developments in biological ecology and theories derived from mathematics, computer modeling, and related sciences. Cultural ecologists do careful research on energy expenditures, use of resources, exchanges of nutrients, population, and interrelations among these factors and with cultural values. As we shall see in later chapters, the research findings of ecological anthropology help to explain sociocultural similarities and differences.

Criticisms of Cultural Ecology

A number of anthropologists have criticized the cultural-ecology approach for a variety of reasons.

Some critics claim that in emphasizing the role of the environment, cultural ecologists do not take into account historical or political factors (Geertz, 1963a; Friedman, 1974; Keesing, 1981; Hefner, 1983). Thus, for example, cultural ecologists can explain how Shoshone culture represents an adaptation to a desert environment, but they cannot explain how or why the Shoshone came to reside in an environment with scarce resources. An explanation of this kind would require detailed historical research examining local and global political factors.

Another criticism is that cultural ecology reduces human behavior to simple adaptations to the external environment. Because of the emphasis on adaptation, cultural ecologists tend to view every cultural element as the best of all possible solutions to the problems of subsistence and energy requirements. In fact, many sociocultural adaptations may involve compromises at the time that turn out later to be maladaptations.

For example, a number of cultural ecologists have used their models to explain the development of warfare in different societies. Some hypothesize that warfare is associated with land ownership, population size, and resource shortages (Vayda, 1961; Sweet, 1965; Meggitt, 1977). As populations expand in areas with scarce resources, societies resort to warfare to secure additional resources and thereby restore stability to the sociocultural system. Critics suggest that this explanation ignores various historical, political, and cultural factors that contribute to warfare, such as conflicting political or religious ideologies. Furthermore, they suggest that this is an extreme form of adaptationism. In most cases, warfare is definitely maladaptive.

Cultural Materialism

The late anthropologist Marvin Harris refined the neoevolutionary approach of White and Steward as a perspective he called cultural materialism. **Cultural materialism** is a research strategy that focuses on technology, environment, and economic factors as key determinants in sociocultural evolution. Cultural materialists divide all sociocultural systems into infrastructure, structure, and superstructure. The *infrastructure* includes the technology and practices used for expanding or limiting the production of basic resources such as food, clothing,

and shelter. The *structure* consists of the domestic economy (family structure, domestic division of labor, age and gender roles) and the political economy (political organization, class, castes, police, military). The *superstructure* includes philosophy, art, music, religion, ideas, literature, advertising, sports, games, science, and values.

According to cultural-materialist theory, the infrastructure largely determines the structure and superstructure of sociocultural systems. As the infrastructure changes, the structure and superstructure may change accordingly. Technology, energy, and environmental factors are crucial to the development of all aspects of society. All societies must devise ways to obtain food and shelter, and they must possess an adequate technology and energy to provide for the survival and continuity of the population. Although cultural materialists do not deny that superstructural and structural components of society may influence cultural evolution, they see infrastructural factors as being far more important. This theoretical perspective represents an extension of the foundations laid down by White and Steward.

Criticisms of Cultural Materialism

A variety of criticisms have been directed at Marvin Harris's theoretical paradigm of cultural materialism. One of the major criticisms is the same one directed at cultural ecology; that is, Harris focuses too exclusively on environmental factors and ignores social, political, and religious values and beliefs. In addition, cultural materialism tends to emphasize the infrastructural mechanisms that strictly "determine" the structure and superstructure of the society. This results in a form of technological determinism that is much too mechanistic in analyzing the social and cultural conditions within a society. As critics of technological determinists note, the level of technological development doesn't tell us anything about the complexity of religion, kinship, family and marriage systems, art, folklore, etc. Finally, Harris's paradigm underplays the importance of symbolism and language and the influence these factors have on people's beliefs and motivations.

Harris replied to all of these criticisms in a number of texts (1979, 1988, 1999). He admitted that he does emphasize infrastructure as the major determinant of the direction in which a society will evolve. However, Harris suggests that his critics neglect his attempt to demonstrate how structural and super-structural aspects of society play a role in influencing conditions for social and cultural evolution. He indicated that when he discusses infrastructural determinism, he means this in a "probabilistic" sense. In other words, he eschews a strict or rigid form of determinism and suggests that a particular infrastructure will result in the probabilities or tendencies to produce certain forms of structure or superstructure within a society. Harris noted that ideas, beliefs, and values can also provide feedback mechanisms and generate change within society.

Marxist Anthropology

Another major theoretical perspective in anthropology stems directly from the writings of Karl Marx (1818–1883). Though most of Marx's writings focus on capitalist societies, he also produced a broad evolutionary scheme of societal development throughout the world. Basing some of his notions on Lewis Henry Morgan's evolutionary thought, Marx theorized that society had evolved through various stages: the tribal, the Asiatic, the feudal, and, finally,

An Indian farmer working in his fields. Marx believed that societies evolved through stages such as the Asiatic, in which the land was cultivated by peasant farmers.

the capitalist stage. Having advanced this far, according to Marx, these societies would then proceed to the socialist and communist stages.

Marx's approach is a form of materialism because it emphasizes how the systems of producing material goods shape all of society. Marx argued that the mode of production in material life determines the general character of the social, political, and spiritual processes of life ([1859] 1959).

Unlike the functionalist anthropologists, who focused on the maintenance of order and stability in society, Marx believed that society is in a state of constant change as a result of class struggles and conflicts among groups within society. Writing at the time of early industrialization and capitalism in Europe, he viewed these developments as causes of exploitation, inequality in wealth and power, and class struggle.

According to Marx, the industrial mode of production had divided society into classes: *capitalists,* those who own the means of production (the factories), and *proletariat* (the workers), those who sell their labor to the owners as a commodity. The capitalist class exploits the labor of workers to produce a surplus for their own profit. This exploitation leads to harsh working conditions and extremely low wages for the proletariat class. This social arrangement sets the stage for a class struggle between these opposing segments of society. Marx suggested that all the major social and cultural transformations since the Industrial Revolution could be seen as a result of this class conflict.

Evaluation of Marxist Anthropology

It must be emphasized that current Marxist anthropologists do not accept the unilineal model of evolution suggested by Marx. For example, most Marxist anthropologists recognize that Marx's prediction regarding the evolution of socialist and communist stages of society from the capitalist stage is wrong. Historically, socialist and communist revolutions occurred in the former Soviet Union and China, which were by no means industrial-capitalist societies. The industrial societies that Marx had focused on, such as Great Britain and Germany, did not develop into what Marx conceived of as socialist or communist societies.

Nevertheless, modern Marxist anthropologists view as valid Marx's analytical approach to understanding societal development and some of the inherent problems of capitalist society. His critical perspective on the institutions of society, the modes of production, and the results of group conflict has inspired many fruitful hypotheses regarding social and cultural evolution and development. Unlike the functionalists, who assumed that society's institutions were balancing conflicting interests, the Marxist anthropologists have demonstrated that conflict is an inherent aspect of human behavior and culture.

Symbolic Anthropology: A Humanistic Method of Inquiry

Another theoretical orientation in anthropology is **symbolic anthropology,** the study of culture through the interpretation of the meaning of the symbols, values, and beliefs of a society. This school of thought focuses on the symbolic rather than the material aspects of culture. Symbolic anthropologists suggest that many cultural symbols cannot be readily reduced to the material conditions and adaptive mechanisms of a society, as proposed by cultural materialists. Rather than viewing values, beliefs, and worldviews as a reflection only of environmental, technological, or economic conditions, symbolic anthropologists argue that these cultural symbols may be completely autonomous from material factors.

From this standpoint, symbolic anthropologists argue that human behavior cannot be explained through the use of the scientific method. The goal of their research is instead to interpret the meaning of symbols within the worldviews of a particular society. For example, recall that in Chapter 10 we discussed the hairstyles of people among the Rastafarians in Jamaican society. We also discussed Mary Douglas's interpretation of the prohibition of different foods, including pork, among the ancient Israelites. She focused on the symbolic classification of various foods as being "clean" or "pure" and "unclean" or "polluted." The symbolic anthropologist tries to discern how such symbols help people produce meaning for themselves. A particular hairstyle or the classification of different foods may become symbolic metaphors, communicating messages.

The methodology of symbolic anthropology focuses on the collection of data—especially data reflecting the point of view of the members of the society studied—on kinship, economy, ritual, myth, and values. Symbolic anthropologists describe this type of data collection as producing a *thick description,* the attempt to interpret the relationships among different symbols within a society. To do this, they must interpret the meanings of the symbolic concepts and metaphors from the point of view of the people in a specific society. The aim of the symbolic anthropologist is to make other people's values, beliefs, and worldviews meaningful and intelligible.

Criticisms of Symbolic Anthropology

A number of criticisms have been directed at symbolic anthropology. One major charge is that symbolic anthropologists focus exclusively on cultural symbols at the expense of other variables that may influence human thought and behavior. Symbolic anthropologists may therefore neglect the conditions and processes that lead to the making of culture (Roseberry, 1982; Fox, 1985). For example, economic and political power may be important factors in the development of cultural values and norms. Dominant groups may be responsible for the emergence of cultural hegemony in a society. Critics emphasize that culture cannot be treated as an autonomous phenomenon separate from historical, political, and economic processes and conditions that affect a society.

Another criticism is that symbolic anthropology substitutes one form of determinism for another. Instead of emphasizing technological or economic variables, symbolic anthropologists stress the meaning of cultural symbols. Despite their rejection of scientific causal explanations, they have been accused of reducing explanations of society and human activity to the "meanings" of cultural symbols.

Materialism versus Culturalism

One major division in anthropology is between those anthropologists who prefer materialist explanations of society and those who prefer culturalist explanations. To some extent, this division reflects the differences between the scientific approach and the humanistic-interpretive perspective in anthropology (see Chapter 1). The scientists and materialists focus on technological, environmental, biological, and economic factors to explain human behavior and society. This group—which includes cultural materialists, some Marxist anthropologists, sociobiologists, and evolutionary psychologists—views many aspects of culture as having a material purpose. Culturalists, including the structuralists and some psychological anthropologists like Ruth Benedict and Margaret Mead (discussed in Chapter 11), and the symbolic anthropologists focus on the symbolic aspect of culture. Their aim is to interpret the meaning of symbols in a society. To the culturalists, symbols and culture may not have a material purpose at all but rather establish meaningfulness for the people in a society.

Anthropologist Richard Barrett (1984) notes that the difference between the materialist and culturalist approaches is related to the nature of society and human existence itself. As Barrett emphasizes, every society must confront the problem of adjusting to the practical circumstances of life. People need food, shelter, clothing, and the necessary technology and energy for survival. This is the material component of culture; it is related to survival. But there is also the nonmaterial aspect of culture: norms, values, beliefs, ideologies, and symbols. These cultural norms and symbols have emotional significance. Symbols may not be related at all to the practical circumstances of life; instead, they may indicate some aesthetic or moral values that are not related to the material conditions of society.

Thus, the distinction between the material and nonmaterial aspects of culture has led to different approaches to the analysis of human behavior and society. In later chapters we learn how anthropologists have employed these approaches in explaining and interpreting human affairs.

Feminist Anthropology

One of the most important developments in anthropological theory was the emergence of a feminist orientation. After the beginning of the twentieth century, a number of women pioneers such as Ruth Benedict, Margaret Mead, Elsie Crews Parsons, Eleanor Leacock, and Phyllis Kaberry began to have a definite impact on the field of anthropology. Margaret Mead popularized the findings of anthropology by writing a monthly article in *Redbook*

magazine, which circulated widely among women in the United States. As we shall see in Chapter 16, Mead was also the first to focus on gender roles within different societies and question a rigid biological determinist view of male and female roles.

With the development of the feminist movement in U.S. society in the 1960s and 1970s (see Chapter 19), many women anthropologists initiated a *feminist perspective*. This feminist perspective challenged the tendency to concentrate on the male role and underestimate the position of women within different societies. Before the 1970s, most anthropologists were male and, for the most part, women were neglected in ethnographic research. As more women became involved in anthropology, they questioned the traditional emphasis on the male position and the invisibility of women in ethnographies. These feminist anthropologists emphasized that gender roles had to be taken into account in ethnographic research (Mascia-Lees & Black, 2000). They also challenged essentialist or stereotypical portrayals of women. As we shall see in later chapters, these feminist anthropologists have produced enormous insights regarding the role of women in societies throughout the world.

Feminist anthropologists have directed their criticisms at a variety of targets that had become prevalent in the discipline. For example, they questioned the underlying assumptions made by the sociobiologists regarding male and female behavioral tendencies. The feminist anthropologists argued that the view of men as sexually promiscuous and females as sexually conservative and desiring monogamy as a reproductive strategy was an overgeneralization and essentialist stereotype. They critiqued the view that males and females were radically different based on biological traits such as hormonal differences. In addition, they directed their criticisms at the physical anthropologists who argued that females had become dependent on males for food and other resources, whereas males were developing tools and other strategies for hunting purposes. They suggested that the female role in human evolution had been overlooked. And feminist anthropologists criticized ethnographic descriptions that presented males as the more active, aggressive agent within the family, and the female as passive and inactive in behavior. These type of descriptions appeared in the ethnographies of the functionalists during the 1930s and 1940s (Mascia-Lees &

Black, 2000). Thus, feminist anthropologists provided new insightful hypotheses and created a more general awareness of gender and women's issues within the discipline.

One of the leading feminist anthropologists is Sherry Ortner, who wrote an important essay in 1974, "Is Female to Male as Nature Is to Culture?" In this essay Ortner tackled the view regarding what appeared to be the universal subordination of women throughout the world. She tried to answer the question of why women were perceived and treated as inferior, second-class citizens in the vast majority of societies. In her analysis, Ortner drew on the structuralist approach in anthropology. Recall that the view of the founder of structuralism, Claude Levi-Strauss (see Chapter 11), was that the fundamental underlying structural binary oppositions of the human mind were "nature" and "culture." Within this structuralist format, Ortner argued that since women gave birth and cared for children, they were perceived as being "closer" to nature. In contrast, men were involved in political affairs and other more symbolic activities and were perceived to be "closer" to the "creative aspect" of culture, and therefore cognitively "superior." According to Ortner, this nature/culture opposition of males and females had structural consequences for the social position of men and women within all societies. Women were regarded as inferior beings and were subjugated within societies all over the world.

This essay was a landmark piece in early feminist anthropology. More recently, Ortner returned to this early essay, which had received a lot of critical attention from other women in anthropology. On the basis of this critical attention, she reexamined her original essay in "So, Is Female to Male as Nature Is to Culture?" in her book *Making Gender: The Politics and Erotics of Culture* (1996). In this essay, she grants that in some societies, the appearance of male superiority and female inferiority is fragmentary and very difficult to determine. She also concurs with her critics that the structuralist explanation regarding the distinction between nature and culture that resulted in the universal subordination of women was not very useful. However, she does think that this nature/culture distinction is something that all of humanity faces. But in different societies and historical conditions, men and women may articulate and respond to these distinctions in enormously variant ways. In general, Ortner suggests that the universal or near-universal male dominance and subordination of women is caused by a complex interaction of functional arrangements in society, power dynamics, and also natural biological differences between males and females. Sherry Ortner has offered some insightful hypotheses for further research on gender and women's issues in anthropology.

Criticisms of Feminist Anthropology

Although feminist anthropology has contributed substantially to the discipline in providing a critical awareness for male anthropologists, some anthropologists argue that this perspective has become too extreme and exaggerated. For example, some feminist anthropologists have put forth the view that biological factors have absolutely nothing to do with male and female differences. An enormous amount of data from various scientifically evaluated fields has demonstrated that both nature and nurture are important in shaping gender and male and female differences. Thus, the view that nature doesn't have anything to do with gender seems to be too extreme.

In addition, some feminist anthropologists have argued that all of the scientific hypotheses and most of science is based on a Western cultural framework and an *androcentric* (male-centered) perspective. Consequently, male anthropologists cannot do research on women in other societies because of their androcentric biases. Therefore, only women can conduct research on women and gender issues. These views also appear to be extreme. At present, most male anthropologists have been attuned to the feminist critique of anthropology and have adjusted to a more sensitive understanding of gender and women's issues. Many male anthropologists today consider themselves to be feminist anthropologists.

Also, as we have emphasized in this book, scientifically based hypotheses are tested by many individuals in both Western and non-Western societies, and as more women come into the field of anthropology, they will become actively involved in testing these hypotheses. Thus, science and scientific hypotheses are not just products of a Western cultural framework and an androcentric perspective. The scientific method used correctly and precisely will weed out any erroneous biases or data and will result in a more comprehensive and refined understanding of the social and cultural world.

Postmodernism and Anthropology

Although ethnographic fieldwork has long been a fundamental aspect of anthropology, one current school is challenging basic ethnographic assumptions and methodologies. This group, known as **postmodernist** anthropologists, includes such figures as James Clifford, George Marcus, and Michael Fischer. The postmodernists suggest that traditional ethnographic research is based on a number of unsound assumptions. One such assumption is that the ethnographer is a detached, scientifically objective observer who is not influenced by the premises and biases of her or his own society. Clifford characterizes one of the models maintained by ethnographers such as Malinowski as that of the "scientific participant-observer" (1983). In his ethnographies, Malinowski eliminated any reference to himself and recorded data that was then written as the documentation of an "objective scientist." Malinowski produced his descriptions as if he did not have any involvement with the Trobriand people. It was as if he were some sort of computing machine without feelings, biases, or emotions, who was simply recording everything about native life.

According to postmodernist critics, ethnographies such as those compiled by Malinowski were intended as a type of scientific study in which the subjects behaved and the ethnographer simply recorded this behavior. From this standpoint, the postmodernists complain that the ethnographers assume they have a thoroughly scientific and objective view of reality, whereas the native view is highly subjective, based on traditional worldviews and cosmologies.

Another type of inquiry criticized by the postmodernists is the interpretive model used by symbolic anthropologists such as Clifford Geertz (Clifford, 1983). In contrast with the "objective" model, the *interpretive model* focuses on the understanding of symbols from the point of view of the members of the society. It assumes that the people in a particular society have a better understanding than others of their own concepts, and the interpretive anthropologist must try to reconstruct these understandings so that others can also understand the meanings of these symbols.

For example, in Clifford Geertz's description of a cockfight in Balinese society, the gambling and the cockfight are viewed as a text that has meaning for the participants (1973). Geertz suggests that the meaning of the cockfight reflects the status rivalries among the Balinese men. He refers to the cockfight as a "status bloodbath." Geertz views the cockfight in relation to the competition among various groups and factions within the Balinese community. The interpretation offered by Geertz suggests that the natives provide cultural meaning for themselves through the activities associated with the cockfight.

Postmodernists critique this type of interpretive ethnology because it is also written as if the ethnologist disappears from the setting through empathy with the subjects. In other words, the people themselves are not described as offering their own interpretations, but instead the ethnologist is looking over their shoulders and reading the cultural meanings and texts of their society and interpreting them.

Postmodernists and Contemporary Research

One of the basic reasons for the postmodernist critiques is that the situation for ethnographic studies has changed substantially. Until recently, most subjects of ethnographic studies were illiterate peoples adjusting to the impact of the West. But as more people throughout the world become educated and familiar with the field of anthropology, Western ethnographers can no longer claim to be the sole authorities regarding anthropological knowledge. Many people in Latin America, Africa, the Middle East, and Asia can, and do, speak and write about their own cultures (some have even become anthropologists), and they are disseminating knowledge about their own societies. The world is no longer dependent on Western anthropologists to gather ethnographic data. Indigenous people are beginning to represent themselves and their societies to the world.

Postmodernists have recommended that ethnographers today adopt a different way of researching and writing. Instead of trying to distance themselves from their subjects, ethnographers should present themselves in dialogue with their subjects. Clifford (1983) argues that an ethnography should consist of many voices from the native population, rather than just a dialogue between the ethnographer and one of his or her informants.

Reaction to this postmodernist critique has varied within the discipline. On the one hand, some ethnographers have charged the postmodernists with characterizing traditional ethnographic methodologies unjustly. Many ethnographers, they contend, were engaged in a form of dialogue with their informants and other members of the societies being studied.

On the other hand, the postmodernist debate has stirred many anthropologists to rethink their roles. Currently, more ethnographers are writing about their actual interactions and relationships with the people they study. Ethnographers must take account of their own political position within the society under investigation. This type of data and personal reflection is no longer pushed into the background, but instead is presented as a vital ingredient of the ethnography. In the 1980s, a number of ethnographies appeared that reflected the postmodernist emphasis on interaction between ethnographers and their subjects. Some of these new ethnographies are based on the life histories of people within the studied population.

Following two periods of fieldwork among the !Kung San or Ju'/hoansi, hunters and gatherers of the Kalahari Desert in southwest Africa, the late Marjorie Shostak completed a life history, *The Life and Words of Nisa, A !Kung Woman* (1981). Shostak interviewed numerous !Kung women to gain a sense of their lives. She focused on the life history of Nisa, who discussed her family, her sex life, marriage, pregnancies, her experiences with !Kung men, and growing older. Shostak cautioned that Nisa does not represent a "typical" !Kung or Ju'/hoansi female because her life experiences are unique (as are all individuals in any society). In addition, Shostak exercised extreme care in discussing with Nisa the material that would go into the book to ensure a faithful representation of Nisa's life.

If we look back over years of ethnographic research, we find many accounts in which anthropologists were scrupulous in their representation of people in other societies. To this extent, the postmodernist critics have exaggerated the past mistakes of ethnographers. However, the postmodernists have alerted ethnographers to some unexamined assumptions concerning their work. Today, most anthropologists do not claim a completely "objective" viewpoint. Anthropologists generally want to maintain empathy with the people they study, yet they usually attempt some critical detachment as well. Otherwise, they could easily become merely the voices and spokespersons of specific political interests and leaders in a community (Errington & Gewertz, 1987).

Collaborative fieldwork, with teams of ethnographers and informants working together to understand a society, is most likely the future direction for ethnographic study. The image of a solitary ethnographer such as Malinowski or Margaret Mead isolated on a Pacific island is outmoded (Salzman, 1989). Collaborative research will lead to more systematic data collection and will offer opportunities to examine hypotheses of both ethnographers and subjects from a variety of perspectives.

Shifts in Anthropological Explanations

We began this chapter with the Hindu legend of the blind men and the elephant. The moral of that story was that we all have partial understandings of the world. As we have sketched a number of different anthropological explanations and critiques in this chapter, it is obvious that no one explanation provides a full understanding of human behavior and culture. However, after more than a century of anthropological research, we do have an improved and more comprehensive understanding of culture, society, and the role of individual behavior than we did in the nineteenth century. Through constant critical evaluation, hypotheses testing, and refinement of explanations by anthropologists, we ought to know even more about these phenomena in the future.

SUMMARY

The first professional anthropologists, notably E. B. Tylor and Lewis Henry Morgan, proposed a theory known as unilineal evolution to explain the differences and similarities in societal evolution. The unilineal evolutionists maintained that societies evolve in one direction from a stage of savagery to one of civilization. In the early twentieth century, another theory proposed diffusionism as the best explanation of the differences and similarities among societies. The British diffusionists argued that all civilization emanated from Egypt, whereas the German diffusionists maintained that there were several original centers of civilization. Although modern anthropologists consider these early views as being of limited value, diffusionism remains important in anthropological thought.

Another early twentieth-century theory, historical particularism, was developed in the United States from the ideas of Franz Boas. Boas criticized the unilineal view that societies could be ranked and compared with one another. Instead, he argued that each society is a unique product of its historical circumstances.

At about the same time, functionalism developed in British anthropology. Anthropologists such as A. R. Radcliffe-Brown and Bronislaw Malinowski focused on cultural institutions as serving societal or individual needs. Although functionalist explanations proved limited in explaining such matters as cultural change, they did provide valuable ethnographic data.

Following World War II, some anthropologists turned to new evolutionary theories. Anthropologists such as Leslie White and Julian Steward began to analyze how environment, technology, and energy requirements led to the evolution of societies. This neoevolutionism avoided the ethnocentric ideas of nineteenth-century unilineal evolution.

As an outgrowth of neoevolutionism, a school of thought known as cultural materialism developed through the writings of Marvin Harris. Harris systematized the analysis of sociocultural systems and maintained that the key determinant of sociocultural evolution is the infrastructure, including technology, environment, and material conditions.

Another anthropological school of thought evolved from the writings of Karl Marx. In the 1970s, a number of anthropologists applied Marxist ideas about the mode of production to the analysis of preindustrial and industrial societies. Marxist anthropologists introduced a global view of societal evolution.

Symbolic anthropology focuses on the study of cultural beliefs, worldviews, and ethos of society. Symbolic anthropologists treat cultural traditions as texts that need to be interpreted by the ethnographer. Symbolic anthropology represents a means of analyzing cultural traditions without reducing them to material conditions.

Feminist anthropology emerged in the 1970s to challenge some of the explanations that males were producing about gender and women's issues. These feminist anthropologists have made an enormous contribution to ethnographic studies by refocusing attention on gender and women's issues.

Postmodern anthropology developed as a critical program that suggested that traditional ethnographic research was Western biased and overly scientific. This postmodern program has produced a much more reflexive type of ethnography that entails examining one's own political position within an ethnographic context.

QUESTIONS TO THINK ABOUT

1. Discuss the principal differences between nineteenth-century models of unilineal evolution and twentieth-century neoevolutionary theories. Who were the principal proponents of each?

2. What are some of the weaknesses of the theory that there was only one source for the development of all civilizations?

3. Define historical particularism. Do you think that this approach can be used along with investigations of cultural evolution? Why or why not?

4. Compare and contrast the perspectives of the neoevolutionists, cultural ecologists, cultural materialists, and Marxists. Are these theoretical views similar in any way, or are they mutually exclusive and contradictory?

5. What are some of the criticisms that have been leveled against the cultural ecological approach? Do you think these criticisms are valid? If so, how would you modify the cultural ecological perspective to take into account the criticism?

6. Discuss the principal effects that the writings of Karl Marx have had on anthropological theory.

Do you think that Marxist anthropology is the same as communist anthropology? Why or why not?

7. Compare and contrast the perspective of the symbolic anthropologists with the Marxists' and cultural materialists' perspectives.

8. Discuss the approach of feminist anthropology. What has feminist anthropology contributed to ethnographic studies?

9. What is postmodern anthropology, and how has it criticized traditional anthropology?

KEY TERMS

cultural ecology

cultural materialism

cultural relativism

diffusionism

functionalism

historical particularism

postmodernists

symbolic anthropology

unilineal evolution

INTERNET EXERCISES

1. Visit the website **http://www.indiana.edu/ ~wanthro/theory.htm**. Click on "Applied Anthropology" by Ann Reed. How does the field of applied anthropology utilize anthropological theory as presented throughout this chapter? Can applied anthropology exist without knowledge of theory, or is applied anthropology the application of theory to various situations? Explain your answer.

2. Read about the life and contributions of Bronislaw Malinowski at **http://emuseum. mnsu.edu/information/biography/klmno/ malinowski_bronislaw.html**. What brought Malinowski to anthropology? What particular skills did he bring to the field? What were his conclusions about the social behavior of people?

SUGGESTED READINGS

BOROFSKY, ROBERT (Ed.). 1994. *Assessing Cultural Anthropology*. New York: McGraw-Hill. A collection of essays representing an overview of the current theoretical issues in anthropology.

CERRONI-LONG, E. L. (Ed.). 1999. *Anthropological Theory in North America*. Westport, CT: Bergin and Garvey. An anthology with some state-of-the-art essays on anthropological theory in the United States.

HARRIS, MARVIN. 1968. *The Rise of Anthropological Theory*. New York: Thomas Y. Crowell. A thorough account of the history of anthropological thought from the perspective of a cultural materialist.

————. 1979. *Cultural Materialism: The Struggle for a Science of Culture*. New York: Random House. A presentation of the cultural-materialist theory in comparison

with contending approaches. Harris tries to show the superiority of this theory when compared with structuralism, Marxist anthropology, sociobiology, and other perspectives.

————. 1999. *Theories of Culture in Postmodern Times*. Walnut Creek, CA: Altamira Press. This book represents the late Marvin Harris's most recent defense of cultural materialism in the midst of postmodernist critiques of theories in anthropology.

HATCH, ELVIN. 1973. *Theories of Man and Culture*. New York: Columbia University Press. A comprehensive summary of anthropological theories from the nineteenth century to the modern era. This book compares and contrasts the major theorists such as Tylor, Boas, Benedict, Malinowski, White, and Steward.

LAYTON, ROBERT. 1997. *An Introduction to Theory in Anthropology*. Cambridge: Cambridge University Press. A recent treatment of theory in anthropology from a British perspective, drawing on a great deal of ethnographic material to illustrate particular orientations.

LETT, JAMES. 1987. *The Human Enterprise: A Critical Introduction to Anthropological Theory*. Boulder, CO: Westview Press. A critical introduction to the basic theories in anthropology using a scientific and materialist focus.

MANNERS, R. A., and D. KAPLAN (Eds.). 1968. *Theory in Anthropology: A Sourcebook*. Chicago: Aldine. An anthology of readings consisting of different theoretical perspectives held by anthropologists.

MASCIA-LEES, FRANCES, and NANCY JOHNSON BLACK. 2000. *Gender and Anthropology*. Prospect Heights, IL: Waveland Press. An excellent overview of feminist anthropology and its approach to gender and women's issues around the world.

MCGEE, JON R., and RICHARD L. WARMS (Eds.). 2000. *Anthropological Theory: An Introductory History*. Mountain View, CA: Mayfield. An excellent anthology of the writings of the leading anthropologists from all the various schools of thought, with extensive footnotes and documentation emphasizing the strengths and weaknesses of various views.

MOORE, HENRIETTA L. 2000. *Anthropological Theory Today*. London: U.K. Polity Press. A collection of essays from leading anthropological theorists for advanced students.

NANDA, SERENA. 2000. *Gender Diversity: Cross-Cultural Variations*. Prospect Heights, IL: Waveland Press. A cross-cultural examination of gender diversity with an emphasis on the acceptance of third-gendered individuals within different societies.

STOCKING, GEORGE. 1995. *After Tylor: British Social Anthropology 1888–1951*. Madison: University of Wisconsin Press. Stocking is the leading historian of anthropology in the world. For a historical view of anthropological theory, see his other books, including *The Ethnographer's Magic and Other Essays in the History of Anthropology; Colonial Situations: Essays on the Contextualization of Ethnographic History;* and *Romantic Motives: Essays on Anthropological Sensibility*.

TERRAY, EMMANUEL. 1972. *Marxism and "Primitive" Societies: Two Studies*. New York: Monthly Review Press. The application of neo-Marxist ideas to the analysis of small-scale societies. This book illustrates the development of Marxist anthropology in the 1970s.

CHAPTER

14

Analyzing Sociocultural Systems

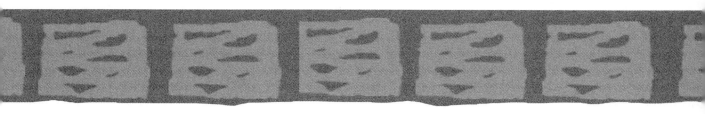

CHAPTER OUTLINE

CHAPTER QUESTIONS

- How do cultural anthropologists study society and culture?

- What are the universals and variables that cultural anthropologists rely on to do their fieldwork?

- What are the strengths and limitations of the cross-cultural approach?

As we discussed in Chapter 10, at times anthropologists use the term *sociocultural system* as a combination of the terms "society" and "culture" in analyzing their data. We also saw that there are some basic cultural universals that are found in all societies (Brown, 1991). This chapter will provide insight on how anthropologists do research on the universal characteristics of sociocultural systems. These universal features of sociocultural systems are usually analyzed by anthropologists as *variables*. Immediately, this terminology suggests that these universals can *vary* within different sociocultural systems, and this is just what anthropologists have discovered in their research. Thus, there are basic universal similarities among all humans, and yet within different societies, these universal features can exhibit tremendous variations. In order to investigate universals and variations, anthropologists must utilize both a scientific and humanistic perspective. In accounting for patterns of relationships found within a sociocultural system, anthropologists use *both* scientific causal explanations and humanistic interpretations of cultural beliefs.

In this chapter we examine the universal conditions and variable features that are investigated by anthropologists, including environmental,

321

demographic, technological, economic, social-organizational (social structure, family, marriage, age, gender relations), political, and religious variables. Anthropologists use the *holistic approach* to analyze sociocultural systems, which means demonstrating how all of these universals and variables interact and influence one another. Although the term *system* is used, it is employed in a highly metaphorical manner. It does not suggest that sociocultural systems are somehow running "above" human affairs. Humans are not just automatons being driven by some mechanical "cultural system." Rather, humans as individuals are actively involved in managing, shaping, and modifying their culture from within these so-called "systems."

In later chapters, we examine different types of sociocultural systems to illustrate the interconnections of these variables. This chapter presents a broad overview of the basic universals and variables that anthropologists investigate when explaining the similarities and differences in societies. Various concepts and terms used by anthropologists to examine variables are also introduced. This will prepare you to evaluate the results of ethnographic findings discussed in later chapters.

Ethnographic Fieldwork

In Chapter 1 we introduced the subfield of anthropology known as cultural anthropology. This subfield focuses on the ethnographic study of contemporary societies all over the world. To prepare for ethnographic fieldwork, the anthropologist must be well grounded in the different theoretical perspectives of anthropology that were discussed in Chapter 13. This background knowledge is especially important for developing a research design for the fieldwork.

A *research design* is the formulation of a strategy to examine a particular topic and specifies the appropriate methods for gathering the richest possible data. The research design must take into account the types of data that will be collected and how those data relate to existing anthropological knowledge. In the research design, the cultural anthropologist has to specify what types of methods will be used for the investigation. Typically, the cultural anthropologist develops the research design, which is then reviewed by other anthropologists, who

recommend it for funding by various government or private research foundations.

Before going into the field for direct research, the cultural anthropologist analyzes available *archival data,* including photos, films, missionary reports, business and government surveys, musical recordings, journalistic accounts, diaries, court documents, medical records, birth, death, marriage, and tax records, and landholding documents. These data help place the communities to be studied in a broad context. Historical material in the archives helps the cultural anthropologist evaluate the usefulness of the observations and interviews he or she will document. Archival data can enrich the sources of information that fieldworkers obtain once they get to the field. They must also read the published anthropological, historical, economic, sociological, and political science literature on the geographic region they are heading toward.

Ethnographic Research and Strategies

After receiving funding and obtaining the proper research clearances from the country in which the subjects of the research are located, the cultural anthropologist takes up residence in that society to explore its institutions and values. This is the basis of the *participant observation* method, which involves learning the language and culture of the group being studied and participating in its daily activities. Language skills are the most important asset that a cultural anthropologist has in the field.

One of the major means of learning about culture and behavior is through direct observation, sometimes referred to as *naturalistic observation.* Naturalistic observation consists of making accurate descriptions of the physical locale and daily activities of the people in the society. This may involve creating maps, or at least being able to read maps, to place the society's physical location in perspective. It may also involve more intensive investigation into soil conditions, rates of precipitation, surveys of crops and livestock, and other environmental factors. Naturalistic observation also involves accurate and reliable records of the cultural anthropologist's direct observations of human social interaction and behavior.

Some cultural anthropologists use what is called *time-allocation analysis* to record how much time the people in the society spend in various activities:

work, leisure, recreation, religious ceremonies, and so on. For example, Allen Johnson (1975) did a systematic time-allocation study of the Machiguenga Indians, who live in the Andes Mountains in Peru. He found that men worked 4.6 hours per day and women worked 4.2 hours per day in the production and preparation of food. Women spent 2.1 hours and men spent 1.4 hours per day in craft production. Men were involved in trade and wage work, and women did housework and child-care activities. The total amount of labor time allocated for this work was 7.6 for men and 7.4 for women. This type of time-allocation study can be useful in assessing how different societies use their time in various activities.

Key Informants   Usually the cultural anthropologist learns about the society through trusted *key informants,* who give the cultural anthropologist insight into the culture's patterns (Powdermaker, 1966; Wax, 1971; Agar, 1980). These informants become the initial source of information and help the cultural anthropologist identify major sources of data. Long-term collaboration with key informants is an integral part of quality ethnographic research.

The cultural anthropologist tries to choose key informants who have a deep knowledge of the community. These informants are usually "native cultural anthropologists" who are interested in their own society. They may serve as tutors or guides, answering general questions or identifying topics that could be of interest to the cultural anthropologist. They often help the cultural anthropologist establish rapport with the people in the community. In many situations, the people may not understand why the cultural anthropologist is interested in their society. The key informant can help explain the cultural anthropologist's role. In some cases, the key informant may become involved in interviewing other people in the community to assist the cultural anthropologist in collecting data. The relationship between the key informant and the cultural anthropologist is a close personal and professional one that usually produces lifelong friendship and collaboration.

Interviews   Cultural anthropologists use a number of *unstructured interviews,* which may involve open-ended conversations with informants, to gain insights into a culture. These unstructured interviews may include the collecting of life histories, narratives, myths, and tales. Through these interviews, the cultural anthropologist may also find out information on dispute settlements, legal transactions, political conflicts, and religious and public events. Unstructured interviewing sometimes involves on-the-spot questioning of informants.

The strength of this type of interviewing is that it gives informants tremendous freedom of expression

Anthropologist Richard Lee interviewing the !Kung San (Ju/'hoansi).

in attempting to explain their culture (Bernard et al., 1986). The informant is not confined to answering a specific question that is designed by the cultural anthropologist. The informant may, for example, elaborate on connections between certain beliefs and political power in the community. Fredrik Barth (1975) discovered through his informant among the Baktaman people of New Guinea that when young males go through their initiation ceremonies, they are introduced to the secret lore and sacred knowledge of the males who are in authority. Thus, cultural beliefs are transmitted along with political authority. Barth found that this secretive sacred knowledge was often arcane and ambiguous. As these young Baktaman males went through each stage of the ritual, the knowledge became much more mysterious and ambiguous. It appeared that the most important feature of the ritual was the reinforcement of elder authority and group bonding. Without his informant's help, Barth might not have paid attention to this relationship between belief and the transmission of authority.

Following this unstructured interviewing, the cultural anthropologist focuses on specific topics of interest related to the research project. In some cases, the cultural anthropologist then begins to develop structured interviews. *Structured interviews* systematically ask the same questions of every individual in a given sample. The cultural anthropologist must phrase the questions in a meaningful and sensitive manner, a task that requires knowledge of both the language and the lifestyle of the people being studied.

By asking the same type of question of every individual in a given sample, the cultural anthropologist is able to obtain more accurate data. If the cultural anthropologist receives uniform answers to a particular question, then the data are more likely to be reliable. If a great deal of variation in responses is evident, then the data may be more unreliable or may indicate a complex issue with many facets. The structured interview helps assess the validity of the collected data. By asking people the same type of question, the cultural anthropologist attempts to gain more quality control over his or her findings. This type of data quality control must be a constant aspect of the cultural anthropologist's research strategy.

To develop an effective questionnaire, the cultural anthropologist must collaborate with her or his informants. This is tedious and difficult methodological work, but it is necessary if the cultural anthropologist is to understand the workings of the society.

If the society is large, the cultural anthropologist must distribute the questionnaire to a random sample of the society. A **random sample** is a representative sample of people of different ages, genders, economic and political status, and other characteristics within the society. In a random sample, all of the individuals in the society have an equal chance of being selected for the survey. If the cultural anthropologist draws information from only one sector of the population—for example, males or young people—the data may be biased. This shortcoming would limit the ability of the cultural anthropologist to develop a well-rounded portrait of the society.

Quantitative and Qualitative Data   Through the structured interviews, the cultural anthropologist gathers basic **quantitative data:** census materials, dietary information, income and household-composition data, and other data that can be expressed as *numbers*. This information can be used as a database for developing a description of the variations in economic, social, political, and other patterns in the society. For example, dietary information can inform the cultural anthropologist about the basic health and nutritional problems that the society may have. Quantitative data provide background for the cultural anthropologist's direct and participant observations and further open-ended interviews with the individuals in the society. Sometimes, this objective, quantitative data is referred to as an aspect of the etic perspective of the anthropologist. The **etic perspective** is the *outsider's* objective, quantifiable data that is used to scientifically analyze the culture of a society. *Etic* is derived from the term *phonetics* in linguistics, which are the sounds of a language.

Much of the data achieved through participant observation and interviewing is **qualitative data,** nonstatistical information that tends to be the most important aspect of ethnographic research. Qualitative data include descriptions of social organization, political activities, religious beliefs, and so on. This qualitative data is often referred to as part of the **emic perspective,** the *insider's* view of their own society and culture. The term *emic* is derived from the word *phonemics* in linguistics, which refers to the sound units of language that have "meaning" for the speakers of the language (see Chapter 12). For example, as we discussed in Chapter 10, the religious beliefs of some societies have influenced their cultural preferences for various foods. Islamic and Jewish cultural traditions prohibit the eating of pork, and orthodox Hindus encourage meatless, vegetarian diets. This type of emic, qualitative data about a society helps the cultural anthropologist understand the etic, quantitative data. Ordinarily, both etic quantitative and emic qualitative data are integral to ethnological research. The anthropologist strives to understand the culture from both the outsider's and insider's perspective.

Cultural anthropologists have a number of different methods for recording qualitative data. The best-known method is *field notes,* which are the systematic recording of observations or interviews into a field notebook. Cultural anthropologists should have some training in how to take useful field notes and how to manage them for more effective coding and recording of data. An increasing number of cultural anthropologists now use the computer as a means of constructing databases to manage their field notes. They select appropriate categories for classifying the data. For example, a cultural anthropologist may set up specific categories for kinship terms, religious taboos, plants, animals, colors, foods, and so on. These data can then easily be retrieved for analysis. Some cultural anthropologists rely on tape recorders for interviews, though they recognize the problems such devices present for producing valid accounts. Most ethnographic fieldworkers utilize photography to record and help document their findings. Cultural anthropologists must use extreme caution when using these technologies, however, for in some cultures people are very sensitive about being recorded or photographed.

Today, many anthropologists use video cameras when gathering primary data. Video recording is one of the most exciting recent developments in anthropology and has stimulated a new area of anthropological research known as *visual anthropology.* The visual documentation of economic, social, political, and ritual behavior sometimes reveals intricate patterns of interaction in a society—interactions that cannot otherwise be described thoroughly. One drawback to video recording, however, is that people who know they are being filmed frequently

behave differently from the way they would normally. This may distort the cultural anthropologist's conclusions. On the other hand, the video can be used to present playbacks to informants for comments on the recorded behaviors. William Rittenberg, who did studies of Buddhist rituals in villages in central Thailand, often played back his video recordings of rituals to members of the community. The informants, including the Buddhist monks, would view the recordings and offer more elaborate explanations of the meanings of the ritual. These strategies frequently help the cultural anthropologist gain a more comprehensive understanding of the culture.

Culture Shock   Ethnographic fieldwork can be a very demanding task. Cultural anthropologists sometimes experience **culture shock,** a severe psychological reaction that results from adjusting to the realities of a society radically different from one's own. Cultural anthropologists enculturated in the United States who may have to eat unfamiliar foods such as reptiles or insects, reside in uncomfortable huts in a rainforest, or observe practices that may not occur within their own society could experience culture shock. Of course, the actual degree of culture shock may vary depending on the differences and similarities between the society studied and the anthropologist's own society. The symptoms may range from mild irritation to surprise or disgust.

Usually after the cultural anthropologist learns the norms, beliefs, and practices of the community, the psychological disorientation of culture shock begins to diminish. Part of the challenge for anthropologists is adjusting to a different society and gaining a much better perspective on one's own society. In fact, most anthropologists report considerable culture shock upon returning from another society to back home. They will never again view their own society and culture in the same light. The adjustment process of culture shock out in the field and returning from the field enables cultural anthropologists to understand themselves and their own society better.

Ethics in Anthropological Research

Cultural anthropologists must not only be trained in appropriate research and analytical techniques, they must also abide by the ethical guidelines of their discipline. In many instances, cultural anthropologists conduct research on politically powerless groups dominated by more powerful groups. When cultural anthropologists engage in participant observation, they usually become familiar with information that might, if made public, become harmful to the community or to individuals in the community. For example, when researching isolated or rural communities, cultural anthropologists might come across certain economic or political behavior or information that could be used by government authorities. This information might include the specific sources of income for people in the community or whether they participate in political opposition to the government. Whenever possible, cultural anthropologists attempt to keep such information confidential so as not to compromise their informants or other sources of data.

Most ethnographic reports do not include the real identities of informants or other people. Cultural anthropologists usually ensure their informants' anonymity, if at all possible, so that these individuals will not be investigated by their governments. Sometimes cultural anthropologists use pseudonyms (fictional names) to make identification difficult. Cultural anthropologists also attempt to be frank and open with the population under study about the aims of the research. At times this is difficult because the community does not understand the role of the cultural anthropologist (Kurin, 1980). Out of courtesy, the cultural anthropologist should give the community a reasonable account of what he or she wants to do.

In general, cultural anthropologists do not accept research funding for projects that are supposed to be clandestine or secretive. Although this type of research has been conducted by some anthropologists in the past (especially during World War II), contemporary anthropologists have adopted a code of ethics that reflects their grave reservations about undercover research.

Analysis of Ethnographic Data

The results of ethnographic research are documented in a descriptive monograph referred to as an *ethnography.* In writing the ethnographic description, the cultural anthropologist must be extremely cautious.

The accumulated field notes, photos, perhaps video or tape recordings, and quantitative data from survey sources must all be carefully managed to reduce bias, distortion, and error. The cultural anthropologist must analyze these data, making sure to cross-check the conclusions from a variety of sources, including informants, censuses, observations, and archival materials. In addition, the cultural anthropologist should plainly distinguish the views of the people being studied from his or her interpretation of those views.

Universals, Independent, and Dependent Variables
Culture, society, and human behavior are not just a random array of occurrences that develop without rhyme or reason. They are the result of universal features and interacting variables that influence the human condition. In analyzing a sociocultural system, anthropologists frequently find that different universals and specific variables *interact* with one another. The interaction of two variables is called a **correlation.** For example, a particular society may experience both population increases and a high incidence of warfare. This does not necessarily mean that the population growth causes the warfare, or vice versa; it simply means that both conditions exist within the society. To determine whether a *causal relationship* exists between these variables would require further investigation, including, in many cases, comparisons with other societies. Further research may indicate that the relationship between population and warfare is a *spurious correlation;* that is, two variables occur together, but each is caused by some third variable.

Alternatively, research may indicate that in a certain society the rate of population growth does influence the frequency of warfare. In such cases the anthropologist might hypothesize that population increases cause the high incidence of warfare. This hypothesis could then be tested and evaluated by other anthropologists.

In determining cause-and-effect relationships, anthropologists distinguish between independent and dependent variables. An **independent variable** is the causal variable that produces an effect on another variable, the **dependent** variable. In the previous example, population growth would be the independent variable because it determines the incidence of warfare, which is the dependent variable.

In actuality, this example of determining causal relationships is far too simplistic. Anthropologists recognize that no aspect of culture and society can be completely explained by any single cause or independent variable. They rely instead on hypotheses that are *multidimensional,* in which many variables interact with one another. This multidimensional approach must be kept in mind when considering the specific variables explored by cultural anthropologists in their study of different societies. The multidimensional approach is linked with the holistic perspective in anthropology; that is, the attempt to demonstrate how sociocultural systems must be understood through the interconnections among universals and specific variables.

Universals and Variables Studied by Cultural Anthropologists

The major variables and universal features of sociocultural systems include subsistence and the physical environment, demography, technology, the economy, social structure (including family and marriage, and gender and age relations), political organization, and religion. Although this is not a complete list of the universals and specific variables studied by cultural anthropologists, it provides the general framework for understanding different societies. An explanation of these universals and specific variables follows, to help you understand the discussions of different types of societies considered in the rest of the book.

Subsistence and the Physical Environment

Living organisms, both plant and animal, do not live or evolve in a vacuum. The evolution and survival of a particular species is closely related to the type of physical environment in which it is located. The speed of a jackal or an arctic fox has evolved in relation to the predators and prey found in East Africa or the Arctic. The physical characteristics of the orchid plant make it highly suitable for surviving in a tropical environment. The environment affects the organism directly and, as Charles Darwin noted, affects the passing on of certain adaptive characteristics that enable these life forms to survive and reproduce in their particular surroundings.

Biologists use the term *adaptation* to refer to the process in which an organism adjusts successfully to a specific environment. Most organisms adapt to the environment through the physical traits that they inherit. Like other creatures, as we have seen in Chapter 6, humans have adapted to their respective environments through physical changes in body size and shape, blood groups, skin coloration, and biological traits. Humans, however, adapt to their specific environments primarily through culture. By any measure, humans have been the most successful living forms in terms of adapting physically and culturally to different types of environments. Humans occupy an extraordinary range of environments, from the tropics to the Arctic, and have developed cultural solutions to the various problems that have arisen in these different regions. Anthropologists have been studying these adaptive strategies and cultural solutions to explain both the similarities and differences among societies.

Modern Cultural Ecology

The term *ecology* was coined by German biologist Ernest Haeckel in the nineteenth century from two Greek words that mean "the study of the home." **Ecology** is the study of living organisms in relationship to their environment. Here we are defining environment broadly, to include both the physical characteristics and the forms of life found in a particular region. In biology, ecological studies focus on how plant and animal populations survive and reproduce in specific environmental niches. An **environmental niche** refers to the given set of ecological conditions that a life form uses to make a living, survive, and adapt.

As noted in Chapter 13, there is a branch of anthropology known as **cultural ecology,** the systematic study of the relationships between the environment and society. Anthropologists recognize that all humans can adjust in extremely creative ways to different environments. Nevertheless, humans, like other organisms, are universally connected to the environment in a number of ways. Just as the environment has an impact on human behavior and society, humans have a major impact on their environment. Modern cultural ecologists examine these dynamic interrelationships as a means of understanding different societies.

Biomes

In their studies of different environments, cultural ecologists use the concept of a biome. A **biome** is an area distinguished by a particular climate and certain types of plants and animals. Biomes may be classified by certain attributes, such as mean rainfall, temperature, soil conditions, and vegetation, which support certain forms of animal life (Campbell, 1983). Cultural ecologists investigate the relationship between specific biomes and human sociocultural systems. Some of the different biomes that will be encountered in this text are listed in Table 14.1.

Subsistence Patterns and Environments

In U.S. society, when we have the urge to satisfy our hunger drive we have many options: We can go to a local fast-food restaurant, place money into a machine to select our choice of food, or obtain food for cooking from a grocery store or supermarket. Other societies have different means of obtaining their food supplies. Cultural anthropologists study **subsistence patterns,** the means by which people in various societies obtain their food supplies. As we shall see in later chapters, the amount of sunlight, the type of soil, forests, rainfall, and mineral deposits all have an effect on the type of subsistence pattern a particular society develops. The specific biome and environmental conditions may limit the development of certain types of subsistence patterns. For example, arctic conditions are not conducive to agricultural activities, nor are arid regions suitable for rice production. These are the obvious limitations of biomes and environmental conditions on subsistence patterns.

The earliest type of subsistence pattern—known as *foraging* or *hunting-gathering*—goes back among early hominids to perhaps 2 million years ago. This pattern of subsistence, along with others such as *horticulture, pastoralism,* various types of *intensive agriculture,* and developments in *agribusiness* in industrial societies, will be introduced in

subsequent chapters. As we shall see, these subsistence patterns are not only influenced by the environment but also directly affect the environment. In other words, as humans transform their subsistence pattern to adapt to the environment, the environment is also transformed to varying degrees depending on the type of subsistence pattern developed. The interaction between subsistence pattern and environment has become an extremely important topic in anthropology and has a direct bearing on how human-environmental relationships may be modified in the future.

Demography

Demography is the study of population and its relationship to society. Demographers study changes in the size, composition, and distribution of human populations. They also study the consequences of population increases and decreases on human societies. *Demographic anthropology* has become an important specialty in anthropology.

Much of the research in demographic anthropology is concerned with the quantitative description of population. Demographic anthropologists design censuses and surveys to collect population statistics on the size, age and sex composition, and increasing or decreasing growth of population of a society. After collecting these data, demographic anthropologists focus on three major variables in a population: fertility, mortality, and migration.

Fertility, Mortality, and Migration

To measure **fertility**—the number of births in a society—demographic anthropologists use the **crude birth rate;** that is, the number of live births in a given year for every thousand people in a population. They also measure **mortality**—the incidence of death in a society's population—by using the **crude death rate;** that is, the number of deaths in a given year for every thousand people. In measuring **migration rate**—the movement of people into and out of a specified territory—demographic anthropologists determine the number of *in-migrants* (people moving into the territory) and the number of *out-migrants* (people moving out of the territory). They then use these numbers to calculate the **net migration,** which indicates the general

Table 14.1	A Listing of the Various Biomes Discussed in the Text, along with Their Major Characteristics

Biome	Principal Locations	Precipitation Range (mm/year)	Temperature Range (hr °C) (daily maximum and minimum)	Soils
Tropical rainforest	Central America (Atlantic Coast) Amazon basin Brazilian coast West African coast Congo basin Malaya	1,270–12,700 Equatorial type: frequent torrential thunderstorms	Little annual variation Max. 29–35 Min. 18–27	Mainly reddish laterites
	East Indies Philippines New Guinea N. E. Australia Pacific islands	Tradewind type: steady, almost daily rains No dry period	No cold period	
Tropical savanna	Central America (Pacific coast) Orinoco basin Brazil, S. of Amazon basin N. Central Africa East Africa S. Central Africa Madagascar India S. E. Asia Northern Australia	250–1900 Warm-season thunderstorms Almost no rain in cool season Long dry period during low sun	Considerable annual variation; no really cold period *Rainy season (high sun)* Max. 24–32 Min. 18–27 *Dry season (low sun)* Max. 21–32 Min. 13–18 *Dry season (higher sun)* Max. 29–40 Min. 21–27	Some laterites; considerable variety
Temperate grasslands	Central North America Eastern Europe Central and Western Asia Argentina New Zealand	300–2000 Evenly distributed through the year or with a peak in summer Snow in winter	*Winter* Max. −18–29 Min. −28–10 *Summer* Max. −1–49 Min. −1–15	Black prairie soils Chestnut and brown soils Almost all have a lime layer
Temperate deciduous forest	Eastern N. America Western Europe Eastern Asia	630–2300 Evenly distributed through year Droughts rare Some snow	*Winter* Max. −12–21 Min. −29–7 *Summer* Max. 24–38 Min. 15–27	Gray-brown Podzolic Red and yellow podzolic
Northern coniferous forest	Northern N. America Northern Europe Northern Asia	400–1000 Evenly distributed Much snow	*Winter* Max. −37– −1 Min. −54– −9 *Summer* Max. 10–21 Min. 7–13	True podzols Bog soils Some permafrost at depth, in places
Arctic tundra	Northern N. America Greenland Northern Eurasia	250–750 Considerable snow	*Winter* Max. −37– −7 Min. −57– −8 *Summer* Max. 2–15 Min. −1–7	Rocky or boggy Much patterned ground permafrost

Source: Adapted from W. D. Billings, *Plants, Man, and the Ecosystem,* 2nd ed. © 1970. Reprinted by permission of Brooks/Cole, an imprint of the Wadsworth Group, a division of Thomson Learning. Fax 800-730-2215.

Fertility trends are studied by anthropologists to determine how populations are increasing or decreasing.

movement of the population in and out of the territory.

To assess overall population change, demographic anthropologists subtract the crude death rate from the crude birth rate to arrive at the *natural growth rate* of a population. The natural growth rate is usually the major indicator of population change in a society. By adding the rate of migration, these anthropologists are able to calculate total population change.

Rates of fertility, mortality, and migration are also influenced by a number of other variables. **Fecundity**—the potential number of children that women in the society are capable of bearing—has an influence on fertility rates. Fecundity varies, however, according to the age of females at puberty and menopause, nutrition, workload, and other conditions in the societies and individuals being studied.

Life expectancy is the number of years an average person can expect to live. A particularly important component of the life expectancy rate in a society is the **infant mortality rate**—the number of babies per thousand births in any year who die before reaching the age of 1. When the infant mortality rate is high, the life expectancy—a statistical average—decreases. In many countries throughout the world, **childhood mortality rates**—the number of children who die before reaching the age of 5—is a major problem. Disease, nutrition, sanitation,

warfare, the general standard of living, and medical care are some of the factors that influence mortality, life expectancy, and infant and child mortality rates.

Migration is related to a number of different factors. In many instances, migration is involuntary. For example, the Cajun people of Louisiana are descendants of French people who were forced out of Canada by the British in the 1700s. Migration can also be voluntary. This type of movement is influenced by what demographers refer to as *push-pull factors*. **Push factors** are those that lead people to leave specific territories; examples are poverty, warfare, and political instability. **Pull factors,** such as economic opportunity, peace, and political freedom, are powerful incentives for people to move to other societies.

Population and Environment

Demographic anthropologists study the relationship between environments (specific biomes) and population. One variable they investigate is **carrying capacity**—the maximum population that a specific environment can support. This concept refers to the environment's potential energy and food resources that can be used to support a certain number of people. Some environments contain food and energy resources that allow for substantial population increases, whereas other environments contain only limited resources. For example, in the past, desert and arctic biomes had carrying capacities that severely limited population increases. In contrast, various river valley regions containing water and fertile soils permitted opportunities for greater population size. As we shall see in later chapters, the development of mechanized agriculture, fertilizers, and synthetic pesticides increases the carrying capacity for many different environments.

Population and Culture

Demographic anthropologists examine not only the relationship between environment and population but also cultural values and practices that affect fertility, mortality, and migration rates. In some societies, religious beliefs encourage high birth rates. In others, political authorities institute programs to increase or decrease population growth. One recent area of anthropological research involves gathering data and developing hypotheses on decisions concerning the "costs and benefits" of having children and the consequences of these individual decisions on fertility. Anthropologists also investigate strategies of population regulation, such as birth control techniques. These topics and others on research in demographic anthropology are introduced in later chapters.

Technology

The term *technology* is derived from the Greek word *techne,* which refers to art or skill. When we hear this term, we usually think of tools, machines, clothing, shelter, and other such objects. As defined by modern anthropologists, however, **technology** consists of all the human techniques and methods of reaching a specific subsistence goal or of modifying or controlling the natural environment. Technology is cultural in that it includes methods for manipulating the environment. But technology is also the product of those methods that are important in changing the environments in which humans live, work, and interact. Thus, technology consists not merely of physical tools but also of cultural knowledge that humans can apply in specific ways. In societies in which people use technologies such as bows and arrows, canoes, plows, penicillin, or computers, the cultural knowledge

needed to construct, design, and use these materials is extremely important.

To sustain life, human societies need to produce and allocate goods and services to provide food, clothing, shelter, tools, and transportation. **Goods** are elements of *material culture* produced from raw materials in the natural environment, ranging from the basic commodities for survival to luxury items. The commodities for survival may include axes and plows for clearing land and cultivating crops. Luxury commodities include such items as jewelry, decorative art, and musical instruments. **Services** are elements of *nonmaterial culture* in the form of specialized skills that benefit others, such as giving spiritual comfort or providing medical care. Goods and services are valued because they satisfy various human needs. To produce these goods and services, societies must have suitable technologies.

Anthropological Explanations of Technology

As stated in Chapter 13, nineteenth-century theorists like E. B. Tylor and Lewis Morgan constructed a unilineal scheme of technological evolution in which societies progressed from the simple, small-scale technology of "savages" to the more complex technology of modern civilizations. In the twentieth century, these simplistic views of technological evolution were rejected through detailed ethnographic research. Anthropologists such as Leslie White, Julian Steward, and the cultural materialists came to view technology as one of the primary factors of cultural evolution. White defined technology as an energy-capturing system made up of energy, tools, and products—that is, all the material means with which energy is harnessed, transformed, and expended (1959). The cultural materialists view technology as a basic and primary source of sociocultural change. They argue that we cannot explain different technological developments in society with reference to "values." Instead, technology must be viewed as a method designed to cope with a particular environment. Therefore, variations in environment, or habitat, could account for the differences between, say, the Inuit (Eskimo) and the Australian aborigine societies.

White's views on technology, as well as the views of other cultural materialists, have been criticized as a rigid form of "technological determinism."

Although the cultural materialists see sociological, ideological, or emotional factors as conditioning or limiting the use or development of technology, these factors exert little influence on sociocultural systems compared to technology's dominant role. Anthropologists are currently evaluating this cultural-materialist hypothesis to determine whether technology is a primary variable in societal development or whether a number of factors work in conjunction with technology to condition societal developments and evolution.

Economy

Like other animals, humans universally require food and shelter. In addition, humans have special needs for other goods and services, ranging from hunting materials to spiritual guidance. As we have seen, these goods and services are produced through technology. The **economy** of a society consists of the social relationships that organize the production, exchange, and consumption of goods and services. **Production** is the organized system for the creation of goods and services. **Exchange** is the process whereby members of society transfer goods and services among one another. **Consumption** is the use of goods and services to satisfy desires and needs. We examine these three different components of the economy in subsequent chapters in various forms of society.

Anthropologists have found that the economy is closely connected with the environment, subsistence base, demographic conditions, technology, and division of labor of the society. The **division of labor** consists of specialized economic roles (occupations) and activities. In small-scale societies, the division of labor is typically simple, and in large-scale societies it is extremely complex. In the twentieth century, ethnographic descriptions of different types of societies have generated two perspectives on economic systems: the formalist and substantivist approaches.

The Formalist Approach

The *formalist view* maintains that all economic systems are fundamentally similar and can be compared with one another. Formalists assume that all people act to maximize their individual gains. In other words, all humans have a psychological inclination to calculate carefully their self-interest. Formalists hypothesize that people do not always choose the cheapest and most efficient strategies to carry out their economic decisions, but they do tend to look for the best "rational" strategy for economic decision making.

Formalists hold that the best method for studying any economy is to employ the same general theories developed by economists. Formalists collect quantitative data and interpret these data by using sophisticated mathematical models developed by economists. They focus on such economic variables as production and consumption patterns, supply and demand, exchange, and investment decisions. One classic formalist study, by anthropologist Sol Tax (1953), focused on economic decision making in Guatemalan Indian communities. Tax analyzed the economic transactions in the traditional markets of these communities. He concluded that although the economy was undeveloped, the people made the same types of economic decisions as people in the developed world. Tax referred to these Indians as "penny capitalists."

The Substantivist Approach

The *substantivist approach* draws its supporting hypotheses from twentieth-century ethnographic studies. Substantivists maintain that the ways of allocating goods and services in small-scale societies differ fundamentally from those of large-scale Western economic systems. Thus, the social institutions found in small-scale societies or larger agricultural societies produce economic systems that are fundamentally different from the market economies of Western societies. According to substantivists, preindustrial economies are not driven by the motive of individual material gain or profit, as are industrial economies. They argue that the economy is *embedded* in the sociocultural system, including the kinship systems, values, beliefs, and norms of the society. These substantivists also argue that modern capitalist societies are embedded within an economy based on market exchange. Other precapitalist societies have other forms of exchange, such as *reciprocity* and *redistribution*. We will focus on these other forms of exchange in later chapters. In general, substantivists emphasize that precapitalist societies had different forms of logic and processes than the market exchange economies of capitalist societies.

Modern Economic Anthropology

Most anthropologists today do not identify exclusively with the formalist or the substantivist perspective; instead, they recognize the contributions of both perspectives to our knowledge of economic systems (Wilk, 1996). Modern anthropologists investigate the different patterns of production, ownership, distribution, exchange, and consumption in relationship to ecological, demographic, and cultural factors. They collect quantitative economic data along with more qualitative cultural data to explain the workings of economic systems. At present, economic anthropologists are not as concerned with how precapitalist societies organized their economies; rather, they are more concerned with how precapitalist economies change as they are influenced by globalization and contact with the global economy. In later chapters we discuss the empirical data gathered by anthropologists about different types of economic systems and how they are affected by global change.

Social Structure

All inorganic and organic things, from planets to living cells, have a *structure;* that is, they consist of interrelated parts in a particular arrangement. Buildings, snowflakes, amoebas, and the human body all have a certain structure. A book has a certain structure consisting of rectangular printed pages, binding, and a cover. All books have a similar structure, although the characteristics of different books can vary significantly.

Anthropologists use the image of structure when they analyze different societies. Societies are not just random, chaotic collections of people who interact with one another. Rather, social interaction in any society takes place in regular patterns. As we discussed in Chapter 11, through the process of enculturation, people learn the norms, values, and behavioral patterns of their society. In the absence of social patterns, people would find social life highly confusing. Anthropologists refer to this pattern of relationships in society as the **social structure.** Social structure provides the framework for all human societies.

Components of Social Structure

One of the most important components of social structure is status. A **status** is a recognized position that a person occupies in society. A person's status determines where he or she fits in society in relationship to everyone else. A status may be based on or accompanied by wealth, power, prestige, or a combination of all of these. Many anthropologists use the term **socioeconomic status** to refer to how a specific position is related to the division of labor, the political system, and other cultural variables.

All societies recognize both ascribed and achieved statuses. An **ascribed status** is one that is attached to a person from birth or that a person assumes involuntarily later in life. The most prevalent ascribed statuses are based on family and kinship relations (for example, daughter or son), sex (male or female), and age. In addition, in some societies ascribed statuses are based on one's race or ethnicity. For example, as we shall see in a later chapter, skin color was used to designate ascribed status differences in South Africa under the system of *apartheid.*

In contrast, an **achieved status** is one based at least in part on a person's voluntary actions. Examples of achieved statuses in the United States are one's profession and level of education. Of course, one's family and kinship connections may influence one's profession and level of education. George W. Bush's or Al Gore's educational level and status are interrelated to their family of birth. However, these individuals had to act voluntarily to achieve their status.

Closely related to status is the concept of social roles. A **role** is a set of expected behavior patterns, obligations, and norms attached to a particular status. The distinction between status and role is a simple one: You "occupy" a certain status, but you "play" a role (Linton, 1936). For example, as a student you occupy a certain status that differs from that of your professor, administrators, and other staff. As you occupy that status, you perform by attending lectures, taking notes, participating in class, and studying for examinations. This concept of role is derived from the theater and refers to the parts played by actors on the stage. If you are a husband, mother, son, daughter, teacher, lawyer, judge, male, or female, you are expected to behave in certain ways because of the norms associated with that particular status.

As mentioned, a society's social statuses usually correspond to wealth, power, and prestige. Anthropologists find that all societies have inequality in statuses, which are arranged in a hierarchy. This inequality of statuses is known as **social stratification.** The degree of social stratification varies from one society to another depending on technological, economic, and political variables. Small-scale societies tend to be less stratified than large-scale societies; that is, they have fewer categories of status and fewer degrees of difference regarding wealth, power, and prestige.

Anthropologists find that in some societies wealth, power, and prestige are linked with ownership of land or the number of animals acquired. In our society, high status is strongly correlated with the amount of wages or salary a person receives or how much property in the form of stocks or other paper assets is held. Exploring the causes of differing patterns of social stratification and how this stratification relates to other facets of society is an important objective of an ethnographic study.

The social structure of any society has several major components that anthropologists look at when analyzing a society. These components are discussed in the following sections on family, marriage, gender, and age.

The Family

In a comprehensive cross-cultural study, George Murdock (1945) found that all societies recognize the family. Thus, the family is a universal feature of humans. Anthropologists define the **family** as a social group of two or more people related by blood, marriage, or adoption who live or reside together for an extended period, sharing economic resources and caring for their young. Anthropologists differentiate between the *family of orientation,* the family into which people are born and receive basic enculturation, and the *family of procreation,* the family within which people reproduce or adopt children of their own (Murdock, 1949). The family is a social unit within a much wider group of relatives, or kin.

Although variations exist in types and forms, Murdock found that the family is a universal aspect of social organization. The reason for the universality of the family appears to be that it performs certain basic functions that serve human needs. The primary function of the family is the nurturing and enculturation of children. The basic norms, values, knowledge, and worldview of the culture are transmitted to children through the family.

Another function of the family is the regulation of sexual activity. Every culture places some restrictions on sexual behavior. Sexual intercourse is the basis of human reproduction and inheritance; it is also a matter of considerable social importance. Regulating sexual behavior is therefore essential to the proper functioning of a society. The family prohibits sexual relations within the immediate family through the incest taboos, as discussed in Chapter 11.

Families also serve to protect and support their members physically, emotionally, and often economically from birth to death. In all societies people need warmth, food, shelter, and care. Families provide a social environment in which these needs can be met. Additionally, humans have emotional needs for affection and intimacy that are most easily fulfilled within the family.

The two major types of families found throughout the world are the nuclear and extended families. A typical **nuclear family** is composed of two parents and their immediate biological offspring or adopted children. George Murdock believed that the nuclear family is a universal feature of all societies (1949). What he meant by this was that all societies have a male and female who reproduce children and are the core of the kinship unit. However, as will be seen in later chapters, the nuclear family is not the principal kinship unit in all societies. In many societies the predominant form is the **extended family,** which is composed of parents, children, and other kin relations bound together as a social unit.

Marriage

In most societies the family is a product of **marriage,** a social bond sanctioned by society between two or more people that involves economic cooperation and culturally approved sexual activity. Two general patterns of marriage exist: **endogamy,** which is marriage between people of the same social group or category; and **exogamy,** marriage between people of different social groups and categories.

A marriage may include two or more partners. **Monogamy** generally involves two individuals in the marriage. Though this is the most familiar form

A wedding ceremony in the United States. Anthropologists study the marital relationships of people and how those ceremonies relate to other aspects of society.

of marriage in Western industrial societies, it is not the only type of marriage practiced in the world. Many societies practice some form of **polygamy,** marriage involving a spouse of one sex and two or more spouses of the opposite sex. There are two forms of polygamy: **polygyny,** marriage between one husband and two or more wives, and **polyandry,** marriage between one wife and two or more husbands. Although the majority of the world's population currently practices monogamy, polygyny is a common form of marriage and is associated with 80 percent of human societies, many of which have relatively small populations (Murdock, 1981a, b). Polyandry is the rarest form of marriage, occurring in only 0.5 percent of all societies. As we shall see, anthropologists have developed hypotheses regarding why certain forms of marriage develop within particular sociocultural systems.

Gender

Gender relationships are another important component of the social structure of a society. When anthropologists discuss relationships between males and females in a society, they distinguish between sex and gender. **Sex** refers to the biological and anatomical differences between males and females. These differences include the primary sexual characteristics—the sex organs—and secondary sexual characteristics, such as breasts and wider hips for females and more muscular development of the upper torso and extensive body hair for males. Note that these are general tendencies, to which many exceptions exist. That is, many males are smaller and lighter and have less body hair than many females. Nevertheless, in general, males and females are universally distinguished by physiological and anatomical differences.

In contrast to sex, **gender** is based on a cultural rather than biological distinction. Gender refers to the specific human traits attached to each sex by a society. As members of a particular society, males and females occupy certain statuses, such as son, daughter, husband, wife, father, and mother. In assuming the gender roles that correspond to these different status positions, males are socialized to be "masculine," and females are socialized to be "feminine." Anthropologists find that definitions of masculine and feminine vary among different societies.

Gender and Enculturation   One major issue regarding gender is the degree to which enculturation influences male and female behavior. To study this issue, anthropologists focus on the values, beliefs, and worldviews that may influence gender roles. They also observe the types of activities associated with young boys and girls. In many societies, boys and girls play different games as an aspect of enculturation. For example, in U.S. society, boys are traditionally encouraged to participate in aggressive, competitive team sports, whereas girls have not traditionally been encouraged to do so. Cultural values and beliefs that affect gender roles are found in other societies as well.

Gender and the Division of Labor A basic component of the division of labor in most societies is the assigning of different tasks to males and females. In studying this phenomenon, anthropologists focus on the issue of whether physical differences between males and females are responsible for these different roles. To address this issue, they ask a number of questions: Is there a universal division of labor based on sex? Does physical strength have anything to do with the work patterns associated with gender? Do child care and pregnancy determine or influence economic specialization for females? To what degree do values and beliefs ascribed to masculine or feminine behavior affect work assignments?

Gender and Status Another important issue investigated by anthropologists is the social and political status of males and females in society. As noted in Chapter 13, some early anthropologists such as Lewis Morgan believed that females at one time had a higher social and political status than males, but through time that pattern was reversed. Anthropologists currently focus on how the status of males and females is related to biology, the division of labor, kinship relations, political systems, and values and beliefs.

Although sex characteristics are biologically determined, gender roles vary in accordance with the technological, economic, and sociocultural conditions of particular types of societies. In later chapters, we explore some recent studies by anthropologists who have broadened our understanding of the variation of gender roles among a wide range of societies.

Age

Like kinship and gender, age is a universal principle used to prescribe social status in sociocultural systems. The biological processes of aging are an inevitable aspect of human life; from birth to death

our bodies are constantly changing. Definite biological changes occur for humans in their progress from infancy to childhood to adolescence to adulthood and to old age. Hormonal and other physiological changes lead to maturation and the onset of the aging process. For example, as we approach old age, our sensory abilities begin to change. Taste, eyesight, touch, smell, and hearing begin to diminish. Gray hair and wrinkles appear, and we experience a loss of height and weight and an overall decline in strength and vitality. Although these physical changes vary greatly from individual to individual and to some extent are influenced by societal and environmental factors, these processes are universal.

The biology of aging, however, is only one dimension of how age is related to the social structure of any specific culture. The human life cycle is the basis of social statuses and roles that have both a physical and a cultural dimension. The cultural meanings of these categories in the life cycle vary among different societies, as do the criteria people use to define age-related statuses. The definitions of the statuses and roles for specific ages have wide-ranging implications for those in these status positions.

Age and Enculturation As people move through the different phases of the human life cycle, they continually experience the process of enculturation. Because of the existence of different norms, values, and worldviews, people in various societies may be treated differently at each phase of the life cycle. For example, the period of enculturation during childhood varies among societies. In the United States and other industrialized societies, childhood is associated with an extensive educational experience that continues for many years. In many preindustrial societies, however, childhood is a relatively short period of time, and children assume adult status and responsibilities at a fairly young age.

Another factor influenced by aging in a society is how individuals are viewed at different ages. How is "old age" defined? For example, in many societies old age is not defined strictly in terms of the passage of time. More frequently, old age is defined in respect to changes in social status, work patterns, family status, or reproductive potential (Cowgill, 1986). These factors influence how people are valued at different ages in a society.

Age and the Division of Labor Another societal factor that is influenced by the aging process is the economic role assumed by a person at different stages of the life cycle. Children everywhere are exposed to the technological skills they will need to survive in their environment. As they mature, they assume specific positions in the division of labor. Just as male and female roles differ, the roles for the young and old differ. For example, in some preindustrial societies, older people occupy central roles, whereas in others they play no important role at all. In industrial societies, the elderly generally do not occupy important occupational roles.

Age and Status Age is one of the key determinants of social status. People are usually assigned a particular status associated with a phase of the life cycle. The result is **age stratification,** the unequal allocation of wealth, power, and prestige among people of different ages. Anthropologists find that age stratification varies in accordance with the level of technological development. For example, in many preindustrial societies, the elderly have a relatively high social status, whereas in most industrial societies, the elderly experience a loss of status.

Anthropologists study the relationship between age and status. Elderly Japanese tend to have a higher status in their society than elderly Americans.

One of the most common ways of allocating the status of people at different ages is through age grades. **Age grades** are statuses defined by age, through which a person moves as he or she ages. For example, the age grades in most industrial societies correspond to the periods of infancy, preschool, kindergarten, elementary school, intermediate school, high school, young adulthood, middle age, young old, and old old (Cowgill, 1986). Each of these grades conveys a particular social status.

Age Status and Rites of Passage Anthropologists have done considerable research on the **rites of passage,** rituals associated with the life cycle and the movement of people between different age-status levels. Almost all cultures have rites of passage to demarcate these different stages of the life cycle. Arnold Van Gennep (1960), a Belgian anthropologist, wrote a classic study of different rites of passage throughout the world. He noted similarities among various rites connected with birth, puberty, marriage, and funerals. According to Van Gennep, these rites of passage are characterized by three interconnected stages: separation, marginality, and aggregation.

The first phase, *separation,* transforms people from one age status to another. In this phase, people leave behind the symbols, roles, and norms associated with their former position. The second phase, referred to as *marginality,* places people in a state of transition or a temporary period of ambiguity. This stage often involves separating individuals from the larger society to undergo traditional ordeals or indoctrination. The final phase is *aggregation,* or incorporation, when individuals assume their new status.

The best-known examples of these rites of passage are various religious rituals associated with adolescence, such as the confirmation rituals associated with Catholicism and the bar mitzvah rituals in Judaism. In later chapters we encounter examples of different rites of passage. The importance of these rites as an aspect of aging, status, and enculturation are explored there.

Political Organization

In the early twentieth century, German sociologist Max Weber introduced definitions of political power and authority that have since been adopted by anthropologists. Weber defined **political power** as the ability to achieve personal ends despite opposition. In this sense, political power can be based on physical or psychological coercion. Weber perceived this type of political power as *illegitimate,* in that it is unacceptable to most members of a society. According to Weber, the most effective and enduring form of political power is based on **authority,** power generally perceived by members of society as legitimate rather than coercive.

A brief example will illustrate the difference between illegitimate and legitimate power. If a large country invades and conquers a smaller one, the occupied people generally will not consider their new rulers to be legitimate. Thus, the rulers must rely on coercion to enforce their laws and to collect payments in the form of taxes or tributes. In contrast, most U.S. citizens voluntarily comply with the tax laws. Although they may complain, they perceive their government as representing legitimate authority. Although physical coercion and force might be used to arrest some people who refuse to pay their taxes, in the majority of cases such actions are not necessary.

Types of Political Systems

As described in Chapter 9, the general categories used by anthropologists to describe political systems are *band, tribe, chiefdom,* and *state.* In Chapter 7 we described band societies associated with hunter-gatherers. A **band** is the least complex—and most likely the oldest—form of political system. Political institutions in band societies are based on close kinship relations within a fairly small group of people. **Tribes** are more complex societies with political institutions that unite larger groupings of people into a political system. Generally tribal societies developed during the early Neolithic societies described in Chapter 8. Tribes do not have centralized, formal political institutions, but they do have **sodalities,** groups based on kinship, age, or gender that provide for political organization. For example, in some tribal societies of Papua New Guinea, secret male societies function as political institutions.

Again, as discussed in Chapter 9, **chiefdom** political systems are more complex than tribal societies in that they are formalized and centralized. Chiefdoms establish centralized, legitimate authority over many communities through a variety of complex economic, social, and religious institutions. Despite their size and complexity, however, chiefdoms are still fundamentally organized by kinship principles. Although chiefdoms have different levels of status and political authority, the people within these levels are related to one another through kinship ties.

Chapter 9 also discusses the evolution of **states,** which are political systems with centralized bureaucratic institutions to establish power and authority over large populations in distinctive territories. State systems are not based on kinship. State bureaucracies govern society on behalf of ruling authorities through procedures that plan, direct, and coordinate highly complex political processes. State political systems range from the early bureaucratic political units of agricultural societies such as Egypt and China to the modern industrial societies of the United States, Japan, the former Soviet Union, and European nations.

These various institutions and practices of these types of societies are going to be discussed in the next five chapters. Nevertheless, it must be emphasized here that this classification does not represent a single scheme of political evolution for the entire world. The archaeological and ethnological data demonstrate again and again that a stage-by-stage development or evolution from band to tribe to chiefdom to state did not occur in all areas. These classifications are to be used only as categories to organize the vast amounts of data accumulated by anthropologists. As with all models, the boundaries separating the various categories are somewhat arbitrary.

Decision Making in a Political System

An important topic in the study of a society is the day-to-day, individual decision making and competition for power and authority. In studying this topic, anthropologists may focus on fields or arenas within a society. A *field* is an area in which political interaction and competition take place (Bourdieu, 1977). It may involve a part of a society, or it may extend beyond the boundaries of a society. For example, a field could be a whole tribe, a chiefdom, a state, or several of these units. A *political arena* is a more local, specific area in which individual actors or small groups compete for power and authority. An arena may be made up of factions, elites, or political parties in a society.

Warfare and Feuds

The study of politics includes political conflicts within and among societies. Two major forms of conflicts are warfare and feuds. Anthropologists define **warfare** as armed combat among territorial or political communities. They distinguish between *internal warfare,* which involves political communities within the same society or culture, and *external warfare,* which occurs among different societal groups. A **feud** is a type of armed combat occurring within a political community and usually involves one kin group taking revenge against another kin group (Otterbein, 1974). Anthropologists examine the different biological, environmental, demographic, economic, social, political, and other cultural variables that influence warfare and feuds.

Law and Social Control

Another aspect of political anthropology is the study of law and social control. As discussed in Chapter 10, one aspect of nonmaterial culture is the normative dimension, sometimes referred to as an *ethos.* All societies maintain an ethos that encourages certain behaviors and prohibits others. This ethos, along with the society's values, makes up the *moral code* that shapes human behavior. The particular ethos of a society represents an attempt to establish social control through various internal and external mechanisms. The internal mechanisms of social control are built into the enculturation process itself. Through enculturation, people learn the specific norms regarding society's expectations. Thereafter, those who violate these norms frequently experience emotional and cognitive discomfort in the form of guilt. Thus, internalized norms can shape and influence people's behavior, even in the absence of constraints from other people.

Despite these internal mechanisms, however, individuals frequently violate norms. For a variety of reasons, enculturation does not bring about perfect social control in a society. Hence, in addition to internal mechanisms, societies use external mechanisms to enforce norms. External mechanisms take the form of *sanctions:* rewards (positive sanctions) for appropriate behaviors, and punishments (negative sanctions) for inappropriate behaviors.

Societies vary with respect to both the nature of their moral code and the types of external sanctions used to enforce the moral code. What one societal group considers deviant or unethical may be acceptable to another group. Divorce is an acceptable solution for severe marital conflicts in the United States. In Italy and Ireland, however, despite recent legislation that allows divorce, many still view it as an unethical pattern of behavior.

Complex societies rely on an organized police or military force to demonstrate political authority.

In large, complex social groups, sanctions are usually highly formalized. Rewards can take the form of public awards, parades, educational or professional degrees, and banquets. Negative sanctions include fines, imprisonment, expulsion, and sometimes death. In small-scale societies, sanctions tend to be informal. Examples of positive sanctions are smiles, handshakes, pats on the back, hugs, and compliments. Negative sanctions include restricted access to certain goods and services, gossip, frowns, impolite treatment, and ostracism.

Law as Formalized Norms and Sanctions   Anthropologists define *laws* as clearly defined norms, violations of which are punished through the application of formal sanctions by ruling authorities. In the 1960s, cultural anthropologist Leopold J. Pospisil attempted to distinguish law from other social norms, based on his research among the Kapaukan tribe of New Guinea. He specified four criteria that must be present for a norm to be considered a law: (1) authority, (2) intention of universal application, (3) obligation, and (4) sanction (1967). To institutionalize legal decisions, a society must have members who possess recognized authority and can therefore intervene to settle disputes. These authorities must be able to enforce a verdict by either persuasion or force. Their verdicts must have universal application; that is, these decisions must be applied in the same manner if a similar situation arises in the future. This distinguishes legal decisions from those based purely on political expediency.

Obligation refers to the status relationships among the people involved in the conflict. If status relationships are unequal, the rights, duties, and obligations of the different parties can vary. Legal decisions must attempt to define the rights and obligations of everyone involved and to restore or create an equitable resolution of the conflict. Finally, punitive sanctions must be applied to carry out the legal decision.

Religion

As we saw in Chapter 7, archaeologists have discovered evidence of religious beliefs and practices associated with archaic *Homo sapiens,* or Neandertals, that date back to 100,000 years ago. Religion is a cultural universal, although specific beliefs and practices vary significantly from one society to another. For example, some religions are based on the worship of an all-knowing, all-powerful supreme being, whereas others have many deities, and some may have no deities at all.

Humans learn their religious traditions through the process of enculturation. Religious convictions are therefore shaped by the historical and social situations in which a person lives. For example, a person enculturated in ancient Greece would most likely have believed in many deities, among whom Zeus was the most powerful.

In studying the anthropology of religion, a critical point must be understood: Anthropologists are not concerned with the "truth" or "falsity" of any particular religious belief. Being based on the scientific method, anthropology is not competent or able to investigate supernatural or metaphysical questions that go beyond empirical data. Rather, anthropological research on religion focuses on the relationship of doctrines, beliefs, and other religious questions to other aspects of society. The major questions posed by anthropologists are: How do religious beliefs become established within a society? and How do religious beliefs affect, relate to, and reflect the sociocultural conditions and concerns of a group of people?

In addition, anthropologists often use the humanistic-interpretive approach when analyzing religious beliefs, symbols, and myths. Clifford Geertz (1973:90) offered a sophisticated definition of religion to use as a tool in this humanistic-interpretive mode of understanding religion:

> *A religion is a system of symbols which acts to establish powerful, pervasive, and long-lasting moods and motivations in men by formulating conceptions of a general order of existence and clothing these conceptions with such an aura of factuality that the moods and motivations seem uniquely realistic.*

Let us examine this definition more closely. Central to any religion is a "system of symbols" that includes all sacred objects, ranging from Christian crucifixes, Native American "medicine pouches," and Buddhist relics, to sacred myths such as "Genesis" or the "Ramayana" of Hinduism. These symbols produce "moods," such as happiness and sadness, and "motivations" that provide direction or ethical goals in a person's life. Hence, religious symbols enhance particular feelings and dispositions, creating an intense sense of awe in individuals. This sense of awe is induced through the use of sacred symbols in rituals and other religious performances to create an atmosphere of mystery going beyond everyday experience. But religious symbols also create and reaffirm a worldview by "formulating conceptions of a general order of existence." This worldview provides meaning or purpose to life and the universe. A religious worldview helps people discern the meaning of pain and suffering in the world. Sacred myths help people make sense of the world and also explain and justify cultural values and social rules.

Myths

The study of the religious worldview includes the analysis and interpretation of myths. **Myths** consist of a people's assumed knowledge about the universe and the natural and supernatural worlds, and humanity's place in these worlds. In Chapter 3, we presented some basic myths or cosmologies regarding the creation of the universe. All societies have such sacred myths. Anthropologists focus on a number of questions regarding myths: Why do myths of a particular type exist in different societies? What is the relationship between myths and other aspects of sociocultural systems? Are myths distortions of historical events? Or as Geertz suggests earlier in the chapter, do myths provide a blueprint for comprehending the natural and social world for a society? What are the functions of myths? How are myths

interpreted and reinterpreted by different people within the society?

Rituals

The final portion of Geertz's definition—that these systems of symbols act to clothe those conceptions in "such an aura of factuality that the moods and motivations seem uniquely realistic"—attempts to deal with the question often asked about religious belief: How do humans come to believe in ideas about spirits, souls, revelations, and many unsupportable or untestable conceptions? Geertz's answer to this question is that religious rituals in which humans participate create an "aura of factuality." It is through ritual that deeper realities are reached. Religion is nonempirical and nonrational in its search for truth. It is not based on conclusions from scientific experience but is "prior" to experience. Religious truth is not "inductive," providing evidence for metaphysical explanations. It symbolically and abstractly evokes the ultimate concerns of humans. Through ritual activities, these symbolic and abstract nonempirical truths are given meaning.

Religious **rituals** consist of repetitive behaviors that communicate sacred symbols to members of society. Examples of religious rituals are the Catholic Mass, Jewish Passover rites, and the Native American sweat lodge rites, which include prayer, meditation, and other spiritual communication. Anthropologist Edmund Leach (1966) emphasized that religious

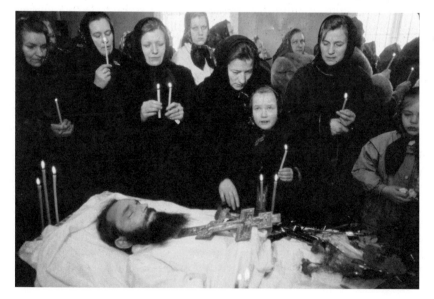

One function of religion is to help people cope with major events and crises, such as death.

rituals communicate these sacred symbols and information in a condensed manner. He noted that the verbal part of a ritual is not separable from the behavioral part, and that rituals can have different symbolic meanings for people in a society. In other words, religious rituals convey a unique, personal, psychological experience for every individual who participates.

Religious Specialists

One important area of research in the anthropology of religion is the study of religious specialists in different societies. Every society has certain individuals who possess specialized, sacred knowledge. Such individuals officiate over rituals and interpret myths. The type of religious specialist varies with the form of sociocultural system. **Shamans** are part-time religious practitioners who are believed to have contact with supernatural beings and powers. They do not have a formalized official status as religious practitioners in their respective societies. As we shall see in later chapters, shamans are involved in various types of healing activities, treating both physical and psychological illnesses. Aside from their religious functions, they participate in the same subsistence activities and functions as anyone else in their society. Anthropologists also use terms such as *native healer, medicine man,* and *medicine woman* to refer to these practitioners.

The terms **priest** and **priestess** refer to full-time religious specialists who serve in an official capacity as the custodians of sacred knowledge. In contrast to shamans, priests and priestesses are usually trained through formal educational processes to maintain religious traditions and rituals. Priests and priestesses are usually associated with more complex sociocultural systems.

Religious Movements

Another topic of interest in the anthropology of religion is the analysis of religious movements. In early approaches of the social sciences, religion was viewed simply as an outcome of certain economic or political conditions in society. It was assumed that as society developed modern economic and political institutions, religious traditions would disappear. Religion was viewed as a peripheral element that served only to conserve society as a static

system. Today, however, some anthropologists have begun to analyze religious beliefs and worldviews as major variables that induce societal change. For example, cultural anthropologists studying Islamic fundamentalist movements have concluded that in the Middle East, religion is a major force for social change. These new modes of understanding and explaining religious movements are analyzed in subsequent chapters.

Cognition and Religion

In Chapter 11 we introduced the fields of cognitive anthropology and evolutionary psychology. Anthropologist Pascal Boyer has drawn on these two fields in order to explore religion in his book *Religion Explained: The Evolutionary Origins of Religious Thought* (2001). Though Boyer recognizes the importance of the humanistic-interpretive approach in understanding religion, he also wants to explore the scientific-causal aspects of religion and the universal aspects of religion everywhere. In his book, Boyer investigates questions such as: Why does religion matter so much in people's lives everywhere? Are there any common features of religion? Why do certain types of religious beliefs develop rather than other types? Drawing on a vast range of cross-cultural data, as well as his own ethnographic studies of the Fang people in Cameroon in West Africa, Boyer suggests that the human mind is designed by evolutionary processes to be "religious." Although there is a tremendous diversity of religious traditions throughout the world, some types of religious beliefs have more resilience and are retained and culturally transmitted by humans more than others. In all societies, children are exposed to various religious beliefs and practices. But, Boyer emphasizes, because of specific predispositions and intuitions within our evolutionary-designed mind, certain forms of religious beliefs and concepts have exceptional relevance and meaning for humans.

Based on an enormous amount of data in experimental psychology, Boyer opens his book by examining what types of intuitive knowledge become evident to children. For example, if children learn that a specific type of animal gives birth to offspring in a particular manner, they will intuitively understand that other types of animals within the same species will give birth in the same manner. They do not have to be exposed to every type of experience in order to develop this intuitive knowledge and make inferences and predictions about various natural phenomena. It appears that, as humans, we build upon mental templates such as ANIMAL, PLANT, PERSON, ARTIFACT, or TOOL. These templates become the basis of inferential and intuitive knowledge that we use to comprehend the world. Children know that objects such as tools or artifacts do not move around or give birth like animals. Boyer does not claim that children are born with these mental templates, but rather, as the mind develops, the child will acquire these templates from an interaction between innate predispositions and a normal environment. Just as children who are not isolated from language acquire their linguistic skills and abilities readily within a normal speaking environment (see Chapter 12), they also develop their intuitive knowledge to make inferences about the world. These inferential systems and intuitive insights do not just enable children to comprehend the natural world. They also provide specialized mechanisms to intuitively understand and empathize with other people's minds and adjust behaviorally and morally to the social world. Children at an early age learn that other persons have thoughts and intentions, and they can rely on these intuitions to engage in social and moral relationships with other people.

In contrast to the intuitive knowledge and inferences that become a reliable basis for comprehending the natural and social world, Boyer emphasizes that religious beliefs and knowledge are mostly *counterintuitive*. Religious spirits and gods have properties that normal people do not have. Although most humans treat religious spirits and gods as persons, they are radically different from what our intuitions tell us about persons. For the most part, they do not eat, grow old, or die; they can even fly through space, become invisible, change shape, and perceive our innermost thoughts. Gods and spirits become invisible partners and friends of people, but these spiritual beings are unlike normal persons. These spiritual agents can be at several places at one time and have full access to our innermost thoughts and specific behaviors and actions. Some societies have a concept of a god that knows everything. Children at an early age and adults understand that normal persons do not have these capacities for knowledge.

These counterintuitive abilities of spirits and gods, including their full access to our thoughts and specific behaviors, are "attention-grabbing" for humans throughout the world. Spiritual agents who have this full access to knowledge become extremely relevant in understanding human social and moral conditions. Beings that can know our innermost thoughts and all of our behaviors resonate with our social and moral intuitions. Thus, religious beliefs and concepts become widespread and plausible in all societies because of the way human cognition is organized and designed. Beliefs in witches, ancestral spirits, and angry or beneficent gods become easily represented in all cultures because they are dependent on our human cognitive capacities and intuitive understandings of the natural and social world. These religious phenomena activate and trigger our human cognitive capacities and intuitive abilities, which results in the universal distribution of certain types of spiritual beliefs and concepts.

In his concluding chapter, Boyer explains why religious beliefs have become so powerful throughout human prehistory and history. He does not suggest that there is a specialized area of the brain or "religious instinct" that is a religious center that handles god-related or spiritual-related thoughts. In addition, he does not suggest that there are specific people who have exceptional religious abilities and are responsible for establishing religious beliefs and practices. Religion, like other everyday matters in our natural and social circumstances, does not require special capacities. Rather, religious beliefs and concepts become relevant to humans everywhere because they readily coincide with our cognitive capacities and intuitive and inferential abilities. These religious beliefs and concepts are likely to have a direct effect on people's thoughts, emotions, and morality. In addition, religious beliefs are different from scientific theories in that they don't easily assimilate with our cognitive dispositions and intuitions.

Religious beliefs have commonalities such as spiritual agents that have full access to our innermost thoughts, concepts of life after death, and concepts of morality all over the world, and most likely have a long evolutionary history. Other religious beliefs may have developed in the past, but they did not have the cognitive resilience or sustaining power of the ones known today, and they disappeared. The religious beliefs that still exist have a central relevance to many people and are extremely powerful and converge with their cognitive capacities and abilities. In some cases, people give up their lives or kill others based on their particular religious beliefs. Boyer's exploration of the interconnection between human cognition and religious expression has contributed toward an anthropological understanding of these phenomena.

Cross-Cultural Research

This chapter has focused on the analysis of universals and variables and their interconnections within specific societies. Although the primary objective of ethnographic research is to improve our understanding of a particular sociocultural system, another aim is to provide a basis for comparing different societies and to offer general explanations for human behavior. Specific ethnographies provide the necessary data for this type of cross-cultural research. This cross-cultural research is usually referred to as *ethnological research*. Anthropologists use ethnological research to further explore the universal and specific cultural conditions that influence the development of societies throughout the world.

Cross-cultural research has been an ongoing project in anthropology for the past hundred years or so. Recently, a great deal of ethnographic data has been computerized in the Human Relations Area Files, commonly known as the HRAF. The HRAF contains descriptive ethnographic data on more than 300 societies. Initiated by George P. Murdock of Yale University, it is made up of original ethnographic descriptions classified for cross-cultural research purposes. Murdock incorporated data on 862 societies in his *Ethnographic Atlas* (1981b) and on 563 societies that cover the major geographic regions of the world in his *Atlas of World Cultures* (1981a). These ethnographic databases enable scholars to retrieve information quickly and can be used for statistical and computerized cross-cultural

research. These databases are extremely valuable sources for assessing the differences and similarities among cultures. Cross-cultural studies allow anthropologists to make distinctions between behaviors that are culture specific and those that are universal. These distinctions help anthropologists provide general explanations for human behavior. In doing so, these studies help fulfill the major goals of anthropological research.

Cross-cultural methods have some limitations, however. One major weakness is that some cultural anthropologists in the past may not have taken historical circumstances into account when describing the particular conditions in a society. This omission may have led to a static, unchanging portrait of the society studied. For example, the description of the economic practices of people in Africa, Asia, or the Pacific islands may not make sense outside of a specific historical context. These societies had historical relationships with other societies outside of their own cultural boundaries, and these relationships resulted in changes in the particular economic practices observed by the cultural anthropologist. In later chapters of this text we explore why cultural anthropologists must understand the historical context of different societies that they study so that they can fully comprehend the behavior being observed.

Another problem with cross-cultural studies lies with faulty ethnographic reporting, which can produce unreliable data, contributing in turn to a distorted image of the society being studied. Consequently, anthropologists approach cross-cultural research with caution. Contemporary anthropologists who use these data must review the work of their predecessors who gathered the basic information to assess its validity. Through careful examination of the original data in the HRAF and other cross-cultural databases, modern anthropologists will make further progress toward formulating sound generalizations regarding the cultures of humankind.

SUMMARY

Cultural anthropologists conduct fieldwork in different societies to examine people's lifestyles. They describe societies in written studies called ethnographies, which focus on behavior and thought among the people studied. Cultural anthropologists must

use systematic research methods and strategies in their examination of society. Their basic research method is participant observation, which involves participating in the activities of the people they are studying.

In their analyses of sociocultural systems, anthropologists investigate cause-and-effect relationships among different variables. They use a multidimensional approach, examining the interaction among many variables to provide explanations for the similarities and differences among societies. Anthropologists explore the interaction between the environment and subsistence practices. They examine the biomes of different regions to determine the influence of environment on societal development. They investigate fertility, mortality, and migration to detect changes in demographic conditions. They also investigate the relationship between cultural values and population. Technological and economic variables are assessed in the analysis of society and culture. The technology and economy of a society produce distinctive differences in the division of labor. Anthropologists find that technology and economic conditions are also influenced by cultural values and norms.

Another area of research is social structure, including the family, marriage, kinship, gender, and age. These components of social structure are related to the division of labor and other cultural conditions. Anthropologists explored different types of political organizations and legal systems. Through detailed ethnological research and cross-cultural comparisons, anthropologists have found that specific types of political and legal systems have been influenced by various societal conditions. To analyze different forms of political systems, anthropologists classify societies into bands, tribes, chiefdoms, and states.

The anthropology of religion is devoted to the examination of diverse religious beliefs and worldviews. Myths, rituals, religious specialists, and religious movements are explored in relationship to other aspects of society. Some anthropologists use the humanistic-interpretive method to understand the symbols, myths, rituals, and meaning of religious practices. Other anthropologists focus on the universality of religion and how it is linked with human psychological processes.

Many ethnographic data have been coded for computer use in cross-cultural studies. These cross-cultural studies can be employed to develop general explanations regarding human behavior in specific societies and across cultural boundaries.

QUESTIONS TO THINK ABOUT

1. What are some of the things that a cultural anthropologist has to do to prepare herself or himself for fieldwork?

2. What are some of the research goals of demographic anthropologists as they relate to fieldwork? Why is a demographic perspective important in anthropological research?

3. Do you think that technology is the primary, basic source of sociocultural change? Do values play any role in sociocultural change?

4. What are the basic components of the economy and the division of labor?

5. What are the basic components or patterns of family and marriage from an anthropological view?

6. Have you ever gone through a rite of passage? If so, what was it? Have you experienced more than one? Pick one rite of passage that you have experienced and describe it in terms of Van Gennep's stages of separation, marginality, and incorporation (aggregation).

7. What is the difference between legitimate and illegitimate political power? Give an example of each.

8. Review Clifford Geertz's definition of religion. What do you think are the strengths or weaknesses of his definition?

9. What are the benefits and limitations of conducting cross-cultural research?

KEY TERMS

achieved status

age grades

age stratification

ascribed status

authority

band

biome	family	production
carrying capacity	fecundity	pull factors
chiefdom	fertility	push factors
childhood mortality rate	feud	qualitative data
consumption	gender	quantitative data
correlation	goods	random sample
crude birth rate	independent variable	rites of passage
crude death rate	infant mortality rate	rituals
cultural ecology	life expectancy	role
culture shock	marriage	services
demography	migration rate	sex
dependent variable	monogamy	shamans
division of labor	mortality	social stratification
ecology	myths	social structure
economy	net migration	socioeconomic status
emic perspective	nuclear family	sodalities
endogamy	political power	state
environmental niche	polyandry	status
etic perspective	polygamy	subsistence patterns
exchange	polygyny	technology
exogamy	priest	tribes
extended family	priestess	warfare

INTERNET EXERCISES

1. Investigate the life of a Vietnamese gang member in Los Angeles by visiting **http://cwis.usc.edu/dept/elab/buidoi/vietgangs.html**. Click on "Introduction to the Project" and read the description. What do you feel is the premise of this website? What is the value of visual anthropology to ethnology?

2. Ethical issues in anthropology are often at the forefront of research. Read the introduction by Joan Cassell and Sue-Ellen Jacobs at the website **http://www.aaanet.org/committees/ethics/intro.htm** How do they think case studies improve anthropological practice? Why are ethical considerations important to anthropological research? How do the views on ethics expressed on this website compare to those in the chapter?

SUGGESTED READINGS

BOHANNON, PAUL (Ed.). 1967. *Law and Warfare: Studies in the Anthropology of Conflict*. Garden City, NY: Natural History Press. A classic introduction to the field of legal anthropology. This series of readings includes descriptive data and hypotheses regarding how anthropologists ought to examine law in different societies.

CAMPBELL, BERNARD. 1983. *Human Ecology: The Story of Our Place in Nature from Prehistory to the Present*. New York: Aldine. A concise introduction to anthropological research in the field of cultural ecology.

COHEN, RONALD, and JOHN MIDDLETON (Eds.). 1967. *Comparative Political Systems: Studies in the Politics of*

Pre-industrial Societies. Garden City, NY: Natural History Press. A collection of readings based on research from the field of political anthropology. It consists of detailed ethnological analyses of political systems in various regions of the world.

DeVita, Philip R. (Ed.). *Stumbling Toward Truth: Anthropologists at Work*. Prospect Heights, IL: Waveland Press. A collection of original essays by cultural anthropologists who describe the painful and humorous situations of fieldwork.

Graburn, Nelson (Ed.). 1971. *Readings in Kinship and Social Structure*. New York: Harper & Row. A collection of fifty-nine essays covering the field of social anthropology from 1860 to the modern period. The readings represent some of the best-known anthropological writings regarding family, marriage, and kinship.

Lehmann, Arthur C., and James E. Myers (Eds.). 1997. *Magic, Witchcraft, and Religion: An Anthropological Study of the Supernatural*, 4th ed. Mountain View, CA:
Mayfield. An anthology containing a good selection of both classic and contemporary essays dealing with the anthropology of religion. The emphasis of the text is on the nonliterate religious traditions.

Oswalt, Wendell. 1976. *An Anthropological Analysis of Food-Getting Technology*. New York: Wiley. A unique overview of the various types of technologies used in preindustrial societies.

Scupin, Raymond (Ed.). 2000. *Religion and Culture: An Anthropological Focus*. Upper Saddle River, NJ: Prentice Hall. This textbook is a reader containing original essays by various anthropologists on most of the indigenous and major religious traditions throughout the world.

Wilk, Richard. 1996. *Economies and Cultures: Foundations of Economic Anthropology*. Boulder, CO: Westview Press. This is an excellent introduction to the field of economic anthropology in a nontechnical manner. It provides examples of different non-Western economies and the difficulties of analyzing those economies.

Band Societies

CHAPTER QUESTIONS

- How are the environments of the modern foraging or band societies different from those of the Paleolithic?

- What are the distinguishing features of the population, economy, social life, political systems, and religious traditions of band societies?

As discussed previously, early societies did not produce their own food but instead survived by hunting and gathering, or foraging. A **hunter-gatherer,** or **foraging, society** is a society whose subsistence is based on the hunting of animals and gathering of vegetation. The basic economic, social, and political unit of hunter-gatherer societies is the **band.**

Food production as a subsistence pattern developed relatively recently, about 12,000 to 10,000 years ago. Thus, for almost 99 percent of humanity's life span, humans lived as foragers. This lifestyle has been the most enduring and persistent adaptation humans have ever achieved. Therefore, band societies have been the basic type of sociocultural system for perhaps as long as one million years. Hence, the study of the foraging way of life has been of particular interest to anthropologists as a means of understanding Paleolithic lifestyles; consequently, anthropologists have studied numerous contemporary hunting-and-gathering societies. Early cultural anthropologists thought that these studies could help provide models for understanding Paleolithic societies.

Unlike some of their nineteenth-century predecessors, however, modern anthropologists do not assume that contemporary hunting-and-gathering societies are representative of this type of society at early stages of human evolution. Paleolithic hunting-and-gathering societies existed in nearly all the major biomes of the world, whereas modern band societies of this type exist only in limited, **marginal environments,** those that are not suitable for intensive agriculture. Therefore, contemporary hunters and gatherers are modern peoples who have adapted to extreme environmental conditions.

In addition, as will be emphasized in Chapter 20, present surrounding societies have altered all of these hunter-gatherer societies. For example, hunter-gatherers in southeast Asia and Africa have carried on continuous economic exchanges with nearby agricultural societies for centuries. More recently, industrial societies have dramatically affected these hunting-and-gathering societies. Many of the hunter-gatherer have been forced by modern nation-states to relocate and adjust to areas not suitable to their traditional subsistence practices. For reasons such as these, studies of modern hunter-gatherer societies do not offer precise comparative data for evaluating Paleolithic societies.

You will notice that in this chapter we refer to hunter-gatherers in both the past and present tenses. As a result of contacts with other peoples, many traditional practices and institutions of band societies have been transformed. The past tense is used to describe these traditional phenomena. Those traditions that have managed to persist into the present are discussed in the present tense.

Modern Foraging Environments and Subsistence

During the last 10,000 years, foraging societies have grown fewer and fewer and are now restricted to marginal environments. Deserts, tropical rain forests, and arctic areas are considered marginal environments, because until recently too much labor and capital were needed to irrigate deserts, plant crops in the Arctic, or slash down tropical forests for agriculture. Consequently, those few foraging or hunter-gatherer societies that adjusted to these marginal environments managed to exist in relative isolation from surrounding groups. Figure 15.1 shows the locations of the major hunter-gatherer societies that still exist.

Deserts

Various cultural-ecological studies have been done with foragers surviving in desert environments. One long-term study focuses on the !Kung San or Ju/'hoansi of the Kalahari Desert in southwestern Africa. The San occupied southern Africa for thousands of years along with another, biologically related population known popularly as the Hottentots, or Khoi. Archaeologist John Yellen (1985) located prehistoric sites in the Kalahari that have been dated to well over 11,000 years ago. This evidence suggests that the !Kung San had been residing in this

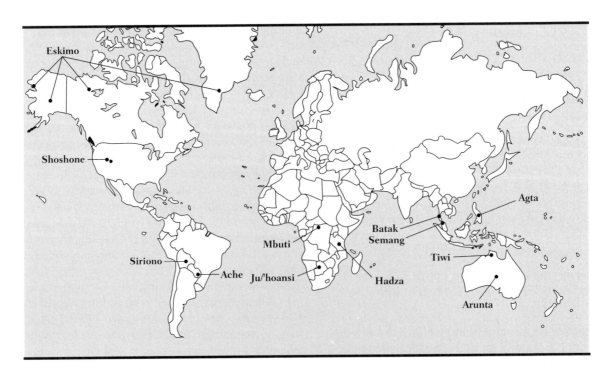

FIGURE 15.1 Hunter-gatherer societies discussed in this chapter.

region before agriculture spread to the surrounding region.

Most historians and archaeologists agree that the processes of migration and culture contact with surrounding societies have affected the !Kung San, and the "modern" !Kung San do not represent a pure remnant of Paleolithic society. The frequency of interaction of the San accelerated with European expansion and settlements throughout southern Africa in the eighteenth century (see Chapter 20). Currently, the population of the Ju/'hoansi or San is estimated at around 100,000 people.

Richard Lee, who studied the Ju/'hoansi or San from the 1960s through the 1990s, gives a comprehensive picture of their food-gathering and dietary practices. At the time he studied them, between 60 and 80 percent of the San diet consisted of nuts, roots, fruit, melons, and berries, which were gathered by the women. Meat from hunting was less common, providing only 20 to 30 percent of the diet. To procure this diet, the San did not need to expend enormous amounts of time and energy. In fact, Lee estimated that San adults spent between two and three days each week finding food.

Photo of the Kalahari Ju/'hoansi people.

Women often were able to gather enough in one or two days to feed their families for a week, leaving time for resting, visiting, embroidering, and entertaining visitors. Males spent much of their leisure time in ritual activities, including curing ceremonies (Lee, 1972b, 1979, 1993).

Other foraging societies existed in various arid and semiarid desert biomes, an example being the Great Basin Shoshone, a Native American group discussed in Chapter 13. Shoshone males hunted and trapped game, and Shoshone females gathered seeds, insects, and assorted vegetation. Both males and females harvested wild pinyon nuts, which the women mixed with seeds and insects and ground into flour for cooking.

Many of the Australian Aborigines were hunter-gatherers living in deserts that made up one-third of the continent. One group, known as the Arunta, lived in the interior desert region. They subsisted on the various species of animals and plants found in their habitat. Women and children gathered seeds, roots, snails, insects, reptiles, burrowing rodents, and eggs of birds and reptiles. Arunta males specialized in hunting larger game such as the kangaroo, the wallaby, the large, ostrichlike emu, and smaller birds and animals. Ethnographic studies indicate that Aborigines spent four to five hours per day per person in gathering food (Sahlins, 1972).

Tropical Rain Forests

Foragers have also adapted to the marginal environments of tropical rain forests. In the central African country of Congo, formerly Zaire, a group of foragers known as the Mbuti Pygmies resides in the luxuriant Ituri rain forest. The first evidence of the Mbuti peoples comes from early Egyptian accounts of an expedition into the Ituri forest. From other archaeological data, it appears that the Mbuti have inhabited this region for at least 5,000 years. The late Colin Turnbull (1983), who did ethnographic research among the Mbuti in the 1960s, suggests that there was no dramatic change in Mbuti culture until about 450 years ago, after Europeans came to Africa.

The division of labor among the Mbuti resembles that of other hunting-and-gathering groups. Males hunt elephants, buffalo, wild pigs, and other game, and females gather vegetation. The entire group, however, is involved in the hunting endeavor. Mbuti males set up nets to capture the game, after which they stand guard with spears. Youths with bows and arrows stand farther back from the nets to shoot any game that escapes, while women and children form semicircles to drive the game into the nets. More independent hunting is done by older males and youths, who may wander off to shoot monkeys and birds.

Another hunting-gathering people, known as the Semang, inhabit the tropical forests of the Malaysian and Thai peninsula. They live in the foothills and lower slopes of dense rain forests that have exceptionally heavy precipitation. Although in the past the Semang may have hunted large game such as elephants and buffalo, they abandoned large-game hunting when they took up the blowgun instead of the bow and arrow (Keyes, 1995). Today, Semang males fish and hunt small game. However, Semang subsistence depends primarily on the gathering of wild fruits and vegetables, including yams, berries, nuts, and shoots collected by females.

Arctic Regions

Survival in arctic conditions has inspired considerable creative adjustments by groups of foragers popularly known as the Eskimo. Most Eskimo refer to themselves as the *Inuit,* as Inuit is the major language of these people. Early Inuit culture has been

dated to at least 2500 B.C. Some Inuit live in northwestern Alaska near the Bering Sea, and others live in the arctic regions of northern Canada, extending eastward all the way to Greenland. The northwestern Alaska Eskimo hunt sea mammals such as bowhead whales, seals, and walruses. Interior groups such as the Netsilik in central Canada, who were studied by cultural anthropologist Asen Balikci, hunt caribou, musk oxen, an occasional polar bear, seals, and birds. They also fish in nearby bays.

Because vegetation historically was scarce in arctic regions, it was a prized food. After killing the caribou, male hunters ate the animal's stomach so as to obtain the valued undigested vegetation. Although their diet consisted primarily of meat, the Inuit generally satisfied their basic nutritional requirements of carbohydrate, protein, and vitamins from eating berries, green roots, fish, and fish oil. They preferred cooked foods, but boiling food over fires fueled by blubber oil was slow and expensive; consequently, the Inuit ate most of their food raw.

The division of labor among the Inuit was unlike that of most other foraging societies. Because of the scarcity of vegetation, women were not specialized collectors. However, during the summer season, males and females gathered larvae, caribou flies, maggots, and deer droppings that contained vegetation.

Inuit hunters in Alaska.

Mobility and Subsistence

No matter what their particular environment, most hunters and gatherers share one characteristic: *mobility*. As food and other resources become scarce in one site, the groups have to move on to another. The Mbuti Pygmies, for example, reside in certain areas during the rainy season and other areas during other seasons, depending on the supply of game (Turnbull, 1983). The Ju/'hoansi or San moved frequently in pursuit of resources. During the winter dry season, they congregated in large groupings around several watering holes, but during the rainy season the groups dispersed into small units. The San moved when subsistence required (Lee, 1969). Most Inuit groups also have to move during different seasons to pursue game and other resources. For example, the northwestern Alaska Eskimos move from the coastal areas into the interior regions during the summer seasons to hunt herds of caribou.

These nomadic behaviors are not arbitrary or spontaneous. Rather, they are carefully planned to minimize labor while providing vital resources. These patterns of mobility represent an admirable appreciation and intimate knowledge of the environment in which these foragers reside.

Optimal Foraging Theory

One of the ways in which anthropologists attempt to study the subsistence and foraging practices of hunter-gatherers is referred to as *optimal foraging theory*. Optimal foraging theory is used to try to predict what potential foods the foragers should exploit, if they are to make the most efficient use of time and energy. It also is used to predict what foods should be avoided because exploiting them would take up time and energy that could be used more efficiently for procuring other foods. The theory assesses the immediate costs and benefits of utlizing different subsistence strategies.

One of the most extensive uses of optimal foraging theory was that of Kristin Hawkes, Kimberly Hill, and James O'Connell, a team of anthropologists who studied the Ache hunter-gatherers of the tropical rain forests of Paraguay in South America (1982). These anthropologists found that optimal foraging theory tended to predict the types of foods procured by the Ache. They started by having the

Ache rank the kinds and types of foods that they foraged. Then, the anthropologists carefully observed what foods were actually procured. For example, they observed that the Ache picked oranges rather than killing monkeys most of the time. Though oranges give a lower yield in calories than monkeys, the processing time was much shorter for oranges than monkeys. The anthropologists calculated that the average return from Ache hunting was 1,115 kilocalories per hour per person. But when they picked oranges, the individuals' average return rose to 4,438 kilocalories per hour. Therefore, oranges were a much more profitable and efficient food to exploit. The Ache told the anthropologists that monkeys were not worth hunting because they were not fat enough. However, when they came across a monkey, they would kill it for food. The Ache tended to make the kinds of decisions one would expect according to optimal foraging calculations. This study, along with other optimal foraging studies, demonstrates that hunter-gatherers make very efficient use of their environment for subsistence purposes.

Foragers and Demographic Conditions

As we have seen, modern foragers live in marginal environments and travel from location to location. The requirement of mobility to procure resources has had a major effect on demographic conditions in these societies. Unlike food producers, hunters and gatherers must depend on the naturally occurring food resources in their territories. These food resources determine and limit excessive population growth. Generally, the population densities of foragers are extremely low as measured in relation to the limited carrying capacity of their environments.

Demographic studies such as those done by cultural anthropologists Richard Lee (1972a) and Nancy Howell (1979) on the Ju/'hoansi or San have enabled anthropologists to make certain generalizations concerning demographic conditions among modern foragers. Population size among the San was carefully controlled in a number of ways. According to Lee (1979), the San knew how many people could be supported in specific territories and how many people were needed to provide sufficient resources. Having too many people leads to shortages of resources, whereas having too few people leads to ineffective foraging strategies.

Fissioning

One of the most important means of limiting population growth for foragers is fissioning. **Fissioning** is the movement of people from one group to another when the population begins to increase and food or other material resources become scarce. Resource scarcity creates population pressure in the form of hardships and problems that emerge as the biome's resources become overtaxed. In such cases, the typical response is for a portion of the population to migrate to other geographic regions. Fissioning was most likely the primary means of population control for Paleolithic foragers and to some extent explains the worldwide expansion of the human species.

Fissioning is practiced by modern foragers to a limited extent. Its success depends on the presence of unoccupied land into which the excess population can expand. In situations where an increasing population is surrounded by other populations and fissioning is not possible, conflict between groups becomes likely, although sometimes *fusion,* or groups combining with one another, occurs (Hammel & Howell, 1987).

Infanticide

Another means of population control in some foraging societies is **infanticide,** the deliberate abandonment or killing of infants, usually immediately after birth. Infanticide has been well documented in foraging societies. Joseph Birdsell (1968) hypothesized that infanticide is a means of spacing children. Because a woman can carry only one child in her arms at a time as a nomadic gatherer, there is a need to space childbirth. Typically, childbirth was spaced at intervals of four years.

Most cases of infanticide in these foraging societies appear to be decisions made by individuals in response to famine conditions or to anticipated food and material scarcities (Harris & Ross, 1987). Infanticide in some of these societies is also associated with the birth of twins (supporting two children might be difficult or impossible) and with genetically abnormal infants.

Fertility Rates

Other lines of demographic research investigate the relatively slow rate of population growth for foraging societies. Some anthropologists are testing demographic hypotheses on the relationship among nutrition, physiological stress, breast-feeding, and rates of fertility (Howell, 1979; Lee, 1979). The purpose of these studies is to determine whether biological factors rather than cultural practices such as infanticide may induce low fertility rates and thus slow population growth for foragers.

For example, Nancy Howell's research on the Ju/'hoansi or San indicates that a low caloric diet and the high energy rate needed for female foraging activities may postpone the occurrence of *menarche,* the onset of menstruation at puberty, which does not appear in San females until a mean age of 16.6 years (Howell, 1979), compared with 12.9 years in the United States (Barnouw, 1985). The low body weight of San females, whose average weight is 90 pounds, also influences the late onset of menarche. This slower rate of maturation may be related to the low fertility of the San.

Other studies have suggested that breast-feeding contributes to low fertility rates. Breast-feeding stimulates the production of prolactin, a hormone that inhibits ovulation and pregnancy (McKenna, Mosko, & Richard, 1999). San women breast-feed their infants for 3 to 4 years. Considering the workload and general ecological conditions San women must deal with, this prolonged nursing may produce a natural, optimal birth interval, or spacing of children (Blurton Jones, 1986, 1987). This factor, along with sexual abstinence, abortion, infanticide, and delayed marriage, may be evidence of early forms of fertility control in prehistoric foraging societies.

Technology in Foraging Societies

In Chapter 7, we discussed the evolution of technology during the Paleolithic period. The crude stone tools of the Lower Paleolithic gave way to the more sophisticated stone tool complex of the Upper Paleolithic. As humans migrated across the continents, technology became specialized, enabling populations to adjust to different types of environments.

Until recently, anthropologists believed that many modern hunter-gatherers had limited technologies.

Nineteenth-century anthropologists thought that these limited technologies reflected a simplicity of mind and lack of skill. Modern anthropologists, in contrast, regard these technologies as highly functional in particular ecological conditions. More important, technology does not refer just to tools or artifacts; it also includes the cultural knowledge that has to be maintained by the society. All foraging peoples have an extensive knowledge of their environmental conditions and of the appropriate means of solving technological problems in these environments.

Desert foragers such as the Ju/'hoansi or San use small bows and arrows and spears. Australian Aborigines did not have the bow and arrow, but they used the well-known boomerang (which did not return to the thrower), spears, and spear-throwers for hunting in desert areas. In tropical rain forests, foragers make traps, snares, and sometimes nets such as those used by the Mbuti. The Mbuti also make fire-hardened wooden spears and arrow tips for hunting. Some foraging groups, like the Semang, use the blowgun for hunting game. Most of the desert and rain forest foragers use natural poisons to make their hunting more efficient. In some cases, the foragers take various types of poisons from plants and place the poisons in streams to kill fish. In other cases, they put poison on the tips of their arrows to kill game.

As we have seen, fruit and vegetable gathering is at least as important as hunting in foraging societies. In the desert and tropical rain forest, the implements for gathering are uncomplicated. The cultural knowledge needed for gathering, however, is profound. The people need to know where to find the plants, when to find them during different seasons, which plants are edible, which plants are scarce or plentiful, and so on. In most cases, gathering food is the responsibility of women and children. The typical tool is a simple sharpened stick for digging up tubers or getting honey out of hives. Sometimes foragers also use net bags, bark, wooden bowls, or other natural objects to carry nuts, seeds, water, or fruit. For example, San women used large ostrich eggs to hold and carry water.

An extremely complex foraging technology was created by the Inuit (Eskimo) to procure animal food resources. The classic Inuit technology has evolved over the past 3,000 years and includes equipment made from bone, stone, skin, wood, and ice. *Umiaks* (large boats) and *kayaks* (canoes) are used for whaling, sealing, and transportation. Inuit technology also includes dogsleds, lances, fish spears, bows and arrows, harpoons with detachable points, traps, fishhooks, and soapstone lamps used with whale and seal oil for heating and cooking. Unlike the desert and rain forest foragers who wear very little clothing, the Eskimo people have developed

A hunter using a blow gun in the rain forest.

sophisticated techniques for curing hides from caribou and seals to make boots, parkas, and other necessary arctic gear.

Economics in Foraging Societies

Despite the vast differences in physical environment, subsistence, and technology, most foraging societies have similar economic systems. The major form of economic system identified with these societies is called the reciprocal economic system (Sahlins, 1972). A **reciprocal economic system** is based on exchanges among family groups as a means of distributing goods and services throughout the society. The basic principle underlying this system is **reciprocity,** the widespread sharing of goods and services in a society. One reason for this system of reciprocal exchange is that the consumption of food and other resources is usually immediate, because there is very little storage capacity for any surplus. Thus, it makes sense to share what cannot be used anyway.

Reciprocity

The many descriptions of economic transactions and exchanges in foraging societies have led Marshall Sahlins to distinguish three types of reciprocity: generalized, balanced, and negative (1965, 1972).

Generalized Reciprocity   This form of exchange is based on the assumptions that an immediate return is not expected and that the value of the exchanges will balance out in the long run. The value of the return is not specified, and no running account of repayment of transactions is calculated. Although **generalized reciprocity** exists in all societies—for example, in the United States when parents pay for their offspring's food, clothing, and shelter—in foraging societies these transactions form the basis of the economic system.

Anthropologists used to refer to generalized reciprocity as a gift, to distinguish it from trade or barter. Neither altruism nor charity, however, accurately describes these transactions. Rather, these exchanges are based on socially recognized family and kinship statuses. Because such behaviors are expected, gratitude or recognition is usually not

required. In fact, in this form of reciprocity it might be impolite or insulting to indicate that a return is expected. For example, among the San and Inuit foragers, a "thank-you" for food or other services is interpreted as an insult (Freuchen, 1961; Lee, 1969). Generosity is required in these small-scale societies to reduce envy and social tensions, promote effective cooperation, distribute resources and services, and create obligations.

Examples of generalized reciprocity occur among foragers like the Ju/'hoansi or San, Mbuti, and Inuit. Aside from food, which is shared with everyone in the group, the San have a generalized exchange system known as *hxaro,* which not only circulates goods but also—and primarily—solidifies social relationships by creating mutual obligations among related kin (Lee, 1993). The *hxaro* system involves exchanging goods ranging from weapons to jewelry. Constant circulation of these material goods not only enhances and maintains kin ties through mutual obligations but also inhibits the accumulation of wealth by any individuals in the society. This enables these societies to remain **egalitarian,** which refers to societies that have very small differences in wealth among individuals. There are no rich or poor in these types of societies.

Balanced Reciprocity   A more direct type of reciprocal exchange with an explicit expectation of immediate return is **balanced reciprocity.** This form of reciprocity is more utilitarian and more like trade and barter than is generalized reciprocity. The material aspect of the exchange is as important as the social aspect. People involved in these transactions calculate the value of the exchanges, which are expected to be equivalent. If an equal return is not given, the original donor may not continue the exchange relationship. Balanced reciprocity is usually found in contexts of more distant kinship relations. Because most exchanges and transactions in modern foraging societies take place among close kin, balanced reciprocity is practiced less frequently than is generalized reciprocity.

Negative Reciprocity   Sahlins (1972) defined **negative reciprocity** as the attempt to get something for nothing. Negative reciprocity means no reciprocity at all. It may involve bargaining, haggling, gambling, cheating, theft, or the outright seizure of goods. In general, negative reciprocity is least common in small-scale foraging societies, in which kinship relations predominate.

Exchange and Altruism In foraging societies, where reciprocity reigns, people may appear to outsiders as naturally generous, altruistic, and magnanimous. But as Lee noted in reference to the economy of the !Kung San or Ju/'hoansi:

> *If I had to point to one single feature that makes this way of life possible, I would focus on sharing. Each Ju is not an island unto himself or herself; each is part of a collective. It is a small, rudimentary collective, and at times a fragile one, but it is a collective nonetheless. What I mean is that the living group pools the resources that are brought into camp so that everyone receives an equitable share. The !Kung and people like them don't do this out of nobility of soul or because they are made of better stuff than we are. In fact, they often gripe about sharing. They do it because it works for them and it enhances their survival. Without this core of sharing, life for the Ju/'hoansi would be harder and infinitely less pleasant. (1993:60)*

It appears that these hunting-and-gathering peoples are no more noble than other people. Rather, the conditions of their existence have led them to develop economic practices that enable them to survive in their particular habitat. As humans, it appears that we reciprocate with one another in all societies. The strategy of "I'll scratch your back and you scratch mine" is found everywhere. And, in a small-scale foraging society where trust can be generated among everyone, reciprocity becomes highly generalized.

Collective Ownership of Property

In the nineteenth century, Lewis Morgan proposed that early economic systems associated with small-scale societies were communistic. In his book *Ancient Society* ([1877] 1964), Morgan claimed that during the early stages of cultural evolution, the productive technology and economic resources were shared by everyone in the society. Today, Morgan's views appear too simplistic to account for the vast range of economic systems found in small-scale societies.

Ethnological data indicate that hunting-and-gathering societies have differing forms of property

relations, which reflect their particular ecological conditions. Among some groups, such as the Ju/'hoansi or San, the Inuit, and the Western Shoshone, where resources are widely distributed, cultural anthropologists report that there are no exclusive rights to territory. Though specific families may be identified with a local camp area, territorial boundaries are extremely flexible, and exclusive ownership of resources within a territory is not well defined. For example, among the Ju/'hoansi San, waterholes were frequently said to be owned by individual families. Yet few restrictions were placed against other families or groups in using these resources. Many foraging groups may have rights of temporary use or rights to claim resources if needed, but not "once-and-for-all" rights that exist in modern capitalist societies (Bloch, 1983).

However, in other foraging societies, such as that of the Owens Valley Paiute Indians who resided near the edge of the Great Basin region in the American West, exclusive rights to territory were well defined and defended against outsiders. The Paiute were heavily dependent on pinyon nuts, which were concentrated in one area and were a more predictable source of food than game animals. Specific territorial ties and exclusive rights to land carrying these resources became important for bands and families. The defense of these resources was economically beneficial to the Paiute. In a comparison of territorial rights among different hunter-gatherers, anthropologists Rada Dyson-Hudson and Eric Smith (1978) found that the greater the predictability and concentration of resources within a particular region, the more pronounced were the conceptions of private ownership and exclusive rights to territory among foragers.

Other forms of private property in foraging societies are associated with individuals—pets, ornaments, clothing, and items of technology such as bows, knives, scrapers, and blowguns. Such items are usually regarded as a form of private personal property over which the person who owns them has certain rights.

The Original Affluent Society?

Until the 1960s, the traditional picture of foraging societies was that of people with limited technologies who were at the mercy of a harsh environment.

It seemed that in these dire environmental circumstances, people had to work constantly to survive. In the 1960s, however, anthropologists began to draw on ethnographic studies to produce a much different image of hunter-gatherer societies. Modern cultural anthropologists gathered basic data on the types of production systems that hunter-gatherers use, the amount of time they spend in production and subsistence, the role of mobility in their adaptation, and how long they live.

The ethnographic data reported in Lee and DeVore's work indicate that contemporary foraging societies usually have an adequate and reliable food base. Lee (1972a, b, 1979, 1993), for example, has argued that the !Kung San or Ju/'hoansi diet was nutritionally adequate. The data also indicate that these foragers expended minimal labor to provide for their basic physical needs. Finally, the life expectancy in these societies turns out to be much greater than was once thought. These findings have led some anthropologists to refer to foragers as "original affluent societies" or "leisured societies" (Sahlins, 1972). Sahlins, for example, argued that the worldview of foragers differs radically from that of capitalist societies. He suggested that the sharing-oriented economy of people such as the Ju/'hoansi or !Kung San demonstrates that the forager's needs are few and are easily satisfied by a relatively meager amount of labor time. In Sahlins's view, foragers do not value the accumulation of material goods in the same way that people in modern capitalist societies do.

It is obvious that for populations that have to maintain a nomadic lifestyle, the accumulation of resources would be unproductive. Material possessions would be burdensome when trekking across the ice of the Arctic or through the dense rain forests. Without a way to store large quantities of food, it would be irrational to accumulate food resources only to have them spoil.

Further evidence of the affluence of foragers is drawn from the demographic conditions for these groups. For example, Lee argued that the composition of the Ju/'hoansi or San population demonstrates that these people were not on the edge of starvation. Ten percent of the individuals surveyed by Lee were over 60 years of age, "a proportion that compares favorably to the percentage of elderly in industrialized populations" (Lee, 1968:36). The blind, senile, or disabled continued to be supported by the Ju/'hoansi. The system of reciprocal exchanges thus ensures the survival of these individuals.

The Affluence Hypothesis Challenged

Some recent anthropological research, however, has challenged the notion of the original affluent societies. Although the San and similar groups may spend only a few hours each day and a few days each week bringing in basic food resources, they must also spend time making tools, weapons, and clothing; processing and cooking food; planning for future foraging activities; solving disputes; healing the sick; and raising children (Konner, 1982). In other words, we can view the San and other foragers as affluent only if we restrict our definition of work to the actual quest for food.

The study of the Ache, foragers mentioned above who live in the rain forest of eastern Paraguay, illustrates the shortcomings of the affluence hypothesis. A team of cultural anthropologists analyzed Ache subsistence activities (Hill et al., 1985). They discovered that Ache males spend forty to fifty hours a week in the quest for special kinds of food. Time-allocation studies such as these challenge the notion that all foragers spend minimal time in pursuit of food resources.

Furthermore, recent medical research has challenged Lee's arguments that the San diet is nutritionally sound. Although the diet is well balanced in respect to carbohydrates, proteins, and fats, the overall caloric intake of the San appears to be inadequate. The small physical size of the San may be due to the fact that mothers usually have not supplemented nursing with additional food intake for infants over six months old. Moreover, the entire San population has suffered from seasonal food shortages and starvation (Konner, 1982).

This recent research on the Ju/'hoansi or San does not totally refute the overall hypothesis regarding the original affluent societies. In general, it appears that in some cases, especially in the tropical rain forest, groups like the Mbuti and the Semang have an abundance of vegetables and fruits. In contrast, groups such as the Shoshone or the Ache have to expend much more time in securing basic resources. When there is a ready presence of resources, relative affluence is possible. But when these items are absent or less plentiful, subsistence becomes much more demanding.

Another factor that influences the relative affluence of foraging societies is the ability to preserve resources over a period of time. Although most of these societies did not store food, groups such as the Inuit had limited storage capacities. Some Inuit groups dug holes beneath the permafrost so that they could store meat. The storage of meat, berries, and greens enabled the Inuit to maintain a certain amount of affluence even in winter. They thus had a steady, reliable source of meat and vegetation as a base for subsistence activities.

Social Organization in Foraging Societies

The fundamental social organization in foraging societies is based on family, marriage, kinship, gender, and age. The two basic elements of social organization for foraging populations are the nuclear family and the band. The **nuclear family** is the small family unit associated with procreation: parents and offspring. The nuclear family appears to be most adaptive for hunting-gathering societies because of the flexibility needed for the location and easy distribution and exchange of food resources, and the other exigencies of hunting (Fox, 1967; Pasternak, 1976).

The most common type of band is made up of a related cluster of nuclear families ranging in size

from twenty to one hundred individuals. At times, in societies such as the desert-dwelling Shoshone Indians, the bands may break up into nuclear families to locate food and other resources. Under other circumstances, several families may cooperate in hunting and other foraging activities. In some instances, bands may contain up to four or five (sometimes more) **extended families,** in which married children and their offspring reside with their parents. These multifamily bands provide the webs of kinship for foraging societies, enabling them to cooperate in subsistence and economic exchanges.

The specific number of people in a band depends on the carrying capacity of the natural environment. Most foraging groups had a range of twenty to one hundred people. Foragers in the desert, the Arctic, and the tropical rain forest all lived in small multifamily bands residing in separate territories. Typically, band organization is extremely flexible, with members leaving and joining bands as circumstances demand. Personal conflicts and shortages of resources may encourage people to move into or out of bands. In some cases, when food or water resources are scarce, whole bands may move into the territories of other bands.

Marriage and Kinship

Although a number of foraging groups practice polygyny, the most common type of marriage found

A Baka pygmy couple in West Africa.

in foraging societies is monogamy. Marriages are an important means of cementing social relationships. In some cases, betrothals are arranged while the future spouses are still young children. Typically, the girl is much younger than the male. For example, Ju/'hoansi or San girls are often married between the ages of 12 and 14, whereas males may be 18 to 25 years old or older.

Though these marital arrangements are regular features of foraging societies, it does not mean the couple easily accepts these arranged marriages. A San woman expressed herself on her first marriage:

> When I married my husband Tsau I didn't fight too hard, but I cried a lot when I was taken to sleep in his hut. When the elders went away I listened carefully for their sleeping. Then, when my husband fell asleep and I heard his breathing, I very quietly sat up and eased my blanket away from his and stole away and slept by myself out in the bush.
>
> In the morning the people came to Tsau's hut and asked, "Where is your wife?" He looked around and said, "I don't know where my wife has gone off to." Then they picked up my tracks and tracked me to where I was sitting out in the bush. They brought me back to my husband. They told me that this was the man they had given to me and that he wouldn't hurt me.
>
> After that we just lived together all right. At first when we slept under the same blanket our bodies did not touch, but then after a while I slept at his front. Other girls don't like their husbands and keep struggling away until the husbands give up on them and their parents take them back. (Lee, 1993:83)

Marriage Rules   Marital arrangements in foraging societies are intended to enhance economic, social, and political interdependence among bands and to foster appropriate band alliances. To do this, rules are established to determine who may marry whom. Many of these rules concern marriages among cousins. A common marriage rule found in foraging societies is referred to as **cross-cousin marriage.** A cross cousin is the offspring of one's father's sister or one's mother's brother. In effect, a cross-cousin marriage means that a male marries a female who is his father's sister's daughter or his mother's brother's daughter.

In addition, foraging societies frequently have rules of residence that specify where the married couple must reside. Most band societies practice **patrilocal residence,** in which the newly married couple resides with the husband's father. Thus, if a man marries a woman from a different band, she must join her husband's band. In such societies, the patrilocal residence rule and cross-cousin marriage combine to create a system called *restricted marital exchange,* in which two groups exchange women (Levi-Strauss, 1969). The purpose of this system is to foster group solidarity by encouraging kinship alliances.

The kinship diagram in Figure 15.2 gives a visual model of the social structure in some foraging societies. In the diagram, Ego is used as a point of reference, and kinship relationships are traced from Ego's offspring, parents, grandparents, and other relatives. Note that Ego has married his father's sister's daughter (his cross cousin on his father's side). Because of the rule of patrilocal residence, Ego's father's sister had to move to another band with her husband. Therefore, Ego is marrying outside his own band.

Like Ego, Ego's wife's brother has married a woman outside his band. In keeping with the cross-cousin rule, their daughter has married Ego's son. Ego's daughter will eventually marry someone from another band. Through the rules of cross cousin marriage and patrilocal residence, this restricted exchange develops strong networks of interfamily and interband kinship relations. These kin networks widen over the generations, expanding economic, social, and political relationships.

Brideservice   Some foraging societies practice **brideservice,** in which a male resides for a specified amount of time with his wife's parents' band. The rule of residence that requires a man to reside with his wife's parents is called **matrilocal residence.** Among the Ju/'hoansi or San, brideservice can last eight to ten years, and the husband and wife don't return to the husband's father's band for residence (the patrilocal rule) until after several children are born (Lee, 1993). The husband will help his wife's band in their subsistence activities, which helps consolidate both economic and social ties between the two bands. Another reason the San practice brideservice is that females are not sexually mature at the time of their marriage. San girls who marry before their menarche are not expected to have sexual intercourse with their husband. Thus, the brideservice period coincides with female maturation. But brideservice also functions to reinforce the kinship and reciprocal ties between bands.

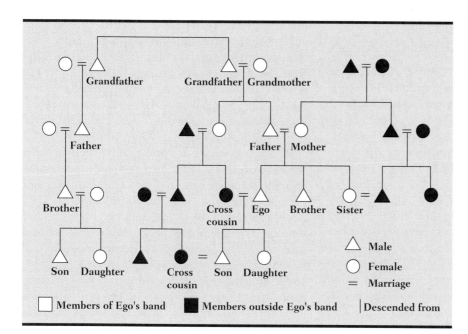

FIGURE 15.2 Kinship and marriage patterns in hunting-and-gathering societies.

Other Marital Patterns among Foragers Not all foraging societies conform to the marital patterns just described. For example, Inuit marriage involved no preferred rules regarding cousin marriage or rituals and ceremonies sanctioning the new couple's relationship. Traditionally, the man and woman simply begin residing with each other. To some extent, the Inuit view this marriage arrangement as a pragmatic and utilitarian relationship for economic and reproductive purposes (Balikci, 1970).

Another aspect of Inuit marriage is the well-known tradition of *wife exchange.* In some cases, males established partnerships with other males that include having sexual intercourse with each other's wives. Usually it is clear that both the men and the women involved make decisions about this. However, cultural anthropologist Ansen Balikci records cases wherein wives were threatened and intimidated if they did not want to participate (1970). One of the most important aspects of wife exchange was the interregional social networks established among these families. In addition, the children produced from these exchanges were considered siblings, which further enhanced the development of kinship obligations and reciprocity.

Divorce In most cases, divorce is easily accomplished in hunting-and-gathering societies. For example, Ju/'hoansi or !Kung San divorces, which are

most frequently initiated by the wife, are simple matters characterized by cordiality and cooperation. The divorced couple may even live next to one another with their new spouses. Because there are no rigid rules or complex kinship relations beyond the nuclear family to complicate divorce proceedings, the dissolution of a San marriage is a relatively easy process (Lee, 1993).

Divorce was also frequent and easily obtained among the Inuit (Balikci, 1970). As with the San, one reason for this was the lack of formal social groups beyond the nuclear family. Another reason was the absence of strict rules governing marriage and postmarital residence. Significantly, divorce did not necessarily lead to the cutting of kin ties. Even if an Inuit couple separated, and this happened for nearly 100 percent of the marriages studied, the kin ties endured (Burch, 1970). Sometimes the couple reunited, and the children of first and second marriages became a newly blended family. Thus, divorce frequently extended kin ties, an important aspect of sociocultural adaptation in severe arctic conditions.

Gender

Gender as an aspect of social structure in foraging societies is an extremely important area of ethnographic research. Cultural anthropologists have been examining the interrelationships among gender, subsistence, economic, and political patterns.

Gender and the Division of Labor Considerable ethnographic research has demonstrated that gender roles in foraging societies are strongly related to the basic division of labor. Prior to recent ethnographic research on foraging societies, anthropologists believed that male subsistence activities, especially hunting and fishing, provided most of the food resources. However, as we have seen, in some of the foraging societies such as the Ju/'hoansi or San, the Semang, and Mbuti, women are providing most of the food, because gathering and collecting vegetation is the primary means of securing food (Martin & Voorhies, 1975; Dahlberg, 1981). One cross-cultural analysis based on all of the available evidence for foraging societies in the past and present indicates that males have typically obtained most of the meat-foods through hunting and fishing (Ember, 1978).

Biological Explanations of the Division of Labor
One question posed by modern cultural anthropologists is: Why is the division of labor in foraging societies so strongly related to gender roles? There are several possible answers to this question. The first is that males hunt and women gather because males

are stronger and have more endurance in the pursuit of large game. Another possibility is that because women bear and nurse children, they lack the freedom of mobility necessary to hunt (Friedl, 1975). A third answer is that gathering, especially near a base camp, is a relatively safe activity that entails no potential dangers for women who are either pregnant or caring for children (Brown, 1970b).

There is evidence for and against each of these theories. We have seen, for example, that in some foraging societies men and women are involved in both hunting and gathering. In addition, women often perform tasks that require strength and stamina, such as carrying food, children, water, and firewood. Thus, gathering resources is not a sedentary or leisurely activity. Based on this evidence, anthropologist Linda Marie Fedigan (1986) has proposed that heavy work and child-care activities may not be mutually exclusive, as was previously thought.

Many research questions pertaining to gender roles and subsistence among foragers remain for future anthropologists. Much of the recent evidence suggests that gender roles and subsistence activities are not as rigid as formerly thought. Among the Batak foragers of the rain forests of Malaysia and the Agta in the Philippines, both men and women perform virtually every subsistence task (Estioko-Griffin & Griffin, 1978; Endicott, 1988). Women among the Agta go out into the forest to kill wild boars just as the men do. The Tiwi of Australia and the Hadza foragers of East Africa demonstrate this same pattern (Goodale, 1971; Woodburn, 1982). In these cases, it appears that the subsistence strategies for both males and females are open, and behavior is flexible.

Ju/'hoansi women carrying their children while gathering vegetation and roots.

Female Status Closely related to gender roles and subsistence is the question of the social status of women. Empirical data suggest that gender relations tend to be more *egalitarian*—men and women having more or less equal status—in foraging societies than in other societies (Friedl, 1975; Martin & Voorhies, 1975; Endicott, 1988). This may reflect the substantial contributions women make in gathering food.

Richard Lee notes, for example, that as a result of their important role in economic activities, Ju/'hoansi or San women participate equally with men in political decision making (1981). San women are treated respectfully, and there is little evidence of male domination or the maltreatment of females. A similar generalization could be applied to the Mbuti, Semang, and Agta as well as to most of the other foragers. This hypothesis suggests, however, that in societies in which female contributions to the food supply are less critical or less valued, female status is lower. For example, among some of the Inuit and other northern foraging groups for whom hunting is the only subsistence activity, females do not gather much in the way of resources for the family. Consequently, those societies tend to be more **patriarchal,** or male dominated, in political and economic matters (Friedl, 1975; Martin & Voorhies, 1975).

Clearly, equality between males and females in foraging societies is not universal. In some groups such as the San and Agta, women have more equality, whereas in others such as the Inuit, females have a lower status. Even in the most egalitarian groups, males tend to have some inherent cultural advantages. In addition, males are more likely to become the political and spiritual leaders in foraging societies. When considering gender relations in a broad, cross-cultural perspective, however, foragers tend to have much more equality than do most other societies.

Age

Like kinship and gender, age is used in virtually all foraging societies as a basis for assigning individuals their particular status in the social hierarchy. Patterns of age stratification and hierarchy vary considerably from society to society, depending on environmental and cultural conditions. Age is also a primary aspect of the division of labor in foraging societies.

Children and Rites of Passage The period of childhood among foragers is a time of playful activity and excitement. But it is also a time when children learn their basic subsistence activities, economic responsibilities, and political roles. In his studies of the Mbuti Pygmies, Turnbull (1963, 1983) has provided us with a thorough account of childhood in a foraging society.

At the age of 3, the Mbuti child enters the *bopi,* a tiny camp about a hundred yards away from the main camp, which might be considered a playground. Older children and adults do not enter the *bopi.* Within the *bopi,* all the children are part of an age grade and are equal to one another and remain so throughout the rest of their lives. It is the area in which children become enculturated and learn the importance of age, kinship, and gender, and the activities associated with these statuses.

Within the *bopi* are noncompetitive play activities for boys and girls. Many of these activities reinforce the rules of hunting and gathering. The elders bring the children out of the *bopi* to show them how to use nets to hunt animals. Children also play house to learn how to take care of their households later in life. Before the age of puberty, boys and girls quit going into the *bopi* and join the main camp with older youths. When they reach puberty, Mbuti males and females have separate, informal rites of passage. The puberty ritual, known as the *Elima* for Mbuti females, occurs at the first menstruation, which is an occasion for great rejoicing because it is a sign that the girl is ready for marriage and motherhood. For a month the girl resides in a special hut with her agemates, and she is watched over by an older female. The girl learns the special songs of the *Elima* and occasionally appears in front of the hut while young men sit outside to admire the girls. At this time, the females sing the *Elima* songs, and the boys sing in response in a form of flirtation. Through their participation in the *Elima* ritual, the Mbuti males demonstrate their readiness for adulthood and marriage.

The Roles of the Elderly In foraging societies, old age tends to be defined less in terms of chronology and more in terms of some change in social status related to involvement in subsistence or work patterns, or becoming grandparents (Glascock, 1981). In all societies, however, the onset of old age is partially defined in terms of the average life span. The general demographic and ethnological data on foraging societies indicate that definitions of "old age" vary from 45 to 75 years old.

An early study of aging hypothesized that in hunting-and-gathering societies, older people wield little power and have low status (Simmons, 1945). This argument was based on the assumption that, because foraging societies had few material goods that older people controlled and could use as leverage with the younger generation, old age represented a loss of status. This hypothesis suggested that the status of older people is correlated with

Older people are taken care of by the group in band societies.

subsistence and economic activities. As foraging people age and decline in strength and energy, their subsistence contribution may be limited, thereby diminishing their status.

Most of the ethnographic data, however, do not support this hypothesis. In an early account of foragers in the Andaman Islands off the coast of India, for example, A. R. Radcliffe-Brown ([1922] 1964) described the reverence and honor given to older males. Among the Mbuti Pygmies, age is a key factor in determining status, and the elders make the most important economic and political decisions for the group. Despite the fact that young people sometimes openly ridicule older people, the elders are able to dominate Pygmy society because of their cultural knowledge (Turnbull, 1983).

Anthropologists who have studied the Ju/'hoansi or San point out that though there was little material security at old age, the elderly were not abandoned and had a relatively high status (Thomas, 1958; Lee, 1979). Despite the fact that older people do not play a predominant productive role in subsistence activities, they are able to remain secure because of close kinship ties. Through reciprocal

exchanges within the economic system of these foraging societies, older people are able to maintain a relatively secure existence.

Anthropologists find that older people in foraging societies generally have a higher status than do younger people. Because of their accumulated knowledge, which is needed for subsistence activities, political decision making, and intellectual and spiritual guidance, older people tend to be respected and are treated with a great deal of deference. Human memory serves as the libraries of these societies and is important for the preservation of culture and the transmission of knowledge. Cultural and historical traditions are memorized and handed down from generation to generation. Control of information is one important basis of esteem for the elderly in nonliterate societies.

In general, the evidence indicates that only in cases of extreme deprivation are the elderly in foraging societies maltreated. In their investigation of the treatment of the elderly in a wide variety of foraging societies, researchers concluded that practices directed against the elderly, such as abandonment, exposure, and killing, occur only under severe environmental circumstances, in which the elderly are viewed as burdens rather than assets (Glascock, 1981). These practices have been documented for groups ranging from the Inuit to the Siriono, but these cases appear to be exceptional. In most foraging societies, the young have moral obligations to take care of the elderly.

Child-Care Activities   Turnbull (1983) has remarked that one of the significant universal roles of elderly grandparents is babysitting. While the parents in foraging societies are involved in subsistence chores like hunting and collecting, grandparents often are engaged in child-care activities. Among the Ju/'hoansi or San and the Mbuti, elderly grandparents care for small children while the children's mothers are away on gathering activities. The elderly teach the grandchildren the skills, norms, and values of the society. Reflecting on the Mbuti Pygmy elders, who spend time in storytelling and reciting myths and legends, Turnbull indicates that this role is the primary function of the Mbuti elderly in the maintenance of culture. In most foraging societies, this is the typical pattern for relationships between the young and the old.

Political Organization in Foraging Societies

Just as the band is the fundamental element of social organization in most hunting-and-gathering societies, it is also the basic political unit. As we saw in the discussion of social organization, bands are tied together through kinship and marriage, creating reciprocal economic and social relationships throughout the community. Each band, however, is politically independent of the others and has its own internal leadership. Most of the leaders in the bands are males, but females also take on some important leadership roles. Leaders are chosen because of their skills in hunting, food collecting, communication, decision making, or other personal abilities.

Political leaders generally do not control the group's economic resources or exercise political power as they do in other societies, and there is little, if any, social stratification between political leaders and others in the band. In other words, band societies are highly egalitarian, with no fundamental differences between those with and those without wealth or political power. Thus, leaders of bands must lead by persuasion and personal influence rather than by coercion or withholding resources. Leaders do not maintain a military or police force and thus have no definitive authority.

In recent extensive cross-cultural studies of the political processes of hunting-gathering societies, Christopher Boehm (1993, 1999) developed an imaginative hypothesis to explain the lack of political power and domination in these egalitarian societies. Boehm suggested that there is a pattern of *reverse dominance* in these societies, which keeps anyone from becoming coercive or politically dominating the group in any manner. Reverse dominance ensures that the whole group will have control over anybody who tries to assert political power or authority over them. Reverse dominance is practiced through criticism and ridicule, disobedience, strong disapproval, execution of offenders or extremely aggressive males, deposing leaders, or outright desertion (an entire group leaving a particularly dominant leader). Boehm finds that reverse dominance and related political processes are widespread in band societies, reinforcing patterns of egalitarianism.

In a related hypothesis, Peter Gardner (1991) suggests that foraging societies tend to have strong cultural values that emphasize individual autonomy. Like Boehm, Gardner suggests that hunter-gatherers dislike being dominated and disdain conforming to norms that restrict their individual freedom. From reviewing many cases of band societies, Gardner indicates that the cultural values promoting individual autonomy enable these people to sustain their egalitarian way of life while promoting flexibility in their behavior, a distinguishing feature of foraging societies.

Characteristics of Leadership

In most cases, individuals in hunting-and-gathering societies do not seek out leadership roles, because there are few benefits or advantages in becoming a leader. Leaders do not accrue power or economic resources in these egalitarian societies. They do, however, have a tremendous responsibility for the management of the band. In a classic essay in political anthropology, Claude Levi-Strauss (1944) described the band leader of the Nambikuara of South America as entirely responsible for selecting the territories for procuring game; ordering and organizing hunting, fishing, and collecting activities; and determining the conduct of the band in relation to other groups in the region. Yet Levi-Strauss emphasized the consensual aspect of this leadership pattern. The leader has no coercive power and must continuously display skill in building consensus within the band to provide political order.

A quotation from a Ju/'hoansi or San leader sums up the pattern of leadership among hunter-gatherer societies: "All you get is the blame if things go wrong." Morton Fried (1967) notes a remark frequently heard from band leaders: "If this is done it will be good." These remarks indicate the lack of authority that leaders of bands have in these societies. Levi-Strauss (1944), however, states that some people in all societies desire the nonmaterial benefits such as prestige that can be gained through assuming leadership responsibilities. Therefore, despite the lack of political power or material benefits, foraging leaders may be motivated by other cultural concerns.

Another characteristic of band political leadership is that it is transient; leaders of bands do not hold permanent positions or offices. This informal leadership pattern adds to the weakness of centralized political authority in band societies. Informal leadership is somewhat situational in that it varies according to circumstances; the band will call on the appropriate type of leader when dealing with a specific type of activity. In some bands, for example, certain individuals may be good at solving disputes within the band or between bands. These individuals may be chosen to deal with such problems when they arise. In general, then, band leadership is diffuse and decentralized.

This minimal pattern of leadership also involves an informal type of political succession. Most hunting-and-gathering societies have no definitive rules for passing leadership from one individual to another. Rather, leadership is based on personal characteristics. It may also be based on supernatural powers that the individual is believed to possess. When an individual dies, his or her influence and authority also die. This lack of rules for succession emphasizes the decentralization of political power and authority in band societies.

Warfare and Violence

Contemporary foraging societies generally engage in very limited warfare. Carol Ember's (1978) cross-cultural research indicates that 64 percent of the worldwide sample of foraging societies engaged in warfare at least once every two years. Most of the ethnographic evidence, however, suggests that warfare among foragers took the form of sporadic violence rather than continual fighting. Because almost the entire population was engaged in the day-to-day hunting and collecting of food, no long-term fighting could be sustained. Also, the lack of centralized political institutions to implement large-scale military mobilization inhibits the development of intense or frequent warfare. No standing armies with specialized warriors can be organized for continual warfare.

The Tiwi of Australia provide a classic case of "restrained" warfare among foraging populations (Hart, Pilling, & Goodale, 1988). War parties of thirty men from two different bands, each armed with spears and wearing white paint symbolizing anger and hostility, met in an adjoining territory. The dispute had originated because some of the males

Australian aborigine children in body paint.

from one band had apparently seduced females from the opposing band. In addition, the senior males of one of the bands had not delivered on their promise to bestow daughters to the other band—a deliberate violation of the norms of reciprocal marital exchange. Both sides first exchanged insults and then agreed to meet with one another on the following day to renew old acquaintances and to socialize. On the third day, the duel resumed, with males throwing spears in all directions, resulting in a chaotic episode in which some people, including spectators, were wounded. Most of the battle, however, involved violent talk and verbal, rather than physical, abuse. Although variations on this type of warfare existed among the Tiwi, warfare generally did not result in great bloodshed.

Richard Lee described conflict among the Ju/'hoansi or San, which involves fights and homicides. Lee (1993) found twenty-two cases of homicide by males and other periodic violence, usually related to internal disputes over women. As Eric Wolf

(1987:130) comments: "Clearly the !Kung are not the 'Harmless People' that some have thought them to be: They fight and sometimes injure other individual !Kung."

Anthropologist Bruce Knauft (1988) has summarized several generalizations concerning violence in foraging societies. First, these societies lack a competitive male-status hierarchy; in fact, there is a strong tendency to discourage this type of interpersonal competition. Status competition among males is a major source of violent conflict in other types of societies. Second, in contrast to many other societies, public displays of interpersonal violence are not culturally valued among foragers. Instead, these societies seek to minimize animosities. Finally, because of the emphasis on sharing food and other resources, rights to property are not restricted. All of these factors serve to reduce the amount of violence in these societies.

Conflict Resolution

Because of the lack of formal government institutions and political authority, social control in foraging societies is based on informal sanctions. One basic mode of conflict resolution that occurs frequently among groups such as the Ju/'hoansi or San is for the people involved to move to another band. Thus, the flexibility of band organization itself is an effective means of reducing conflict. Furthermore, the economic and social reciprocities and the frequent exchanges among bands also serve to reduce conflicts. These reciprocal ties create mutual obligations and interdependencies that promote cooperative relationships.

Nevertheless, violations of norms do lead to more structured or more ritualized means of conflict resolution in foraging societies. Among the Mbuti, for example, age groups play specific roles in the conflict resolution process. Children play an essential role in resolving conflicts involving misbehavior such as laziness, quarreling, or selfishness. Children ridicule people who engage in these behaviors, even if these people are adults. Young children excel at this form of ridicule, which usually is sufficient to resolve the conflict.

When these measures do not succeed, the elders in the group assert their authority. They try to evaluate the dispute carefully and show why things went wrong. If necessary, they walk to the center of the camp and criticize individuals by name, although they frequently use humor to soften their criticism. Through this process, elders reinforce the norms and values of Mbuti society (Turnbull, 1983).

The Inuit (Eskimo) Song Duel Another example of dispute resolution is the Inuit song duel. The song duel was often used to resolve conflicts between males over a particular female. Because Inuit society lacks specific rules of marriage, males would sometimes accuse others of wife stealing. In these types of conflicts, the two males encountered each other in front of a large public meeting. They then insulted each other through improvised songs, and the crowd resolved the conflict by selecting a winner. With the declaration of a winner, the dispute was resolved without the use of any formal court system or coercion (Hoebel, [1954] 1968).

Religion in Foraging Societies

The religions associated with modern foragers are based on oral traditions referred to by Mircea Eliade (1959) as "cosmic religions." Cosmic religions are intimately associated with nature. The natural cycle of seasons; inorganic matter such as rocks, water, and mountains; and other features of the natural environment are invested with sacred significance. Spirit and matter are inseparable. In addition, cosmic religions are not identified with any particular historical events or individuals, as are the "literate" religious traditions of Judaism, Islam, Christianity, Buddhism, and Hinduism.

The sacredness of the natural environment is sometimes expressed in a form of **animism,** the belief that spirits reside within all inorganic and organic substances. Yet, as applied to the metaphysical conceptions in the Ju/'hoansi or San, the Australian Aborigine, or Mbuti cultural systems, the label *animism* appears too simplistic. Concepts of a god or gods are found in combination with animistic beliefs.

The Dreamtime

An illuminating example of a cosmic religion among foragers is the Australian Aborigine notion of *dreamtime* (Stanner, 1979). The dreamtime exists in the "other world," the world associated with the time of creation, where a person goes in dreams and visions and after death. It is believed that at the time of creation, the ancestors deposited souls of all living forms near watering holes, and eventually these souls or spirits were embedded in all matter, from rocks and water to trees and humans. The unification of all substance and spirit was a byproduct of the work of these ancestral beings. All of these spirits come to the world from the dreamtime; the birth of the universe is like a fall from the dreamtime.

The Aborigines believe that the ancestral beings still exist in the dreamtime, where they act as intermediaries between that world and the profane, everyday world of human affairs. The ancestral beings intervene in life, controlling plant, animal, and human life, and death. This fundamental belief provides explanations for pain, joy, chaos, and order in human life. The dreamtime is a fundamental and complex conception that embraces the creative past and has particular significance for the present and future.

According to Aborigine conceptions, life without the dreamtime is extremely unsatisfactory. The invisible side of life can become visible through rituals, ceremonies, myths, art, and dreams. Aborigines believe that through these activities they can communicate with their ancestral beings. This belief is reflected in Aborigine rites of passage. In initiation ceremonies, it is believed that the individual moves farther and farther back into the dreamtime. In puberty rituals—which for males included circumcision, subincision (the cutting of the penis lengthwise to the urethra), and other bloodletting actions—the individual is dramatically moved from one status to another through contact with the dreamtime. The rite of passage at death moves the individual into the invisibility of the dreamtime.

The dreamtime also conveys certain notions of morality. According to Aborigine traditions, the ancestral beings originally lived like other humans and had the capacity for being both moral and immoral, both good and evil (Stanner, 1979). The immoral behavior of the dreamtime beings is highlighted to accentuate what is proper and moral in human affairs. Thus, this religion creates a moral order that functions to sustain social control in the physical world. Although the dreamtime ancestors do not directly punish human wrongdoers, they have provided a blueprint for proper behavior with respect to obligations, reciprocities, and social behavior in general.

Inuit (Eskimo) Religion

The Inuit maintain a traditional religious belief system that involves curers or healers who control and manipulate the supernatural world. In contrast to some of the "literate" religious traditions, Inuit religion did not assume the existence of an omnipotent supreme being. The Inuit did believe that every living creature possessed a soul or spirit that is reincarnated after death. They believed that the souls of deceased individuals remain in the vicinity of the living. The Inuit did not maintain a belief in an afterworld, or heaven, in which these souls congregate after death. Rather, they believed that these souls remained close to the natural world. The spirits of animals allow themselves to be hunted and are constantly reincarnated in other animal forms, to be hunted again to ensure the Inuit way of life.

Within these general conceptions of spirituality, the Inuit believed in *soul loss,* in which a person's soul is taken from the body as a result of unforeseen circumstances. Soul loss causes mental and physical illness for the individual. It is often believed that the soul has been stolen by another spirit. The Inuit coped with these situations through *shamanism.*

Two different forms of shamanism are found in Inuit culture: one form is hereditary, passed on through either parent; the more common variety involves people who receive shamanistic powers through direct contact with the supernatural, usually through dreams, visions, or hallucinations.

People usually go through an extensive training period before they can begin practicing as a shaman. Inuit shamans learn various relaxation techniques to induce trance states. They also learn methods of healing, curing, and exorcism. These techniques are used to produce group emotional experiences to enhance spiritual growth. In many cases, the shamanistic performances work effectively in curing illnesses or resolving emotional problems. Undoubtedly, in certain instances the Inuit beliefs and cultural conceptions surrounding shamanism trigger certain states of mind that produce positive psychological and even physical consequences, such as overcoming illness and injuries.

An example of Australian aborigine rock painting illustrating mythical themes regarding how an individual was transformed into a turtle after violating the incest taboo.

Art, Music, and Religion

The art of foraging societies is intimately related to nature. Animals, plants, humans, and other components of the natural environment are the major subjects. This naturalistic art also has a religious significance, as nature and spirit are viewed as inseparable. Rock paintings with highly symbolic images of natural phenomena are found in most foraging societies. It is believed that this art is sacred and can be used to make contact with supernatural sources.

Traditional Inuit art products include many items made from ivory, one of the few rigid materials available in the Arctic. Human and animal figurines, which were worn as amulets to enhance supernatural powers and practices, dominate Inuit artistic output. The Inuit also carve masks in ivory (or sometimes wood) for use by their shamans.

The music of foraging societies is generally divided into recreational (folk or popular) and religious music. The Mbuti, for example, have no instrumental music, but they have many songs and dances. In their vocal music they have a precise sense of harmony, giving each singer one note to produce at a given moment. This leads to a harmonic pattern that is passed around a circle of people. This technique is often used in Mbuti recreational music.

The sacred music of the Mbuti is much more important than their recreational music, and much of it is linked to the *Elima* rites of passage discussed earlier. In the *Elima,* young girls and boys sing back and forth to one another in harmony. Other sacred songs are sung by males only. The intensity of the singing builds in order that it may reach the spirit of the rain forest. One of the hunters goes off into the forest to echo the song of his fellows, so that the spirit may be sure to hear it. As in most societies, Mbuti ritual music usually follows a standardized form, with little improvisation allowed. Ritual music helps sustain the cultural and spiritual traditions of the people. The lyrics of the music emphasize the sacred symbols that are maintained in Mbuti society. As the group chants the music together, a sense of sacredness is created in the community.

Music and religion are inextricably bound within the shamanistic rituals of the Inuit. In the shamanistic performances, a drum is used to enhance the rhythmic songs. The shaman's songs are simple, chantlike recitations that have no actual words. Short phrases are repeated again and again. The drumming and song chants are used to establish contact with the spirits. Anthropologist Rodney Needham (1967) suggested that the use of instruments such as the drum in shamanistic rituals not only heightens the spiritual atmosphere of the ceremony but also affects psychological (and neurological) processes that produce altered states of consciousness in individuals.

SUMMARY

Unlike the hunter-gatherers, or foragers, of the Paleolithic period, modern foraging societies have adapted to marginal environments: deserts, tropical rain forests, and arctic regions. The subsistence patterns of band societies in these environments require a mobile, nomadic lifestyle. Foragers must move frequently to procure their basic food resources.

Population growth among foragers within specific territories is minimal. This slow growth rate is due to fissioning and other practices that minimize the number of individuals within a territory. Cultural anthropologists have been studying foragers to determine whether low fertility rates are due to biological or cultural factors. The technology of foragers is refined to enable adjustments to the practical needs of their environmental conditions. They have developed economic patterns that depend on reciprocity and resource sharing to produce cooperative behavior. Generally, a foraging economy does not depend on private property but rather on kinship and family ownership.

The social organization of foraging societies is based on kinship, age, and gender. Kinship relations are maintained among different multifamily bands through marriage. Generally, people marry outside their own band. Gender relations are related to the division of labor; in most societies men hunt and women gather. To some extent, this division of labor determines the status of females. Age is also an important determinant of status in foraging societies. As individuals move through the life cycle, they learn more about their society. When they reach old age, they are respected for their knowledge and teaching skills.

Political organization is limited in foraging societies. There is no formal, centralized political authority. Leadership is based on personal qualities and is not permanent. Although violence exists, usually among males, warfare is infrequent and restrained because of the limited political organization.

Religion in foraging societies is based on a unity between spiritual and material forces. Healers and shamans are the religious specialists who serve the people's spiritual needs. The art forms found among foragers reflect the spiritual aspects of their culture. The most common subjects are components of the natural environment, including plants, animals, and human beings.

QUESTIONS TO THINK ABOUT

1. What can we learn from studying hunter-gatherer societies that might help us understand and interpret life in industrial societies today?

2. How can the study of contemporary foragers provide us with an understanding of Paleolithic lifestyles?

3. What types of economic exchange would you expect to find in hunter-gatherer societies? Are the individuals in foraging societies more altruistic, magnanimous, and generous, or are they no more noble than other peoples?

4. Is private ownership of land a universal concept that applies to all societies? How much variation in "ownership" is found among forager groups?

5. Evaluate the hypothesis that in societies in which female contributions to the food supply are less critical or less valued than male contributions, female status is lower.

6. Would you rather be involved in warfare as a member of a forager society or as a member of an industrial nation? Why?

7. How are forager religions different from your own? Are there any similarities?

KEY TERMS

animism
balanced reciprocity

band
brideservice

cross-cousin marriage
egalitarian

extended families

fissioning

foraging society

generalized reciprocity

hunter-gatherer society

infanticide

marginal environments

matrilocal residence

negative reciprocity

nuclear family

patriarchal

patrilocal residence

reciprocal economic system

reciprocity

INTERNET EXERCISES

1. Read over the website **http://www.ucalgary. ca/~walde/paleo.html**. How can the movement of Paleoindians across Beringia be compared to band societies presented in this chapter? What are the problems identified here that archaeologists face when studying this overall problem?

2. Look at the ecological model described by Flannery at **http://www.unl.edu/rhames/ courses/for97notes.htm**. What is meant by the phrase "ingenious team of lay botanists"? How does Flannery's view vary from that of Lubbock? Why do you think the differences between the two views are so great?

SUGGESTED READINGS

BICCHIERI, M. G. (Ed.). 1972. *Hunters and Gatherers Today*. New York: Holt, Rinehart & Winston. A collection of eleven ethnographic portraits of foraging societies that exist in different parts of the world.

INGOLD, TIM, DAVID RICHES, and JAMES WOODBURN (Eds.). 1991. *Hunters and Gatherers: History, Evolution and Social Change*, Vol. 1. New York: Berg.

———. 1992. *Hunters and Gatherers: Property, Power and Ideology*, Vol. 2. New York: Berg. A two-volume collection of state-of-the-art essays on hunters and gatherers worldwide.

KATZ, RICHARD. 1982. *Boiling Energy: Community Healing among the Kalahari !Kung*. Cambridge, MA: Harvard University Press. An excellent descriptive account of the healers among the !Kung San and how they serve both spiritual and material needs.

SHOSTAK, MARJORIE. 1981. *Nisa: The Life and Words of a !Kung Woman*. New York: Vintage Books. An extensive biography of a San woman. It has become a modern classic of anthropology.

TURNBULL, COLIN. 1961. *The Forest People: A Study of the Pygmies of the Congo*. New York: Simon & Schuster. A wonderfully written book that evokes the personal lives of the Mbuti people of the Ituri rain forest.

16

Tribes

CHAPTER OUTLINE

CHAPTER QUESTIONS

- What problems do anthropologists encounter in trying to use the term *tribe* to classify various societies?

- What are the basic environmental, demographic, technological, and economic features associated with tribal societies?

- Compare the complexities of social organization in tribal societies with those in band societies.

- What are the differences in gender relations in tribal societies compared to those in band societies?

- What are the characteristics of tribal political relationships?

- What are the unique expressions of religion, art, and music among tribal peoples?

In Chapter 14 we introduced the typologies that anthropologists use to classify different forms of political systems. For example, hunter-gatherer societies are classified as *band* political systems. The term *tribe* is used loosely to characterize two different types of subsistence systems: horticulturalist and pastoralist. Unlike hunting-and-gathering societies, tribal societies are food-producing groups that depend on the limited domestication of plants and animals. Figure 16.1 shows the distribution of tribal societies around the world. Politically, tribes are noncentralized sociocultural systems in which authority is diffused among a number of kinship groups and associations. These characteristics are explored in this chapter.

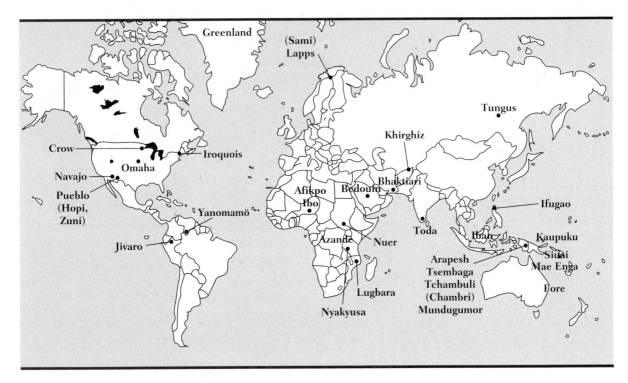

FIGURE 16.1 This map highlights many tribal societies, including those discussed in this chapter.

Some anthropologists, most notably the late Morton Fried (1967, 1975), have objected to the use of the term *tribe* to characterize these societies. The word *tribe* is derived from the Latin term *tribus,* which was used by the Romans to refer to certain peoples who were not technologically advanced. Fried claimed that the term is often applied to a particular group by a more powerful group and usually has a pejorative connotation.

One aspect of Fried's criticism has created some theoretical controversy in anthropology. Fried argued that tribal organization is not an evolutionary stage emerging from the simpler stage represented by the foraging society, as most anthropologists had maintained. He suggested that, for the most part, tribes are usually "secondary" developments that evolve through contacts with other societies. This contact occurs when large, complex state societies, both agricultural and industrial, create tribal groups through the process of subjugation and domination. In many cases, these tribal groups become subjugated ethnic minorities in state societies.

We examine these processes later in the text, especially in Chapter 20.

Fried's criticisms have sensitized most anthropologists to the vagueness of the term *tribe*. In the past and sometimes currently, the term has been used haphazardly to refer to an enormous range of societies that have almost nothing in common. Despite these reservations, the term is still used to categorize the many different types of horticulturalist and pastoralist societies and to denote a form of political complexity and evolutionary development that bridges the gap between bands and centralized societies (Lewellen, 1983).

Environment and Subsistence for Horticulturalists

Horticulture is a form of agriculture in which people use a limited, nonmechanized technology to cultivate plants. One major type of horticulture is known as *slash-and-burn cultivation*. This system was once widespread but today is found primarily in tropical rain forests. Approximately 250 million people throughout the world currently engage in slash-and-burn cultivation (Moran, 1982).

Slash-and-burn cultivation involves the production of food without the intensive use of land, a large labor force, or complex technology. As generally practiced, it is a cyclical process that begins with clearing a tract of land by cutting down the trees and then setting fire to the brush. The burned vegetation and ashes remain, and the nutrients from them are unlocked and sink into the soil. After the land is cleared and burned, various crops are planted. In most cases, women and children spend a great deal of time weeding and tending the gardens. Typically, after the crops are planted and harvested for several years, the garden plot is left fallow (unplanted) for three to fifteen years, and the cultivators must shift to a new location.

People who practice slash-and-burn cultivation must maintain a delicate balance with their environment. If the plot is not left fallow and is cultivated too often, grasses and weeds may colonize the area at the expense of forest regrowth. The land then becomes useless or overexploited. Some horticulturalists have recleared their land too often and brought devastation to some forest environments; others

have been able to reside in one location for almost a century (Carneiro, 1961). In general, compared with foragers, slash-and-burn horticulturalists are less nomadic and more sedentary.

Amazon Horticulturalists: The Yanomamö

One South American tribal group, known as the Yanomamö, practices slash-and-burn cultivation. Napoleon Chagnon studied the Yanomamö for more than thirty years. Approximately 80 to 90 percent of their diet comes from their gardens (Chagnon, 1997). Yanomamö males clear the forest, burn the vegetation, and plant the crops; the females (and sometimes children) weed the garden and eventually harvest the crops. Generally, the Yanomamö do not work on subsistence activities for food production more than three to four hours per day. A Yanomamö garden lasts for about three years from the time of the initial planting; after this period, the garden is overrun with scrub vegetation, and the soil becomes depleted.

Early cultural ecologists assumed that slash-and-burn cultivators are forced to relocate because the soil becomes exhausted. Chagnon, however, has shown that Yanomamö decisions to move are not based simply on soil depletion. In fact, as the soil begins to lose its capacity to support crops, the

A tropical forest in the first stages of slash-and-burn horticulture.

Yanomamö make small adjustments, such as extending a previous garden or clearing a new tract of land near the old one. Chagnon discovered that major population movements of the Yanomamö are due instead to warfare and conflict with neighboring groups. Thus, a sedentary life in these Amazonian societies is not simply a product of ecological conditions; it also involves strategic alliances and political maneuvers designed to deal with human populations in nearby communities (Chagnon, 1997).

Although horticulture is the primary subsistence activity of many Amazonian tribes, hunting, fishing, and gathering typically supplement this activity. The Yanomamö gather wild foods, especially palm fruits and a variety of nuts, pods, tubers, mushrooms, and honey. They hunt game birds and a number of animals. In addition, they collect toads, frogs, and many varieties of insects.

New Guinea Horticulturalists: The Tsembaga

The Papua New Guinea highlands contain many horticulturalist populations, some of whom were not contacted by Western society until the 1950s and 1960s. Archaeologists have traced early horticultural developments in highland New Guinea to 7000 B.C. (White & O'Connell, 1982). One group, the Tsembaga Maring, has been studied thoroughly by anthropologist Roy Rappaport (1984).

The Tsembaga live in two river valley areas surrounded by mountains. They cultivate the mountain slopes with their subsistence gardens. Tsembaga males and females clear the undergrowth from the secondary forest, after which the men cut down the trees. When the cut vegetation dries out, it is stacked up and burned. The women then plant and harvest crops, especially sweet potatoes, taro, manioc, and yams; 99 percent of the Tsembaga diet by weight consists of vegetables, particularly these root crops. The Tsembaga also domesticate pigs, but these animals are usually consumed only during certain ritual occasions.

Horticulturalists in Woodland Forest Areas: The Iroquois

In the past, many Native American groups such as the Iroquois, who resided in the eastern woodland region of North America, practiced horticulture. Rivers such as the St. Lawrence drain into the area,

providing fertile ground for horticultural activities. These horticultural practices probably appeared between 2300 and 1000 B.C. The native peoples of this region began to raise maize and other crops along with local wild species. Most archaeologists have concluded that this horticultural pattern of maize, beans, and squash originated in Mesoamerica and then extended across the Gulf of Mexico and up the Mississippi River, spreading out to the Ohio River valley areas and eastward to Native American groups such as the Iroquois.

The Iroquois constructed their villages with longhouses in the center of the settlement. (*Longhouses* were large, multifamily housing built with upright posts that supported horizontal poles for rafters. Large slabs of bark, laced together with cords of plant fiber, covered the framework.)

Iroquois males cleared the primary forest around the village and burned the cut litter. In the spring the women planted fifteen varieties of maize, beans, squash, and other crops, which females later harvested and processed. The Iroquois left part of the primary forest standing so that deer, squirrels, fox, and bear were available for hunting. The forest also provided nuts, berries, and many species of wild plants.

After harvesting the crops in the fall, the men would concentrate their subsistence activities on game such as deer and bear. In the spring, while the women planted crops, the men fished in the many lakes and rivers and also captured birds. Like many other slash-and-burn cultivators, the Iroquois farmed their fields until the fields were no longer fertile, after which they cleared new fields while the old ones lay fallow. After a generation or so, depending on local conditions, the fertile fields were located far enough away from the village that the entire community moved so that it could be closer to the gardens.

Environment and Subsistence for Pastoralists

In central Asia, the Middle East, North and East Africa, and the subarctic regions, there were—and, in some cases, still are—**pastoralists,** groups whose subsistence activities are based on the care of domesticated animals. The use of herd animals differs

Bedouin pastoralist with camels in the Middle East.

from group to group. The Bedouins of Arabia, for example, use the camel mainly for transportation and other purposes and only sometimes consume the meat. Other pastoralist groups, such as the Sami (Lapps) of Scandinavia, have in the past completely depended on caribou, deriving most of their food and other vital resources from them. Although some pastoralists may have small gardens, most of them have only their herd animals for subsistence purposes.

The care of herd animals requires frequent moves from camp to camp and sometimes involves long migrations. Some groups such as the Tungus of Siberia, who are reindeer pastoralists, trek more than 1,000 miles annually. The Basseri of southern Iran, who keep goats, sheep, horses, and donkeys, migrate seasonally through mountainous regions in a strip of land 300 miles long, an area of about 2,000 square miles (Barth, 1961). These pastoralist migrations are not aimless; the groups know the layout of the land and move to territories that contain specific grazing pastures or waterholes during different seasons.

East African Cattle Complex

In an area stretching from southern Sudan through Kenya, Uganda, Rwanda, Burundi, Tanzania, Mozambique, and into parts of South Africa, various pastoralists herd cattle as their means of subsistence.

Most of these groups do not depend entirely on their cattle for subsistence needs, but they plant gardens to supplement their food resources.

The Nuer Anthropologist E. E. Evans-Pritchard (1940, 1951, 1956) conducted a classic study of a pastoralist group called the Nuer. The Nuer reside along the upper Nile River and its tributaries in southern Sudan. Because of the flatness of this region, the annual flooding of the Nile during the rainy season, and the heavy clay soils, the Nuer spend the wet season on high, sandy ground, where they plant sorghum, a cereal grass used for grain. This horticulture is very limited, however, because strong rainfall, as well as elephants, birds, and insects, destroy the crops. Therefore, cattle are the most important subsistence resource for the Nuer.

The Nuer view cattle herding with a great deal of pride. In the dry season they move with their cattle into the grassland areas. The cattle transform the energy stored in the grasses, herbs, and shrubs into valuable subsistence products. Yet, as is true of other herders in this area, the basis of the Nuer subsistence is not consumption of cattle. Rather, they depend heavily on the blood and milk of their animals. Every few months during the dry season, the cattle are bled by making small incisions that heal quickly. The Nuer boil the blood until it gets thick, then roast it and eat it. The cows are milked morning and night; some of the milk is used to make butter. The Nuer slaughter their old cattle, which then calls for elaborate ceremonies or sacrifices.

Demographics and Settlement

Generally, as humans developed the capacity to produce food through the domestication of animals and plants, the carrying capacity of particular territories increased to support a greater population density than had been possible for band societies. Whereas foraging populations had to live in small bands, tribal societies became much more densely populated. According to Murdock's (1967) cross-cultural tabulations, the median size of horticulturalist societies ranges from 100 to more than 5,000 people in specific territories, and pastoralists have a median size of 2,000 people in particular niches. Some tribal populations have denser populations in large regions in which villages are connected through economic, social, and political relationships.

Compared with most foraging societies, tribal societies are relatively settled within fairly well-defined territories. As mentioned earlier, horticulturalists are somewhat mobile, having to move to fertile lands every so often, but they generally settle in one locale for a number of years.

Of course, pastoralist societies are nomadic, but their wanderings are limited to specific pastures and grasslands to care for their animals. Because pastoralists move seasonally from pasture to pasture, they place less intense population pressure on each area. Population densities for pastoralists range from 1 to 5 persons per square mile of land; however, in the richly endowed grassland environment of central Asia, the Kalmuk Mongols maintain an average density of about 18 people per square mile. In general, pastoralist populations are denser than are those of foragers, but both are spread thinly over the land (Sahlins, 1968b).

Like foraging societies, both horticulturalist and pastoralist societies experience only slow population growth because of limited resources. To regulate their populations, tribal societies have adopted the same strategies as bands, especially fissioning. Other cultural practices designed to control population growth include sexual abstinence, infanticide, abortion, and a prolonged period of nursing.

Technology

The whole range of tribal technologies is extremely broad and varies among differing populations depending on whether they are horticulturalists or pastoralists and to what types of environments they have had to adapt. Technological innovations found in tribal societies include woodworking, weaving, leather working, and the production of numerous copper ornaments, tools, and weapons.

Horticulturalist Technology

Horticulturalist groups used sharpened digging sticks and sometimes wooden hoes to plant small gardens. Slash-and-burn horticulturalists such as the Yanomamö and the Iroquois used crude stone or wooden axes to fell the primary forest. It sometimes took weeks for a small group of males to cut down a wooded area for a garden.

Many horticultural societies have also developed technologies to aid in hunting and fishing to supplement their horticultural activities. For example, some Amazonian peoples such as the Jivaro of Ecuador and Peru often use blowguns, which propel poison darts up to 45 yards, to kill monkeys and birds deep in the forest (Harner, 1972). The Yanomamö use large, powerful bows, sometimes 5 to 6 feet long, and long arrow shafts with a splintered point dipped in curare, a deadly poison (Chagnon, 1997). Amazonian horticulturalists also pour poisons into local waters, causing the fish to rise to the surface in a stupefied condition; they are then gathered for food (Harner, 1972; Chagnon, 1997).

The woodland Iroquois used both the blowgun and the bow (called the *self-bow*) and arrow to hunt game in surrounding forests. The Iroquois carefully selected light wooden branches for arrow shafts, dried them to season the wood, and then smoothed them with stone and bone tools. To make the arrow twist in flight, they took feathers from eagles, turkeys, and hawks, which they then attached with a glue made from animal tissues, sinew, or horns. Arrowheads were made from wood, stone, horn, antler, shell, or raw copper (Garbarino, 1988).

Horticulturalists such as the Pacific islanders, who were not slash-and-burn farmers and resided in more permanent locations, tended to have a more elaborate technology. In addition to the simple digging stick used to cultivate the irrigated gardens, they had many other sophisticated tools and utensils. Although the Pacific islanders had no metals or clay for pottery, they had many specialized kinds of shell and woodworking tools for making jewelry, knives, rasps, and files.

Pastoralist Technology

The mobility required by the pastoralist lifestyle prevented these groups from using an elaborate technology. Pastoralists such as the Mongols and the Bedouins carried all of their belongings with them in their yearly migrations. Their technologies aided them in these mass movements; for example, they had saddles for their horses and camels, weapons for hunting, equipment for taking care of their livestock and processing food, and tents that could be moved during migrations. Other pastoralists such as the Nuer of East Africa constructed huts of thatch in permanent locations that served as home bases where a certain number of people remained during the migration season.

Economics

As in hunting-and-gathering societies, reciprocity is the dominant form of exchange of economic resources in tribal economic systems. All three forms of reciprocity—generalized, balanced, and negative—are used by tribal societies. Generalized reciprocity tends to occur within close kinship groupings. Balanced and negative reciprocity occur among more distant kinship groupings. One example of balanced reciprocity occurs among the Yanomamö, who maintain a system of trade and feasting activities with other villages. One village will host a feast, inviting another village to attend. During the feast, the villagers exchange tools, pots, baskets, arrows, dogs, yarn, and hallucinogenic drugs. The feast activities sustain intervillage cooperation, marital exchanges, and political and military alliances (Chagnon, 1997). The villagers calculate these transactions and exchanges very carefully to determine exact equivalencies. If an equal return is not given, then the original donor village will discontinue the exchange relationship. This may lead to hostilities and perhaps warfare between the villages.

Money

Unlike foragers, some tribal societies engage in monetary exchange, that is, transactions that involve money. **Money** is a medium of exchange based on a standard value. According to economists, money has four functions:

1. It enables people to pay for a good or service, and then it circulates to allow for subsequent purchases.

2. It serves as a uniform standard of value for goods and services within a society.

3. It has a store of value; that is, its standard of value does not fluctuate radically from one time to another.

4. It serves as a form of deferred payment; that is, it can express a promise to pay in the future with the same standard value. (Neale, 1976)

Economic anthropologists classify money into two types: general-purpose money (or multipurpose money) and limited-purpose money (or special-purpose money). *General-purpose money* serves all four of the above functions. It can be used as a medium of exchange for most of the goods and services in society. *Limited-purpose money,* in contrast, is restricted for the purchase of certain goods and services. The paper currencies used in the United States and other industrial societies are examples of general-purpose money. In contrast, most tribal societies that practice monetary exchange use limited-purpose money.

Peoples in some of the Pacific islands and other coastal areas have used a variety of shells to conduct trade relations. In other tribal societies, livestock, cloth, salt, feathers, animal teeth, and, sometimes, women functioned as money. This type of money was used for specialized exchange circumstances. For example, the Siane of New Guinea exchanged food for other subsistence goods, and luxury items such as bird feathers were exchanged only for other luxury items. Another separate level of exchange took place with respect to prestige items such as certain forms of shell necklaces (Salisbury, 1962).

Property Ownership

Ownership of property—especially land for horticulturalists and animals for pastoralists—takes on significance in tribal societies that it does not have in band societies. The concept of property ownership becomes more clearly defined in tribal societies and is based on a web of social relations involving rights, privileges, and perhaps duties and obligations regarding the use of a particular piece of land, a herd of animals, or other objects.

In tribal societies, exclusive right to use property is rare. With some exceptions, property rights in tribal societies are generally invested in family and wider kinship groupings. Usually tribal families have *use rights* to farmland, pastures, animals, and other items. The property of tribal societies is transferred to families through inheritance; individual access to property, however, is largely determined by *status*. In other words, in tribal societies, an individual gains certain rights, privileges, and obligations with respect to property through inheriting a particular status position. Status in tribal societies is usually determined by kinship, age, and gender, as we shall discuss later in the chapter.

Property rights in tribal societies are not completely static with respect to statuses. Rather, they may fluctuate according to the availability of basic resources. If land is plentiful in a specific tribe, for example, outsiders who need land may be granted rights to use the land. On the other hand, if there is a shortage of land, rights to that property may become more narrowly defined and may be defended if the land is intruded on. Grazing land for pastoralists or arable land for horticulturalists may become limited, and, if so, use rights may be defined more exclusively for particular family and kinship groupings. In contrast to foraging societies, in tribal societies warfare frequently results from encroachments on more narrowly defined property.

Tribal societies generally possess certain types of personal property. Horticulturalists typically have more personal property than do pastoralists, because they are more sedentary. Because of the demands of a nomadic life, pastoralist property tends to be portable (saddles, tents, and similar objects), whereas much horticultural property tends to be immovable, like housing structures and land. Because families based on large kin groupings owned most tribal property, individuals generally do not have the opportunity to amass concentrations of wealth. The limited technological capabilities and reciprocal economic system of tribal societies also restrict the capacity of individuals to accumulate large stores of wealth. Consequently, tribal societies tend to be egalitarian with respect to the ownership of property.

Social Organization

Tribal societies differ from foraging societies in that tribal peoples produce most of their subsistence foods through small-scale cultivation and the domestication of animals. The evolution of food-producing subsistence corresponds to the development of new forms of social organization. As is true among foragers, social organization among tribes is largely based on kinship. Rules concerning kinship, marriage, and other social systems, however, are much more elaborate in tribal societies, which have to resolve new types of problems including denser populations, control of land or livestock, and, sometimes, warfare.

New and diverse forms of social organization have enabled tribal societies to adjust to the new conditions of food production. Unlike foragers, who sometimes have to remain separate from one another in small, flexibly organized bands, food producers have had to develop social relationships that are more fixed and permanent. Tribal social organization is based on family, the descent group, gender, and age. The social organization of tribal societies is much more complex than that of band societies.

Families

The most common social grouping among tribal societies is the extended family. Most extended families consist of three generations—grandparents, parents, and children—although they can also contain married siblings with their spouses and children. Compared with the nuclear family, the extended family is a larger and more stable social unit that is more effective in organizing and carrying out domestic economic and subsistence activities (Pasternak, 1976). Even the extended family, however, cannot satisfy the complex needs of tribal

A depiction of a traditional Iroquois person.

Unilineal Descent Groups

Unilineal descent groups are lineage groups that trace their descent through only one side of the lineage or through only one sex. The most common type of unilineal descent group is a **patrilineal descent group,** or *patrilineage,* composed of people who trace their descent through males from a common, known male ancestor (see Figure 16.2 top). Patrilineal descent groups are the predominant form of lineage in tribal societies (Pasternak, 1976).

Another form of unilineal descent group is the **matrilineal descent group,** or *matrilineage,* whose members calculate descent through the female line from a commonly known female ancestor (see Figure 16.2 bottom). Matrilineal descent groups occur most frequently in horticultural societies, although they are not the most common organization. Matrilineal descent is found among a small number of North American tribal societies such as the Iroquois, Hopi, and Crow; among a number of tribes in central and south Africa; and among a few peoples in the Pacific islands.

One very rare type of unilineal grouping is based on *double descent,* a combination of patrilineal and matrilineal principles. In this type of social organization, an individual belongs to both his or her father's and mother's lineal descent groups. Several African tribal societies, such as the Afikpo Igbo in Nigeria, have a double-descent type of social organization (Ottenberg, 1965).

Ambilineal Descent Groups   One other form of descent group is known as ambilineal descent. An **ambilineal descent group** is formed by tracing an individual's descent relationships through either a male or a female line. The members of these groups are not all related to each other through a particular male or female. Therefore, technically, this form of descent group is not unilineal. Usually, once an individual chooses to affiliate with either the father's or mother's descent group, he or she remains with that descent group. Because each individual may choose his or her descent group, the ambilineal system offers more opportunity for economic and political strategizing. This choice frequently takes into account the relative economic resources or political power of the two family groups.

societies for cooperation, labor, and reciprocity. To meet these needs, tribal groups have developed even more "extended" types of social organization, based on both kinship and nonkinship principles.

Descent Groups

One of the more extended social groupings that exist in tribal societies is the descent group. A **descent group** is a social group identified by a person to trace actual or supposed kinship relationships. Descent groups are the predominant social unit in tribal societies.

One major type of descent group is based on lineage. Anthropologists define **lineages** as descent groups composed of relatives, all of whom trace their relationship through *consanguineal* (blood) or *affinal* (marriage) relations to an actual, commonly known ancestor. Everyone in the lineage knows exactly how she or he is related to this ancestor.

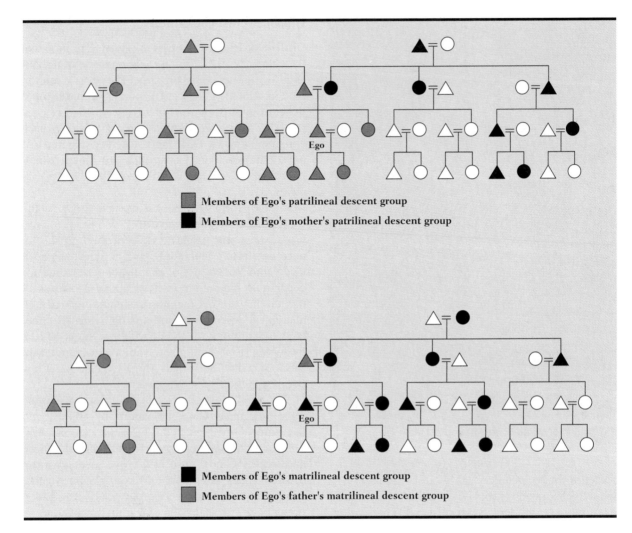

FIGURE 16.2 (*top*) A patrilineal descent system; (*bottom*) a matrilineal descent system.

Bilateral Descent A number of tribal societies practice **bilateral descent,** in which relatives are traced through both maternal and paternal sides of the family simultaneously. This type of descent system does not result in any particular lineal descent grouping. For that reason, it is not common in tribal societies. In those cases in which bilateral descent is found among tribes, a loosely structured group known as a *kindred* is used to mobilize relatives for economic, social, or political purposes. **Kindreds** are overlapping relatives from both the mother's and father's side of a family that an individual recognizes as important kin relations (see Figure 16.3). In U.S. society, for example, when a

person refers to all of his or her relatives, that person is designating a type of bilateral kindred. This bilateral kindred, however, has no functional significance in U.S. society compared to its role in a tribal society.

Clans A **clan** is a form of descent group whose members trace their descent to an unknown ancestor or, in some cases, to a sacred plant or animal. Members of clans usually share a common name but are not able to specify definitive links to an actual genealogical figure. Some clans are *patriclans,* a group distinguished by a male through whom descent is traced. Other clan groupings are

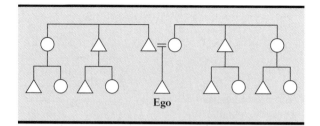

Ego

FIGURE 16.3   A kindred consists of relatives from both sides of a family that Ego recognizes as important kin relations.

matriclans, whose descent is traced through a female. Some tribal societies have both clans and lineages. In many cases, clans are made up of lineages that link their descent to an extremely vague person or sacred spirit. In such a system, clans are larger groupings consisting of several different lineages.

Phratries and Moieties   Other, more loosely structured groups found in tribal societies include phratries and moieties. **Phratries** are social groupings that consist of two or more clans combined. Members of phratries usually believe they have some loose genealogical relationship to one another. **Moieties** (derived from the French word for "half") are composed of clans or phratries that divide the entire society into two equal divisions. In some cases, such as among the Hopi, the moiety divisions divide the village in half. People have to marry outside their own moiety. In addition, each moiety has specific functions related to economic and political organization and religious activities. Wherever phratries and moieties are found in tribal societies, they provide models for organizing social relationships.

Functions of Descent Groups

Descent groups provide distinctive organizational features for tribal societies. They may become *corporate social units,* meaning that they endure beyond any particular individual's lifetime. Thus, they can play a key role in regulating the production, exchange, and distribution of goods and services over a long period of time. Family rights to land, livestock, and other resources are usually defined in relation to these corporate descent groups.

Descent Groups and Economic Relationships
Descent groups enable tribal societies to manage their economic rights and obligations. Within the descent groups, individual nuclear families have rights to particular land and animals. For example, among patrilineal horticulturalist peoples, land is sometimes transmitted from generation to generation through an eldest male, an inheritance pattern known as **primogeniture.** Another, less common, pattern is **ultimogeniture,** in which property and land are passed to the youngest son.

In horticultural societies, separate families within patrilineages have joint rights to plots of land for gardening. For example, among the Yanomamö, villages are usually made up of two patrilineages; families within these lineages cultivate their own plots of land (Chagnon, 1997). In this sense, the Yanomamö patrilineage is an economic and territorial corporate group. The transmission of status, rights, and obligations through these patrilineages occurs without constant disputes and conflicts. In these tribal societies, land is usually not partitioned into individual plots and cannot be sold to or exchanged with other descent groups.

Iroquois tribal society was based on matrilineal corporate groupings. Matrilineages among the Iroquois resided together in longhouses and had collective rights over tools and garden plots. These matrilineages were also the basic units of production in the slash-and-burn cultivation for maize and other crops. Property was inherited through matrilineal lines from the eldest woman in the corporate group. She had the highest social status in the matrilineage and influenced decision making regarding the allocation of land and other economic rights and resources (Brown, 1970a).

Sometimes in societies with bilateral descent, kindreds are the basic labor-cooperative groups for production and exchange. People living in bilateral societies can turn to both the mother's and father's side of the family for economic assistance. The kindred is thus a much more loosely structured corporate group. The kindred is highly flexible and allows for better adaptation in certain environmental circumstances.

Marriage

Corporate descent groups play a role in determining marital relations in tribal societies. Like foragers,

A Yanomamö married couple.

most tribal peoples maintain *exogamous* rules of marriage with respect to different corporate groups, meaning people generally marry outside their lineage, kindred, clan, moiety, or phratry. Marriages in tribal societies are guided by rules that ensure the perpetuation of kinship ties and group alliances.

Some tribal societies practice different forms of cousin marriage, which are illustrated in Figure 16.4. For example, among the Yanomamö, cross-cousin marriage and patrilocal residence, in which a newly married couple resides with the husband's parents, are practiced among patrilineages in different villages. Males in one patrilineage, in effect, exchange sisters, whom they may not marry, with males of other patrilineages. When the sons of the next generation repeat this form of marriage, each is marrying a woman to whom he is already related by kinship. The woman whom the man marries is both his father's sister's daughter and his mother's brother's daughter. The woman is marrying a man who is both her mother's brother's son and her father's sister's son. This form of patrilineal exogamous marriage is common in many

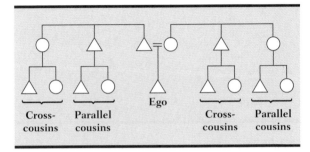

FIGURE 16.4   Different types of cousin marriage.

tribal societies. It is a type of restricted marriage exchange that helps provide for the formation of economic and political alliances among villages.

Some patrilineal tribal societies, including several in Southeast Asia, prefer a more specific rule of matrilateral cross-cousin marriage. In this system, males consistently marry their mother's brothers' daughters. This produces a marital system in which females move from one patrilineage to another. More than two lineages are involved in this system. The patrilineages become specialized as either wife givers or wife takers. In an example with three lineages—A, B, and C—anthropologists have noted cycles of marital exchange. Lineage B always gives women to lineage A but takes its wives from lineage C (see Figure 16.5). Claude Levi-Strauss (1969) refers to this type of marital system as *general exchange,* in contrast to *restricted exchange,* which is practiced between two lineages.

Another form of cousin marriage found in some patrilineal societies is **parallel-cousin marriage,** in

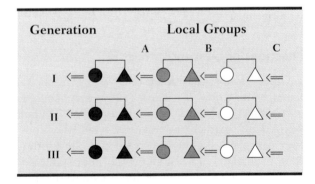

FIGURE 16.5   Matrilateral cross-cousin marriages among three lineages.

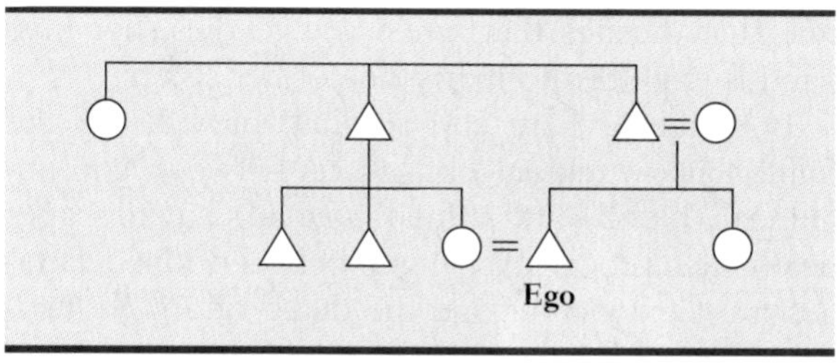

FIGURE 16.6   Patrilateral parallel-cousin marriage.

which a male marries his father's brother's daughter. Unlike the other forms of cousin marriage, parallel-cousin marriage results in *endogamy*—marriage within one's own descent group (see Figure 16.6). This form of marriage is found among the Bedouin and other tribes of the Middle East and North Africa.

Polygyny   Cross-cultural research has demonstrated that *polygyny,* in which a male marries two or more females, occurs most frequently in tribal societies. Anthropologists Kay Martin and Barbara Voorhies (1975) emphasized that polygyny is an ecologically and economically adaptive strategy for tribal populations. The more wives an individual male has, the more land or livestock he will control for allocation and exchange. This leads to an increase in both the labor supply and the overall productive value of the household. In addition, wealth in many of these tribal societies is measured in the number of offspring. Reproducing children for one's descent group is viewed as prestigious, and the children also become productive members of the household.

Anthropologist Douglas White (1988) has done extensive cross-cultural research on polygyny. He described one widespread type of polygyny as a wealth-enhancing form of marriage in which elder males accumulate several wives for productive labor, which increases their wealth. Strongly correlated with this wealth-enhancing polygyny is the ability to acquire new land for expansion. As new land becomes available, the labor produced by co-wives is extremely valuable. According to White, this wealth-enhancing form of polygyny is also related to warfare and the capture of wives. In his cross-cultural research, White found that tribal warfare often involved the capture of women from other groups as a major means of recruiting new co-wives for elder males.

In addition to increasing wealth, polygyny enables certain individuals and lineages to have a large number of children. For example, roughly 25 percent of Yanomamö marriages are polygynous. One sample group of twenty Yanomamö political leaders had 71 wives and 172 children among them (Chagnon & Irons, 1979). One Yanomamö individual named Shinbone had 11 wives and 43 children (Chagnon, 1997).

Bridewealth Exchange   Among many tribal societies, marriages are accompanied by an exchange of wealth. The most common type of exchange, particularly among patrilineal societies, is called **bridewealth,** which involves the transfer of some form of wealth, sometimes limited-purpose money like shells or livestock, from the descent group of the groom to that of the bride. Bridewealth is not a commercial exchange that reduces a bride to a commodity; that is, the bride's family does not "sell" her to her husband's family. Bridewealth serves to symbolize and highlight the reciprocities and rights established between two descent groups through marriage. In a patrilineal society, the bride becomes a member of a new corporate group that acquires access to her labor and, eventually, to her offspring. In return, the husband's kin group has certain responsibilities toward the wife. The bridewealth reflects these mutual rights and obligations and compensates the bride's family for the loss of her labor and her reproductive potential. Once the bridewealth is paid, any children she has belong to the groom's family. Thus, it helps to forge an alliance between the two kin groups. One cross-cultural study of marriage transactions suggests that bridewealth exchanges in tribal societies relate to the need to introduce new female labor into the household, the transmission of property, and the enhancement of status for males (Schlegel & Eloul, 1988). Failure to pay the bridewealth usually leads to family conflicts, including the possible dissolution of the marriage.

Polyandry   Not all tribal societies are polygynous. Some practice monogamy, and a few practice polyandry. Polyandrous marriage appears as a systematic pattern only in formerly tribal societies in the Himalayan regions of northern India and Tibet, and, until recently, among the Todas of southern India. The most common type of polyandry is *fraternal polyandry,* in which brothers share a wife.

The Toda were a buffalo-herding, pastoralist tribe of approximately 800 people. Traditionally, parents arranged the marriages when the partners were young children. When a Toda girl married a specific individual, she automatically became a wife of his brothers, including those who were not yet born. Through patrilocal residence rules, the wife joined the household of the husband. There was little evidence of sexual jealousy among the co-husbands. If the wife became pregnant, the oldest male claimed paternity rights over the child. The other co-husbands were "fathers" in a sociological sense and had certain rights regarding the child, such as labor for their households. Biological paternity was not considered important. The most prevalent explanation for the development of polyandry among the Toda was that female infanticide was practiced, leading to a scarcity of females (Rivers, [1906] 1967; Oswalt, 1972; Walker, 1986).

Among other cases of polyandry such as in the Himalyan areas, a lack of land and resources fostered this practice. Nancy Levine found that among the Nyinba of northwestern Nepal, the ideal form of marriage is a woman who marries three brothers from another family (1988). This enables one husband to farm the land, another to herd livestock, and a third to engage in trade. Levine discovered that the males in these marriages were very concerned about the paternity of their own children in these polyandrous marriages and favored close relationships with their own offspring, just as would be predicted by a sociobiological hypothesis (see Chapter 4).

The Levirate and Sororate The corporateness of descent groups in some tribal societies is exemplified by two rules of marriage designed to preserve kin ties and fulfill obligations following the death of a spouse. These rules are known as the levirate and the sororate. The **levirate** is the rule that a widow is expected to marry one of her deceased husband's brothers. In some societies, such as the ancient Israelites of biblical times or the contemporary Nuer tribe, the levirate rule requires a man to cohabit with a dead brother's widow so that she can have children, who are then considered to be the deceased husband's. The essential feature of the levirate is that the corporate rights of the deceased husband and the lineage endure even after the husband's death. The **sororate** is a marriage

rule that dictates that when a wife dies, her husband is expected to marry one of her sisters.

Both the levirate and sororate provide for the fulfillment of mutual obligations between consanguineal (blood) and affinal (marital) kin ties after death. Reciprocal exchanges between allied families must extend beyond the death of any individual. These marital practices emphasize the crucial ties among economic, kinship, and political factors in tribal societies.

Postmarital Residence Rules in Tribal Societies Anthropologists find that the rules for residence after marriage in tribal societies are related to the forms of descent groups. For example, the vast majority of tribal societies have *patrilineal descent* groups and *patrilocal rules of residence.* Another, less frequent, pattern of postmarital residence is *matrilocal residence,* in which the newly wedded couple lives with or near the wife's parents. Yet another rule of residence found in matrilineal societies is known as *avunculocal,* in which a married couple resides with the husband's mother's brother.

Causes of Postmarital Residence Rules From studying the relationships between postmarital residence rules and forms of descent groups in tribal societies, anthropologists have found that residence rules often represent adaptions to the practical conditions a society faces. The most widely accepted hypothesis states that rules of postmarital residence usually develop before the form of descent groups in a society (Fox, 1967; Keesing, 1975; Martin & Voorhies, 1975). For example, limited land and resources, frequent warfare with neighboring groups, population pressure, and the need for cooperative work may have been important factors in developing patrilocal residence and patrilineal descent groups. The purpose of these male-centered rules of residence and descent may have been to keep fathers, sons, and brothers together to pursue common interests in land, animals, and people.

What, then, creates matrilocal rules and matrilineal descent? One explanation, based on cross-cultural research by Melvin and Carol Ember (1971), proposes that matrilocal rules developed in response to patterns of warfare. The Embers suggested that societies that engage in *internal warfare*—warfare with neighboring societies close to home—have patrilocal rules of residence. In contrast, societies involved in *external warfare*—warfare a long distance from home—develop matrilocal residence rules. In societies in which external warfare takes males from the home territory for long periods of time, there is a strong need to keep the women of kin groups together. The classic example used by the Embers is the Iroquois, whose males traveled hundreds of miles away from home to engage in external wars, and this produced matrilocal residence and matrilineal descent.

Marvin Harris (1979) has extended the Embers' hypothesis to suggest that matrilocal rules and matrilineal descent emerge in societies in which males are absent for long periods, for whatever reason. For example, among the Navajo, females tended sheep near their own households, and males raised horses and participated in labor that took them away from their homes. The Navajo had matrilocal residence and matrilineal descent.

Generalizations on Marriage in Tribal Societies   It must be emphasized that descent, marriage, and residence rules are not static in tribal societies. Rather, they are flexible and change as ecological, demographic, economic, and political circumstances change. For example, tribal groups with rules of preference for marriage partners make exceptions to those rules when the situation calls for it. If a tribal society has norms that prescribe cross-cousin or parallel-cousin marriage, and an individual does not have a cousin in the particular category, various options will be available for the individual.

There are usually many other candidates available for an arranged marriage. As anthropologist Ward Goodenough (1956) demonstrated long ago, much strategizing goes on in tribal societies in determining marital choice, residence locales, and descent. Factors such as property and the availability of land, animals, or other resources often influence decisions about marital arrangements. Often, tribal elders will be involved in lengthy negotiations regarding marital choices for their offspring. These people, like others throughout the world, are not automatons responding automatically to cultural norms. Kinship and marital rules are ideal norms, and these norms are often violated.

Divorce   Among tribal peoples, especially those with patrilineal descent groups, divorce rates may be related to bridewealth exchanges. One traditional view suggested that in patrilineal descent societies with a high bridewealth amount, marriages tend to

be stable. In Evans-Pritchard's (1951) account of Nuer marriage, he noted that one of the major reasons for bridewealth is to ensure marital stability. In lineage societies, the man's family pays a bridewealth in exchange for the rights to a woman's economic output and fertility. The greater the bridewealth, the more complete is the transfer of rights over the woman from her own family to that of her husband. The dissolution of a marriage, which requires the return of bridewealth, is less likely to occur if the bridewealth is large and has been redistributed among many members of the wife's family (Gluckman, 1953; Leach, [1953] 1954; Schneider, 1953). In contrast, when the bridewealth is low, marriages are unstable, and divorce is frequent.

As Roger Keesing (1981) has pointed out, however, this hypothesis raises a fundamental question: Is marriage stable because of high bridewealth costs, or can a society afford to have high bridewealth only if it has a stable form of marriage? Keesing's own theories concerning divorce focus on rules of descent. In general, societies with matrilineal descent rules have high divorce rates, whereas patrilineal societies have low rates. In matrilineal societies, a woman retains the rights to her children and so is more likely to divorce her husband if he misbehaves. Among the matrilineal Hopi or Zuni, for example, a woman has only to put a man's belongings outside her house door to secure a divorce. The husband then returns to his mother's household, and the wife and children remain in the wife's household (Garbarino, 1988).

Marriages in matrilineal descent groups tend to be less enduring than those in patrilineal groups because of the clash of interests (or corporate rights) over children. When a woman's primary interests remain with her lineage at birth and the people of her descent group have control over her and her children, her bond to her husband and his lineage tends to be fragile and impermanent (Keesing, 1975). In contrast, in patrilineal societies, the wife has been fully incorporated into the husband's lineage. This tends to solidify patrilineal rights over children, leading to more durable marital ties.

Gender

Gender is an extremely important element of social structure in tribal societies. Cross-cultural ethnographic research on tribal societies has contributed to a better understanding of male-female relations. Anthropologists are interested in the interrelationships among gender roles, subsistence practices, female status, patriarchy, and sexism in tribal societies.

Gender and Enculturation: Margaret Mead's Study

Although nineteenth-century anthropologists addressed the question of gender roles, their conclusions were largely speculative and were not based on firsthand research. In the twentieth century, anthropologists went into the field to collect information concerning the roles of males and females. The first landmark ethnographic study of gender roles was carried out by Margaret Mead and involved three New Guinea societies: the Arapesh, the Mundugumor, and the Tchambuli. Mead's study was published in 1935 and was titled *Sex and Temperament in Three Primitive Societies.*

Mead described these three tribes as having totally different types of gender roles. Among the Arapesh, males and females had similar attitudes and behavior. Mead described both sexes as unaggressive, cooperative, passive, and sensitive to the needs of others. Based on U.S. standards of the time, Mead described the Arapesh as feminine. In contrast, Mead described Mundugumor males and females as aggressive, selfish, insensitive, and uncooperative, much like the U.S. stereotype of masculinity. The Tchambuli, according to Mead, represented a complete reversal of U.S. conceptions of gender roles. Tchambuli females were dominant politically and economically, whereas males were submissive, emotionally dependent, and less responsible. Females were the breadwinners and the political leaders, and they engaged in warfare. Males stayed near the domestic camp and cared for children. One of their primary activities was artistic work such as dancing, painting, and jewelry making. Hence, by U.S. standards, Tchambuli women were masculine, and Tchambuli men were feminine.

Mead concluded that societies can both minimize and exaggerate social and cultural differences between males and females. She argued that gender differences are extremely variable from society to society. Mead's study challenged the status quo in U.S. society regarding gender-role stereotypes. It also appealed strongly to the emerging feminist movement because it asserted that culture, rather than biology, determines (and limits) gender roles.

Deborah Gewertz with the Chambri people.

Tchambuli women became an important symbol for the feminist movement in the United States during the 1960s.

Mead's Study Reappraised   After restudying the Tchambuli (who actually call themselves the Chambri) during the 1970s, anthropologist Deborah Gewertz (1981) concluded that Mead's description of the reversal of gender roles was not accurate. Though Gewertz concludes that Mead was essentially valid in her descriptions and observations, she didn't stay long enough to see what was happening to the Chambri. According to Gewertz, Mead had viewed the Chambri at a time when they were going through a unique transition. For example, in the 1930s the Chambri had been driven from their islands by an enemy tribe. All of their physical structures and artwork had been burned. Consequently, the Chambri men were engaged near the domestic camps in full-time artwork and rebuilding at the time Mead conducted her study. Mead assumed that these were typical activities for males, when, in fact, they were atypical. After assessing her ethnographic data carefully, Gewertz concludes that the Chambri are not the complete reverse of male and female gender roles that Mead had described. Gewertz found that the Chambri males allocate and control the distribution of goods and valuables and hence are dominant politically and economically, despite the fact that females produce most of the goods.

Gewertz's reevaluation of Chambri gender-role patterns challenges the hypothesis presented by

Mead regarding the tremendous flexibility of gender roles in human societies. Although Gewertz notes that cultural values do influence gender roles, a complete reversal of the male-female role was not evident in the Chambri case. Like many anthropologists of the era of the 1930s, Mead did not take account of the complex regional histories that influenced gender roles in these New Guinea tribal societies.

Patriarchy Despite Mead's conclusions concerning gender roles among the Tchambuli, most modern anthropologists agree that a pattern of matriarchy, in which females regularly dominate males economically and politically, is not part of the archaeological, historical, and ethnographic record (Bamberger, 1974; Friedl, 1975; Martin & Voorhies, 1975; Ortner, 1974). With some exceptions, most tribal societies tend to be patriarchal. Anthropologists have offered many hypotheses to explain the prevalence of patriarchy.

Sociobiologists view patriarchy in tribal societies as a consequence of innate reproductive strategies, leading to enhanced reproductive fitness. In this view, males are unconsciously motivated to reproduce with as many females as possible to increase their chances of reproductive success. As we have seen, some tribal males have many more children than others. These reproductive strategies involve competition among males for females. According to this model, this male competition, in turn, leads to political conflict and increases in warfare. These factors produce the patterns of patrilocality, patrilineality, polygyny, and patriarchy in tribal societies (Van den Berghe & Barash, 1977; Chagnon & Hames, 1979; Chagnon, 2000). Another biologically based view suggested by Steven Goldberg is that males are always dominant in society because male hormones cause them to compete more strongly than women for high status and dominance (1993).

Instead of referring to supposed innate biological drives, cultural materialists like William Divale and Marvin Harris (1976) maintain that patriarchy and gender hierarchy are caused by the scarcity of resources and recurring warfare in tribal societies. In general, when material resources are scarce, especially in horticultural societies, warfare between competitive tribes is prevalent. Because most warriors are male, both the status and the power of males in these societies become intensified. For

example, warfare is an endemic feature of life for some tribes in the Amazon and in New Guinea. For these reasons, a male-supremacy complex develops.

Patriarchy and Sexism in Tribal Societies Other anthropologists emphasize that although biological or material considerations may contribute to male domination, the cultural values used to define "female" are extremely important in the maintenance of tribal patriarchies. In other words, in many tribal societies, female roles have much less prestige than male roles. Many tribal societies adhere to mythologies, beliefs, and ideologies that justify male domination and female subordination. These mythologies, beliefs, and ideologies reinforce **sexism**—prejudice and discrimination against people based on their sex. Many patrilineal horticultural societies of New Guinea, for example, seclude females from males during menstruation because they believe that menstruating females are unclean and will harm the community. Menstrual blood was often associated with witchcraft or the production of harmful potions; therefore, precautions, taboos, and regular contacts with women were prohibited. Women were often thought to be radically different physically and psychologically from males, and their bodily fluids and essences were dangerous and evil (Lindenbaum, 1972; Keesing, 1981). These male anxieties, mythical beliefs, and prejudices frequently led to discriminatory practices against females. For example, most tribes in New Guinea have rules of residence that separate husbands and wives into different houses, and young boys are taken from their mothers and segregated into men's houses.

In many of these tribal societies, women are excluded from political and sacred ritual activities, as well as from military combat. This limitation results in the cultural definition of males as the primary gender that ensures the survival of society. Because of these views, women in many of these tribal societies are often subjected to social subordination, sexual segregation, excessive domination, and systematic physical abuse (Lindenbaum, 1972; Chagnon, 1997). At times, they are deprived of material resources during pregnancy, denied the same access to food as males, and physically mutilated. Sexist ideologies are often used to justify these practices.

Yet there is variation among tribal societies. Based on ethnographic research among the Vanatinal tribal people of Papua New Guinea, Maria Lepowsky reports that there is very little ideology of male dominance and no prohibitions regarding contact with women who are menstruating (1993). Lepowsky argues that the women among the Vanatinal are respected and treated as equals with the men. Vanatinal women can gain prestige through trading and exchanging valuables. Nevertheless, these women are not allowed to hunt, fish, or make war. Vanatinal men control and retain power over the mobilization of warfare and threats of violence. Thus, Vanatinal society is not a perfectly egalitarian society.

Gender, Subsistence, and Female Status A number of anthropologists have proposed that, as in foraging societies, the status of women in tribal societies depends on their contributions to subsistence activities. As we have seen, both males and females are involved in horticultural production. Males usually clear the ground for the gardens, whereas women weed and harvest the crops. In a survey of more than five hundred horticultural societies, Martin and Voorhies (1975) found that women actually contribute more to cultivation activities in horticultural societies than do men. Nevertheless, patriarchy reigns in conjunction with a sexist ideology in most of these tribal groups. In some matrilineal horticultural societies, however, the status of females tends to be higher.

Female Status in Matrilineal Societies In matrilineally organized societies such as the Iroquois, Hopi, and Zuni of North America, women have considerable influence in economic and political decision making. Also, the mother and sisters of the wives in matrilineages can often offer support in domestic disputes with males. In addition, rights to property—including land, technology, and livestock—are embodied in the matrilineages. In general, however, males in matrilineal societies hold the influential positions of political power and maintain control over economic resources. In most matrilineal societies, the mother's brother has political authority and economic control within the family. Thus, matrilineality does not translate into matriarchy.

The Iroquois: Women in a Matrilineal Society The Iroquois offer a good example of the status of females in matrilineal societies. The families that occupied the Iroquois longhouses were related through matrilineages. The senior women, their daughters, and the daughters' children, the brothers, and the unmarried sons built the longhouses. Although husbands lived in the longhouses, they were considered outsiders. The matrilineages of the longhouse maintained the garden plots and owned the tools in common. These matrilineages planted, weeded, and harvested the corn, beans, and squash. The Iroquois women processed, stored, and distributed all of the food and provisioned the men's war parties. The men were highly dependent on the food supplies of the women.

The elder matrons in these matrilineages had the power to appoint the *sachem,* a council leader of the Iroquois political system. A council of fifty sachems governed the five different tribes of the Iroquois confederacy. Often they appointed their younger sons to this position and would rule until their sons were older. Women could also influence decisions about peace and warfare and determine whether prisoners of war should live or die (Brown, 1970a).

Clearly, as the Iroquois case indicates, women influenced the political and economic dynamics in some matrilineal societies. In their cross-cultural survey, Martin and Voorhies (1975) found that the status of women is higher in horticultural societies that practice matrilineal descent. In many of these matrilineal societies, males developed political power only if they had strong support from the relatives of their wives. Nevertheless, these findings also indicate that in the matrilineal societies, males still exercise political authority and assume control over key economic resources. In these societies, women may be held in high regard, but they are still economically and politically subordinate to men.

Age

As mentioned in Chapter 14, all societies have *age grades,* groupings of people of the same age. Within an age grade, people learn specific norms and acquire cultural knowledge. In some tribal societies, age grades have become specialized as groupings that have many functions.

Age Sets In certain tribal societies of East Africa, North America, Brazil, India, and New Guinea, specialized age groupings emerged as multifunctional institutions. In some tribal societies, age grades become much more formalized and institutional-ized as age sets. **Age sets** are corporate groups of people of about the same age who share specific rights, obligations, duties, and privileges within their community. Typically, people enter an age set when they are young and then progress through various life stages with other members of the set. The transition from one stage of life to the next stage of life within the age set is usually accompa-nied by a distinctive rite of passage. The corporate units provide for permanent mutual obligations that continue through time.

Age Sets among the Nyakyusa

The best-known age-set system is found among the Nyakyusa, an East African tribe that cultivates land and tends live-stock. Nyakyusa men strive to accumulate many cattle and many wives. Cattle and wives are not only symbols of status; they are also instruments of power and security in old age. The Nyakyusa have age sets that influence their entire social organization. Young males reside in their father's home until the age of 10. From that time until they are 25, they reside with their own age mates in separate villages, although they still visit and eat meals at their father's house. When they are about 25 they are allowed to marry.

After marriage, a Nyakyusa man is allowed to set up his household and accumulate land for horticul-tural production. Approximately ten years after marrying, these males undergo a series of elaborate rituals to enter a new status within their age set that grants them senior status and political authority over the entire range of Nyakyusa affairs (Wilson, 1951). The age sets produce enduring social and political units that allow the Nyakyusa to manage, control, and organize their society without substan-tial conflict and disruption.

Age Grades among the Sebei Pastoralists

A num-ber of tribal pastoralists of East Africa, such as the Karimojong, the Masai, the Nuer, the Pokot, the Samburu, and the Sebei, have specialized age-set and age-grade systems that structure social organi-zation. The Sebei, for example, have eight age-set groups, each of which is divided into three subsets. The eight groups are given a formal name, and the subsets have informal nicknames. Sebei males join an age set through initiation, in which they are cir-cumcised and exposed to tribal secret lore and indoctrination.

The Sebei initiations are held approximately every six years, and the initiation rituals extend over a period of six months. Those who are initiated to-gether develop strong bonds. Newly initiated males enter the lowest level of this system, the junior war-riors. As they grow older, they graduate into the next level, the senior warriors, while younger males enter the junior levels. Groups of males then progress from one level to the next throughout the course of their lifetime (Goldschmidt, 1986).

The most important function of the Sebei age sets is military. The members of the age set are re-sponsible for protecting livestock and for conduct-ing raids against other camps. In addition, age sets are the primary basis of status in these societies. Among the most basic social rankings are junior and senior military men and junior and senior elders. All social interaction, political activities, and ceremonial events are influenced by the age-set system. In the absence of a centralized govern-ment, age sets play a vital role in maintaining social cohesion.

The Elderly

Among tribal pastoralists and horticul-turalists, older people make use of ownership or control of property to reinforce their status. Soci-eties in which the elderly control extensive re-sources appear to show higher levels of deference toward the aged (Silverman & Maxwell, 1983). The control of land, women, and livestock and their al-location among the younger generations are the primary means by which the older men (and some-times older women, in matrilineal societies) exer-cise their power over the rest of society. In many cases, this dominance by the elderly leads to age stratification or inequalities.

The system in which older people exercise ex-ceptional power is called **gerontocracy**—rule by elders (usually male) who control the material and reproductive resources of the community. In geron-tocracies, elderly males tend to monopolize not only the property resources but also the young women in the tribe. Access to human beings is the greatest source of wealth and power in these tribal societies. Additionally, older males benefit from the accumu-lation of bridewealth. Through these processes, older men tend to have more secure statuses and economic prerogatives. They retire from subsistence and economic activities and often assume political leadership in tribal affairs. In this capacity they make important decisions regarding marriage ties, resource exchanges, and other issues.

Gerontocratic tribal societies have been prominent in the past as well as in the present. Among the ancient Israelites—once a pastoralist tribe—the elders controlled the disposition of property and marriages of their adult children, and the Bible mentions many examples of tribal patriarchs who were involved in polygynous marriages. In a modern pastoralist tribe—the Kirghiz of Afghanistan—the elderly enjoy extensive political power and status gained partially through the control of economic resources. In addition, the elders are thought to be wise, possessing extensive knowledge of history and local ecological conditions as well as medical and veterinary skills crucial to the group's survival (Shahrani, 1981). Thus, the possession of cultural knowledge may lead to the development of gerontocratic tendencies within tribal societies.

Political Organization

Like band societies, tribal societies have decentralized political systems in which authority is distributed among a number of individuals, groups, and associations. Political leadership is open to any male (especially older males) in the society and is usually based on personal abilities and qualities.

Sodalities

Although anthropologists recognize that tribes are the most varied of all small-scale societies, Elman Service ([1962] 1971) attempted to distinguish the tribe from the band by referring to the existence of *sodalities* (associations). In tribal societies, two types of sodalities exist: *kinship sodalities,* including lineages and clans, and *nonkin sodalities,* voluntary and involuntary associations. Kinship sodalities are the primary basis for political organization in tribal societies. Nonkin sodalities, such as age sets, village councils of elders, male secret societies, and military societies, also have political functions and are mostly voluntary associations that cut across kinship ties by creating alliances outside the immediate kin groups.

In both horticulturalist and pastoralist societies, descent groups such as lineages and clans are the most common political sodalities. Intravillage and intervillage politics are based on these groups, through which alliances are created that assist in maintaining peaceful and harmonious relationships within the tribe. As we have seen, these descent groups are instrumental in carrying out reciprocal exchanges involving bridewealth, women, and other goods, and they are often the only basis for maintaining order. Kinship is the primary basis for political activities and processes in tribal societies.

How Leaders Are Chosen

In horticulturalist and pastoralist societies, political leaders are recruited from within descent groups. As in band societies, however, these leaders do not have much coercive power and formal authority. Although many tribes engage in warfare, political leadership tends to be almost as weak and diffuse as it is in band societies. A number of anthropologists hypothesize that this decentralized and limited form of political leadership is due to the constant movement involved in slash-and-burn cultivation and to the nomadism associated with pastoralism (Vayda, 1961; Sahlins, 1968b). They suggest that permanent, long-term settlement in one locale is needed for the development of an effective, centralized form of political authority.

Village Headman Some horticultural groups like the Yanomamö select a village headman. To become an effective leader, this individual must be "generous" and be able to motivate feasting and exchange activities among different lineages in the village. To become generous, the individual must cultivate more land, which requires more productive labor. One way to be more productive is to have more wives. As we have seen, the Yanomamö leaders are polygynous. Thus, polygynous marital relations enable a Yanomamö headman to sustain his generosity and political status.

The Yanomamö headman has no recognized authority to enforce political decisions in the group; he has to lead more by example than by coercion (Chagnon, 1997). He must persuade people to obey the norms of the village, and he gives advice and suggestions on subsistence, economic, and ritual matters. Among the Ndembu horticulturalist tribe studied by Victor Turner, a village headman has to be aggressive, but it has to be balanced by tact, generosity, and the ability to serve as a mediator of conflicts (1957).

Big Man   Another style of political leadership and organization found among some horticultural groups, particularly in Melanesia, is the "big-man" system. One of the most detailed descriptions of this system was compiled by anthropologist Douglas Oliver (1955), who did fieldwork in the Solomon Islands among the Siuai tribe. According to Oliver, the aspiring Siuai big man has to collect as many wives as possible to form kinship alliances with other descent groups. In addition, he must accumulate a large number of pigs and grow taro (an edible root crop) to feed them. Most of this productive labor is carried out by the man's wives. When a man has enough pigs, he has a pig feast in which he attracts followers while humiliating rival big men. If the leader is able to recruit a few hundred men through the "generosity" demonstrated by the feast, these followers may begin to build a "clubhouse" to

demonstrate their political commitment to the big man.

The big-man political organization of the Siuai is both formidable and fragile. It is formidable in that the pig feasts can enable a man to attract more and more followers, and thus more power. This system provides the basis for political and war-making alliances. The big man is also able to command and sometimes coerce other people. At the same time, the political loyalties of the followers of the big man are not long-lasting; the lineage of the big man does not assume any of his political power or authority. With the death of the big man, the entire political organization collapses, and loyalties and allegiances shift to another or several other big men, who compete through pig feasts for political supporters. Hence, the big man, like the hunter-gatherer leader, cannot pass on power or build permanent structures of authority.

Pastoralist Tribal Politics

Pastoralist tribal groups tend to have similar political organizations, depending on the degree of their nomadic lifestyle. Some pastoralist societies depend on the agricultural societies within their region and are not completely self-sufficient. In these groups, leadership tends to become more permanent and centralized. For example, among the Basseri, a nomadic pastoralist group in Iran, leadership was vested in the *khan,* who was a strong force in decision making within the tribe (Barth, 1961). Yet in reality, the power and authority of the *khan* was extremely limited, and they had to rule from consensus (Salzman, 2000). It appears that in tribal pastoralist societies, the greater the degree of nomadic independence, isolation, and self-sufficiency of a group, the more diffuse and egalitarian is its political leadership (Lindholm, 1986).

Segmentary Lineage Systems   One traditional form of political organization found among such groups as the Nuer of East Africa and the Bedouins is the segmentary lineage system. A **segmentary lineage system** is a type of political organization in which multiple descent groups (usually patrilineages) form at different levels and serve political functions. This system reflects a complex yet flexible arrangement of lineage groups. Among the Nuer, for example, the patrilineages are identified

A "Big Man" of a tribe in New Guinea.

with particular territories in the tribal area. These patrilineages have both *maximal lineages,* which include descendants who trace their ancestors back through many generations, and *minimal lineages,* segments of the maximal lineage whose descendants trace their ancestry back only one or two generations. Minimal lineages are nested within the maximal lineage, and all members of the lineage can link themselves directly to the same maximal blood ancestor.

Complementary Opposition   The segmentary lineage system is composed of the various patrilineages, both maximal and minimal, that can be united for military or political purposes. The process by which alliances are formed and conflicts are resolved in this system is referred to as complementary opposition. **Complementary opposition** is the formation of groups that parallel one another as political antagonists. To understand this process, imagine a village with two different maximal lineages. We will call the maximal lineages A and B; the minimal lineages within A we will call A1 and A2; and the minimal lineages within B we will call B1 and B2 (see Figure 16.7).

Now imagine that a member of B2 commits an offense against a member of B1. A feud may erupt, but it will usually be settled within the maximal lineage (B) to which both minimal lineages belong. However, should B2 commit an offense against A2, a different process unfolds. Both A2 and A1 will unite in opposition to B2, which in turn will join with B1. The result is a large-scale feud between

maximal lineages A and B. This process can extend beyond the lineages to an entire population. For example, in the event of an outside attack, all of the maximal lineages will unite to defend the tribe.

In the process of complementary opposition, then, kinspeople may be allies under one set of circumstances and enemies under another. Through this process, the segmentary lineage system can achieve political goals without any definitive type of centralized leadership, such as kings, chiefs, or headmen. The philosophy behind complementary opposition is summarized in an old Bedouin proverb:

> *Me against my brother*
> *I and my brother against our cousins*
> *I and my brother and my cousins against non-*
>   *relatives*
> *I and my brother and my cousins and friends against*
>   *the enemies in our village*
> *All of these and the whole village against another*
>   *village. (Murphy & Kasdan, 1959)*

Many other pastoralist societies have maintained segmentary lineage systems. For example, during their nomadic pastoralist existence prior to the establishment of the kingdom of Israel, the ancient Israelites appear to have been organized on the basis of segmentary lineages without any centralized political institutions. (In the Bible, patrilineal groups are referred to as *families.*)

Among segmentary lineage societies, feuds frequently erupt between lineages and result in retaliation or compensation without the imposition of force by a centralized authority. If a member of a particular lineage kills a member of another lineage, the victim's lineage may seek blood revenge. To prevent this blood revenge, the Nuer attempt to reduce the tension between the victim's and the murderer's lineages. In Nuer society, an individual known as the *leopard skin chief* sometimes provides sanctuary for a murderer and attempts to negotiate compensation with the victim's lineage. In some instances, compensation takes the form of cattle, a desired possession that can be used as bridewealth.

Explaining Tribal Warfare

Both internal and external warfare are far more common among tribes than among foragers. This does not suggest that all tribal societies were

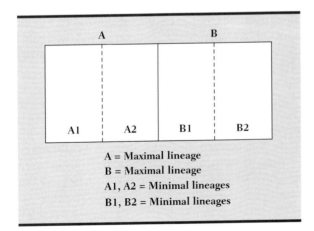

FIGURE 16.7   Model of segmentary lineage system.

engaged in warfare, and there very well may have been long interludes in which tribes did not engage in warfare (Otterbein, 2000). Apparently, at least in some cases, tribal warfare was exacerbated by external political processes resulting from globalization (Ferguson & Whitehead, 1992). We shall return to these globalization pressures and their consequences for some of these tribal societies in Chapter 20. Generally, anthropologists reject the notion that humans are by nature aggressive and warlike, possessing a definitive biological instinct for violence (see box on Human Aggression). Instead, most theories of warfare focus on environmental, demographic, and other external political and cultural factors.

Among horticulturalist societies, members of one village frequently raid other villages for territory, women, or, occasionally, headhunting (removing the head of a slain enemy and preserving it as a trophy). In a detailed analysis of warfare among the Mae Enga of highland New Guinea, anthropologist Mervyn Meggitt (1977) noted that land shortages and ecological conditions are the most important causes of warfare. The Mae Enga, numbering more than thirty thousand, are organized into phratries, clans, and localized patrilineal groups. Meggitt distinguishes among different types of warfare involving phratries, clans, and patrilineages.

Phratry warfare involving the entire tribe is mostly ceremonial and serves to display status and prestige between big men and males. Phratry warfare is extremely limited. Interclan and interlineage internal warfare, however, is vicious and ongoing, with conquering kin groups seizing the land of the conquered patrilineages. Meggitt noted that 58 percent of cases of internal warfare were over land, and in 74 percent of the cases, the victors incorporated some or all of the land of the victims. The Mae Enga themselves interpret their internal warfare as a consequence of population growth in relation to the scarcity of land for cultivation.

The Yanomamö and Protein Shortages Cultural materialists Divale and Harris (1976) explain warfare among the tribal Yanomamö in terms of ecological factors. They view the internal warfare of the Yanomamö as an indirect means of regulating population growth. Divale and Harris suggest that the Yanomamö institutions and values that relate to intervillage warfare emerge from the group's cultivation practices and nutritional deficiencies. They hypothesize that the Yanomamö expand their cultivation because they experience protein shortages. Thus, the intensification of warfare in which villages raid one another's game reserves is an adaptive Yanomamö response or mechanism that indirectly and unintentionally serves to inhibit population growth. The limited protein supplies are inadequate to support larger populations.

Other anthropologists have rejected the protein shortage explanation of Yanomamö warfare. Napoleon Chagnon and Raymond Hames (1979) measured the amount of protein consumed in different Yanomamö villages and encountered no clinical signs of shortages. Furthermore, they discovered that some villages that consumed high amounts of protein engaged in warfare as frequently as villages that consumed low amounts.

Sociobiological Hypotheses of Tribal Warfare
Anthropologist William Durham (1976) offered an evolutionary sociobiological hypothesis of tribal warfare. An example of his model is his study of the Mundurucu of the Amazon, who had a reputation for continual warfare and headhunting against other tribes. Although Durham did not rule out competition for resources and land as explanations for warfare, he hypothesized that, ultimately, warfare is an adaptive reproductive strategy. In Durham's view, tribal warfare is a means of increasing inclusive fitness on a tribal level in competition with other tribal populations in the region. (Inclusive fitness was discussed in Chapter 13.) If the population of a rival tribe is reduced, one's own tribe may increase its rate of survival and reproduction. Durham believed that increasing the number and survival of offspring (one's own genes) into the next generation is the underlying motivation for tribal warfare. He is not suggesting that this was a conscious evolutionary process, but rather an underlying strategy that resulted in reproductive success for various tribal populations.

Multidimensional Explanations of Tribal Warfare
All of the hypotheses above view tribal warfare as having in some way an adaptive function for society or individuals within society. But many critics say that although population pressure, competition for land and livestock, and reproductive success may help explain tribal warfare, these variables need to

CRITICAL PERSPECTIVES

HUMAN AGGRESSION: BIOLOGICAL OR CULTURAL?

Throughout history, humans have been confronted with questions about violence and aggression. Enlightenment philosophers such as Thomas Hobbes and Jean-Jacques Rousseau wrote about primitive societies in the state of nature, which they believed revealed the "natural" inclinations of humans. In *Leviathan* ([1651] 1958) by Hobbes, humans were characterized as naturally violent, and life in primitive societies was described as "nasty, brutish, and short." Hobbes believed that the cultural lifestyle of primitives was devoted to a "war of all men against all men." He argued that only a strong state could coerce people to be peaceful. In contrast, Rousseau, in *Social Contract* (1762), argued that primitive societies were peaceful, harmonious communities. He classified these people as "Noble Savages." He claimed that the onset of civilization was the corrupting force that resulted in warfare and conflict within these societies.

One of the problems with both of these competing frameworks for understanding human nature is that they were based on superficial, fragmentary, and stereotypical depictions of small-scale societies. They drew on the stories, myths, and legends of explorers, missionaries, and government officials of that time to describe the native peoples of America and elsewhere. During the twentieth century, with the development of systematic ethnographic studies of indigenous societies, anthropologists began to build a better understanding of violence, aggression, and warfare in these societies.

In today's world of mass media, we are constantly confronted with accounts of violence and aggression, ranging from sports brawls to assaults and murders to revolutions and wars. The seeming universality of aggression has led some people to conclude with Hobbes that humans are "naturally" violent. Or is Rousseau more correct in his view that the development of civilization and its various corruptions caused once-peaceful societies to become war-like and aggressive? What are the causes of human aggression? Is violence inbred, or is it learned? Not surprisingly, anthropologists and other social scientists have been examining these questions for decades, often arriving at conflicting conclusions. Some tend to be more Hobbesian, whereas others are more Rousseauian. To some extent, these disputes concerning the origins of violence reflect the biology-versus-culture debate.

Some psychologists and ethologists attribute warfare and violence to humans' psychobiological genetic heritage. For example, ethologist Konrad Lorenz developed an elaborate biological hypothesis based on comparisons

Napoleon Chagnon

of human with animal behaviors. In his widely read book, *On Aggression* (1966), Lorenz proposed that during humanity's long period of physical evolution, certain genes were selected that provide humans with an aggressive instinct, which has survival value for the species. He argued that this instinct evolved through natural selection because of inter-group warfare and competition. Lorenz noted that nonhuman animals usually do not kill within their species, and that aggression among males within species is highly ritualized and rarely leads to death. Male deer, wolves, and other social animals fight each other, but this fighting establishes a hierarchy of dominant and submissive males and therefore helps to ensure order within the group. Thus, nonhuman animals have an instinct for inhibiting aggression that is activated by ritualized fighting behavior.

Humans, in contrast, have evolved as physically weak creatures without sharp teeth, claws, beaks, or tremendous strength. Therefore, the instinct for inhibiting violence was not selected for the human species. According to Lorenz, this accounts for the prevalence of warfare in human societies and makes humans highly dangerous animals. Compounding this loss of instinctual inhibitions against violence is the human technological capacity to produce deadly weapons.

Many anthropologists challenged this concept of a universal instinct for aggression. Citing ethnographic evidence from sociocultural systems that experienced little violence, Ashley Montagu, Marshall Sahlins, and others proposed that cultural factors are more important than biological instincts in determining aggression (Montagu, 1968; Sponsel, 1998). They argued that human behavior can be shaped and influenced in many ways. Humans can be extremely violent or extremely pacific, depending on the prevailing cultural values and norms. In general, these anthropologists were more Rousseauian in their approach, arguing that external forces such as industrial societies and globalization had an effect on tribal or small-scale societies.

During the 1980s, the controversial anthropologist Napoleon Chagnon hypothesized that aggression is related to strategies that have to do with reproduction and increasing one's ability to have more children. This sociobiological view of warfare and aggression has been challenged by other anthropologists (see box on Controversy in El Dorado in Chapter 20). Though anthropologists such as Chagnon, influenced by sociobiology or evolutionary psychology, denied the existence of an aggressive instinct, they agreed that humans possess an innate capacity or predisposition for violence. Violent behavior can be triggered by a number of factors that threaten humans' capacity to survive and reproduce, including scarcities of resources, excessive population densities, and significant ecological developments. Sociologists and evolutionary psychologists do, however, acknowledge that the norms and values of a particular sociocultural system can either inhibit or enhance aggressive tendencies. Thus, the same pressures that would lead to warfare in one society might be resolved without violence in a society with a different set of values.

In this chapter, we saw that warfare is much more prevalent in tribal societies than in the hunter-gathering bands of the last chapter. Tribal societies such as the horticulturalist Yanomamö or the pastoralist Nuer are more frequently involved in violence and aggression. And this violence and warfare appears to have developed prior to the influence of colonialism and outside global pressures. This fact suggests that the cultivation of crops and the domestication of animals as food sources by these tribal societies is related to the origins of warfare. Territories and land become more important within these tribal societies. Yanomamö lineages are important as social units that defend territories against raids and thefts of crops. Likewise, Nuer lineages defend their cattle against theft or raids. Most of the tribal societies are engaged in these defensive strategies involving warfare.

Anthropologists today generally concur that human aggression results from both biological and cultural factors, although they continue to disagree about the relative importance of each. Meanwhile, research into the origins of aggression has raised some basic questions concerning human behavior.

POINTS TO PONDER

1. If cultural norms and values can promote violence, can they also eliminate or sharply reduce it?

2. Can you foresee a society (or a world) in which conflicts and problems are resolved peacefully? Or will violence always be with us?

3. Given the complex relationships among various cultural and biological factors, what concrete steps can a society take to reduce the level of aggressive behavior?

be combined with cultural factors such as honor, prestige, and the enhancement of male status.

Anthropologist Walter Goldschmidt (1989) noted in an essay that males in tribal societies are induced to go to war against other groups through institutionalized religious and cultural indoctrination. Although in some tribal societies warriors are given material rewards such as women or land, in most cases, nonmaterial rewards such as prestige, honor, and spiritual incentives are just as important. Most likely, this generalization applies to all societies that engage in warfare.

Law and Conflict Resolution

Tribal societies that have no centralized political institutions for addressing internal conflicts must, for the most part, rely primarily on informal and formal sanctions to resolve conflicts. Because tribes have larger, more settled populations and more complex kinship networks than do bands, they cannot resolve disputes merely by having people move to another location. Thus, many tribal groups have developed more formalized legal techniques and methods of conflict resolution.

In general, tribal societies have no formal courts and no lawyers. However, ethnologists have found in such societies some individuals, usually older males, who are highly skilled in negotiation and conflict resolution. These individuals may become *mediators* who help resolve disputes among clans, lineages, and other descent groups. One example of a mediator is the Nuer leopard skin chief, who attempts to restore amicable relations between Nuer patrilineages after a homicide. It is important to note that the chief has no authority to enforce legal decisions, a pattern typical of mediators in tribal societies. These mediators preside over the litigation procedures, but the final decision can be reached only when a consensus is achieved among the different descent groups.

Ordeals   Another, more formalized, legal mechanism found in some tribal societies is known as the *ordeal.* Anthropologist R. F. Barton described a classic case of an ordeal among the Ifugao, a horticulturalist tribe of the Philippines (1919). An Ifugao individual accused of a transgression who wanted to claim innocence might submit to an ordeal. Barton described several types of ordeals found

A Nuer leopard skin chief. These individuals are basically mediators who help resolve conflicts by building a consensus. They do not have the power to coerce other people.

among the Ifugao. In one type, referred to as the hot-water ordeal, a person had to reach into a pot of boiling water to pull out a pebble and then replace it. In another, a red-hot knife was lowered onto a person's hand. If the party were guilty, his or her hand would be burned badly; if innocent, it would not be. If there were two disputants, they both had the hot knife lowered onto their hands. The one burned more severely was judged to be the guilty party. A third type of ordeal among the Ifugao involved duels or wrestling matches between the disputants.

A *monkalun,* or arbiter, supervised all of these ordeals. The Ifugao assumed, however, that spiritual or supernatural intervention was the ultimate arbiter in these cases, and that moral transgressions would be punished, not by the *monkalun,* but by cosmic religious forces and beings who oversee the social and moral order of Ifugaoan life. The *monkalun* interpreted the evidence and acted as an umpire in deciding the guilt or innocence of an individual.

Oaths and Oracles   Some tribal societies use oaths and oracles to arrive at legal decisions. An **oath** is an attempt to call on a supernatural source of power to sanction and bear witness to the truth or falseness of an individual's testimony. Some tribal groups are rely on **oracles,** individuals or sacred objects believed to have special prophetic abilities, to help resolve legal matters. Individuals who are believed to have oracular or prophetic powers are empowered to make legal decisions. One example is the Azande, a tribal group in East Africa described by Evans-Pritchard (1937). The Azande used oracles to help decide criminal cases.

In general, ordeals, oaths, and oracles are more common among tribal societies with weak authority structures, in which power is widely diffused throughout the society. Individuals in these societies lack the authority to enforce judicial rulings and therefore do not want to accept the full responsibility for making life-and-death decisions that would make them politically vulnerable (Roberts, 1967).

Religion

Given the immense diversity from tribe to tribe, it is very difficult to generalize about tribal religions. Like hunter-gatherer religions, tribal religions tend to be *cosmic religions;* that is, the concepts, beliefs, and rituals of these religions are integrated with the natural environment, seasonal cycles, and all living organisms. *Animism* and *shamanism* are common religious traditions.

Animism and Shamanism in South America

The mingling of animism and shamanism is evident among some South American tribes. Some of these tribes use the extracts of certain plants for shamanistic practices. The Yanomamö, for example, use a hallucinogenic snuff called *ebene* to induce a supernatural state of ecstasy during which it is believed an individual will have direct contact with the spirit world. The *ebene* powder is blown through a bamboo tube into the nostrils to gain contact with the *hekura* spirits. These spirits, numbering in the thousands, are believed to reside in trees, rocks, and even within people's chests. Through the use of *ebene,* Yanomamö shamans fall into trances, enabling them to attract and control the *hekura* for various purposes.

The Jivaro of Ecuador use a tealike drink, *natema,* which enables almost anyone to achieve a trance state. *Natema* is concocted by boiling vines to produce a hallucinogenic drink containing alkaloids, which are somewhat similar to LSD and mescaline. Among the Jivaro, approximately one out of every four males is a shaman. Any adult, male or female, who desires to become such a practitioner simply gives a gift to an experienced shaman, who, in turn, gives the apprentices a drink of *natema* as well as some of his own supernatural power in the form of spirit helpers. The spirit helpers, or *darts,* are believed to be the major causes of illness and death. Some Jivaro shamans send these spirit helpers to infect enemies. Others gain the ability to cure illnesses through the use of their clairvoyant powers (Harner, 1972).

Witchcraft and Sorcery

Many tribal societies practice witchcraft and sorcery. Evans-Pritchard, in a classic ethnographic study of the Azande tribe, referred to **witchcraft** as a belief in an innate, psychic ability of some people to harm others, whereas **sorcery** is a magical strategy in which practitioners manipulate objects to bring about either harmful or beneficial effects (1937). Contemporary anthropologists regard this distinction as too clear-cut and view the belief in occult powers to be much more culturally variant, ambivalent, and diffuse in meaning to be subject to this type of precise definition.

Anthropologists perceive witchcraft and sorcery as strategies for people to understand bad luck, illness, injustice, and other misfortunes that they cannot otherwise explain. Sorcerers and witches in tribal societies of Africa and Melanesia are often described as insatiably hungry individuals who eat others by absorbing their reproductive powers, children, sexual fluids, and flesh (Patterson, 2000). Witches and sorcerers are usually connected with kinship and descent, as these are all-important aspects of tribal society. In many cases, families are directing supernatural assaults upon one another. Witches and sorcerers may manipulate spirits to inflict diseases or use poisons on other individuals or families. Many tribal peoples perceive the cosmos as composed of various spirits that can affect human lives. Although these peoples accept cause-and-effect explanations for most occurrences, certain phenomena such as pain and suffering do not seem to have "natural" causes. These phenomena are therefore explained in terms of witchcraft and sorcery.

The Role of Witchcraft   In Evans-Pritchard's study of the Azande, witchcraft played a role in all aspects of life. Any misfortunes that could not be explained by known causes, such as the lack of game or fish, or crop failure, were attributed to witchcraft. The Azande believed that a person became a witch because of an inherited bodily organ or blackish substance known as *mangu*. The identity of a witch was even unknown to the individual who had this *mangu*. A male could inherit it only from another male, a female only from another female. The identity of a witch was determined by a "poison oracle." A carefully prepared substance called *benge* was fed to a bird, and a yes-or-no question was put to the oracle. Whether the bird survived or died constituted the answer to whether someone was a witch. After a witch died, the Azande performed autopsies to determine whether witchcraft was carried in a family line.

Anthropologist Clyde Kluckhohn (1967) analyzed witchcraft beliefs among the Navajo Indians of the southwestern United States. Navajo witches were considered despicable monsters. The Navajo believed that the witches could transform themselves into animals. In these werewolf-like transformations, they ate the meat of corpses and made poisons from dried and ground human flesh, especially that of children. These poisons were thrown into houses of enemies, buried in cornfields, or placed on victims. Fatal diseases were believed to result from the poisons. The Navajo had antidotes (the gall of an eagle, bear, mountain lion, or skunk) to forestall witchcraft activity, and they usually carried these antidotes with them into public situations.

Kluckhohn learned that the Navajo believed witchcraft was related to economic differences. The Navajo thought that those who had more wealth had gained it through witchcraft activities such as grave robbing and stealing jewelry from the dead. The only way a person could refute such an accusation was to share his or her wealth with friends and relatives. Thus, Kluckhohn hypothesized that the belief in witchcraft had the effect of equalizing the distribution of wealth and promoting harmony in the community.

The Role of Sorcery   In tribal groups in Africa, New Guinea, and North America, sorcery is also used to influence social relationships. Among many tribes, one form of sorcery is used to promote fertility and good health and to avert evil spells. Another type is used to harm people whom the sorcerer hates and resents. In some cases, sorcery is used to reinforce informal sanctions.

One example of how societies use sorcery to explain misfortunes is provided by Shirley Lindenbaum's (1972) study of various New Guinea tribes. Among the Fore people, sorcery is often used to explain severe illnesses and death, whereas in other tribal groups, such as the Mae Enga, sorcery is not important. In particular, the Fore accuse sorcerers of trying to eliminate all women in their society, thereby threatening the group's survival. At the time of Lindenbaum's fieldwork, the Fore were faced with an epidemic disease that was devastating their population. This epidemic disease was found to be a variant of Creutzfeld–Jakob's disease (mad cow disease), which the Fore were infected with as a result of eating human brains (Diamond, 1997). In this traumatic situation, Diamond found that sorcery aided in explaining fundamental survival questions.

Familistic Religion

In addition to animism, shamanism, witchcraft, and sorcery, tribal religions are intertwined with corporate descent groupings, particularly clans and lineages. Recall that clans are descent groups with fictive ancestors. Many of these clan ancestors are spiritual beings, symbolically personified by a deceased ancestor, animal, or plant found in specific environments. For example, among many Native American tribes, lineage groupings such as clans, moieties, and phratries divide the society into different groupings. Each group is symbolized by a particular animal spirit, or **totem,** which the group recognizes as its ancestor. Among the various totems are eagles, bears, ravens, coyotes, and snakes. There are as many tribal spirits or deities as there are constituent kin groupings. Although each grouping recognizes the existence of all the deities in the entire tribe, the religious activities of each group are devoted to that group's particular spirit.

Ghost Lineage Members among the Lugbara   The Lugbara of Uganda, Africa, illustrate the familistic aspect of tribal religion (Middleton, 1960). The Lugbara believe that the dead remain as an integral part of the lineage structure of their society. Ancestors include all the dead and living forebears of a person's lineage. The spirits of the dead regularly commune with the elders of the lineages. Shrines are erected to the dead, and sacrifices are offered to ensure that the ancestors will not harm people. At the shrines it is believed that people have direct contact with their ancestors, especially during the sacrifices.

A Lugbara elder explained the relationship between the dead and the living:

> *A ghost watches a man giving food at a sacrifice to him. A brother of that ghost begs food of him. The other will laugh and say "Have you no son?" Then he thinks, "Why does my child not give me food? If he does not give me food soon I shall send sickness to him." Then later that man is seized by sickness, or his wife and his children. The sickness is that of the ghosts, to grow thin and to ache throughout the body; these are the sicknesses of the dead. (Middleton, 1960:46)*

A Katchina *doll. The* Katchina *dolls represent some of the forms of artistic production of the Pueblo Indians of the Southwest.*

Art and Music

Art in tribal societies has both utilitarian and ceremonial functions. The expressive art of the tribes of Papua New Guinea and of the U.S. southwest is used to decorate utensils such as baskets, bowls, and other tools. It is also deeply connected with religious and sacred phenomena. Various tribes in the interior highlands of Papua New Guinea use body decorations as their principal art form, whereas the tribal peoples in the coastal regions make large, impressive masks that symbolize male power. These tribes also use various geometric designs to decorate their ceremonial war shields and other paraphernalia.

The Pueblo Indians of the U.S. southwest, such as the Hopi and Zuni, use distinctive designs in their artworks to represent a harmonious balance among humans, nature, and the supernatural. The

groups create colorful sand paintings that are erased after the ceremony is completed. In addition, they make masks and dolls to be used in the *katchina* cult activities. *Katchinas* are spiritual figures that exercise control over the weather, especially rainfall, which is particularly important in this arid region. *Katchina* art is used in various dance ceremonies and is believed to help produce beneficial weather conditions. Because clay is abundant in the southwest, the Pueblo Indians developed elaborate pottery with complex geometric motifs and animal figures representing different tribal groups in the area.

Musical Traditions

Music and musical instruments vary from one region to another. For example, various sub-Saharan African tribes produce a vast range of musical instruments, including drums, bells, shells, rattles, and hand pianos. The musical instruments are heard solo and in ensembles. The hand piano, or *mbira,* is a small wooden board onto which a number of metal keys are attached. The keys are arranged to produce staggered tones so that certain melodic patterns can be improvised. Along with the instrumentation, singing is used in many cases to invoke specific moods: sadness, happiness, or a sense of spirituality (Mensah, 1983).

Native American tribal musical traditions also vary from region to region. The musical instruments consist primarily of percussive rattles and drums. The drumming is done with a single drumstick, although several drum players may accompany the drummer. The traditional tribal music includes spiritual hymns, game songs, recreational dance music, war dance music, and shamanistic chanting. Most of the songs, even the game and recreational songs, are inseparable from sacred rituals related to crop fertility, healing, and other life crises. Nearly all of the music is vocal, sung by choruses. Many of the song texts contain extensive use of syllables such as "yu-waw, yu-waw, hi hi hi, yu-wah hi." These songs help to create a hypnotic spiritual consciousness that produces an appropriate sacred atmosphere (McAllester, 1983, 1984).

SUMMARY

Most anthropologists use the term *tribe* to refer to peoples who rely on horticulture, which is a limited form of agriculture, or pastoralism, which involves the maintenance of animals, for their basic subsistence. Most horticulturalists reside in tropical rain forests, whereas most pastoralists reside in eastern and northern Africa and the Middle East.

The population of tribal societies is larger than that of foragers because they have more abundant food supplies. The economic patterns of tribal societies are based on reciprocal exchanges, although some groups have developed special-purpose forms of monetary exchanges for certain goods. Property ownership is based on large kinship groups.

Social organization varies widely from region to region. Large extended families are the norm. Anthropologists generally find that tribal societies have extensive descent groups consisting of many extended families known as lineages (patrilineages and matrilineages), clans, phratries, and moieties that are multifunctional and corporate in nature.

Marriage in tribal societies tends to be polygynous and usually involves bridewealth exchanges. Marriage bonds are the basis of descent-group alliances among villages. Marital practices such as the levirate and sororate tend to cement social ties among descent groups in tribes.

Despite some early research that indicated women had a fairly high status in tribal societies, modern anthropologists find that patriarchy prevails in most tribes. At times, patriarchy is associated with sexism and the maltreatment of women. Anthropologists have been investigating the relationship among subsistence, warfare, and biology to explain the prevalence of patriarchy in tribal societies.

Age is another important feature of social organization in tribal society. In some tribes, age sets are the basis of economic, political, and religious organization. As people age in tribal societies, they often become more powerful, and in some cases gerontocratic societies arise.

Tribal political organization is usually decentralized and lacks permanent political offices. In horticulturalist tribes, village headmen and big men often organize and arrange intervillage political activities. In pastoralist tribes, the lack of centralized leadership often leads to segmentary lineage systems based on the consolidation of kinship principles to resolve feuds and disputes.

Warfare tends to be more prevalent among tribal societies than among foragers. Anthropologists have investigated the causes of tribal warfare by drawing on ecological, demographic, economic, and biological factors. Most anthropologists agree that no one of these factors explains tribal warfare, and they must use cultural variables such as honor, status, and glory to offer comprehensive explanations.

Religion in tribal society consists of animism, shamanism, witchcraft, and sorcery. These practices and beliefs help to explain illness, bad luck, and various crises. In addition, tribal religion is often familistic, with beliefs in ancestor worship and spirits that commune with the living members of descent groups.

QUESTIONS TO THINK ABOUT

1. What are some of the demographic differences one finds between foragers and food producers such as pastoralists and horticulturalists? Why do you think these differences exist?

2. Discuss the concept of property ownership in tribal societies. How does it differ from what generally occurs in band societies?

3. What is a descent group? What forms do descent groups take? What are some of their functions?

4. Discuss the functions of a descent group in managing the economic rights and obligations of a tribal society. Use specific examples to illustrate your points.

5. Why do you think a society would have marriage rules such as the levirate and sororate?

6. What are some of the explanations given for the fact that anthropologists have not found any truly matriarchal societies in the archaeological, historical, or ethnographic records?

7. What forms of political organization are found in tribal societies? What are some of the reasons that have been offered to explain these types of organization? How do these types of political organization differ from those found in forager groups?

8. How are descent groups associated with tribal religious practices?

KEY TERMS

age sets	levirate	phratries
ambilineal descent group	lineages	primogeniture
bilateral descent	matrilineal descent group	segmentary lineage system
bridewealth	moieties	sexism
clan	money	sorcery
complementary opposition	oath	sororate
descent group	oracles	totem
gerontocracy	parallel-cousin marriage	ultimogeniture
horticulture	pastoralists	unilineal descent groups
kindred	patrilineal descent group	witchcraft

INTERNET EXERCISES

1. Visit the website **http://www.head-hunter.com/jivaro.html** and review the information on the Jivaro. What unique and unusual practice did they perform? Why would a horticultural people be so fierce? Compare them to the Yanomamö also mentioned in this chapter.

2. Read the website **http://www.fao.org/News/FOTOFILE/PH9819-e.htm** to determine the United Nations Food and Agriculture Organization's view of pastoralism. How does this view compare to that of the chapter? How can camels help support desert-living people?

SUGGESTED READINGS

BARTH, FREDRICK. 1961. *Nomads of South Persia*. New York: Humanities Press. An ethnography of the Basseri, a pastoralist group of southern Iran.

CHAGNON, NAPOLEON. 1997. *The Yanomamö*, 5th ed. New York: Holt, Rinehart & Winston. This frequently cited account of a tribal horticulturalist society has become a modern classic.

EVANS-PRITCHARD, E. E. 1940. *The Nuer*. Oxford: Clarendon Press. The classic ethnography of pastoralist life. It summarizes the ecological, economic, social, and political organization of this eastern African tribe.

FRIEDL, ERNESTINE. 1975. *Women and Men: An Anthropologist's View*. New York: Holt, Rinehart & Winston. A study of gender relations that focuses on tribal societies. Friedl examines how subsistence, economy, family, kinship, and politics influence gender relationships.

GLUCKMAN, MAX. 1965. *Politics, Law and Ritual in Tribal Society*. Chicago: Aldine. A comprehensive account of different political institutions and legal techniques developed in tribal societies. The focus of the text is on law.

HAAS, JONATHAN (Ed.). 1990. *The Anthropology of War*. Cambridge: Cambridge University Press. An excellent series of readings dealing with the various causes of warfare, plus detailed cases of warfare among tribal peoples.

HARNER, MICHAEL, J. 1972. *The Jivaro: People of the Sacred Waterfall*. Garden City, NY: Natural History Press. A fascinating ethnography of horticultural Indians of Ecuador.

KEESING, ROGER M. 1971. *Kin Groups and Social Structure*. New York: Holt, Rinehart & Winston. A thorough summary of the different types of descent groupings and kinship relationships in tribal and nontribal societies.

KLUCKHOHN, CLYDE. 1967. *Navaho Witchcraft*. Boston: Beardon Press. An account of witchcraft among the Navajo emphasizing the positive benefits of witchcraft for the tribe.

OTTERBEIN, KEITH (Ed.). 1994. *Feuding and Warfare: Selected Works of Keith F. Otterbein*. Langborn, PA: Gordon and Breach. A collection of papers by an anthropologist who has devoted his lengthy career to the understanding of feuds and warfare.

SAHLINS, MARSHALL D. 1968. *Tribesmen*. Englewood Cliffs, NJ: Prentice Hall. An overall summary of the different forms of tribal groups and institutions found throughout the world. Although contemporary anthropologists have criticized many of the author's generalizations, this work remains valuable.

SOUTHALL, AIDAN. 1996. "Tribes," in *Encyclopedia of Cultural Anthropology*, Vol. 4 (Ed.) David Levinson and Melvin Ember. New York: Henry Holt. A recent critical essay that surveys the concept of tribes among many different regions of the world.

CHAPTER

17

Chiefdoms

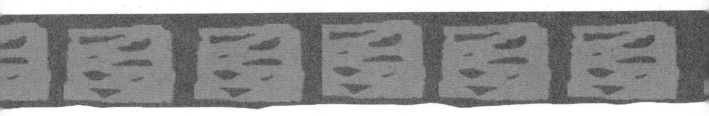

CHAPTER QUESTIONS

- What are the characteristics of an environment that are conducive to the development of chiefdom societies?

- How is the political system of chiefdoms related to the economic system?

- How does the social structure of chiefdom societies compare to egalitarian societies?

- In what ways are the legal and religious traditions of chiefdoms different from those of tribal and band societies?

Like the term *tribe,* the term *chiefdom* has caused a certain amount of confusion outside anthropology. A major reason for this confusion is that chiefdoms have little to do with what people commonly refer to as "chiefs." For example, in Chapter 16 we discussed the Nuer leopard skin chief. The Nuer, however, are not classified as a chiefdom society. In addition, many Native American societies had leaders who were usually referred to as "chiefs," although these societies were usually tribes rather than chiefdoms. In the past, Western explorers, missionaries, and government officials used the label "chief" to describe any individual who held a leadership role in a non-Western, stateless society. But as we have learned in our previous discussions of band and tribal societies, political leadership was widely diffused in these groups, and many of these societies did not have permanent systems of leadership.

In contrast to this common usage, anthropologists use *chiefdom* to refer to a form of complex society that is intermediate between the band and tribal societies (discussed in Chapters 15 and 16) and the formally organized bureaucratic state societies (discussed in Chapters 18 and 19). A **chiefdom** is a political economy that organizes regional populations in the thousands or tens of thousands through a hierarchy of leaders, or chiefs. **Chiefs** own, manage, and control the basic productive factors of the economy and have privileged access to strategic and luxury goods. These leaders are set off from the rest of society by various cultural practices and symbols, such as clothing, jewelry, specialized language, and social status. Thus, chiefdom societies are *not egalitarian* in the sense that band and tribal societies are.

Another reason that the term *chiefdom* is often unclear is that chiefdom societies vary greatly with respect to political, economic, and cultural forms. Hence, even anthropologists frequently disagree about which societies should be classified as chiefdoms. Some consider the chiefdom to be a subcategory of the tribe, whereas others view it as qualitatively different from tribes and bands (Service, [1962] 1971; Sahlins, 1968b). Anthropologists have designated two different forms of chiefdoms: one is a *centralized* political system with localized chiefs who control economic, social, political, and religious affairs; a second is more *decentralized,* with centers of political power and authority distributed throughout a region, and chiefs having control over different local arenas. Although most anthropologists now recognize the limitations of the term *chiefdom* as it is applied to a vast range of societies in different circumstances, most also consider it a valuable category for cross-cultural and comparative research.

As with tribal and foraging societies, hundreds of chiefdoms existed during at least the past 12,000 years of human history. Chiefdoms were widespread throughout Polynesia, including the islands of Hawaii, Tahiti, and Tonga. They also flourished in parts of North, Central, and South America, sub-Saharan Africa, the Caribbean, Southeast Asia, and in Europe until the Roman Empire. Today, however, very few of these chiefdoms remain as autonomous societies. Therefore, the past tense is used to discuss these societies. Not surprisingly, a great deal of the research on chiefdoms is based on archaeological and historical documentation.

The transition to a chiefdom society from a prior form of society is not well documented in any part of the world. But through comparisons with tribal and foraging societies, anthropologists have developed various hypotheses to explain this transition. The central question is how one particular descent group (or several descent groups) managed to gain advantages or monopolies of resources over other descent groups. In other words, how did social stratification and economic inequality emerge from the egalitarian economic and political processes found in tribal or foraging societies? As we shall see in the descriptions of chiefdoms, ecological, demographic, economic, social, political, and religious factors all influenced the development of chiefdom societies. We begin with a description of the environments and subsistence activities of different chiefdoms.

Environment, Subsistence, and Demography

Most chiefdom societies have occupied ecological regions that contain abundant resources, usually more abundant than the resources in the areas inhabited by band and tribal societies.

Pacific Island Chiefdoms

In the area known as Polynesia, which extends eastward from Hawaii to New Zealand and includes Samoa, Tahiti, and Tonga (see Figure 17.1), various chiefdoms existed. The arable land on these Pacific islands is very fertile, and the soil is covered by a dense forest growth. Rainfall is plentiful, and the average temperature is 77°F year-round. Tahiti is a typical example of a Polynesian island on which most of the people resided on the coastal flatlands.

One important aspect of subsistence for the Tahitian people was the bountiful harvest from the sea. Fish and shellfish accounted for a substantial portion of their diet. The coconut palm, which grows abundantly even in poor soil, provided nourishment from its meat and milk, as well as oil for cooking. The breadfruit plant was another important foodstuff; if fermented, breadfruit can be stored in pits for long periods of time.

Like many other chiefdom societies, the Tahitians practiced *intensive horticulture,* in which one improves crop production by irrigating, fertilizing, hoeing, and terracing the land. Through intensive horticulture (and near-perfect weather conditions), the Tahitians were able to make efficient use of small parcels of arable land. Although this type of agriculture demanded labor, time, and energy, the agricultural yields it produced were much greater than those produced by tribal peoples who practiced slash-and-burn horticulture.

The Tahitians' most important crops were taro, yams, and sweet potatoes. Supplementing these crops were bananas, plantains, sugar cane, and gourds. Protein requirements were met by the consumption of seafood and such animals as domesticated pigs, chickens, and, on occasion, dogs. (The Polynesians did distinguish between dogs that were

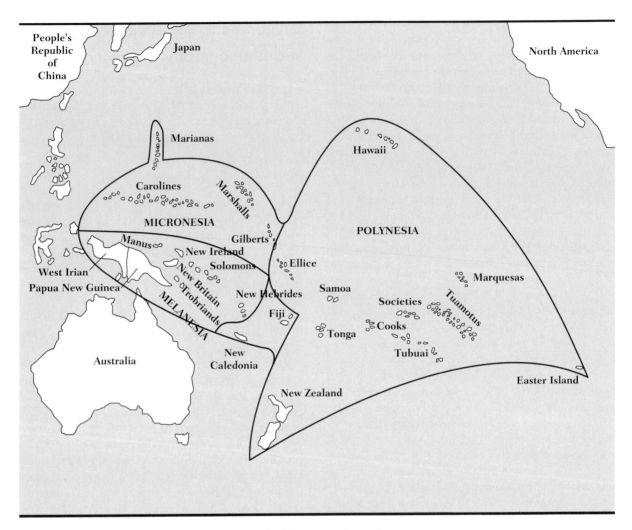

FIGURE 17.1   The Pacific islands, where many chiefdoms were located.

kept as pets and those that were used for food.) The native peoples of Hawaii, Samoa, Easter Island, and Cook Island had essentially the same ecological setting for the development of a highly productive subsistence strategy.

African Chiefdoms

Anthropologist Jacques Maquet (1972) suggested that a very high proportion of precolonial African societies were chiefdoms. These savanna chiefdom societies included peoples such as the Kpelle of Liberia, the Bemba of Zambia, and the Luba and Songhe of central Africa. These chiefdoms developed in the dry forest, the woodland savanna, and the grassy savanna. In the savanna regions, the use of intensive horticulture, including the use of hoes, produced a surplus of crops consisting of cereals such as sorghum, millet, cassava, and maize, and legumes such as peas and beans. Archaeologists have determined that sorghum, rice, and millet were cultivated as far back as 1000 B.C. (McIntosh & McIntosh, 1993). Generally, these chiefdoms were more decentralized and power was diffused widely throughout wide-ranging areas by localized leadership (McIntosh, 1999).

Native American Chiefdoms

The Mississippi Region   One prehistoric ecological region in North America where various chiefdom societies flourished was the region along the Mississippi River extending from Louisiana northward to Illinois. One of the primary cultural centers of the North American chiefdoms was the Cahokian society, located near where the Mississippi and Missouri rivers come together. This area contained extremely fertile soil and abundant resources of fish, shellfish, and game animals. The Cahokian people also practiced intensive horticulture, using hoes and fertilizers to produce their crops. The Cahokian chiefdom society emerged around A.D. 950 and reached its peak by about 1100. At that point, it had evolved into an urban center with a population of about twenty thousand people.

The Northwest Coast   Another region in North America that contains a vast wealth of natural resources is the area of the Northwest Coast. This area is bounded by the Pacific Ocean on the west and mountain ranges on the east. Numerous groups such as the Haida, Tlingit, Tsimshian, Kwakiutl, Bella Coola, Bella Bella, Nootka, Makah, and Tillamook lived in this region (see Figure 17.2). These societies are usually categorized as chiefdoms, although they do not fit the ideal pattern as neatly as do the Polynesian societies (Lewellen, 1983). Although

there were some differences in respect to subsistence and adaptation for each group, the patterns were very similar for the entire region.

One of the major reasons the Northwest Coast groups do not fit as well into the chiefdom category is that they were essentially hunters and gatherers and did not practice any horticulture or agriculture. Because of their economic, social, and political features, however, they have been traditionally characterized as chiefdoms. The unique ecological conditions of the northwest region enabled these societies to develop patterns not usually associated with the hunters and gatherers discussed in Chapter 15. Instead of residing in marginal environments as did many foragers, these peoples lived in environments rich with resources.

The ecological conditions on the Northwest Coast were as ideal as those of the Pacific islands. The climate was marked by heavy rainfall, and the mountain barrier to the east sheltered the region from cold winds from the continent. The region could therefore support rich forests of cedar, fir, and other trees. Game such as deer, bears, ducks, and geese were plentiful, and berries, roots, and other plants were easily harvested. The most important food resources, however, came from the coastal and inland waters. Streams and rivers were filled every fall with huge salmon, which were smoked and dried for storage, providing a year-round food

An artist's recreation of the Cahokia Mound around A.D. 1200.

FIGURE 17.2 Map of the Northwest Coast showing where various chiefdoms were located.

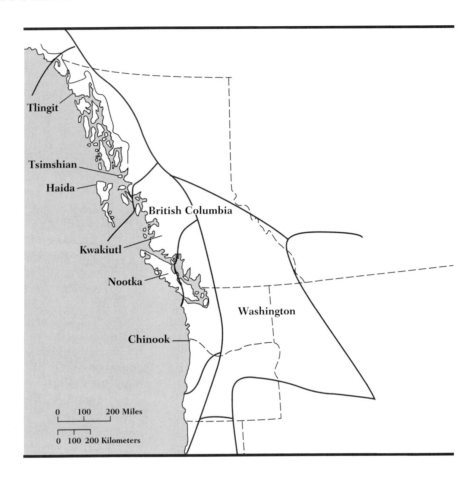

source. The coastal waters supplied these groups with shellfish, fish, and sea mammals such as seals, sea otters, and porpoises.

The environments of the Pacific islands, the Mississippi region, and the Northwest Coast of North America produced what is known as regional symbiosis. In **regional symbiosis,** a people reside in an ecological habitat divided into different resource areas; groups living in these different areas become interdependent. People in one region may subsist on fishing, in another region on hunting, and in a third region on cultivation. These groups exchange products, thus establishing mutual dependency.

Demography

Anthropologists hypothesize that population growth is an important factor in the centralized administration and social complexity associated with chiefdoms (Carneiro, 1967; Dumond, 1972). Chiefdom populations, which range from 5,000 to

50,000 people, frequently exceed the carrying capacity of the region (Drennan, 1987; Johnson & Earle, 2000). Population growth leads to an increased risk of shortages of food and other resources. To maintain adequate resources, these societies give certain individuals the power and authority to organize systematically the production and accumulation of surplus resources (Sahlins, 1958; Johnson & Earle, 2000).

Technology

Chiefdom societies developed technologies that reflected their abundant and varied natural resources. Although the Polynesians relied primarily on digging sticks for intensive horticulture, they also had many specialized tools—including tools to cut shells and stones—for making jewelry, knives, fishhooks, harpoons, nets, and large canoes. Likewise, the Cahokian society had an elaborate technology consisting of fishhooks, grinding stones, mortars and pestles, hoes, and many other tools.

Housing

The dwellings used in chiefdom societies varied over regions, depending on materials available. The traditional Pacific island housing of Tahiti and Hawaii was built with poles and thatched with coconut leaves and other vegetation. The island houses needed repair from time to time but generally were long-lasting dwellings. Similarly, the Cahokian people built firm housing by plastering clay over a wood framework. In the Northwest Coast villages, people lived in houses made of cedar planks, which were some of the most solid housing construction in all of America before European colonization. In all of these chiefdom societies, the housing structures of the chief's family were much more elaborate, spacious, and highly decorated than those of other people.

Political Economy

Because the economic and political aspects of chiefdom societies are so strongly interrelated, we discuss the variables together. As we shall see, as political centralization emerged in chiefdom societies, the economic system came under control of the chiefly elite.

Food Storage

One aspect of the economy that often played a key role in chiefdom societies was the storage of food. For chiefdoms to exist, resources had to be abundant, and people needed a technology for storing and preserving these resources. Food storage was a key variable in the ability of a society to become economically productive, creating the potential for economic and political stratification. Although there were occasional instances of food storage in some nomadic hunter-gatherer societies in marginal environments, food storage was not common among foragers or tribal societies (Testart, 1988).

The Northwest Coast Native Americans provide an example of food storage methods practiced by chiefdoms. These societies experienced two different seasonal cycles: in the summer, the groups engaged in fishing, hunting, and gathering; during the winter season, little subsistence activity occurred. During the winter these peoples lived on stored food, particularly smoked and preserved salmon. In these circumstances, certain descent groups and individuals accumulated surpluses, thereby acquiring a higher position in the society.

Property Ownership

Property ownership developed when a powerful individual, a chief, who was the head of a lineage, a village, or a group of interrelated villages, claimed exclusive ownership of the territory within the region. To use the land, other people had to observe certain restrictions on their production and turn over some of their resources to the chief.

In chiefdom societies, property ownership tended to become more closely identified with particular descent groups and individuals. For example, on the Northwest Coast, fishing sites with large and predictable runs of salmon tended to be owned and inherited by particular corporate kin groups. As another example, specific chiefs among the Trobriand Islands owned and maintained more or less exclusive rights to large canoes that were important in regional trade.

Political Aspects of Property Ownership Anthropologists differ over how much exclusive ownership the chiefs had over their realm. As we shall see later in the chapter, the political authority of a chief did have some limitations. Accordingly, the claim to exclusive rights over the territories may, in some cases, have been restricted. For example, among the Kpelle of Liberia in West Africa, the land was said to be owned formally by the paramount chief (the highest-ranking chief), who divided it into portions for each village in the chiefdom. These portions were then distributed in parcels to families of various lineages. Once land was parceled out, it remained within the lineage until the lineage died out. In this sense, the paramount chief was only a steward holding land for the group he represented (Gibbs, 1965). Among the Trobriand Islands, in theory, a *dala,* a corporate matrilineal kin group comprised of some sixty-five persons, owned their own land for cultivating yams and other crops for exchange. However, a *dala* leader (a son within the matrilineage) had effective control over the access and allocation of crops from the land (Weiner, 1976).

The Evolution of Chiefdoms

A number of anthropologists, including Elman Service, hypothesize that in some cases chiefdom societies emerged because of regional symbiosis (Service, [1962] 1971). Because particular descent groups were strategically located among territories with different resources, these groups played a key role in the exchange and allocation of resources throughout the population. Eventually, some of the leaders of these descent groups became identified as the chiefs or centralized leaders. In other words, by regulating the exchange of resources, the chiefs held these formerly autonomous regions together under a centralized administration. In a detailed account of the evolution of chiefdoms, Service (1975) used cultural ideology as well as ecological variables to identify certain individuals and descent groups as chiefs. He argued that particular individuals and their descent group were recognized as having more prestige and status. A consensus thus emerged within the society regarding who became chiefs.

Based on his research of Polynesian chiefdoms, archaeologist Timothy Earle (1977, 1997) challenged the hypothesis that chiefdoms emerged through regional symbiosis. By analyzing the ecological conditions and reconstructing exchange networks in Hawaii and other Polynesian locations, Earle found that commodity exchanges were much more limited and did not involve large-scale exchanges among specialized ecological regions as described by Service and others. Exchanges were localized, and most households appear to have had access to all critical resources.

Earle (1987, 1997) suggested that the key factor in the evolution of chiefdoms was the degree of control over vital productive resources and labor. In the case of Hawaii, with population growth, land became a scarce commodity, and competition for the limited fertile land developed. Chiefs conquered certain agricultural lands over which they claimed exclusive rights. Other people received use rights to small subsistence plots in return for their work on the chief's lands. This system permitted the chiefs to exercise much more extensive control over resources and labor. According to Earle, in contrast to the paramount chief as the steward of the land, these chiefs not only had "title" to the land but also effectively controlled the labor on the land.

Economic Exchange

Chiefdom societies practiced a number of different types of economic exchange. Two basic types of exchange are *reciprocal exchanges* and *redistributional exchanges*.

Reciprocal Exchange Like all societies, chiefdoms engaged in reciprocal exchanges. One classic case of balanced reciprocal exchange occurred among the Trobriand Islanders, as described by Bronislaw Malinowski ([1922] 1961). The Trobrianders, intensive horticulturalists who raised yams and depended heavily on fishing, maintained elaborate trading arrangements with other island groups. They had large sea canoes, or outriggers, and traveled hundreds of miles on sometime dangerous seas to conduct what was known as the *kula exchange*.

The Kula Exchange The **kula** was the ceremonial trade of valued objects that took place among a number of the Trobriand Islands. In his book *Argonauts of the Western Pacific* ([1922] 1961), Malinowski described how red-shell necklaces and white-shell armbands were ritually exchanged from island to island through networks of male traders. The necklaces traditionally traveled clockwise, and the armbands traveled counterclockwise. These necklaces and armbands were constantly circulating, and the size and value of these items had to be perfectly matched (hence, *balanced reciprocity*). People did not keep these items very long; in fact, they were seldom worn. There was no haggling or discussion of price by any of the traders.

Trobriand males were inducted into the trading network through elaborate training regarding the proper etiquette and magical practices of the *kula*. The young men learned these practices through their fathers' or mothers' brothers and eventually established trading connections with partners on other islands.

A more utilitarian trade accompanied the ceremonial trade. Goods such as tobacco, pottery, coconuts, fish, baskets, and mats were exchanged through the Trobriand trading partners. In these exchanges, the partners haggled and discussed price. Malinowski referred to this trade as *secondary trade*, or **barter**, the direct exchange of one commodity for another. He argued that the ceremonial *kula* trade created emotional ties among trading partners and that the utilitarian trade was secondary and incidental. Because of this argument, Malinowski is often referred to as one of the first substantivist economic anthropologists (see Chapter 14). He hypothesized that the economic production and exchange of utilitarian goods were embedded in the social practices and cultural norms of the *kula* exchange, which was noneconomic.

Some anthropologists, however, hypothesized that the ceremonial trade was only the ritual means for conducting the more utilitarian transactions for material goods. Annette Weiner (1987) reanalyzed the *kula* trade and, in her interviews with older informants, found that Malinowski had overlooked the fact that certain armbands or necklaces, known as *kitomu,* were owned by the chiefs. The *kitomu* could be used for bridewealth payments, funeral expenses, or to build a canoe. In other words, they were more like money. At times, a chief would add some *kitomu* into the *kula* transactions to attract new partners and new wealth. These chiefs would take economic risks with these shells to accumulate valuable private profits. If a chief gained a new partner through these transactions, he would be able to gain more wealth. If he was not able to gain new partners, however, he could lose some of his investments.

Thus, Weiner viewed the *kula* not as a system of *balanced reciprocity* but rather as a system of *economic competition* in which certain traders tried to maximize social and political status and to accumulate profits. Although the *kula* exchanges emphasized the notions of equality and reciprocity, this was, in fact, an illusion. In actuality, trading partners tried to achieve the opposite—to gain ever-larger profits and status.

Malinowski overlooked the fact that the trade items of the *kula* exchange, referred to as "wealth finances," were critically important in establishing a chief's social status and personal prestige. For example, only the chiefs were able to control the extensive labor needed to construct outrigger canoes, by means of which the trade was conducted. Thus, the chiefs benefited enormously from the *kula* exchange (Earle, 1987; Johnson & Earle, 2000).

Redistributional Exchange   The predominant form of economic exchange in chiefdom societies, and one that is not usually found in band and tribal societies, is **redistributional economic exchange,** which involves the exchange of goods and resources through a centralized organization. In the redistributional system, food and other staples, such as craft goods, are collected as a form of tax or rent. The chiefs (and subsidiary chiefs) redistribute some of these goods and food staples back to the population at certain times of the year. This system thus assures the dispersal of food and resources throughout the community through a centralized agency.

Potlatch   A classic example of a chiefdom redistributional system was found among the Native

Many of the Northwest Coast chiefdoms use the potlatch for redistributing goods and resources.

Americans of the Northwest Coast. Known as the **potlatch,** it was described at length among the Kwakiutl by Franz Boas (1930) and was later interpreted by Ruth Benedict (1934).

The term *potlatch* is a Chinook word translated loosely as "giveaway." In a potlatch, local leaders gave away large quantities of goods and resources in what appeared to be a highly wasteful manner. Potlatches were held when young people were introduced into society or during marriage or funeral ceremonies. Families would prepare for these festive occasions by collecting food and other valuables such as fish, berries, blankets, and animal skins, which were then given to local leaders in many different villages. In these potlatch feasts, the leaders of different villages competed in giving away or sometimes destroying more food than their competitors. Northwest Coast Indians believe that the more gifts that were bestowed on the people or destroyed by a chief, the higher the status of that chief.

Benedict interpreted the potlatch feasts and rivalry among chiefs as the result of their megalomaniacal personalities. To substantiate this view, she presented this formal speech made by a Kwakiutl chief (1934:191):

> I am the first of the tribes, I am the only one of the tribes. The chiefs of the tribes are only local chiefs. I am the only one among the tribes. I search among all the invited chiefs for greatness like mine. I cannot find one chief among the guests. They never return feasts. The orphans, poor people, chiefs of the tribes! They disgrace themselves. I am he who gives these sea otters to the chiefs, the guests, the chiefs of the tribes. I am he who gives canoes to the chiefs, the guests, the chiefs of the tribes.

Despite the apparent wastefulness, status rivalry, and megalomaniacal personalities suggested by Benedict, contemporary anthropologists view the potlatch feasts as having served a redistributional exchange process. For example, despite the abundance of resources in the Northwest Coast region, there were regional variations and periodic fluctuations in the supply of salmon and other products. In some areas people had more than they needed, whereas in other regions, people suffered from frequent scarcities. Given these circumstances, the potlatch helped distribute surpluses and special local products to other villages in need (Piddocke, 1965).

Marvin Harris (1977) argues that the potlatch also functioned to ensure the production and distribution of goods in societies that lacked ruling classes. Through the elaborate redistributive feasts and conspicuous consumption, the chiefs presented themselves as the providers of food and security to the population. The competition among the chiefs meant that both the haves and the have-nots benefited from this system. According to Harris, this form of competitive feasting enabled growing chiefdom populations to survive and prosper by encouraging people to work harder and accumulate resources.

Redistribution in Polynesia   Another classic example of redistribution appears in the historical records of native Polynesian societies. In societies such as Tahiti and Hawaii, people who were able to redistribute goods and resources among various villages and islands emerged as leaders. After crops were harvested, a certain portion (the "first fruits of the harvest") was directed to local village leaders and then given to higher-level subsidiary chiefs who were more centrally located. These goods were eventually directed toward the paramount chiefs, who redistributed some of them back to the population during different periods of the year (Sahlins, 1958; Kirch, 1984). Along with coordinating exchanges, the chiefs could also decree which crops were to be planted and how they were to be used.

Redistributional exchange economies are similar to reciprocal economic systems in that they involve transfers of goods and other resources among related villagers. A major difference between the two systems is that the latter is predominant in societies that are highly egalitarian, whereas in the chiefdom societies that have redistributional economic systems, rank and status are unequal.

Within a redistributional system, local leaders and related individuals not only have a higher status and rank but are also able to siphon off some of the economic surplus for their own benefit. This inequality creates a **hierarchical society** in which some people have access to more wealth, rank, status, authority, and power than do other people. This redistributional exchange system among the

Polynesian chiefdoms has been referred to as an early form of taxation (Johnson & Earle, 2000).

Political Authority among Chiefdoms Whereas the political structures of bands and tribes were impermanent and indefinite, chiefdom political structures were well defined, permanent, and corporate. In chiefdoms the leadership functions were formalized in the institutionalized office of chief, with the personal qualities of the chief being unrelated to the responsibilities and prerogatives of the office. (An **office** refers to the position of authority assigned to a person.) In most cases, the chief's office had clearly defined rules of succession. The office of the chief existed apart from the man who occupied it, and on his death, the office had to be filled by a man from a similar chiefly family. This system differed markedly from the big-man system found in some tribes, in which leadership positions were attached to particular individuals based on personal characteristics. Tribal societies had no hereditary rules of succession; the big man's authority could not be passed on to his sons or to other kin.

In many of the Polynesian chiefdoms, the rule of succession was based on **primogeniture,** in which the eldest son assumed the status (and realm) of the father. This form of political succession is prevalent in other chiefdom societies as well. The rule of primogeniture helped to avoid a power struggle when the chief died, and it provided for continuity for the overall political (and economic) system (Service, 1975).

As is evident from our previous discussions, the chiefs had a great deal of control over both surplus prestige goods and strategic resources, including food and water. This control enhanced chiefly status, rank, and authority, ensuring both loyalty and deference on the part of those from lower descent groups. In addition, it enabled the chiefs to exercise a certain amount of coercion. They could recruit armies, distribute land and water rights to families, and sentence someone to death for violating certain societal norms.

Limits on Chiefly Power Nevertheless, chiefs did not maintain absolute power over their subjects. They ruled with minimal coercion based on their control over economic production and redistribution, rather than on fear or repression. This political

legitimacy was buttressed by religious beliefs and rituals, which will be discussed later.

A Case Study: The Trobriand Islands The political systems of the Pacific island societies had varying degrees of chiefly authority. Chiefly authority was more limited among the Trobrianders than among the Hawaiians and Tahitians. The Trobriand chief had to work to expand his arena of power and status and prevent other chiefs from destroying or diminishing his ancestral rights (Weiner, 1987). Much economic and political competition existed among the chiefs of matrilineal descent groups. A Trobriand chief gained rights, legitimacy, and authority through descent. That authority, however, also depended on what the chief accomplished in the way of redistribution and giving feasts to furnish food and other resources. Generosity was therefore one of the most important aspects of Trobriand chieftaincy. If generosity was not demonstrated, the chief's power, authority, and legitimacy diminished. Chiefs were frequently replaced by other, more generous people within the chiefly family.

A Case Study: Hawaii and Tahiti The aboriginal Hawaiian and Tahitian chiefdoms tended to be more fully developed than those of the Trobrianders. For example, Hawaiian society was divided into various social strata composed of descent groups. The highest-ranking noble strata, known as *ali'i,* were district chiefs and their families. Within the highest-ranking descent groups, the eldest son (or daughter) inherited the political and social status of the father. Above the *ali'i* were the paramount chiefs, or *ali'i nui,* who ruled over the islands.

The paramount chiefs and district chiefs were treated with reverence and extreme deference. They were carried around on litters, and the "commoners"—farmers, fishermen, craftsworkers, and "inferiors"—had to prostrate themselves before the nobles. Thus, political legitimacy and authority were much more encompassing than in the Trobriand case.

This does not mean, however, that the Hawaiian or Tahitian chiefs had absolute or despotic power. In fact, most of the evidence indicates that the political stability of Tahitian and Hawaiian chiefdoms was somewhat delicate. There were constant challenges to the paramount and district chiefs by rival leaders who made genealogical claims for rights to succession. These rivals would marry women of chiefly families, combined with the manipulation of genealogical status, to challenge a paramount chief's leadership. In many cases, paramount chiefs had to demonstrate their authority and power not only through the redistribution of land, food, and prestige goods but also through warfare against rival claimants. If a paramount chief was unable to hold his territorial area, challengers could increase their political power, and the political legitimacy of the paramount chief might diminish substantially. Permanent conquest by rival chiefs over a paramount chief resulted in a new ranking system in which the lineage of the conquering group supplanted that of the paramount chief. When this occurred in Hawaii, the paramount chief's descent group became sacrificial victims to the new ruler's deities (Valeri, 1985). Thus, conquest did not result in the complete overthrow of the society's political structure. Rather, it consisted of revolts that minimally reordered the social and political ranking order. The basic fabric of the chiefdoms was not transformed; one noble lineage simply replaced another.

In some cases, the chiefs tried to institutionalize a more permanent basis of power and authority. For example, chiefs occasionally meted out a death sentence for those accused of treason or of plotting to overthrow a chief. Yet this use of force was rarely displayed. Despite the fact that authority was centralized, political legitimacy was based ultimately on consensus and goodwill from the populace rather than military coercion. Polynesian chiefs could normally expect to command a majority of the labor and military needed in their domains simply by occupying their political office. But if things were going badly, if the chief was not fair and generous in redistribution or settling disputes, armed revolts could begin, or political struggles would erupt—not to overthrow the political or social order but to substitute one chief for another.

Warfare Warfare among chiefdom societies was more organized than among bands or tribes, primarily because the political and economic mechanisms in chiefdoms were more centralized and formalized. In many cases, chiefs were able to recruit armies and conduct warfare in a systematic manner.

Anthropologist Robert Carneiro (1970) views warfare as one of the decisive factors in the evolution of chiefdoms. The objective of many chiefs was to extend their chiefdom regionally so as to dominate the populations of surrounding communities and thereby control those communities' surplus production. As chiefdoms expanded through warfare and conquest, many of the people in the conquered territories were absorbed into the chiefdom. In certain cases, these chiefdoms succeeded because of their technological superiority. In many other cases, such as in Polynesia, they succeeded because the surrounding communities were circumscribed by oceans and had no choice but to become absorbed by the conquering chiefdom.

Social Organization

In Chapter 14, we discussed the concept of *social stratification,* the inequality among statuses within society. Chiefdom societies exhibit a great deal of stratification. They are divided into different **strata** (singular: stratum), a group of equivalent statuses based on ranked divisions in a society. Strata in chiefdom societies are not based solely on economic

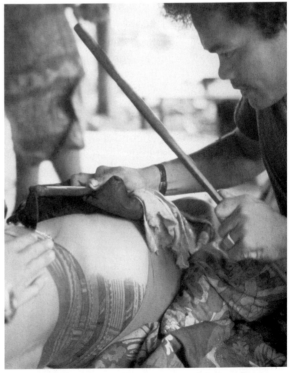

Tattooing in the Pacific islands was used frequently to symbolize status relationships.

factors but rather cut across society based on prestige, power, and generalized religious conceptions.

Rank and Sumptuary Rules

Chiefdom societies are hierarchically ranked societies. The various families and descent groups—households, lineages, and clans—have a specific ascribed rank in the society and are accorded certain rights, privileges, and obligations based on that rank. Social interaction between lower and higher strata is governed by sumptuary rules. **Sumptuary rules** are cultural norms and practices used to differentiate the higher-status groups from the rest of society. In general, the higher the status and rank, the more ornate the jewelry, costumes, and decorative symbols. Among the Natchez, Native Americans of the Mississippi region, the upper-ranking members were tattooed all over their bodies, whereas lower-ranking people were only partially tattooed.

Some of the Pacific chiefdoms had sumptuary rules requiring that a special orator chief instead of the paramount chief speak to the public. The highest paramount chiefs spoke a noble language with an archaic vocabulary containing words that commoners could not use with one another. Other sumptuary rules involved taboos against touching or eating with higher-ranking people. Sumptuary rules also set standards regarding dress, marriage, exchanges, and other cultural practices. In many of the chiefdoms, social inferiors had to prostrate themselves and demonstrate other signs of deference in the presence of their "social superiors." Symbols of inequality and hierarchy were thoroughly ingrained in most of these societies.

A Case Study: Polynesia and Stratified Descent Groups   The ethnohistoric data on the Polynesian Islands contain some of the most detailed descriptions of social stratification within chiefdom societies. The ideal basis of social organization was the *conical clan* (see Figure 17.3), an extensive descent group having a common ancestor who was usually traced through a patrilineal line (Kirchoff, 1955; Sahlins, 1968b; Goldman, 1970). Rank and lineage were determined by a person's kinship distance to the founding ancestor, as illustrated in Figure 17.3. The closer a person was to the highest-ranking senior male in direct line of descent to the ancestor, the higher his or her rank and status. In

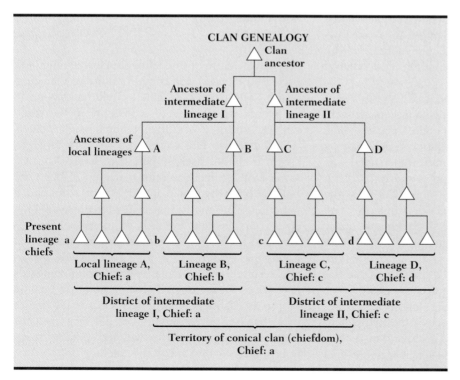

FIGURE 17.3   Model of a conical clan.

Source: From *Tribesmen* by Marshall D. Sahlins, © 1968. Reprinted by permission of Prentice-Hall, Inc., Upper Saddle River, NJ.

fact, as Marshall Sahlins (1985) suggested, the Hawaiians did not trace *descent* but *ascent* toward a connection with an ancient ruling line.

Although Polynesian societies reflected a patrilineal bias, most had ambilineal descent groups (Goodenough, 1955; Firth, 1957). Senior males headed local descent groups in the villages. These local groups were ranked in relation to other larger, senior groups that were embedded in the conical clan. Because of ambilateral rules, people born into certain groups had the option of affiliating with either their paternal or maternal linkages in choosing their rank and status. In general, beyond this genealogical reckoning, these chiefdom societies offered little in the way of upward social mobility for achieved statuses.

Marriage

As in tribal societies, most marriages in chiefdoms were carefully arranged affairs, sometimes involving cousin marriages from different descent groups. People who married outside of their descent group usually married within their social stratum. In some chiefdom societies, however, marriages were sometimes arranged between higher-strata males and females of lower strata. Anthropologist Jane Collier (1988) noted that women in chiefdom societies that emphasized hereditary rank tended to avoid low-ranking males and tried to secure marriages with men who possessed more economic and political prerogatives.

One chiefdom in North America illustrates a situation in which marriage provided a systematic form of social mobility for the entire society. The Natchez Indians of the Mississippi region were a matrilineal society divided into four strata: the Great Sun chief (the eldest son of the top-ranking lineage) and his brothers; the noble lineages; the honored lineages; and the inferior "stinkards." All members of the three upper strata had to marry down to a stinkard. This resulted in a regular form of social mobility from generation to generation. The children of the upper three ranks took the status of their mother, unless she was a stinkard.

If a woman of the Great Sun married a stinkard, their children became members of the upper stratum. If a noble woman married a stinkard man, their children became nobles. However, if a noble man married a stinkard, their children would drop to the stratum of the honored status. Through marriage, all of the stinkard children moved up in the status hierarchy.

Although this system allowed for a degree of mobility, it required the perpetuation of the stinkard stratum so that members of the upper strata would have marriage partners. One way the stinkard stratum was maintained was through marriage between two stinkards; their children remained in the inferior stratum. In addition, the stinkard category was continually replenished with people captured in warfare.

Endogamy Marriages in chiefdom societies were both exogamous and endogamous. Although marriages might be exogamous among descent groupings, the spouses were usually from the same stratum (endogamy). These endogamous marriages were carefully arranged so as to maintain genealogically appropriate kinship bonds and descent relations in the top-ranking descent group. Frequently, this involved cousin marriage among descent groups of the same stratum. Among Hawaiian chiefs, rules of endogamy actually resulted in sibling marriages, sometimes referred to as *royal-incest marriage*. One anthropologist categorized these sibling marriages as attempts to create alliances between chiefly households among the various Hawaiian Islands (Valeri, 1985).

Polygyny Many of the ruling families in chiefdom societies practiced polygyny. Among the Tsimshian of the Northwest Coast, chiefs could have as many as twenty wives, usually women from the high-ranking lineages of other groups. Lesser chiefs would marry several wives from lower-ranking lineages. In some cases, a Tsimshian woman from a lower-ranking lineage could marry up through the political strategies of her father. For example, a father might arrange a marriage with a high-ranking chief and his daughter. All of these polygynous marriages were accompanied by exchanges of goods that passed to the top of the chiefly hierarchy, resulting in accumulations of surplus resources and wives (Rosman & Rubel, 1986). Among the Trobriand Islanders, male chiefs traditionally had as many as sixty wives drawn from different lineages. High rates of polygyny in the high-ranking strata flourished in many chiefdom societies.

General Social Principles

Among chiefdom societies, the typical family form was the extended family, with three generations living in a single household. In the Pacific region, for example, the basic domestic unit was usually made up of a household with three generations; in some cases, two or three brothers with their offspring were permanent residents of the household. The households in a specific area of a village were usually part of one lineage. The extended-family household was usually the basic economic unit for subsistence production and consumption in chiefdom societies.

Postmarital residence varied among chiefdoms. Patrilocal, matrilocal, and ambilocal types of residence rules were found in different areas. The ambilocal rule, found in many chiefdoms of the Pacific, enabled people to trace descent to ancestors (male or female) who had the highest rank in the society. This flexibility enabled some individuals to attain access to property, privileges, and authority in spite of the inherent restrictions on status mobility in chiefdom societies (Goodenough, 1956).

Gender

Typically, gender relations were highly unequal in chiefdom societies, with males exercising economic and political dominance over females. Bridewealth payments, along with arranged marriages, enabled men to claim rights to the labor of children and women. This practice was particularly significant among the highest-status descent groups. A woman's chances of success depended entirely on the rank of her siblings and parents. Higher-ranking males frequently married women with low-ranking brothers who wanted to control and manage their marital relations, labor, and potential offspring.

If a woman was fortunate enough to be born or marry into a high-ranking descent group, her ascribed or achieved status was secured. Anthropologist Laura Klein described how some high-ranking women among the Tsimshian Indians were able to maintain considerably high status in their society (1980). According to Sahlins (1985), some wives of high-ranking chiefs in traditional Hawaiian society married as many as forty males (a type of royal polyandry) to maintain their high status. Thus, the women of the ruling stratum had a higher status than men or women from other strata. Yet, generally, men controlled and dominated economically and politically in chiefdom societies.

Age

In many chiefdom societies, senior males had much more authority, rank, and prestige than other people. As in some tribal societies, this form of inequality produced *gerontocratic systems.* As people—especially in the higher-ranking descent groups—aged, they received more in the way of status, privileges, and deference from younger people. Because senior males controlled production, marriages, labor, and other economic activities, they became the dominant political authorities. Senior males also possessed special knowledge and controlled sacred rituals, reinforcing their authority. One of their major responsibilities was to perpetuate the beliefs that rank depended on a person's descent group and that status was hereditary. As in some of the tribal societies, the combination of patriarchy and gerontocracy resulted in *cultural hegemony,* the imposition of norms, practices, beliefs, and values that reinforced the interests of the upper stratum. This cultural hegemony will become more apparent in the discussion of law and religion in chiefdom societies.

Slavery

Earlier in the chapter, we noted that chiefdoms frequently engaged in systematic, organized warfare. One consequence of this warfare was the taking of captives, who were designated as slaves. Slavery in chiefdoms generally did not have the same meaning or implications that it did in more complex state societies, and it usually did not involve the actual ownership of a human being as private property. In this sense, it was very different from the plantation slavery that developed later in the Americas. With some exceptions, most of the slaves in chiefdoms were absorbed into kin groups through marriage or adoption and performed essentially the same type of labor that most people did. Nevertheless, in contrast to the more egalitarian band and tribal societies, chiefdom societies did show the beginnings of a slave stratum.

We have already mentioned an example of a chiefdom slave system in our discussion of the Natchez. Recall, however, that upper-ranking members were obliged to marry members of the stinkard stratum; thus the Natchez did not have a hereditary slave population.

One exception to these generalizations involves some of the Northwest Coast Indians, who maintained a hereditary slave system. Because marrying a slave was considered debasing, slavery became an inherited status (Kehoe, 1995). The children of slaves automatically became slaves, producing a permanent slave stratum. These slaves—most of them war captives—were excluded from ceremonies and on some occasions were killed in human sacrifices. In addition, they were sometimes exchanged, resulting in a kind of commercial traffic of humans. Even in this system, however, slaves who had been captured in warfare could be ransomed by their kinfolk or could purchase their own freedom (Garbarino, 1988).

Law and Religion

Legal and religious institutions and concepts were inextricably connected in chiefdom societies. These institutions existed to sanction and legitimize the political economy and social structure of chiefdoms. They played a critical role in maintaining the cultural hegemony discussed earlier.

Law

As with political economy, mechanisms of law and social control were more institutionalized and centralized in chiefdom societies. As we discussed earlier, in bands and tribes social norms were unwritten, and social conflicts were resolved through kinship groups, often with the intervention of a leader who was respected but lacked political authority. In contrast, the authority structure in chiefdoms enabled political leaders to act as third-party judges above the interests of specific kin groupings and to make definitive decisions without fear of vengeance. Chiefs had the power to sanction certain behaviors by imposing economic fines or damages, by withholding goods and services, and by publicly reprimanding or ridiculing the offending parties. Chiefs could use their economic and political power

to induce compliance. They were not just mediators; rather, they engaged in **adjudication,** the settling of legal disputes through centralized authority.

Within chiefdoms, a dispute between kin groups was handled in the same way it was handled in band and tribal societies—through mediation by the groups. Chiefdoms differed substantially from these other societies, however, in their treatment of crimes against authority. These crimes were of two general types: direct violations against a high-ranking chief, and violations of traditional customs, norms, or beliefs, injuring the chief's authority (Service, 1975). Such crimes carried severe punishments, including death. The reason for such severe punishments is that these crimes were perceived as threatening the basis of authority in the chiefdom system.

Religion

Religious traditions in chiefdom societies were in some respects similar to the cosmic religions described for the band and tribal societies. That is, they reflected the belief that the spiritual and material aspects of nature could not be separated from one another. Religious worldviews were oriented to the cyclical pattern of the seasons and all other aspects of nature. The natural order was also the moral and spiritual order. The religious concepts in chiefdom societies were based on oral traditions perpetuated from generation to generation through elaborate cosmological myths. The most dramatic difference between chiefdom religions and band and tribal religions is the degree to which chiefdom religions legitimized the social, political, and moral status of the chiefs.

A Case Study: Law and Religion In Polynesia
Nowhere was the relationship between law and religion clearer than among the Polynesian Island chiefdoms. Hawaiian chiefs, for example, were believed to be either gods or sacred intermediaries between human societies and the divine world. Hawaiian chiefdoms have been referred to as **theocracies,** societies in which people rule not because of their worldly wealth and power but because of their place in the moral and sacred order. The political and legal authority of Hawaiian, Tonga, and Tahitian chiefs was reinforced by a religious and ideological system known as the **tabu** system, which was based on social inequalities.

Social interaction in these societies was carefully regulated through a variety of *tabus*. Elaborate forms of deference and expressions of humility served to distinguish various strata, especially those of commoners and chiefs.

Religious beliefs buttressed the tabu system. The Polynesians believed that people are imbued with cosmic forces referred to as **mana.** These spiritual forces were powerful and sometimes dangerous. They were inherited and distributed according to a person's status and rank. Thus, paramount chiefs had a great deal of *mana,* subsidiary chiefs had less, and commoners had very little. Violations of certain *tabus*—for example, touching a member of a chiefly family—could bring the offender into contact with the chief's *mana,* which was believed to cause death.

These magical forces could also be gained and lost through a person's moral actions. Thus, the success or failure of a chief was attributed to the amount of *mana* he controlled. This was also reflected in the economic and political spheres, in that a chief who was a good redistributor and maintained order was believed to possess a great amount of *mana.* On the other hand, if things went badly, this reflected a loss of magical powers. When one chief replaced another, the deposed chief was believed to have lost his powers.

Shamanism

Shamanism was practiced in many chiefdoms and has been thoroughly described among the Native American groups of the Northwest Coast. Like other social institutions, shamanism reflected the hierarchical structure of these societies. The shamans became the personal spiritual guides and doctors of the chiefs and used their knowledge to enhance the power and status of high-ranking chiefs. For example, it was believed that the shamans had the ability to send diseases into enemies and, conversely, to cure and give spiritual power to the chief's allies.

In addition, shamans danced and participated in the potlatch ceremonies on behalf of the chiefs (Garbarino, 1988). One widespread belief throughout the Northwest Coast was in a "man-eating spirit." These groups believed that an animal spirit could possess a man, which transformed him into a cannibal. During the potlatch ceremonies, shamans would dance, chant, and sing, using masks to enact the

transformation from human to animal form to ward off the power of the man-eating spirit. Through these kinds of practices, shamans could help sanction the power and authority of the high-ranking chiefs. The chiefs demonstrated their generosity through the potlatch, whereas the shamanistic ceremonies exhibited the supernatural powers that were under the control of the chiefs.

By associating closely with a chief, a shaman could elevate both his own status and that of the chief. The shaman collected fees from his chiefly clients, which enabled him to accumulate wealth. In some cases, low-ranking individuals became shamans by finding more potent spirits for a chief. No shaman, however, could accumulate enough wealth to rival a high-ranking chief (Garbarino, 1988).

Human Sacrifice

Another practice that reflected the relationships among religion, hierarchy, rank, and the legitimacy of chiefly rule was human sacrifice, which existed in some—but not all—chiefdoms. Among the Natchez Indians, for example, spectacular funerary rites were held when the Great Sun chief died. During these rites, the chief's wives, guards, and attendants were expected to sacrifice their lives, feeling privileged to follow the Great Sun into the afterworld. Parents also offered their children for sacrifice, which, they believed, would raise their own rank. The sacrificial victims were strangled, but they were first given a strong concoction of tobacco, which made them unconscious. They were then buried alongside the Great Sun chief in an elaborate burial mound.

Human sacrifice was also practiced in the Polynesian region. In Hawaii there were two major rituals: the *Makahiki,* or so-called New Year's festival, and the annual rededication of the Luakini temple, at which human sacrifices were offered (Valeri, 1985). Some of the sacrificial victims had transgressed or violated the sacred *tabus.* These victims frequently were brothers or cousins of the chiefs who were their political rivals. It was believed that these human sacrifices would help perpetuate the fertility of the land and the people. Human sacrifice was the prerogative of these chiefs and was a symbolic means of distinguishing these divine rulers from the rest of the human population. Such rituals effectively sanctioned the sacred authority of the chiefs.

Art, Architecture, and Music

Compared with band and tribal societies, chiefdom societies had more extensive artwork, which reflected two different tendencies in chiefdom societies: a high degree of labor organization, and the status symbols associated with high-ranking chiefs. One of the most profound examples of the artwork of a chiefdom society is found on Easter Island. Between 800 and 1,000 monumental stone figures known as *moai* have been discovered there. These figures vary in height from less than 2 meters to almost 10 meters (about 30 feet) and weigh up to 59 metric tons. After sculpting these figures in quarries, laborers dragged them over specially constructed transport roads and erected them on platforms. This project called for an extensive, region-wide labor organization. The symbolic design of the Easter Island statuaries evokes the power, status, and high rank of the chiefs of Easter Island (Kirch, 1984).

The large mounds associated with the Cahokian chiefdom complex also represented extensive labor projects and a hierarchical society. Different types of earthen mounds surrounded the city of Cahokia. In the center of the city was a large, truncated, flat-top mound. This mound is 100 feet high, covers 16 acres, and is built of earth, clay, silt, and sand. It took perhaps 200 years to construct. This flat-top mound is surrounded by hundreds of smaller mounds, some conical in shape, others flat-topped. Although the Cahokian society collapsed around A.D. 1450 (before European contact), archaeologists know from other remaining Mississippian chiefdom societies such as the Natchez Indians that the flat-topped mounds were used chiefly for residences and religious structures, whereas the conical mounds were used for burials.

Another example of the labor and status associated with chiefdom art forms comes from the Northwest Coast Native Americans. These groups produced totem poles, along with decorated house posts and wooden dance masks. The carved, wooden totem poles and house posts were the ultimate status and religious symbols, indicating the high social standing and linkages between the chiefs and the ancestral deities. Typically, a totem pole was erected on the beach in front of a new chief's house, which had decorated house posts. The symbolic messages transmitted through these poles expressed the status hierarchies in these societies.

A totem pole of the Kwakiutl, a Native American group of the Northwest Coast.

Music

We have already mentioned the important shamanic dances that accompanied the potlatch activities of the Northwest Coast chiefdoms. Most of the traditional music of chiefdom societies exemplified the interconnections among sociopolitical structure, religion, and art. The traditional music of Polynesia is a good example of these interconnections. Although work songs, recreational songs, and mourning songs were part of everyday life, formal music was usually used to honor the deities and chiefs (Kaeppler, 1980). In western Polynesia, on the islands of Tonga, Tikopia, and Samoa, much of the traditional music consisted of stylized poetry accompanied by bodily movements and percussion instruments such as drums.

In some ceremonies, formal poetic chants were sung in verses. In other contexts, people sang narrative songs, or *fakaniua*, describing famous places, past events, and legends, accompanied by hand clapping in a syncopated, complex rhythmic pattern.

The traditional formal musical style of eastern Polynesia, including the Hawaiian Islands, also consisted of complex, integrated systems of poetry, rhythm, melody, and movement that were multifunctional but were usually related to chiefly authority. The Hawaiians had a variety of musical instruments, including membranophones made of hollow wooden cylinders covered with sharkskin, mouth flutes, rhythm sticks, and bamboo tubes. In contrast to performers of the other islands, traditional Hawaiian musical performers and dancers were highly organized and trained in specially built schools under the high priests. The major function of the Hawaiian performers was to pay homage to the chiefs and their ancestral deities through religious chants and narrative songs.

SUMMARY

Chiefdoms are intermediate forms of societies between tribal and large-scale state societies. They tend to consist of more centralized economic and political sociocultural systems than those of foragers or tribes. In the past, they existed in many parts of the world, including the Pacific islands, Africa, the Americas, and Europe.

Chiefdoms usually had greater populations and more extensive technologies than did tribes. The political economy of chiefdoms was based on redistributional economic exchanges, in which the upper stratum, the chiefly families, had greater access to wealth, power, and political authority than did other people. There were, however, many limitations on chiefly political authority and property ownership. Because many of these chiefdoms did not have regular police or a recruited military, the chiefs had to rule through popular acceptance rather than through coercion.

The social organization of chiefdom societies consisted of lineages, clans, and other descent groups. Yet unlike tribal societies, these descent groups were ranked in strata based on their relationship to a chiefly family. Marriages were frequently endogamous within a particular stratum. Many chiefdoms practiced polygyny, especially in the upper stratum. Gender relations in chiefdom societies tended to be patriarchal, although females in the chiefly stratum often had a high status. Senior males, especially in the upper stratum, often dominated chiefdom societies, resulting in a form of gerontocracy. Although slavery emerged in some chiefdom societies, it generally was not based on commercial exchanges of humans.

Law and religion were intertwined with the sociopolitical structure of chiefdom societies. Law was based on adjudication of disputes by chiefly authorities, especially in cases that threatened the chief's legitimacy. These laws were backed by supernatural sanctions such as the *tabu* system of Polynesia, which reaffirmed chiefly authority.

The traditional art and music in chiefdom societies were also intended as a form of homage to the legitimacy of the chiefs and their ancestral deities.

QUESTIONS TO THINK ABOUT

1. How and why did chiefdoms come into existence? That is, how did economic inequality and social stratification arise from egalitarian foraging and tribal societies? What factors may have been involved in this change?

2. Aside from the prestige factors associated with the potlatch among the Northwest Coast Indians, what other functions did these ceremonies have, and what were the implications?

3. What role did kinship and descent play in the social structure of a chiefdom?

4. What was the role of trade and exchange in chiefdom societies? Give some specific examples of how goods were acquired and transferred from one individual to another.

5. How and why did the practices of reciprocity and redistribution in chiefdoms differ from the way they functioned in bands and tribes? What factors affected the way exchanges took place?

6. Describe the social structure of a chiefdom. What were the specific social rankings, and how were they determined?

7. What was the role of supernatural forces in legitimizing the power of the chief? Illustrate your answer with specific concepts from ethnographic case studies.

KEY TERMS

adjudication

barter

chiefdom

chief

hierarchical society

intensive horticulture

kula

mana

office

potlatch

primogeniture

redistributional economic
    exchange

regional symbiosis

strata

sumptuary rules

tabu

theocracies

INTERNET EXERCISES

1. Read the summary report of the Great Salt Spring site by Jon Muller at **http://www.siu. edu/~anthro/muller/Salt/salt.html**.   How does the specialized economic behavior described in this article relate to the concept of the chiefdom as described in this chapter? What unusual environmental factors play into this discussion?

2. Explore the web site **http://www.uapress. arizona.edu/samples/sam1493.htm**, which discusses the Hohokam culture of the Phoenix Basin (Gila and Salt Rivers). What comparisons can you make between this society and the chiefdoms described in this chapter? What importance to the overall political structure did the Hohokam irrigation system have? Why are the Hohokam not classified as a civilization?

SUGGESTED READINGS

DRUCKER, PHILIP. 1965. *Cultures of the North Pacific*. San Francisco: Chandler. One of the first attempts to classify and analyze the different types of chiefdoms of the Northwest Coast of North America.

EARLE, TIMOTHY K. 1997. *How Chiefs Come to Power: The Political Economy in Prehistory*. Stanford: Stanford University Press. An excellent account of the many variables that affected the development of chiefdoms. Earle is anthropology's foremost expert on chiefdoms.

GOLDMAN, I. 1970. *Ancient Polynesian Society*. Chicago: University of Chicago Press. The classic discussion of the entire range of chiefdoms in Polynesia.

HARDING, THOMAS G., and BEN J. WALLACE (Eds.). 1970. *Cultures of the Pacific*. Garden City, NY: Free Press. A good collection of essays dealing with the multiplicity of societies in the Pacific, including chiefdoms.

KIPP, RITA SMITH, and EDWARD M. SCHORTMAN. 1989. "The Political Impact of Trade in Chiefdoms." *American Anthropologist* 91 (2):370–385. A sophisticated and thorough discussion of the relationship between trade and the development of the political economy in chiefdom societies.

MALINOWSKI, BRONISLAW. 1922. *Argonauts of the Western Pacific*. New York: Dutton. This classic ethnography gives a full description of the *kula* exchange among the Trobriand Islanders. It is the first substantivist (versus formalist) treatment of economic behavior in anthropology.

———. [1926] 1959. *Crime and Custom in Savage Society*. Paterson, NJ: Littlefield, Adams. A classic treatment of law among the Trobriand Islanders, dealing with a number of cases, such as suicide. Malinowski treats law as an aspect of exchange and reciprocity between individuals in society.

SAHLINS, MARSHALL D. 1958. *Social Stratification in Polynesia*. Seattle: University of Washington Press. A classic treatise comparing the different types of chiefdoms and their institutions with other societies in Polynesia.

18

Agricultural States

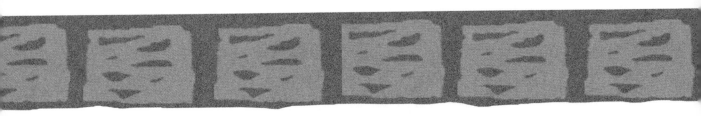

CHAPTER OUTLINE

CHAPTER QUESTIONS

- How do the demographic characteristics of agricultural societies differ from those of small-scale societies?

- What are the features of the different forms of political economy that can be found in agricultural societies?

- What is the relationship among family, gender, and subsistence in agricultural societies?

- How does social stratification in agricultural societies differ from that in more egalitarian societies?

- What are the characteristics of law, warfare, and religion in agricultural state societies?

As discussed in earlier chapters, throughout much of their prehistory humans have relied on hunting wild animals and gathering wild plants. This period of primary hunting-and-gathering is referred to as the Paleolithic, as discussed in Chapter 7. During the Neolithic, as discussed in Chapter 8, beginning about 12,000 years ago, new patterns of subsistence developed. Following the Neolithic, many former hunter-gatherers made a transition to a dependence on domesticated plants and animals, becoming tribal and chiefdom societies. The Neolithic period saw increasing technological, political, and social complexity. As a result, many peoples developed **intensive agriculture,** the cultivation of crops by preparing permanent fields year after year, often using irrigation and fertilizers. In contrast to *horticulture,* intensive agriculture enables a population to produce enormous food surpluses to sustain dense populations in large, permanent settlements.

In some regions, as discussed in Chapter 9, beginning as much as 5,500 years ago, the intensification of agriculture was accompanied by the appearance of complex agricultural states. Anthropologists use the term *state* to describe a wide range of societies that differ structurally from bands, tribes, and chiefdoms. The major difference between state and pre-state societies is a bureaucratic organization (or government). The first states developed with the intensification of agriculture and are referred to as *agricultural states.* The other type of state society—*industrial states*—will be examined in Chapter 19.

As discussed in Chapter 9, major agricultural states are sometimes referred to as *agricultural civilizations.* Although anthropologists disagree on the precise scientific meaning of **civilization,** the term loosely implies a complex society with a number of characteristics, including dense populations located in urban centers; extensive food surpluses; a highly specialized division of labor with economic roles other than those pertaining to agricultural production; a bureaucratic organization or government; monumental works, including art and engineering projects that involve massive labor; and writing systems for record keeping and religious texts. Figure 18.1 shows the location of some early agricultural states.

A number of important geographical and ecological features resulted in large-scale agricultural civilizations in some areas of the world, whereas other areas did not have those features. For example, agriculture developed around the major river valleys of the Near East in Mesopotamia and Egypt, but there

were no such areas in sub-Saharan Africa. In addition, some areas, such as the Near East and Europe, had domesticated animals such as sheep, cattle, goats, and horses, whereas neither sub-Saharan Africa nor the Americas had many domesticated animals (Diamond, 1997). Therefore, geographical and ecological advantages have played an important role in whether agricultural civilizations developed. Also, some areas did not have geographical barriers such as mountains, rain forests, or deserts that inhibited the flow of agricultural patterns from one area to another. The Near East and Europe were contiguous with one another, and technology and agricultural patterns diffused quickly throughout these regions. The Mediterranean Sea enabled the cultures of Greece and Rome to have considerable contact with the diffusion of ideas and agricultural patterns from Egypt and the Near East. Other areas of the world were not as fortunately located.

In this chapter, we examine some of the general characteristics associated with traditional agricultural states. Contemporary developments in specific

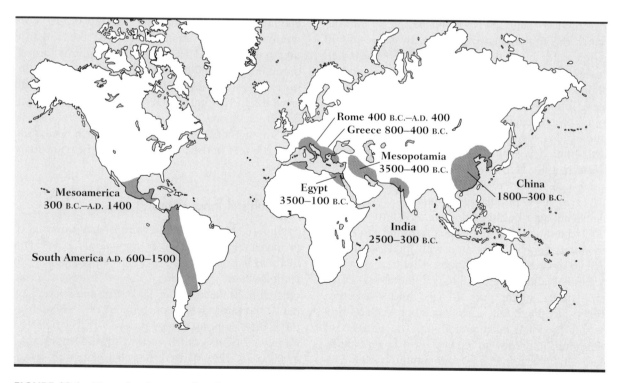

FIGURE 18.1 Map of major agricultural states.

world areas are explored in later chapters on globalization in Latin America, Africa, the Caribbean, the Middle East, and Asia. Once traditional agricultural states, these areas are now undergoing significant change. As with bands, tribes, and chiefdoms, the agricultural states discussed in this chapter no longer exist in the same form as in the past. The political economy, social organization, and religious traditions that emerged, however, have had consequences that persist up to the present.

Demography

After the transition to intensive agriculture, population began to increase dramatically along with an increase in agricultural production, enabling people to settle in large urban areas. These population increases produced conditions that led to higher mortality rates. Poor sanitation coupled with the domestication of confined animals led to frequent epidemics that affected both animals and humans. The overwhelming evidence from fossil and ethnographic evidence suggests that pre-Neolithic or Paleolithic peoples had fewer health problems and less disease than did Neolithic peoples. This debunks the notion that evolution always results in progress for humans—a nineteenth-century belief. Disease, warfare, and famines all contributed to higher mortality rates in agricultural societies than those found in bands, tribes, or chiefdoms. The majority of paleoanthropological and archaeological studies also suggest that life expectancy decreased with the development of intensive agriculture (Hassan, 1981; Harris & Ross, 1987; Cohen, 1994).

Despite increased mortality rates and decreased life expectancy, populations continued to grow at a significant rate because of increased fertility rates. Undoubtedly, higher birth rates reflected the socioeconomic benefits associated with increased family size in agricultural civilizations. Children provided additional labor for essential agricultural tasks, such as planting, caring for animals, and harvesting, thereby freeing adults for other labor, such as processing food and making clothing. The actual costs of rearing children were relatively low in agricultural states in which increased agricultural yields produced surplus foods to support large families. Clothing and shelter were manufactured domestically and were therefore inexpensive.

In addition, high mortality rates, particularly infant mortality rates, encouraged parents to have more children to ensure that some would survive into adulthood. Moreover, children were viewed as future assets who could take care of their parents in later life. In addition to the socioeconomic motives of parents, the political dynamics in agricultural civilizations encouraged high fertility rates. All of the agricultural states promoted the ideal of having large families (Harris & Ross, 1987). These societies depended on a large labor force to maintain their extensive agricultural production and military operations. Policies favoring high birth rates frequently were backed up by religious ideologies.

Technology

One major factor that contributed to the evolution of agricultural states was the development of a more sophisticated technology. To some extent, this represented modifications of existing technologies. For example, stone tools such as axes, hammers, knives, and scrapers were refined for more prolonged use. Increased knowledge of metallurgy enabled some agricultural peoples to create more durable tools. For example, copper, tin, and iron ores were smelted and cast into weapons, armor, ornaments, and other tools. Many technological innovations were dramatically expressed in myriad artwork and monumental constructions, exemplified by such massive structures as the Pyramid of the Sun at Teotihuacan in Mexico, which rises more than 200 feet in the air and covers some 650 square feet.

Agricultural Innovations

Technological innovations were of key importance in increasing crop yields in agricultural states. Humans in various world areas developed specialized techniques to exploit local natural resources more efficiently. Initially, water had to be transported by hand, but later civilizations crafted devices such as the *shaduf,* a pole-and-lever device that is believed to have originated in southwest Asia more than 4,000 years ago. Many of the civilizations in southwest Asia, the Nile Valley, India, and the Americas created complicated irrigation systems that extended the amount of land that could be cultivated.

Large-scale monument building, like this Teotihuacan pyramid, required a ruling elite that organized peasants to provide labor to the state.

Old World agricultural civilizations reached a pivotal point with the advent of the plow, with which farmers could turn soil to a much greater depth than had previously been possible, radically transforming it by reaching deeper into the soil to replenish it with nutrients. The plow thus enabled agricultural peoples to utilize fields on a more permanent basis and occupy the same land for many generations.

The first plows were modifications of the hoe and were probably pulled by the farmers themselves. Eventually, oxen were harnessed to the plows, and farmers gained the ability to cultivate large plots. Then, as people forged innovations in metallurgy, wooden-tipped plows were replaced by plows made first of bronze and then of iron. Oxen-drawn, iron-plowed agriculture spread widely, transforming civilizations throughout the Old World.

Early New World civilizations never used the plow. Instead, they devised a wide variety of other agricultural innovations in response to particular environmental settings. For example, in the Oaxacan Valley in Mexico, the people practiced *pot irrigation,* in which farmers planted their crops near small, shallow wells and used pots to carry water to their fields (Flannery, 1968). More complicated irrigation techniques undergirded agriculture in other American agricultural states. In both the highland and lowland regions of Mesoamerica, the Mayan civilization (300 B.C.–A.D. 1500) created agricultural technology to support densely populated urban centers. Because no evidence of intensive agriculture had been discovered, archaeologists initially hypothesized that the Maya lived in widely dispersed villages with ritual centers consisting of relatively few inhabitants. However, using more careful study techniques, researchers have proved that the Maya devised sophisticated irrigation systems throughout lowland areas, which provided food for the large urban centers.

The Diffusion of Technology

In today's multicultural societies, we take the diffusion, or exchange, of technological innovations for granted and, indeed, archaeologists have uncovered evidence that certain ideas—such as iron technology and plow agriculture—diffused over large areas during ancient times. However, the fact remains that before A.D. 1500, most regions of the world were comparatively isolated, and technological innovations were not spread as readily as today.

Certain areas experienced greater technological advances than did others. For example, the Near East, China, and parts of India had made remarkable technological and scientific achievements compared with those of Europe (Lenski & Lenski, 1982).

Pot irrigation. These women are carrying pots of water for irrigation.

Among the major innovations identified with China alone were paper making, movable-type printing, paper money, guns and gunpowder, compasses, underwater mining, umbrellas, hot-air balloons, multi-stage rockets, and scientific ideas concerning the circulation of blood and the laws of motion (Frank, 1998). Little was known of these technological and scientific developments in Western societies until much later.

Political Economy

The scale of state organization varied in agricultural civilizations. In some areas there existed large-scale bureaucratic empires that organized and controlled wide-ranging territories. Examples are centralized governments in the Near Eastern empires such as Mesopotamia and Egypt; Rome, which controlled an empire that incorporated more than 70 million people throughout its long period of domination; China, in which a large centralized bureaucracy managed by government officials ruled over perhaps as many as 100 million people; and American empires such as those of the Mayas and Aztecs, which ruled over millions of people.

In contrast, state societies in Africa, India, and Southeast Asia were much less centralized and had less authority over adjacent regions. Anthropologist

Aidan Southall (1956) applied the term *segmentary states* to African states in which the ruler was recognized as belonging to an appropriate royal segmentary lineage but had only symbolic and ritual authority over outlying regions. Centralized bureaucratic structures in such states did not effectively control peripheral areas. Anthropologist Clifford Geertz (1980) used the term *theater state* to refer to the limited form of state society in Southeast Asia. The power of the theater state was mostly symbolic and theatrical, with many ceremonies to demonstrate the political legitimacy of the regime. The power and authority of the theater state have been compared with the light of a torch, radiating outward from the center and gradually fading into the distance, merging imperceptibly with the ascending power of a neighboring sovereign (Geertz, 1980).

Feudalism, a decentralized form of political economy based on landed estates, existed in agricultural civilizations during different historical periods. To some extent, these feudal regimes were very similar to the chiefdom societies discussed in Chapter 17. Usually, feudal regimes resulted from the breakdown of large-scale centralized states. Feudal political economies emerged at various times in western Europe and Japan. In these systems, lords, like chiefs, were autonomous patrons who owned land and maintained control over their own military (knights and *samurai*) and demanded labor and tribute from their serfs. Political power varied from a decentralized form of authority (the nobles) to a more centralized form (a king or emperor). For example, during the Tokugawa period in Japan (1600–1868), the *daimyo* (lords) had to reside in the central capital, Edo (present-day Tokyo), for a year to demonstrate loyalty to the ruler, or *shogun*. This represented a more centralized form of feudalism.

The Division of Labor

The creation of substantial food surpluses, along with better food-storing technologies, led to new forms of economic relations in agricultural states. Many people could be freed from working in the fields to pursue other specialized functions. Hundreds of new occupations developed in the urban centers of agricultural states. Craftsworkers produced tools, clothing, jewelry, pottery, and other accessories. Other workers engaged in commerce, government, religion, education, the military, and other sectors of the economy.

This new division of labor influenced both rural and urban areas. Farm laborers were not only involved in essential food production; they also turned to craft production to supplement their income. Over time, some agricultural villages began to produce crafts and commodities not just for their own consumption, but for trade with other villages and with the urban centers. Through these activities, rural villages became involved in widespread trading alliances and marketing activities.

Property Rights

Despite the complex division of labor in agricultural states, the major source of wealth was arable land. In effect, the ownership of land became the primary basis for an individual's socioeconomic position. The governing elite in most of the agricultural states claimed ownership over large landholdings, which included both the land and the peasant or slave labor that went with it (Lenski & Lenski, 1982).

Two forms of property ownership predominated in agricultural states, depending on whether they were large-scale centralized states or decentralized feudal states. Eric Wolf (1966) identified one type of property ownership in which a powerful government claimed ownership of the land, appointed officials to supervise its cultivation, and collected the surplus agricultural production. In the other type of system, a class of landlords who owned the land privately inherited it through family lines and oversaw its cultivation. In certain cases, peasants could own land directly and produce surpluses for the elites. Agricultural states thus developed major inequalities between those who owned land and those who did not. Bureaucratic and legal devices were developed by the elite to institute legal deeds and titles, and land became a resource that was bought, sold, and rented.

A new form of economic system known as the **tributary form** became predominant. **Tribute,** in the form of taxes, rent, or labor services, replaced economic exchanges based on kinship reciprocity or chiefdom redistribution. Wolf (1997) referred to this as a *tributary mode of production,* in contrast to the *kin-ordered mode of production* of nonstate societies. Under these conditions, a hierarchy emerged in which the elite who resided in the urban centers or on landed estates collected tribute, and the peasants, who cultivated the land, paid tribute to this elite (Wolf, 1966, 1997).

The Command Economy versus the Entrepreneur

In the large-scale centralized states, a form of **command economy** emerged, wherein the political elite controlled production, prices, and trading. Some agricultural states became expansive world empires that extracted tribute and placed limits on people's economic activities. State authorities controlled the production, exchange, and the consumption of goods within the economies of these bureaucratic empires. Although private trade and entrepreneurial activities did occur at times within these bureaucratic empires, it was rare (Adams, 1974). For example, China and Rome attempted to organize and control most aspects of their economy by monopolizing the production and sale of items like salt and iron.

In the less centrally organized agricultural states, more independent economic activity was evident. For example, during the feudal periods in western Europe and Japan, the lack of a dominating elite that organized and managed the economic affairs of the society enabled more autonomous economic production and exchange to occur at the local level. Entrepreneurs had freedom to develop and innovate within the context of feudal political economies. This was a key factor in the later economic development of these regions.

The Peasantry

Peasants are people who cultivate land in rural areas for their basic subsistence and pay tribute to elite groups. The socioeconomic status of the peasantry, however, varied in agricultural societies. As we have seen, rights to land differed between the bureaucratic empires and the less centralized societies. In most agricultural states, elites claimed rights to most of the land, and the peasantry in the rural areas paid tribute or taxes as a type of rent (Wolf, 1966). In other cases, the peasants owned the land they cultivated; nevertheless, they still paid tribute from their labor surplus or production. In the case of feudal Europe, the peasants, or serfs, were bound to the estates owned by lords, or nobles.

Whatever their status, all peasants had to produce a surplus that flowed into the urban centers. It is estimated that this surplus, including fines, tithes, and obligatory gifts, represented at least half of the peasants' total output (Lenski & Lenski, 1982). Also, in the bureaucratic civilizations such as Egypt and Teotihuacan, the peasantry provided much of the compulsory labor for large-scale government projects such as massive irrigation works and pyramids. Although research on peasants has demonstrated that they were often able to evade some of these obligations or contrived to hide some of their surpluses, most were subject to burdensome demands from the elites.

The Moral Economy   Despite the domination of the peasantry by the agricultural state or by landlords, the peasantry developed norms that emphasized community cooperation in production, distribution, consumption, and exchange in the village. These norms led to what some anthropologists have referred to as a moral economy for the peasantry. This **moral economy** involved sharing food resources and labor with one another in a reciprocal manner to provide a form of social and economic insurance so that individual families would not fall into destitution (Scott, 1976). Peasant families would exchange labor with each other to aid production of crops. In addition, rituals and festivals occurred at which peasants were encouraged to donate and exchange food and

goods to be distributed throughout the community. Although the moral economy of the peasantry was not always successful, and individual families did become impoverished, in many cases it did help sustain the viability of the village community.

Trade and Monetary Exchange

As previously discussed, the production of agricultural surpluses and luxury items in agricultural states led to internal and external trade. This trade included raw materials for production, such as copper, iron ore, obsidian, and salt. Long-distance trade routes over both land and sea spanned immense geographical areas. Through constant policing, governing elites enforced political order and military security over these trade routes. In turn, this protection led to the security and maintenance of extensive road networks that aided commercial pursuits. For example, the Romans constructed roads and bridges that are still in use (Stavrianos, 1995).

Extensive caravan routes developed in areas such as the Near East and North Africa. The Bedouins, Arabic-speaking pastoralists, used camels to conduct long-distance trade, carrying goods from port cities in the Arabian peninsula across the desert to cities such as Damascus, Jerusalem, and Cairo. In Asia, other caravan routes crossed the whole of China and central Asia, with connections to the Near East. In the Americas, long-distance trade developed between Teotihuacan and the Mayan regions.

In conjunction with long-distance trade, monetary exchange became more formalized. In the Near East (and probably elsewhere), foodstuffs such as grains originally could be used to pay taxes, wages, rents, and other obligations. Because grains are perishable and bulky, however, they were not ideal for carrying out exchanges. Thus, general-purpose money, based on metals, especially silver and copper, came into use. The sizes and weights of these metals became standardized and were circulated as stores of value. At first, bars of metal were used as money, but eventually smaller units of metal, or *coins,* were manufactured and regulated. After developing printing, the Chinese began to produce paper money as their medium of exchange.

The Rise of Merchants and Peripheral Markets
One result of the development of a formalized monetary system was the increased opportunity for merchants to purchase goods not for their own

consumption but to be sold to people who had money. *Merchants* made up a new status category of people who, although below the elites, often prospered by creating demands for luxury goods and organizing the transportation of those goods across long distances. Much of the trade of the Near Eastern empires, followed by the Greek, Roman, Byzantine, and Islamic Mediterranean commercial operations, was stimulated by merchants who furnished imported luxury goods from foreign lands for consumption by internal elites (Wolf, 1997). Sometimes, as in the case of the Aztecs, the merchants of these empires also doubled as spies, providing information to governing authorities regarding peoples in outlying regions.

With increasing long-distance trade and other commercial developments, regional and local marketplaces as well as marketplaces in the urban areas began to emerge. Foodstuffs and other commodities produced by peasants, artisans, and craftsworkers were bought and sold in these marketplaces. In early cities such as Ur, Memphis, Teotihuacan, and Tikal, markets were centrally located, offering both imported and domestically manufactured items as well as food. In addition, marketplaces arose throughout the countryside. A steady flow of goods developed from villages to counties to regional and national capitals.

Women play an important role in markets in agricultural societies.

Although many goods were bought and sold in these regional markets, the vast majority of people—that is, the peasantry—did not receive their subsistence items from these markets. Nor were people engaged full time in producing or selling in these marketplaces (Bohannon & Dalton, 1962). The regional and local markets existed only as a convenient location for the distribution of goods. In many cases, the activity was periodic. For example, in medieval Europe, traveling fairs that went from city to city enabled merchants to bring their local and imported goods to be bought and sold.

Goods were bought and sold in markets through a system known as haggling. *Haggling* is a type of negotiation between buyer and seller that establishes the price of an item. The buyer asks a seller how much he or she wants for an item, the seller proposes a figure, and the buyer counters with a lower price, until a price is finally agreed on.

Social Organization

Because agricultural states were more complex and highly organized than pre-state societies, they could not rely solely on kinship for recruitment to different status positions. Land ownership and occupation became more important than kinship in organizing society. In highly centralized agricultural societies, the state itself replaced kin groups as the major integrating principle in society.

Kinship and Status

Nevertheless, family and kinship remained an important part of social organization. In elite and royal families, kinship was the basic determination of status. Royal incest in brother-sister marriages by both the Egyptian and Incan royalty shows the importance of kinship as a distinctive means of maintaining status in agricultural societies. The typical means of achieving the highest statuses was through family patrimony, or the inheritance of status. Access to the highest ranks was generally closed to those who did not have the proper genealogical relationships with the elite or the nobility.

The Extended Family The extended family was the predominant family form in both urban and rural areas in most agricultural states. Family ties remained critical to most peasants; typically, the peasant extended family held land in common, and the members of the family cooperated in farm labor. To some extent, intensive agricultural production required the presence of a large extended family to provide the necessary labor to plant, cultivate, and harvest crops (Wolf, 1966). Large domestic groups had to pool their resources and labor to maintain economic production. To induce this cooperation, generalized reciprocal economic exchanges of foodstuffs, goods, and labor were maintained in these families.

Other Kinship Principles   In a cross-cultural survey of fifty-three agricultural civilizations, Kay Martin and Barbara Voorhies (1975) found that 45 percent had patrilineal kin groupings, another 45 percent had bilateral groupings, and 9 percent had matrilineal groupings. In some Southeast Asian societies, such as Burma, Thailand, and Cambodia, bilateral descent existed along with kindred groupings. In some circumstances, these kindreds provided domestic labor for agricultural production through reciprocal labor exchanges. Families connected through kindreds would regularly exchange labor for the transplanting or harvesting of rice crops.

Family Structure among the Nayar   One matrilineal society, the Nayar of southern India, had unusual marriage practices that produced a remarkably different type of family structure. They practiced a visiting ritualized mating system called the *sambandham*. Once every few years, the Nayar would hold this ceremony to "marry" females to males. At the ceremony, the male would tie a gold ornament around the neck of his ritual bride. After seclusion for three days, sexual intercourse might or might not take place, depending on the girl's age. After this the couple would take a ritual bath to purify themselves of the pollution of this cohabitation. After the ceremony, the male had no rights regarding the female. Later, the female could enter a number of marriages with males of her same caste and have children. The Nayar system was unusual because none of the husbands resided with the female. The matrilineal group assumed the rights over her and her children. Thus, the household family unit consisted of brothers and sisters, a woman's daughter and granddaughters, and their children. The

bride and her children were obliged to perform a ceremony at the death of her "ritual" husband.

From the Western viewpoint, the Nayar marital arrangement might not seem like a family because it does not tie two families together. This system, however, was a response to historical circumstances in southern India. Traditionally, most Nayar males joined the military. In addition, the land owned by the matrilineal group was worked by lower-caste, landless peasants. Therefore, young Nayar males had no responsibilities to the matrilineal group and were free to become full-time warriors (Mencher, 1965).

Marriage

The significance of social ties in agricultural states is evident in the form of marriage practices found in these societies, all of which have economic and political implications. Because of these implications, the selection of marital partners was considered too important to be left to young people. Marriages were usually arranged by parents, sometimes with the aid of brokers, who assessed the alliances between the extended families with respect to landed wealth or political connections to the elite. In some cases (for example, China), arranged marriages were contracted when the children were young (see Chapter 11). As in chiefdom societies, elite marriages were frequently endogamous. Peasants, however, generally married outside their extended families and larger kin groups.

Dowry and Bridewealth   Most agricultural states practiced some form of marital exchange involving land, commodities, or foodstuffs. In Asia and some parts of Europe, the most common type of exchange was the **dowry**—goods and wealth paid by the bride's family to the groom's family. In this sense, the dowry appears to be the reverse of *bridewealth,* in which the groom's family exchanges wealth for the bride. The dowry was used as a social exchange between families to arrange a marriage contract. Upon marriage, the bride in an Indian or Chinese family was expected to bring material goods into her marriage.

In a cross-cultural comparison, Jack Goody (1976) found that bridewealth occurs more frequently in horticultural societies, whereas the dowry is found in complex, agricultural societies. In Europe and Asia, intensive agriculture was associated with the use of plows and draft animals, high population densities, and a scarcity of land. Goody hypothesized that one result of the dowry system was to consolidate property in the hands of elite groups. As commercial and bureaucratic families expanded their wealth and increased their status, these groups began to move from bridewealth to dowry. As bridewealth was a means of circulating wealth among families through creating alliances between the groom's and bride's families, the dowry served to concentrate property and wealth within the patrilineal line of families. Elites in India, China, and Greece relied on this form of marital exchange.

Although dowry exchanges were most significant in the upper socioeconomic groups in which wealth and status were of central significance, they were also supposed to be customary among the peasantry. Bridewealth was not unknown in peasant society. In both northern and southern India, bridewealth became more common among the lower socioeconomic classes. In the poorest families, there was little to be inherited anyway, and the actual exchanges were mainly for the costs of the wedding feast and for simple household furnishings.

Polygyny   In contrast to pre-state societies, polygyny was rare in agricultural states, except among the elite. In some cases, the rulers of these societies would have large *harems,* in which many different women were attached to one ruler. The royal households of many agricultural states had hundreds of women at the disposal of the rulers. Elite males who were wealthy were able to keep mistresses or concubines in addition to their wives. For example, many Chinese males kept concubines or secondary wives, despite laws against this practice. Other agricultural states had similar polygynous practices for individuals in high-ranking socioeconomic positions.

For most of the populace, however, monogamy was the primary form of marriage. Economist Ester Boserup (1970) has argued that the general absence of polygyny in societies with plow agriculture is due to the lack of land that could be accumulated by adding wives to one's family. Similarly, Goody (1976) hypothesized that in agricultural societies where land is a scarce commodity, peasants cannot afford the luxury of polygyny. Obviously, wealth and status influenced the type of marriage patterns found in agricultural civilizations.

Divorce   For the most part, divorce was rare in agricultural civilizations. The corporate nature of the extended family and the need for cooperative agricultural labor among family members usually led to normative constraints against divorce. In addition, marriage was the most important vehicle for the transfer of property and served as the basis for alliances between families and kin groups. Thus, families tended to stay together, and enormous moral, political, and social weight was attached to the marriage bond. In India, marriage was considered sacred, and therefore divorces were not legally permitted. Similar norms were evident in the feudal societies of Europe, where Christianity reinforced the sanctity of the family and the stability of marriage.

For women, however, marriage offered the only respectable career or means of subsistence. Most women faced destitution if a marriage were terminated. Thus, few women wanted to dissolve a marriage, regardless of the internal conflicts or problems. This pattern reflects the unequal status of males and females.

Gender, Subsistence, and Status

The transition to intensive agriculture affected the subsistence roles of both males and females. Martin and Voorhies (1975) noted that in agricultural systems the amount of labor that women contributed to actual production of food declined. For example, the adoption of plow agriculture greatly diminished the need for weeding, a task that was primarily taken care of by women. They hypothesized that as women's role in agriculture decreased, their social status decreased accordingly. Thus, agricultural civilizations were even more patriarchal than were tribes or chiefdoms. Women were viewed as unable to contribute toward the household economy, and for the most part they were confined to cooking, child rearing, and caring for the domestic animals. They had little contact outside their immediate families.

Martin and Voorhies (1975) emphasized that a definite distinction arose in agricultural states between men's and women's roles. Women were restricted to inside (domestic) activities, whereas males were allowed to participate in outside (public) activities. In general, women were not allowed to own property, engage in politics, pursue education, or participate in any activity that would take them outside the domestic sphere. Since Martin and Voorhies did their research, a number of feminist anthropologists have questioned the simplistic dichotomy between the domestic and public realms for gender roles. In some cases, the domestic domain encompassed some of the activities of the public sphere, and vice versa. However, they have agreed that this distinction has helped analyze gender in most agricultural societies (Lamphere, 1997; Ortner, 1996). Generally, most studies concur that the female role was restricted in many of these societies.

Female Seclusion   This highly restricted female role was reflected in a number of cultural practices. For example, China adopted the tradition of *foot binding,* which involved binding a young female child's feet so the feet would not grow. Although this practice was supposed to produce beautiful feet (in the view of Chinese males), it had the effect of immobilizing women. Less of a handicap for upper-class females, who did not have to participate in the daily labor requirements of most women and were carried around by servants, foot binding was also practiced by the peasantry during

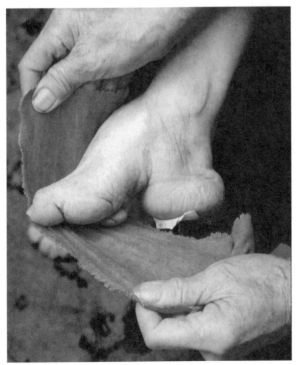

The binding of women's feet in traditional agricultural China led to results shown in this photo.

various periods, which meant that peasant women had to work with considerable disabilities.

Similarly, many areas of the Near East, North Africa, and southern Asia practiced **purdah,** a system that restricted women to the household. *Purdah* is a Persian word translated as "curtain" or "barrier." In this system, women had to obtain permission from their husbands to leave the house to visit families and friends. In some of these regions, a woman had to cover her face with a veil when in public (Beck & Keddie, 1978; Fernea & Fernea, 1979). Female seclusion was one of the ways in which males tried to control the paternity of the children that they are raising.

Patriarchy and Sexism   Sexist ideology developed in agricultural states as a means of reinforcing the seclusion of women. Females were viewed as inherently inferior and dependent on males. The so-called "natural superiority" of males was reinforced in most of the legal, moral, and religious traditions in agricultural states, including Confucianism, Islam, Hinduism, Judaism, and Christianity. Males were viewed as more intelligent, stronger, and more emotionally mature. In addition, many of these societies viewed women as sexually dangerous; women caught having premarital or extramarital sex were punished severely, in some cases by execution. In contrast, males were permitted to engage in extramarital affairs.

Variations in the Status of Women   The role and status of women in agricultural civilizations varied by region. In some areas where soil conditions were poor, both male and female peasants had to work together in the fields to produce for the household, which tended to create more gender equality. In most southeast Asian countries, such as Thailand and Cambodia, both males and females worked together in rice cultivation. In some cases, land was divided equally among all children, regardless of gender, indicating that in these societies females had relative equality with males. Although in these countries, women were mostly confined to the domestic sphere and to household tasks, they played an important role in decision making and financial matters within the rural communities (Keyes, 1995; Van Esterik, 1996; Winzeler, 1996).

Anthropologists have discovered other exceptions regarding the role and status of peasant women in public in some agricultural civilizations. In China, Mesoamerica, and West Africa, many women participated as sellers in the marketplaces, taking some of the surplus produce or crafts made in the village to the marketplaces. However, this activity was generally restricted to older women whose children were grown, but in some cases the role of market woman did lead to higher status. Many of these women participated in the public sphere but were still segregated from male political activities. Moreover, these women had to perform their domestic chores as well as their marketplace activities.

Social Stratification

As previously mentioned, agricultural civilizations were highly stratified, and social mobility was generally restricted to people with elite family or kinship backgrounds. Thus, anthropologists classify these societies as **closed societies,** in that social status was generally ascribed rather than achieved. For example, in traditional Chinese society, people born outside the emperor's family had two paths to upward mobility. One route was to be born into the *gentry*—the land-owning class that made up about 2 percent of Chinese families. The second route was to become a *mandarin*—a Chinese bureaucrat and scholar—by becoming a student and passing rigorous examinations based on classical Confucian texts. Although in theory this option existed for all males, in fact it was restricted to families or clans that could afford to spend resources for educating a son.

The Caste System

India developed a much more restrictive form of social inequality known as the caste system. A **caste** is an endogamous social grouping into which a person is born and in which the person remains throughout his or her lifetime. Thus, an individual's status in a caste system is ascribed, and movement into a different caste is impossible. The Indian caste system evolved from four basic categories, or *varnas,* that were ranked in order from Brahmans (priests) to Ksaitryas (warriors) to Vaisyas (merchants) to Sudras (laborers). Hence, the caste into which a person was born determined that person's occupation. In addition, people were required to

marry within their caste. Although contact among members of different castes was generally discouraged, the castes were interrelated through various mutual economic exchanges and obligations known as the *jajmani system* (discussed in Chapter 22).

Slavery   Another form of social inequality and ascribed status was slavery. Slavery tends to increase as a society increases its productive technology, as trade expands, and as states become more centrally organized (Goody, 1980; Van den Berghe, 1981). For example, the Mediterranean empires of the Greeks, Romans, Arabs, and Turks used vast numbers of slaves in galleys, monument construction, irrigation works, plantation agriculture, and major public works projects.

Slave systems differed from one society to another. The Greeks and Romans reduced the status of the slave to a subhuman "thing" that was considered an instrument or tool, differing from inanimate tools only by the faculty of speech (Worsley, 1984). Indigenous African kingdoms practiced large-scale slavery in which nobles owned hundreds of slaves (Goody, 1980). Most of these slaves worked on plantations or in the household, although some became advisers and administrators for nobles. Although African slavery involved the capture and sale of human beings, eventually the slaves could be incorporated into the kinship groups.

In a comprehensive review of indigenous Asian and African slavery, anthropologist James Watson (1980) referred to *open* and *closed* forms of slavery. The indigenous African form of slavery was open, in that slaves could be incorporated into domestic kinship groups and even become upwardly mobile. In contrast, the slave systems of China, India, Greece, and Rome were closed, with no opportunities for upward mobility or incorporation into kinship groups.

The two different types of slavery were correlated with specific demographic conditions and political economies. In societies such as Africa or Thailand, where land was relatively abundant and less populated, more open forms of slavery developed (Goody, 1971; Turton, 1980). In these societies, the key to power and authority was control over people rather than land. In political economies such as Greece, Rome, China, and India, where land was scarce and populations much more dense, closed forms of slavery emerged. The key to power

CRITICAL PERSPECTIVES

WERE THERE MATRIARCHAL STATES?

As mentioned in earlier chapters, anthropologists have not found any substantive archaeological or ethnographic evidence for the existence of matriarchal societies. There are, of course, societies that have *matrilineal* social organization, in which one traces descent through the mother's side of the family. But as we have discussed (see Chapter 16), matriliny does not translate into a *matriarchal society* in which women would have economic and political dominance over males. Within societies organized by matrilineal descent, such as the Iroquois Indian societies discussed in Chapter 16, males tend to dominate in political and economic affairs. Women may have a more active role in these areas, but *patriarchy* exists as the prevalent gender pattern in these matrilineal societies.

However, the belief that there were once matriarchal societies that were overcome by male-dominated, warlike societies has a long history in the West. For example, after examining Greek and Roman mythology, law, religion, and history, the German lawyer Johann Jacob Bachofen wrote an influential book called *Das Mutterrecht (The Mother-Right)* published in 1861. Bachofen suggested that matrilineal kinship combined with matriarchy was the first form of human evolutionary development. He reasoned that since no child could determine its paternity, kinship, descent, and inheritance could

only be recognized through women. Bachofen argued that women dominated these early primitive societies both economically and politically. Anthropologist John MacLellan developed this same theme in his book *Primitive Marriage: An Inquiry into the Origin of the Form of Capture in Marriage Ceremonies* (1865). A number of other scenarios of this evolution from matriarchy to patriarchy were published in books in Europe.

Using similar reasoning, Lewis Henry Morgan, an early American anthropologist (see Chapter 13), reinforced this Victorian view of ancient matriarchal societies. Based on his ethnographic study of Iroquois Indian society and other sources, Morgan argued in his famous book *Ancient Society* (1877) that there must have been an early stage of matriarchal society. He studied kinship terms from different areas of the world to substantiate this view. Morgan suggested that a patriarchal stage of evolution replaced an earlier form of matriarchy as more advanced forms of agriculture developed. In his understanding, matriarchal societies were based on the communal ownership of property and polyandry (females married to two or more males). He argued that patriarchy evolved along with the concept of private property and ownership. Morgan suggested that males invented the institution of monogamy in order to ensure their paternity of their

children. This enabled them to pass their private property on to their male heirs.

Europeans Karl Marx and Friedrich Engels became enthusiastic about Morgan's ideas in *Ancient Society*. Engels wrote about the connection between the evolution of private property and the emergence of patriarchal societies in his book *The Origin of the Family, Private Property, and the State* in 1884. This book, along with other writings by Marx and Engels, provided the intellectual foundation of the socialist and communist movement in the nineteenth and twentieth centuries. Following Morgan, Marx and Engels believed that revolutionary change in the economy caused by the evolution of advanced forms of agriculture resulted in men taking control of the politics from women. As men gained control over herd animals and farmland, they also instituted the marriage pattern of monogamy, in which females pledged lifetime fidelity to one man. This institution assured males of the paternity of their own children. Engels referred to this commitment as "the world historical defeat of the female sex." He and Marx argued that the institution of the patriarchal family and monogamy became the basis of treating females as property and commodities, demonstrated in existing rituals such as the "giving away of the bride by the father to the groom" in Western wedding ceremonies. Women became servants of men and provided sustenance to support male authority and wealth accumulation in capitalist societies. Marx and Engels believed that Victorian sexist attitudes and male chauvinism had been developed to assure male authority and paternity. They believed that the global transformation from matrilineal and matriarchal societies into patrilineal and patriarchal societies established one of the integral components resulting in exploitative capitalist societies.

Other important thinkers of the twentieth century such as Sigmund Freud (see Chapter 11) transmitted these ideas regarding early matriarchal societies. One European archaeologist, the late Maria Gimbutas, proposed that early "matristic" societies were once the predominant form of society in ancient Europe (1982, 1991). She argued that in the period she calls "Old Europe" (between 6500 and 3500 B.C.), peaceful, sedentary villages existed where men and women formed equal partnerships with one another. Gimbutas drew upon a number of types of artifacts to make her case. Based on art, architecture, figurines, ceramic pottery, marble, gold, grave goods, and other artifacts, she suggested that the culture of "Old Europe" was based on the belief in a Great Mother Goddess and other goddesses. According to Gimbutas, a "queen-priestess" ruled and maintained control over this matri-

focused religious tradition. She found no evidence of weapons or warfare from that time period. Thus, she challenged the assumption that warfare is endemic and universal in human societies. In addition, Gimbutas argued that these societies were completely egalitarian, with no classes, castes, slaves, and, of course, no male rulers.

According to Gimbutas, "Old Europe" began to be invaded by tribal horse-riding pastoralists known as the Kurgan by 4400 B.C. These Kurgan pastoralists were male-dominated and were associated with the earliest forms of Indo-European languages. These Indo-European Kurgans from the Eurasiatic steppes developed religious traditions and mythologies that reflected a warrior cult. They maintained a pantheon of male gods representing the sun, stars, thunder, and lightning, and they were associated with warrior-like artifacts such as daggers and axes. Eventually, the Kurgan introduced iron plows that were used to cultivate the land. This technological innovation altered forever the relationship between males and females in European society. Males with plows and draft animals supplanted the female-oriented forms of cultivation. As the Kurgan society replaced the "Old Europe," women were relegated to the domestic aspect of subsistence activities. According to Gimbutas, the mythical and ideological culture perpetuated by the Kurgans continued until the beginnings of Christianity in Europe and beyond.

Recently, archaeologist Lynn Meskell has criticized the picture of Old Europe and the Kurgan culture presented by Maria Gimbutas (1995). Meskell notes that since the nineteenth century, there has been a recurrent interest in the notion of original, matriarchal Mother Goddess societies. This view has been perpetuated in some of the ecofeminist and "New Age" religious literature. Meskell argues that these "New Age" feminists utilize Gimbutas to ground their movement in a utopian vision of the past. She suggests that the current interest in the Mother Goddess "gynocentric" theories of prehistory serve as vehicles for attempting to overturn patriarchal institutions in today's societies. However, Meskell suggests that these gynocentric views are based on inadequate scholarship and actually damage the positive aspects of gender research in anthropology. She and many other archaeologists note that Gimbutas neglected a tremendous amount of data and artifacts that would demonstrate the fallibility of her thesis. Numerous artifacts such as artwork indicating the prevalence of male deity figurines were dismissed in Gimbutas's data collection. Artifacts indicating warfare, human sacrifice, and fortifications are abundant throughout the archaeological record dated within Gimbutas's "Old Europe" period. And the view of Kurgan patriarchal domination of this once-peaceful matristic society is too simplistic to explain the

(continued on page 440)

CRITICAL PERSPECTIVES

WERE THERE MATRIARCHAL STATES?—CONTINUED

complexities of European archaeology. Meskell concludes that the belief that there were distinctive stages of matriarchal and patriarchal societies is a remnant of the Victorian past. She argues that these simplistic views do not do justice to interpretations in archaeology or feminist anthropological and gender studies in the twenty-first century.

Of course there were agricultural societies that worshipped female goddesses and maintained mythologies about matriarchal societies. In fact, there were agricultural societies that had females who held important leadership and political roles, such as the famed Cleopatra. Yet the evidence from archaeology and ethnography suggests that female political supremacy and domination over the economy did not exist. Despite Cleopatra's political

authority, a male elite clearly controlled the economy and politics in ancient Egypt.

As seen in this chapter, the status of women in most of the agricultural societies in the past, including the goddess-worshipping ones, was very low. Both males and females have used mythologies and beliefs about early matriarchies throughout history. Nineteenth-century males used these beliefs to justify the status and authority of what they believed to be more evolved and advanced "patriarchal" institutions. Today, some women in the ecofeminist and "New Age" movements use these myths to perpetuate their vision of a utopian society.

One of the major goals of anthropology is to enhance and improve the rights of women and men throughout the world (see

Chapter 25). But to do so, we must have an accurate assessment of what the archaeological and ethnographic record tell us. Without this accurate assessment, we cannot either further our knowledge of humanity or aid in the improvement of the human condition.

POINTS TO PONDER

1. What kind of data would be needed to infer a true matriarchal society in the past?

2. What are the strengths and weaknesses of the belief in an early matriarchal society?

3. Could there ever be a truly matriarchal society? If so, how could one develop?

4. What has this Critical Perspectives box taught you about analyzing anthropological data?

and wealth in these societies was control over land and labor.

Racial and Ethnic Stratification

Related to slavery and a rigid social hierarchy was a pattern not found in nonstate societies: *racial and ethnic stratification*. Although "race" is not a scientifically useful concept (see Chapters 6 and 23), the term is often used to differentiate people according to skin color or other physical characteristics. In contrast, **ethnicity** refers to the cultural differences among populations, usually based on attributes such as language, religion, clothing, lifestyle, and ideas regarding common descent or specific territory.

As agricultural states expanded into surrounding environments, a variety of racially and ethnically different peoples were incorporated into the growing empires. Some of these groups were band, tribal, or chiefdom societies that spoke different languages and maintained different cultural or ethnic traditions. Once conquered or absorbed, they frequently found themselves under the rule of a particular dominant ethnic group. In many cases, the dominant group ascribed subordinate statuses to them. Sometimes the conquered group became slaves. In other cases its members were viewed as racially or ethnically inferior and were given only limited opportunities for upward mobility. Thus, many ethnic and racial minorities were identified as

An Aztec scene painting.

subordinate classes and stigmatized as inherently inferior.

With the intensification of social stratification in agricultural states, social distance between the ruling elite and the rest of the population was accentuated not only by rights to land, wealth, and power but also by restrictive sumptuary laws. For example, among the Aztecs, patterns of deference and demeanor between the rulers and the ruled were highly formalized. The Aztec nobility were distinguished by clothing and jewelry, and they were believed to be vested with divine status (Berdan, 1982). Aztec commoners were required to prostrate themselves before the emperor and were not permitted to speak to him or look at him. Similar patterns of deference and social etiquette developed throughout the agricultural societies in the Old and New World.

Law

Agricultural states formalized legal decisions and punishments not only through laws but also through court systems, police, and legal specialists such as judges. In many of these societies, law became highly differentiated from customs, norms, tradition, and religious dogma (Vago, 1995). Writing systems enabled many of these societies to keep records of court proceedings.

The first recognized codified laws originated in the Near Eastern civilization of Babylon. The Babylonian code of law, known as the *Laws of Hammurabi,* was based on standardized procedures and precedents for dealing with civil and criminal offenses. Other agricultural states such as China, Rome, and India developed formalized legal systems, including court systems. Morton Fried (1978) used evidence from the Hammurabi codes to demonstrate that these laws reinforced a system of inequality by protecting the rights of the governing class while keeping the peasants in a subordinate status. In other words, the codes of Hammurabi were designed to allow those in authority to have access to scarce resources.

In contrast, anthropologists who adhere to the functionalist perspective emphasize the benefits of codified laws for the maintenance of society (Service, 1978b). They argue that the maintenance of social and political order was crucial for agricultural states. Serious disruptions would have led to the neglect of agricultural production, which would have had devastating consequences for all members of society. Thus, legal codes such as the Hammurabi codes, the Talmudic laws of the Israelites, the laws of Manu of India, the Confucianist codes of China, and the Roman imperial laws benefitted the peasants by maintaining social order, which made possible greater agricultural production.

Obviously, both of these perspectives provide useful insights into the role of law in agricultural states. Ruling elites developed these codified legal systems, but they also functioned to control crime and institute political order.

Mediation and Self-Help

Despite the emergence of codified systems, the practice of mediation and self-help in the redress of criminal offenses did not completely disappear. Rolando Tamayo demonstrated, for example, that these practices continued centuries after the development of the Greek state (Claessen et al., 1985). In addition, oaths, oracles, and ordeals remained as methods for determining legal decisions in many agricultural civilizations.

A Case Study: Law in China   The legal system of China evolved through various dynasties, culminating in the complex legal codes of the Han dynasty (206 B.C.–A.D. 220). Chinese criminal codes specified punishments for each offense, ranging from blows with a cane to execution by strangulation, by decapitation, or even by slow slicing. Punishments also included hard labor and exile. Chinese civil law included rules on agricultural property, family, and inheritance.

Decisions involving civil law frequently were left to arbitration between the disputants in the local community. In this sense, many legal decisions depended on self-regulation of small groups. Use of written laws and the court system was generally restricted to cases that affected society as a whole. County magistrates familiar with the legal codes administered the law and recorded the decisions, which served as precedents for future cases. A hierarchy of judicial bodies from the county magistrates to the imperial court served as courts of appeal for serious cases. Despite the existence of a highly formalized court system, however, most scholars concur that Chinese law was weak. Because local magistrates had hundreds of thousands of people under their jurisdiction and the police force was weak, law enforcement was ineffective at the local level. Basic law enforcement relied instead on informal processes and sanctions administered by community leaders (Clayre, 1985).

Warfare

Warfare was an integral aspect of agricultural state development. The state emerged, in most cases, as a result of conflict and competition among groups that eventually led to domination by a ruling group. Thus, with the emergence of state societies, warfare increased in scale and became much more organized. As governing elites accumulated more wealth and power, warfare became one of the major means of increasing their surpluses. Archaeologist Gordon Childe (1950), a conflict theorist, maintained that the ruling class in agricultural societies turned its energies from the conquest of nature to the conquest of people.

One cross-cultural study of external warfare by Keith Otterbein found that the capacity for organized warfare is much greater in agricultural state societies than in band and tribal societies. State societies usually have a centralized political and military leadership as well as professional armies and military training. In addition, surpluses of foodstuffs and luxury items frequently attract outside invaders, particularly nomadic pastoralists. Otterbein (1994) concluded that the primary motivation for warfare in state systems was to gain political control over other people. In the feudal societies of western Europe and Japan, professional classes of knights and samurai protected the interests and resources of nobles. In addition, these warrior classes were used to wage offensive warfare against neighboring estates to increase landholdings and the supply of manpower.

Religion

As state societies emerged, cultural elements such as political power, authority, and religion became much more closely intertwined. The religious traditions that developed in most of the agricultural states are referred to as **ecclesiastical religions,** in which there is no separation between state and religious authority. Generally, all people in the political jurisdiction are required to belong to the religion, and there is little toleration for other belief systems.

Ecclesiastical Religions

Major ecclesiastical religious traditions emerged in agricultural civilizations around the world. Mesopotamia, Egypt, China, Greece, Rome, Mesoamerica, and South America developed some of the earliest ecclesiastical religions. These religious traditions were limited to the specific territory of these societies and were intimately tied to their particular state organization. For example, the Mesopotamian, Egyptian, Confucian (Chinese), Greek, Roman, Mayan, Aztec, and Incan religious traditions integrated both political and religious functions for their own people. State officials were often the priests who managed the rituals and maintained the textual traditions for these people.

Universalistic Religions

Other religious traditions that developed in early agricultural societies became **universalistic religions,** consisting of spiritual messages that apply to all of humanity rather than just to their own cultural heritage. There are two major branches of universalistic religions: one emerged in the Near East and led to the formation of the historically related religions of Judaism, Christianity, and Islam; the other developed in southern Asia and resulted in Hinduism and Buddhism.

These universalistic religious traditions are known as the great religious traditions. Although they began as universalistic traditions, in many cases they evolved into ecclesiastical religions identified with specific political regions. For example, many European nations established particular Christian denominations as state religions.

Divine Rulers, Priests, and Religious Texts

Most of the early ecclesiastical religions taught that their rulers have divine authority. For example, the rulers of Mesopotamia and the pharaohs of Egypt were believed to be divine rulers upholding the moral and spiritual universe. Various Greek and Roman rulers attempted to have themselves deified during different historical periods. In India and Southeast Asia, political rulers known as *rajahs* were thought to have a semidivine status that was an aspect of their religious traditions.

Ecclesiastical religious traditions are based on written texts interpreted by professionally trained, full-time priests, who became the official custodians of the religious cosmologies and had official roles in the political hierarchy. They presided over state-organized rituals called **rites of legitimation,** which reinforced the divine authority of the ruler. In these rituals, the priests led prayers, chants, and hymns addressed to the kings and the various deities (Parrinder, 1983). As in chiefdom societies, religion sanctified and legitimized the authority of political leaders.

One of the major functions of the priests was to standardize religious beliefs and practices for the society. Individualistic religious practices and beliefs were viewed as threatening to state authorities. For example, among the Maya, state authorities perceived the shamanistic practice of taking hallucinogens to control spirits as too individualistic. As the ecclesiastical religion developed, only the Mayan priests were allowed to take mind-altering drugs. Priests managed the use of these hallucinogens on behalf of state-organized ritual activities (Dobkin de Rios, 1984).

SUMMARY

The transition from hunting and gathering to food production is known as the Neolithic. The Neolithic involved the domestication of plants and animals, which provided a more reliable food supply and thus allowed for population growth, the emergence of cities, the specialization of labor, technological complexity, and many other features that are characteristic of agricultural states.

States are societies that have bureaucratic organizations, or governments. State societies emerged with the development of intensive agriculture.

The demographic conditions of agricultural civilizations included a rise in mortality rates along with increases in fertility rates. Agricultural states often encouraged high fertility rates to raise population levels for political purposes. The technological developments associated with agricultural societies represented dramatic innovations in metallurgy, shipbuilding, paper making, printing, and many scientific ideas.

The political economy of agricultural states varied from region to region. In some areas, large-scale, centralized empires emerged, such as in China and Egypt. In other areas, smaller-scale states developed that did not have complete political control over outlying regions. After the fall of some centralized states in Europe and Japan, a type of decentralized political economy known as feudalism developed.

Different forms of property relations developed, depending on whether an agricultural state was centralized or feudal. In the centralized states, property was owned and administered by the government, whereas in feudal regimes, lords and nobles owned their estates. Long-distance trade and government-regulated monetary-exchange systems developed in agricultural societies. Within the context of long-distance trade and monetary exchange, merchants and markets emerged.

The social organization of agricultural states consisted of extended families and other descent groups, including lineages, clans, and kindreds. Marriages in agricultural societies were arranged by parents and based on political and economic considerations. In contrast to pre-state societies, polygyny and bridewealth were not widespread among agricultural state societies. Instead, monogamy and dowry exchanges were the major patterns. Divorce was infrequent.

Gender relations became more patriarchal in agricultural societies, possibly reflecting the reduced participation of females in agricultural labor. Females were largely confined to the domestic sphere, and various patterns of female seclusion developed in many of these societies, although variations in the status of women appeared in some of these agricultural states.

Social stratification in agricultural societies was based on class, caste, slavery, and racial and ethnic stratification. Some of these societies have been described as closed societies, with little opportunity for social mobility. Formalized legal systems developed, codifying laws administered by courts and government authorities. However, self-help and mediation were also used to resolve disputes.

Ecclesiastical religions developed in agricultural societies, with full-time priests, religious texts, and concepts of divine rulers associated with particular state societies. Some universalistic religious traditions developed in the Near East and Asia.

QUESTIONS TO THINK ABOUT

1. How do agricultural states differ demographically from small-scale societies such as bands, tribes, and chiefdoms?

2. Discuss some of the technological innovations developed in agricultural states.

3. How do segmentary states and theater states differ from the Aztec, Roman, and Chinese empires?

4. How do property rights differ in agricultural states from those in forager and tribal societies?

5. What are some of the advantages of having an extended family organization in an agricultural state, as opposed to an autonomous nuclear family?

6. Are marriage patterns and social ties in agricultural states independent of economic and political considerations? If so, why? If not, what are some of the economic and political implications of marriage patterns and other social ties?

7. Discuss the relationships among gender, subsistence, and status in agricultural states. How does the picture that emerges differ from the one for any of the following groups: (1) foragers, (2) tribes, or (3) chiefdoms?

8. According to Morton Fried, codified laws reinforce a system of inequity by keeping peasants subordinate while allowing those in power to have access to scarce resources. Elman Service provides a different perspective. What is Service's perspective?

9. How does religion interact with state power and bureaucratic authority in agricultural civilizations? Give examples of the relationship between the state and religion in these agricultural societies.

KEY TERMS

caste

closed societies

civilization

command economy

dowry

ecclesiastical religions

ethnicity

feudalism

intensive agriculture

moral economy

peasants

purdah

rites of legitimation

tributary form

tribute

universalistic religions

INTERNET EXERCISES

1. While visiting the website **http://www.chass.utoronto.ca:8080/~reak/hist/earlyag.htm**, determine the meaning of the phrase "agricultural frontier." What is it? What is the basic industry of all modern countries? Why? What is the French "Physiocrats'" view of all of this? Why did Thomas Jefferson equate farming with independence?

2. Review Hinduism's concept of the caste system at **http://www.friesian.com/caste.htm**. In the introductory chart, examine the section on the "twice born." Who are the "twice born"? What is the meaning of the term? How does skin color enter into Hindu caste structure? How does the caste system differ from open slavery?

SUGGESTED READINGS

ADAMS, ROBERT MCC. 1966. *The Evolution of Urban Society: Early Mesopotamia and Prehispanic Mexico.* Chicago: Aldine. A classic discussion by an archaeologist comparing Southwest Asian and American agricultural societies.

FAGAN, BRIAN. 1999. *Floods, Famines and Emperors: El Niño and the Fate of Civilizations.* New York: Basic Books. A new book by a well-known archaeologist who looks at the powerful effects of El Niño, a climatological pattern that had devastating effects on many of the ancient agricultural civilizations, such as those in Egypt, India, and Peru.

GOODY, JACK. 1971. *Technology, Tradition and the State in Africa.* London: Oxford University Press. A cross-cultural comparison of agricultural states in Africa and other regions. This work contains many insightful, thought-provoking hypotheses regarding state development in different societies.

SERVICE, ELMAN. 1975. *Origins of the State and Civilization: The Process of Cultural Evolution.* New York: Norton. A good introduction to the various theories of state formation.

TAINTER, JOSEPH A. 1990. *The Collapse of Complex Societies.* New York: Cambridge University Press. A seminal attempt to provide a general model of collapse in complex societies. Although Tainter addressed mainly his own theoretical position, the volume provides an excellent survey and critique of previous work on the subject.

CHAPTER

19

Industrial States

CHAPTER OUTLINE

CHAPTER QUESTIONS

- What were some of the historical changes that resulted in the Industrial Revolution?

- What are some of the energy use patterns and technological changes associated with industrial societies?

- What are the characteristics of the economy in industrial societies?

- How did the Industrial Revolution influence the status and role of family, gender, and age?

- Why are industrial societies considered to be more "open" in social stratification than preindustrial societies?

- What are the characteristics of politics, law, and warfare in industrial societies?

- What are the consequences of industrialization for religion in industrial societies?

The *Industrial Revolution* is the term used to describe the broad changes that occurred during the latter part of the eighteenth century in Europe. However, the roots of these dramatic changes in the structure and organization of society were there much earlier. This chapter considers the causes of the Industrial Revolution and its consequences for the states in which it occurred. This is an extremely important topic, because it emphasizes how anthropologists interpret and explain the development of the Industrial Revolution in Europe, rather than in other regions of the world. Traditionally, most cultural anthropologists did research on preindustrial societies, as covered in Chapter 15 through Chapter 18. However, many cultural anthropologists have turned their attention to doing ethnography in the industrial regions of the world, including Europe, Russia, the United States, Canada, Australia, and Japan. These cultural anthropologists have to take a highly interdisciplinary approach, drawing on the work of historians, economists, political scientists, and sociologists. The chapter uses much of the research of these other disciplines, as well as the studies of cultural anthropologists.

An **industrial society** uses sophisticated technology based on machinery powered by advanced fuels to produce material goods. A primary feature of industrial societies in comparison with preindustrial societies is that most productive labor involves factory and office work, rather than agricultural or foraging activities. This pattern has produced new forms of economic organization and social-class arrangements. In terms of political organization, industrial societies became the first well-developed **nation-states**—political communities that have clearly defined territorial borders dividing them from one another. All modern industrial nation-states exercise extensive political authority over many aspects of the lives of their citizenry through the application of formalized laws and a centralized government.

The Commercial, Scientific, and Industrial Revolution

One of the traditional explanations of why Europe succeeded in developing the Industrial Revolution and that other societies did not is that Europeans were superior to other people mentally and intellectually. Anthropologists do not accept this claim of European mental and intellectual superiority. This idea has a long history that is connected with racist beliefs that go back deep into Western history (see Chapter 23). These racists believe that other races of people were incapable of developing advanced technology, and that is why Europe was the center of the rise of industrial society. Again, anthropologists have refuted the basis of these racist arguments through systematic biological, archaeological, and cultural research throughout the world.

An influential book by Jared Diamond called *Guns, Germs, and Steel: The Fate of Human Societies* (1997), which draws on an enormous amount of geographical, archaeological, and anthropological research, demonstrates that the European Industrial Revolution did not develop as the result of the genius and intelligence of Europeans, but as an unpredictable sequence of historical processes. As mentioned in Chapter 18, most of the plants and large mammals that could be domesticated existed in the Near East by chance, and this pattern diffused into Europe. Europe, the Near East, and the Asian land mass were contiguous with one another. Harvests were abundant, and domesticated animals enabled the Near Easterners, Europeans, and Asians to develop cities with large populations, governments, specialized economic systems, and writing systems, as described in Chapter 9. Centuries later, they had the technological knowledge and political power to conquer other areas of the world that did not have these resources. For example, as mentioned in Chapter 18, Africa and the Americas lacked easily domesticated species of animals for agriculture. The Near Easterners, Europeans, and Asians developed resistance to certain diseases as a result of living with domesticated animals such as cattle and pigs for many years. The diffusion of agriculture and domesticated animals happened quickly in Europe and Asia because, unlike Africa and the Americas, there were no substantial geographic barriers such as oceans, deserts, and rain forests. This gave Europe the edge in the initial beginnings of the Industrial Revolution. China was almost to the same point of development in the 1600s, but for historical reasons they did not begin to expand beyond their boundaries. Consequently, Europe, not China, became the center of the Industrial Revolution during that period.

Anthropologists address the question of why Europe was the center of the Industrial Revolution by drawing on a wide range of historical sources from many regions of the world. A global perspective is the only way of trying to answer this question. Anthropologists such as Jack Goody (1996) and Eric Wolf (1997) have adopted this global perspective and have examined the interrelationships between the non-European world and Europe to provide answers to this question.

A major factor leading to the emergence of industrial states in European society was the increased contact among different societies, primarily through trade. Although, as discussed in the last chapter, long-distance trade was present in agricultural states, the major regions of the world were relatively isolated from one another. Trade was conducted in Asia, the Near East, Europe, Africa, and internally within the Americas before A.D. 1500, but the difficulties of transportation and communication inhibited the spread of ideas, values, and technology among these regions. Although Europeans had contact with non-Europeans through religious wars such as the Crusades and the travels of adventurers such as Marco Polo, they did not engage in systematic relations with non-Europeans until after the year 1500.

The upper class and royalty of agricultural European society encouraged long-distance trade as a means of accumulating wealth. Their principal motivation was to build a self-sufficient economy as a basis for extending their centralized government. This type of economic system is often referred to as mercantilism. **Mercantilism** is a system in which the government regulates the economy of a state to ensure economic growth, a positive balance of trade, and the accumulation of gold and silver. One key mercantilist strategy was for the government to grant *monopolies* to trading companies so that these companies could accumulate wealth for the home country. The European upper classes were also attempting to compete with the Islamic and Asian trade that predominated in the East. These elites formed an alliance with merchants to support their endeavors (Wolf, 1997). Thus, for example, during the fifteenth and sixteenth centuries, the rulers of Spain and Portugal sponsored private traders who explored the world to search for wealth. These expeditions eventually established ports of trade in Africa, the Americas, and Asia.

Eventually European countries such as the Netherlands, Great Britain, France, and Russia became mercantile competitors with Spain and Portugal. They formed private trading companies such as the British East India Company, which were subsidized by the government. These companies were given special rights to engage in trade in specific regions. In turn, they were expected to find both sources of wealth and luxury goods that could be consumed by the ruling classes.

One result of this mercantilist trade was the beginning of global unity (Chirot, 1986; Wolf, 1997). European explorers visited every part of the globe. An enormous diffusion of plants, animals, humans, technology, and ideas took place among Europe, America, and the rest of the world. Cultures from every region of the world began to confront each other. These encounters led to new patterns of trade, political developments, and the transmission of beliefs, ideas, and practices. European traders backed by military force began to compete with other traders from the Middle East and Asia. Soon, through the use of military force, European trade came to displace the Asian and Islamic trading empires. As economic wealth began to amass in Europe, through the accumulation of gold, silver, and other commodities from the Americas, Asia, Africa, and the Middle East, the political center of power also swung to Europe. These economic and political changes were accompanied by major transformations in non-Western societies. These changes in non-Western societies will be discussed in later chapters.

The global diffusion of philosophical and practical knowledge provided the basis for the scientific revolution in the West. Ideas and technology that were developed in the civilizations of China, India, the Middle East, Africa, and the Americas provided the stimulus for the emergence of scientific enterprise in Europe. Eventually, scientific methods based on deductive and inductive logic (see Chapter 1) were allied with practical economic interests to provide the basis for the Industrial Revolution in Europe. But again, many of the ideas and technological developments that gave rise to the Industrial Revolution in Europe had emerged earlier in agricultural civilizations in other regions of the world. The scientific revolution would not have developed in Europe without the knowledge of scientific and mathematical concepts previously developed in India, the Middle East, and Asia.

The notion that there was a unique European miracle that was associated with the so-called White Race is a fallacy. The idea that Europeans were superior geniuses who were capable of developing the industrial civilization is also a fallacy. Without the diffusion of knowledge and technologies from other regions of the world, Europe would not have been able to develop the Industrial Revolution. Slowly and gradually, over a period of some four hundred years, the combination of scientific and commercial alliances in Europe produced dramatic consequences that transformed economic, social, and political structures through the process of **industrialization**—the adoption of a mechanized means of production to transform raw materials into manufactured goods.

Modernization

The overall consequences of the Industrial Revolution are often referred to as **modernization**—the economic, social, political, and religious changes related to modern industrial and technological change. Modernization was not an overnight occurrence. It took more than four hundred years, from 1600 on, to develop in the West, and it remains an ongoing process. It depended on the commercial transformations brought about through years of mercantilism that led to the accumulation of capital for investment and the gradual diffusion of practical knowledge and scientific methods that engendered technological innovations.

Environment and Energy Use

In earlier chapters, we saw how the availability of resources affects levels of political and economic development. States and chiefdoms emerged in areas with abundant resources, whereas other environments could support only bands and tribes. Environmental conditions also had an influence on the early phases of industrialization. Industrial societies still depended heavily on agricultural production to meet basic food requirements, but through industrialization, agricultural production itself was transformed. The major natural-resource requirements for industrial societies are based on harnessing new sources of energy, especially fossil-fuel energy.

In industrial societies such as Japan, most couples prefer small families.

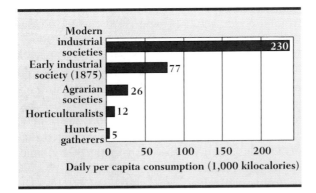

FIGURE 19.1 Energy consumption among the various types of societies. Note the dramatic increase in consumption in the modern industrial societies.

Source: Adapted from Earl Cook, "The Flow of Energy in an Industrial Society," *Scientific American* 224(3) (1971):136. Reprinted by permission of the Estate of Bunji Tagawa.

In Chapter 13 we discussed Leslie White's attempt to explain sociocultural evolution in terms of energy use. He suggested that sociocultural evolution progressed in relationship to the harnessing of energy. Anthropologist John Bodley (1985) attempted to quantify White's ideas. He suggested that sociocultural systems can be divided into *high-energy cultures* and *low-energy cultures*, and that these categories have implications for the evolution of society. For example, before the Industrial Revolution, no states used more than 26,000 kilocalories per capita daily, and tribal hunters and farmers used between 4,000 and 12,000. These societies are classified as low-energy cultures. In contrast, early industrial societies using fossil fuels almost tripled their consumption of energy to 70,000 kilocalories. Later phases of industrialization in high-energy cultures such as the United States experienced a quadrupling of energy consumption. Energy use and expenditure have risen dramatically in all industrial societies (see Figure 19.1).

In the low-energy, preindustrial societies, human and nonhuman animal labor was the chief source of energy, supplemented by firewood, wind, and sometimes waterpower. In contrast, in high-energy societies, fossil fuels such as coal, natural gas, and petroleum became the primary energy sources. During the early phases of the Industrial Revolution, societies in Europe and America relied on fossil fuels found in their own territories, but they eventually began to exploit resources from other regions. In later chapters we examine the consequences of these patterns of high-energy use on the different environments of the world.

Demographic Change

One major consequence of the early phases of the Industrial Revolution was a dramatic increase in population. The major reasons for this were technological developments in agriculture and transportation that enabled farmers to grow more food and transport it to areas with food scarcities. In addition, scientific advances led to the control of some infectious diseases, such as the bubonic plague, diphtheria, typhus, and cholera, which had kept death rates high in preindustrial societies. As death rates declined, birth rates remained high. The combination of lower death rates with high birth rates produced major population increases of about 3 percent annually. Europe's population grew from about 140 million in 1750 to 463 million in 1914 (Stavrianos, 1995).

The Demographic Transition

During later phases of industrialization (especially since the 1960s), population growth began to decline in societies like England, Western Europe, the United States, and Japan (Population Reference Bureau, 1986). Demographers refer to this change as the **demographic transition,** in which birth rates and death rates decline. In contrast to preindustrial societies, in which high birth rates were perceived as beneficial, in industrial societies many people no longer see large families as a benefit. One reason for this view is the higher costs of rearing children in industrial societies. In addition, social factors such as changing gender relations—more women in the work force and the reduction in family size—have contributed to lower fertility rates. (These social factors are discussed later in this chapter.) Increased knowledge of, and access to, contraceptives helped people to control family size.

Urbanization

Population increases, coupled with the movement of workers from farms to factories, resulted in the unprecedented growth of urban centers (see Table 19.1). During the nineteenth century, the populations of cities such as London, Paris, and Chicago soared into the millions. By 1930, one-fifth of all humanity, or approximately 415 million people, lived in urban areas (Mumford, 1961; Stavrianos, 1995). One of the major factors causing rapid urban growth was the increasing need for labor in the machine-based factory system. Factory towns like Manchester, England, grew into large industrial centers connected to financial and communications districts.

Table 19.1	Population in Selected Industrial Cities	
City	1995 (thousands)	2015 (projected) Density
Tokyo	26,959	28,887
New York	16,332	17,602
Los Angeles	12,410	14,217

Source: **Reprinted from** *The World Almanac and Book of Facts 1999.* **Copyright © 1998 World Almanac Education Group. All rights reserved.**

Urbanization is a trend in industrial societies as seen in this photo of New York City.

Technology and Economic Change

Industrialization was fueled by a series of technological innovations that occurred after the middle of the eighteenth century. The major change was a movement from human and animal labor to mechanical, or machine, labor. More recently, through science, engineering, and commerce, technological innovations ranging from automobiles to electronics to computers have continued to transform industrial societies. These technologies have not only made communication and transportation more efficient but have also contributed to a vast international global economic network in which all societies can interact. Through the Internet, the World Wide Web, e-mail, fax, telephones, television, and satellite transmissions, societies are increasingly linked to a global economy.

Technology and Work

The technological revolution transformed basic work conditions. The factory system imposed a new work pace and led to a new form of discipline for laborers. Factory and mine workers were organized around the machine's schedule, and work became increasingly time-oriented. Most work in the early factories was highly routinized and repetitious.

Preindustrial workers had some control over the quantity and quality of their products and the pace of their labor, but early industrial workers had little control over these matters. Karl Marx, a major critic of industrial capitalism, saw that industrial workers were estranged and alienated from their work conditions and that they viewed their labor as meaningless and beyond their control.

The Division of Labor

The division of labor in industrial economies is much more complex than it is in preindustrial economies. Industrial economies have three identifiable sectors, which correspond to the division of labor. The **primary sector** represents the part of the industrial economy devoted to the extraction of raw materials and energy; it includes agriculture, lumber, fishing, and mining. The **secondary sector** includes the factories that take the raw materials and process them for consumption. The **tertiary sector,** sometimes referred to as the *service sector,* includes the financial and banking industries and other industries, such as automobile repair, communications, health care, computer services, government, and education.

In the first phases of industrialization, most of the labor force was engaged in the primary sector, extracting raw materials for industrial production. Further mechanization of industry led to an increase of the labor force in the secondary, or manufacturing, sector. These workers are the manual, or "blue-collar," workers. Finally, in the advanced phases of industrialization, an increasing percentage of the labor force has become located in the various service industries.

Currently, in the most advanced industrial societies—such as the United States, the United Kingdom, Japan, Germany, Canada, and Australia—the tertiary sector is the largest and most rapidly expanding component of the economy. Some sociologists refer to these societies as *postindustrial societies*, because more people are employed in service and technical occupations than in manufacturing. Information is the key component of a postindustrial economy, since people must acquire a great deal of technical knowledge to function effectively, and educational requirements for many jobs have increased substantially. To meet the demands of a postindustrial economy, an increasing percentage of the population attends college (and graduate and professional schools), and computer skills have been integrated into the educational curriculum. With their capacity to process and manipulate vast amounts of data, computers have become essential in these societies.

Economic Exchange

Like other types of societies, industrial states engage in reciprocal and redistributional economic exchanges. Reciprocal exchanges, such as Christmas gifts and gifts of funds for college tuition, frequently occur within the family. The graduated income tax in U.S. society represents one form of redistributional exchange in which income is collected from some people and flows back to society. Taxes also represent a form of tributary economic exchange, which is characteristic of agricultural states.

Market Economies   In addition to these activities, industrial states developed a new pattern of exchange based on a market economy. A **market economy** is a pattern of economic exchange based on the value of goods and services determined by the *supply and demand* of these items. The evolution of the market economy, linked with industrial technological developments, radically changed the way goods and services were produced and exchanged in industrial societies. Goods and services are assigned monetary value and are bought and sold with general-purpose money. The prices of these goods and services depend on the supply and demand of the goods and services on the world market.

Moreover, in the market economy the basic factors of production—land, labor, and capital—are assigned monetary prices and are bought and sold freely in the marketplace. Thus, rather than kinship or prominent leaders, market forces determine the general process of economic exchange.

In agricultural societies, goods and services were bought and sold in regional or local markets. These markets, however, were not based on market

The New York Stock Exchange represents the peak development of a market-driven economy.

APPLYING ANTHROPOLOGY

STUDYING INDUSTRIAL CORPORATIONS

The image of cultural anthropologists is changing. The typical image of a cultural anthropologist is of a person dressed in a safari jacket copying detailed notes from an informant in a tropical region of the world. However, another role for cultural anthropologists has developed recently. In attempting to cut costs and improve productivity and competitiveness, many American and multinational corporations have begun to hire cultural anthropologists to do studies of the "natives" in the factory or in middle and upper management. In the past, corporations usually hired efficiency experts such as industrial engineers and industrial psychologists to help design their policies and work systems. But those programs usually involved little input and feedback from the employees themselves. In many cases, the implementation of the policies resulted in inefficient and unproductive practices (Garza, 1991).

Cultural anthropologists study corporate life through participant observation and in-depth interviews with employees. These studies focus on gathering information about the corporate culture: the corporate norms, values, and practices that can be described

only through these anthropological techniques. John Seely Brown, former director of Xerox Corporation's Palo Alto Research Center, has admitted that the cultural anthropologist of corporate life can deliver dramatic improvements in productivity. He goes on to say that "companies have to go beyond industrial psychology and reengineer the business process. They have to work from the bottom up. And anthropology is the field most attuned to that" (Garza, 1991).

In the mid 1980s, Xerox set out to devise more efficient and less costly methods to train its service technicians. Julian Orr, an anthropologist, was hired to determine whether Xerox could do its training more productively. Orr used participant-research methods, taking the service training and going out on jobs himself to discover factors that affected the job. In the field, Orr found that the repair work was not the main job. Instead, he discovered that most of the service calls stemmed from customers who did not know how to run the machines rather than from technical breakdowns. Thus, the most important part of the job involved communication skills. Orr reasoned that service

technicians ought to be trained as teachers who can explain the technicalities of the new machines to customers who are using them. Through participant-observation research methods, cultural anthropologists such as Orr can suggest remedies for improving relationships between companies and their clients.

Cultural anthropologists are also being hired to bring their understanding of different cultures and their specialized research techniques to bear on the problems of multinational corporations. One study by anthropologist Margo L. Smith (1986) observed fifteen multinational corporations based in Chicago to determine what types of employees were selected for overseas assignments in foreign cultural environments and what types of cross-cultural skills these employees needed. She found that very few of the companies recognized the need for cross-cultural training for employees to be sent overseas on short-term assignments. Companies usually provided culture and language training for upper-management personnel who were going to be assigned for more lengthy periods. Smith advised that the companies underestimated the importance of language and culture skills, even for short-term assignments. Employees with short-term assignments represent the company's interests abroad as much as do those with longer-term assignments and may jeopardize the success of various projects by behaving improperly and saying something that could be interpreted as offensive to the local people.

General Motors hired anthropologists Elizabeth Briody and Marietta L. Baba to do research on overseas assignments. These anthropologists found that whereas upper management was promoting overseas assignments as a means of achieving improved business skills and managerial techniques, executives in the North American car and truck units discouraged the idea. The cultural anthropologists discovered that GM's North American operation was run separately from the company's overseas subsidiaries, and that within GM's corporate culture, employees perceived the North American operation as GM's elite. Therefore, a position overseas was perceived as a lower-status position. Many of the people who worked overseas were placed on slower career paths. In contrast, in some component divisions of GM such as Delco, top executives were frequently assigned overseas and were viewed as valuable assets to the company.

Briody and Baba recommended that GM adopt a policy whereby managers assigned overseas would be given specific agendas that would lead to improvements in domestic car operations. For example, they could learn techniques from Europe on design, engineering, and manufacturing that could improve U.S. plants. They also suggested an exchange program to replace those sent overseas with a foreign counterpart. These exchanges would result in an improved understanding of global manufacturing, productivity, and competition.

A number of anthropologists are now directly employed in corporations or with market research firms to find out about consumer preferences for different products. A company may want to know which type of advertising has successfully attracted consumers and which segment of a population represents the most promising market for future sales. Why do certain products appeal to some ethnic, age, or sex groups and not others? Why do some advertising campaigns result in higher sales than others?

Anthropologist Steve Barnett, who headed a cultural-analysis group at Planmetrics, a Chicago consulting firm, directs a number of projects related to business research (Lewin, 1986). Aside from directing research on management-union relations and other business-related topics for various corporations, Barnett also does marketing research and gathers information on consumer preferences. He emphasizes participant observation in his research methods. For example, to report on consumer patterns of teenagers for fast-food chains, Barnett directs student researchers who participate in teen activities.

As corporations become more experienced with international business and strive to become more productive and competitive both domestically and internationally, anthropologists will increasingly be drawn into consulting and research roles. Anthropological research techniques and cultural knowledge have helped corporations throughout the world solve some of their practical problems. Perhaps future anthropologists may want to think about combining their course-work with some business and management courses to prepare for these new projects in anthropology.

exchange; instead, buyers and sellers met and haggled over the price of goods. This is a type of nonmarket price determination. In contrast, in industrial societies, buyers and sellers do not have to meet face to face. Buyers can compare prices from different sellers, and the prices are then established according to supply and demand. Impersonality and lack of haggling between buyer and seller are the general patterns in market exchanges.

Perspectives on Market Economies

Market forces based on the supply and demand of land, labor, and capital began to drive economic production, exchange, and consumption in industrial societies. The market process, which determined the prices of these factors of production, exerted tremendous influence over all aspects of these industrializing societies. The new economic forces and processes were described by the "father of modern economics," Adam Smith. In his book *An Inquiry into the Nature and Causes of the Wealth of Nations* ([1776] 1937), Smith argued that both buyers and sellers would reap rewards from market exchange and competition, because prices would be lower for consumers and profits higher for sellers. The result would be increased prosperity for all segments of society. Smith viewed the market economy as a mechanism for promoting progress.

In contrast, one hundred years later, Karl Marx offered a gloomier picture of industrial societies. Marx focused on how the market economy determined the price and organization of human labor, bringing about misery for millions of people. Marx believed that industrial capitalist societies must be transformed to a new form of socialist society in which the factors of production would not be driven by the market but would be controlled by the state to ensure an even division of profits among all classes.

Eventually, both capitalist and socialist forms of industrial societies developed in different regions of the world. To highlight some of the variations of industrial societies, we next examine the development of capitalism and socialism in some of these regions.

Capitalism   As is evident from the previous discussion, the Industrial Revolution was intricately connected with the emergence of capitalism in Western societies. **Capitalism** is an economic system in which natural resources as well as the means of producing and distributing goods and services are privately owned. Capitalist societies share three basic ideals: first, the factors of production are privately owned, and an emphasis on private property has become the standard incorporated into all economic, legal, and political documents of capitalist societies; second, companies are free to maximize profits and accumulate as much capital as they can; third, free competition and consumer sovereignty are basic to all economic activities. Ideally, people are free to buy and sell at whatever prices they can to satisfy their own interests. Also, government regulation of economic affairs is usually discouraged.

Capitalism in the United States   Capitalism spread into North America following the settling of colonies by British and other European peoples. The English had incorporated major portions of North America as a colony during the mercantile period. But eventually, the English colonists began to control their own economic and political destinies, which led to the American Revolution of the late eighteenth century. Following independence, capitalist economic development and industrialization proceeded rapidly in the United States. Bountiful natural resources provided the raw materials for factory production, and millions of immigrants arrived from Europe, providing a source of cheap labor for factories. The U.S. economy grew quickly, and by 1894 the nation had the world's fastest-growing economy.

Despite the ideals of pure capitalism, which discouraged government regulation of the economy, the U.S. government actively encouraged industrial economic expansion through state subsidies, protective tariffs, and other policies. For example, the government promoted the development of a nationwide railroad system by providing large financial incentives, rights to land, and subsidies to individual capitalists. In addition, free land was given to people who wanted to settle frontier regions through the Homestead Act of 1862.

By the late nineteenth century, rapid economic expansion had produced a new moneyed class that held a great proportion of assets. A relatively small number of people controlled a large number of industries and other commercial enterprises of finance and capital. The wealthiest 1 percent of the population owned about one-third of all *capital assets* (wealth in land or other private property). Economic expansion also spurred the growth of a large middle class that exerted a powerful influence on both the economic and political structure of U.S. society.

Capitalism in Japan Japan was an agricultural feudal society from the period of the first shogunate in the twelfth century until about 1870, after which it rapidly industrialized. Following a period of historical isolation from the West during the Tokugawa period (1600–1870), Japan was forced to open its doors to outside powers such as the United States. The Japanese recognized the technological advancements of the Western world, and, to avoid being colonized like other Asian countries, they rapidly modified their society to accommodate industrial capitalism. But the socioeconomic and political conditions that made possible rapid capitalist development existed before Japan's intensive contact with the West.

During the Tokugawa period, internal trade and entrepreneurial developments flourished in highly developed urban centers such as Tokyo and Kyoto. Moreover, Japan had a highly educated class of *samurai*, who were in a position to bring about innovations in society (Befu, 1971).

Following the opening of Japan to the West, the Japanese abandoned the feudal system and centralized their government under the Meiji emperor. With help from Western advisers (1868–1911), the Meiji government introduced a mandatory education system and modern military technology. The government also took concrete steps to help introduce capitalism (Geertz, 1963b). It taxed the peasants to raise money for industrialization and subsidized certain entrepreneurial families, the *zaibatsu*, who gained control of the major industrial technologies. Families such as the Mitsubishi family were encouraged to invest in needed industries to compete with Western interests. Thus, the government developed key industries in Japan by cooperating with private interests and families.

Socialism A different type of economic system developed in some industrial societies as a historical response to capitalism. **Socialism** is an economic system in which the state, ideally as the representative of the people, owns the basic means of production. Although individuals may own some

consumer goods such as housing and automobiles, they are not allowed to own stock in corporations or wealth-generating property related to the production of capital goods. Socialism evolved as a response to the considerable economic inequalities that existed in capitalist societies. To create more economic equality and less exploitation of working people, socialist philosophers promoted ideals that contrasted with those of capitalism. Socialist ideals maintained that meeting the population's basic needs takes precedence over the enrichment of a small number of people.

Socialism in the Former Soviet Union In contrast to Marx's predictions that socialist revolutions would occur in industrial societies, socialism initially developed in Russia, which was primarily agricultural and feudal. From about A.D. 1000, the basic form of land tenure in Russia was based on the *mir,* or peasant commune, which was linked to feudal estates to which the serfs provided labor (Dunn & Dunn, 1988). During the nineteenth century, feudalism was abolished, and the serfs were freed from the estates. The Russian economy, however, remained largely dependent on wheat exports and Western capital (Chirot, 1986).

As in Japan, the Russian elites realized that they had to industrialize quickly if they were to survive. The central government subsidized industrialization by taxing the peasantry heavily and importing European industrial technology. As a result, Russia gradually began to industrialize. However, the new economic burdens on peasant society, a military defeat by the Japanese in 1905, and the widespread suffering produced by World War I severely weakened the government of the emperor, or *czar*. The result was the Russian Revolution of 1917.

Under the leadership of Vladimir Lenin, the new Soviet state implemented a number of policies designed to create a more egalitarian society that would meet the basic needs of all the people. All wealth-generating property (the means of production) was placed under government control. The government collectivized agriculture by taking land from landowners and distributing the peasant population on collective, state-controlled farms. State authorities systematically regulated all prices and wages. In addition, the government initiated a policy of rapid industrialization to try to catch up with the West.

Soviet factory workers in the 1930s were mobilized by the state to develop heavy industry.

Hybrid Economic Systems   To some extent, neither capitalism nor socialism exists in pure form according to the ideals espoused by their leading theorists. Government intervention in the economy exists in both types of economic systems. In some industrial societies such as Sweden, and to a lesser extent in Western Europe and England, a hybrid form of economic system referred to as *democratic socialism* developed. In these societies, the key strategic industries that produce basic capital goods and services are government owned, as are certain heavy industries such as steel and coal and utilities such as telephone companies. At the same time, much of the economy and technology is privately owned, and production takes place for private profit.

The Evolution of Economic Organizations

As industrial economies developed in capitalist, socialist, and democratic-socialist societies, the major economic organizations increased in size and complexity. In capitalist societies, family businesses grew into corporations, which were established as legal entities to raise capital through the sale of *stocks and bonds.* Eventually, these corporations increased their economic holdings and were able to concentrate their ownership of the society's major technology. Through expansion and mergers, they came to dominate economic production and exchange. The result was **oligopoly,** in which a few giant corporations control production in major industries. For example, in the United States in the early 1900s, there were thirty-five domestic automobile companies, but by the 1950s only three remained. This process of corporate expansion ushered in a phase of capitalism known as **monopoly capitalism,** a form of capitalism dominated by large corporations that can reduce free competition through the concentration of capital. This concentration of capital enables oligopolies to control prices and thereby dominate the markets.

In socialist societies such as the former Soviet Union, in which private ownership of technology was prohibited, the government controls and manages the major economic organizations. The equivalent of the large capitalist corporation is the state-owned enterprise that has some degree of financial autonomy, although government authorities establish production goals. The majority of state enterprises were still small or medium in size, but the enterprises of the former Soviet state became more concentrated (Kerblay, 1983). These enterprises followed the production aims established by the various ministries, which were ultimately controlled by Communist Party officials.

Multinational Corporations   In the capitalist, socialist, and hybrid economic systems, corporations increased in size to become large multinational corporations with enormous assets. **Multinational corporations** are economic organizations that operate in many different regions of the world. Multinational corporations are based in their home countries but own subsidiaries in many other countries. For example, American-based I.T.T., a multinational corporation with more than 400,000 employees, has offices in 68 different countries. Although approximately 300 of the 500 largest multinational corporations are based in the United States, others, such as Unilever, Shell, and Mitsubishi, are based in England, Western Europe, and Japan, respectively. The socialist societies of the former Soviet Union and former

Eastern European countries had large state-owned multinational corporations that coordinated their activities through what was known as *Comecon* (a committee that coordinated multinational activities worldwide).

The evolution of the multinational corporation has had tremendous consequences for the global economy. Anthropologist Alvin Wolfe proposed that multinational corporations are beginning to evolve into supranational organizations that are stronger than the nation-state (1977, 1986). Reed Riner (1981) described how various multinational corporations are interconnected in the world global economy. The top CEOs in the various multinational corporations sit on one another's boards of directors. In addition, the multinational corporations are increasingly involved in joint ventures, consolidating their capital assets and technologies to produce goods and services throughout the world. We consider the effects of these multinational corporations in different societies in later chapters.

Capitalist Consumer Societies

Another major change in industrial capitalist societies and the development of multinational corporations is the extent of production and consumption of consumer goods. After the twentieth century, and especially after World War II, corporations in the United States and other capitalist countries began to engage in extensive marketing to create demand for a plethora of consumer goods, including automobiles, home appliances, televisions, and electronic products. Corporations launched advertising campaigns targeting children and young people as potential consumers for these products. Major investment in advertising and marketing campaigns to create demand for consumer goods was promoted through the media, especially television. Eventually, cartoons and amusement parks such as Disneyland for children became the vehicle for promoting toy products and other goods for young people. Television and media advertising, along with easy credit, created enormous demand for various consumer goods in these capitalist societies. These patterns of consumption have resulted in extensive global ecological, economic, and cultural changes. We discuss some of the global consequences of capitalist consumer societies in Chapter 24.

Social Structure

The impact of industrialization on kinship, family, gender, aging, and social status has been just as dramatic as it has been on demography, technology, and economic conditions.

Kinship

Kinship is less important in industrialized states than in preindustrial societies. New structures and organizations perform many of the functions associated with kinship in preindustrial societies. For example, occupational and economic factors replace kinship as the primary basis of social status; a person no longer has to be part of an aristocratic or elite family to have access to wealth and political power.

As states industrialized, newly emerging middle-class families began to experience upward economic and social mobility, and economic performance, merit, and personal achievement, rather than ascribed kinship relationships, became the primary basis of social status. Of course, kinship and family background still have a definite influence on social mobility. Families with wealth, political power, and high social status can ensure that their children will have the best education. These families provide their offspring with professional role models and values that emphasize success. They also maintain economic and political connections that enhance their offspring's future opportunities. Hence, their children have a head start over children from lower socioeconomic categories. But kinship alone is not the fundamental determinant of social status and rank that it had been in most preindustrial societies.

Family

In Chapter 14 we discussed the various functions of the family: socializing children, regulating sexual behavior, and providing emotional and economic security. In industrial societies, some of these functions have been transformed. The major transformation has been the diminishing importance of the extended family and the emergence of the smaller nuclear family. Some basic functions, such as reproduction and the primary care and socialization of children, are still performed in the nuclear family.

The family's economic role has changed dramatically. In industrial societies the family is no longer an economic unit linked to production. The prevalence of wage labor in industrial societies has been one of the principal factors leading to the breakdown of the extended family and the emergence of the nuclear family (Wolf, 1966). The extended family in peasant societies maintained cooperative economic production on the land. When employers began to hire individual workers for labor in mines, factories, and other industries, the extended family as a corporate unit no longer had any economically productive function.

Another factor leading to the diminishing importance of the extended family has been the high rate of geographical mobility induced by industrialization. Because much of the labor drawn into factories and mines initially came from rural areas, workers had to leave their families and establish their own nuclear families in the cities. Land tenure based on the extended family was no longer the

During the early phases of industrialization, rural women, including these women who worked in the Lowell textile mill, often had to leave their rural extended families and, when married, formed nuclear families residing in urban areas.

driving force it had been in preindustrial societies. In addition, as manufacturing and service industries expanded, they frequently moved or opened new offices, requiring workers to relocate. Thus, the economic requirements of industrializing societies have had the effect of dissolving the extended family ties that had been so critical in preindustrial societies.

Historians and sociologists have studied the disintegration of the extended family in industrial England, Europe, and North America for decades (Goode, 1963, 1982). A similar process occurred in Russia and Japan. In Russia, the nuclear family began to replace the extended family following the emancipation of the serfs (Kerblay, 1983). Yet anthropologists have noted that the nuclear family is not the ideal norm in Russian society. Surveys indicate that the Russians do not consider it proper for older parents to live alone, and that many consider the grandfather to be the head of the family. These ideal norms reflect the older traditions of the extended peasant family in Russia (Dunn & Dunn, 1988).

In Japanese society, the traditional family was based on the *ie* (pronounced like the slang term "yeah" in American English). The *ie* is a patrilineal extended family that had kinship networks based on blood relations, marriage, and adoption (Befu, 1971; Shimizu, 1987). The *ie* managed its assets in land and property as a corporate group and was linked into a hierarchy of other branch *ie* families, forming a *dozoku*. The *dozoku* maintained functions similar to those of the peasant families of other agricultural societies. With industrialization, the rurally based *ie* and *dozoku* began to decline, and urban nuclear families called the *kazoku* began to develop (Befu, 1971; Kerbo & McKinstry, 1998). The shift from the *ie* and *dozuku* to the *kazoku* has been very sudden and recent, and many older people in Japan have not adjusted to this recent change.

Despite the general tendency toward the breakup of the extended family in industrialized societies, specific groups and regions in these societies may still retain extended family ties. For example, extended, peasant-type families exist in the rural regions such as Uzbekistan, Azerbaijan, and Georgia, which were formerly part of the Soviet Union (Kerblay, 1983). Similar tendencies can be found in rural British, European, and Japanese societies. Even in the urban areas of nations such as the United States and Great Britain, some ethnic groups maintain extended family ties. In the United States, some African Americans and Latinos enjoy the loyalty and support of extended family ties to enhance their economic and social organization within the larger society (Stack, 1975; Macionis, 2001).

Marriage

One of the major changes in marriage in industrialized societies is that it has become much more *individualized;* that is, the establishment of the union has come to involve personal considerations more than family arrangements. This individualistic form of marriage is usually based on *romantic love,* which entails a blend of emotional attachment with physical and sexual attraction. Romantic love existed in preindustrial societies (Fisher, 1992; Jankowiak & Fischer, 1992), and there are many ethnographic descriptions of couples falling in love in both pre-state and agricultural state societies. The classical literature of China, India, Greece, and Rome, as well as various religious texts such as the Bible, are filled with stories about romantic love. Shakespeare's play *Romeo and Juliet* underscores the conflict between romantic love and the familistic and practical considerations of marriage.

Prior to about 150 years ago and industrialization, however, most couples were married through the intervention of parents, who arranged their relationships. Romantic love may have existed in preindustrial societies (and in many cases it was the basis for extramarital relationships), but it did not become the primary basis of marriage until after the Industrial Revolution. This change first took place in England, the center of industrialized commercialization. As the extended family declined in significance, important decisions such as selection of a marriage partner increasingly were made by individuals rather than by families.

Though individuals select their own marriage partners in most industrialized societies, parents in these societies often attempt to enhance marital choices in certain categories. For example, parents of the upper and upper-middle class often choose certain colleges for their children so that they will meet suitable marriage partners. Many parents sponsor social activities for their children to meet potential marriage partners of their own socioeconomic, ethnic, and religious affiliations. Thus, to some extent, even in industrialized societies, individual choice of marriage partners is circumscribed by

parental guidance. However, many people in an industrialized society such as the United States find that because of the breakdown in family and community ties, individuals find it more difficult to meet prospective spouses. Many individuals are from homes where their parents have been divorced at least once, and consequently this reduces the possibility of meeting someone through their family. For that reason, there has been an increase in dating and match-making services in industrialized societies such as the United States. Thousands of these dating and match-making services, along with websites aimed at helping singles find a spouse, have developed within the past decades.

One exception needs to be noted with respect to the relationships between industrialization and commercialization and individualized decision making in the selection of marriage partners. In Japanese society, the traditional form of marriage was arranged through a go-between, a *nakoda,* who set up a meeting for a couple to get to know each other (Hendry, 1987). The *nakoda* would establish an alliance between two extended households. This pattern is known as the *samurai* form of marriage because the warrior-scholars practiced it during the Tokugawa period.

With industrialization in Japanese society, romantic love has had an effect on the selection of marriage partners, and currently many Japanese individuals choose their own mates. But anthropologist Joy Hendry (1987) notes that "love marriages" are still suspect and go against the serious practical concerns of marital ties and the traditional obligations felt by people toward their parents. In many cases, *nakoda* are still used to arrange marriages in this highly modern society.

Approximately one-third of the marriages in Japan are the result of arranged marriages. A couple of marriageable age is brought together in a formal meeting called an *omiai,* arranged by the *nakoda.* "Love marriages" based on romantic love, called *renai kekkon,* may result in marriage, but in most cases parents still have veto power over who their children marry (Kerbo & McKinstry, 1998). Marriage in Japan is still very much a family consideration, rather than just an individual's own choice or decision.

Divorce   All but a few industrialized societies have legalized divorce, and obtaining a divorce has become easier. In general, little social stigma is associated with divorce in industrialized societies (Quale, 1988). Divorce rates tend to be higher in industrial societies than in preindustrial societies. Among the many factors that contribute to high divorce rates in industrialized societies is the dissatisfaction that some people experience in their marital relationships. People who contract a marital bond primarily on the ideals and expectations of romantic love may experience a conflict between those ideals and the actualities of marital life. Women who are more financially independent in industrialized societies are much less likely to remain in a bad marriage. In preindustrial societies, in which marriages were actually alliances between corporate kin groups, individuals typically did not have the freedom to dissolve the marital bond. As individualistic decision making increased with the emergence of industrialization, however, partners in an unsatisfying relationship were more willing to consider divorce.

Divorce rates of most Western industrialized societies have ballooned during the last century. For example, the U.S. rate increased tenfold between 1890 and 1970 (Macionis, 2001). The same pattern is evident in Russia, where traditional taboos regarding divorce have been replaced by more tolerant attitudes (Kerblay, 1983).

In Japan, however, the divorce rate has decreased since industrialization (Befu, 1971). In contrast to most agricultural societies, prior to the Meiji period Japan had a fairly high divorce rate. This was not due to conflicts between husband and wife; instead, divorce resulted because elders in the husband's family rejected a young bride because she did not conform easily enough to family norms, did not bring enough of a dowry, or other reasons. The traditional postmarital rule of residence was patrilocal, with the wife moving in with the husband's father's household (Goode, 1982). With industrialization and the breakdown of these traditional patterns, the divorce rate began to fall. More recently, however, the divorce rate has begun to increase in Japan, as industrialization creates the tensions experienced in all industrial societies. Yet the divorce rate in Japan is still only one-fifth of that of the United States (Kerbo & McKinstry, 1998). To some extent, the traditional norms and expectations regarding the female gender role in Japanese society have undoubtedly had an influence on this lower divorce rate. Traditionally, Japanese women are not

supposed to threaten the primacy of the husband's role as head of the family. The Japanese woman is supposed to dedicate herself to the husband and children. Work outside of the home should only be undertaken to boost family income when it is necessary, and upon having children, the Japanese woman is expected to be a full-time homemaker (Kerbo & McKinstry, 1998). Consequently, many fewer Japanese women have the financial capability to sustain themselves outside of a marriage.

Gender

Industrialization has had a profound impact on gender relationships, particularly in England, Europe, and North America. The transition from an agricultural economy to an industrial wage economy drew many women from the domestic realm into the workplace. Women have thus become more economically self-sufficient and less dependent on men for support.

Gender and the Division of Labor   Although women in Western industrial societies have entered

Women are joining the work force in industrial societies in increasing numbers.

the work force in considerable numbers in the last several decades, most women work in a small number of occupations within the service economy, especially in underpaid clerical positions. In addition, women in industrial societies perform the majority of domestic tasks, such as household chores and child care, which are still considered by many the primary responsibility of women. Male occupations and the husband's income are usually considered the primary source of family income. Consequently, women in these societies have a dual burden of combining their domestic role with employment outside the home (Bernard, 1981).

Female Status in Industrial Societies   To some degree, industrialization undermined the traditional form of patriarchy. In most preindustrial societies, males held considerable authority and control over females. This authority diminished in industrial societies as women gained more independence, and gender relations became more egalitarian. As we have seen, however, women are still restricted in the workplace and have a dual burden of combining outside work and domestic chores. This indicates that the cultural legacy of patriarchy still persists in most industrial societies.

As their economic role has changed, women have attempted to gain equal economic and political rights. The call for gender equality began with women from upper- and middle-class families. Unlike working-class women, these early women's rights advocates were financially secure and had much leisure time to devote to political activism. They eventually secured the right to vote in the United States and in other industrialized nations. In addition, with increasing educational levels and economic opportunities, more women entered the work force. For example, by the middle of the twentieth century, nearly 40 percent of all adult females in the United States were in the work force; by 1990 that number was almost 60 percent, as illustrated in Figure 19.2.

Feminism   During the 1960s, a combination of economic and social forces fueled the feminist movement in many industrialized societies. **Feminism** is the belief that women are equal to men and should have equal rights and opportunities. The contemporary feminist movement has helped many women discover that they have been denied equal rights and dignity. This movement

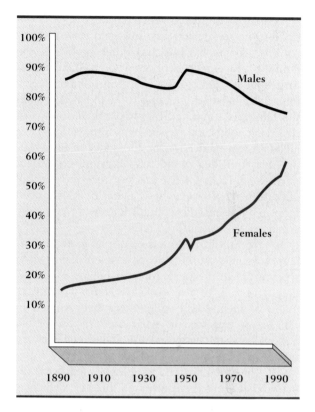

FIGURE 19.2   The labor force participation rates of women in the United States over the past century. What does this say about the effects of industrialization on traditional gender roles?

Source: Adapted from Francine D. Blau and Marianne A. Ferber, *The Economics of Women, Men, and Work* (Upper Saddle River, NJ: Prentice Hall, 1986), p. 70; and *Statistical Abstract of the United States, 1991* (Washington DC: Government Printing Office, 1991), Table 635.

has a much broader base of support than the early women's rights movement. Among its supporters are career women, high school and college students, homemakers, senior citizens, and even many men.

Feminists have secured some concrete gains and helped change certain attitudes in the United States. For example, in a landmark legal decision in 1972, the American Telephone and Telegraph Company (AT&T), the world's largest employer of women, was forced to pay $23 million in immediate pay increases and $15 million in back pay to employees who had suffered sex discrimination. In addition, women have been admitted to many formerly all-male institutions, such as the U.S. Military Academy at West Point.

Despite these gains, many female workers continue to be segregated into low-paid service occupations. To resolve this and other problems, the feminist movement supported the Equal Rights Amendment (ERA) to the U.S. Constitution to prohibit discrimination because of gender. Although the ERA was supported by almost three-fourths of American adults and passed by Congress in 1972, it failed to win ratification by the states in time. Apparently, the idea of full equality and equivalent pay for equivalent work has not received the full endorsement of U.S. society. Even in an advanced industrial society, the cultural legacy of patriarchy remains a persistent force.

In Japan the cultural legacy of patriarchy has retained its grip on the role of women. Even when women are in the work force in Japanese society, they tend to have a second-class status when compared to men. Many college-educated women in offices are expected to wear uniforms, serve tea and coffee to the men, and are treated as if they are office servants (Hendry, 1987; Kerbo & McKinstry, 1998). They are expected to defer to men in the office and present themselves as infantile, which is interpreted as cute and polite. Most men in Japan perform almost no domestic chores and expect to be waited on by their wives. Despite this tradition of patriarchy in Japan, the Japanese woman has a powerful position within the domestic household. She manages the household budget, takes charge of the children's education, and makes long-term financial investments for the family. Thus, the outside-of-the-home, and the inside-of-the-home roles for women in Japan are still strongly influenced by patriarchal traditions. There are some women active in a growing feminist movement in Japan that wants to transform gender roles, but traditional cultural expectations based on patriarchy are resistant to change.

Age

Another social consequence of industrialization is the loss experienced by the elderly of traditional status and authority. This trend reflects the changes in the family structure and the nature of knowledge in industrial societies. As the nuclear family replaced the extended family, older people no longer lived with their adult children. Pension plans and government support programs such as Social Security replaced the family as the source of economic support for the elderly. At the same time, exchanges of resources between elders and offspring became less important in industrial societies (Halperin, 1987). Thus, elderly family members lost a major source of economic power.

The traditional role of the elderly in retaining and disseminating useful knowledge has also diminished. Sociologist Donald O. Cowgill (1986) hypothesizes that as the rate of technological change accelerates in industrial societies, knowledge quickly becomes obsolete, which has an effect on the status of elderly people. Industrialization promotes expanding profits through new products and innovative services, all of which favor the young, who, through formal education and training, have greater access to technological knowledge. In addition, the amount of cultural and technical information has increased to the point where the elderly can no longer store all of it. Instead, libraries, databases, and formalized educational institutions have become the storehouses of cultural knowledge.

Although many elderly people in industrial societies have substantial economic resources, they no longer possess the political and social status they did in preindustrial societies.

The result of these changes, according to Cowgill, has been the rapid disengagement of the elderly from their roles in industrial societies. Although many elderly people remain active and productive, they no longer possess the economic, political, and social status they did in preindustrial societies. In some cases, the elderly are forced to retire from their jobs in industrial societies to make way for the younger generation. For example, in industrial Japan, the elderly are forced to retire at the age of 55 and often have difficulties adjusting to their senior years.

The status and roles of the elderly have changed much more dramatically in the West than in Japan and the former Soviet Union, where the elderly retain a great deal of authority and prestige in the family (Palmore, 1975; Kerblay, 1983). In Japanese society, the tradition of family obligations influenced by Confucian values and ethos serves to foster the veneration of the elderly. In addition, about three-fourths of the elderly reside with their children, which encourages a greater sense of responsibility on the part of children toward their parents.

Theorists such as Cowgill suggest that because Japan and the former Soviet Union industrialized much later than Western societies, there has been less time to transform family structures and the status of the elderly. This view is supported by a comparison between the most modern industrialized urban sectors of these societies and the rural regions. For example, in the more rural regions in Russia and Japan, the extended family is still the norm, and the elderly remain influential and esteemed. Thus, the high status of the aged in Japan and Russia may represent delayed responses to industrialization (Cowgill, 1986).

Social Stratification

In earlier chapters we discussed the type of social stratification that existed in preindustrial societies. Bands and tribes were largely egalitarian, whereas chiefdoms and agricultural states had increased social inequality based on ascribed statuses. Chiefdoms and agricultural states are classified as *closed societies* because they offer little, if any, opportunity for social mobility. In contrast, industrial states are classified as **open societies** in which social status can be achieved through individual efforts. The achieve-ment of social status is related to the complex division of labor, which is based on specialized occupational differences. Occupation becomes the most important determinant of status in industrial states. Societal rewards such as income, political power, and prestige all depend on a person's occupation.

This is not to say that industrial states are egalitarian. Rather, like some agricultural states, they have distinctive classes that consist of somewhat equivalent social statuses. The gaps among these classes in terms of wealth, power, and status are actually greater in industrial than in preindustrial societies. Thus, although people in industrial states have the opportunity to move into a different class from that into which they were born, the degree of stratification in these societies is much more extreme than it is in preindustrial societies. Let's examine the types of stratification systems found in some industrial states.

The British Class System

Some industrial states continue to reflect their agricultural past. Great Britain, for example, is made up of a class system that retains some of its feudal-like social patterns. It has a symbolic monarchy and nobility based on ascribed statuses passed down from generation to generation. The monarchy and nobility have titles such as "prince," "princess," "knight," "peer," and "earl." These individuals have to be addressed with the appropriate form: "sir," "lord," "lady." The British political system reflects its feudal past in the structure of the House of Lords, in which membership is traditionally inherited through family. This contrasts with the House of Commons, to which individuals are freely elected. Although the monarchy and the House of Lords have relatively little power today, they play an important symbolic role in British politics.

Class divisions in modern Britain are similar to those in many other European societies. They include a small upper class that maintains its position through inheritance laws and the education of children in elite private schools; a larger middle class that includes physicians, attorneys, businesspeople, and other occupations in the service sector; and a large working class employed in the primary and secondary sectors of the economy. Yet social mobility in Great Britain is open, and people can move from one class to another.

The degree of social mobility in Great Britain, as well as in other industrial states, is to some extent a result of recent changes in the industrial economy. With advanced industrialization, an increasing percentage of jobs are found in the tertiary (service) sector, whereas the primary and secondary sectors have declined. Therefore, the number of white-collar workers has grown, and the number of blue-collar workers has decreased. Consequently, many of the sons and daughters of blue-collar workers have a higher social status than that of their parents. For example, in Great Britain approximately 40 percent of the sons of manual workers have moved into the middle class since the 1950s (Robertson, 1990). Sociologists refer to this as *structural mobility,* a type of social mobility resulting from the restructuring of the economy, producing new occupational opportunities. Technological innovations, economic booms or busts, wars, and other events can affect this mobility.

Class in the United States

Most research demonstrates that the rate of social mobility in the United States is about the same as in other industrial states (Macionis, 2001). Although the United States differs from Great Britain in that it has never had an official class system with a titled aristocracy, it is not a classless society. The class structure of the United States consists of five basic categories based on equivalent social statuses, which are largely determined by occupation, income, and education (see Table 19.2).

One of the principal cultural ideals of the United States is that any person can move up the social ladder through effort and motivation. For this reason, upper-class and upper-middle-class Americans tend to believe that economic and social inequalities arise primarily from differences in individual abilities and work habits. They believe that equal opportunities are available to any individual. These cultural beliefs therefore help justify social inequity.

In fact, many factors besides individual efforts—such as family background and the state of the national and world economy—affect a person's location on the socioeconomic ladder. In addition, people's ethnic and racial backgrounds can inhibit or enhance their chances of social mobility. African Americans, Native Americans, and Hispanics have lower rates of mobility than do Asian Americans and white, middle-class Americans.

Class in Japan and the Former Soviet Union

Most research indicates that, despite the cultural emphasis on group harmony, class divisions and conflicts exist in Japan. Sociologist Rob Steven (1983) has identified five major classes in Japanese society: the bourgeoisie or capitalist class (the owners of the major industries), the petty bourgeoisie (small-business owners), the middle class (professional and other service workers), the peasantry (rural farmers), and the working class. The primary means of social mobility in Japanese society is the educational system, which is highly regimented and rigorous from the elementary years through high school. Higher education is limited to those students who excel on various achievement exams, a system that to some extent reflects class background. As in other industrial societies, middle- and upper-class students have better opportunities. The rate of social mobility in Japan is similar to that of other industrial states (Lipset & Bendix, 1967).

Ever since the Russian Revolution in 1917, the former Soviet Union claimed to be a classless society, because its system was not based on the private ownership of the means of production. In fact, however, it had a stratified class system based on occupation. Occupations were hierarchically ranked into four major status groups, based on income, power, and prestige. The highest-ranking statuses consisted of upper-level government officials—Politburo members who were recruited from the Communist Party. The second tier consisted of professional workers such as engineers, professors, physicians, and scientists, as well as lower-level government workers. The third tier was made up of the manual workers in the industrial economy, and the bottom rung was composed of the rural peasantry (Kerblay, 1983; Dunn & Dunn, 1988). Most sociologists agree that this hierarchy of statuses reflects a class-based society.

Ethnic and Racial Stratification

In addition to social stratification based on occupation, many industrial states have a system of stratification based on ethnic or racial descent. For example, in the United States, various ethnic and racial groups such as African Americans, Native Americans, and Hispanics have traditionally occupied a subordinate status and have experienced a

Table 19.2	The American Class System in the Twenty-First Century: A Composite Estimate					
Class and Percentage of Total Population	Income	Property	Occupation	Education	Personal and Family Life	Education of Children
Upper class (1–3%)	Very high income, most of it from wealth	Great wealth old wealth, control over investment	Managers, professionals, high civil and military officials	Liberal arts education at elite schools Graduate training	Stable family life Autonomous personality	College education by right for both sexes Educational
Upper-middle class (10–15%)	High income	Accumulation of property through savings	Lowest unemployment		Better physical and mental health and health care	system biased in their favor
Lower-middle class (30–35%)	Modest income	Few assets Some savings	Small-business people and farmers, lower professionals, semiprofessionals, sales and clerical workers	Some college High school or some high school	Longer life expectancy	Greater chance of college than working-class children
Working class (40–45%)	Low income	Few to no assets No savings No assets	Skilled labor Unskilled labor	Grade school	Unstable family life One-parent homes Conformist personality	Educational system biased against them Tendency toward vocational programs
Lower class (20–25%)	Poverty income	No savings	Highest unemployment Surplus labor	Illiteracy, especially functional illiteracy	Poorer physical and mental health Lower life expectancy	Little interest in education, high dropout rates

Source: Daniel W. Rossides, *Social Stratification: The Interplay of Class, Race, and Gender,* 2nd ed. © 1997. Adapted by permission of Pearson Education, Inc., Upper Saddle River, NJ.

more restricted type of social mobility. In contrast, most Western European countries traditionally have been culturally homogeneous, without many minority ethnic groups.

Recently, however, this situation has begun to change, as many formerly colonized peoples, such as Indians, Pakistanis, and Africans, have moved to Great Britain, and other non-Western peoples have migrated to other European nations. This has led to patterns of ethnic and racial stratification and discrimination in these countries.

In the former Soviet Union, many ethnic minorities resided in Estonia, Lithuania, the Ukraine, and Turko-Mongol areas such as Azerbaijan and Uzbekistan. These ethnic minorities lived outside the central Soviet territory, the heartland of the dominant Russian majority. Historically, the Soviet state had attempted to assimilate these national minorities by making the Russian language a compulsory subject in the educational system (Eickelman, 1993; Maybury-Lewis, 1997; Scupin, 2003). Although the Soviet state prided itself on its principles of equality and autonomy applied to its national minorities, the outbreak of ethnic unrest and rebellion in these non-Russian territories in the mid-1990s demonstrated that these populations viewed themselves as victimized by the dominant ethnic Russian populace. Thus, ethnic stratification has been a component of industrial Soviet society.

Japan is one of the most homogeneous societies in the world; however, cultural anthropologists have noted some patterns of ethnic stratification. For example, a small minority of Japanese of Korean ancestry have experienced widespread discrimination, even though they have adopted Japanese language, norms, and values. In addition, a native-born Japanese population known as the *eta* or *burakumin,* consisting of about 3 million people, also occupies a lower status. Despite the fact that the *burakumin* are physically indistinguishable from most other Japanese, they reside in separated ghetto areas in Japan. They are descendants of peoples who worked in the leather-tanning industries, traditionally considered low-status professions. Most of the *burakumin* still work primarily in the shoe shops and other leather-related industries. Marriages between *burakumin* and other Japanese are still restricted, and other patterns of ethnic discrimination against this group continue (Befu, 1971; Hendry, 1987; Ohnuki-Tierney, 1998; Scupin, 2003). This ethnic discrimination has resulted in poverty, lower education attainment, delinquency, and other social problems for the *burakumin,* just as it has for some ethnic minorities in the United States. As indicated in Chapter 6 in our discussion of IQ and race, the *burakumin* also score lower on IQ tests in Japan. As was emphasized in that discussion, since these people are not biologically or racially different from other Japanese people, this fact indicates that ethnic discrimination, poverty, and related environmental conditions are more responsible for differences in intelligence than any purported biological differences.

Political Organization

As European and American societies began to industrialize, the nature of their political organization was transformed. Members of the middle class grew economically powerful and were drawn to idea of *popular sovereignty*—that is, that the people, rather than the rulers, were the ultimate source of political authority. In addition, because the middle classes (particularly the upper-middle class) were the primary beneficiaries of industrial capitalism, they favored a type of government that would allow them economic freedom to pursue profits without state interference. The feudal aristocratic patterns were thus eventually replaced with representative, constitutional governments. The overriding ideal in these democratic states is freedom or personal liberty, which includes freedom of expression, the right to vote, and the right to be represented in the government. Representation is based on the election of political leaders selected from various political parties that engage in competition for offices.

Though representative governments emerged in earlier centuries, their political ideals were not immediately realized. For example, in the United States, political rights, including the right to vote, were not extended to women and other minorities until the twentieth century.

Another aspect of political change was the growth of **nationalism,** a strong sense of loyalty to the nation-state based on shared language, values, and culture. Before the development of nationalism, the primary focus of loyalty was to the local community, religion, and the family (Anderson, 1983; Scupin, 2003). For example, in agricultural states, peasants rarely identified with the interests of the ruling elites. In industrial states, however, with the increase in literacy and the development of a print technology, nationalism became a unifying force. Print technology was used to create what political scientist Benedict Anderson (1983) refers to as "imagined communities," an allegiance to a nation-state that is often far removed from everyday family or local concerns. As a literate populace began to read about their history and culture in their own language, they embarked on a new self-identification, and eventually people began to express pride and loyalty to these newly defined countries.

Anderson, though, is not suggesting that nationalism is just "invented," but holds that people who begin to define themselves as members of a nation will never know most of their fellow members, meet them, or even hear of them (1983). He notes that the fact that people are willing to give up their lives for their nation or country means that nationalism has a powerful influence on people's

This Nazi rally demonstrates an extreme form of nationalism in German society in the 1940s.

emotions and sentiments. This loyalty to a nation is a byproduct of literacy and the proliferation of the media in promoting specific ideas regarding one's nation.

Michael Herzfeld, an anthropologist who has written extensively about nationalism, notes that nationalism parallels religious cosmologies in that it creates distinctive differences between the believers and nonbelievers, insiders and outsiders, and it reaffirms that the world is meaningful and sacred to people (1992). Herzfeld did ethnographic research in Greece, and in his book *Ours Once More: Folklore, Ideology, and the Making of Modern Greece* (1986) he focused on how Greek nationalism was created and managed by state authorities. One of the themes in his book is how nineteenth- and twentieth-century Greek intellectuals drew on folklore from rural areas to present an image of modern Greece as a continuation of their classical past. The Greek state has drawn on a classical past that has been imagined as the root of all Western civilization to produce a contemporary source of nationalism for its citizens. The bureaucrats and intellectuals selected certain images and neglected other aspects of the past to develop this sense of nationalism for Greek citizens. For example, they selectively underplayed the role of the Ottoman empire and the Turkish influence on Greek society

for centuries. The Turks were considered outsiders, and not an integral part of Greek national culture. The manufacture of nationalism by state authorities and intellectuals who romanticized the classical past and rural villages produced a culture of loyalty and sacredness for Greek national culture. Many other industrialized societies, such as England, Japan, or Russia, could be used to illustrate this same pattern and the production of nationalism, a contemporary trait of modern nation-states.

Political Organization in Socialist States

The former Soviet Union was the first nation to declare that it had a socialist government that would be dominated by the working class—the proletariat—rather than the upper or middle classes. According to Marxist theory, this socialist government was to be only a transitional stage of state development, to be followed by a true form of communism in which the state would wither away. In Marx's view, in the communist stage there would be no need for the state, or government, because everyone's needs would be completely taken care of through people who would be free to produce and create for the community.

In the ensuing years, the ideals of the socialist state ruled by the proletariat and the movement

ANTHROPOLOGISTS AT WORK

THE JAPANESE CORPORATION: AN ANTHROPOLOGICAL CONTRIBUTION FROM HARUMI BEFU

During the past several decades, Japan became one of the world's major economic powers. Many social scientists have investigated the organization and management techniques of Japanese corporations to determine how the Japanese economy has grown so rapidly.

One of the major conclusions of most of these studies is that Japanese corporations are run much differently from corporations in Western capitalist countries. According to these studies, Japanese corporations emphasize traditional values such as group harmony, or *wa*, and collective rather than individual performance (Ouichi, 1981; Lincoln & McBride, 1987). For example, rather than hiring managers based on their individual performance as indicated by grades in college, Japanese corporations recruit managers as groups from different universities. Japanese firms are more interested in how groups and teams of managers work together than they are in each person's individual effort or performance. Managers are hired, trained, and promoted as groups by the corporation, based on their ability to cooperate in teams. In contrast to Western countries, which emphasize individualism and independence, the Japanese stress mutual dependence and teamwork.

To ensure this collective performance, large Japanese corporations offer lifetime employment and a concern for their employees' general welfare. Employees are rarely fired or laid off. Corporations provide recreational facilities, parties, child care and other family-related services, and other benefits to enhance corporate loyalty. Corporate decision making is also based on collective principles. Typically, several younger managers are responsible for talking to sixty or seventy people who will be affected by a decision. Proposals for a new plan or policy are discussed and then redrafted until a consensus is achieved. A decision requiring one or two phone calls to a division manager in a U.S. company

Harumi Befu

may take two or three weeks in a Japanese corporation. Once a decision is reached, however, everyone involved becomes committed to the plan.

Japanese anthropologist Chia Nakane (1970) believed that this collective orientation results from the hierarchical nature of Japanese social organization. Nakane viewed Japanese society as consisting of hierarchically organized groups with paternalistic leaders at the top who serve group needs. She believed that the psychological process supporting this group

---

toward an egalitarian communism were not realized in the Soviet Union. Instead, the Communist Party of the Soviet Union, with about 18 million members out of a total population of about 300 million, dominated the government, selecting the bureaucratic elite (the *apparatchiki*) of about 1 million to rule over the society. The former Soviet Union became a totalitarian state that controlled the economy, the political process, the media, the educational system, and other social institutions. During certain periods of extreme repression, as under Joseph Stalin in the 1930s, millions of people were killed or exiled to forced labor camps. Citizens were prohibited from organizing politically, and official opposition to state policies was not tolerated. This form of totalitarian government also existed in

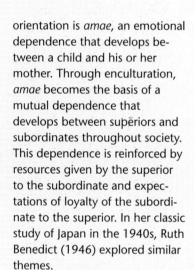

orientation is *amae*, an emotional dependence that develops between a child and his or her mother. Through enculturation, *amae* becomes the basis of a mutual dependence that develops between superiors and subordinates throughout society. This dependence is reinforced by resources given by the superior to the subordinate and expectations of loyalty of the subordinate to the superior. In her classic study of Japan in the 1940s, Ruth Benedict (1946) explored similar themes.

Stanford anthropologist Harumi Befu (1980) has questioned this group model of Japanese society. Befu has a unique background and perspective from which to view this issue. He was born in the United States in 1930 but moved to Japan when he was six years old to receive his primary and secondary education. He returned to the United States in 1947 to carry out his undergraduate and graduate studies in anthropology. He subsequently remained in the United States and specialized in

the ethnological study of Japanese society.

Befu criticized the group model of Japanese society for its tendency to overlook social conflict, individual competition, self-interest, and exploitation. Regarding the purported internal harmony of Japanese groups and society, Befu believed that many proponents of the group model have lost sight of various aspects of Japanese society. Befu believed that many of these theorists failed to distinguish between the real and ideal norms of Japanese society. Although a president of a corporation may refer to his or her company as a harmonious, happy family at an induction ceremony for new recruits, he or she acts differently at a collective bargaining session in dealing with union demands.

Befu averred that not only Western scholars but the Japanese themselves have accepted this group-model concept as an integral aspect of their cultural identity. He argued that the group model is not really a social model for Japanese society as much as

a cultural model or belief system. He suggested that the group model as a social model is too simplistic to explain comprehensively a complex, postindustrial society such as Japan. Befu did not reject the group model entirely, however. Rather, he contended that the group model as well as a model based on individualism could be applied to both Japanese and Western institutions and bureaucracies. For example, at various times in both Japanese and Western corporations, individuals are in competition and conflict with one another over wealth, power, and status, while simultaneously working on group projects that will benefit the corporation as a whole. Individual competition and conflict may take a different form in Japan than it does in Western countries; nevertheless, Befu emphasized that it does exist in both regions. To that extent, Befu suggested that Japanese corporations and social life may not be as unique as either the Japanese or Westerners think they are.

the socialist countries of Eastern Europe that were dominated by the Soviet Union.

Industrialism and State Bureaucracy

One similarity among the governments of the West, Japan, and the Soviet Union is the degree to which the state has become a highly developed

bureaucracy. It appears that when an industrial economy becomes highly specialized and complex, a strong, centralized government develops to help coordinate and integrate the society's complicated political and economic affairs. Of course, as previously discussed, in socialist societies such as the Soviet Union, this growth and centralization of the state is more extreme.

Law

Legal institutions are more formalized in industrial states. In general, the more complex the society, the more specialized the legal system (Schwartz & Miller, 1975). As discussed in Chapter 18, legal institutions became formalized in some of the intensive agricultural states with the emergence of codified written law, records of cases and precedents, courts and government officials such as judges, procedures for deciding cases, and a police force to enforce legal decisions. These innovations in legal systems have been expanded in modern industrial societies.

In industrial states, laws become more complex and bureaucratically formalized with the development of national and local statutes, private and public codes, the differentiation between criminal and civil laws, and more specialized law enforcement agencies. With the development of centralized national governments, a hierarchy of legal codes was formulated that ranged from national constitutions to regional and local codes. One of the most distinctive features of law in industrial societies is the proliferation of public and procedural law, referred to as administrative law (Vago, 1995).

Administrative law reflects the emerging bureaucratic rules and technical requirements in the various legal institutions and agencies in industrial states. Courts in modern industrial states play an important role not only in adjudication but also in mediation and other methods of conflict resolution. In addition, the legal system is the most important means of inducing social change in complex industrial societies. For example, legislation was used to gain civil rights for ethnic minorities such as African Americans in the United States.

Japanese Law

The unique configuration of Japanese values and norms, in comparison with Western or Soviet society, has produced a different form of legal system in Japan. The Confucian ethos and traditional Japanese norms emphasizing group harmony have deeply influenced legal processes and institutions. The Japanese generally adopt extra-judicial, informal means of resolving disputes and prefer legal compromises as opposed to assigning moral blame or deciding on the rightness or wrongness of an action. When a dispute arises, a mediator is usually employed to bring about a reconciliation. The Japanese prefer the mediator to a lawyer, who is less likely to know the parties or to have a personal relationship with them. In this sense, the Japanese mediation system resembles those of small-scale tribal societies (Hendry, 1987).

In Japanese society, there tends to be no legal or societal pressure for absolute justice. The proper, moral action is to accept blame for a wrongdoing and resign oneself to the consequences. Conflict resolution outside the court system and codified law tends to be the rule with respect to civil law. Obviously, one of the differences between Japan and the United States is the overwhelming cultural homogeneity of Japan. In contrast, the United States is a highly heterogeneous society with many different ethnic groups and cultural backgrounds. The relative homogeneity of Japanese society facilitates resolving conflicts through informal means rather than through the legal system, as in the United States. However, a recent study indicates that Japan's rate of litigation is beginning to increase (Vago, 1995).

Warfare and Industrial Technology

We noted in Chapter 18 that warfare increased with the territorial expansion of agricultural empires such as China, Rome, the Aztec, and India. To some extent, this increase in warfare was linked to technological developments such as the invention of iron weapons. In addition, the nature of warfare began to change with the development of centralized state systems that competed with rival territories. These general tendencies were accelerated with the evolution of industrial states.

Industrial states began to develop military technologies that enabled them to carry on fierce nationalistic wars in distant regions. One of the prime motivations for these wars was to establish economic and political hegemony over foreign peoples. The industrial nation-states became much more involved in economic rivalry over profits, markets, and natural resources in other territories. Most historians conclude that these imperialist rivalries were the principal reasons for World War I.

World War I marked a watershed in the evolution of military warfare. It was a global war in

Pablo Picasso, Guernica, *1937, oil on canvas. 11'5½ × 25'5¾. Museo Nacional Centro de Arte Reina Sofia/©1998 Estate of Pablo Picasso/Artists Rights Society (ARS), New York. This painting by Picasso symbolizes the destructiveness of industrial warfare.*

which nation-states mobilized a high proportion of their male populations and reoriented their economic systems toward military production and support. The numbers of combatants and noncombatants killed far outnumbered those of any previous war in any type of society.

The combination of technological advances and centralized military organizations dramatically changed the nature of warfare. Tanks, airplanes, and other modern weapons enabled industrial states to wage tremendously destructive global warfare, as witnessed by World War II. This expanding military technology was inextricably linked to industrial technology. The rise of industries such as airlines, automobiles, petroleum and plastics, and electronics and computers were all related to the development of war technology. And, of course, the atomic era began in 1945, when the United States dropped atomic bombs on Hiroshima and Nagasaki.

Religion

Ever since the Enlightenment, Western industrial states have experienced extensive **secularization,** the historical decline in the influence of religion in society. Scientists such as Galileo and Charles Darwin developed ideas that challenged theological doctrines. Secular philosophies increasingly proposed naturalistic (nonsupernatural), scientific explanations of both the natural and social worlds. Secularization has influenced all industrialized states. For example, most people in these societies do not perceive illness as the result of supernatural forces; rather, they rely on physicians trained in scientific medical practices to diagnose and cure diseases.

Despite the increase of secularization, however, religion has not disappeared from industrial states. For example, the United States has experienced a great deal of secularization, and yet it remains one of the most religious societies in the world. Polls indicate that almost 88 percent of all Americans profess a belief in some sort of divine power. Nearly two-thirds of Americans are affiliated with a religious organization, and many of them identify with a particular religion (National Opinion Research Center, 1999). Most sociologists who have studied the question of how religious Americans are have concluded that this question is extremely complex because it relates to ethnic, political, and social-class issues. Many Americans claim religious affiliation in relationship to their communal or ethnic identity; others may belong to religious organizations to gain a sense of identity and belonging or as

CRITICAL PERSPECTIVES

GRADUATION: A RITE OF PASSAGE IN U.S. SOCIETY

As the United States continues to change from an industrial to a postindustrial society, more people are attending college to gain the skills and knowledge necessary to prepare them for careers. Consequently, one rite of passage that people increasingly look forward to is graduation from college. This rite of passage is similar to those in many other societies. Following an intensive four or five years of study, examinations, and research papers, students face the climactic rite of passage known as the commencement ceremony.

The commencement ceremony dates back to the twelfth century at the University of Bologna in what is now Italy. Shortly thereafter, it spread to other European universities. The first U.S. graduates went through their commencement in 1642 at Harvard University. These first commencement ceremonies lasted several days and were accompanied by entertainment, wrestling matches, banquets, and dances.

The academic costumes worn by graduates come directly from the late Middle Ages and the Renaissance. The black gowns and square caps, called "mortarboards," were donned to celebrate the change in status. A precise ritual dictates that the tassel that hangs off the cap should be moved from the right side to the left side when the degree is conferred.

Like rituals of passage in other societies, graduation from college represents a transition in status. In Latin, *gradus* means a step, and *degradus* means a rung on a ladder. From the first we get the word *graduation*; from the second, *degree*. Both words are connected to a stage in life—the end of one period of life and the beginning of another. To graduate means to change by degrees.

Typically, the college graduate moves from the status of a receiver to that of a giver. Up to the point of graduation, many students are subsidized and nurtured by society and especially by parents. After graduation, a person becomes a giver in all sorts of ways. A degree qualifies graduates to get jobs and to contribute to the workplace. In addition, degree holders will begin to subsidize others through taxes. Many will marry and accept such responsibilities as raising children and paying mortgages. This movement from receiver to giver represents a fundamental life-cycle transition for many U.S. students.

POINTS TO PONDER

1. As you move toward your degree in college, do you believe that what you are learning has any relationship to what you will need after your change in status?

2. In what ways would you change the educational process so that it would help you to develop your potential?

3. Do you think the grading system used by most colleges and universities is a fair means of assessing your acquisition of knowledge and skills?

4. What would you suggest as a better means of evaluating students?

5. What kinds of expectations do you have about your change in status after you receive your degree?

a source of social prestige. Whatever the reasons, secularization has not substantially eroded religious beliefs and institutions in the United States.

Religion in Socialist States

In the former Soviet Union, secularization had been an aspect of the ideological apparatus of the state. According to Marxist views, religion is a set of beliefs and institutions used by the upper classes to control and regulate the lower classes. The ultimate aim of socialist societies is to eradicate religion, thereby removing a major obstacle to equality. For this reason, the former Soviet Union and socialist Eastern European nations repressed religious organizations and officially endorsed atheism.

Despite these policies, however, in the former Soviet Union 15 percent of the urban population and 30 percent of the rural population practiced religion. There are about 40 million Russian Orthodox Catholics, 600,000 Protestants, and up to 45 million Muslims in a country that has proclaimed itself as atheistic for five decades (Kerblay, 1983; Eickelman, 1993). Thus, religious beliefs appear to have been a continuing source of inspiration and spiritual comfort for many citizens of the former Soviet state.

Religion in Japan

Japan has also experienced a great deal of secularization as it has industrialized. Traditional Japanese religion was an amalgamation of beliefs based on an indigenous animistic form of worship referred to as Shintoism, combined with Confucianism, Taoism, and Buddhism, which spread from China. Most Japanese and Western observers agree that secularization has diminished the influence of these traditional faiths. Although the majority of Japanese still turn to Shinto shrines and Buddhist ceremonies for life-cycle rituals or personal crises, most modern Japanese confess that they are not deeply religious (Befu, 1971; Hendry, 1987).

Most anthropologists concur, however, that religious beliefs and practices are so thoroughly embedded in Japanese culture that religion cannot easily be separated from the national identity and way of life. For example, many Japanese refer to *nihondo* (the Japanese way) as the basis of their national, ethnic, and cultural identity. *Nihondo* refers to Japanese cultural beliefs and practices, including traditional religious concepts. Thus, it appears that religion is intimately bound up with Japanese identity.

SUMMARY

The changes associated with the Industrial Revolution dramatically transformed the technologies, economies, social structures, political systems, and religions of various nations. The center of the first Industrial Revolution was in Europe. However, when taking a global perspective, anthropologists agree that this Industrial Revolution could not have occurred without the substantial influence of many other non-Western regions of the world.

These changes brought about by the Industrial Revolution are referred to collectively as modernization. The use of industrial technology required increasing amounts of fossil fuels and other non-renewable energy sources. In contrast to preindustrial societies, industrial societies are high-energy consumers. These societies also experienced decreasing fertility and mortality rates. This pattern is known as demographic transition. With the expansion of the factory system, people increasingly came to reside in dense urban areas.

The technological and economic changes of industrial societies led to a new, complex division of labor. Industrial economies consist of the primary, secondary, and tertiary sectors, with jobs increasingly located in the tertiary sector, consisting of white-collar, service industries. Industrialization also stimulated new exchange patterns, resulting in the development of the market economy. Both capitalist and socialist systems developed in industrial societies.

Industrial expansion transformed the social structure. Occupation replaced kinship as the most important determiner of status, and the nuclear family largely replaced the extended family. Marriage and divorce increasingly reflected personal choice rather than family arrangements. Gender relationships became more egalitarian, and a majority of women entered the work force. Still, the legacy of patriarchy and male domination continued to influence female status and the division of labor.

The status of the elderly declined in most industrial societies as a result of rapid technological change and new methods of acquiring and storing knowledge. Social stratification increased as class systems based on wealth and occupation emerged. Class systems developed in both capitalist and socialist societies. In addition, ethnicity and race influenced the patterns of stratification.

New forms of political systems, including democratic and totalitarian governments, took root in industrial societies. In both democratic-capitalist and totalitarian-socialist societies, state bureaucracies grew in size and complexity. New, complex forms of legal processes and court systems emerged.

Finally, scientific and educational developments influenced religious traditions in industrial states. Secularization has affected all of these societies, yet religion has not disappeared, and it remains an important component of all industrial societies.

QUESTIONS TO THINK ABOUT

1. Characterize the types of changes that led to the Industrial Revolution.
2. Compare high and low energy-using technologies.
3. What form does the division of labor take in industrial states? Where do you think the United States falls in this scheme?
4. Compare the principal tenets of capitalism and socialism. Would it be possible to create a functional economy that combined these two systems?
5. What is meant by the terms *market economy* and *capitalism*? What are the principal advantages and disadvantages of these systems for individual participants?
6. Using a specific example, describe what is meant by a multinational corporation. What are the processes by which this multinational corporation can affect the processes of both individual countries and the global economy?
7. How has industrialization affected the family, kinship, marriage, and divorce?
8. What is the difference between a closed society and an open society? Is the United States a closed or open society? What about Japan, the former Soviet Union, and Great Britain?
9. What are some of the characteristics of Japanese industrial corporations?
10. Define the term *feminism*. What are the goals of feminists in industrialized states? Do you agree with these goals? Why or why not?
11. What are the processes whereby industrialization affects the status of elderly individuals? How can we explain the higher status of the aged in societies like Japan and Russia?
12. How do political systems differ in industrial societies compared to preindustrial societies?
13. In your experience, has secularization had an impact on your religious beliefs and practices?

KEY TERMS

capitalism
demographic transition
feminism
industrialization
industrial society
market economy
mercantilism

modernization
monopoly capitalism
multinational corporations
nationalism
nation-states
oligopoly
open societies

primary sector
secondary sector
secularization
socialism
tertiary sector

INTERNET EXERCISES _____

1. Visit the website **http://www.fatbadgers.co.uk/Britain/revolution.htm** and note the changes to British economics and social life brought about by the Industrial Revolution. List and describe several of each. What invention did James Watt improve and what did it do for British industrialism? Can one invention really make a difference to an economy? Explain your answer.

2. After reading the section of this chapter subtitled "Religion in Japan," go to **http://www.askasia.org/frclasrm/readings/r000009.htm**. What is Shintoism? What is the Shinto worldview? How does Shintoism integrate into Buddhism? Are the Japanese really as irreligious as this subsection of the chapter implies? Why or why not?

SUGGESTED READINGS _____

BERNARD, JESSIE. 1981. *The Female World*. New York: Free Press. A comprehensive account of the changes in gender patterns and female status that have occurred in the industrial world.

CHIROT, DANIEL. 1986. *Social Change in the Modern Age*. San Diego, CA: Harcourt Brace Jovanovich. A global perspective on industrial change and its consequences for economic, social, and political development.

GOODE, WILLIAM J. 1982. *The Family*, 2d ed. Englewood Cliffs, NJ: Prentice Hall. A broad-based classic sociological analysis of the changes in family, marriage, and divorce that accompanied modernization.

GOODY, JACK. 1996. *The East in the West*. Cambridge: Cambridge University Press. A global analysis of how much influence non-Western societies, especially China and the Islamic world, had on the development of the Industrial Revolution in Europe. Goody critically examines the Eurocentric notions of how Europe was the first to develop science, industry, and other institutions that led to the Industrial Revolution.

HARRIS, MARVIN. 1987. *Why Nothing Works: The Anthropology of Daily Life*. New York: Simon & Schuster. A fascinating account by a prominent anthropologist of the transformations accompanying modern industrial change in contemporary U.S. society.

MUMFORD, LEWIS. 1961. *The City in History*. San Diego, CA: Harcourt Brace and World. A classic account of urbanization and its consequences for modern humans.

CHAPTER

20

Globalization and Aboriginal Peoples

CHAPTER OUTLINE

CHAPTER QUESTIONS

- How are modernization and globalization interconnected?

- What are the differences between modernization and dependency theory?

- What are the advantages and disadvantages of using world-systems theory to understand globalization?

- How has globalization affected foragers, tribes, and chiefdom societies?

- In what ways have native societies tried to resist globalization?

- Why should we care about the plight of indigenous societies?

In Chapter 19 we discussed the emergence of industrial states. The rise of industrial states has led to what is referred to as *global industrialism,* or **globalization,** the impact of industrialization and its socioeconomic, political, and cultural consequences on the nonindustrialized societies of the world. Globalization has created substantial economic and political interconnections between the Western and non-Western worlds. The globalization process began with the expansion of Western industrial societies into the non-Western world through colonialism. Through this process, an interconnected global economy emerged with the spread of capital, labor, technology, and culture across national borders. Globalization continues to occur today through the increasing spread of industrial technology, including electronic communications, television, the Internet, and the expansion of multinational corporations into the non-Western world.

The next three chapters focus on these interconnections. This chapter introduces some of the theoretical perspectives used to understand globalization. It also explores the influence of global-industrial expansion on small-scale aboriginal societies.

Globalization: Theoretical Approaches

Three major theoretical approaches have been used to examine globalization: modernization theory, dependency theory, and world-systems theory. Each provides a model for analyzing the impact of globalization on industrial and nonindustrial societies.

Modernization Theory

Modernization theory, which was developed in the United States during the 1950s, is concerned with the process of economic, social, political, and cultural change that accompanies industrial-technological change. Although modernization theory had its roots in Enlightenment ideas as espoused by anthropologists such as E. B. Tylor and later theorists such as Max Weber, it became the leading model of societal evolution in the 1950s in the context of the Cold War between the United States and the former Soviet Union. During that period, the two superpowers were competing for economic resources and the political allegiance of different nations. Modernization theory provided a model to explain how social and cultural change could take place in all societies through industrial capitalism.

One of the most influential proponents of modernization is the American economist W. W. Rostow. Rostow argued that although modernization occurred first in the West, it can occur in all societies, provided those societies meet certain preconditions. According to Rostow (1978), evolution from traditional preindustrial societies to modern industrial societies takes place through five general stages:

1. *Traditional stage.* Premodern societies are unlikely to become modernized because of *traditionalism*—persisting values and attitudes that represent obstacles to economic and political development. According to modernization theorists, traditionalism creates a form of "cultural inertia" that keeps premodern societies backward and underdeveloped. Traditionalism places great significance on maintaining family and community relationships, which inhibit individual freedom and initiative.

2. *Culture-change stage.* One of the preconditions for modernization involves cultural and value changes. People must accept the belief that progress is both necessary and beneficial to society and the individual. This belief in progress is linked to an emphasis on individual achievement, which leads to the emergence of individual entrepreneurs who will take the necessary risks for economic progress. Modernization theorists insist that these changes in values can be brought about through education and will result in the erosion of traditionalism.

3. *Takeoff stage.* As traditionalism begins to weaken, rates of investment and savings begin to rise. These economic changes provide the context for the development of industrial-capitalist society. England reached this stage by about 1783, and the United States by about 1840. Modernization theorists believe that this stage can be reached only through foreign aid to support the diffusion of education and technology from industrial-capitalist societies into premodern societies. Many premodern societies have not yet achieved this stage of development.

4. *Self-sustained growth.* At this stage, the members of the society intensify economic progress through the implementation of industrial technology. This process involves a consistent reinvestment of savings and capital in modern technology. It also includes a commitment to mass education to promote advanced skills and modern attitudes. As the population becomes more educated, traditionalism will continue to erode.

5. *High economic growth.* This last stage involves the achievement of a high standard of living, characterized by mass production and consumption of material goods and services. Western Europe and the United States achieved this stage in the 1920s, and Japan reached it in the 1950s.

This model includes both economic and noneconomic factors such as cultural values as preconditions for modernization. In fact, as seen in Stage 2, the changes in attitudes and cultural values are the most important prerequisites for eliminating traditionalism and generating patterns of achievement. Thus, modernization theorists view cultural values and traditionalism as the primary reasons for the lack of economic development. The practical implication that derives from this model is that before a country should receive foreign aid, traditionalism and the values that support it must be transformed.

Like Rostow, theorist David McClelland (1973) maintained that a need for achievement represents the most important variable in producing the process of modernization. McClelland argued that this need for achievement is not just a desire for more material goods, but rather an intrinsic need for satisfaction in achieving success. He believed that this desire for achievement leads to increased savings and accumulation of capital. McClelland claimed to have found evidence for this need in some non-Protestant countries such as Japan, Taiwan, and Korea, as well as in Western countries.

First, Second, and Third Worlds

The modernization model led to the categorization of societies into three "worlds": the First, Second, and Third Worlds. According to the modernization theorists, the **First World** is composed of modern industrial states with predominantly capitalist or hybrid economic systems. These societies became industrialized "first." Included in this group are Great Britain, Western Europe, Australia, Canada, New Zealand, Japan, and the United States. The **Second World** consists of industrial states that have predominantly socialist economies. It includes the former Soviet Union and many of the former socialist countries of Eastern Europe—for example, Poland and Hungary. The **Third World** refers to premodern agricultural states that maintain traditionalism. The Third World encompasses the vast majority of the people in the world, including most of Latin America, Africa, the Middle East, and Asia.

Criticisms of Modernization Theory Modernization theory enabled anthropologists and other social scientists to identify various aspects of social and cultural change that accompany globalization. By the 1960s, however, modernization theory had come under attack by a number of critics. One of the major criticisms is that the applied model of modernization has failed to produce technological and economic development in Third World countries. Despite massive injections of foreign aid and education projects sponsored by First World countries, most Third World countries remain underdeveloped. An **underdeveloped society** has a low

gross national product (GNP), the total value of goods and services produced by a country.

Some critics view modernization theory as ethnocentric or "Westerncentric." They believe that this theory promotes Western industrial-capitalist society as an ideal that ought to be encouraged universally. These critics argue that Western capitalist societies have many problems, such as extreme economic inequality and the dislocation of community and family ties, and they question whether a Western model of modernization is suitable or beneficial for all societies. They do not agree that all societies must emulate the West to progress economically.

Modernization theorists have also been criticized for citing traditional values as obstacles to technological and economic development in the Third World. Critics consider this an example of blaming the victim. They charge that this argument oversimplifies both the conditions in Third World countries and the process of industrialization as it occurred in the West. For example, recall from Chapter 19 that

Many people in underdeveloped countries such as Peru have the same need to achieve as other people in the West, but they lack basic economic opportunities.

individual entrepreneurs in the West and in Japan had a great deal of economic freedom, which encouraged independent initiative. Under feudalism, governments did not have systematic control over independent economic activities in local regions. Consequently, entrepreneurs had freedom to develop their technologies and trading opportunities. In contrast, many Third World people have a so-called "need to achieve" but lack the necessary economic and political institutions and opportunities for achievement.

Another criticism of modernization theory is that it neglects the factors of global economic and political power, conflict, and competition within and among societies. For example, the wealthier classes in Third World countries that have benefited from the new technology and other assets from the First World often exploit the labor of the lower classes. This conflict and division between classes may inhibit economic development. Modernization theorists also tend to view First, Second, and Third World countries as existing in isolation from one another.

One other major problem with the modernization theorists is that the terminology First, Second, and Third World countries is too simplistic today to account for the great diversity that anthropologists actually discover in these societies. Modernization theory was a product of Cold War politics, in which the capitalist West (the First World) was in global competition with the socialist East (the Second World); and the rest of the world (the Third World) was influenced by Cold War politics. However, as we shall see in Chapter 24, sweeping changes have been transforming the Eastern bloc countries, including those of the former Soviet Union, resulting in the dissipation of most Second World socialist societies. In addition, the phrase "Third World societies" tends to lump together many societies that are at different levels of socioeconomic development. For example, Saudi Arabia, rich in oil resources, cannot be compared with Bangladesh, which has very little natural resource wealth on which to draw. Some countries in the so-called Third World are much better off economically, with ten to twenty times the national wealth of other countries. Although the terms First, Second, and Third Worlds are still used in the media and elsewhere, we should be aware that this terminology is a legacy of the Cold War and is no longer relevant to an understanding of present-day societies.

Dependency Theory

Criticism of modernization theory led to a new approach that emerged primarily from the underdeveloped world. Known as **dependency theory**, this approach is a model of socioeconomic development that explains global inequality as resulting from the historical exploitation of poor, underdeveloped societies by rich, developed societies. Dependency theory was influenced by Marxism and is associated with theorists such as Andre Gunder Frank, who denied that underdevelopment is the product of the persistence of traditionalism in preindustrial societies. These theorists instead contend that wealthy industrialized capitalist countries exploit underdeveloped precapitalist societies for the cheap labor and raw materials needed to maintain their own industrial technologies. Through this process, impoverished underdeveloped countries became economic and political dependencies of wealthy industrialized capitalist countries.

Dependency theorists suggest that mercantilism increased the prosperity and economic and political power of Western nations at the expense of poor nations. Especially after 1870, following the early phases of industrialism, a new type of relationship developed between industrialized and nonindustrialized societies. As manufacturing expanded, the industrial nations' needs for raw materials increased. Also, changing patterns of consumption created more demands for new foodstuffs and goods such as tea, coffee, sugar, and tobacco from nonindustrialized regions. The availability of cheap labor in underdeveloped countries contributed to increasing wealth and profits in industrial nations. Thus, according to dependency theorists, the wealth and prosperity of the industrial capitalist countries was due largely to the exploitation of the underdeveloped world.

The need for raw materials, consumer goods, cheap labor, and markets led to increasing **imperialism**, the economic and political control of a particular nation or territory by an external nation. Although imperialism had developed among preindustrial agricultural states, it did not involve the whole world. In contrast, industrial countries like Great Britain, the United States, France, Germany, the Netherlands, Belgium, Russia, and Japan divided the nonindustrialized areas into "spheres of economic and political influence." Most of the nonindustrialized regions became **colonies** that exported raw materials and provided labor and other commodities for the industrialized nations.

Dependency theorists categorize the industrial capitalist countries as the *metropole* societies that maintain dependent *satellite* countries in the underdeveloped world. Through the organization of the world economy by the industrial capitalist societies, the surpluses of commodities produced by cheap labor flow from the satellites to the metropole. The satellites remain underdeveloped because of economic and political domination by the metropole. Despite the fact that many satellite countries have become politically independent from their former colonial rulers, the emergence of multinational corporations based in the industrialized capitalist societies has produced a new form of imperialism, *neoimperialism*. The industrial capitalist societies control foreign aid, international financial institutions such as the World Bank and the International Monetary Fund (IMF), and international political institutions such as the United Nations, all of which function to maintain their dominant position.

Criticisms of Dependency Theory   Unlike modernization theory, the dependency approach demonstrates that no society evolves in isolation. By examining the political economy in industrial capitalist and precapitalist countries, theorists showed conclusively that some aspects of underdevelopment are related to the dynamics of power, conflict, class relations, and exploitation.

Critics, however, have noted a number of flaws in the dependency approach. Generally, dependency theory tends to be overly pessimistic. It suggests that dependency and impoverishment can be undone only by a radical restructuring of the world economy to reallocate wealth and resources from wealthy industrial capitalist countries to impoverished precapitalist countries. Economic development, however, has occurred in some countries that have had extensive contact with industrial capitalist societies. Notably, Japan moved from an underdeveloped society to a wealthy industrial capitalist position after the 1950s. Other countries such as Taiwan and South Korea have also developed. In contrast, some poor societies that have had less contact with the industrial capitalist societies remain highly undeveloped.

Critics also point out that dependency theorists neglect the internal conditions of underdeveloped countries that may inhibit economic development. Rapid population growth, famine and hunger, the excessive control of the economy by centralized governments, and, in some instances, traditional cultural values may inhibit economic development.

World-Systems Theory

The perspective known as **world-systems theory** maintains that the socioeconomic differences among various societies are a result of an interlocking global political economy. The world-systems model represents a response to both modernization and dependency theories. Sociologist Immanuel Wallerstein, who developed the world-systems approach, agrees with the dependency theorists that the industrial nations prosper through the economic domination and exploitation of nonindustrial peoples. His world-systems model (1974, 1979, 1980) places all countries in one of three general categories: core, peripheral, and semiperipheral. **Core societies** are the powerful industrial nations that exercise economic domination over other regions. Most nonindustrialized countries are classified as **peripheral societies,** which have very little control over their own economies and are dominated by the core societies. Wallerstein notes that between the core and peripheral countries are the **semiperipheral societies,** which are somewhat industrialized and have some economic autonomy but are not as advanced as the core societies (see Figure 20.1).

Unlike dependency theorists, Wallerstein believes that under specific historical circumstances a peripheral society can develop economically. For example, during the worldwide depression of the 1930s, some peripheral Latin American countries, such as Brazil and Mexico, advanced to a semiperipheral position. Wallerstein also explains the recent rapid economic development of countries such as Taiwan and South Korea in terms of their favored status by core societies. Because the United States was in competition with the former Soviet Union and feared the emergence of communism in Asia, it invested huge amounts of technology and capital in Taiwan and South Korea.

Criticisms of World-Systems Theory   Although Wallerstein's world-systems theory has some advantages over modernization and dependency theories,

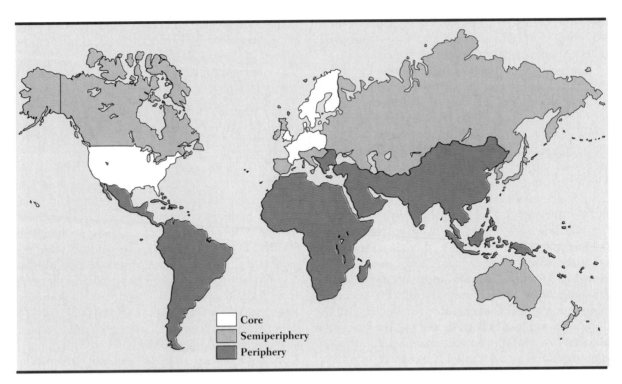

FIGURE 20.1(a)   The world system around 1900.

Source: From *Macrosociology: An Introduction to Human Societies,* 4th ed., by Stephen K. Sanderson.
Copyright © 1999. All rights reserved. Reprinted by permission of Allyn & Bacon.

critics note some weaknesses (Shannon, 1988). One criticism is that the theory focuses exclusively on economic factors at the expense of noneconomic factors such as politics and cultural traditions. In addition, it fails to address the question of why trade between industrial and nonindustrial nations must always be exploitative. Some theorists have noted that in certain cases, peripheral societies benefit from the trade with core societies in that, for example, they may need Western technology to develop their economies (Chirot, 1986).

Although world-systems theory has been helpful in allowing for a more comprehensive and flexible view of global economic and political interconnections, it is not a perfected model. However, the terms used by Wallerstein, such as *core, semiperipheral,* and *peripheral,* have been adopted widely by the social sciences. These terms offer an improvement by helping to classify different types of global interrelationships and substitute for the older terminology of *First, Second,* and *Third Worlds.*

Anthropological Analysis and Globalization

Ethnographic research has uncovered limitations to all the approaches to globalization. Such labels as *traditional, modern, metropole-satellite,* and *peripheral* are too simplistic to classify realistically the diverse economic and cultural traditions in the world. Anthropologists find that there are no predictable, unilineal, or unalterable patterns of societal evolution. They criticize the modernization, dependency, and world-systems theorists for neglecting the diverse precapitalist economic systems, specific histories, internal class relations, ethnic differences, political conditions, and dynamic cultural traditions.

Before the 1960s, many anthropologists were influenced by the modernization approach, which tended to view societies in isolation. Since the development of the dependency and world-systems perspectives, however, anthropologists have become more attuned to the global perspective. For

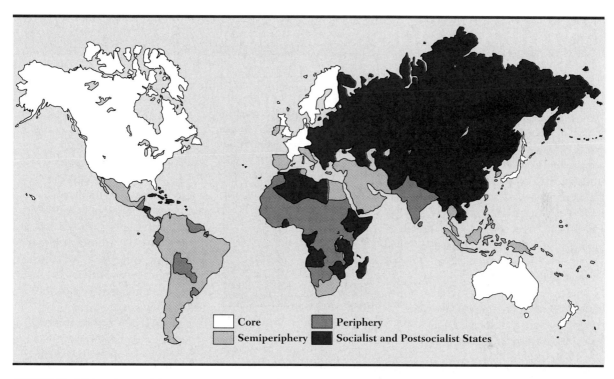

FIGURE 20.1(b) The world system, 2000.

Source: From *Macrosociology: An Introduction to Human Societies,* 4th ed., by Stephen K. Sanderson. Copyright © 1999. All rights reserved. Reprinted by permission of Allyn & Bacon.

example, a book by Eric Wolf, *Europe and the People without History* (1997), reflected these developments in anthropological thought. Wolf espoused a global perspective by drawing on modernization, dependency, and world-systems approaches while criticizing all of them for their weaknesses. Anthropologists today evaluate the claims of all three approaches by combining in-depth historical information with cultural data gathered through ethnological research. This strategy contributes to a more comprehensive understanding of the internal and external conditions that influence societal changes arising from globalization.

Globalization and Prestate Societies

In Chapters 15, 16, and 17 we discussed the major types of prestate societies studied by anthropolo-gists: bands, tribes (horticultural and pastoral), and chiefdoms. Contrary to some popular stereotypes, these societies have never been entirely isolated, nor are they static. Since coming into contact with industrial societies and globalization, however, they have undergone dramatic transformations. These prestate societies are sometimes referred to as the "Fourth World," as an additional classification to the First, Second, and Third World categories. Other terms for these societies include *native, indigenous, aboriginal,* or *first nation.* Extensive ethnological research has provided us with considerable documentation concerning the changes in these nonstate societies.

The expansion of globalization produced traumatic and violent changes in many prestate societies. These peoples were absorbed as subordinate ethnic groups in larger nation-states or in some cases became extinct. When absorbed, they usually were forced to abandon their traditional language and culture, a process known as **ethnocide.** In other

ANTHROPOLOGISTS AT WORK

ERIC WOLF: A GLOBAL ANTHROPOLOGIST

Eric Wolf was born in Vienna, Austria, in 1923. After elementary school he went to *gymnasium*, a combined middle school and high school, in Czechoslovakia. At an early age, he was exposed to many diverse ethnic groups and nationalistic movements. His parents later sent him to England, where he first discovered the natural sciences. In 1940, he came to the United States to attend Queens College. He majored in a variety of subjects until he finally settled on anthropology. In 1943, he joined the U.S. Army and saw combat in Italy, returning with a Silver Star and a Purple Heart. After the war, he completed his studies at Queens College and then went on to graduate from Columbia University, where he studied with Ruth Benedict and Julian Steward. He did ethnological fieldwork in Puerto Rico, Mexico, and the Italian Alps.

Having been exposed to peasant groups during his childhood in Europe, Wolf focused his studies on the peasantry in different parts of the world. Through his

Eric Wolf

fieldwork in areas such as Puerto Rico and Mexico, he became interested in how peasants adjust to global change. In a number of essays, he refined the analytical approach to understanding the peasantry. His early books include *Sons of the Shaking Earth* (1959), an overview of the historical transformations in Mesoamerica caused by Spanish colonialism; *Peasants* (1966), an analytic treatment of peasants throughout the world; and *Peasant Wars of the Twentieth Century* (1969), an examination of peasant revolutions.

Because of the success of his early books and his global perspective in his comprehensive *Europe and the People without History* ([1982] 1997), Wolf has exerted a tremendous influence on many anthropologists and other social scientists. *Europe and the People without History* won several awards. Wolf was awarded a grant from the MacArthur Foundation, frequently called the "genius" award. Candidates are recommended by one hundred anonymous nominators, whose selections are reviewed by panels of experts. Recipients can spend the grant money as they wish on their own research projects. Wolf wrote another influential text called *Envisioning Power* (1999) about ideology and its relationship to political economy, global developments, and culture.

Unfortunately, Eric Wolf died in March 1999. His contributions to anthropological thought and his emphasis on the global perspective will endure forever within the profession.

situations, aboriginal peoples faced **genocide,** the physical extermination of a particular group or race of people. People such as the Tasmanians of Australia and some Native American groups were deliberately killed so that colonists could take their lands and resources. The following sections focus on the impact of globalization on some first nation peoples.

Vanishing Foragers

As described in Chapter 15, contemporary bands, or foraging societies, have survived in marginal environments: deserts, tropical rain forests, and arctic regions. Because these lands are not suitable for agriculture, foragers lived in relative isolation from surrounding populations. Following the emergence of industrial states, however, these marginal areas became attractive as unsettled frontiers with low population densities and bountiful natural resources such as land, timber, energy resources, minerals, and other valuable products. Industrial states have expanded into these regions in search of energy supplies and resources such as oil and minerals in the deserts and arctic areas, and land and timber from the tropical rain forests. One result of this process has been increased contact between industrial and foraging societies, often with tragic results.

The Ju/'hoansi Foragers

The bands of the African deserts and tropical rain forests have been devastated by confrontations with expanding industrial states. The Ju/'hoansi or San people of the Kalahari Desert, who, before the 1950s, had little contact with industrial nations, are now caught in the midst of forced change. Many of the Ju/'hoansi live in Namibia, which for many years was controlled by South Africa. Beginning in the 1960s, the South African government began to expand into the Kalahari Desert. In the process it restricted the Ju/'hoansi hunting territories and attempted to resettle them in a confined reservation. It further attempted to introduce the Ju/'hoansi to agriculture—the cultivation of maize, melons, sorghum, and tobacco—and cattle raising. Because of the unsuitability of the land and inadequate water supplies, however, these activities have not succeeded. Consequently, the Ju/'hoansi have become increasingly dependent on government rations of corn, salt, sugar, and tobacco.

In Namibia, the only economic opportunities for Ju/'hoansi males are menial chores, clearing fields, and building roads. The government initially paid Ju/'hoansi laborers with *mealie* (ground corn), sugar, or tobacco, but eventually switched to money. The introduction of this cash economy transformed traditional relationships in Ju/'hoansi society. People who previously had embraced a reciprocal exchange system that enhanced their kinship and social ties now had to adjust to a system in which resources were managed for one's own family. Conflicts arose between those who wanted to share and others who were forced to become self-interested and hide resources even from their own kin.

In some of the areas where the Ju/'hoansi were settled, population began to increase. This is a typical consequence of a shift from a foraging to a settled life. With increased crowding came epidemics, particularly tuberculosis, that claimed many lives. Moreover, in response to the rapid transformation of their lifestyle, many Ju/'hoansi resorted to frequent drinking. Much of their newly acquired cash from employment went into alcohol consumption, and alcoholism became a problem for many.

Other Ju/'hoansi males were recruited by the South African military to engage in campaigns during the 1960s and 1970s against the South-West African People's Organization (SWAPO), guerrilla insurgents who opposed the South African regime. The Ju/'hoansi were valued as soldiers because they were good trackers and courageous fighters. Most of them, however, were unaware of the geopolitical strategies and racist policies of the South African government. They were simply attracted to military service by the promise of high wages.

Richard Lee believed that this involvement in the South African military increased the amount of violence in Ju/'hoansi society. Lee documented only twenty-two cases of homicide among all the Ju/'hoansi between 1922 and 1955. In contrast, seven murders were recorded in a single village known as Chum!kwe during the brief period from 1978 to 1980, a major increase (Lee, 1993). According to Lee, the aggressive values and norms associated with militarism increased the tendency toward violence in Ju/'hoansi society.

In 1998 the Ju/'hoansi established what is known as a *conservancy* to oversee the wild life resources in the region. It is a block of communal land on which people can utilize the wild life resources and make decisions about land use. This conservancy called NYAE NYAE has been successful in producing income for the group and giving assistance for conservation projects. Recently, however, a number of refugees are flooding into Namibia from an ongoing war in neighboring Angola, which has created problems for resettling these populations in the Kalahari region. These refugees may threaten the conservancy projects in Namibia (Hitchcock & Biesle, 2002a).

The Dobe Ju/'hoansi

Lee (1993) also studied the situation of the Ju/'hoansi of the Dobe area in the country of Botswana, who have not had to make the same types of adjustments as the Ju/'hoansi of Namibia. Generally, the nation of Botswana has not been subject to the same expansive South African policies as Namibia. Therefore, the Ju/'hoansi in Dobe have not been recruited into the South African army, nor has the government funded settlement reservations. However, Lee found that by the 1970s, the Ju/'hoansi Dobe were beginning to adopt agriculture and herding. Although agriculture continues to be a very risky proposition in the desert area, herding and livestock production is beginning to become a viable source of income for the Dobe Ju/'hoansi.

Lee described how Ju/'hoansi Dobe males also began to migrate outside their own territories to work in South African mines for $18 to $25 a month. Upon returning home after months of working in the mines, they spent much of their cash wages on a home brew. This pattern of drinking increased the tendency toward alcoholism among some Ju/'hoansi Dobe.

The introduction of a cash economy disrupted traditional Ju/'hoansi Dobe patterns of egalitarianism and reciprocity. The availability of manufactured goods such as soap, foodstuffs, kerosene, and clothing led to the decline of indigenous technologies and crafts. Drinking, violence, and conflict increased. These problems heightened anxieties among the Ju/'hoansi Dobe, as they realized how dramatically their traditional lifestyle had changed. However, even in the late 1990s, much of the ethos of sharing and egalitarianism endured in spite of all the changes, giving some indications of the resilience of this way of life.

In 2001, the Botswana government moved toward restricting the land use rights of the San people. The government announced that the local people would no longer have legal rights to exploit natural resources in the Central Kalahari. They have taken steps to cut off the San water supplies and are restricting their subsistence hunting activities. The native people have said they will resist this intrusion with their bows and arrows. Some suspect that that the area's rich diamond deposits are the real motivation for moving these people off their land (Hitchcock & Biesle, 2002b).

The Mbuti Pygmies

The late Colin Turnbull examined two cases of African foragers who have faced decimation through forced cultural change. Turnbull did the major ethnographic study, discussed in Chapter 15, of the Mbuti Pygmies of the Ituri rain forest of the Congo, formerly Zaire. He noted (1963, 1983) that the Pygmies had been in contact with outsiders for centuries but had chosen to retain their traditional hunting-and-gathering way of life. During the colonial period in what was then the Belgian Congo, however, government officials tried to resettle the Mbuti on plantations outside the forest.

Following the colonial period, the newly independent government of Zaire continued the same policies of forced resettlement. In the government's view, this move would "emancipate" the Pygmies, enabling them to contribute to the economy and to participate in the national political process (Turnbull, 1983). The Pygmies would become national citizens and would also be subject to taxation. Model villages were built outside the forest with Mbuti labor. Convinced by government officials that they would benefit, many Mbuti at first supported these relocation projects.

The immediate results of this resettlement, however, were disastrous. Turnbull visited the model villages and found many of the Mbuti suffering from various diseases. Because the Mbuti were unaccustomed to living a sedentary life, they lacked knowledge of proper sanitation. Turnbull found that the Mbuti water had become contaminated, and the change of diet from forest products to cultivated crops had created nutritional problems.

More recently, globalization has had other effects on many of the Mbuti people. In 1992, international pressure resulted in the government creating an area called Okapi Faunal Reserve or "green zone" to conserve the rain forest and indirectly to preserve the Mbuti way of life. The law protecting the reserve decreed that poaching protected animals like elephants, leopards, chimpanzees, and gorillas was forbidden (Tshombe, 2001). However, the "green zone" has not been protected due to the extreme political and institutional crises faced by the Democratic Republic of the Congo. This region has been besieged by civil wars and the erosion of political control and stability. Due to this weakening of the state, immigrants began to flow into the

The Mbuti Pygmies have been traumatically influenced by globalization processes.

Ituri forest to clear land for agriculture, which resulted in the rapid deterioration of the soil. Multinational companies continued logging throughout the forest area, and elephant poaching increased with the killing of about one hundred elephants between 1998 and 2000.

One of the most devastating consequences in the Ituri forest came from the introduction of coltan mining (Harden, 2001). Coltan is a mineral that is found in the forests of the Congo near where the Mbuti live. Coltan is refined in the United States and Europe into tantalum, which is a metallic element that is used in capacitors and other electronic components for computers, cell phones, and pagers. The electronics and computer industries are heavily dependent on coltan. Many of the Mbuti have been recruited by the mining industry to dig for coltan. They chop down great swaths of the rain forest and dig large holes in the forest floor to dig out this vital mineral, which is used in electronic equipment far away from the Ituri forest. The Mbuti use pick and shovel to dig out this mineral, which was worth $80 a kilogram in the early part of 2001. They could earn as much as $2,000 a month, which represented more cash wages than the Mbuti had ever seen. Thousands of other immigrants began to pour into the area to take advantage of this new profitable mineral needed by the high-tech businesses of the postindustrial societies.

This encounter between the high-tech world and the Ituri forest resulted in painful circumstances for the Mbuti people. First, the mining created major environmental damage to the rain forest where these people depended on hunting and gathering. The streams of the forest were polluted, trees were cut down, and the large holes in the ground for coltan mining ruined the environment. The growing migrant population began to poach and kill the lowland gorillas and other animals for food. Lowland gorillas have been reduced to fewer than one thousand, and other forest animals were overhunted. Along with the increase of the population in the mining camps came prostitution, the abuse of alcohol, conflict, exploitation by outside groups, and the spread of diseases such as gonorrhea.

Additionally, by the spring of 2001, the price of coltan fell from $80 to $8.00 a kilogram. A slump in cell phone sales and the decrease in the high tech economy created a glut of coltan on the global market, which had consequences for the people of the rain forest. Mining camps that had ravaged the rain forest were still filled with migrants, prostitutes, and some of the Mbuti people, but many of the people abandoned these mining camps. However, many of the Mbuti have not returned to their traditional hunting-and-gathering way of life. Many of them lost the land that sustained their way of life. The weakness of the state, civil wars, and ethnic conflict surrounding the Mbuti enabled outsiders to take over their forest land. Globalization resulted in ecological damage and social and cultural dislocations for the Mbuti people in a very short period of time.

The Siriono

Many other hunter-gatherer societies are facing similar situations in their confrontation with industrializing societies and global processes. Allan Holmberg described the Siriono foragers of eastern Bolivia in an ethnography entitled *Nomads of the Long Bow* (1950). In contrast to the portrait of foragers elsewhere, Holmberg described the Siriono as living at the edge of starvation. He presented the Siriono as so focused on food and hunger that they were ungenerous and did not have the same patterns of reciprocity practiced in other foraging societies. He further described them as having a rudimentary culture with little technology and no games, music, cosmology, myths, folk tales, and ritual ceremonies. He hypothesized that the Siriono were so concerned with their immediate biological needs that they had no time for a reflective life.

Barry Isaac (1977) subsequently studied the historical conditions that affected the Siriono and challenged Holmberg's conclusions. As Isaac noted, Holmberg had underestimated the consequences of contact with outsiders. The Spanish had been in the region for more than four hundred years. Some of the Siriono observed by Holmberg were escapees from missions and plantations. In addition, the Siriono population had been decimated by smallpox and influenza, as well as by raids from other Indian groups. The Siriono had become so dependent on European technology such as steel axes and knives that they had completely abandoned their traditional foraging activities for several generations.

In other words, the situation observed by Holmberg was that of a foraging society attempting to adapt to outside pressures while undergoing a traumatic transition. Instead of representing a rudimentary culture existing in the rain forest, the Siriono were adjusting to epidemics, exploitation, and warfare. The resulting depopulation accelerated the process of **deculturation,** the loss of traditional patterns of culture. In the case of the Siriono, the lost cultural elements included technology and subsistence practices as well as religious practices such as shamanism. Isaac maintained that the Siriono represented a fragile foraging society that, when confronted with external pressures, was easily tipped toward disintegration.

Tribes in Transition

The process of globalization has adversely affected many horticulturalist and pastoralist tribes. For example, many Native American societies suffered serious disruptions as a result of European colonization. The Spanish, French, Dutch, and British came to the Americas in search of precious metals, furs, and land for settlement. Each of these countries had different experiences with the indigenous peoples of North America. But wherever the Europeans settled, indigenous tribes were usually devastated through depopulation, deculturation, and, in many cases, physical extinction.

North American Horticulturalists

The collision of cultures and political economies between Native Americans and Europeans can be illustrated by the experiences of the Iroquois of New York State. The traditional horticulturalist system of the Iroquois was described in Chapter 16. British and French settlers established a fur trade with the Iroquois and nearby peoples during the late 1600s. French traders offered weapons, glass beads, liquor, and ammunition to the Iroquois in exchange for beaver skins. Eventually, the Iroquois abandoned their traditional economy of horticulture supplemented by limited hunting to supply the French with fur pelts. The French appointed various *capitans* among the Iroquois to manage the fur trade. This resulted in the decline of the tribe's traditional social and political order (Kehoe, 1995).

Meanwhile, the intensive hunting of beaver led to a scarcity of fur in the region, which occurred just as the Iroquois were becoming more dependent on European goods. The result was increased competition between European traders and various Native Americans who were linked to the fur trade. The Iroquois began to raid other tribal groups, such as the Algonquins, who traded with the British. Increasing numbers of Iroquois males were drawn into more extensive warfare (Blick, 1988). Many other Native American tribal peoples also became entangled in the economic, political, and military conflicts between the British and French over land and resources in North America.

The Relocation of Native Americans   Beginning in the colonial period, many Native American tribes were introduced to the European form of intensive agriculture, with plows, new types of grains, domesticated cattle and sheep, fences, and individual plots of land. The white settlers rationalized this process as a means of introducing Western "civilization" to indigenous peoples. However, whenever Native Americans became proficient in intensive agriculture, many white farmers viewed them as a threat. Eventually, following the American Revolution, the government initiated a policy of removing Native Americans from their lands to open the frontier for white settlers. A process developed in which Native Americans were drawn into debt for goods and then

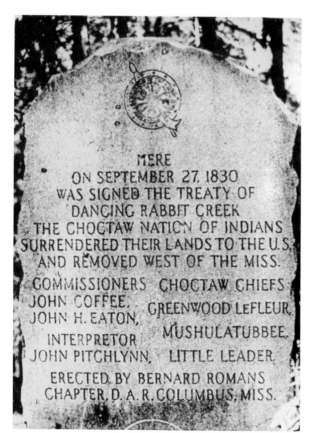

Many Native Americans such as the Choctaw Indians signed treaties with the U.S. government giving up their rights to land.

pressured to cede their lands as payment for these debts.

Ultimately, the U.S. government developed the system of reservations for resettling the Native American population. Under Andrew Jackson in the 1830s, many southeastern tribal groups were resettled into western regions such as Oklahoma. In many cases, Native Americans were forcibly removed from their land, actions that colonists justified as a way of bringing Western civilization and Christianity to these peoples. The removal policies led to brutal circumstances such as the Trail of Tears, in which thousands of Shawnees and Cherokees living in Georgia and North Carolina were forced to travel hundreds of miles westward to be resettled. Many died of starvation and other physical deprivations on this forced march.

The patterns of land cession were repeated as white settlers moved westward. European Americans justified these behaviors through the concept of *Manifest Destiny,* the belief that they were responsible for extending the benefits of Western civilization throughout the continent. Military force frequently was used to overcome Indian resistance.

In 1890, Native Americans held title to 137 million acres of land. By 1934, these holdings had been reduced to 56 million acres. After suffering the dispossession of most of their lands, the majority of Native Americans were forced to live on reservations, most of which were unsuitable for agriculture. Lack of employment opportunities led to increased impoverishment for many of these people. The Bureau of Indian Affairs (BIA) oversees the reservations. Before 1934, Native Americans were viewed as wards of the state, and the BIA established Indian schools to introduce "civilization" to Native American children. The BIA was empowered to decide whether Native Americans could sell or lease their land, send their children to boarding schools, or practice their traditional religion.

Native Americans in the Twentieth Century   Based on a survey of archaeological materials and fossil evidence, Douglas Ubelaker (1988) estimated how dramatic the population decline precipitated by colonization and settlement was. The survey indicates that at the time of initial European contact, the Native American population ranged from 1.2 million to more than 2.6 million. This is an extremely conservative estimate. But by 1890, when

Native Americans made their last stand at Wounded Knee, South Dakota, their population had declined to about 250,000. This trend reflects the effects of warfare, forced marches, loss of traditional lands, and diseases such as smallpox, measles, influenza, and tuberculosis, to which Native Americans lacked immunity.

In the twentieth century, the Native American population increased to about 2 million. Approximately two-thirds of the Native Americans live on reservations, and most of the remaining one-third reside in major metropolitan areas. Native Americans are far below the average American in income and education.

Today, multinational corporations want to develop the reserves of coal, oil, natural gas, and uranium on Native American reservation lands, such as the Hopi and Navajo territories. Other companies have been making lucrative offers to lease Native American lands to be used as garbage landfills and toxic-waste dumps. These monetary offers have produced splits within Native American communities. Some favor the offers as a means of combating poverty, whereas others condemn mining or any other commercial activity as a desecration of their sacred land. Many other Native American communities have developed gambling casinos as a source of income for their people. These issues have caused splits in the communities and present difficult decisions for Native Americans.

South American Horticulturalists

In the Amazon rain forests of South America, tribal peoples such as the Yanomamö, the Jivaro, and the Mundurucu are facing dramatic changes resulting from globalization. Beginning in the 1950s, European and American missionaries representing different Christian denominations began to settle in the Amazon region and competed to "civilize" peoples such as the Yanomamö. In Venezuela the major missionary group is the Salesians, a Catholic mission. The missionaries attempted to persuade Yanomamö communities to reside in their mission stations. Those who did so became completely dependent on the missionaries, gradually abandoning their traditional means of subsistence and social life. The missionaries set up schools to teach the Yanomamö new methods of agriculture and train them to spread these ideas among others. With the

building of highways and increased settlement in the Amazon rain forest—developments sponsored by the Venezuelan and Brazilian governments—the Yanomamö became increasingly exposed to influenza, dysentery, measles, and colds. In some regions, almost 50 percent of the population have fallen victim to these diseases (Kellman, 1982).

One consequence of contact with the outside world was the Yanomamö's adoption of the shotgun for hunting in the forest. The Yanomamö originally obtained shotguns from the missionaries or other employees on the missions. Initially, Yanomamö hunters who knew the forest very well became proficient in obtaining more game. In time, however, the game in the rain forest grew more scarce. Consequently, the Yanomamö had to hunt deeper and deeper into the rain forest to maintain their diet. In addition, as indicated by cultural anthropologist Raymond Hames (1979a), the Yanomamö had to expend much more labor in the cash economy to be able to purchase shotguns and shells to continue hunting. Additionally, some Yanomamö began to use the shotgun as a weapon in warfare and political intimidation and raiding each other.

Recent Developments among the Yanomamö   The Amazon rain forest is experiencing new pressures. Prospectors, mining companies, energy companies, and government officials interested in industrial development are eager to obtain the gold, oil, tin, uranium, and other minerals in the 60,000 square miles of forest straddling the Brazilian and Venezuelan borders, where the Yanomamö live. A 1987 gold rush led to the settlement of at least 40,000 prospectors in Yanomamö territory. The prospectors hunt game in the forest, causing scarcities and increased malnutrition among the Yanomamö. Clashes between prospectors and the Yanomamö have led to many deaths. In August 1993, gold miners massacred Yanomamö men, women, and children in Venezuela. After the attack, a Yanomamö leader described the massacre: "Many miners surrounded the lodge and started to kill Yanomamö. The women were cut in the belly, the breasts and the neck. I saw many bodies piled up" (Brooke, 1993; Chagnon, 1997).

In Brazil, the drive toward economic development and industrialization has stimulated rapid and tragic changes affecting the Yanomamö. The survival of the 9,000 Yanomamö in Brazil is in question.

Their population has declined by one-sixth since the gold rush began in 1987. Alarmed by these developments, concerned anthropologists, missionaries, and Brazilians formed a committee to reserve an area for the Yanomamö to practice their traditional way of life. The Brazilian government and business leaders opposed this proposal, but eventually, the government allotted 8,000 square miles of land, which became known as Yanomamö Park. The land, however, was subdivided into small parcels that were impossible to defend against outsiders. In 1995 officials of the National Brazilian Indian Foundation (FUNAI) assured Napoleon Chagnon that there were no more than a few hundred illegal miners in the Yanomamö area, and they were systematically trying to find and expel them (Chagnon, 1997). However, there are still news reports from Brazil indicating that more gold miners are infiltrating the area.

In contrast to Brazil, the Venezuelan government has been developing more humane and effective policies toward the Yanomamö natives. In 1991, Venezuelan President Carlos Andres Perez took action to develop a reserve for the Yanomamö of some 32,000 square miles of rain forest as a "special biosphere" or national park that would be closed to mining and other development (Chagnon, 1997). Then, in 1992, the Venezuelan government designated the Venezuelan Amazonas as a new state in its national political structure. State governments are being given more control over their own populations and resources. The resources of the new Amazonas state will probably include mineral wealth and tourism. Thus, the Yanomamö of Venezuela will become increasingly drawn into contact with outsiders. Whether this will mean more tragedy and epidemic diseases and economic problems for these natives is a question that can only be answered in the future (see the box, "Controversy in El Dorado").

Pastoralist Tribes

Pastoralists have also been subjected to expanding industrial societies. The adaptive objectives of pastoralists tend to be at odds with the primary aims of state societies. Because of their nomadic way of life, pastoralists cannot be easily incorporated and controlled by state societies. They are not usually subject to the same processes of enculturation as settled peoples. They don't attend schools, and they may place their tribal loyalties above their loyalties to the state. Rapid change among pastoralist societies is evident in some Middle Eastern countries.

Middle Eastern Pastoralists: The Bedouins Anthropologist Donald Cole (1984) conducted research on the Bedouins of Saudi Arabia, groups of nomadic pastoralists. Cole focused on one particular group, the Al-Murrah, a tribe of 15,000 who live in the

Bedouins of Arabia have been influenced by global economic and political developments in their societies.

CRITICAL PERSPECTIVES

CONTROVERSY IN EL DORADO

In this chapter we discussed the ethnographic research conducted by Napoleon Chagnon on the Yanomamö tribe in the Amazon. Recently, a controversial book by an investigative journalist with some background in anthropology has been written about Chagnon's research among the Yanomamö.

Napoleon Chagnon was born in Port Austin, Michigan, in 1938. As a physics major at the University of Michigan, he chose to take a few anthropology courses to fulfill some of his liberal arts requirements. These courses so captivated him that he changed his major and ultimately earned B.A., M.A., and Ph.D. degrees in anthropology at Michigan. After completing his Ph.D. in 1966, he joined the Department of Human Genetics at the University of Michigan Medical School and participated in a multidisciplinary study of the Yanomamö Indians of Venezuela and Brazil along with the geneticist James Neel.

Chagnon returned to do fieldwork among the Yanomamö almost every year since 1966, enabling him to conduct a long-term, systematic study of change within this population. Chagnon's ethnographic studies and the many educational films that he and colleague Timothy Asch have produced have made the Yanomamö well-known around the world.

Chagnon's description of his first fieldwork experience with the Yanomamö demonstrates how culture shock can affect cultural

anthropologists who encounter a society radically different from their own. He describes his initial experience with the Yanomamö after a long voyage up the Orinoco River, arriving at a river-bank near the village:

I looked up and gasped when I saw a dozen burly, naked, sweaty, hideous men staring at us down the shafts of their arrows! Immense wads of green tobacco were stuck between their lower teeth and lips, making them look even more hideous, and strands of dark green slime dripped or hung from their nostrils—so long that they clung to their [chests] or drizzled down their chins. (1983:10) [The dark green slime was the remains of a hallucinogenic drug that the Yanomamö had taken.]

Eventually Chagnon adjusted to his new environment and conducted a thorough, systematic ethnographic study. In a book about his fieldwork, *Studying the Yanomamö* (1974), he describes both his analytical techniques and his immersion into Yanomamö society. Over the years, Chagnon has written dozens of books and hundreds of articles about Yanomamö society and culture.

In 2000 the investigative journalist Patrick Tierney had a book published called *Darkness in El Dorado: How Scientists and Journalists Devastated the Amazon* that accuses Chagnon and James Neel of seriously disrupting the

Yanomamö society and in some cases increasing death rates among these people. Tierney alleges that the geneticist James Neel improperly used a measles vaccine among the Yanomamö that resulted in a measles epidemic causing "hundreds, perhaps thousands of deaths." Tierney suggests that Neel did this to experiment in a natural laboratory, and to observe an epidemic for scientific reasons. In other words, he accused Neel and his accomplice Chagnon of carrying out genocide among these people. He also claimed that Neel was conducting secret radiation experiments among the Yanomamö.

Darkness in El Dorado also indicts Chagnon for nefarious misdeeds in his role as an anthropologist. Tierney argues that Chagnon staged warfare and violence among the Yanomamö for filmmaker Timothy Asch in order to project an image of a warlike, violent people. In addition, Tierney argues that Chagnon fraudulently manipulated his analysis of warfare and violence among the Yanomamö to support his sociobiological views. Tierney goes on to allege that Chagnon himself is directly or indirectly responsible for the endemic warfare found among the Yanomamö. By introducing trade items such as machetes, metal goods, and imported foods to these tribal people, Tierney suggests that Chagnon created conditions for competition among villages for these goods, and consequently this competition resulted in intergroup warfare and violence. Tierney argues that Chagnon perpetuated an image of the Yanomamö as a naturally violent and warlike people, and as a result of this stereotype, 40,000 gold miners invaded Yanomamö territory between 1980 and 1987 and used violence against them (see page 492). He also alleges that Chagnon colluded with some Venezuelan politicians to gain control of Yanomami land for illegal gold mining concessions to benefit himself.

Tierney's book created a well-publicized controversy that was carried internationally in leading newspapers, the Internet, and other media. Tierney had worked on this book for 11 years, and it contained 18 chapters, 398 sources, and 1,599 footnotes. The book also led to a lot of investigations and soul-searching among anthropologists. Many anthropologists began to ask themselves if this book was going to unhinge their whole discipline. Immediately, the University of Michigan, the University of California at Santa Barbara (both helped sponsor the research of Chagnon), the National Academy of Science, and the American Anthropological Association launched investigations into the possible malfeasance of Neel and Chagnon. Teams of researchers began to assess every one of the allegations that Tierney made and to follow up every claim and every footnote in his book.

The most serious allegation—that Neel had improperly introduced a measles vaccine resulting in loss of life among the Yanomamö—has been thoroughly refuted by leading scientists who investigated the medical documents of Neel concerning the vaccination process. The co-developer of the actual measles vaccine, Dr. Samuel Katz, has stated that the vaccine was not virulent and could not cause measles, and had never done so in millions of applications. In addition, researchers found in medical reports that Brazilian missionaries had introduced the initial measles outbreak among the Yanomamö in November 1967, prior to the Chagnon-Neel expedition in 1968. Chagnon, Neel, and the medical team were actively trying to vaccinate the population to reduce the incidence of measles. Through investigation of Neel's field journals and daily logs, the allegation that he was using radiation experiments among the Yanomamö was also refuted.

Researchers also investigated Tierney's claims regarding Chagnon's misdeeds in his role as an anthropologist. Although Timothy Asch, the filmmaker, had died before the publication of Tierney's book, many of his assistants who had helped edit and did research for the films on the Yanomamö, insist that the films were not staged productions, but rather were authentic portrayals of the life of these people.

Tierney's claim that Chagnon was directly or indirectly responsible for the endemic warfare among these people has also been examined carefully. Archaeologists have exhumed an enormous amount of evidence of warfare in this region of the Amazon going back at least 3,500 years. Prior to Chagnon's ethnographic studies, missionaries and other explorers had been publishing accounts of warfare among the Yanomamö since the sixteenth century. The Yanomamö describe themselves as *waitiri*, and Chagnon translated this term into English as "fierce and valiant."

Tierney's thesis that Chagnon's characterization of these people as fierce and violent resulted in the gold miners' attacks and invasions does not appear valid when examined historically. The treatment of indigenous Native American peoples by gold miners in the gold rush in California or the Black Hills of the Dakota region parallels the behavior of the gold miners in the Amazon. These gold miners often brutalized Native Americans. It didn't take an anthropological description to motivate these misbehaviors, just as it didn't take Chagnon's depictions to motivate the behavior of gold miners in the Amazon to invade, attack, and attempt to take over Yanomamö land.

As for the charge that Chagnon manipulated or "cooked" his data to support his sociobiological view that warlike, violent Yanomamö males were likely to have more wives and to be more reproductively successful, other anthropologists such as Clayton and Carole Robarchek have found a similar correlation in their ethnographic data among the Waorani Indians of Ecuador (1998). However, the Robarcheks interpret this data differently from Chagnon and offer a different hypothesis. Their data

(continued on page 496)

CRITICAL PERSPECTIVES

CONTROVERSY IN EL DORADO—CONTINUED

indicates that the longer a man lives, the more children he will have, and in that context, Waorani males will more frequently be associated with warfare and homicides. Thus, the number of a man's wives and his offspring was a function of his longevity. This conclusion indicates that more research needs to be done on this ethnographic issue to provide more testable hypotheses.

One of the negative consequences of the publication of Tierney's book is that politicians, scholars, and journalists in various countries have been calling for a boycott of further anthropological and medical research on populations in their regions. Without assessing Tierney's claims, many countries have claimed their populations "off limits" to research or medical care from outsiders. Surely, this will have negative effects on the indigenous peoples who will be invaded by gold miners, infected by diseases from the outside, and experience the downside of globalization, without having their conditions ameliorated or improved by research and medical care.

Although most of the allegations in Tierney's book have been refuted, the final report of the American Anthropological Association (AAA) is not completed yet. Worldwide, anthropologists have been shaken by the publication of this book. The AAA has appointed a task force that will assess the ethics of anthropological research

in light of the allegations in the book. Thus, in some sense, aside from the negative aspersions that have tarnished the reputations of Chagnon and Neel, this book has produced a more critical awareness of how anthropologists and researchers conduct their research, and how they portray the various peoples they describe in their ethnographies. Retrospectively, Chagnon should not have used violence and warfare as his principal theme for the Yanomamö, and not have subtitled his ethnography "The Fierce People." (Eventually that subtitle was dropped on newer editions of the text as Chagnon recognized his error.) He described thoroughly the society and culture of the Yanomamö, which has a lot of different activities such as ritual, myth, child care, subsistence practices, marriage, as do all peoples. Warfare is not prevalent all the time. Thus, these people are not unique and are like most other humans in the world. But many journalists and others in the media focused on the sensational aspects of sex and violence among the Yanomamö to accelerate demand and ratings for their outlets.

Looking back on the early stages of Chagnon's research, most anthropologists today would not conduct themselves in the same manner. Chastened by some of the postmodern critiques about fieldwork in anthropology (see Chapter 13), anthropologists today would be more sensitive to

their own role and activities among the people they were studying. Anthropologists today are active in obtaining informed consent from the people they study.

To be fair to Chagnon, over the years he developed many close ties and friendships among the Yanomamö, and organized a Yanomamö Survival fund to help protect these people from external forces who wanted to take their land. If it were not for the thorough pioneering research on the Yanomamö by Chagnon, we would probably not be aware of the conditions and problems that these people face today. Ethnographic research and anthropological explanations and interpretations have to proceed, despite the negative publicity that they sometimes entail. Without them, we are not going to be able to gain a comprehensive picture of humanity's diversity throughout the world.

POINTS TO PONDER:

1. How would you assess the biases in Tierney's book?

2. Do you think that Chagnon was guilty of disrupting Yanomamö society?

3. Do you think that the investigations of the claims made by Tierney in his book were biased?

4. How do you weigh the moral claims versus the scientific research in this controversy?

extreme desert conditions of Rub al-Khali. Traditionally, Al-Murrah subsistence was based on caravan trade, which depended on the care of camels and other animals. The Al-Murrah traded commodities with oasis centers for dates, rice, and bread. On average, they traveled about 1,200 miles annually during their migrations across the desert. They were also an autonomous military force, conducting raids and warfare.

The attempt to incorporate the Bedouin population into the Saudi state has been an ongoing process, going back to the early phases of state formation in the Arabian peninsula during the age of Muhammad (A.D. 622–632). As Cole indicates, this process of settling and controlling the Bedouins accelerated following the emergence of the modern petroleum industry. To facilitate this process, the Saudi government drafted Al-Murrah males into their national guard. The principal leader of the Al-Murrah, the *emir,* has been recognized by the Saudi government as the commander of this national guard unit. The government gives the emir a share of the national budget, and he distributes salaries to the tribespeople. Thus, the emir has become a dependent government official of the Saudi state.

The traditional subsistence economy based on nomadism and the care of herds of animals appears to be at an end. Camels are being replaced by pickup trucks. Bedouins are settling in cities and participating in the urban economy. All of the formerly self-sufficient Bedouin communities are being absorbed into nation-states throughout the Arabian peninsula.

The Qashqa'i Cultural anthropologist Lois Beck (1986) has written an in-depth study of the Qashqa'i pastoralist tribe of Iran. The Qashqa'i reside in the southern part of the Zagros Mountains. Beck emphasized that the Qashqa'i were to some degree a creation of state processes within Iran. In other words, the Qashqa'i tribe was not a self-contained entity but rather was formed through the long-term process of incorporating tribal leaders into the Iranian nation-state. During different historical periods, the state offered land and political protection to the Qashqa'i in exchange for taxes. Through that process, the Qashqa'i leadership was able to maintain some autonomy. Eventually, the Qashqa'i political system became increasingly centralized around an economic and political elite. This is an example

of how tribes may be formed as a result of an expansionist state political system.

As with other pastoralist societies, the Qashqa'i relationship with the central government in Iran was not always beneficial. During the 1960s, the Iranian government under Shah Pahlavi wanted to modernize and industrialize Iran rapidly with Western support (see Chapter 22). The government viewed the Qashqa'i as resisting modernization and used military force to incorporate them. This policy resulted in the establishment of strong ethnic boundaries between the Iranians and the Qashqa'i. The Qashqa'i began to emphasize their own ethnic identity and to demand more autonomy.

In the initial stages of the Iranian Revolution led by Ayatollah Khomeini, the Qashqa'i joined demonstrations against the shah. Following the revolution, however, the Qashqa'i found themselves subject to patterns of discrimination and repression similar to those they had endured under the shah. Because they never accepted the revolutionary doctrines of the Khomeini regime, they were considered a threat to the ideals of the state. Consequently, Khomeini's Revolutionary Guards harassed the Quasha'i. Thus, Qashqa'i autonomy and local authority continued to erode under the pressures of the nation-state of Iran.

East African Pastoralists and Globalization

In Chapter 16 we discussed pastoralists of East Africa such as the Nuer, the Maasai, Dinka, and others who maintain cattle-keeping on the savannah. Many of these East African tribes are now caught within the interregional net of globalization and disaster. A series of regional wars have broken out in East Africa as a byproduct of colonialism, ethnic rivalry, and political competition within the last decade. For example, in the Republic of Sudan, a war between the Muslim north and the Christian south has affected the Nuer and Dinka tribes that reside in the southern area. Nuer tribal peoples have been recruited into the Sudanese People's Liberation Army to fight against the north. Weapons have flowed into their society and have become new luxury items. Instead of cows being exchanged through reciprocal ties between kinsmen, weapons were now used as a source of wealth and money (Hutchinson, 1996). These guns began to displace the traditional power relationships within the communities as the Nuer and other groups used their cattle to obtain guns and ammunition from different military factions. If these tribal people survived the warfare, many of them became displaced migrants living in poverty in urban areas and refugee camps. Globalization has brought tragedy to most of these once self-sufficient autonomous tribal pastoralists.

Chiefdoms in Transition

Some chiefdoms experienced a fate similar to that of many of the other nonstate societies we have just discussed. However, certain chiefdoms, most likely because they were more centrally organized, developed state organizations themselves following Western contact. The historical development of Polynesian chiefdoms such as in Tahiti and Hawaii illustrates the evolution of state organization that occurred as a result of contact with the global economy.

The Hawaiian Islands

Before contact with the West, Hawaii contained eight inhabited islands with a population of about 600,000. As described in Chapter 17, paramount chiefs, who maintained a redistributional exchange economy, ruled through a belief in their divine authority. The Hawaiian islands were contacted by the English expedition of Captain Cook in 1778, and the islands were eventually penetrated by traders, whalers, missionaries, and other outsiders. The impact of the Western encounter resulted in a unique religious "revolution" when compared with other aboriginal societies we have discussed in earlier sections.

Cook's expedition on the part of the British, which began in the 1760s, set the stage for the colonization of the Pacific. At the time of Captain Cook's discovery of Hawaii, the major paramount chief on the island of Hawaii was engaged in warfare with the chief of the island of Maui, who had already incorporated the islands of Oahu and Molokai under his chieftaincy. The reaction to Cook's arrival during this period was shaped by the aboriginal religious culture. He appeared during the time of Makahiki, a time of religious-based

human sacrifices (see Chapter 17), and he was perceived as someone extremely powerful, perhaps as a god or at the least an important foreign chief. For a variety of different reasons, the Hawaiians ended up killing Captain Cook at this time (Sahlins, 1985, 1995; Obeyesekere, 1992).

Later, a man by the name of Kamehameha, who was a nephew of the Hawaiian chief, gained a considerable reputation as a fearless warrior in the Maui campaign. When the chief of Hawaii died, Kamehameha became his successor. Because the island of Hawaii offered good anchorage and became a vital strategic point of contact with Europeans, Kamehameha had an advantage over any other rivals in trading with European ships. The Hawaiians began to trade their products such as sandalwood with Europeans, and in exchange, Kamehameha received guns and light cannon. Eventually, he was able to employ European help in conquering most of the other islands of Hawaii and transformed the Hawaiian chiefdoms into a unified, centralized military kingdom or state.

Kamehameha died in 1819 and was succeeded by his son Liholiho, later known as Kamehameha II. After Western contact, Hawaii continued to be heavily influenced by Western culture. A number of traditional taboos of the Hawaiian culture were being violated on a regular basis. Some of the Hawaiian women became involved in sexual and romantic relationships with Westerners and openly ate with men, violating traditional taboos (Ortner, 1996). Some of the commoners began to trade openly with Europeans, which also violated traditional norms and taboos, causing tension between the rulers and commoners. Seeing practical advantages for trade with the Europeans and rule over their kingdom, in 1819 Liholiho, the new ruler, and other members of the royal family began to deliberately flout the most sacred traditional taboos of their ancient religion. The royal family began to systematically dismantle the aboriginal religious traditions and practices, which represented a revolutionary transformation in religious thought and culture for Hawaiian society. This transformation of religion was accomplished prior to the coming of Christian missionaries to Hawaii. This religious revolution was resisted by some of the more conservative people of Hawaii, and Liholiho had to arm his forces to defeat the more conservative faction within the kingdom. This Hawaiian revolution appeared to be an intentional strategy on the part of the ruling family to enhance their political control over the military kingdom.

The sandalwood trade declined in the 1830s and was replaced by the whaling industry, which began to dominate commerce in Hawaii. Since the island was located in the vicinity of a major whaling area of the Pacific, New England whalers used Hawaii as an important base for provisioning and relaxation. However, during the 1830s, various companies began to develop sugar plantations in Hawaii, which eventually became successful, resulting in the influx of more Europeans, including various Christian missionaries from the United States. Many of the missionaries were themselves sugar planters or were connected with sugar planters. Private property was introduced, and land was commodified for sale. As the sugar plantations were developed, substantial native Hawaiian land was lost to the planters. Additionally, the native Hawaiians were subjected to devastating epidemics introduced by the Westerners; whooping cough, measles, influenza, and other diseases led to rapid depopulation among the native peoples. As Hawaii became increasingly incorporated into the U.S. political economy during the nineteenth and twentieth centuries, the native population declined to a small minority of about forty thousand people. This depopulation resulted in a labor shortage for the sugar planters, who began to import labor from the Philippines, Japan, and China. In 1893, the United States, backed by American Marines, who represented the families of the missionaries and plantation owners such as Sanford Dole (founder of Dole pineapples), overthrew the Hawaiian monarchy. Five years later Hawaii was annexed as a colony of the United States.

Following U.S. colonization, the Hawaiian islands were dominated by U.S. political and economic interests, and the native Hawaiian population became a marginal group in their own islands. Eventually, through more contact with Western societies, the Pacific islands such as Hawaii and Tahiti experienced depopulation, deculturation, forced labor, and increased dependency on the global economy. The American and European settlers imported labor from Asia, introduced the system of private property, abolished the traditional patterns of authority, and incorporated the islands into colonial empires. As these islands were integrated into colonial systems, the people were forced to adjust to the conditions of the global economy.

Through missionary schooling and activities, the native Hawaiian people were forbidden to speak their native language or practice any of their traditional religious or cultural activities, which were deemed to be barbaric and uncivilized. These policies led to societal and cultural disintegration for the native population. Combined with the growing Asian population and new settlers from North America who were rapidly developing the sugar economy, and the expansion of mass tourism to Hawaii from the mainland United States, the small modern Hawaiian population began to lose not only its native lands but also its cultural and ethnic identity (Friedman, 1992).

Forms of Resistance in Native Societies

As is evident from the preceding discussion, many nonstate societies resisted becoming incorporated into industrial states and colonial empires and engaged in resistance movements, also known as revitalization movements. A **revitalization movement** is an attempt to reestablish the traditional cultural values and beliefs of a group faced with dramatic changes. In some cases, revitalization movements take the form of violent military or political resistance. Generally, however, prestate peoples have lacked the technological capabilities to sustain armed resistance against more powerful societies. In most cases, therefore, these movements are nonviolent and have a strong religious element.

Revitalization among Native Americans

Native American societies developed a number of revitalization movements. One type of movement was associated with a particular prophet who was able to mobilize the population both politically and spiritually. In the Pueblo groups of the southwest, a prophet leader known as Popé organized a rebellion against the Spanish rulers in 1680. The Pueblo tribes attacked the Spanish, killed the Catholic priests in the missions, and attempted to reinstitute Pueblo traditions. Twenty years later, Spanish troops based in Mexico defeated this movement and reasserted their authority over the region.

Other Native American prophets, such as Handsome Lake, Pontiac, Tecumseh, and Chief Joseph, combined traditional religious values with military activities to resist European and American expansion into their territories. Eventually the U.S. military defeated all of these leaders.

The Ghost Dance One of the best-known revitalization movements was the Ghost Dance movement of the late 1800s. The Ghost Dance spread through the region of Nevada and California, across the Rocky Mountains to Plains groups such as the Cheyenne, Arapaho, and Sioux. The movement became associated with the prophet Wovoka, a Paiute who was believed to have received spiritual visions of the future during an eclipse of the sun. Wovoka taught that if the Native American people did the Ghost Dance, a hypnotic dance with spiritual meanings, the whites would disappear, and a train would come from the east with the ghosts of recently deceased Native Americans, signaling the restoration of Native American autonomy and traditions. Wovoka stressed nonviolent resistance and nonaccommodation to white domination (Kehoe, 1989).

Among the groups influenced by the Ghost Dance were the Lakota Sioux, who had been forced to reside on five reservations in South Dakota. In 1890, the Lakota Sioux leader, Kicking Bear, introduced a special shirt, called a "ghost shirt," that he claimed would protect the Sioux from the bullets of the white soldiers. The wearing of the ghost shirts precipitated conflicts between the U.S. military and the Sioux, culminating in a massacre of almost two hundred Sioux at Wounded Knee, South Dakota, on December 29, 1890. Following that confrontation, Sioux leaders such as Kicking Bear surrendered to the U.S. military.

Among the most common refrains of the Ghost Dance songs were:

My children,/When at first I liked the whites,/I gave them fruits,/I gave them fruits. (Southern Arapaho)
The father will descend/The earth will tremble/ Everybody will arise,/Stretch out your hands. (Kiowa)
We shall live again./We shall live again. (Apache)
(Rothenberg, 1985:109–10)

These Ghost Dance songs and dances are heard among Native Americans up to the present. For example, in February 1973, Wounded Knee once again became the site for a violent confrontation between the Plains Indians and the U.S. military forces. Led by the Lakota Indians, Russel Means, and spiritual leader Leonard Crow Dog, the Pine Ridge Indian reservation at Wounded Knee was taken over by the organization known as AIM, the American Indian Movement. AIM accused the tribal government leaders of political and economic corruption, and demanded justice and civil rights for all Native Americans. Leonard Crow Dog led a Ghost Dance ritual during the seventy-day occupation to create solidarity and spiritual renewal among the Sioux at Wounded Knee. In addition, the Sun Dance ritual was also conducted at Pine Ridge in 1973. Fire fights between AIM and the FBI and U.S. forces were common throughout the longest siege in American history since the Civil War. The events of 1973 at Wounded Knee represented the frustration and resentment of many Native Americans regarding their conditions after a century of subordination by the U.S. government. The Ghost Dance led by Leonard Crow Dog symbolized the spiritual resurgence and religious renewal of contemporary Native Americans on the Plains.

The Peyote Cult Another form of revitalization movement developed among Native Americans on one Oklahoma reservation in the 1880s. It too was a nonviolent form of resistance, based on a combination of Christian and Native American religious beliefs. The movement is referred to as the *peyote cult*. Peyote, the scientific name of which is *Lophophora*

Big Foot's frozen body after the Battle of Wounded Knee in 1890.

williamsii, is a mild hallucinogenic drug contained in the bud of a cactus, which is either chewed or drunk as tea. It is a nonaddictive drug. Traditionally, for thousands of years peyote had been used in some Native American rituals for inducing spiritual visions, especially in the southwest desert areas around the Rio Grande in both Mexico and North America. A number of Navajo Indians in the southwest became involved in the ritual use of peyote (Aberle, 1966). During their incarceration on the Oklahoma reservation, some of the Comanche, Kiowa, and other Plains Indians began to combine biblical teachings with the peyote ritual (Steinmetz, 1980). The ritual took place in a tepee, where the participants surrounded a fire and low altar and took peyote as a form of communal sacrament to partake of the "Holy Spirit." Eventually, the peyote cult grew in membership and was legalized on the Oklahoma reservation as the Native American Church in 1914. It has spread throughout at least fifty other Native American tribes, and approximately 250,000 Indians are associated with the NAC.

Melanesia and New Guinea: The Cargo Cults

As various Europeans colonized the islands of Melanesia, the native peoples' lives were forever transformed. The Dutch, French, British, and Germans claimed different areas as colonies. The Dutch, from their colonial base in Indonesia, took over the western half of New Guinea. It is now known as Irian Jaya and is a province of the country of Indonesia. In the 1880s, German settlers occupied the northeastern part of New Guinea. In the 1890s, gold was discovered in New Guinea, and many prospectors from Australia and other places began to explore the region. At the beginning of World War I in 1914, the Australians conquered the German areas. During World War II, Japanese, Australian, and U.S. troops fought bitter battles in New Guinea. After the war, Australia resumed administrative control over the eastern half of the island until 1975, when Papua New Guinea was granted political independence. Today, the country of Papua New Guinea (PNG) occupies the eastern half of the island of New Guinea and has about 4 million people.

The colonization of Melanesia and Papua New Guinea was both a dramatic and traumatic experience for the native peoples as they faced new systems of economics with the introduction of cash wages, indentured labor, plantations, taxation, new forms of political control, and the unfathomable technologies and apparently fabulous riches of the Europeans. Prospectors, traders, and soldiers during the world wars created a highly unstable and unpredictable environment for Melanesian natives. One of the reactions to this rapid change took a religious and spiritual form. These Melanesian religious responses to Western impact were often loosely labeled as revitalization movements and were called **cargo cults,** which was a form of millenarian religious movement. Many native peoples referred to the European or Australian goods that were loaded off ships or aircraft as *kago,* translated by anthropologists as "cargo."

Beginning in the nineteenth century and continuing up to the present, these millenarian cult movements spread throughout many areas of Melanesia. Generally, in New Guinea the coastal or seaboard peoples were contacted first by Europeans, and by the end of the nineteenth century, they were subjected to intensive pressures from the outside world. The highland peoples were contacted much later and were not fully penetrated by the Europeans and Australians until after the 1930s. The native peoples became aware of a dazzling array of goods, such as steel axes, matches, medicines, soft drinks, umbrellas, and eventually jet planes and helicopters. Because these native peoples had no exposure to industrial production, they did not see how these Western goods were manufactured. Many, therefore, believed that these goods were generated through spiritual forces, which delivered cargo to humans through spiritual means. Many of the tribal groups of this region attempted to discover the identity of the cargo spirits and the magical-ritual techniques used by Westerners to induce the spirits to deliver the particular commodities.

One New Guinean man who led a millenarian cult movement is known as Yali. Yali had lived in the coastal area of New Guinea, and in the 1950s the Australians recognized him as an important future leader of his people. He had been a World War II war hero fighting with the Allies against the Japanese. The Australians took Yali to Australia to show him how the industrial goods were produced. Nevertheless, Yali maintained the belief that there must be a supernatural cause or divine intervention for the ability of Westerners to be able to produce cargo. He originated a millenarian cult movement known as Wok bilong Yali (Lawrence, 1964) and began to preach in hundreds of villages throughout New Guinea about the need to develop spiritual techniques to duplicate the white man's delivery of cargo. Over the years of this movement, Yali's teaching ranged from recommending close imitation of the Europeans to opposing white culture and returning to traditional rituals to help deliver the cargo. Although Yali openly rejected the millenarian cult movements' beliefs, after his death in 1973 many of his followers began to teach that Yali was a messiah equivalent to the white man's Jesus. In their religious literature they propagated these ideas of messiahship by using Yali's sayings to help develop a religious movement that was an alternative to Christianity.

However, some of the millenarian cult movements combined traditional rituals with Christian beliefs in the hope of receiving the material benefits they associated with the white settlers. One movement, described by Paul Roscoe (1993), developed among the Yangoru Boiken of Papua New Guinea. It merged some of the millennial teachings of Canadian missionaries from the Switzerland-based New Apostolic Church (NAC). Roscoe describes how those in the movement believed that on Sunday, February 15, 1981, Yaliwan, a leading spiritual and political leader, was going to be crucified, ushering in the millennium. The villagers believed that the earth would rumble, hurricanes would arrive, the mountains would flash with lightning and thunder, and a dense fog would cover the earth. Afterwards, Yaliwan would be resurrected as the native counterpart of Jesus, and the two Jesuses would judge the living and the dead. They believed that the whites and native members of the NAC would usher in a new "Kingdom of Rest," described as an earthly utopian paradise with an abundance of material goods and peaceful harmony between native peoples and whites. The millennial teachings of the NAC were interpreted and integrated with traditional Yangoru beliefs of spirits of the dead and other magical practices. Some of the traditional aboriginal beliefs had millenarian aspects, promising the Yangoru economic prosperity and political autonomy. Therefore the NAC missionary teachings based on millenarian views were easily integrated with the traditional beliefs of the

Yangoru. Though the crucifixion did not take place, millenarian movements continue to have some influence on religious and political affairs in Papua New Guinea.

Various anthropologists have attempted to explain the development of the millenarian cult movements of Melanesia. One early explanation by anthropologist Peter Worsley (1957) viewed these millenarian cults as rational attempts at explaining unknown processes that appeared chaotic to the natives. The myths and religious beliefs of the cults also helped mobilize political resistance against colonialism. The cults provided an organizational basis for political action for the various Melanesian tribes. Groups who spoke different languages and maintained separate cultures joined the same religious cult, which enabled them to form political organizations to challenge European and Australian colonial rule. Other explanations rely on more spiritually based phenomena emphasizing how the cargo cults represent the resurgence of aboriginal religious thought, which is more creative and authentic than that of the newer missionary religions that came to Melanesia.

Today most anthropologists recognize that these millenarian cult phenomena are extremely varied. As they learn more about cult movements in different regions of Melanesia, they discover that some have millenarian aspects while others do not. Some integrate aboriginal beliefs and practices with the teachings of Christianity, a form of syncretism, while others feature a revival of the aboriginal elements and a rejection of the Christian teachings. A few of the movements have developed into vital political movements and even violent rebellions, whereas others tend to have a purely spiritual influence. Anthropologists agree that the analysis of these cults is a fruitful area of investigation, and much more needs to be documented through interviews, historical examination, and intensive ethnographic research.

A Hawaiian Religious Renaissance

As U.S. corporate capitalism and tourism became the dominant form of economy in Hawaii, every aspect of the traditional Hawaiian culture was affected. At present, the tourist industry generates close to 40 percent of Hawaii's income. Tourists crowd the hotels, restaurants, streets, highways, beaches, golf courses, and parks throughout Hawaii. The advertising industry attempts to promote the image of Hawaii as a romantic and exotic paradise setting where tourists can enjoy the traditional dancing, music, and culture of "primitive" peoples. Ads show skimpily clad women and men dancing before fires on near-deserted beaches. The tourist industry is trying to preserve the traditional culture of Hawaii because it is "good for business."

However, native Hawaiians have begun to resist the marketing of their culture. Beginning in the 1970s, with a growing awareness of their marginal status in the U.S. political economy and more familiarity with the civil rights movement in the mainland United States led by various minorities, Hawaiians launched a movement known as the *Hawaiian Renaissance*. The Hawaiian Renaissance manifested itself as a resurgence of interest in aboriginal Hawaiian culture, including the traditional language and religious beliefs. The movement is fundamentally anti-tourist. Many contemporary native Hawaiians who are part of the new movement understand that their traditional culture has been mass-marketed and mass-consumed. They feel that their traditional culture has been commercialized, and they resent the tourist industry for selling the Hawaiian tradition.

Some of the spiritual elements of the native religious beliefs have been reintroduced and revitalized in the context of the Hawaiian Renaissance movement. For example, a number of native Hawaiians have become involved in environmental activism. In doing so, they draw on traditional religious beliefs. They are attempting to prohibit the destruction of the rain forests and other natural settings by developers. The native peoples emphasize a spiritual renewal and refer to traditional Hawaiian gods and goddesses that are associated with the natural areas in order to protect these areas from destructive tourist and commercial forces. In some areas, the native Hawaiians are restoring some of the ancient temples, or *heiaus*. Native Hawaiians can be seen making offerings to the god Pele at the rim of Halemaumau Crater in the Hawaii Volcanoes National Park. Some aboriginal young people complain about their parents' conversion to Christianity and the negative views expressed by Westerners about their traditional culture and religion. However, most important, the revitalization of their religious culture is part of an overall attempt to preserve their heritage and reclaim their cultural identity and selfhood. As these native peoples of Hawaii were subjected to overwhelming and traumatic cultural change, they found that they were marginalized in their own land. After losing their land, their autonomy, and their culture, these native Hawaiians have been involved in reconstructing and reinvigorating some of their aboriginal spiritual beliefs as a means of repossessing their cultural identity (Friedman, 1995).

Many Native Hawaiians are beginning to emphasize their traditional ethnic heritage. In 1993, a march was held to commemorate the 100th anniversary of the Native Hawaiian monarchy.

APPLYING ANTHROPOLOGY

MARKETING PRODUCTS OF THE RAIN FOREST

Anthropologists use their cultural knowledge of different societies to solve some of the problems faced by indigenous peoples. One anthropologist actively engaged in trying to develop techniques to help native peoples cope with the changes induced by globalization is Jason Clay. Clay is director of research at Cultural Survival, the major anthropological organization committed to aiding indigenous peoples in their adaptation to the processes of globalization.

Clay has recently developed a project to expand the market for products from tropical rain forests. Under his leadership, Cultural Survival has established a nonprofit trading company, Cultural Survival Imports. The major objective of this project is to use the world market to save the rain forest. Destroying the forests leads to global problems such as the greenhouse effect and the disruption of indigenous societies. Cultural Survival Imports has funded management projects for indigenous peoples who produce goods for the world market. These goods include nuts, roots, fruits, pigments, oils, and fragrances that can be regularly harvested without harming the rain forest.

One of the major clients of Cultural Survival Imports is Ben & Jerry's Homemade, an American ice cream company. In 1990, Ben & Jerry's ordered 200,000 pounds of Brazil nuts and 100,000 pounds of cashews. It set up a separate company, Community Products, to manufacture a nut brittle for Ben & Jerry's and other distributors to use in ice cream, cookies, and candy. The ice cream, called "Rainforest Crunch," is available in Ben & Jerry's stores. The company also markets rain forest sherbets and

A Lost Opportunity?

As Brian Fagan noted in his book *Clash of Cultures* (1984b), which surveys the disappearance of many nonstate societies, the same confrontations between incompatible cultural systems were played out in many parts of the world during the late nineteenth century and continue to this day in the Amazon rain forests and other remote areas. Some government officials and businesspeople in industrial countries view the drastic modifications that took place and are taking place among prestate societies as necessary for the achievement of progress. This view is, of course, a continuation of the nineteenth-century unilineal view of cultural evolution, which overestimates the beneficial aspects of industrial societies. Depopulation, deculturation, fragmentation of the social community, increasingly destructive warfare, unemployment, and increases in crime, alcoholism, and degradation of the environment are only some of the consequences of this so-called "progress." As Fagan (1984b:278) emphasized:

> *Progress has brought many things: penicillin, the tractor, the airplane, the refrigerator, radio, and television. It has also brought the gun, nuclear weapons, toxic chemicals, traffic deaths, and environmental pollution, to say nothing of powerful nationalisms and other political passions that pit human being against human being, society against society. Many of these innovations are even more destructive to non-Western societies than the land grabbing and forced conversion of a century and a half ago.*

As was discussed in previous chapters, prestate societies were not idyllic, moral communities in which people lived in perfect harmony with one another and their environment. Warfare, sexism, infanticide, slavery, stratification, and other harmful practices existed in many of these societies.

fruit ice creams, rotating flavors every four to six weeks to coincide with the seasons of the rain forest.

Another client of Cultural Survival Imports is the Body Shops, a cosmetic firm based in England. The company is interested in marketing oils, flours, nuts, fibers, fruits, and fragrances for developing organic cosmetic products. For example, in 1990, the company ordered 80 tons of copaiba oil, a product to be used for shampoos, face creams, lotions, soaps, and massage creams.

These orders for sustainable commodities have immediate benefits for the peoples of the rain forest. For example, in 1989, the nut collectors of Brazil received only 3 to 4 cents per pound for nuts that sold for more than $1.50 a pound wholesale in New York City. Cultural Survival is using grants from international aid groups to help gatherers of forest products to form marketing and processing cooperatives. Through strengthening this marketing system, Cultural Survival can guarantee producers higher, more stable prices for these commodities.

Jason Clay has taken 350 product samples from Brazil to exhibit to about forty companies in the United States and Europe. He predicts that American and European consumers will soon be using such products from the rain forest in sherbets, yogurts, oils, shampoos, and perfumes. In addition, Clay wants to expand the markets in the countries where these rain forests are located. Many people in cities such as São Paulo and Rio de Janeiro in Brazil have never eaten the most common fruits of the Amazon. Increased marketing in these nations will contribute to the preservation of the rain forests and also lead to improvements for the native populations of these areas, which will ultimately benefit all of humanity.

Nonstate societies are not inherently good, and industrial societies are not inherently evil. Both types of societies have advantages and disadvantages, strengths and weaknesses. There are benefits associated with industrial societies, such as hospitals, better sanitation, and consumer goods, that bring comfort and enjoyment, but nonstate societies also have benefits to offer to industrial societies.

Anthropological research has begun to alert the modern industrial world to the negative implications of the rapid disappearance of first nation peoples—specifically, the loss of extensive practical knowledge that exists in these populations. In the nineteenth-century view (and sometimes even in twenty-first-century discourse), nonstate societies were described as backward, ignorant, and nonscientific. Ethnological research, however, demonstrates that these peoples have developed a collective wisdom that has contributed practical benefits for all of humankind.

Native American Knowledge

In a book titled *Indian Givers,* anthropologist Jack Weatherford (1988) summarized the basic knowledge, labor, and experience of Native American peoples that have contributed to humankind's collective wisdom. Native Americans introduced three hundred food crops to the world, including potatoes and corn. Their experiments with horticultural diversity generated knowledge regarding the survival of crops in different types of environments. They recognized that planting a diversity of seeds would protect the seeds from pests and diseases. Only recently have farmers in the industrialized world begun to discover the ecological lessons developed by Native Americans.

The medical knowledge of Native Americans, which is based on experience with various plants and trees, has benefited people throughout the world. Weatherford uses the example of quinine, derived from the bark of the South American cinchona tree, which is used to treat malaria. Ipecac was made from the roots of an Amazonian tree as a cure for amoebic dysentery. Native Americans treated scurvy with massive doses of vitamin C, using a tonic made from the bark and needles of an evergreen tree. They also developed treatments for goiter, intestinal worms, headaches (with a medication similar to aspirin), and skin problems.

The lesson from Weatherford's book is that without the contributions of Native American societies, humankind may not have acquired this knowledge for years. As globalization brings about the disappearance of nonstate societies, humanity risks losing a great deal of knowledge. For example, as the Amazon rain forests are invaded and destroyed by governments and multinational interests, not only do we lose hundreds of species of plants and animals, but we also lose the indigenous societies with their incalculable knowledge of those species. Thus, it is in humanity's best interests to abandon the view that deculturation, subjugation, and—sometimes—the extinction of nonstate societies represent a form of progress.

The most difficult issue that faces anthropologists, government officials, and aboriginal peoples is how best to fit traditional patterns in with the modern, industrial world. The fact that these nonstate societies were, and are, almost powerless to resist the pressures from global economic and political forces creates enormous problems. Multinational corporations, national governments, missionaries, prospectors, and other powerful groups and institutions place these indigenous societies in vulnerable circumstances. How will nonstate societies withstand these pressures and continue to contribute to humankind?

Preserving Indigenous Societies

Most anthropologists argue that indigenous peoples should be able to make free and informed choices regarding their destiny, instead of being coerced into assimilating (Hitchcock, 1988; Bodley, 1990). As previously discussed, many nonstate societies have tried to resist domination by outside powers but generally lacked the power to do so successfully. In some cases, anthropologists assisted these peoples in their struggles. Anthropologists such as Napoleon Chagnon have set up foundations to collect money to aid indigenous peoples in their struggles against governments and economic interests who demand their territory. At Harvard University, anthropologists under the guidance of David Maybury-Lewis formed an organization known as Cultural Survival that seeks to aid nonstate societies in their confrontations with industrial and global pressures. Robert Hitchcock, a student of Richard Lee, has become an internationally known advocate of the rights of indigenous peoples such as the Ju/'hoansi.

Since the 1970s, many indigenous peoples themselves have become active in preserving their way of life. At a 1975 assembly on Nootka tribal lands on Vancouver Island, the World Council of Indigenous Peoples was founded. Fifty-two delegates representing indigenous peoples from nineteen countries established this council, which has become a nongovernmental organization of the United Nations (Fagan, 1984b). The council endorsed the right of indigenous peoples to maintain their traditional economic and cultural structures. It emphasized that native populations have a special relationship to their languages and should not be forced to abandon them. It further stressed that land and natural resources should not be taken from native populations. Perhaps this new political awareness and activism will enable these cultures to exercise greater control over their future economic, political, and cultural adjustments in the modern world.

SUMMARY

Social scientists have developed three basic models for understanding the process of globalization. The first, known as modernization theory, maintains that traditionalism retards industrial expansion and social change in underdeveloped societies. Modernization theorists propose education and change in cultural values as prerequisites for economic and social development. Modernization theorists developed the terms First, Second, and Third Worlds.

The second perspective, dependency theory, developed as a critique of modernization. Dependency theorists view global change as the consequence of relationships between the industrial capitalist societies and underdeveloped precapitalist societies. They focus on the spread of the capitalist world economy and the political domination of the poor underdeveloped societies by wealthy nations.

The third approach is world-systems theory, which divides the world into core, peripheral, and semiperipheral nations, based on economic criteria. The world-systems approach has helped social scientists to understand worldwide changes based on the interconnections among different societies. Anthropologists evaluate these different models by collecting empirical data through ethnological studies.

Globalization has directly affected nonstate societies, or indigenous peoples. Ever since industrialist expansion began, foragers, tribes, and chiefdoms have undergone rapid changes. Among the negative consequences of globally induced change are depopulation, deculturation, the disintegration of social communities, and, in some cases, genocide.

Many nonstate peoples developed forms of resistance known as revitalization movements as they confronted the industrialized nations. Movements such as the Ghost Dance, the peyote cult, and the various cargo cults represented attempts at reinstituting traditional cultural patterns.

Anthropologists have warned that the disappearance of native societies leads to the loss of beneficial knowledge. Thus, it is in the interest of all of humanity to see that these populations do not become extinct. Recently, anthropologists have focused their activities on trying to give native peoples a choice in preserving their cultural heritage, land, and resources. Indigenous peoples are becoming politically aware and active in demanding their autonomy and human rights.

QUESTIONS TO THINK ABOUT

1. Describe the five stages by which a traditional society undergoes modernization to reach a level of high economic growth.

2. As the head of state of an underdeveloped nation, what are the public policies that you would implement if you wished to modernize your society?

3. Given a choice between modernization theory and dependency theory, which model do you prefer to explain the existence of vast inequities between industrialized capitalist societies and the precapitalist societies? What are the strengths of the model you prefer? What are its weaknesses?

4. What are the principal elements of Immanuel Wallerstein's world-systems theory? How has the theory been used in anthropology?

5. Describe some of the changes that have occurred in the Ju/'hoansi society as a result of global industrialization. What are some of the ways that the negative effects of industrialization can be reversed?

6. Discuss the principal factors that result in deculturation. What are some of the risks that deculturation poses for a traditional society?

7. What governmental policies contributed to the decline of Native American populations in the United States?

8. What do you think ought to be the policies of governments toward native peoples? Why?

KEY TERMS

cargo cults
colonies

core societies
deculturation

dependency theory
ethnocide

First World
genocide
globalization
imperialism

modernization theory
peripheral societies
revitalization movement
Second World

semiperipheral societies
Third World
underdeveloped society
world-systems theory

INTERNET EXERCISES

1. Read an account of the Trail of Tears, titled "Samuel's Memory," at **http://cherokeehistory.com/samuel.html**. How does this story relate to the overall theme of the chapter? How does ethnocentrism allow for this behavior by the United States Army? What is the purpose of the Army? How does the Army function as a tool of the overall society?

2. Compare this chapter's view of globalization to that of the following website: **http://econ.worldbank.org/prr/subpage.php?sp=2477**. What are the similarities? What are the differences? How does the process of globalization build an inclusive world economy?

SUGGESTED READINGS

BODLEY, JOHN H. (Ed.). 1988. *Tribal Peoples and Development Issues: A Global Overview.* Mountain View, CA: Mayfield. A collection of essays dealing with human rights, development, health conditions, conservation, and policies affecting Fourth World peoples.

———. 1990. *Victims of Progress,* 3rd ed. Mountain View, CA: Mayfield. The most comprehensive treatment of the impact of globalization on Fourth World societies. Bodley details the plight of nonstate societies everywhere as they confront the industrialized world. He summarizes the different approaches taken by government officials and anthropologists in trying to aid indigenous peoples.

CHIROT, DANIEL. 1986. *Social Change in the Modern Era.* Orlando, FL: Harcourt Brace Jovanovich. A comprehensive account of the impact of the Western capitalist world economy; it draws on modernization, dependency, and world-systems approaches.

JOSEPHY, ALVIN M., JR. 1976. *The Patriot Chiefs: A Chronicle of American Indian Resistance.* New York: Penguin Books. A good historical account of different Native American resistance leaders, including Handsome Lake, Popé, Pontiac, Tecumseh, Crazy Horse, and Chief Joseph.

WEYLER, REX. 1982. *Blood of the Land: The Government and Corporate War against the American Indian Movement.* New York: Vintage Books. A detailed account of how Native American peoples are deprived of their rights to land and resources by the U.S. government and multinational corporations.

The organization Cultural Survival Inc., located at 11 Divinity Avenue, Cambridge, MA 02138, publishes newsletters and studies on first nation peoples.

21

Globalization in Latin America, Africa, and the Caribbean

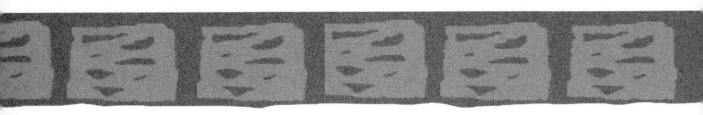

CHAPTER OUTLINE

CHAPTER QUESTIONS

- What were the early phases of Western colonialism like for Latin America, Africa, and the Caribbean?

- What were the demographic, economic, political, and religious changes associated with globalization in Latin America, Africa, and the Caribbean?

- Why did independence, nationalist, and revolutionary movements develop in Latin America, Africa, and the Caribbean?

- How are the Latin American, African, and Caribbean countries situated in the global economy today?

- What have anthropologists learned about the peasantry in Latin America, Africa, and the Caribbean countries?

- What are the characteristics of family and gender relationships in Latin America, Africa, and the Caribbean countries?

- How has urbanization influenced Latin America, Africa, and the Caribbean countries?

Most anthropologists have focused on non-Western countries for their ethnographic research. To understand how globalization processes have influenced local conditions and cultures, they have had to adopt a broad global perspective in their research. The non-Western countries of Latin America, the Caribbean, and Africa comprise a complex of diversified regions and cultures that cannot be characterized easily. The various countries in these regions are located in different types of environmental zones, ranging from highland mountain areas, to lowland river valleys, to small island regions, to complex urban centers (see Figure 21.1). Each country is made up of various ethnic groups in different proportions. As a result of globalization, all of these countries are at different stages of political and economic development.

In Chapter 20 we discussed various band, tribal, and chiefdom societies that exist in these different

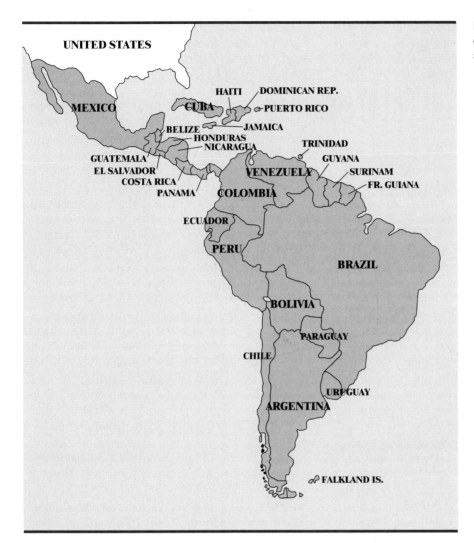

FIGURE 21.1 A map of contemporary Latin America and the Caribbean.

regions and how globalization has had an impact on their development. This chapter begins with an overview of the spread of globalization and colonialism in Latin America, Africa, and the Caribbean. We proceed with a discussion of some consequences of globalization processes on these regions. Finally, we discuss various ethnographic studies that have illuminated the effects of globalization on various institutions in these countries.

One of the points that we want to stress is that globalization is always a painful process for any society to experience. When Europe, the United States, and Japan went through industrialization, as discussed in Chapter 19, it brought dislocation and

disruption of families through rapid urbanization and other changes. People were torn away from their traditional communities of support, and ethnic and religious communities no longer provided the source of security they once did. Extensive migration, urban congestion, increases in deviance and crime, political corruption, population growth, pollution, and other social problems accompanied industrialization in these so-called First World countries.

But the countries that we will be discussing in this chapter and the next are facing these globalization processes in a much different way from the First World countries. The industrialized countries, such as Europe or the United States, had centuries to adjust to these processes, whereas other areas of the world have been experiencing aspects of globalization for a short period of time. Though these processes began during the time of colonization for most of these countries, it is only within the past few decades that globalization has penetrated deeply into the fabric of these societies.

Globalization and Colonialism

Latin America

Following Columbus's explorations in the 1400s, Spanish and Portuguese *conquistadores* led expeditions to the Americas. Recall that this was the period of mercantilism (see Chapters 19 and 20), when European states were competing to accumulate wealth to build their national treasuries. The Portuguese and Spanish were the first Europeans to engage in this mercantilist competition. Columbus believed that he had reached islands off Asia, and the Spanish and Portuguese were anxious to acquire access to this new trade route, in part to cut off the Muslim monopoly of trade in the Mediterranean and Asia. Thus, the primary objectives of the *conquistadores* were to find wealth and conquer the Americas.

The indigenous societies of Latin America consisted of three major types of sociocultural systems: small-scale hunting-and-gathering bands; horticulturalist tribes, who lived in permanent or semipermanent villages and supplemented their diet by hunting, fishing, and gathering; and chiefdoms and agricultural empires, such as the Aztec and Inca, with great achievements in technology, architecture, economic organization, and statecraft.

In 1494, the Spanish and Portuguese governments agreed to the Treaty of Tordesillas, which divided the world into two major mercantilist spheres of influence. As a result, in the Americas the Portuguese took control of what is now Brazil, and the Spanish gained access to most of the remainder of Latin America.

Cortés and the Aztec Empire   The first major collision between the Spanish and the indigenous peoples occurred in 1519, when Hernando Cortés confronted the Aztec Empire in Mexico. After landing at Veracruz, Cortés encouraged many native groups who had been conquered and subjugated by the Aztecs to revolt against the Aztecs and their ruler, Montezuma. Besieged by these rebellious peoples and the superior weaponry of the Spaniards—especially guns and cannon—the Aztec state quickly crumbled. In 1521, Cortés and his Native American allies captured Tenochtitlan, establishing Spanish domination over the entire empire.

The Spanish then went on to conquer Mesoamerica, including Mexico, Honduras, and Guatemala, and areas in southeastern and southwestern North America. Similar conquests occurred in various regions of South America, such as Francisco Pizarro's conquest of the Incas. The Spanish ransacked these civilizations, taking the gold, silver, precious stones, and other valuables these people had accumulated. After this first phase of conquest and occupation, the Spanish began to exploit this wealth for the benefit of their home country. They developed systems of mining, commercial agriculture, livestock raising, and trading. These new forms of economic organization drastically transformed the sociocultural systems of the Americas.

The region of Brazil in South America contained no productive agricultural states such as those of the Aztecs or Incas, and the native population consisted of only about 1 million people. Therefore, instead of searching for wealth in gold, silver, and other precious goods, the Portuguese turned immediately to developing commercial agriculture and introduced sugar plantations. The plantation system initially relied on local labor, but because there were few natives in this area, the Portuguese also imported African slaves.

Africa

Mercantilist expansion into Africa began with the Portuguese, who came seeking gold; their explorers reached the West African coast in the second half of the fifteenth century. Although they did not find in Africa the vast amounts of gold that the Americas had yielded, they discovered another source of wealth: slaves.

Slave Trade   In earlier chapters, we noted that slavery was an accepted institution in some chiefdoms and agricultural states around the world. Slavery existed throughout much of the ancient agricultural world, including Egypt, Greece, Rome, the Middle East, and parts of Africa. Until the twentieth century, various Middle Eastern empires maintained an extensive slave trade based on African labor (Hourani, 1991). In Africa, agricultural states such as the Asante kingdom kept war captives and criminals as slaves. This slavery, however, was much different from that of later Western societies (Davidson, 1961; Goody, 1980). In Chapter 18 we discussed the "open" forms of slavery associated with societies with abundant land and low populations. In Africa, this open system included slaves who were attached to extended families and became part of the domestic social unit. They could own property and marry, and they were protected from mutilation and murder by formalized norms or legal institutions.

The Portuguese initiated the major European slave trade around 1440. They took slaves from coastal areas of West Africa to Portugal and to some islands in the Mediterranean. African slaves became the major source of labor for the expanding plantation systems in North and South America. Portugal, Holland, and, by the 1700s, England and France became the dominant slave-trading nations.

Unlike the "open" forms of slavery found in Africa, these Western countries classified slaves as property, with no personal rights, who could never be incorporated into the owner's domestic family or social system. These countries traded goods and weapons with certain African groups, who, in turn, supplied the Europeans with slaves. Sometimes African leaders simply relied on the local institutions of slavery to sell their own slaves to the Europeans. In many cases, however, coastal Africans raided inland villages for slaves. These practices had emerged in the earlier slave trade with the Islamic empires to the north.

Millions of slaves were taken from Africa and transported to Latin America and the Caribbean. The Atlantic slave trade declined in the early nineteenth century, when antislavery movements in Britain and France led to the prohibition of slave trading. British ships patrolled the coasts of Africa to capture slave traders, although many ships eluded this blockade. Slave trade to the United States ended in 1808, but the complete abolition of the slave trade was not possible until countries such as Brazil and the United States abandoned their plantation systems. The United States made slavery illegal in 1865, and Brazil did so in 1888 (Stavrianos, 1995). The devastating effects of the slave trade, however, continue to plague Africa to the present.

Colonization in Africa Europeans generally did not venture into the interior of Africa for colonization during the mercantilist phase of 1500 and 1600 A.D. The threat of malaria and military resistance kept them in the coastal regions. During the late nineteenth century, however, European nations began to compete vigorously for African territories. To serve their needs for raw materials and overseas markets, the British, French, Dutch, Belgians, and Germans partitioned different areas of Africa into colonies, as reflected in the boundaries of present-day countries.

In West Africa, the difficult climate and the presence of diseases such as malaria discouraged large-scale European settlement. The British, French, and Germans, however, established commercial enterprises to control the production and exportation of products such as palm oil (used in soap making) and cocoa (Wolf [1982] 1997).

In central Africa, King Leopold of Belgium incorporated the 900,000 acres of the Congo as a private preserve. He controlled the basic economic assets of the region through stock ownership in companies that were allowed to develop the rubber and ivory trade. In doing so, the king used brutal methods of forced labor that caused the population to decline by one-half (from 20 million to 10 million) during his reign, from 1885 to 1908 (Stavrianos, 1995).

In East Africa during the 1880s, the Germans and the British competed for various territories to develop plantations and other enterprises. This rivalry eventually resulted in treaties that gave the British the colony of Kenya and the Germans a large territory known as Tanganyika. British and German settlers flocked to these countries and took possession of lands from the native peoples.

The colonization of southern Africa began in the late seventeenth century, when Dutch explorers built a refueling station for their ships at Cape Town. From that site, Dutch settlers, called first "Boers" and later "Afrikaners," penetrated into the region. The Boers displaced, and often enslaved, the native peoples, including foragers such as the Ju/'hoansi or San and tribal peoples such as the Hottentots. They eventually adopted a racially based, hierarchical system in which the Boers held the highest ranks, followed by the *coloreds* (people of mixed parentage), the Bantu-speaking agriculturalists, and people like the Ju/'hoansi and Hottentots. Each group was segregated from the others and treated differently. The Boers eventually decimated most of the Hottentots through genocidal policies.

As the Dutch were settling these lands, the British were also penetrating into southern Africa. They incorporated several kingdoms, which they transformed into native reservations under British control. Fearful of British expansion, the Boers migrated north into lands that had long been inhabited by the Bantu-speaking Zulus. This migration became known as the "Great Trek." Although the Zulus fought bitterly against this encroachment, they were defeated in 1838 by the superior military technology of the Boers.

As the Boers moved north, they established the republics of Natal, the Orange Free State, and the Transvaal. In the meantime, gold and diamonds had been discovered in these areas, leading to intense competition between the British and the Boers. In the Boer War of 1899–1902, the British defeated the Boers and annexed all of their republics. In 1910, the British established the Union of South Africa (see Figure 21.2).

FIGURE 21.2 A map of Sub-Saharan Africa, highlighting some of the peoples discussed in the chapter.

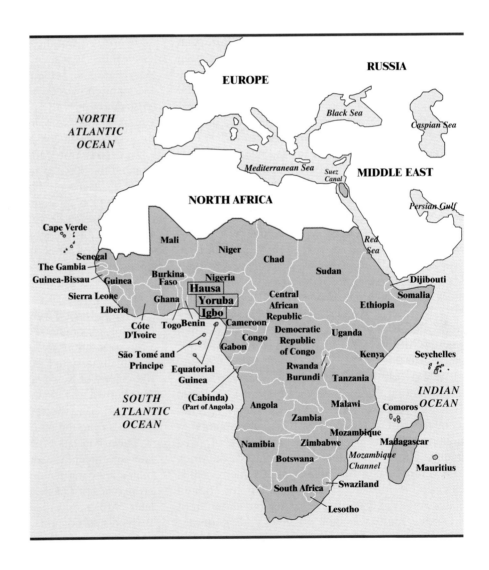

The Caribbean

The Caribbean islands consist of four distinct geographical regions: the first contains the Bahamas, nearest to the coast of North America; the second, called the Greater Antilles, consists of Cuba and Hispaniola (Haiti and the Dominican Republic), Jamaica, the Cayman Islands, Puerto Rico, and the Virgin Islands; the third, the Lesser Antilles, includes Antigua, Barbuda, Dominica, St. Lucia, St. Vincent, the Grenadines, Grenada, and St. Christopher-Nevis (St. Kitts); the fourth, off the coast of South America, includes Trinidad, Tobago, Barbados, Aruba, Curaçao, and Bonaire. Some of the islands, such as Cuba, Haiti, and Puerto Rico, came under Spanish rule by 1500. Others were divided up by other European powers, such as the British, French, and Dutch.

Unlike the mainland regions, these islands did not have large, complex agricultural states with accumulated treasures. Therefore, the colonial powers introduced commercialized agriculture, usually in the form of sugar plantations, an agricultural system that had been developing in the Mediterranean region. As these sugar plantations were developed, large numbers of African slaves were imported by the Europeans to labor on these plantations. When the African slave trade began to decline, the British replaced slave labor with East Indian workers on some of the islands. Thus, the islands of the Caribbean are an extremely diverse region with Hispanic, French, Dutch, African, and East Indian cultural influences.

An example of the strong traditional African influence is evident in Haiti, Jamaica, and other islands. For example, Carriacou, a small island located in the eastern Caribbean between Grenada and St. Vincent, provides an example of the retention and reformulation of African beliefs and practices in the context of New World slavery. Most residents of Carriacou are descendants of African slaves brought to the island in the seventeenth and eighteenth centuries, first by French and later by British planters. After emancipation of the slaves in the 1830s, most of the European planters left; the former slaves developed a relatively egalitarian society based on subsistence activities such as farming and fishing, supplemented by market activity and also by migration to places offering opportunities for wage labor. This relative isolation allowed Carriacou people to maintain their connections to their African past in ways not available to former slaves in other places. For example, Carriacouans continue to trace their descent from particular African ethnic groups, some of which are Igbo, Yoruba, Mandingo, Congo, and Kromanti (Asante). Along with this knowledge, talented musicians keep alive the traditional drumming patterns associated with each group, and these have been combined over the years with new songs in Creole French and Creole English.

The songs and drumming patterns are the central feature of the ritual known as the Big Drum or Nation Dance, which is held to celebrate special occasions such as the launching of a boat, a marriage, the placing of a permanent tombstone, or a bountiful harvest. A Big Drum ceremony may also be held to honor a request for food from the ancestors; such requests come to the living through dreams and are considered very important.

The Big Drum ceremony usually takes place at night in the yard of the ceremony's sponsor. An important feature of the ceremony, in addition to the drumming and singing, is food, which is prepared in sufficient quantity to be shared with all who attend the ceremony. Some of the food is set aside for the ancestors; this food, called the *saraka* or "parents plate," is placed on a table inside the house and watched over by an elder woman called a *gangan*. This woman has "special sight" and can tell when the ancestors have come and eaten their fill; the *saraka* is then distributed among the children at the ceremony.

The ceremony, including the drumming and the sharing of food, might be considered an example of egalitarian redistribution similar to that which takes place in some tribal societies, as it serves to reinforce the Carriacouan values of egalitarianism and sharing (Hill, 1977; McDaniel, 1998).

Consequences of Globalization and Colonialism

Demographic Change

The immediate impact of the West on Mesoamerica, South America, Africa, and the Caribbean was disastrous for local populations. In Mesoamerica, South America, and the Caribbean, the native population began to decline drastically. One of the major reasons for this decline was the introduction of diseases—smallpox, typhoid fever, measles, influenza, the mumps—to which the Indians had no resistance, because they had never been exposed to them before. In Brazil and the Caribbean, the importation of African slaves led to the introduction of diseases such as malaria and yellow fever. Although the numbers vary, archaeologists estimate that at least 25 million people lived in Mesoamerica when the Europeans arrived; by 1650, only 1.5 million remained (Wolf, 1997).

Rapid depopulation was also due to the stresses induced by the new forms of labor to which these peoples were subjected. Large-scale slave raiding decimated native populations. The rigorous forms of enforced labor—including slavery—in mining, plantations, and livestock raising created serious health problems and caused numerous deaths. In addition, the collapse of the indigenous patterns of intensive agriculture brought about famines and food shortages. All of these factors increased the social and biological stresses that aided the spread of disease in these populations (Wolf, 1997).

The demographic consequences of the slave trade in Africa were also immense. Historians estimate that as many as 40 million Africans were captured from the interior between 1440 and 1870 (Stavrianos, 1995). During this period, about 30 million Africans perished on their march from the inland regions or during the voyage to the New World. Approximately 12 million Africans were imported forcibly to the Americas. Many of them were in their prime reproductive years, which, in conjunction with the wars between the coastal and interior regions, may account for the slow growth of Africa's population during this period (Wolf, 1997).

In the long run, however, Western expansion and colonialism in non-Western countries brought unprecedented demographic growth to the populations of these agricultural states. For example, the population of Mexico tripled in the nineteenth century from 2.5 million to 9 million, and Cuba's population increased from 550,000 to 5.8 million in 1953. Apparently, as Europeans began to change the indigenous population from traditional subsistence peasant farming to the production of cash crops, fertility rates began to rise in the traditional

villages. There were labor shortages in the villages, and peasants responded by having larger extended families to try to maintain their subsistence peasant farming (Robbins, 1999). And, generally, fertility rates remain high in most of the countries of Latin America, Africa, and the Caribbean.

Eventually, new medical and sanitation practices introduced by modernization led to a tremendous reduction in death rates through the control of smallpox, plague, yellow fever, and malaria. Meanwhile, birth rates remained high. The combination of reduced death rates and high birth rates led to dramatic population increases. In Chapter 24 we discuss some of the global effects of these population trends.

Economic Change

The economic changes that occurred with globalization in Latin America, Africa, and the Caribbean countries wrought a dramatic transformation in these societies. In Latin America, the Spanish developed large-scale mining operations that used forced labor. In addition to gold, the Spanish discovered vast supplies of silver in Mexico and Bolivia. The American mines eventually became the major source of bullion accumulated by mercantile Spain. For example, of the 7 million pounds of silver extracted from these mines, the Spanish Crown collected 40 percent.

New patterns of economic organization in Latin America and the Caribbean were introduced after the Iberian (Portuguese and Spanish) conquest. In the Spanish areas, the Crown rewarded the *conquistadores* with the *encomienda,* or grants of Indian land, tribute, and labor, which, because it was based on forced labor, reduced the Indians to dependents.

Eventually, the *encomienda* system was superseded by the *hacienda* (in Brazil, *fazenda*), or large-scale plantation. Established during the colonial period, *haciendas* and *fazendas* remained the major economic institutions in Latin America until the mid-twentieth century. The owners, called *hacendados* or *fazendieros,* acquired status, wealth, and power by owning the land and subjugating the tenants, or *peons,* who were tied to the *haciendas* through indebtedness and lived in shacks. In certain respects, the *haciendas* and *fazendas* were similar to the feudalistic manors of European societies described in Chapter 18.

Although the *haciendas* and *fazendas* were self-sufficient economic units providing the essential resources for the owners and tenants, they were not efficient (Wolf, 1969, 1997). The *hacendados,* preoccupied with their social prestige and comfortable lifestyle, did not attempt to produce cash crops for the world market or use their land productively. This pattern of inefficient, localized production and marketing of the *haciendas* is still visible in much of Latin America.

After three centuries of Iberian rule, much of Latin America consisted of these inefficient *haciendas,* economically deprived Indian communities with limited land, and a native population that was undernourished, maltreated, overworked, and reduced to bondage. An enormous social gap developed between the Indian peons and a class of individuals who identified with Iberian political and economic interests.

In Africa during the first phase of colonialism, the different European powers attempted to make their colonies economically self-sufficient. African labor was recruited for work on the commercialized plantations and in the gold and diamond mines. Native workers received substandard wages and were forced to pay head taxes to the colonial regimes. Head taxes were assessed for each individual and had to be paid in cash. By requiring cash payments, the colonial governments forced villagers to abandon subsistence agriculture and become wage laborers. In eastern and southern Africa, many choice agricultural lands were taken from the native peoples and given to British and Dutch settlers. As the demand for exports from Africa began to increase in the world-market system, the colonial powers began to develop transportation and communication systems linking coastal cities with inland regions. The purpose of these systems was to secure supplies of natural resources and human labor.

A major consequence of these colonial processes was the complete disruption of the indigenous production and exchange systems. Africans were drawn into the wage economy. Monetary systems based on European coinage were introduced, displacing former systems of exchange. The price of African labor and goods came to be determined by the world market. Global economic conditions began to shape the sociocultural systems and strategies of native peoples throughout Africa.

Another consequence of Western colonialism was the integration of many agricultural village communities into wider regional and global economic patterns. Although the precolonial traditional villages were probably never entirely self-sufficient and were tied to regional and national trading networks through Western colonialism, the village peasantry was no longer isolated from cities, and the global market determined the prices for agricultural goods. The transformation of agricultural economies

An Indian peasant woman in Peru.

triggered dramatic changes in traditional peasant rural communities. Because few peasants had enough capital to own and manage land, much of the land fell into the hands of colonial settlers, large landowners, and money lenders. In many cases, these changes encouraged absentee landownership and temporary tenancy. Long-term care of the land by the peasantry was sacrificed for immediate profits. Land, labor, and capital were thus disconnected from the village kinship structures of reciprocity and redistribution, or what has been referred to as the *moral economy* (see Chapter 18). Peasants were incorporated into the global capitalist cash economy.

Religious Change

Numerous religious changes occurred with globalization. The Catholic church played a major role in Latin American society during the colonial period. Initially, the *conquistadores* were not sure whether the native peoples were fully human; that is, they were not certain that the natives had souls. After the Spanish authorities, backed by the pope, ruled that the Indians did indeed have souls and could be saved, various missionaries began to convert the Indians to Catholicism. The missionaries established the pueblos and villages where the Indians were relocated and attempted to protect the Indians from the major abuses of colonialism, but were too few and too spread out to do so.

In general, the Indians of Latin America readily accepted Catholicism. The indigenous religions of Mesoamerica, for example, were able to absorb foreign deities without giving up their own (Berdan, 1982). Many local religious conceptions were somewhat analogous to Catholic beliefs. A process of religious **syncretism** developed, in which indigenous beliefs and practices blend with those of Christianity. For example, the central theological tenet of Christianity, that Jesus sacrificed his life for the salvation of humanity, was acceptable to people whose religious traditions formerly included human sacrifices for the salvation of Mesoamerican peoples (see Chapter 18). The Indians were also attracted to the elaborate rituals and colorful practices associated with the Virgin Mary and the saints. Catholic beliefs and practices were assimilated into traditional indigenous cosmologies to become powerful symbolic images and rituals.

One well-known tradition that has endured in Mexico, representing a combination of pre-Hispanic and Spanish Catholic religious beliefs and practices, is the *Día de los Muertos* (the Day of the Dead). The *Día de los Muertos* takes place on November 2nd, the day after All Saints' Day (*Todos Santos*). This is the time when the souls of the dead return to earth to visit their living relatives. *Día de los Muertos* is a time when families get together for feasting. They construct altars to the dead and offer food and drink and prayers to the souls of their dead relatives. The altars usually have a photo of the dead person, along with an image of Jesus or the Virgin Mary. For those who died as children, there may be toys or sugar treats made in the shape of animals on the altar. Mexicans prepare for this day many months ahead of time. They prepare candy skulls (*calaveras*), which are given out to

Candy skulls, called calaveras, are given to family and friends to celebrate the Day of the Dead in Mexico.

everyone in the family and friends. A substantial expense goes into preparing the foods, chocolate sauces (*mole*), and drinks, along with flowers, candles, and incense for the festivities. Food, drinks, and gifts of *calaveras* are exchanged to symbolize strong linkages among family members both living and dead. It is the most important ritual in Mexico exemplifying the crucial links between the past pre-Hispanic symbolic culture and the present. The *Día de los Muertos* represents the persistence of cultural traditions despite the globalizing processes induced by colonialism (Norget, 1996; Garciagodoy, 1998).

Despite the official position of the Catholic church in Latin America and the Caribbean, indigenous religious traditions have survived for centuries, partly because Catholicism had evolved over a long period in Europe, during which it absorbed a number of indigenous pagan traditions. Thus, Catholicism was predisposed to accommodate pagan traditions in the Americas (Ingham, 1986).

In addition, the slaves that were imported from Africa to Latin America and the Caribbean brought traditional religious ideas and practices that were also absorbed into Catholicism. In Brazil these religious traditions are referred to as *Umbanda* and *Macumba;* in northeast Brazil, these traditions are known as *Candomble.* In Cuba these syncretic traditions are called *Santeria.*

On the island of Haiti the vast majority of the people believe in the tradition known as *Vodoun.* Vodoun is a similar combination of African and a blend of other traditions. Vodounists believe that they communicate directly with spirits. Vodoun traditions have evolved into a code of ethics, education, and a system of politics that are evident throughout Haitian society. Secret vodoun societies control everyday life in Haiti. These secret societies trace their origins to escaped slaves that organized revolts against the French colonizers. They meet at night and use traditional African drumming and celebrations. The vodounists have a complex belief system that involves practices of priests or priestesses that can do harm to people. One practice is known as *zombification.* Using the poison of a puffer fish, they can cause an individual to appear to die, and then recover several days later. The victims of the poisoning remain conscious, but are not able to speak or move. Zombification and the threat of zombification were used by the secret societies to police the Haitian rural communities and maintain order (Metraux et al., 1989; Davis, 1997) All of these syncretic traditions combining traditional African religions and Catholicism are sometimes called *spiritism* and are evident in many parts of Latin America and the Caribbean.

With European colonization in Africa came missionaries who established schools to spread

A Voodoo altar and celebration in Haiti.

ANTHROPOLOGISTS AT WORK

KRISTIN NORGET: RESEARCH IN MEXICO

Kristin Norget's involvement with anthropology was never a single, conscious choice but rather a result of a series of decisions concerning how she preferred to live her life and what was meaningful to her. When she was a child growing up in the prairie city of Winnipeg, in central Canada, the subject of anthropology was embodied by the big, thick book that sat on the living room table, filled with photos of apes and of archaeologists unearthing treasures from ruins in far-off places. It was not something to which she could relate readily. However, she always had the urge to travel, to see the possibility for ways of viewing and being in the world that were different from her immediate world of experience.

Her first "fieldwork" was during her last year of high school, when she spent two weeks in Jamaica doing research on Rastafarianism for a paper in a course on comparative politics. This experience, though brief, left a strong impact and inspired her to seek ways to find the same kind of connection with, and understanding about, people and culture not accessible through books and formal education alone.

Norget's first direct contact with anthropology as a more encompassing body of ideas about humanity and culture came in her first year at the University of Victoria, when anthropology was just one of several courses that she took as part of a general arts program that included languages, art history, philosophy, and English literature. In a course on cultural anthropology, she was intrigued by what anthropology offered for an immersion in themes that had always captivated her interest: art, symbolism, religion, and other creative domains of culture; also people's ways of making sense of their worlds and their innovation and richness of spirit in situations of material impoverishment. After completing her undergraduate degree in anthropology, she moved to England to begin her graduate studies at Cambridge University. There she was exposed to the classical works of British social anthropology and experienced the culture shock that came from living within a particularly privileged and rare slice of English society. Although her time in Cambridge was overwhelming in some respects, it was also highly stimulating and enriching.

Kristin Norget

Norget chose as the focus of her master's research the Mexican festival of the Day of the Dead, a topic she saw could encompass her real interests in anthropology related to religion, ritual, art, and the expressive realms of culture. She had already visited Mexico as a tourist and had been fascinated by its history, art, and literature, and moved by the warmth and generosity of the Mexicans she had met. Her master's dissertation was the first stage of her exploration of the Day of the Dead (the Mexican commemoration of the Catholic festival and All Souls' and All Saints' Days), which later

Christianity. As in Latin America, many of the missionaries in Africa were paternalistic toward the native peoples and tried to protect them from the worst abuses of colonialism. Mission schools served as both hospitals and education centers. Many people sent their children to the Christian schools because this education offered opportunities for better jobs and higher social status, and many people educated in the mission schools became part of the elite.

At the same time, however, the missionaries attempted to repress traditional religious beliefs and

evolved into a doctoral research project. She was already familiar with the Day of the Dead from museum exhibitions she had attended in England and Mexico and from the colorful popular art and iconography inspired by the festival that she had come across during her travels. Much of what she had previously seen and read about the Day of the Dead struck her as a rather one-dimensional, romanticized portrayal of the festival as simply a folkloric tradition with strong roots in pre-Hispanic religiosity and in a supposed quintessentially "Mexican" obsession with death. She wanted to explore the significance of the festival in a more contemporary framework, as well as to learn more about the ritualization of death in Mexico.

She chose as her fieldsite the southern Mexican city of Oaxaca, located in one of the poorest and most indigenous regions of the country. The urban milieu of Oaxaca enabled her to examine the Day of the Dead in a dynamic setting in which traditional lifeways came into direct interaction with tourism, commercialization, and other influences. Norget

situated her investigation of the Day of the Dead in the context of Oaxacan urban popular culture, popular Catholicism, and other rituals concerned with death. During her fieldwork, she immersed herself in the local community of the neighborhood in which she lived, especially in the religious dimension of people's everyday lives, taking part in Bible discussion groups, masses, and other church activities, but especially in funerals and other death-related rituals. She discovered that death in Oaxaca is the inspiration for an elaborate series of ritual events and cultural discourses concerned with the reinvigoration of traditional ideas of collectivism and community in a rapidly changing and unstable social context in which such norms and values are being severely eroded. Her research deepened her fascination with the very practical way in which people use ritual for the imaginative and creative reconstruction of their social world.

Since completing her doctorate in 1993, Norget has been teaching anthropology at McGill University in Montreal. While she

finds teaching very rewarding, she is most content when she is in Mexico, immersed in research, writing, and spending time with the wide community of friends she has amassed there over the past ten years. In 1995, she was able to extend her interests in popular religiosity and Catholicism into a new research project investigating the relation between liberation theology and indigenous movements in southern Mexico. Through her work on this project, she finds an avenue for her continuing fascination with the ways that people use religion as a powerful means for articulating and actualizing their desires for a transformation of their social environment. It has also brought her into practical involvement with the human rights struggle in Mexico as well as in Montreal, where she is an active member of various local Mexican human rights and refugee rights organizations. Norget has published articles based on her research in various international journals and is currently in the final stages of writing a book on death and its ritualization in Oaxacan popular culture.

practices. The missionaries believed that to be "saved," the Africans had to abandon their customary practices and embrace the Christian faith. To some extent, the ethnocentrism of the missionaries in Africa had tragic consequences for many native peoples. Through the educational system, Africans were taught that their traditional culture was shameful, something to be despised. In many cases, this led to a loss of ethnic and cultural identity and sometimes induced feelings of self-hatred.

As various Christian denominations missionized throughout Africa, a number of syncretistic movements began to emerge among the indigenous peoples. They became known as Independent African Church denominations referred to as "Zionist," "Spiritual," or "Prophet." The leaders of these churches are often called prophets and are known for their charismatic powers of healing. Facing the crisis created by colonialism and the loss of their traditional culture, many indigenous Africans turned to these traditions for relief. In some cases, these syncretic traditions combining traditional spiritual beliefs and Christianity have played a pivotal role in political movements throughout Africa (Comaroff, 1985).

Political Changes: Independence and Nationalist Movements

One important consequence of globalization and colonialism in various Latin American, African, and Caribbean areas was the development of political movements that emphasized independence and nationalistic ideas. Some of the indigenous peoples became educated under the colonial regime and began to assert their independence. After approximately three hundred years of European domination, the various regions of Latin America and the Caribbean began to demand political autonomy from the colonial regimes. An educated descendant of the ancient Incans, Tupac Amaru, led a rebellion in Peru against the Spanish rulers. Simón Bolívar (1783–1830), a national hero among both Venezuelans and Colombians, led a broad-based independence/nationalist movement. In the French colony of Saint Domingue (modern-day Haiti), a slave uprising became a warning for all the various colonial regimes in the region.

During the decades following World War II, European colonial rule ended in Africa; by the 1970s, no fewer than thirty-one former colonies had won their independence. The first country to do so, the West African nation of Ghana, became independent of Britain in 1957. Kwame Nkrumah, a charismatic leader who mobilized workers, youths, professionals, and farmers to speed up the pace of decolonization, led the Ghanian independence movement. Ghana's success intensified independence movements elsewhere. By the early 1960s, all of the West African countries, including the French colonies of Niger, Mali, Senegal, and Dahomey, had gained their independence, making a fairly smooth transition to independent political control.

In the Congo region, however, because of the Belgians' rigid exploitative political and economic policies, the independence movement was much more difficult. Belgian colonial policies had brutalized the native population, and the inadequate educational system had failed to produce an elite, affording Africans in the Belgian colonies little opportunity to gain political training for self-rule or nation building. When Belgium finally granted independence to the Congo in 1960, it was due more to international pressure than to nationalist movements.

In East Africa, the large numbers of white settlers vigorously resisted nationalist movements. In Kenya, for example, hostility between the majority Kikuyu tribe and white settlers who had appropriated much of the best farmland contributed to the Mau Mau uprisings, which resulted in thousands of deaths and the imprisonment of thousands of Kikuyu in detention camps. Jomo Kenyatta, a British-educated leader who had completed an anthropological study of the Kikuyu, led Kenya to independence in 1963 with his call for *uhuru* ("freedom" in Swahili). In the colony of Tanganyika, nationalist leader Julius Nyerere organized a mass political party insisting on self-rule. Tanganyika achieved independence in 1961, and in 1964 merged with Zanzibar to form the nation of Tanzania.

In South Africa, colonization and independence eventually produced a system of racial stratification known as **apartheid,** in which different populations were assigned different statuses with varying social and political rights based on racial criteria. Dutch settlers, or Afrikaners, inaugurated the apartheid system when they came to power after World War II, and apartheid was the official policy of South Africa until recently.

Apartheid was based on white supremacy and assumed that the culture and values of nonwhite Africans rendered them incapable of social, political, and economic equality with whites. The government enforced this system through legal policies designed to bring about strict segregation among the different "races." The population was stratified into a hierarchy with whites, who number about 4.5 million, at the top. Approximately 60 percent of the whites are Afrikaners, and the rest are English-speaking. An intermediate category consists of *coloreds*—the 2.6 million people of mixed European and African ancestry—and Asians, primarily immigrants from India and Malaysia, who number about 800,000.

At the bottom of the hierarchy were the approximately 21 million black South Africans, who were divided into four major ethnic groupings: the Nguni, which includes the Xhosa, the Zulu, the Swazi, and the Ndebele; the Sotho; the Venda; and the Tsonga (Crapanzano, 1986). Important cultural and linguistic differences exist among these groups.

The policies of apartheid affected every aspect of life in South Africa. Blacks were segregated socially and forced into lower-paying—and frequently hazardous—occupations. They could not vote or take part in strikes, and until recently they had to carry passes and observe curfews. In 1963, the South African government created a series of black states called Bantustan homelands, to which millions of black South Africans were forcibly removed.

Opposition to apartheid led to the emergence of various resistance and liberation movements, including the major resistance group, the African National Congress (ANC), formed in 1912. Although the ANC began as a moderate political organization calling for a unified South Africa representing all races in the government, it turned to armed struggle in response to ruthless suppression by the government. Many people were killed, and resistance leaders such as Nelson Mandela were imprisoned.

Forced by international pressures, the government implemented some reforms in the 1980s and early 1990s: abolished laws that had once confined blacks to the rural homelands, forbade them to join legal trade unions, reserved skilled jobs for whites, and prohibited interracial marriages. Black nationalist groups and the clergy, led by Archbishop Desmond Tutu, negotiated with the government for other political reforms.

In April 1994, all South Africans participated in a national election for the first time, electing Nelson Mandela's African National Congress (ANC) with a solid majority. Mandela, who became president, agreed to share power with whites during a five-year transitional period and tried to implement an economic blueprint for South Africa that included providing new homes, electrification projects, free and mandatory education, and millions of new jobs. In June 1999, South Africa's parliament chose

Nelson Mandela, the first black elected president of South Africa.

Thabo Mbeki as the nation's second freely elected president. Mbeki, also a member of the ANC, is striving to carry out Nelson Mandela's programs.

Explaining Revolution

In some of the countries of Latin America, Africa, and the Caribbean, revolutionary movements emerged as a response to the consequences of globalization and colonialism. Anthropologists have been examining the causes of revolution in Latin America and other non-Western countries. A **revolution** is a dramatic, fundamental change in a society's political economy brought about by the overthrow of the government and the restructuring of the economy. The classical understanding of revolution is derived from the writings of Karl Marx, who explained revolutions as the product of the struggle between the propertied and non-propertied classes. For example, Marx predicted that the discontented proletariat would rise up against their bourgeois masters and overthrow capitalism (see Chapter 13). The revolutions in most non-Western countries, however, have not followed the Marxist model. Most countries in Latin America, Africa, or the Caribbean did not have a substantial proletariat and bourgeoisie. Rather, their revolutions were identified with the peasants.

Social scientists have found, however, that the poorest peasants did not organize and participate in peasant revolutions. People living in extreme poverty were too preoccupied with everyday subsistence to become politically active. Severe poverty tends to generate feelings of fatalism and political apathy. Consequently, anthropologists and other social scientists turned from the traditional Marxist model to find alternative models to explain revolutions. These models involve the concepts of *rising expectations* and *relative deprivation.*

Rising expectations refers to how a particular group experiences improvements in economic and political conditions. Often these improvements stimulate the desire for even more improvements. For example, revolutions sometimes occur in the midst of political and economic reform. Groups that experience improvements brought about by their governments may become politically active and protest for even broader changes. **Relative deprivation** refers to a group's awareness that it lacks economic opportunities and political rights in comparison with other groups in a society. Even though a particular group may have experienced improved economic and political conditions, it still perceives it is suffering from injustice and inequality compared with other groups. The combination of rising expectations and relative deprivation helps explain revolutionary movements in areas such as Latin America, Africa, and the Caribbean.

Although the first independence movements in Latin America brought about certain reforms, some groups were affected by rising expectations and relative deprivation. The emerging middle class, which consisted of intellectuals and businesspeople, as well as some peasants who were benefiting from the introduction of the global economy, began to organize against the *hacendados* and the governing elite. For example, the Indians and peasants played a vital role in the Mexican Revolution of 1910–1920. At that time, 1 percent of the Mexican population owned 85 percent of the land, whereas 95 percent owned no land at all (Wolf, 1969; Chirot, 1986). Peasant leaders such as Emiliano Zapata, who called for the redistribution of land, carried out guerrilla campaigns against the *hacendados.* Although the revolution did not establish an egalitarian state, it did bring about the redistribution of land to many of the Indian communities.

In Latin American and Caribbean countries where power remained in the hands of the elites, revolutionary movements continued to develop throughout the twentieth century. From the Cuban Revolution of the 1950s through the Nicaraguan Revolution of the 1980s, peasants joined with other dissatisfied elements in overthrowing elite families. Countries such as El Salvador continue to experience peasant revolutions. The *hacienda* system produced tenant farmers, sharecroppers, and day laborers on large estates, a situation that will inevitably make peasant guerrillas a continuing presence in some Latin American nations.

Uneven Development

Throughout the twentieth century, the countries of Latin America, Africa, and the Caribbean have increasingly been incorporated into the global economy. These countries, however, differ in the degree of integration into this global economy. Some nations are *peripheral* agricultural states that produce a few cash crops for the international market. Others, such as Mexico, Venezuela, Brazil, and Nigeria, have a significant industrial sector and are clearly *semiperipheral.* In some regions, small-scale industrialists produce manufactured goods alongside the crops and cattle of the plantations. In many cases, however, these industrialists have to depend on Europe and North America for their machinery. They also discover that the internal market for their products is extremely limited because their own societies lack a consuming middle class.

Peripheral Societies

Anthropologists find that many countries in Latin America, Africa, and the Caribbean remain peripheral societies. The core societies developed these countries as *export platforms,* that is, nations whose economies concentrate almost exclusively on the export of raw materials and agricultural goods to the core nations. Through economic aid and military assistance, core countries such as the United States supported elite families and local capitalists in these peripheral countries. The elites minimized restrictions on foreign investments and encouraged the production of cash crops for the export economy. The entire economy in these peripheral societies was reorganized to produce profits and commodities for the core societies.

A Case Study: The United Fruit Company An example of the development of a peripheral country by a multinational corporation involves the U.S.–based United Fruit Company in Central America. United Fruit obtained rights to thousands of acres of empty tropical lowlands in Central America for banana plantations. It enlisted local Indians, *mestizos,* and blacks from the Caribbean islands to work the plantations. Anthropologist Philippe Bourgois (1989b) studied one of the plantations operated by United Fruit, which expanded in 1987 to become the multinational Chiquita Brands. He investigated the archival records of United Fruit to determine how the North Americans managed the plantations.

Focusing on the Bocas Del Toro plantation, Bourgois observed the interactions among the various ethnic groups on the plantation. He discovered that the North Americans used race and ethnicity as a form of manipulation. He described the relationship between management and labor as based on a hierarchy in which each of the four ethnic groups—blacks, *mestizos,* Indians, and white North Americans—worked at different tasks. Indian workers were used to spread corrosive fertilizers and dangerous pesticides. The management rationale for this practice was that "the Indian skin is thicker, and they don't get sick." Indians were not paid a full wage because, according to superiors, "the Indian has low physiological needs. . . . The Indian only thinks of food; he has no other aspirations. He works to eat" (1989b:x).

Blacks worked in the maintenance department's repair shops and electrical division because, Bourgois was told, they are "crafty and don't like to sweat." The *mestizo* immigrants from Nicaragua were worked as hard as the Indians because they "are tough, have leathery skin [*cueron*], and aren't afraid of sweating under the hot sun" (1989b:xi). The white North Americans were the top management because "they are the smartest race on earth." Management used these stereotypes to classify the workers, thereby segregating each ethnic group in a separate occupation and preventing the workers from uniting to organize labor unions. Bourgois found that racism, ethnicity, inequality, exploitation, and class conflict were all interrelated in a continuing process in the day-to-day realities of a banana-plantation economy.

Semiperipheral Societies

A number of countries in Latin America and Africa, because of their valuable strategic resources, have emerged as semiperipheral societies. Two examples of peripheral societies that have become semiperipheral are Mexico and Nigeria.

Mexico Following a political revolution, Mexico gradually achieved stability under the control of a single political party, the Party of the Institutionalized Revolution (PRI). One-party rule, however, fostered corruption and inefficiency, resulting in personal enrichment for political officials. The government nationalized the key industries, including the important oil industry, which had been developed by foreign multinational corporations. Despite political authoritarianism and corruption, the Mexican economy continued to grow with gradual industrialization.

During the 1970s, as the industrial world experienced major oil shortages, the Mexican government implemented a policy of economic growth through expanded oil exports. International lending agencies and financial institutions in the core countries offered low-interest loans to stimulate industrial investment in Mexico. As a result, Mexico initially experienced an impressive growth rate of 8 percent annually and moved from a peripheral to a semiperipheral nation.

This progress was short-lived, however. Surpluses on the petroleum market in the early 1980s led to falling prices for Mexican oil. Suddenly Mexico faced difficulties in paying the interest on the loans that came due. The government had to borrow more money, at higher interest rates, to cover its international debt, which exceeded $100 billion. This excessive debt began to undermine government-sponsored development projects. Foreign banks and lending organizations such as the International Monetary Fund (IMF) demanded that the government limit its subsidies for social services, food, gasoline, and electricity. These policies led to inflation and a new austerity that adversely affected the standard of living of the poor and the middle classes of Mexico.

Another development influencing Mexico's economic status was the expansion of U.S. multinational corporations into Mexico. Since the 1980s, thousands of U.S. companies have established plants

Many of the workers in the maquiladoras *in Mexico are women.*

inside Mexico to take advantage of the low wage rates, lax environmental standards, and favorable tax rates there. These plants, known as *maquiladoras,* have drawn hundreds of thousands of peasants and workers from rural communities to expanding cities such as Juarez, a border city (Shirk & Mitchell, 1989). Among the companies that have established plants in Mexico are Fisher-Price, Ford, Emerson Electric, Zenith, Sara Lee, and General Electric.

Faced with mounting debts and unemployment, the Mexican government did everything possible to attract multinational corporations. This was also seen as a solution to the problem of the migration of Mexican workers to the United States as illegal aliens. The *maquiladoras* employ approximately 500,000 people and account for 17 percent of the Mexican economy. Although many *maquiladora* workers appear satisfied with their jobs, the *maquiladoras* have created a number of problems for Mexico. Because they pay such low wages, they do not transform workers into consumers, which restricts economic expansion. Other problems include occupational health hazards, the taxing of

sewer systems and water supplies, and high turnover rates among workers.

Nigeria   Under British rule, Nigeria developed an export economy centered on palm oil and peanut oil, lumber, cocoa, and metal ores. As in Mexico, after independence, a new commodity was discovered that had major consequences for Nigerian society—petroleum. The discovery of oil appeared to be an economic windfall for Nigeria, and the government saw it as the foundation for rapid economic growth. Many Africans from other nations immigrated to Nigeria in search of opportunity.

By the 1980s, over 90 percent of Nigeria's revenues came from the sale of petroleum. These monies were used to fuel ambitious economic development schemes. Unfortunately, the Nigerian economy fell into disarray when oil prices dropped during the first half of the 1980s. In spite of tremendous economic expansion during the 1970s, unemployment rose, and the Nigerian government expelled virtually all non-Nigerian workers and their families, forcing millions of Africans to return to their former homelands, where the local economies could not absorb them.

By the late 1980s, cocoa was the only important Nigerian agricultural export. Oil production and the vast wealth that it represented for Nigeria had actually contributed to the decline of agriculture because the government invested heavily in the petroleum industry, neglecting the agricultural sector (Rossides, 1990a). Consequently, Nigeria now depends on core countries for imported foods. In addition, much of its oil wealth was spent on imported goods such as automobiles, motorcycles, and televisions, which fueled inflation and did not benefit an underdeveloped industrial sector. Today, the industrial sector accounts for only 10 percent of Nigeria's economic production. In 1995, Nigeria's annual per capita income was $970, one of the highest figures of any African country but far below that of many other semiperipheral societies (Ramsay, 2001).

South Africa: An Economy in Transition

The country of South Africa, as described above, is going through a painful transition following the abolishment of apartheid and the development of a democratic society in which every citizen has equality in voting rights. However, the legacy of apartheid is still apparent, with inequalities among the various groups that were classified as races in South Africa. The official black unemployment rate is more than six times that of the white minority population. More than 50 percent of the black population under 30 are unemployed (Gay, 2001). Black education, housing, and other material conditions are far behind the white population in South Africa. With the rise of the ANC and the election of Nelson Mandela and Thabo Mbeki as presidents, a new direction is being forged in stimulating the South Africa economy.

The ANC is trying to develop opportunities to close the gap between the black and white populations in education, health, and economic prospects. The South African economy was in recession before the abolishment of apartheid due to the international economic boycott and withdrawal of investments from its major corporations, which imposed a burden on the new leaders in their attempt to develop economic opportunities. The white population still holds the dominant positions within the South African economy, but a number of government policies are being enacted to further the education of black entrepreneurs to develop greater incentives for participation in economic ventures. The government is also publicizing its stability in order to attract foreign investment and venture capital into South Africa.

High crime rates, high unemployment rates, and the low educational levels of the black population continue to be the most pressing problems for maintaining stability and economic growth in South Africa. The ANC government can take pride in accelerating the rate of education among the black population. It knows that more educated and literate South Africans means more trained, skilled workers to take advantage of and create new economic opportunities for its future.

Ethnographic Studies of the Peasantry

As Latin American, African, and Caribbean countries were drawn increasingly into the global economy, the status and lifestyles of the peasantry were transformed. Anthropologists have been studying this

transformation of the peasantry for many decades. For example, cultural anthropologists such as Redfield (1930), Villa Rojas (Redfield & Villa Rojas, 1934), Lewis (1951), and Goldkind (1965) have been studying peasant communities in Latin America and the Caribbean since the 1920s.

A problem in generalizing about behavior in rural communities of non-Western countries is the tremendous variation from one community to another, although as these countries became integrated into the global economy, the peasantry became more heterogeneous. This variation is due to the different historical processes that have influenced these communities. For example, research by Eric Wolf (1955b, 1959) led to some important insights regarding the different types of peasant communities in some regions of Latin America and Asia. Wolf distinguished between closed peasant communities and open peasant communities. The **closed peasant community** is made up of peasants who lived in the highland regions of Mexico and Guatemala or in more isolated areas. In these communities, a person had ascribed economic and social status, and there was a great deal of internal solidarity and homogeneity. The peasants produced primarily for subsistence rather than for the world market. Many closed peasant communities in Central America, such as Chan Kom, consisted of Indian refugees who attempted to isolate themselves from the disruptive effects of Spanish colonial policies. They held their land in common, but much of this land was marginal.

An **open peasant community** consisted primarily of peasants who were directly drawn into the world market. These communities were located in the lowland areas of Latin America and Indonesia. Land was owned individually rather than held in common. The open peasant community evolved in response to the intrusion of colonialism, which engendered the development of plantations and the production of commodities for the core societies. In open communities, some peasants sold as much as 90 to 100 percent of their produce to outside markets, which enabled them to achieve some economic stability; however, they were subject to the fluctuations in the global economy.

Most recently, because of the global consequences of NAFTA (the North American Free Trade Agreement), which was signed by the United States, Mexico, and Canada in 1994, peasant lives are being transformed. Responding to the demands of NAFTA, the Mexican government has been trying to reform the agricultural system. Mexico is flooded with imported crops such as corn from the United States, and the small landholding peasants cannot compete with the prices of U.S.-produced corn. In addition, the peasants who produce sugar cane cannot export to the United States, because of a clause in the NAFTA agreement that protects the U.S. sugar industry. And the less costly U.S.-produced fructose corn syrup for soda preferred by the soft drink industry in Mexico is also affecting the sugar cane producers.

Anthropologist James McDonald has been studying small farmers in different areas of Mexico to investigate the consequences of NAFTA and globalization (1997, 1999, 2001). Since the 1990s, after years of neglect, the Mexican government, influenced by the NAFTA agreement, has been attempting to privatize and introduce the free market into the agricultural economy. Small farmers were encouraged to reorganize and form larger producer groups to take advantage of the newer, high-tech agricultural methods and make their farms more competitive, productive, and efficient.

McDonald focused on a study of dairy farmers in Guanajuato and Michoacan, Mexico, who managed cows in the production of milk. In Guanajuato, the size of the dairy ranches ranged from under twenty cows to larger ranches with as many as two hundred head. Guanajuato has been successful in integrating its dairy farmers into the global economy. This region is close to the U.S. border and has a more open political system, and its economy is also dependent on remittances from migrants to the United States.

In Michoacan, the dairy farms were smaller, with only twenty head of cattle. Following NAFTA, large private commercial dairies supported by state and federal government reorganized these dairy farmers and gave them limited training to enhance productivity and efficiency. The result of these new organizations was to create alliances between private businesspeople and politicians, who began to displace the older rural elites. These new elites concentrated their wealth and authority and dictated the policies and economic conditions for the rural farmers. In some cases, even when these new entrepreneurs had failing businesses, they managed to maintain their rewards and privileges.

Politicians benefited from these arrangements and supported policies and legislation that profited the entrepreneurs.

McDonald concludes that with further privatization and the new free market policies in Mexico, extensive economic inequalities, political corruption, and continuing dislocations of the small independent farmer were bound to occur.

African Peasants: A Unique Phenomenon?

Anthropologists David Brokensha and Charles Erasmus (1969) maintained that Africans were not typical peasants because of the distinctive nature of precolonial African states. They suggested that most precolonial states had very limited control over their populations, and that Africans were able to retain control over their land and their economic production. Other anthropologists suggested that sub-Saharan Africans could not be characterized as peasants because in many cases they were still horticulturalists (Goldschmidt & Kunkel, 1971).

Anthropologists Godfrey Wilson and Max Gluckman of the Rhodes-Livingstone Institute in southern Africa have engaged in detailed studies of African society. They distinguished six types of regions based on an array of factors, such as degree of urbanization and industrialization, relative importance of subsistence and cash cropping, and nature of the work force. They also examined such related phenomena as rural-to-urban migration, depopulation, unionization, and prevailing political issues. These and other studies helped produce an improved understanding of how the global economy directly affected the African people (Vincent, 1990).

Most anthropologists now agree that the general term *peasants* does not apply to the diverse conditions found in the African agricultural states. In some regions there were rural peoples who could be designated "peasants," whereas in other regions the term was not applicable. The historical experience of Africa was much different from that of medieval Europe, Latin America, or Asia. Environmental, economic, and political circumstances varied from region to region, involving different types of societal adaptations. In addition, the presence of so many colonial powers in Africa created greater diversity than was the case in Latin America, which was colonized almost exclusively by the Spanish and Portuguese. Thus, the current political economy of Africa is more heterogenous than that of many other regions.

Social Structure

Ethnographic studies have illuminated aspects of the social structure, including family and gender relations, of various countries of Latin America, Africa, and the Caribbean. As in most rural agricultural societies, the traditional family unit was an extended family that provided aid for people living in marginal subsistence conditions. But with the growth of industry and wage labor and the redistribution of land from communities to individuals, many large extended families were forced to break up. Thus, the typical family in many urban areas today is the nuclear family. Ethnographers, however, have found some unique features of kinship and social structure in these countries.

Latin American Social Relationships

Many peasant communities maintain **fictive kinship ties**—that is, extrafamilial social ties that provide mutual-aid work groups for the planting and harvesting of crops and for other economic and political activities. George Foster described one type of fictive kinship tie in Mexican peasant communities that is known as the **dyadic contract,** a reciprocal exchange arrangement between two individuals (a *dyad*). According to Foster (1967), to compensate for the lack of voluntary organizations or corporate groups beyond the nuclear family in these communities, males and females established dyadic contracts to exchange labor, goods, and other needed services. These extra-kin social ties help sustain peasants who are vulnerable to the new demands of the unpredictable global market economy. Dyadic contracts can be established with people of equal or superior status or with supernatural beings such as Jesus, the Virgin Mary, and the saints. People develop dyadic contracts with these supernatural sources in hopes of inducing specific spiritual and material benefits. They care for the shrines of Jesus, the Virgin Mary, and the saints to demonstrate their loyalty and obedience.

Dyadic contracts between individuals of equal status are based on generalized reciprocal exchanges: continuing exchanges that are not short term but rather bind two people in cooperative relationships for many years. This is an attempt to develop the older forms of the moral economy that existed prior to globalization.

The dyadic contracts between people of unequal status, known as **patron-client ties,** are informal contracts between peasant villagers and nonvillagers (including supernatural beings). The patron is an individual who combines status, power, influence, and authority over the client. Patrons include politicians, government employees, town or city friends, and local priests.

One type of dyadic contract found in Latin America is known as the *compadrazgo,* associated with the rite of passage of baptism and Catholicism. Cultural anthropologists have investigated *compadrazgo* relationships extensively (Redfield, 1930; Wolf & Mintz, 1950; Foster, 1967). This institution, brought to the Americas with Catholicism, has become an integral aspect of Latin American social relationships. During the colonial period, the *hacendado* often served as godparent to the children of peons. The result was a network of patron-client ties involving mutual obligations and responsibilities. The godparent had to furnish aid in times of distress such as illness or famine. In return, the peon had to be absolutely loyal and obedient to the *hacendado*.

The *compadrazgo* system eventually spread throughout peasant and urban areas. Every individual has a *padrino* (godfather) and *madrina* (godmother) who are sponsors at baptismal rituals. The sponsors become the co-parents (*compadres, comadres*) of the child (Davila, 1971; Romanucci-Ross, 1973). The most important social relationship is the one between the *compadres* and the parents, who ideally will assist one another in any way possible. The *compadrazgo* is a remarkably flexible extra-kin relationship that sometimes reaches across class lines to help peasants cope with the tensions and anxieties of globalization and modern life in Latin America.

Machismo   Gender relationships in Latin America have been strongly influenced by the Spanish and Portuguese colonial experience. The basic traditional values affecting gender relations are known as *machismo,* the explicit code for the behavior of Latin American males. As a part of this code, the "true man" (*macho*) is supposed to be courageous, sexually virile and aggressive, and superior to women. A woman, in contrast, is supposed to be passive, sexually conservative and faithful, obedient, and completely devoted to her mate. These ideals and values have affected gender relations throughout Latin America.

Yet many cultural anthropologists who have done research in Latin American peasant communities have observed that the actual behaviors of males and females do not conform completely to the ideals of *machismo*. Lewis (1951) observed that in Tepotztlan males were not the dominant authoritarian figures in the family that they wanted to be, and wives were not completely submissive. Instead, in many families he found conflict between the spouses over authority. Most families tended to follow a middle course. The wife did little to challenge the authority of her husband, and the husband was not too overbearing toward his wife. May Diaz (1966) also showed that the ideals of *machismo* conflict with the actual behavioral realities of gender relations in Mexico. She observed in her study of Tonala, a small town near Guadalajara, that females often effectively opposed male domination within the family and the community.

African Social Relationships

Because many African societies are composed of horticulturalist or pastoralist peoples in transition to different forms of peasantry, their social organization largely centers on lineages and extended families. But as in other regions of the world, as globalization, industrialization, and the commercialization of agriculture develop, social organization inevitably changes.

Some cultural anthropologists have challenged basic concepts regarding the African family. For example, Niara Sudarkasa (1989), an anthropologist who did ethnographic research on the Yoruba and other West African groups, has challenged anthropologists such as George Murdock, who believe that all families worldwide can be reduced to the nuclear family (see Chapter 14). Murdock (1949) had argued that the extended family, or polygamous African family, really consists of multiple nuclear families with a common husband and father.

Sudarkasa saw this hypothesis as a distortion of the basic elements of the African family. She argued that the male-female dyad and offspring do not perform the basic functions of the family in African society. That is, the nuclear family is not the unit of economic production or consumption, not the unit of socialization, and not the unit providing emotional support. A typical African family such as that of the Yoruba consists of a group of brothers, their wives, their adult sons and grandsons and their wives, and any unmarried children. Marriages usually are polygynous, and the husband has a room separate from his wives. Every wife has a separate domain, with her own cooking utensils and other furnishings. Co-wives depend on the senior wife to be a companion and confidante. Sudarkasa concluded that the nuclear family is not the basic "building block" of the African family. She further maintained that Western cultural anthropologists misunderstand and distort the practice of polygyny in African society. She noted that most of the anthropological literature emphasizes the negative characteristics of polygyny, such as rivalry and discord

A Yoruban man and family members.

among co-wives. Her research demonstrated that co-wives develop important emotional and social bonds with one another that create a nurturing environment for both co-wives and children.

Although not all anthropologists have accepted Sudarkasa's views, most concur that there are many variations of the African family, depending on sociocultural conditions. In the urban areas of Africa, the extended family and polygyny are declining in influence. Several factors are responsible for these changes. As employment opportunities develop outside agriculture, prompting migration from rural to urban areas, extended family ties break down. Wage employment in mines and industrial firms tends to disrupt extended families that are tied to agricultural land. In addition, African governments often promote "modern" family and marriage practices to alter traditional ways of behavior, which they perceive as impeding economic development. To some extent, the elites of these societies accept Western conceptions of the family, romantic love, and monogamy.

Gender in Africa   Most African societies tend to be patriarchal, placing women in a subordinate status. In 1988, for example, women provided approximately 60 to 80 percent of the household food needs in many parts of Africa (Smith-Ivan, 1988). They often worked ten to twelve hours a day, and in many instances their workload increased after colonization and independence. As colonial regimes forced males to migrate to mines for employment, women were forced to assume the major subsistence roles for the family. Because their husbands' wages were meager, women had to grow and collect food for their families. In most cases, the lack of formal education prevented females from entering the wage-labor economy, so they were unable to buy property and send their children to school.

Despite providing much of the agricultural labor and household food needs, women in rural Africa tend to be the poorest people on the world's poorest continent. The European colonial powers often allocated land to males, but African women were given rights to land only through their relationship to males (Henn, 1984; Tandon, 1988). This tended to decrease the status of females in African society. Males were considered the head of the household and earned income, whereas females were viewed as the providers of the family's social needs (such as child care) and the producers of the future labor force. Following independence, males were given access to credit, training, and new skills to improve agricultural production. Because females did not have collateral through land ownership, they were denied the credit and training needed for commercialized agriculture.

African women have had difficult problems in both rural and urban areas.

Urban Women African women in the urban regions often receive a formal education and tend to have more independence than do rural women. In West Africa, where females have traditionally been employed in urban markets, some educated women have become prominent self-employed entrepreneurs. In general, however, even highly educated women are confined to the service sector of the urban economy, working in clerical or secretarial occupations (Robertson, 1984; Smith-Ivan, 1988). Urban women without formal education who lack the support of extended families and village communities are especially vulnerable to exploitation and alienation. Without extended family ties to assist in child care, women often are restricted to unskilled, low-wage occupations, such as making clothing, that require them to remain at home.

Because South Africa was largely a settler colony and possesses a strong economy, the role of women there is somewhat different from that in other parts of Africa. Some African women are employed as domestics in white homes or as clerical and textile workers in the industrial sector. Despite their valuable contribution to these sectors of the economy, however, they earn 20 percent less than the minimum wage (Smith-Ivan, 1988).

One positive development in many African countries is the increasing attention given to women. The pivotal role of women in agriculture and the urban areas is increasingly being recognized and supported by various governments. Prenatal and health care for mothers and babies have improved. New cooperatives for women in rural agriculture and improvements for women working in factories have been established by government policies. Women are also beginning to play a more important role in politics. Yet these advances could be subject to economic declines and political instability (Ramsey, 2001). Thus, the role of women in both rural and urban Africa depends on the adjustment to the new demands and opportunities of globalization.

Patterns of Ethnicity

As a result of European conquest and colonization, the ethnicity of Latin America, Africa, and the Caribbean became increasingly diverse and heterogeneous.

Ethnicity in Latin America

In Latin America, a small minority of Spanish and Portuguese rulers, never exceeding more than 5 percent of the total population, dominated the native population. Following the conquest, people born in Spain and Portugal went to Latin America to improve their social status. The Europeans eventually intermarried with native Indian women. The offspring of these marriages were called *mestizos,* a new social class in Latin America. After three centuries, the *mestizo* population grew to become the majority in Latin America, representing approximately 60 percent of the population. In addition, in Brazil and the Caribbean, the intermarriages of Africans and Europeans produced a group known as *mulattos.*

Gradually, in certain regions of Latin America and the Caribbean, the new populations of mestizos and mulattos began to outnumber the indigenous peoples. The relative populations of these different groups vary from region to region. For example, only about 10 percent of the Mexican population speaks an Indian language, as opposed to about 50 percent in Guatemala, which is more geographically isolated. Brazil's population is about 11 percent black and 33 percent mulatto. Other areas in Bolivia, Peru, and Ecuador that are farther from the commercial coastal regions are primarily mestizo and Indian; only 10 percent of their populations are European or white. In contrast, in the coastal areas of Argentina and Uruguay, the European component of the population is more prominent.

In countries such as Mexico and Guatemala, the Indian population as a minority has faced obstacles in attaining economic and political opportunities. Ethnographers have found that one of the only routes to upward social and economic mobility for the Indian population was **assimilation,** the adoption of the culture and language of the dominant group in society (Nash, 1989). Some Indians did assimilate by adopting the Spanish language, clothing, and culture of the dominant majority and thereby becoming *ladino.* The ethnic distinction between a *ladino* and Indian was based on a cultural boundary. However, many Indians have tried to maintain their ethnic distinctiveness and have recently been involved in asserting their Indian ethnic identity in an attempt to attain economic and political rights.

For example, in southern Mexico, especially in the province of Chiapas, the Mayan Indians have been mobilized politically into what is referred to as the Zapatista movement. The Zapatista movement is named after Emiliano Zapata and has been using armed guerilla warfare tactics against Mexican government forces to attain political and economic rights from the state. In this area, the Maya Indian population is dominated economically and politically by a wealthy group of landowners and ranchers. Traditionally, the Maya Indians had a certain amount of communal land, or *ejidos,* that they could share. In the 1980s, in order to encourage private enterprise and capitalism in agriculture, the Mexican government declared that *ejido* land could be sold. The Maya lost their communal land, which they had been using for their basic subsistence. For these reasons, the Zapatistas, led by a mysterious charismatic leader known as Sub-Comandante Marcos, declared war on the Mexican government. This movement has drawn on their traditional ethnic roots as a means of mobilizing a political struggle against a dominant majority in the midst of globalization (Nash, 1997).

Ethnicity in Africa

In Africa, as another example, the term *tribe* has negative connotations and is seldom used. Consequently, peoples of different language groupings and culture refer to themselves as *ethnic groups.* Anthropologist Herbert Lewis (1992) has estimated that there are no fewer than 1,000 distinct ethnic groups among the more than fifty countries in Africa. As independence movements spread, many people hoped that the new African nations would develop as plural societies in which diverse ethnic groups would share power and tolerate cultural differences. These plural societies, however, generally have not developed. Anthropologists find that political parties are linked with specific ethnic groups. As one ethnic group assumes power, it usually forms a one-party state and establishes a military government that dominates other groups. This has become one of the major problems in African society.

One country that has been the subject of much ethnological research on ethnic relationships is Nigeria. The resolution of ethnic problems in Nigeria may provide a model for other African countries. Nigeria is the most populous nation of Africa, with about 98 million people, consisting of many different ethnic groups. Approximately 300 different languages are recognized by the Nigerian government. The three major ethnic divisions, which make up two-thirds of the Nigerian population, are the Yoruba, the Hausa, and the Igbo (Ibo).

More than 12 million Yoruba live in the southwest region of Nigeria and across its borders in neighboring Benin. The Yoruba were the most highly organized precolonial urban people in West Africa. The majority of the Yoruba were subsistence peasant farmers. The men traditionally supplemented their diet through hunting and fishing.

British colonialism changed the political economy of Nigeria. Aside from commercialized agriculture that emphasized cocoa production, railways, automobiles, new manufactured goods, Christian churches and schools, and industry entered Yoruban society. One-fifth of the people live in the urban areas of Nigeria such as Lagos and Ibadan. Wage employment and industrialization are rapidly transforming the society of the Yoruba, creating new class structures and integrating the traditional kingdom into the Nigerian nation and the global economy.

To the north of the Yoruba live the Hausa, who number about 20 million. Like the Yoruba, the Hausa had developed large, urban areas with extensive trade routes. Hausa cities had elaborate markets that offered different types of foodstuffs and crafts produced by peasants and craftspeople. British anthropologist M. G. Smith (1965) conducted extensive ethnological and historical research on Hausa society.

The Hausa made their home in a savanna where the peasants cultivated various crops and maintained cattle for trade and consumption. Hausa craftsmen smelted iron and crafted iron tools for farming, sewing, leather work, and hunting. As with the Yoruba, most Hausa peasants were engaged in subsistence agriculture, but cash crops such as cotton and peanuts were introduced by the British and changed the nature of economic production and consumption.

The third major ethnic group in Nigeria is the Igbo people of the southeastern region. Igbo anthropologist Victor Uchendu (1965) completed a major ethnological study of the Igbo. His descriptions of Igbo society are extremely insightful because he blends an anthropological focus with an insider's perspective.

APPLYING ANTHROPOLOGY

FAMINES AND FOOD PROBLEMS IN AFRICA

Although Africa has the land and resources to produce more food than its current population requires, many African countries face famine conditions. A *famine* is starvation that is epidemic in scale and causes death from starvation-related diseases. Agencies of the United Nations estimate that more than 14 million people continually face starvation in Africa. In the 1980s, widespread famines occurred in twenty-two African nations. Ethiopia confronted famines in 1984 and 1989. In 1992, six countries were suffering from severe famine, including Somalia and the Sudan. Despite international relief and tens of millions of dollars of food aid, African agricultural production has been stifled.

A number of anthropologists have been researching famines to provide a knowledge base for countries that face these conditions. One area that has been investigated concerns the causes of famine conditions (Shipton, 1990). Researchers have found that many factors are responsible for the widespread famines in Africa. Climatic conditions, particularly droughts, decimate crops and diminish the fertility of the land. In some cases, political instability and civil war prevent food from reaching hungry people. For example, the Sudan has been destabilized by a civil war between the Muslim north and the Christian south. Both sides use food as a weapon, withholding needed grains to weaken the opposition. Similar conditions exist in Somalia, where rival tribes compete for political power by using food. In addition, in impoverished regions such as the Sudan, Somalia, and Ethiopia, poor transportation and communication facilities inhibit the shipment and distribution of food. Despite the work of international relief agencies, food frequently does not reach the famine-stricken population.

In addition, the colonial heritage of these nations contributes to the abysmal state of agricultural production. In substituting export crops for subsistence agriculture, the colonial powers promoted the growing of a single crop. This practice resulted in the loss of cultivable land, which, combined with population growth, led to problems in food production. In addition, the decrease in the availability of land resulted in fewer economic opportunities in rural regions and increased migration to overcrowded cities.

The growth of a single crop also led to widespread environmental deterioration, including soil erosion, desertification, and deforestation. This agricultural pattern depletes the soil, turning grazing land into desert. Since the late 1970s, the Sahara Desert has been expanding southward at a rate of about 12 miles per year. The country of Ethiopia loses about a billion tons of topsoil annually as a result of intensive cultivation for cash crops. The use of firewood for fuel in Africa has resulted in severe deforestation. All of these developments have impeded food production.

As African countries became integrated into the world economy,

---

Most of the Igbo were primarily root-crop subsistence farmers who grew yams, cassava, and taro. Unlike some of the other West African peoples in the area, both Igbo males and females were engaged in agricultural production. Like most other traditional West African societies, the Igbo used some of their agricultural production for exchanges within the villages and trade outside the region. Women dominated trade in the rural village markets, whereas men dominated trade with other regions.

Uchendu described the traditional political system of the Igbo as unique. Igbo villages were essentially autonomous. At the village level, a form of direct democracy operated in which all adult males

Harvesting sugarcane.

food problems were intensified by declining commodity prices. Western industrial nations with large-scale mechanized agriculture have produced huge surpluses of wheat, corn, rice, and soybeans. Large multinational companies based in Minneapolis and Chicago have been able to dominate the world grain trade. These companies are able to lower the prices of

these grains, which has driven thousands of African farmers out of business. In many cases, government officials living in African cities support low prices for food to gain political loyalty from urban residents. Yet falling prices lower the export earnings of African states, which were already confronted with rising interest rates and debts to core nations. These developments negated government plans to increase food production. As a result, food imports have increased throughout Africa. For example, wheat imports rose by 250 percent from 1969 to 1982, just before the widespread Ethiopian famine (Connell, 1987).

To resolve this food crisis, some Africans have called for increased regional trade within Africa and less reliance on the world market and global economy (Okigbo, 1988). Both anthropological researchers and Africans have called for production of underutilized African food plants that would broaden their food base. They suggest growing a variety of different plant species to improve the productive capacity of the

land. In addition, anthropologists suggest restoring some traditional, small-scale subsistence production to provide a more balanced system of agriculture. This would involve providing credit and education to peasant farmers. Moreover, African governments must devote greater resources to research on land use and technology.

Western and African anthropologists, in cooperation with other specialists, have been working to resolve these problems. For example, in 1984, the American Anthropological Association set up a Task Force on African Famine, which included anthropologists with fieldwork experience in Africa, specialists in food security, and members of private voluntary organizations such as Oxfam, which deal with famine.

Anthropologists have a great deal of knowledge that is needed by agencies dealing with famine and food supply. The ethnographic data on local conditions in different communities are extremely valuable in famine relief and development planning to prevent future famines in Africa.

participated in decision making. Leadership was exercised by male and female officeholders who had developed power and influence gradually. Executive, legislative, and judicial functions were divided among leaders, lineages, and age-grade associations.

After Nigeria became independent in 1960, it was confronted with the types of ethnic problems

that beset many other African nations. The British had drawn political boundaries without respect to the traditional territorial areas of indigenous kingdoms or ethnic groups. For example, the Yoruba live in both Benin and Nigeria, and the Hausa reside in both Niger and Nigeria. Consequently, when Nigeria achieved independence, the presence of various ethnic groups inhibited the political unification of the new nation. Most of the Hausa, Igbo, and Yoruban peoples identified with their own ethnic group and territories.

Cultural anthropologist Abner Cohen, who examined the role of ethnicity and political conflict in Nigeria, focused on Hausa traders in the Yoruban city of Ibadan. Cohen (1969, 1974) described how ethnic distinctions between the Hausa and Yoruba became the basis of political and economic competition. Cohen used the term *retribalization* to refer to the Hausa strategy of using ethnic affiliations as an informal network for economic and political purposes. These networks were in turn used to extend and coordinate Hausa cattle-trading activities in Ibadan. Cohen's ethnographic research in Ibadan has become a model for analyzing ethnic trends in urban areas throughout the world. Cohen demonstrated how ethnic processes and the meaningful cultural symbols used by ethnic groups can mobilize political and economic behavior. These cultural symbols aided ethnic groups in Nigeria in their struggle to attain a decent livelihood and political power in the urban communities. This process, however, generated tensions among the various ethnic groups.

Nigeria's multicultural society was racked by interethnic, religious, and political competition and conflict. In the mid-1960s, these conflicts erupted into civil war. Because the Igbo people had had no historical experience with a centralized state, they resented the imposition of political authority over them. This led to conflict among the Igbo, the Yoruba, and the Hausa. Following the collapse of a civilian government in the 1960s, the Igbo were attacked and massacred in northern Nigeria. The Igbo fled as refugees from the north and called for secession from Nigeria. In 1967, under Igbo leadership, eastern Nigeria seceded and proclaimed itself the independent Republic of Biafra. The result was a civil war in which non-African powers assisted both sides. After three years of bitter fighting and a loss of about 2 million people, Biafra was defeated, and the Igbo were reincorporated into Nigeria.

Under a series of military-dominated regimes, Nigeria has succeeded in healing the worst wounds of its civil war. One strategy was to incorporate all ethnic and religious groups into the military leadership. In addition, the country was carved into nineteen states, the boundaries cutting through the territories of the Yoruba, Hausa, and Igbo. This encouraged the development of multiethnic coalitions and a federalist political system (Ramsay, 2001). Nigerians hope that when ethnic and religious factions develop new social ties based on education, class backgrounds, and new forms of nationalism, older forms of association will weaken. Currently, however, ethnic loyalties and identities appear to be very powerful bases for social and political life in Africa. This has produced the potential for political disintegration in many African states (Lewis, 1992). Nation-building projects that unify different ethnic groups remain the most formidable challenge facing Nigeria and other African countries.

Ethnicity in the Caribbean

Ethnicity in the Caribbean is a complex, diverse mixture of imported African slaves, East Indian laborers, and various Europeans. One conventional ethnic classification is based on skin color, especially the distinction between black and brown. Beginning with the illicit offspring of European whites and slave women, a category of mulattoes began to gain certain advantages. At present, "brown" in many Caribbean islands such as Jamaica is synonymous with middle class, and these people are associated with the professional occupations (Eriksen, 1993).

After the arrival of East Indians in the Caribbean, new ethnic relations began to develop. In contrast to the blacks, East Indians were free to develop their own ethnic communities. Thus, in the Caribbean, the East Indian descendants are divided among different linguistic and cultural groups. There are Hindu and Muslim ethnic communities, as well as Tamil and other language communities. Many of the Indians have used these ethnic ties to form effective career networks to enhance their professional careers. In response to the large Indian communities in islands such as Trinidad, the black community began to strengthen its own ethnic identity. The blacks began to develop stereotypes, such as the "backwardness" of the Indian communities and the "progressive" Europeanized black communities. Many of the black, brown, and Indian communities have been revitalizing their own ethnic identity in the context of globalization within the Caribbean region.

Patterns of Urban Anthropology

Urban anthropologists who have done research in Latin America, Africa, and the Caribbean have helped improve our understanding of issues such as poverty and rural-to-urban migration. These topics are of vital interest to government officials and urban planners, economists and development technicians, and other international agencies. Population growth and urbanization in non-Western underdeveloped nations have posed global problems that urgently need to be resolved. Urban anthropologists working in these regions are providing data that can be used to help resolve these global problems.

The mass movement of people from rural areas to the cities is a major trend in these regions. Between 1950 and 1980, the proportion of the population living in urban areas increased from 41 to 65 percent. Cities such as Mexico City, Rio de Janeiro (Brazil), Buenos Aires (Argentina), San Juan (Puerto Rico), and Lagos (Nigeria) are among the largest metropolitan areas in the world. For example, it is predicted that by 2015, the population of Mexico City will exceed 20 million (*World Almanac,* 2001). It is projected that if growth rates remain the same, the metropolitan area of Mexico City will have more than 28 million inhabitants.

Much of this urban growth is due to internal migration. Migrants are *pushed* from the countryside by population growth, poverty, lack of opportunity, and the absence of land reform. They are *pulled* to the city by the prospects of regular employment, education and medical care for their children, and the excitement of urban life. Rapid urbanization has led to the development of illegal squatter settlements, or high-density shantytowns, in and outside urban areas. Shantytowns provide homes for the impoverished and unskilled migrants. Anthropologists have found that in some of these settlements, some people are optimistic about finding work and improving their living conditions. In the shantytowns, the new migrants take advantage of city services such as running water, transportation, and electricity. However, in the worst slums in non-Western cities, many of these new migrants are so poor that they are forced to live in the streets.

Some anthropologists have focused their research on the poverty conditions of many of the

A squatter settlement in Santo Domingo, the Dominican Republic. Wealth and poverty coexist throughout the Caribbean.

non-Western urban centers. One well-known pioneer is Oscar Lewis, who studied families of slum dwellers in Mexico City (1961) and San Juan and New York (1966). From these studies, and from other evidence collected by urban anthropologists, Lewis concluded that the cultural values of the slum dwellers inhibited them from pursuing economic opportunities. He referred to these values as the **culture of poverty.**

Lewis described the people who maintained this culture of poverty as having a sense of fatalism, apathy, and hopelessness with respect to aspirations for economic or social mobility. They tended to be suspicious and fearful, disdained authority, and did not plan for the future. Alcoholism, violence, and unstable marriages were common. According to Lewis, these values were passed on to children through the enculturation process. Thus, poverty and hopelessness were perpetuated from generation to generation.

To be fair, Lewis stressed that the culture of poverty was a result of the lack of economic opportunities in the slum neighborhoods. Moreover, he carefully noted that these attitudes affected only about 20 percent of the people living in these areas. Nevertheless, many critics have charged that Lewis's hypothesis is an example of *blaming the victim;* that is, it attributes poverty to the negative attitudes of poor people themselves rather than to the economic and social stratification of their society. Some anthropologists have challenged the assertion that these attitudes are widespread among slum residents. For example, Helen Safa (1974) conducted research on a shantytown in San Juan and did not find the hopelessness and apathy that were portrayed in Lewis's studies. Safa found that the poor in the shantytowns have values emphasizing hard work, thrift, and determination. Her data contained little to confirm Lewis's characterization of the poor as having a pathological culture.

Safa and other anthropologists emphasize that these culture-of-poverty values are not perpetuated from generation to generation as Lewis suggested.

Rather, each individual develops attitudes and strategies toward achievement depending on the availability of real economic opportunities. According to Safa, a sense of achievement based on individual initiative had relatively little effect on real economic and social mobility. She observed that, because of rapid economic growth in Puerto Rico, a few privileged people were able to achieve upward mobility. This limited mobility led poor people to believe that economic and social advancement was due to individual and personal initiative rather than socioeconomic factors. In fact, Safa contends, socioeconomic conditions in Puerto Rico are, to a great extent, a consequence of global economic processes beyond the control of individuals in the shantytowns.

Other anthropologists are investigating the patterns of rural to urban migrations in non-Western countries. For example, during the 1970s, a comprehensive study of highland Guatemalan Mayan Indians of San Pedro La Laguna by anthropologists William Demarest and Benjamin Paul (1981) found a significant pattern of rural-to-urban mobility among Indian males. Although the Indians were extremely resourceful in gaining employment in urban areas such as Guatemala City, the low wages did not allow them to support families. Consequently, many of them resettled in San Pedro, where they looked for wives.

SUMMARY

Globalization has had a major effect on the countries of Latin America and the Caribbean, Africa, the Middle East, and Asia. These countries were either directly or indirectly affected by Western colonialism. Demographically, diseases or slavery devastated the countries of Latin America, the Caribbean, and Africa. In the long run, all of these countries were affected by declining death rates brought about by Western colonialism, but populations began to increase rapidly because of high birth rates.

Economically, these societies were drawn into the global economy and were transformed by producing commodities that were demanded by the wealthier core societies. Patterns of land ownership were reordered, and many peasants were producing

for economic elites. Religious changes occurred in all of these countries because of Western expansion and missionary influence.

Western colonialism eventually gave way to political movements based on nationalist, independence, and, sometimes, revolutionary tendencies. These movements represented anticolonial sentiments and resulted in many new countries around the world.

These countries were absorbed into the global economy at different levels, depending on the resources that were available in their regions. Some countries remain poor and underdeveloped because their economies are heavily dependent on the wealthy core countries. Other countries, including

Mexico and Nigeria, have oil resources that could be used to help develop their economies. Despite oil resources, these non-Western countries still find themselves with various obstacles to developing their economies.

Ethnographers have conducted research on the peasantry, social structures, family life, and gender in these countries. Each region has unique structures based on its cultural beliefs and practices. The peasantry differs in various countries based on the people's traditional relations and new global relationships to the world market. Family structures and gender relations are illuminated by cultural anthropologists as they study patterns that develop in relationship to the emergence of new urban areas and the changing rural areas.

Cultural anthropologists are also studying the overall patterns and consequences of urbanization in these societies, including the issues of poverty and rural-to-urban migration. They find that people throughout these countries, despite their hardships, continue to adapt their traditional social and cultural mechanisms to help them adjust to the effects of globalization.

QUESTIONS TO THINK ABOUT

1. Compare and contrast the effects of colonialism on Latin America, Africa, and the Caribbean.

2. How did globalization impinge on the traditional economies of Latin America, Africa, and Caribbean countries?

3. What were some of the religious changes that came with Western expansion into Latin America, Africa, and the Caribbean?

4. Compare the independence movements in Latin America and Africa.

5. What are some of the differences between the peripheral and semiperipheral countries in Latin America, Africa, and the Caribbean?

6. What do you think will enable the peripheral and semiperipheral countries in Latin America, Africa, and the Caribbean to sustain their economies in the future?

7. How is the peasantry different in various Latin American, African, and Caribbean countries?

8. Compare and contrast the social structure of Latin America with that of Africa.

9. How have family and gender patterns in Latin America, Africa, and the Caribbean been influenced by globalization?

10. What are the effects of urbanization in Latin America, Africa, and the Caribbean?

KEY TERMS

apartheid	dyadic contract	relative deprivation
assimilation	fictive kinship ties	revolution
closed peasant community	open peasant community	rising expectations
culture of poverty	patron-client ties	syncretism

INTERNET EXERCISES

1. Read about the 1954 overthrow of the president of Guatemala, Jacobo Arbenz, at **http://www.english.upenn.edu/~afilreis/50s/zinn-chap16.html#guatemala**. What was the purpose of the overthrow? Why was the United States involved? How does this type of practice by the United States subvert the needs of the people of the region? Why were human rights of so little concern to the United States government in this situation?

2. Review the website titled "CIA Involved in Guatemala Coup, 1954" at **http://www. english.upenn.edu/~afilreis/50s/guatemal a.html**. Why was simple land reform such a threat to the United States? How does the United Fruit Company play into this? How is Guatemala (and many other countries in Central America) a peripheral nation?

SUGGESTED READINGS

COMAROFF, JEAN. 1985. *Body of Power, Spirit of Resistance.* Chicago: University of Chicago Press. An incisive and moving anthropological analysis of a religious-based resistance movement among the Tshidi of South Africa.

CRAPANZANO, VINCENT. 1986. *Waiting: The Whites of South Africa.* New York: Random House. A fascinating ethnological study that examines the deep convictions, fears, and religious fervor mixed with racism of white South Africans as they assess their dilemma.

GIBBS, JAMES L., JR. (Ed.). 1965. *Peoples of Africa.* New York: Holt, Rinehart & Winston. An anthology containing some classic descriptions of African societies, including the Igbo, the Swazi, and the Yoruba.

KOTTAK, CONRAD. 1983. *Assault on Paradise: Social Change in a Brazilian Village.* New York: Random House. This is a detailed description of a Brazilian community responding to the changes brought about by the modern global economy.

KUPER, LEO, and M. G. SMITH (Eds.). 1971. *Pluralism in Africa.* Berkeley: University of California Press. A classic theoretical attempt at understanding ethnicity, colonialism, and social change in various African societies.

LEWIS, OSCAR. 1959. *Five Families: Mexican Case Studies in the Culture of Poverty.* New York: Wiley.

———. 1961. *The Children of Sanchez.* New York: Random House. These two books by Oscar Lewis are based on in-depth interviews with rural migrants who face problems in urban Mexico. They remain worthwhile descriptions of people coping with poverty, although the culture-of-poverty thesis has been challenged by many anthropologists.

OLMOS, MARGARITE FERNANDEZ (Ed.). 1997. *Sacred Possessions: Vodoun, Santeria, Obeah, and the Caribbean.* New Brunswick, NJ: Rutgers University Press. A broad overview of the various syncretic religious movements such as Vodoun and Santeria that have influenced the people of the Caribbean islands.

RICH, EVELYN JONES, and IMMANUEL WALLERSTEIN. 1972. *Africa: Tradition and Change.* New York: Random House. A dated but useful introduction to the peoples of Africa. It includes many Africans speaking for themselves about their condition.

SMITH, CAROL (Ed.). 1990. *Guatemalan Indians and the State: 1540–1988.* Austin: University of Texas Press. An anthology of readings on the relationship between the Indian communities and economic and political developments in Guatemala.

CHAPTER 22

Globalization in the Middle East and Asia

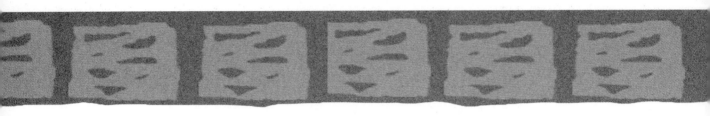

CHAPTER OUTLINE

CHAPTER QUESTIONS

- What were the most important consequences of colonialism in the Middle East and Asia?

- What creates uneven development in the Middle East and Asia?

- What are the basic features of family and gender relations in the Middle East and Asia?

- How does globalization result in ethnic tensions in the Middle East and Asia?

- What is the link between globalization and Islamic movements?

As in Latin America, Africa, and the Caribbean, the process of globalization has been going on in the Middle East and Asia since the exploration of these regions by Europeans. The Middle East and Asia are vast heterogeneous regions with different ethnic groups and cultures that have had contact with each other through trade and exploration since the first millennium. For the purposes of this chapter, the Middle East includes the area of both North Africa and Southwest Asia (Figure 22.1). Many of the countries of these regions were influenced by the development of Islamic culture and the Arabic language. Traditionally, this area was referred to as the "Near East" to distinguish it from the "Far East." At other times, it has been mistakenly labeled the "Arab world." The term *Arab* refers to people who speak the Arabic language; included within this category of Arabic-speaking regions are the countries of Jordan, Syria, Iraq, Saudi Arabia, Yemen, Oman, and the Persian Gulf states such as Kuwait and the United Arab Emirates. The Middle Eastern region, however, also contains non-Arabic-speaking countries such as Israel, Turkey, and Iran. Thus, the Middle East as described in this chapter comprises peoples with different histories, languages, ethnicities, and religions.

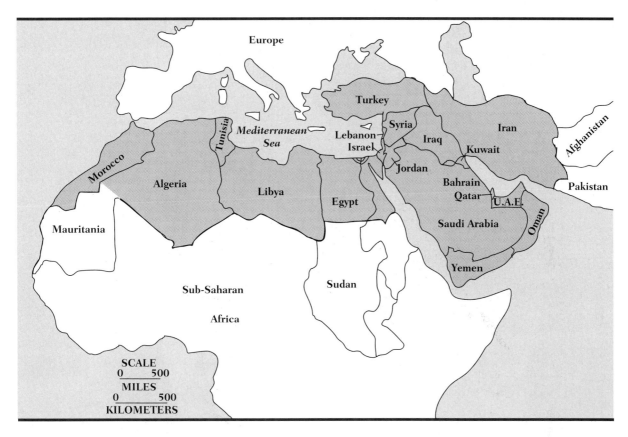

FIGURE 22.1 The Middle East.

Source: Adapted from *The Middle East and Central Asia: An Anthropological Approach*, 4th ed., by Dale F. Eickelman.
© 1998. Reprinted by permission of Prentice Hall, Upper Saddle River, NJ.

Asia too is a culturally diverse continent with a wide variety of sociocultural systems. This chapter focuses on three regions: South Asia, East Asia, and Southeast Asia (Figure 22.2). These regions contain most of the world's population—over 3 billion people. Different forms of societies have developed in these regions, ranging from hunter-gatherer and horticultural societies of the tropical rain forests to the pastoral nomads of northern China to the advanced industrial society of Japan. We have already discussed Japanese society in Chapter 19 on industrial societies. This chapter focuses primarily on the agricultural societies in Asia that have been transformed by globalization processes and discusses the findings of anthropologists who use a global perspective that reflects the ongoing changes and transitions in the societies of the Middle East and Asia.

Colonialism and Globalization

The Middle East

Aside from the Portuguese, most Europeans did not have much direct contact with the Middle East until the 1800s. As European countries industrialized, however, they came to view the Middle East as an area ripe for imperial control. In the European view, the Middle East could supply raw materials and serve as markets for manufactured goods. Napoleon Bonaparte led an expedition to Egypt in 1798, bringing it under French rule for a brief period. He planned to incorporate Egypt as a colony that would complement French economic interests. Because of British rivalry following the Napoleonic Wars, the French had to evacuate Egypt; nevertheless,

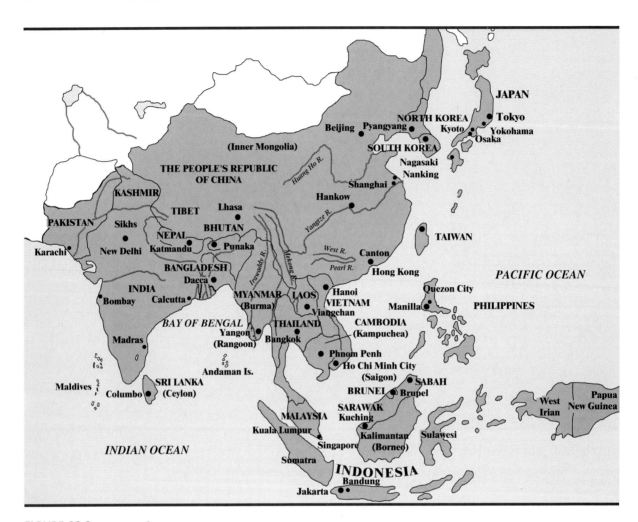

FIGURE 22.2   A map of contemporary Asia.

Europeans gradually attained more influence in the region.

Although the British did not directly colonize Egypt until 1882, various European advisers influenced Egyptian rulers to develop specific products for the world market. Egyptian rulers and the upper classes cooperated with Western interests in these activities to induce economic growth. Factories were built for processing sugar, and cotton became the most important agricultural commodity in the country. The most important development project that affected ties between the Middle East and the West was the Suez Canal, which connects the Mediterranean Sea with the Gulf of Suez. Completed in 1869, the Suez Canal was financed through capital supplied by French and British interests. The canal shortened the distance between East and West, thereby drawing the Middle East into the orbit of the core nations.

To offset British expansion in the Middle East, the French began to build a North African empire, taking control of Algeria, Tunisia, and Morocco. Morocco was considered the most "perfect" French colony, in which, through indirect rule, the French devised a "scientific colony" that required only a small number of French officials to supervise a vast territory. Thus, the French ruled through urban elites, rural leaders, and Moroccan religious officials. They developed large commercial enterprises such as railroads and mining, as well as various agricultural operations. These commercial enterprises enabled the colony to pay for itself, a definite asset for the French.

European expansion in the Middle East continued throughout the nineteenth and early twentieth centuries. Although not directly colonized, Turkey, which was then the center of the Ottoman Empire, came under the economic control of Western interests. To reduce the disparity in economic development between their country and Europe, Turkish rulers gave concessions to French and British interests to develop industries and services in Turkey. These enterprises produced cheap goods that undermined native Turkish businesses. By the end of the nineteenth century, Turkey had become a peripheral society, exporting raw materials, providing cheap labor, and depending on core societies for manufactured goods. This led to the end of the Ottoman Empire.

Although not as industrialized as many other European countries, Russia began to expand toward the Middle East during the mid-1800s and eventually assumed control over various regions of central Asia, absorbing the Muslim populations of Samarkand, Tashkent, and Turkestan. To secure access to the warm waters of the Persian Gulf, Russia also moved into Iran (formerly Persia), taking control of the northern half of the country. The British, who maintained control of commerce in the Persian Gulf through their naval fleet, were thus threatened by this Russian expansion. As a countermeasure, they moved into southern Iran and funneled capital into the region by developing a tobacco monopoly and financing other economic projects. Eventually, in 1907, the British and Russians agreed to divide Iran into three spheres, with northern and central Iran, including Tehran, in the Russian sphere; southeastern Iran in the British sphere; and an area between in the neutral zone. The Iranians were neither consulted nor informed about the terms of this agreement (Keddie, 1981).

Another area that was contested between the Russians and the British was Afghanistan. Geographically, Afghanistan is situated between the Middle East and South Asia. It is a country made up of various Muslim ethnic groups who were involved in agricultural practices and also nomadic pastoralism in the rugged mountains and deep valleys, deserts, and arid plateaus. Afghanistan was a remnant of one of the major Muslim empires founded in the seventeenth century.

In the nineteenth century, the Russians tried to colonize Afghanistan by completing a railway to the Afghan border, and the British countered by building a railway from their colonized portion of South Asia northward. This "Great Game" played out between the British and Russians left Afghanistan as a buffer state between these colonial powers. Various Afghan leaders had to negotiate between these powers and give concessions to them to maintain their independence.

Following World War I, the European powers divided the Middle East into different *spheres of influence*. In addition to their North African empire, the French gained the countries of Lebanon and Syria as direct colonies. Other areas such as Turkey and the Arabian peninsula remained politically independent but became peripheral states.

The British took Egypt, Iraq, and Palestine as direct colonies. The British also allowed European Jews to immigrate to Palestine. Because Jewish communities had faced discrimination and persecution for centuries in European society, Jewish leaders in Europe called for the resettlement of Jews in their original homeland in Palestine. This movement, known as *Zionism,* influenced British policy, which led to the immigration of thousands of Jews to Palestine, with dramatic consequences for the Middle East.

Asia

Intensive economic and political contact between Asia and the West began during the period of European mercantilism. The first phase of Western expansion into Asia began with the Portuguese trade in India, China, and Southeast Asia. The next phase involved the Dutch, French, and British, who established private trading companies in Asia to secure access to exportable goods.

India, Burma, and Malaysia Western nations resorted to direct colonization in Asia following the Industrial Revolution. For example, Britain colonized India, gaining control over the production of export cash crops such as jute, oil seeds, cotton, and wheat. Because India did not have a strong centralized state, it could not resist British colonization.

The opening of the Suez Canal facilitated Britain's management of its Asian colonies, and by 1900, the British had established direct economic and political control over 300 million South Asians (Warshaw, 1989b).

From their base in India, the British initiated a series of wars to incorporate Burma as a direct colony. Eventually, the British expanded their colonial domination southward to the region of Malaysia. To satisfy industrial societies' increasing demand for commodities such as tin (for the canning industry) and rubber, the British developed mining and plantations in both Burma and Malaysia. In addition, as the demand for rice grew in the world market, the British commercialized rice production for export.

China   The industrial nations also attempted to carve out colonies in China. Although that country had been open to European trade ever since the Portuguese established ports in Macao in the sixteenth century, China successfully resisted direct colonization by the West, for several reasons. First, it was farther from the West than were other Asian countries. Second, China had a highly centralized state empire in which mandarin officials controlled local regions and thus was a more formidable empire than were other Asian countries. Third, the Chinese government was not impressed with Western goods and technology. Chinese officials had been familiar with Western products from the time of Marco Polo in the fifteenth century and forbade the importation of Western commodities.

Despite this resistance, the British eventually gained access to China through the introduction of opium. Attempts by the Chinese government to prohibit the illegal smuggling of this drug into the country led to the Opium Wars of 1839–1842 between Great Britain and China. Britain defeated China, subsequently acquiring Hong Kong as a colony and securing other business concessions. Eventually, international settlements were established in cities such as Shanghai, which became sovereign city-states outside the Chinese government's control (Tweddell & Kimball, 1985).

The Dutch Empire   The Dutch expanded into the East Indies, eventually incorporating the region— now known as Indonesia—into their colonial empire. By the nineteenth century, the Dutch had

developed what they referred to as the *Kultur-System,* which lasted until 1917. Through this system, Indonesian peasants were allowed to grow only certain cash crops, such as sugar, coffee, tobacco, and indigo, for the world market. These crops were developed at the expense of subsistence crops such as rice. The policy of coerced labor and exploitation of the peasantry held back the economic development of the Indonesian islands (Geertz, 1963a).

French Indo-China   French imperial rivalry with Britain had direct consequences for Southeast Asia. By 1893, the French had conquered and established direct colonial rule over Cambodia, Vietnam, and Laos—a region that became known as Indochina. In northern Vietnam, French settlers directed the production of coal, zinc, and tin; in the southern areas near the Mekong River, they developed the land to produce rubber and rice exports.

Thailand: An Independent Country   One country in Southeast Asia that did not become directly colonized was Thailand. The Thai monarchy, which had some experience with Western interests, developed economic and political strategies to play European rivals against one another while adopting Western innovations. European business interests were allowed to aid in the development of some goods, but not to exercise direct political control. To some extent, this suited the geopolitical strategies of both the British and the French, who preferred Thailand as a buffer state between their colonial domains (Slagter & Kerbo, 2000).

The Philippines   The Philippines were directly colonized first by Spain, then by the United States. Spain took control of most of the Philippine Islands during the sixteenth century. As in Latin America, the Spanish established *pueblos* (towns) in which colonial officials directed Filipino peasant labor and collected tribute. Eventually, *encomiendas*—land grants to Spanish settlers—developed into *haciendas,* on which tobacco, sugar, and indigo were planted for export to the world market. Aside from these agricultural enterprises, the Spanish encouraged few commercial developments. During the Spanish-American War of 1898, the United States defeated Spanish forces in both the Philippines and the Caribbean. Many Filipinos sided with the United

States in hopes of achieving independence from
Spain. When the United States refused to recognize
Philippine independence, numerous Filipinos redirected their resistance efforts against the United
States. After a protracted war in which 600,000 Filipinos lost their lives and many more were placed
in concentration camps, the Philippines were directly colonized by the United States. The United
States continued to organize native Filipino labor to
produce cash crops such as tobacco, sugar, and indigo as export commodities for the world market
(Warshaw, 1988).

Consequences of Colonialism

Demographic Change

Western expansion and colonialism in non-Western
countries brought unprecedented demographic
growth to the populations of these agricultural
states. As in Latin America, Africa, and the
Caribbean, the development of intensive cash-crop
cultivation often resulted in rapid population
growth. As labor shortages developed in subsistence agriculture as a result of moving labor into
cash-cropping agriculture for the European market,
peasant farmers began to increase their family size
(Robbins, 1999). This increase in fertility led to
rapid population growth in many of the Middle
East and Asian societies. Eventually, Europeans introduced new medical and sanitation practices that
led to a tremendous reduction in death rates
through the control of smallpox, plague, yellow
fever, and malaria. Meanwhile, birth rates remained
high. The combination of reduced death rates and
high birth rates led to dramatic population increases. For example, the population of India increased by one-third between 1881 and 1931 and
then doubled between 1931 and 1971. In Chapter
24 we will discuss some of the global effects of
these population trends.

Unlike the situation in the West, population
growth in colonized non-Western countries was not
coupled with sustained and rapid industrialization.
The expanding Middle Eastern and Asian populations therefore had to be absorbed by the intensification of agricultural production. For example,
population growth in Indonesia under the Dutch
led to what Clifford Geertz has referred to as

"agricultural involution" (1963a). The commercialization of agriculture and the use of coerced labor
increased production somewhat, but the rates of increase could not keep pace with population
growth. Agricultural yields per day of labor actually
decreased. In addition, as the population grew,
land became more scarce. Thus, the system of intensified agriculture was increasingly unable to
feed the growing population.

As a result of colonialism, major urban centers
grew quickly in the Middle East and Asia. For example, the cities of Cairo in Egypt and Tehran in
Iran began to grow at tremendous rates. In India,
the British created port cities such as Calcutta,
Bombay, and Madras that became international
trading and financial centers. In China, Shanghai
and Nanking developed into major urban centers
as a result of the expansion of Western businesses.
Southeast Asian cities such as Rangoon, Bangkok,
Saigon, Jakarta, Kuala Lumpur, Singapore, and
Manila expanded rapidly. These cities attracted
rural migrants who crowded into squatter settlements and slums.

Economic Change

The economies of the countries of the Middle East
and Asia during the nineteenth century were directed toward the production of agricultural goods
such as tea, sugar, tobacco, cotton, rice, tin, and
rubber for export. Prices of these goods were subject to fluctuations in the world market. Land that
had been converted to growing these export crops
could no longer support peasant villages. Native
handicrafts declined dramatically in importance in
comparison with export-oriented commodity production. In addition, as in other colonized areas of
the world, imported Western manufactured goods
flowed into Middle Eastern and Asian nations.
Thus, these societies became more dependent on
core industrial societies.

As in Latin America, Africa, and the Caribbean,
one major consequence of Western colonialism was
the integration of many agricultural village communities into wider regional and global economic
patterns. The precolonial traditional villages were
probably never entirely self-sufficient and were tied
to regional and national trading networks. However,
under Western colonialism, the village peasantry in
the Middle East and Asia was no longer isolated

from cities, and the global market determined the prices for agricultural goods. This global transformation of agricultural economies triggered dramatic changes in non-Western rural communities. Because few peasants had enough capital to own and manage land, much of the land fell into the hands of colonial settlers, large landowners, and money lenders. In many cases, these changes encouraged absentee landownership and temporary tenancy. Long-term care of the land by the peasantry was sacrificed for immediate profits. As in the case of the peasants of Latin America, Africa, and the Caribbean, land, labor, and capital were thus disconnected from the village kinship structures of reciprocity and redistribution, or what has been referred to as the *moral economy* (see Chapter 18). As globalization occurred, these peasants were incorporated into the global cash economy. Their lives were now dependent on the fluctuations of a global economy that determined their success or failure as farmers.

Religious Change

The major religious traditions of most of the societies in the Middle East and Asia are Islam, Hinduism, and Buddhism. The Islamic tradition dates to the life of Muhammad, who was born in A.D. 570 in the city of Mecca, which is now in Saudi Arabia. Muslims believe that Muhammad is the final prophet in the long line of prophets referred to in the Bible. They share with Christians and Jews the faith that Abraham was the founder and first prophet of their tradition. Unlike Christians and Jews, however, they believe that Muhammad began receiving revelations from God that culminated in the major religious text known as the *Qur'an* (Koran). The traditions of Islam spread widely throughout areas of the Middle East and Asia.

Two other southern Asian religions—Hinduism and Buddhism—have influenced civilizations throughout the region. Both developed in India and are associated with three major doctrines. The first doctrine is known as *samsara,* or reincarnation, which refers to how an individual's soul transmigrates and is reborn in a new organism in a new cycle of existence. The second doctrine is *karma,* the belief that an individual's destiny is affected by his or her behavior in previous lives. Hinduism emphasizes that an individual must live a dutiful

and ethical life to produce good *karma* for future existences. The third doctrine is *moksha,* or *nirvana*—spiritual enlightenment—the ultimate aim and spiritual goal for all Hindus and Buddhists. Enlightenment represents the final escape from the cycle of life, death, rebirth, and suffering into an ultimate spiritual state of existence.

The Middle East and Asia already had the highly literate religious traditions of Islam, Hinduism, and Buddhism, which meant that Western missionaries had a much more difficult time trying to convert native populations in these regions. However, in many cases, the Western missionaries in these Middle Eastern and Asian countries were instrumental in teaching some of the basic cultural values of the Western world, including political ideas regarding democratic institutions, civil liberties, and individual freedom.

Political Change: Independence and Nationalism

During the nineteenth and twentieth centuries, the extension of Western power into the Middle East and Asia elicited responses ranging from native reformist activities to nationalist independence movements. Because most people in these regions were Muslims, Hindus, or Buddhists, many of the anti-colonial responses reflected a religious orientation. In response to Western colonialism, Muslim, Hindu, and Buddhist leaders called for a rethinking of their religious traditions to accommodate pressures from the West. Reformers such as Muhammad Abduh in Egypt and Tagore in India argued that the sources of Western strength evolved in part from early Eastern contributions to science, medicine, and scholarship. Thus, the reformists exhorted believers to look to their own religious traditions as a source of inspiration to overcome Western domination. Reformist movements spread throughout the Muslim world, especially among the urban, educated classes, paving the way for later nationalist and independence movements throughout the region.

Similarly, most of the anti-colonial, nationalist, and independence movements that emerged in Asia were linked to local religious or political developments. They were also associated with the rise of Western-educated groups that articulated nationalist demands.

A Nationalist and Independence Movement in India

As in other colonies, the British desired an educated class of Indians to serve as government clerks and cultural intermediaries between the British and the colonized people. The British sponsored a national educational system that included universities and training colleges, which educated thousands of Indians. These educated people became part of a literate middle class, familiar with Western liberal thought regarding human rights and self-determination. A small, powerful merchant class that benefited from British economic policies also emerged.

Whereas India formerly had been fragmented into separate language groups, the colonial educational system provided the educated middle classes with a common language—English. Improved transportation and communication media such as railroads, print technology, and the telegraph accelerated the movement for national unity. In addition, the educated classes became increasingly aware of the hypocrisy of British "values" such as equality and democracy, as they were exposed to racism and discrimination in the form of exclusion from British private hotels, clubs, and parks.

The majority of the Indian population, however, was not middle class but was made up of peasants who lived in rural village communities and did not speak English. Thus, the middle-class nationalist movement did not directly appeal to them. This gulf between the middle classes and the peasants was bridged by a remarkable individual, Mohandas Gandhi, later called the Mahatma, or "great soul." Although from the middle class, Gandhi fused Hindu religious sentiments with Western political thought to mobilize the peasantry against British domination. Anthropologist Richard Fox contributed an extensive analysis of Gandhi's role in the anticolonial struggle (1989). In his study, Fox emphasized the role of an individual with charismatic abilities to bring about major social and cultural change within a society.

Hindu traditions provided the model for Gandhi's strategies of *nonviolent resistance*. He called for the peaceful boycott of British-produced goods, telling the villagers to maintain their traditional weaving industries to spin their own cloth. Through his protests and boycotts, he rallied

Mohandas Gandhi rallied the Indian nation toward independence from the British.

millions of Indians in a mass movement that eventually could not be resisted. In 1947, two years after the end of World War II, the British were forced to relinquish their empire in South Asia (Warshaw, 1989b).

Revolutionary Movements in Asia

As in Latin America, Africa, and the Caribbean, a number of revolutionary movements developed in the Middle East and Asia as a result of globalization and contact with Western colonialism and power. The revolutions that developed in Asia had worldwide repercussions. In China, a grassroots revolutionary movement developed out of anti-Western, nationalistic movements. In the early twentieth century, Sun Yat-sen, a doctor educated in Hawaii and Hong Kong, championed the formation of a democratic republic in China, gaining support among the peasants by calling for the redistribution of land. The movement toward democracy failed, however. Instead, the military under Chiang Kai-shek, who did not sympathize with peasant resistance

Mao Zedong

movements or democratic reforms, assumed control of China. These developments encouraged the growth of the Chinese Communist Party under Mao Zedong. Mao's guerrillas engaged in a protracted struggle against Chiang Kai-shek's forces in the 1940s.

Mao Zedong was familiar with Karl Marx's prediction that the urban proleteriat would direct revolutions toward socialism and communism. Mao, in contrast, believed that the peasantry could become the backbone of a communist revolution (Wolf, 1969). Through the Chinese Communist Party, Mao began to mobilize the peasantry. Calling for the overthrow of the landlords and Western forms of capitalism that he blamed for social and economic inequality, Mao made Marxism comprehensible to Chinese peasants. By 1949, after two decades of struggle, Mao and his peasant-based armies gained control of the country, renaming it the People's Republic of China.

Vietnam experienced the most dramatic nationalist and revolutionary movement of any of the French colonies of Southeast Asia. After World War II, the French attempted to reestablish their colonial regime in Indochina. Leading the opposition was Ho Chi Minh, who like many other Vietnamese, was frustrated by French colonialism and its negative impact on his society. Ho believed in the communist ideal but, like Mao Zedong, adapted

Marxist ideology to the particular concerns of his nationalist struggle (Wolf, 1969). His well-organized peasant army, the Vietminh, defeated the French forces at Dien Bien Phu in 1954. This defeat led to the withdrawal of the French from Vietnam.

Following Dien Bien Phu, the French and the Vietminh agreed to a temporary division of the country into North Vietnam under Ho Chi Minh and South Vietnam under Ngo Dinh Diem. The nation was to be unified through elections in 1956, but the elections were never held. As a Cold War strategy, the United States, meanwhile, committed itself to the survival of an independent, noncommunist South Vietnam, supplying Diem with massive economic, political, and military support. Diem lacked widespread support among the South Vietnamese population, however, and he brutally repressed dissent against his regime. He was overthrown in a military coup in 1963.

As communist opposition, supported by North Vietnam, escalated in the South, the United States dramatically increased its level of military involvement. By 1967, more than 500,000 U.S. troops were stationed in Vietnam. Unable to defeat the Vietnamese guerrillas, the United States entered into a long period of negotiation with the Vietnamese communists, finally signing a peace treaty in January 1973. Two years later, North Vietnam overran the South, thereby unifying the nation.

Ho Chi Minh

Uneven Development

By redirecting economic development toward an export-oriented global economy, Western colonialism and globalization transformed most of the formerly agricultural countries into peripheral, dependent economies. The wealthy core industrial societies of the West provided economic and political support to those elites who instituted policies to promote economic growth. Many of those elites in the Middle East and Asia minimized restrictions on foreign investment and opened their borders to multinational corporations. In addition, some of these societies had vital resources that enabled them to develop a special type of relationship with the wealthy industrialized core societies. However, a number of these societies, especially in Asia, began to attempt to withdraw from globalization and capitalism and develop self-sufficient economies.

Oil and the Middle East

The discovery of vast sources of oil—60 percent of the world's known reserves—in the Middle East has revolutionized trade and politics and has brought tremendous social change to the region. Oil became the major energy source for the industrial world. Multinational corporations based in the core societies developed these resources, controlling both oil production and prices, to maintain economic growth in their home countries. As nationalist independence movements spread, however, many countries demanded control over their oil. Nations such as Libya, Iran, Saudi Arabia, Iraq, and Kuwait began to nationalize their oil industries, and the multinational corporations eventually lost their controlling interests in the region.

The rapid increase in the price of oil since the 1970s enabled the oil-producing countries of the region to accumulate vast wealth and fueled worldwide inflation that raised the costs of all goods and raw materials. The per capita incomes of some Middle Eastern countries eventually surpassed those of many core countries. Realizing that they were dependent on a single export commodity, however, Middle Eastern countries took certain steps to diversify their economies. Smaller countries, such as Saudi Arabia, with a population of 15 million people, and Kuwait, with only 2 million—both ruled by

Oil production in countries such as Saudi Arabia has had global consequences.

royal families—financed some capital-intensive industries such as cement and detergent manufacturing and food processing. In doing so, these small Arab countries ensured high incomes for most of their population, which enhanced their political legitimacy and stability.

Larger oil-rich countries such as Iran and Iraq pursued rapid economic development to increase national wealth and legitimize their political regimes. Shah Muhammad Reza Pahlavi of Iran and Saddam Hussein of Iraq invited multinational corporations and consultants from core countries to help diversify their industries and develop their military forces. In contrast to the smaller countries, however, Iraq and Iran, with their larger populations (18 million and 42 million, respectively), had more difficulty raising economic standards for everyone immediately.

The vast majority of the people of the Middle East, however, do not live in oil-rich countries. These nations include Egypt, Syria, Jordan, Lebanon, and Morocco; although they have developed some industries to diversify their economies, they remain peripheral societies dependent on the wealthier industrial core societies.

Withdrawal from the Global Economy

Some countries, by adopting a socialist form of economic system, tried to develop economically outside of the capitalist global economy. In China following his victory in 1949, Mao Zedong implemented an economic development plan modeled on that of the former Soviet Union. He collectivized agriculture by appropriating the land owned by the elite and giving it to the peasants. Mao established cooperatives in which a number of villages owned agricultural land in common, and he also sponsored the development of heavy industries to stimulate economic growth. Communist Party officials, known as cadres, managed both the agricultural cooperatives and industrial firms.

When these policies failed to generate economic growth, Mao launched a radically different effort in 1958 favoring a decentralized economy. This plan, known as the Great Leap Forward, established locally based rural and urban communes that organized the production and distribution of goods and services. Each commune, consisting of 12,000 to 60,000 people, was subdivided into brigades of 100 to 700 households, production teams of about 35 households, and work teams of eight to ten households. Each commune was supposed to be self-sufficient, containing a banking system, police force, schools, day-care centers, mess halls, hospitals, and old-age centers. The communes established their own production goals and reinvested their profits in the commune.

Although some aspects of the Great Leap Forward were successful, especially those involving health care and literacy, the program failed to promote agricultural and industrial development. In fact, it was marked by famine, political corruption, and economic retardation. Mao then initiated an ideological campaign to eliminate corruption and political "deviance" while restoring revolutionary consciousness. This campaign, known as the Cultural Revolution, lasted from 1966 to 1976. Mao

organized young people into groups called the Red Guards to purify China of any capitalist, traditional Confucianist, or Western tendencies. Millions of people, primarily the educated classes, were arrested and forced to work on rural communes as punishment for their deviance from the communist path. By 1976, at the time of Mao's death, the Cultural Revolution had paralyzed economic development by eliminating the most skilled and educated classes, those who could have contributed to the nation's growth.

Vietnam also tried to withdraw from the world capitalist system, implementing a socialist government based on Marxist-Leninist principles. After the end of the Vietnam War, the government instituted a five-year plan that collectivized agriculture and relocated people from urban to rural communities. By 1978, 137 collective farms had been established; four million people, including half the population of Ho Chi Minh City (formerly Saigon), were resettled in what were called "new economic zones." These zones were organized to produce crops and light industry as a means of encouraging economic self-sufficiency. They were managed by Communist Party officials, many of whom had no direct experience in agriculture or industry.

By 1981, Vietnam had become one of the poorest peripheral nations in the world. While food production and labor productivity decreased, inflation and unemployment rose. Military expenditures drained the economy of needed funds for capital development. Part of the reason that Vietnam was underdeveloped was the war itself. For example, the defoliation of forests as a result of U.S. bombing and the use of Agent Orange impeded the growth of timber. At the same time, however, many of the problems were a direct result of inflexible ideological commitments and lack of expertise on the part of Communist Party bureaucrats (Pike, 1990).

Ethnographic Studies

A Middle Eastern Village in Transition

Studies of peasant villages in the Middle East have contributed to a more comprehensive understanding of the interconnections between peripheral and core nations. Cultural anthropologist Hani Fakhouri (1972) studied the Egyptian village of Kafr El-Elow, which at the time of Fakhouri's study (1966–1968) was undergoing substantial changes. About 80 percent of the Egyptian population lived in about 4,000 rural villages, many of which were being drawn into the global economy through rapid industrialization and the commercialization of agriculture.

Kafr El-Elow is located 18 miles south of Cairo. Before the 1920s, it was a relatively small farming community in which the *fellaheen* (peasants) practiced small-scale subsistence agriculture. After British colonization in the nineteenth century, the *fellaheen* began to grow cotton as an export commodity. By the 1920s, water pumps had been introduced into the village, and several industries had begun to develop. Roads were constructed, linking Kafr El-Elow with nearby industrializing communities. After the 1950s, industrialization accelerated, and subsistence farming was no longer the primary aspect of the Kafr El-Elow economy. Instead, many nearby industries related to steel, natural gas, cement, textiles, railways, aircraft, and other products drew increasing numbers of *fellaheen* into the industrial work force; however, many villagers continued cultivating their crops after factory hours and on weekends to supplement their incomes.

By the 1960s, only about 10 percent of the community was made up of peasants. Although the remaining fellaheen continued to plow their fields with draft animals, they also used some modern machinery such as crop sprayers and irrigation pumps. At the time of Fakhouri's study, agricultural productivity was very high, and the *fellaheen* were able to harvest three or four crops a year. Wheat and corn were cultivated for domestic consumption, primarily for making bread, and vegetables were grown for cash crops and home consumption. Cash crops became important enough that the Egyptian government built refrigerated bins to store the farmers' seeds and cuttings for replanting.

Industrialization brought to Kafr El-Elow new patterns of social mobility, an influx of migrants for urban labor, and rising incomes, which created new socioeconomic classes. These new classes demanded a variety of consumer goods and services not familiar to the traditional population. Bicycles, wristwatches, radios, and electricity for households became increasingly common. Preferences for Western clothing, housing, entertainment, and other commodities contributed to the decline of traditional handicraft industries and the rise of new businesses. Six businesses existed in 1930; in 1966, Fakhouri counted seventy-eight.

Middle Eastern Family, Marriage, and Gender

An enormous amount of ethnographic research is available on family, marriage, and gender in Arab, Turkish, and Iranian societies. In all of these societies, the ideal form of the family has been patrilineal, endogamous, polygynous, and patriarchal. The main sources for the ideals of the Muslim family are Islamic religious texts, principally the *Qur'an* and

Traditional Egyptian peasants.

the *Sharia*. Cultural anthropologists have discovered, however, that the ideals of the Muslim family do not always coincide with the realities of social life in the Middle East and North Africa.

In some parts of the Arab world, such as among the Palestinian communities, the term **hamula** is used to refer to an idealized descent group (a patrilineage or patriclan) that members view as a kinship group. The *hamula* is associated with a patronym, the name of a particular male who is thought to be a paternal ancestor. In rural areas, the typical *hamula* is a clan that embraces various patrilineages. The head of the clan is referred to as a *sheik*, a hereditary position. He resolves disputes and encourages cooperation among members of the clan. The *hamula* has always been a source of pride and loyalty in rural Arab communities.

Despite the descriptions of the *hamula* as a patrilineal descent grouping and its association with a particular patronym, cultural anthropologists find that it is frequently a loosely structured group combining patrilineal, affinal, matrilineal, and neighborhood relations (Eickelman, 1998). Nevertheless, it serves to coordinate economic, political, and ceremonial affairs. Research on urban and rural communities in Lebanon, Kuwait, and other Arab countries suggests that loyalty to the *hamula* remains a basic aspect of social organization throughout the Muslim world (Al-Thakeb, 1985).

The Family   As in most other agricultural states, the extended family is the ideal in the Middle East. The traditional household espoused by Arabs, Turks, and Iranians is made up of the patriarch, his wife, one or more married sons and their families, and unmarried daughters and sons. Yet, as in the case of the *hamula*, these ideals are often not realized (Bates & Rassam, 1983). Economic and demographic conditions such as landlessness, poverty, and geographical mobility frequently influence the size and dimension of the Muslim family.

As industrialization and consequent urbanization influence the Middle East, the nuclear family is becoming the normative pattern. Survey research on the Muslim family from Egypt, Syria, Libya, Jordan, Lebanon, Iraq, Bahrain, and Kuwait suggests that the nuclear family has become the predominant form in both rural and urban areas (Al-Thakeb, 1981, 1985). Variability in family type is often related to socioeconomic status. The ideal of the nuclear family appears to be most prevalent among the middle and upper classes, which are most influenced by globalization. Among the lower socioeconomic classes, especially families involved in agriculture, the extended family retains its importance. Yet even when the nuclear family predominates, wider kinship relations, including the *hamula*, remain important (Al-Thakeb, 1985; Eickelman, 1998).

Marriage   Marriage is a fundamental obligation in the Islamic tradition. Unless financially or physically unable, every Muslim male and female is required to be married. Marriage is regarded as a sacred contract between two families that legalizes intercourse and the procreation of children. In the Islamic tradition, there are no cultural beliefs or practices such as monasticism that sanction any form of life outside of marriage.

Islamic societies are known for practicing polygyny. Polygyny is mentioned once in the *Qur'an* (iv:3):

Marry of the women, who seem good to you, two, three, or four, and if ye fear that ye cannot do justice [to so many] the one [only].

Although polygynous marriage is permitted and to some extent represents the ideal norm in Muslim societies, cultural anthropologists find that most marriages are monogamous. For example, less than 10 percent of married Kuwaiti males and about 1 percent of married Egyptian males are involved in polygynous marriages (Al-Thakeb, 1985; Eickelman, 1998). In Kafr El-Elow, Fakhouri (1972) found that only a few males had multiple wives. In questioning males involved in polygynous marriages, Fakhouri noted that the major rationales for taking a second wife were either the first wife's infertility or poor health or the desire of wealthy males to demonstrate their high status.

Wealthy males in both urban and rural areas contract polygynous marriages. In the traditional pattern found in rural communities, a wealthy male from the landed elite contracts a parallel-cousin marriage and then takes a wife from another family (Bates & Rassam, 1983). Polygyny is also found among the new elite in some of the wealthy oil-producing countries. However, economic limitations and the fact that the Islamic tradition prescribes equal justice for all wives encourage monogamous marriages among the majority of Muslims.

Arranged marriage based on parental decision making still predominates in Islamic societies. Until recently, for example, Saudi Arabian males did not even view their wives until their wedding day. Some indicators suggest, however, that a degree of individual choice in marriage may become more prevalent. Anthropological research from Kuwait in the mid-1980s indicates that an individual's freedom to select a spouse varies according to education, socioeconomic status, age, and sex (Al-Thakeb, 1985). As males become more educated and achieve greater economic independence from their parents, they enjoy greater freedom in mate selection. Females generally have much less choice.

Divorce Like polygyny, divorce in traditional Islamic societies was a male prerogative. To obtain a divorce, a male does not need much justification; Islamic law specifies several means whereby a male can easily repudiate his wife. It also empowers a husband to reclaim his wife without her consent within a four-month period after the divorce. Traditionally, a Muslim wife did not have the same rights to obtain a divorce. A woman could, however, divorce her husband for reasons such as impotence, insanity, and lack of economic support; but to prove these accusations, she would need a very sympathetic judge (Esposito, 1998).

Cultural anthropologists find it difficult to generalize about divorce and marriage in the Muslim world. In countries such as Egypt, Turkey, and Morocco, which have greater exposure to outside influences, divorce laws for women have become liberalized. These countries have educated middle classes that support reform. In conjunction with these reform movements, along with the modification of divorce laws, some Muslim feminists have called for the abolition of polygyny. Certain countries—for example, Tunisia and Turkey—have prohibited this practice, and others have restricted it (Eickelman, 1998).

Gender The Western image of the Arab or Muslim woman is frequently that of a female hidden behind a veil and completely dominated by the demands of a patriarchal society. Early Western scholars painted a grim and unwholesome portrait of the female in the Muslim household. Cultural anthropologists find that this image obscures the complexity of gender relations in the Middle East.

The patriarchal ideal and the status of the female in the Muslim world cannot be understood without reference to two views in the Islamic doctrine. First, according to the Islamic tradition, before the origins of Islam, females were treated negatively. For example, in the pre-Islamic period, the Bedouins regularly practiced female infanticide by burying the unwanted child in sand. The *Qur'an* explicitly forbids this practice. Thus, Islam was viewed as having had a progressive influence on the role of women. Second, Islam condemns all sexual immorality, prescribing severe penalties for adultery. The *Qur'an* enjoins both males and females to be chaste and modest.

Islamic religious texts prescribe a specific set of statuses and corresponding roles for females to play in the Muslim family as daughter, sister, wife, and mother. Each of these statuses carries certain obligations, rights, privileges, and duties. These statuses are influenced by the patriarchal ideals of the Islamic texts. One passage of the *Qur'an* (iv:34) is often cited when referring to the role of women:

Men are in charge of women, because god hath made the one of them to excel the other, and because they spend of their property (for the support of women). So good women are the obedient.

This passage provides the context for the development of various laws that have influenced the status of Muslim women. For example, traditionally a woman could inherit only a one-half share of her parents' estate, whereas her brothers inherited full shares. This law assumed that a woman is fully cared for by her family, and when she marries, her husband's family will provide for her material needs. Thus, a Muslim woman does not need the full share of inheritance.

Another traditional code in Islamic law illustrates the patriarchal attitudes toward women with respect to political and legal issues. In legal cases, a woman is granted half the legal status of a man. For example, if a crime is committed, two women as opposed to one man are needed as legal witnesses for testimony. This legal equation of "two females equals one male" reflects the traditional Islamic image of women as less experienced and less capable than men in political and legal affairs.

Ethnographic research since the 1970s has demonstrated that male-female relations in these societies are far more complex than the religious texts might imply. By focusing exclusively on Islamic texts and laws, early researchers distorted and misunderstood actual practices and relations between males and females. Moreover, before the 1970s, much of the ethnographic research in Muslim societies was done by males, resulting in a skewed understanding of the position of women, because male cultural anthropologists did not have the same access to female informants as did female cultural anthropologists. Eventually, female cultural anthropologists such as Lois Beck, Lila Abu Lughod, Soraya Altorki, and Elizabeth Fernea began to study the Muslim female world.

Female cultural anthropologists discovered that the position of Muslim women cannot be categorized uniformly. One major reason for variation is the extent to which Islamic countries have been exposed to the West. Some, like Tunisia, Egypt, and Turkey, have adopted legal reforms that have improved the status of women. For example, Egyptian women have had access to secondary education since the early 1900s and have had career opportunities in medicine, law, engineering, management, and government. The Egyptian constitution accords women full equality with men, and—ideally—prohibits sexual discrimination in career opportunities. Muslim feminist movements dedicated to improving the status of women have emerged in those countries most affected by the West.

In contrast to Egypt, religiously conservative Saudi Arabia has highly restrictive cultural norms regarding women. Saudi Arabia was not colonized and thus was more isolated from Western values. The Saudi Arabian government has interpreted Islamic law to declare that any mingling of the sexes is morally wrong. Saudi women are segregated from men; they attend separate schools, and upon finishing their education can seek employment only in exclusively female institutions such as women's hospitals, schools, and banks. Saudi women are forbidden by law to drive cars, and when riding on public buses they have to sit in special closed sections. All Saudi public buildings must have separate entrances and elevators for men and women (May, 1980).

Despite legal reforms and access to education in some Muslim societies, the notion that women are subordinate to men remains firmly entrenched. For example, in Egypt a woman trained in law cannot become a judge or hold any position with legislative authority. Also, in Egypt polygyny remains legal, and men can obtain divorces with minimal justification (May, 1980). In many respects, the patriarchal family remains the center of Islamic social organization. Hence, in some cases attempts to reform women's status have been perceived as heretical assaults on the Islamic family and morality. Some of the recent Islamic revival movements have reactivated conservative, patriarchal cultural norms.

The Veil and Seclusion   To many Westerners, the patriarchal order of the Islamic societies is most conspicuously symbolized by the veil and the other shapeless garments worn by Muslim women. As a female approaches puberty, she is supposed to be restricted and kept from contact with males. The veil is an outward manifestation of a deep cultural pattern (Beck & Keddie, 1978; Fernea & Fernea, 1979). The wearing of the veil and the enforced seclusion of the Muslim woman are known as **purdah.** These practices reinforce a separation between the domestic private sphere of women and the male-dominated public sphere.

Veiling and *purdah* tend to be associated with urban Muslim women. Most scholars believe that the tradition of veiling originated in urban areas among upper-class women (Beck & Keddie, 1978). Many peasant and Bedouin women in the Middle East and North Africa do not wear the veil and generally have more freedom to associate with men than do Muslim women who live in towns and cities. Many urban Muslim women report that the veil and accompanying garments offer practical protection from strangers, and that when in public they would feel naked and self-conscious without these garments (Fernea & Fernea, 1979).

In countries such as Egypt, Turkey, and Iran that had formerly abandoned traditional dress codes, many educated, middle-class women have opted to wear the veil and the all-enveloping garments. To some extent, this return to traditional dress reflects the revival movements now occurring throughout the Islamic world. For many Muslim women, returning to the veil is one way in which they can affirm their Islamic religious and cultural identity and make a political statement of resistance to Western power and influence.

An Afghan woman with child.

Social Structure, Family, and Gender in India and South Asia

In the aftermath of independence and the retreat of Western colonial authority in South Asia, cultural anthropologists began to explore the various societies of the region. Much ethnographic research centered on rural communities of India, with cultural anthropologists such as McKim Marriott, Oscar Lewis, Milton Singer, and Alan Beals investigating the Indian peasantry.

Origins of the Caste System The caste system of India was briefly introduced in Chapter 18. Most

scholars associate the origins of the caste system with the Aryan peoples who settled in northern India after 1500 B.C. Various social divisions in Aryan society developed into broad ideological categories known as *varnas*. At the top were the *brahmins* (priests), followed by the *kshatriyas* (warriors), the *vaisyas* (merchants), and the *sudras* (commoners). This fourfold scheme provided the ideological framework for organizing thousands of diverse groups.

The functional groupings in the *varna* categories are the subcastes, or, more precisely, what Indians refer to as **jatis,** of which there are several thousand, hierarchically ranked. Jatis are based on marital, economic, and ritual relations. Marriages are endogamous (marriage within a group) with respect to *jati; jatis* are thus ranked endogamous descent groups. In addition, each *jati* is a specific hereditary occupational group. A person's *jati* places him or her within a rigid form of social stratification.

Cultural anthropologists have found that *jati* relationships are intimately linked with what is known as the **jajmani** economy of rural Indian villages. The typical Indian village consists of many different castes, with one caste dominating the village both economically and politically. Traditionally, all of these castes were interconnected through economic exchanges within the *jajmani* economy. The dominant caste controlled the land and exchanged land-use rights for other goods and services. For example, members of the dominant caste would have their hair cut and fingernails trimmed by a barber. Then, at harvest time, the barber would get a stipulated amount of grain from his client. In addition, the barber, carpenter, potter, and water carrier would exchange their goods and services with one another in a type of barter system. Every caste, even the lowest ranking, had access to housing, furniture, food, credit, and other goods and services through these exchanges.

More recent ethnographic studies have concluded that the *jajmani* system is collapsing because of globalization and the introduction of new consumer goods and technology into Indian villages. When people can use safety razors to shave, buy imported dishware and glasses, and use electric pumps to obtain water, many of the old occupations become superfluous. Consequently, many artisans and service workers leave their villages to

CRITICAL PERSPECTIVES

THE SACRED COW

From the Western perspective, the Hindu conception of the cow as a sacred animal seems irrational. Because India has severe economic problems, including malnutrition and underdeveloped agricultural production, Westerners are usually critical of Hindu norms prohibiting the consumption of cattle. Cattle wander the streets unharmed, and elderly cows sometimes are kept in government-sponsored "old-age homes." Western peoples often consider these practices to be the primary source of poverty in India.

Anthropologists, however, have studied these practices in terms of the needs of the Indian population. Marvin Harris (1985), for example, has used a cultural ecology approach in analyzing Hindu norms concerning cattle. He hypothesized that there are highly practical reasons for these norms. First, cows generally don't consume the same kinds of foods as humans and therefore don't compete with humans for scarce resources. More important, cows produce oxen (neutered offspring of cows), which are used for

plowing fields. Peasant farmers who sold or killed their cows for food would be destroying the "factories" for producing their natural "tractors." In many cases, farmers would have to abandon their farms or increase production. Thus, the short-term benefits of consuming the cow would be more than offset by the long-term consequences of increased land-lessness and starvation. In addition, cows produce manure, which is used for both fertilizer and cooking fuel.

Thus, in Harris's analysis, living cows are sound, long-term investments. In the context of the traditional labor-intensive agricultural system of India, Hindu attitudes toward cows make good practical sense. Harris went on to explain that while the development of an Indian beef industry would strain the ecological relationships in the country, in the United States, for example, over three-quarters of all crop lands are used to feed cattle. To produce these cattle, the U.S. farmer depends on very expensive, energy-consuming

machinery, fertilizers, and pesticides. If this highly inefficient, capital-intensive form of agriculture were introduced into India, the economy would be severely shaken. India would have to depend on high-cost petrochemicals and other expensive capital technology. Developing a beef industry in India would be a highly irrational decision.

POINTS TO PONDER

1. Do you find Harris's arguments convincing?

2. When examined in anthropological terms, do Hindu attitudes toward cattle seem more rational?

3. Why, in your opinion, do Westerners perceive these attitudes as irrational?

4. Is the maintenance of a large-scale cattle industry in the United States a rational response to U.S. needs and resource availability?

5. What can you conclude about cross-cultural analysis from this study of the sacred cow?

market their skills elsewhere or, in many cases, to join the increasing number of unskilled migrants flooding the cities.

Although the *jajmani* system is disappearing, cultural anthropologists find that the caste system persists. Contemporary India has caste hotels, banks, hospitals, and co-ops. Caste organization continues to delineate political factions in India. Most elections are decided by caste voting blocs,

and politicians must therefore appeal to caste allegiances for support. Thus, caste remains one of the most divisive factors facing the democratic process in India.

Cultural anthropologists find that the caste system is reinforced by the worldview of Hinduism. The doctrines of *karma* and reincarnation reinforce concepts of purity and pollution that correlate with caste hierarchy. An individual's *karma* is believed to determine his or her status and ritual state. It is believed that individuals born into low castes are inherently polluted, whereas higher-caste individuals such as *brahmins* are ritually pure. This state of purity or pollution is permanent.

The late French anthropologist Louis Dumont (1970) argued that, from the Hindu viewpoint, humans have to be ranked in a hierarchy; egalitarian relationships are inconceivable. Dumont asserted that in this worldview, caste relations produce interdependency and reciprocity through exchanges and ritual relationships. He concluded that the cultural understandings of caste rules and ritual purity and pollution have created a system of stratification based on widespread consensus.

In contrast, cultural materialists ground caste relationships in prevailing economic and political conditions, maintaining that Hindu beliefs about caste were primarily ideological justifications for a system that emerged from long-standing inequalities in which a dominant group accumulated most of the land and other resources. They deny that a consensus exists concerning the appropriateness of caste relationships, citing as evidence the situation of the *harijans,* or untouchables, at the bottom of the caste hierarchy, who daily face discrimination and exploitation. Based on her research in southern India, anthropologist Joan Mencher (1974) reported that the *harijans* resent, rather than accept, this treatment.

Other anthropologists have refined their analyses of caste relations by combining both material and cultural variables. For example, cultural anthropologists such as Jonathan Parry and Gloria Raheja have described the complex interplay of material interests and cultural meanings of exchanges among castes in the *jajmani* system. They note how upper-caste *brahmins* accept gifts and other material items from lower-caste members, but in this exchange they ritually absorb the sins of the donors (Parry, 1980; Raheja, 1988). Raheja emphasizes that in these *jajmani* exchanges, the lower- and upper-caste groups become equal, and strict hierarchy is undermined. Thus, the exchanges are based on material factors and on the symbolic conceptions of Hinduism.

Family and Marriage in South Asia   The most typical form of family in South Asia is the extended family, which consists of three generations: grandparents, parents, and children. It may also include brothers and their wives and children within the same household. The extended family is the ideal norm for South Asian villages because it provides a corporate structure for landowning, labor, and other functions. Cultural anthropologists find, however, that families actually go through development cycles—an extended family at one point, a large extended family at another time, and a nuclear family at still other times. But despite modernizing influences, the cultural ideal of the joint family persists, even in most urban areas (Maloney, 1974; Tyler, 1986).

Parents arrange the marriages in South Asia. As noted, in northern India people marry outside their patrilineage and village but inside their caste grouping. A married woman must switch allegiance from her father's descent group to that of her husband. After marriage, a woman moves into her husband's joint family household and must adjust to the demands of her mother-in-law. In Pakistan and Bangladesh, parallel-cousin marriage is often preferred, and polygynous marriages, in accordance with Muslim practices, are sometimes found.

The Dowry   Another marital practice, found especially in northern India, is the dowry. The Indian bride brings to the marriage an amount of wealth that to some extent represents her share of the household inheritance. Typically, the dowry includes clothing and jewelry that the bride retains for her personal property, household furnishings, and prestige goods (Tambiah, 1989). Upper-caste families try to raise a large dowry payment as a sign of their elevated status. In these cases, the dowry creates alliances between elite families.

Gender and Status in South Asia   The status of women in South Asia varies from one cultural area to another. In Pakistan and Bangladesh, which are influenced by the Islamic tradition, women are secluded according to the prescriptions of *purdah*. Until recently, Hindu women of northern India were subject to similar norms. Today, however, many do not wear the veil and accompanying clothing, thereby distinguishing themselves from Muslims. Traditionally, in both Islamic and Hindu regions, a woman was expected to obey her father, her husband, and, eventually, her sons. Women ate after the men were finished and walked several paces behind them.

ANTHROPOLOGISTS AT WORK

SUSAN BROWNELL: ETHNOGRAPHY IN CHINA

Susan Brownell traces her interest in China back to the stories told by her grandmother. Her grandmother's father, Earl Leroy Brewer, was governor of Mississippi, a civil rights proponent, and lawyer for the Mississippi Chinese Association in the 1910s and 1920s. Brownell's love of anthropology began as an undergraduate at the University of Virginia, where she took Victor Turner's famous seminar, in which the participants reenacted different rituals from around the world. She wrote her first paper on sports for Turner's seminar in 1981, and his ideas continued to inspire her over the years. She was also a nationally ranked track and field athlete (in the pentathlon and heptathlon) from 1978 to 1990. She was a six-time collegiate All-American while at Virginia, and competed in the 1980 and 1984 U.S. Olympic Trials. In 1980 she also worked for six weeks as a stunt double for the feature film *Personal Best*, which depicted four years in the life of a young pentathlete played by Mariel Hemingway.

After starting the Ph.D. program at the University of California, Santa Barbara, she decided to try to combine her various interests in a dissertation on Chinese sports. While at Beijing University in 1985–1986 for a year of Chinese language studies, she joined the track team. She was chosen to represent Beijing in the 1986 Chinese National College Games, where she won a gold medal and set a national record in the heptathlon, earning fame throughout China as the American girl who won glory for Beijing University. She returned to China to study sport theory at the Beijing University of Physical Education (1987–1988). She was awarded her Ph.D. in 1990. After teaching at Middlebury College, the University of Washington, and Yale University, she joined the Department of Anthropology at the

Susan Brownell

University of Missouri, St. Louis, in the fall of 1994 and was promoted to associate professor in 1998. In 1995–1996, Brownell began a new project on "The Body in Consumer Culture in Beijing." She did fieldwork on cosmetic surgery, fashion models, and upscale fitness clubs as a way of gauging how concepts of beauty, health, and fitness are changing under the growth of global consumerism.

Brownell drew on her direct experience of Chinese athletics in *Training the Body for China: Sports in the Moral Order of the People's*

Older women, particularly mothers-in-law, gained more respect and status in the family. In certain cases, older women became dominant figures in the extended family, controlling the household budget. As some urban South Asian women have become educated, they have begun to resist the patriarchal tendencies of their societies. Some have even participated in emerging feminist political activities. As industrialization and urbanization continue, an increase in feminist activity would be expected.

However, because about 80 percent of the population still resides in rural communities, patriarchal tendencies remain pervasive.

Family and Gender in China

Ethnographic research in China was severely restricted by the Chinese communist government. During the 1970s, the United States and China developed a more formal cooperative relationship, and

Republic (University of Chicago Press, 1995), an insightful look at the culture of sports and the body in China. This was the first book on Chinese sports based on field-work in China by a Westerner. Most recently, Brownell and Jeffrey N. Wasserstrom edited a volume entitled *Chinese Femininities, Chinese Masculinities: A Reader* (University of California Press, 2002). Brownell is an internation-ally recognized expert on Chinese sports and has acted as a consul-tant and expert on the topic for different media, including *Sports Illustrated, The Los Angeles Times, The Atlanta Journal and Constitu-tion, The Asian Wall Street Journal, The Sports Factor* on Australian Broadcasting Corporation Radio, *The Ultimate Athlete* on The Discovery Channel, the NBC Sports Olympic Unit, China Central Television, National Public Radio, and many others.

She has participated in national and international conferences bringing together officials of the International Olympic Committee, the International Olympic Academy, the U.S. Olympic Committee, the Atlanta Commit-tee for the Olympic Games, the Amateur Athletic Foundation, sports journalists, sports scholars, and others. On these occasions, she has spoken on topics such as women in Chinese sports, doping in Chinese sports, sports television broadcasting in China, and Western misconceptions of the world record-setting female long-distance runners.

Most recently, Brownell was appointed by the International Olympic Committee (IOC) to the seven-member Research Council of the Olympic Studies Centre. She also actively argued on behalf of Beijing's bid to host the 2008 Olympics, which succeeded when the IOC awarded the games to Beijing in July 2001. Dr. Brownell argues that the increasing global media attention that the Olympics will bring to China will create greater openness to the outside world and also give human rights activists a platform from which to make their voices heard. She believes that this international ex-posure will accelerate the develop-ment of democracy in China. In all of these settings, her goal has been to promote a deeper under-standing of Chinese sports that moves beyond the stereotype of the "Big Red Machine" with a centralized doping system. She has attempted to nudge members of the Olympic Movement and the press toward comprehending that Chinese sports people are "like us" in the problems they face due to sexism, commercialization, the complexities of international telecasting, and drug use; but that they are "unlike us" in the cultural background they bring to sports, which includes different senti-ments about gender, nationalism, "fair play," and—more generally—the meaning of sports.

China began to allow some cultural anthropologists to conduct research within its borders. In the 1970s, Norman Chance became the first American cultural anthropologist allowed to conduct fieldwork in both rural and urban communes. His detailed ethnogra-phy of Half Moon Village in Red Flag Commune, near Beijing, offers important insights into the eco-nomic, social, political, and cultural developments of that period. Half Moon Village was one sector of the Red Flag Commune, which was one of the largest communes in China when it was formed in 1958. Red Flag occupied 62 square miles and con-tained 85,000 inhabitants in 17,000 households, or-ganized into production brigades and work teams. The state owned the land and the sideline industries associated with the commune. The commune work force consisted of more than 40,000 people, most of whom did agricultural work. Many of the com-mune's crops were sent to Beijing markets, provid-ing a steady income for the villagers. Approximately

15 percent of the labor force worked in the commune's industrial sector.

The Family, Marriage, and Kinship in Red Flag Commune Following the Chinese Revolution, the government initiated a campaign to eradicate the patriarchal nature of the Chinese family and clan. The communist leadership viewed the traditional family, clan, and male dominance as remnants of precommunist "feudal" China, as well as major sources of inequality. The Chinese Communist Party passed legislation such as the marriage laws of 1950 to destroy the traditional clan and extended-family ties and create more equal relationships between males and females. The marriage laws required free choice in marriage by both partners, guaranteed monogamy, and established a woman's right to work and obtain a divorce without losing her children.

Norman Chance's (1984) research indicated, however, that despite government attempts to alter family and kinship relations, Half Moon Village residents sought to maintain strong kinship ties for economic security. Chance discovered that many decisions concerning access to various jobs in the commune were based on kinship relationships. To ensure kinship ties, families maneuvered around government officials and decisions. In addition, younger family members looked to their elders for knowledge and advice. Chance found that within the family, harmonious relationships were emphasized according to the centuries-old Confucianist traditions.

The role and the status of women have been strongly influenced by the ideals of the Chinese Communist Party leadership. Based on his study of Half Moon Village, Chance (1984) concluded that the status of women had improved under the communist regime, and that in general the new marriage laws had disrupted the Confucian pattern of rigid patriarchy. Young girls were no longer married off or sold. Women were no longer confined to the home; rather, they were encouraged to work along with the men in agriculture and industry.

Chance noted some other changes in the status of women. He regularly observed young men taking care of their children and doing tasks such as cooking, chores that were previously performed only by women. In addition, women had assumed decision-making roles in certain areas, especially in respect to family planning—a high priority for the Chinese government after 1976. After China adopted the well-known one-child policy, the Communist Party paid bonuses to families that had only one child (see Chapter 24). Families had to return the bonus to the government if they had a second child. Women were responsible for administering and monitoring this policy.

A sign advertising the importance of the one-child policy and family planning in the People's Republic of China.

Despite these changes, however, Chance found that some remnants of the older patriarchal norms were still evident. For example, peasant women engaged in agricultural labor were unable to develop skills that would lead to better job opportunities in the factories and other sideline occupations of the commune. In contrast to men, women were restricted to unskilled jobs. In addition, women did not hold administrative positions on commune committees.

Chance also found that women's role in the family did not change dramatically. Typically, patrilocal residence rules prevailed at Half Moon Village. Chance noted that this often led to conflicts between the mother-in-law and daughter-in-law in the modern Chinese family, just as it had for centuries in the traditional Chinese family. In addition, despite the passage of the marriage laws, matchmaking and arranged marriages remained the norm, and villagers strongly disapproved of divorce. Couples still preferred male over female children to perpetuate family interests. Party officials frequently postponed efforts to alter these patriarchal patterns because such changes might cause stress and conflicts in the family unit.

Ethnic Tensions

Ethnic tensions divide some Middle Eastern countries. Anthropologist Dale Eickelman notes how difficult it is to maintain a rigid primordialist perspective on ethnicity when viewing the population known as the Kurds (1995). Kurdish ethnic identity is constructed and shifted to adjust to many different circumstances and conditions. The Kurdish minority crosses several international borders. About 20 percent live in Turkey (about 10 million), several million live in Iran and Iraq, and others live in Syria. Their Kurdish identity is constructed and treated differently within these various countries of the Middle East. In general, the Kurds view themselves as an oppressed ethnic minority in all of the countries in which they live and have faced considerable persecution and discrimination by all of these countries. They have struggled within all of these different countries to form an autonomous country called Kurdistan, but thus far they have not succeeded.

Cultural anthropologists have studied the ethnic problems that confront some Asians. One such problem involves the Sikhs, a population of about 18 million who live in the Punjab region bordering India and Pakistan. The Sikh religion developed in the fifteenth century as a syncretic blend of Hindu and Islamic beliefs. Sikhism is a mystical religious tradition centered on venerated leaders who founded a military fraternity that offered protection from both Muslims and Hindus. The Sikhs pride themselves on their warrior spirit. Every male carries the name Singh, which translates as "lion." The Sikhs have built a major house of worship—the golden Temple of Amritsar in the Punjab.

Anthropologist Richard Fox (1985) conducted ethnographic research among the Sikhs in 1980–1981. Using historical material and ethnographic data, he focused on the development of Sikh ethnic and religious identity as a response to external pressures. The Sikhs, who had freed themselves from Muslim and Hindu domination, were confronted with colonialism and the capitalist world system that penetrated the Punjab. The British viewed the Sikhs as an important military shield that could be used for extending their control over India. They therefore treated the Sikhs as a separate

Many Sikhs in India would like to have their own country.

race, which reinforced Sikh separateness from Muslims, Hindus, and other groups.

Eventually, the Sikhs recognized that the incorporation of their territory into the British empire would reduce their political and economic autonomy. They therefore initiated reform movements that sought to unify urban workers and rural peasants. These movements led to violent resistance against the British and, following India's national independence in 1947, to secessionist movements against the Indian government.

In 1984, a group of militant armed Sikhs occupied the golden Temple of Amritsar, demanding political autonomy from India. The government responded by sending military troops into the Punjab, some of whom entered the temple. This violation of their sacred temple outraged many Sikhs. Later in 1984, as resistance to Hindu domination grew, a Sikh militant assassinated Prime Minister Indira Gandhi. Conflict between Sikhs and Hindus will probably remain a problem in the twenty-first century.

Another South Asian country facing severe ethnic problems is Sri Lanka. Prior to independence from the British in 1948, this island country was called Ceylon. Under colonialism, Tamil-speaking Hindus were imported from southern India to work on rubber plantations. (Although Tamil-speaking Hindus were already in residence in Sri Lanka, British policies increased their population.) The indigenous population of Sri Lanka are Sinhalese-speaking Buddhists. By 1980, the Tamil Hindus made up 18 percent of the population and constituted a majority in northern Sri Lanka. They considered themselves victims of discrimination by the Sinhalese.

Tamil militants formed an organized paramilitary group, the Tamil Tigers, who called for the liberation of northern Sri Lanka as an independent Tamil state. Violence broke out between Tamils and Sinhalese in the north. The Sinhalese army responded with an invasion and indiscriminate killings in the Tamil communities, and the Tamils responded in kind. In 1987, India sent soldiers to quell the violence. Pressured by the Sri Lankan government, India withdrew in 1989. Meanwhile, the violence continues. As anthropologist Stanley Tambiah notes, the ethnic fratricide that is ongoing in Sri Lanka is exacerbated by the continuing delivery of strategic arms from the industrialized world into the hands of these various ethnic groups (1991).

As is obvious, in the Middle East and Asia many different ethnic and cultural traditions are colliding with the process of globalization. The process of globalization is disrupting the traditional values and practices within the regions, and in some cases, the overall reaction to this rapid process of change is to revert to a nostalgic past in which the traditional rural communities maintain the moral economy, the extended family, and other communal practices. This reaction to the process of rapid globalizing has at times led to tensions among political, religious, and ethnic groups throughout these regions. Continuing ethnographic research is needed in these regions to help people understand each other's traditions as one major step in helping to reduce these tensions.

Islamic Revitalization

One pervasive trend throughout the Muslim world since the 1970s has been Islamic fundamentalism. Contemporary fundamentalist movements have their roots in earlier reformist movements that sought to combine Islam with Western values as a means of coping with colonialism and industrialism. In countries such as Egypt, however, fundamentalist groups such as the Muslim Brotherhood rejected reform in favor of the total elimination of secular Western influences. These movements encouraged the reestablishment of an Islamic society based on the *Qur'an* and *Sharia* (Islamic law). Some groups sought to bring about these changes peacefully, whereas others believed that an Islamic state could be established only through violent revolution.

Ethnographic studies have contributed to a better understanding of the sources of Islamic revival movements. One critical factor was the 1967 Arab-Israeli War, which resulted in the crushing defeat of the Arab states and the loss of Arab territories to Israel. This event symbolized the economic and political weakness of the Islamic nations and inspired many Muslims to turn to their faith as a source of communal bonds and political strength.

Another significant factor was the oil boom. Many fundamentalists believed that by bestowing rich oil reserves on these societies, Allah was shifting power from the materialist and secular civilizations of the West to the Islamic world (Esposito, 1998). The oil revenues of countries such as Libya,

Iran, Saudi Arabia, and Kuwait have been used to support fundamentalist movements throughout the Muslim world.

Islamic Revolution in Iran

Islamic revivalistic movements in the Middle East surprised many Western social scientists. They assumed that with modernization and globalization these societies would become increasingly secularized, and that the role of religion in economic, social, and political affairs would be reduced. Instead, most Muslim countries experienced Islamic movements that were linked to national, political, and economic issues.

One of the regions of the Middle East most affected by Islamic fundamentalist tendencies has been Iran. Through ethnographic, historical, and comparative research, anthropologists Mary Hegland, Michael Fischer, William Beeman, Henry Munson, and others have contributed to an understanding of the Islamic revival in Iran. They cite a number of factors that converged to produce this revival.

Iran is predominantly a Shi'a Islamic society. After the death of the prophet Muhammad, the Islamic community was divided into the Sunni versus the Shi'a sect. In the sixteenth century, Shah Ismail of the Safavid dynasty proclaimed Shi'ism as the official religion of Iran. From that time, many Shi'a migrated to Iran for protection from the dominant Sunni rulers elsewhere. Traditional Shi'a theology does not distinguish between religion and politics; instead, based on the doctrine of the *imamate,* the Shi'a maintain that their religious leaders have both theological and political authority. Consequently, Shi'a religious leaders constantly emphasize that Islamic beliefs and doctrine show no separation between religion and politics.

During the nineteenth century, the Iranian rulers, or shahs, offered a large number of concessions to British and Russian bankers and private companies and also attempted to modernize Iran's military and educational system along Western lines. These policies generated internal opposition. The newly educated classes, who had acquired Western ideals of democracy and representative government, opposed the shahs' absolute power. The clergy opposed secularization and Western education, which interfered with traditional education, which they controlled.

In 1925, the Pahlavi dynasty came to power in Iran. Reza Shah Pahlavi viewed the Shi'a religious leaders as obstacles to his plans for rapid modernization. He attempted to reduce their power by appropriating their lands, thus depriving them of income. Reza Shah decreed that secular laws would replace the Sharia and that women would no longer have to wear the veil.

During World War II, Muhammad Reza Pahlavi, supported by Russian and Western interests, replaced his father as ruler. The new shah continued the modernization and secularization policies of his father. By the 1960s, he had centralized all political authority in his hands. Many Western multinational corporations were attracted to Iran because of its vast oil reserves and growing gross national product. By the 1970s, about 43,000 Americans were living in Iran. The Iranian economy became increasingly dependent on Western imported goods, while internally, aside from oil production, few native industries were developed.

In 1963, the shah announced the White Revolution, which included the commercialization of agriculture through land reforms and the expansion of capitalism. It also included public ownership of companies and voting rights for women. The land reforms disrupted the traditional peasant economy,

Ayatollah Khomeini

creating a class of landless peasants. These peasants flocked to Iranian cities in search of scarce opportunities. The White Revolution further mobilized the opposition of the religious clergy, who saw the plight of the peasants. The shah was perceived as a puppet of the United States ("the Great Satan") and Western imperialism. One of the major critics was the Ayatollah Khomeini, who was arrested and exiled in 1963.

The Shah's policies alienated many other sectors of Iranian society. To buttress his power, the shah—along with his secret police, the SAVAK—brutally crushed any opposition to his regime. The Westernized middle classes, the university students, the merchants in the bazaars, and the urban poor began to sympathize with any opposition to the shah's regime. These groups allied themselves with the Muslim clergy and heeded the clergy's call for an Islamic revolution. For fifteen years, Khomeini continued to attack the shah in pamphlets and taped sermons smuggled into Iran.

Although united in their opposition to the shah, various segments of Iranian society viewed the Islamic revolution in different terms. The rural migrants who flooded into the Iranian cities steadfastly supported the Islamic clergy. The Westernized middle class viewed the Islamic revolution in terms of its own democratic aspirations, believing that the religious leaders would play a secondary role in the actual administration of the Iranian state. Many university students had been influenced by the writings of Ali Shariati, who interpreted Shi'a Islam as a form of liberation theology that would free their society from foreign domination. These elements in Iranian society formed a coalition that encouraged the social and political revolution led by Khomeini and the religious clerics. A cycle of demonstrations, violent protests, and religious fervor led to the downfall of the shah, and in 1979, Khomeini returned to Iran to lead the revolution.

Ever since the overthrow of the shah, religious clerics have assumed nearly all of the important political positions. Khomeini announced the establishment of the Islamic Republic of Iran, a theocratic state ruled by the Shi'a clergy, who used the mosques as the basic building blocks of political power. All Iranians were forced to register at a mosque, which functioned as an amalgam of government office, place of worship, and local police force. A systematic campaign was waged to purge

Iranian society of Western influences: alcohol, gambling, prostitution, and pornography were strictly forbidden; women were required to wear head scarves; and those who refused were sent to "reeducation centers." The Shi'a regime believed it had a religious duty to export its revolution to other areas of the Islamic world.

Since the Islamic revolution, most ethnographic research has been forbidden in Iran, so collecting data on recent trends has been difficult. From press reports, it is clear that the revolution has radically changed the nature of Iranian society. The revolution was not only political but also a total social and cultural transformation. Iran is, however, racked with internal conflicts among different classes, religious factions, and political groups. Economic problems exacerbated by the reduction in oil prices and a ten-year war against Iraq led to infighting among radical militants, conservative fundamentalists, and moderates.

In May 1997, Mohammad Khatami, a moderate Muslim cleric, won Iran's presidential election in a landslide victory over more conservative candidates. Khatami attracted a broad coalition of centrists, women, youth of both genders, and middle-class intellectuals to his cause. He is believed to be a direct descendant of the Prophet Muhammad, which helped him consolidate support. While Khatami's victory did not result in immediate changes in the country's Islamic fundamentalist path, he has tried to restrain the more conservative faction of the clergy that ruled the country since 1979.

Five years later, in 2001, Khatami again won a national election for president. The reform movement within Iran is trying to overcome the more conservative factions associated with the Islamic revolution. Although the conservative political factions have retained the controlling political force in Iran, Khatami and the reformists have inspired many of the young people, especially women, democratic media, and other elements. Increases in education and the transnational flow of information, people, and cultures accompanying globalization have fostered the development of a more democratically oriented populace. These changes have resulted in a loosening of the grip of the conservative Islamic clergy in Iran.

Although Khatami has not been able to produce a new version of a reformed society in Iran, free speech and new forms of Islamic interpretation have challenged the conservative clergy. One leading ayatollah, Hussein Ali Montazeri, has been openly questioning the legitimacy of Iran's clerical rule. Only time will tell whether Iran will be able to overcome factionalism and resolve its political and economic problems.

Islamic Revitalization in Afghanistan

Another region in which Islamic revitalization has played a profound role is in Afghanistan. Afghanistan has a troubled history. As we have seen, the British and Russians tried to colonize the area during the nineteenth century in the so-called "Great Game" between these powers. During the nineteenth century, with British support, Afghan leaders such as Abdul Rahman attempted to modernize and unify its many ethnic groups by building roads and pacifying fractious tribes throughout the country. During the 1920s and 1930s, with increased education, many Afghan intellectuals were exposed to ideas based on constitutional democracy and nationalism. Some of these leaders tried to institute democratic processes; however, economic development programs were failing. Consequently, class-based Marxist movements began to emerge in Afghanistan, with the support of the Soviet Union. In 1973, a pro-Soviet Marxist leader staged a military coup and proclaimed himself president of the Republic of Afghanistan. Five years later, another military coup installed a communist government with the patronage of the Soviet Union.

The communist leadership and the Soviet Union underestimated the strength of the Islamic traditions and multiethnic assertiveness of Afghanistan. The ethnic groups of Afghanistan include the Pashtuns (the largest group comprising about 47 percent of the population), Tajiks, Uzbeks, Turkmen, Kirghiz, Hazara, Baluchis, and others. The Sunni Muslims constitute about 88 percent of the population, and the Shi'a comprise about 12 percent (Dupree, 1980; Shahrani & Canfield, 1984). These ethnic and religious coalitions began to resist the Soviet Union and the Marxist communist government. A nationwide Islamic struggle was launched, referred to as a **jihad,** or "holy war," by a group of "holy warriors" called the **Mujahidin.**

The former Soviet Union invaded Afghanistan in 1979 to repress this Islamic resistance led by the Mujahidin. Cold War politics began to influence this struggle against the Russians, with many Western governments offering financial and military assistance to the Mujahidin. Many Afghans were driven out of their country into neighboring Pakistan. However, with increasing internal weaknesses within the USSR and the fierce resistance of the Mujahidin, the Soviets withdrew from Afghanistan in 1989.

Following the withdrawal of the Soviet Union, ethnic differences and varying Islamic traditions and movements presented obstacles to the unification of the Afghans. Local Islamic and ethnic factions that had developed during the Soviet occupation began to fight for power, resulting in years of warfare in Afghanistan during the 1980s and 1990s. The Western governments that had patronized the Mujahidin during the Cold War withdrew support, fearing an Islamic revolution similar to the Iranian one. Consequently, the factional fighting among ethnic and religious groups resulted in political disorder and chaos in Afghanistan.

The Islamic faction that emerged in Afghanistan in 1994 was known as the Taliban. Anthropologist David Edwards has described the social and religious background of the Taliban (1998). The majority of the Taliban are Afghan religious students recruited from Islamic religious schools. (The term *Taliban* refers to religious students.) The Taliban served as a militia that scored a series of victories over other ethnic and religious factions and consolidated control over most of the regions in Afghanistan.

The Taliban imposed stringent Islamic guidelines and norms: men were forbidden to trim their beards; Afghan women were strictly secluded from any contact with men, were not allowed to work outside of the home, and had to wear the traditional Islamic full veil and covering known as the *burqa*. Edwards emphasizes that many of the Taliban had been socialized and trained in Pakistan, outside the confines of traditional ethnic and tribal affinities within Afghanistan. Therefore, young men from different backgrounds were able to unify an Islamic revitalization movement based on a sense of frustration over twenty years of conflict, factionalism, and political disorder. The Taliban did manage to provide order and stability throughout Afghanistan, and many Afghans supported them, despite their attempt to impose a purified Islamic culture on the country. However, in order to provide political order they received support from terrorist organizations such as

ANTHROPOLOGISTS AT WORK

DAVID EDWARDS: ETHNOGRAPHY IN AFGHANISTAN

David Edwards became interested in Afghanistan before he ever thought about anthropology. As a child growing up in the Midwest, he was captivated by stories of travel, especially those his grandmother would tell him. Edwards's grandmother was widowed at a relatively young age and thereafter set off to see as much of the world as she could, often aboard inexpensive freighters that took on a half-dozen or so paying passengers. One of the stories she told her grandson was about watching camel caravans unloading their wares in the central bazaar in Kabul, Afghanistan. The story caught his imagination, and he was determined to make his way to Central Asia, which he managed to do right after graduating from Princeton University in 1975.

After spending two years teaching English in Afghanistan, Edwards went back to the United States with the idea of going to graduate school in a field that would allow him to delve more fully into Afghan culture. Never having taken an anthropology course as an undergraduate, he stumbled upon this field as the right one for his interests when he read a book by Clifford Geertz. The book's blend of elegant writing and insightful cultural analysis captured for him a sense of what

David Edwards

he hoped to accomplish in his own research and writing, and he began graduate school in that discipline in the fall of 1977.

While he initially hoped and expected to return to Afghanistan to conduct fieldwork in a small mountain village, Edwards had to change course after the Marxist revolution, which happened toward the end of his first year of graduate school. Thereafter, Edwards redirected his research primarily toward studies of refugees and guerrilla movements, which became the focus of his fieldwork, the first stint of which took place in and around Peshawar, Pakistan, between 1982 and 1984. Peshawar is right across the border from Afghanistan and was the headquarters for most of the Islamic political parties that worked to dislodge the Marxist regime in Afghanistan from power. Edwards's research dealt

mostly with the internal dynamics of these parties and their conduct of the war inside Afghanistan, but also included an extended study of a camp of some 30,000 Afghan refugees located on the outskirts of Peshawar. Subsequent fieldtrips in 1986 and 1995 have taken him back to Pakistan and Afghanistan and have allowed him to follow Afghan political developments, including the takeover by the Taliban militia.

The publications that resulted from his field research have focused mostly on the evolution of Islamic political authority in Afghanistan and the social transformations brought about by the Islamic political parties in their quest for power. These publications include a book published by the University of California Press, *Heroes of the Age: Moral Fault Lines on the Afghan Frontier* (1996), and a second book, *Before Taliban: Genealogies of the Afghan Jihad* (2002), which he is completing for publication while enjoying a year's sabbatical at the School of American Research in Santa Fe, New Mexico. In between sabbatical leaves and research trips to Pakistan and Afghanistan, Edwards lives in Williamstown, Massachusetts, with his wife and two children and teaches anthropology at Williams College.

The Taliban asserted political control in Afghanistan beginning in 1994.

Al Qaeda, which was headed by Osama bin Laden, the Saudi multimillionaire who directed terrorist activities against the United States.

In 2001, following the September 11 attack on the World Trade Center and Pentagon, the United States military began a campaign to subvert the political control of the Taliban and root out *Al Qaeda* and other terrorists in Afghanistan. Most of the international community supported this effort to dethrone the Taliban and provide a more effective and humane political order in Afghanistan.

After a brief period of U.S. bombing and other military operations, the Taliban were routed from their bases of power and a new pro-democratic government was formed to help stabilize Afghanistan. Women's rights were restored and other reforms were instituted with the advent of the new government. Western powers including the United States have been providing support for the development of the infrastructure and political structure of Afghan society. The United States, Western powers, and the global community have a large stake in promoting stability in this region so that it will not revert to a haven for terrorist activity in the future.

Islam Interpreted   One conclusion resulting from the many ethnographic studies of Islam in the Middle East and Asia is that this religious tradition, like all religious traditions, can have different interpretations depending on the context. The Islamic religion can be combined with diverse types of political activity. It can provide ideological support for revolutionary change, as the case of Iran suggests, or it can help sustain a specific socioeconomic and political order, as in contemporary Saudi Arabia, where some two thousand princes control the entire political economy. Thus, political and religious leaders can use Islam to advance social justice, justify political oppression, or further the goals of one particular political group.

SUMMARY

As in Latin America, Africa, and the Caribbean, globalization has had dramatic consequences for the countries in the Middle East and Asia. These countries were either directly or indirectly affected by Western colonialism. Demographically, in the long run, all of these countries experienced declining death rates brought about by Western colonialism, and populations began to increase rapidly because of economic circumstances and the maintenance of high birth rates.

Economically, these societies were drawn into the global economy and were transformed by producing commodities that were demanded by the wealthier core societies. Patterns of landownership were reordered, and many peasants were producing for economic elites.

Religious changes occurred; however, since most of the population in the Middle East and Asia were committed to the traditions of Islam, Hinduism, or Buddhism, Christianity did not make significant inroads into these colonized areas.

Western colonialism eventually gave way to political movements based on nationalist, independence, and sometimes revolutionary tendencies.

These movements represented anti-colonial sentiments and resulted in many new countries in the Middle East and Asia. Some leaders in the Middle East, such as Gamal Nasser in Egypt, tried to develop a Pan-Arabic movement directed against Western colonialism. Countries such as India were led by charismatic leaders such as Mahatma Gandhi, who mobilized millions of people to develop a national identity and notions of self-determination. In China and Vietnam, revolutionary leaders such as Mao Zedong and Ho Chi Minh organized millions of peasants to bring about new social and political orders based on Marxist ideals mixed with indigenous cultural ideals.

These countries were absorbed into the global economy at different levels, depending on the resources available in their regions. Some countries remain poor and underdeveloped because their economies are heavily dependent on the wealthy core countries. In the Middle East, some countries have tremendous oil resources that could be used to help develop their economies. Despite oil resources, these Middle Eastern countries still find themselves dependent on the wealthy core industrialized nations. Many of the countries in both the Middle East and Asia face internal population problems and underdeveloped economic systems that tend to make them marginal to the global economy. Countries such as China, Burma, and Vietnam tried to withdraw from the global economy through a commitment to a socialist program.

Ethnographers have conducted research on the peasantry, social structures, family life, and gender in these countries. The peasantry is rapidly changing in the Middle East and Asia, as globalization introduces the cash economy, new consumer goods, and other changes. The peasantry differs in various countries based on the people's traditional relations and new global relationships to the world market. Family structures and gender relations are illuminated by ethnographers as they study patterns that develop in response to the emergence of new urban areas and the changing rural areas. Each region has unique structures based on its cultural beliefs and practices.

In the Middle East, the Islamic tradition and Arab cultural practices influence the patterns of family life and gender. However, ethnographers find a great deal of variation within these Islamic societies based on the contact these societies have had with Western countries. In addition, there are some basic misconceptions and stereotypes of the Islamic family, marriage, and gender practices that have been debunked through systematic ethnographic research.

Ethnographers in Asia have focused on some of the traditional practices regarding family and gender that have remained, despite globalization and revolutionary movements in countries such as China. However, globalization is having a transformative effect on all of these institutions throughout Asia.

One of the consequences of globalization is the resurgence of Islamic movements in countries such as Iran and Afghanistan. Ethnographers have employed their analytical skills to try to comprehend and explain Islamic revitalization movements in these countries of the Middle East and Asia.

QUESTIONS TO THINK ABOUT

1. Compare and contrast the Western impact on India and on China.

2. How did demographic change occur as a result of globalization in the Middle East and Asia?

3. How did globalization impinge on the traditional economies of the Middle East and Asia?

4. How did religion change as a result of colonialism and Western influence in the Middle East and Asia?

5. Compare the independence movements in India with the revolutionary movement in China.

6. What are some of the differences between the oil-producing countries of the Middle East and non-oil producers?

7. How has the peasantry changed as a result of globalization in the Middle East and Asian countries?

8. What are some of the stereotypes of family, marriage, and gender patterns in the Middle Eastern Islamic countries?

9. Discuss some of the problems of ethnicity in the Middle East and Asia that have been influenced by globalization.

10. What are some of the factors discovered by ethnographers that have influenced the Islamic revitalization movement in the Middle East?

KEY TERMS

hamula	*jatis*	*Mujahidin*
jajmani	*jihad*	*purdah*

INTERNET EXERCISES

1. Read the article by W. Judd Peak on the U.S. strategic interests in the Middle East at **http://www.is.rhodes.edu/modus/95/Peak. html**. How are the United States interests in the Middle East different from the earlier imperialist goals of Britain and France? How have our strategic interests changed since the fall of the Soviet Union? How do these concepts relate to the current chapter?

2. Examine the Amnesty International report on Algeria at **http://www.web.amnesty.org/ai. nsf/index/MDE280021999**. Why would a country that had escaped colonial rule (Algeria won independence from France in 1962) use such terror techniques on its citizenry? Look at the section on the Algerian economy in the CIA Fact Book page (**http://www.odci.gov/ cia/publications/factbook/geos/ag.html**) and see if you can see any reasons for this behavior. Support your opinion using examples from this chapter and the Fact Book.

SUGGESTED READINGS

BECK, LOIS, and NIKKI KEDDIE (Eds.). 1978. *Women in the Muslim World.* Cambridge, MA: Harvard University Press. A fine collection of essays dealing with the role of women in Middle Eastern societies.

EICKELMAN, DALE F. 1989. *The Middle East: An Anthropological Approach,* 2d ed. Upper Saddle River, NJ: Prentice Hall. An excellent summary of the ethnographic and historical research on the Middle East.

FERNEA, ELIZABETH WARNOCK. 1965. *Guests of the Sheik.* Garden City, NY: Doubleday Anchor. A classic ethnography of an Iraqi village. It is one of the first accounts by a female cultural anthropologist of the role of women in an Islamic society.

SPENCER, WILLIAM. 2002. *The Middle East,* 9th ed. Guilford, CT: McGraw-Hill/Dushkin Publishing Group. A country-by-country survey of the Middle East, containing recent general data on the political economies of the region. It also includes articles from the world press on various topical issues.

TAMBIAH, STANLEY J. 1976. *World Conqueror and World Renouncer: A Study of Buddhism and Polity in Thailand against a Historical Background.* Cambridge: Cambridge University Press. An investigation of how religion interconnects with politics in the development of Thailand as a modern nation.

CHAPTER

23

Race and Ethnicity

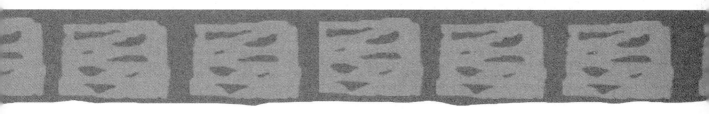

CHAPTER QUESTIONS

- How did racism develop in Western thought?

- What are the basic criticisms of racism developed by anthropologists?

- How is race socially constructed?

- How do race and ethnicity differ?

- How do the primordialist and circumstantialist perspectives on ethnicity differ?

- What are the different patterns of ethnic relations described by anthropologists?

- How have different ethnic groups adapted in U.S. society?

- Why have ethnonationalist movements developed recently?

Race, Racism, and Culture

As we saw in Chapter 6, physical characteristics such as skin pigmentation, nose shape, and hair texture have prompted people throughout history to classify humans into different "races." The word *race* is a loaded term in part because people use the word differently in different contexts to mean different things (MacEachern, 2003). It can be used in census data or in other senses to refer to certain styles of music, dance, or literature. Biologists may employ the term *race* to refer to different species of plants and animals.

The term *race* appears to have been derived from the Latin root *ratio*, with a meaning similar to species or kind (of thing). However, as seen in Chapter 6, attempts to employ racial classifications for humans based on "scientific criteria" have foundered because they were too rigid to account for the tremendous variation within different so-called "races." The majority of anthropologists today find dividing different populations into distinctive racial categories or classifications extremely problematic. Clearly, bounded racially distinct populations are not found in the real world. However, it cannot be denied that humans in both the past and present have used various racial classifications to categorize people and develop stereotypes about the behavior and mental abilities of different "racial categories." These categories have often been used throughout human history as the basis and justification of **racism,** the belief that some races are superior to other races. Racism can often result in discrimination and hostile acts toward different peoples and societies.

Some fascinating research by cognitive anthropologists Larry Hirschfeld (1996) and Francisco Gil-White (2001) indicates that all humans categorize races and ethnic groups in a similar manner. We saw how people throughout time and in different cultures classified different races and ethnic groups in *essentialist categories,* categories that assumed that there were physical and cultural features that were similar. Hirschfeld did laboratory studies of cognition of children in the United States and France and found that at very early ages children constructed prototypical, essentialist categories of different races. He concluded that these categories become more salient and are utilized more frequently if the society emphasizes racial differences within their culture. Francisco Gil-White found that when he gave cognitive tasks to Mongols in China to elicit thought about the differences among ethnic groups, they used essentialist categories to think about ethnic differences.

Both of these anthropologists emphasize that *there are no biological, essential features of distinctive races among human populations.* Yet despite these scientific findings, most people tend to utilize essentialist categories to categorize racial and ethnic groups. Based on this research and other similar cognitive research, it appears that humans everywhere tend to classify different populations in essentialist, stereotypical ways (Boyer, 1994).

Ancient Classification Systems

The conceptual idea that one's physical characteristics are linked to mental abilities and behaviors was inherent within ancient Greek society. Philosophers such as Plato (427–347 B.C.) argued that there were different "essences" for different types of people. According to Plato, people were born with different types of souls, which gave them particular dispositions, or essences. For example, he claimed that certain categories of people who had the specific essences were suited to be rulers, soldiers, farmers, or slaves.

Another Greek, Hippocrates (460–377 B.C.), the well-known medical specialist of ancient Greek society, developed a "humoral-environmental" essentialist theory to classify various peoples throughout the world. According to Hippocrates, there were four elements that constituted the universe: fire, air, earth, and water. These four elements were transformed into *humors,* or essences, that were present in all forms of life. One of the primary humors in humans was the type of blood inherited, which contained different distributions of the four elements that produced varying personality and behavioral dispositions among populations. Hippocrates maintained that the different populations of humanity had different essences and temperaments. For example, he claimed that the people of Asian descent were "gentle, well-fed, courageous," and could endure suffering. However, Asian people would not develop industrious habits because pleasure dominated their lives.

This type of classification based on the idea of inherited blood, essences, and humors continued to influence people during the medieval period in Western society and resulted in simplified stereotypes of behavior and temperament of people around the world. In the medieval period, it was accepted that there was a "Great Chain of Being," which posited natural essential categories based on a hierarchy established by God and nature. Eventually, social groupings based on blood, essences, and humors were placed within this hierarchy. By correlating physical characteristics with cultural differences, classification systems such as these assumed erroneously that populations that shared certain physical traits also exhibited similar patterns of behavior. These beliefs gave rise to popular misconceptions and generalizations concerning the values, traditions, and behaviors of differing peoples.

Modern Racism in Western Thought

Later, after the period of the 1500s in European society when explorers began to make contact with many peoples and cultures outside of Europe, various forms of "scientific racism" began to replace the earlier medieval conceptions. The prior conceptual frameworks based on blood and humors influenced these models of scientific racism. As Europeans began to discover civilizations and cultures in the Americas, Africa, the Middle East, and

Asia, they associated the skin color of many of the people in these non-Western societies with certain forms of essences, behavior, and mental developments. Europeans measured these civilizations in comparison with their own, and thus designated them as "savage" and "barbaric." Since many of these people had a different skin color, they began to assume that the level of these civilizations had something to do with the skin color, essence, or race of these populations. Europeans began to rank the people they discovered according to skin color differences, with non-white peoples at the bottom. Thus, colonizing their lands and using them as slaves could occur freely. It was assumed by the Europeans that these people were no better than animals, and that they needed Europeans to help civilize them.

The Spanish used the term *Negro* to describe the Africans in the 1500s. They used *claro* or "light" for themselves. Following exploration and colonization by northern Europeans such as the Dutch, British, and Belgians, the term *white* was used to apply to their own skin color. Eventually, these folk classifications began to creep into the scientific attempts to classify different peoples.

As we saw in Chapter 6, the Swedish scientist Carolus Linnaeus constructed a taxonomy in 1758 that divided *Homo sapiens* into four races based on skin color: Europeans (white), North American Indians (red), Asiatics (yellow), and Africans (black). Yet his classification of humans was influenced by ancient and medieval theories and various ideas about European superiority. For example, he classified the American Indians with reddish skin as "choleric," with a need to be regulated by customs. Africans with black skin were relaxed, indolent, negligent, and governed by caprice. In contrast, Europeans with white skin were described as gentle, acute, inventive, and governed by laws (Lieberman, 2003).

In Chapter 6 we also discussed how in 1781, a German scientist, Johann Blumenbach, devised a racial classification system that is still sometimes used in popular, unscientific discussions of race. He divided humans into five distinct groups— Caucasian, Mongolian, Malay, Ethiopian, and Native American—corresponding to the colors white, yellow, brown, black, and red, respectively. Blumenbach based his racial typology primarily on skin color, but he considered other traits as well, including facial features, chin form, and hair color. Later, a number of physical anthropologists in the United States and Europe began to assert that the Caucasian race had larger brains and higher intellectual capacities than non-Caucasians.

Eventually, these "scientific racist" beliefs were used to rationalize slavery and the political oppression of various groups around the world. Following

Neo-Nazi groups promote hatred against minorities in the United States and elsewhere.

Darwin's publications on human evolution, many writers supported allegedly "scientific" racist philosophies based on misinterpretations of his theory. In nineteenth-century England, thinkers such as Herbert Spencer and Francis Galton believed that social evolution worked by allowing superior members of society to rise to the top, while inferior ones sank to the bottom. These views reinforced the false belief that particular groups of people, or "races," had quantifiably different intellectual capacities.

In 1853 the French aristocrat Joseph Arthur de Gobineau published a work entitled *Essai sur l'inégalité des races humaines* (*Essay on the Inequality of the Races of Humanity*). In this work, Gobineau described the whole of human history as a struggle among the various "races" of humanity. He argued that each race had its own intellectual capacity, either high or low, and that there were stronger and weaker races. Gobineau promoted the conquest of so-called weaker races by allegedly stronger ones. He opened the book with the statement that everything great, noble, and fruitful in the works of humanity springs from the *Aryan family,* the so-called "super race." The Aryans spread out to create, first, the Hindu civilization, then the Egyptian, Assyrian, Greek, Chinese, Roman, German, Mexican, and Peruvian civilizations (Banton, 1998; Montagu, 1997). Gobineau argued that these civilizations declined because of "racial mixing." These so-called "scientific" views of racism were later taken up by writers such as Houston Stewart Chamberlain in twentieth-century Europe, whose writings, in turn, influenced Adolph Hitler. Gobineau's ideas were the philosophical progenitors of Hitler's *Mein Kampf,* which promoted the notions of racial superiority and inferiority. In the 1930s, the Nazi "scientific racist" ideology, based on the presumed superiority of a pure "Aryan race," was used to justify the annihilation of millions of Jews and other "non-Aryan" peoples, such as Slavs and Gypsies in Europe.

Critiques of Scientific Racism

A number of scholars within the field of anthropology were subjecting these scientific racist beliefs to rigorous testing and evaluation. In the United States, anthropologist Franz Boas (1858–1943), who had migrated from Germany, led a concerted effort to assess these scientific racist ideas (see Chapter 13).

Boas and his students took precise assessments of the physical characteristics of different populations, including cranial capacity and brain size. His research began to challenge the scientific racist views. The research demonstrated conclusively that brain size and cranial capacities of modern humans differ widely within all so-called "races." This anthropological research resulted in findings that conclusively showed that there were no so-called "superior" or "inferior" races. Boas's research also confirmed that there was no direct link between race, brain size, cranial capacity, and intelligence levels.

This pioneering research initiated a program of research among the four fields of anthropology, which continues to challenge scientific racist beliefs wherever they appear. This research has demonstrated time and time again that racist beliefs have no basis in fact. Human groups never fit into such neat categories. For example, many Jewish people living in Europe during the Holocaust possessed the same physical features as those associated with the so-called Aryans. The physical anthropologists of Nazi ideology who advocated Aryan racist ideology found it difficult to define precisely which

Timothy McVeigh was motivated by racist beliefs to bomb the Federal Building in Oklahoma City.

physical characteristics supposedly distinguished one "race" from another (Schafft, 1999). At present, a number of groups such as the Pioneer Fund persist in supporting research that purports to demonstrate scientifically that races differ in brain size, mental abilities, and intelligence. Anthropologists are actively criticizing these erroneous views with sound, scientifically based research (Lieberman, 2001, 2003).

The Cultural and Social Significance of Race

Even though race does not have the biological foundations it is assumed to have, not only is the concept of race very important in the United States, but it is found to resonate in many societies. For example, in Puerto Rico, an island colonized by the Spanish and later by the United States, racial classifications are used to categorize different people by skin color. Puerto Ricans use *blanco* to refer to whites, *prieto* to refer to blacks, and *trigueño* to refer to tan-skinned people. In Brazil, a complex racial classification uses different criteria with which to categorize people than those used in the United States. Brazilians do not see or define races in the same way as people in the United States. An individual categorized as "black" in the United States might be categorized as "white" in Brazil (Harris, 1964).

Since the nineteenth century in the United States, there is what has been termed the **hypodescent concept** of racial classification. This means that in cases of racial mixture, offspring have the race of the parent with the lowest racial status. Since black Americans were considered to be a lower "race," a person is considered black if he or she has a black ancestor anywhere in the family history. This is known as the **one-drop rule** of racial classification because it is based on the myth that one drop of "black blood" is sufficient to determine racial blackness. Thus, Americans with both white and black ancestry are usually classified as black and often encouraged to identify as black in personal and social contexts. In contrast, a person is classified as white if he or she has no black ancestry anywhere in his or her family history. This means that in order to be white, a person has to prove a negative, the absence of black ancestors.

Other racial categories such as *mulatto* (half black and half white), *quadroon* (one-quarter black

and three-quarters white), and *octoroon* (one-eighth black and seven-eighths white) were developed to go along with this one-drop rule. Until the 1950s, in Louisiana it was illegal for a doctor to give a blood transfusion from a black person to a white person. Despite the fact that this notion of the one-drop rule is mythical and is based on false notions of "racial essences," these ideas still persist in some circles.

In contrast to the one-drop rule, Native Americans are treated differently in the United States. Because Native Americans have entitlements based on treaties and legislation, the U.S. federal government has sometimes imposed blood quanta rules of at least 50 percent ancestry from a particular tribe in order to be classified as a Native American. This rule has created considerable confusion both legally and socially for many Native American peoples.

The one-drop rule and blood quanta tests emphasize that the mythical ideas of racial essences are deeply embedded within the folk wisdom and culture of U.S. society. Similar folk conceptions are held about race in other societies. In Northern Ireland, both Protestants and Catholics say that they can identify members of the other group based on physical differences, despite their obvious physical similarities. Anthropologists have long recognized that although these folk conceptions of race are obviously based on arbitrary categories, they have a profound social and cultural significance in many societies.

Ethnicity

In Chapter 10 we discussed the concept of an *ethnic group,* which is a collectivity of people who believe they share a common history, culture, or ancestry. We also discussed how ethnicity is based on perceived differences in ancestral origins or descent and shared historical and cultural heritage. However, the terms *ethnicity* and *ethnic group* have had a long history of misinterpretation in Western culture. For example, anthropologist David Maybury-Lewis has noted that "ethnicity has a will-o'-the wisp quality that makes it extremely hard to analyze and not much easier to discuss" (1997:59). He goes on to say that everyone knows that ethnicity has something to do with a kind of "fellow-feeling" that binds people together and makes them feel distinct from others. Yet it is difficult, if not impossible, he says, to say precisely what kind of feeling it is and why and when people will be affected by it. Under some circumstances, some people are willing to die on behalf of their ethnic group, whereas other people are not strongly pre-occupied by their ethnicity in their everyday lives. In some circumstances, people will be classified as members of a particular ethnic group without feeling it or recognizing it themselves. Maybury-Lewis refers to the example of Native American "Indians," who were a diverse group of people before receiving the ethnic label "Indians" from Europeans.

The criteria for distinguishing ethnic groups require a complex interpretive process. At times, an ethnic group may be distinguished by language, in other cases by religion, and in other situations by skin color or a shared historical past. But it is also recognized that an ethnic group's shared past is open to reconstruction and reinterpretation in a variety of ways. This chapter will introduce the conceptions of ethnicity that have driven anthropological research and have led to a variety of insights into these complex questions.

One of the fundamental misconceptions in early Western perspectives on race and culture and later "scientific racist" views was the confusion between *race* and *culture*. Purported racial characteristics such as skin color, nose shape, or other traits were associated with particular "essences," which determined behavior and cultural attributes. These misunderstandings were also prevalent in the early usages of the word *ethnicity*. The Greek term *ethnos* (derived from *ethnikos*) was used to refer to non-Greeks, or to other peoples who share some biological and cultural characteristics and a common way of life. Later, the word *ethnos*, as used in the Greek New Testament, was associated with non-Jewish and non-Christian peoples and nations referred to as pagans, heathens, and idolaters (Simpson & Weiner, 1989).

Eventually, in various European languages, the words *ethnic, ethnical, ethnicity, ethnique,* and *ethnie* corresponded to an association with "race" (Simpson & Weiner, 1989). As the field of anthropology (including cultural anthropology or ethnology) developed in the nineteenth century, the usage of ethnology or ethnicity was associated with race. Thus, ethnological studies focused on the scientific investigation of the different "races of mankind."

Race, language, and ethnicity were perceived as a fusion of physical and cultural traits by the Western scientists and anthropologists of the nineteenth century.

However, as emphasized above, one of the basic findings based on the research of Franz Boas and later anthropologists is that the "physical characteristics" of a specific group of people are not associated with any particular behavior or culture or language. In other words, one's language or culture is not inherited through biological transmission or genetics. Boas stressed that culture was far more significant in explaining how people in different ethnic groups behaved than any biological factors. One acquires his or her language and culture through *enculturation,* by learning the various language, symbols, values, norms, and beliefs in the environment to which one is exposed.

Since the 1960s, anthropologists and other social scientists have generally used the term *ethnicity* or *ethnic group* to refer to an individual's cultural heritage, which is separate from one's physical characteristics.

In the modern definition, we emphasize both the objective and subjective aspect of ethnicity. The *objective aspect* of ethnicity is the observable culture and shared symbols of a particular group. It may involve a specific language or religious tradition that is maintained by the group, or it may be particular clothing, hairstyles, preferences in food, or other conspicuous characteristics. The *subjective aspect* of ethnicity involves the internal beliefs of the people regarding their shared ancestry. They may believe that their ethnic group has a shared origin, or family ancestry, or a common homeland in the past. In some cases, they may believe that their ethnicity has specific physical characteristics in common. This subjective aspect of ethnicity entails a "we-feeling," and a sense of community or oneness, or a distinction between one's own "in-group" versus an "out-group." It doesn't matter whether these beliefs are historically or scientifically accurate, genuine, or fictional. This subjective identification of individuals with an ideology of an (at least imagined) shared history, unique past, and symbolic attachment with a homeland are often the most important expressions of ethnicity (Smith, 1986).

Thus, one's ethnicity is not innately determined by biology or purported racial characteristics. Despite early classifications of the "European race" or the "English, German, French, or Polish races," these differences among Europeans were not based on physical differences, but rather on linguistic and cultural variation. Likewise, there is no "African race." Rather, Africa is a continent or area of the world where hundreds of different ethnic groups reside that vary from region to region. The descendants of African slaves residing in the United States have a very different ethnicity than descendants of African slaves who live in the Caribbean islands. In Asia, the differences among the Chinese, Japanese, Koreans, Thais, Indonesians, Vietnamese, Cambodians, or Laotians are not based on racial differences, but rather on ethnic differences. Though there may be some minor genetic differences among these populations, these genetic differences are slight and do not result in distinctive races. These ethnic groups have different languages, histories, and cultural traditions that create variation among them. Since ethnicity is based on cultural characteristics, it is much more variable, modifiable, changeable, and as we shall see, more situational, than an identity based on physical characteristics.

Major Anthropological Perspectives

The Primordialist Model Anthropologists have employed a number of different theoretical strategies to study ethnic groups and processes of ethnicity. One early model that developed in the 1960s is known as the *primordialist* model. The primordialist model of ethnicity is associated with anthropologist Clifford Geertz. Geertz attempted to describe how many Third World countries were trying to build nations and integrate their political institutions based on a "civil order"—a political system based on democratic representation processes rather than traditional ties of kinship or religion. However, as he indicates in the essay "The Integrative Revolution," this new civil order clashed with older traditional or "primordial" aspects of kinship, race, ethnicity, language, and religion (1963c).

Geertz suggests that ethnic attachments based on assumed kinship and other social ties and religious traditions are deeply rooted within the individual through the enculturation process. He maintains that ethnic affiliation persists because it is fundamental to a person's identity. In this view, as people are enculturated into a particular ethnic group, they form deep emotional attachments to it.

These sentiments are sometimes evident through **ethnic boundary markers,** which distinguish one ethnic group from another. These ethnic boundary markers include religion, dress, language or dialect, or other visible symbols. But Geertz tends to focus on the intense internal aspects of ethnicity, and the deep subjective "feeling of belonging" to a particular ethnic group. This is one of the strengths of the primordialist perspective on ethnicity. It emphasizes the meaning and significance that people invest in their ethnic attachments. Geertz emphasizes how the "assumed givens" are subjective perceptions of attributes such as blood ties and ancestry, which may or may not coincide with the actual circumstances of one's birth. Geertz goes on to say that the primordial ties are experienced by the people of new Third World nations, and that despite the introduction of new forms of civil political institutions and ideologies, these ethnic attachments endure and are at times obstacles, as new nations attempt to integrate their societies based on a new political civil order. He suggests that there is a basic conflict between the modern state and one's personal identity based on these primordial ties.

Another proponent of the primordialist model is Joshua Fishman. In an essay entitled "Social Theory and Ethnography," he says:

Ethnicity has always been experienced as a kinship phenomenon, a continuity within the self and within those who share an intergenerational link to common ancestors. Ethnicity is partly experienced as being "bone of their bone, flesh of their flesh, and blood of their blood." The human body itself is viewed as an expression of ethnicity, and ethnicity is commonly felt to be in the blood, bones, and flesh. It is crucial that we recognize ethnicity as a tangible, living reality that makes every human a link in an eternal bond from generation to generation—from past ancestors to those in the future. Ethnicity is experienced as a guarantor of eternity." (1980:84–97)

The Circumstantialist Model Another model of ethnicity began to surface within anthropology during the 1960s based on research on multiethnic societies. *Ethnic Groups and Boundaries,* a book by anthropologist Frederick Barth, described a new approach to ethnicity (1969). In a number of case studies in this book, Barth noted the fluidity of ethnic relations in different types of multiethnic societies. Although ethnic groups maintain boundaries such as language to mark their identity, people may modify and shift their language and ethnic identity in different types of social interaction. He criticized a view of culture based on earlier anthropological research in small-scale societies that tended to treat ethnic groups as having discrete, impermeable boundaries. Barth emphasized the interaction between ethnic groups and how people identify with different elements of their own ethnicity and express or repress these elements and characteristics in different circumstances for economic, political, or other practical interests. This approach is sometimes referred to as the *instrumentalist approach* to ethnicity, but it has become known widely in anthropology as the *circumstantialist model* of ethnicity.

In the circumstantialist approach, Barth emphasizes how ethnic boundary markers such as language, clothing, or other cultural traits are not based on deeply rooted, enduring aspects of ethnicity. Ethnic boundaries are continually being revised, negotiated, and redefined according to the practical interests of actors. Ethnic boundaries are generated by the varying contexts and circumstances in which people find themselves. For example, in the United States, people of German descent may refer to themselves as "German Americans" to distinguish themselves from "Irish Americans" or "Italian Americans." Should they happen to be among Europeans, however, these same people might refer to themselves simply as "Americans." The circumstantialist model explains how people draw on their ethnic identity for specific economic, social, and political purposes. People strategically use their ethnic affiliations as the basis of collective political mobilization or to enhance their economic interests. Barth demonstrates how some people modify and change their ethnic identity when it is perceived to be advantageous for their own interests. They may emphasize the ethnic or racial identities of others, or establish boundaries between themselves and others, in order to define themselves differently and interact with others for political or economic purposes. Thus, in Barth's view, ethnicity is not fixed and unchanging but is instead fluid and contingent, as people strategically use, define, and redefine their ethnicity to respond to their immediate basic needs.

Barth's analysis of ethnicity illustrates how individuals within ethnic groups that adapt to specific types of economic and political circumstances in a multiethnic society may emphasize their shared identity as a means of enhancing cooperation with other members of the group. Throughout the world, individuals migrating to different areas often use ethnic ties as a means of social adjustment. Individuals may pursue political interests through ethnic allegiances. In numerous situations, people may manipulate ethnic traditions and symbols to their advantage.

This circumstantialist view of ethnicity also asserts that ethnicity will be displayed to a different degree by various ethnic groups. Ethnic traits will vary from one historical time to another, and group identity may shift from one generation to another. Ethnic groups are not stable collective entities. They may appear and vanish within a generation or less than a generation. Ethnic groups will come into being during different historical periods.

Ethnogenesis refers to the origins of an ethnic group. Ethnogenesis has taken place throughout the world in many different historical circumstances. For example, the English, Germans, French, and other major ethnic groups went through this process in Europe. They began to define themselves as distinctive ethnic groups, which is what is meant by ethnogenesis. Ethnogenesis is a continual, ongoing sociocultural and political process that began in prehistory and continues today for many people.

Over the years, most contemporary anthropologists have drawn from both the primordialist and circumstantialist models to explain or interpret ethnicity. Both models have clarified the nuances of ethnic identity throughout the world. The primordialist model has been extremely useful in substantiating the persistence of ethnicity, whereas the circumstantialist model has helped demonstrate how ethnic identity can be altered and constructed in various economic and political conditions. Today, many contemporary anthropologists occupy a middle ground between these positions, as they pay close attention to the detailed manner in which ethnicity may be both primordial and circumstantial.

Anthropologists today investigate how societal conditions may impinge on how people define themselves ethnically. What are the ethnic categories that have enduring meaningfulness and purpose for people, and under what circumstances are those categories asserted, negotiated, reaffirmed, or repressed? Also, to what extent and to what ends are the elements of ethnicity "invented" and "imagined" by ethnic groups? Anthropologists have to provide a detailed understanding of the ethnogenesis of a particular ethnic group. How does an ethnic group come to construct a shared sense of identity? What are the particulars of this ethnic identity? Is most ethnicity tied to religion? Or is it based on common ancestors or shared myths of common history and territory? Furthermore, anthropologists find it necessary to understand the global and local economic and political dynamics and processes that affect ethnic relations in continually changing societies. Globalization, government policies, the labor market, urbanization, and other aspects of the political economy have a profound influence on how ethnicity is expressed in different societies.

Patterns of Ethnic Relations

Pluralism

In a book *Pluralism in Africa,* a number of anthropologists described a **plural society** as one in which different groups are internally distinguished from each other by institutional and cultural differences (Kuper & Smith, 1969). Instead of one identical system of institutions shared within a society, a plural society consists of ethnic groups that differ in social organization, beliefs, norms, and ideals. Building on this framework, anthropologists have utilized the phrase *cultural pluralism* to describe how various ethnic groups maintain diverse cultures within one society. The example of the Amish in U.S. society would exemplify cultural pluralism. In contrast, *institutional pluralism* is the phrase used to refer to how different ethnic groups may have a similar culture but maintain separate institutions, including schools, churches, businesses, and other organizations within a society. These ethnic groups may share the same language, dietary practices, and subscribe to the same values and beliefs, but have minimal social interaction with other ethnic groups. In the United States the Mormon religious community exemplifies this type of institutional pluralism.

Different forms of plural societies are based on the political order and legal institutions. In some forms of plural societies, ethnic groups are not only divided culturally and structurally, but they also are organized in highly unequal political relationships.

We term such societies *radically plural societies.* In radically plural societies, a minority ethnic group rules other ethnic groups through coercion. The state or government rules as an agent to protect the interests of the dominant ethnic group. The subordinate ethnic groups are treated as "subjects" rather than "citizens." This results in an ethnic hierarchy with the dominant ethnic group in control of the political, economic, and prestigious social positions within the society. Some radically plural societies evolved in early ancient agricultural civilizations. However, these forms of radically plural societies developed in more recent times under European colonialism in many parts of Latin America, the Caribbean, Africa, the Middle East, and Asia, as described in Chapters 21 and 22. These radically plural societies had a European elite that ruled through control of the political economy and the legal institutions of these colonized regions. Typically, these inegalitarian plural societies usually resulted in divisive ethnic conflict and strained ethnic relationships.

Other forms of plural societies, sometimes referred to as *consociational plural societies,* are based on more egalitarian relationships among ethnic groups. In these plural societies, the government protects the structural and cultural differences among the ethnic groups. These ethnic groups are formally recognized by the state and legal institutions to allocate political rights and economic opportunities proportionally. Each ethnic group has a great deal of political autonomy, and, in theory, there is no politically dominant ethnic group. In Europe, Switzerland is often used as an example of a plural society where different ethnic groups have distinctive cultures, but they have parity or equality with each other. Switzerland consists of French, Italian, German, and Romansh ethnic groups, and they all have relatively similar political and economic opportunities. Another European country, Belgium, is also known as an egalitarian plural society in which the population is divided into two major ethnic groups: the Dutch-speaking Flemish and the French-speaking Walloons. In such plural societies, ethnic groups have the legal and political right to maintain their own language, educational systems, and culture. A balance of power is often reached among the different ethnic groups according to a political formula that grants each group a proportional representation of the multiethnic population. As expected, cultural pluralism endures and remains stable in these ethnically egalitarian societies, resulting in relatively amicable relationships.

Many plural societies today fall between the inegalitarian radically plural and egalitarian consociational forms. Following decolonization in most of the countries of Latin America, Africa, the Middle East, and Asia, the radically plural forms of society were dislodged. The European elites were replaced by indigenous elites in these post-colonial societies. However, as seen in Chapters 21 and 22, these societies remained pluralistic as they were comprised of many different ethnic groups. In some cases, the indigenous elites represented one particular ethnic group and perpetuated a continuation of radically plural politics. In other situations, new indigenous-based governments developed policies to manage competition and rivalry among different ethnic groups. This resulted, under some conditions, in another form and pattern of interethnic relations known as assimilation.

Assimilation

Assimilation is a process of ethnic boundary reduction that may come about when two or more ethnic groups come into contact with each other. One or more ethnic groups adopt the culture, values, beliefs, and norms of another ethnic group. The process of assimilation results in similarity of culture and homogeneity among ethnic groups. As would be expected, assimilation occurs more easily when the physical and cultural characteristics of the different ethnic groups are more similar from the beginnings of contact. Anthropologists have been engaged in research to determine whether these general factors are valid in different societal and cultural contexts. But in order to refine their research, anthropologists distinguish different forms of assimilation: cultural assimilation and biological assimilation.

Cultural assimilation involves one ethnic group's adoption of the culture traits including language, religion, clothing styles, diet, and other norms, values, and beliefs of another group. Sometimes anthropologists use the term *acculturation* to refer to the tendency of distinct cultural groups to borrow words, technology, clothing styles, foods, values, norms, and behavior from each other. Generally, cultural assimilation and acculturation have

slightly different meanings to anthropologists. Cultural assimilation involves a subordinate ethnic minority adopting some of the culture of another ethnic group, whereas acculturation refers to the overall adjustment and adaptation of the group to the dominant ethnic group. Obviously, the process of cultural assimilation or acculturation has been going on since the earliest days of humanity and continues today.

As groups came in contact with one another, they borrowed from each other's cultures. Anthropologists, however, find that cultural assimilation and acculturation can be a very complex process for many ethnic groups. These processes may vary depending on government policies and other societal conditions. For example, some cultural assimilation may be voluntary, wherein a particular ethnic group may choose to embrace the culture of another group. Many ethnic groups who immigrate into a particular society adopt the culture of the ethnically dominant group to secure their political rights and economic prospects. In some societies, government and educational policies may encourage groups to assimilate the culture of the dominant ethnic group. During different historical periods, the policies of many governments, such as the United States, France, Mexico, Nigeria, Israel, and China, have promoted cultural assimilation on a voluntary basis within their societies.

Conversely, under some historical conditions, governments may require nonvoluntary or *forced* cultural assimilation. This is where the government forces ethnic groups to take on the culture of the dominant ethnic group of the society. Anthropologists sometimes refer to forced cultural assimilation as *ethnocide,* which implies the killing of the culture of a particular ethnic group (see Chapter 20). Ethnocide demands an ethnic group to abandon their language, religion, or other cultural norms, values, and beliefs and adopt the culture of the dominant group. This process of ethnocide occurred in various ancient agricultural civilizations, such as Egypt, India, China, Rome, and the Aztecs. As these agricultural civilizations expanded and conquered territories and other ethnic groups, at times they forced these other ethnic groups to assimilate and adopt the culture of the dominant ethnic group.

This pattern of induced ethnocide was also prevalent during more modern forms of colonialism. For example, as Europeans colonized areas of

Guatemalan women wear particular types of clothing to exhibit their ethnic traditions.

Latin America, or the Japanese colonized areas in Asia such as Taiwan, or the United States colonized the region of North America, indigenous peoples were often forced to assimilate. This type of forced assimilation is usually extremely difficult for individuals. They have to forsake their own language and cultural traits to become a part of a different, often antagonistic set of values and beliefs. As was seen in earlier chapters, forced cultural assimilation and ethnocide continues to influence many contemporary patterns of ethnic relations.

Biological assimilation refers to the process of intermarriage and reproduction among different ethnic groups resulting in the development of a new ethnic group. This is also known as *amalgamation,* or the biological merging of formerly distinct ethnic groups. The process of biological assimilation has been taking place for thousands of years as different groups have been intermarrying and reproducing with each other. Usually intermarriage among ethnic groups occurs after a great deal of cultural and

structural assimilation following extensive inter-ethnic contact. Thus, usually ethnic boundaries have been extensively reduced, if not eliminated, when intermarriage takes place. The degree of biological assimilation may range from a society where there are no longer any cultural and biological distinctions among the population to societies where new forms of ethnicity develop. Historically, in the United States intermarriage among different European Americans (descendants of English, Irish, German, Italian, Polish) have reduced most meaningful ethnic boundaries. On the other hand, as was seen in Chapter 21 on Latin America and the Caribbean, new forms of ethnicity emerged as intermarriage took place among Europeans, native populations, and African slaves.

Anthropologists have identified three other patterns of ethnic interaction. One is **segregation,** or the physical and social separation of categories of people. Segregation was the policy of many southern states in the United States following the abolition of slavery until the civil rights movements of the 1950s and 1960s. **Jim Crow laws** were developed that resulted in the creation of separate facilities and institutions for African Americans and white Americans. There were segregated schools, restaurants, drinking fountains, restrooms, parks, neighborhoods, and other areas. Until recently, South Africa's constitution had similar laws to segregate races and ethnic groups.

Another pattern of ethnic interaction is *ethnic cleansing,* the attempt to remove an ethnic group from its location and territory within a society. Recently, the Serbs attempted to bring about ethnic cleansing and remove ethnic groups such as the Bosnians from different regions of Yugoslavia. In East Africa, former ruler Idi Amin expelled East Indian immigrants from Uganda for economic and political reasons. Following the Vietnam War, in 1975 the Vietnamese government encouraged the migration of more than one million ethnic Chinese from their country. These people were abruptly eliminated as an ethnic minority, despite the fact that many had assimilated into Vietnamese society. In the past, the U.S. government removed Native Americans from their territories, a process of ethnic cleansing that resulted in reservation life for these ethnic groups.

Finally, the third pattern of ethnic interaction is known as *genocide,* the systematic attempt to kill and totally eliminate a particular ethnic group. Genocide may overlap with ethnic cleansing. In both the cases of the U.S. government and Native Americans, and the Serbs and the Bosnians, removal policies were often combined with more deadly policies of genocide. When the British colonized Australia, native populations such as the Tasmanians were exterminated. There were 5,000 Tasmanians in 1800, but as a result of being attacked by the British, the last full-blooded Tasmanian died in 1876. In the settling of South Africa by the Dutch, indigenous populations such as the Hottentots were systematically killed off. In the twentieth century, the most horrific forms of genocide befell European Jews and other ethnic groups under Adolf Hitler's reign of terror. The Nazi Party murdered about 6 million Jews and millions of people belonging to other ethnic groups, including European gypsies. In Cambodia, the communist ruler Pol Pot killed as many as 2 million people (one-fourth of the population) in what has become known as the "killing fields." Ethnic minorities, such as people with Chinese ancestry or Muslims, were favored targets in this genocidal campaign (Kiernan, 1988). In 1994, in the country of Rwanda in Central Africa, the majority ethnic group (the Hutus) slaughtered some half a million ethnic Tutsis within a few weeks. Though genocidal policies have been condemned by recognized moral standards throughout the world, they have occurred time and again in human history.

Ethnic Relations in the United States

To illustrate the dynamics of ethnic relations, we will focus on U.S. society. We begin with an overview of the early English settlers to America, or the so-called WASP ethnic group, which provided the basic cultural heritage for U.S. society. In addition, we examine the patterns of non-WASP immigration from Europe in the nineteenth century and the consequences of this immigration for U.S. society.

WASP Dominance

The early European colonization of what was to become the United States begins with the so-called "WASPs," or White Anglo-Saxon Protestants. The term *WASP* has come to refer to the ethnic group with a particular cultural and institutional complex that dominated U.S. society for generations. The British settlers were able to overcome their rivals—the French, Spanish, and Dutch in colonial America—and were free to develop their own form of culture. With the exception of the Native Americans and enslaved African Americans, four out of five colonial settlers in America were British Protestants. Smaller groups of settlers included Scots and Welsh, as well as Scotch-Irish (Protestants from Northern Ireland), Dutch, Germans, and Scandinavians. Yet by the end of the seventeenth century, these early non-Anglo settlers assimilated, culturally and structurally, becoming a part of the core WASP ethnic group that became dominant.

WASP ethnicity became preeminent in the United States through the establishment of its language, symbols, and culture. The English language was the fundamental underpinning of the cultural legacy that was bestowed by the WASPs on American society. It became the acceptable written and spoken language for the building of the nation-state and country, and it represented the standard for creating ethnic identity in colonial America. English was the institutional language of education, politics, and religion among the WASPs. From the early establishment of WASP culture, the expectation held that any subsequent ethnic groups that came to America would have to learn the English language. This was the first stage of what has sometimes been referred to as *Anglo-conformity*.

Along with the English language, the WASPs brought their basic fabric of the economic, legal, and political institutional framework for U.S. society. One of the primary reasons for colonization of North America by the British settlers was to extract raw materials and to produce new markets for England. Commercial capitalism, including the right to own private property, was brought to America by the English settlers. The initiatives for taking land from Native Americans, for developing European forms of agriculture—including the importation of slaves—and for sending raw materials across the Atlantic were all aspects of the market-oriented capitalism that was transported from England to America. Following the American Revolution, this market-oriented capitalism became the cornerstone of the expansion of the Industrial Revolution in the

United States. As the principal ethnic group engaged in the development of commercial capitalism and the Industrial Revolution, the WASPs were able to dominate and manage the major economic capitalist institutions in U.S. society. At present, some 33 million people trace their descent to these English settlers.

New Ethnic Challenges for U.S. Society

The nineteenth century was to see an enormous number of non-Anglos flowing in from other areas of the world that would begin to challenge the Anglo dominance of U.S. society. Over 30 million non-Anglo European immigrants would come to the United States in the nineteenth century. Many were non-Protestants, maintaining either Catholic or Jewish religious traditions. In addition, especially in respect to those ethnic groups from southern and eastern Europe, these people spoke different languages that were historically far removed from the English language.

German and Irish Americans

Since the seventeenth century, approximately 7 million people born in the area now known as Germany settled in North America. Currently, more Americans trace their ancestry to Germany than any other country. Although it is difficult to assess these numbers precisely, some 50 to 60 million Americans are descendants of Germans (U.S. Census Bureau, 2000). Many of the German migrants entering the United States were urban-based peoples skilled in crafts, trades, or the professions. Some of these immigrants were German Jewish migrants who were adapting along with other Germans to the booming cities of New York, Cincinnati, St. Louis, Chicago, Pittsburgh, Milwaukee, Indianapolis, and Louisville. Located along waterways or railways, these were attractive sites for urban skills (Glazier, 2003). Breweries, bakeries, distilleries, flour millers, tailor shops, print shops, surveying businesses, and plumbing stores were developed by these immigrants. A number of well-educated immigrants who had fled Germany for political reasons became important political activists and officials of the

U.S. government. Thus, nineteenth-century German American ethnic communities included both skilled and unskilled laborers. Because of their numbers and the occupational diversity of their population, German Americans could develop extremely self-sufficient communities.

As the numbers of immigrants from Germany increased, rather than assimilate quickly into American society, many attempted to retain their ethnic identity, including their language, culture, and religious traditions. Many of these German immigrants wanted to conserve their ethnic and nationalist identity within the United States. Aside from German language schools and churches, they began to establish ethnically based organizations such as music societies, theater clubs, beer halls, lodges, and political clubs. Through these organizations and institutions, as well as the private schools and churches in specific neighborhoods, various "Little Germanies" emerged in major cities such as St. Louis, Cincinnati, and Milwaukee. The endeavor to preserve German culture in the United States even led to a proposal to establish an exclusive German state in the Union (Adams, 1993; Cornell & Hartmann, 1998).

During World War I and World War II, extensive anti-German prejudice and discrimination emerged within American society. As a reaction to these anti-German sentiments, rapid cultural assimilation began to dominate the German American communities. For example, German surnames and German business names were Anglicized.

The major influx of Irish immigrants into the United States came during the nineteenth century. Today, some 40 million persons in the United States trace their ancestry to the Irish (U.S. Census Bureau, 2000). As the Irish Catholics settled in the United States, they adapted within many different types of occupations, skilled and professional. Because many of the Irish came with little education and capital, they were forced to take the lowest wage jobs in factories, mines, mills, construction of railways and canals, and other unskilled occupations. For example, large numbers of Irish workers were employed in the construction of the Erie Canal in New York state. Later, Irish labor was used to build the intercontinental railroad across the United States. Others worked in foundries, railway locomotive factories and repair shops, furniture factories, boat-building shops, breweries, and other unskilled industries. Many Irish women began to work as domestic servants for WASP households or in the textile mills and factories in eastern cities such as New York and Boston.

As Irish and German immigration increased in the nineteenth century, *xenophobic* sentiments (fear of foreigners) helped usher in nativistic movements among the WASPs. In particular, Roman Catholicism associated with the Irish was perceived to be untrustworthy. A political party known as the Know-Nothings developed. (They were known as Know-Nothings because party members were instructed to divulge nothing about their political program and to say they knew nothing about it.) Much of the Know-Nothing party activity was aimed at the Irish, who were unwelcome because they were non-WASP and Roman Catholic. The Know-Nothing program aimed to elect only WASPs to political office, to fight against Roman Catholicism, and to restrict citizenship and voting rights to immigrants who had resided in the United States twenty-one years instead of the five years required by law. The Irish Catholics were perceived to be a "separate race" and were purported to have a distinctive biology that made them different from the WASPs. The "Irish race" was perceived by the WASPs as undesirables who were immoral, unintelligent, uncouth, dirty, lazy, ignorant, temperamental, hostile, and addicted to alcohol. In cities such as Boston and New York,

there were signs in storefronts, housing complexes, and factories saying "No Irish Need Apply."

Italian and Polish Americans

Many southern and eastern European ethnic groups—Greeks, Italians, Serbians, Hungarians, Bulgarians, Russians, Ukrainians, and Poles—began to immigrate to the United States between 1880 and 1915. The United States was undergoing an unprecedented economic and industrial transformation that demanded large reserves of labor. Industrial expansion in the garment industries, food processing, mining, construction, and other manufacturing and services offered opportunities for people from southern and eastern Europe. Approximately two-thirds of the foreign-born population that came into the United States during this period were from these regions.

Unlike northern European groups such as the Germans or Irish, these new immigrants had languages and cultures that were far and away much different from those of prior immigrants. Today, over 15 million Americans trace their ancestry to Italy (U.S. Census Bureau, 2000). Many of the early Italian immigrants had come through a form of indentured labor known as the *padrone system*. A *padrone*, or boss, would recruit laborers in Italy, pay for their passage to the United States, and

An Italian American family.

arrange work for them, mostly in construction. Other Italian immigrants came through "chain-migration," relying on kinship networks. As Roman Catholics, they used the church organizations and other voluntary mutual-aid societies to help them adapt to the new conditions in America. Because of these ties, eventually these immigrants began to perceive themselves as having a common identity as Italian Americans (Alba, 1985). This new identity created the foundation for "Little Italys" in different urban areas such as New York, Boston, Chicago, and St. Louis.

Like many others from Europe, people from Poland were pushed and pulled by economic, political, and religious factors that influenced their decision to immigrate to America. Polish peasants (together with some members of the Polish middle class and intelligentsia) began to seek a new way of life in the United States. Letters from relatives and friends in America advertised high wages and employment opportunities in America. In addition, class, political, and religious oppression from occupying ruling empires propelled Polish immigration to America. Poles with sufficient funds could buy transatlantic tickets, while others depended on their relatives to provide kinship connections through the process of chain migration for their resettlement in America.

Although about 3 of every 10 migrants returned to Poland, today about 9 million Americans trace their descent to Polish ancestry (U.S. Census Bureau, 2000). Many of the Polish immigrants were taken to coal-mining towns like Scranton, Wilkes-Barre, Windber, and Hazelton in Pennsylvania, or the steel manufacturing cities of Pittsburgh and Cleveland. Other midwestern cities like Toledo, Milwaukee, Minneapolis, St. Louis, Chicago, and Detroit attracted Poles who were seeking work in the mills, slaughter-houses, foundries, refineries, and factories. In 1920 Chicago had 400,000 Poles, New York 200,000, Pittsburgh 200,000, Buffalo 100,000, Milwaukee 100,000, and Detroit 100,000 (Greene, 1980). In these towns and cities, Polish immigrants founded neighborhoods and communities known individually and collectively as "Polonia" (Latin for Poland).

With the unprecedented immigration into the United States from southern and eastern Europe in the first two decades of the twentieth century, Italians and the Poles were subjected to severe discrimination and prejudice from many Americans.

As we saw above, nativistic movements, beliefs in the superiority of the Anglo-Saxons, and anti-Catholicism were developing at this time. Like the Irish, the Italians and Poles were categorized by many WASPs as a different "race" that was inferior intellectually and morally to the Anglo-Saxons. But this construction of an "Italian race" or "Polish race" was even more severely restrictive than that applied to the Irish. An Anglo-Saxon-based racism, which was linked to "scientific racism" in the 1880s and 1890s, grew in the United States as a reaction to the immigration of southern and eastern European peoples. The "Italian race" and "Polish race," as well as other southern and eastern European "races" such as Jews were classified as inferior in contrast to the northern European "races."

As mentioned in Chapter 6, IQ tests and literacy tests were also given to these early Italian and Polish migrants; and, as expected, these people scored lower than the "average" American. These IQ and literacy tests were used as purported "scientific proof" of these new immigrants' inferior intellect (Kamin, 1974). These racist beliefs were promoted by the media and "scientific" works of the time. Anglo-Saxon Americans were warned not to intermarry with Italians and Poles because it would cause the degeneration of the "race." The Italian and Polish "races" were identified with correlates of behavior such as jealous, overly emotional, rough, mean, dirty, lazy, and other negative characteristics.

Despite the racial prejudice and discrimination they faced, the German, Irish, Italian, and Polish American communities were able to adjust to their circumstances through organized efforts in economic and political activities. They joined unions and organized political parties to cope with discrimination and prejudice, and the second and third generation of these non-Anglo immigrants began to assimilate culturally into U.S. society.

The Melting Pot: Assimilation or Pluralism?

As we saw above, U.S. society was challenged dramatically by the massive immigration of non-Anglo populations in the nineteenth and early twentieth centuries. Questions were raised about whether German, Jewish, Irish, Italian, or Polish immigrants could really become "Americans." Nativistic groups such as the Know-Nothings and the American Protective Association directed prejudice and discrimination at these immigrants. This prejudice against Catholicism and other ethnic traits, including language and purported "race," eventually resulted in restrictive immigration policies. During this same period, state and local authorities began to restrict the use of languages other than English in schools and to require all teachers to be U.S. citizens. Government policies promoted the use of the public school system to "Americanize" and assimilate the various non-Anglo immigrants.

One of the popular manifestations of these policies of assimilation evolving in U.S. society was the concept of the "melting pot." This became the popular symbol of ethnic interaction in the United States during the early twentieth century. The term *melting pot* was associated with a play by a Jewish immigrant, Israel Zangwill, called *The Melting Pot,* which had a long run in New York in 1909. Zangwill's play focused on the life of a Jewish immigrant who believes that the Old World nationalities and languages ought to be forgotten in the United States, and that all ethnic elements should fuse together in the creation of a new and superior American nationality and ethnicity (Gleason, 1980). This was not a new idea, but it was popularized at this time as a response to anti-immigration and anti-foreign attitudes of the nativist movements. The melting pot ideal implied that the new "American ethnicity" would represent only the best qualities and attributes of the different cultures contributing to U.S. society. It became a plea for toleration of the different immigrants, as they poured into American society. It was assumed that the American ideals of equality and opportunity for material improvement would automatically transform foreigners into Americans. It also suggested that the Anglo or WASP ethnicity was itself being transformed into a more comprehensive, global type of an American ethnic identity.

Despite the tolerant tone, universal appeal, and openness of the metaphor of the melting pot, it still emphasized assimilation. The belief that immigrants must shed their European ethnic identity and adopt a "Yankee" ethnic identity was at the heart of this concept. The second generation of Germans, Jews, Irish, Italians, and Poles thus tended to assimilate into the Anglo-American culture of the majority. Economic, social, and political benefits accrued to these "white ethnics" upon assimilation. To pursue the American Dream, the white ethnics assimilated culturally and structurally into the fabric of American society. As older ethnic neighborhoods and communities declined, most white ethnics abandoned their traditional languages and cultures. The metaphor of the melting pot appeared to have some validity, at least for most of these white ethnics. A substantial number of white ethnics had sloughed off their ethnic traditions to adapt to American society. For example, many Jewish celebrities changed their names, including Tony Curtis (Bernie Schwartz), Doris Day (Doris Kapplehoff), and Kirk Douglas (Issur Daneilovitch) (Glazier, 2003).

Along with this assimilationist trend in U.S. society, the crystallization of the race concept of "whiteness" was reinforced. Eventually, the people who came from Ireland, Germany, Italy, Poland, and other European countries became "white Caucasians," in contrast to other ethnic minorities (Jacobson, 1998). For many Americans, "whiteness" became a new socially constructed category of race that differentiated these Europeans from non-Europeans in the United States. Native Americans, African Americans, Hispanic Americans, and Asian Americans were non-whites, and thereby were excluded from the institutional benefits and privileges of people with white identities. Although there were some who still referred to the Anglo-WASP racial category, the enlarged category of a "white identity" assigned to Europeans tended to become part of the racial consciousness of U.S. society.

African Americans

Although people of African descent have been involved in peopling and building civilization in the United States for as long as Europeans, there are various misrepresentations and stereotypes about African Americans that have been perpetuated by the media and held by many U.S. citizens. For example, contrary to these stereotypes, two-thirds of African Americans are working class and middle class and above and are not living in poverty conditions. Today, African Americans constitute about 13 percent of the population, or about 36 million people (U.S. Census Bureau, 2000).

The majority of African Americans trace their ethnic history to the slave-trading activities that brought approximately 500,000 West and Central

An African American family.

Africans to the United States beginning in the seventeenth century. As seen in Chapter 21, millions more were brought to Latin America and the Caribbean. Slaves were chained together on sailing ships for a trip across the Atlantic Ocean, and many were killed by disease and filthy conditions aboard the European ships. The first slaves were auctioned off in 1619 in Jamestown, Virginia. Slavery was the foundation of the plantation system. Slavery was used in both the north and south United States prior to the American Revolution due to labor shortages. The first colony to legalize slavery was Massachusetts in 1641. The people of West and Central Africa were experienced farmers, skilled at iron smelting, cattle herding, and textile manufacture, and thus were viewed as valuable "commodities" by plantation owners (Brown, 2003). Slave labor was used for the benefit of the white plantation owners to plant and harvest their crops from daybreak to sunset and even longer. Slave families were often divided, as these humans were bought and sold in public auctions. Despite this attack

against the family unit, most slaves practiced marriage and attempted to maintain the family as much as possible (Brown, 2003). The southern laws enabled owners to treat their slaves as property and to discipline them in any way they desired to produce obedience and productivity. Although some slaves managed to resist and rebel against such oppression, the military and political power mustered by their owners disallowed the slaves to have any real control over their destinies.

Anthropologist Melville Herskovits did extensive studies of African Americans in the United States. As a student of Franz Boas, he debunked many racist notions that maintained that African Americans were an inferior race (Brown, 2003). Herskovits had a deep knowledge of African cultures and societies, and demonstrated that African Americans were neither inferior nor a people without a past. He and other anthropologists provided a foundation for understanding the unique and substantial contribution that African Americans have made for U.S. society.

Not all African Americans were slaves. Some were "free blacks" who had earned their freedom by working in nonagricultural professions in the urban areas, primarily in the north. Many free blacks were descendants of runaway slaves or had purchased their freedom through their own labor. Many African Americans managed to adapt to their condition in the United States by maintaining their own Christian churches, which became the center for social life in their communities. Thus, the culture of African Americans was forged in both slave and free conditions (Brown, 2003). They developed their own unique music and gospel singing that persists until the present, and they introduced many foods and agricultural and skilled techniques, such as cattle herding, that were brought from Africa.

Post-Slavery and Segregation   Following the Civil War in 1865, the Thirteenth Amendment to the U.S. Constitution outlawed slavery. The Fourteenth Amendment granted citizenship to all people born in the United States. The Fifteenth Amendment, ratified in 1870, stated that neither race nor previous condition of slavery should deprive anyone of the right to vote. Despite these amendments to the Constitution, African Americans found that obstacles were created to prevent them from becoming equal citizens under the law. In particular, southern states began to disenfranchise blacks legally by passing state laws denying them access to equal education.

If African Americans resisted segregation laws that upheld separate schools, restaurants, drinking fountains, restrooms, parks, churches, and other institutions, they would be beaten and sometimes lynched. Between 1882 and 1927, almost 3,500 African Americans were lynched. Southern whites justified these lynchings as a form of social control. Organizations such as the Klu Klux Klan and the White Citizens Councils conducted lynchings, violence, and intimidation against African Americans. Tired of suffering these deprivations in the southern areas, many African Americans began to move to northern cities for newly developing jobs in industry and other enterprises. However, even in northern cities, African Americans often found prejudice and discrimination awaited them.

The Civil Rights Movement   Returning home from World War II, many African American males who had fought in segregated divisions for U.S. society recognized that they did not have the individual freedoms and equal opportunities that they had fought for. In the 1950s and 1960s many African Americans, sometimes assisted by white Americans, began to participate in a massive civil rights movement for individual freedoms and equal opportunities as idealized in the American Constitution. In southern towns and cities African Americans began what were called "sit-ins" in segregated restaurants, bus boycotts against segregated buses, and other protests led by leaders such as the Reverend Martin Luther King, Jr. The civil rights movement was often faced by brutal violence, bombings of black churches, arrests, and intimidation. Some African American leaders such as Malcolm X of the Nation of Islam and Eldridge Cleaver of the Black Panthers called for armed defense against police brutality and violence against their communities. As a result of the civil rights movements and other protests, a number of civil rights bills were passed that provided for more individual rights, equal opportunity, and the breakdown of the Jim Crow laws.

African Americans Today   Despite the considerable gains of African Americans following the civil rights movement, a disproportionate number of their communities are in poverty when compared to white U.S. citizens. During the 1980s, earnings declined for many African Americans as factory jobs and other industries closed in the United States (Wilson, 1980). Thus, African American unemployment, especially among young black teenagers, rose considerably. Although African Americans have made tremendous strides in educational achievement since the 1960s, black college graduates are still half of the average national standard in the United States. These factors have left many young African Americans in inner cities susceptible to crime, drug addiction, and other dysfunctional behaviors. The destiny of the African American community in the twenty-first century will inevitably be influenced by a continued struggle for equality and individual rights, and against racism.

Hispanic Americans

The 2000 Census reported that the Hispanic/Latino population has had the largest demographic increase compared with any other ethnic group in the United States. The Hispanic/Latino population is approximately 37 million people, or 12.5 percent of the U.S. population, which compares roughly in size to the African American populace.

The terms *Hispanic* or *Latino* are umbrella terms that include many diverse people (Bigler, 2003). They include descendants of Mexican Americans (20 million), Puerto Rican Americans (3.4 million), Cuban Americans (1.2 million), and smaller groups of Dominican Americans, Mayan Indians, Peruvians, and other Central and South American immigrants and their descendants. These Hispanics or Latinos comprise a cluster of distinct populations, each of which identifies with groups that are associated with different countries or regions of origin. Hispanics or Latinos do not constitute a particular "racial" group. Skin coloration, hair texture, facial features, and physical appearance vary considerably among and within these different populations.

Most of the U.S. Hispanic or Latino population live in the southwest. Following the Mexican American War (1846–1848), the U.S. government annexed the areas now known as California, Colorado, New Mexico, Nevada, Utah, most of Arizona, and Texas. This area was known as *Aztlan* (home of the original Aztecs) to the Mexican population and represented half of Mexican territory. The influx of Anglos into these regions following the gold rush and the development of ranching, mining,

A Hispanic American family.

and other activities rapidly made the Mexicans minorities in these new states of the United States. Though these Mexican minorities were promised equal rights if they chose to become American citizens, they were discriminated against by laws enacted by Anglo-dominated legislatures (Takaki, 1990a). They also faced assaults and lynchings similar to those abuses faced by African Americans. Many Mexican Americans lost their lands and found themselves surrounded by Anglo Americans who maintained racist and ethnocentric views about the superiority of their own race and culture.

Eventually, as ranching and industrial development expanded in the southwest, many Mexican nationals were encouraged to immigrate to these U.S. regions to work as low-wage labor. Mexicans were paid much lower wages than Anglos to work in the mines or to plant and harvest the various crops of the region. The industries and ranches became dependent on this Mexican labor, and people moved back and forth across the border very easily. The unstated policy of the U.S. ranchers and industrialists was to have the Mexicans fulfill the demands of the labor market, but to return to Mexico when the economy went sour. Thus, during the Great Depression of the 1930s, many Mexicans were rounded up and deported back to Mexico so that Euro-Americans could have their jobs. However, following World War II, Mexican labor was

again in demand. This shortage resulted in what is known as the *Bracero* program, which allowed the United States to import Mexican labor to meet the demands of the economy (Bigler, 2003).

Following the war, the U.S. government organized "Operation Wetback," which captured and deported some 3.8 million people to Mexico who looked Mexican. This was done without any formal legal procedures. Yet many U.S. ranchers and industrialists continued to encourage the movement of Mexican labor back and forth across the border. As a result of the *Bracero* program and the importation of temporary workers, the Mexican American population, both legal and illegal, began to increase after World War II.

Puerto Rican Americans   In contrast to Mexican Americans in the southwest, New York City and the northeast became the center for the Puerto Rican American community. Puerto Rico came under U.S. control following the Spanish-American War of 1898. In 1917, Puerto Ricans became U.S. citizens. As U.S. citizens, Puerto Ricans were eligible to migrate to the United States without any restrictions. Following World War II, as industrial expansion increased, many Puerto Ricans were recruited and enticed to work in the low-wage sector vacated by Euro-Americans who were moving to the suburbs. Most of them settled in New York and sometimes refer to themselves as "Nuyoricans," many of whom reside in "Spanish Harlem." They believed that they were going to participate in the American Dream of upward mobility. Manufacturing jobs and related industries, however, were declining in the 1970s and 1980s in New York and other regions. Like many African Americans, Puerto Rican Americans were caught in the industrial and urban decline of this period. Better-paying unionized manufacturing jobs were disappearing, and faced with racism and discrimination, the Puerto Rican community encountered difficulties in achieving the American Dream of upward mobility.

Cuban Americans Prior to the Cuban revolution in 1959 led by Fidel Castro, a number of Cubans had migrated to the United States for economic opportunities. However, following the Cuban revolution, some 400,000 Cubans immigrated to the United States. The first wave of Cubans after the revolution comprised middle- and upper-class families who were threatened by the Castro government. These people were highly educated professionals, government officials, and businesspeople who brought capital and skills with them to the United States. Most of them settled in Miami, Florida, and became extremely successful in their adjustment to U.S. society. Many of them thought that they would return to Cuba to reestablish themselves after Castro was defeated (Bigler, 2003).

During the Cold War, these Cubans were welcomed by the U.S. government as political refugees fleeing a communist regime. A second wave of Cuban refugees came during the 1980s, as Castro allowed people to freely leave Cuba to go to the United States. About 10 percent of these refugees were ex-convicts and mental patients, and they had a much more difficult time adapting to conditions in U.S. society. Overall, though many Cuban Americans speak both English and Spanish, they have maintained the Spanish language and Cuban culture within the boundaries of U.S. society.

Hispanic Americans Today As indicated earlier, aside from the Mexican, Puerto Rican, and Cuban Americans, many other individuals are included within the terms *Hispanic* or *Latino*. These Hispanic/Latino people were influenced by the civil rights movements of the 1960s. Although African Americans were at the center of the civil rights

struggle, many Hispanic/Latino populations became involved in what some called the "Brown Power Movement." Civil rights activists such as Cesar Chavez, who led the United Farm Workers (UFW) struggle for Mexican American workers, began to challenge the inherent racism, prejudice, and discrimination against Hispanic/Latino Americans. Some Mexican Americans began to call themselves "Chicanos" as a means of challenging the hyphenated-American ethnic policies of assimilation and "melting pot" orientation of U.S. society. Mexican American activists began to refer to *Aztlan* as their original homeland. Puerto Rican American political activists also joined in many of the civil rights struggles against the assimilationist policies of the United States.

Today, the three largest Hispanic/Latino populations are concentrated in the southwest, northeast, and Miami, Florida. Four out of five Mexican Americans reside in the southwest, one-third of the Puerto Rican Americans live in New York City, and two-thirds of Cuban Americans live in the Miami area. But many others from the Dominican Republic, Nicaragua, El Salvador, Guatemala, Colombia, and other areas of the Caribbean, Central, and South America are arriving in U.S. cities. Many of these migrants are poor and unskilled and have taken low-wage jobs in the informal labor sector of the economy. Over one-quarter of all Hispanic/Latino Americans live below the poverty level, and the median family income of Hispanics is roughly half of that of Euro-Americans (Bigler, 2003). Thus, the Hispanic/Latino communities face challenges as they confront this twenty-first century in the United States.

Asian and Arab Americans

Asian and Arab Americans represent highly diverse populations that arrived during the nineteenth and twentieth centuries in the United States. Asian Americans include people from China, Japan, Korea, the Philippines, Vietnam, India, Pakistan, and other countries. Arab Americans include people from Lebanon, Syria, Iraq, Egypt, Jordan, Yemen, and other Middle Eastern countries. The 2000 U.S. Census reports that there are approximately 10 million Asian Americans and about two million Arab Americans.

During the mid-nineteenth century, Chinese immigrants came during the gold rush economic boom in California. Many of the Chinese worked as "coolie labor" building railways and in other lower-status jobs shunned by whites. Japanese immigrants followed in the 1880s and found jobs as agricultural laborers, first in Hawaii and then in California (Benson, 2003). Nativist white Americans viewed the immigration of the Chinese as a threat, resulting in mob violence against them. The Chinese were viewed as "The Yellow Peril" by these nativist white Americans. Eventually, the Chinese Exclusion Act was passed, the first federal law ever enacted solely on the basis of race or nationality. Though the numbers of Japanese immigrants were smaller and did not engender similar hostile legislation, in 1913 laws were passed in California restricting the amount of land that could be purchased by the Japanese.

Japanese Americans faced their greatest challenge after December 7, 1941, when Japan bombed Pearl Harbor. President Franklin D. Roosevelt signed laws that resulted in the internment of 110,000 Japanese Americans in military detention camps. This relocation meant selling their homes, furniture, and businesses on very short notice, and much of their property was confiscated. They were placed in crowded and dirty military prisons sur-rounded by barbed wire and armed guards. Not one of the Japanese Americans had been accused of any disloyal act, and two-thirds of the population were *Nisei*—U.S. citizens by birth. Very little action was taken against German or Italian citizens at this time. Thus, this legislation and its implementation were based partially on the racist views held by many white Americans.

Koreans and Filipinos came to Hawaii to work on the sugar and pineapple plantations. Following World War II and the Korean War of the 1950s, Koreans came as wives to U.S. military personnel and as independent businesspeople. Because the Philippines were acquired as a colony by the United States following the Spanish–American War of 1898, Filipinos were not subject to the same anti-immigrant, discriminatory laws faced by Chinese and Japanese populations. Thus, many Filipinos came to work in the agricultural fields in California and other West Coast states. Despite the lack of discriminatory legislation, a number of race riots directed at Filipinos broke out during the depression of the 1920s and 1930s. Several states also passed legislation against Filipino-white intermarriages (Benson, 2003).

South Asians from India, Pakistan, and Bangladesh migrated to the United States during the twentieth century. In the early 1900s, Punjabi Sikhs

An Asian American family.

migrated to northern and central California to work as agricultural laborers. Anthropologist Karen Leonard has studied these Sikh migrants and found that many Sikh men intermarried with Mexican American women (1997). It was next to impossible to get a white Justice of the Peace to recognize a Sikh and white marriage. The first generation of children of these Sikh-Mexican American marriages learned Spanish and identified with their mother's cultural heritage. In the second generation, however, many of these children are beginning to identify with their father's Sikh traditions.

Following the Immigration and Nationality Act of 1965, which opened the doors for Asian immigration, Chinese, Korean, Filipino, Vietnamese (following the Vietnam War after 1975), and South Asian and Southeast Asian peoples arrived on U.S. shores. Aside from the Vietnamese, who came as political refugees, these Asian immigrants were seeking opportunities in the booming U.S. economy. Some were working-class people who did not know English and encountered problems in adjusting to their new homes. Others were highly skilled professionals or independent businesspeople who had a very successful adaptation to the U.S. way of life. Because of the success and higher incomes of this latter group than most other immigrants, Asian Americans have been labeled a "model minority." Many Asian Americans, however, resent this stereotype, as it tends to neglect the hard work and determination of these families despite racist attitudes and discrimination against them. This stereotype also neglects the problems and difficulties faced by working-class Asian Americans in U.S. society.

The Arab American communities are smaller than other nonwhite minorities and are often marginalized in discussions of ethnicity in the United States. The major problem encountered by Arab Americans is a monolithic negative stereotype of Arabs and the Islamic tradition. Despite the tremendous diversity within this population of 2 million people, many of whom are Christians, the prevalent stereotype of Arab Americans is based on fears of international terrorism. This stereotype became heightened as a result of the September 11, 2001 attack on the World Trade Center. Following that event, many Arab Americans became alarmed that they would all be lumped together as threats to U.S. society, and there was some violence directed at Arab Americans and Islamic mosques. Many Arab Americans were arrested following 9/11 and were detained and released without substantial evidence of any links with terrorist networks. The negative stereotype of the Arab and a misunderstanding of their religion and history, as depicted in textbooks and the Western media, is the major problem that affects the Arab American communities in the United States.

An Arab American family.

Cultural Pluralism

Beginning in the late 1950s and 1960s, the melting pot metaphor was challenged by many non-European ethnic groups. African Americans, Hispanic Americans, Native Americans, Asian Americans, and other non-European ethnic groups demanded equal rights and opportunities for their respective communities. Non-European ethnic groups asserted that, because of their skin color and other cultural elements, they were not as "meltable" as European ethnic groups. Some civil rights leaders, such as Martin Luther King, Jr., rejected the assimilationist policies of U.S. society and called for a plural society, where different ethnic groups could retain their culture and heritage, but have equal rights and opportunities like other Americans.

The demand for cultural pluralism became a dominant trend in ethnic relations in the 1960s in U.S. society. Various non-European ethnic groups emphasized pride in their own unique history, experience, and culture. "Black Power" among African Americans, "Brown Power" among Hispanic Americans, and "Red Power" among Native Americans became the rallying anthems for cultural pluralism in America. Rather than emphasizing the melting pot as an ideal, non-European groups suggested that America should be a "salad bowl" or better yet, a "stir fry," which implies that everyone can maintain his or her own distinctive culture and ethnicity and still contribute to American society.

Multiculturalism in the United States

In the 1950s during the Cold War, the United States opened its doors for political refugees from communist countries such as Hungary and Cuba. Later, during the civil rights movement and demands for more cultural pluralism in the United States, a new immigration law in 1965 opened the doors once again for immigration into the United States from different areas of the world. During the past forty years there has been a significant growth in the population of peoples of non-European ancestry. A decline in the birth rate of the majority of the white population of European descent, coupled with new trends in immigration and higher birth rates of ethnic minorities, is changing the ethnic landscape of U.S. society.

As indicated by Figure 23.1, recent immigration from Europe to the United States represents a tiny fraction compared with immigration from Latin America and Asia. The ethnic diversity of non-European immigrants to the United States is remarkable. Among the Asians are Filipinos, Koreans, Chinese, Japanese, Vietnamese, Laotians, Cambodians, Thais, Indians, and Pakistanis. From Latin America come Central Americans from El Salvador, Guatemala, and Mexico, and people from the countries of South America. And from the Middle East and Africa come Palestinians, Iraqis, Iranians, Lebanese, Syrians, Israelis, Nigerians, and Egyptians.

Like the nineteenth-century immigrants from Europe, the majority of these immigrants have come to the United States seeking economic opportunities, political freedom, and improved social conditions. The United States has truly become much more of a multicultural society. A movement known as **multiculturalism** developed as an extension of the demand for cultural pluralism in U.S. society. As a result of this multiculturalist movement, federal, state, and local governments in the United States have encouraged the development of educational programs to prepare people to live in this new type of society.

Multiculturalism has led to revision of the curricula in educational programs throughout the United States. Instead of focusing narrowly on a Eurocentric or an Anglo-centric version of history, history texts were revised to include discussions of non-European ethnic groups and their contributions to U.S. history. Bilingual education was developed to extend equal education for those students not proficient in English. The ongoing multicultural movement emphasizes that there is no one model type of "American."

The movement for multiculturalism views cultural and ethnic differences as positive. It downplays any kind of competition or conflict among ethnic groups. Rather, the emphasis is on encouraging tolerance and cooperation among different ethnic groups. The hope is that as students become more ethnically literate, and more educated about ethnic groups, they will be able to appreciate and tolerate other people from different ethnic backgrounds. In

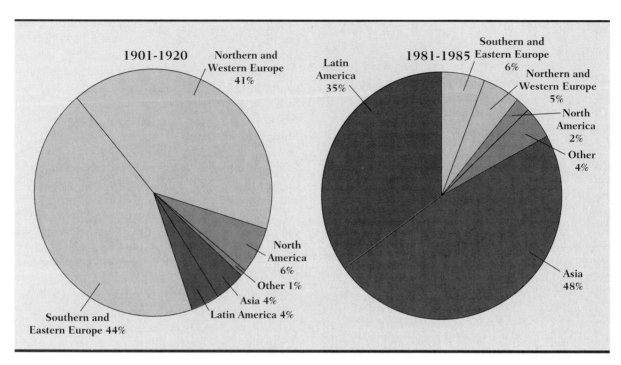

FIGURE 23.1   Legal immigrants admitted to the U.S. by region of birth.

Source: Leon F. Bauvier and Robert W. Gardner, "Immigration to the U.S.: The Unfinished Story," *Population Bulletin,* *40*(4). Washington, D.C.: Population Reference Bureau, Inc., 1986; and U.S. Census Bureau, *Statistical Abstract of the United States: 1998*. Reprinted by permission of the Population Reference Bureau.

addition, they will be able to make personal decisions that would affect public policy, promoting a more harmonious form of ethnic and race relations in the United States.

Ethnonationalism

In Chapter 19 we discussed how *nationalism*—a set of symbols and beliefs providing the sense of belonging to a single political community—developed along with industrialism in Europe and elsewhere. Before the development of nationalism, the primary focus of loyalty was to the local community, a particular ruler, ethnicity, religion, and the family (Gellner, 1983; Anderson, 1991).

However, as nationalism has emerged in these societies, minority ethnic groups sometimes view the imposition of language, culture, and the political system of the majority ethnic group as a form of cultural hegemony. To contest and resist this cultural hegemony, these ethnic groups may want to secede

and develop their own ethnically based nation-states. These ethnic secessionist developments are often called **ethnonationalist movements.** Many indigenous people and ethnic minorities have expressed their identity in nationalistic terms, without actually having an existing nation-state.

As seen in Chapters 21 and 22, many ethnonationalist movements emerged in areas of the world that were once colonized by Europeans. Ethnonationalist movements played a role in the struggle against European colonialism. Leaders such as Mohandas Gandhi in India, Jomo Kenyatta in East Africa, or Simon Bolivar in Latin America mobilized new forms of ethnonationalism in order to free themselves from European colonialism. After independence, these new, postcolonial societies had to form nation-states that incorporated disparate ethnic communities and cultures. In some instances, during the colonial period some ethnic groups had prospered more than others, and this disparity often resulted in postcolonial states in which the dominant ethnic group imposed their particular

APPLYING ANTHROPOLOGY

MULTICULTURALISM IN U.S. SOCIETY

As we have seen in this chapter, since the nineteenth century, the population of the United States has become more ethnically and culturally diverse. In addition, during the past forty years, there has been a significant growth in the population of peoples of non-European ancestry. The population of the United States is approximately 284 million, and ethnic minorities are increasing their proportion of this total very rapidly.

As a response to this multiculturalism, federal, state, and local governments in the United States have encouraged the development of programs to prepare people to live in this new type of society. For example, at least twenty-two states have developed guidelines to implement a multicultural approach in their educational systems. These guidelines have resulted in changes in curriculum and the content of textbooks to attempt to fairly portray the ethnic and cultural groups that compose the country's multicultural heritage.

Anthropologists have become involved in trying to solve some of the problems that resulted from these new ethnic and demographic trends. These applied anthropologists have been using knowledge about different cultures to educate people in various types of institutions in the United States. For example,

applied anthropologists have been providing intercultural training workshops in schools, hospitals, police departments, businesses, and other community settings where different ethnic groups are interacting with one another. These anthropologists are using their ethnographic knowledge about different cultures of the world to help people from different ethnic and religious backgrounds understand one another.

For example, one of the authors of this textbook was called on to help direct an intercultural workshop for a police department in a rural area of Missouri that had recently experienced the immigration of ethnic minorities from urban areas. The police department had had no experience in dealing with African Americans and Hispanic Americans. The workshop was intended to overcome some of the problems that had developed between the police department and the new ethnic communities. It included an introduction to what anthropologists have discovered regarding prejudice and discrimination on a worldwide basis and how some societies have resolved these problems. It also provided cultural background about ethnic minorities in the United States and demonstrated examples of communication and value differences that can create conflict between ethnic groups.

Applied anthropologists have been working with educators and education researchers in a number of areas regarding multiculturalism in U.S. society. They have contributed to curriculum development projects aimed at multicultural education and have also provided cultural background information to help educators adapt their teaching to the specific needs of ethnic minority children.

However, many applied anthropologists have become aware of some inherent problems with these multicultural education programs. Cultural ideas can be applied overzealously by educators. Anthropologist Jacquetta Hill-Burnett discovered that teachers would sometimes use cultural information regarding Puerto Rican Americans to stereotype children in the classroom (1978). Another researcher found a similar tendency in teachers of Eskimo and Indian children in Alaska (Kleinfeld, 1975). Thus, anthropologists have to provide cultural information for use in the multicultural settings, but they must also be extremely cautious to avoid broad generalizations about cultural differences that can be used as the basis of ethnic stereotypes. One of the major lessons that anthropology has to teach is that despite being part of an ethnic or cultural group, individuals differ from one another.

culture and language. Many of these postcolonial states still have a very weakly developed sense of nationalism because ethnic minorities perceive their own local interests and culture as being undermined by the dominant ethnic group.

Another variation of the postcolonial ethnonationalist movements occurred with the downfall of the former Soviet Union and its satellite countries in Eastern Europe. Various ethnic minorities—Latvians, Estonians, Lithuanians, Belarusians, Ukrainians, Georgians, Turkmens, Uzbeks, Tajiks, and others—began to accentuate their ethnic identities and regional nationalism as the Soviet empire began to collapse in the late 1980s. Historically, the Soviet Union was administered by fifteen Soviet Socialist Republics that contained "Autonomous Republics" that were defined by ethnic groups or nationalities. However, under the orthodox Marxist ideology that provided the foundation for Soviet political policies, ethnic groups were supposed to "wither away" and be replaced by a Soviet "super ethnicity." This was an attempt by the Soviet political elite to use its own version of nationalism, based on a political creed, to produce a civil polity (Banks, 1996; Gellner, 1988). In reality, none of these autonomous regions were allowed political rights and were strictly controlled by Soviet authorities in Moscow. Members of ethnic groups were subject to deportation or exile, and their boundaries were manipulated by the Soviet state.

In most cases, contrary to Marxist dogma, the various ethnic minorities did not abandon their cultural, linguistic, and religious traditions as expected. As the Soviet system began to disintegrate, a variety of ethnonationalist movements developed among these various ethnic minorities throughout the empire. In the aftermath of the dissolution of the Soviet Union, these ethnonationalist aspirations resulted in myriad newly independent countries. In Eastern Europe, as the communists lost their authority over Hungary, Czechoslovakia, Bulgaria, Romania, Poland, Yugoslavia, and East Germany, ethnonationalist movements materialized, which have had major consequences for these regions. For example, deep tensions between the ethnic Czechs and Slovaks led to the division of the former Czechoslovakia. Much more tragic results transpired in Yugoslavia, when Serbs, Croats, Bosnians, and other ethnic groups turned against one another in genocidal warfare.

In general, globalization processes have been a major factor in the appearance of many of these ethnonationalist movements (Friedman, 1994). At times, regional and ethnic identities are accentuated in a response to, and as a defense against, the growing impact of the wider world on their lives. Through the globalization process, dominant forms of culture and identity—most notably those of Western society—are disseminated around the world and imposed on local regions and ethnic groups. The communications media—including television, film, and the Internet—play a huge role in this process. Some theorists have referred to this globalization process as the "McWorld" tendency—the distribution of McDonald's, Macintosh computers, and Mickey Mouse throughout the world (Barber, 2001). One response to these globalizing trends is a reassertion and revitalization of one's own ethnic and local identity, leading to ethnonationalist movements. Many ethnic groups view these globalizing trends as a menacing process that tends to obliterate their own cultural traditions. Today, as we have seen in prior chapters, there are various ethnonationalist movements: Mayan ethnonationalism in Mexico, and similar movements among the Igbo, Yoruba, and Hausa in Nigeria, the Sikhs in India, and Native Hawaiians in the United States. Undoubtedly, these ethnonationalist movements will become a prevalent aspect of social and political life in the twenty-first century.

SUMMARY

Race and culture were misunderstood for many centuries in Western society. As Europeans explored the world, they confused the culture and behavior of different peoples with superficial physical traits such as skin color. Eventually, this led to distortions in the early scientific classifications of human racial groups. In addition, scientific racist beliefs began to dominate Western society, resulting in tragic human events such as the Holocaust in Nazi Germany. Anthropologists have been engaged in criticizing scientific racist beliefs in the past and the present by using sound evidence and rigorous examination of indicators such as IQ tests. Despite the useless scientific enterprise of classifying races throughout the world, societies continue to use folk taxonomies of race to distinguish different people. These folk taxonomies have profound social and cultural meaning for societies around the world.

Another confusion that developed in Western societies and other areas of the world is the identification of race with culture. Anthropologists have used the term *ethnic group* or *ethnicity* to distinguish ethnicity from race and are actively engaged in studying ethnic relations in different regions of the world.

Contemporary anthropologists have been doing research on race and ethnic relations in U.S. society. The history of U.S. race and ethnic relations was defined by the WASPs (White Anglo-Saxon Protestants) who instituted the language, the political culture, and the religious culture of American society. Other Europeans who immigrated to the United States included Irish, Germans, Italians, and Polish ethnic groups. These groups became known as the "white ethnics." African Americans arrived in the United States as slaves and have struggled for their political rights for centuries. Hispanic Americans are a diverse group that includes Mexican, Cuban, and Puerto Rican Americans, all of whom maintain distinctive cultural traditions in the United States. Asian and Arab Americans are also represented in multiethnic America. Though the myth of the "melting pot" has worked better for white Americans, policies involving multicultural practices and values aimed at recognizing the contributions of all Americans now permeate U.S. society.

QUESTIONS TO THINK ABOUT

1. What was the basis of race classification in ancient societies?

2. What were the basic criticisms of racism developed by anthropology?

3. What are some examples that represent the difference between race and ethnicity?

4. What can we learn from primordialist and circumstantialist approaches to ethnicity?

5. How do patterns of assimilation and pluralism differ in various societies?

6. What can we learn from the ethnic group adaptations in U.S. society?

7. What is the basis of ethnonationalist movements today?

KEY TERMS

assimilation
biological assimilation
cultural assimilation
ethnic boundary markers
ethnogenesis

ethnonationalist movements
hypodescent concept
Jim Crow Laws
multiculturalism
one-drop rule

plural society
racism
segregation

INTERNET EXERCISES

1. Review the article "The Death of Scientific Racism" at **http://shadow.autono.net/ sin001/race.htm**. How does the author of this article dismiss the concept of the inheritability of IQ? How do his conclusions compare to those expressed in this chapter?

2. How does the U.S. Census Bureau define race and ethnicity? For the answer to this question go to that section in the Census Bureau's website at **http://www.census.gov/Press-Release/www/2001/raceqandas.html**. How does this definition compare to anything you have read in the book? Could this legal definition used by the United States government cause any harm to groups or individuals? Why does our government classify people in such a way?

SUGGESTED READINGS

BAKER, L. 1998. *From Savage to Negro: Anthropology and the Construction of Race, 1896–1954*. Berkeley: University of California Press. An excellent historical overview of how anthropologists treated the concept of race up until the 1950s.

BRACE, LORING C. 2000. "Does Race Exist? An Antagonist's Perspective." Nova Online: (*http://www.pbs.org/wgbh/nova/first/brace.html*). An excellent critique of the concept of race as it was utilized in anthropology for many years.

ERIKSEN, THOMAS HYLLAND. 1993. *Ethnicity and Nationalism: Anthropological Perspectives*. London: Pluto Press. This text is an overview of ethnicity and the study of ethnicity through an anthropological viewpoint. It contains many ethnographic examples of ethnic change and ethnic persistence in different regions of the world.

MONTAGU, ASHLEY. 1997. *Man's Most Dangerous Myth: The Fallacy of Race*, 6th ed. Walnut Creek, CA: Altamira Press. This book is the classic statement by a trained physical anthropologist regarding the abuse of racial classification and the problems these classifications have created in the world. The first edition was published in 1942 at the height of the Nazi period. It represented the most fundamental attack on Nazi racist theories by American anthropologists. The most recent edition critiques the fallacies of the IQ studies that show supposed correlations between race and IQ.

SCUPIN, RAYMOND (Ed.). 2003. *Race and Ethnicity: An Anthropological Focus on the United States and the World*. Upper Saddle River, NJ: Prentice Hall. An introduction to race and ethnicity, with state-of-the-art essays on the these concepts and illustrations from ethnographic research in the United States, Africa, Latin America and the Caribbean, the Middle East, Asia, the Pacific islands, Canada, and Europe.

SMEDLEY, AUDREY. 1999. *Race in North America: Origin and Evolution of a Worldview*, 2d ed. Boulder, CO: Westview Press. A good overview of how the race concept was developed and used in the United States and Canada.

CHAPTER

'24

Contemporary Global
Trends

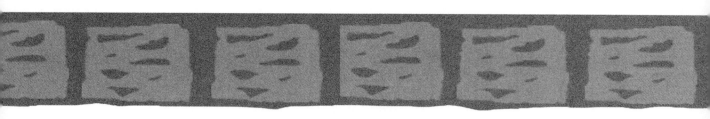

CHAPTER QUESTIONS

- What are some of the environmental trends that are a consequence of globalization?

- How do demograpic trends differ in various societies?

- What are the results of globalization on technology and energy use?

- How does the logic-of-growth model compare with the sustainability model?

- What are some of the economic consequences of globalization?

- What are some of the political, ethnic, and religious tendencies resulting from globalization?

As we have seen throughout this text, global interdependence, or what we have called *globalization,* has become an undeniable fact in the contemporary world. This process began after the Neolithic revolution, when small-scale societies were either absorbed into larger states or became dependent on those states. Ever since the Industrial Revolution, the trend toward global interdependence has escalated, especially through the process of colonialism. As the world shrinks and industrial societies continue to expand, interconnections are developing among different societies, creating a *global village*. The global village has been described as a world in which all regions are in contact with one another through the mass media, instantaneous communication, and highly integrated economic and political networks. This chapter reviews some of the recent trends associated with the development of this global village.

Environmental Trends

Hunting-and-gathering, horticulturalist, pastoralist, and intensive agriculture societies survived by extracting natural resources from a particular biome. In these societies, people were directly linked with nature and the environment, and they lived in relative harmony with the natural environment. This is not to suggest that humans in preindustrial societies did not harm their environments in any manner.

Slash-and-burn horticulture, intensive agriculture, pastoralism, and sometimes even foraging caused some environmental damage. Overgrazing, soil erosion, and the depletion of certain species have always been part of humankind's evolution.

With the development of globalization, however, the negative consequences for the environment have multiplied rapidly. Ironically, many people in industrial societies came to believe that they had gained mastery over the natural environment and were therefore free from its constraints. But in recent decades, people have become more aware that they are as dependent on the natural environment as were preindustrial peoples. It has become evident that the pollution created by global industrialization is threatening the ecological balance of the planet and the health of plant and animal species, including the human species.

Mechanized Agriculture and Pollution

One major source of pollution is commercialized, mechanized agriculture, known as **agribusiness.** Mechanized agriculture, or agribusiness, depends on the use of fossil fuels, chemical fertilizers, large tracts of land, and toxic poisons such as herbicides and pesticides to increase agricultural yields. This form of agriculture is not only prevalent in the industrialized world; it is also becoming common in developing countries. For example, some farmers in societies such as Mexico, India, and Indonesia have adopted mechanized agriculture. The spread of mechanized agriculture has been labeled the **Green Revolution** (Schusky, 1990). Through biotechnology research, sometimes known as *genetic engineering,* and other methods, scientists have produced hybrid species of wheat and rice seeds that generate higher agricultural yields. To take advantage of these yields, however, farmers must use expensive, capital-intensive technology for irrigation and cultivation; nonrenewable fossil fuels such as gasoline and oil; synthetic chemical fertilizers; and toxic weed killers, or herbicides, and pesticides.

The use of capital-intensive agriculture, however, can have negative consequences for the global environment. One of the most tragic cases resulting from the Green Revolution occurred in 1984 in Bhopal, India, where toxic fumes leaking from a chemical-fertilizer plant killed or injured thousands of people. Many of the consequences of mechanized agriculture, however, are much less dramatic (and therefore less publicized), although perhaps just as dangerous. For example, research has shown that much of the food produced in both industrialized and developing countries contains traces of pesticides and other poisons. Even when governments ban the use of chemicals, the residues may remain in the food chain for many years. Because many new synthetic chemicals are being produced for agribusiness every year, the danger to the environment continues to increase.

Air Pollution

Air pollution, especially from the emissions of motor vehicles, power generators, and waste incinerators, continues to be a major problem for industrializing

Globalization creates dense traffic problems in major cities such as Bangkok.

societies. As less developed countries industrialize, the degree of global air pollution steadily multiplies. It appears that atmospheric pollution is depleting the earth's ozone layer, which absorbs 99 percent of the ultraviolet radiation from the sun. These pollutants could irreversibly alter the earth's ability to support life. Satellite data show that during the period from 1978 to 1984, the ozone layer eroded at an average annual rate of 0.5 percent. In addition, acid rain produced by the burning of fossil fuels such as coal and gasoline has become a global problem, spreading across national boundaries and wreaking havoc on forests, lakes, and various species of aquatic life.

Scientific data suggest that the increased levels of carbon dioxide produced primarily by the burning of fossil fuels and tropical rain forests, methane, and nitrous oxide will create a **greenhouse effect,** or global warming. According to this hypothesis, after solar rays reach the earth's surface, the carbon dioxide (CO_2) in the atmosphere traps the heat and prevents it from radiating back into space. This process could eventually melt the polar ice caps, which would raise sea levels, flood major coastal cities, create violent weather patterns, and turn the tropics into deserts. An enormous amount of scientific data has accumulated that confirms the greenhouse effect hypothesis and global warming. Emissions of these greenhouse gases are likely to increase in the future. Predictions based on present-day estimates suggest that CO_2 emissions from industrialized countries will reach levels of 50 to 70 percent above 1990 levels by 2020. However, as more countries such as China begin to emit more greenhouse gases, global warming could proceed even more quickly. China accounts for 13 percent of the CO_2 emissions today. At this level, it is becoming the world's second largest emitter of CO_2 after the United States, which generates 23 percent (Wang, 1999). Stabilizing atmospheric concentrations of greenhouse gases will require reversing current emission trends.

Population Trends

As discussed in Chapter 19, with industrialization, new demographic trends have arisen. A recent model used to measure population trends is based on the **demographic-transition theory,** which assumes a close connection between fertility and mortality rates and socioeconomic development (Figure 24.1). According to the demographic-transition model, societies pass through three major phases of population change. During Phase 1, a high fertility rate is counterbalanced by a high mortality rate, resulting in minimal population growth. Phase 1 describes preindustrial societies. At first, societies used various methods of population regulation, such as self-induced abortions, postpartum abstinence, infanticide, or migration to limit population growth. As preindustrial societies developed

FIGURE 24.1 The demographic-transition model.

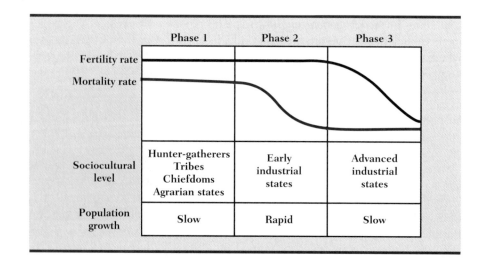

	Phase 1	Phase 2	Phase 3
Fertility rate **Mortality rate**			
Sociocultural level	Hunter-gatherers Tribes Chiefdoms Agrarian states	Early industrial states	Advanced industrial states
Population growth	Slow	Rapid	Slow

intensive agriculture, the population began to increase, but disease, famine, and natural disasters kept mortality rates fairly high, thus limiting growth.

In Phase 2, population tends to increase rapidly because of continued high fertility rates coupled with lower mortality rates. Mortality rates decline because of increases in the food supply, the development of scientifically based medical practices, and improved public sanitation and health care. Improvements in nutrition and health care enable people to control certain diseases, thus diminishing infant mortality rates and increasing life expectancy. Consequently, during Phase 2, population growth is dramatic. Growth of this magnitude was associated with the early phases of industrialization in Western Europe and North America, but it is also visible in many Third World societies that are now in the early stages of industrialization.

Phase 3 of the demographic-transition model represents the stage in which fertility rates begin to fall along with mortality rates. According to the model, as industrialization proceeds, family planning is introduced, and traditional institutions and religious beliefs supporting high birth rates are undermined. Values stressing individualism and upward mobility lead couples to reduce the size of their families. Phase 3 describes the stage of advanced industrial societies such as Western Europe, the United States, and Japan. Other trends, such as geographic mobility and the increased expense of rearing children, also affect reproductive decisions in industrial societies. Hence, in advanced industrial societies, as the birth rate, or fertility rate, falls, population growth begins to decline.

The Demographic-Transition Model Applied

The demographic-transition model seems to have some validity when applied to global population trends. World population during the Paleolithic period (Phase 1) is estimated to have been about 10 million (Hassan, 1981). Following the agricultural revolution, around the year A.D. 1, global population was approximately 300 million. But after the early stages of industrialization (Phase 2), from 1650 to 1900, world population tripled from 510 million to 1.6 billion. By 1950, the global population had risen to 2.5 billion, and by 1970, another billion people

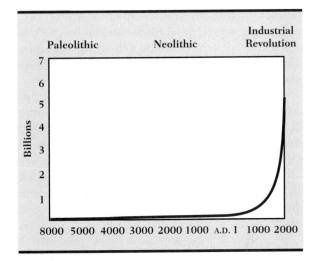

FIGURE 24.2 Global population growth. From about ten million people in the Paleolithic period, world population reached one billion by 1850. Following the Industrial Revolution and decreases in mortality rates, world population increased to over five billion people.

had been added. By 1990, the world population was approximately 5.4 billion, with 150 babies being born every minute (Figure 24.2). By the year 2000, world population exceeded 6 billion, and by 2050, global population will reach 10.2 billion.

Thomas Robert Malthus (1766–1834), a British clergyman and economist, is known as the father of demography. Malthus predicted that human populations would increase at a rapid, or exponential, rate, but the production of food and other vital resources would increase at a lower rate. Thus, populations would always grow more quickly than the food supply to support them. As a result, human societies would constantly experience hunger, increases in warfare, resource scarcities, and poverty.

To measure the exponential growth rate, demographers use the concept of **doubling time,** the period it takes for a population to double. For example, a population growing at 1 percent will double in 70 years; one growing at 2 percent will take 35 years to double; and one growing at 3 percent will double in 23 years.

The industrial nations of Western Europe, the United States, and Japan have reached Phase 3 of the demographic-transition model. The U.S. population is growing at only 0.7 percent. Countries such as

Germany, Hungary, and Japan actually have negative growth rates, which means that they are not replacing the number of people dying with new births. For a society to maintain a given level of population, each woman must give birth to an average of 2.1 children. At this point, the society has achieved **zero population growth (ZPG),** meaning that the population is simply replacing itself. When the average number of births falls below 2.1, a society experiences negative growth. Thus, Japan, with an average of 1.8 births, is actually experiencing a population decline (Martin, 1989). Decreased growth rates in industrialized nations have helped lower the global growth rate from 2 to 1.7 percent.

The demographic-transition model provides a conceptual scheme for evaluating global population trends, especially for the core industrial societies, yet it must be used carefully as a hypothesis. Although the industrial societies of North America, Western Europe, and Japan have reached Phase 3, the vast majority of the world's people reside in societies that are in Phase 2, with exponential growth rates. Population growth in African countries such as Kenya is almost 4 percent (doubling every 15 years), and Mexico's growth rate is 2.6 percent (doubling every 27 years). Thus, the demographic-transition hypothesis explains population trends in industrial societies, but it may not accurately predict population growth elsewhere for Phase 3. Suggesting that all societies will follow the path of development of the advanced industrial societies is somewhat naive. As we have seen from our discussion of industrial societies in Chapter 19, it took at least 500 years of historical experience for these countries to become fully industrialized societies and reach Phase 3 of the demographic model.

Most peripheral societies maintain high birth rates related to their agricultural lifestyles. As these societies become industrialized, however, death rates fall, leading to dramatic population increases. These societies have not had an extended time period to adjust to the demographic trends related to industrialization. Consequently, predicting a movement to Phase 3 is problematic. Most underdeveloped countries can attain population decline only through changes in technology, political economy, and social and cultural practices.

The One-Child Policy in China   One developing country that has taken steps to drastically reduce

its population growth is China. In the 1950s Mao Zedong perceived China's revolution as being based on peasant production and small-scale, labor-intensive technology. For this reason, he encouraged population growth among the peasantry. After Mao's death, however, a new leadership group emerged that reversed his policies regarding population growth.

In 1979, a demographic study was presented at the Second Session of the Fifth National People's Congress that indicated that if the existing average of three children per couple were maintained, China's population would reach 1.4 billion by the year 2000 and 4.3 billion by the year 2080. Alarmed by the implications of these statistics, the government introduced a one-child policy designed to achieve zero population growth (ZPG), with a target of 1.6 children per couple by the year 2000. Families that restricted their family size to one child were given free health care and free plots of land. In addition, their children would receive free education and preferential employment treatment. Families that had more than one child would be penalized through higher taxes and nonpreferential treatment. The one-child policy was enforced by neighborhood committees at the local level, and contraceptives, sterilization, and abortion services were provided free of charge. Neighborhood committees monitored every woman's reproductive cycle to determine when she was eligible to have her one child.

With some exceptions, the one-child policy has been remarkably effective. Between 1980 and 1990, the birth rate in China was reduced, and the annual growth rate fell from 2.0 percent to 1.4 percent, a record unmatched by any developing nation. This rate is similar to those of the most advanced industrial societies (World Population Data Sheet, 1991). Incentives, propaganda campaigns, and government enforcement combined to produce a new image of the Chinese family, one that had only a single child. Billboards and TV ads throughout China showed radiant mothers nurturing their one child.

Because the one-child policy is an attempt to reverse Chinese family patterns that have existed for thousands of years, it created controversies and problems. In the agricultural areas, it generated a great deal of resentment. Many Chinese prefer sons to daughters—a long-established Confucian tradition. In some cases, couples that have a daughter may practice female infanticide so that they may have a son to assume family responsibilities. Although infanticide is a criminal offense in China, it appears to be increasing in rural areas. Moreover, anthropologist Steven Mosher (1983) has reported that government officials sometimes forced women to undergo abortions to maintain the one-child policy. More recently, anthropologist Susan Greenhalgh, a Chinese population policy expert, reported that one out of every eight Chinese women married in the 1970s had suffered the trauma of a second or third-term abortion (Evans, 2000). There were many reports of full-term abortions, involuntary sterilization, forcible insertion of IUDs, the abandonment of female children, and female infanticide.

In response to some of these conflicts, the Chinese government relaxed the one-child policy in 1989. Rural families could have two children, but urban families were still restricted to one. This policy, known colloquially as "the one son or two child policy," placed a burden on second children who were females. Second-born daughters were subject to being placed in orphanages so that a family might have a son. China's orphanages are struggling to keep up with the number of female children. Additionally, the various minority groups have no restrictions on the number of children they can have. The minorities argued that through the one-child policy, the majority would quickly become the dominant group in their regions. They viewed the policy as an attempt to reduce their population and pressured the government to relax restrictions on their population growth. Recently, in April 2000, the Chinese government ruled that all the children of "only children" can have two children. But the government still offers higher rewards to those couples that have only one child. The Chinese government believes that the key to the success of its population-control efforts is the system of rewards offered to compliant families. Whether the people are willing to transform their fundamental cultural traditions to conform to government regulations is a question to be answered in the future.

Technological Change

Ever since the Industrial Revolution, the scale of technological change has become global rather than local. Industrial technology—computers, electronics, and advances in global communications—has spread from the core nations to the developing countries. For example, as previously discussed, the Green Revolution has altered the nature of food production. Technical information on agricultural production is spread through television and satellites to villages in countries such as India and Pakistan.

Energy-Consumption Patterns

High energy consumption is not only creating environmental hazards; it has also led to increased depletion of resources. High-energy, industrialized societies such as the United States consume a major portion of the world's nonrenewable energy and resources. For example, in 1987, the United States used over 2 billion tons of energy (the equivalent of coal), and the former Soviet Union used 1.8 billion. In contrast, Mexico used 140 million; Egypt, 33 million; Bangladesh, 6.8 million; and the Sudan, 1.5 million (*Information Please Almanac,* 1991). In 1997 the United States, Russia, and China were the leading producers and consumers of energy. These three countries produced 39 percent and consumed 41 percent of world energy. In that same year, the United States, representing 5 percent of the world's population, consumed 18.6 million barrels of petroleum per day—almost 26 percent of world consumption (*Time Almanac,* 2000). The U.S. Geological Survey estimates that there are about 3 trillion barrels of proven reserves of oil worldwide. The entire world should reach its peak levels of oil production in 2037, after which output is expected to fall precipitously. The 23 percent of the world's population residing in industrialized countries is consuming about 58 percent of the energy reserves that the planet is capable of producing.

Were semiperipheral and peripheral countries, with 77 percent of the world's population, to adopt the same consumption patterns as the core nations, nonrenewable energy supplies and resources might not be sufficient to support global economic development (Schusky, 1990). For example, as peripheral countries adopted mechanized farming, they increased their consumption of fossil fuels, leading to a worldwide jump in energy use. Between 1950 and 1985, the energy used to produce a ton of grain increased from 0.44 barrels of oil per ton to 1.14 barrels. By 1985, fossil-fuel energy used in farming totaled 1.7 billion barrels, about one-twelfth of the world oil output of 21 billion barrels per year (Brown, 1988).

Loss of Biodiversity

One of the major concerns regarding the consequences of globalization on the planet is the loss of biodiversity. **Biodiversity** is the genetic and biological variation within and among different species of plants and animals. Biologists are not exactly certain of how many species of plants and animals exist; new species are discovered every day. Some biologists think that there may be as many as 30 to 100 million species, or even more. Approximately 250,000 flowering plant species, 800,000 lower-plant species, and 1.5 million animal species have been identified (Raven, Berg, & Johnson, 1993). About 50 percent of these species live in tropical rain forests. As humans, we are dependent on these living organisms for survival; in both preindustrial and industrial societies, people rely on plant and animal species for basic foodstuffs and medicinal applications.

Many plant and animal species are threatened with extinction, causing a loss of biodiversity. Biologists estimate that at least one species becomes extinct each day. And as globalization continues, it is estimated that perhaps as many as a dozen species will be lost per day. Biologist E. O. Wilson writes in *In Search of Nature* (1996) that each year an area of rain forest half the size of Florida is cut down. If that continues, by 2020 the world will have lost forever 20 percent of its existing plant species. That is a loss of 30,000 species per year, 74 per day, 3 per hour. He goes on to say that we know almost nothing about the majority of plants and animals that the rain forest comprises. We haven't even named 90 percent of them, much less studied their properties or tapped their potential value. Wilson suggests that it is likely that a substantial portion of the planet's biodiversity will be eliminated within the next few decades. With the increase of industrialism, mechanized agriculture, and deforestation, as many as one-fourth of the world's higher-plant families may become extinct by the end of the next century.

Wilson believes that we are entering the greatest period of mass extinction in the planet's history. We have very limited knowledge of the world's plant and animal species. For example, there are approximately 250,000 different flowering plant species, but 225,000 of them have never been evaluated with respect to their agricultural, medicinal, or industrial potential (Raven, Berg, & Johnson, 1993). One out of every four prescription drugs comes from flowering plants, yet less than 1 percent has been studied for pharmacological potential. Many of these plants could be exploited as new food crops, pharmaceuticals, fibers, or petroleum substitutes. As long as biodiversity can be preserved, it represents a wealth of information and potential resources that can be extremely beneficial for humanity. In addition, with the new developments in genetic engineering, which depend on biodiversity (genetic variation), humanity may be able to find new resources that provide solutions for food and health problems.

Pessimists versus Optimists on Global Issues

Two basic perspectives—one negative, one positive—have influenced the analyses of global trends affecting the environment, population, and technology.

The Doomsday Model

The negative perspective is sometimes referred to as the Doomsday Model, or the neo-Malthusian approach. This model predicts that if current population, environmental, and technological trends continue, they will produce a series of ecological disasters that will threaten human existence. In the 1970s, a group of scientists and academics known as the Club of Rome assessed these global trends and predicted worldwide scarcities and a global economic collapse. Using elaborate computer models developed at the Massachusetts Institute of Technology, these scientists concluded that current global trends in population growth, energy-consumption patterns, and environmental pollution will exhaust the world's natural resources within the next 100 years.

The Optimists: The Logic-of-Growth Model

The Doomsday Model has been challenged by optimists such as Julian Simon (1981), who foresee a more promising future for humankind. Simon noted that health improvements, including a decrease in infant mortality and an increase in life expectancy, are a global trend. Simon also argued that pollution has abated in most societies that have experienced economic growth. Simon believed that as development and economic improvements continue in different societies, people will spend money to solve pollution problems.

Sometimes this perspective is referred to as the logic-of-growth model. This **logic-of-growth model** assumes that natural resources are infinite, and that economic growth can continue indefinitely without long-term harm to the environment. For example, this model notes that Malthus had not foreseen the biotechnological revolution in agriculture that made land much more productive than was true in eighteenth-century England. Economists such as Simon believe that food-production problems in regions such as Africa can be attributed to farm collectivization, government attempts to control the prices of agricultural commodities, and other institutional problems. Simon cites statistics indicating that on a worldwide level, food prices per person are decreasing, and food production per person is increasing.

The logic-of-growth theorists cite evidence showing that the costs of energy and other natural resources have actually fallen over time because humans have found creative technological solutions for producing and extracting these resources. For example, Simon argues that the increase in the price of oil in the 1970s was purely political. The cost of producing a barrel of oil is still about 15 to 25 cents. He notes how people in the past responded to shortages of firewood used for heating by turning to coal, and from coal shortages by using oil. Simon believed that this ongoing process of creative innovation will continue.

Simon and other logic-of-growth theorists further suggest that population growth is a stimulus for, rather than a deterrent to, economic progress. The title of Simon's major book is *The Ultimate Resource* (1981), which he considers to be the human mind. Productivity and solutions for economic and environmental problems come directly from the human mind. In the long run, therefore, population growth helps to raise the standard of living in society by utilizing creative ideas and technologies to devise solutions. Although Simon and other logic-of-growth theorists admit that, in the short term, population growth may inhibit economic development, they conclude that countries ought not restrict population growth forcibly, and that eventually technological innovations and human creativity will solve our problems, just as they have in the past.

The Pessimists and the Optimists: An Assessment

Most likely, both the pessimistic and the optimistic predictions regarding global problems are exaggerated. Predicting the future is risky for any social scientist, and to project complex global trends regarding population growth, environmental destruction, and technological change over many decades is highly problematic. The optimists believe that, ever since the beginnings of civilization, humanity has benefited from technological progress. A comprehensive view of the past, however, challenges this assumption. For example, we saw in Chapter 18 that the emergence of intensive agriculture—one of the major developments in human history—produced benefits for small segments of the population but adversely affected the majority of people by contributing to higher disease rates, increased inequality, and other problems. Conversely, the pessimists tend to underestimate the human capacity to devise technological solutions to global problems.

Anthropological research may help assess these global issues in a more cautious and analytic manner. With its holistic approach, anthropology has always been concerned with precisely those aspects of human interaction with the environment that are now being recognized widely by scientists studying global environmental change. The U.S. Committee on Global Change (1988) called for the development of an interdisciplinary science for understanding global change. The discipline of anthropology represents a prototype or model for the interdisciplinary science that would be needed to understand these changes (Rayner, 1989). Anthropological data can help assess the causes of such phenomena as the greenhouse effect by examining land-use choices and the impacts of economic activities. Anthropology may assist in the development of policies on matters such as agriculture, biotechnology, pollution, and population growth by providing information on the links between local practices and global processes.

Ethnographic Research on the Green Revolution

An example of how ethnographic research can illuminate global problems involves studies of the Green Revolution in underdeveloped countries. Optimists such as Simon cite the Green Revolution as one of the advancements made through technology and human creativity. In their view, the Green Revolution contradicts the basic assumptions made by the neo-Malthusians that population will outgrow the finite resources (food) of a particular area of land. Use of hybrid species of high-yield wheat and rice and highly mechanized agricultural techniques have increased food production to a degree that could not have been anticipated by Malthusians of past ages.

However, many cultural anthropologists who have studied the adoption of mechanized agriculture

Vaccinating cattle before they are shipped to a feedlot. Industrial societies have changed the nature of agricultural production. Large corporate farming that depends on expensive energy and heavy capital investment has resulted in the decline of family farming.

in developing countries have found that these innovations have created unintended economic and social problems. In most cases, only wealthy farmers have the capital to invest in irrigation equipment, chemical fertilizers, and large tracts of land. To extend their landholdings, wealthy farmers buy out smaller farmers, creating a new class of landless peasants and a small group of wealthy farmers, which intensifies patterns of inequality and related economic and social problems (Schusky, 1990).

In addition, cultural anthropologists find that in areas such as Mexico, where the Green Revolution was adopted enthusiastically, the increased agricultural yields in grains are often used to feed animals raised for human consumption. Anthropologist Billie Dewalt (1984) discovered that more than 50 percent of the annual grain production in Mexico was used to feed animals such as pigs, chickens, and cattle. His research indicates that people who can afford meat have benefitted from the Green Revolution. By increasing inequalities, however, the Green Revolution has reduced the percentage of the population that can afford meat. Dewalt concluded that the commercialization and industrialization of agriculture has not only widened the gap between rich and poor in Mexico; it has led to the underutilization of food, energy, and labor, thus hindering rather than promoting agricultural development.

Case Study: The Green Revolution in Shahidpur

One ethnographic study has shown that when the Green Revolution is carried out under the right conditions, it can be successful. Cultural anthropologist Murray Leaf (1984) studied the effects of the Green Revolution in the Punjab region of northern India. Leaf conducted research in a Sikh village called Shahidpur from 1964 to 1966 and then returned in 1978. The years 1965 and 1978 mark the onset and complete adoption, respectively, of the Green Revolution in Shahidpur. Thus, Leaf was able to view the beginning and end of the process. During this period, the village switched from subsistence to mechanized agriculture.

The villagers adopted new strains of wheat, tractors, insecticides, and an irrigation technology on an experimental basis to determine whether this would increase their yields. Wealthy farmers adopted the technology readily, investing their capital in equipment and land. Poor peasants, however, also took the needed capital investment risks (with the support of government development agencies), and the risks paid off. Leaf's research demonstrates that, in contrast to modernization theory, poor peasants are not constrained by traditional cultural patterns that might inhibit rational strategies of investment and savings. When these peasants saw they would directly benefit from these investments, they were willing to accept the economic risks.

More important, the villagers were willing to acquire the knowledge and technical skills needed to manage and ensure the continuity of their agricultural production. Through a university extension center, new plant varieties and technologies were adopted on an experimental basis. The people could directly see the results of their agricultural experiments and respond appropriately to various conditions. The education was a low-cost investment with government-subsidized tuition even for the poorest families. Furthermore, the university center provided training in the maintenance and repair of farm equipment and in other nonagricultural employment fields.

Leaf suggested that a key to the success of the Green Revolution in this region (in contrast to many other rural areas) is that government officials were more interested in development than in control. Government advice was always linked to the actual reactions among the villagers. Channels of communication were always open between local and regional levels. Leaf's valuable ethnographic study has some suggestive insights for those interested in furthering the Green Revolution in the Third World. Much more ethnographic research needs to be done, however, to evaluate the successes and problems in implementing the Green Revolution.

Case Study: The Conservation of Wood in Haiti

Another area in which ethnographic research has increased our understanding of a global problem is the growing shortage of wood for fuel and construction in developing societies. This problem is most acute in regions where growing populations practice intensive agriculture. Peasant farmers spend several hours each day searching for firewood, the principal cooking fuel in poor households. This practice results in the cutting of forests, which take a long time to grow back. Deforestation has become a worldwide ecological challenge.

A Haitian farmer.

Anthropologist Gerald Murray (1989), who conducted research among the rural peasants in Haiti, helped design a plan to solve the problem. European powers such as the French had developed Haiti as a sugar-exporting colony. They found it profitable to cut forests to clear land for sugar cane, coffee, and indigo for European consumers. After Haiti became independent in the nineteenth century, foreign lumber companies continued to cut and export most of the nation's hardwoods. These activities, combined with population growth that created land scarcities, greatly reduced the amount of forest area. The Haitian government tried to develop a reforestation project but failed to secure the cooperation of most of the peasants. The government blamed traditional peasant attitudes and patterns of land use for the project's failure.

In contrast, Murray argued that neither traditional land-use patterns nor peasant attitudes were responsible for the failure of reforestation. He discovered that the peasants did not cooperate with the project because they did not see any immediate benefits. Most of the trees with which the peasants were familiar took many years to grow. Moreover, the peasants believed that planting trees on their small tracts of land would interfere with crop cultivation. They also feared that even if they reforested the land, the government would assume ownership of the trees and thereby deprive them of the use of the land.

Because of his study, Murray was invited to help design a reforestation plan. With assistance from other anthropologists and development specialists, he designed a program that introduced fast-growing hardwood trees as an additional cash crop for peasant farmers. The increasing demand for this type of wood for charcoal and construction made it an ideal commodity. Thousands of trees were planted all across Haiti. In addition, the plan called for the trees to be completely owned and managed by the peasantry rather than by the government. The peasants could harvest the trees whenever needed, and they knew that they would receive the direct benefits from the project. After several years, the peasants constructed their houses and sold charcoal from the new woods. Murray views this type of peasant-managed, cash-crop production as a feasible option for many Third World peasant communities.

A Global Solution for Global Problems

In June 1992 in Rio de Janiero, Brazil, representatives of 178 nations gathered at what was known as the Earth Summit. These representatives tried to set the stage for managing the Planet Earth through global cooperation. The issues were the environment, climate change induced by the greenhouse effect and global warming, population growth, deforestation, the loss of biodiversity, air and water pollution, and the threats of globalization throughout the world. Although the Earth Summit was successful because it received so much international attention and created worldwide awareness of global issues, the specifics of how soon problems were going to be solved, how much it would cost, and who was going to pay became extremely complicated.

A follow-up summit on climate change was held in Kyoto, Japan, in December 1997. The Kyoto Summit was organized by the Organization for Economic Co-operation and Development (OECD), which represents most industrialized countries of the world. The OECD is committed to helping its member countries move toward sustainable development for the planet's life-support system. The Kyoto Summit resulted in a protocol agreement endorsed by 110 countries to try to reduce greenhouse gases and stabilize atmospheric changes that would mitigate increasing global warming.

The Kyoto Protocol established targets and set the stage for international monitoring of greenhouse gas emissions from various countries. The Kyoto agreement set a target of overall reduction of 5.2 percent in greenhouse gases from 1990 levels by the year 2012. The European countries set a target of reducing their emissions by 8 percent; the United States by 7 percent; and Japan by 6 percent. The United Kingdom took it upon itself to set higher targets and committed itself to a 20 percent reduction of emissions by 2010. Part of the agreement encouraged the industrial countries to become partners with the developing countries to help curb greenhouse gas emissions throughout the world.

Not surprisingly, many leaders of developing countries blamed the industrialized countries for the problems. Leaders of developing countries view themselves as victims of industrialized countries. For example, the Rio Declaration was going to contain a statement of principles on deforestation that would legally prohibit developing countries from burning their tropical rain forests. The developing countries objected to this statement because it was unfairly focused on the tropical forests and included nothing regarding the deforestation of the old-growth forests in the United States, Canada, and Europe. When a compromise could not be reached, the legally binding statement was scrapped for a weaker statement with no legal implications.

In addition, the industrialized countries, including the United States, were very reluctant to participate in some issues. For example, with respect to global warming, Japan and the European community had established limits on carbon dioxide emissions. In 2001, with the election of George W. Bush as president, the U.S. administration dropped out of the Kyoto Summit agreement. The Bush administration claimed that the treaty was unacceptable because it would harm the U.S. economy. They contended that the cost of curbing greenhouse emissions from coal-burning power plants and automobiles was too great a burden on the U.S. economy and would result in the loss of jobs and profits. The U.S. administration argued that the Kyoto agreement made exceptions for countries such as China and India, who did not have to reduce their emissions although these countries were emitting substantial amounts of greenhouse gases. Thus, the Bush administration opted out of the agreement, stating that it was unfair because it did not hold developing countries to the same strict emissions standards as the developed countries.

Many of the developing countries at the Rio de Janeiro summit felt that their number-one priority was economic survival rather than saving the environment. Developing countries wanted to adopt industrialization as rapidly as possible to induce economic development. Although they agreed to some of the environmental mandates of industrialized countries, they did so only by requiring the industrialized countries to contribute large sums of money toward those efforts. This resulted in various conflicts between the have and have-not countries.

The Sustainability Model

Obviously, the problems resulting from globalization are extremely complex and are not going to be resolved without some sort of global unity. Anthropological research in countries throughout the world has resulted in a perspective sometimes known as the sustainability model. The **sustainability model** suggests that societies throughout the world need environments and technologies that provide sustenance, not only for the present generation, but also for future generations. This model encourages resource management that does not degrade the environment for future generations. The sustainability model is opposed to the logic-of-growth model, which assumes that economic and technological growth will inevitably bring progress. The sustainability model is more realistic in assessing environmental and technological change, and recommends policy changes to inhibit problems that are induced by globalization. Some countries are beginning to adopt this sustainability model of development by limiting their emissions, curbing population growth, and cleaning up pollution. However, these global problems cannot be solved by country-by-country solutions. The challenge for this generation is to provide a global, internationally based organizational context for the resolution of these problems. Neglecting these global problems is bound to result in massive difficulties for the future of humanity. Anthropological research can help in assessing these problems and thereby promote the model of sustainability.

Economic Trends

As indicated in earlier chapters, the contemporary global economy began with European expansion in the mercantilist and colonialist periods. Ever since World War II, this world economic system has been divided into core, semiperipheral, and peripheral countries, with the United States the leading core country. Trading and financial institutions in the capitalist countries controlled the international organizations such as the World Bank and the International Monetary Fund. The industrial-socialist countries of Eastern Europe and the former Soviet Union tried not to participate directly in the capitalist world economic system and also tried to create their own client states in areas such as Cuba, Angola, and Afghanistan. By the 1980s, however, new developments in the world economy were producing a radical restructuring of the world economic system.

Multinational Corporations

One of the major factors behind the emergence of the global economic network is the multinational corporation. In Chapter 19, we discussed multinational corporations as they have evolved in both the capitalist and socialist world. In many ways, multinational corporations have opened the door for globalization by promoting the spread of technical and cultural knowledge to non-Western societies. In the modern era, multinational corporations have expanded to the point that some anthropologists consider them a new societal institution beyond the state. For example, anthropologist Alvin Wolfe (1977, 1986) discussed how multinational corporations have integrated the manufacturing processes at a supranational level. Multinational corporations have reorganized the electronics industry, garment manufacturing, and the automobile industry. Today, products might be manufactured in several different countries, and the financing and organization of labor carried out by the multinational corporation. Wolfe suggested that this process will continue. The multinational corporations will eventually assume the management of global affairs, and the nation-state will disappear.

Jobs and Growth: A Positive Assessment Given their power and influence, multinational corporations have become highly controversial. With their tremendous capital assets, they can radically alter a society. Some theorists believe that multinational corporations can enhance global economic development, thereby reducing poverty and hunger. As these corporations expand into Latin America, Africa, the Middle East, and Asia, they bring capital and technology and provide employment. From this vantage point, they create jobs and spur both short- and long-term economic growth.

Neocolonialism: A Negative Assessment Dependency theorists, however, suggest that multinational corporations have actually intensified the problems of developing countries. They contend that these corporations create benefits for a wealthy elite and a small, upwardly mobile middle class, while the vast majority of the population remains in desperate poverty. Because the multinational corporations tend to invest in capital-intensive commodities, the majority of the population does not participate in the modernization of the economy. Furthermore, the entire society becomes dependent on corporations that are based outside the region, which inhibits self-sufficiency and the development of a more diversified economy.

According to this view, multinational corporations are simply the forerunners of a new form of neocolonialism, aimed at supplying the industrial world with natural resources and cheap labor. Multinational corporations based in core societies encourage peripheral societies to incur loans to produce a limited number of export-oriented commodities, a process that creates a cycle of economic indebtedness and increased dependency. In contrast to the older forms of colonialism, the core countries do not incur the expenses of maintaining direct political control over these societies; rather, they keep the peripheral nations in a state of dependency and maintain indirect political control by making contributions and paying bribes to politicians. In certain cases, however, when core countries feel threatened by political developments in peripheral nations, they resort to direct military intervention.

Case Study: The Potlatch Corporation As with other global developments, these issues can benefit from ethnographic research. In one example, anthropologist Paul Shankman (1975, 1978) researched the changes generated by a multinational corporation on

the island of Western Samoa. The corporation studied by Shankman was a large wood-product firm called the Potlatch Corporation, based in the northwest coast region of the United States and named after the famed redistributional exchanges of Native Americans in that region (see Chapter 17). The Potlatch Corporation surveyed the tropical hardwood trees in a portion of Western Samoa and found a dozen species that could be used for furniture and veneers. To facilitate the leasing of large amounts of land in Western Samoa (bypassing traditional landholding arrangements), the Potlatch Corporation requested that the Samoan government set up an agency to act as a broker on behalf of the corporation. Potlatch eventually won a number of concessions from the Samoan parliament.

Although Potlatch claimed to be committed to the economic development of Western Samoa, Shankman found that the monetary rewards from leasing the land did not prove as great as the people had expected. For example, Potlatch leased 28,000 acres of land for $1.40 an acre. In one project in which it leased land from a group of seven villages, the average yearly income from leasing amounted to less than $11 per person. Royalties paid on cut timber were also low, amounting to 4 cents per cubic foot, part of which was to go back to the government for reforestation.

The Potlatch Corporation did provide jobs for three hundred people in Western Samoa, making it one of the island's largest employers. Shankman discovered, however, that most of these people were formerly employed in agriculture, civil service, and light industry. Through the Potlatch projects, labor was simply shifted from other sectors of the economy to forestry. Thus, Potlatch did not really create jobs; rather, it simply shifted them to new sectors.

Shankman believed that Potlatch's leasing policies would ultimately create a scarcity of land, and more peasants would be forced to produce on marginal land. Moreover, Shankman suggested that the inflated cost of living generated by the company, through increased debt of workers, in addition to the negative consequences such as erosion of the rain forest caused by rapid lumbering, may result in long-term negative costs to the people of Samoa.

Shankman also noted that the risks assumed by the people of Western Samoa were much greater than those of the multinational corporation. If

Potlatch were successful, it could recoup its initial investments very quickly. Were it to lose revenue, it could simply leave the area. In contrast, the peasants did not have any capital to fall back on were they to lose their land. Moreover, they had to live permanently with the economic, social, and ecological changes brought about by Potlatch's policies. Eventually, the Potlatch Corporation pulled out of the region. As Shankman (1990, 2000) concluded: "So much for the commitment to economic development of Western Samoa."

Other anthropologists are conducting research similar to Shankman's. The consensus at this point appears to confirm his charges that the expansion of multinational corporations has created new forms of economic dependency and neocolonialism. Thus, in the short run, the global changes wrought by multinational corporations appear to have had negative consequences for developing societies. Whether this will be true over the long run remains to be seen.

Emerging Economic Trends

Driven by new technological and scientific developments in areas such as biotechnology, telecommunications, microprocessor information systems, and other high-tech industrialization, the world economy continues to undergo rapid changes. The globalization of the world economy has produced a vast array of products and services in interlocking markets. World trade has accelerated over the last few decades, stimulating greater economic interdependency. These trends have resulted in a restructuring of the world economic system.

Changes in Socialist Countries The globalization of the economy has had traumatic consequences for the industrial, socialist-based economies of the former Soviet Union, Eastern Europe, and other peripheral socialist economies such as China and Vietnam. These state-administered economies did not produce the extensive economic development that they had promised. Government officials in these countries promoted five-year plans for economic development, but these plans did not lead to the production of prized consumer goods or a higher standard of living.

Anthropologist Marvin Harris (1992) advocated a cultural-materialist approach in explaining the downfall of the former Soviet Union and Eastern European communism. Harris suggested that the infrastructure, which encompasses the technological, economic, demographic, and environmental activities directed at sustaining health and well-being, has a primary, determinant role in the functioning of a sociocultural system. The serious deficiencies and weaknesses in the infrastructure of the former Soviet Union and Eastern Europe undermined the entire fabric of society. For example, the basic energy supply based on coal and oil production became stagnant, and the generating plants for electricity were antiquated, leading to periodic blackouts and frequent breakdowns.

Harris described how the agricultural and marketing system for the production and distribution of food resulted in severe shortages, delays in delivery, hoarding, and rationing. In addition, increasing problems with, and costs incurred by, industrial pollution led to the deterioration of the socialist economies. According to Harris, the infrastructural deficiencies of these socialist systems had fundamental consequences for the basic health, safety, and ultimate survival of the people in these societies. These deficiencies eventually led to the societies' systemic breakdown.

The industrial-socialist societies faced major economic crises. Repeated failures in agriculture and industry led to frustration and unrest among the populace. Global communications with other societies, particularly those with much greater access to consumer goods, caused many people in socialist states to become frustrated with the inadequacy of their systems. These people began to question the aims and policies of their leaders.

The Soviet Union: Perestroika and Glasnost In the former Soviet Union, Communist Party leader Mikhail Gorbachev responded to the people's criticisms and the economic crisis facing the country by instituting a series of reforms and economic restructuring known as *perestroika*. In effect, this policy involved the reintegration of the former Soviet Union into the world-capitalist system. New joint ventures with capitalist firms were undertaken; McDonald's and other multinational corporations from the West and Japan were invited to participate in the Soviet economy. Soviet industrial corporations were reorganized to emphasize competition and the maximization of private profits for individual firms.

McDonald's restaurants are one sign of globalization in non-Western countries.

Wages and salaries in Soviet industries were no longer to be controlled by the government; rather, they would reflect market conditions and individual productivity.

To carry out *perestroika,* Gorbachev had to confront the bureaucratic elite that dominated the Soviet political economy (see Chapter 19). Because these reforms directly threatened the bureaucratic control of the political economy, he faced much resistance by government officials. Some of these bureaucrats were ideologically committed to the Marxist–Leninist model of communism and did not want the Soviet Union integrated into the world-capitalist economy. Others believed that tinkering with the economy with these reforms would induce more hardship for the Soviet people. For example, after the introduction of *perestroika* and the removal of government-controlled price restraints, the costs of food and other basic commodities skyrocketed.

As a means of implementing his economic reforms, Gorbachev also called for *glasnost,* usually translated as "openness," which involved the freedom to criticize government policies and officials. Newspapers and other media were allowed to express views that were in opposition to Communist Party dictates. *Glasnost* also permitted greater political freedom of expression as well as democratic elections and a multiparty political system. The policy of *glasnost* led to mass demonstrations against the former Soviet government and eventually to criticism and the downfall of Gorbachev himself.

As a result of the severe economic difficulties and subsequent political crises in the Soviet Union, many of the non-Russian republics began to declare sovereignty and independence. Regions such as Estonia, Lithuania, the Ukraine, Kazakhstan, Uzbekistan, Turkmenistan, and Azerbaijan cut their political ties with the Soviet Union. Although Gorbachev attempted to frustrate these developments, sometimes with a show of military force, the Soviet empire began to collapse. Eventually, all of the non-Russian regions formed their own independent republics. The independent republics not only cut political ties, leaving the Russian republic by itself; they also began to restrict the export of their domestic commodities into Russia. This exacerbated the difficult economic conditions within the Russian state itself.

The successor to Mikhail Gorbachev, Boris Yeltsin, attempted to further the *perestroika* and *glasnost* policies of his predecessor. Yeltsin's primary goal was to transform the remains of the state-managed centralized economy of Russia into an economy in which managerial and consumer decisions are based on market forces and the economy is in private hands. The Yeltsin government tried to radically restructure the political economy by ending price and wage controls, reducing or eliminating subsidies to factories and farms, slashing military expenditures, introducing new taxes, and balancing the national budget.

The United States and other European economic leaders supported these policies, which became known as *shock therapy*. This economic shock therapy had some positive consequences, but most economists agree that the peculiarities of the Soviet system were bound to prolong the process of economic reform. In the meantime, many Russians who were accustomed to subsidies and government benefits had to endure substantial hardships. A number of Russian bureaucrats began to use their positions to acquire economic assets through illegal maneuvers. *Ponzi schemes,* which used fake banks and financial institutions to gain large sums of capital from government organizations and the general population, were prevalent during this shock therapy period (Titma and Tuma, 2001). In addition, a lack of knowledge of how capitalism, free labor, and the market economy operate has resulted in major economic declines in agriculture and industry. In 2000, Vladimir Putin, Yeltsin's prime minister, was elected president of Russia, promising to continue the economic reforms and democratization of Russian society. The question for future developments in Russia is whether the people can be patient enough to endure these economic difficulties.

Eastern Europe Stimulated by the policies of *perestroika* and *glasnost,* the Eastern European nations of East Germany, Poland, Czechoslovakia, Hungary, Romania, Bulgaria, and Yugoslavia began reforms of their socialist political economies. These countries had been restricted to trading primarily with the Soviet Union and among themselves. In the German Democratic Republic (East Germany), mass demonstrations and migrations of people to West Germany led to the fall of the communist government and the destruction of the Berlin Wall. Solidarity, a popular outlawed labor union led by Lech Walesa, toppled the government of Poland. Polish workers demanded economic reforms and a better standard of living than that offered by the socialist model. Democratic elections led to Walesa's becoming prime minister. Walesa subsequently visited the United States and other Western countries in search of foreign investment. Many of the Eastern European socialist-bloc societies actively sought reintegration into the world-capitalist economy as a means of stimulating both economic growth and democratic freedom.

In a book entitled *What Was Socialism and What Comes Next?* (1996), anthropologist Katherine Verdery, who did most of her ethnographic work in the East European country of Romania, summarizes some of the problems and dilemmas facing this region. She writes about how a different sense of time prevailed during the socialist period in Eastern Europe, and the new forms of capitalism and its industrial work rhythms based on progress and linear models are disrupting these societies. Verdery notes that new resurgent patterns of gender inequality based on older patriarchal forms are reemerging in these postsocialist Eastern European countries. During the socialist period, gender relations were supposed to have been equalized. However, Verdery describes how the socialist government in Romania reconfigured gender roles, making women dependent on a patrilineal-paternalistic state. After the downfall of socialism, Romania, as well as Poland, Hungary, and other postsocialist countries, have been emphasizing a return to "traditional values" regarding gender, which positions the woman once again in the home doing household chores. To some extent, this gender organization of postsocialist society defines housework as "nonwork." As these Eastern European economies become more capitalistic, women will probably be drawn into the work force, but in the meantime, these women are returning to the older patriarchal forms of family life.

In the final chapter of her book, Verdery comments on how the transformation of Eastern Europe and Russian societies may take a much different path toward capitalism than the Western European or U.S. societies have taken. The privatization of property is likely to involve very different processes than in Western societies. Former socialist leaders will undoubtedly use the legal and political process to develop economic opportunities for themselves, as they transfer the state enterprises into private hands. Verdery suggests that black markets, organized crime, and the manipulation of the legal and state apparatus by former socialist bureaucrats will all have consequences for these postsocialist societies. The future of these postsocialist societies cannot be predicted based on models of how Western capitalist states developed.

China Since Mao Zedong's death, China, under leaders such as Deng Xiaoping, introduced many tenets of capitalism. Instead of relying on Communist Party cadre who wanted to instill egalitarian ideals, the new leadership sought to develop leaders with technical, agricultural, and scientific expertise. They encouraged students to obtain education in the United States and other Western nations. They abolished the commune system and reorganized agricultural and industrial production based on individual profits and wages for farmers and workers. The Chinese government called for modernization in agriculture, industry, science, and defense.

Although promoting economic change, the Chinese government has not endorsed political reform. Party bureaucrats remain entrenched in power and resist all pressure to relinquish their authority. The absence of political freedom resulted in mass demonstrations by students and others in Tiananmen Square in Beijing in 1989. The Chinese government crushed this freedom movement with military force and has continued to repress any form of political dissent that threatens its authority. Whether economic development and reintegration into the world economic system can work in China without corresponding political freedom is a question that remains to be answered.

Vietnam Confronted with being one of the poorest countries in the world, the Vietnamese government in 1981 introduced a series of economic reforms called *doi moi* (Pike, 1990). Some of the younger politicians in Vietnam are calling for greater participation in the world economic system, the introduction of private enterprise, and individual material benefits in the form of wages and salaries. The Vietnamese reformers face the same problem as those in China and the Soviet Union. With their memories of their colonial experience and wars against the capitalist nations, conservative bureaucrats who are committed to Marxist–Leninist ideology oppose reintegration into the world economic system. Reformers, in contrast, actively seek support from capitalist countries and the international community to pursue their economic liberalization policies and democratization. Recently, it appears that reformers are having the stronger influence regarding state policies. For example, they were instrumental in the negotiations that resulted in the United States lifting its trade embargo against Vietnam in January 1994. This shift in U.S. policy

Vietnamese boat people.

will undoubtedly lead to increasing trade and capitalist economic activity in Vietnam.

Changes in the Core Societies: The United States and Japan   The globalization of the world economy has also had dramatic effects on the core industrial societies, such as the United States and Japan. The United States currently exports about one-fifth of its industrial production. This is double what it was exporting in the 1950s, and that proportion is rapidly increasing. About 70 percent of those exported goods compete directly with goods produced by other nations. Some U.S. states depend heavily on the international economy. For example, approximately one-half of the workers in Ohio work directly on exports such as tires and automobiles. Honda, the major automobile company in Japan, has a large plant in Marion, Ohio. Most American corporations now conduct business on a global level. Although the United States remains the world's largest economy, with a gross national product twice the size of that of its nearest competitor, it no longer dominates as it did in the past. In fact, at the beginning of the twenty-first century, the United States had one of the largest trade deficits and the largest foreign debt of any nation.

In contrast, Japan has maintained a trade surplus. During the past several decades, the United States and Japan have engaged in global economic competition. This competition needs to be considered in the context of the world economic system.

In the 1920s, in the early phases of Japanese industrialization, Japan's population began to expand. Lacking adequate natural resources such as fertile land, raw materials, and energy supplies, Japan became increasingly dependent on imported food and other raw materials. To secure a food supply to support its growing population, the Japanese began to act as an imperial power in Asia, colonizing Korea and Taiwan and expanding into China. Japanese imperialism in Asia was one of the direct causes of World War II.

During its occupation of Japan following World War II, the United States encouraged the development of corporate capitalism. The U.S. government viewed Japan as a capitalist center that could be used to forestall the spread of communism in Asia. Some of Japan's *zaibatsu,* wealthy family conglomerates, were broken up into smaller concerns. Others, such as the Mitsui and Mitsubishi families, were

encouraged to invest in new equipment and technologies to induce rapid capitalist growth. Large sums of U.S. capital were funneled into corporations such as Sony to stimulate corporate capitalism. These policies led to the "economic miracle" in Japan that occurred in the 1960s. By the end of that decade, Japan had become one of the world's leading exporters.

The Japanese government, however, realized that it was still dependent on energy and food from other regions of the world. The government constantly reminded its population that Japan must "develop exports or die." The government organized the Ministry of International Trade and Industry (M.I.T.I.) to mobilize industrial firms to export products such as automobiles and electronics to ensure a balance of funds to pay for its heavy imports of food and energy. The M.I.T.I. helps finance Japan's huge exporting corporations so that it can maintain a favorable balance of trade. By the late 1980s, Japan had a large trade surplus. However, it imported approximately 8 tons of fuel, food, wood, and other raw materials for every ton of goods it exported.

Both Japan and the United States, as well as other core capitalist countries, have become postindustrial societies, with a large component of their economy devoted to the service sector (see Chapter 19). At the same time, many of the basic manufacturing plants of these industrial economies are relocating into developing countries to exploit the cheaper labor supply. Japanese multinational corporations have relocated auto factories and other industries to developing Asian countries such as Indonesia and Thailand. Ford Motor Company has relocated an engine manufacturing plant in Mexico. As the core countries become increasingly internationalized, economic interdependency accelerates. Some theorists believe that this interdependency may become a key component in resolving conflict among nations in the global village.

The Semiperipheral NICs   Another result of the globalization of the economy is the rise of the *newly industrializing countries* (NICs) from a peripheral to a semiperipheral status in the world economic system. Included here are the nations of South Korea, Hong Kong, Singapore, and Taiwan. Popularly known as the "Little Dragons of Asia," they compete with the economic might of Japan. Both Taiwan and Korea were colonies of Japan, whereas Hong Kong and Singapore were colonies of Great Britain. As with other colonized nations, they became peripheral dependencies. These countries, however, are rapidly industrializing and have broken their bonds of dependency. In some industries, such as electronics, these nations have marketed products that compete with core countries like Japan.

The success of the NICs reflects the changing division of labor in the world economic system. As the multinationals relocated some of their labor-intensive industries to low-wage regions, the NICs were able to absorb some of these jobs. Like Japan, their success is partially due to U.S. economic support. In particular, during the 1950s and 1960s, the United States viewed South Korea and Taiwan as part of the capitalist bloc in Asia. The United States invested large sums of capital and foreign aid into these countries, thereby enabling them to develop as capitalist centers. In addition, as in Japan, the governments in these countries directed the modernization of the economy through massive investment into export industries.

The NICs have changed the context of the world economy through low-cost production methods and aggressive marketing. They have created a unique niche in the world economic system by exporting products that compete directly with those produced by the core countries. In many cases, they have expanded their overseas markets through joint ventures with multinational firms based in core countries. In other cases, they have created their own multinational corporations. For example, NIC multinational corporations have become global competitors as producers of semiconductors for electronic and computer equipment. The world's largest plastic firm is Formosa Plastics, based in Taiwan. The best-selling imported car in Canada is the Pony, made by Hyundai in South Korea.

Political Trends

As the world economy becomes more integrated, major political changes are taking place in the global network. During the 1950s, some modernization theorists (Chapter 20) predicted that the various nations would become very similar as they were brought closer together in the global economy. People everywhere would share the same goods and services and eventually the same cultural values. This similarity would set the stage for a unified world government. Certain current trends indicate that such a movement may be taking place; for example, in 1999, fifteen European countries agreed to accept the "Euro" as the form of currency exchange in order to facilitate trade and to help develop a unified European economy. The EU (European Union) covers some 1.2 million square

Japanese factories are moving to new areas of the world such as Indonesia.

miles and contains 375 million people speaking 11 different languages. It is currently the largest market in the world, and its gross domestic product (GDP) rivals that of the United States.

In addition, a unified European parliament has been established, and Europeans no longer need passports to travel among the fifteen different countries. Some Europeans are beginning to think of themselves as "Europeans" rather than Italians, Greeks, Germans, Irish, or British. The nation-state may be giving way to larger political organizations and processes. At the same time, however, other political tendencies seem to indicate movement in the opposite direction; in many areas the nation-state appears to be fragmenting along linguistic, ethnic, and religious lines.

In considering these global political trends, many anthropologists suggest that the nation-state is too small for the immense problems in the world political economy: capital flows, economic development, management of technology, environmental and demographic trends, production of commodities, and labor problems. Organizations such as the United Nations, International Monetary Fund, World Bank, World Trade Organization (WTO), NAFTA, the EU, and the multinational corporations appear to be in the process of displacing the nation-state in the management of the global economy. Although the United Nations has not been effective in producing an international consensus on global problems, it may become more important in the future.

At the same time, the nation-state may be too large to care for the different needs of people at the local level. Government officials representing the nation-state may not have enough contact with the populace in local areas to respond to their needs, which can range from housing and food to the opportunity to express their cultural values. One sign of the fragmentation of the nation-state into smaller components is the increase of ethnic and religious tensions at the local level.

Ethnic Trends

Ethnic unrest and tension are prevalent in today's world. Newspapers and television news are rife with stories about ethnic violence among the peoples of the former Soviet Union and Eastern Europe, Africa, Sri Lanka, India, Ireland, the Middle East, and the United States.

Anthropologists have been systematically examining ethnicity since the 1960s. As we saw in Chapters 10 and 23, an ethnic group is a collectivity of people who believe they share a common history and origins. Members of ethnic groups often share cultural traits such as language, religion, dress, and food. Today, as we saw in Chapters 21 and 22, the countries of Latin America, Africa, the Caribbean, the Middle East, and Asia are plural societies that contain many ethnic groups.

As globalization occurs, with its rapid integration of nation-states, markets, and information technology, and as the management of economic and political development goes to the World Bank, the International Monetary Fund, the EU, the United Nations, and large multinational corporations, many peoples at the local level feel threatened by these global processes. Citizens of various countries lose faith in their government's ability to represent their interests in these pluralistic societies. These globalization processes often exacerbate ethnic tensions and conflicts.

In previous chapters, we looked at the development of ethnonationalist movements in Latin America, the Caribbean, Africa, the Middle East, and Asia. As we saw, these ethnonationalist movements were, to some extent, a result of earlier colonial policies and new post-Cold War trends in globalization. Many ethnic groups have expressed a desire to return to a more simple way of life and traditional culture and behavior. They distrust the new global managers, and ethnonationalism is a reaction to these globalization tendencies. Restoring ethnic autonomy is sometimes seen as a strategy to rectify the globalization process.

The revival of local ethnic tendencies and identities is developing in the West as well as in non-Western countries. Anthropologists are studying the ethnic resurgence of the Scots and why they want more independence in the United Kingdom, and why Quebec wants to separate from the rest of Canada (Handler, 1988; Cohen, 1996). These local ethnic movements for autonomy and separatism are a response to the weakening of older nation-state loyalties, induced by globalization. As globalization is fraught with anxieties and produces

APPLYING ANTHROPOLOGY

WORLD MIGRATION AND REFUGEES

It has been estimated that some 100 million people are migrating from their homelands to other countries; of this number, about 17 million are refugees and another 20 million have fled violence, drought, and environmental destruction (Popline, 1993). The vast majority of the migration and refugee problems involve Africa, Latin America, the Middle East, and Asia. However, during the 1990s, thousands of refugees in Europe, primarily from Bosnia and Kosovo, began a forced migration out of their homelands. Although some of the migrants and refugees come to wealthier countries in North America or Europe, the majority are marking time or trying to carve out a new existence in underdeveloped regions. Approximately 87 percent of the 17 million refugees are residing in underdeveloped countries, countries that have rapidly growing populations and severe economic and environmental problems.

A number of anthropologists are actively engaged in research projects and planning activities directed at resolving some of the basic problems that confront refugee populations. An organization known as the Committee on Refugee Issues (CORI) has developed as a division of the American Anthropological Association to sponsor and encourage research and problem-solving projects among refugee populations. Various anthropologists are studying the Southeast Asian migrants who came to the United States in the aftermath of the Vietnam War from Vietnam, Laos, and Kampuchea (Cambodia). Most of these anthropologists are attempting to help these refugees adapt to conditions in the United States.

Anthropologist Pamela DeVoe (1992) has been doing research among Southeast Asian refugees in the St. Louis area. DeVoe has found that Southeast Asian refugees enter the work force at the unskilled and semiskilled level within the first six months of their arrival in the United States. She found that the key problem for these refugees is the lack of adequate health benefits to cover their families. DeVoe found a lack of federal planning for a comprehensive refugee health program and an inadequate, uncoordinated state network of health services for them. Consequently, these refugees, who have to cope with traumatic experiences as a result of the stresses of migration and relocation, have few opportunities for adequate health care.

After interviewing the employers of the refugees, DeVoe discovered that many of the Southeast Asian refugee workers quit their jobs suddenly, for no apparent reason. She found that absenteeism and abrupt quitting occurred frequently, indicating that these refugees were having difficulties adjusting to U.S. society. DeVoe found that in some cases the refugees did not understand the system of health care and the benefits available to them. Hospitals treat illnesses and bill patients over time, using a sliding scale to determine how much a person has to pay for a service. Because of the lack of language skills, however, these refugees did not understand what the health care system could do for them or what it would cost, which caused delays in health care treatment. Generally, when these delays occurred, the refugees bought over-the-counter medications or used folk remedies to treat themselves. In some cases this resulted in more severe illnesses or dangerous treatments.

DeVoe found that only about 40 percent of the refugees employed in metropolitan St. Louis have work-related health insurance. Generally, as for other Americans, the expense of buying private health insurance is too

costly for most refugees. Thus, health insurance is the critical problem for many of the Southeast Asian refugees in the work force in the St. Louis area. DeVoe suggested that a national comprehensive health care system would eliminate many of the problems for these refugees and help them become more self-sufficient, productive members of American society.

Other anthropologists have been using their research skills and problem-solving techniques to assist migrants who have been detained in refugee camps in different parts of the world. Anthropologist Nancy Donnelly (1992) studied the Vietnamese refugees who had been confined in detention centers in Hong Kong. Vietnamese refugees have been coming to Hong Kong as asylum seekers since the end of the Vietnam War. Since 1979, about 180,000 men, women, and children have arrived in Hong Kong by boat. Approximately 64,000 remain in refugee detention camps awaiting acceptance by other countries. In 1989, Hong Kong attempted to force some of the refugees to return to Vietnam, but international pressure forced Hong Kong to reverse its policy, and it has focused instead on assisting refugees to return voluntarily, if they wish to do so.

Donnelly conducted her research in 1991, visiting thirteen detention camps and agency offices that manage the camps in Hong Kong. She found that most of the camps are much like prisons and are strictly controlled by the Correctional Services Department in Hong Kong. As many as three hundred people live together in Quonset huts that are surrounded by double chain-link fences topped by barbed wire. These camps contain Vietnamese who are waiting for screening to determine their eligibility for resettlement. They have little to do most of the time. Camp life is described as rule-bound and boring, punctuated by occasional violent episodes. In general, Donnelly found that these refugees are treated as criminals. On the other hand, Donnelly found that for most of the refugees, their status in the camps was preferable to their lives in Vietnam. Everyone expressed hopes regarding freedom and a better life.

Drawing on anthropological research, Holly Ann Williams (1990) attempted to highlight general trends for family situations of people detained in refugee camps. In the initial decision-making stages of choosing to flee one's country, refugee families often face upheaval, disruption, disorientation, and possible death

for friends and family members. The breakdown of customary family roles and the new, unfamiliar patterns of social organization often result in multiple stresses. In some cases, extended family units fragment into smaller nuclear units to safeguard resources and food. In other cases, when families are fleeing war conditions, males stay behind as resistance fighters. This leads to the development of many female-headed households in the refugee camps. The vast majority of the refugees in camps in Third World societies are women and children.

Once they are situated in the camps, scarce resources, limited food, communicable diseases, minimal health care, and overcrowding place more stress on the families. Families are crowded into living quarters with little privacy, often leading to increased marital and family conflicts, including wife and child abuse. In the camps, refugee families experience a loss of control over their destiny; they describe camp life as a waste of time, meaningless, and depressing.

Despite this loss of autonomy and self-determination and the consequent disintegration of the family unit, Williams reported that in many cases the individuals often try to re-create the family structure as a basis of social

(continued on page 624)

APPLYING ANTHROPOLOGY

WORLD MIGRATION AND REFUGEES—CONTINUED

support. Women begin to develop the new leadership roles, economic responsibilities, and coping skills required for family maintenance in the camps. Although women experience more hardship than men in refugee camps, often being subjected to personal violence, rape, and abduction, they are sometimes able to assume leadership roles and create social support for family members. Williams, who completed her

specific research on Cambodian refugees, called on anthropologists to do more research on family dynamics in refugee camps, to better understand these coping mechanisms.

The United Nations High Commissioner for Refugees (UNHCR) is the organization responsible for ensuring that refugee camps maintain minimum standards of health and safety conditions.

Anthropologists are engaged in studies that provide information and problem-solving strategies that can be used by various voluntary agencies and UN officials to help improve the lives of refugees confined to these camps. This has become an increasingly important project for anthropologists who can use their knowledge and research techniques in solving various global problems.

---

uncertainties in structures and institutions, and as it develops in anarchic, haphazard fashion carried along by economic, technological, and cultural imperatives, the ethnic group becomes the refuge for people who feel as if they have no control over these new forces.

Religion and Secularization

Just as ethnic trends have created contradictory political trends, there are ongoing, contradictory religious trends in the context of globalization. In Chapter 19, on industrial societies, we discussed the process of secularization. Generally, traditional religious beliefs and rituals become separated from economic, social, and political institutions in industrial societies, and religion becomes a private affair for most people.

After the Enlightenment, social thinkers such as Auguste Comte and Karl Marx, as well as early anthropologists, predicted that as societies became increasingly industrialized and modernized, secularization would eradicate religious institutions and beliefs. Though secularization has occurred, however,

religion has not disappeared in these societies. Even in places such as the former Soviet Union and Poland, where government authorities prohibited religious beliefs and institutions, religion remained a vital force.

To some extent, religious institutions have survived in industrial societies because religious leaders have emphasized many of the cultural values—for example, nationalism—espoused by other institutions. In addition, the persistence of religion may also be a product of the secularization process itself. Many recent religious revivals have occurred in those societies that have been most affected by modernization. We saw this in Chapter 22 in the case of the Iranian Islamic revolution. As globalization introduces sweeping political, social, and ideological changes, many traditional beliefs and values are challenged. To cope with these destabilizing transformations, many people are reemphasizing traditional cultural values, including religion. For example, the fundamentalist movements in North America, whether Catholic, Jewish, or Protestant, can be partially understood as a reaction against secularization and modernization. The same can be said of Buddhist, Hindu, and Islamic fundamentalism in other parts of the world.

The Role of Anthropology

Although the political, ethnic, and religious trends discussed in this chapter are essentially global, they also obviously affect people on the local level. Not surprisingly, therefore, cultural anthropologists are actively documenting the local responses to global political and religious trends of people in the agricultural regions of Latin America, Africa, the Middle East, Asia, and nonstate societies, as well as in industrialized societies. Cultural anthropologists have recorded the various dislocations of global political and religious processes in these societies and the ways in which people have attempted to cope with these global changes. The continuing agony of separatist, ethnic, and religious conflicts in Bosnia, Kosovo, Sri Lanka, and elsewhere threatens people throughout the world. Existing institutions such as the nation-state have not been able to manage this local conflict. Perhaps by understanding the specific aspirations of these different peoples, national governments and the international community will be more responsive to their diverse needs and interests.

As anthropologists identify the cultural variations that hamper international coordination, they may help to contribute to the reduction of ethnic and religious tensions worldwide. Anthropologist John Bennett (1987) recommended that anthropologists synthesize their local studies (the micro level) with studies of global conditions (the macro level) to identify trends that militate against international cooperation. Anthropologists should make a concerted effort to understand the underlying historical and cultural motivations that contribute to ethnic and religious conflicts. In doing so, they may aid in humankind's understanding of its existence and the need for cooperation in the global village.

Jerry Falwell has been a leader of fundamentalist Christianity in the United States.

As people recognize that globalization is not incidental to their lives but rather a recognizable transformation in their everyday circumstances, they draw on religious substance as a means of restoring power over their lives. The reconstruction and reinvigoration of their religious identity gives some people a sense of greater control in what appears to be a runaway world. Fundamentalist religious movements articulate the uncertainties and distress brought about by expanding globalization and advocate alternative ways of organizing life on a more localized level.

SUMMARY

Numerous global trends are altering the way of life in all societies. Environmental changes induced by globalization—the greenhouse effect, the depletion of the ozone layer, and atmospheric pollution—are creating new problems that may threaten the existence of our planet. Population growth has declined in the core countries but has risen in many Third World societies because of a combination of reduced mortality rates and continued high birth rates. Technological changes resulting from industrialism have increased the consumption of energy and other raw materials.

Global environmental, demographic, and technological changes have led to two different perspectives: one pessimistic and the other optimistic. Pessimists predict that population growth and expanded industrialism will result in global economic collapse. Optimists tend to see human creativity and technological solutions as the salvation for humanity. Both the pessimistic and optimistic views are probably exaggerated. Anthropologists have examined specific cases regarding the adoption of mechanized agriculture and reforestation projects to better understand these worldwide problems.

Various global economic trends have developed in recent decades. Multinational corporations are creating more economic interdependency among nations. Ethnographic research, however, indicates that the changes introduced by multinational corporations may not always generate economic development in Third World societies. Other global economic trends include the reintegration of socialist societies into the world-capitalist system. Russia, Eastern Europe, China, and Vietnam are abandoning orthodox forms of socialism to join the world-market system.

The core countries such as the United States and Japan compete with one another in the global economy. This competition has resulted in the expansion of multinational corporations into various areas, leading to a new global division of labor. Countries such as South Korea and Taiwan have been moving from peripheral to semiperipheral status in the world-market system.

In contrast to global economic interdependency and modernization, political, ethnic, and religious trends often move in the opposite direction. Ethnic separatist movements often divide people, making the promotion of national goals difficult. Religious fundamentalist movements often result from the rapid modernization processes that erode traditional cultural beliefs. Anthropological studies of these trends improve our understanding of both local aspirations and global processes.

QUESTIONS TO THINK ABOUT

1. In your view, what are the positive and negative consequences of globalization?

2. What is demographic-transition theory? Do you think that this model applies to all cultures in the world?

3. Why is there concern over the loss of biodiversity?

4. What is the Doomsday Model (neo-Malthusian approach)? How does it differ from the logic-of-growth model?

5. How can an anthropologist make a difference in the changing world of today? Or is the world in need of engineers and technicians who can invent new ways of solving problems? That is, how can the anthropological perspective be used to examine global issues such as overpopulation, deforestation, global warming, and the loss of biodiversity?

6. What types of unanticipated problems has the implementation of the Green Revolution caused in areas where it was introduced? Are there any success stories, or is the verdict all negative?

7. What is the global economy? What types of changes have occurred in the world recently that are related to the globalization of the world economy?

8. What types of contributions can anthropologists make by studying ethnic conflict and religious movements?

KEY TERMS

agribusiness	doubling time	logic-of-growth model
biodiversity	Green Revolution	sustainability model
demographic-transition theory	greenhouse effect	zero population growth (ZPG)

INTERNET EXERCISES

1. While reading **http://www.converge.org.nz/ pirm/dtoxgrev.htm** please note that alternative forms of agriculture are now being developed for hybrid crops that require a large amount of pesticides and fertilizers. What makes these newer organic approaches better? Do you think that the world will be able to feed itself with organic methods? Why or why not?

2. Look at the following website on Hungary: **http://www.interlog.com/~photodsk/ magyar/negbirth.html**. What is the concern expressed here? How does Hungary's birthrate problem compare to that of Japan as described in this chapter? Are these serious concerns or are they just driven by group pride? Explain your answer.

SUGGESTED READINGS

BERNARD, H. R., and P. J. PELTO (Eds.). 1987. *Technology and Social Change,* 2d ed. Prospect Heights, IL: Waveland Press. A fine series of essays by anthropologists examining the consequences of technological change in different societies.

BODLEY, JOHN H. 1985. *Anthropology and Contemporary Human Problems,* 2d ed. Palo Alto, CA: Mayfield. A broad overview of how an anthropological perspective can be brought to bear on problems such as environmental pollution, population growth, energy consumption, and political problems.

HUTCHINSON, JOHN, and ANTHONY SMITH (Eds.). 1996. *Ethnicity.* Oxford, UK: Oxford University Press. A comprehensive collection of essays, both classic and contemporary, on the topic of ethnicity. Many of the essays are by anthropologists.

ROBBINS, RICHARD H. 2002. *Global Problems and the Culture of Capitalism,* 2d ed. Boston: Allyn & Bacon. An interesting and comprehensive review of problems that have been created by the global capitalist economy and the culture of consumerism.

WILSON, E. O. (Ed.). 1989. *Biodiversity.* Washington, DC: National Academy Press. A comprehensive series of essays by distinguished scientists on the topic of biodiversity and threats to it.

CHAPTER

25

Applied Anthropology

CHAPTER QUESTIONS

- What types of projects are conducted by applied anthropologists?

- What are the different roles of applied anthropologists in various projects?

- What type of research is identified with medical anthropology?

- How are archaeologists involved in applied anthropology?

- How have applied anthropologists become involved in human rights research?

As the preceding chapters illustrated, anthropologists are engaged in extensive research in the four basic subfields of the discipline: physical anthropology, archaeology, linguistics, and ethnology. Within these fields, different specializations have emerged that allow for the in-depth gathering of data and the testing and evaluation of specific hypotheses regarding human societies and behavior. As mentioned in Chapter 1, however, one of the most important developments in the field of anthropology is **applied anthropology,** the use of data from the research in anthropology to offer practical solutions to problems faced by a society. This chapter introduces some of the issues that are relevant to applied anthropologists in solving practical problems.

The Roles of the Applied Anthropologist

The popular, if not accurate, images of anthropologists vary from the adventurous explorer seeking out lost treasure to the absent-minded academic working away in the dusty halls of a university or museum. These perspectives do not provide a valid picture of the modern physical anthropologist or archaeologist. Anthropologists are increasingly engaged in a variety of activities that have direct relevance to the modern world. Rather than being confined to the halls of the university, an increasing number of anthropologists have become practitioners of anthropology. Indeed, according to a 1990 survey, 50 percent of individuals with doctorates in anthropology develop careers outside the academic area (Givens & Fillmore, 1990). Similarly, a 1994 survey indicated that only 35 percent of the membership of the Society for American Archaeology, the primary national organization for archaeologists working in North America, was made up of researchers employed in academic positions, while approximately 8 percent were employed in museums (Zeder, 1997:47–48). Of the remainder of the membership, the largest portion, 23 percent, were employed by federal, state, or local governments, followed by 18 percent who worked in private businesses. Comparable trends can be seen in the membership of other archaeological organizations. Many physical anthropologists work with or are employed by public agencies such as the United States Agency for International Development (USAID) and the National Institutes of Health (NIH). Some also work for private firms.

Distinguishing applied anthropology from other anthropological pursuits in many respects presents a false dichotomy. Methodical and theoretical concerns are shared by all; the difference lies in perceptions of the practitioners' objectives, an arbitrary division based on the practicality of the intended outcomes. As Bronislaw Malinowski observed more than a half-century ago: "Unfortunately, there is still a strong but erroneous opinion in some circles that practical anthropology is fundamentally different from theoretical or academic anthropology. The truth is that science begins with application. . . . What is application in science and when does 'theory' become practical? When it first allows us a definite grip on empirical reality" (Malinowski, 1945:5).

The work of many anthropologists can be seen as applied in some sense. In an overview of applied anthropology, Erve Chambers (1985) classified the different roles of applied anthropologists. While he was primarily concerned with the applied aspects of cultural anthropology, his observations are equally relevant to the work of physical anthropologists and archaeologists. One role noted by Chambers is that of *representative,* in which the anthropologist becomes the spokesperson for the particular group being studied. Anthropologists at times have represented Native American communities in negotiations with state and federal authorities, mining companies, and development organizations. Anthropologists can also be seen as *facilitators*. In this capacity, anthropologists actively help bring about change or development in the community being researched. For example, they may take a proactive, participatory role in economic or social change to improve medical care, education, or public facilities. An alternative position is the *informant* role, in which the

applied anthropologist transfers cultural knowledge obtained from anthropological research to the government or other agency that wants to promote change in a particular area. The U.S. government has employed anthropologists as on-site researchers to provide data on how local-level service clients and delivery agencies respond to government policy. Informally, many archaeologists and anthropologists become involved in local activities and educational programs that present anthropological findings to the public.

Yet another role of applied anthropologists is that of *analyst*. Rather than being just a provider of data, the practicing anthropologist sometimes becomes engaged in the actual formulation of policy. In archaeology, in particular, this has become an important area with the passage of the National Historic Preservation Act in 1966, the Native American Graves Repatriation Act of 1990, and other related legislation. These laws have afforded increased protection to some archaeological resources and mandated the consideration of archaeological resources in planning development. Archaeologists have increasingly found employment in federal, state, or local governments reviewing proposals for development and construction projects that impact cultural resources and archaeological sites.

Another role Chambers identified is that of *mediator,* which involves the anthropologist as an intermediary among different interest groups that are participating in a development project. This may include private developers, government officials, and the people who will be affected by the project. As mediator, the anthropologist must try to reconcile differences among these groups, facilitating compromises that ideally will benefit all parties involved in the project. The following discussions highlight some of the applied work that physical anthropologists and archaeologists are engaged in.

Physical Anthropology

As seen in the preceding chapters, physical anthropologists deal with the biological aspects of humans and human ancestors in the past and the present. Much of the basic information gathered consists of the measurement, observation, and explanation of various physical characteristics.

ANTHROPOLOGISTS AT WORK

CLYDE SNOW: FORENSIC ANTHROPOLOGIST

Clyde Collins Snow obtained a master's degree in zoology from Texas Technical University and planned to pursue a Ph.D. in physiology, but his career plans were interrupted by military service. While stationed at Lackland Air Force Base near San Antonio, he was introduced to the field of archaeology and became fascinated with the ancient artifacts discovered in the surrounding area.

After leaving the military, Snow attended the University of Arizona, where his zoological training and archaeology interests led him to a Ph.D. in physical anthropology. He became skilled at identifying old bones and artifacts. With his doctoral degree completed, he joined the Federal Aviation Administration as a consulting forensic anthropologist, providing technical assistance in the identification of victims of aircraft accidents. Snow also lent his expertise to the design of safety equipment to prevent injuries in aircraft accidents.

As word of Snow's extraordinary skill in forensic anthropology spread, he was called to consult on and provide expert testimony in many criminal cases. His testimony was crucial at the sensational murder trial of John Wayne

Dr. Clyde Snow

Gacy, accused of murdering more than thirty teenagers in the Chicago area. Snow also collaborated with experts in the reinvestigation of President John F. Kennedy's assassination. These experts built a full-scale model of Kennedy's head to determine whether Lee Harvey Oswald could have inflicted all of Kennedy's wounds. They did not uncover any scientific evidence to contradict the Warren Commission's conclusion that Oswald was the sole assassin.

More recently, Snow and his team have been recognized for their contributions to human rights issues. Snow served as a consultant to the Argentine government's National Commission on Disappeared Persons in its efforts to determine the fate of thousands of Argentineans who were abducted and murdered by military death squads between 1976 and 1983, when the country was under the rule of a military dictatorship. As a result of his investigations, Snow was asked to testify as an expert witness in the trial of the nine junta members who ruled Argentina during the period of military repression. He also assisted people in locating their dead relatives.

Snow stresses that in his human rights investigative work he is functioning as an expert, not necessarily as an advocate. He must maintain an objective standpoint in interpreting his findings. The evidence he finds may then be presented by lawyers (as advocates) in the interests of justice. Snow's human rights work is supported by various agencies, such as the American Association of Advanced Sciences, the Ford Foundation, the J. Roderick MacArthur Foundation, Amnesty International, Physicians for Human Rights, and Human Rights Watch.

Anthropometry, for example, concerns the measurement of human body parts, and osteometry is the measurement of skeletal elements. This information is basic to the interpretation of fossil hominids as well as human remains recovered from archaeological sites. However, some of this information has immediate relevance to the present. Such information may be used in combination with engineering data to design ergonomically efficient airplane cockpits, work environments, or equipment. Such data may also provide an important aid to police in investigations of murders or the identification of disaster victims. Physical anthropological study of the causes of diseases, when combined with knowledge of cultural anthropology, offers important insight into perceptions of medical treatment in different cultural settings. Some of these examples of practicing anthropologists are considered in this section.

Forensic Anthropology

A fragmentary skeleton is accidentally found in a desolate part of the desert. Through a series of twists and turns, an enterprising detective pieces together clues to a twenty-year-old murder and brings a fugitive to justice. Such a scenario is the stuff of mystery novels, but real-life criminal investigations often do depend on the identification of fragmentary skeletal remains. **Forensic anthropology** can be defined as the application of physical anthropological data to law. Physical anthropologists in this area of specialization are often called to assist police when unidentified humans remains are found. Whereas medical doctors focus on the soft tissues, forensic anthropologists study the hard tissues—the skeletal remains (Isçan & Kennedy, 1989). Analysis of such material would begin by reconstructing the skeleton and joining together the often fragmentary and broken remains. Missing pieces might be reconstructed or estimated. The materials are then carefully measured and compared to anthropological data. Such research can yield the sex, approximate age, height, and physical characteristics of an individual.

The skeleton also provides a record of medical problems, illnesses, and the overall health of a person. The bones may preserve information about a person's health at the time of death, as well as the living conditions and health problems the individual faced during his or her lifetime. For example, broken bones, although healed, still leave a trace on the skeleton. Arthritis, certain infections, dietary stress, and nutrition may also be in evidence. This kind of information may provide insight into living conditions in the distant human past, as, for example, when considering the consequences of domestication (see Chapter 8), but it also provides details that may be very helpful to the police in identifying victims. Unidentified skeletal remains from a white female, 5'4" to 5'6", 40 to 45 years of age, with a healed fracture of the left leg and traces of arthritis in the hands, would dramatically reduce the number of potential fits with reported missing persons files.

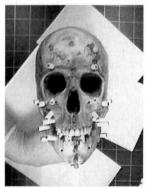 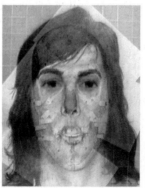  

A specialized area of forensic anthropology deals with the reconstruction of facial features. The photographs illustrate (from left) the victim's skull, a reconstruction of the face, a sketch based on the reconstruction, and a photograph of how the victim actually appeared in life.

Source: Courtesy of Gene O'Donnell, FBI.

A specialized area within forensic anthropology deals specifically with the reconstruction of faces (Prag & Neave, 1997). Using average skin depth, muscle patterns, and knowledge about the skeleton, the researcher can create an image of what a person looked like when alive. This interdisciplinary work draws on information from anatomy, facial surgery, pathology, dentistry, and the skills of an artist, as well as physical anthropology. Reconstruction of a face based solely on information provided by the skull may be done using a computer or may be sketched by an artist, but researchers also rely on a detailed model of a skull, which they then cover with clay. Muscles of clay are sculpted over the skull, which are then covered with clay representing the overlying tissues. The thickness of the skin covering the skull is based on average thickness at different points of the skull, estimated for individuals of different ages, sexes, body builds, and ethnic groups. A final model is prepared using plaster of Paris, which is colored and given hair. Although the final products may not be exact portraits, their resemblance to the living individuals has proven remarkable.

Forensic anthropology may also offer important clues about the circumstances of a person's death and the treatment of the body after death (Haglund & Sorg, 1997). Damage or trauma to the bones may provide a primary indicator of the cause of death. For example, bullet wounds, stabbings, and blunt force trauma may be identified in skeletal remains. Careful study of the skeleton may also indicate whether an individual was killed where the body was found or at another location and then transported to the site. Forensic anthropologists may be able to determine whether the body was disturbed or transported after burial. Such information may be extremely important in determining the cause of death. As in the case of archaeological and paleontological investigations, the *context* of the findings is very important. Hence, physical anthropologists with archaeological training can help ensure that all of the remains are recovered.

Because the cause of death may be central to a murder investigation and trial, the forensic anthropologist is often called upon to testify as an expert witness. In such cases the forensic anthropologist impartially presents his or her findings, which may prove or disprove the identity or cause of death of the victim. The ultimate concern of the forensic anthropologist is not the outcome of the trial but the evidence provided by the skeletal remains.

The amount of information extracted from skeletal remains can be surprising. Many illustrations from actual criminal cases can be recounted (Stewart, 1979; Rathbun & Buikstra, 1984). For example, fractures of the hyoid or the thyroid, a small bone and ossified cartilage of the throat, may indicate strangulation. The location and kind of breaks may offer clues to the type of weapon used, as well as the position of the attacker relative to the victim. In the vein of a Sherlock Holmes novel, it may actually be possible to determine that a fatal blow was struck from behind by a right-handed assailant.

Forensic anthropologists have also played important roles in the identification of victims of natural disasters, airplane crashes, war, and genocide

Excavation of the burial site of civilians who were killed by government troops at El Morote, El Salvador, during the country's civil war in the 1980s. Forensic anthropologists often play an important role in the identification of victims of natural disasters, airplane crashes, wars, and genocide.

(Stewart, 1970; Stover, 1981, 1992; Snow et al., 1989; Snow & Bihorriet, 1992). Many of the methods and techniques used by modern forensic anthropologists were needed during and after World War II to assist with the identification and repatriation of the remains of soldiers killed in battle. This remained an important role for forensic anthropologists during the Korean and Vietnam wars (Stewart, 1979: 11–12). In these cases the physical remains recovered are matched against the life histories provided by medical and dental records. In some instances the positive identification may be dependent on relatively minor variation in bony structures. The role of physical anthropologists in locating and identifying American soldiers killed or missing in action in Vietnam continues to this day. Forensic anthropologists and archaeologists have assisted in the documentation of human rights abuses and recovery of victims from mass graves in Argentina, Brazil, Croatia, El Salvador, Haiti, Iraq, Rwanda, and other world areas.

Medical Anthropology

Another subfield of anthropology, **medical anthropology,** represents the intersection of cultural anthropology with physical anthropology. Medical anthropologists may study disease, medicine, curing, and mental illness in cross-cultural perspective. Some focus specifically on **epidemiology,** which examines the spread and distribution of diseases and how they are influenced by cultural patterns. For example, these anthropologists may be able to determine whether coronary (heart) disease or cancer is related to particular cultural or social dietary habits, such as the consumption of foods high in sodium or saturated fats. They also study cultural perceptions of illness and their treatment. These studies can often help health providers to design more effective means for delivering health care and formulating health care policies.

An illustration of medical anthropology is the work of Louis Golomb (1985), who conducted ethnological research on curing practices in Thailand. Golomb did research on Buddhist and Muslim medical practitioners who rely on native spiritualistic beliefs to diagnose and cure diseases. These practices are based on earlier Hindu, magical, and animistic beliefs that had been syncretized with Buddhist and Muslim traditions. Practitioners draw on astrology, faith healing, massage, folk psychotherapy, exorcism, herbs, and charms and amulets to treat patients. The most traditional practitioners are curer-magicians, or *shamans,* who diagnose and treat every illness as an instance of spirit possession or spirit attack. Other practitioners are more skeptical of the supernatural causation of illness and diagnose health problems in reference to natural or organic causes. They frequently use herbal medicines to treat illnesses.

Medical anthropologists do studies to help improve basic health care delivery in countries around the world.

Golomb discovered that although Western-based scientific forms of medicine may be available, many Thais still rely on traditional practitioners. He found that even urban-educated elite, including those who had studied in the United States and other Western countries, adhered to both supernatural and scientific views. Golomb referred to this as **therapeutic pluralism.** He observed that patients do not rely on any single therapeutic approach but rather use a combination of therapies that include elements of ritual, magic, and modern scientific medications. Parasites or germs are rarely seen as the only explanations of disease; a sick person may go to a clinic to receive medication to relieve symptoms but may then seek out a traditional curer for a more complete treatment. Golomb emphasized that the multiplicity of alternative therapies encourages people to play an active role in preserving their health.

In Thailand, as in many other countries undergoing modernization, modern medical facilities have been established based on the scientific treatment of disease. Golomb found that personnel in these facilities are critical of traditional medical practices. Nevertheless, he discovered that although the people in the villages often respect the modern doctor's ability to diagnose diseases and prescribe medications to relieve symptoms, in most cases they don't accept the scientific explanation of the disease. In addition, villagers feel that modern medical methods are brusque and impersonal, because doctors do not offer any psychological or spiritual consolation. Doctors also do not make house calls and rarely spend much time with patients. This impersonality in the doctor–patient relationship is also due to social status differences based on wealth, education, and power. Golomb found that many public health personnel expected deference from their rural clientele. For these reasons, many people preferred to rely on traditional curers.

Through his study of traditional medical techniques and beliefs, Golomb isolated some of the strengths and weaknesses of modern medical treatment in Thailand. His work contributed to a better understanding of how to deliver health care services to rural and urban Thais. For example, the Thai Ministry of Public Health began to experiment with ways of coordinating the efforts of modern and traditional medical practitioners. Village midwives and traditional herbalists were called on to dispense modern medications and pass out information about nutrition and hygiene. Some Thai hospitals have established training sessions for traditional practitioners to learn modern medical techniques. Golomb's studies in medical anthropology offer a model for practical applications in the health field for other developing societies.

Interventions in Substance Abuse

Another area of research and policy formulation for applied medical anthropologists is substance abuse, many of the causes of which may be explained by social and cultural factors. For example, Michael Agar (1973, 1974) did an in-depth study of heroin addicts based on the addicts' description of U.S. society and its therapeutic agencies in particular. His research involved taking on the role of a patient himself so that he could participate in some of the problems that exist between patients and staff. From that perspective he was better able to understand the "junkie" worldview.

Through his research, Agar isolated problems in the treatment of heroin addiction. He found that when the drug methadone was administered by public health officials as a substitute for heroin, many heroin addicts not in treatment became addicted to methadone, which was sold on the streets by patients. This street methadone would often be combined with wine and pills to gain a "high." In some cases, street methadone began to rival heroin as the preferred drug, being less expensive than heroin, widely available, and in a form that could be taken orally rather than injected. By providing this information, Agar helped health officials monitor their programs more effectively.

In a more recent study, Philippe Bourgois spent three and a half years investigating the use of crack cocaine in Spanish Harlem in New York City. In his award-winning ethnography, *In Search of Respect: Selling Crack in El Barrio* (1996), Bourgois noted that policy makers and drug-enforcement officials minimize the influences of poverty and low status in dealing with crack addiction. Through his investigation of cultural norms and socioeconomic conditions in Spanish Harlem, Bourgois demonstrated that crack dealers are struggling to earn money and status in the pursuit of the American Dream. Despite the fact that many crack dealers have work experience, they find that many of the potential jobs in construction and factory work are reserved

Some applied anthropologists have been doing studies of drug addiction to assist agencies in the prevention of drug use.

for non-Hispanics. In addition, unpleasant experiences in the job world lead many to perceive crack dealing as the most realistic route to upward mobility. Most of the inner-city youths who deal crack are high school dropouts who do not regard entry-level, minimum-wage jobs as steps to better opportunities. In addition, they perceive the underground economy as an alternative to becoming subservient to the larger society. Crack dealing offers a sense of autonomy, position, and rapid short-term mobility.

Bourgois compared the use of crack to the feelings that people have in millenarian movements or other spiritual movements:

> *Substance abuse in general, and crack in particular, offer the equivalent of a millenarian metamorphosis. Instantaneously, users are transformed from being unemployed, depressed high school dropouts, despised by the world—and secretly convinced that their failure is due to their own inherent stupidity, "racial laziness," and disorganization—into being a mass of heart-palpitating pleasure, followed only minutes later by a jaw-gnashing crash and wide-awake alertness that provides their life with concrete purpose: get more crack—fast! (1989b:11)*

Bourgois's depictions of the culture and economy of crack dealers and users provided useful policy suggestions. He concluded that most accounts of crack addiction deflect attention away from the economic and social conditions of the inner city, and that by focusing on the increases of violence and terror associated with crack, U.S. society is absolved

from responsibility for inner-city problems. He suggested that rather than use this "blame-the-victim" approach, officials and policymakers need to revise their attitudes and help develop programs that resolve the conditions that encourage crack use.

Applied Archaeology

One of the problems that humanity faces is how to safeguard the cultural heritage preserved in the archaeological record. Although archaeology may address questions of general interest to all of humanity, it is also important in promoting national heritage, cultural identity, and ethnic pride. Museums the world over offer displays documenting a diversity of local populations, regional histories, important events, and cultural traditions. The number of specialized museums focusing on particular peoples, regions, or historic periods has become increasingly important. Archaeologists must be concerned with the preservation of archaeological sites and the recovery of information from sites threatened with destruction, as well as the interpretation and presentation of their findings to the more general public.

Preservation of the past is a challenge to archaeologists, government officials, and the concerned public alike, as archaeological sites are being destroyed at an alarming rate. Archaeological materials naturally decay in the ground, and sites are constantly destroyed through geological processes, erosion, and animal burrowing (see Chapter 2). Yet while natural processes contribute to the disappearance of archaeological sites, by far the greatest threat to the archaeological record is human activity. Construction projects such as dams, roads, buildings, and pipelines all disturb the ground and can destroy archaeological sites in the process. In many instances, archaeologists work only a few feet ahead of construction equipment, trying to salvage any information they can before a site disappears forever.

Some archaeological sites are intentionally destroyed by collectors searching for artifacts that have value in the antiquities market, such as arrowheads and pottery. Statues from ancient Egypt, Mayan terra cotta figurines, and Native American pottery may be worth thousands of dollars on the antiques market. To fulfill the demands, archaeological sites in many world areas are looted by pothunters, who dig to retrieve artifacts for collectors, ignoring the traces of ancient housing, burials, and cooking hearths. Removed from their context, with no record of where they came from, such artifacts are of limited value to archaeologists. The rate of destruction of North American archaeological sites is such that some researchers have estimated

that 98 percent of sites predating the year 2000 will be destroyed by the middle of the twenty-first century (Herscher, 1989; Knudson, 1989).

The rate at which archaeological sites are being destroyed is particularly distressing because the archaeological record is an irreplaceable, *nonrenewable* resource. That is, after sites are destroyed, they are gone forever, along with the unique information about the past that they contained. In many parts of the world, recognition of this fact has led to legislation aimed at protecting archaeological sites (Table 25.1). The rational for this legislation is that the past has value to the present and, hence, should be protected and interpreted for the benefit of the public.

Preserving the Past

Recognition of the value and nonrenewable nature of archaeological resources is the first step in a planning process. Archaeological resources can then be systematically identified and evaluated. Steps can be taken to preserve them by limiting development or designing projects in a way that will preserve the resource. For example, the projected

Table 25.1	Major Federal Legislation for the Protection of Archaeological Resources in the United States
Antiquities Act of 1906	Protects sites on federal lands
Historic Sites Act of 1935	Provides authority for designating National Historic Landmarks and for archaeological survey before destruction by development programs
National Historic Preservation Act of 1966 (amended 1976 and 1980)	Strengthens protection of sites via National Register and integrates state and local agencies into national program for site preservation
National Environmental Policy Act of 1969	Requires all federal agencies to specify impact of development programs on cultural resources
Archaeological Resources Protection Act of 1979	Provides criminal and civil penalties for looting or damaging sites on public and Native American lands
Convention on Cultural Property of 1982	Authorizes U.S. participation in 1970 UNESCO convention to prevent illegal international trade in cultural property
Cultural Property Act of 1983	Provides sanctions against U.S. import or export of illicit antiquities
Federal Abandoned Shipwreck Act of 1988	Removes sunken ships of archaeological interest from marine salvage jurisdiction; provides for protection under state jurisdiction
Native American Graves Protection and Repatriation Act of 1990 (NAGRA)	Specifies return of Native American remains and cultural property to Native American groups by U.S. museums

Source: From *Discovering Our Past: A Brief Introduction to Archaeology* by Wendy Ashmore and Robert J. Sharer. Copyright © 2003 by Mayfield Publishing Company. Reprinted by permission of the publisher.

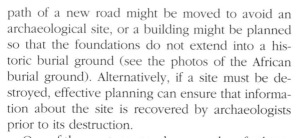

Located just blocks from Wall Street in New York City, an eighteenth-century African burial ground was accidentally uncovered during construction of a federal office building in 1991. The 427 burials excavated at the site are testament to the enslaved Africans that made up the second largest slave population in colonial America. As many as 20,000 individuals may have been buried at the site. Following discovery, local community protests over the treatment and interpretation of the remains led to a delay in construction, modification of the construction plan, and the increased involvement of African-American researchers in the analysis of the finds.

Source: Courtesy of the General Services Administration.

path of a new road might be moved to avoid an archaeological site, or a building might be planned so that the foundations do not extend into a historic burial ground (see the photos of the African burial ground). Alternatively, if a site must be destroyed, effective planning can ensure that information about the site is recovered by archaeologists prior to its destruction.

One of the most spectacular examples of salvage archaeology arose as a result of the construction of a dam across the Nile River at Aswan, Egypt, in the 1960s. The project offered many benefits, including water for irrigation and the generation of electricity. However, the rising water behind the dam threatened thousands of archaeological sites that had lain undisturbed and safely buried by desert sand for thousands of years. The Egyptian government appealed to the international community and archaeologists from around the world to mount projects to locate and excavate the threatened sites.

Among the sites that were to be flooded by the dam was the temple of Pharaoh Rameses II at Abu Simbel, a huge monument consisting of four colossal figures carved from a cliff face on the banks of the Nile River. With help from the United Nations

Educational, Scientific, and Cultural Organization (UNESCO), the Egyptian government was able to cut the monument into more than a thousand pieces, some weighing as much as 33 tons, and reassemble them above the floodwaters. Today the temple of Rameses can be seen completely restored only a few hundred feet from its original location. Numerous other archaeological sites threatened by the flooding of the Nile were partly salvaged or recorded. Unfortunately, countless other sites could not be located or even recorded before they were flooded.

The first legislation in the United States designed to protect historic sites was the Antiquities Act of 1906, which safeguarded archaeological sites on federal lands (see Table 25.1). Other, more recent legislation, such as the National Historic Preservation Act passed in 1966, has extended protection to sites threatened by projects that are funded or regulated by the government. The federal Abandoned Shipwreck Act of 1988 gives states jurisdiction over shipwreck sites. This legislation has had a dramatic impact on the number of archaeologists in the United States and has created a new area of specialization, generally referred to as **cultural**

resource management (CRM). Whereas most archaeologists had traditionally found employment teaching or working in museums, many are now working as applied archaeologists, evaluating, salvaging, and protecting archaeological resources that are threatened with destruction. Applied archaeologists conduct surveys before construction begins to determine if any sites will be affected. Government agencies such as the Forest Service have developed comprehensive programs to discover, record, protect, and interpret archaeological resources on their lands (Johnson & Schene, 1987).

Unfortunately, current legislation in the United States leaves many archaeological resources unprotected. In many countries, excavated artifacts, even those located on privately owned land, become the property of the government. This is not the case in the United States. One example of the limitations of the existing legislation is provided by the case of Slack Farm, located near Uniontown, Kentucky (Arden, 1989). Archaeologists had long known that an undisturbed Native American site of the Late Mississippian period was located on the property. Dating roughly to between 1450 and 1650, the site was particularly important because it was the only surviving Mississippian site from the period of first contact with Europeans. The Slack family, who had owned the land for many years, protected the site and prevented people from digging (Arden, 1989). When the property was sold in 1988, however, conditions changed. Anthropologist Brian Fagan described the results:

> Ten pot hunters from Kentucky, Indiana, and Illinois paid the new owner of the land $10,000 for the right to "excavate" the site. They rented a tractor and began bulldozing their way through the village midden to reach graves. They pushed heaps of bones aside and dug through dwellings and potsherds, hearths, and stone tools associated with them. Along the way, they left detritus of their own—empty pop-top beer and soda cans—scattered on the ground alongside Late Mississippian pottery fragments. Today Slack Farm looks like a battlefield—a morass of crude shovel holes and gaping trenches. Broken human bones litter the ground, and fractured artifacts crunch underfoot. (1988:15)

The looting at the site was eventually stopped by the Kentucky State Police, using a state law that prohibits the desecration of human graves. Archaeologists went to the site attempting to salvage what

information was left, but there is no way of knowing how many artifacts were removed. The record of America's prehistoric past was irrevocably damaged.

Regrettably, the events at Slack Farm are not unique. Many states lack adequate legislation protecting archaeological sites on private land. For example, Arkansas had no laws protecting unmarked burial sites until 1991. As a result, Native American burial grounds were systematically mined for artifacts. In fact, one article written about the problem was titled "The Looting of Arkansas" (Harrington, 1991a). Although Arkansas now has legislation prohibiting the unauthorized excavation of burial grounds, the professional archaeologists of the Arkansas Archaeological Survey face the impossible job of trying to locate and monitor all of the state's archaeological sites. This problem is not unique. Even on federal lands, the protection of sites is dependent on a relatively small number of park

Although many countries have legislation protecting their archaeological resources, enforcing the laws is often difficult. Here a farmer in Mali displays artifacts looted from an archaeological site. Removed from their archaeological context, such finds have limited value to archaeologists.

rangers and personnel to police large areas. Even in national parks such as Mesa Verde or Yellowstone, archaeological sites are sometimes vandalized or looted for artifacts. Much of the success that there has been in protecting sites is largely due to the active involvement of amateur archaeologists and concerned citizens who bring archaeological remains to the attention of professionals.

The preservation of the past needs to be everyone's concern. Unfortunately, however well intended the legislation and efforts to provide protection for archaeological sites may be, they are rarely integrated into comprehensive management plans. For example, a particular county or city area might have a variety of sites and resources of historic significance identified using a variety of different criteria and presented in different lists and directories. These might include National Historic sites, designated through the National Historic Preservation office; state files of archaeological sites; data held by avocational archaeological organizations and clubs; and a variety of locations of historical importance identified by county or city historical societies. Other sites of potential historical significance might be identified through documentary research or oral traditions. Ideally, all of these sources of information should be integrated and used to plan development. Such comprehensive approaches to cultural resource management plans are rare rather than the norm.

Important strides have been taken in planning and coordinating efforts to identify and manage archaeological resources. Government agencies, including the National Park Service, the military, and various state agencies, have initiated plans to systematically identify and report sites on their properties. There have also been notable efforts to compile information at the county, state, and district levels. Such efforts are faced with imposing logistical concerns. For example, by the mid-1990s, over 180,000 historic and prehistoric archaeological sites had been identified in the American southeast (including the states of Alabama, Arkansas, Florida, Georgia, Kentucky, Louisiana, Mississippi, North Carolina, South Carolina, and Tennessee). In addition, an estimated 10,000 new sites are discovered each year (Anderson & Horak, 1995). A map of these resources reveals a great deal of variation in their concentration. On one hand, this diversity reflects the actual distribution of sites; on the other, it reflects the areas where archaeological research has

and has not been undertaken. Incorporating the thousands of new site reports into the database requires substantial commitment of staff resources. What information should be recorded for each site? What computer resources are needed? The volume of information is difficult to process with available staff, and massive backlogs of reports waiting to be incorporated into the files often exist. Nevertheless, this kind of holistic perspective is needed to ensure effective site management and the compliance of developers with laws protecting archaeological sites. It also provides a holistic view of past land use that is of great use to archaeologists.

The Study of Garbage

The majority of archaeological research deals with the interpretation of past societies. Whether the focus is on the Stone Age inhabitants of Australia or the archaeology of nineteenth-century mining

Archaeological study of modern garbage has provided important insights into waste management procedures, marketing, food wastage, and recycling.

Source: Courtesy of C. R. DeCorse.

communities in the American west, the people being examined lived at a time somewhat removed from the present. There are, however, some archaeologists who are concerned with the study of the refuse of modern society and the application of archaeological methods and techniques to concerns of the present—and the future. The focus for these researchers is not the interpretation of past societies but the immediate application of archaeological methods and techniques to the modern world. The topics examined range from the use of archaeological data in marketing strategies to the best methods for marking nuclear waste sites. Archaeologists who routinely examine artifacts thousands of years old can, for example, provide important perspectives of the suitability of different materials and burial strategies that can be used to bury nuclear waste (Kaplan & Mendel, 1982).

One of the more interesting examples of this kind of applied archaeology is *Le Projet du Garbage,* or the Garbage Project, that grew out of an archaeological method and theory class at the University of Arizona in 1971 (Rathje & Ritenbaugh, 1984; Rathje, 1992). Archaeologists William L. Rathje and Fred Gorman were so intrigued by the results of the student projects that they established the Garbage Project the following year, and the project is still ongoing. The researchers gather trash from households with the help of the City of Tucson sanitation foremen, who tag the waste with identification numbers that allow the trash bags to be identified with specific census tracts within the city. The trash bags are not identified with particular households, and personal items and photographs are not examined. Over the years research has been broadened to the study of trash from other communities, including Milwaukee, Marin County, and Mexico City, and also to the excavation of modern landfills in Chicago, San Francisco, and Phoenix using archaeological methods.

The Garbage Project has provided a surprising amount of information on a diversity of topics. On one hand, the study provides data that are extremely useful in monitoring trash disposal programs. As Rathje observed, study of waste allows the effective evaluation of current conditions, the anticipation of changing directions in waste disposal, and, therefore, more effective planning and policy making (1984:10). Reviewing data on the project, Rathje noted a number of areas in which

this archaeological research dispelled some common notions about trash disposal and landfills. Despite common perceptions, items such as fast-food packaging, polystyrene foam, and disposable diapers do not account for a substantial percentage of landfills. Rathje observed:

> *Of the 14 tons of garbage from nine municipal landfills that the Garbage Project has excavated and sorted in the past five years, there was less than a hundred pounds of fast-food packaging—that is, containers or wrappers for hamburgers, pizzas, chicken, fish and convenience-store sandwiches, as well as the accessories most of us deplore, such as cups, lids, straws, sauce containers, and so on. (Rathje, 1992:115)*

Hence, fast-food packaging makes up less than one-half of 1 percent of the weight of landfills. The percentage by volume is even lower. Rathje further noted that despite the burgeoning of materials made from plastic, the amount of plastic in landfills has remained fairly constant since the 1960s, or even decreased. The reason for this, he believes, is that while more things are made of plastic, many objects are now made with less plastic. A plastic milk bottle that weighed 120 grams in the 1960s, today weighs 65 grams.

Rathje found that the real culprit in landfills remains plain old paper. A year's subscription to *The New York Times* is roughly equivalent to the volume of 18,660 crushed aluminum cans or 14,969 flattened Big Mac containers. While some predicted that computers would bring about a paperless office, the photocopier and millions of personal printers ensure that millions of pounds of paper are discarded each year: "Where the creation of paper waste is concerned, technology is proving to be not so much a contraceptive as a fertility drug" (Rathje, 1992:116). He also observed that despite popular perception, much of the paper in landfills is not biodegrading. Because of the limited amount of moisture, air, and biological activity in the middle of a landfill, much of the nation's newsprint is being preserved for posterity.

The Garbage Project has also provided information on a diversity of issues connected with food waste, marketing, and the disposal of hazardous materials. In these studies, archaeology has provided a unique perspective. Much of the available data on such topics has typically been provided by questionnaires, interviews, and data collection methods that rely on the cooperation of informants. The problem is that informants often present biased responses, consistently providing lower estimates of the alcohol, snack food, or hazardous waste that they dispose of than is actually the case. Archaeology, on the other hand, presents a fairly impartial material record. While there are sampling problems in archaeological data—some material may be sent down the garbage disposal and not preserved in a landfill—the material record can provide a fairly unambiguous record of some activities.

The Garbage Project has examined the discard of food and food wastage for the U.S. Department of Agriculture; the recycling of paper and aluminum cans for the Environmental Protection Agency; studies of candy and snack food consumption for dental associations and manufacturers; and the impact of a new liquor store on alcohol consumption in a Los Angeles neighborhood. In the latter case, researchers conducted both interviews and garbage analysis before and after the liquor store opened. The interview data suggested no change in consumption patterns before and after the store's opening. Study of the trash, however, showed a marked increase in the discard of beer, wine, and liquor cans and bottles. Studies such as these have wide applications both for marketing and policy makers.

Who Owns the Past?

A critical issue for modern archaeologists and physical anthropologists is **cultural patrimony,** that is, who owns the human remains, artifacts, and associated cultural materials that are recovered in the course of research projects. Are they the property of the scientists who collected or excavated them? The descendants of the peoples discovered archaeologically? The owners of the land on which the materials were recovered? Or the public as a whole? Resolution of this issue has at times been contentious, and the position taken by anthropologists has not always been the best. Prior to the twentieth century, laws governing the deposition of antiquities were nonexistent or unclear at best, and the owner often became the person, institution, or country with the most money or the strongest political clout. Colonial governments amassed tremendous collections from their territories throughout the world. The spoils of war belonged to the victors. Such a position remained the norm until after the turn of the century. Rights of conquest were only outlawed by the Hague Convention of 1907 (Shaw, 1986; Fagan, 1992).

Prior to the twentieth century, there was also little or no legislation governing human remains. Researchers appropriated excavated skeletal material, medical samples, and even cadavers of the recently deceased (Blakely & Harrington, 1997). Native American remains from archaeological sites were displayed to the public, despite the fact that some of the descendant communities found such displays inappropriate or sacrilegious. Scientific value was the underlying rational for ownership, though until the latter half of the twentieth century there was little discussion of this issue. As in the case of antiquities, value and ownership were vested in the politically stronger, whether a colonial government or the politically enfranchised within a country. Such remains had scientific value, and this was viewed as more important than the interests of other groups or cultural values.

Ironically, such views would seem to fly in the face of some of the basic tenets of modern anthropology, which underscore sensitivity and openness to other cultural perspectives and beliefs. In fact, archaeological resources and human remains at times do provide unique, irreplaceable information that cannot be obtained through any other source. Archaeologists and physical anthropologists have provided information extremely important in documenting the past of Native Americans and indigenous peoples throughout the world, at times serving to underscore their ties to the land and revealing cultural practices forgotten from memory. But what is the cost of such information if the treatment and methods of obtaining the artifacts and remains are abhorrent to the populations whose history is represented? Researchers of the present cannot afford to ignore the views and concerns of the focus of their research.

Recognition of the validity of different concerns and perspectives of cultural patrimony has not made resolution of debate easier. Artifacts now in museums were, in some instances, obtained hundreds of years ago in ways that were consistent with the moral and legal norms of that time (see the box "The Elgin Marbles"). Many antiquities have legitimately changed ownership numerous times. Not infrequently, information about the original origins may be unclear, and there are differences of opinion or uncertainty about the cultural associations of some artifacts or cultural remains. These issues aside, there remain fundamentally different perspectives about the role of the descendant population.

Native American Graves Protection and Repatriation Act

Perhaps the most important legislation affecting the treatment and protection of archaeological and physical anthropological resources in the United States is the Native American Graves Protection and Repatriation Act (NAGPRA), passed on November 16, 1990 (McKeown, 1998). This legislation is the most comprehensive of a series of recent laws dealing with the deposition of Native American burials and cultural properties. NAGPRA and related legislation require that federal institutions consult with the lineal descendants of Native American groups and Native Hawaiians prior to the initial excavation of Native American human remains and associated artifacts on federal or tribal lands. Under this legislation, federal agencies and institutions receiving federal funding are also required to **repatriate**—or return—human remains and cultural items in their collections at the request of the descendant populations of the relevant Native American group. NAGPRA also dictates criminal penalties for trade in Native American human remains and cultural properties.

The impact of NAGPRA has been profound, not only on the way in which many archaeological projects are conducted, but also on the way in which museums and institutions inventory, curate, and manage their collections. The law has, at times, placed very different worldviews in opposition. For many Native Americans, the past is intricately connected to the present, and the natural world— animals, rocks, and trees, as well as cultural objects—may have spiritual meaning (Naranjo, 1995). This perspective is fundamentally different from that of most museums, where both human remains and cultural artifacts are treated as nonliving entities, and the continuing spiritual links with the present are, at least at times, unrecognized. Museums are traditionally concerned with the collection and exhibition of objects. Reburial or repatriation

of collections is the antithesis of their mission. As one scholar noted: "No museum curator will gladly and happily relinquish anything which he has enjoyed having in his museum, of which he is proud, which he has developed an affection for, and which is one of the principal attractions of his museum" (Shaw, 1986:46).

NAGPRA and repatriation also raise pragmatic concerns. Return of objects or remains is dependent on complete and accurate inventory of all of a museum's holdings. Yet often museums have amassed collections over many decades, and the full extent of their collections may not be in a readily assessable form. While records may be accurate, the number of human remains or Native American artifacts from a particular tribal group may not be known, not because of poor records but because such information was not a priority.

A case in point is the collection of the Peabody Museum of Archaeology and Ethnology at Harvard University. Founded in 1866, the Peabody has a massive collection from all over the world, including substantial Native American and ancient Mesoamerican holdings. In the 1970s and 1980s, before the passage of NAGPRA, the museum repatriated several burials, collections, and objects at the request of various constituencies. NAGPRA spurred the museum to complete a detailed inventory. They found that the estimated 7,000 human remains grew to an inventory of about 10,000, while the amount of archaeological objects grew from 800,000 to 8 million (Isaac, 1995). Following NAGPRA guidelines, the Peabody sent out summaries of collections to the 756 recognized tribal groups in the United States. Determining the cultural affiliations, the relevant descendant communities, and the need for repatriation of all of these items is a daunting task.

Many museums have undertaken major inventories, revamped storage facilities, and hired additional staff specifically to deal with the issue of repatriation. Impending repatriation of collections and human remains has also spurred many institutions and researchers to reexamine old collections. Such study is necessary to ensure that the presumed age and cultural attribution of individual remains are correct. Of course, all of these concerns have serious budgetary considerations.

While NAGPRA has produced conflicts, it has also provided an avenue for new cooperation

CRITICAL PERSPECTIVES

THE ELGIN MARBLES

The story of the Parthenon sculptures—or Elgin marbles as they came to be called—is a twisted tale of the nineteenth-century quest for antiquities, international politics, and the complexities of cultural heritage. The Parthenon, perched on a hilltop overlooking Athens, is a striking symbol of both ancient Greece and the modern Greek nation-state. It was built by the Greek ruler Pericles to commemorate the Greek victory over the Persians at Plataea in 479 B.C. A temple to Athena, the patron goddess of Athens, the Parthenon was deemed by Pericles to be one of the most striking edifices in the city. The Parthenon is clearly the most striking of the buildings in the Acropolis, the cluster of classical structures that cover Mount Athena. It is regarded by some to be one of the world's most perfect buildings. It was distinguished by a full surrounding colonnade, and the exterior walls were decorated with a processional frieze. The pediments, or peaked eaves, in the east and west also had strikingly detailed sculptures.

The structure has endured for centuries, and it has come to embody classical civilization to the world. In recent years, the Parthenon has been the focus of several restoration efforts that have stabilized the structure, removed more recent additions, and replaced some of the fallen masonry.

Two young horsemen join a procession of sculpted figures on the Parthenon frieze. The marbles were taken from Greece in the early nineteenth century and are now on display in the British Museum, London.

Source: © Copyright The British Museum.

The Parthenon still overlooks Athens and it hopefully will for years to come. But while the Parthenon is an architectural treasure, today only traces of the magnificent art that once adorned it remain. To view its friezes and sculptures, you have to go to the British Museum in London, where they are beautifully displayed in a specially designed room. To understand why statuary of such clear cultural significance to Greece is to be found in England, one has to go back to the early nineteenth century and the exploits of Thomas Bruce, the 7th Earl of Elgin (Jackson, 1992). By the early nineteenth century, Britain was in the midst of a classical revival. The country's well-to-do traveled to Europe to visit the historic ruins of ancient Greece and Rome. The wealthier purchased statuary and antiquities for their estates. Patterns and illustrations from classical Greek and Roman motifs were reproduced and incorporated into architectural features, jewelry, and ceramic designs. Within this setting, Lord Elgin, a Scottish nobleman, set out to obtain sketches and casts of classical sculptures that might be used at his estate, then being built near the Firth of Forth.

In 1799, Elgin was appointed British ambassador to the Ottoman Empire, which extended over much of the eastern Mediterranean from western Europe to Egypt. By the late eighteenth century, the Ottomans had ruled Greece for 350 years.

A major military power and one-time masters of the Mediterranean, the Ottomans have been viewed by historians in a variety of ways, but one thing is certain: They were not overly concerned with the glories of ancient Greece. During their rule the Parthenon was used as a mosque, then as an ammunition dump; also, various Turkish structures were built on the site. Much of the north colonnade was destroyed in the Venetian bombardment of 1687. Some of the Parthenon marble was ground to make lime, and bits of statuary were broken off (Jackson, 1992). In 1800, one of the world's most perfect buildings was in a sorry state.

Elgin initially proposed that the British government finance a survey of the art of the Acropolis as a resource for British art. When this initiative was turned down, Elgin made his own plans and contracted laborers. Initially, his workers were to make copies of the Parthenon sculptures. In 1801, however, Britain defeated Napoleon's forces in Egypt, saving the Ottoman Empire. Coincidentally, Elgin soon obtained a permit from the Ottomans not only to copy and make molds of the Parthenon art but also to "take away any pieces of stone with old inscriptions or sculptures thereon" (Jackson, 1992:137). During 1801 and 1802, scaffolding was erected, and hundreds of laborers went to work on the Parthenon with blocks and tackles and

marble saws. Some sculptures broke or crashed to the ground. Twenty-two ships conveyed the marbles, loaded in hundreds of crates, back to England.

The marbles hardly proved to be good fortune for Elgin. The expense of obtaining them ruined his credit, and he discarded the idea of installing them at his estate. Totaling all of his expenses, Elgin estimated that he had spent over £60,000. To recoup his costs, he began negotiations for sale of the marbles to the government for display in the British Museum. After long parliamentary debate, they were sold for £35,000 in 1816. More than half of this amount went to clear Elgin's debt.

Elgin's treatment of the Parthenon's marbles had its contemporary critics. Among the most vocal opponents was none other than the Romantic poet and celebrator of Greek art and culture, Lord Byron, who immortalized the story of the Elgin marbles in the poems "Childe Harold's Pilgrimage" and "Curse of Minerva." Disgusted by what he saw as the desecration of the Parthenon, Byron asked by what right Elgin had removed these treasures of national cultural significance.

Greece gained independence from Turkey in 1830, and the Parthenon became integrally tied to the new nation's identity. The first restoration efforts began soon after independence. In the years since their installation in the British

Museum, the ownership of the Parthenon's marbles and demands for their return have periodically been raised by Greeks and Britons alike, but to no avail. In the 1980s, then Greek Minister of Culture Melina Mercouri charged the British with vandalism and argued that the continued possession of the marbles by the British Museum was provocative. Although garnering substantial international support from ministers of culture from around the world, these efforts also proved unsuccessful.

In his defense of his actions, Elgin pointed to the poor conditions of the Parthenon and the ill treatment that the sculptures had received. If left in place they would surely have continued to deteriorate. Why not remove them and have them cared for and appreciated by those who could afford to preserve them? Despite criticism, Elgin believed he was saving the sculptures from the ravages of time and neglect. Time has proven Elgin at least somewhat correct. The Parthenon continues to present a complex and continuous preservation problem. Time has ravaged the remains of the sculptures that were not removed, and deterioration of the monument accelerated rather than diminished throughout the twentieth century. Stonework and architectural detail have been eaten away by erosion, pollution, and acid rain, as well as by early and poorly conceived restoration efforts. As recently as 1971, a UNESCO report stated

(continued on page 646)

CRITICAL PERSPECTIVES

THE ELGIN MARBLES—CONTINUED

that the building itself was so weakened that it was in danger of collapse. Recent supporters of retaining the marbles argue that the marbles were obtained honestly with the permission of the government then in power. Other ancient Greek treasures such as the Venus de Milo (currently on display in the Louvre in Paris)

have also been removed from the country. Are these to be returned as well? For the time being it seems that the marbles remain in London.

POINTS TO PONDER

1. Do you feel Elgin was right or wrong to remove the marbles?

2. Should the Elgin marbles be returned to Greece? On what basis did you make your decision?

3. The conservation of the Parthenon and the preservation of the sculptures are valid concerns. How can these concerns be reconciled with the question of ownership?

---

between Native Americans and researchers. Native claims will in some instances necessitate additional research on poorly documented groups. Indeed, anthropological or archaeological research may be critical to assessing the association and ownership of cultural materials and human remains. On the other hand, anthropologists are given the opportunity to share their discoveries with those populations for whom the knowledge is most relevant.

The Roles of Applied Anthropologists in Planning Change

Over the years, many applied cultural anthropologists have worked in helping to improve societies through planning change. To assist governments, private developers, or other agencies, applied anthropologists are hired because of their ethnological studies of particular societies. Government and private agencies often employ applied anthropologists to prepare **social-impact studies,** research on the possible consequences that change will have on a community. Social-impact studies involve indepth interviews and ethnological studies in local communities to determine how various policies and developments will affect social life in those communities.

One well-known social-impact study was carried out by Thayer Scudder and Elizabeth Colson (1979) in the African country of Zambia. Scudder and Colson had conducted long-term ethnological research for about thirty years in the Gwembe Valley in Zambia. In the mid-1950s, the Zambian government subsidized the development of a large-scale dam, which would provide for more efficient agricultural activities and electrification. Because of the location of the dam, however, the people in the Gwembe Valley would be forced to relocate. Scudder and Colson used their knowledge from their long-term research and subsequent interviews to study the potential impact of this project on the community.

From their social-impact study, Scudder and Colson concluded that the forced relocation of this rural community would create extreme stresses that would result in people clinging to familiar traditions and institutions during the period of relocation. Scudder did social-impact studies of other societies in Africa experiencing forced relocation from dams, highways, and other developments. These studies enabled Scudder and Colson to offer advice to the various African government officials, who could then assess the costs and benefits of resettling these populations and could plan their development projects taking into consideration the impact on the people involved.

Applied anthropologists often serve as consultants to government organizations, such as the

Agency for International Development (AID), that formulate policies involving foreign aid. For example, anthropologist Patrick Fleuret (1988), a full-time employee of AID, studied the problems of farmers in Uganda after the downfall of Idi Amin in 1979. Fleuret and other AID anthropologists discovered that, on the heels of the political turmoil in Uganda, many of the peasants had retreated into subsistence production rather than participate in the market economy. They also found that subsistence production was affected by a technological problem—a scarcity of hoes for preparing the land for cultivation. In response, AID anthropologists helped design and implement a system to distribute hoes through local cooperative organizations.

This plan for the distribution of hoes reflects the development of new strategies on the part of AID and the facilitator role for applied anthropology. Most of the development work sponsored by AID and applied anthropology in the 1950s and 1960s was aimed at large-scale development projects such as hydroelectric dams and other forms of mechanized agriculture and industrialism. Many of these large-scale projects, however, have resulted in unintended negative consequences. In the preceding chapter, we saw how the Green Revolution frequently led to increasing inequality and a mechanized agriculture system that was expensive, inefficient, and inappropriate. Often these large-scale projects were devised in terms of the modernization views proposed by economists such as Walt Rostow (see Chapter 20) and were designed to shift an underdeveloped country to industrialism very rapidly.

Most recently, AID and applied anthropologists have modified their policies on development projects in many less developed countries. They now focus on projects that involve small-scale economic change with an emphasis on the development of appropriate technologies. Rather than relying on large-scale projects to have "trickle-down" influences on local populations, applied anthropologists have begun to focus more realistically on determining where basic needs must be fulfilled. After assessing the needs of the local population, the applied anthropologist can help facilitate change by helping people learn new skills.

One project that placed applied anthropologists in decision-making and analytical roles was run by Allan Holmberg of Cornell University. In the 1950s and 1960s, Holmberg and Mario Vasquez, a Peruvian

Applied anthropologists often act as consultants for farmers in underdeveloped areas such as rural India.

anthropologist, developed what is known as the Vicos Project in the Andean highlands. Vicos is the name of a *hacienda* that was leased by Cornell in 1952 as part of a program to increase education and literacy, improve sanitation and health care, and teach new agricultural methods to the Andean Indians. Prior to the Vicos Project, these Indians were peasant farmers who were not able to feed themselves. Their land on the *hacienda* was broken into small plots that were insufficient to raise potato crops. The Indians were indebted to the *hacendado* (owner) and were required to work on the hacendado's fields without pay to service their debts.

Although the applied anthropologists took on the role of a new patron to the Indians, the overall aim was to dissolve historic patterns of exploitation and to guide the Indians toward self-sufficiency (Holmberg, 1962; Chambers, 1985). The Indians were paid for their labor and were also introduced to new varieties of potatoes, fertilizers, and pesticides. New crops such as leafy vegetables and foods such as eggs and fruit were introduced into their diet.

Through an educational program, the Indians became acquainted with forms of representative democratic organization. Developing more independence, they eventually overturned the traditional authority structure of the *hacienda*. In 1962, the Indians purchased the land of the *hacienda* from its former owners, which gave the Indians a measure of self-sufficiency. Overall, the Vicos Project led to

ANTHROPOLOGISTS AT WORK

JOHN MCCREERY: APPLYING ANTHROPOLOGY IN JAPAN

This chapter has some examples of anthropologists who work outside the academic setting. John McCreery is an anthropologist who has lived in Japan since 1980 and has developed a productive and fruitful career in advertising. For a number of years, he worked as a copywriter and creative director for Hakuhodo Incorporated, Japan's second largest advertising agency. In 1984, he and his wife and business partner, Ruth McCreery, founded The Word Works, a supplier of translation, copywriting, and presentation support services to Japanese and other clients with operations in Japan. While earning his living as vice president and managing director of The Word Works, he is also a lecturer in the Graduate Program in Comparative Culture at Sophia University in Tokyo. There he teaches seminars on "The Making and Meaning of Advertising" and "Marketing in Japan." When asked, "How did an anthropologist get into advertising?" he replies, "In Taiwan I studied magicians. In Japan I joined the guild."

As an undergraduate in the honors college at Michigan State University, McCreery had studied philosophy and medieval history. In the summer after his junior year, a friend recommended that he take a course in East African

ethnography taught by anthropologist Marc Swartz. The course and the thought of doing research that involved travel to exotic places were fascinating. Another friend was studying Chinese, and noting that an anthropologist should have some experience with a non-Indo-European language, McCreery decided to study Chinese as well. One thing led to another, and he wound up in graduate school at Cornell University, doing a Ph.D. in anthropology and preparing to do research in Chinese anthropology. McCreery's first field research was in Puli, a market town in central Taiwan, where he and Ruth McCreery lived and worked from September 1969 to August 1971. He returned to Taiwan in 1976 to 1977, the summer of 1978, and again in 1983.

At Cornell University McCreery studied with Victor Turner. In Taiwan, McCreery focused his ethnographic study on religious traditions and worked with a Taoist master, Tio Se-lian. Both Victor Turner and Tio Se-lian were teachers with a willingness to listen, a flair for the dramatic, a passion for detail, and a breadth of humanity that moved all those with whom they came in contact. They and senior creative director Kimoto Kazuhiko, who shared

John McCreery

these earlier mentors' traits and gave McCreery his job at Hakuhodo, are the models he tries to emulate in his work.

McCreery's essays on Chinese religion and ritual have appeared in *The Journal of Chinese Religions* and *American Ethnologist*. He is also the author of a book titled *Japanese Consumer Behavior: From Worker Bees to Wary Shoppers*. McCreery maintains his contact with other anthropologists through an Internet listserve, Anthro-list, which provides lively discussions on ethnographic and theoretical issues in the field. Anthropologists from many backgrounds participate on this listserve. As a student you may want to become involved in lurking or participating on this listserve yourself.

basic improvements in housing, nutrition, clothing, and health conditions for the Indians. It also served as a model for similar projects in other parts of the world.

Problems sometimes arise between applied anthropologists and private developers or government officials. Many developers and governments want to induce modernization and social change as rapidly as possible with capital-intensive projects, hydroelectric dams, and manufacturing facilities. In many cases, anthropologists have recommended against these innovations because of their expense and inefficient use of labor resources and the heavy cost to communities. For example, as discussed in Chapter 24, anthropologist Billie DeWalt argued that the majority of Mexicans were not receiving benefits from the adoption of mechanized agriculture, which was being encouraged by the government. Political officials, however, often ignore these recommendations because they are committed to programs that serve their political and personal interests. In these circumstances, applied anthropologists are often forced to take an advocacy approach, or the representative role, which means supporting the interests of the people who will be directly affected by policies and projects.

In Chapter 20, we discussed the activities of advocacy organizations such as Cultural Survival, founded by David Maybury-Lewis in 1972, which is actively engaged in trying to reduce the costs imposed by globalization on small-scale societies. Driven by trade deficits and gigantic foreign debts, many governments in developing countries want to extract as much wealth as possible from their national territories. Highway expansion, mining operations, giant hydroelectric projects, lumbering, mechanized agriculture, and other industrial developments all intrude on the traditional lifestyle and territory of small-scale societies. Applied anthropologists connected with groups such as Cultural Survival try to obtain input from the people themselves and help them represent their interests to the government or private developers.

Maybury-Lewis (1985) admits that the advocacy role in anthropology is extremely difficult, requiring great sensitivity and complex moral and political judgments. Most recently, as discussed in Chapter 20, many small-scale societies and minority groups in developing countries are organizing themselves to represent their own interests. This

has resulted in the diminished role of the applied anthropologist as advocate or representative. Generally, anthropologists are pleased when their role as advocates or representatives is diminished, because these roles are called for only when native people are dominated by forces from globalization that are beyond their control.

Applied Anthropology and Human Rights

Cultural Relativism and Human Rights

A recent development that has had wide-ranging consequences for applied anthropology and ethnographic research involves the ways in which anthropologists assess and respond to the values and norms of other societies. Recall our discussion of *cultural relativism,* the method used by anthropologists to understand another society through their own cultural values, beliefs, norms, and behaviors. In order to understand another society's culture and practices, anthropologists must strive to temporarily suspend their judgement of the indigenous culture (Maybury-Lewis, 1998). This difficult procedure will help anthropologists gain insights into other cultures. Some critics have charged that anthropologists and other people who adopt this position cannot (or will not) make value judgments concerning values, norms, and practices of any society. If this is the case, then how can anthropologists encourage any conception of human rights that would be valid for all of humanity? Must anthropologists accept such practices as infanticide, caste and class inequalities, and female subordination out of fear of forcing their own values on other people?

Relativism Reconsidered These criticisms have led some anthropologists to reevaluate the basic assumptions regarding cultural relativism. In his 1983 book *Culture and Morality: The Relativity of Values in Anthropology,* Elvin Hatch recounted the historical acceptance of the cultural-relativist view. As we saw in Chapter 13, this was the approach of Franz Boas, who challenged the unilineal-evolutionary models of nineteenth-century anthropologists like E. B. Tylor, with their underlying assumptions of Western cultural superiority. Boas's approach, with its emphasis on tolerance and equality, appealed to many liberal-minded Western scholars.

However, belief in cultural relativism led to the acceptance by some early twentieth-century anthropologists of **ethical relativism,** the notion that we cannot impose the values of one society on other societies. Ethical relativists argued that because anthropologists had not discovered any universal moral values, each society's values were valid with respect to that society's circumstances and conditions. No society could claim any superior position over another regarding ethics and morality.

As many philosophers and anthropologists have noted, the argument of ethical relativism is a circular one that itself assumes a particular moral position. It is, in fact, a moral theory that encourages people to be tolerant toward *all* cultural values, norms, and practices. Hatch notes that in the history of anthropology, many who accepted the premises of ethical relativism could not maintain these assumptions in light of their data. Ethical relativists would have to tolerate practices such as homicide, child abuse, human sacrifice, torture, warfare, racial discrimination, and even genocide. In fact, even anthropologists who held the ethical-relativist position in the early period of the twentieth century condemned many cultural practices. For example, Ruth Benedict condemned the practice of the Plains Indians, who cut off the nose of an adulterous wife. Boas himself condemned racism, anti-Semitism, and other forms of bigotry. Thus, these anthropologists did not consistently adhere to the ethical-relativist paradigm.

The horrors associated with World War II eventually led most scholars to reject ethical relativism. The argument that Nazi Germany could not be condemned because of its unique moral and ethical standards appeared ludicrous to most people. In the 1950s, some anthropologists such as Robert Redfield suggested that general standards of judgment could be applied to most societies. However, these anthropologists were reluctant to impose Western standards on prestate societies. In essence, they suggested a double standard in which they could criticize large-scale, industrial state societies but not prestate societies.

This double standard of morality poses problems, however. Can anthropologists make value judgments about homicide, child abuse, warfare, torture, rape, and other acts of violence in a small-scale society? Why should they adopt different standards in evaluating such behaviors in prestate societies as compared with industrial societies? In both types of societies, human beings are harmed. Don't humans in all societies have equal value?

A Resolution to the Problem of Relativism   There is a resolution to these philosophical and moral dilemmas. First, we need to distinguish between *cultural relativism* and *ethical relativism*. In other words, to understand the values, the reasoning and logic, and the worldviews of another people does not mean to accept all of their practices and standards (Salmon, 1997). Second, we need to realize that the culture of a society is not completely homogeneous or unified. In Chapter 10, we noted how culture was distributed differentially within any society. For example, men and women do not share the same "culture" in any society. Ethnographic experience tells anthropologists that there are always people who may not agree with the content of the moral and ethical values of a society. Treating cultures as "uniform united wholes" is a conceptual mistake. For one thing, it ignores the power relationships within a society. Elites within society can maintain cultural hegemony and use harmful practices against their own members to produce conformity. In some cases, governments use the concept of relativism to justify their repressive policies and deflect criticism of these practices by the international community. Those who impose harmful practices upon others may be the beneficiaries of those practices.

To get beyond the problem of ethical relativism, we ought to adopt a humanitarian standard that would be recognized by all people throughout the world. This standard would not be derived from any particular cultural values—such as the U.S. Declaration of Independence—but rather would involve the basic principle that every individual is entitled to a certain standard of "well-being." For example, no individual ought to be subjected to bodily harm through violence or starvation.

Of course, we recognize certain problems with this solution. Perhaps the key problem is that people in many societies accept—or at least appear to accept—behaviors that we would condemn as inhumane. For example, what about the Aztec practice of human sacrifice? The Aztecs firmly believed that they would be destroyed if they did not sacrifice victims to the sun deity. Would an outside group have been justified in condemning and abolishing this practice? A more recent case involves the West Irian tribe known as the Dani, who engaged in constant warfare with neighboring tribes. They believed that through revenge they had to placate the ghosts of their deceased kin killed in warfare, because unavenged ghosts bring sickness and disaster to the tribe. Another way of placating the ghosts was to bring two or three young girls related to the deceased victim to the funeral site and chop two fingers off their hands. Until recently, all Dani women lost from two to six fingers in this way (Heider, 1979; Bagish, 1981). Apparently these practices were accepted by Dani males and females.

In some Islamic countries women have been accused of sexual misconduct and then executed by male members in what are called "honor killings." The practice of honor killings, which victimizes women, has been defended in some of these societies as a means to restore harmony to the society. The males argue that the shedding of blood washes away the shame of sexual dishonor. There have been a number of cases of "honor killings" among immigrant Middle Eastern families within the United States. In both Africa and the Middle East, young girls are subjected to female circumcision, a polite term for the removal of the clitoris and other areas of the vagina. One of the purposes of this procedure is to reduce the pleasure related to sexual intercourse and thereby induce more fidelity from women in marriage. Chronic infections are a common result of this practice. Sexual intercourse is painful and childbirth is much more difficult for these women. However, the cultural ideology may maintain that an uncircumcised woman is not respectable, and few families want to risk their daughter's chances of marriage availability by not having her circumcised (Fluehr-Lobban, 1995). The right of a male to discipline, hit, or beat his wife is often maintained in a male-dominated culture (Tapper, 1992, 1993). Other examples of these types of practices—such as headhunting, slavery, female subordination, torture, and unnecessarily dangerous child labor—also fall into this category. According to a universal humanitarian standard suggested here, all of these practices could be condemned as harmful behaviors.

The Problem of Intervention

The condemnation of harmful cultural practices with reference to a universal standard is fairly easy.

The abolition of such practices, however, is not. Anthropologists recommend that one should take a pragmatic approach in reducing these practices. Sometimes intervention in the cultures in which practices such as genocide are occurring would be a moral imperative. This intervention would not proceed from the standpoint of specific Western values but from the commonly recognized universal standards of humanitarianism. Such intervention, however, must proceed cautiously and be based on a thorough knowledge of the society. In addition, the cultural practice must be shown to clearly create pain and suffering for people. When these elements are present, intervention should take place in the form of a dialogue.

As is obvious, these suggestions are based on the highly idealistic standards of a universal humanitarianism. In many cases, intervention may not be possible, and in some cases, intervention to stamp out a particular cultural practice may cause even greater problems. In Chapter 20, we saw how outside intervention adversely affected such peoples as the Ju/'hoansi, the Mbuti, and the Yanomamö. Communal riots, group violence, or social chaos may result from the dislocation of certain cultural practices. Thus caution, understanding, and dialogue are critical to successful intervention. We need to be sensitive to cultural differences but not allow them to produce severe harm to individuals within a society.

A Successful Intervention

An illustration of this type of research and effort by applied anthropologists is the work of John Van Willigen from the United States and V. C. Channa of India, who together researched the harmful consequences of the dowry in India (1991). As discussed in Chapter 22, India, like some other primarily agricultural societies, has the cultural institution known as the *dowry*, in which the bride's family gives a certain amount of cash or other goods to the groom's family upon marriage. Recently, the traditions of the dowry have led to increasing cases of what has been referred to as "dowry death" or "bride burning." Some husbands or their families have been dissatisfied with the amount of the dowry that the new wife brings into the family. Following marriage, the family of the groom begins to make additional demands for more money and goods from the wife's family. These demands result in harassment and abuse of the wife, culminating in murder. The woman is typically burned to death after being doused with kerosene, hence the use of the term "bride burning."

Dowry deaths have increased in recent years. In 1998, 6,917 cases were reported nationally in India. Feminist organizations and other groups say the number is much higher, since many incidents go unreported. By one estimate, there are 15,000 deaths per year (South Asia Online Briefing Program, 2000). In addition, another negative result of the burdens imposed by the dowry tradition has led many pregnant women to pay for amniocentesis (a medical procedure to determine the health status of the fetus) as a means to determine the sex of the fetus. If the fetus is female, in many cases Indian women have an abortion partly because of the increasing burden and expense of raising a daughter and developing a substantial dowry for her marriage. Thus, male children are preferred, and female fetuses are selectively aborted.

National laws established against the institution of the dowry (the Dowry Prohibition Act of 1961, amended in 1984 and 1986) are very tough. The laws make it illegal to give or take a dowry, but they are ineffective in restraining the practice. In addition, a number of public education groups have been organized in India. Using slogans such as "Say No to Dowry," they have been advertising and campaigning against the dowry practices. Yet the problem continues to plague India.

After carefully studying the dowry practices of different regions and local areas of India, Van Willigen and Channa concluded that the increase in dowry deaths was partially the result of the rapid inflationary pressures of the Indian economy as well as the demands of a consumer-oriented economy. Consumer price increases have resulted in the increasing demands for more dowry money to buy consumer goods. It has become increasingly difficult to save for a substantial dowry for a daughter or sister that is satisfactory to the groom's family. Van Willigen and Channa found that aside from wealth, family "prestige" that comes with wealth expenditures is sought by the groom's family.

From the perspective of the bride's family, dowry payments provide for present consumption and future earning power for their daughter through acquiring a husband with better connections and future earning potential. In a less developed society such as India, with extremely high unemployment and rapid inflation, the importance of investing in a husband with high future earning potential is emphasized. When asked why they give a dowry when their daughters are being married, people respond, "because we love them." The decision by the groom's family to forgo the dowry would also be very difficult.

There appears to be a very positive commitment to the institution of the dowry in India. Most people have given and received a dowry. Thus, declaring dowry a crime technically makes many people criminals. Van Willigen and Channa recommended that to be effective, the anti-dowry practices must be displaced by other, less problematic practices, and that the apparent causes of the practice be attacked. Women's property rights must be examined so as to increase their economic access. Traditional Hindu cultural norms regarding inheritance, which give sons the right from birth to claim the so-called "ancestral properties," must be reformed. At present, male descendants inherit property, but females must pay for marriage expenses and dowry gifts. Van Willigen and Channa assert that a gender-neutral inheritance law in which women and men receive equal shares ought to be established to help reduce the discrepancy between males and females in India.

In addition, Van Willigen and Channa recommended the establishment of universal marriage registration and licenses throughout India. This may enable the government to monitor dowry abuses so that anti-dowry legislation could be more effective. These anthropologists conclude that a broad program to increase the social and economic status of women, along with more rigorous control of marriage registration and licensing, will be more effective than anti-dowry legislation in solving the dowry death problem in Indian society.

This example of applied anthropology, based on the collaboration between Western and non-Western anthropologists to solve a fundamental human rights issue, represents a commendable strategy for applied anthropologists in the future. It is hoped that through better cross-cultural understanding aided by ethnographic research, and through applied anthropology, universally recognized and humanitarian standards will become widely adopted throughout the world.

Applied anthropologists utilize their research to help develop human rights for women in India and in other areas of the world.

Universal Human Rights

The espousal of universally recognized standards to eradicate harmful practices is a worthwhile, albeit idealistic, goal. Since the time of the Enlightenment, Western societies have prided themselves on extending human rights. Many Western theorists emphasize that human rights have spread to other parts of the world through globalization, thus providing the catalyst for social change, reform, and political liberation. At the same time, as people from other non-Western societies can testify, the West has also promoted intolerance, racism, and genocide. Western society has not always lived up to the ideals of its own tradition.

Cultural anthropologists and applied anthropologists have a role in helping to define the universal standards for human rights in all societies. By systematically studying community standards, applied anthropologists can determine whether practices are harmful and then help provide solutions for reducing these harmful practices. This may involve consultation with local government officials and dialogue with members of the community to resolve the complex issues regarding the identified harmful practices. The exchange of ideas across cultures through anthropological research is beginning to foster acceptance of the universal nature of some human rights regardless of cultural differences.

Many anthropologists are promoting *advocacy anthropology,* the use of anthropological knowledge to further human rights. Universal human rights would include the right to life and freedom from physical and psychological abuse, including torture; freedom from arbitrary arrest and imprisonment; freedom from slavery and genocide; the right to nationality; freedom of movement and departure from one's country; the right to seek asylum in other countries because of persecution in one's own country; rights to privacy, ownership of property, freedom of speech, religion, and assembly; the rights of self-determination; and the right to adequate food, shelter, health care, and education (Sponsel, 1996). Obviously, not all of these rights exist in any society at present. However, most people will probably agree that these rights ought to be part of any society's obligations to its people.

As people everywhere are brought closer together with the expansion of the global village, different societies will experience greater pressures to treat one another in sensitive and humane ways. We live in a world in which our destinies are tied to one another more closely than they have ever been. Yet it is a world containing many different societies with varied norms and practices. Sometimes this leads to mutual distrust and dangerous confrontations.

Anthropologists may be able to play a role in helping to bring about mutual understanding, to help to understand one another's right to existence. Perhaps through this understanding we may be able to develop a worldwide, **pluralistic metaculture,** a global system emphasizing fundamental human rights, with a sense of political and global responsibility. This cross-cultural understanding and mutual respect for human rights may be the most important aspect of anthropological research today.

SUMMARY

Applied anthropology is one of the specializations that has offered new opportunities for physical anthropologists, archaeologists, and ethnologists to serve as consultants to public and private agencies to help solve local and global human problems. Applied anthropologists cooperate with government officials and others in establishing economic development projects, health care systems, and substance abuse programs. They serve in a variety of roles to help bring about solutions to human problems.

Physical anthropologists help solve problems related to the design of physical environments for the human body. They also provide assistance in solving crimes using their knowledge in the growing field of forensic anthropology. A recent development in the field of archaeology is cultural resource management, or applied archaeology. Legislation passed by state and federal authorities in the United States requires the preservation of both prehistoric and historic materials. Applied archaeologists are involved in identifying important sites that may be endangered by development. They conduct surveys and excavations to preserve data that are important to understanding the cultural heritage of the United States. Cultural resource management offers new career opportunities for archaeologists in government agencies, universities, and consulting firms.

Early ethnologists who accepted the tenets of cultural relativism sometimes also embraced ethical relativism, the idea that a person should not make value judgments about other societies. Although most anthropologists reject ethical relativism, the issue of universal standards to evaluate values and harmful cultural practices is still problematic. Proposing universal standards to make value judgments and help reduce harmful cultural practices remains one of the most important tasks for applied anthropology and future ethnological research.

QUESTIONS TO THINK ABOUT

1. What is applied anthropology? Erve Chambers suggests that there are different roles that applied anthropologists play. Discuss each of these roles as they apply to present-day applied anthropological studies.

2. Forensic anthropology may offer information of critical importance in a police investigation. Consider the different types of information that can and cannot be provided.

3. What is medical anthropology? What are some of the types of things that medical anthropologists do?

4. What is cultural resource management? What resources are being evaluated and preserved?

5. Examine the concepts of cultural relativism and ethical relativism. Can an anthropologist be involved in applied anthropology and adhere to either of these principles or views? Are there any problems associated with an ethical relativist perspective?

6. Is it possible to understand the values and worldview of another culture and not accept all of their practices and standards? In other words, can one be a cultural relativist and not an ethical relativist at the same time?

7. Do you think it is possible to adopt a humanitarian standard that would be accepted by everyone in the world? What might this view entail?

8. Is there such a thing as universal human rights?

KEY TERMS

applied anthropology
cultural patrimony
cultural resource management
epidemiology

ethical relativism
forensic anthropology
medical anthropology

pluralistic metaculture
repatriate
social-impact studies

INTERNET EXERCISES

1. Visit the website **http://www.ulster.net/ ~hrmm/hvrr/lindner.htm** to read about the cultural landscape of the Hudson River. How have prehistoric and historical archaeologists "discovered" the various land uses in this area? What is the purpose of this type of study? Why is historical archaeology necessary as history records events during periods covered by these studies?

2. Review the World Health Organization report "1997–1999 World Health Statistics Annual" at **http://www3.who.int/whosis/menu.cfm? path=whosis,whsa&language=english**. Look at the tables of life expectancies for several countries (This is Table 3). How can the field of applied anthropology help in understanding the differences in life expectancy between countries and the great variation in the causes of death around the world?

SUGGESTED READINGS

CHAMBERS, ERVE. 1985. *Applied Anthropology: A Practical Guide*. Englewood Cliffs, NJ: Prentice Hall. A thorough introduction to the field of applied anthropology, with many examples of how anthropologists resolve social problems.

JOHNSON, RONALD W., and MICHAEL G. SCHENE. 1987. *Cultural Resources Management*. Malabar, FL: Robert E. Krieger. A compilation of essays focusing on the management of archaeological resources and the preservation of standing historic monuments. The work serves as a useful introduction to cultural resource management and the diverse problems confronting archaeologists in their efforts to preserve the past.

PARTRIDGE, WILLIAM (Ed.). 1984. *Training Manual in Development Anthropology*. Special publication of the American Anthropological Association and the Society for Applied Anthropology, no. 17. A series of essays by applied anthropologists who served as consultants for development projects. These essays identify the potential conflicts that arise in planning and consulting on such projects and provide illustrations of how the conflicts were resolved.

PODOLEFSKY, AARON, and PETER J. BROWN (Eds.). 1997. *Applying Cultural Anthropology: An Introductory Reader,* 3rd ed. Mountain View, CA: Mayfield. A reader containing state-of-the-art essays on how cultural anthropologists apply their research skills and knowledge to solve problems in health care, economic development, business, agricultural development, and law.

Glossary

acclimatization The physiological process of being or becoming accustomed to a new physical environment.

Acheulian The technology associated with *Homo erectus*.

achieved status A status that results at least in part from a person's specific actions.

adaptation The process in which an organism makes a successful adjustment to a specific environment.

adaptive radiation The relatively rapid evolution of a species in a new environmental niche.

adjudication The settling of legal disputes through a formal, centralized authority.

aerial photography Photographs taken from the air of archaeological sites and the landscape. Helpful to archaeologists in mapping and locating sites.

age grades Statuses, defined by age, through which a person moves in the course of his or her lifetime.

age sets Corporate groups of people who are about the same age and share specific rights, obligations, duties, and privileges in their community.

age stratification The unequal allocation of wealth, power, and prestige among people of different ages.

agribusiness Commercialized, mechanized agriculture.

agricultural states States in which the power of the ruling elite was vested in the control of agricultural surpluses. This type of control typifies early states.

alleles The alternate forms of a gene.

ambilineal descent group A corporate kinship group formed by choosing to trace relationships through either a male or a female line.

amino acids The chemical compounds that form protein molecules.

analogy Similarities in organisms that have no genetic relatedness.

anatomically modern *Homo sapiens* The most recent form of human, distinguished by a unique anatomy that differs from that of earlier, archaic *Homo sapiens*.

animism The belief that the world is populated by spiritual beings such as ghosts, souls, and demons.

anthropology The systematic study of humankind.

antiquaries Collectors whose interest lies in the object itself, not in where the fossils might have come from or what the artifact and associated materials might tell about the people that produced them. Collectors of this kind characterized the early history of archaeology.

apartheid A political, legal, and social system developed in South Africa in which the rights of different population groups were based on racial criteria.

applied anthropology The use of data gathered from the other subfields of anthropology to find practical solutions to problems in a society.

arboreal Living in trees.

archaeological sites Places of past human activity that are preserved in the ground.

archaeology The discipline that focuses on the study of the artifacts from past societies to determine the lifestyles, history, and evolution of those societies.

Archaic A post-Pleistocene hunting-and-gathering adaptation in the Americas characterized by tools suitable for broad-spectrum collecting and more intensive exploitation of localized resources. Corresponds in terms of general trends with the Mesolithic of Europe.

archaic *Homo sapiens* The earliest form of *Homo sapiens*, dating back more than 200,000 years.

artifacts The material products of past societies.

artificial selection The process in which people select certain plants and animals for breeding.

ascribed status A status that is attached to a person from birth; for example, sex, caste, and race.

assimilation The adoption of the language, culture, and ethnic identity of the dominant group in a society by other groups.

authority Power generally perceived by members of society as legitimate rather than coercive.

balanced polymorphism The mixture of homozygous and heterozygous genes of a population in a state of equilibrium.

balanced reciprocity A direct type of reciprocal exchange with an explicit expectation of immediate return.

band The least complex and, most likely, the oldest form of a political system.

barter The direct exchange of one commodity for another; it does not involve the use of money.

baton method   A method of percussion flaking of tools that involves the use of bone or antler. This provides more precise control than is possible with a hammer stone.

beliefs   Specific cultural conventions concerning true or false assumptions shared by a particular group.

bilateral descent   A descent system that traces relatives through both maternal and paternal sides of the family simultaneously.

biodiversity   The genetic and biological variation within and among different species of plants and animals.

biological assimilation   The process by which formerly distinct groups merge through marriage and reproduction.

biome   An area dominated by a particular climate and distinguished by the prevalence of certain types of plants and animals.

bipedalism   The ability to walk erect on two hind legs.

brachiation   An arm-over-arm suspensory locomotion used by some primates to move in trees.

brideservice   A male resides with his wife's family for a specified amount of time.

bridewealth   Transfer of some form of wealth from the descent group of the groom to that of the bride.

broad-spectrum collecting   The exploitation of varied food resources in local environments.

capitalism   An economic system in which natural resources as well as the means of producing and distributing goods and services are privately owned.

cargo cult   Revitalization movements in Papua New Guinea that involve beliefs that Western goods are produced by supernatural forces.

carrying capacity   The upper limit of the size of a population that a specific environment can support.

caste   A social grouping into which a person is born and remains throughout his or her lifetime.

catastrophism   A theory that suggests that many species have disappeared since the time of creation because of major catastrophes such as floods, earthquakes, and other major geological disasters.

central place theory   The theory in geography and archaeology that, given uniform topography, resources, and opportunities, the distribution of sites within a region should be perfectly regular. Political and economic centers would be located an equal distance from one another, and each in turn would be surrounded by a hierarchical arrangement of smaller settlements, all evenly spaced. Developed by the German geographer Walter Christaller in the 1930s.

chief   A person who owns, manages, and controls the basic productive factors of the economy and has privileged access to strategic and luxury goods.

chiefdom   A political system with a formalized and centralized leadership, headed by a chief.

chromosomes   Structures within the cell nucleus that contain the hereditary information.

circumstantialist model   A model of ethnicity that focuses on the situations and circumstances that influence ethnic interaction.

civilization   A form of society that has a complex government, dense urban centers, extensive food surpluses, a specialized division of labor, monumental art, and usually a writing system.

clan   A form of descent group in some societies whose members trace their descent to an unknown ancestor or, in some cases, to a sacred plant or animal.

clinal distribution   Plotting the varying distribution of physical traits in various populations on maps by clines, or zones.

clines   The zones on a map used to plot physical traits of populations.

closed instincts   Genetically encoded behaviors that are not open to learning.

closed peasant communities   Indian communities in highland areas of Latin America that were isolated from colonialism and the market economy.

closed society   A society in which social status is generally ascribed rather than achieved.

Clovis culture   A Paleo-Indian tool tradition in the Americas characterized by distinctive spear points and associated with the hunting of late Pleistocene megafauna.

Clovis-first hypothesis   The theory that maintains that the Clovis culture represents the initial human settlement of the Americas.

cognitive anthropology   The study of human psychological thought processes based on computer modeling.

colonies   Societies that are controlled politically and economically by a dominant society.

command economy   An economic system in which a political elite makes the decisions concerning production, prices, and trade.

communication   The act of transferring information.

complementary opposition   A system in which kinship groups within a segmentary lineage organization can be allies or antagonists.

composite tools   Tools, such as harpoons or spears, made from several components.

conflict theories   Theories that argue that state-level organization is beneficial only to the ruling elite and is generally costly to subordinate groups such as the peasantry.

context   The specific location in the ground of an artifact or fossil and all associated materials.

continental drift   The separation of continents that occurred over millions of years as a result of the geological process of plate tectonics.

consumption   The process of using natural and human-made resources within a particular economic system.

continuous variation   A phenomenon whereby variation in a particular trait or characteristic cannot be divided into discrete, readily definable groups but varies continuously from one end of the spectrum to the other.

core societies   Powerful industrial nations that have exercised economic hegemony over other regions.

correlation   The simultaneous occurrence of two variables.

cosmologies   Ideas that present the universe as an orderly system, including answers to basic questions about the place of humankind.

cross-cousin marriage   A system in which a person marries the offspring of parental siblings of the opposite sex; for example, a male marries his mother's brother's daughter.

crude birth rate   The number of live births in a given year for every thousand people in a population.

crude death rate   The number of deaths in a given year for every thousand people.

cultivation   The systematic planting and harvesting of plants to support the subsistence activities of a population.

cultural anthropology   The subfield of anthropology that focuses on the study of contemporary societies.

cultural assimilation   The process by which ethnic groups adopt the culture of another ethnic group.

cultural ecology   The systematic study of the relationships between the environment and society.

cultural hegemony   The control over values and norms exercised by the dominant group in a society.

cultural materialism   A research strategy that focuses on technoenvironmental and economic factors as key determinants in sociocultural evolution.

cultural patrimony   The ownership of cultural properties, such as human remains, artifacts, monuments, sacred sites, and associated cultural materials.

cultural relativism   The view that cultural traditions must be understood within the context of a particular society's responses to problems and opportunities.

cultural resource management   The attempt to protect and conserve artifacts and archaeological resources for the future.

cultural universals   Essential behavioral characteristics of humans found in all societies.

culture   A shared way of life that includes material products, values, beliefs, and norms that are transmitted within a particular society from generation to generation.

culture of poverty   The hypothesis that sets of values sustaining poverty are perpetuated generation after generation within a community.

culture shock   A severe psychological reaction that results from adjusting to the realities of a society radically different from one's own.

datum point   A reference point in an archaeological excavation, often some permanent feature or marker, from which all measurements of contour, level, and location are taken.

deculturation   The loss of traditional patterns of culture.

deductive method   A scientific research method that begins with a general theory, develops a specific hypothesis, and tests it.

demographic-transition theory   A model used to understand population changes within a society through different stages, concluding in the decline of fertility and mortality rates in advanced industrial societies.

demography   The study of population and its relationship to society.

dendrochronology   A numerical dating technique based on the varying pattern of environmental conditions preserved in the annual growth rings of trees.

dentition   The number, form, and arrangement of teeth.

deoxyribonucleic acid (DNA)   A chain of chemicals contained in each chromosome that produces physical traits that are transmitted to the offspring during reproduction.

dependency theory   The theory that underdevelopment in Third World societies is the result of domination by capitalist, industrial societies.

dependent variable   A variable whose value changes in response to changes in the independent variable.

descent group   A corporate group identified by a person that traces his or her real or fictive kinship relationships.

dialect   Linguistic patterns involving differences in pronunciation, vocabulary, or syntax that occur within a common language family.

diffusionism   The spread of cultural traits from one society to another.

diurnal   Active during the day.

division of labor   The specialization of economic roles and activities within a society.

domestication   The systematic, artificial selection of traits in plants or animals to make them more useful to human beings.

dominance hierarchy   The relative social status or ranking order found in some primate social groups.

dominant The form of a gene that is expressed in a heterozygous pair.

doubling time The period of time required for a population to double.

dowry Goods and wealth paid by the bride's family to the groom's family.

drives Basic, inborn, biological urges that motivate human behavior.

dyadic contract A reciprocal exchange arrangement between two individuals.

ecclesiastical religions Religious traditions that develop in state societies and combine governmental and religious authority.

ecofacts Archaeological finds that have cultural significance, but that are not artifacts manufactured or produced by humans. Examples of ecofacts would be botanical, faunal, and shell remains recovered from an archaeological site.

ecological niche The specific environmental setting to which an organism is adapted.

ecology The study of living organisms in relationship to their environment.

economy The social relationships that organize the production, distribution, and exchange of goods and services.

egalitarian A type of social structure that emphasizes equality among different statuses.

emic perspective A study of a culture from an insider's point of view.

enculturation The process of social interaction through which people learn their culture.

endogamy Marriage between two people of the same social group or category.

environmental niche A locale that contains various plants, animals, and other ecological conditions to which a species must adjust.

epidemiology The study of disease patterns in a society.

ethical relativism The belief that the values of one society should never be imposed on another society.

ethnic boundary marker The distinctions of language, clothing, or other aspects of culture that emphasize ethnicity.

ethnic group A group that shares a culture.

ethnicity Cultural differences among populations usually based on attributes such as language, religion, lifestyle, and cultural ideas about common descent or specific territory.

ethnocentrism The practice of judging another society by the values and standards of one's own.

ethnocide A process in which a dominant group or society forces other groups to abandon their traditional language and culture.

ethnogenesis The emergence of a new ethnic group.

ethnography A description of a society written by an anthropologist who conducted field research in that society.

ethnology The subfield of anthropology that focuses on the study of different contemporary cultures throughout the world.

ethnomusicology The study of the practices and culture of musical traditions of different societies.

ethnonationalist movements The process of emphasizing the cultural distinctions of a particular group for political purposes.

ethnopoetics The study of poetry traditions and practices in different societies.

ethologist A scientist who studies the behaviors of animals in their natural setting.

ethos Socially acceptable norms in a society.

etic perspective The study of a culture from an outsider's point of view.

evolution Process of change within the genetic makeup of a species over time.

evolutionary psychology The study of the mind using evolutionary findings.

exchange The transfer of natural and human-made resources from one person to another.

exogamy Marriage between people of different social groups and categories.

experimental studies Studies involving the replication of tools or activities to infer how ancient tools may have been made and used.

extended family A type of family made up of parents, children, and other kin relations residing together as a social unit.

family A social group of two or more people related by blood, marriage, or adoption who reside together for an extended period, sharing economic resources and caring for their young.

faunal correlation The dating of fossils through the comparison of similar fossils from better-dated sequences.

faunal succession Literally, "animal" succession; recognizes that life forms change through time. First noted by the English geologist William Smith.

features Nonmovable artifacts or traces of past human activity, such as an ancient fire hearth, a pit dug in the ground, or a wall.

fecundity The potential number of children women are capable of bearing.

feminism The belief that women are equal to men and should have equal rights and opportunities.

fertility The number of births in a society.

feud A type of armed combat between groups in a community.

feudalism   A decentralized form of political economy based on landed estates, which existed during different historical periods in agrarian societies.

fictive kinship ties   Extrafamilial social ties that provide mutual-aid work groups.

First World   The sector of the global economy that is composed of modern industrialized capitalist societies.

fissioning   The movement of people from one group to another area when their population begins to increase and food or other resources become scarce.

fission-track dating   A numerical dating method based on the decay of an unstable isotope of uranium. Used to date volcanic rocks.

flotation   A specialized recovery technique in archaeology in which material from an excavation is placed in water to separate soil from organic remains such as plants, seeds, and charcoal.

folkways   Norms guiding ordinary usages and conventions of everyday life.

foraging society   Another classification used for a hunting-and-gathering society.

foramen magnum   The opening in the base of the skull through which the spinal cord passes.

forensic anthropology   The identification of human skeletal remains for legal purposes.

fossil   The preserved remains of bones and living materials from earlier periods.

fossil localities   Places where fossils are found. These may be locations where predators dropped animals they killed, places where creatures were naturally covered by sediments, or sites where early humans or primates actually lived.

founder effect   A type of genetic drift resulting from the randomly determined genetic complement present in the founders of an isolated population.

functionalism   An anthropological perspective based on the assumption that society consists of institutions that serve vital purposes for people.

gametes   Sex cells (such as egg and sperm in humans). They contain only half of the chromosomes found in ordinary body, or somatic, cells.

gender   Specific behavioral traits attached to each sex by a society and defined by culture.

gene flow   The exchange of genes between populations as a result of interbreeding.

gene pool   The total collection of all the alleles within a particular population.

generalized reciprocity   A type of reciprocal exchange based on the assumption that an immediate return is not expected and that the value of the exchange will balance out in the long run.

genes   Discrete units of hereditary information that determine specific physical characteristics of organisms.

genetic drift   Change in allele frequencies within a population as a result of random processes of selection.

genocide   The physical extermination of a particular ethnic group in a society.

genotype   The specific genetic constitution of an organism.

gerontocracy   Rule by elders (usually males) who control the material and reproductive resources within the community.

gestation period   The length of time the young spend in the mother's womb.

globalization   The worldwide impact of industrialization and its socioeconomic, political, and cultural consequences on the world.

goods   Elements of material culture produced from raw materials in the natural environment, ranging from the basic commodities for survival to luxury items.

gradualistic theory, or gradualism   A theory suggesting that the rate of evolutionary change is relatively constant and occurs gradually over a long time.

grammar   A finite set of rules that determines how sentences are constructed to produce meaningful statements.

greenhouse effect   Global warming caused by the trapping of heat from solar rays by carbon dioxide, preventing it from radiating back into space.

Green Revolution   The use of bioengineering and industrial technology for agricultural purposes.

hamula   Arabic term for clan-like organization.

Hardy-Weinberg theory of genetic equilibrium   An idealized mathematical model that sets hypothetical conditions under which no evolution is taking place. Developed independently by G. H. Hardy and W. Weinberg, the model is used to evaluate evolutionary processes operating on a population.

heterozygous   Having two different alleles in a gene pair.

hierarchical society   A society in which some people have greater access than others to wealth, rank, status, authority, and power.

hieroglyphic writing   *Hiero* meaning "sacred," and *gyphein* meaning "carving." An early pictographic writing system in which symbols denoted the ideas and concepts.

historical linguistics   The comparison and classification of different languages to explore the historical links among them.

historical particularism   An approach to studying human societies in which each society has to be understood as a unique product of its own history.

holistic   A broad comprehensive approach to the study of humankind drawing on the four fields of anthropology, integrating both biological and cultural phenomena.

home bases Archaeological sites that, according to some theoretical interpretations, were locations where early hominids gathered for food sharing, child care, and social interaction.

hominid The family of primates that includes modern humans and their direct ancestors who share distinctive types of teeth, jaws, and bipedalism.

hominoids Members of the primate superfamily *Hominoidea*, which includes all apes and hominids.

homology Traits that have a common genetic origin but may differ in form and function.

homozygous Having the same alleles in a gene pair.

horticulture A form of agriculture in which a limited, nonmechanized technology is utilized to cultivate plants.

hunter-gatherer A society that depends on hunting animals and gathering vegetation for subsistence.

hypodescent concept A system in which children of mixed parentage acquire the social and racial status of the parent whose social and racial status is lower.

hypothesis A testable proposition concerning the relationship among different variables within the collected data.

ideal culture What people say they do or should do.

ideographic writing system An early form of writing in which simple pictures are used to communicate ideas, an individual picture expressing each idea. In actuality, this system involves neither language nor writing.

ideology Cultural symbols and beliefs that reflect and support the interests of specific groups in a society.

imperialism Economic and political domination and control over other societies.

incest Sexual relations or marriage between certain relatives.

incest avoidance Avoidance of sexual relations and marriage with members of one's own family.

incest taboo Strong cultural norms that prohibit sexual relations or marriage with members of one's own family.

independent variable Causal variable that produces an effect on another variable, the dependent variable.

inductive method A method of investigation in which a scientist first makes observations and collects data and then formulates a hypothesis.

industrial society A society that uses sophisticated technology based on machinery powered by advanced fuels to produce material goods.

industrialization The use of machines and other sophisticated technology to satisfy the needs of society.

infanticide Deliberate abandonment or killing of infants 1 year of age or younger.

infant mortality rate The number of babies per thousand births in any year who die before reaching the age of 1.

instincts Fixed, complex, genetically based, unlearned behaviors that promote the survival of a species.

integrationist theories A variety of theories that argue that state organization is, on the whole, advantageous and beneficial to all members of a society.

intelligence The general ability to process information and adapt to the world.

intensive agriculture The cultivation of crops by preparing permanent fields year after year, often including the use of irrigation and fertilizers.

intensive horticulture A method of crop production by irrigating, fertilizing, hoeing, and terracing hillsides.

jajmani Hindi term for traditional caste-based economy in India.

jati Hindi term for caste.

jihad the Arabic word that refers to "struggle" against immorality or the destroyer of one's own religion and culture.

Jim Crow laws Laws that were used to segregate African Americans from white Americans in the southern United States prior to the Civil Rights era.

kindred Overlapping relatives from both sides of a family whom an individual recognizes as being part of his or her descent group.

kinesics The study of body motion and gestures used in nonverbal communication.

knowledge The storage and retrieval of learned information.

knuckle walking A quadrupedal form of locomotion using the hind limbs and the knuckles of the front limbs.

kula A form of reciprocal exchange involving ceremonial items in the Trobriand Islands.

lactase deficiency The inability to digest lactose, the sugar found in milk.

language A system of symbols with standard meanings through which members of a society communicate with one another.

law of supraposition States that in any succession of rock layers, the lowest rocks were deposited first and the upper rocks have been in place for progressively shorter periods. This assumption forms the basis of stratigraphic dating.

Levalloisian technique A refined type of percussion flaking used during the Middle Paleolithic.

levirate The rule that a widow is expected to marry one of her deceased husband's brothers.

life expectancy The average number of years a person can expect to live.

lineages Descent groups comprised of relatives, all of whom trace their relationship through consanguineal or affinal relations to an actual, commonly known ancestor.

linguistic anthropology The subdiscipline of anthropology dealing with the study of language.

linguistic relativism The theory that language molds habits of both cognition and perception.

linguistics The study of language.

logic-of-growth model The model and set of values that suggest that economic growth and technological developments will always represent progress for society.

Lower Paleolithic The earliest stage of the Stone Age characterized by the Oldowan and Acheulian stone tool industries, roughly spanning the period between 2.4 million and 200,000 years ago and including the tools produced by pre-*Homo sapiens* hominids.

mana The Polynesian term referring to supernaturally significant powers.

marginal environment An environment that is not suitable for intensive agriculture.

market economy A pattern of economic exchange based on the value of goods and services as determined by the worldwide supply and demand of these items.

marriage A social bond between two or more people sanctioned by society that involves economic cooperation and culturally approved sexual activity.

material culture Tangible products of human society.

matrilineal descent group A corporate descent group within which members calculate descent through the female line from a commonly known female ancestor.

matrilocal residence A rule of postmarital residence in which a man resides with his wife's parents.

medical anthropology The study of disease, health care systems, and theories of disease and curing in different societies.

megaliths Large stone complexes such as those found at Stonehenge that were used for burial chambers or astronomical observations. Such structures are the principal defining characteristic of the Megalithic, a Neolithic tradition found in western Europe and Britain.

meiosis The process by which gametes, which contain only half the number of chromosomes present in the original cell, are formed.

mercantilism A system in which the government regulates the economy of a state to ensure economic growth, a positive balance of trade, and the accumulation of wealth, usually gold and silver.

Mesolithic The Middle Stone Age of the Old World. A post-Pleistocene hunting-and-gathering adaptation characterized by tools suitable for broad-spectrum collecting and more intensive exploitation of localized resources. Corresponds in terms of general trends with the Archaic of the Americas.

microliths Small flakes of stone probably used for harpoon barbs and specialized cutting tools during the Mesolithic.

middens Artifacts often found in sites of ancient dumps or trash heaps.

Middle Paleolithic A stage within the Paleolithic characterized by innovations in tool technology, particularly the Levalloisian technique. Dated to approximately 200,000 to 40,000 years ago and associated with archaic *Homo sapiens.*

migration rate The rate at which people move into and out of a specific territory.

mitosis The process by which somatic cells divide to produce new cells with the full number of chromosomes present in the original cell.

modernization Economic, social, political, and religious change that is interrelated with modern industrial and technological developments.

modernization theory A theory that the forces associated with industrialization will eventually transform all societies into modern industrial states.

moieties Descent groups made up of clans or phratries that form two groups, dividing the entire society into equal divisions.

money A durable medium of exchange, based on a standard value, that is used to purchase goods and services.

monogamy A form of marriage that involves one spouse of each sex.

monopoly capitalism A form of capitalism dominated by oligopolies that can reduce free competition through the concentration of capital.

moral economy An economy that involves reciprocity and redistribution among close kin and other villagers in an agricultural society.

mores Stronger norms than folkways; violators are usually punished severely.

morphemes The smallest units of a language that convey meaning.

morphology The study of morphemes.

mortality The incidence of death in a society's population.

Mousterian A Middle Paleolithic stone tool tradition associated with Neandertals in Europe.

mujahedin The Arabic term for "holy warrior."

multiculturalism Policies adopted by governments to be inclusive to multiple ethnic groups within a society.

multinational corporation A transnational economic organization that operates in many different regions and is not necessarily associated with any one country.

multiregional evolutionary model The view that *Homo sapiens* evolved from *Homo erectus* concurrently in different regions of the world.

multivariate analysis A complex form of analysis that examines the distributions and interrelations among multiple variables or characteristics as, for example, patterns of disease, blood groups, and demographics in human populations.

mutation   A change in the genotype of an individual through the alteration of the chromosomes or DNA.

myth   Assumed knowledge about the universe, the natural and supernatural worlds, and humanity's place therein.

narratives   The oral or written representation of an event or a story.

nationalism   Strong sense of loyalty to the nation-state based on shared language, values, and culture.

nation-states   Political communities that have clearly defined territorial borders with centralized authority.

natural selection   A theory presented by Darwin and Wallace that nature or environmental circumstances determine which characteristics are essential for survival. Individuals with these characteristics survive and pass them on to their offspring.

negative reciprocity   The opposite of reciprocity, involving getting something for nothing.

Neolithic   Literally the "New Stone Age," it was first categorized by polished stone tools. Later it came to refer to the shift from food gathering to food production, as well as a suite of other characteristics and cultural features such as sedentary village life, animal husbandry, and pottery production. Though the term is still used, this package of characteristics is clearly not associated in many cultural settings.

net migration   The total movement of a population into and out of a territory.

nocturnal   Active during the night.

nonmaterial culture   Intangible products of human society, including values, beliefs, and knowledge.

norms   Shared rules that define how people are supposed to behave under certain circumstances.

nuclear family   A family that is composed of two parents and their immediate biological offspring or adopted children.

oath   The attempt to call on a supernatural source of power to sanction and bear witness to the truth or falseness of an individual's testimony.

office   A formal, corporate position of authority in a group or society.

Oldowan   The oldest stone tool industry, dating back 2.4 million years in Africa, characterized by simple hammerstones, choppers, and cutting tools.

oligopoly   Economic organizations that merge and dominate a society.

omnivorous   Possessing a diverse, generalized diet consisting of plants, fruits, nuts, seeds, insects, and animals.

one-drop rule   American social and legal custom of classifying anyone with one black ancestor, regardless of how far back, as black.

open instincts   Genetically based predispositions for behavior that are subject to modification through learning.

open peasant communities   Communities in which peasants are involved in producing some of their crops for the world market.

open society   A society in which social status can be achieved through individual efforts.

opposable thumb   A highly flexible thumb that can touch the tips of the fingers; it is characteristic of the human primate.

oracle   A person, sacred object, or shrine believed to have special or supernatural abilities.

paleoanthropology   The study of human evolution and the behavior of early human ancestors through the analysis of fossil remains, the ancient environment, and associated artifacts.

paleoecology   *Paleo*, meaning "old," and *ecology*, meaning "study of environment." The area of research focusing on the reconstruction and interpretation of ancient environments.

paleoethnobotany   The field of study that specializes in the interpretation of the relationship between plants and ancient human populations.

Paleolithic   The period of time characterized by the use of stone tools. Often divided on the basis of innovations in tool technology. (*See* Lower, Middle, and Upper Paleolithic.)

palynology   The study of pollen grains, the minute male reproductive part of plants. It may provide a means of reconstructing past environments and of relative dating.

parallel-cousin marriage   A system in which a person marries the offspring of parental siblings of the same sex; for example, a male marries his father's brother's daughter.

participant observation   The method by which the ethnologist learns the culture of the group being studied by participating in the group's daily activities.

pastoralists   Groups whose subsistence activities center on the care of domesticated animals.

patriarchal   Male-dominated societies.

patrilineal descent group   A corporate group made up of people who trace their descent through males from a common, known male ancestor.

patrilocal residence   A postmarital residence rule in which a newly married couple must reside with the husband's father.

patron-client ties   Informal contracts between people of unequal status.

peasants   People who cultivate land in the rural areas for their basic subsistence and pay tribute to elite groups.

percussion flaking The production of tools by striking a stone with a hammerstone or other strong object to remove chips or flakes.

peripheral societies Societies that exercise little control over their own economies and are dominated by the core industrial societies.

personality Stable patterns of thought, feeling, and action associated with a specific person.

phenotype The external, observable physical characteristics of an organism that result from the interaction of the organism's genetic make-up (the genotype) and its distinctive life history.

phoneme A basic unit of sound that distinguishes meaning in a language.

phones Units of sound in a language.

phonology The study of the sounds made in speech.

phratries Umbrella-like social groupings that consist of two or more clans.

plate tectonics The gradual movement of plates on the earth's surface as a result of geological processes, one consequence of which is the movement of continents or continental drift.

plural society A society made of different ethnic groups.

political power The ability to achieve personal ends in spite of opposition.

polyandry Marriage between a female and more than one male.

polygamy Marriage involving a spouse of one sex and two or more spouses of the opposite sex.

polygyny Marriage between one male and two or more females.

polymorphism A trait that exhibits variation within a species.

polytypic A species exhibiting physical variation in different regional populations.

population A group of organisms that interbreeds and occupies a given territory at the same time.

postmodernism A viewpoint that is critical of modern scientific and philosophic perspectives.

postorbital constriction A feature of *Homo erectus* in which the front portion of the skull is narrow and the forehead is low.

potassium-argon dating A numerical dating method based on the decay of an unstable isotope of potassium into the inert gas argon. It is used by paleoanthropologists to date volcanic rocks.

potlatch A form of redistributional exchange found among many northwest Native American groups.

pre-Clovis hypothesis The hypothesis that the initial settlement of the Americas took place prior to the arrival of the populations represented by Clovis spear points and associated artifacts.

priest A full-time, formally trained, male religious specialist.

priestess A full-time, formally trained, female religious specialist.

primary sector The sector of an industrial economy that is devoted to the extraction of natural resources.

primates A diverse order of mammals, including humans, monkeys, and apes, that share similar characteristics.

primatology The study of primates.

primogeniture An inheritance pattern in which land or other wealth is transmitted from generation to generation through the eldest male.

primordialist model A model of ethnicity emphasizing the fundamental determinants of language, descent, locale, or religion.

production The human process of producing goods, works, or services.

protolanguage The parent language for many ancient and modern languages.

proton magnetometer A sensor that can detect differences in the soil's magnetic field caused by buried features and artifacts.

proxemics The study of how people in different societies perceive and use space.

psychological anthropologist An anthropologist who studies the interrelationship between the individual and culture, or enculturation.

pull factors The incentives that lead to the migration of people of one area to another.

punctuated equilibrium The theory of evolution that species remain relatively stable for long periods, with major changes (punctuations) and new species arising very rapidly as a result of mutations or changes in selective pressures.

purdah Arabic term for seclusion of women from men in public.

push factors The conditions that force people to migrate from one area to another.

quadrupeds Species that use all four limbs for locomotion.

qualitative data Nonstatistical information that tends to be the most important aspect of ethnological research.

quantitative data Data that can be expressed as numbers, including census materials, dietary information, and income and household-composition data.

races Divisions within a species based on identifiable hereditary traits.

racism Beliefs and practices that advocate the superiority of certain races and the inferiority of others.

radiocarbon dating A numerical dating technique based on the decay of the unstable isotope carbon-14. Can be used to date organic material such as charcoal, wood fragments, or skeletal material as much as 80,000 years old.

random sample A nonobjective representative sample of people of various ages or statuses in a society.

real culture People's actual behaviors, as opposed to ideal culture.

recessive Designating a gene that is unexpressed when occurring in a heterozygous pair with a dominant form.

reciprocal economic system An exchange system based on transactional exchanges among family groups that allocate goods and services throughout the community.

reciprocity The exchange of goods and services among people.

redistributional economic exchange A system that involves the exchange of goods and services through a centralized organization.

regional symbiosis The pattern in which a particular society resides in an ecological habitat divided into different resource areas that become interdependent.

relative dating A variety of dating methods that can be used to establish the age of a fossil, artifact, or geological feature relative to another.

relative deprivation A group's awareness of the absence of economic opportunities and political rights for its members in contrast to those for other groups.

repatriation The return of human remains or cultural property to a descendant community or interest group.

replacement model The paleoanthropological theory that *Homo sapiens* evolved in one world area and then expanded, replacing regional populations of earlier hominids.

research design A proposal in which the objectives of a project are set out and the strategy for recovering the relevant data is outlined.

resistivity The measurement of variation in the electrical current passing between electrodes placed in the ground that indicates differences in the soil's moisture content, which in turn reflects buried ditches, foundations, or walls that retain moisture to varying degrees.

revitalization movement A social movement by people faced with dramatic changes that is designed to reinstitute traditional cultural values and beliefs.

revolution Sudden, dramatic, sweeping change that usually involves the overthrow of a government.

rising expectations The process in which a particular group begins to experience improvements in living conditions, stimulating the desire for further improvements.

rites of legitimation Rituals that reinforce the authority of a ruler.

rites of passage Rituals associated with the life cycle and the movement of people between different age-status levels.

rituals Repetitive behaviors that communicate sacred symbols to members of society.

role A set of expected behavior patterns, obligations, and norms attached to a particular status.

sagittal crest A bony ridge along the top of the skull.

Sapir–Whorf hypothesis A hypothesis that assumes a close relationship between language and culture; it claims that language defines people's experiences.

schema The mental codification of experience that includes a particular organized way of perceiving cognitively and responding to a complex situation or set of stimuli.

scientific method A method used to investigate the natural and social world that relies on critical thinking, logical reasoning, and skeptical thought.

secondary sector The sector of an industrial economy that is devoted to processing raw materials into manufactured goods.

Second World In the terminology of the Cold War, the industrial socialist societies in the global economy.

secularization The decline in the influence of religion in a society.

segmentary lineage system A type of political organization in which multiple descent groups form at different levels and serve political functions.

segregation The institutional separation of human populations or ethnic groups from one another.

semantics The meaning of words, phrases, and sentences.

semiperipheral societies Societies that have some degree of industrialization and some economic autonomy in the world economy but are not as advanced as core societies.

seriation A relative dating method based on the assumption that any particular artifact, attribute, or style will appear, gradually increase in popularity until it reaches a peak, and then progressively decrease.

services Elements of nonmaterial culture derived from cultural knowledge in the form of specialized skills that benefit others, such as giving spiritual comfort or medical care.

sex Biological and anatomical differences between males and females.

sexism Prejudice and discrimination against people based on their sex.

sexual dimorphism The presence of different characteristics in males and females of the same species.

shamans Part-time religious specialists who are believed to be linked with supernatural beings and powers.

signs Meanings that are directly associated with concrete physical phenomena.

silica gloss A distinctive residue left on stone blades used by people to harvest plants.

situational learning A type of learning in which organisms adjust their behavior in response to direct experience.

social grooming A social activity of many primates that involves removing ticks, fleas, dirt, and debris from one another. It may serve as an important means of maintaining sociality.

social-impact studies Research on the possible consequences of change in a society.

socialism An economic system in which the state owns the basic means of production.

social learning A type of learning in which an organism observes another organism's response to a stimulus and then adds that response to its own collection of behaviors.

social stratification Inequality of statuses in a society.

social structure The sum of the patterns of relationships in a society.

society A group of people who reside within a specific territory and share a common culture.

socioeconomic status A composite ranking (SES) based on various social and economic variables.

sociolinguistics The systematic study of language use in various social settings to explore the links between language and social behavior.

sodalities Groups based on kinship, age, gender, or other principles that provide for political organization.

somatic cells Body cells; unlike gametes (sex cells), they have the full number of chromosomes.

sorcery A conscious magical strategy, often using different objects, that is believed to bring about either harmful or beneficial results.

sororate The marriage rule requiring a widower to marry one of his deceased wife's sisters.

speciation The development of new species.

species Groups of organisms with similar physical characteristics that can potentially interbreed successfully.

state A form of political system with centralized bureaucratic institutions to establish power and authority over large populations in clearly defined territories.

status A recognized position that a person occupies in a society.

strata A group of equivalent statuses based on ranked divisions within a society.

stratigraphic dating A form of relative dating by assessing whether a layer of rock is recent or old.

structural linguistics An area of research that investigates the structure of language patterns as they presently exist.

subsistence patterns The means by which people obtain their food supply.

sumptuary rules Cultural norms and practices that are used to differentiate higher-status groups from lower-status groups.

survey An examination of a particular area, region, or country to locate archaeological sites or fossil localities.

sustainability model A model that emphasizes the conservation and preservation of environmental resources for future generations.

symbolic anthropology The study of culture through the interpretation of a society's symbols, values, beliefs, and ethos.

symbolic learning The ability to use and understand symbols.

symbols Arbitrary units of meaning that can stand for different concrete or abstract phenomena.

syncretism The blending of indigenous religious beliefs and practices with those introduced by outside groups.

syntax Rules for phrase and sentence construction in a language.

tabu The Polynesian term for a prohibition of specific behaviors.

taphonomy The study of the variety of natural and behavioral processes that led to the formation of a fossil locality. This may include traces of the activities of early human ancestors, as well as natural agencies such as erosion, decay, and animal activities.

taxonomy The science of classification, which provides scientists a convenient way of referring to, and comparing, living and extinct organisms.

technology All the human techniques and methods of reaching a specific goal in subsistence or in modifying or controlling the natural environment.

terrestrial Living on land.

tertiary sector The sector of an industrial economy devoted to services.

theocracy A society in which people are believed to rule not because of their worldly wealth and power but because of their place in the moral and sacred order.

theories General, overarching statements that explain hypotheses about natural or social phenomena.

therapeutic pluralism Health care that involves the use of traditional and modern healing practices and beliefs.

Third World In the terminology of the Cold War, premodern, nonindustrialized societies in the global economy.

totem   A mythical ancestor, usually a plant or animal, that symbolizes a particular group.

trace element analysis   The study of elements in artifacts that may provide a distinctive signature of the artifacts' origin.

transitional forms   The hominid fossils that are either advanced *Homo erectus* or early *Homo sapiens.*

tribe   Complex societies having political institutions that unite horticulturalist or pastoralist groups into a political system.

tribute   The payment of labor, taxes, or other services from one group to another.

tributary form   The type of agricultural society that uses tribute to extract labor, taxes, or other services from peasants.

ultimogeniture   An inheritance system in which property and land are passed to the youngest son.

underdeveloped society   A country with a low gross national product.

uniformitarianism   The geological view that the earth's geological features are the result of gradual, natural processes that can still be observed.

unilineal descent group   A lineage group that traces its descent through only one side of the lineage or through only one sex.

unilineal evolution   The belief, widespread during the nineteenth century, that societies were evolving in a single direction toward complexity and industrial progress.

universalistic religions   Religions whose spiritual messages apply to all of humanity.

Upper Paleolithic   The late Stone Age, dating back to about 40,000 years ago.

use-wear   Studies of the damage or traces of use present on tools. Such traces may provide indications of how a tool was used.

values   Standards by which a society defines what is desirable and undesirable.

variable   Specific characteristics or phenomena that vary from case to case, such as temperature, age, size, color, and the like.

vegiculture   The propagation of plants by selectively dividing and replanting living plants.

warfare   Armed combat among territorial or political communities.

witchcraft   The innate, unconscious psychic ability of some people, which is believed to bring about harmful effects.

world-systems theory   The view that core societies dominate peripheral and semiperipheral societies to create a global economic system.

worldview   An integrated system of beliefs and cosmologies about natural and supernatural realities.

zero population growth   The level of reproduction that maintains population at a steady state.

References

ABERLE, DAVID F. 1961. "'Arctic Hysteria' and Latah in Mongolia." In Yehudi Cohen, ed., *Social Structure and Personality. A Casebook.* New York: Holt, Rinehart and Winston.

———. 1966. *The Peyote Religion Among the Navajo.* New York: Wenner-Gren Foundation for Anthropological Research, Inc.

ABU-LUGHOD, JANET. 1961. "Migrant Adjustment to City Life: The Egyptian Case." *The American Journal of Sociology* 62:22–32.

ABU-LUGHOD, LILA. 1987. *Veiled Sentiments: Honor and Poetry in a Bedouin Society.* Berkeley: University of California Press.

ADAMS, ROBERT MCC. 1966. *The Evolution of Urban Society.* Chicago: Aldine.

———. 1974. "Anthropological Perspectives on Ancient Trade." *Current Anthropology* 15(3):239–58.

———. 1981. *Heartland of Cities.* Chicago: Aldine.

ADAMS, WILLI PAUL. 1993. *The German Americans: An Ethnic Experience,* L. J. Rippley and Eberhard Reichmann, trans. Indianapolis, IN: Indiana University–Purdue University at Indianapolis.

ADOVASIO, JAMES M. and JAKE PAGE. 2002. *The First Americans: In Pursuit of Archaeology's Greatest Mystery.* Random House: New York, NY.

AGAR, MICHAEL. 1973. *Ripping and Running.* New York: Academic Press.

———. 1974. *Cognition and Ethnography.* Minneapolis: Burgess.

———. 1980. *The Professional Stranger: An Informal Introduction to Ethnography.* New York: Academic Press.

AIKENS, C. MELVIN, and TAKAYASU HIGUCHI. 1981. *Prehistory of Japan.* New York: Academic Press.

ALBA, RICHARD. 1985. *Italian Americans: Into the Twilight of Ethnicity.* Englewood Cliffs, NJ: Prentice Hall.

ALGAZE, GUILLERMO. 1993. "Expansionary Dynamics of Some Early Pristine States." *American Anthropologist* 95(2): 304–33.

AL-THAKEB, FAHAD. 1981, July–December. "Size and Composition of the Arab Family: Census and Survey Data." *International Journal of Sociology of the Family* 2:171–78.

———. 1985. "The Arab Family and Modernity: Evidence from Kuwait." *Current Anthropology* 25(5):575–580.

ALVAREZ, L. W., et al. 1980. "Extraterrestrial Cause for the Cretaceous-Tertiary Extinction." *Science* 208:1095–1108.

ALVERSON, HOYT. 1994. *Semantics and Experience: Universal Metaphors of Time in English, Mandarin, Hindi, and Sesotho.* Baltimore, MD: Johns Hopkins University Press.

AMERICAN ANTHROPOLOGICAL ASSOCIATION. [1976] 1983. *Professional Ethics: Statements and Procedures of the American Anthropological Association.* Washington, DC: American Anthropological Association.

ANDERSON, BENEDICT. 1991. *Imagined Communities: Reflections on the Origin and Spread of Nationalism.* London: Verso.

ANDERSON, DAVID G., and VIRGINIA HORAK, eds. 1995. *Archaeological Site File Management: A Southeastern Perspective.* Readings in Archaeological Resource Protection Series No. 3. Atlanta, GA: Interagency Archaeological Service Division.

ANDERSON, RICHARD L. 1989. *Art in Small-Scale Societies.* Upper Saddle River, NJ: Prentice Hall.

ANDRESEN, JOHN M., BRIAN F. BYRD, MARK D. ELSON, RANDALL H. MCGUIRE, RUBEN G. MENDOZA, EDWARD STASKI, and J. PETER WHITE. 1981. "The Deer Hunters: Star Carr Reconsidered." *World Archaeology* 13(1):31–46.

ANDREWS, PETER, and LAWRENCE MARTIN. 1987. "Cladistic Relationships of Extant and Fossil Hominoid Primates." *Journal of Human Evolution* 16:101–18.

ANUMAN-RAJADHON, PHYA. 1961. "Thai Traditional Salutation." *Journal of the Siam Society* 49(2):161–71.

ARDEN, HARVEY. 1989. "Who Owns Our Past?" *National Geographic* 75(3):378.

ARDREY, ROBERT. 1961. *African Genesis.* New York: Dell.

AUEL, JEAN M. 1981. *The Clan of the Cave Bear.* New York: Bantam.

ASWAD, BARBARA. 2003. "Arab Americans." In Raymond Scupin, ed., *Race and Ethnicity: An Anthropological Focus on the U.S. and the World.* Upper Saddle River, NJ: Prentice Hall.

ATRAN, SCOTT. 1990. *Cognitive Foundations of Natural History.* Cambridge: Cambridge University Press.

———. 1998. "Folk Biology and the Anthropology of Science: Cognitive Universals and Cultural Particulars." *Behavioral and Brain Sciences* 21(4): 547–609.

BACHOFEN, JOHANN JAKOB. [1861] 1992. *Das Mutterecht.* In Ralph Manheim, trans., *Myth, Religion and Mother Right: Selected Writings of J. J. Bachofen.* Princeton: Princeton University Press.

BAGISH, HENRY H. 1981. *Confessions of a Former Cultural Relativist.* Santa Barbara, CA: Santa Barbara City College Publications.

BAILEY, R. C., G. HEAD, M. JENIKE, B. OWN, T. RECHTMAN, and E. ZECHENTER. 1989. "Hunting and Gathering in Tropical Rain Forests: Is It Possible?" *American Anthropologist* 91(1):59–82.

BAKER, LESLIE. 1989. "Cultural Survival Imports: Marketing the Rain Forest." *Cultural Survival Quarterly* 13(3):64–67.

BALIKCI, ASEN. 1970. *The Netsilik Eskimo.* Garden City, NY: Natural History Press.

BAMBERGER, JOAN. 1974. "The Myth of Matriarchy: Why Men Rule in Primitive Society." In Michelle Zimbalist Rosaldo and Louise Lamphere, eds., *Women,*

Culture, and Society. Stanford, CA: Stanford University Press.

BANKS, MARCUS. 1996. *Ethnicity: Anthropological Constructions.* London: Routledge.

BANTON, MICHAEL. 1998. *Racial Theories.* Cambridge: Cambridge University Press.

BARASH, DAVID P. 1987. *The Hare and the Tortoise: Culture, Biology, and Human Nature.* New York: Penguin.

BARBER, BENJAMIN R. 2001. *Jihad vs. McWorld: Terrorism's Challenge to Democracy.* New York: Ballantine Books.

BARKOW, J. H., L. COSMIDES, and J. TOOBY, eds. 1992. *The Adapted Mind: Evolutionary Psychology and the Generation of Culture.* New York: Oxford University Press.

BARNOUW, VICTOR. 1985. *Culture and Personality,* 4th ed. Homewood, IL: Dorsey Press.

BARRETT, LEONARD E. 1977. *Rastafarians: Sounds of Cultural Dissonance.* Boston: Beacon Press.

BARRETT, RICHARD A. 1984. *Culture and Conduct: An Excursion in Anthropology.* Belmont, CA: Wadsworth.

BARRET, RICHARD E., and FANG LI. 1999. *Modern China.* New York: McGraw-Hill.

BARTH, FREDERICK. 1961. *Nomads of South Persia: The Basseri Tribe of the Khamseh Confederacy.* Boston: Little, Brown.

———. 1969. *Ethnic Groups and Boundaries.* Boston: Little, Brown.

———. 1975. *Ritual and Knowledge Among the Baktaman of New Guinea.* Oslo: Universitets Forlaget; New Haven, CT: Yale University Press.

BARTON, R. F. 1919. "Ifugao Law." *Publications in American Archeology and Ethnology,* Vol. 15, No. 1, pp. 92–109. Berkeley: University of California Press.

BASCOM, WILLIAM. 1969. *The Yoruba of Southwestern Nigeria.* New York: Holt, Rinehart and Winston.

BASS, GEORGE FLETCHER. 1963. "Underwater Archaeology: Key to History's Warehouse." *National Geographic* 124(1): 138–56.

———. 1973. *Archaeology Beneath the Sea.* New York: Harper & Row.

BASSIS, MICHAEL S., RICHARD J. GELLES, and ANN LEVINE. 1991. *Sociology: An Introduction,* 4th ed. New York: McGraw-Hill.

BATES, DANIEL G., and AMAL RASSAM. 2000. *Peoples and Cultures of the Middle East,* 2nd ed. Upper Saddle River, NJ: Prentice Hall.

BEALS, K. L. 1972. "Head Form and Climatic Stress." *American Journal of Physical Anthropology* 37:85–92.

BEARD, K. C., M. F. TEAFORD, and A. WALKER. 1986. "New Wrist Bones of *Proconsul africanus* and *P. nyanzae* from Rusinga Island, Kenya." *Folia Primatology* 47:97–118.

BEAUDRY, MARY C., ed. 1988. *Documentary Archaeology in the New World.* Cambridge: Cambridge University Press.

BECK, LOIS. 1986. *The Qashqa'i of Iran.* New Haven, CT: Yale University Press.

BECK, LOIS, and NIKKI KEDDIE, eds. 1978. *Women in the Muslim World.* Cambridge, MA: Harvard University Press.

BEEMAN, WILLIAM O. 1986. *Language, Status, and Power in Iran.* Bloomington: Indiana University Press.

BEFU, HARUMI. 1971. *Japan: An Anthropological Introduction.* San Francisco: Chandler.

———. 1980. "A Critique of the Group Model of Japanese Society." *Social Analysis* 5(6):205–25.

BELL, DANIEL. 1973. *The Coming of the Post-Industrial Society: A Venture into Social Forecasting.* New York: Basic Books.

BELLAH, R., R. MADSEN, W. SULLIVAN, A. SWIDLER, and S. M. TIPTON. 1985. *Habits of the Heart: Individualism and Commitment in American Life.* New York: Harper & Row.

BENEDICT, RUTH. 1928. "Psychological Types in the Cultures of the Southwest." Reprinted in Margaret Mead, ed., *An Anthropologist at Work: Writings of Ruth Benedict.* Boston: Houghton Mifflin.

———. 1934. *Patterns of Culture.* Boston: Houghton Mifflin.

———. 1946. *The Chrysanthemum and the Sword.* Boston: Houghton Mifflin.

BENNETT, JOHN W. 1987. "Anthropology and the Emerging World Order: The Paradigm of Culture in an Age of Interdependence." In Kenneth Moore, ed., *Waymarks: The Notre Dame Inaugural Lectures in Anthropology.* Notre Dame, IN: University of Notre Dame Press.

BENSON, JANET. 2003. "Asian Americans." In Raymond Scupin, ed., *Race and Ethnicity: An Anthropological Focus on the U.S. and the World.* Upper Saddle River, NJ: Prentice Hall.

BENTLEY, JEFFERY W., and GONZALO RODRÍGUEZ. 2001. "Honduran Folk Entomology." *Current Anthropology* 42(2): 285–300.

BENTON, M. J. 1986. "More Than One Event in the Late Triassic Mass Extinction." *Nature* 321:857–61.

BERDAN, FRANCES F. 1982. *The Aztecs of Central Mexico: An Imperial Society.* New York: Holt, Rinehart and Winston.

BERLIN, BRENT, and PAUL KAY. 1969. *Basic Color Terms: Their Universality and Evolution.* Berkeley: University of California Press.

BERNARD, JESSIE. 1981. *The Female World.* New York: Free Press.

BERNARD, RUSSELL H. 1992. "Preserving Language Diversity." *Human Organization* 51(1):82–89.

BERNARD, RUSSELL H., and JESÚS SALINAS PEDRAZA. 1989. *Native Ethnography: A Mexican Indian Describes His Culture.* Newbury Park, CA: Sage.

BERNARD, R. H., PERTTI PELTO, O. WERNER, J. BOSTER, K. A. ROMNEY, A. JOHNSON, C. EMER, and A. KASAKOTT. 1986. "The Construction of Primary Data in Cultural Anthropology." *Current Anthropology* 27(4):382–96.

BICKERTON, DEREK. 1985. *Roots of Language.* Ann Arbor, MI: Karoma Publishing.

———. 1999. *Language and Human Behavior.* Seattle: University of Washington Press.

BIGLER, ELLEN. 2003. "Hispanic Americans/ Latinos." In Raymond Scupin, ed., *Race and Ethnicity: An Anthropological Focus on the U.S. and the World.* Upper Saddle River, NJ: Prentice Hall.

BINFORD, LEWIS. 1968. "Post-Pleistocene Adaptations." In Lewis R. Binford and Sally Binford, eds., *New Perspectives in Archaeology,* pp. 313–41. New York: Academic Press.

———. 1985. "Human Ancestors: Changing Views of Their Behavior." *Journal of Anthropological Archaeology* 1:5–31.

BINFORD, LEWIS R., and SALLY BINFORD. 1966. "A Preliminary Analysis of Functional Variability in the Mousterian of Levallois Facies." *American Anthropologist* 68(2):238–95.

BINFORD, LEWIS R., and CHUAN KUN HO. 1985. "Taphonomy at a Distance: Zhoukoudian, the Cave Home of Beijing Man?" *Current Anthropology* 26:413–42.

BIRDSELL, JOSEPH B. 1968. "Some Predictions for the Pleistocene Based on Equilibrium Systems Among Recent Hunter-Gatherers." In Richard B. Lee and Irven Devore, eds., *Man the Hunter*. Chicago: Aldine.

———. 1981. *Human Evolution*, 3rd ed. Boston: Houghton Mifflin.

BIRDWHISTLE, RAY. 1970. *Kinesics and Context*. Philadelphia: University of Pennsylvania Press.

BISCHOF, N. 1972. "The Biological Foundations of the Incest Taboo." *Social Science Information* 2:7–36.

BLAKELY, ROBERT L., and JUDITH M. HARRINGTON. 1997. *Bones in the Basement: Postmortem Racism in Nineteenth-Century Medical Training*. Washington, DC: Smithsonian Institution Press.

BLICK, JEFFREY P. 1988. "Genocidal Warfare in Tribal Societies as a Result of European-Induced Culture Conflict." *Man* 23:654–70.

BLINDERMAN, C. 1986. *The Piltdown Inquest*. Buffalo, NY: Prometheus Books.

BLOCH, MAURICE. 1977. "The Past and the Present." *Man* 12:278–92.

———. 1983. *Marxism and Anthropology*. Oxford: Oxford University Press.

———. 1985. "From Cognition to Ideology." In R. Fardon, ed., *Power and Knowledge: Anthropological and Sociological Approaches*. Edinburgh: Scottish Academic Press.

BLURTON JONES, NICHOLAS. 1986. "Bushman Birth Spacing: A Test for Optimal Intervals." *Ethology and Sociobiology* 7(2):91–106.

———. 1987. "Bushman Birth Spacing: Direct Tests of Some Simple Predictions." *Ethology and Sociobiology* 8(3): 183–204.

BOAS, FRANZ. 1930. *The Religion of the Kwakiutl*, Vol. 10, Part II. Contributions to Anthropology. New York: Columbia University.

———. [1940] 1966. *Race, Language, and Culture*. New York: Free Press.

BOAZ, NOEL T., and ALAN J. ALMQUIST. 1997. *Biological Anthropology: A Synthetic Approach to Human Evolution*. Upper Saddle River, NJ: Prentice Hall.

BODLEY, JOHN H. 1985. *Anthropology and Contemporary Human Problems*, 2nd ed. Mountain View, CA: Mayfield.

———. 1990. *Victims of Progress*, 3rd ed. Mountain View, CA: Mayfield.

BOEHM, CHRISTOPHER. 1993. "Egalitarian Behavior and Reverse Dominance Hierarchy." *Current Anthropology* 34(3): 227–54.

———. 1999. *Hierarchy in the Forest: The Evolution of Egalitarian Behavior*. Cambridge, MA: Harvard University Press.

BOGIN, B. A. 1978. "Seasonal Pattern in the Rate of Growth in Height of Children Living in Guatemala." *American Journal of Physical Anthropology* 49:205–10.

BOHANNON, PAUL, and GEORGE DALTON. 1962. *Markets in Africa*. Evanston, IL: Northwestern University Press.

BORDES, FRANÇOIS. 1968. *The Old Stone Age*. New York: McGraw-Hill.

BOSERUP, ESTER. 1965. *The Conditions of Agricultural Growth: The Economics of Agrarian Change Under Population Pressure*. Chicago: Aldine.

———. 1970. *Women's Role in Economic Development*. London: Allen & Unwin.

BOSTER, JAMES. 1987. "Agreement Between Biological Classification Systems Is Not Dependent on Cultural Transmission." *American Anthropologist* 89(4):914–19.

BOURDIEU, PIERRE. 1977. *Outline of a Theory of Practice*. Cambridge: Cambridge University Press.

BOURGOIS, PHILIPPE. 1989a. "Crack in Spanish Harlem: Culture and Economy in the Inner City." *Anthropology Today* 5(4):6–11.

———. 1989b. *Ethnicity at Work: Divided Labor on a Central American Banana Plantation*. Baltimore: Johns Hopkins University Press.

———. 1996. *In Search of Respect: Selling Crack in El Barrio*. Cambridge, England: Cambridge University Press.

BOURGUIGNON, ERIKA. 1979. *Psychological Anthropology: An Introduction to Human Nature and Cultural Differences*. New York: Holt, Rinehart and Winston.

BOWER, BRUCE. 1990. "Biographies Etched in Bone." *Science News* 138:106–8.

———. 1991. "Fossil Finds Expand Early Hominid Anatomy." *Science News* 139:182.

BOYER, PASCAL. 1994. "Cognitive Constraints on Cultural Representations: Natural Ontologies and Religious Ideas." In L. A. Hirschfeld and S. Gelman, eds., *Mapping the Mind: Domain-Specificity in Culture and Cognition*. New York: Cambridge University Press.

———. 1998. "Cognitive Tracks of Cultural Inheritance: How Evolved Intuitive Ontology Governs Cultural Transmission." *American Anthropologist* 100:876–889.

———. 2001. *Religion Explained: The Evolutionary Origins of Religious Thought*. New York: Basic Books.

BRACE, C. L. 1964. "The Fate of the 'Classic' Neanderthals: A Consideration of Hominid Catastrophism." *Current Anthropology* 5:3–43.

———. 1967. *The Stages of Human Evolution: Human and Cultural Origins*. Englewood Cliffs, NJ: Prentice Hall.

———. 1989. "Medieval Thinking and the Paradigms of Paleoanthropology." *American Anthropologist* 91(2):442–46.

BRACE, C. L., and M. F. A. MONTAGU. 1965. *Man's Evolution: An Introduction to Physical Evolution*. New York: Macmillan.

BRAIDWOOD, ROBERT J. 1960. "The Agricultural Revolution." *Scientific American* 203:130–41.

BRILL, R. H. 1964. "Applications of Fission-Track Dating to Historic and Prehistoric Glasses." *Archaeometry* 7:51–57.

BROKENSHA, DAVID, and CHARLES ERASMUS. 1969. "African 'Peasants' and Community Development." In David Brokensha and Marion Pearsall, eds., *The Anthropology of Development in Sub-Saharan Africa*. Society for Applied Anthropology Monograph No. 10, pp. 85–100.

BROOKE, JAMES. 1993. "Brazil's Outrage Intensifies as Toll in Massacre Hits 73." *The New York Times*, August 23, p. A6.

BROOM, ROBERT. 1938. "The Pleistocene Anthropoid Apes of South Africa." *Nature* 142:377–79.

———. 1949. "Another New Type of Fossil Ape Man." *Nature* 163:57.

BROWN, CECIL H. 1984. *Language and Living Things: Uniformities in Classification and Naming*. New Brunswick, NJ: Rutgers University Press.

BROWN, DONALD E. 1976. *Principles of Social Structure: Southeast Asia*. London: Duckworth Press.

———. 1991. *Human Universals*. New York: McGraw-Hill.

————. 2003. "Ethnicity and Ethnocentrism: Are They Natural?" In Raymond Scupin, ed., *Race and Ethnicity: An Anthropological Focus on the U.S. and the World.* Upper Saddle River, NJ: Prentice Hall.

BROWN, JAMES A., ed. 1971. "Approaches to the Social Dimensions of Mortuary Practices." *Memoirs of the Society for American Archaeology* No. 25.

BROWN, JUDITH K. 1970a. "Economic Organization and the Position of Women Among the Iroquois." *Ethnohistory* 17: 151–67.

————. 1970b. "A Note on the Division of Labor by Sex." *American Anthropologist* 72:1073–78.

BROWN, KAREN MCCARTHY. 1992. *Mama Lola: A Voodoo Priestess in Brooklyn.* Comparative Studies in Religion and Society, No. 4. Berkeley: University of California Press.

BROWN, LESTER R. 1988. "The Vulnerability of Oil-Based Farming." *World Watch,* March/April. Reprinted in Robert Jackson, ed., *Global Issues 90/91.* Sluice Dock, Guilford, CT: Dushkin Publishing Group, 1990.

BROWN, MICHAEL H. 1990. *The Search for Eve.* New York: HarperCollins.

BROWN, SUSAN LOVE. 2003. "African Americans." In Raymond Scupin, ed., *Race and Ethnicity: An Anthropological Focus on the U.S. and the World.* Upper Saddle River, NJ: Prentice Hall.

BROWN, T. M., and K. D. ROSE. 1987. "Patterns of Dental Evolution in Early Eocene Anaptomorphine Commomyodael from the Bighorn Basin, Wyoming." *Journal of Paleontology* 61:1–62.

BRUES, A. M. 1977. *People and Races.* New York: Macmillan.

BRUMFIEL, ELIZABETH. 1983. "Aztec State Making: Ecology, Structure, and the Origin of the State." *American Anthropologist* 85(2):261–84.

————. 1991. "Weaving and Cooking: Women's Production in Aztec Mexico." In Joan M. Gero and Margaret Conkey, eds., *Engendering Archaeology: Women and Prehistory,* pp. 224–51. Cambridge: Blackwell.

BURCH, ERNEST J., JR. 1970. "Marriage and Divorce Among the North Alaskan Eskimos." In Paul Bohannon, ed., *Divorce and After,* pp. 152–81. Garden City, NY: Doubleday.

BUTZER, KARL W. 1984. "Long-Term Nile Flood Variation and Political Discontinuities in Pharaonic Egypt." In J. Desmond Clark and Steven A. Brandt, eds., *From Hunters to Farmers: The Causes and Consequences of Food Production in Egypt,* pp. 102–12. Berkeley: University of California Press.

BYARD, P. J. 1981. "Quantitative Genetics of Human Skin Color." *Yearbook of Physical Anthropology* 24:123–37.

CALLENDER, CHARLES, and L. KOCHEMS. 1983. "The North-American Berdache." *Current Anthropology* 24:443–70.

CAMPBELL, BERNARD G. 1983. *Human Ecology: The Story of Our Place in Nature from Prehistory to the Present.* Chicago: Aldine.

————. 1987. *Humankind Emerging,* 5th ed. Glenview, IL: Scott, Foresman.

CANN, R. L., W. M. BROWN, and A. C. WILSON. 1987. "Mitochondrial DNA and Human Evolution." *Nature* 325:31–36.

CARLISLE, R., ed. 1988. *Americans Before Columbus: Perspectives on the Archaeology of the First Americans.* Pittsburgh: University of Pittsburgh Press.

CARLISLE, R. C., and J. M. ADAVASIO. 1982. *Collected Papers on the Archaeology of Meadowcroft Rockshelter and the Cross Creek Drainage.* Pittsburgh: Department of Anthropology, University of Pittsburgh.

CARNEIRO, ROBERT. 1961. "Slash and Burn Cultivation Among the Kuikura and Its Implications for Cultural Development in the Amazon Basin." In Johannes Wilbert, ed., *The Evolution of Horticultural Systems in Native South America, Causes and Consequences: A Symposium. Anthropologica,* Supplement Publication No. 2, pp. 47–67.

————. 1967. "On the Relationship Between Size of Population and Complexity of Social Organization." *Southwestern Journal of Anthropology* 23: 234–43.

————. 1970, August 21. "A Theory of the Origin of the 'State.'" *Science,* pp. 733–38.

————. 1988. "Indians of the Amazonian Forest." In Julie Sloan Denslow and Christine Padoch, eds., *People of the Tropical Rain Forests.* Berkeley: University of California Press.

CARR, K. W., J. M. ADOVASIO, and D. R. PEDLER. 1996. "Paleoindian Populations in Trans-Applachia: the View from Pennsylvania." Paper Presented at the Integrating Appalachian Archaeology Conference. Albany: New York State Museum.

CARTER, GEORGE F. 1988. "Cultural Historical Diffusion." In Peter J. Hugill and Bruce D. Dickson, eds., *The Transfer and Transformation of Ideas and Material Culture.* College Station: Texas A&M University Press.

CATON, STEVEN C. 1986. "Salam Tahiyah: Greetings from the Highlands of Yemen." *American Ethnologist* 13(2):290–308.

CHAGNON, NAPOLEON A. 1974. *Studying the Yanomamö.* New York: Holt, Rinehart and Winston.

————. 1997. *Yanomamö,* 5th ed. Fort Worth, TX: Harcourt Brace College Publishers.

————. 2000. "Manipulating Kinship Rules: A Form of Male Yanomamö Reproductive Competition." In Lee Cronk, Napoleon Chagnon, and William Irons, eds., *Adaptation and Human Behavior: An Anthropological Perspective.* New York: Aldine De Gruyter.

CHAGNON, NAPOLEON, and RAYMOND HAMES. 1979. "Protein Deficiency and Tribal Warfare in Amazonia: New Data." *Science* 20(3):910–13.

CHAGNON, NAPOLEON, and WILLIAM IRONS. 1979. *Evolutionary Biology and Human Social Behavior.* North Scituate, MA: Duxbury Press.

CHAMBERS, ERVE. 1985. *Applied Anthropology: A Practical Guide.* Englewood Cliffs, NJ: Prentice Hall.

CHANCE, NORMAN. 1984. *China's Urban Villagers: Life in a Beijing Commune.* New York: Holt, Rinehart and Winston.

CHANG, KWANG-CHIH. 1970. "The Beginnings of Agriculture in the Far East." *Antiquity* 44(175):175–85.

————. 1975. "From Archaeology to History: The Neolithic Foundations of Chinese Civilization." In Chang Chunshu, ed., *The Making of China: Main Themes in Premodern Chinese History,* pp. 38–45. Englewood Cliffs, NJ: Prentice Hall.

————. 1976. *Early Chinese Civilization: Anthropological Perspectives.* Cambridge, MA: Harvard University Press.

————. 1986. *The Archaeology of Ancient China,* 4th ed. New Haven, CT: Yale University Press.

CHAPMAN, ROBERT, IAN KINNES, and KLAVS RANDSBORG, eds. 1981. *The Archaeology of Death*. Cambridge: Cambridge University Press.

CHASE, P. G., and H. L. DIBBLE. 1987. "Middle Paleolithic Symbolism: A Review of Current Evidence and Interpretations." *Journal of Anthropological Archaeology* 6:263–93.

CHILDE, V. GORDON. 1936. *Man Makes Himself*. London: Watts.

———. 1950. "The Urban Revolution." *Town Planning Review*, 21:3–17.

———. 1952. *New Light on the Most Ancient East*. London: Routledge & Kegan Paul.

CHIROT, DANIEL. 1986. *Social Change in the Modern Era*. San Diego, CA: Harcourt Brace Jovanovich.

CHOMSKY, NOAM. 1980. *Rules and Representation*. New York: Columbia University Press.

———. 1995. *The Minimalist Program*. Cambridge, MA: MIT Press.

CHRISTALLER, WALTER. 1933. *Die Zentralen Orte in Suddeuyschland*. Jena, Germany: Karl Zeiss.

CIOCHON, R. L., and R. CORRUCCINI, eds. 1983. *New Interpretations of Ape and Human Ancestry*. New York: Plenum Press.

CIOCHON, R. L., J. OLSEN, and J. JAMES. 1990. *Other Origins: The Search for the Giant Ape in Human Prehistory*. New York: Bantam Books.

CLAESSON, H. J. M., P. VAN DE VELDE, and E. M. SMITH. 1985. *Development and Decline: The Evolution of Sociopolitical Organization*. South Hadley, MA: Bergin & Garvey.

CLARK, GRAHAME, and STUART PIGGOTT. 1965. *Prehistoric Societies*. New York: Knopf.

CLARK, J. DESMOND. 1970. *The Prehistory of Africa*. New York: Praeger.

CLARK, J. DESMOND. 1979. *Mesolithic Prelude*. Edinburgh: Edinburgh University Press.

CLARK, J. DESMOND, and STEVEN A. BRANDT. 1984. *From Hunters to Farmers: The Causes and Consequences of Food Production in Africa*. Berkeley: University of California Press.

CLARK, J. DESMOND, and J. W. K. HARRIS. 1985. "Fire and Its Roles in Early Hominid Lifeways." *African Archaeological Review* 3:3–27.

CLAYRE, ALASDAIR. 1985. *The Heart of the Dragon*. Boston: Houghton Mifflin.

CLEMENS, W. A. 1974. "Purgatorius, an Early Paromomyid Primate Mammalia." *Science* 184:903–6.

CLIFFORD, JAMES. 1983. "On Ethnographic Authority." *Representations* 1:118–146.

COE, MICHAEL. 1977. *Mexico,* 2nd ed. New York: Praeger.

COE, MICHAEL, DEAN SNOW, and ELIZABETH BENSON. 1986. *Atlas of Ancient America*. New York: Facts on File.

COHEN, ABNER. 1969. *Custom and Politics in Urban Africa*. Berkeley: University of California Press.

———. 1974. *Urban Ethnicity*. London: Tavistock.

COHEN, ANTHONY. 1996. "Personal Nationalism: A Scottish View of Some Rites, Rights, and Wrongs." *American Ethnologist* 23(4):802–15.

COHEN, MARK NATHAN. 1977. *The Food Crisis in Prehistory*. New Haven, CT: Yale University Press.

———. 1994. "Demographic Expansion: Causes and Consequences." In Tim Ingold, ed., *Companion Encyclopedia of Anthropology*. New York: Routledge.

COHEN, MARK NATHAN, and GEORGE J. ARMELAGOS. 1984. *Paleopathology at the Origins of Agriculture*. New York: Academic Press.

COHEN, RONALD. 1978. "Introduction." In R. Cohen and E. Service, eds., *Origins of the State: The Anthropology of Political Evolution*. Philadelphia: Institute for the Study of Human Issues.

COHEN, RONALD, and ELMAN SERVICE, eds. 1978. *Origins of the State: The Anthropology of Political Evolution*. Philadelphia: Institute for the Study of Human Issues.

COLE, DONALD POWELL. 1984. *Nomads of the Nomads: The Al-Murrah Bedouin of the Empty Quarter*. Prospect Heights, IL: Waveland Press.

COLE, MICHAEL, and SYLVIA SCRIBNER. 1974. *Culture and Thought: A Psychological Introduction*. New York: Wiley.

COLLIER, JANE FISHBURNE. 1988. *Marriage and Inequality in Classless Societies*. Stanford, CA: Stanford University Press.

COMAROFF, JEAN. 1985. *Body of Power, Spirit of Resistance*. Chicago. University of Chicago Press.

CONNAH, GRAHAM. 1987. *African Civilizations: Precolonial Cities and States in Tropical Africa: An Archaeological Perspective*. Cambridge: Cambridge University Press.

CONNELL, DAN. 1987. "The Next African Famine." *Dollars and Sense*. Reprinted in Robert Jackson, 1990. *Global Issues 90/91*, 6th ed. Sluice Dock, Guilford, CT: Dushkin Publishing Group.

———. 1997. *Reconstructing Human Origins: A Modern Synthesis*. New York: Norton Press.

CONROY, GLENN C. 1990. *Primate Evolution*. New York: W. W. Norton.

CONROY, GLENN C., and MICHAEL VANIER. 1990. "Endocranial Features of *Australopithecus africanus* Revealed by 2- and 3-D Computer Tomography." *Science* 247:839–41.

CORNELL, STEPHAN, and DOUGLAS HARTMANN. 1998. *Ethnicity and Race: Making Identities in a Changing World*. Thousand Oaks, CA: Pine Forge Press.

COWAN, C. WESLEY, and PATTY JO T. B. WATSON, eds. 1992. *The Origins of Agriculture: An International Perspective*. Washington, DC: Smithsonian Institution Press.

COWGILL, DONALD O. 1986. *Aging Around the World*. Belmont, CA: Wadsworth.

CRAPANZANO, VINCENT. 1986. *Waiting: The Whites of South Africa*. New York: Random House.

CRAWFORD, G. W. 1992. "Prehistoric Plant Domestication in East Asia." In C. Wesley Cowan and Patty Jo Watson, *The Origins of Agriculture: An International Perspective*, pp. 7–38. Washington, DC: Smithsonian Institution Press.

CRONK, LEE. 1999. *That Complex Whole: Culture and the Evolution of Human Behavior*. Boulder, CO: Westview Press.

DAGOSTO, M. 1988. "Implications of Postcranial Evidence for the Origin of Euprimates." *Journal of Human Evolution* 17:35–56.

DAHLBERG, FRANCES, ed. 1981. *Woman the Gatherer*. New Haven, CT: Yale University Press.

D'ANDRADE, ROY G. 1989. "Cultural Cognition." In M. Posner, *Foundations of Cognitive Science*. Cambridge, MA: MIT Press.

———. 1995. *The Development of Cognitive Anthropology*. Cambridge: Cambridge University Press.

DANIEL, GLYN. 1981. *A Short History of Archaeology*. New York: Thames and Hudson.

DANIELS, PETER T., and WILLIAM BRIGHT, eds. 1995. *The World's Writing Systems*. New York: Oxford University Press.

DART, RAYMOND A. 1967. *Adventures with the Missing Link*. Philadelphia: Institutes Press.

———. 1925. "*Australopithecus africanus:* The Man-Ape of South Africa." *Nature* 115:195–99.

DARWIN, CHARLES. 1979. *The Illustrated Origin of Species*. New York: Hill & Wang.

DARWIN, CHARLES, and E. MAYR. [1859] 1966. *The Origin of Species* (Facsimile of the 1st ed.). Cambridge, MA: Harvard University Press.

DAVIDSON, BASIL. 1961. *The African Slave Trade*. Boston: Atlantic; Little, Brown.

DAVILA, MARIO. 1971. "Compadrazgo: Fictive Kinship in Latin America." In Nelson Graburn, ed., *Readings in Kinship and Social Structure*. New York: Harper & Row.

DAVIS, WADE. 1997. *The Serpent and the Rainbow*. New York: Touchstone Books.

DAWKINS, RICHARD. 1976. *The Selfish Gene*. Oxford, England: Oxford University Press.

DAY, MICHAEL H. 1986. *Guide to Fossil Man,* 4th ed. Chicago: University of Chicago Press.

DEACON, H. J. 1992. "Southern Africa and Modern Human Origins." *Philosophical Transactions of the Royal Society of London,* B 337:177–83.

DEBLIJ, HARM J., and PETER O. MULLER. 1985. *Geography: Regions and Concepts,* 4th ed. New York: John Wiley.

DECORSE, CHRISTOPHER. 1998. "Culture Contact and Change in West Africa." In James G. Cusick, ed., *Studies in Culture Contact: Interaction, Culture Change, and Archaeology.* Occasional Paper 25, pp. 358–77. Bloomington, IN: Center for Archaeological Investigations.

———. 2001. *An Archaeology of Elmina: Africans and Europeans on the Gold Coast, 1400–1900.* Washington, DC: Smithsonian Institution Press.

DEETZ, JAMES. 1996. *In Small Things Forgotten: An Archaeology of Early American Life.* New York: Anchor Books.

DEGLER, CARL N. 1991. *In Search of Human Nature: The Decline and Revival of Darwinism in American Social Thought.* New York: Oxford University Press.

DE LUMLEY, H. 1969. "A Paleolithic Camp at Nice." *Scientific American* 220:42–59.

DEMAREST, WILLIAM J., and BENJAMIN D. PAUL. 1981. "Mayan Migrants in Guatemala City." *Anthropology, UCLA* 11(12):43–73.

D'EMILIO, JOHN. 1988. *Intimate Matters: A History of Sexuality in America.* New York: Harper & Row.

DE MUNCK, VICTOR. 2000. *Culture, Self, and Meaning.* Prospect Heights, IL: Waveland Press.

DENNELL, ROBIN W. 1992. "The Origins of Crop Agriculture in Europe." In C. Wesley Cowan and Patty Jo Watson, eds., *The Origins of Agriculture: An International Perspective,* pp. 71–100. Washington, DC: Smithsonian Institution Press.

DEVOE, PAMELA. 1992. "Refugee Work and Health in Mid-America." In Pamela DeVoe, ed., *Selected Papers on Refugee Issues.* Arlington, VA: American Anthropological Association.

DEWALT, BILLIE. 1984. "Mexico's Second Green Revolution: Food for Feed." *Mexican Studies/Estudios Mexicanos* 1: 29–60.

DIAMOND, JARED. 1987. "The Worst Mistake in the History of the Human Race." *Discover* (May), pp. 64–66.

———. 1993. "Speaking with a Single Tongue." *Discover* (February), pp. 78–85.

———. 1997. *Guns, Germs, and Steel: The Fates of Human Societies.* New York: W. W. Norton & Co.

DIAZ, MAY N. 1966. *Tonala: Conservatism, Responsibility and Authority in a Mexican Town.* Berkeley: University of California Press.

DICKEMANN, MILDRED. 1979. "Female Infanticide, Reproductive Strategies, and Social Stratification." In N. Chagnon and W. Irons, eds., *Evolutionary Biology and Human Social Behavior: An Anthropological Perspective,* pp. 321–67. North Scituate, MA: Duxbury Press.

DILLEHAY, THOMAS D. 1989. *Monte Verde: A Late Pleistocene Settlement in Chile,* Vol. 1. Washington, DC: Smithsonian Institution Press.

———. 1997a. "The Battle of Monte Verde." *The Sciences* (January/February): 28–33.

———. 1997b. *Monte Verde: A Late Pleistocene Settlement in Chile,* Vol. 2. Washington, DC: Smithsonian Institution Press.

———. 2000. *The Settlement of the Americas.* Basic Books: New York, NY.

DILLEHAY, THOMAS D., and DAVID J. MELTZER. 1991. *The First Americans: Search and Research.* Boca Raton, FL: CRC Press.

DIVALE, WILLIAM, and MARVIN HARRIS. 1976. "Population, Warfare, and the Male Supremacist Complex." *American Anthropologist* 78:521–38.

DOBKIN DE RIOS, MARLENE. 1984. *Hallucinogens: Cross-Cultural Perspectives.* Albuquerque: University of New Mexico Press.

DONNAN, CHRISTOPHER B., and DONNA MCCLELLAND. 1979. *The Burial Theme in Moche Iconography.* Washington, DC: Dunbarton Oaks.

DONNAN, CHRISTOPHER, and LUIS JAIME CASTILLO. 1992. "Finding the Tomb of a Moche Priestess." *Archaeology* 45(6): 38–42.

DONNELLY, NANCY D. 1992. "The Impossible Situation of Vietnamese in Hong Kong's Detention Centers." In Pamela DeVoe, ed., *Selected Papers on Refugee Issues.* Arlington, VA: American Anthropological Association.

DORN, R., et al. 1986. "Cation Ratio and Accelerator Radiocarbon Dating of Rock Varnish on Archaeological Artifacts and Land Forms in the Mojave Desert." *Science* 213:830–33.

DORN, R. and D. WHITLEY. 1988. "Cation-Ratio Dating of Petroglyphs Using PIXE." *Nuclear Instruments and Methods in Physics Research* 35:410–14.

DOUGLAS, MARY. 1966. *Purity and Danger: An Analysis of the Concepts of Pollution and Taboo.* London: Routledge and Kegan Paul.

DRENNAN, ROBERT D. 1987. "Regional Demography in Chiefdoms." In Robert D. Drennan and Carlos A. Uribe, eds., *Chiefdoms in the Americas.* New York: University Press of America.

DUBOIS, E. 1894. "*Pithecanthropus erectus,* Transitional Form Between Man and the Apes." *Scientific Transactions of the Royal Dublin Society* 6:1–18.

DUMOND, DON E. 1972. "Population Growth and Political Centralization." In Brian Spooner, ed., *Population Growth: Anthropological Implications.* Cambridge, MA: MIT Press.

DUMONT, LOUIS. 1970. *Homo Hierarchicus: An Essay on the Caste System,* trans. Mark Sainsburg. Chicago: University of Chicago Press.

DUNN, STEPHEN P., and ETHEL DUNN. 1988. *The Peasants of Central Russia*. Prospect Heights, IL: Waveland Press.

DUPREE, LOUIS. 1980. *Afghanistan*. Princeton: Princeton University Press.

DURHAM, WILLIAM H. 1976. "Resource Competition and Human Aggression. Part I: A Review of Primitive War." *Quarterly Review of Biology* 51:385–415.

DYSON-HUDSON, RADA, and ERIC ALDEN SMITH. 1978. "Human Territoriality: An Ecological Reassessment." *American Anthropologist* 80(1):21–41.

EARLE, TIMOTHY. 1977. "A Reappraisal of Redistribution: Complex Hawaiian Chiefdoms." In T. Earle and J. Ericson, eds., *Exchange Systems in Prehistory*. New York: Academic Press.

———. 1987. "Chiefdoms in Archaeological and Ethnohistorical Perspective." *Annual Review of Anthropology* 16:299–308.

———. 1997. *How Chiefs Come to Power: The Political Economy in Prehistory*. Stanford: Stanford University Press.

EARLE, T., and J. ERICSON, eds. 1977. *Exchange Systems in Prehistory*. New York: Academic Press.

EBERT, J. I. 1984. "Remote Sensing Application in Archaeology." In Michael Schiffer, ed., *Advances in Archaeological Method and Theory*, Vol. 7, pp. 293–362. New York: Academic Press.

EDWARDS, DAVID. 1998. "Learning from the Swat Pathans: Political Leadership in Afghanistan, 1978–97." *American Ethnologist* 25(4):712–28.

———. 1996. *Heroes of the Age: Moral Fault Lines on the Afghan Frontier*. Berkeley: University of California Press.

———. 2002. *Before Taliban: Genealogies of the Afghan Jihad*. Berkeley: University of California Press.

EHRET, CHRISTOPHER, and MERRICK POSNANSKY. 1982. *The Archaeological and Linguistic Reconstruction of African History*. Berkeley: University of California Press.

EICKELMAN, DALE F. 1976. *Moroccan Islam: Tradition and Society in a Pilgrimage Center*. Modern Middle East Series, Vol. 1. Austin and London: University of Texas Press.

———. 1982. "The Study of Islam in Local Contexts." *Contributions to Asian Studies* 17:1–16.

———, ed. 1993. *Russia's Muslim Frontiers: New Directions in Cross-Cultural Analysis*. Bloomington and Indianapolis: Indiana University Press.

———. 1995. "Ethnicity." In John L. Esposito, ed., *The Oxford Encyclopedia of the Modern Islamic World*, Vol. I. New York: Oxford University Press.

———. 1998. *The Middle East and Central Asia: An Anthropological Approach*. Upper Saddle River, NJ: Prentice Hall.

EKMAN, PAUL. 1973. "Cross-Cultural Studies of Facial Expressions." In P. Ekman, ed., *Darwin and Facial Expression: A Century of Research in Review*. New York: Academic Press.

EKMAN, PAUL, WALLACE V. FRIESEN, and JOHN BEAR. 1984. "The International Language of Gestures." *Psychology Today*, pp. 64–69.

ELIADE, MIRCEA. 1959. *The Sacred and the Profane: The Nature of Religion*. New York: Harper & Row.

EMBER, CAROL. 1978. "Myths About Hunter-Gatherers." *Ethnology* 17:439–48.

EMBER, MELVIN. 1975. "On the Origin and Extension of the Incest Taboo." *Behavior Science Research* 10:249–81.

EMBER, MELVIN, and CAROL EMBER. 1971. "The Conditions Favoring Matrilocal versus Patrilocal Residence." *American Anthropologist* 73:371–574.

———. 1979. "Male-Female Bonding: A Cross-Species Study of Mammals and Birds." *Behavior Science Research* 14:37–56.

Engels, Frederick. [1884] 1972. *The Origin of the Family, Private Property, and the State*. New York: Pathfinder Press.

ENDICOTT, KIRK. 1988. "The Basis of Egalitarian Social Relations Among the Batak Foragers of Malaysia." Paper read at the Eighty-Seventh Annual Meeting of the American Anthropological Association, Phoenix, AZ.

ERICKSON, MARK T. 1999. "Incest Avoidance: Clinical Implications of the Evolutionary Perspective." In Wenda R. Trevathan, E. O. Smith, and James J. McKenna, eds., *Evolutionary Medicine*. New York and Oxford: Oxford University Press.

ERIKSEN, THOMAS HYLLAND. 1993. *Ethnicity and Nationalism: Anthropological Perspectives*. London: Pluto Press.

ERRINGTON, FREDERICK, and DEBORAH GEWERTZ. 1987. "Of Unfinished Dialogues and Paper Pigs." *American Ethnologist* 14(2):367–76.

ESPOSITO, JOHN. 1998. *Islam: The Straight Path*, 3rd ed. London: Oxford University Press.

ESTIOKO-GRIFFIN, AGNES, and BION P. GRIFFIN. 1978. "Woman the Hunter: The Agta." In Frances Dahlberg, ed., *Woman the Gatherer*, pp. 121–52. New Haven, CT: Yale University Press.

EVANS, KARIN. 2000. "The One-Child, Maybe-One-More Policy." In Elvio Angeloni, ed., *Anthropology 2001/2002*. New York: McGraw-Hill, Dushkin.

EVANS, ROBERT K., and JUDITH A. RASSON. 1984. "Ex Balkanis Lux? Recent Developments in Neolithic and Chalcolithic Research in Southeastern Europe." *American Antiquity* 49:713–41.

EVANS-PRITCHARD, E. E. 1937. *Witchcraft, Oracles and Magic Among the Azande*. Oxford: Clarendon Press.

———. 1940. *The Nuer*. Oxford: Clarendon Press.

———. 1951. *Kinship and Marriage Among the Nuer*. Oxford: Clarendon Press.

———. 1956. *Nuer Religion*. New York: Oxford University Press.

FAGAN, BRIAN. 1984a. *The Aztecs*. New York: W. H. Freeman.

———. 1984b. *Clash of Cultures*. New York: W. H. Freeman.

———. 1988. "Black Day at Slack Farm." *Archaeology* 41(4):15–16, 73.

———. 1992. *Rape of the Nile*. Providence, RI: Moyer-Bell.

———. 2000. *People of the Earth: An Introduction to World Prehistory*, 10th ed. New York: HarperCollins.

———. 2001. *Grahame Clark: An Intellectual Life of an Archaeologist*. Cambridge, MA: Westview.

FAKHOURI, HANI. 1972. *Kafr El-Elow: An Egyptian Village in Transition*. New York: Holt, Rinehart and Winston.

FALK, D. 1983. "A Reconsideration of the Endocast of *Proconsul africanus*: Implications for Primate Brain Evolution." In R. L. Ciochon and R. Corruccini, eds., *New Interpretations of Ape and Human Ancestry*. New York: Plenum Press.

———. 2000. *Primate Diversity*. New York: W. W. Norton.

FARB, PETER. 1974. *Word Play: What Happens When People Talk*. New York: Knopf/Bantam.

FARLEY, JOHN E. 1990. *Sociology*. Upper Saddle River, NJ: Prentice Hall.

FARR, GRANT M. 1999. *Modern Iran*. McGraw-Hill.

FEDER, KENNETH L. 2002. *Frauds, Myths, and Mysteries: Science and*

Pseudoscience in Archaeology. New York: McGraw-Hill.

FEDIGAN, LINDA M. 1983. "Dominance and Reproductive Success in Primates." *Yearbook of Physical Anthropology* 26: 91–129.

———. 1986. "The Changing Role of Women in Models of Human Evolution." *Annual Review of Anthropology* 15: 25–66.

FELL, BARRY. 1980. *Saga America.* New York: Times Mirror.

FERGUSON, R. BRIAN. 1997. "Review of War Before Civilization: The Myth of The Peaceful Savage." *American Anthropologist* 99:424–25.

FERGUSON, R. BRIAN, and NEIL L. WHITEHEAD, eds. 1992. *War in the Tribal Zone: Expanding States and Indigenous Warfare.* Seattle, WA: University of Washington Press.

FERNEA, ELIZABETH W., and ROBERT A. FERNEA. 1979. "A Look Behind the Veil." In *Human Nature.* Reprinted in *Anthropology 1989/90.* 1989. Sluice Dock, Guilford, CT: The Dushkin Publishing Group.

FESSLER, DANIEL M. T. 1999. "Toward an Understanding of the Universality of Second Order Emotions." In Alexander Laban Hinton, ed., *Biocultural Approaches to the Emotions.* Cambridge: Cambridge University Press.

FIRTH, RAYMOND. 1957. "A Note on Descent Groups in Polynesia." *Man* 57:4–8.

FISHER, HELEN E. 1992. *Anatomy of Love: The Natural History of Monogamy, Adultery, and Divorce.* New York: W. W. Norton.

FISHMAN, JOSHUA. 1980. "Social Theory and Ethnography." In Peter Sugar, ed., *Ethnic Diversity and Conflict in Eastern Europe.* Santa Barbara: ABC-CLIO.

FLANNERY, KENT. 1965. "The Ecology of Early Food Production in Mesopotamia." *Science* 147:1247–56.

———. 1968. "Archaeological Systems Theory and Early Mesoamerica." In Betty Meggars, ed., *Anthropological Archaeology in the Americas,* pp. 67–87. Washington, DC: Anthropological Society of Washington.

———. 1972. "The Cultural Evolution of Civilizations." *Annual Review of Ecology and Systematics* 4:399–426.

———. 1973. "The Origins of Agriculture." *Annual Review of Anthropology* 2: 271–310.

———. 1985. "Los Origenes de la Agricultura en Mexico: Las Teorias y la Evidencia." In T. Rojas-Rabiela and W. T. Sanders, eds., *Historia de la Agricultura: Epoca Prehispanica-Siglo XVI,* pp. 237–65. Coleccion Biblioteca del INAH, Instituto Nacional de Antropologia e Historia.

FLEAGLE, JOHN G. 1983. "Locomotor Adaptations of Oligocene and Miocene Hominoids and Their Phyletic Implications." In R. Ciochon and R. Corruccini, eds., *New Interpretations of Ape and Human Ancestry,* pp. 301–24. New York: Plenum Press.

———. 1988. *Primate Adaptations and Evolution.* New York: Academic Press.

FLEAGLE, J. G., T. M. BOWN, J. O. OBRADOVICH, and E. L. SIMONS. 1986. "How Old Are the Fayum Primates?" In J. G. Else and P. C. Lee, eds., *Primate Evolution,* pp. 133–42. Cambridge: Cambridge University Press.

FLEAGLE, J. G., and R. F. KAY. 1987. "The Phyletic Position of the *Parapithecidae.*" *Journal of Human Evolution* 16:483–531.

FLEURET, PATRICK. 1988. "Farmers, Cooperatives, and Development Assistance in Uganda: An Anthropological Perspective." In David Brokensha and Peter D. Little, eds., *Anthropology of Development and Change in East Africa.* Boulder, CO: Westview Press.

FLUEHR-LOBBAN, CAROLYN. 1998. "Cultural Relativism and Universal Rights." (http://www.cs.org/publications/featuredarticles/1998/fluehrlobban.htm).

FORD, RICHARD I. 1985. "Prehistoric Food Production in North America." University of Michigan, Museum of Anthropology, Paper 75.

FOSSEY, DIAN. 1983. *Gorillas in the Mist.* Boston: Houghton Mifflin.

FOSTER, GEORGE M. 1967. *Tzintzuntzan: Mexican Peasants in a Changing World.* Boston: Little, Brown.

FOUTS, R. S., and R. L. BUDD. 1979. "Artificial and Human Language Acquisition in the Chimpanzee." In D. A. Hamburg and E. R. McCown, eds., *The Great Apes,* pp. 374–92. Menlo Park, CA: Benjamin/Cummings.

FOWLER, BRENDA. 2000. *Iceman: Uncovering the Life and Times of a Prehistoric Man Found in an Alpine Glacier.* Chicago: Chicago University Press.

FOX, RICHARD G. 1985. *Lions of the Punjab: Culture in the Making.* Berkeley: University of California Press.

———. 1989. *Gandhian Utopia: Experiments with Culture.* Boston: Beacon Press.

FOX, ROBIN. 1967. *Kinship and Marriage: An Anthropological Perspective.* Baltimore: Penguin.

FRANK, ANDRE GUNNER. 1993. "Bronze Age World System Cycles." *Current Anthropology* 34(4):383–429.

———. 1998. *Reorient: Global Economy in the Asian Age.* Berkeley: University of California Press.

FRAYER, DAVID W., MILFORD H. WOLPOSS, ALAN G. THORNE, FRED H. SMITH, and GEOFFREY G. POPE. 1993. "Theories of Modern Human Origins: The Paleontological Test." *American Anthropologist* 95(1):14–50.

FREEMAN, DEREK. 1983. *Margaret Mead and Samoa: The Making and Unmaking of an Anthropological Myth.* Cambridge, MA: Harvard University Press.

———. 1997. *Margaret Mead and the Heretic: The Making and Unmaking of an Anthropological Myth.* New York: Penguin.

———. 1999. *The Fateful Hoaxing of Margaret Mead,* 2nd ed. Boulder, CO: Westview.

FREUCHEN, PETER. 1961. *Book of the Eskimos.* Cleveland: World Publishing Co.

FREUD, SIGMUND. 1913. *Totem and Taboo: Some Points of Agreement Between the Mental Lives of Savages and Neurotics,* trans. James Strachey. New York: W. W. Norton.

FRIED, MORTON. 1953. *Fabric of Chinese Society: A Study of the Social Life of a Chinese County Seat.* New York: Praeger.

———. 1967. *The Evolution of Political Society: An Essay in Political Anthropology.* New York: Random House.

———. 1975. *The Notion of Tribe.* Menlo Park, CA: Cummings.

———. 1977. "First Contact and Political Theory." In Ronald K. Wetherington, ed., *Colloquia in Anthropology,* Vol. 1. Taos, NM: Fort Burgwin Research Center, Southern Methodist University.

———. 1978. "The State, the Chicken and the Egg: Or What Came First?" In R. Cohen and E. R. Service, eds., *Origins of the State: The Anthropology of Political Evolution,* pp. 35–48. Philadelphia: Institute for the Study of Human Issues.

FRIEDL, ERNESTINE. 1975. *Women and Men: An Anthropologist's View.* New York: Holt, Rinehart and Winston.

FRIEDMAN, JONATHAN. 1974. "Marxism, Structuralism, and Vulgar Materialism." *Man* 9:444–69.

———. 1992. "Narcissism, Roots, and Postmodernity: The Constitution of Selfhood in the Global Crisis." In Scott Lash and Jonathan Friedman, eds., *Modernity and Identity.* Oxford: Basil Blackwell.

———. 1995. *Culture Identity and Global Process.* London: Sage Publications.

FRISANCHO, A. R. 1979. *Human Adaptation: A Functional Interpretation.* St. Louis, MO: C. V. Mosby.

FUTUYMA, D. J. 1995. *Science on Trial: The Case for Evolution.* New York: Pantheon Books.

GARBARINO, MERWYN. 1988. *Native American Heritage,* 2nd ed. Prospect Heights, IL: Waveland Press.

GARCIAGODOY, JUANITA. 1998. *Digging the Days of the Dead: A Reading of Mexico's Dias De Muertos.* Niwot, CO: University Press of Colorado.

GARDNER, HOWARD. 1983. *Frames of Mind: The Theory of Multiple Intelligences.* New York: Basic Books.

GARDNER, PETER. 1991. "Foragers Pursuit of Individual Autonomy." *Current Anthropology* 32:543–58.

GARDNER, R. A., and B. T. GARDNER. 1969. "Teaching Sign Language to a Chimpanzee." *Science* 16:664–72.

GARN, STANLEY. 1971. *Human Races,* 3rd ed. Springfield, IL: Chas. C Thomas.

GARZA, CHRISTINA ELNORA. 1991. "Studying the Natives on the Shop Floor." *Business Week,* September 30, pp. 74–78.

GAY, PHILLIP T. 2001. *Modern South Africa.* Boston: McGraw-Hill.

GEERTZ, CLIFFORD. 1960. *The Religion of Java.* Glencoe, IL: Free Press.

———. 1963a. *Agricultural Involution: The Processes of Ecological Change in Indonesia.* Berkeley and Los Angeles: University of California Press.

———. 1963b. *Peddlars and Princes: Social Change and Modernization in Two Indonesian Towns.* Chicago: University of Chicago Press.

———. 1966. "Religion as a Cultural System." In Michael Banton, ed., *Anthropological Approaches to the Study of Religion.* Association of Social Anthropologists Monographs, No. 3.

———. 1973. *The Interpretation of Cultures: Selected Essays by Clifford Geertz.* New York: Basic Books.

———. 1980. *Negara: The Theatre State in Nineteenth-Century Bali.* Princeton, NJ: Princeton University Press.

———. 1983. "Common Sense as a Cultural System." In Clifford Geertz, ed., *Local Knowledge: Further Essays in Interpretive Anthropology.* New York: Basic Books.

GELLNER, ERNEST. 1983. *Nations and Nationalism.* Oxford: Oxford University Press.

———. ed., [1977] 1988. *State and Society in Soviet Thought.* Oxford: Basil Blackwell.

GEWERTZ, DEBORAH. 1981. "A Historical Reconsideration of Female Dominance Among the Chambri of Papua New Guinea." *American Ethnologist* 8(1): 94–106.

GIBBS, JAMES L. 1965. "The Kpelle of Liberia." In James L. Gibbs, ed., *Peoples of Africa.* New York: Holt, Rinehart and Winston.

GILKEY, LANGDON. 1986. "The Creationism Issue: A Theologian's View." In Robert W. Hanson, ed., *Science and Creation: Geological, Theological, and Educational Perspectives.* New York: Macmillan.

GIL-WHITE, FRANCISCO. 2001. "Are Ethnic Groups Biological 'Species' to the Human Brain?" *Current Anthropology* 42(4):515–54.

GIMBUTAS, MARIJA. 1982. "Old Europe in The Fifth Millenium B.C.: The European Situation on The Arrival of Indo-Europeans." In Edgar C Polome, ed., *The Indo-Europeans in the Fourth and Third Millennia.* New York: Karoma Press.

———. 1991. *The Civilization of the Goddess: The World of Old Europe.* San Francisco: Harper Collins.

GINGERICH, P. D. 1986. "Plesiadapis and the Delineation of the Order Primates." In B. Wood, L. Martin, and P. Andrews, eds., *Major Topics in Primates and Human Evolution,* pp. 32–46. Cambridge: Cambridge University Press.

———. 1990. "African Dawn for Primates." *Nature* 346:411.

GIVENS, DAVID, and RANDOLPH FILLMORE. 1990. "AAA Pilot Survey of Nonacademic Departments: Where the MAs Are." *Anthropology Newsletter* 31(5), May.

GLADKIH, M. I., N. KORNEITZ, and O. SEFFER. 1984. "Mammoth-Bone Dwelling on the Russian Plain." *Scientific American* 251(5):164–75.

GLASCOCK, ANTHONY P. 1981. "Social Assets or Social Burden: Treatment of the Aged in Nonindustrial Societies." In C. L. Fry, ed., *Dimensions: Aging, Culture and Health.* New York: Praeger.

GLAZIER, JACK. 2003. "Jewish Americans." In Raymond Scupin, ed., *Race and Ethnicity: An Anthropological Focus on the U.S. and the World.* Upper Saddle River, NJ: Prentice Hall.

GLEASON, PHILIP. 1980. "American Identity and Americanization." In Stephan Thernstrom, ed., *Harvard Encyclopedia of American Ethnic Groups,* pp. 31–59. Cambridge, MA: Harvard University Press.

GLUCKMAN, MAX. 1953. "Bridewealth and the Stability of Marriage." *Man* 53: 141–42.

GOBINEAU, JOSEPH-ARTHUR. [1966] 1854. *Essays on the Inequality of Human Races.* Adrian Collins, trans. Los Angeles: Noontide Press.

GOLDBERG, STEVE. 1993. *Why Men Rule: A Theory of Male Dominance.* London: Open Court.

GOLDING, WILLIAM G. 1981. *The Inheritors.* New York: Harcourt Brace Jovanovich.

GOLDKIND, VICTOR. 1965. "Social Stratification in a Peasant Community: Redfield's Chan Kom Reinterpreted." *American Anthropologist* 67:863–84.

GOLDMAN, IRVING. 1970. *Ancient Polynesian Society.* Chicago: University of Chicago Press.

GOLDSCHMIDT, WALTER. 1986. *The Sebei: A Study in Adaptation.* New York: Holt, Rinehart and Winston.

———. 1989. "Inducement to Military Participation in Tribal Societies." In Paul R. Turner, David Pitt, et al., eds., *The Anthropology of War and Peace: Perspectives on the Nuclear Age,* pp. 15–29. Granby, MA: Bergin & Garvey.

GOLDSCHMIDT, WALTER, and EVELYN J. KUNKEL. 1971. "The Structure of the Peasant Family." *American Anthropologist* 73:1058–76.

GOLOMB, LOUIS. 1985. *An Anthropology of Curing in Multiethnic Thailand.* Urbana: University of Illinois Press.

GOODALE, JANE. 1971. *Tiwi Wives: A Study of the Women of Melville Island, North Australia.* Seattle: University of Washington Press.

GOODALL, JANE VAN LAWICK. 1971. *In the Shadow of Man.* New York: Dell.

———. 1986. *The Chimpanzees of Gombe.* Cambridge, MA: Harvard University Press.

———. 1990. *Through a Window: Thirty Years Observing the Chimpanzees of Gombe.* Boston: Houghton Mifflin.

GOODE, WILLIAM J. 1963. *World Revolution and Family Patterns.* New York: Free Press.

———. 1982. *The Family,* 2nd ed. Englewood Cliffs, NJ: Prentice Hall.

GOODENOUGH, WARD H. 1955. "A Problem in Malayo-Polynesian Social Organization." *American Anthropologist* 57: 71–83.

———. 1956. "Residence Rules." *Southwestern Journal of Anthropology* 12: 22–37.

GOODLUCK, HELEN. 1991. *Language Acquisition: A Linguistic Introduction.* Oxford: Blackwell.

GOODMAN, ALAN H., DEBRA L. MARTIN, and GEORGE J. ARMELAGOS. 1984. "Indications of Stress from Bone and Teeth." In Mark Nathan Cohen and George J. Armelagos, eds., *Paleopathology at the Origins of Agriculture,* pp. 13–49. New York: Academic Press.

GOODMAN, JEFFREY. 1981. *American Genesis.* New York: Berkley.

GOODMAN, M., M. L. BABA, and L. L. DARGA. 1983. "The Bearings of Molecular Data on the Cladogenesis and Times of Divergence of Hominoid Lineages." In R. L. Ciochon and R. Corruccini, eds., *New Interpretations of Ape and Human Ancestry,* pp. 67–86. New York: Plenum Press.

GOODMAN, M., and G. W. LASKER. 1975. "Molecular Evidence as to Man's Place in Nature." In R. H. Tuttle, ed., *Primate Functional Morphology and Evolution,* pp. 70–101. The Hague: Mouton.

GOODY, JACK. 1971. *Technology, Tradition, and the State in Africa.* London: Oxford University Press.

———. 1976. *Production and Reproduction: A Comparative Study of the Domestic Domain.* Cambridge: Cambridge University Press.

———. 1980. "Slavery in Time and Space." In James L. Watson, ed., *Asian and African Systems of Slavery,* pp. 17–42. Berkeley and Los Angeles: University of California Press.

———. 1987. *The Interface Between the Written and the Oral.* Cambridge: Cambridge University Press.

———. 1996. *The East in the West.* Cambridge: Cambridge University Press.

GOODY, JACK, and STANLEY J. TAMBIAH. 1973. *Bridewealth and Dowry.* Cambridge: Cambridge University Press.

GOODYEAR, ALBERT C. 1999. "Results of the 1999 Allendale Paleoindian Expedition." *Legacy* 4(1–3):8–13.

GORMAN, CHESTER A. 1969. "Hoabhinian: A Pebble-Tool Complex with Early Plant Associations in Southeast Asia." *Science* 163:671–73.

———. 1977. "A Priori Models and Thai Prehistory: A Reconsideration of the Beginning of Agriculture in Southeast Asia." In Charles A. Reed, ed., *Origins of Agriculture,* pp. 321–55. The Hague: Mouton.

GOSSETT, THOMAS F. 1963. *Race, The History of an Idea in America.* Dallas: Southern Methodist University Press.

GOUCHER, CANDICE L. 1981. "Iron Is Iron 'til It Is Rust!: Trade and Ecology in the Decline of West African Iron Smelting." *Journal of African History* 22(1): 179–84.

GOUGH, KATHLEEN. 1975. "The Origin of the Family." In Rayna Reiter, ed., *Towards an Anthropology of Women.* New York: Monthly Review.

GOULD, JAMES L. 1986. "The Locale Map of Honey Bees: Do Insects Have Cognitive Maps?" *Science* 232:861–63.

GOULD, JAMES L., and PETER MARLER. 1987. "Learning by Instinct." *Scientific American* 256:74–85.

GOULD, R. A. 1980. *Living Archaeology.* Cambridge: Cambridge University Press.

GOULD, S. J. 1977. *Ever Since Darwin.* New York: W. W. Norton.

———. 1985. *The Flamingo's Smile.* New York: W. W. Norton.

———. 1987. "Bushes All the Way Down." *Natural History* 87(6):12–19.

GOULD, S. J., and NILES ELDREDGE. 1972. "Punctuated Equilibrium: The Tempo and Mode of Evolution Reconsidered." *Paleobiology* 3:115–51.

GOULD, S. J., and R. C. LEWONTIN. 1979. "The Spandrels of San Marco and the Panglossian Paradigm: A Critique of the Adaptionist Programme." *Proceedings of the Royal Society of London,* B205: 581–98.

GRABER, ROBERT B., and PAUL B. ROSCOE. 1988. "Introduction: Circumscription and the Evolution of Society." *American Behavioral Scientist* 31:405–15.

GRANT, P. R. 1999. *Ecology and Evolution of Darwin's Finches.* Princeton, NJ: Princeton University Press.

GREEN, ERNESTINE, ed. 1984. *Ethics and Values in Archaeology.* New York: Free Press.

GREENBERG, JOSEPH H. 1986. "The Settlement of the Americas." *Current Anthropology* 27:477–97.

GREENBERG, JOSEPH H., KEITH DENNING, and SUZANNE KEMMER, eds. 1990. *On Language: Selected Writings of Joseph H. Greenberg.* Palo Alto, CA: Stanford University Press.

GREENE, JEREMY. 1990. *Maritime Archaeology: A Technical Handbook.* London: Academic Press.

GREENE, VICTOR. 1980. "Poles." In Stephan Thernstrom, ed. *Harvard Encyclopedia of American Ethnic Groups,* pp. 787–803. Cambridge, MA: Harvard University Press.

GRIFFIN, DONALD. 1985. *Animal Thinking.* Cambridge, MA: Harvard University Press.

GUHA, ASHOK S. 1981. *An Evolutionary View of Economic Growth.* Oxford: Clarendon Press.

HAAS, JONATHAN. 1982. *The Evolution of the Prehistoric State.* New York: Columbia University Press.

HABGOOD, PHILLIP. 1985. "The Origin of the Australian Aborigines." In Phillip Tobias, ed., *Hominid Evolution: Past, Present, and Future.* New York: Alan R. Liss.

HAGLUND, K., and M. H. SORG. 1997. *Forensic Taphonomy: The Postmortem Fate of Human Remains.* Boca Raton, FL: CRC Press.

HAILE-SELASSIE, Y. 2001 "Late Miocene Hominids from the Middle Awash, Ethiopia." *Nature* 412:178–81.

HALL, EDWARD T. 1969. *The Hidden Dimension.* New York: Anchor Press.

———. 1981. *The Silent Language.* New York: Anchor Press.

HALL, MARTIN. 1988. "Archaeology Under Apartheid." *Archaeology* 41(6):62–64.

HALPERIN, RHODA. 1987. "Age in Cross-Cultural Perspective: An Evolutionary Approach." In Philip Silverman, ed., *The Elderly as Modern Pioneers.* Bloomington: Indiana University Press.

HALVERSON, JOHN. 1987. "Art for Art's Sake in the Paleolithic." *Current Anthropology* 28:63–89.

HAMES, RAYMOND B. 1979a. "A Comparison of the Efficiencies of the Shotgun and the Bow in Neotropical Forest Hunting." *Human Ecology* 7(3):219–52.

———. 1979b. "Relatedness and Interaction Among the Ye'Kwana: A Preliminary Analysis." In N. Chagnon and W. Irons, eds., *Evolutionary Biology and Human Social Behavior: An Anthropological Perspective,* pp. 238–51. North Scituate, MA: Duxbury Press.

HAMILTON, D. L., and ROBYN WOODWARD. 1984. "A Sunken 17th Century City: Port Royal, Jamaica." *Archaeology* 37(1): 38–45.

HAMMEL, E. A., and NANCY HOWELL. 1987. "Research in Population and Culture: An Evolutionary Framework." *Current Anthropology* 28(2):141–60.

HANDLER, RICHARD. 1988. *Nationalism and the Politics of Culture in Quebec.* Madison, WI: Wisconsin University Press.

HARDEN, BLAINE. 2001. "The Dirt in the New Machine." *The New York Times Magazine,* August 12, pp. 35–39.

HARDMAN-DE-BAUTISTA, M. 1978. "Linguistic Postulates and Applied Anthropological Linguistics." In V. Honsa and M. Hardman-de-Bautista, eds. *Papers on Linguistics and Child Language.* The Hague: Mouton.

HARLAN, J. R. 1971. "Agricultural Origins: Centers and Noncenters." *Science* 174: 468–74.

———. 1992. "Indigenous African Agriculture." In C. Wesley Cowan and Patty Jo Watson, eds., *The Origins of Agriculture: An International Perspective,* pp. 59–70. Washington, DC: Smithsonian Institution Press.

HARLOW, HARRY F., and MARGARET K. HARLOW. 1961. "A Study of Animal Affection." *Natural History* 70:48–55.

HARNER, MICHAEL J. 1972. *The Jivaro: People of the Sacred Waterfalls.* Garden City, NY: Natural History Press.

———. 1977. "The Ecological Basis for Aztec Sacrifice." *American Ethnologist* 4:117–35.

HARRINGTON, SPENCER P. M. 1991a. "The Looting of Arkansas." *Archaeology* 44(3):22–30.

———. 1991b. "Shoring Up the Temple of Athena." *Archaeology* 45(1):30–43.

HARRIS, MARVIN. 1964. *Patterns of Race in the Americas.* New York: Norton Press.

———. 1977. *Cannibals and Kings: The Origins of Cultures.* New York: Random House.

———. 1979. *Cultural Materialism: The Struggle for a Science of Culture.* New York: Random House.

———. 1985. *The Sacred Cow and the Abominable Pig: Riddles of Food and Culture.* New York: Simon & Schuster.

———. 1988. *Culture, People, Nature: An Introduction to General Anthropology,* 5th ed. New York: Harper & Row.

———. 1992. "Distinguished Lecture: Anthropology and the Theoretical and Paradigmatic Significance of the Collapse of Society and East European Communism." *American Anthropology* 94(2): 295–305.

———. 1999. *Theories of Culture in Postmodern Times.* Walnut Creek, CA: Altamira Press.

HARRIS, MARVIN, and ERIC ROSS. 1987. *Death, Sex, and Fertility: Population Regulation in Preindustrial and Developing Societies.* New York: Columbia University Press.

HARROLD, FRANCIS B. AND RAYMOND A. EVE. 1987. *Cult Archaeology and Creationism: Understanding Pseudoscientific Beliefs about the Past.* Iowa City: University of Iowa Press.

HART C. W. M., ARNOLD PILLING, and JANE GOODALE. 1989. *The Tiwi of North Australia,* 3rd. ed. New York: Holt, Rinehart and Winston.

HARTWIG, WALTER CARL, ed. 2002. *The Primate Fossil Record.* Cambridge: New York: Cambridge University Press.

HASSAN, FEKRI A. 1981. *Demographic Archaeology.* New York: Academic Press.

HATCH, ELVIN. 1973. *Theories of Man and Culture.* New York: Columbia University Press.

———. 1983. *Culture and Morality: The Relativity of Values in Anthropology.* New York: Columbia University Press.

HAWKES, K., K. HILL, and J. F. O'CONNELL. 1982. "Why Hunters Gather: Optimal Foraging and the Ache of Eastern Paraguay." *American Ethnologist,* 9: 379–98.

HAWKINS, GERALD S. 1965. *Stonehenge Decoded.* New York: Doubleday.

HAYNES, C. V., JR. 1991. "Geoarchaeological and Paleohydrological Evidence for a Clovis-Age Drought in North America and Its Bearing on Extinction." *Quartinary Research* 35:438–50.

HEFNER, ROBERT W. 1983. "The Culture Problem in Human Ecology: A Review Article." *Comparative Studies in Society and History* 25(3):547–56.

HEIDER, KARL. 1979. *Grand Valley Dani: Peaceful Warriors.* New York: Holt, Rinehart and Winston.

———. 1991. *Landscapes of Emotion: Mapping Three Cultures of Emotion in Indonesia.* Cambridge: Cambridge University Press.

HENDRY, JOY. 1987. *Understanding Japanese Society.* London: Croom Helm.

———. 1992. "Introduction and Individuality: Entry into a Social World." In Roger Goodman and Kirsten Refsing, eds., *Ideology and Practice in Modern Japan.* London: Routledge Press.

HENN, JEANNE K. 1984. "Women in the Rural Economy: Past, Present, and Future." In Margaret Jean Hay and Sharon Stichter, eds., *African Women South of the Sahara,* pp. 1–19. London: Longman.

HENRY, DONALD O. 1984. "Preagricultural Sedentism: The Natufian Example." In Douglas T. Price and James A. Brown, eds., *Prehistoric Hunter-Gatherers: The Emergence of Cultural Complexity,* pp. 365–84. New York: Academic Press.

HERDT, GILBERT. 1987. *The Sambia: Ritual and Custom in New Guinea.* New York: Holt, Rinehart and Winston.

HERDT, GILBERT, and ROBERT J. STOLLER. 1990. *Intimate Communications: Erotica and the Study of Culture.* New York: Columbia University Press.

HERRING, GEORGE C. 1979. *America's Longest War: The United States and Vietnam.* New York: John Wiley.

HERRNSTEIN, RICHARD J. and CHARLES MURRAY. 1994. *The Bell Curve: Intelligence and Class Structure in American Life.* New York: Free Press.

HERSCHER, ELLEN. 1989. "A Future in Ruins." *Archaeology* 42(1):67–70.

HERZFELD, MICHAEL. 1986. *Ours Once More: Folklore, Ideology, and the Making of Modern Greece.* New York: Pella Publishing Co.

———. 1992. *The Social Production of Indifference: Exploring the Symbolic Roots of Western Bureaucracy.* Chicago: University of Chicago Press.

HICKERSON, NANCY PARROTT. 1980. *Linguistic Anthropology.* New York: Harper & Row.

HILL, D. 1977. *The Impact of Migration on the Metropolitan and Folk Society of Carriacou, Grenada.* New York: American Museum of Natural History.

HILL, K., H. KAPLAN, K. HAWKES, and A. M. HURTADO. 1985. "Men's Time Allocation to Subsistence Work Among the Ache of Eastern Paraguay." *Human Ecology* 13:29–47.

HILL-BURNETT, JAQUETTA. 1978. "Developing Anthropological Knowledge Through Application." In E. Eddy and W. Partridge, eds., *Applied Anthropology in America*. New York: Columbia University Press.

HINDE, ROBERT A., and JOAN STEVENSON-HINDE. 1987. *Instinct and Intelligence*, 3rd ed. Burlington, NC: Scientific Publications Department, Carolina Biological Supply Company.

HINTON, ALEXANDER LABAN, ed. 1999. *Biocultural Approaches to the Emotions*. Cambridge: Cambridge University Press.

HIRSCHFELD, LAWRENCE. 1986. "Kinship and Cognition: Geneology and the Meaning of Kinship Terms." *Current Anthropology* 27:217–42.

———. 1989. "Rethinking the Acquisition of Kinship Terms." *International Journal of Behavioral Development* 12: 541–68.

———. 1996. *Race in the Making: Cognition, Culture, and the Child's Construction of Human Kinds*. Cambridge, MA: MIT Press.

HITCHCOCK, ROBERT. 1988. *Monitoring Research and Development in the Remote Areas of Botswana*. Gaborone: Government Printer.

HITCHCOCK, ROBERT, and MEGAN BIESLE. 2002a. "Namibia." (forthcoming).

HITCHCOCK, ROBERT, and MEGAN BIESLE. 2002b. "Botswana." (forthcoming).

HOBBES, THOMAS. [1651] 1958. *Leviathan*. New York: Liberal Arts Press.

HOCKETT, CHARLES F., and R. ASCHER. 1964. "The Human Revolution." *Current Anthropology* 5:135–68.

HOEBEL, E. ADAMSON. [1954] 1968. *The Law of Primitive Man*. New York: Atheneum.

HOLLOWAY, R. L. 1985. "The Poor Brain of *Homo sapiens neanderthalensis*: See What You Please." In E. Delson, ed., *Ancestors: The Hard Evidence*, pp. 319–24. New York: Alan R. Liss.

HOLMBERG, ALLAN R. [1950] 1969. *Nomads of the Long Bow: Siriono of Eastern Bolivia*. Garden City, NY: Natural History Press.

———. 1962. "Community and Regional Development: The Joint Cornell-Peru Experiment." *Human Organization* 17:12–16.

HOLMES, LOWELL D. 1987. *Quest for the Real Samoa: The Mead/Freeman Controversy and Beyond*. South Hadley, MA: Bergin & Garvey.

HOPKINS, KEITH. 1982. "Aspects of the Paleogeography of Beringia During the Late Pleistocene." In D. M. Hopkins, J. Matthews, C. Schweger, and S. Young, eds., *The Paleoecology of Beringia*, pp. 3–28. New York: Academic Press.

HOSTETLER, JOHN A. 1980. *Amish Society*, 3rd ed. Baltimore, MD: Johns Hopkins University.

HOURANI, ALBERT. 1991. *A History of the Arab Peoples*. Cambridge: Cambridge University Press.

HOWELL, NANCY. 1976. "The Population of the Dobe Area !Kung." In Richard B. Lee and Irven DeVore, eds., *Kalahari Hunter-Gatherers*. Cambridge, MA: Harvard University Press.

———. 1979. *Demography of the Dobe !Kung*. New York: Academic Press.

HOWELLS, W. W. 1976. "Explaining Modern Man: Evolutionists versus Migrationists." *Journal of Human Evolution* 5: 477–96.

HOYLE, FRED. 1977. *On Stonehenge*. San Francisco: W. H. Freeman.

HSU, FRANCIS. 1948. *Under the Ancestor's Shadow: Chinese Culture and Personality*. New York: Columbia University Press.

———. 1981. *Americans and Chinese: Passage to Differences*, 3rd ed. Honolulu: University of Hawaii Press.

HUNTINGTON, ELSWORTH. 1924. *Civilization and Climate*. New Haven, CT: Yale University Press.

HUTCHINSON, SHARON. 1996. *Nuer Dilemmas: Coping with Money, War, and the State*. Berkeley: University of California Press.

HUTTON, JAMES. 1785. *Theory of the Earth: Or an Investigation of the Laws Observable in the Composition, Dissolution and Restoration of Land Upon the Globe*. London.

INGHAM, JOHN. M. 1986. *Mary, Michael, and Lucifer: Folk Catholicism in Central Mexico*. Austin: University of Texas Press.

INFORMATION PLEASE ALMANAC. 1991. "Energy, Petroleum, and Coal, by Country," pp. 146–47. Boston: Houghton Mifflin.

IRWIN, G. 1993. *Prehistoric Exploration and Colonization of the Pacific*. Cambridge: Cambridge University Press.

ISAAC, BARBARA. 1995. "An Epimethean View of the Future at the Peabody Museum of Archaeology and Ethnology at Harvard University." *Federal Archaeology*. Offprint Series, Fall/Winter, pp. 18–22.

ISAAC, BARRY L. 1977. "The Siriono of Eastern Bolivia: A Reexamination." *Human Ecology* 5:137–54.

ISAAC, G. L. 1978. "The Food-Sharing Behavior of Protohuman Hominids." *Scientific American* 238(4):90–108.

———. 1984. "The Archaeology of Human Origins: Studies of the Lower Pleistocene in East Africa, 1971–1981." In Fred Wendorf and Angela E. Close, eds., *Advances in World Archaeology*, Vol. 3, pp. 1–87. New York: Academic Press.

ISCAN, M. Y. S., and K. A. R. KENNEDY. 1989. *Reconstruction of Life from the Skeleton*. New York: Alan R. Liss.

JABLONSKI, NINA, AND GEORGE CHAPLIN. 2000. "The Evolution of Skin Color." *Journal of Human Evolution* 39(1): 57–106.

JACKSON, DONALD DALE. 1992. "How Lord Elgin First Won—and Lost—His Marbles." *Smithsonian* 23(9):135–46.

JACOBSON, MATTHEW FRYE. 1998. *Whiteness of Different Color: European Immigrants and the Alchemy of Race*. Cambridge, MA: Harvard University Press.

JANKOWIAK, WILLIAM R., and EDWARD F. FISCHER. 1992. "A Cross-Cultural Perspective on Romantic Love." *Ethnology* 3(2):149–55.

JENNINGS, JESSE D. 1989. *Prehistory of North America*. Mountain View, CA: Mayfield.

JENSEN, ARTHUR. 1980. *Bias in Mental Testing*. New York: Free Press.

JETT, STEPHEN C. 1978. "Precolumbian Transoceanic Contacts." In Jesse D. Jennings, ed., *Ancient North Americans*. San Francisco: W. H. Freeman.

JOHANSON, DONALD, and MAITLAND EDEY. 1981. *Lucy: The Beginnings of Humankind*. New York: Simon & Schuster.

JOHANSON, DONALD C., and JAMES SHREEVE. 1989. *Lucy's Child: The Discovery of a Human Ancestor*. New York: Avon Books.

JOHANSON, DONALD, and TIMOTHY WHITE. 1979. "A Systematic Assessment of Early African Hominids." *Science* 203:321–30.

JOHANSON, D. C., T. D. WHITE, and Y. COPPENS. 1978. "A New Species of the Genus *Australopithecus* (Primates: Hominidae) from the Pliocene of Eastern Africa." *Kirtlandia* 28:1–14.

JOHANSON, DONALD C., et al. 1982. "Pliocene Hominid Fossils from Hadar, Ethiopia. *American Journal of Physical Anthropology* 57(4):1–719.

JOHNSON, ALLEN W. 1975. "Time Allocation in a Machiguenga Community." *Ethnology* 14:301–10.

JOHNSON, ALLEN, and TIMOTHY EARLE. 2000. *The Evolution of Human Societies: From Foraging Group to Agrarian State,* 2d ed. Stanford, CA: Stanford University Press.

JOHNSON, RONALD W., and MICHAEL G. SCHENE. 1987. *Cultural Resources Management.* Malabar, FL: Robert E. Krieger.

JOLLY, ALISON. 1985. *The Evolution of Primate Behavior,* 2nd ed. New York: Macmillan.

JURMAIN, ROBERT, HARRY NELSON, and WILLIAM A. TURNBAUGH. 1990. *Understanding Physical Anthropology and Archaeology,* 4th ed. St. Paul, MN: West.

KAEPPLER, ADRIENNE L. 1980. "Polynesian Music and Dance." In Elizabeth May, ed., *Musics of Many Cultures.* Berkeley: University of California Press.

KAMIN, LEON. *The Science and Politics of I.Q.* New York: Wiley.

KAPLAN, MAUREEN F., and JOHN E. MENDEL. 1982. "Ancient Glass and the Disposal of Nuclear Waste." *Archaeology* 35(4): 22–29.

KARNOW, STANLEY. 1984. *Vietnam: A History.* New York: Penguin.

KAY, R. F., M. PLAUKIN, P. C. WRIGHT, K. GLANDER, and G. H. ALBRECHT. 1988. "Behavioral and Size Correlates of Canine Dimorphism in Platyrrhine Primates." *American Journal of Physical Anthropology* 88:385–97.

KEDDIE, NIKKI R. 1981. *Roots of Revolution: An Interpretive History of Modern Iran.* New Haven, CT: Yale University Press.

KEEGAN, WILLIAM F., ed. 1987. *Emergent Horticultural Economies of the Eastern Woodlands.* Occasional Publications No. 7. Carbondale: Southern Illinois University, Center for Archaeological Investigations.

KEELEY, LAWRENCE H. 1996. *War before Civilization.* New York: Oxford University Press.

KEELEY, L. H., and N. TOTH. 1981. "Microwear Polishes on Early Stone Tools from Koobi Fora, Kenya." *Nature* 293: 464–65.

KEESING, ROGER M. 1975. *Kin Groups and Social Structure.* New York: Holt, Rinehart and Winston.

———. 1981. *Cultural Anthropology: A Contemporary Perspective.* New York: Holt, Rinehart and Winston.

KEHOE, ALICE BECK. 1989. *The Ghost Dance: Ethnohistory and Revitalization.* New York: Holt, Rinehart and Winston.

———. 1995. *North American Indians: A Comprehensive Account,* 2nd ed. Upper Saddle River, NJ: Prentice Hall.

KELLMAN, SHELLY. 1982. "The Yanomamös: Portrait of a People in Crisis." *New Age Journal,* May. Reprinted in *Anthropology 88/89.* 1988. Sluice Dock, Guilford, CT: Dushkin Publishing Group.

KENNEDY, G. E. 1984. "The Emergence of Homo sapiens: The Postcranial Evidence." *Man* 19:94–110.

KENYON, KATHLEEN M. 1972. "Ancient Jericho." In *Old World Archaeology: Foundations of Civilization, Readings from Scientific American.* San Francisco: W. H. Freeman.

KEPHART, WILLIAM M., and WILLIAM ZELLNER. 1994. *Extraordinary Groups: The Sociology of Unconventional Life Styles,* 4th ed. New York: St. Martin's Press.

KERBLAY, BASILE. 1983. *Modern Soviet Society.* New York: Pantheon.

KERBO, HAROLD R. and JOHN A. MCKINSTRY. 1998. *Modern Japan.* New York: McGraw-Hill.

KEYES, CHARLES F. 1995. *The Golden Peninsula: Culture and Adaptation in Mainland Southeast Asia.* Honolulu: University of Hawaii Press.

KIERNAN, BEN. 1988. "Orphans of Genocide: The Cham Muslims of Kampuchea under Pol Pot." *Bulletin of Concerned Asian Scholars* 20(4):2–33.

KINSEY, WARREN G., ed. 1987. *The Evolution of Human Behavior: Primate Models.* Albany: State University of New York Press.

KIRCH, PATRICK V. 1984. *The Evolution of the Polynesian Chiefdoms.* Cambridge: Cambridge University Press.

KIRCHOFF, PAUL. 1955. "The Principles of Clanship in Human Society." *Davidson Anthropological Journal* 1:1. Reprinted in Morton H. Fried, ed., 1958. *Readings in Anthropology,* 2 vols. New York: Thomas Y. Crowell.

KITCHER, PHILLIP. 1982. *Abusing Science: The Case Against Creationism.* Cambridge, MA: MIT Press.

KLEIN, LAURA. 1980. "Contending with Colonization: Tlingit Men and Women in Charge." In Mona Etienne and Eleanor Leacock, eds., *Women and Colonization.* New York: Praeger.

KLEIN, RICHARD G. 1992. "The Archaeology of Modern Human Origins." *Evolutionary Anthropology* 1(1):5–14.

KLEINFELD, JUDITH. 1975. "Positive Stereotyping: The Cultural Relativism in the Classroom." *Human Organization* 34(3):269–74.

KLUCKHORN, CLYDE. 1967. *Navajo Witchcraft.* Boston: Beacon Press.

KNAUFT, BRUCE 1985. *Good Company and Violence: Sorcery and Social Action in Lowland New Guinea Society.* Berkeley: University of California Press.

———. 1988. "Reply to Betzig, Laura. On Reconsidering Violence in Simple Human Societies." *Current Anthropology* 29(4):629–33.

———1993. *South Coast New Guinea Cultures: History, Comparison, Dialectic.* Cambridge: Cambridge University Press.

———1996. *Genealogies for the Present in Cultural Anthropology.* London and New York: Routledge Press.

———1999. *From Primitive to Postcolonial in Melanesia and Anthropology.* Ann Arbor: University of Michigan Press.

———, ed. 2002. *Critically Modern: Alternatives, Alterities, Anthropologies.* Bloomington: Indiana University Press.

KNUDSON, RUTHANN. 1989. "North America's Threatened Heritage." *Archaeology* 42(1):71–75.

KONDO, DORINNE. 1990. *Crafting Selves: Power, Gender, and Discourses of Identity in a Japanese Workplace.* Chicago: University of Chicago Press.

KONNER, MELVIN. 1982. *The Tangled Wing: Biological Constraints on the Human Spirit.* New York: Holt, Rinehart and Winston.

KRINGS, M., A. STONE, R. W. SCHMITZ, H. KRAINITSKI, M. STONEKING, and S. PAABO. 1997. "Neandertal DNA Sequences and the Origins of Modern Humans." *Cell* 90: 19–30.

KRUCKMAN, L. 1987. "The Role of Remote Sensing in Ethnohistorical Research." *Journal of Field Archaeology* 14: 343–351.

KUPER, ADAM. 1988. *The Invention of Primitive Society.* London: Routledge Press.

KUPER, LEO, and M. G. SMITH. 1969. *Pluralism in Africa.* Berkeley and Los Angeles: University of California Press.

KURIN, RICHARD. 1980. "Doctor, Lawyer, Indian Chief." *Natural History* 89(11): 6–24.

KURTZ, DONALD V. 1982. "The Virgin of Guadalupe and the Politics of Becoming Human." *Journal of Anthropological Research* 38:194–210.

LAHR, MARTA MIRAZON, and ROBERT FOLEY. 1994. "Multiple Dispersals and Modern Human Origins." *Evolutionary Anthropology* 3(2):48–60.

LAITMAN, JEFFREY T. 1984. "The Anatomy of Human Speech." *Natural History* 93(8):20–27.

LAKOFF, GEORGE. 1987. *Women, Fire, and Dangerous Things.* Chicago: University of Chicago Press.

LAKOFF, GEORGE, and MARK JOHNSON. 2000. *Philosophy in the Flesh: The Embodied Mind and Its Challenge to Western Thought.* New York: Basic Books.

LAMBERG-KARLOVSKY, C. C. 1989. *Archaeological Thought in America.* Cambridge: Cambridge University Press.

LAMPHERE, LOUISE. 1997. "The Domestic Sphere of Women and the Public World of Men: The Strengths and Limitations of an Anthropological Dichotomy." In C. Brettel and C. Sargent, eds., *Gender in Cross-Cultural Perspective,* 2nd ed. Upper Saddle River, NJ: Prentice Hall.

LARSEN, CLARK SPENCER. 1995. "Biological Changes in Human Populations with Agriculture." *Annual Review of Anthropology* 24:185–213.

LAVILLE, H., J. RIGUAD, and J. SACKETT. 1980. *Rock Shelters of the Perigord.* New York: Academic Press.

LAWRENCE, PETER. 1964. *Road Belong Cargo: A Study of the Cargo Movement in the Southern Madang District, New Guinea.* Manchester: Manchester University Press.

LEACH, EDMUND. [1953] 1954. "Bridewealth and the Stability of Marriage." *Man* 53: 179–80; *Man* 54:173.

———. 1966. "Ritualization in Man in Relation to Conceptual and Social Development." *Philosophical Transactions of the Royal Society of London,* Series B 251(772):403–8.

———. 1988. "Noah's Second Son." *Anthropology Today* 4(4):2–5.

LEAF, MURRAY J. 1984. *Song of Hope: The Green Revolution in a Punjab Village.* New Brunswick, NJ: Rutgers University Press.

LEAKEY, L. S. B. 1959. "A New Fossil Skull from Olduvai." *Nature* 201:967–70.

———. 1961. "Exploring 1,750,000 Years into Man's Past." *National Geographic* 120(4):564–89.

LEAKEY, M. D. 1971. *Olduvai Gorge,* Vol. 3. Cambridge: Cambridge University Press.

LEAKEY, M. D. and R. L. HAY. 1979. "Pliocene footprints in Laetoli Beds at Laetoli, Northern Tanzania." *Nature* 278:317–23.

LEAKEY, MEAVE G., et al. 1995. "New Four-Million-Year-Old Hominid Species from Kanapoi and Allia Bay, Kenya." *Nature* 376:565–71.

LEAKEY, M.G., et al. 2001. "New Hominin Genus from Eastern Africa Shows Diverse Middle Pliocene Lineages." *Nature* 410:433–40.

LEAP, WILLIAM. 1988. "Indian Language Renewal." *Human Organization* 47(4): 283–91.

LEE, RICHARD B. 1968. "What Do Hunters Do for a Living, Or How to Make Out on Scarce Resources." In R. B. Lee and Irven DeVore, eds., *Man the Hunter,* pp. 30–43. Chicago: Aldine.

———. 1969. "Kung Bushman Subsistence: An Input-Output Analysis." In A. P. Vayda, ed., *Environment and Cultural Behavior: Ecological Studies in Cultural Anthropology.* Garden City, NY: Natural History Press.

———. 1972a. "The Intensification of Social Life Among the !Kung Bushmen." In Brian Spooner, ed., *Population Growth: Anthropological Implications,* pp. 343–50. Cambridge, MA: MIT Press.

———. 1972b. "Population Growth and the Beginning of Sedentary Life Among the !Kung Bushmen." In Brian Spooner, ed., *Population Growth: Anthropological Implications,* pp. 330–42. Cambridge, MA: MIT Press.

———. 1979. *The !Kung San: Men, Women, and Work in a Foraging Society.* Cambridge: Cambridge University Press.

———. 1981. "Politics, Sexual and Nonsexual in an Egalitarian Society: The !Kung San." In Gerald Berreman, ed., *Social Inequality: Comparative and Developmental Approaches,* pp. 83–101. New York: Academic Press.

———. 1993. *The Dobe Ju/'hoansi.* Fort Worth, TX: Harcourt Brace College Publishers.

LEE, RICHARD B., and IRVEN DEVORE, eds. 1968. *Man the Hunter.* Chicago: Aldine.

LEGROS CLARK, W. E. 1962. *The Antecedents of Man.* Edinburgh: Edinburgh University Press.

LENSKI, GERHARD E. 1966. *Power and Privilege: A Theory of Social Stratification.* New York: McGraw-Hill.

LENSKI, GERHARD, and JEAN LENSKI. 1982. *Human Societies: An Introduction to Macrosociology.* New York: McGraw-Hill.

LEONARD, KAREN ISAKSEN. 1997. *The South Asian Americans.* Westport, CT: Greenwood Press.

LEONE, MARK P., and PARKER B. POTTER. 1988. *The Recovery of Meaning: Historical Archaeology in the Eastern United States.* Washington, DC: Smithsonian Institution Press.

LEPOWSKY, MARIA. 1993. *Fruit of the Motherland: Gender in an Egalitarian Society.* New York: Columbia University Press.

LEVINE, NANCY. 1988. *The Dynamics of Polyandry.* Chicago: University of Chicago Press.

LEVINTON, JEFFREY. 1988. *Genetics, Paleontology, and Macroevolution.* New York: Cambridge University Press.

LEVI-STRAUSS, CLAUDE. 1944. "The Social and Psychological Aspects of Chieftainship in a Primitive Tribe: The Nambikuara of Northwestern Matto Grosso." *Transactions of the New York Academy of Sciences* 7:16–32.

———. 1966. *The Savage Mind,* trans. George Weidenfeld and Nicholson, Ltd. Chicago: University of Chicago Press.

———. 1969. *The Elementary Structures of Kinship,* rev. ed., trans. J. H. Bell. Boston: Beacon Press.

LEWELLEN, TED C. 1983. *Political Anthropology: An Introduction.* South Hadley, MA: Bergin & Garvey.

LEWIN, TAMAR. 1986. "Profile of an Anthropologist Casting an Anthropological Eye on American Consumers." *The New York Times,* May 11.

LEWIS, HERBERT. 1992. "Ethnic Loyalties Are on the Rise Globally." *Christian Science Monitor,* December 28. Reprinted in

Jeffress Ramsay, ed. 1993. *Africa,* 5th ed. Guilford, CT.: Dushkin Publishing Group.

LEWIS, OSCAR. 1951. *Life in a Mexican Village: Tepotzlan Restudied.* Urbana: University of Illinois Press.

———. 1961. *The Children of Sanchez: Autobiography of a Mexican Family.* New York: Random House.

———. 1966. *La Vida: A Puerto Rican Family in the Culture of Poverty—San Juan and New York.* New York: Random House.

LEWONTIN, R. 1972. "The Apportionment of Human Diversity." In Theodore Dobzhansky and William C. Steere, eds., *Evolutionary Biology,* Vol. 6, pp. 381–98. New York: Plenum Press.

LI, WEN-HSIUNG, and MASAKO TANIMURA. 1987. "The Molecular Clock Runs More Slowly in Man Than in Apes and Monkeys." *Nature* 326:93–96.

LIEBERMAN, LEONARD. 2001. "How Caucasoids Got Such Big Crania and Why They Shrank: From Morton to Rushton." *Current Anthropology* 42:69–95.

———. 2003. "A History of 'Scientific' Racialism." In Raymond Scupin, ed., *Race and Ethnicity: An Anthropological Focus on the U.S. and the World.* Upper Saddle River, NJ: Prentice Hall.

LIEBERMAN, PHILIP. 1984. *The Biology and Evolution of Language.* Cambridge, MA: Harvard University Press.

LINCOLN, JAMES R., and KERRY MCBRIDE. 1987. "Japanese Industrial Organization in Comparative Perspective." *Annual Review of Sociology* 13:289–312.

LINDENBAUM, SHIRLEY. 1972. "Sorcerers, Ghosts, and Polluting Women: An Analysis of Religious Belief and Population Control." *Ethnology* 2(3):241–53.

LINDHOLM, CHARLES. 1986. "Kinship Structure and Political Authority: The Middle East and Central Asia." *Comparative Study of Society and History* 28(2): 334–55.

LINDHOLM, CHARLES, and CHERRY LINDHOLM. 1980. "What Price Freedom?" *Science Digest,* November-December, pp. 50–55.

LINTON, RALPH. 1936. *The Study of Man.* New York: Appleton-Century-Crofts.

———. 1942. "Age and Sex Categories." *American Sociological Review* 7: 589–603.

LIPSET, SEYMOUR MARTIN, and REINHARD BENDIX. 1967. *Social Mobility in Industrial Society.* Berkeley: University of California Press.

LIVINGSTON, FRANK B. 1971. "Malaria and Human Polymorphisms." *Annual Review of Genetics* 5:33–64.

LORENZ, KONRAD. 1966. *On Aggression.* New York: Harcourt, Brace & World.

LOVEJOY, OWEN C. 1981. "The Origin of Man." *Science* 211:341–50.

———. 1984. "The Natural Detective." *Natural History* 93(10):24–28.

———. 1988. "Evolution of Human Walking." *Scientific American* 259(5):118–25.

LOVEJOY, OWEN C., and R. S. MEINDL. 1972. "Eukaryote Mutation and the Protein Clock." *Yearbook of Physical Anthropology* 16:18–30.

LOWE, JOHN W. G. 1985. *The Dynamics of Apocalypse: Systems Simulation of the Classic Maya Collapse.* Albuquerque: University of New Mexico Press.

LUCY, JOHN. 1992. *Grammatical Categories and Cognition: A Case Study of the Linguistic Relativity Hypothesis.* Cambridge: Cambridge University Press.

LUTZ, CATHERINE. 1988. *Unnatural Emotions: Everyday Sentiments on a Micronesian Atoll and Their Challenge to Western Theory.* Chicago: University of Chicago Press.

LYELL, CHARLES. 1830–1833. *Principles of Geology* (3 volumes). London.

MACLENNAN, JOHN FERGUSON. 1865. *Primitive Marriage: An Inquiry into the Origin of the Form of Capture in Marriage Ceremonies.* Edinburgh: A. and C. Black.

MACEACHERN, SCOTT. 2003. "Race." In Raymond Scupin, ed., *Race and Ethnicity: An Anthropological Focus on the U.S. and the World.* Upper Saddle River, NJ: Prentice Hall.

MACIONIS, JOHN. 2001. *Society: The Basics,* 6th ed. Upper Saddle River, NJ: Prentice Hall.

MACNEISH, RICHARD. 1970. *The Prehistory of the Tehuacan Valley.* Austin: University of Texas Press.

MALINOWSKI, BRONISLAW. [1922] 1961. *Argonauts of the Western Pacific.* New York: Dutton.

———. 1927. *Sex and Repression in Savage Society.* New York: Meridian Books.

———. 1945. Foreward In P. Kaberry, ed., *The Dynamics of Culture Change: An Inquiry into Race Relations in Africa.* New Haven, CT: Yale University Press.

MALONEY, CLARENCE. 1974. *Peoples of South Asia.* New York: Holt, Rinehart and Winston.

MALOTKI, EKKEHART. 1983. *Hopi Time: A Linguistic Analysis of the Temporal Concepts in the Hopi Language.* Berlin: Mouton.

MAQUET, JACQUES. 1972. *Civilizations of Black Africa.* London: Oxford University Press.

MARANO, LOU. 1982. "Windigo Psychosis: The Anatomy of an Emic-Etic Confusion." *Current Anthropology* 23:385–412.

MARINATOS, SPIRIDON. 1939. "The Volcanic Destruction of Minoan Crete." *Antiquity* 13:425–39.

MARSELLA, ANTHONY J. 1979. "Cross-Cultural Studies of Mental Disorders." In Anthony J. Marsella, Ronald G. Tharp, and Thomas J. Cibrowski, eds., *Perspectives on Cross-Cultural Psychology.* New York: Academic Press.

MARTIN, KAY, and BARBARA VOORHIES. 1975. *Female of the Species.* New York: Columbia University Press.

MARTIN, LINDA G. 1989. "The Graying of Japan." Population Reference Bureau, *Population Bulletin* 44(July):1–43. Washington, DC: U.S. Government Printing Office.

MARTIN, SAMUEL. 1964. "Speech Levels in Japan and Korea." In Dell Hymes, ed., *Language in Culture and Society: A Reader in Linguistics and Anthropology.* New York: Harper & Row.

MARX, KARL. [1859] 1959. *A Contribution of the Critique of Political Economy.* New York: International Publishers.

MASCIA-LEES, FRANCES, and NANCY JOHNSON BLACK. 2000. *Gender and Anthropology.* Prospect Heights, IL: Waveland Press.

MAUSS, MARCEL. 1985. "A Category of the Human Mind: The Notion of Person; the Notion of Self," trans. W. D. Halls. In Michael Carrithers, Steven Collins, and Steven Lukes, eds., *The Category of the Person: Anthropology, Philosophy, History.* Cambridge: Cambridge University Press.

MAY, DARLENE. 1980. "Women in Islam: Yesterday and Today." In Cyriac Pullapilly, ed., *Islam in the Contemporary World.* Notre Dame, IN: Cross Roads Books.

MAYBURY-LEWIS, DAVID. 1985. "A Special Sort of Pleading: Anthropology at the Service of Ethnic Groups." In

R. Paine, ed., *Advocacy and Anthropology.* St. John's, Newfoundland: Institute of Social and Economic Research, Memorial University of Newfoundland.

———. 1997. *Indigenous Peoples, Ethnic Groups, and the State.* Needham Heights, MA: Allyn & Bacon.

———. 1998. "Cultural Survival, Ethics and Political Expediency: The Anthropology of Group Rights." (http:\\www.cs.org/publications/featuredarticles/1998/mayburylewis.htm).

MCALLESTER, DAVID P. 1983. "North American Native Music." In Elizabeth May, ed., *Music of Many Cultures: An Introduction.* Berkeley: University of California Press.

———. 1984. "North America/Native America." In Jeff Todd Titon, ed., *Worlds of Music: An Introduction to the Music of the World's Peoples.* New York: Schirmer Books.

MCCLELLAND, DAVID. 1973. "Business Drive and National Achievement." In A. Etzioni and E. Etzioni-Halevy, eds., *Social Change.* New York: Basic Books.

MCCLUNG DE TAPIA, EMILY. 1992. "The Origins of Agriculture in Mesoamerica and Central America." In C. Wesley Cowan and Patty Jo Watson, eds., *The Origins of Agriculture: An International Perspective,* pp. 143–72. Washington, DC: Smithsonian Institution Press.

MCCREERY, JOHN. 2000. *Japanese Consumer Behavior: From Worker Bees to Wary Shoppers.* Honolulu: University of Hawaii Press.

MCDANIEL, L. 1998. *The Big Drum Ritual of Carriacou: Praise Songs in Memory of Flight.* Gainesville: University Press of Florida.

MCDONALD, JAMES, H. 1997. "Privatizing the Private Family Farmer: NAFTA and the Transformation of the Mexican Dairy Sector." *Human Organization* 56(1):321–32.

———. 1999. "The Neoliberal Project and Governmentality in Rural Mexico: Emergent Farmer Organization in the Michoacan Highlands." *Human Organization* 58(3):274–84.

———. 2001. "Reconfiguring the Countryside: Power, Control, and the (Re)Organization of Farmers in West Mexico." *Human Organization* 60(3):247–58.

MCHENRY, HENRY M. 1982. "The Pattern of Human Evolution Studies on Bipedalism, Mastication, and Encephalization."

Annual Review of Anthropology 11: 151–73.

———. 1988. "New Estimates of Body Weight in Early Hominids and Their Significance to Encephalization and Megadentia in Robust Australopithecines." In F. E. Grine, ed., *Evolutionary History of the Robust Australopithecines,* pp. 133–48. Hawthorne, NJ: Aldine.

MCINTOSH, SUSAN. 1999. *Beyond Chiefdoms: Pathways to Complexity in Africa.* Cambridge: Cambridge University Press.

MCINTOSH, S. K., and R. J. MCINTOSH. 1993. "Current Directions in West African Prehistory." *Annual Review of Anthropology,* 12:215–58.

MCKENNA, JAMES, SARAH MOSKO, and CHRIS RICHARD. 1999. "Breastfeeding and Mother-Infant Cosleeping in Relation to SIDS Prevention." In Wenda R. Trevathan, E. O. Smith, and James J. McKenna, eds., *Evolutionary Medicine.* New York and Oxford: Oxford University Press.

MCKEOWN, C. TIMOTHY. 1998. "Ethical and Legal Issues, Complying with NAGPRA." In Rebecca A. Buck, Amanda Murphy, and Jennifer Schansberg, eds., *The New Museums Registration Methods.* American Association of Museums.

MCMAHON, FRANK, and JUDITH H. MCMAHON. 1983. *Abnormal Behavior: Psychology's View.* Homewood, IL: Dorsey Press.

MEAD, MARGARET. 1928. *Coming of Age in Samoa.* New York: Morrow.

———. 1935. *Sex and Temperament in Three Primitive Societies.* New York: Mentor.

MEGGITT, MERVYN. 1977. *Blood Is Their Argument: Warfare Among the Mae Enga Tribesmen of the New Guinea Highlands.* Palo Alto, CA: Mayfield.

MELLAART, JAMES. 1975. *The Earliest Civilizations of the Near East.* London: Thames and Hudson.

MELLARS, P. A. 1988. "The Origin and Dispersal of Modern Humans." *Current Anthropology* 29:186–88.

———. 1989. "Major Issues in the Emergence of Modern Humans." *Current Anthropology* 30(3):349–85.

MELTZER, D. J. 1993. "Pleistocene Peopling of the Americas." *Evolutionary Anthropology* 1(5):157–69.

MENCHER, JOAN P. 1965. "The Nayars of South Malabar." In M. F. Nimkorr, ed.,

Comparative Family Systems, pp. 162–91. Boston: Houghton Mifflin.

———. 1974. "The Caste System Upside Down: Or the Not-So-Mysterious East." *Current Anthropology* 15:469–94.

MENSAH, ATTA ANNAM. 1983. "Music South of the Sahara." In Elizabeth May, ed., *Music of Many Cultures: An Introduction.* Berkeley: University of California Press.

MERNISSI, FATIMA. 1975. *Beyond the Veil: Male-Female Dynamics in a Modern Muslim Society.* Cambridge, MA: Schenkman.

MESKELL, LYNN. 1995. "Goddesses, Gimbutas and 'New Age Archaeology,' " *Antiquity* (March).

MESSENGER, JOHN. 1971. "Sex and Repression in an Irish Folk Community." In Donald S. Marshall and Robert C. Suggs, eds., *Human Sexual Behavior: Variations in the Ethnographic Spectrum.* New York: Basic Books.

METRAUX, AFRED, HUGO CHARTERIS, and SIDNEY MINTZ. 1989. *Voodoo in Haiti.* New York: Schocken Books.

MIDDLETON, JOHN. 1960. *Lugbara Religion.* London: Oxford University Press.

———. 1978. *Peoples of Africa.* New York: Arco.

MILLER, N. F. 1992. "The Origins of Plant Cultivation in the Near East." In C. Wesley Cowan and Patty Jo Watson, eds., *The Origins of Agriculture: An International Perspective,* pp. 39–58. Washington, DC: Smithsonian Institution Press.

MILLON, RENÉ. 1976. "Social Relations in Ancient Teotihuacán." In Eric R. Wolf, ed., *The Valley of Mexico: Studies in Prehispanic Ecology and Society.* Albuquerque: University of New Mexico Press.

MILLON, RENÉ, R. BRUCE DREWITT, and GEORGE COWGILL. 1974. *Urbanization at Teotihuacán, Mexico.* Austin: University of Texas Press.

MOLNAR, STEPHEN. 1997. *Human Variation: Races, Types, and Ethnic Groups,* 4th ed. Upper Saddle River, NJ: Prentice Hall.

MONAGHAN, L, L. HINTON, and R. KEPHART. 1997. "Can't Teach a Dog to Be a Cat?: A Dialogue on Ebonics." *Anthropology Newsletter* 38(3):1,8,9.

MONTAGU, ASHLEY, ed. 1968. *Man and Aggression.* London: Oxford University Press.

———. 1997. *Man's Most Dangerous Myth: The Fallacy of Race,* 6th ed. Walnut Creek, CA: Altamira Press.

MORAN, EMILIO F. 1982. *Human Adaptability: An Introduction to Ecological Anthropology.* Boulder, CO: Westview Press.

MORGAN, LEWIS HENRY. [1877] 1964. *Ancient Society.* Cambridge, MA: Harvard University Press.

MORRIS, DESMOND. 1967. *The Naked Ape.* New York: McGraw-Hill.

MOSELEY, MICHAEL E., and JAMES B. RICHARDSON. 1992. "Doomed by Natural Disaster." *Archaeology* 45(6):44–45.

MOSHER, STEVEN W. 1983. *The Broken Earth: The Rural Chinese.* Glencoe, IL: Free Press.

MOTULSKY, ARNO. 1971. "Metabolic Polymorphisms and the Role of Infectious Diseases in Human Evolution." In Laura Newell Morris, ed., *Human Populations, Genetic Variation, and Evolution.* San Francisco: Chandler.

MOUNTAIN, JOANNA L. 1998. "Molecular Evolution and Modern Human Origins." *Evolutionary Anthropology* 7(1):21–38.

MUMFORD, LEWIS. 1961. *The City in History: Its Origins, Its Transformations, and Its Prospects.* New York: Harcourt, Brace & World.

MURDOCK, GEORGE. 1945. "The Common Denominator of Cultures." In Ralph Linton, ed., *The Science of Man in the World Crisis,* pp. 123–42. New York: Columbia University Press.

———. 1949. *Social Structure.* New York: Macmillan.

———. 1967. "Ethnographic Atlas: A Summary." *Ethnology* 6:109–236.

———. 1968. "The Current Status of the World's Hunting and Gathering Peoples." In Richard Lee and Irven DeVore, eds., *Man the Hunter,* pp. 13–20. Chicago: Aldine.

———. 1981a. *Atlas of World Cultures.* Pittsburgh: University of Pittsburgh Press.

———. 1981b. *Ethnographic Atlas.* Pittsburgh: University of Pittsburgh Press.

MURPHY, R. F., and L. KASDAN. 1959. "The Structure of Parallel Cousin Marriage." *American Anthropologist* 61:17–29.

MURRAY, GERALD F. 1989. "The Domestication of Wood in Haiti: A Case Study in Applied Evolution." *Anthropological Praxis.* Reprinted in Aaron Podelfsky and Peter J. Brown, eds., 1994. *Applying*

Anthropology: An Introductory Reader. Mountain View, CA: Mayfield.

MURRAY, R. D., and SMITH, E. O. 1983. "The Role of Dominance and Intrafamilial Bonding in the Avoidance of Close Inbreeding." *Journal of Human Evolution* 12:481–86.

MYERS, DAVID G. 1998. *Psychology,* 5th ed. New York: Worth Publishers.

NAKANE, CHIA. 1970. *Japanese Society.* Rutland, VT: Charles Tuttle.

NANDA, SERENA. 1990. *Neither Man nor Woman: The Hijras of India.* Belmont, CA: Wadsworth.

———. 2000. *Gender Diversity: Crosscultural Variations.* Prospect Heights, IL: Waveland Press.

NARANJO, TESSIE. 1995. "Thoughts on Two Worldviews." *Federal Archaeology.* Offprint Series, Fall/Winter, 8.

NASH, JUNE. 1997. "The Fiesta of the Word: The Zapatista Uprising and Radical Democracy in Mexico." *American Anthropologist* 99(2):261–74.

NASH, MANNING. 1989. *The Cauldron of Ethnicity in the Modern World.* Chicago: University of Chicago Press.

NATIONAL OPINION RESEARCH CENTER. 1999. *General Social Surveys. 1972–1999: Cumulative Codebook.* Chicago: University of Chicago.

NEALE, WALTER. 1976. *Monies in Societies.* San Francisco: Chandler.

NEEDHAM, RODNEY. 1967. "Percussion and Transition." *Man* 2:606–14.

NELSON, HARRY, and ROBERT JURMAIN. 1988. *Introduction to Physical Anthropology,* 4th ed. St. Paul, MN: West.

NEWMAN, R. W., and E. H. MUNRO. 1955. "The Relation of Climate and Body Size in U.S. Males." *American Journal of Physical Anthropology* 13:1–17.

NOEL HUME, IVOR. 1983. *Historical Archaeology: A Comprehensive Guide.* New York: Knopf.

NORGET, KRISTIN. 1996. "Beauty and the Feast: Aesthetics and the Performance of Meaning in the Day of the Dead, Oaxaca, Mexico." *Journal of Latin American Lore* 19:53–64.

OAKLEY, KENNETH P. 1964. *Man the Tool Maker.* Chicago: University of Chicago Press.

OBEYESKERE, GANANATH. 1992. *Apotheosis of Captain Cook: European Mythmaking in the Pacific.* Princeton, NJ: Princeton University Press.

OFFICER, C. B. 1990. "Extinctions, Iridium, and Shocked Minerals Associated with the Cretaceous/Tertiary Transition." *Journal of Geological Education* 38: 402–25.

OHNUKI-TIERNEY, EMIKO. 1998. "A Conceptual Model for the Historical Relationship Between the Self and the Internal and External Others: The Agrarian Japanese, the Ainu, and the Special Status People." In Dru Gladney, ed., *Making Majorities: Constituting the Nation in Japan, Korea, China, Malaysia, Fiji, Turkey, and the United States.* Stanford: Stanford University Press.

OKIGBO, BEDE N. 1988. "Food: Finding Solutions to the Crisis." *Africa Report,* September-October.

OLIVER, DOUGLAS. 1955. *A Solomon Island Society: Kinship and Leadership Among the Siuai of Bougainville.* Cambridge, MA: Harvard University Press.

———. 1974. *Ancient Tahitian Society,* 3 vols. Honolulu: University of Hawaii Press.

OLMOS, M. F. 1997. *Sacred Possessions: Vodou, Santeria, Obeah, and the Caribbean.* New Brunswick, NJ: Rutgers University Press.

O'MEARA, TIM J. 1990. *Samoan Planters: Tradition and Economic Development in Polynesia.* New York: Holt, Rinehart and Winston.

OMOHUNDRO, JOHN. 1998. *Careers in Anthropology.* Mountain View, CA: Mayfield.

ORTNER, SHERRY. 1974. "Is Female to Male as Nature Is to Culture?" In Michelle Zimbalist Rosaldo and Louise Lamphere, eds., *Woman, Culture, and Society,* pp. 67–87. Stanford, CA: Stanford University Press.

———. 1996. *Making Gender: The Politics and Erotics of Culture.* Boston: Beacon Press.

OSWALT, WENDELL H. 1972. *Other Peoples, Other Customs: World Ethnography and Its History.* New York: Holt, Rinehart and Winston.

———. 1976. *An Anthropological Analysis of Food-Getting Technology.* New York: John Wiley.

OTTENBERG, PHOEBE. 1965. "The Afikpo Ibo of Eastern Nigeria." In James L. Gibbs, ed., *Peoples of Africa.* New York: Holt, Rinehart and Winston.

OTTERBEIN, KEITH. 1970. *The Evolution of War.* New Haven, CT: HRAF Press.

————. 1974. "The Anthropology of War." In John Honigmann, ed., *Handbook of Social and Cultural Anthropology*. Chicago: Rand McNally.

————. 1994. *Feuding and Warfare: Selected Works of Keith F. Otterbein*. Langhorne, PA: Gordon and Breach.

————. 1999. "Historical Essay: A History of the Research on Warfare in Anthropology." *American Anthropologist* 101(4): 794–805.

————. 2000. "The Doves Have Been Heard From, Where Are the Hawks?" *American Anthropologist* 102(4):841–44.

OUICHI, WILLIAM G. 1981. *Theory Z: How American Business Can Meet the Japanese Challenge*. New York: Avon Books.

PAIGEN, B., L. R. GOLDMAN, J. H. MAGNANT, J. H. HIGHLAND, and A. T. STEEGMAN. 1987. "Growth and Children Living Near the Hazardous Waste Site, Love Canal." *Human Biology* 59:489–508.

PALAKORNKUL, ANGKAB. 1972. *A Sociolinguistic Study of Pronominial Strategy in Spoken Bangkok Thai*. Doctoral Dissertation, University of Texas, Austin.

PALMORE, ERDMAN BALLAGH. 1975. *The Honorable Elders: A Cross-Cultural Analysis of Aging in Japan*. Durham, NC: Duke University Press.

PARRINDER, GEOFFREY. 1983. *World Religions: From Ancient History to the Present*. New York: Hamlyn Publishing Group.

PARRY, JONATHAN. 1980. "Ghosts, Greed and Sin: The Occupational Identity of the Benares Funeral Priests." *Man* 21: 453–73.

PASSINGHAM, R. E. 1982. *The Human Primate*. San Francisco: W. H. Freeman.

PASTERNAK, BURTON. 1976. *Introduction to Kinship and Social Organization*. Englewood Cliffs, NJ: Prentice Hall.

PATTERSON, FRANCINE, and DONALD COHN. 1978. "Conversations with a Gorilla." *National Geographic* 154:454–62.

PATTERSON, FRANCINE, and EUGENE LINDEN. 1981. *The Education of Koko*. New York: Holt, Rinehart and Winston.

PATTERSON, MARY. 2000. "Sorcery and Witchcraft." In Raymond Scupin, *Religion and Culture: An Anthropological Focus*. Upper Saddle River, NJ: Prentice Hall.

PAUL, ROBERT A. 1989. "Psychoanalytic Anthropology." *Annual Review of Anthropology* 18:177–202.

————. 1996. *Moses and Civilization: The Meaning Behind Freud's Myth*. New Haven: Yale University Press.

PEACOCK, JAMES. 1986. *The Anthropological Lens: Harsh Light, Soft Focus*. Cambridge: Cambridge University Press.

PEARSALL, D. M. 1992. "The Origins of Plant Cultivation in South America." In C. Wesley Cowan and Patty Jo Watson, eds., *The Origins of Agriculture: An International Perspective*, pp. 173–205. Washington, DC: Smithsonian Institution Press.

PERKINS, DEXTER. 1964. "The Prehistoric Fauna from Shanidar, Iraq." *Science* 144:1565–66.

PFEIFFER, JOHN. 1985. *The Emergence of Man*, 4th ed. New York: Harper & Row.

PHILLIPSON, DAVID W. 1993. *African Archaeology*. Cambridge University Press: New York, NY.

PIDDOCKE, STUART. 1965. "The Potlatch System of the Southern Kwakiutl: A New Perspective." *Southwestern Journal of Anthropology* 21:244–64.

PIKE, DOUGLAS. 1990. "Change and Continuity in Vietnam." *Current History* 89(545):117–34.

PILBEAM, DAVID. 1972. *The Ascent of Man*. New York: Macmillan.

PINKER, STEVEN. 1994. *The Language Instinct: How the Mind Creates Language*. New York: HarperCollins.

POIRER, FRANK E., WILLIAM A. STINI, and KATHY B. WREDEN. 1990. *In Search of Ourselves: An Introduction to Physical Anthropology*, 4th ed. Upper Saddle River, NJ: Prentice Hall.

POLEDNAK, ANTHONY P. 1974. "Connective Tissue Responses in Negroes in Relation to Disease." *American Journal of Physical Anthropology* 41:49–57.

POLYANI, KARL. 1944. *The Great Transformation*. New York: Rinehart.

POPLINE: WORLD POPULATION NEWS SERVICE. 1993. "1993 State of World Population Edition," Vol. 15, July–August.

POPULATION REFERENCE BUREAU. 1986. *Population Data Sheet*. Washington, DC: Population Reference Bureau.

————. 1991. *World Population Data Sheet*. Washington, DC: Population Reference Bureau.

POSNANSKY, MERRICK. 1984. "Early Agricultural Societies in Ghana." In J. Clark and Steven A. Brandt, eds., *From Hunter to Farmer*, pp. 147–51. Berkeley: University of California Press.

POSPISIL, LEONARD. 1963. *The Kapauku Papuans of West New Guinea*. New York: Holt, Rinehart and Winston.

————. 1967. "The Attributes of Law." In Paul Bohannon, ed., *Law and Warfare: Studies in the Anthropology of Conflict*. Garden City, NY: Natural History Press.

POST, P. W., F. DANIELS, and R. T. BINFORD. 1975. "Cold Injury and the Evolution of White Skin." *Human Biology* 47:65–80.

POTTS, RICHARD. 1988. *Early Hominid Activities at Olduvai*. New York: Aldine de Gruyter.

————. 1991. "Why the Oldowan? Plio-Pleistocene Toolmaking and the Transport of Resources." *Journal of Anthropological Research* 47:153–76.

————. 1993. "Archaeological Interpretations of Early Hominid Behavior and Ecology." In D. Tab Rasmussen, ed., *The Origins and Evolution of Humans and Humanness*, pp. 49–74. Boston: Jones and Barlett Publisher.

POTTS, RICHARD and PAT SHIPMAN. 1981. "Cutmarks Made by Stone Tools from Olduvai Gorge, Tanzania." *Nature* 291: 577–80.

POWDERMAKER, HORTENSE. 1966. *Stranger and Friend: The Way of an Anthropologist*. New York: W. W. Norton.

PRAG, JOHN, and RICHARD NEAVE. 1997. *Making Faces*. College Station: Texas A&M University Press.

PRICE, DOUGLAS T., and JAMES A. BROWN. 1985. *Prehistoric Hunter-Gatherers: The Emergence of Cultural Complexity*. New York: Academic Press.

PROTHERO, DONALD R. 1989. *Interpreting the Stratigraphic Record*. New York: W. H. Freeman.

QUALE, ROBIN G. 1988. *A History of Marriage Systems*. New York: Greenwood Press.

QUINN, NAOMI, and DOROTHY HOLLAND. 1987. "Culture and Cognition." In D. Holland and N. Quinn, eds., *Cultural Models in Language and Thought*. Cambridge: Cambridge University Press.

RADCLIFFE-BROWN, A. R. [1922] 1964. *The Andaman Islanders*. New York: Free Press.

RADINSKY, LEONARD. 1967. "The Oldest Primate Endocast." *American Journal of Physical Anthropology* 27:358–88.

RAHEJA, GLORIA. 1988. *The Poison in the Gift: Ritual, Prestation, and the Dominant Caste in a North Indian Village*. Chicago: University of Chicago Press.

RAMSAY, JEFFRESS F., ed. 2001. *Africa,* 9th ed. Guilford, CT: McGraw-Hill/Dushkin Publishing Group.

RAPPAPORT, ROY. 1979. *Ecology, Meaning, and Religion.* Richmond, VA: North Atlantic Books.

———. 1984. *Pigs for the Ancestors: Ritual in the Ecology of a New Guinea People.* New Haven, CT: Yale University Press.

RASMUSSEN, TAB D., and ELWYN L. SIMONS. 1988. "New Species of *Oligopithecus savagei,* Early Oligocene Primate from the Fayum, Egypt." *Folia Primatology* 51:182–208.

RATHBUN, T. A., and J. E. BUIKSTRA. 1984. *Human Identification: Case Studies in Forensic Anthropology.* Springfield, IL: Charles C Thomas.

RATHJE, WILLIAM. 1971. "The Origin and Development of Lowland Classic Maya Civilization." *American Antiquity* 36: 275–85.

———. 1984. "The Garbage Decade." *American Behavioral Scientist* 28(1): 9–29.

———. 1992. "Five Major Myths about Garbage, and Why They Are Wrong." *Smithsonian* 23(4):113–22.

RATHJE, WILLIAM L., and CHERYL K. RITENBAUGH. 1984. "Household Refuse Analysis: Theory, Method, and Applications in Social Science." *American Behavioral Scientist* 28(1):5–153.

RAUP, DAVID M. 1986. *The Nemesis Affair: A Story of the Death of the Dinosaurs and the Ways of Science.* New York: W. W. Norton.

RAVEN, PETER H., LINDA R. BERG, and GEORGE B. JOHNSON. 1993. *Environment.* Fort Worth, TX : Saunders College Publishing.

RAYNER, STEVE. 1989. "Fiddling While the Globe Warms." *Anthropology Today* 5(6):1–2.

REDFIELD, ROBERT. 1930. *Tepotzlan: A Mexican Village: A Study of Folk Life.* Chicago: University of Chicago Press.

REDFIELD, ROBERT, and ALFONSO VILLA ROJAS. 1934. *Chan Kom, A Maya Village.* Washington, DC: Carnegie Institute.

RELETHFORD, JOHN H. 1997. *The Human Species: An Introduction to Biological Anthropology,* 3rd ed. Mountain View, CA: Mayfield.

RENFREW, COLIN. 1989. *Archaeology and Language: The Puzzle of Indo-European Origins.* Cambridge: Cambridge University Press.

RENFREW, COLIN, and PAUL BAHN. 2000. *Archaeology: Theories, Methods and Practice,* 3rd ed. New York: Thames & Hudson.

RENFREW, COLIN, and K. L. COOKE. 1979. *Transformations: Mathematical Approaches to Culture Change.* New York: Academic Press.

RICE, PRUDENCE M. 1987. *Pottery Analysis: A Sourcebook.* Chicago: University of Chicago Press.

RICHARD, ALISON F. 1985. *Primates in Nature.* New York: W. H. Freeman.

RICKFORD, JOHN R. 1997. "Suite for Ebony and Phonics." *Discovery* 18(2):82–87.

RIDLEY, MATT. 1996. *The Origins of Virtue: Human Instincts and the Evolution of Cooperation.* New York: Viking Press.

RIESENFELD, ALPHONSE. 1973. "The Effect of Extreme Temperatures and Starvation on the Body Proportions of the Rat." *American Journal of Physical Anthropology* 39:427–59.

RIGHTMIRE, G. P. 1981. "Patterns in the Evolution of *Homo erectus.*" *Paleobiology* 7:241–46.

RINDOS, DAVID. 1984. *The Origins of Agriculture: An Evolutionary Perspective.* New York: Academic Press.

RINER, REED. 1981. "The Supranational Network of Boards of Directors." *Current Anthropology* 22(2):167–72.

RIVERS, W. H. O. [1906] 1967. *Todas.* London: Macmillan.

ROBARCHEK, C. A., and C. J. ROBARCHEK. 1998. *Waorani: The Contexts of Violence and War.* Fort Worth: Harcourt Brace.

ROBBINS, RICHARD H. 1999. *Global Problems and the Culture of Capitalism.* Boston: Allyn and Bacon.

ROBERTS, JOHN M. 1967. "Oaths, Autonomic Ordeals, and Power." In Clellan S. Ford, ed., *Cross-Cultural Approaches: Readings in Comparative Research.* New Haven, CT: HRAF Press.

ROBERTSON, CLAIRE C. 1984. "Women in the Urban Economy." In Margaret Jean Hay and Sharon Stichter, eds., *African Women South of the Sahara.* London: Longman.

ROBERTSON, IAN. 1990. *Sociology,* 4th ed. New York: Worth Publishers.

ROGERS, J. DANIEL, and SAMUEL M. WILSON. 1988. *Ethnohistory and Archaeology: Approaches to Postcontact Change in the Americas.* New York: Plenum Press.

ROMANUCCI-ROSS, LOLA. 1973. *Conflict, Violence and Morality in a Mexican Village.* Palo Alto, CA: National Press Books.

ROOSEVELT, ANNA CURTENIUS. 1984. "Population, Health, and the Evolution of Subsistence: Conclusions from the Conference." In Mark Nathan Cohen and George J. Armelagos, eds., *Paleopathology at the Origins of Agriculture,* pp. 559–84. New York: Academic Press.

ROSCOE, PAUL B. 1993. "The Brokers of the Lord: The Ministrations of a Christian Faith in the Sepik Basin of Papua New Guinea." In V. Lockwood, T. Harding, and B. Wallace, eds. *Contemporary Pacific Societies: Studies in Development and Change.* Upper Saddle River, NJ: Prentice Hall.

——— 1994. "Amity and Aggression: A Symbolic Theory of Incest." *Man* 28: 1–28.

ROSEBERRY, WILLIAM. 1982. "Balinese Cockfights and the Seduction of Anthropology." *Social Research* 49:1013–38.

ROSENBERG, MICHAEL. 1990. "The Mother of Invention: Evolutionary Theory, Territoriality, and the Origins of Agriculture." *American Anthropologist* 92(2): 399–415.

ROSMAN, ABRAHAM, and PAULA G. RUBEL. 1986. *Feasting with Mine Enemy: Rank and Exchange Among Northwest Coast Societies.* Prospect Heights, IL: Waveland Press.

ROSSIDES, DANIEL W. 1990a. *Comparative Societies: Social Types and Their Interrelations.* Upper Saddle River, NJ: Prentice Hall.

———. 1990b. *Social Stratification: The American Class System in Comparative Perspective.* Upper Saddle River, NJ: Prentice Hall.

ROSTOW, WALTER W. 1978. *The World Economy: History and Prospect.* Austin: University of Texas Press.

ROTHENBERG, JEROME. 1985. *Technicians of the Sacred: A Range of Poetries from Africa, Asia, Europe, and Oceania.* Berkeley: University of California Press.

ROUSSEAU, JEAN JACQUES. [1762] 1973. *The Social Contract.* London: Dent.

ROWLEY-CONWY, PETER. 1993. "Was There a Neanderthal Religion?" In G. Burenhult, ed., *The First Humans: Human Origins and History to 10,000 BC,* p. 70. New York: HarperCollins.

RUMBAUGH, DUANE M., ed. 1977. *Language Learning by a Chimpanzee.* New York: Academic Press.

RUSELL, D. E. H. 1986. *The Secret Trauma: Incest in the Lives of Girls and Women.* New York: Basic Books.

SABLOFF, JEREMY, and C. C. LAMBERG-KARLOVSKY, eds. 1975. *Ancient Civilization and Trade.* Albuquerque: University of New Mexico Press.

SACKETT, JAMES R. 1982. "Approaches to Style in Lithic Archaeology." *Journal of Anthropological Archaeology* 1:59–112.

SAFA, HELEN I. 1974. *The Urban Poor of Puerto Rico: A Study in Development and Inequality.* New York: Holt, Rinehart and Winston.

SAHLINS, MARSHALL. 1958. *Social Stratification in Polynesia.* Monograph of the American Ethnological Society. Seattle: University of Washington Press.

———. 1965. "On the Sociology of Primitive Exchange." In M. Banton, ed., *The Relevance of Models for Social Anthropology,* pp. 139–227. London: Tavistock.

———. 1968b. *Tribesmen.* Englewood Cliffs, NJ: Prentice Hall.

———. 1972. *Stone Age Economics.* Chicago: Aldine.

———. 1976. *The Use and Abuse of Biology: An Anthropological Critique of Sociobiology.* Ann Arbor: University of Michigan Press.

———. 1985. *Islands of History.* Chicago: University of Chicago Press.

———. 1995 *How 'Natives' Think, About Captain Cook, For Example.* Chicago: University of Chicago Press.

SALISBURY, R. F. 1962. *From Stone to Steel: Economic Consequences of a Technological Change in New Guinea.* Cambridge: Cambridge University Press.

SALMON, MERRILEE H. 1997. "Ethical Considerations in Anthropology and Archaeology, or Relativism and Justice for All." *Journal of Anthropological Research* 53:47–63.

SALZMAN, PHILIP. 1989. "The Lone Stranger and the Solitary Quest." *Anthropology Newsletter* 30(5):16, 44.

———. 2000. "Hierarchical Image and Reality: The Construction of a Tribal Chiefship." *Comparative Study of Society and History* 42(1):49–66.

SANDERS, WILLIAM T., and BARBARA J. PRICE. 1968. *Mesoamerica: The Evolution of a Civilization.* New York: Random House.

SARDESAI, D. R. 1989. *Southeast Asia: Past and Present.* Boulder, CO: Westview Press.

SARICH, V. M., and A. C. WILSON. 1967. "Rates of Albumen Evolution in Primates." *Proceedings of the National Academy of Sciences* 58:142–48.

SAUER, CARL O. 1952. *Agricultural Origins and Dispersals.* New York: American Geographical Society.

SAVAGE-RUMBAUGH, SUE E. 1986. *Ape Language from Conditioned Response to Symbol.* New York: Columbia University Press.

SCARR, S. and R. A. WEINBERG. 1978. "Attitudes, Interests, and IQ." *Human Nature* 1(4):29–36.

SCHAFFT, GRETCHEN. 1999. "Professional Denial." *Anthropology Newsletter* 40(1): 56–54 (January).

SCHALLER, GEORGE. 1976. *The Mountain Gorilla—Ecology and Behavior.* Chicago: University of Chicago Press.

SCHIEFFELIN, BAMBI B. 1990. *The Give and Take of Everyday Life: Language Socialization of Kaluli Children.* New York: Cambridge University Press.

SCHIEFFELIN, BAMBI, and ELINOR OCHS, eds. 1987. *Language Socialization Across Cultures.* Studies in the Social and Cultural Foundations of Languages, No 3. Cambridge: Cambridge University Press.

SCHIFFER, MICHAEL B. 1987. *Formation Processes of the Archaeological Record.* Albuquerque: University of New Mexico Press.

SCHLEGEL, ALICE, and ROHN ELOUL. 1988. "Marriage Transactions: Labor, Property, and Status." *American Anthropologist* 90(2):291–309.

SCHNEIDER, DAVID. 1953. "A Note on Bridewealth and the Stability of Marriage." *Man* 53:55–57.

SCHUSKY, ERNEST L. 1990. *Culture and Agriculture.* New York: Bergin and Garvey.

SCHWARTZ, RICHARD, and JAMES C. MILLER. 1975. "Legal Evolution and Societal Complexity." In Ronald L. Akers and James C. Miller, eds., *Law and Control in Society.* Englewood Cliffs, NJ: Prentice Hall.

SCOTT, JAMES. 1976. *The Moral Economy of the Peasant: Rebellion and Subsistence in Southeast Asia.* New Haven: Yale University Press.

SCUDDER, THAYER, and ELIZABETH COLSON. 1979. "Long-Term Research in Gwembe Valley, Zambia." In G. Foster, ed., *Long Term Field Research in Social Anthropology.* New York: Academic Press.

SCUPIN, RAYMOND. 1988. "Language, Hierarchy and Hegemony: Thai Muslim Discourse Strategies." *Language Sciences* 10(2):331–51.

———, ed. 2003. *Race and Ethnicity: An Anthropological Focus on the U.S. and the World.* Upper Saddle River, NJ: Prentice Hall.

SEBEOK, THOMAS A., and JEAN UMIKER-SEBEOK, eds. 1980. *Speaking of Apes: A Critical Anthology of Two-Way Communication with Man.* New York: Plenum Press.

SENUT, B., M. PICKFORD, D. GOMMERY, P. MEIN, K. CHEBOI, and Y. COPPENS. 2001. "Premier Hominidé du Miocène (Formation de Lukeino, Kenya)" *Comptes Rendus de l'Académie des Sciences,* Série IIa, 332:137–44.

SERVICE, ELMAN. 1960. "The Law of Evolutionary Potential." In Marshall D. Sahlins and Elman R. Service, eds., *Evolution and Culture,* pp. 93–122. Ann Arbor: University of Michigan Press.

———. [1962] 1971. *Primitive Social Organization: An Evolutionary Perspective.* New York: Random House.

———. 1975. *Origins of the State and Civilization: The Process of Cultural Evolution.* New York: W. W. Norton.

———. 1978a. "Classical and Modern Theories of the Origin of Government." In Ronald Cohen and E. R. Service, eds., *Origins of the State: The Anthropology of Political Evolution.* Philadelphia: Institute for Study of Human Issues.

———. 1978b. *Profiles in Ethnology.* New York: Harper & Row.

———. 1979. *The Hunters,* 2nd ed. Englewood Cliffs, NJ: Prentice Hall.

SHAHRANI, M. NAZIF. 1981. "Growing in Respect: Aging Among the Kirghiz of Afghanistan." In P. Amoss and S. Harrell, eds., *Other Ways of Growing Old: Anthropologist Perspectives.* Stanford, CA: Stanford University Press.

SHAHRANI, M. NAZIF, and ROBERT CANFIELD, eds. 1984. *Revolutions and Rebellions in Afghanistan: Anthropological Perspectives.* Berkeley: University of California Press.

SHANKMAN, PAUL. 1975. "A Forestry Scheme in Samoa." *Natural History* 84(8):60–69.

———. 1978. "Notes on a Corporate 'Potlatch': The Lumber Industry in Samoa." In A. Idris-Soven, E. Idris-Soven, and M. K. Vaugh, eds., *The*

World as a Company Town: Multinational Corporations and Social Change. The Hague: Mouton World Anthropology Series.

———. 1990. Personal correspondence.

———. 1998. "Margaret Mead, Derek Freeman, and the Issue of Evolution." *Skeptical Inquirer* 22(6):35–39.

———. 2000. "Development, Sustainability, and the Deforestation of Samoa." *Pacific Studies.*

———. 2001. "Requiem for a Controversy: Whatever Happened to Margaret Mead?" *Skeptic* 9:48–53.

SHANNON, THOMAS RICHARD. 1988. *An Introduction to the World-System Perspective.* Boulder, CO: Westview Press.

SHAW, THURSTAN. 1986. "Whose Heritage?" *Museum* 149:46–48.

SHEA, B. T., and A. M. GOMEZ. 1988. "Tooth Scaling and Evolutionary Dwarfism: An Investigation of Allometry in Human Pygmies." *American Journal of Physical Anthropology* 77:117–32.

SHEPHER, JOSEPH. 1983. *Incest: A Biosocial View.* New York: Academic Press.

SHIMIZU, AKITOSHI. 1987. "*Ie* and *Dozuku*: Family and Descent in Japan." *Current Anthropology* 28(4):S85–S90.

SHIPMAN, PAT. 1984. "Scavenger Hunt." *Natural History* 4(84):20–27.

———. 1986a. "Baffling Limb on the Family Tree." *Discover* 7(9):86–93.

———. 1986b. "Scavenging or Hunting in Early Hominids: Theoretical Frameworks and Tests." *American Anthropologist* 88:27–43.

SHIPTON, PARKER. 1990. "African Famines and Food Security: Anthropological Perspectives." *Annual Review of Anthropology* 19:353–94.

SHIRK, MARTHA, and O'DELL MITCHELL, JR. 1989. "One Company Evolving in Two Lands." *St. Louis Post-Dispatch,* June 25.

SHOSTAK, MARJORIE. 1981. *Nisa: The Life and Words of a !Kung Woman.* New York: Vintage Books, Random House.

SHWEDER, RICHARD. 1991. *Thinking Through Cultures: Expeditions in Cultural Psychology.* Cambridge, MA: Harvard University Press.

SIGNOR, PHILIP W., and JERE H. LIPPS. 1982. "Sampling Bias, Gradual Extinction Patterns and Catastrophes in the Fossil Record." *Geological Society of America,* Special Paper 190.

SILBY, CHARLES G., and JON E. ALQUIST. 1984. "The Phylogeny of the Hominoid Primates as Indicated by DNA-DNA Hybridization." *Journal of Molecular Evolution* 20:2–15.

SILVERMAN, PHILIP, and ROBERT J. MAXWELL. 1983. "The Role and Treatment of the Elderly in 95 Societies." In Jay Sokolovsky, ed., *Growing Old in Different Cultures,* pp. 43–55. Belmont, CA: Wadsworth.

SIMMONS, LEO. 1945. *The Role of the Aged in Primitive Society.* London: Oxford University Press.

SIMON, JULIAN L. 1981. *The Ultimate Resource.* Princeton, NJ: Princeton University Press.

SIMONS, ELWYN L. 1972. *Primate Evolution: An Introduction to Man's Place in Nature.* New York: Macmillan.

———. 1984. "Ancestor: Dawn Ape of the Fayum." *Natural History* 93(5):18–20.

———. 1989a. "Description of Two Genera and Species of Late Eocene Anthropoidea from Egypt." *Proceedings of the National Academy of Science* 86: 9956–60.

———. 1989b. "Human Origins." *Science* 245:1343–50.

———. 1990. "Discovery of the Oldest Known Anthropoidean Skull from the Paleogene of Egypt." *Science* 247: 1567–69.

SIMONS, ELWYN L., and D. RASMUSSEN. 1990. "Vertebrate Paleontology of the Fayum: History of Research, Faunal Review, and Future Prospects." In R. Said, ed., *The Geology of Egypt,* pp. 627–638. Rotterdam: Balkema Press.

SIMPSON, J. A., and E. S. C. WIENER. 1989. "Ethnic." *Oxford English Dictionary,* 2d ed., Vol. 5. Oxford: Clarendon Press.

SINGLETON, THERESA A., ed. 1985. *The Archaeology of Slavery and Plantation Life.* New York: Academic Press.

———. 1999. "I, Too, Am America." *Archaeological Studies in African American Life.* Charlottesville: University of Virginia Press.

SLAGTER, ROBERT, and HAROLD R. KERBO. 2000. *Modern Thailand.* Boston: McGraw-Hill.

SMITH, ADAM. [1776] 1937. *An Inquiry into the Nature and Causes of the Wealth of Nations.* New York: The Modern Library.

SMITH, ANDREW B. 1984. "Origins of the Neolithic in the Sahara." In Desmond J. Clark and Steven A. Brandt, eds., *From Hunter to Farmer,* pp. 84–92. Berkeley: University of California Press.

SMITH, ANTHONY. 1986. *The Ethnic Origins of Nations.* Oxford: Blackwell.

SMITH, BRUCE D. 1989. "Origins of Agriculture in Eastern North America." *Science* 246:1566–71.

———. 1995. *The Emergence of Agriculture.* New York: Scientific American Library.

SMITH, F. H. 1984. "Fossil Hominids from the Upper Pleistocene of Central Europe and the Origin of Modern Europeans." In F. H. Smith and F. Spencer, eds., *The Origins of Modern Humans: A World Survey of Fossil Evidence,* pp. 137–210. New York: Alan R. Liss.

SMITH, HUSTON. *The Religions of Man.* New York: Harper & Row.

SMITH, MARGO L. 1986. "Culture in International Business: Selecting Employees for Expatriate Assignments." In Hendrick Serrie, ed., *Anthropology and International Business.* Williamsburg, VA: Department of Anthropology, William and Mary University.

SMITH, M. G. 1965. "The Hausa of Northern Nigeria." In James L. Gibbs, Jr., ed., *Peoples of Africa.* New York: Holt, Rinehart, and Winston.

SMITH, NEIL. 1999. *Chomsky: Ideas and Ideals.* Cambridge: Cambridge University Press.

SMITH, STUART T. 1990. "Administration at the Egyptian Middle Kingdom Frontier: Sealings from Uronarti and Askut." *Aegaeum* 5:197–219.

SMITH-IVAN, EDDA. 1988. "Introduction." In Edda Smith-Ivan, Nidhi Tandon, and Jane Connors, eds., *Women in Sub-Saharan Africa,* Report No. 7. London: Minority Rights Group.

SMUTS, BARBARA. 1987. "What Are Friends For?" *Natural History* 96(2).

SNOW, C. C., E. STOVER, and K. HANNIBAL. 1989. "Scientists as Detectives Investigating Human Rights." *Technology Review* 92:2.

SNOW, C. C., and M. J. BIHURRIET. 1992. "An Epidemiology of Homicide: Ning'n Nombre Burials in the Province of Buenos Aires from 1970 to 1984." In T. B. Jabine and R. P. Claude, eds., *Human Rights and Statistics: Getting the Record Straight.* Philadelphia: University of Pennsylvania Press.

SOLECKI, RALPH S. 1991. *Shanidar: The First Flower People.* New York: Knopf.

SOLHEIM, WILLIAM. 1971. "An Earlier Agricultural Revolution." *Scientific American* 133(11):34–51.

SOUTHALL, AIDAN. 1956. *Alur Society: A Study in Processes and Types of Domination.* Cambridge: Heffer.

South Asia Online Briefing Program. 2000. June/August. Accessed at http://www.thp.org/sac/unit4/cycle.htm.

SOWELL, THOMAS. 1994. *Race and Culture.* New York: Basic Books.

———. 1995. "Ethnicity and IQ." In Steven Fraser, ed., *The Bell Curve Wars: Race, Intelligence and the Future of America.* New York: Basic Books.

SPERBER, DAN. 1996. *Explaining Culture: A Naturalistic Approach.* Oxford: Blackwell Publishers.

SPIRO, MELFORD. 1952. "Ghosts, Ifaluk, and Teleological Functionalism." *American Anthropologist* 54:497–503.

———. 1971. *Buddhism and Society: A Great Tradition and Its Burmese Vicissitudes.* Berkeley: University of California Press.

———. 1982. *Oedipus in the Trobriands.* Chicago: University of Chicago Press.

SPONSEL, LESLIE. 1996. "Human Rights and Advocacy Anthropology." In M. Ember and D. Levinson, eds., *Encyclopedia of Cultural Anthropology,* Vol. 2. New York: Henry Holt and Company.

———. 1998. "Yanomamin: An Arena of Conflict and Aggression in the Amazon." *Aggressive Behavior* 24: 97–122.

STACK, CAROL B. 1975. *All Our Kin: Strategies for Survival in a Black Community.* New York: Harper & Row.

STANNER, W. E. H. 1979. "The Dreaming." In W. A. Lessa and E. Z. Vogt, eds., *Reader in Comparative Religion,* 4th ed., pp. 513–23. New York: Harper & Row.

STAVENHAGEN, RODOLFO. 1975. *Social Classes in Agrarian Societies.* Garden City, NY: Anchor Press.

STAVRIANOS, L. S. 1995. *A Global History: From Prehistory to the Present,* 6th ed. Upper Saddle River, NJ: Prentice Hall.

STEINMETZ, PAUL. 1980. *Pipe, Bible and Peyote Among the Oglala Lakota.* Stockholm: Almquist and Wiksell International.

STEVEN, ROB. 1983. *Classes in Contemporary Japan.* Cambridge: Cambridge University Press.

STEWARD, JULIAN H. 1955. *Theory of Culture Change: The Methodology of Multilinear Evolution.* Urbana: University of Illinois Press.

STEWART, T. D., ed. 1970. *Personal Identification in Mass Disasters.* Washington, DC: Smithsonian Institution Press.

———. 1979. *Essentials of Forensic Anthropology.* Springfield, IL: Charles C. Thomas.

STIEBING, WILLIAM H., JR. 1984. *Ancient Astronauts: Cosmic Allusions and Popular Theories About Man's Past.* Buffalo, NY: Prometheus Books.

STINI, WILLIAM A. 1975. *Ecology and Human Adaptation.* Dubuque, IA: William C. Brown.

STONEKING, M., K. BHATIA, and A. C. WILSON. 1987. "Rate of Sequence Divergence Estimated from Restricted Maps of Mitochondrial DNAs from Papua, New Guinea." *Cold Spring Harbor Symposia on Quantitative Biology* 51:433–39.

STOVER, E. 1981. "Scientists Aid Search for Argentina's 'Ëdesaparacidos.'" *Science* 211(4486):6.

———. 1992. "Unquiet Graves: The Search for the Disappeared in Iraqi Kurdistan." A report published by Middle East Watch and Physicians for Human Rights.

STRASSER, ELIZABETH, and MARIAN DAGOSTO, eds., 1988. *The Primate Postcranial Skeleton: Studies in Adaptation and Evolution.* New York: Academic Press.

STRAUSS, CLAUDIA. 1992. "Models and Motives." In R. D'Andrade and C. Strauss, eds., *Human Motives and Cultural Models.* Cambridge: Cambridge University Press.

STRINGER, C. B. 1985. "Middle Pleistocene Hominid Variability and the Origin of Late Pleistocene Humans." In E. Delson, ed., *Ancestors: The Hard Evidence,* pp. 289–95. New York: Alan R. Liss.

STRINGER, C. B., and P. ANDREWS. 1988. "Genetic and Fossil Evidence for the Origin of Modern Humans." *Science* 239:1263–68.

STRIER, KAREN B. 2003. *Primate Behavioral Ecology,* 2nd ed. New York: Allyn and Bacon.

STRUEVER, STUART, ed. 1970. *Prehistoric Agriculture.* Garden City, NY: Natural History Press.

STRUG, DAVID L. 1986. "The Foreign Politics of Cocaine: Comments on a Plan to Eradicate the Coca Leaf in Peru." In Deborah Pacini and Christine Franquemont, eds., *Coca and Cocaine: Effects on People and Policy in Latin America,* Cultural Survival Report 23. Cambridge, MA:

Cultural Survival, Inc.; Latin American Studies Program, Cornell University.

STRUM, SHIRLEY C., and WILLIAM MITCHELL. 1987. "Baboon Models and Muddles." In Warren G. Kinsey, ed., *The Evolution of Human Behavior,* pp. 87–114. Albany: State University of New York Press.

SUDARKASA, NIARA. 1989. "African and Afro-American Family Structure." In Johnetta Cole, ed., *Anthropology for the Nineties: Introductory Readings,* pp. 132–60. New York: Free Press.

SUSSMAN, R. W. 1993. "A Current Controversy in Human Evolution: Overview." *American Anthropologist* 95:9–13.

SWADESH, MORRIS. 1964. "Linguistics as an Instrument of Prehistory." In Dell H. Hymes, ed., *Language and Society.* New York: Harper & Row.

SWEET, LOUISE. 1965. "Camel Raiding of North Arabian Bedouin: A Mechanism of Ecological Adaptation." *American Anthropologist* 67:1132–50.

SWISHER, C. C., G. H. CURTIS, T. JACOB, A. G. GETTY, and A. SUPRIJO WIDIASMORO. 1994. "Age of the Earliest Known Hominids in Java, Indonesia." *Science* 263:1118–21.

SYMONS, DONALD. 1979. *The Evolution of Human Sexuality.* Oxford: Oxford University Press.

SZABO, G. 1967. "The Regional Anatomy of the Human Integument with Special Reference to the Distribution of Hair Follicles, Sweat Glands and Melanocytes." *Philosophical Transactions of the Royal Society of London* 252B:447–85.

TAINTER, JOSEPH A. 1990. *The Collapse of Complex Societies.* Cambridge: Cambridge University Press.

TAKAKI, RONALD. 1990a. *Iron Cage: Race and Culture in 19th Century America.* New York: Oxford University Press.

———. 1990b. *Strangers from a Different Shore: A History of Asian Americans.* New York: Penguin.

TALMON, YONINA. 1964. "Mate Selection in Collective Settlements." *American Sociological Review* 29:491–508.

TAMBIAH, STANLEY J. 1989. "Bridewealth and Dowry Revisited: The Position of Women in Sub-Saharan Africa and North India." *Current Anthropology* 30(4):413–35.

———. 1991. *Sri Lanka: Ethnic Fratricide and the Dismantling of Democracy.* Chicago: University of Chicago Press.

TANDON, NIDHI. 1988. "Women in Rural Areas." In Edda Smith-Ivan, Nidhi Tandon, and Jane Connors, eds., *Women in Sub-Saharan Africa,* Report No. 77. London: Minority Rights Group.

TANNER, NANCY M. 1981. *On Becoming Human.* London: Cambridge University Press.

———. 1987. "Gathering by Females: The Chimpanzee Model Revisited and the Gathering Hypothesis." In Warren G. Kinsey, ed., *The Evolution of Human Behavior,* pp. 3–27. Albany: State University of New York Press.

TAPPER, RICHARD, and NANCY TAPPER. 1992, 1993. "Marriage, Honor, and Responsibility: Islamic and Local Models in the Mediterranean and Middle East." *Cambridge Anthropology* 16(2).

TARLING, D. H. 1985. *Continental Drift and Biological Evolution.* Burlington, NC: Carolina Biological Supply Co.

TATTERSALL, IAN. 1986. "Species Recognition in Human Paleontology." *Journal of Human Evolution* 15:165–75.

TAX, SOL. 1953. *Penny Capitalism: A Guatemalan Indian Economy.* Smithsonian Institution, Institute of Social Anthropology, Publication No. 16. Washington, DC: U.S. Government Printing Office.

TAYLOR, R. E. 1995. "Radiocarbon Dating: The Continuing Revolution." *Evolutionary Anthropology* 4(5):169–81.

TEMPLETON, ALAN R. 1993. "The 'Eve' Hypothesis: A Genetic Critique and Reanalysis." *American Anthropologist* 95(1):51–72.

———. 1998. "Human Races: A Genetic and Evolutionary Perspective." *American Anthropologist* 100(3):632–50.

TERRACE, HERBERT S. 1986. *Nim: A Chimpanzee Who Learned Sign Language.* New York: Columbia University Press.

TESTART, ALAIN. 1988. "Some Major Problems in the Social Anthropology of Hunter-Gatherers," trans. Roy Willis. *Current Anthropology* 29(1):1–31.

THOMAS, E. M. 1958. *The Harmless People.* New York: Random House.

THOMASON, SARAH G., and TERRENCE KAUFMAN. 1988. *Language Contact, Creolization, and Genetic Linguistics.* Berkeley: University of California Press.

THORNE, A., and M. H. WOLPOFF. 1992. "The Multiregional Evolution of Humans." *Scientific American* 266:76–83.

THROCKMORTON, PETER. 1962. "Oldest Known Shipwreck Yields Bronze Age Cargo." *National Geographic* 121(5): 697–711.

THROCKMORTON, PETER, ed. 1987. *The Sea Remembers: Shipwrecks and Archaeology from Homer's Greece to the Rediscovery of the Titanic.* New York: Weidenfeld & Nicholson.

TIERNEY, PATRICK. 2000. *Darkness in El Dorado: How Scientists and Journalists Devastated the Amazon.* New York: W. W. Norton.

TIME ALMANAC. 2000. Boston: Information Please.

TITMA, MIKK, and NANCY BRANDON TUMA. 2001. *Modern Russia.* Boston: McGraw-Hill.

TRIGGER, BRUCE. 1989. *A History of Archaeological Thought.* New York: Cambridge University Press.

———. 1993. *Early Civilizations: Ancient Egypt in Context.* Cairo: American University in Cairo Press.

TRINKAUS, ERIK, and PAT SHIPMAN. 1994. *The Neandertals.* New York: Random House.

TSHOMBE, RICHARD KEY. 2001. "The Case of the Okapi Faunal Reserve in the Northeastern Democratic Republic of Congo." *People and Natural Resources: Changes in Times of Crisis.* Okapi Faunal Reserve Zoning Program. (http://www.cerc.Columbia.edu/elf/ ELF2001CS/TshombeCS)

TURNBULL, COLIN. 1963. *The Forest People: A Study of the Pygmies of the Congo.* New York: Simon & Schuster.

———. 1983. *The Mbuti Pygmies: Change and Adaptation.* New York: Holt, Rinehart and Winston.

TURNER, VICTOR. 1957. *Schism and Continuity in an African Society: A Study of Ndembu Village Life.* Manchester: Manchester University Press.

———. 1967. *The Forest of Symbols: Aspects of Ndembu Ritual.* Ithaca, NY: Cornell University Press.

———. 1974. *Dramas, Fields, and Metaphors: Symbolic Action in Human Society.* Ithaca, NY: Cornell University Press.

TURTON, ANDREW. 1980. "Thai Institutions of Slavery." In James L. Watson, ed., *Asian and African Systems of Slavery,* pp. 251–92. Berkeley: University of California Press.

TWEDDELL, COLIN E., and LINDA AMY KIMBALL. 1985. *Introduction to the Peoples and Cultures of Asia.* Englewood Cliffs, NJ: Prentice Hall.

TYLER, STEPHEN A. 1986. *India: An Anthropological Perspective.* Prospect Heights, IL: Waveland Press.

TYLOR, EDWARD B. 1871. *Primitive Culture.* London: J. Murray.

———. 1889. "On a Method of Investigating the Development of Institutions, Applied to Laws of Marriage and Descent." *Journal of the Royal Anthropological Institute* 18:245–72.

UBELAKER, DOUGLAS H. 1988. "North American Indian Population Size, A.D. 1500 to 1985." *American Journal of Physical Anthropology* 77:289–94.

UCHENDU, VICTOR C. 1965. *The Igbo of Southeast Nigeria.* New York: Holt, Rinehart and Winston.

UCKO, PETER J., and G. W. DIMBLEBY. 1969. *The Domestication and Exploitation of Plants and Animals.* Chicago: Aldine.

U.S. CENSUS BUREAU. 2000. *Statistical Abstracts of the United States,* 2000.

U.S. COMMITTEE ON GLOBAL CHANGE. 1988. *Toward an Understanding of Global Change.* Washington, DC: National Academy Press.

VAGO, STEVEN. 1995. *Law and Society,* 2nd ed. Upper Saddle River, NJ: Prentice Hall.

VALERI, VALERIO. 1985. *Kingship and Sacrifice: Ritual and Society in Ancient Hawaii,* trans. Paula Wissing. Chicago: University of Chicago Press.

VAN DEN BERGHE, PIERRE. 1979. *Human Family Systems: An Evolutionary View.* New York: Elsevier Science Publishing Co.

———. 1980. "Incest and Exogamy: A Sociobiological Reconsideration." *Ethology and Sociobiology* 1:151–62.

———. 1981. *The Ethnic Phenomenon.* New York: Elsevier Science Publishing Co.

VAN DEN BERGHE, PIERRE, and DAVID BARASH. 1977. "Inclusive Fitness Theory and the Human Family." *American Anthropologist* 79:809–23.

VAN ESTERIK, PENNY, ed. 1996. *Women of Southeast Asia.* DeKalb, IL: Northern Illinois University.

VAN GENNEP, ARNOLD. 1960. *The Rites of Passage.* Chicago: University of Chicago Press.

VAN WILLIGEN, JOHN, and V. C. CHANNA. 1991. "Law, Custom, and Crimes Against Women: The Problem of Dowry Death in India." *Human Organization* 50(4): 369–77.

VAYDA, ANDREW P. 1961. "Expansion and Warfare Among Swidden Agriculturalists." *American Anthropologist* 63: 346–58.

VAYDA, ANDREW P., ed. 1969. *Environment and Cultural Behavior.* Garden City, NY: Natural History Press.

VERDERY, KATHERINE. 1996. *What Was Socialism, and What Comes Next?* Princeton: Princeton University Press.

VIANNA, N. J., and A. K. POLAN. 1984. "Incidence of Low Birth Weight Among Love Canal Residents." *Science* 226:1217–19.

VIGILANT, L., M. STONEKING, H. HARPENDING, K. HAWKES, and A. C. WILSON. 1991. "African Populations and the Evolution of Human Mitochondrial DNA." *Science* 233:1303–7.

VILLA, PAOLA. 1983. *Terra Amata and the Middle Pleistocene Archaeological Record of Southern France.* Berkeley: University of California Press.

VON DANIKEN, ERICH. 1970. *Chariots of the Gods.* New York: Bantam.

VON FRISCH, KARL. 1967. *The Dance Language and Orientation of Bees,* trans. L. E. Chadwick. Cambridge, MA: Harvard University Press.

VON HUMBOLDT, W. [1836] 1972. *Linguistic Variability and Intellectual Development,* trans. C. G. Buck and F. Raven. Philadelphia: University of Pennsylvania Press.

WAFER, JIM. 1991. *The Taste of Blood: Spirit Possession in Brazilian Candomble.* Contemporary Ethnography Series. Philadelphia: University of Pennsylvania Press.

WALKER, ANTHONY. 1986. *The Toda of South India: A New Look.* Delhi: Hindustan Publishing Company.

WALKER, A. C., and M. PICKFORD. 1983. "New Post-Cranial Fossils of *Proconsul africanus* and *Proconsul nyanzae*." In R. L. Ciochon and R. Corruccini, eds., *New Interpretations of Ape and Human Ancestry,* pp. 325–52. New York: Plenum Press.

WALKER, A. R., E. LEAKEY, J. M. HARRIS, and F. H. BROWN. 1986. "2.5 MYR *Australopithecus boisei* from West of Lake Turkana, Kenya." *Nature* 322:517–22.

WALLACE, ANTHONY K. C. 1972. "Mental Illness, Biology, and Culture." In Francis Hsu, ed., *Psychological Anthropology.* Cambridge, MA: Schenkman.

WALLERSTEIN, IMMANUEL. 1974. *The Modern World-System: Capitalist Agriculture and the Origins of the European World-Economy in the Sixteenth Century.* New York: Academic Press.

———. 1979. *The Capitalist World-Economy.* New York: Cambridge University Press.

———. 1980. *The Modern World-System: II. Mercantilism and the Consolidation of the European World-Economy, 1600–1750.* New York: Academic Press.

———. 1986. *Africa and the Modern World.* Trenton, NJ: Africa World Press.

WANG, CHENG GANG. 1999. "China's Environment in the Balance." In Susan Ogden, ed., *China,* 9th ed. Guilford, CT: McGraw-Hill/Dushkin.

WARSHAW, STEVEN. 1988. *Southeast Asia Emerges.* Berkeley, CA: Diablo Press.

———. 1989b. *India Emerges.* Berkeley, CA: Diablo Press.

WASHBURN, SHERWOOD. 1960. "Tools and Human Evolution." *Scientific American* 203(3):67–75.

WASSERMAN, H. P. 1965. "Human Pigmentation and Environmental Adaptation." *Archives of Environmental Health* 11: 691–94.

WATSON, JAMES L. 1980. "Slavery as an Institution, Open and Closed Systems." In James L. Watson, ed., *Asian and African Systems of Slavery.* Berkeley: University of California Press.

WATSON, PATTY JO. 1984. *Archaeological Explanation: The Scientific Method in Archaeology.* New York: Columbia University Press.

WATSON, PATTY JO, STEVEN A. LEBLANC, and CHARLES L. REDMAN. 1971. *Explanation in Archaeology: An Explicitly Scientific Approach.* New York: Columbia University Press.

WAX, ROSALIE. 1971. *Doing Fieldwork: Warnings and Advice.* Chicago: University of Chicago Press.

WEATHERFORD, JACK. 1988. *Indian Givers: How the Indians of the Americas Transformed the World.* New York: Crown.

WEINER, ANNETTE B. 1976. *Women of Value, Men of Renown.* Austin: University of Texas Press.

———. 1987. *The Trobrianders of Papua New Guinea.* New York: Holt, Rinehart and Winston.

WEINER, J. 1994. *The Beak of the Finch.* New York: Knopf.

WEINER, J. S. 1955. *The Piltdown Forgery.* London: Oxford University Press.

WENDORF, FRED, and ROMUALD SCHILD. 1981. "The Earliest Food Producers." *Archaeology* 34(5):30–36.

———. 1984. "The Emergence of Food Production in the Egyptian Sahara." In Desmond J. Clark and Steven A. Brandt, eds., *From Hunter to Farmer,* pp. 93–101. Berkeley: University of California Press.

WEST, FRED. 1975. *The Way of Language: An Introduction.* New York: Harcourt Brace Jovanovich.

WHITE, DOUGLAS. 1988. "Rethinking Polygyny: Co-Wives, Codes, and Cultural Systems." *Current Anthropology* 29(4):529–53.

WHITE, JOHN PETER. 1993. "The Settlement of Ancient Australia." In G. Burenhult, ed., *The First Humans: Human Origins and History to 10,000 BC,* pp. 147–70. New York: HarperCollins.

WHITE, JOHN PETER, and JAMES F. O'CONNELL. 1982. *A Prehistory of Australia, New Guinea and Sahul.* New York: Academic Press.

WHITE, LESLIE. [1949] 1971. "The Symbol: The Origin and Basis of Human Behavior." In Leslie White, ed., *The Science of Culture: A Study of Man and Civilization.* New York: Farrar, Straus & Giroux.

———. 1959. *The Evolution of Culture.* New York: McGraw-Hill.

WHITE, RANDALL. 1982. "Rethinking the Middle/Upper Paleolithic Transition." *Current Anthropology* 23:169–92.

WHITE, T. D., G. SUWA, and B. ASFAW. 1994. "*Australopithecus ramidus,* a New Species of Early Hominid from Aramis, Ethiopia." *Nature* 37:306–12.

WHITLEY, DAVID S., and RONALD I. DORN. 1993. "New Perspectives on the Clovis vs. Pre-Clovis Controversy." *American Antiquity* 58(4):626–47.

WHORF, BENJAMIN. 1956. *Language, Thought, and Reality: The Selected Writings of Benjamin Lee Whorf.* Cambridge, MA: MIT Press.

WIKAN, UNNI. 1991. *Behind the Veil in Arabia: Women in Oman.* Chicago: University of Chicago Press.

WILK, RICHARD R. 1996. *Economies and Cultures: Foundations of Economic Anthropology.* Boulder, CO: Westview Press.

WILLIAMS, HOLLY ANN. 1990. "Families in Refugee Camps." *Human Organization* 49(2):100–9.

WILLIAMS, ROBIN M., JR. 1970. *American Society: A Sociological Interpretation,* 3rd ed. New York: Knopf.

WILLIAMS-BLANGERO, S., and J. BLANGERO. 1992. "Quantitative Genetic Analysis of Skin Reflectance: A Multivariate Approach." *Human Biology* 64:35–49.

WILSON, A. C., and R. L. CANN. 1992. "The Recent African Genesis of Humans." *Scientific American* 266(4):68–73.

WILSON, B., C. GRIGSON, and S. PAYNE, eds. 1982. *Aging and Sexing Animal Bones from Archaeological Sites.* Oxford: British Archaeological Reports, International Series 109.

WILSON, E. O. 1975. *Sociobiology: The New Synthesis.* Cambridge, MA: Harvard University Press.

———. 1978. *On Human Nature.* Cambridge, MA: Harvard University Press.

———. ed. 1988. *Biodiversity.* Washington, DC: Smithsonian Institution, National Academy of Sciences.

———. ed. 1989. *Biodiversity.* Washington, DC: National Academy Press.

———. 1992. *The Diversity of Life.* Cambridge, MA: Harvard University Press.

WILSON, E. O., and LAURA SIMONDS SOUTHWORTH. 1996. *In Search of Nature.* New York: Island Press.

WILSON, MONICA. 1951. *Good Company: A Study of Nyakyusa Age-Villages.* Boston: Beacon Press.

WINZELER, ROBERT L. 1996. "Sexual Status in Southeast Asia: Comparative Perspectives on Women, Agriculture and Political Organization." In Penny Van Esterik, ed., *Women of Southeast Asia.* Occasional Paper No. 17. DeKalb, IL: Northern Illinois University, Center for Southeast Asian Studies.

WITTFOGEL, KARL W. 1957. *Oriental Despotism: A Comparative Study of Total Power.* New Haven, CT: Yale University Press.

WOLF, ARTHUR. 1970. "Childhood Association and Sexual Attraction: A Further Test of the Westermarck Hypothesis." *American Anthropologist* 72:503–15.

WOLF, ERIC R. 1955a. "Closed Corporate Communities in Mesoamerica and Java." *Southwestern Journal of Anthropology* 13(1):1–18.

———. 1955b. "Types of Latin American Peasantry: A Preliminary Discussion." *American Anthropologist* 57(3), Part 1: 452–71.

———. 1958. "The Virgin of Guadalupe: A Mexican National Symbol." *Journal of American Folklore* 71:34–39.

———. 1959. *Sons of the Shaking Earth.* Chicago: University of Chicago Press.

———. 1964. *Anthropology.* Englewood Cliffs, NJ: Prentice Hall.

———. 1966. *Peasants.* Englewood Cliffs, NJ: Prentice Hall.

———. 1969. *Peasant Wars of the Twentieth Century.* New York: Harper & Row.

———. 1987. "Cycles of Violence: The Anthropology of War and Peace." In Kenneth Moore, ed., *Waymarks: The Notre Dame Inaugural Lectures in Anthropology,* pp. 127–51. Notre Dame, IN: University of Notre Dame Press.

———. [1982] 1997. *Europe and the People Without History.* Berkeley: University of California Press.

———. 1999. *Envisioning Power: Ideologies of Domination and Crisis.* Berkeley: University of California Press.

WOLF, E. R., and S. MINTZ. 1950. "An Analysis of Ritual Coparenthood (*Compadrazgo*)." *Southwestern Journal of Anthropology* 6. Reprinted in Jack A. Potter, May Diaz, and George Foster, eds., 1967 *Peasant Society: A Reader,* pp. 174–99. Boston: Little, Brown.

WOLFE, ALVIN. 1977. "The Supranational Organization of Production: An Evolutionary Perspective." *Current Anthropology* 18:615–35.

———. 1986. "The Multinational Corporation as a Form of Sociocultural Integration Above the Level of the State." In Hendrick Serrie, ed., *Anthropology and International Business,* Publication No. 28. Williamsburg, VA: Studies in Third World Societies.

WOLPOFF, MILFORD H. 1980. *Paleoanthropology.* New York: Knopf.

———. 1983. "Ramapithecus and Human Origins: An Anthropologist's Perspective of Changing Interpretations." In R. L. Ciochon and R. Corruccini, eds., *New Interpretations of Ape and Human Ancestry,* pp. 651–76. New York: Plenum Press.

WOODBURN, JAMES. 1982. "Egalitarian Societies." *Man* 17:431–51.

WORKMAN, P. L., B. S. BLUMBERG, and A. J. COOPER. 1963. "Selection, Gene Migration and Polymorphic Stability in a U.S. White and Negro Population." *American Journal of Human Genetics* 15:71–84.

WORLD ALMANAC and BOOK OF FACTS. 2001. New York: Scripps Howard Company.

WORSLEY, PETER. 1957. *The Trumpet Shall Sound.* New York: Schocken.

———. 1984. *The Three Worlds: Culture and World Development.* Chicago: University of Chicago Press.

WRIGHT, HENRY T. 1977. "Recent Researches of the Origin of the State." *Annual Review of Anthropology* 6: 355–70.

WRIGHT, HENRY T., and G. JOHNSON. 1975. "Population, Exchange, and Early State Formation in Southwestern Iran." *American Anthropologist* 77:267–89.

YELLEN, JOHN. 1985. "Bushmen." *Science* 85:40–48.

YENGOYAN, ARAM A. 1986. "Theory in Anthropology: On the Demise of the Concept of Culture." *Comparative Studies in Society and History* 28(2):357–74.

YOFFEE, NORMAN. 1979. "The Decline and Rise of Mesopotamian Civilization." *American Antiquity.* 44:5–35.

ZEDER, MELINDA A. 1997. *The American Archaeologist: A Profile.* Walnut Creek, CA: Altamira Press.

Photo Credits

Index